6th Workshop on Statistical Machine Translation 2011

(WMT 2011)

Held at EMNLP 2011

Edinburgh, Scotland, UK
30-31 July 2011

ISBN: 978-1-61839-255-8

Printed from e-media with permission by:

Curran Associates, Inc.
57 Morehouse Lane
Red Hook, NY 12571

Some format issues inherent in the e-media version may also appear in this print version.

Printed by Curran Associates, Inc. (2011)

For permission requests, please contact the Association for Computational Linguistics at the address below.

Association for Computational Linguistics
209 N. Eighth Street
Stroudsburg, Pennsylvania 18360

Phone: 1-570-476-8006
Fax: 1-570-476-0860

acl@aclweb.org

Additional copies of this publication are available from:

Curran Associates, Inc.
57 Morehouse Lane
Red Hook, NY 12571 USA
Phone: 845-758-0400
Fax: 845-758-2634
Email: curran@proceedings.com
Web: www.proceedings.com

Introduction

The EMNLP 2011 Workshop on Statistical Machine Translation (WMT-2011) took place on Saturday and Sunday, July 30–31 in Edinburgh, Scotland, immediately following the Conference on Empirical Methods on Natural Language Processing (EMNLP) 2011, which was hosted by the University of Edinburgh.

This is the seventh time this workshop has been held. The first time was in 2005 as part of the ACL 2005 Workshop on Building and Using Parallel Texts. In the following years the Workshop on Statistical Machine Translation was held at HLT-NAACL 2006 in New York City, US, ACL 2007 in Prague, Czech Republic, ACL 2008, Columbus, Ohio, US, EACL 2009 in Athens, Greece, and ACL 2010 in Uppsala, Sweden.

The focus of our workshop was to use parallel corpora for machine translation. Recent experimentation has shown that the performance of SMT systems varies greatly with the source language. In this workshop we encouraged researchers to investigate ways to improve the performance of SMT systems for diverse languages, including morphologically more complex languages, languages with partial free word order, and low-resource languages.

Prior to the workshop, in addition to soliciting relevant papers for review and possible presentation, we conducted a shared task that brought together machine translation systems for an evaluation on previously unseen data. The results of the shared task were announced at the workshop, and these proceedings also include an overview paper for the shared task that summarizes the results, as well as provides information about the data used and any procedures that were followed in conducting or scoring the task. In addition, there are short papers from each participating team that describe their underlying system in some detail.

Like in previous years, we have received a far larger number of submission than we could accept for presentation. This year we have received 42 full paper submissions (not counting withdrawn submissions) and 47 shared task submissions. In total WMT-2011 featured 18 full paper oral presentations and 47 shared task poster presentations.

The invited talk was given by William Lewis (Microsoft Research), Robert Munro (Stanford University), and Stephan Vogel (Carnegie Mellon University).

We would like to thank the members of the Program Committee for their timely reviews. We also would like to thank the participants of the shared task and all the other volunteers who helped with the evaluations.

Chris Callison-Burch, Philipp Koehn, Christof Monz, and Omar F. Zaidan

WMT 5-year Retrospective Best Paper Award

Since this is the Sixth Workshop on Statistical Machine Translation, we have decided to create a WMT 5-year Retrospective Best Paper Award, to be given to the best paper that was published at the first Workshop on Statistical Machine Translation, which was held at HLT-NAACL 2006 in New York. The goals of this retrospective award are to recognize high-quality work that has stood the test of time, and to highlight the excellent work that appears at WMT.

The WMT11 program committee voted on the best paper from a list of six nominated papers. Five of these were nominated by high citation counts, which we defined as having 10 or more citations in the ACL anthology network (excluding self-citations), and more than 30 citations on Google Scholar. We also opened the nomination process to the committee, which yielded one further nomination for a paper that did not reach the citation threshold but was deemed to be excellent.

The program committee decided to award the WMT 5-year Retrospective Best Paper Award to:

Andreas Zollmann and Ashish Venugopal. 2006. *Syntax Augmented Machine Translation via Chart Parsing*. In Proceedings of the Workshop on Statistical Machine Translation. Pages 138–141.

This short paper described Zollmann and Venugopal's entry into the WMT06 shared translation task. Their system introduced a parsing-based machine translation system. Like David Chiang's Hiero system, Zollmann and Venugopal's system used synchronous context free grammars (SCFGs). Instead of using a single non-terminal symbol, X, Zollmann and Venugopal's SCFG rules contained linguistically informed non-terminal symbols that were extracted from a parsed parallel corpus.

This paper was one of the first publications to demonstrate that syntactically-informed approaches to statistical machine translation could achieve translation quality that was comparable to – or even better than – state-of-the-art phrase-based and and hierarchical phrase-based approaches to machine translation. Zollmann and Venugopal's approach has influenced a number of researchers, and has been integrated into open source translation software like the Joshua and Moses decoders.

In many ways this paper represents the ideals of the WMT workshops. It introduced a novel approach to machine translation and demonstrated its value empirically by comparing it to other state-of-the-art systems on a public data set.

Congratulations to Andreas Zollmann and Ashish Venugopal for their excellent work!

Organizers:

Chris Callison-Burch (Johns Hopkins University)
Philipp Koehn (University of Edinburgh)
Christof Monz (University of Amsterdam)
Omar F. Zaidan (Johns Hopkins University)

Invited Talk:

William Lewis (Microsoft Research)
Robert Munro (Stanford University)
Stephan Vogel (Carnegie Mellon University)

Program Committee:

Lars Ahrenberg (Linköping University)
Nicola Bertoldi (FBK)
Graeme Blackwood (University of Cambridge)
Michael Bloodgood (University of Maryland)
Ondrej Bojar (Charles University)
Thorsten Brants (Google)
Chris Brockett (Microsoft)
Nicola Cancedda (Xerox)
Marine Carpuat (National Research Council Canada)
Simon Carter (University of Amsterdam)
Francisco Casacuberta (University of Valencia)
Daniel Cer (Stanford University)
Mauro Cettolo (FBK)
Boxing Chen (National Research Council Canada)
Colin Cherry (National Research Council Canada)
David Chiang (ISI)
Jon Clark (Carnegie Mellon University)
Stephen Clark (University of Cambridge)
Christophe Costa Florencio (University of Amsterdam)
Michael Denkowski (Carnegie Mellon University)
Kevin Duh (NTT)
Chris Dyer (Carnegie Mellon University)
Marc Dymetman (Xerox)
Marcello Federico (FBK)

Andrew Finch (NICT)
Jose Fonollosa (University of Catalonia)
George Foster (National Research Council Canada)
Alex Fraser (University of Stuttgart)
Michel Galley (Microsoft)
Niyu Ge (IBM)
Dmitriy Genzel (Google)
Ulrich Germann (University of Toronto)
Kevin Gimpel (Carnegie Mellon University)
Adria de Gispert (University of Cambridge)
Spence Green (Stanford University)
Nizar Habash (Columbia University)
Keith Hall (Google)
Greg Hanneman (Carnegie Mellon University)
Kenneth Heafield (Carnegie Mellon University)
John Henderson (MITRE)
Howard Johnson (National Research Council Canada)
Doug Jones (Lincoln Labs MIT)
Damianos Karakos (Johns Hopkins University)
Maxim Khalilov (University of Amsterdam)
Roland Kuhn (National Research Council Canada)
Shankar Kumar (Google)
Philippe Langlais (Univeristy of Montreal)
Adam Lopez (Johns Hopkins University)
Wolfgang Macherey (Google)
Nitin Madnani (Educational Testing Service)
Daniel Marcu (Language Weaver)
Yuval Marton (IBM)
Lambert Mathias (Nuance)
Spyros Matsoukas (Raytheon BBN Technologies)
Arne Mauser (RWTH Aachen)
Arul Menezes (Microsoft)
Bob Moore (Google)
Smaranda Muresan (Rutgers University)
Kemal Oflazer (Carnegie Mellon University)
Miles Osborne (University of Edinburgh)
Matt Post (Johns Hopkins University)
Chris Quirk (Microsoft)
Antti-Veikko Rosti (Raytheon BBN Technologies)
Salim Roukos (IBM)
Anoop Sarkar (Simon Fraser University)
Holger Schwenk (University of Le Mans)

Jean Senellart (Systran)
Khalil Simaan (University of Amsterdam)
Michel Simard (National Research Council Canada)
David Smith (University of Massachusetts Amherst)
Matthew Snover (Raytheon BBN Technologies)
Joerg Tiedemann (Uppsala University)
Christoph Tillmann (IBM)
Dan Tufis (Romanian Academy)
Jakob Uszkoreit (Google)
Masao Utiyama (NICT)
David Vilar (RWTH Aachen)
Clare Voss (Army Research Labs)
Taro Watanabe (NTT)
Andy Way (Dublin City University)
Jinxi Xu (Raytheon BBN Technologies)
Sirvan Yahyaei (Queen Mary, University of London)
Daniel Zeman (Charles University)
Richard Zens (Google)
Bing Zhang (Raytheon BBN Technologies)

Table of Contents

Conference Program

Saturday, July 30, 2011

Session 1: Shared Tasks and Evaluation

9:00–9:20 *A Grain of Salt for the WMT Manual Evaluation*
Ondřej Bojar, Miloš Ercegovčević, Martin Popel and Omar Zaidan

9:20–9:40 *A Lightweight Evaluation Framework for Machine Translation Reordering*
David Talbot, Hideto Kazawa, Hiroshi Ichikawa, Jason Katz-Brown, Masakazu Seno and Franz Och

9:40–10:30 *Findings of the 2011 Workshop on Statistical Machine Translation*
Chris Callison-Burch, Philipp Koehn, Christof Monz and Omar Zaidan

10:30–11:00 Coffee

Session 2: Shared Metrics and System Combination Tasks

11:00–12:40 Poster Session Metrics

Evaluate with Confidence Estimation: Machine ranking of translation outputs using grammatical features
Eleftherios Avramidis, Maja Popović, David Vilar and Aljoscha Burchardt

AMBER: A Modified BLEU, Enhanced Ranking Metric
Boxing Chen and Roland Kuhn

TESLA at WMT 2011: Translation Evaluation and Tunable Metric
Daniel Dahlmeier, Chang Liu and Hwee Tou Ng

Meteor 1.3: Automatic Metric for Reliable Optimization and Evaluation of Machine Translation Systems
Michael Denkowski and Alon Lavie

Approximating a Deep-Syntactic Metric for MT Evaluation and Tuning
Matouš Macháček and Ondřej Bojar

Evaluation without references: IBM1 scores as evaluation metrics
Maja Popović, David Vilar, Eleftherios Avramidis and Aljoscha Burchardt

Saturday, July 30, 2011 (continued)

Morphemes and POS tags for n-gram based evaluation metrics
Maja Popović

E-rating Machine Translation
Kristen Parton, Joel Tetreault, Nitin Madnani and Martin Chodorow

TINE: A Metric to Assess MT Adequacy
Miguel Rios, Wilker Aziz and Lucia Specia

Regression and Ranking based Optimisation for Sentence Level MT Evaluation
Xingyi Song and Trevor Cohn

MAISE: A Flexible, Configurable, Extensible Open Source Package for Mass AI System Evaluation
Omar Zaidan

11:00–12:40 Poster Session System Combination

MANY improvements for WMT'11
Loïc Barrault

The UPV-PRHLT combination system for WMT 2011
Jesús González-Rubio and Francisco Casacuberta

CMU System Combination in WMT 2011
Kenneth Heafield and Alon Lavie

The RWTH System Combination System for WMT 2011
Gregor Leusch, Markus Freitag and Hermann Ney

Expected BLEU Training for Graphs: BBN System Description for WMT11 System Combination Task
Antti-Veikko Rosti, Bing Zhang, Spyros Matsoukas and Richard Schwartz

The UZH System Combination System for WMT 2011
Rico Sennrich

Description of the JHU System Combination Scheme for WMT 2011
Daguang Xu, Yuan Cao and Damianos Karakos

12:40–14:00 Lunch

Session 3: Language Models and Document Alignment

14:00–14:25 *Multiple-stream Language Models for Statistical Machine Translation*
Abby Levenberg, Miles Osborne and David Matthews

14:25–14:50 *KenLM: Faster and Smaller Language Model Queries*
Kenneth Heafield

14:50–15:15 *Wider Context by Using Bilingual Language Models in Machine Translation*
Jan Niehues, Teresa Herrmann, Stephan Vogel and Alex Waibel

15:15–15:40 *A Minimally Supervised Approach for Detecting and Ranking Document Translation Pairs*
Kriste Krstovski and David A. Smith

15:40–16:10 Coffee

Session 4: Syntax and Semantics

16:10–16:35 *Agreement Constraints for Statistical Machine Translation into German*
Philip Williams and Philipp Koehn

16:35–17:00 *Fuzzy Syntactic Reordering for Phrase-based Statistical Machine Translation*
Jacob Andreas, Nizar Habash and Owen Rambow

17:00–17:25 *Filtering Antonymous, Trend-Contrasting, and Polarity-Dissimilar Distributional Paraphrases for Improving Statistical Machine Translation*
Yuval Marton, Ahmed El Kholy and Nizar Habash

17:25–17:50 *Productive Generation of Compound Words in Statistical Machine Translation*
Sara Stymne and Nicola Cancedda

Sunday, July 31, 2011

Session 5: Machine Learning and Adaptation

9:00–10:25 *SampleRank Training for Phrase-Based Machine Translation*
Barry Haddow, Abhishek Arun and Philipp Koehn

9:25–10:50 *Instance Selection for Machine Translation using Feature Decay Algorithms*
Ergun Bicici and Deniz Yuret

9:50–10:15 *Investigations on Translation Model Adaptation Using Monolingual Data*
Patrik Lambert, Holger Schwenk, Christophe Servan and Sadaf Abdul-Rauf

10:15–10:40 *Topic Adaptation for Lecture Translation through Bilingual Latent Semantic Models*
Nick Ruiz and Marcello Federico

10:40–11:00 Coffee

Session 6: Shared Translation Task

11:00–12:40 Poster Presentations

Personal Translator at WMT2011
Vera Aleksic and Gregor Thurmair

LIMSI @ WMT11
Alexandre Allauzen, Hélène Bonneau-Maynard, Hai-Son Le, Aurélien Max, Guillaume Wisniewski, François Yvon, Gilles Adda, Josep Maria Crego, Adrien Lardilleux, Thomas Lavergne and Artem Sokolov

Shallow Semantic Trees for SMT
Wilker Aziz, Miguel Rios and Lucia Specia

RegMT System for Machine Translation, System Combination, and Evaluation
Ergun Bicici and Deniz Yuret

Improving Translation Model by Monolingual Data
Ondřej Bojar and Aleš Tamchyna

Sunday, July 31, 2011 (continued)

UPM system for the translation task
Verónica López-Ludeña and Rubén San-Segundo

Two-step translation with grammatical post-processing
David Mareček, Rudolf Rosa, Petra Galuščáková and Ondřej Bojar

Influence of Parser Choice on Dependency-Based MT
Martin Popel, David Mareček, Nathan Green and Zdenek Zabokrtsky

The LIGA (LIG/LIA) Machine Translation System for WMT 2011
Marion Potet, Raphaël Rubino, Benjamin Lecouteux, Stéphane Huet, Laurent Besacier, Hervé Blanchon and Fabrice Lefèvre

Factored Translation with Unsupervised Word Clusters
Christian Rishøj and Anders Søgaard

The BM-I2R Haitian-Créole-to-English translation system description for the WMT 2011 evaluation campaign
Marta R. Costa-jussà and Rafael E. Banchs

The Universitat d'Alacant hybrid machine translation system for WMT 2011
Víctor M. Sánchez-Cartagena, Felipe Sánchez-Martínez and Juan Antonio Pérez-Ortiz

LIUM's SMT Machine Translation Systems for WMT 2011
Holger Schwenk, Patrik Lambert, Loïc Barrault, Christophe Servan, Sadaf Abdul-Rauf, Haithem Afli and Kashif Shah

Spell Checking Techniques for Replacement of Unknown Words and Data Cleaning for Haitian Creole SMS Translation
Sara Stymne

Joshua 3.0: Syntax-based Machine Translation with the Thrax Grammar Extractor
Jonathan Weese, Juri Ganitkevitch, Chris Callison-Burch, Matt Post and Adam Lopez

DFKI Hybrid Machine Translation System for WMT 2011 - On the Integration of SMT and RBMT
Jia Xu, Hans Uszkoreit, Casey Kennington, David Vilar and Xiaojun Zhang

CEU-UPV English-Spanish system for WMT11
Francisco Zamora-Martinez and Maria Jose Castro-Bleda

Hierarchical Phrase-Based MT at the Charles University for the WMT 2011 Shared Task
Daniel Zeman

12:40–14:00 Lunch

Invited Talk

14:00–15:40 *Crisis MT: Developing A Cookbook for MT in Crisis Situations*
William Lewis, Robert Munro and Stephan Vogel

15:40–16:10 Coffee

Session 7: Translation Models

16:10–16:35 *Generative Models of Monolingual and Bilingual Gappy Patterns*
Kevin Gimpel and Noah A. Smith

16:35–17:00 *Extraction Programs: A Unified Approach to Translation Rule Extraction*
Mark Hopkins, Greg Langmead and Tai Vo

17:00–17:25 *Bayesian Extraction of Minimal SCFG Rules for Hierarchical Phrase-based Translation*
Baskaran Sankaran, Gholamreza Haffari and Anoop Sarkar

17:25–17:50 *From n-gram-based to CRF-based Translation Models*
Thomas Lavergne, Alexandre Allauzen, Josep Maria Crego and François Yvon

A Grain of Salt for the WMT Manual Evaluation*

Ondřej Bojar, Miloš Ercegovčević, Martin Popel
Charles University in Prague
Faculty of Mathematics and Physics
Institute of Formal and Applied Linguistics
{bojar,popel}@ufal.mff.cuni.cz
ercegovcevic@hotmail.com

Omar F. Zaidan
Department of Computer Science
Johns Hopkins University
ozaidan@cs.jhu.edu

Abstract

The Workshop on Statistical Machine Translation (WMT) has become one of ACL's flagship workshops, held annually since 2006. In addition to soliciting papers from the research community, WMT also features a shared translation task for evaluating MT systems. This shared task is notable for having *manual evaluation* as its cornerstone. The Workshop's overview paper, playing a descriptive and administrative role, reports the main results of the evaluation without delving deep into analyzing those results. The aim of this paper is to investigate and explain some interesting idiosyncrasies in the reported results, which only become apparent when performing a more thorough analysis of the collected annotations. Our analysis sheds some light on how the reported results should (and should not) be interpreted, and also gives rise to some helpful recommendation for the organizers of WMT.

1 Introduction

The Workshop on Statistical Machine Translation (WMT) has become an annual feast for MT researchers. Of particular interest is WMT's shared translation task, featuring a component for manual evaluation of MT systems. The friendly competition is a source of inspiration for participating teams, and the yearly overview paper (Callison-Burch et al., 2010) provides a concise report of the state of the art. However, the amount of interesting data collected every year (the system outputs and, most importantly, the annotator judgments) is quite large, exceeding what the WMT overview paper can afford to analyze with much depth.

In this paper, we take a closer look at the data collected in last year's workshop, WMT10[1], and delve a bit deeper into analyzing the manual judgments. We focus mainly on the English-to-Czech task, as it included a diverse portfolio of MT systems, was a heavily judged language pair, and also illustrates interesting "contradictions" in the results. We try to explain such points of interest, and analyze what we believe to be the positive and negative aspects of the currently established evaluation procedure of WMT.

Section 2 examines the primary style of manual evaluation: system ranking. We discuss how the interpretation of collected judgments, the computation of annotator agreement, and document that annotators' individual preferences may render two systems effectively incomparable. Section 3 is devoted to the impact of embedding reference translations, while Section 4 and Section 5 discuss some idiosyncrasies of other WMT shared tasks and manual evaluation in general.

2 The *System Ranking* Task

At the core of the WMT manual evaluation is the system ranking task. In this task, the annotator is presented with a source sentence, a reference translation, and the outputs of five systems over that source sentence. The instructions are kept minimal: the annotator is to rank the presented translations from best to worst. Ties are allowed, but the scale provides five rank labels, allowing the annotator to give a total order if desired.

The five assigned rank labels are submitted at once, making the 5-tuple a unit of annotation. In the following, we will call this unit a *block*. The blocks differ from each other in the choice of the

* This work has been supported by the grants EuroMatrixPlus (FP7-ICT-2007-3-231720 of the EU and 7E09003 of the Czech Republic), P406/10/P259, MSM 0021620838, and DARPA GALE program under Contract No. HR0011-06-2-0001. We are grateful to our students, colleagues, and the three reviewers for various observations and suggestions.

[1] http://www.statmt.org/wmt10

Proceedings of the 6th Workshop on Statistical Machine Translation, pages 1–11,
Edinburgh, Scotland, UK, July 30–31, 2011. ©2011 Association for Computational Linguistics

Language Pair	Systems	Blocks	Labels	Comparisons	Ref $\geq$ others	Intra-annot. κ	Inter-annot. κ
German-English	26	1,050	5,231	10,424	0.965	0.607	0.492
English-German	19	1,407	6,866	13,694	0.976	0.560	0.512
Spanish-English	15	1,140	5,665	11,307	0.989	0.693	0.508
English-Spanish	17	519	2,591	5,174	0.935	0.696	0.594
French-English	25	837	4,156	8,294	0.981	0.722	0.452
English-French	20	801	3,993	7,962	0.917	0.636	0.449
Czech-English	13	543	2,691	5,375	0.976	0.700	0.504
English-Czech	18	1,395	6,803	13,538	0.959	0.620	0.444
Average	19	962	4,750	9,471	0.962	0.654	0.494

Table 1: Statistics on the collected rankings, quality of references and kappas across language pairs. In general, a block yields a set of five rank labels, which yields a set of $\binom{5}{2} = 10$ pairwise comparisons. Due to occasional omitted labels, the Comparisons/Blocks ratio is not exactly 10.

source sentence and the choice of the five systems being compared. A couple of tricks are introduced in the sampling of the source sentences, to ensure that a large enough number of judgments is repeated across different screens for meaningful computation of inter- and intra-annotator agreement. As for the sampling of systems, it is done uniformly – no effort is made to oversample or undersample a particular system (or a particular pair of systems together) at any point in time.

In terms of the interface, the evaluation utilizes the infrastructure of Amazon's Mechanical Turk (MTurk)[2], with each MTurk HIT[3] containing three blocks, corresponding to three consecutive source sentences.

Table 1 provides a brief comparison of the various language pairs in terms of number of MT systems compared (including the reference), number of blocks ranked, the number of pairwise comparisons extracted from the rankings (one block with 5 systems ranked gives 10 pairwise comparisons, but occasional unranked systems are excluded), the quality of the reference (the percentage of comparisons where the reference was better or equal than another system), and the κ statistic, which is a measure of agreement (see Section 2.2 for more details).[4]

We see that English-to-Czech, the language pair on which we focus, is not far from the average in all those characteristics except for the number of collected comparisons (and blocks), making it the second most evaluated language pair.

[2] `http://www.mturk.com/`

[3] "HIT" is an acronym for *human intelligence task*, which is the MTurk term for a single screen presented to the annotator.

[4] We only use the "expert" annotations of WMT10, ignoring the data collected from paid annotators on MTurk, since they were not part of the official evaluation.

2.1 Interpreting the Rank Labels

The description in the WMT overview paper says: "Relative ranking is our official evaluation metric. [Systems] are ranked based on how frequently they were judged to be **better than or equal to any other system**." (Emphasis added.) The WMT overview paper refers to this measure as "$\geq$ others", with a variant of it called "$>$ others" that does not reward ties.

We first note that this description is somewhat ambiguous, and an uninformed reader might interpret it in one of two different ways. For some system A, each block in which A appears includes four implicit pairwise comparisons (against the other presented systems). How is A's score computed from those comparisons?

The correct interpretation is that A is rewarded once for **each** of the four comparisons in which A wins (or ties).[5] In other words, A's score is the number of pairwise comparisons in which A wins (or ties), divided by the total number of pairwise comparisons involving A. We will use "$\geq$ others" (resp. "$>$ others") to refer to this interpretation, in keeping with the terminology of the overview paper.

The other interpretation is that A is rewarded only if A wins (or ties) **all** four comparisons. In other words, A's score is the number of *blocks* in which A wins (or ties) all comparisons, divided by the number of *blocks* in which A appears. We will use "$\geq$ all in block" (resp. "$>$ all in block") to refer to this interpretation.[6]

[5] Personal communication with WMT organizers.

[6] There is yet a third interpretation, due to a literal reading of the description, where A is rewarded at most once per block if it wins (or ties) *any one* of its four comparisons. This is probably less useful: it might be good at identifying the bottom tier of systems, but would fail to distinguish between all other systems.

	REF	CU-BOJAR	CU-TECTO	EUROTRANS	ONLINEB	PC-TRANS	UEDIN
$\geq$ others	95.9	65.6	60.1	54.0	**70.4**	62.1	62.2
$>$ others	90.5	45.0	44.1	39.3	49.1	**49.4**	39.6
$\geq$ all in block	93.1	32.3	30.7	23.4	**37.5**	32.5	28.1
$>$ all in block	81.3	13.6	**19.0**	13.3	15.6	18.7	10.6

Table 2: Sentence-level ranking scores for the WMT10 English-Czech language pair. The "$\geq$ others" and "$>$ others" scores reproduced here exactly match numbers published in the WMT10 overview paper. A boldfaced score marks the best system in a given row (besides the reference).

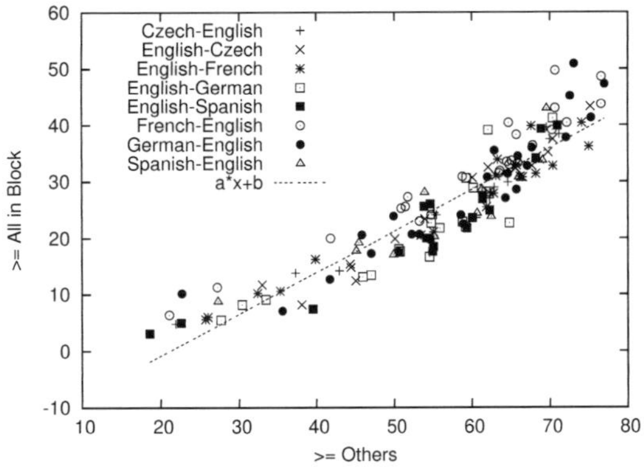

Figure 1: "$\geq$ all in block" and "$\geq$ others" provide very similar ordering of systems.

For quality control purposes, the WMT organizers embed the reference translations as a 'system' alongside the actual entries (the idea being that an annotator clicking randomly would be easy to detect, since they would not consistently rank the reference 'system' highly). This means that the reference is as likely as any other system to appear in a block, and when the score for a system A is computed, pairwise comparisons with the reference *are* included.

We use the publicly released human judgments[7] to compute the scores of systems participating in the English-Czech subtask, under both interpretations. Table 2 reports the scores, with our "$\geq$ others" (resp. "$>$ others") scores reproduced exactly matching those reported in Table 21 of the WMT overview paper. (For clarity, Table 2 is abbreviated to include only the top six systems of twelve.)

Our first suggestion is that **both** measures could be reported in future evaluations, since each tells us something different. The first interpretation gives partial credit for an MT system, hence distinguishing systems from each other at a finer level. This is especially important for a language pair with relatively few annotations, since "$\geq$ others" would produce a larger number of data points (four per system per block) than "$\geq$ all in block" (one per system per block). Another advantage of the official "$\geq$ others" is greater robustness towards various factors like the number of systems in the competition, the number of systems in one block or the presence of the reference in the block (however, see Section 3).

As for the second interpretation, it helps identify whether or not a single system (or a small group of systems) is strongly dominant over the other systems. For the systems listed in Table 2, "$>$ all in block" suggests its potential in the context of system combination: CU-TECTO and PC-TRANS win almost one fifth of the blocks in which they appear, despite the fact that either a reference translation or a combination system already appears alongside them. (See also Table 4 below.)

Also, note that if the ranking task were designed specifically to cater to the "$\geq$ all in block" interpretation, it would only have **two** 'rank' labels (basically, "top" and "non-top"). In that case, annotators would spend *considerably* less time per block than they do now, since all they need to do is identify the top system(s) per block, without distinguishing non-top systems from each other.

Even for those interested in distinguishing non-state-of-the-art systems from each other, we point out that the "$\geq$ all in block" interpretation ultimately gives a system ordering that is very similar to that of the official "$\geq$ others" interpretation, **even** for the lower-tier systems (Figure 1).

2.2 Annotator Agreement

The WMT10 overview paper reports inter- and intra-annotator agreement over the pairwise comparisons, to show the validity of the evaluation setup and the "$\geq$ others" metric. Agreement is quantified using the following formula:

$$\kappa = \frac{P(A) - P(E)}{1 - P(E)} \tag{1}$$

where $P(A)$ is the proportion of times two annotators are observed to agree, and $P(E)$ is the expected proportion of times two annotators would agree by chance. Note that κ has a value of at most 1, with higher κ values indicating higher rates of agreement. The κ measure is more meaningful

[7] `http://statmt.org/wmt10/results.html`

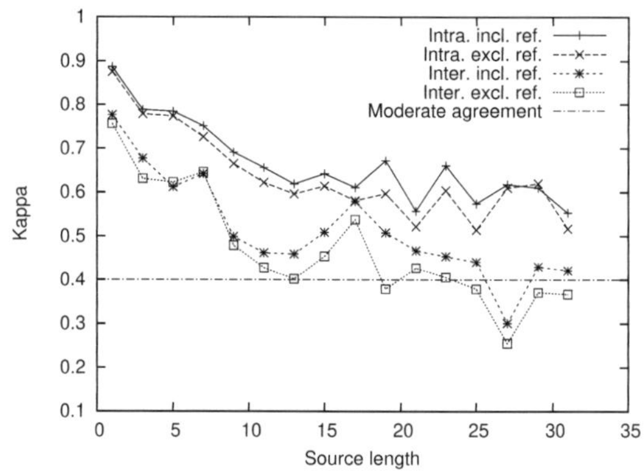

Figure 2: Intra-/inter-annotator agreement with/without references, across various source sentence lengths (lengths of n and $n+1$ are used to plot the point at $x = n$). This figure is based on all language pairs.

than reporting $P(A)$ as is, since it takes into account, via $P(E)$, how 'surprising' it is for annotators to agree in the first place.

In the context of pairwise comparisons, an agreement between two annotators occurs when they compare the same pair of systems (S_1,S_2), and both agree on their relative ranking: either $S_1 > S_2$, $S_1 = S_2$, or $S_1 < S_2$. $P(E)$ is then:

$$P(E) = P^2(s_1{>}s_2) + P^2(s_1{=}s_2) + P^2(s_1{<}s_2) \quad (2)$$

In the WMT overview paper, all three categories are assumed equally likely, giving $P(E) = \frac{1}{9} + \frac{1}{9} + \frac{1}{9} = \frac{1}{3}$. For consistency with the WMT overview paper, and unless otherwise noted, we also use $P(E) = \frac{1}{3}$ whenever a κ value is reported. (Though see Section 2.2.2 for a discussion about $P(E)$.)

2.2.1 Observed Agreement for Different Sentence Lengths

In Figure 2 we plot the κ values across different source sentence lengths. We see that the inter-annotator agreement (when excluding references) is reasonably high only for sentences up to 10 words in length – according to Landis and Koch (1977), and as cited by the WMT overview paper, not even 'moderate' agreement can be assumed if κ is less than 0.4. Another popular (and controversial) rule of thumb (Krippendorff, 1980) is more strict and says that $\kappa < 0.67$ is not suitable even for tentative conclusions.

For this reason, and given that a majority of sentences are indeed more than 10 words in length (the median is 20 words), we suggest that future evaluations either include fewer outputs per block, or divide longer sentences into shorter segments (e.g. on clause boundaries), so these segments are more easily and reliably comparable. The latter suggestions assumes word alignment as a preprocessing and presenting the annotators the context of the judged segment.

2.2.2 Estimating $P(E)$, the Expected Agreement by Chance

Several agreement measures (usually called kappas) were designed based on the Equation 1 (see Artstein and Poesio (2008) and Eugenio and Glass (2004) for an overview and a discussion). Those measures differ from each other in how to define the individual components of Equation 2, and hence differ in what the expected agreement by chance ($P(E)$) would be:[8]

- The S measure (Bennett et al., 1954) assumes a uniform distribution over the categories.
- Scott's π (Scott, 1955) estimates the distribution empirically from *actual annotation.*
- Cohen's κ (Cohen, 1960) estimates the distribution empirically as well, and further assumes *a separate distribution for each annotator.*

Given that the WMT10 overview paper assumes that the three categories ($S_1 > S_2$, $S_1 = S_2$, and $S_1 < S_2$) are equally likely, it is using the S measure version of Equation 1, though it does not explicitly say so – it simply calls it "the kappa coefficient" (K).

Regardless of what the measure should be called, we believe that the uniform distribution itself is not appropriate, even though it seems to model a "random clicker" adequately. In particular, and given the design of the ranking interface, $\frac{1}{3}$ is an overestimate of $P(S_1 = S_2)$ for a random clicker, and should in fact be $\frac{1}{5}$: each system receives one of five rank labels, and for two systems to receive the same rank label, there are only five (out of 25) label pairs that satisfy $S_1 = S_2$. Therefore, with $P(S_1 = S_2) = \frac{1}{5}$,

[8]These three measures were later generalized to more than two annotators (Fleiss, 1971; Bartko and Carpenter, 1976), Thus, without loss of generality, our examples involve two annotators.

"≥ Others"		S	π
Inter	incl. ref.	0.487	0.454
	excl. ref.	0.439	0.403
Intra	incl. ref.	0.633	0.609
	excl. ref.	0.601	0.575

Table 3: Summary of two variants of kappa: S (or K as it is reported in the WMT10 paper) and our proposed Scott's π. We report inter- vs. intra-annotator agreement and collected from all comparisons ("incl. ref.") vs. collected only from comparisons without the reference ("excl. ref.") because it is generally easier to agree that the reference is better than the other systems. This table is based on all language pairs.

we have $P(S_1 > S_2) = P(S_1 < S_2) = \frac{2}{5}$, and therefore $P(E) = 0.36$ rather than 0.333.

Taking the discussion a step further, we actually advocate following the idea of Scott's π, whereby the distribution of each category is estimated *empirically from the actual annotation*, rather than assuming a random annotator – these frequencies are easy to compute, and reflect a more meaningful $P(E)$.[9]

Under this interpretation, $P(S_1 = S_2)$ is calculated to be 0.168, reflecting the fraction of pairwise comparisons that correspond to a tie. (Note that this further supports the claim that setting $P(S_1 = S_2) = \frac{1}{3}$ for a random clicker, as used in the WMT overview paper, is an overestimate.) This results in $P(E) = 0.374$, yielding, for instance, $\pi = 0.454$ for "≥ others" inter-annotator agreement, somewhat lower than $\kappa = 0.487$ (reported in Table 3).

We do note that the difference is rather small, and that our aim is to be mathematically sound above all. Carefully defining $P(E)$ would be important when comparing kappas across different tasks with different $P(E)$, or when attempting to satisfy certain thresholds (as the cited 0.4 and 0.67). Furthermore, if one is interested in measuring agreement for individual annotators, such as identifying those who have unacceptably low intra-annotator agreement, the question of $P(E)$ is quite important, since annotation behavior varies noticeably from one annotator to another. A 'conservative' annotator who prefers to rank systems as being tied most of the time would have a high $P(E)$, whereas an annotator using ties moderately would have a low $P(E)$. Hence, two annotators with equal agreement rates ($P(A)$) are not necessarily equally proficient, since their $P(E)$ might differ considerably.[10]

2.3 The ≥ variant vs. the > variant

Even within the same interpretation of how systems could be scored, there is a question of whether or not to reward ties. The overview paper reports both variants of its measure, but does not note that there are non-trivial differences between the two orderings. Compare for example the "≥ others" ordering vs. the "> others" ordering of CU-BOJAR and PC-TRANS (Table 2), showing an unexpected swing of 7.9%:

	≥ others	> others
CU-BOJAR	**65.6**	45.0
PC-TRANS	62.1	**49.4**

CU-BOJAR seems better under the ≥ variant, but loses out when only strict wins are rewarded. Theoretically, this could be purely due to chance, but the total number of pairwise comparisons in "≥ others" is relatively large (about 1,500 pairwise comparisons for each system), and ought to cancel such effects.

A similar pattern could be seen under the "all in block" interpretation as well (e.g. for CU-TECTO and ONLINEB). Table 4 documents this effect by looking at how often a system is the sole winner of a block. Comparing PC-TRANS and CU-BOJAR again, we see that PC-TRANS is up there with CU-TECTO and DCU-COMBO as the most frequent sole winners, winning 71 blocks, whereas CU-BOJAR is the sole winner of only 53 blocks. This is in spite of the fact that PC-TRANS actually appeared in slightly fewer blocks than CU-BOJAR (385 vs. 401).

One possible explanation is that the two variants ("≥" and ">") measure two subtly different things about MT systems. Digging deeper into Table 2's values, we find that CU-BOJAR is tied with another system $65.6 - 45.0 = 20.4\%$ of the time, while PC-TRANS is tied with another system only $62.1 - 49.4 = 12.7\%$ of the time. So it seems that PC-TRANS's output is *noticeably different* from another system more frequently than CU-BOJAR, which reduces the number of times that annotators

[9] We believe that $P(E)$ should not reflect the chance that two *random* annotators would agree, but the chance that two **actual** annotators would agree *randomly*. The two sound subtly related but are actually quite different.

[10] Who's more impressive: a psychic who correctly predicts the result of a coin toss 50% of the time, or a psychic who correctly predicts the result of a *die roll* 50% of the time?

Blocks	Sole Winner
305	Reference
73	CU-TECTO
71	PC-TRANS
70	DCU-COMBO
57	RWTH-COMBO
54	ONLINEB
53	CU-BOJAR
46	EUROTRANS
41	UEDIN
41	UPV-COMBO
175	One of eight other systems
409	No sole winner
1395	Total English-to-Czech Blocks

Table 4: A breakdown of the 1,395 blocks for the English-Czech task, according to which system (if any) is the sole winner. On average, a system appears in 388 blocks.

mark PC-TRANS as tied with another system.[11] In that sense, the "≥" ranking is hurting PC-TRANS, since it does not benefit from its small number of ties. On the other hand, the ">" variant would not reward CU-BOJAR for its large number of ties.

The "≥ others" score may be artificially boosted if several very similar systems (and therefore likely to be "tied") take part in the evaluation.[12] One possible solution is to completely disregard ties and calculate the final score as $\frac{\text{wins}}{\text{wins}+\text{losses}}$. We recommend to use this score instead of "≥ others" ($\frac{\text{wins}+\text{ties}}{\text{wins}+\text{ties}+\text{losses}}$) which is biased toward often tied systems, and "> others" ($\frac{\text{wins}}{\text{wins}+\text{ties}+\text{losses}}$) which is biased toward systems with few ties.

2.4 Surprise? Does the Number of Evaluations Affect a System's Score?

When examining the system scores for the English-Czech task, we noticed a surprising pattern: it seemed that the more times a system is sampled to be judged, the lower its "≥ others" score ("≥ all in block" behaving similarly). A scatter plot of a system's score vs. the number of blocks in which it appears (Figure 3) makes the pattern obvious.

We immediately wondered if the pattern holds in other language pairs. We measured Pearson's correlation coefficient within each language pair, reported in Table 5. As it turns out, English-Czech happened to be the one language pair where the 'correlation' is strongest, with only English-Spanish also having a somewhat strong correlation. Overall, though, there is a consistent trend that can be seen across the language pairs. Could it really be the case that the more often a system is judged, the worse its score gets?

Examining plots for the other language pairs makes things a bit clearer. Consider for example the plot for English-Spanish (Figure 4). As one would hope, the data points actually come together to form a cloud, **indicating a lack of correlation**. The reason that a hint of a correlation exists is the presence of two outliers in the bottom right corner. In other words, the **very** worst systems are, indeed, the ones judged quite often. We observed this pattern in several other language pairs as well.

The correlation naturally does not imply causation. We are still not sure how to explain the artifact. A subtle possibility lies in the MTurk interface: annotators have the choice to accept a HIT or skip it before actually providing their la-

Source	Target	Correlation of Block Count vs. "≥ Others"
English	Czech	-0.558
English	Spanish	-0.434
Czech	English	-0.290
Spanish	English	-0.240
English	French	-0.227
English	German	-0.161
French	English	-0.024
German	English	0.146
Overall		-0.092

Table 5: Pearson's correlation between the number of blocks where a system was ranked and the system's "≥ others" score. (The reference itself is not included among the considered systems).

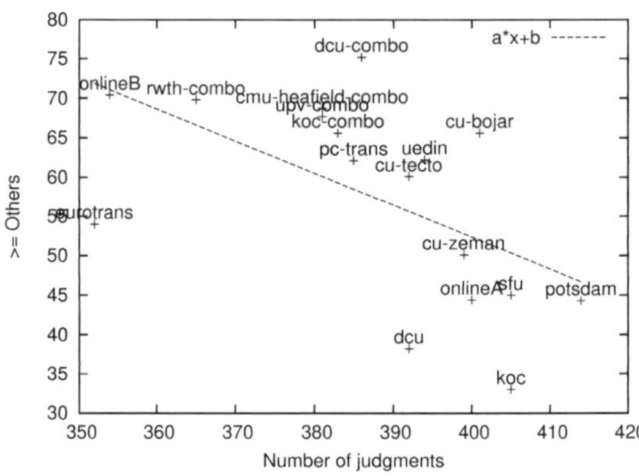

Figure 3: A plot of "≥ others" system score vs. times judged, for English-Czech.

[11] Indeed, PC-TRANS is a commercial system (manually) tuned over a long period of time and based on resources very different from what other participants in WMT use.

[12] In the preliminary WMT11 results, this seems to happen to four Moses-like systems (UEDIN, CU-BOJAR, CU-MARECEK and CU-TAMCHYNA) which have better "≥ others" score but worse "> others" score than CU-TECTO.

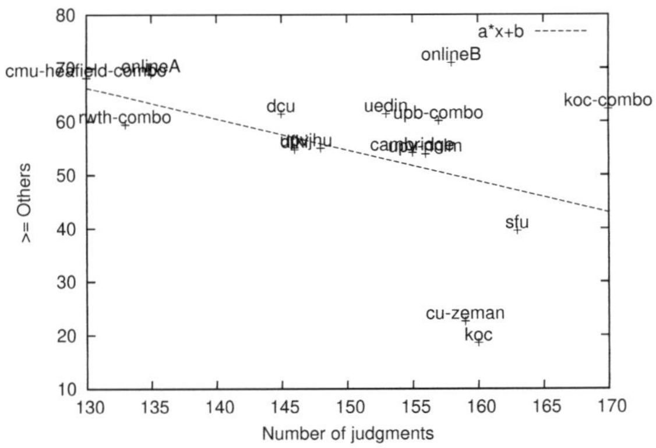

Figure 4: A plot of "≥ others" system score vs. times judged, for English-Spanish.

bels. It might be the case that some annotators are more willing to accept HITs when there is an obviously poor system (since that would make their task somewhat easier), and who are more prone to skipping HITs where the systems seem hard to distinguish from each other. So there might be a causation effect after all, but in the reverse order: a system gets judged more often if it is a bad system.[13] A suggestion from the reviewers is to run a pilot annotation with deliberate inclusion of a poor system among the ranked ones.

2.5 Issues of Pairwise Judgments

The WMT overview paper also provides pairwise system comparisons: each cell in Table 6 indicates the percentage of pairwise comparisons between the two systems where the system in the column was ranked better (>) than the system in the row. For instance, there are 81 ranking responses where both CU-TECTO and CU-BOJAR were present and indeed ranked[14] among the 5 systems in the block. In 37 (45.7%) of the cases, CU-TECTO was ranked better, in 29 (35.8%), CU-BOJAR was ranked better and there was a tie in the remaining 15 (18.5%) cases. The ties are not explicitly shown in Table 6 but they are implied by the total of 100%. The cell is in bold where there was a win in the pairwise comparison, so 45.7 is bold in our example.

An interesting "discrepancy" in Table 6 is that CU-TECTO wins pairwise comparisons with CU-BOJAR and UEDIN but it scores worse than them in the official "≥ others", cf. Table 2. Similarly, UEDIN outperformed ONLINEB in the pairwise comparisons but it was ranked worse in both > and ≥ official comparison.

[13] No pun intended!

[14] The users sometimes did not fill any rank for a system. Such cases are ignored.

	REF	CU-BOJAR	CU-TECTO	EUROTRANS	ONLINEB	PC-TRANS	UEDIN
REF	-	4.3	4.3	5.1	3.8	3.6	2.3
CU-BOJAR	**87.1**	-	**45.7**	28.3	**44.4**	39.5	**41.1**
CU-TECTO	**88.2**	35.8	-	38.0	**55.8**	**44.0**	36.0
EUROTRANS	**88.5**	**60.9**	**46.8**	-	**50.7**	**53.8**	**48.6**
ONLINEB	**91.2**	31.1	29.1	32.8	-	43.8	**39.3**
PC-TRANS	**88.0**	**45.3**	42.9	28.6	**49.3**	-	36.6
UEDIN	**94.3**	39.3	**44.2**	31.9	32.1	**49.5**	-

Table 6: Pairwise comparisons extracted from sentence-level rankings of the WMT10 English-Czech News Task. Re-evaluated to reproduce the numbers published in WMT10 overview paper. Bold in column A and row B means that system A is pairwise better than system B.

In the following, we focus on the CU-BOJAR (B) and CU-TECTO (T) pair because they are interesting competitors on their own. They both use the same parallel corpus for lexical mapping but operate very differently: CU-BOJAR is based on Moses while CU-TECTO transfers at a deep syntactic layer and generates target text which is more or less grammatically correct but suffers in lexical choice.

2.5.1 Different Set of Sentences

The mismatch in the outcomes of "≥ others" and pairwise comparisons could be caused by different set of sentences. The pairwise ranking is collected from the set of blocks where both CU-BOJAR and CU-TECTO appeared (and were indeed ranked). Each of the systems however competes in other blocks as well, which contributes to the official "≥ others".

The set of sentences underlying the comparison is very different and more importantly that the basis for pairwise comparisons is much smaller than the basis of the official "≥ others" interpretation. The outcome of the official interpretation however depends on the random set of systems your system was compared to. In our case, it is impossible to distinguish, whether CU-TECTO had just bad luck on sentences and systems it was compared to when CU-BOJAR was not in the block and/or whether the 81 blocks do not provide a reliable picture.

2.5.2 Pairwise Judgments Unreliable

To complement WMT10 rankings for the two systems and avoid the possible lower reliability due to 5-fold ranking instead of a targeted compari-

		Author of B says:				
		B>T	T>B	both fine	both wrong	Total
T says:	B>T	9	-	1	1	11
	T>B	2	13	-	3	18
	both fine	2	-	2	3	7
	both wrong	10	5	1	11	27
	Total	23	18	4	18	63

Table 7: Additional annotation of 63 CU-BOJAR (B) vs. CU-TECTO (T) sentences by two annotators.

	Better		Both	
Annotator	B	T	fine	wrong
A	**24**	23	5	11
C	10	**12**	5	36
D	**32**	20	2	9
M	11	**18**	7	27
O	**23**	18	4	18
Z	25	**27**	2	9
Total	**125**	118	25	110

Table 8: Blurry picture of pairwise rankings of CU-BOJAR vs. CU-TECTO. Wins in bold.

son, we asked the main authors of both CU-BOJAR and CU-TECTO to carry out a *blind* pairwise comparison on the exact set of 63 sentences appearing across the 81 blocks in which both systems were ranked. As the totals in Table 7 would suggest, each author unwittingly recognized his system and slightly preferred it. The details however reveal a subtler reason for the low agreement: one of the annotators was less picky about MT quality and accepted 10+5 sentences completely rejected by the other annotator. In total, these two annotators agreed on $9 + 13 + 2 + 11 = 35$ (56%) of cases and their pairwise κ is 0.387.

A further annotation of these 63 sentences by four more people completes the blurry picture: the pairwise κ for each pair of our five annotators ranges from 0.242 to 0.615 with the average 0.407 ± 0.106. The multi-annotator κ (Fleiss, 1971) is 0.394 and all six annotators agree on a single label only in 24% of cases. The agreement is not better even if we merge the categories "Both fine" and "Both wrong" into a single one: The pairwise κ ranges from 0.212 to 0.620 with the average 0.405 ± 0.116, the multi-annotator κ is 0.391. Individual annotations are given in Table 8.

Naturally, the set of these 63 sentences is not a representative sample. Even if one of the systems

		Ranks	
SRC	It's not completely ideal.		
REF	Není to úplně ideální.		
PC-TRANS	To není úplně ideální.	2	5
CU-BOJAR	To není úplně ideální.	5	4

Table 9: Two rankings by the same annotator.

SRC	FCC awarded a tunnel in Slovenia for 64 million
REF	FCC byl přidělen tunel ve Slovinsku za 64 milionů
Gloss	FCC **was** awarded a tunnel in Slovenia for 64 million
HYP1	FCC přidělil tunel ve Slovinsku za 64 miliónů
HYP2	FCC přidělila tunel ve Slovinsku za 64 milionů
Gloss	FCC awarded$^{masc}_{/fem}$ a tunnel in Slovenia for 64 million

Figure 5: A poor reference translation confuses human judges. The SRC and REF differ in the active/passive form, attributing completely different roles to "FCC".

actually won, such an observation could not have been generalized to other test sets. The purpose of the exercise was to check whether we are *at all* able to agree which of the systems translates this specific set of sentences better. As it turns out, even a simple pairwise ranking can fail to provide an answer because different annotators simply have different preferences.

Finally, Table 9 illustrates how poor the WMT10 rankings can be. The exact same string produced by two systems was ranked differently each time – by the same annotator. (The hypothesis is a plausible translation, only the information structure of the sentence is slightly distorted so the translation may not fit well it the surrounding context.)

3 The Impact of the Reference Translation

3.1 Bad Reference Translations

Figure 5 illustrates the impact of poor reference translation on manual ranking as carried out in Section 2.5.2. Of our six independent annotations, three annotators marked the hypotheses as "both fine" given the match with the source and three annotators marked them as "both wrong" due to the mismatch with the reference. Given the construction of the WMT test set, this particular sentence comes from a Spanish original and it was most likely translated directly to both English and Czech.

Source	Target	Correlation of Reference vs. "≥ others"
Spanish	English	0.341
English	French	0.164
French	English	0.098
German	English	0.088
Czech	English	-0.041
English	Czech	-0.145
English	Spanish	-0.411
English	German	-0.433
Overall		-0.107

Table 10: Pearson's correlation of the relative percentage of blocks where the reference was included in the ranking and the final "≥ others" of the system (the reference itself is not included among the considered systems).

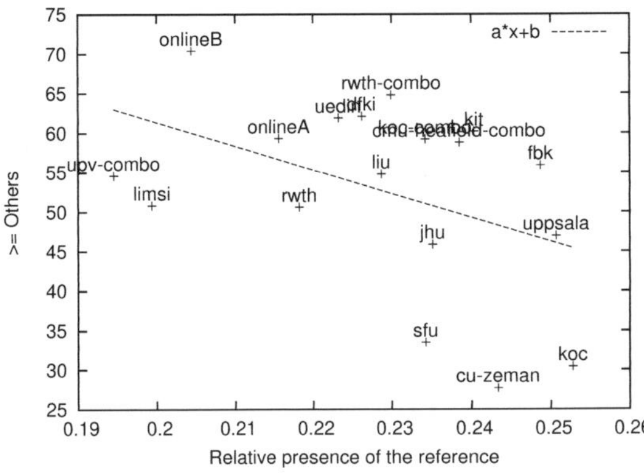

Figure 6: Correlation of the presence of the reference and the official "≥ others" for English-German evaluation.

3.2 Reference Can Skew Pairwise Comparisons

The exact set of competing systems in each 5-fold ranking in WMT10 evaluation is random. The "≥ others" however is affected by this: a system may suffer more losses if often compared to the reference, and similarly it may benefit from being compared to a poor competitor.

To check this, we calculate the correlation between the relative presence of the reference among the blocks where a system was judged and the system's official "≥ others" score. Across language, there is almost no correlation (Pearson's coefficient: -0.107). However, for some language pairs, the correlation is apparent, as listed in Table 10. Negative correlation means: the more often the system was compared along with the reference, the worse the score of the system.

Figure 6 plots the extreme case of English-German evaluation.

Source	Target	Min	Avg±StdDev	Max
English	Czech	40	65±19	115
English	French	40	66±17	110
English	German	10	40±16	80
English	Spanish	30	54±15	85
Czech	English	5	38±13	60
French	English	5	37±15	70
German	English	10	32±12	65
Spanish	English	35	56±11	70

Table 11: The number of post-edits per system for each language pair to complement Figure 3 (page 12) of the WMT10 overview paper.

4 Other WMT10 Tasks

4.1 Blind Post-Editing Unreliable

WMT often carries out one more type of manual evaluation: "Editing the output of systems without displaying the source or a reference translation, and then later judging whether edited translations were correct." (Callison-Burch et al., 2010). We call the evaluation "blind post-editing" for short.

We feel that blind post-editing is more informative than system ranking. First, it constitutes a unique comprehensibility test, and after all, MT should aim at comprehensible output in the first place. Second, blind post-editing can be further analyzed to search for specific errors in system output, see Bojar (2011) for a preliminary study.

Unfortunately, the amount of post-edits collected in WMT10 varied a lot across systems and language pairs. Table 11 provides the minimum, average and maximum number of post-edits of outputs of a particular MT system. We see that e.g. while English-to-Czech has many judgments of this kind per system, Czech-to-English is one of the worst supported directions.

It is not surprising that conclusions based on 5 observations can be extremely deceiving. For instance CU-BOJAR seems to produce 60% of outputs comprehensible (and thus wins in Figure 3 on page 12 in the WMT overview paper), far better than CMU. This is not in line with the ranking results where both rank equally (Table 5 on page 10 in the WMT overview paper). In fact, CU-BOJAR was post-edited 5 times and 3 of these post-edits were acceptable while CMU was post-edited 30 times and 5 of these post-edits were acceptable.

4.2 A Remark on System Combination Task

One results of WMT10 not observed in previous years was that system combinations indeed performed better than individual systems. Previous

Sententes	Dev Set 455	Test Set 2034	Diff
GOOGLE	17.32±1.25	16.76±0.60	↘
BOJAR	16.00±1.15	16.90±0.61	↗
TECTOMT	11.48±1.04	13.19±0.58	↗
PC-TRANS	10.24±0.92	10.84±0.46	↗
EUROTRAN	9.64±0.92	11.04±0.48	↗

Table 12: BLEU scores of sample five systems in English-to-Czech combination task.

years failed to show this clearly, because Google Translate used to be included among the combined systems, making it hard to improve. In WMT10, Google Translate was excluded from system combination task (except for translations involving Czech, where it was accidentally included).

Our Table 12 provides an additional explanation why the presence of Google among combined systems leads to inconclusive results. While the test set was easier (based on BLEU) than the development set for most systems, it was much harder for Google. All system combinations were thus likely to overfit and select Google n-grams most often. Without access to Google powerful language models, the combination systems were likely to underperform Google in final fluency of the output.

5 Further Issues of Manual Evaluation

We have already seen that the comprehensibility test by blind post-editing provides a different picture of the systems than the official ranking. Berka et al. (2011) introduced a third "quiz-based evaluation". The quiz-like evaluation used the English-to-Czech WMT10 systems, applied to different texts: short text snippets were translated and annotators were asked to answer three yes/no questions complementing each snippet. The order of the systems was rather different from the official WMT10 results: CU-TECTO won the quiz-based evaluation despite being the fourth in WMT10.

Because the texts were different in WMT10 and the quiz-based evaluation, we asked a small group of annotators to apply the ranking technique on the text snippets. While not exactly comparable to the WMT10 ranking, the WMT10 ranking was confirmed: CU-TECTO was again among the lowest-scoring systems and Google won the ranking.

Bojar (2011) applies the error-flagging manual evaluation by Vilar et al. (2006) to four systems of WMT09 English-to-Czech task. Again, the overall order of the systems is somewhat different when ranked by the number of errors flagged. Mireia Farrús and Fonollosa (2010) use a coarser but linguistically motivated error classification for Catalan-Spanish and suggest that differences in ranking are caused by annotators treating some types of errors as more serious.

In short, different types of manual evaluations lead to different results even when identical systems and texts are evaluated.

6 Conclusion

We took a deeper look at the results of the WMT10 manual evaluation, and based on our observations, we have some recommendations for future evaluations:

- We propose to use a score which ignores ties instead of the official "$\geq$ others" metric which rewards ties and "$>$ others" which penalizes ties. Another score, "$\geq$ all in block", could help identify which systems are more dominant.
- Inter-annotator agreement decreases dramatically with sentence length; we recommend including fewer sentences per block, at least for longer sentences.
- We suggest agreement be measured based on an empirical estimate of $P(E)$, or at least using a more correct random clicking $P(E) = 0.36$.
- There is evidence of a negative correlation between the number of times a system is judged and its score; we recommend a deeper analysis of this issue.
- We recommend the reference be sampled at a lower rate than other systems, so as to play a smaller role in the evaluation. We also recommend better quality control over the production of the references.

And to the readers of the WMT overview paper, we point out:

- Pairwise comparisons derived from 5-fold rankings are sometimes unreliable. Even a targeted pairwise comparison of two systems can shed little light as to which is superior.
- The acceptability of post-edits is sometimes very unreliable due to the low number of observations.

References

R. Artstein and M. Poesio. 2008. Inter-coder agreement for computational linguistics. *Computational Linguistics*, 34(4):555–596.

John J. Bartko and William T. Carpenter. 1976. On the methods and theory of reliability. *Journal of Nervous and Mental Disease*, 163(5):307–317.

E. M. Bennett, R. Alpert, and A. C. Goldstein. 1954. Communications through limited questioning. *Public Opinion Quarterly*, 18(3):303–308.

Jan Berka, Martin Černý, and Ondřej Bojar. 2011. Quiz-Based Evaluation of Machine Translation. *Prague Bulletin of Mathematical Linguistics*, 95:77–86, March.

Ondřej Bojar. 2011. Analyzing Error Types in English-Czech Machine Translation. *Prague Bulletin of Mathematical Linguistics*, 95:63–76, March.

Chris Callison-Burch, Philipp Koehn, Christof Monz, Kay Peterson, Mark Przybocki, and Omar Zaidan. 2010. Findings of the 2010 joint workshop on statistical machine translation and metrics for machine translation. In *Proceedings of the Joint Fifth Workshop on Statistical Machine Translation and MetricsMATR*, pages 17–53, Uppsala, Sweden, July. Association for Computational Linguistics.

Jacob Cohen. 1960. A coefficient of agreement for nominal scales. *Educational and Psychological Measurement*, 20(1):37–46.

Barbara Di Eugenio and Michael Glass. 2004. The kappa statistic: A second look. *Computational linguistics*, 30(1):95–101.

J. L. Fleiss. 1971. Measuring nominal scale agreement among many raters. *Psychological Bulletin*, 76(5):378–382.

Klaus Krippendorff. 1980. *Content Analysis: An Introduction to Its Methodology*. Sage Publications, Beverly Hills, CA. Chapter 12.

J. Richard Landis and Gary G. Koch. 1977. The measurement of observer agreement for categorical data. *Biometrics*, 33:159–174.

José B. Mariño Mireia Farrús, Marta R. Costa-jussà and José A. R. Fonollosa. 2010. Linguistic-based evaluation criteria to identify statistical machine translation errors. In *Proceedings of the 14th Annual Conference of the Euoropean Association for Machine Translation (EAMT'10)*, pages 167–173, May.

William A. Scott. 1955. Reliability of content analysis: The case of nominal scale coding. *Public Opinion Quarterly*, 19(3):321–325.

David Vilar, Jia Xu, Luis Fernando D'Haro, and Hermann Ney. 2006. Error Analysis of Machine Translation Output. In *International Conference on Language Resources and Evaluation*, pages 697–702, Genoa, Italy, May.

A Lightweight Evaluation Framework for Machine Translation Reordering

David Talbot[1] and **Hideto Kazawa**[2] and **Hiroshi Ichikawa**[2]
Jason Katz-Brown[2] and **Masakazu Seno**[2] and **Franz J. Och**[1]

[1] Google Inc.
1600 Amphitheatre Parkway
Mountain View, CA 94043
{talbot, och}@google.com

[2] Google Japan
Roppongi Hills Mori Tower
6-10-1 Roppongi, Tokyo 106-6126
{kazawa, ichikawa}@google.com
{jasonkb, seno}@google.com

Abstract

Reordering is a major challenge for machine translation between distant languages. Recent work has shown that evaluation metrics that explicitly account for target language word order correlate better with human judgments of translation quality. Here we present a simple framework for evaluating word order independently of lexical choice by comparing the system's reordering of a source sentence to reference reordering data generated from manually word-aligned translations. When used to evaluate a system that performs reordering as a preprocessing step our framework allows the parser and reordering rules to be evaluated extremely quickly without time-consuming end-to-end machine translation experiments. A novelty of our approach is that the translations used to generate the reordering reference data are generated in an *alignment-oriented* fashion. We show that how the alignments are generated can significantly effect the robustness of the evaluation. We also outline some ways in which this framework has allowed our group to analyze reordering errors for English to Japanese machine translation.

1 Introduction

Statistical machine translation systems can perform poorly on distant language pairs such as English and Japanese. Reordering errors are a major source of poor or misleading translations in such systems (Isozaki et al., 2010). Unfortunately the standard evaluation metrics used by the statistical machine translation community are relatively insensitive to the long-distance reordering phenomena encountered when translating between such languages (Birch et al., 2010).

The ability to rapidly evaluate the impact of changes on a system can significantly accelerate the experimental cycle. In a large statistical machine translation system, we should ideally be able to experiment with separate components without retraining the complete system. Measures such as perplexity have been successfully used to evaluate language models independently in speech recognition eliminating some of the need for end-to-end speech recognition experiments. In machine translation, alignment error rate has been used with some mixed success to evaluate word-alignment algorithms but no standard evaluation frameworks exist for other components of a machine translation system (Fraser and Marcu, 2007).

Unfortunately, BLEU (Papineni et al., 2001) and other metrics that work with the final output of a machine translation system are both insensitive to reordering phenomena and relatively time-consuming to compute: changes to the system may require the realignment of the parallel training data, extraction of phrasal statistics and translation of a test set. As training sets grow in size, the cost of end-to-end experimentation can become significant. However, it is not clear that measurements made on any single part of the system will correlate well with human judgments of the translation quality of the whole system.

Following Collins et al. (2005a) and Wang (2007), Xu et al. (2009) showed that when translating from English to Japanese (and to other SOV languages such as Korean and Turkish) applying reordering as

Proceedings of the 6th Workshop on Statistical Machine Translation, pages 12–21,
Edinburgh, Scotland, UK, July 30–31, 2011.

a preprocessing step that manipulates a source sentence parse tree can significantly outperform state-of-the-art phrase-based and hierarchical machine translation systems. This result is corroborated by Birch et al. (2009) whose results suggest that both phrase-based and hierarchical translation systems fail to capture long-distance reordering phenomena.

In this paper we describe a lightweight framework for measuring the quality of the reordering components in a machine translation system. While our framework can be applied to any translation system in which it is possible to derive a token-level alignment from the input source tokens to the output target tokens, it is of particular practical interest when applied to a system that performs reordering as a preprocessing step (Xia and McCord, 2004). In this case, as we show, it allows for extremely rapid and sensitive analysis of changes to parser, reordering rules and other reordering components.

In our framework we evaluate the reordering proposed by a system separately from its choice of target words by comparing it to a reference reordering of the sentence generated from a manually word-aligned translation. Unlike previous work (Isozaki et al., 2010), our approach does not rely on the system's output matching the reference translation lexically. This makes the evaluation more robust as there may be many ways to render a source phrase in the target language and we would not wish to penalize one that simply happens not to match the reference.

In the next section we review related work on reordering for translation between distant language pairs and automatic approaches to evaluating reordering in machine translation. We then describe our evaluation framework including certain important details of how our reference reorderings were created. We evaluate the framework by analyzing how robustly it is able to predict improvements in subjective translation quality for an English to Japanese machine translation system. Finally, we describe ways in which the framework has facilitated development of the reordering components in our system.

2 Related Work

2.1 Evaluating Reordering

The ability to automatically evaluate machine translation output has driven progress in statistical machine translation; however, shortcomings of the dominant metric, BLEU (Papineni et al., 2001) , particularly with respect to reordering, have long been recognized (Callison-burch and Osborne, 2006). Reordering has also been identified as a major factor in determining the difficulty of statistical machine translation between two languages (Birch et al., 2008) hence BLEU scores may be most unreliable precisely for those language pairs for which statistical machine translation is most difficult (Isozaki et al., 2010).

There have been many results showing that metrics that account for reordering are better correlated with human judgements of translation quality (Lavie and Denkowski, 2009; Birch and Osborne, 2010; Isozaki et al., 2010). Examples given in Isozaki et al. (2010) where object and subject arguments are reversed in a Japanese to English statistical machine translation system demonstrate how damaging reordering errors can be and it should therefore not come as a surprise that word order is a strong predictor of translation quality; however, there are other advantages to be gained by focusing on this specific aspect of the translation process in isolation.

One problem for all automatic evaluation metrics is that multiple equally good translations can be constructed for most input sentences and typically our reference data will contain only a small fraction of these. Equally good translations for a sentence may differ both in terms of lexical choice and word order. One of the potential advantages of designing a metric that looks only at word order, is that it may, to some extent, factor out variability along the dimension of the lexical choice. Previous work on automatic evaluation metrics that focus on reordering, however, has not fully exploited this.

The evaluation metrics proposed in Isozaki et al. (2010) compute a reordering score by comparing the ordering of unigrams and bigrams that appear in both the system's translation and the reference. These scores are therefore liable to overestimate the reordering quality of sentences that were poorly translated. While Isozaki et al. (2010) does propose a work-around to this problem which combines the reordering score with a lexical precision term, this clearly introduces a bias in the metric whereby poor translations are evaluated primarily on their lexical choice and good translations are evaluated more on the basis of their word order. In our experience word order is particularly poor in those sentences that have the lowest lexical overlap with reference translations; hence we would like to be able to compute the quality of reordering in all sentences independently of the quality of their lexical choice.

Birch and Osborne (2010) are closer to our approach in that they use word alignments to induce a permutation over the source sentence. They compare a source-side permutation generated from a word alignment of the reference translation with one generated from the system's using various permutation distances. However, Birch and Osborne (2010) only demonstrate that these metrics are correlated with human judgements of translation quality when combined with BLEU score and hence take lexical choice into account.

Birch et al. (2010) present the only results we are aware of that compute the correlation between human judgments of translation quality and a reordering-only metric independently of lexical choice. Unfortunately, the experimental set-up there is somewhat flawed. The authors 'undo' reorderings in their reference translations by permuting the reference tokens and presenting the permuted translations to human raters. While many machine translation systems (including our own) assume that reordering and translation can be factored into separate models, e.g. (Xia and McCord, 2004), and perform these two operations in separate steps, the latter conditioned on the former, Birch et al. (2010) are making a much stronger assumption when they perform these simulations: they are assuming that lexical choice and word order are entirely *independent*. It is easy to find cases where this assumption does not hold and we would in general be very surprised if a similar change in the reordering component in our system did not also result in a change in the lexical choice of the system; an effect which their experiments are unable to model.

Another minor difference between our evaluation framework and (Birch et al., 2010) is that we use a reordering score that is based on the minimum number of chunks into which the candidate and reference permutations can be concatenated similar to the reordering component of METEOR (Lavie and Denkowski, 2009). As we show, this is better correlated with human judgments of translation quality than Kendall's τ. This may be due to the fact that it counts the number of 'jumps' a human reader has to make in order to parse the system's order if they wish to read the tokens in the reference word order. Kendall's τ on the other hand penalizes every pair of words that are in the wrong order and hence has a quadratic (all-pairs) flavor which in turn might explain why Birch et al. (2010) found that the square-root of this quantity was a better predictor of translation quality.

2.2 Evaluation Reference Data

To create the word-aligned translations from which we generate our reference reordering data, we used a novel *alignment-oriented* translation method. The method (described in more detail below) seeks to generate reference reorderings that a machine translation system might reasonably be expected to achieve. Fox (2002) has analyzed the extent to which translations seen in a parallel corpus can be broken down into clean phrasal units: they found that most sentence pairs contain examples of reordering that violate phrasal cohesion, i.e. the corresponding words in the target language are not completely contiguous or solely aligned to the corresponding source phrase. These reordering phenomena are difficult for current statistical translation models to learn directly. We therefore deliberately chose to create reference data that avoids these phenomena as much as possible by having a single annotator generate both the translation and its word alignment. Our word-aligned translations are created with a bias towards simple phrasal reordering.

Our analysis of the correlation between reordering scores computed on reference data created from such alignment-oriented translations with scores computed on references generated from standard professional translations of the same sentences suggests that the alignment-oriented translations are more useful for evaluating a current state-of-the-art system. We note also that while prior work has conjectured that automatically generated alignments are a suitable replacement for manual alignments in the context of reordering evaluation (Birch et al., 2008), our results suggest that this is not the case at least for the language pair we consider, English-Japanese.

3 A Lightweight Reordering Evaluation

We now present our lightweight reordering evaluation framework; this consists of (1) a method for generating reference reordering data from manual word-alignments; and (2) a reordering metric for scoring a sytem's proposed reordering against this reference data; and (3) a stand-alone evaluation tool.

3.1 Generating Reference Reordering Data

We follow Birch and Osborne (2010) in using reference reordering data that consists of permuations of source sentences in a test set. We generate these from word alignments of the source sentences to reference translations. Unlike previous work, however, we have the same annotator generate both the reference translation and the word alignment. We also explicitly encourage the translators to generate translations that are easy to align even if this does result in occasionally unnatural translations. For instance in English to Japanese translation we require that all personal pronouns are translated; these are often omitted in natural Japanese. We insist that all but an extremely small set of words (articles and punctuation for English to Japanese) be aligned. We also disprefer non-contiguous alignments of a single source word and require that all target words be aligned to at least one source token. In Japanese this requires deciding how to align particles that mark syntactic roles; we choose to align these together with the content word (*jiritsu-go*) of the corresponding constituent (*bunsetsu*). Asking annotators to translate and perform word alignment on the same sentence in a single session does not necessarily increase the annotation burden over stand-alone word alignment since it encourages the creation of *alignment-friendly* translations which can be aligned more rapidly. Annotators need little special background or training for this task, as long as they can speak both the source and target languages.

To generate a permutation from word alignments we rank the source tokens by the position of the first target token to which they are aligned. If multiple source tokens are aligned to a single target word or span we ignore the ordering within these source spans; this is indicated by braces in Table 2. We place unaligned source words immediately before the next aligned source word or at the end of the sentence if there is none. Table 2 shows the reference reordering derived from various translations and word alignments.

3.2 Fuzzy Reordering Score

To evaluate the quality of a system's reordering against this reference data we use a simple *reordering metric* related to METEOR's reordering component (Lavie and Denkowski, 2009) . Given the reference permutation of the source sentence σ_{ref} and the system's reordering of the source sentence σ_{sys} either generated directly by a reordering component or inferred from the alignment between source and target phrases used in the decoder, we align each word in σ_{sys} to an instance of itself in σ_{ref} taking the first unmatched instance of the word if there is more than one. We then define C to be the number chunks of contiguously aligned words. If M is the number of words in the source sentence then the *fuzzy reordering score* is computed as,

$$\mathbf{FRS}(\sigma_{\text{sys}}, \sigma_{\text{ref}}) = 1 - \frac{C-1}{M-1}. \quad (1)$$

This metric assigns a score between 0 and 1 where 1 indicates that the system's reordering is identical to the reference. C has an intuitive interpretation as the number of times a reader would need to jump in order to read the system's reordering of the sentence in the order proposed by the reference.

3.3 Evaluation Tool

While the framework we propose can be applied to any machine translation system in which a reordering of the source sentence can be inferred from the translation process, it has proven particularly useful applied to a system that performs reordering as a separate preprocessing step. Such *pre-ordering* approaches (Xia and McCord, 2004; Collins et al., 2005b) can be criticized for greedily committing to a single reordering early in the pipeline but in practice they have been shown to perform extremely well on language pairs that require long distance reordering and have been successfully combined with other more integrated reordering models (Xu et al., 2009).

The performance of a parser-based pre-ordering component is a function of the reordering rules and parser; it is therefore desirable that these can be evaluated efficiently. Both parser and reordering rules may be evaluated using end-to-end automatic metrics such as BLEU score or in human evaluations. Parsers may also be evaluated using intrinsic treebank metrics such as labeled accuracy. Unfortunately these metrics are either expensive to compute or, as we show, unpredictive of improvements in human perceptions of translation quality.

Having found that the fuzzy reordering score proposed here is well-correlated with changes in human judgements of translation quality, we established a stand-alone evaluation tool that takes a set of reordering rules and a parser and computes the reordering scores on a set of reference reorderings. This has become the most frequently used method for evaluating changes to the reordering component in our system and has allowed teams working on parsing, for instance, to contribute significant improvements quite independently.

4 Experimental Set-up

We wish to determine whether our evaluation framework can predict which changes to reordering components will result in statistically significant improvements in subjective translation quality of the end-to-end system. To that end we created a number of systems that differ only in terms of reordering components (parser and/or reordering rules). We then analyzed the corpus- and sentence-level correlation of our evaluation metric with judgements of human translation quality.

Previous work has compared either quite separate systems, e.g. (Isozaki et al., 2010), or systems that are artificially different from each other (Birch et al., 2010). There has also been a tendency to measure corpus-level correlation. We are more interested in comparing systems that differ in a realistic manner from one another as would typically be required in development. We also believe sentence-level correlation is more important than corpus-level correlation since good sentence-level correlation implies that a metric can be used for detailed analysis of a system and potentially to optimize it.

4.1 Systems

We carried out all our experiments using a state-of-the-art phrase-based statistical English-to-Japanese machine translation system (Och, 2003). During both training and testing, the system reorders source-language sentences in a preprocessing step using a set of rules written in the framework proposed by (Xu et al., 2009) that reorder an English dependency tree into target word order. During decoding, we set the reordering window to 4 words. In addition to the regular distance distortion model, we incorporate a maximum entropy based lexicalized phrase reordering model (Zens and Ney, 2006). For parallel training data, we use an in-house collection of parallel documents. These come from various sources with a substantial portion coming from the web after using simple heuristics to identify potential document pairs. We trained our system on about 300 million source words.

The reordering rules applied to the English dependency tree define a precedence order for the children of each head category (a coarse-grained part of speech). For example, a simplified version of the precedence order for child labels of a verbal head HEADVERB is: advcl, nsubj, prep, [other children], dobj, prt, aux, neg, HEADVERB, mark, ref, compl.

The dependency parser we use is an implementation of a transition-based dependency parser (Nivre, 2008). The parser is trained using the averaged perceptron algorithm with an early update strategy as described in Zhang and Clark (2008).

We created five systems using different parsers; here *targeted self-training* refers to a training procedure proposed by Katz-Brown et al. (2011) that uses our reordering metric and separate reference reordering data to pick parses for self-training: an n-best list of parses is generated for each English sentence for which we have reference reordering data and the parse tree that results in the highest fuzzy reordering score is added to our parser's training set. Parsers P3, P4 and P5 differ in how that framework is applied and how much data is used.

- P1 Penn Treebank, perceptron, greedy search
- P2 Penn Treebank, perceptron, beam search
- P3 Penn Treebank, perceptron, beam search, targeted self-training on web data

- P4 Penn Treebank, perceptron, beam search, targeted self-training on web data
- P5 Penn Treebank, perceptron, beam search, targeted self-training on web data, case insensitive

We also created five systems using the fifth parser (P5) but with different sets of reordering rules:

- R1 No reordering
- R2 Reverse reordering
- R3 Head final reordering with reverse reordering for words before the head
- R4 Head final reordering with reverse reordering for words after the head
- R5 Superset of rules from (Xu et al., 2009)

Reverse reordering places words in the reverse of the English order. Head final reordering moves the head of each dependency after all its children. Rules in R3 and R4 overlap significantly with the rules for noun and verb subtrees respectively in R5. Otherwise all systems were identical. The rules in R5 have been extensively hand-tuned while R1 and R2 are rather naive. System P5R5 was our best performing system at the time these experiments were conducted.

We refer to systems by a combination of parser and reordering rules set identifiers, for instance, system P2R5, uses parser P2 with reordering rules R5. We conducted two subjective evaluations in which bilingual human raters were asked to judge translations on a scale from 0 to 6 where 0 indicates nonsense and 6 is perfect. The first experiment (Parsers) contrasted systems with different parsers and the second (Rules) varied the reordering rules. In each case three bilingual evaluators were shown the source sentence and the translations produced by all five systems.

4.2 Meta-analysis

We perform a meta-analysis of the following metrics and the framework by computing correlations with the results of these subjective evaluations of translation quality:

1. Evaluation metrics: BLEU score on final translations, Kendall's τ and fuzzy reordering score on reference reordering data
2. Evaluation data: both manually-generated and automatically-generated word alignments on both standard professional and *alignment-oriented* translations of the test sentences

The automatic word alignments were generated using IBM Model 1 in order to avoid directional biases that higher-order models such as HMMs have.

Results presented in square parentheses are 95 percent confidence intervals estimated by bootstrap resampling on the test corpus (Koehn, 2004).

Our test set contains 500 sentences randomly sampled from the web. We have both professional and *alignment-friendly* translations for these sentences. We created reference reorderings for this data using the method described in Section 3.1. The lack of a broad domain and publically available Japanese test corpus makes the use of this non-standard test set unfortunately unavoidable.

The human raters were presented with the source sentence, the human reference translation and the translations of the various systems simultaneously, blind and in a random order. Each rater was allowed to rate no more than 3 percent of the sentences and three ratings were elicited for each sentence. Ratings were a single number between 0 and 6 where 0 indicates nonsense and 6 indicates a perfectly grammatical translation of the source sentence.

5 Results

Table 2 shows four reference reorderings generated from various translations and word alignments. The automatic alignments are significantly sparser than the manual ones but in these examples the reference reorderings still seem reasonable. Note how the alignment-oriented translation includes a pronoun (translation for 'I') that is dropped in the slightly more natural standard translation to Japanese.

Table 1 shows the human judgements of translation quality for the 10 systems (note that P5R5 appears in both experiments but was scored differently as human judgments are affected by which other translations are present in an experiment). There is a clear ordering of the systems in each experiment and

1. Parsers	Subjective Score (0-6)	2. Rules	Subjective Score (0-6)
P1R5	2.173 [2.086, 2.260]	P5R1	1.258 [1.191, 1.325]
P2R5	2.320 [2.233, 2.407]	P5R2	1.825 [1.746, 1.905]
P3R5	2.410 [2.321, 2.499]	P5R3	1.849 [1.767, 1.931]
P4R5	2.453 [2.366, 2.541]	P5R4	2.205 [2.118, 2.293]
P5R5	2.501 [2.413, 2.587]	P5R5	2.529 [2.441, 2.619]

Table 1: Human judgements of translation quality for 1. Parsers and 2. Rules.

Metric	Sentence-level correlation	
	r	ρ
Fuzzy reordering	0.435	0.448
Kendall's τ	0.371	0.450
BLEU	0.279	0.302

Table 6: Pearson's correlation (r) and Spearman's rank correlation (ρ) with subjective translation quality at sentence-level.

Translation	Alignment	Sentence-level	
		r	ρ
Alignment-oriented	Manual	0.435	0.448
Alignment-oriented	Automatic	0.234	0.252
Standard	Manual	0.271	0.257
Standard	Automatic	0.177	0.159

Table 7: Pearson's correlation (r) and Spearman's rank correlation (ρ) with subjective translation quality at the sentence-level for different types of reordering reference data: (i) alignment-oriented translation vs. standard, (ii) manual vs. automatic alignment.

we see that both the choice of parser and reordering rules clearly effects subjective translation quality.

We performed pairwise significance tests using bootstrap resampling for each pair of 'improved' systems in each experiment. Tables 3, 4 and 5 shows which pairs were judged to be statistically significant improvements at either 95 or 90 percent level under the different metrics. These tests were computed on the same 500 sentences. All pairs but one are judged to be statistically significant improvements in subjective translation quality. Significance tests performed using the fuzzy reordering metric are identical to the subjective scores for the Parsers experiment but differ on one pairwise comparison for the Rules experiment. According to BLEU score, however, none of the parser changes are significant at the 95 percent level and only one pairwise comparison (between the two most different systems) was significant at the 90 percent level. BLEU score appears more sensitive to the larger changes in the Rules experiment but is still in disagreement with the results of the human evaluation on four pairwise comparisons.

Table 6 shows the sentence-level correlation of different metrics with human judgments of translation quality. Here both the fuzzy reordering score and Kendall's τ are computed on the reference reordering data generated as described in Section 3.1. Both metrics are computed by running our lightweight evaluation tool and involve no translation whatsoever. These lightweight metrics are also more correlated with subjective quality than BLEU score at the sentence level.

Table 7 shows how the correlation between fuzzy reordering score and subjective translation quality degrades as we move from manual to automatic alignments and from alignment-oriented translations to standard ones. The automatically aligned references, in particular, are less correlated with subjective translation scores then BLEU; we believe this may be due to the poor quality of word alignments for languages such as English and Japanese due to the long-distance reordering between them.

Finally we present some intrinsic evaluation metrics for the parsers used in the first of our experiments. Table 8 demonstrates that certain changes may not be best captured by standard parser benchmarks. While the first four parser models improve on the WSJ benchmarks as they improve subjective translation quality the best parser according to subjective translation qualtiy (P5) is actually the worst under both metrics on the treebank data. We conjecture that this is due to the fact that P5 (unlike the other parsers) is case insensitive. While this helps us significantly on our test set drawn from the web, it

Standard / Manual	
Source	How Can I Qualify For A Mortgage Tax Deduction ?
Reordering	A Mortgage {{ Tax Deduction }} For I Qualify How Can ?
Translation	住宅 ローン 減税 に 必要 な 資格 を 得る に は どう すれ ば よい です か ？
Alignment	6,6,7_8,4,3,3,3,3,3,0,0,0,0,0,1,1,9,9

Alignment-oriented / Manual	
Source	How Can I Qualify For A Mortgage Tax Deduction ?
Reordering	I How A Mortgage {{ Tax Deduction }} For Qualify Can ?
Translation	私 は どう し たら 住宅 ローン の 減税 の 資格 に 値する こと が でき ます か ？
Alignment	2,2,0,0,0,6,6,6,7_8,4,3,3,3,1,1,1,1,1,9

Standard / Automatic	
Source	We do not claim to cure , prevent or treat any disease .
Reordering	any disease cure , prevent or treat claim to We do not .
Translation	いかなる 病気 の 治癒 ， 防止 ， または 治療 も 断言 する もの で は あり ませ ん ．
Alignment	10,11,,5,6,7,,8,9,,,4,,,,2,2,2,12

Alignment-oriented / Automatic	
Source	We do not claim to cure , prevent or treat any disease .
Reordering	We any disease cure , prevent or treat claim to do not .
Translation	私 達 は あらゆる 疾患 の 治癒 ， 予防 あるいは 治療 を 行う と 主張 し ませ ん ．
Alignment	0,0,,10,11,,5,6,7,8,9,,,,3,4,2,2,12

Table 2: Reference reordering data generated via various methods: (i) alignment-oriented vs. standard translation, (ii) manual vs. automatic word alignment

	Exp. 1 Parsers					Exp. 2 Reordering Rules			
	P2R5	P3R5	P4R5	P5R5		P5R2	P5R3	P5R4	P5R5
P1R5	+**	+**	+**	+**	P5R1	+**	+**	+**	+**
P2R5		+**	+**	+**	P5R2		0	+**	+**
P3R5				+**	P5R3			+**	+**
P4R5				0	P5R4				+**

Table 3: Pairwise significance in subjective evaluation (0 = not significant, * = 90 percent, ** = 95 percent).

	Exp. 1 Parsers					Exp. 2 Reordering Rules			
	P2R5	P3R5	P4R5	P5R5		P5R2	P5R3	P5R4	P5R5
P1R5	+**	+**	+**	+**	P5R1	0	+**	+**	+**
P2R5		+**	+**	+**	P5R2		+**	+**	+**
P3R5			+**	+**	P5R3			+**	+**
P4R5				0	P5R4				+**

Table 4: Pairwise significance in fuzzy reordering score (0 = not significant, * = 90 percent, ** = 95 percent).

	Exp. 1 Parsers					Exp. 2 Reordering Rules			
	P2R5	P3R5	P4R5	P5R5		P5R2	P5R3	P5R4	P5R5
P1R5	0	0	+*	+*	P5R1	+**	+**	+**	+**
P2R5		0	0	0	P5R2		0	+**	+**
P3R5			0	0	P5R3			0	+*
P4R5				0	P5R4				0

Table 5: Pairwise significance in BLEU score (0 = not significant, * = 90 percent, ** = 95 percent).

Parser	Labeled attachment	POS accuracy
P1	0.807	0.954
P2	0.822	0.954
P3	0.827	0.955
P4	0.830	0.955
P5	0.822	0.944

Table 8: Intrinsic parser metrics on WSJ dev set.

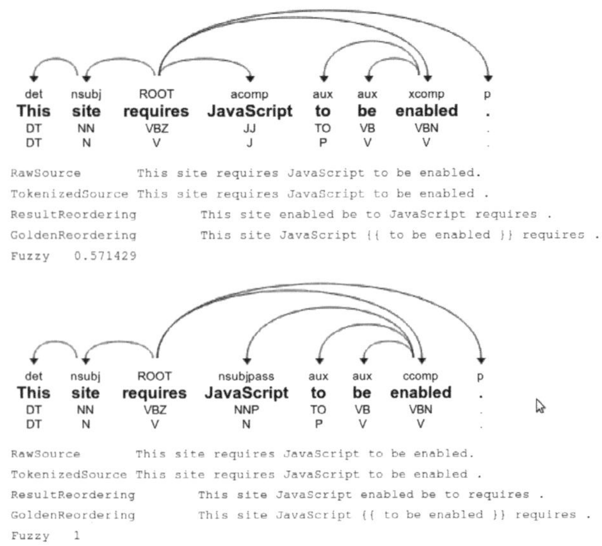

Figure 1: P1 and P5's parse trees and automatic reordering (using R5 ruleset) and fuzzy score.

hurts parsing performance on cleaner newswire.

6 Discussion

We have found that in practice this evaluation framework is sufficiently correlated with human judgments of translation quality to be rather useful for performing detailed error analysis of our English-to-Japanese system. We have used it in the following ways in simple error analysis sessions:

- To identify which words are most frequently reordered incorrectly
- To identify systematic parser and/or POS errors
- To identify the worst reordered sentences
- To evaluate individual reordering rules

Figures 1 and 2 show pairs of parse trees together with their resulting reorderings and scores against

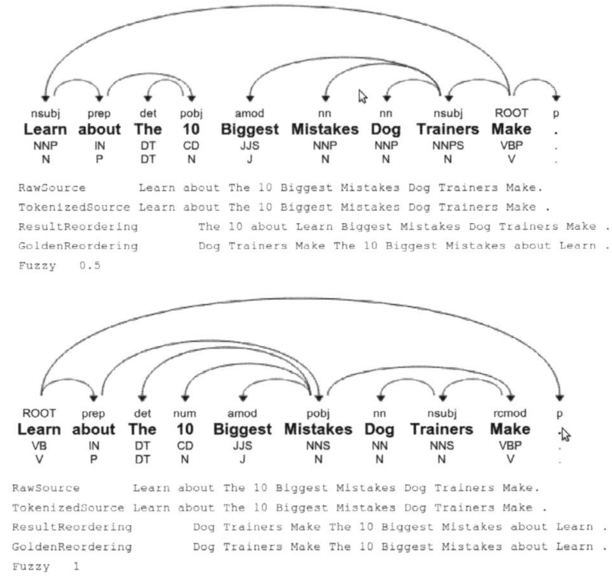

Figure 2: P1 and P5's parse trees and automatic reordering (using R5 ruleset) and fuzzy score.

the reference. These are typical of the parser errors that impact reordering and which are correctly identified by our framework. In related joint work (Katz-Brown et al., 2011) and (Hall et al., 2011), it is shown that the framework can be used to optimize reordering components automatically.

7 Conclusions

We have presented a lightweight framework for evaluating reordering in machine translation and demonstrated that this is able to accurately distinguish significant changes in translation quality due to changes in preprocessing components such as the parser or reordering rules used by the system. The sentence-level correlation of our metric with judgements of human translation quality was shown to be higher than other standard evaluation metrics while our evaluation has the significant practical advantage of not requiring an end-to-end machine translation experiment when used to evaluate a separate reordering component. Our analysis has also highlighted the benefits of creating focused evaluation data that attempts to factor out some of the phenomena found in real human translation. While previous work has provided meta-analysis of reordering metrics across quite independent systems, ours is we believe the first to provide a detailed comparison of systems that differ only in small but realistic aspects such as parser quality. In future work we plan to use the framework to provide a more comprehensive analysis of the reordering capabilities of a broad range of machine translation systems.

References

Alexandra Birch and Miles Osborne. 2010. Lrscore for evaluating lexical and reordering quality in mt. In *Proceedings of the Joint Fifth Workshop on Statistical Machine Translation and MetricsMATR*, pages 327–332, Uppsala, Sweden, July.

Alexandra Birch, Miles Osborne, and Philipp Koehn. 2008. Predicting success in machine translation. In *Proceedings of the 2008 Conference on Empirical Methods in Natural Language Processing*, pages 745–754, Honolulu, Hawaii, October. Association for Computational Linguistics.

Alexandra Birch, Phil Blunsom, and Miles Osborne. 2009. A quantitative analysis of reordering phenomena. In *Proceedings of the Fourth Workshop on Statistical Machine Translation*, pages 197–205, Athens, Greece, March.

Alexandra Birch, Miles Osborne, and Phil Blunsom. 2010. Metrics for mt evaluation: evaluating reordering. *Machine Translation*, 24:15–26, March.

Chris Callison-burch and Miles Osborne. 2006. Reevaluating the role of bleu in machine translation research. In *In EACL*, pages 249–256.

Michael Collins, Philipp Koehn, and Ivona Kucerova. 2005a. Clause restructuring for statistical machine translation. In *Proceedings of the 43rd Annual Meeting of the Association for Computational Linguistics (ACL'05)*, pages 531–540, Ann Arbor, Michigan, June. Association for Computational Linguistics.

Michael Collins, Philipp Koehn, and Ivona Kučerová. 2005b. Clause restructuring for statistical machine translation. In *Proceedings of the 43rd Annual Meeting on Association for Computational Linguistics*, ACL '05, pages 531–540, Stroudsburg, PA, USA. Association for Computational Linguistics.

Heidi Fox. 2002. Phrasal cohesion and statistical machine translation. In *Proceedings of the 2002 Conference on Empirical Methods in Natural Language Processing*, pages 304–3111, July.

Alexander Fraser and Daniel Marcu. 2007. Measuring word alignment quality for statistical machine translation. *Comput. Linguist.*, 33:293–303, September.

Keith Hall, Ryan McDonald, and Jason Katz-Brown. 2011. Training dependency parsers by jointly optimizing multiple objective functions. In *Proc. of EMNLP 2011*.

Hideki Isozaki, Tsutomu Hirao, Kevin Duh, Katsuhito Sudoh, and Hajime Tsukada. 2010. Automatic evaluation of translation quality for distant language pairs. In *Proceedings of the 2010 Conference on Empirical Methods in Natural Language Processing*, pages 944–952, Cambridge, MA, October. Association for Computational Linguistics.

Jason Katz-Brown, Slav Petrov, Ryan McDonald, Franz Och, David Talbot, Hiroshi Ichikawa, Masakazu Seno, and Hideto Kazawa. 2011. Training a Parser for Machine Translation Reordering. In *Proc. of EMNLP 2011*.

Philipp Koehn. 2004. Statistical significance tests for machine translation evaluation. In *EMNLP*, pages 388–395.

Alon Lavie and Michael J. Denkowski. 2009. The meteor metric for automatic evaluation of machine translation. *Machine Translation*, 23(2-3):105–115.

J. Nivre. 2008. Algorithms for deterministic incremental dependency parsing. *Computational Linguistics*, 34(4):513–553.

F. Och. 2003. Minimum error rate training in statistical machine translation. In *ACL '03*.

Kishore Papineni, Salim Roukos, Todd Ward, and Wei-Jing Zhu. 2001. Bleu: a method for automatic evaluation of machine translation. In *ACL '02: Proceedings of the 40th Annual Meeting on Association for Computational Linguistics*, pages 311–318, Morristown, NJ, USA. Association for Computational Linguistics.

Chao Wang. 2007. Chinese syntactic reordering for statistical machine translation. In *In Proceedings of EMNLP*, pages 737–745.

Fei Xia and Michael McCord. 2004. Improving a statistical mt system with automatically learned rewrite patterns. In *Proceedings of the 20th international conference on Computational Linguistics*, COLING '04, Stroudsburg, PA, USA. Association for Computational Linguistics.

Peng Xu, Jaeho Kang, Michael Ringgaard, and Franz Och. 2009. Using a dependency parser to improve SMT for subject-object-verb languages. In *Proceedings of Human Language Technologies: The 2009 Annual Conference of the North American Chapter of the Association for Computational Linguistics*, pages 245–253, Boulder, Colorado, June.

Richard Zens and Hermann Ney. 2006. Discriminative reordering models for statistical machine translation. In *Proceedings of the Workshop on Statistical Machine Translation*, pages 55–63.

Y. Zhang and S. Clark. 2008. A Tale of Two Parsers: Investigating and Combining Graph-based and Transition-based Dependency Parsing. In *Proc. of EMNLP*.

Findings of the 2011 Workshop on Statistical Machine Translation

Chris Callison-Burch
Center for Language and Speech Processing
Johns Hopkins University

Philipp Koehn
School of Informatics
University of Edinburgh

Christof Monz
Informatics Institute
University of Amsterdam

Omar F. Zaidan
Center for Language and Speech Processing
Johns Hopkins University

Abstract

This paper presents the results of the WMT11 shared tasks, which included a translation task, a system combination task, and a task for machine translation evaluation metrics. We conducted a large-scale manual evaluation of 148 machine translation systems and 41 system combination entries. We used the ranking of these systems to measure how strongly automatic metrics correlate with human judgments of translation quality for 21 evaluation metrics. This year featured a Haitian Creole to English task translating SMS messages sent to an emergency response service in the aftermath of the Haitian earthquake. We also conducted a pilot 'tunable metrics' task to test whether optimizing a fixed system to different metrics would result in perceptibly different translation quality.

1 Introduction

This paper presents the results of the shared tasks of the Workshop on statistical Machine Translation (WMT), which was held at EMNLP 2011. This workshop builds on five previous WMT workshops (Koehn and Monz, 2006; Callison-Burch et al., 2007; Callison-Burch et al., 2008; Callison-Burch et al., 2009; Callison-Burch et al., 2010). The workshops feature three shared tasks: a translation task between English and other languages, a task to combine the output of multiple machine translation systems, and a task to predict human judgments of translation quality using automatic evaluation metrics. The performance for each of these shared tasks is determined through a comprehensive human evaluation. There were a two additions to this year's workshop that were not part of previous workshops:

- **Haitian Creole featured task** – In addition to translation between European language pairs, we featured a new translation task: translating Haitian Creole SMS messages that were sent to an emergency response hotline in the immediate aftermath of the 2010 Haitian earthquake. The goal of this task is to encourage researchers to focus on challenges that may arise in future humanitarian crises. We invited Will Lewis, Rob Munro and Stephan Vogel to publish a paper about their experience developing translation technology in response to the crisis (Lewis et al., 2011). They provided the data used in the Haitian Creole featured translation task. We hope that the introduction of this new dataset will provide a testbed for dealing with low resource languages and the informal language usage found in SMS messages.

- **Tunable metric shared task** – We conducted a pilot of a new shared task to use evaluation metrics to tune the parameters of a machine translation system. Although previous workshops have shown evaluation metrics other than BLEU are more strongly correlated with human judgments when ranking outputs from multiple systems, BLEU remains widely used by system developers to optimize their system parameters. We challenged metric developers to tune the parameters of a fixed system, to see if their metrics would lead to perceptibly better translation quality for the system's resulting output.

Proceedings of the 6th Workshop on Statistical Machine Translation, pages 22–64,
Edinburgh, Scotland, UK, July 30–31, 2011.

The primary objectives of WMT are to evaluate the state of the art in machine translation, to disseminate common test sets and public training data with published performance numbers, and to refine evaluation methodologies for machine translation. As with previous workshops, all of the data, translations, and collected human judgments are publicly available.[1] We hope these datasets form a valuable resource for research into statistical machine translation, system combination, and automatic evaluation of translation quality.

2 Overview of the Shared Translation and System Combination Tasks

The recurring task of the workshop examines translation between English and four other languages: German, Spanish, French, and Czech. We created a test set for each language pair by translating newspaper articles. We additionally provided training data and two baseline systems.

2.1 Test data

The test data for this year's task was created by hiring people to translate news articles that were drawn from a variety of sources from early December 2010. A total of 110 articles were selected, in roughly equal amounts from a variety of Czech, English, French, German, and Spanish news sites:[2]

Czech: aktualne.cz (4), Novinky.cz (7), iHNed.cz (4), iDNES.cz (4)

French: Canoe (5), Le Devoir (5), Le Monde (5), Les Echos (5), Liberation (5)

Spanish: ABC.es (6), Cinco Dias (6), El Periodico (6), Milenio (6), Noroeste (7)

English: Economist (4), Los Angeles Times (6), New York Times (4), Washington Post (4)

German: FAZ (3), Frankfurter Rundschau (2), Financial Times Deutschland (3), Der Spiegel (5), Süddeutsche Zeitung (3)

The translations were created by the professional translation agency CEET.[3] All of the translations were done directly, and not via an intermediate language.

Although the translations were done professionally, in some cases errors still cropped up. For instance, in parts of the English-French translations, some of the English source remains in the French reference as if the translator forgot to delete it.

2.2 Training data

As in past years we provided parallel corpora to train translation models, monolingual corpora to train language models, and development sets to tune system parameters. Some statistics about the training materials are given in Figure 1.

2.3 Baseline systems

To lower the barrier of entry for newcomers to the field, we provided two open source toolkits for phrase-based and parsing-based statistical machine translation (Koehn et al., 2007; Li et al., 2010).

2.4 Submitted systems

We received submissions from 56 groups across 37 institutions, as listed in Tables 1, 2 and 3. We also included two commercial off-the-shelf MT systems, two online statistical MT systems, and five online rule-based MT systems. (Not all systems supported all language pairs.) We note that these nine companies did not submit entries themselves, and are therefore anonymized in this paper. Rather, their entries were created by translating the test data via their web interfaces.[4] The data used to construct these systems is not subject to the same constraints as the shared task participants. It is possible that part of the reference translations that were taken from online news sites could have been included in the online systems' models, for instance. We therefore categorize all commercial systems as unconstrained when evaluating the results.

2.5 System combination

In total, we had 148 primary system entries (including the 46 entries crawled from online sources), and 60 contrastive entries. These were made available to

[1] `http://statmt.org/wmt11/results.html`

[2] For more details see the XML test files. The `docid` tag gives the source and the date for each document in the test set, and the `origlang` tag indicates the original source language.

[3] `http://www.ceet.eu/`

[4] We would like to thank Ondřej Bojar for harvesting the commercial entries (2), Christian Federmann for the statistical MT entries (14), and Hervé Saint-Amand for the rule-based MT entries (30)!

Europarl Training Corpus

	Spanish ↔ English		French ↔ English		German ↔ English		Czech ↔ English	
Sentences	1,786,594		1,825,077		1,739,154		462,351	
Words	51,551,370	49,411,045	54,568,499	50,551,047	45,607,269	47,978,832	10,573,983	12,296,772
Distinct words	171,174	113,655	137,034	114,487	362,563	111,934	152,788	56,095

News Commentary Training Corpus

	Spanish ↔ English		French ↔ English		German ↔ English		Czech ↔ English	
Sentences	132,571		115,562		136,227		122,754	
Words	3,739,293	3,285,305	3,290,280	2,866,929	3,401,766	3,309,619	2,658,688	2,951,357
Distinct words	73,906	53,699	59,911	50,323	120,397	53,921	130,685	50,457

United Nations Training Corpus

	Spanish ↔ English		French ↔ English	
Sentences	10,662,993		12,317,600	
Words	348,587,865	304,724,768	393,499,429	344,026,111
Distinct words	578,599	564,489	621,721	729,233

10^9 Word Parallel Corpus

	French ↔ English	
Sentences	22,520,400	
Words	811,203,407	668,412,817
Distinct words	2,738,882	2,861,836

CzEng Training Corpus

	Czech ↔ English	
Sentences	7,227,409	
Words	72,993,427	84,856,749
Distinct words	1,088,642	522,770

Europarl Language Model Data

	English	Spanish	French	German	Czech
Sentence	2,032,006	1,942,761	2,002,266	1,985,560	479,636
Words	54,720,731	55,105,358	57,860,307	48,648,697	10,770,230
Distinct words	119,315	176,896	141,742	376,128	154,129

News Language Model Data

	English	Spanish	French	German	Czech
Sentence	30,888,595	3,416,184	11,767,048	17,474,133	12,333,268
Words	777,425,517	107,088,554	302,161,808	289,171,939	216,692,489
Distinct words	2,020,549	595,681	1,250,259	3,091,700	2,068,056

News Test Set

	English	Spanish	French	German	Czech
Sentences	3003				
Words	75,762	79,710	85,999	73,729	65,427
Distinct words	10,088	11,989	11,584	14,345	16,922

Figure 1: Statistics for the training and test sets used in the translation task. The number of words and the number of distinct words (case-insensitive) is based on the provided tokenizer.

ID	Participant
ALACANT	University of Alicante (Sánchez-Cartagena et al., 2011)
CEU-UPV	CEU University Cardenal Herrera & Polytechnic University of Valencia (Zamora-Martinez and Castro-Bleda, 2011)
CMU-DENKOWSKI	Carnegie Mellon University - Denkowski (Denkowski and Lavie, 2011b)
CMU-DYER	Carnegie Mellon University - Dyer (Dyer et al., 2011)
CMU-HANNEMAN	Carnegie Mellon University - Hanneman (Hanneman and Lavie, 2011)
COPENHAGEN	Copenhagen Business School
CST	Centre for Language Technology @ Copenhagen University (Rishøj and Søgaard, 2011)
CU-BOJAR	Charles University - Bojar (Mareček et al., 2011)
CU-MARECEK	Charles University - Mareček (Mareček et al., 2011)
CU-POPEL	Charles University - Popel (Popel et al., 2011)
CU-TAMCHYNA	Charles University - Tamchyna (Bojar and Tamchyna, 2011)
CU-ZEMAN	Charles University - Zeman (Zeman, 2011)
DFKI-FEDERMANN	Deutsches Forschungszentrum für Künstliche Intelligenz - Federmann (Federmann and Hunsicker, 2011)
DFKI-XU	Deutsches Forschungszentrum für Künstliche Intelligenz - Xu (Xu et al., 2011b)
HYDERABAD	IIIT-Hyderabad
ILLC-UVA	Institute for Logic, Language and Computation @ University of Amsterdam (Khalilov and Sima'an, 2011)
JHU	Johns Hopkins University (Weese et al., 2011)
KIT	Karlsruhe Institute of Technology (Herrmann et al., 2011)
KOC	Koc University (Bicici and Yuret, 2011)
LATL-GENEVA	Language Technology Laboratory @ University of Geneva (Wehrli et al., 2009)
LIA-LIG	Laboratoire Informatique d'Avignon @ The University of Avignon & Laboratoire d'Informatique de Grenoble @ University of Grenoble (Potet et al., 2011)
LIMSI	LIMSI (Allauzen et al., 2011)
LINGUATEC	Linguatec Language Technologies (Aleksic and Thurmair, 2011)
LIU	Linköping University (Holmqvist et al., 2011)
LIUM	University of Le Mans (Schwenk et al., 2011)
PROMT	ProMT
RWTH-FREITAG	RWTH Aachen - Freitag (Huck et al., 2011)
RWTH-HUCK	RWTH Aachen - Huck (Huck et al., 2011)
RWTH-WUEBKER	RWTH Aachen - Wübker (Huck et al., 2011)
SYSTRAN	SYSTRAN
UEDIN	University of Edinburgh (Koehn et al., 2007)
UFAL-UM	Charles University and University of Malta (Corbí-Bellot et al., 2005)
UOW	University of Wolverhampton (Aziz et al., 2011)
UPM	Technical University of Madrid (López-Ludeña and San-Segundo, 2011)
UPPSALA	Uppsala University (Koehn et al., 2007)
UPPSALA-FBK	Uppsala University & Fondazione Bruno Kessler (Hardmeier et al., 2011)
ONLINE-[A,B]	two online statistical machine translation systems
RBMT-[1–5]	five online rule-based machine translation systems
COMMERCIAL-[1,2]	two commercial machine translation systems

Table 1: Participants in the shared translation task (European language pairs; individual system track). Not all teams participated in all language pairs. The translations from commercial and online systems were crawled by us, not submitted by the respective companies, and are therefore anonymized.

ID	Participant
BBN-COMBO	Raytheon BBN Technologies (Rosti et al., 2011)
CMU-HEAFIELD-COMBO	Carnegie Mellon University (Heafield and Lavie, 2011)
JHU-COMBO	Johns Hopkins University (Xu et al., 2011a)
KOC-COMBO	Koc University (Bicici and Yuret, 2011)
LIUM-COMBO	University of Le Mans (Barrault, 2011)
QUAERO-COMBO	Quaero Project* (Freitag et al., 2011)
RWTH-LEUSCH-COMBO	RWTH Aachen (Leusch et al., 2011)
UOW-COMBO	University of Wolverhampton (Specia et al., 2010)
UPV-PRHLT-COMBO	Polytechnic University of Valencia (González-Rubio and Casacuberta, 2011)
UZH-COMBO	University of Zurich (Sennrich, 2011)

Table 2: Participants in the shared system combination task. Not all teams participated in all language pairs.
* The Quaero Project entry combined outputs they received directly from LIMSI, KIT, SYSTRAN, and RWTH.

participants in the system combination shared task. Continuing our practice from last year's workshop, we separated the test set into a tuning set and a final held-out test set for system combinations. The tuning portion was distributed to system combination participants along with reference translations, to aid them set any system parameters.

In the European language pairs, the tuning set consisted of 1,003 segments taken from 37 documents, whereas the test set consisted of 2,000 segments taken from 73 documents. In the Haitian Creole task, the split was 674 segments for tuning and 600 for testing.

Table 2 lists the 10 participants in the system combination task.

3 Featured Translation Task

The featured translation task of WMT11 was to translate Haitian Creole SMS messages into English. These text messages were sent by people in Haiti in the aftermath of the January 2010 earthquake. In the wake of the earthquake, much of the country's conventional emergency response services failed. Since cell phone towers remained standing after the earthquake, text messages were a viable mode of communication. Munro (2010) describes how a text-message-based emergency reporting system was set up by a consortium of volunteer organizations named "Mission 4636" after a free SMS short code telephone number that they established. The SMS messages were routed to a system for reporting trapped people and other emergencies. Search and rescue teams within Haiti, including the US Military, recognized the quantity and reliability of actionable information in these messages and used them to provide aid.

The majority of the SMS messages were written in Haitian Creole, which was not spoken by most of first responders deployed from overseas. A distributed, online translation effort was established, drawing volunteers from Haitian Creole- and French-speaking communities around the world. The volunteers not only translated messages, but also categorized them and pinpointed them on a map.[5] Collaborating online, they employed their local knowledge of locations, regional slang, abbreviations and spelling variants to process more than 40,000 messages in the first six weeks alone. First responders indicated that this volunteer effort helped to save hundreds of lives and helped direct the first food and aid to tens of thousands. Secretary of State Clinton described one success of the Mission 4636 program:"The technology community has set up interactive maps to help us identify needs and target resources. And on Monday, a seven-year-old girl and two women were pulled from the rubble of a collapsed supermarket by an American search-and-rescue team after they sent a text message calling for help." Ushahidi@Tufts described another:"The World Food Program delivered food to an informal camp of 2500 people, having yet to receive food or water, in Diquini to a location that 4636 had identi-

[5]A detailed map of Haiti was created by a crowdsourcing effort in the aftermath of the earthquake (Lacey-Hall, 2011).

ID	Participant
BM-I2R	Barcelona Media & Institute for Infocomm Research (Costa-jussà and Banchs, 2011)
CMU-DENKOWSKI	Carnegie Mellon University - Denkowski (Denkowski and Lavie, 2011b)
CMU-HEWAVITHARANA	Carnegie Mellon University - Hewavitharana (Hewavitharana et al., 2011)
HYDERABAD	IIIT-Hyderabad
JHU	Johns Hopkins University (Weese et al., 2011)
KOC	Koc University (Bicici and Yuret, 2011)
LIU	Linköping University (Stymne, 2011)
UMD-EIDELMAN	University of Maryland - Eidelman (Eidelman et al., 2011)
UMD-HU	University of Maryland - Hu (Hu et al., 2011)
UPPSALA	Uppsala University (Hardmeier et al., 2011)

Table 3: Participants in the featured translation task (Haitian Creole SMS into English; individual system track). Not all teams participated in both the 'Clean' and 'Raw' tracks.

fied for them."

In parallel with Rob Munro's crowdsourcing translation efforts, the Microsoft Translator team developed a Haitian Creole statistical machine translation engine from scratch in a compressed timeframe (Lewis, 2010). Despite the impressive number of translations completed by volunteers, machine translation was viewed as a potentially useful tool for higher volume applications or to provide translations of English medical documents into Haitian Creole. The Microsoft Translator team quickly assembled parallel data from a number of sources, including Mission 4636 and from the archives of Carnegie Mellon's DIPLOMAT project (Frederking et al., 1997). Through a series of rapid prototyping efforts, the team improved their system to deal with non-standard orthography, reduced pronouns, and SMS shorthand. They deployed a functional translation system to relief workers in the field in less than 5 days – impressive even when measured against previous rapid MT development efforts like DARPA's surprise language exercise (Oard, 2003; Oard and Och, 2003).

We were inspired by the efforts of Rob Munro and Will Lewis on translating Haitian Creole in the aftermath of the disaster, so we worked with them to create a featured task at WMT11. We thank them for generously sharing the data they assembled in their own efforts. We invited Rob Munro, Will Lewis, and Stephan Vogel to speak at the workshop on the topic of developing translation technology for future crises, and they recorded their thoughts in an invited publication (Lewis et al., 2011).

3.1 Haitian Creole Data

For the WMT11 featured translation task, we anonymized the SMS Haitian Creole messages along with the translations that the Mission 4636 volunteers created. Examples of these messages are given in Table 4. The goal of anonymizing the SMS data was so that it may be shared with researchers who are developing translation and mapping technologies to support future emergency relief efforts and social development. We ask that any researcher working with these messages to be aware that they are actual communications sent by people in need in a time of crisis. Researchers who use this data are asked to be cognizant of the following:

- Some messages may be distressing in content.
- The people who sent the messages (and who are discussed in them) were victims of a natural disaster and a humanitarian crisis. Please treat the messages with the appropriate respect for these individuals.
- The primary motivation for using this data should be to understand how we can better respond to future crises.

Participants who received the Haitian Creole data for WMT11 were given anonymization guidelines

mwen se [FIRSTNAME] mwen gen twaset ki mouri mwen mande nou ed pou nou edem map tan repons	I am [FIRSTNAME], I have three sisters who have died. I ask help for us, I await your response.
Ki kote yap bay manje	Where are they giving out food?
Eske lekol kolej marie anne kraze?mesi	Was the College Marie Anne school destroyed? Thank you.
Nou pa ka anpeche moustik yo mòde nou paske yo anpil.	We can't prevent the mosquitoes from biting because there are so many.
tanpri kèm ap kase mwen pa ka pran nouvel manmanm.	Please heart is breaking because I have no news of my mother.
4636:Opital Medesen san Fwontiè delmas 19 la fèmen. Opital sen lwi gonzag nan delma 33 pran an chaj gratwitman tout moun ki malad ou blese	4636: The Doctors without Borders Hospital in Delmas 19 is closed. The Saint Louis Gonzaga hospital in Delmas 33 is taking in sick and wounded people for free
Mwen résévoua mesaj nou yo 5 sou 5 men mwen ta vle di yon bagay kilè e koman nap kapab fèm jwin èd sa yo pou moune b la kay mwen ki sinistwé adrès la sé	I received your message 5/5 but I would like to ask one thing when and how will you be able to get the aid to me for the people around my house who are victims of the earthquake? The address is
Sil vous plait map chehe [LASTNAME][FIRSTNAME].di yo relem nan [PHONENUMBER].mwen se [LASTNAME] [FIRSTNAME]	I'm looking for [LASTNAME][FIRSTNAME]. Tell him to call me at [PHONENUMBER] I am [LASTNAME] [FIRSTNAME]
Bonswa mwen rele [FIRSTNAME] [LASTNAME] kay mwen krase mwen pagin anyin poum mange ak fanmi-m tampri di yon mo pou mwen fem jwen yon tante tou ak mange. .mrete n	Hello my name is [FIRSTNAME] [LASTNAME]my house fell down, I've had nothing to eat and I'm hungry. Please help me find food. I live
Mwen viktim kay mwen kraze èskem ka ale sendomeng mwen gen paspò	I'm a victim. My home has been destroyed. Am I allowed to go to the Dominican Republic? I have a Passport.
KISAM DWE FE LEGEN REPLIK,ESKE MOUN SAINT MARC AP JWENN REPLIK.	What should I do when there is an aftershock? Will the people of Saint Marc have aftershocks?
MWEN SE YON JEN ETIDYAN AN ASYANS ENFOMATIK KI PASE ANPIL MIZE NAN TRANBLEMAN DE TE 12 JANVYE A TOUT FANMIM FIN MOURI MWEN SANTIM SEL MWEN TE VLE ALE VIV	I'm a young student in computer science, who has suffered a lot during and after the earthquake of January 12th. All my family has died and I feel alone. I wanted to go live.
Mw rele [FIRSTNAME], mw fè mason epi mw abite laplèn. Yo dim minustah ap bay djob mason ki kote pou mw ta pase si mw ta vle jwenn nan djob sa yo.	My name is [FIRSTNAME], I'm a construction worker and I live in La Plaine. I heard that the MINUSTAH was giving jobs to construction workers. What do I have to go to find one of these jobs?
Souple mande lapolis pou fe on ti pase nan magloire ambroise prolonge zone muler ak cadet jeremie ginyin jen gason ki ap pase nan zone sa yo e ki agresi	please ask the police to go to magloire ambroise going towards the "muler" area and cadet jeremie because there are very aggressive young men in these areas
KIBO MOUN KA JWENN MANJE POU YO MANJE ANDEYO KAPITAL PASKE DEPI 12 JANVYE YO VOYE MANJE POU PEP LA MEN NOU PA JANM JWENN ANYEN. NAP MOURI AK GRANGOU	Where can people get food to eat outside of the capital because since January 12th, they've sent food for the people but we never received anything. We are dying of hunger
Mwen se [FIRSTNAME][LASTNAME] mwen nan aken mwen se yon jèn ki ansent mwen te genyen yon paran ki tap ede li mouri pòtoprens, mwen pral akouye nan kòmansman feviye	I am [FIRSTNAME][LASTNAME] I am in Aquin I am a pregnant young person I had a parent who was helping me, she died in Port-au-Prince, I'm going to give birth at the start of February

Table 4: Examples of some of the Haitian Creole SMS messages that were sent to the 4636 short code along with their translations into English. Translations were done by volunteers who wanted to help with the relief effort. Prior to being distributed, the messages were anonymized to remove names, phone numbers, email addresses, etc. The anonymization guidelines specified that addresses be retained to facilitate work on mapping technologies.

Training set	Parallel sentences	Words per lang
In-domain SMS data	17,192	35k
Medical domain	1,619	10k
Newswire domain	13,517	30k
Glossary	35,728	85k
Wikipedia parallel sentence	8,476	90k
Wikipedia named entities	10,499	25k
The bible	30,715	850k
Haitisurf dictionary	3,763	4k
Krengle dictionary	1,687	3k
Krengle sentences	658	3k

Table 5: Training data for the Haitian Creole-English featured translation task. The in-domain SMS data consists primarily of raw (noisy) SMS data. The in-domain data was provided by Mission 4636. The other data is out-of-domain. It comes courtesy of Carnegie Mellon University, Microsoft Research, Haitisurf.com, and Krengle.net.

alongside the SMS data. The WMT organizers requested that if they discovered messages with incorrect or incomplete anonymization, that they notify us and correct the anonymization using the version control repository.

To define the shared translation task, we divided the SMS messages into an in-domain training set, along with designated dev, devtest, and test sets. We coordinated with Microsoft and CMU to make available additional out-of-domain parallel corpora. Details of the data are given in Table 5. In addition to this data, participants in the featured task were allowed to use any of the data provided in the standard translation task, as well as linguistic tools such as taggers, parsers, or morphological analyzers.

3.2 Clean and Raw Test Data

We provided two sets of testing and development data. Participants used their systems to translate two test sets consisting of 1,274 unseen Haitian Creole SMS messages. One of the test sets contains the "raw" SMS messages as they were sent, and the other contains messages that were cleaned up by human post-editors. The English side is the same in both cases, and the only difference is the Haitian Creole input sentences.

The post-editors were Haitian Creole language informants hired by Microsoft Research. They provided a number of corrections to the SMS messages, including expanding SMS shorthands, correcting spelling/grammar/capitalization, restoring diacritics that were left out of the original message, and cleaning up accented characters that were lost when the message was transmitted in the wrong encoding.

Original Haitian Creole messages:

> Sil vou plé éde mwen avek moun ki viktim yo nan tranbleman de té a,ki kité potoprins ki vini nan provins- mwen ede ak ti kob mwen te ginyin kounié a
> 4636: Manje vin pi che nan PaP apre tranbleman te-a. mamit diri ap van'n 250gd kounye, sete 200gd avan. Mayi-a 125gd, avan sete 100gd

Edited Haitian Creole messages:

> Silvouple ede mwen avèk moun ki viktim yo nan tranblemanntè a, ki kite Pòtoprens ki vini nan pwovens, mwen ede ak ti kòb mwen te genyen kounye a
> 4636: Manje vin pi chè nan PaP apre tranblemanntè a. Mamit diri ap vann 250gd kounye a, sete 200gd avan. Mayi-a 125gd, avan sete 100gd.

For the test and development sets the informants also edited the English translations. For instance, there were cases where the original crowdsourced translation summarized the content of the message instead of translating it, instances where parts of the source were omitted, and where explanatory notes were added. The editors improved the translations so that they were more suitable for machine translation, making them more literal, correcting disfluencies on the English side, and retranslating them when they were summaries.

Crowdsourced English translation:

> We are in the area of Petit Goave, we would like .... we need tents and medication for flu/colds...

Post-edited translation:

> We are in the area of Petit Goave, we would like to receive assistance, however,

it should not be the way I see the Minustah guys are handling the people. We need lots of tents and medication for flu/colds, and fever

The edited English is provided as the reference for both the "clean" and the "raw" sets, since we intend that distinction to refer to the form that the source language comes in, rather than the target language.

Tables 47 and 48 in the Appendix show a significant difference in the translation quality between the clean and the raw test sets. In most cases, systems' output for the raw condition was 4 BLEU points lower than for the clean condition. We believe that the difference in performance on the raw vs. cleaned test sets highlight the importance of handling noisy input data.

All of the in-domain training data is in the raw format. The original SMS messages are unaltered, and the translations are just as the volunteered provided them. In some cases, the original SMS messages are written in French or English instead of Haitian Creole, or contain a mixture of languages. It may be possible to further improve the quality of machine translation systems trained from this data by improving the quality of the data itself.

3.3 Goals and Challenges

The goals of the Haitian Creole to English translation task were:

- To focus researchers on the problems presented by low resource languages
- To provide a real-world data set consisting of SMS messages, which contain abbreviations, non-standard spelling, omitted diacritics, and other noisy character encodings
- To develop techniques for building translation systems that will be useful in future crises

There are many challenges in translating noisy data in a low resource language, and there are a variety of strategies that might be considered to attempt to tackle them. For instance:

- Automated cleaning of the raw (noisy) SMS data in the training set.
- Leveraging a larger French-English model to translate out of vocabulary Haitian words, by creating a mapping from Haitian words onto French.
- Incorporation of morphological and/or syntactic models to better cope with the low resource language pair.

It is our hope that by introducing this data as a shared challenge at WMT11 that we will establish a useful community resource so that researchers may explore these challenges and publish about them in the future.

4 Human Evaluation

As with past workshops, we placed greater emphasis on the human evaluation than on the automatic evaluation metric scores. It is our contention that automatic measures are an imperfect substitute for human assessment of translation quality. Therefore, we define the manual evaluation to be primary, and use the human judgments to validate automatic metrics.

Manual evaluation is time consuming, and it requires a large effort to conduct on the scale of our workshop. We distributed the workload across a number of people, including shared-task participants, interested volunteers, and a small number of paid annotators (recruited by the participating sites). More than 130 people participated in the manual evaluation, with 91 people putting in more than an hour's worth of effort, and 29 putting in more than four hours. There was a collective total of 361 hours of labor.

We asked annotators to evaluate system outputs by ranking translated sentences relative to each other. This was our official determinant of translation quality. The total number of judgments collected for the different ranking tasks is given in Table 6.

We performed the manual evaluation of the individual systems separately from the manual evaluation of the system combination entries, rather than comparing them directly against each other. Last year's results made it clear that there is a large (expected) gap in performance between the two groups. This year, we opted to reduce the number of pairwise comparisons with the hope that we would be more likely to find statistically significant differences between the systems in the same groups. To that same end, we also eliminated the editing/acceptability task that was featured in last year's evaluation, instead we had annotators focus solely on the system ranking task.

4.1 Ranking translations of sentences

Ranking translations relative to each other is a reasonably intuitive task. We therefore kept the instructions simple:

> *You are shown a source sentence followed by several candidate translations.*
> *Your task is to rank the translations from best to worst (ties are allowed).*

Each screen for this task involved judging translations of three consecutive source segments. For each source segment, the annotator was shown the outputs of five submissions, and asked to rank them.

With the exception of a few tasks in the system combination track, there were many more than 5 systems participating in any given task—up to 23 for the English-German individual systems track. Rather than attempting to get a complete ordering over the systems, we instead relied on random selection and a reasonably large sample size to make the comparisons fair.

We use the collected rank labels to assign each system a score that reflects how highly that system was usually ranked by the annotators. The score for some system A reflects how frequently it was judged to be better than or equal to other systems. Specifically, each block in which A appears includes four implicit pairwise comparisons (against the other presented systems). A is rewarded once for each of the four comparisons in which A wins or ties. A's score is the number of such winning (or tying) pairwise comparisons, divided by the total number of pairwise comparisons involving A.

The system scores are reported in Section 5. Appendix A provides detailed tables that contain pairwise **head-to-head** comparisons between pairs of systems.

4.2 Inter- and Intra-annotator agreement in the ranking task

We were interested in determining the inter- and intra-annotator agreement for the ranking task, since a reasonable degree of agreement must exist to support our process as a valid evaluation setup. To ensure we had enough data to measure agreement, we purposely designed the sampling of source segments and translations shown to annotators in a way that ensured some items would be repeated, both within the screens completed by an individual annotator, and across screens completed by different annotators.

We did so by ensuring that 10% of the generated screens are exact repetitions of previously generated screen within the same batch of screens. Furthermore, even within the other 90%, we ensured that a source segment appearing in one screen appears again in two more screens (though with different system outputs). Those two details, intentional repetition of source sentences and intentional repetition of system outputs, ensured we had enough data to compute meaningful inter- and intra-annotator agreement rates.

We measured pairwise agreement among annotators using Cohen's kappa coefficient (κ) (Cohen, 1960), which is defined as

$$\kappa = \frac{P(A) - P(E)}{1 - P(E)}$$

where $P(A)$ is the proportion of times that the annotators agree, and $P(E)$ is the proportion of time that they would agree by chance. Note that κ is basically a normalized version of $P(A)$, one which takes into account how meaningful it is for annotators to agree with each other, by incorporating $P(E)$. Note also that κ has a value of at most 1 (and could possibly be negative), with higher rates of agreement resulting in higher κ.

The above definition of κ is actually used by several definitions of agreement measures, which differ in how $P(A)$ and $P(E)$ are computed.

We calculate $P(A)$ by examining all pairs of systems which had been judged by two or more judges, and calculating the proportion of time that they agreed that $A > B$, $A = B$, or $A < B$. In other words, $P(A)$ is the empirical, observed rate at

	Inividual System Track			System Combination Track		
Language Pair	# Systems	Label Count	Labels per System	# Systems	Label Count	Labels per System
Czech-English	8	2,490	276.7	4	1,305	261.0
English-Czech	10	8,985	816.8	2	2,700	900.0
German-English	20	4,620	220.0	8	1,950	216.7
English-German	22	6,540	284.4	4	2,205	441.0
Spanish-English	15	2,850	178.1	6	2,115	302.1
English-Spanish	15	5,595	349.7	4	3,000	600.0
French-English	18	3,540	186.3	6	1,500	214.3
English-French	17	4,590	255.0	2	900	300.0
Haitian (Clean)-English	9	3,360	336.0	3	1,200	300.0
Haitian (Raw)-English	6	1,875	267.9	2	900	300.0
Urdu-English (tunable metrics task)	8	3,165	351.7	N/A	N/A	N/A
Overall	**148**	**47,610**	**299.4**	**41**	**17,775**	**348.5**

Table 6: A summary of the WMT11 ranking task, showing the number of systems and number of labels collected in each of the individual and system combination tracks. The system count does not include the reference translation, which was included in the evaluation, and so a value under "Labels per System" can be obtained only after adding 1 to the system count, before dividing the label count (e.g. in German-English, $4,620/21 = 220.0$).

which annotators agree, in the context of pairwise comparisons. $P(A)$ is computed similarly for *intra*-annotator agreement (i.e. self-consistency), but over pairwise comparisons that were annotated more than once by a *single* annotator.

As for $P(E)$, it should capture the probability that two annotators would agree randomly. Therefore:

$$P(E) = P(\text{A>B})^2 + P(\text{A=B})^2 + P(\text{A<B})^2$$

Note that each of the three probabilities in $P(E)$'s definition are squared to reflect the fact that we are considering the chance that *two* annotators would agree by chance. Each of these probabilities is computed empirically, by observing how often annotators actually rank two systems as being tied. We note here that this empirical computation is a departure from previous years' analyses, where we had assumed that the three categories are equally likely (yielding $P(E) = \frac{1}{9} + \frac{1}{9} + \frac{1}{9} = \frac{1}{3}$). We believe that this is a more principled approach, which faithfully reflects the motivation of accounting for $P(E)$ in the first place.[6]

Table 7 gives κ values for inter-annotator and intra-annotator agreement across the various evaluation tasks. These give an indication of how often different judges agree, and how often single judges are consistent for repeated judgments, respectively.

There are some general and expected trends that can be seen in this table. First of all, intra-annotator agreement is higher than inter-annotator agreement. Second, reference translations are noticeably better than other system outputs, which means that annotators have an artificially high level of agreement on pairwise comparisons that include a reference translation. For this reason, we also report the agreement levels when such comparisons are excluded.

The exact interpretation of the kappa coefficient is difficult, but according to Landis and Koch (1977), $0-0.2$ is slight, $0.2-0.4$ is fair, $0.4-0.6$ is moderate, $0.6-0.8$ is substantial, and $0.8-1.0$ is almost perfect. Based on these interpretations, the agreement for sentence-level ranking is moderate to substantial for most tasks.

[6]Even if we wanted to assume a "random clicker" model, setting $P(E) = \frac{1}{3}$ is still not entirely correct. Given that annotators rank five outputs at once, $P(A = B) = \frac{1}{5}$, not $\frac{1}{3}$, since there are only five (out of 25) label pairs that satisfy $A = B$. Working this back into $P(E)$'s definition, we have $P(A > B) = P(A < B) = \frac{2}{5}$, and therefore $P(E) = 0.36$ rather than 0.333.

INTER-ANNOTATOR AGREEMENT (I.E. ACROSS ANNOTATORS)

	ALL COMPARISONS			NO REF COMPARISONS		
	$P(A)$	$P(E)$	κ	$P(A)$	$P(E)$	κ
European languages, individual systems	0.601	0.362	0.375	0.561	0.355	0.320
European languages, system combinations	0.671	0.335	0.505	0.598	0.342	0.389
Haitian-English, individual systems	0.691	0.362	0.516	0.639	0.350	0.446
Haitian-English, system combinations	0.761	0.358	0.628	0.674	0.335	0.509
Tunable metrics task (Urdu-English)	0.692	0.337	0.535	0.641	0.363	0.437
WMT10 (European languages, all systems)	0.658	0.374	0.454	0.626	0.367	0.409

INTRA-ANNOTATOR AGREEMENT (I.E. SELF-CONSISTENCY)

	ALL COMPARISONS			NO REF COMPARISONS		
	$P(A)$	$P(E)$	κ	$P(A)$	$P(E)$	κ
European languages, individual systems	0.722	0.362	0.564	0.685	0.355	0.512
European languages, system combinations	0.787	0.335	0.680	0.717	0.342	0.571
Haitian-English, individual systems	0.763	0.362	0.628	0.700	0.350	0.539
Haitian-English, system combinations	0.882	0.358	0.816	0.784	0.335	0.675
Tunable metrics task (Urdu-English)	0.857	0.337	0.784	0.856	0.363	0.774
WMT10 (European languages, all systems)	0.755	0.374	0.609	0.734	0.367	0.580

Table 7: Inter- and intra-annotator agreement rates, for the various manual evaluation tracks of WMT11. See Tables 49 and 50 below for a detailed breakdown by language pair.

However, one result that is of concern is that agreement rates are noticeably lower for European language pairs, in particular for the individual systems track. When excluding reference comparisons, the inter- and intra-annotator agreement levels are 0.320 and 0.512, respectively. Not only are those numbers lower than for the other tasks, but they are also lower than last year's numbers, which were 0.409 and 0.580.

We investigated this result a bit deeper. Tables 49 and 50 in the Appendix break down the results further, by reporting agreement levels for each language pair. One observation is that the agreement level for some language pairs deviates in a non-trivial amount from the overall agreement rate.

Let us focus on inter-annotator agreement rates in the individual track (excluding reference comparisons), in the top right portion of Table 49. The overall κ is 0.320, but it ranges from 0.264 for German-English, to 0.477 for Spanish-English.

What distinguishes those two language pairs from each other? If we examine the results in Table 8, we see that Spanish-English had two very weak systems, which were likely easy for annotators to agree on comparisons involving them. (This is the converse of annotators agreeing more often on comparisons involving the reference.) English-French is similar in that regard, and it too has a relatively high agreement rate.

On the other hand, the participants in German-English formed a large pool of more closely-matched systems, where the gap separating the bottom system is not as pronounced. So it seems that the low agreement rates are indicative of a more competitive evaluation and more closely-matched systems.

5 Results of the Translation Tasks

We used the results of the manual evaluation to analyze the translation quality of the different systems that were submitted to the workshop. In our analysis, we aimed to address the following questions:

- Which systems produced the best translation quality for each language pair?
- Which of the systems that used only the provided training materials produced the best translation quality?

Czech-English
1023–1166 comparisons/system

System	C?	≥others
UEDIN •⋆	Y	0.69
ONLINE-B •	N	0.68
CU-BOJAR	N	0.60
JHU	N	0.57
UPPSALA	Y	0.57
SYSTRAN	N	0.51
CST	Y	0.47
CU-ZEMAN	Y	0.44

Spanish-English
583–833 comparisons/system

System	C?	≥others
ONLINE-B •	N	0.72
ONLINE-A •	N	0.72
KOC ⋆	Y	0.67
SYSTRAN •	N	0.66
ALACANT •	N	0.66
RBMT-1	N	0.63
RBMT-3	N	0.61
RBMT-2	N	0.60
RBMT-4	N	0.60
RBMT-5	N	0.51
UEDIN	Y	0.51
UPM	Y	0.50
UFAL-UM	Y	0.47
HYDERABAD	Y	0.17
CU-ZEMAN	Y	0.16

French-English
608–883 comparisons/system

System	C?	≥others
ONLINE-A •	N	0.66
LIMSI •⋆	Y+G	0.66
ONLINE-B •	N	0.66
LIA-LIG	Y	0.64
KIT •⋆	Y+G	0.64
LIUM	Y+G	0.63
CMU-DENKOWSKI ⋆	Y	0.62
JHU	Y+G	0.61
RWTH-HUCK	Y+G	0.58
RBMT-1 •	N	0.58
CMU-HANNEMAN	Y+G	0.58
RBMT-3	N	0.55
SYSTRAN	N	0.54
RBMT-4	N	0.53
RBMT-2	N	0.52
UEDIN	Y	0.50
RBMT-5	N	0.45
CU-ZEMAN	Y	0.37

English-Czech
3126–3397 comparisons/system

System	C?	≥others
ONLINE-B •	N	0.65
CU-BOJAR	N	0.64
CU-MARECEK •	N	0.63
CU-TAMCHYNA	N	0.62
UEDIN ⋆	Y	0.59
CU-POPEL ⋆	Y	0.58
COMMERCIAL2	N	0.51
COMMERCIAL1	N	0.51
JHU	N	0.49
CU-ZEMAN	Y	0.43

English-Spanish
1300–1480 comparisons/system

System	C?	≥others
ONLINE-B •	N	0.74
ONLINE-A •	N	0.72
RBMT-3 •	N	0.71
PROMT •	N	0.70
CEU-UPV ⋆	Y	0.65
UEDIN ⋆	Y	0.64
UPPSALA ⋆	Y	0.61
RBMT-4	N	0.61
RBMT-1	N	0.60
UOW	Y	0.59
RBMT-2	N	0.57
KOC	Y	0.56
RBMT-5	N	0.54
CU-ZEMAN	Y	0.49
UPM	Y	0.34

English-French
868–1121 comparisons/system

System	C?	≥others
LIMSI •⋆	Y+G	0.73
ONLINE-B •	N	0.70
KIT •⋆	Y+G	0.69
RWTH-HUCK	Y+G	0.65
LIUM	Y+G	0.64
RBMT-1	N	0.61
ONLINE-A	N	0.60
UEDIN	Y	0.58
RBMT-3	N	0.58
RBMT-5	N	0.55
UPPSALA	Y	0.55
JHU	Y	0.55
UPPSALA-FBK	Y	0.54
RBMT-4	N	0.49
RBMT-2	N	0.46
LATL-GENEVA	N	0.39
CU-ZEMAN	Y	0.20

German-English
741–998 comparisons/system

System	C?	≥others
ONLINE-B •	N	0.72
CMU-DYER •⋆	Y+G	0.66
ONLINE-A •	N	0.66
RBMT-3	N	0.64
LINGUATEC	N	0.63
RBMT-4	N	0.61
RBMT-1	N	0.60
DFKI-XU	N	0.60
RWTH-WUEBKER ⋆	Y+G	0.59
KIT	Y+G	0.57
LIU	Y	0.57
LIMSI	Y+G	0.56
RBMT-5	N	0.56
UEDIN	Y	0.55
RBMT-2	N	0.54
CU-ZEMAN	Y	0.47
UPPSALA	Y	0.47
KOC	Y	0.45
JHU	Y+G	0.43
CST	Y	0.37

English-German
1051–1230 comparisons/system

System	C?	≥others
RBMT-3 •	N	0.73
ONLINE-B •	N	0.73
RBMT-1 •	N	0.70
DFKI-FEDERMANN •	N	0.68
DFKI-XU	N	0.67
RBMT-4 •	N	0.66
RBMT-2 •	N	0.66
ONLINE-A •	N	0.65
LIMSI ⋆	Y+G	0.65
KIT ⋆	Y	0.64
UEDIN	Y	0.60
LIU	Y	0.59
RBMT-5	N	0.58
RWTH-FREITAG	Y	0.56
COPENHAGEN ⋆	Y	0.56
JHU	Y	0.54
KOC	Y	0.53
UOW	Y	0.53
CU-TAMCHYNA	Y	0.50
UPPSALA	Y	0.49
ILLC-UVA	Y	0.48
CU-ZEMAN	Y	0.38

C? indicates whether system is constrained: trained only using supplied training data, standard monolingual linguistic tools, and, optionally, LDC's English Gigaword. Eentries that used the Gigaword are marked with +G.

• indicates a **win**: no other system is statistically significantly better at p-level≤0.10 in pairwise comparison.

⋆ indicates a ***constrained* win**: no other *constrained* system is statistically better.

Table 8: Official results for the WMT11 translation task. Systems are ordered by their ≥others score, reflecting how often their translations won or tied pairwise comparisons. For detailed head-to-head comparisons, see Appendix A.

Czech-English
1036–1042 comparisons/combo

System	≥others
CMU-HEAFIELD-COMBO •	0.64
BBN-COMBO •	0.62
JHU-COMBO	0.58
UPV-PRHLT-COMBO	0.47

English-Czech
1788–1792 comparisons/combo

System	≥others
CMU-HEAFIELD-COMBO •	0.48
UPV-PRHLT-COMBO	0.41

German-English
811–927 comparisons/combo

System	≥others
CMU-HEAFIELD-COMBO •	0.70
RWTH-LEUSCH-COMBO	0.65
BBN-COMBO	0.61
UZH-COMBO •	0.60
JHU-COMBO	0.56
UPV-PRHLT-COMBO	0.52
QUAERO-COMBO	0.46
KOC-COMBO	0.45

English-German
1746–1752 comparisons/combo

System	≥others
CMU-HEAFIELD-COMBO •	0.61
UZH-COMBO •	0.58
UPV-PRHLT-COMBO	0.56
KOC-COMBO	0.46

Spanish-English
1132–1249 comparisons/combo

System	≥others
RWTH-LEUSCH-COMBO •	0.71
CMU-HEAFIELD-COMBO •	0.67
BBN-COMBO •	0.64
UPV-PRHLT-COMBO	0.64
JHU-COMBO	0.62
KOC-COMBO	0.56

English-Spanish
2360–2378 comparisons/combo

System	≥others
CMU-HEAFIELD-COMBO •	0.69
UOW-COMBO	0.63
UPV-PRHLT-COMBO	0.59
KOC-COMBO	0.58

French-English
820–916 comparisons/combo

System	≥others
BBN-COMBO •	0.67
RWTH-LEUSCH-COMBO •	0.63
CMU-HEAFIELD-COMBO	0.62
JHU-COMBO •	0.59
LIUM-COMBO	0.53
UPV-PRHLT-COMBO	0.53

English-French
586–587 comparisons/combo

System	≥others
CMU-HEAFIELD-COMBO •	0.51
UPV-PRHLT-COMBO	0.43

• indicates a **win**: no other system combination is statistically significantly better at p-level≤0.10 in pairwise comparison.

Table 9: Official results for the WMT11 system combination task. Systems are ordered by their ≥others score, reflecting how often their translations won or tied pairwise comparisons. For detailed head-to-head comparisons, see Appendix A.

Haitian Creole (Clean)-English
(individual systems)
1256–1435 comparisons/system

System	≥others
BM-I2R •	0.71
CMU-DENKOWSKI	0.66
CMU-HEWAVITHARANA	0.64
UMD-EIDELMAN	0.63
UPPSALA	0.57
LIU	0.55
UMD-HU	0.52
HYDERABAD	0.43
KOC	0.31

Haitian Creole (Raw)-English
(individual systems)
1065–1136 comparisons/system

System	≥others
BM-I2R •	0.65
CMU-HEWAVITHARANA	0.60
CMU-DENKOWSKI	0.59
LIU	0.55
UMD-EIDELMAN	0.52
JHU	0.41

Haitian Creole (Clean)-English
(system combinations)
896–898 comparisons/combo

System	≥others
CMU-HEAFIELD-COMBO •	0.52
UPV-PRHLT-COMBO	0.48
KOC-COMBO	0.38

Haitian Creole (Raw)-English
(system combinations)
600–600 comparisons/combo

System	≥others
CMU-HEAFIELD-COMBO	0.47
UPV-PRHLT-COMBO	0.43

• indicates a **win**: no other system is statistically significantly better at p-level$\leq$0.10 in pairwise comparison.

Table 10: Official results for the WMT11 featured translation task (Haitian Creole SMS into English). Systems are ordered by their ≥others score, reflecting how often their translations won or tied pairwise comparisons. For detailed head-to-head comparisons, see Appendix A.

Tables 8–10 show the system ranking for each of the translation tasks. For each language pair, we define a system as 'winning' if no other system was found statistically significantly better (using the Sign Test, at $p \leq 0.10$). In some cases, multiple systems are listed as winners, either due to a large number of participants or a low number of judgments per system pair, both of which are factors that make it difficult to achieve statistical significance.

We start by examining the results for the individual system track for the European languages (Table 8). In Spanish↔English and German↔English, unconstrained systems are observed to perform better than constrained systems. In other language pairs, particularly French↔English, constrained systems are found to be able to be on the same level or outperform unconstrained systems. It also seems that making use of the Gigaword corpora is likely to yield better systems, even when translating out of English, as in English-French and English-German. For English-German the rule-based MT systems performed well.

Of the participating teams, there is no individual system clearly outperforming all other systems across the different language pairs. However, one of the crawled systems, ONLINE-B, performs consistently well, being one of the winners in all eight language pairs.

As for the system combination track (Table 9), the CMU-HEAFIELD-COMBO entry performed quite well, being a winner in seven out of eight language pairs. This performance is carried over to the Haitian Creole task, where it again comes out on top (Table 10). In the *individual* track of the Haitian Creole task, BM-I2R is the sole winner in both the 'clean' and 'raw' tracks.

6 Evaluation Task

In addition to allowing us to analyze the translation quality of different systems, the data gathered during the manual evaluation is useful for validating automatic evaluation metrics. Our evaluation shared task is similar to the MetricsMATR workshop (Metrics for MAchine TRanslation) that NIST runs (Przybocki et al., 2008; Callison-Burch et al., 2010). Table 11 lists the participants in this task, along with their metrics.

A total of 21 metrics and their variants were submitted to the evaluation task by 9 research groups. We asked metrics developers to score the outputs of the machine translation systems and system combinations at the system-level and at the segment-level. The system-level metrics scores are given in the Appendix in Tables 39–48. The main goal of the evaluation shared task is not to score the systems, but instead to validate the use of automatic metrics by measuring how strongly they correlate with human judgments. We used the human judgments collected during the manual evaluation for the translation task and the system combination task to calculate how well metrics correlate at system-level and at the segment-level.

This year the strongest metric was a new metric developed by Columbia and ETS called MTeRater-Plus. MTeRater-Plus is a machine-learning-based metric that use features from ETS's e-rater, an automated essay scoring engine designed to assess writing proficiency (Attali and Burstein, 2006). The features include sentence-level and document-level information. Some examples of the e-rater features include:

- Preposition features that calculate the probability of prepositions appearing in the given context of a sentence (Tetreault and Chodorow, 2008)
- Collocation features that indicate whether the collocations in the document are typical of native use (Futagi et al., 2008).
- A sentence fragment feature that counts the number of ill-formed sentences in a document.
- A feature that counts the number of words with inflection errors
- A feature that counts the the number of article errors in the sentence citeHan2006.

MTeRater uses only the e-rater features, and measures fluency without any need for reference translations. MTeRater-Plus is a meta-metric that incorporates adequacy by combining MTeRater with other MT evaluation metrics and heuristics that take the reference translations into account.

Please refer to the proceedings for papers providing detailed descriptions of all of the metrics.

Metric IDs	Participant
AMBER, AMBER-NL, AMBER-IT	National Research Council Canada (Chen and Kuhn, 2011)
F15, F15G3	Koç University (Bicici and Yuret, 2011)
METEOR-1.3-ADQ, METEOR-1.3-RANK	Carnegie Mellon University (Denkowski and Lavie, 2011a)
MTERATER, MTERATER-PLUS	Columbia / ETS (Parton et al., 2011)
MP4IBM1, MPF, WMPF	DFKI (Popović, 2011; Popović et al., 2011)
PARSECONF	DFKI (Avramidis et al., 2011)
ROSE, ROSE-POS	The University of Sheffield (Song and Cohn, 2011)
TESLA-B, TESLA-F, TESLA-M	National University of Singapore (Dahlmeier et al., 2011)
TINE	University of Wolverhampton (Rios et al., 2011)
BLEU	provided baseline (Papineni et al., 2002)
TER	provided baseline (Snover et al., 2006)

Table 11: Participants in the evaluation shared task. For comparison purposes, we include the BLEU and TER metrics as baselines.

	EN-CZ - 10 SYSTEMS	EN-DE - 22 SYSTEMS	EN-ES - 15 SYSTEMS	EN-FR - 17 SYSTEMS	AVERAGE	AVERAGE W/O CZ
System-level correlation for translation out of English						
TESLA-M		.90	**.95**	**.96**		**.94**
TESLA-B		.81	.90	.91		.87
MPF	.72	.63	.87	.89	**.78**	.80
WMPF	.72	.61	.87	.89	.77	.79
MP4IBM1	**-.76**	**-.91**	-.71	-.61	.75	.74
ROSE	.65	.41	.90	.86	.71	.73
BLEU	.65	.44	.87	.86	.70	.72
AMBER-TI	.56	.54	.88	.84	.70	.75
AMBER	.56	.53	.87	.84	.70	.74
AMBER-NL	.56	.45	.88	.83	.68	.72
F15G3	.50	.30	.89	.84	.63	.68
METEOR$_{rank}$	.65	.30	.74	.85	.63	.63
F15	.52	.19	.86	.85	.60	.63
TER	-.50	-.12	-.81	-.84	.57	.59
TESLA-F		.86	.80	-.83		.28

Table 12: System-level Spearman's rho correlation of the automatic evaluation metrics with the human judgments for translation out of English, ordered by average absolute value. We did not calculate correlations with the human judgments for the system combinations for the out of English direction, because none of them had more than 4 items.

6.1 System-Level Metric Analysis

We measured the correlation of the automatic metrics with the human judgments of translation quality at the system-level using Spearman's rank correlation coefficient ρ. We converted the raw scores assigned to each system into ranks. We assigned a human ranking to the systems based on the percent of time that their translations were judged to be better than or equal to the translations of any other system in the manual evaluation. The reference was not included as an extra translation.

When there are no ties, ρ can be calculated using the simplified equation:

$$\rho = 1 - \frac{6 \sum d_i^2}{n(n^2-1)}$$

where d_i is the difference between the rank for system$_i$ and n is the number of systems. The possible values of ρ range between 1 (where all systems are ranked in the same order) and -1 (where the systems are ranked in the reverse order). Thus an automatic evaluation metric with a higher absolute value for ρ is making predictions that are more similar to the human judgments than an automatic evaluation metric with a lower absolute ρ.

The system-level correlations are shown in Table 13 for translations into English, and Table 12 out of English, sorted by average correlation across the language pairs. The highest correlation for each language pair and the highest overall average are bolded. This year, nearly all of the metrics

	CZ-EN - 8 SYSTEMS	DE-EN - 20 SYSTEMS	DE-EN - 8 COMBOS	ES-EN - 15 SYSTEMS	ES-EN - 6 COMBOS	FR-EN - 18 SYSTEMS	FR-EN - 6 COMBOS	AVERAGE (EUROPEAN LANGS)	HT-EN (CLEAN) - 9 SYSTEMS	HT-EN (RAW) - 6 SYSTEMS	AVERAGE (ALL LANGS)
System-level correlation for metrics scoring translations into English											
MTERATER-PLUS	-.95	-.90	-.93	-.91	-.94	-.93	-.77	**.90**	-.82	-.54	.85
TINE-SRL-MATCH	.95	.69	.95	.95	**1.00**	.87	.66	.87			
TESLA-F	.95	.70	**.98**	**.96**	.94	.90	.60	.86	.93	.83	**.87**
TESLA-B	**.98**	.88	**.98**	.91	.94	.91	.31	.84	.93	.83	.85
MTERATER	-.91	-.88	-.91	-.88	-.89	-.79	-.60	.83	.13	.77	.55
METEOR-1.3-ADQ	.93	.68	.91	.91	.83	.93	.66	.83	**.95**	.77	.84
TESLA-M	.95	**.94**	.95	.82	.94	.87	.31	.83	.95	.83	.84
METEOR-1.3-RANK	.91	.71	.91	.88	.77	.93	.66	.82	.95	.83	.84
AMBER-NL	.88	.58	.91	.88	.94	.94	.60	.82			
AMBER-TI	.88	.63	.93	.85	.83	.94	.60	.81			
AMBER	.88	.59	.91	.86	.83	**.95**	.60	.80			
MPF	.95	.69	.91	.83	.60	.87	.54	.77	.95	.77	.79
WMPF	.95	.66	.86	.83	.60	.87	.54	.76	.93	.77	.78
F15	.93	.45	.88	.96	.49	.87	.60	.74			
F15G3	.93	.48	.83	.94	.49	.88	.60	.74			
ROSE	.88	.59	.83	.92	.60	.86	.26	.70	.93	.77	.74
BLEU	.88	.48	.83	.90	.49	.85	.43	.69	.90	.83	.73
TER	-.83	-.33	-.64	-.89	-.37	-.77	**-.89**	.67	-.93	-.83	.72
MP4IBM1	-.91	-.56	-.50	-.12	-.43	-.08	.14	.35			
DFKI-PARSECONF		.31	.52								

Table 13: System-level Spearman's rho correlation of the automatic evaluation metrics with the human judgments for translation into English, ordered by average absolute value for the European languages. We did not calculate correlations with the human judgments for the system combinations for Czech to English and for Haitian Creole to English, because they had too few items (≤ 4) for reliable statistics.

	FR-EN (6337 PAIRS)	DE-EN (8950 PAIRS)	ES-EN (5974 PAIRS)	CZ-EN (3695 PAIRS)	AVERAGE
Segment-level correlation for translations into English					
MTERATER-PLUS	**.30**	**.36**	**.45**	**.36**	**.37**
TESLA-F	.28	.24	.39	.32	.31
TESLA-B	.28	.26	.36	.29	.30
METEOR-1.3-RANK	.23	.25	.38	.28	.29
METEOR-1.3-ADQ	.24	.25	.37	.27	.28
MPF	.25	.23	.34	.28	.28
AMBER-TI	.24	.26	.33	.27	.28
AMBER	.24	.25	.33	.27	.27
WMPF	.24	.23	.34	.26	.27
AMBER-NL	.24	.24	.30	.27	.26
MTERATER	.19	.26	.33	.24	.26
TESLA-M	.21	.23	.29	.23	.24
TINE-SRL-MATCH	.20	.19	.30	.24	.23
F15G3	.17	.15	.29	.21	.21
F15	.16	.14	.27	.22	.20
MP4IBM1	.15	.16	.18	.12	.15
DFKI-PARSECONF	n/a	.24	n/a	n/a	

Table 14: Segment-level Kendall's tau correlation of the automatic evaluation metrics with the human judgments for translation into English, ordered by average correlation.

had stronger correlation with human judgments than BLEU. The metrics that had the strongest correlation this year included two metrics, MTeRater and TINE, as well as metrics that have demonstrated strong correlation in previous years like TESLA and Meteor.

6.2 Segment-Level Metric Analysis

We measured the metrics' segment-level scores with the human rankings using Kendall's tau rank correlation coefficient. The reference was not included as an extra translation.

We calculated Kendall's tau as:

$$\tau = \frac{\text{num concordant pairs - num discordant pairs}}{\text{total pairs}}$$

where a concordant pair is a pair of two translations of the same segment in which the ranks calculated from the same human ranking task and from the corresponding metric scores agree; in a discordant pair, they disagree. In order to account for accuracy- vs. error-based metrics correctly, counts of concordant vs. discordant pairs were calculated specific to these two metric types. The possible values of τ range between 1 (where all pairs are concordant) and -1 (where all pairs are discordant). Thus an automatic evaluation metric with a higher value for τ is making predictions that are more similar to the human judgments than an automatic evaluation metric with a lower τ.

	EN-FR (6934 PAIRS)	EN-DE (10732 PAIRS)	EN-ES (8837 PAIRS)	EN-CZ (11651 PAIRS)	AVERAGE
Segment-level correlation for translations out of English					
AMBER-TI	**.32**	.22	**.31**	.21	**.27**
AMBER	.31	.21	**.31**	**.22**	.26
MPF	.31	**.22**	.30	.20	.26
WMPF	.31	**.22**	.29	.19	.25
AMBER-NL	.30	.19	.29	.20	.25
METEOR-1.3-RANK	.31	.14	.26	.19	.23
F15G3	.26	.08	.22	.13	.17
F15	.26	.07	.22	.12	.17
MP4IBM1	.21	.13	.13	.06	.13
TESLA-B	.29	.20	.28	n/a	
TESLA-M	.25	.18	.27	n/a	
TESLA-F	.30	.19	.26	n/a	

Table 15: Segment-level Kendall's tau correlation of the automatic evaluation metrics with the human judgments for translation out of English, ordered by average correlation.

We did not include cases where the human ranking was tied for two systems. As the metrics produce absolute scores, compared to five relative ranks in the human assessment, it would be potentially unfair to the metric to count a slightly different metric score as discordant with a tie in the relative human rankings. A tie in automatic metric rank for two translations was counted as discordant with two corresponding non-tied human judgments.

The correlations are shown in Table 14 for translations into English, and Table 15 out of English, sorted by average correlation across the four language pairs. The highest correlation for each language pair and the highest overall average are

ID	Participant	Metric Name
CMU-METEOR	Carnegie Mellon University	METEOR (Denkowski and Lavie, 2011a)
CU-SEMPOS-BLEU	Charles University	SemPOS/BLEU (Macháček and Bojar, 2011)
NUS-TESLA-F	National University of Singapore	TESLA-F (Dahlmeier et al., 2011)
RWTH-CDER	RWTH Aachen	CDER (Leusch and Ney, 2009)
SHEFFIELD-ROSE	The University of Sheffield	ROSE (single reference) (Song and Cohn, 2011)
STANFORD-DCP	Stanford	DCP (based on Liu and Gildea (2005))
BLEU	provided baseline	BLEU
BLEU-SINGLE	provided baseline	BLEU (single reference)

Table 16: Participants in the tunable-metric shared task. For comparison purposes, we included two BLEU-optimized systems in the evaluation as baselines.

bolded. There is a clear winner for the metrics that score translations into English: the MTeRater-Plus metric (Parton et al., 2011) has the highest segment level correlation across the board. For metrics that score translation into other languages, there is not such a clear-cut winner. The AMBER metric variants do well, as do MPF and WMPF.

7 Tunable Metrics Task

This year we introduced a new shared task that focuses on using evaluation metrics to tune the parameters of a statistical machine translation system. The intent of this task was to get researchers who develop automatic evaluation metrics for MT to work on the problem of using their metric to optimize the parameters of MT systems. Previous workshops have demonstrated that a number of metrics perform better than BLEU in terms of having stronger correlation with human judgments about the rankings of multiple machine translation systems. However, most MT system developers still optimize the parameters of their systems to BLEU. Here we aim to investigate the question of whether better metrics will result in better quality output when a system is optimized to them.

Because this was the first year that we ran the tunable metrics task, participation was limited to a few groups on an invitation-only basis. Table 16 lists the participants in this task. Metrics developers were invited to integrate their evaluation metric into a MERT optimization routine, which was then used to tune the parameters of a fixed statistical machine translation system. We evaluated whether the system tuned on their metrics produced higher-quality output than the baseline system that was tuned to BLEU, as is typically done. In order to evaluate whether the quality was better, we conducted a manual evaluation, in the same fashion that we evaluate the different MT systems submitted to the shared translation task.

We provide the participants with a fixed MT system for Urdu-English, along with a small parallel set to be used for tuning. Specifically, we provide developers with the following components:

- **Decoder** - the Joshua decoder was used in this pilot.
- **Decoder configuration file** - a Joshua configuration file that ensures all systems use the same search parameters.
- **Translation model** - an Urdu-to-English translation model, with syntax-based SCFG rules (Baker et al., 2010).
- **Language model** - a large 5-gram language model trained on the English Gigaword corpus
- **Development set** - a development set, with 4 English reference sets, to be used to optimize the system parameters.
- **Test set** - a test set consisting of 883 Urdu sentences, to be translated by the tuned system (no references provided).
- **Optimization routine** - we provide an implementation of minimum error rate training that allows new metrics to be easily integrated as the objective function.

Tunable Metrics Task
1324–1484 comparisons/system

System	$\geq$**others**	>others
BLEU •	**0.79**	0.28
BLEU-SINGLE •	**0.77**	0.27
CMU-METEOR •	**0.76**	0.27
RWTH-CDER	**0.76**	0.26
CU-SEMPOS-BLEU •	**0.74**	0.29
STANFORD-DCP •	**0.73**	0.27
NUS-TESLA-F	**0.68**	0.28
SHEFFIELD-ROSE	**0.05**	0.00

- indicates a **win**: no other system combination is statistically significantly better at p-level$\leq$0.10 in pairwise comparison.

Table 17: Official results for the WMT11 tunable-metric task. Systems are ordered by their $\geq$others score, reflecting how often their translations won or tied pairwise comparisons. The > column reflects how often a system strictly won a pairwise comparison.

	REF	BLEU	BLEU-SINGLE	CMU-METEOR	CU-SEMPOS-BLEU	NUS-TESLA-F	RWTH-CDER	SHEFFIELD-ROSE	STANFORD-DCP
REF	–	.15‡	.11‡	.13‡	.09‡	.09‡	.10‡	.00‡	.11‡
BLEU	**.78**‡	–	.15	**.11**	.20	.19†	.13*	.01‡	.14
BLEU-SINGLE	**.82**‡	**.20**	–	.11	.16	.21	.11	.00‡	**.20**
CMU-METEOR	**.84**‡	.09	**.15**	–	**.21**	.20	**.19**	.00‡	.19
CU-SEMPOS-BLEU	**.82**‡	**.23**	**.21**	.21	–	.12‡	.18	.00‡	.21
NUS-TESLA-F	**.80**‡	**.32**†	**.31**	**.28**	**.28**‡	–	**.31**	.00‡	.28
RWTH-CDER	**.79**‡	**.22***	**.16**	.16	**.22**	.23	–	.00‡	.15
SHEFFIELD-ROSE	**.98**‡	**.93**‡	**.93**‡	**.96**‡	**.95**‡	**.95**‡	**.93**‡	–	**.94**‡
STANFORD-DCP	**.82**‡	**.17**	.18	**.26**	**.27**	.28	.15	.00‡	–
> others	.83	.28	.27	.27	**.29**	.28	.26	.00	.27
>= others	.90	**.79**	.77	.76	.74	.68	.76	.05	.73

Table 18: Head to head comparisons for the tunable metrics task. The numbers indicate how often the system in the column was judged to be better than the system in the row. The difference between 100 and the sum of the corresponding cells is the percent of time that the two systems were judged to be equal.

We provided the metrics developers with Omar Zaidan's Z-MERT software (Zaidan, 2009), which implements Och (2003)'s minimum error rate training procedure. Z-MERT is designed to be modular with respect to the objective function, and allows BLEU to be easily replaced with other automatic evaluation metrics. Metric developers incorporated their metrics into Z-MERT by subclassing the EvaluationMetric.java abstract class. They ran Z-MERT on the dev set with the provided decoder/models, and created a weight vector for the system parameters.

Each team produced a distinct final weight vector, which was used to produce English translations of sentences in the test set. The different translations produced by tuning the system to different metrics were then evaluated using the manual evaluation pipeline.[7]

7.1 Results of the Tunable Metrics Task

The results of the evaluation are in Table 18. The scores show that the entries were quite close to each other, with the notable exception of the SHEFFIELD-ROSE-tuned system, which produced overly-long and erroneous output (possibly due to an implementation issue). This is also evident from the fact that 38% of pairwise comparisons indicated a **tie** between the two systems, with the tie rate increasing to a full 47% when excluding comparisons involving the reference. This is a very high tie rate – the corresponding figure in, say, European language pairs (individual systems) is only 21%.

What makes the different entries appear even more closely-matched is that the ranking changes significantly when ordering systems by their >others score rather than the $\geq$others score (i.e. when rewarding only wins, and not rewarding ties). NUS-TESLA-F goes from being a bottom entry to being a top entry, with CU-SEMPOS-BLEU also benefiting, changing from the middle to the top rank.

Either way, we see that a BLEU -tuned system is performing just as well as systems tuned to the other metrics. This might be an indication that some work remains to be done before a move away from BLEU-tuning is fully justified. On the other hand, the close results might be an artifact of the language pair choice. Urdu-English translation is still a relatively difficult problem, and MT outputs are still of a relatively low quality. It might be the case that human annotators are simply not very good at distin-

[7]We also recased and detokenized each system's output, to ensure the outputs are more readable and easier to evaluate.

guishing one bad translation from another bad translation, especially at such a fine-grained level.

It is worth noting that the designers of the TESLA family replicated the setup of this tunable metric task for three European language pairs, and found that human judges *did* perceive a difference in quality between a TESLA-tuned system and a BLEU -tuned system (Liu et al., 2011).

7.2 Anticipated Changes Next Year

This year's effort was a pilot of the task, so we intentionally limited the task to some degree, to make it easier to iron out the details. Possible changes for next year include:

- More language pairs / translations into languages other than English. This year we focus on Urdu-English because the language pair requires a lot of reordering, and our syntactic model has more parameters to optimize than the standard Hiero and phrase-based models.
- Provide some human judgments about the model's output, so that people can experiment with regression models.
- Include a single reference track along with the multiple reference track. Some metrics may be better at dealing with the (more common) case of there being only a single reference translation available for every source sentence.
- Allow for experimentation with the MIRA optimization routine instead of MERT. MIRA can scale to a greater number of features, but requires that metrics be decomposable.

8 Summary

As in previous editions of this workshop we carried out an extensive manual and automatic evaluation of machine translation performance for translating from European languages into English, and vice versa.

The number of participants grew slightly compared to previous editions of the WMT workshop, with 36 groups from 27 institutions participating in the translation task of WMT11, 10 groups from 10 institutions participating in the system combination task, and 10 groups from 8 institutions participating in the featured translation task (Haitian Creole SMS into English).

This year was also the first time that we included a language pair (Haitian-English) with non-European source language and with very limited resources for the source language side. Also the genre of the Haitian-English task differed from previous WMT tasks as the Haitian-English translations are SMS messages.

WMT11 also introduced a new shared task focusing on evaluation metrics to tune the parameters of a statistical machine translation system in which 6 groups have participated.

As in previous years, all data sets generated by this workshop, including the human judgments, system translations and automatic scores, are publicly available for other researchers to analyze.[8]

Acknowledgments

This work was supported in parts by the EuroMatrixPlus project funded by the European Commission (7th Framework Programme), the GALE program of the US Defense Advanced Research Projects Agency, Contract No. HR0011-06-C-0022, the US National Science Foundation under grant IIS-0713448, and the CoSyne project FP7-ICT-4-248531 funded by the European Commission. The views and findings are the authors' alone. A big thank you to Ondřej Bojar, Simon Carter, Christian Federmann, Will Lewis, Rob Munro and Hervé Saint-Amand, and to the shared task participants.

References

Vera Aleksic and Gregor Thurmair. 2011. Personal Translator at WMT2011. In *Proceedings of the Sixth Workshop on Statistical Machine Translation*.

Alexandre Allauzen, Hélène Bonneau-Maynard, Hai-Son Le, Aurélien Max, Guillaume Wisniewski, François Yvon, Gilles Adda, Josep Maria Crego, Adrien Lardilleux, Thomas Lavergne, and Artem Sokolov. 2011. LIMSI @ WMT11. In *Proceedings of the Sixth Workshop on Statistical Machine Translation*.

Yigal Attali and Jill Burstein. 2006. Automated essay scoring with e-rater v.2.0. *Journal of Technology, Learning, and Assessment*, 4(3):159–174.

Eleftherios Avramidis, Maja Popović, David Vilar, and Aljoscha Burchardt. 2011. Evaluate with confidence

[8] `http://statmt.org/wmt11/results.html`

estimation: Machine ranking of translation outputs using grammatical features. In *Proceedings of the Sixth Workshop on Statistical Machine Translation.*

Wilker Aziz, Miguel Rios, and Lucia Specia. 2011. Shallow semantic trees for SMT. In *Proceedings of the Sixth Workshop on Statistical Machine Translation.*

Kathryn Baker, Michael Bloodgood, Chris Callison-Burch, Bonnie Dorr, Scott Miller, Christine Piatko, Nathaniel W. Filardo, and Lori Levin. 2010. Semantically-informed syntactic machine translation: A tree-grafting approach. In *Proceedings of AMTA.*

Loïc Barrault. 2011. MANY improvements for WMT'11. In *Proceedings of the Sixth Workshop on Statistical Machine Translation.*

Ergun Bicici and Deniz Yuret. 2011. RegMT system for machine translation, system combination, and evaluation. In *Proceedings of the Sixth Workshop on Statistical Machine Translation.*

Ondřej Bojar and Aleš Tamchyna. 2011. Improving translation model by monolingual data. In *Proceedings of the Sixth Workshop on Statistical Machine Translation.*

Chris Callison-Burch, Cameron Fordyce, Philipp Koehn, Christof Monz, and Josh Schroeder. 2007. (Meta-) evaluation of machine translation. In *Proceedings of the Second Workshop on Statistical Machine Translation (WMT07)*, Prague, Czech Republic.

Chris Callison-Burch, Cameron Fordyce, Philipp Koehn, Christof Monz, and Josh Schroeder. 2008. Further meta-evaluation of machine translation. In *Proceedings of the Third Workshop on Statistical Machine Translation (WMT08)*, Colmbus, Ohio.

Chris Callison-Burch, Philipp Koehn, Christof Monz, and Josh Schroeder. 2009. Findings of the 2009 workshop on statistical machine translation. In *Proceedings of the Fourth Workshop on Statistical Machine Translation (WMT09)*, Athens, Greece.

Chris Callison-Burch, Philipp Koehn, Christof Monz, Kay Peterson, Mark Przybocki, and Omar F. Zaidan. 2010. Findings of the 2010 joint workshop on statistical machine translation and metrics for machine translation. In *Proceedings of the Fourth Workshop on Statistical Machine Translation (WMT10)*, Uppsala, Sweden.

Boxing Chen and Roland Kuhn. 2011. Amber: A modified bleu, enhanced ranking metric. In *Proceedings of the Sixth Workshop on Statistical Machine Translation.*

Jacob Cohen. 1960. A coefficient of agreement for nominal scales. *Educational and Psychological Measurment*, 20(1):37–46.

Antonio M. Corbí-Bellot, Mikel L. Forcada, Sergio Ortiz-Rojas, Juan Antonio Pérez-Ortiz, Gema Ramírez-Sánchez, Felipe Sánchez-Martínez, Iñaki Alegria, Aingeru Mayor, and Kepa Sarasola. 2005. An open-source shallow-transfer machine translation engine for the romance languages of Spain. In *Proceedings of the European Association for Machine Translation*, pages 79–86.

Marta R. Costa-jussà and Rafael E. Banchs. 2011. The BM-I2R Haitian-Créole-to-English translation system description for the WMT 2011 evaluation campaign. In *Proceedings of the Sixth Workshop on Statistical Machine Translation.*

Daniel Dahlmeier, Chang Liu, and Hwee Tou Ng. 2011. TESLA at WMT 2011: Translation evaluation and tunable metric. In *Proceedings of the Sixth Workshop on Statistical Machine Translation.*

Michael Denkowski and Alon Lavie. 2011a. Meteor 1.3: Automatic metric for reliable optimization and evaluation of machine translation systems. In *Proceedings of the Sixth Workshop on Statistical Machine Translation.*

Michael Denkowski and Alon Lavie. 2011b. METEOR-Tuned Phrase-Based SMT: CMU French-English and Haitian-English Systems for WMT 2011. Technical Report CMU-LTI-11-011, Language Technologies Institute, Carnegie Mellon University.

Chris Dyer, Kevin Gimpel, Jonathan H. Clark, and Noah A. Smith. 2011. The CMU-ARK German-English translation system. In *Proceedings of the Sixth Workshop on Statistical Machine Translation.*

Vladimir Eidelman, Kristy Hollingshead, and Philip Resnik. 2011. Noisy SMS machine translation in low-density languages. In *Proceedings of the Sixth Workshop on Statistical Machine Translation.*

Christian Federmann and Sabine Hunsicker. 2011. Stochastic parse tree selection for an existing RBMT system. In *Proceedings of the Sixth Workshop on Statistical Machine Translation.*

Robert Frederking, Alexander Rudnicky, and Christopher Hogan. 1997. Interactive speech translation in the DIPLOMAT project. In *Proceedings of the ACL-1997 Workshop on Spoken Language Translation.*

Markus Freitag, Gregor Leusch, Joern Wuebker, Stephan Peitz, Hermann Ney, Teresa Herrmann, Jan Niehues, Alex Waibel, Alexandre Allauzen, Gilles Adda, Josep Maria Crego, Bianka Buschbeck, Tonio Wandmacher, and Jean Senellart. 2011. Joint WMT submission of the QUAERO project. In *Proceedings of the Sixth Workshop on Statistical Machine Translation.*

Yoko Futagi, Paul Deane, Martin Chodorow, and Joel Tetreault. 2008. A computational approach to detecting collocation errors in the writing of non-native speakers of English. *Computer Assisted Language Learning Journal.*

Jesús González-Rubio and Francisco Casacuberta. 2011. The UPV-PRHLT combination system for WMT 2011.

In *Proceedings of the Sixth Workshop on Statistical Machine Translation*.

Greg Hanneman and Alon Lavie. 2011. CMU syntax-based machine translation at WMT 2011. In *Proceedings of the Sixth Workshop on Statistical Machine Translation*.

Christian Hardmeier, Jörg Tiedemann, Markus Saers, Marcello Federico, and Mathur Prashant. 2011. The Uppsala-FBK systems at WMT 2011. In *Proceedings of the Sixth Workshop on Statistical Machine Translation*.

Kenneth Heafield and Alon Lavie. 2011. CMU system combination in WMT 2011. In *Proceedings of the Sixth Workshop on Statistical Machine Translation*.

Teresa Herrmann, Mohammed Mediani, Jan Niehues, and Alex Waibel. 2011. The Karlsruhe Institute of Technology translation systems for the WMT 2011. In *Proceedings of the Sixth Workshop on Statistical Machine Translation*.

Sanjika Hewavitharana, Nguyen Bach, Qin Gao, Vamshi Ambati, and Stephan Vogel. 2011. CMU Haitian Creole-English translation system for WMT 2011. In *Proceedings of the Sixth Workshop on Statistical Machine Translation*.

Maria Holmqvist, Sara Stymne, and Lars Ahrenberg. 2011. Experiments with word alignment, normalization and clause reordering for SMT between English and German. In *Proceedings of the Sixth Workshop on Statistical Machine Translation*.

Chang Hu, Philip Resnik, Yakov Kronrod, Vladimir Eidelman, Olivia Buzek, and Benjamin B. Bederson. 2011. The value of monolingual crowdsourcing in a real-world translation scenario: Simulation using Haitian Creole emergency SMS messages. In *Proceedings of the Sixth Workshop on Statistical Machine Translation*.

Matthias Huck, Joern Wuebker, Christoph Schmidt, Markus Freitag, Stephan Peitz, Daniel Stein, Arnaud Dagnelies, Saab Mansour, Gregor Leusch, and Hermann Ney. 2011. The RWTH Aachen machine translation system for WMT 2011. In *Proceedings of the Sixth Workshop on Statistical Machine Translation*.

Maxim Khalilov and Khalil Sima'an. 2011. ILLC-UvA translation system for EMNLP-WMT 2011. In *Proceedings of the Sixth Workshop on Statistical Machine Translation*.

Philipp Koehn and Christof Monz. 2006. Manual and automatic evaluation of machine translation between European languages. In *Proceedings of NAACL 2006 Workshop on Statistical Machine Translation*, New York, New York.

Philipp Koehn, Hieu Hoang, Alexandra Birch, Chris Callison-Burch, Marcello Federico, Nicola Bertoldi, Brooke Cowan, Wade Shen, Christine Moran, Richard Zens, Chris Dyer, Ondrej Bojar, Alexandra Constantin, and Evan Herbst. 2007. Moses: Open source toolkit for statistical machine translation. In *Proceedings of the ACL-2007 Demo and Poster Sessions*, Prague, Czech Republic.

Oliver Lacey-Hall. 2011. The guardian's poverty matters blog: How remote teams can help the rapid response to disasters, March.

J. Richard Landis and Gary G. Koch. 1977. The measurement of observer agreement for categorical data. *Biometrics*, 33:159–174.

Gregor Leusch and Hermann Ney. 2009. Edit distances with block movements and error rate confidence estimates. *Machine Translation*, 23:129–140.

Gregor Leusch, Markus Freitag, and Hermann Ney. 2011. The RWTH system combination system for WMT 2011. In *Proceedings of the Sixth Workshop on Statistical Machine Translation*.

William Lewis, Robert Munro, and Stephan Vogel. 2011. Crisis MT: Developing a cookbook for MT in crisis situations. In *Proceedings of the Sixth Workshop on Statistical Machine Translation*.

William D. Lewis. 2010. Haitian Creole: How to build and ship an MT engine from scratch in 4 days, 17hours, & 30 minutes. In *Proceedings of EAMT 2010*.

Zhifei Li, Chris Callison-Burch, Chris Dyer, Juri Ganitkevitch, Ann Irvine, Sanjeev Khudanpur, Lane Schwartz, Wren Thornton, Ziyuan Wang, Jonathan Weese, and Omar Zaidan. 2010. Joshua 2.0: A toolkit for parsing-based machine translation with syntax, semirings, discriminative training and other goodies. In *Proceedings of the Joint Fifth Workshop on Statistical Machine Translation and MetricsMATR*, Uppsala, Sweden, July.

Ding Liu and Daniel Gildea. 2005. Syntactic features for evaluation of machine translation. In *Proceedings of the ACL Workshop on Intrinsic and Extrinsic Evaluation Measures for Machine Translation and/or Summarization*, pages 25–32.

Chang Liu, Daniel Dahlmeier, and Hwee Tou Ng. 2011. Better evaluation metrics lead to better machine translation. In *Proceedings of EMNLP*.

Verónica López-Ludeña and Rubén San-Segundo. 2011. UPM system for the translation task. In *Proceedings of the Sixth Workshop on Statistical Machine Translation*.

Matouš Macháček and Ondřej Bojar. 2011. Approximating a deep-syntactic metric for MT evaluation and tuning. In *Proceedings of the Sixth Workshop on Statistical Machine Translation*.

David Mareček, Rudolf Rosa, Petra Galuščáková, and Ondřej Bojar. 2011. Two-step translation with grammatical post-processing. In *Proceedings of the Sixth Workshop on Statistical Machine Translation*.

Robert Munro. 2010. Crowdsourced translation for emergency response in Haiti: the global collaboration of local knowledge. In *Proceedings of the AMTA Workshop on Collaborative Crowdsourcing for Translation*.

Douglas W. Oard and Franz Josef Och. 2003. Rapid-response machine translation for unexpected languages. In *Proceedings of MT Summit IX*.

Douglas W. Oard. 2003. The surprise language exercises. *ACM Transactions on Asian Language Information Processing*, 2(2):79–84.

Franz Josef Och. 2003. Minimum error rate training for statistical machine translation. In *Proceedings of the 41st Annual Meeting of the Association for Computational Linguistics (ACL-2003)*, Sapporo, Japan.

Kishore Papineni, Salim Roukos, Todd Ward, and Wei-Jing Zhu. 2002. Bleu: A method for automatic evaluation of machine translation. In *Proceedings of the 40th Annual Meeting of the Association for Computational Linguistics (ACL-2002)*, Philadelphia, Pennsylvania.

Kristen Parton, Joel Tetreault, Nitin Madnani, and Martin Chodorow. 2011. E-rating machine translation. In *Proceedings of the Sixth Workshop on Statistical Machine Translation*.

Martin Popel, David Mareček, Nathan Green, and Zdeněk Žabokrtský. 2011. Influence of parser choice on dependency-based MT. In *Proceedings of the Sixth Workshop on Statistical Machine Translation*.

Maja Popović, David Vilar, Eleftherios Avramidis, and Aljoscha Burchardt. 2011. Evaluation without references: IBM1 scores as evaluation metrics. In *Proceedings of the Sixth Workshop on Statistical Machine Translation*.

Maja Popović. 2011. Morphemes and POS tags for n-gram based evaluation metrics. In *Proceedings of the Sixth Workshop on Statistical Machine Translation*.

Marion Potet, Raphaël Rubino, Benjamin Lecouteux, Stéphane Huet, Laurent Besacier, Hervé Blanchon, and Fabrice Lefèvre. 2011. The LIGA (LIG/LIA) machine translation system for WMT 2011. In *Proceedings of the Sixth Workshop on Statistical Machine Translation*.

Mark Przybocki, Kay Peterson, and Sebastian Bronsart. 2008. Official results of the NIST 2008 "Metrics for MAchine TRanslation" challenge (MetricsMATR08). In *AMTA-2008 workshop on Metrics for Machine Translation*, Honolulu, Hawaii.

Miguel Rios, Wilker Aziz, and Lucia Specia. 2011. TINE: A metric to assess MT adequacy. In *Proceedings of the Sixth Workshop on Statistical Machine Translation*.

Christian Rishøj and Anders Søgaard. 2011. Factored translation with unsupervised word clusters. In *Proceedings of the Sixth Workshop on Statistical Machine Translation*.

Antti-Veikko Rosti, Bing Zhang, Spyros Matsoukas, and Richard Schwartz. 2011. Expected BLEU training for graphs: BBN system description for WMT11 system combination task. In *Proceedings of the Sixth Workshop on Statistical Machine Translation*.

Víctor M. Sánchez-Cartagena, Felipe Sánchez-Martínez, and Juan Antonio Pérez-Ortiz. 2011. The Universitat d'Alacant hybrid machine translation system for WMT 2011. In *Proceedings of the Sixth Workshop on Statistical Machine Translation*.

Holger Schwenk, Patrik Lambert, Loïc Barrault, Christophe Servan, Sadaf Abdul-Rauf, Haithem Afli, and Kashif Shah. 2011. LIUM's SMT machine translation systems for WMT 2011. In *Proceedings of the Sixth Workshop on Statistical Machine Translation*.

Rico Sennrich. 2011. The UZH system combination system for WMT 2011. In *Proceedings of the Sixth Workshop on Statistical Machine Translation*.

Matthew Snover, Bonnie Dorr, Richard Schwartz, Linnea Micciulla, and John Makhoul. 2006. A study of translation edit rate with targeted human annotation. In *Proceedings of the 7th Biennial Conference of the Association for Machine Translation in the Americas (AMTA-2006)*, Cambridge, Massachusetts.

Xingyi Song and Trevor Cohn. 2011. Regression and ranking based optimisation for sentence level MT evaluation. In *Proceedings of the Sixth Workshop on Statistical Machine Translation*.

Lucia Specia, Dhwaj Raj, and Marco Turchi. 2010. Machine translation evaluation versus quality estimation. *Machine Translation*, 24(1):39–50.

Sara Stymne. 2011. Spell checking techniques for replacement of unknown words and data cleaning for Haitian Creole SMS translation. In *Proceedings of the Sixth Workshop on Statistical Machine Translation*.

Joel Tetreault and Martin Chodorow. 2008. The ups and downs of preposition error detection. In *Proceedings of COLING*, Manchester, UK.

Jonathan Weese, Juri Ganitkevitch, Chris Callison-Burch, Matt Post, and Adam Lopez. 2011. Joshua 3.0: Syntax-based machine translation with the Thrax grammar extractor. In *Proceedings of the Sixth Workshop on Statistical Machine Translation*.

Eric Wehrli, Luka Nerima, and Yves Scherrer. 2009. Deep linguistic multilingual translation and bilingual dictionaries. In *Proceedings of the Fourth Workshop on Statistical Machine Translation*, pages 90–94.

Daguang Xu, Yuan Cao, and Damianos Karakos. 2011a. Description of the JHU system combination scheme for WMT 2011. In *Proceedings of the Sixth Workshop on Statistical Machine Translation*.

Jia Xu, Hans Uszkoreit, Casey Kennington, David Vilar, and Xiaojun Zhang. 2011b. DFKI hybrid machine translation system for WMT 2011 - on the integration of SMT and RBMT. In *Proceedings of the Sixth Workshop on Statistical Machine Translation*.

Omar F. Zaidan. 2009. Z-MERT: A fully configurable open source tool for minimum error rate training of machine translation systems. *The Prague Bulletin of Mathematical Linguistics*, 91:79–88.

Francisco Zamora-Martinez and Maria Jose Castro-Bleda. 2011. CEU-UPV English-Spanish system for WMT11. In *Proceedings of the Sixth Workshop on Statistical Machine Translation*.

Daniel Zeman. 2011. Hierarchical phrase-based MT at the Charles University for the WMT 2011 shared task. In *Proceedings of the Sixth Workshop on Statistical Machine Translation*.

A Pairwise System Comparisons by Human Judges

Tables 19–38 show pairwise comparisons between systems for each language pair. The numbers in each of the tables' cells indicate the percentage of times that the system in that column was judged to be better than the system in that row. Bolding indicates the winner of the two systems. The difference between 100 and the sum of the complementary cells is the percent of time that the two systems were judged to be equal.

Because there were so many systems and data conditions the significance of each pairwise comparison needs to be quantified. We applied the Sign Test to measure which comparisons indicate genuine differences (rather than differences that are attributable to chance). In the following tables $\star$ indicates statistical significance at $p \leq 0.10$, † indicates statistical significance at $p \leq 0.05$, and ‡ indicates statistical significance at $p \leq 0.01$, according to the Sign Test.

B Automatic Scores

Tables 39–48 give the automatic scores for each of the systems.

C Meta-evaluation

Tables 49 and 50 give a detailed breakdown of intra- and inter-annotator agreement rates for all of manual evaluation tracks of WMT11, broken down by language pair.

	REF	CST	CU-BOJAR	CU-ZEMAN	JHU	ONLINE-B	SYSTRAN	UEDIN	UPPSALA
REF	–	.02‡	.04‡	.01‡	.04‡	.04‡	.04‡	.05‡	.04‡
CST	**.88**‡	–	**.49**‡	**.36**	**.49**†	**.59**‡	**.41**	**.58**‡	**.44**†
CU-BOJAR	**.91**‡	.27‡	–	.27‡	.30	**.48**‡	.28‡	**.41**†	**.41**
CU-ZEMAN	**.94**‡	.31	**.49**‡	–	**.47**‡	**.67**‡	**.47**†	**.64**‡	**.49**‡
JHU	**.89**‡	.29†	**.39**	.28‡	–	**.47**‡	.36	**.41**†	.36
ONLINE-B	**.84**‡	.20‡	.27‡	.19‡	.28‡	–	.24‡	.30	.27‡
SYSTRAN	**.91**‡	.31	**.49**‡	.30†	**.39**	**.59**‡	–	**.56**‡	.37
UEDIN	**.89**‡	.16‡	.25†	.16‡	.27†	**.36**	.23‡	–	.25†
UPPSALA	**.84**‡	.28†	.40	.24‡	**.37**	**.49**‡	**.38**	**.45**†	–
> others	.89	.23	.36	.23	.33	**.46**	.31	.43	.33
>= others	.96	.47	.60	.44	.57	.68	.51	**.69**	.57

Table 19: Ranking scores for entries in the Czech-English task (individual system track).

	REF	COMMERCIAL-1	COMMERCIAL-2	CU-BOJAR	CU-MARECEK	CU-POPEL	CU-TAMCHYNA	CU-ZEMAN	JHU	ONLINE-B	UEDIN
REF	–	.05‡	.04‡	.04‡	.04‡	.05‡	.05‡	.04‡	.03‡	.04‡	.04‡
COMMERCIAL-1	**.91**‡	–	.36	**.53**‡	**.50**‡	**.47**‡	**.44**⋆	.33‡	.33†	**.55**‡	**.45**†
COMMERCIAL-2	**.87**‡	**.42**	–	**.52**‡	**.47**⋆	**.47**‡	**.50**‡	.30‡	.40	**.50**‡	**.43**
CU-BOJAR	**.89**‡	.31‡	.31‡	–	**.29**	.41	.21†	.19‡	.27‡	**.42**⋆	.31⋆
CU-MARECEK	**.88**‡	.31‡	.37⋆	.27	–	.35†	.28	.21‡	.30‡	.39	.28†
CU-POPEL	**.85**‡	.33‡	.29‡	**.43**	**.45**†	–	**.41**	.27‡	.31‡	**.50**‡	.39
CU-TAMCHYNA	**.87**‡	.34⋆	.35‡	**.30**†	**.32**	.40	–	.22‡	.25‡	**.45**‡	.32
CU-ZEMAN	**.91**‡	**.47**‡	**.52**‡	**.56**‡	**.56**‡	**.55**‡	**.55**‡	–	**.44**‡	**.64**‡	**.54**‡
JHU	**.91**‡	**.43**†	**.41**	**.50**‡	**.47**‡	**.51**‡	**.51**‡	.31‡	–	**.52**‡	**.48**‡
ONLINE-B	**.86**‡	.27‡	.32‡	.33⋆	**.39**	.33‡	.29‡	.18‡	.23‡	–	.31‡
UEDIN	**.85**‡	.34†	.40	**.40**⋆	**.37**†	**.42**	**.36**	.24‡	.25‡	**.44**‡	–
> others	.88	.33	.34	.39	.39	.40	.36	.23	.28	**.44**	.35
>= others	.96	.51	.51	.64	.63	.58	.62	.43	.49	**.65**	.59

Table 20: Ranking scores for entries in the English-Czech task (individual system track).

	REF	CMU-DYER	CST	CU-ZEMAN	DFKI-XU	JHU	KIT	KOC	LIMSI	LINGUATEC	LIU	ONLINE-A	ONLINE-B	RBMT-1	RBMT-2	RBMT-3	RBMT-4	RBMT-5	RWTH-WUEBKER	UEDIN	UPPSALA
REF	–	.05‡	.02‡	.03‡	.04‡	.00‡	.08‡	.04‡	.00‡	.07‡	.05‡	.07‡	.14‡	.02‡	.08‡	.00‡	.06‡	.08‡	.02‡	.10‡	.08‡
CMU-DYER	**.95**‡	–	.18‡	.17‡	.33	.26⋆	.22‡	.12‡	.29⋆	.43	.23⋆	.43	**.54**	.32	.20†	.40	**.43**	**.48**	.31	.19†	.18‡
CST	**.96**‡	**.74**‡	–	**.42**	**.62**‡	**.35**	**.68**‡	**.44**‡	**.47**⋆	**.78**‡	**.62**‡	**.77**‡	**.73**‡	**.81**‡	**.70**‡	**.74**‡	**.67**‡	**.53**⋆	**.65**‡	**.47**	**.51**
CU-ZEMAN	**.97**‡	**.67**‡	.22	–	**.56**†	.26†	**.41**	.22⋆	**.48**	**.66**‡	**.46**	**.60**‡	**.62**‡	**.73**‡	**.57**†	**.60**†	**.62**‡	**.53**⋆	**.40**	**.44**	**.48**
DFKI-XU	**.94**‡	**.44**	.06‡	.24†	–	.10‡	.26	.17‡	**.49**†	**.47**	.21⋆	.42	**.45**	**.52**	.42	**.45**	**.51**	.39	**.40**	**.48**	.29
JHU	**1.00**‡	**.61**⋆	.33	**.55**†	**.64**‡	–	**.59**†	**.45**	**.51**⋆	**.59**	**.52**⋆	**.68**‡	**.63**†	**.62**‡	**.64**†	**.65**‡	**.58**†	**.46**	**.61**‡	**.44**	.38
KIT	**.87**‡	**.65**‡	.12‡	.21	**.44**	.23†	–	.34	**.40**	**.54**	.30	**.43**	**.57**†	.44	.43	.47	**.50**	**.53**	**.40**	.28	.17‡
KOC	**.96**‡	**.64**‡	.09‡	**.49**⋆	**.66**‡	.36	**.43**	–	**.43**	**.69**‡	**.57**†	**.69**‡	**.63**‡	**.62**†	.41	**.63**‡	**.59**	**.52**⋆	**.51**	**.59**⋆	**.40**
LIMSI	**.96**‡	**.54**⋆	.24⋆	.30	.22†	.25⋆	.38	.27	–	**.63**†	**.52**	**.43**	**.55**†	.43	**.43**	**.59**†	**.47**	.40	.41	.32	**.44**
LINGUATEC	**.91**‡	**.45**	.13‡	.24‡	.38	.32	.34	.18‡	.27†	–	.26†	**.45**	**.62**†	**.46**	.20‡	**.49**	**.53**	.36	.41	.32⋆	.29†
LIU	**.89**‡	**.49**⋆	.14‡	.29	**.54**⋆	.25⋆	**.48**	.24†	.31	**.64**†	–	**.47**	**.61**†	**.52**	**.46**	**.48**	**.50**	.23‡	**.48**	.37	.36
ONLINE-A	**.88**‡	**.47**	.12‡	.25‡	.42	.18‡	.41	.19‡	.39	.39	.30	–	.32	.26†	.28	.46	.36	.35	.42	.19‡	.27‡
ONLINE-B	**.78**‡	.38	.16‡	.23‡	.33	.28†	.26†	.16‡	.26†	.29†	.22†	**.38**	–	.23‡	.23†	.29⋆	.29⋆	.22‡	.27	.22†	.18‡
RBMT-1	**.96**‡	**.42**	.09‡	.18‡	.35	.21‡	**.51**	.23†	.43	.41	.38	**.56**†	**.62**‡	–	.31	**.46**	**.39**	.13	**.48**	**.50**	.30⋆
RBMT-2	**.86**‡	**.54**†	.15‡	.28†	**.48**	.29†	.43	.41	.39	**.55**‡	.44	**.51**	**.64**†	**.43**	–	**.55**⋆	**.47**	**.54**⋆	**.44**	**.41**	.29⋆
RBMT-3	**.92**‡	**.42**	.11‡	.27†	.32	.23‡	.47	.18‡	.19†	.34	.38	**.49**	**.55**⋆	.38	.26⋆	–	.36	.29⋆	.34	.33	.28†
RBMT-4	**.88**‡	.36	.19‡	.24‡	.38	.29†	.43	.38	.45	.32	.37	**.44**	**.56**⋆	.33	.34	**.45**	–	.35	.29⋆	**.51**	.24†
RBMT-5	**.92**‡	.45	.27⋆	.27⋆	**.45**	.32	.37	.27⋆	**.47**	**.47**	**.61**‡	**.55**	**.67**‡	**.26**	.24⋆	**.53**⋆	**.46**	–	.45	**.47**	.39
RWTH-WUEBKER	**.93**‡	**.50**	.23‡	.26	.33	.20‡	.24	.36	.41	**.44**	.39	**.47**	**.55**	.44	.38	**.53**	**.56**⋆	.45	–	.21	**.39**
UEDIN	**.88**‡	**.59**†	.24	.28	.28	.33	**.50**	.24⋆	**.45**	**.65**⋆	**.40**	**.67**‡	**.62**†	.34	.39	**.52**	.41	.36	**.43**	–	**.48**
UPPSALA	**.92**‡	**.64**‡	.27	.29	**.39**	**.44**	**.58**‡	.32	.41	**.66**†	**.53**	**.68**‡	**.69**‡	**.59**⋆	**.59**⋆	**.58**†	**.61**†	**.54**	.36	.31	–
> others	.92	.50	.17	.28	.40	.26	.40	.26	.38	.51	.40	.51	**.57**	.43	.38	.49	.47	.39	.41	.36	.32
>= others	.95	.66	.37	.47	.60	.43	.57	.45	.56	.63	.57	.66	**.72**	.60	.54	.64	.61	.56	.59	.55	.47

Table 21: Ranking scores for entries in the German-English task (individual system track).

	REF	COPENHAGEN	CU-TAMCHYNA	CU-ZEMAN	DFKI-FEDERMANN	DFKI-XU	ILLC-UVA	JHU	KIT	KOC	LIMSI	LIU	ONLINE-A	ONLINE-B	RBMT-1	RBMT-2	RBMT-3	RBMT-4	RBMT-5	RWTH-FREITAG	UEDIN	UOW	UPPSALA
REF	–	.08‡	.06‡	.00‡	.13‡	.02‡	.05‡	.05‡	.02‡	.02‡	.16‡	.06‡	.11‡	.07‡	.14‡	.14‡	.19‡	.11‡	.11‡	.16‡	.07‡	.07‡	.08‡
COPENHAGEN	**.85‡**	–	.31	.09‡	**.60‡**	**.39**	.25	.32	**.41**	.27	**.36**	**.34**	**.49†**	**.61‡**	**.56‡**	**.61‡**	**.64‡**	**.64‡**	**.60**	.26	**.49**	.30	.16
CU-TAMCHYNA	**.92‡**	**.37**	–	.13†	**.61‡**	**.48†**	.30	**.38**	**.58†**	.33	**.39**	**.41⋆**	**.55†**	**.57‡**	**.72‡**	**.69‡**	**.81‡**	**.49**	**.59†**	**.47**	**.39**	**.40**	**.43**
CU-ZEMAN	**1.00‡**	**.60‡**	**.41†**	–	**.76‡**	**.78‡**	**.51†**	**.47⋆**	**.64‡**	**.53‡**	**.66‡**	**.49⋆**	**.77‡**	**.68‡**	**.69‡**	**.64‡**	**.70‡**	**.64‡**	**.72‡**	**.55‡**	**.47**	**.44**	**.50**
DFKI-FEDERMANN	**.72‡**	.19‡	.17‡	.16‡	–	**.39**	.25‡	.38	.38	.24‡	.32	.29	.35	.40	**.43**	.33	**.39**	.19	.33⋆	.22†	.31	.11‡	.30
DFKI-XU	**.84‡**	.31	.21†	.08‡	.37	–	.25†	.32	.34	.12‡	**.37**	.30	.35	**.47**	**.54⋆**	.30	**.51⋆**	**.43**	.37	.20†	.22†	.25†	.14‡
ILLC-UVA	**.90‡**	**.39**	**.37**	.25†	**.63‡**	**.50†**	–	**.41⋆**	**.58‡**	.35	**.56‡**	**.38**	**.55†**	**.63‡**	**.61‡**	**.63‡**	**.71‡**	**.75‡**	**.62†**	**.33**	**.56‡**	**.38**	**.41**
JHU	**.91‡**	**.45**	.27	.27⋆	**.41**	**.40**	.20⋆	–	.37	.27	**.43**	**.50‡**	**.58†**	**.59‡**	**.43**	**.55†**	**.72‡**	**.50**	**.50**	**.50⋆**	**.47**	**.46**	.22†
KIT	**.87‡**	.24	.23†	.17‡	**.41**	**.43**	.26‡	.37	–	.16‡	**.51**	.27†	.37	**.45⋆**	**.47**	.39	**.58†**	**.53**	**.47**	.23‡	.24	.21‡	.17‡
KOC	**.95‡**	**.35**	**.35**	.13‡	**.61‡**	**.65‡**	**.38**	**.42**	**.57‡**	–	**.47⋆**	.33	**.47⋆**	**.62‡**	**.61†**	**.53†**	**.64‡**	**.63‡**	**.45**	.20	**.38**	**.37**	.18†
LIMSI	**.77‡**	.31	.26	.11‡	**.48**	.35	.18‡	.30	.33	.23⋆	–	.36	**.39**	**.50†**	**.52**	**.47**	**.48**	.39	.42	.18‡	.22†	.28	.14‡
LIU	**.84‡**	.32	.20⋆	.25⋆	**.51**	**.38**	.26	.21‡	**.51†**	**.35**	**.39**	–	**.51**	**.49⋆**	**.63†**	**.52⋆**	**.56**	**.48⋆**	**.56**	.29	**.38**	.25	.25
ONLINE-A	**.75‡**	.21†	.24†	.09‡	**.48**	**.41**	.22†	.30†	.37	.25⋆	.37	.37	–	**.46**	.37	**.41**	**.47**	.33	.44	.27⋆	.28	.22‡	.16‡
ONLINE-B	**.91‡**	.17‡	.15‡	.13‡	**.44**	.22	.17‡	.16‡	.20⋆	.15‡	.24†	.25⋆	.27	–	**.43**	.35	**.48**	.33	.17‡	.17‡	.26	.12‡	.20‡
RBMT-1	**.80‡**	.23‡	.11‡	.20‡	.37	.28⋆	.18‡	.29	.38	.25†	.36	.30†	**.41**	.38	–	.34	**.45**	.36	.02‡	.17‡	.17‡	.28⋆	.24†
RBMT-2	**.80‡**	.20‡	.10‡	.16‡	**.43**	**.38**	.20‡	.27†	**.45**	.22†	.36	.30⋆	.38	**.51**	**.43**	–	**.48**	**.40**	**.42**	.31⋆	.28⋆	.16‡	.25‡
RBMT-3	**.65‡**	.18‡	.14‡	.15‡	.37	.29⋆	.17‡	.22‡	.25†	.20‡	.27	.33	.33	.29	.30	.31	–	.34	.16‡	.24†	.35	.20‡	.11‡
RBMT-4	**.80‡**	.21‡	.28	.22‡	.19	.26	.09‡	.32	.29	.27‡	.39	.27⋆	**.43**	**.44**	**.38**	.38	**.45**	–	**.42**	.29⋆	.36	.27‡	.31⋆
RBMT-5	**.88‡**	.35	.31†	.15‡	**.54⋆**	**.51**	.26†	.34	.36	.36	**.44**	.35	.44	**.59‡**	**.37‡**	.33	**.62‡**	.38	–	.29	**.45**	.38	.30
RWTH-FREITAG	**.80‡**	**.31**	.27	.17‡	**.62†**	**.55†**	.19	.25⋆	**.56‡**	**.30**	**.49‡**	**.41**	**.53⋆**	**.59‡**	**.56‡**	**.53⋆**	**.62†**	**.57⋆**	**.45**	–	**.36**	**.38**	.24
UEDIN	**.82‡**	.27	.27	.27	**.46**	**.47†**	.17‡	.28	**.36**	.33	**.48†**	.27	**.47**	**.43**	**.75‡**	**.55⋆**	**.52**	**.50**	.43	.21	–	.35	.27
UOW	**.86‡**	**.39**	.21	.23	**.74‡**	**.53†**	.36	.38	**.64‡**	.20	**.38**	**.41**	**.74‡**	**.61‡**	**.56⋆**	**.64‡**	**.57‡**	**.65‡**	.38	.26	**.41**	–	.31
UPPSALA	**.79‡**	**.32**	.35	.29	**.54**	**.57‡**	.34	**.51†**	**.51‡**	**.45†**	**.53‡**	**.43**	**.73‡**	**.70‡**	**.55†**	**.64‡**	**.77‡**	**.57⋆**	**.55**	**.43**	**.33**	**.41**	–
> others	.84	.29	.24	.17	.48	.42	.24	.31	.42	.27	.40	.34	.46	.51	.51	.47	**.56**	.46	.41	.29	.34	.29	.25
>= others	.91	.56	.50	.38	.68	.67	.48	.54	.64	.53	.65	.59	.65	**.730**	.70	.66	**.732**	.66	.58	.56	.60	.53	.49

Table 22: Ranking scores for entries in the English-German task (individual system track).

	REF	ALACANT	CU-ZEMAN	HYDERABAD	KOC	ONLINE-A	ONLINE-B	RBMT-1	RBMT-2	RBMT-3	RBMT-4	RBMT-5	SYSTRAN	UEDIN	UFAL-UM	UPM
REF	–	.03‡	.02‡	.00‡	.02‡	.03‡	.12‡	.15‡	.04‡	.07‡	.05‡	.02‡	.03‡	.03‡	.03‡	.07‡
ALACANT	**.86‡**	–	.07‡	.08‡	.30	**.52**	.31	.27⋆	.29⋆	**.54**	**.49**	.32⋆	**.51**	.27†	.26†	.26⋆
CU-ZEMAN	**.98‡**	**.89‡**	–	**.48**	**.84‡**	**.85‡**	**.94‡**	**.90‡**	**.83‡**	**.87‡**	**.85‡**	**.78‡**	**.97‡**	**.79‡**	**.79‡**	**.91‡**
HYDERABAD	**.98‡**	**.86‡**	.27	–	**.88‡**	**.95‡**	**.92‡**	**.85‡**	**.96‡**	**.74‡**	**.82‡**	**.80‡**	**.88‡**	**.91‡**	**.80‡**	**.86‡**
KOC	**.93‡**	**.48**	.06‡	.06‡	–	.28	.39	.40	.34	.44	.38	.26†	**.59†**	.22‡	.20‡	.18‡
ONLINE-A	**.90‡**	.28	.02‡	.02‡	**.48**	–	**.32**	.34	.34	.26⋆	.34	.19‡	.35	.20‡	.11‡	.20‡
ONLINE-B	**.79‡**	**.33**	.04‡	.00‡	**.47**	.30	–	.24†	.31⋆	.31⋆	.27†	.25‡	.33	.27†	.21‡	.07‡
RBMT-1	**.81‡**	**.52⋆**	.05‡	.11‡	**.50**	**.57**	**.62†**	–	**.50**	.36	.34	.17	.40	.39	.34	.30⋆
RBMT-2	**.96‡**	**.61⋆**	.09‡	.04‡	**.52**	**.47**	**.59⋆**	.37	–	**.39**	**.46**	.27	**.58†**	.29†	.24†	.45
RBMT-3	**.88‡**	.31	.09‡	.13‡	.44	**.56⋆**	**.60⋆**	**.53**	.37	–	**.47**	.14‡	**.52**	.40	.23†	.31
RBMT-4	**.90‡**	.38	.08‡	.16‡	**.50**	**.53**	**.60†**	**.41**	.43	.38	–	**.43**	**.52**	.33⋆	.18‡	.22‡
RBMT-5	**.94‡**	**.61⋆**	.06‡	.10‡	**.54†**	**.70‡**	**.63‡**	**.37**	**.45**	**.59‡**	.41	–	**.66‡**	.42	**.50**	**.43**
SYSTRAN	**.92‡**	.33	.02‡	.10‡	.25†	**.53**	**.53**	**.42**	.30†	.36	.38	.27‡	–	.21‡	.41	.24‡
UEDIN	**.95‡**	**.63†**	.13‡	.02‡	**.63‡**	**.67‡**	**.59†**	**.47**	**.61†**	**.53**	**.59⋆**	.42	**.53‡**	–	.32†	**.45**
UFAL-UM	**.94‡**	**.63†**	.10‡	.11‡	**.56‡**	**.70‡**	**.74‡**	**.51**	**.61†**	**.59†**	**.74‡**	.36	**.47**	**.61†**	–	**.44**
UPM	**.85‡**	**.54⋆**	.02‡	.03‡	**.62‡**	**.61‡**	**.81‡**	**.59⋆**	.45	**.55**	**.68‡**	.40	**.60‡**	.42	.38	–
> others	.91	.51	.07	.10	.52	.56	**.59**	.48	.48	.47	.48	.35	.54	.39	.34	.36
>= others	.96	.66	.16	.17	.67	**.723**	**.723**	.63	.60	.61	.60	.51	.66	.51	.47	.50

Table 23: Ranking scores for entries in the Spanish-English task (individual system track).

	REF	CEU-UPV	CU-ZEMAN	KOC	ONLINE-A	ONLINE-B	PROMT	RBMT-1	RBMT-2	RBMT-3	RBMT-4	RBMT-5	UEDIN	UOW	UPM	UPPSALA
REF	–	.06‡	.03‡	.09‡	.09‡	.09‡	.05‡	.03‡	.06‡	.04‡	.08‡	.02‡	.08‡	.02‡	.03‡	.04‡
CEU-UPV	**.84**‡	–	.21‡	.20†	**.43**	**.36**	**.42**	.37	.34⋆	**.50**†	.31	.34	**.32**	.21†	.13‡	.22
CU-ZEMAN	**.87**‡	**.56**‡	–	**.38**⋆	**.56**‡	**.56**‡	**.58**‡	**.46**⋆	**.40**	**.70**‡	**.46**⋆	**.49**†	**.51**‡	**.45**‡	.19‡	**.49**‡
KOC	**.84**‡	**.41**†	.22⋆	–	**.56**‡	**.51**‡	**.48**†	**.54**‡	**.39**	**.55**‡	**.42**	.35	**.51**‡	**.44**	.11‡	**.34**
ONLINE-A	**.72**‡	.31	.24‡	.15‡	–	**.36**	.37	.28†	.23‡	.35	.25‡	.20‡	.29⋆	.25†	.08‡	.09‡
ONLINE-B	**.72**‡	.30	.17‡	.18‡	.26	–	.29	.23‡	.20‡	**.37**	.20‡	.19‡	.19‡	.22‡	.02‡	.23⋆
PROMT	**.76**‡	.29	.21‡	.25†	**.42**	**.43**	–	.24‡	.24	.19	.27⋆	.26†	.32	.25‡	.18‡	.21‡
RBMT-1	**.85**‡	.37	.29⋆	.23‡	**.51**†	**.54**‡	**.48**‡	–	.35	**.45**‡	**.40**†	.05‡	**.47**	.39	.25‡	.39
RBMT-2	**.86**‡	**.50**⋆	.35	.38	**.51**‡	**.48**‡	**.35**	**.39**	–	**.41**†	.34	.36	**.45**	.36	.23‡	**.41**
RBMT-3	**.86**‡	.26†	.18‡	.22‡	**.40**	.35	.19	.20‡	.22†	–	.25†	.23‡	.24‡	.33	.10‡	.22†
RBMT-4	**.80**‡	**.45**	.29⋆	.34	**.53**‡	**.51**‡	**.43**⋆	.21†	**.38**	**.43**†	–	.24‡	.34	.30	.20‡	**.45**⋆
RBMT-5	**.96**‡	**.43**	.29†	**.42**	**.57**‡	**.61**‡	**.46**†	**.22**‡	**.38**	**.49**‡	**.47**‡	–	**.50**	**.46**	.27†	**.47**
UEDIN	**.74**‡	.28	.20‡	.21‡	**.46**⋆	**.48**‡	**.43**	.37	.31	**.49**‡	**.45**	.35	–	.20†	.14‡	.23
UOW	**.90**‡	**.44**†	.18‡	.32	**.46**†	**.52**‡	**.56**‡	.39	**.39**	**.44**	**.45**	.36	**.38**†	–	.10‡	**.32**
UPM	**.93**‡	**.65**‡	**.53**‡	**.67**‡	**.74**‡	**.71**‡	**.69**‡	**.59**‡	**.51**‡	**.74**‡	**.60**‡	**.51**†	**.64**‡	**.68**‡	–	**.62**‡
UPPSALA	**.84**‡	**.36**	.21‡	.32	**.49**‡	**.42**⋆	**.45**‡	.39	.35	**.45**†	.29⋆	.41	**.35**	.30	.15‡	–
> others	.83	.38	.24	.30	**.47**	.46	.41	.33	.32	.43	.35	.29	.38	.33	.14	.31
>= others	.94	.65	.49	.56	.72	**.74**	.70	.60	.57	.71	.61	.54	.64	.59	.34	.61

Table 24: Ranking scores for entries in the English-Spanish task (individual system track).

	REF	CMU-DENKOWSKI	CMU-HANNEMAN	CU-ZEMAN	JHU	KIT	LIA-LIG	LIMSI	LIUM	ONLINE-A	ONLINE-B	RBMT-1	RBMT-2	RBMT-3	RBMT-4	RBMT-5	RWTH-HUCK	SYSTRAN	UEDIN
REF	–	.10‡	.18‡	.06‡	.03‡	.14‡	.15‡	.14‡	.14‡	.12‡	.05‡	.12‡	.09‡	.05‡	.06‡	.05‡	.05‡	.07‡	.02‡
CMU-DENKOWSKI	**.79**‡	–	.35	.12‡	.34	.32	**.41**	**.35**	.21⋆	**.47**⋆	**.46**	**.49**	.32	.33	.36	.35	.25	**.45**	.29
CMU-HANNEMAN	**.79**‡	.35	–	.17‡	.29	**.44**⋆	**.43**	**.52**⋆	**.45**	**.45**	**.49**	**.51**	**.39**	**.44**	**.38**	.35	.35	**.43**	.37
CU-ZEMAN	**.94**‡	**.61**‡	**.67**‡	–	**.54**†	**.66**‡	**.66**†	**.58**†	**.60**‡	**.59**†	**.88**‡	**.62**‡	**.59**⋆	**.63**‡	**.60**†	**.56**	**.68**‡	**.64**†	.40
JHU	**.82**‡	.34	.29	.22†	–	.26	**.54**⋆	**.40**	.36	**.43**	.40	**.49**	**.42**	.40	.34	.35	.36	**.47**	.20†
KIT	**.79**‡	**.39**	.20⋆	.16‡	**.40**	–	.26⋆	**.46**	.34	**.38**	**.52**	.38	.35	.39	.28	.38	.15†	.32	.30
LIA-LIG	**.75**‡	.24	.31	.28†	.24⋆	**.59**⋆	–	**.49**	.27	**.40**	**.46**	.35	.26	.31⋆	.29	.32	.32	.33⋆	.35
LIMSI	**.86**‡	.30	.25⋆	.21†	.31	.26	.26	–	.38	**.40**	**.42**	.35	.18†	.43	.34	.16‡	.34	.34	.33
LIUM	**.78**‡	**.45**⋆	.33	.16‡	**.38**	.34	**.44**	**.40**	–	.38	.30	.44	.26†	.33⋆	.38	.28	.29	.33	.28
ONLINE-A	**.80**‡	.23⋆	.21	.22†	.37	.35	.36	.33	**.46**	–	**.43**	.35	.16‡	.33	.24†	.20‡	.26	.34	.27†
ONLINE-B	**.86**‡	.37	.31	.04‡	**.46**	.22	.36	.33	**.43**	.26	–	.40	.20†	.16‡	**.44**	.20‡	.41	.38	.22†
RBMT-1	**.87**‡	.44	.35	.23‡	.46	**.44**	**.54**	**.48**	.44	**.53**	**.54**	–	.39	.37	.33	.11†	.39	.17†	.35
RBMT-2	**.84**‡	**.47**	.37	.26⋆	.40	**.50**	**.45**	**.52**†	**.54**†	**.58**‡	**.67**†	**.45**	–	**.51**	.35	.22†	**.51**	**.57**	**.41**
RBMT-3	**.89**‡	**.44**	.42	.19‡	.40	**.43**	**.54**⋆	**.46**	**.61**⋆	**.50**	**.71**‡	.37	.32	–	.42	.35	.42	**.47**	.40
RBMT-4	**.85**‡	**.53**	.36	.26†	**.51**	**.47**	**.55**	**.52**	**.46**	**.59**†	.40	**.43**	**.50**	.42	–	.34	**.46**	.44	**.41**
RBMT-5	**.93**‡	**.58**	**.55**	.33	**.54**	**.54**	**.59**	**.70**‡	**.56**	**.66**‡	**.65**‡	**.36**†	**.54**†	**.46**	**.37**	–	**.50**	**.54**⋆	**.54**
RWTH-HUCK	**.92**‡	**.43**	**.38**	.14‡	.36	**.59**†	**.41**	**.44**	.29	**.53**	**.48**	**.46**	.30	**.46**	.32	.38	–	.37	.17†
SYSTRAN	**.93**‡	.39	.38	.24†	.44	**.48**	**.60**⋆	**.50**	**.40**	**.55**	**.57**	**.45**†	.36	.29	.44	.21⋆	**.49**	–	.36
UEDIN	**.93**‡	**.48**	**.41**	.40	**.51**†	**.48**	**.54**	**.49**	**.46**	**.60**†	**.57**†	**.52**	.37	**.47**	.39	.39	**.51**†	**.52**	–
> others	.85	.39	.36	.21	.39	.41	.46	.46	.41	.46	**.50**	.41	.33	.39	.35	.28	.37	.39	.32
>= others	.91	.62	.58	.37	.61	.64	.64	**.661**	.63	**.661**	.66	.58	.52	.55	.53	.45	.58	.54	.50

Table 25: Ranking scores for entries in the French-English task (individual system track).

	REF	CU-ZEMAN	JHU	KIT	LATL-GENEVA	LIMSI	LIUM	ONLINE-A	ONLINE-B	RBMT-1	RBMT-2	RBMT-3	RBMT-4	RBMT-5	RWTH-HUCK	UEDIN	UPPSALA	UPPSALA-FBK
REF	–	.07‡	.06‡	.25‡	.07‡	.13‡	.20‡	.15‡	.20‡	.10‡	.09‡	.18‡	.11‡	.12‡	.14‡	.18‡	.16‡	.16‡
CU-ZEMAN	**.92**‡	–	**.83**‡	**.86**‡	**.63**†	**.85**‡	**.90**‡	**.86**‡	**.81**‡	**.89**‡	**.70**‡	**.75**‡	**.75**‡	**.61**‡	**.78**‡	**.79**‡	**.81**‡	**.81**‡
JHU	**.91**‡	.07‡	–	**.55**†	.30⋆	**.60**‡	**.50**⋆	**.55**⋆	**.59**‡	**.45**	.41	.34⋆	.30†	**.50**	**.40**	**.42**	**.42**	**.44**
KIT	**.63**‡	.04‡	.29†	–	.18‡	**.47**	.37	.30⋆	.37	.38	.30†	.37	.24‡	.34	.28	.34	.24†	.13‡
LATL-GENEVA	**.86**‡	.29†	**.54**⋆	**.73**‡	–	**.77**‡	**.67**‡	**.71**‡	**.79**‡	**.55**†	**.39**	**.66**‡	**.52**	**.58**‡	**.58**‡	**.51**	**.52**	**.58**†
LIMSI	**.75**‡	.04‡	.21‡	.29	.13‡	–	.23⋆	.28⋆	.37	.27†	.27‡	.24‡	.24‡	.21‡	.27†	.28⋆	.25†	.31
LIUM	**.76**‡	.04‡	.26⋆	**.44**	.24‡	**.46**⋆	–	.33	**.52**	**.48**	.25‡	.36	.25‡	.28†	**.43**	**.40**	.35	.32
ONLINE-A	**.78**‡	.10‡	.31⋆	**.51**⋆	.22‡	**.51**⋆	**.46**	–	**.44**	.39	.36	.41	.30⋆	.41	**.41**	.32⋆	.46	.33
ONLINE-B	**.70**‡	.06‡	.27‡	**.41**	.13‡	**.39**	.32	.30	–	**.47**	.22‡	.26†	.13‡	.28†	.32	.26†	.33	.27†
RBMT-1	**.83**‡	.07‡	.38	**.46**	.23†	**.56**†	.39	**.41**	.42	–	.17‡	.34	.36	.13	**.52**	.33⋆	.40	.40
RBMT-2	**.88**‡	.25‡	**.47**	**.59**†	.37	**.65**‡	**.63**‡	**.51**	**.57**‡	**.54**‡	–	**.58**‡	.39	**.54**⋆	**.63**‡	**.61**†	**.47**	.42
RBMT-3	**.80**‡	.19‡	**.54**⋆	**.42**	.20‡	**.60**‡	**.47**	**.44**	**.52**†	**.42**	.18‡	–	.21†	**.43**	**.51**	**.55**	.41	.39
RBMT-4	**.82**‡	.22‡	**.54**†	**.63**‡	.33	**.63**‡	**.64**‡	**.54**⋆	**.59**‡	**.41**	**.44**	**.46**†	–	**.47**	**.68**‡	**.53**	**.42**	.39
RBMT-5	**.86**‡	.18‡	.46	**.53**	.20‡	**.62**‡	**.56**†	**.46**	**.61**†	**.22**	.33⋆	.40	.34	–	**.43**	**.52**	.40	**.53**⋆
RWTH-HUCK	**.76**‡	.08‡	.33	**.38**	.21‡	**.60**†	.40	.38	**.43**	.36	.18‡	.37	.21‡	.38	–	.39	.22‡	.29
UEDIN	**.78**‡	.15‡	.37	**.46**	.34	**.49**⋆	.38	**.53**⋆	**.58**†	**.56**⋆	.33†	.35	.36	.37	**.47**	–	.38	.31
UPPSALA	**.77**‡	.07‡	.36	**.53**†	.36	**.49**†	**.46**	.46	**.56**	**.46**	.38	**.42**	.39	**.55**	**.57**‡	**.39**	–	**.47**
UPPSALA-FBK	**.80**‡	.10‡	.40	**.71**‡	.27†	**.50**	**.47**	**.51**	**.53**†	**.42**	**.48**	**.41**	**.52**	.29⋆	**.50**	**.47**	.40	–
> others	.80	.12	.39	.51	.25	**.55**	.48	.45	.52	.43	.32	.41	.33	.39	.46	.43	.39	.38
>= others	.86	.20	.55	.69	.39	**.73**	.64	.60	.70	.61	.46	.58	.49	.55	.65	.58	.55	.54

Table 26: Ranking scores for entries in the English-French task (individual system track).

	REF	BM-I2R	CMU-DENKOWSKI	CMU-HEWAVITHARANA	HYDERABAD	KOC	LIU	UMD-EIDELMAN	UMD-HU	UPPSALA
REF	–	.03‡	.01‡	.03‡	.02‡	.01‡	.00‡	.01‡	.01‡	.02‡
BM-I2R	**.91**‡	–	.28†	.27†	.13‡	.08‡	.19‡	.30†	.30‡	.24‡
CMU-DENKOWSKI	**.93**‡	**.44**†	–	.25	.22‡	.15‡	.28†	.33	.29‡	.31†
CMU-HEWAVITHARANA	**.91**‡	**.40**†	**.31**	–	.21‡	.16‡	.29†	.35	.39	.30
HYDERABAD	**.96**‡	**.71**‡	**.59**‡	**.58**‡	–	.27‡	**.56**‡	**.57**‡	**.42**	**.52**‡
KOC	**.94**‡	**.78**‡	**.75**‡	**.64**‡	**.55**‡	–	**.65**‡	**.69**‡	**.62**‡	**.64**‡
LIU	**.92**‡	**.56**‡	**.42**†	**.44**†	.27‡	.24‡	–	**.43**	.41	.39
UMD-EIDELMAN	**.94**‡	**.44**†	**.35**	.35	.17‡	.17‡	.34	–	.37	.31⋆
UMD-HU	**.90**‡	**.50**‡	**.57**‡	**.45**	.35	.21‡	**.46**	**.45**	–	**.42**
UPPSALA	**.93**‡	**.48**‡	**.47**†	**.39**	.31‡	.20‡	**.40**	**.43**⋆	.37	–
> others	.93	**.49**	.42	.39	.25	.17	.35	.40	.36	.35
>= others	.98	**.71**	.66	.64	.43	.31	.55	.63	.52	.57

Table 27: Ranking scores for entries in the Haitian Creole (Clean)-English task (individual system track).

	REF	BM-I2R	CMU-DENKOWSKI	CMU-HEWAVITHARANA	JHU	LIU	UMD-EIDELMAN
REF	–	.05‡	.03‡	.04‡	.02‡	.02‡	.03‡
BM-I2R	**.83**‡	–	.29†	.25‡	.22‡	.30‡	.30‡
CMU-DENKOWSKI	**.89**‡	**.44**†	–	**.37***	.23‡	.37	.30†
CMU-HEWAVITHARANA	**.86**‡	**.43**‡	.26*	–	.27‡	**.37**	.32
JHU	**.96**‡	**.62**‡	**.53**‡	**.49**‡	–	**.52**‡	**.47**‡
LIU	**.92**‡	**.48**‡	**.38**	.34	.31‡	–	.36
UMD-EIDELMAN	**.92**‡	**.48**‡	**.44**†	**.42**	.29‡	**.41**	–
> others	.90	**.43**	.34	.33	.23	.34	.30
>= others	.97	**.65**	.59	.60	.41	.55	.52

Table 28: Ranking scores for entries in the Haitian Creole (Raw)-English task (individual system track).

	REF	BBN-COMBO	CMU-HEAFIELD-COMBO	JHU-COMBO	UPV-PRHLT-COMBO
REF	–	.01‡	.02‡	.01‡	.01‡
BBN-COMBO	**.91**‡	–	**.25**	.18*	.16‡
CMU-HEAFIELD-COMBO	**.90**‡	.24	–	.17‡	.12‡
JHU-COMBO	**.92**‡	**.27***	**.29**‡	–	.20‡
UPV-PRHLT-COMBO	**.94**‡	**.41**‡	**.42**‡	**.36**‡	–
> others	.92	.23	**.24**	.18	.12
>= others	.99	.62	**.64**	.58	.47

Table 29: Ranking scores for entries in the Czech-English task (system combination track).

	REF	CMU-HEAFIELD-COMBO	UPV-PRHLT-COMBO
REF	–	.04‡	.04‡
CMU-HEAFIELD-COMBO	**.86**‡	–	.17‡
UPV-PRHLT-COMBO	**.88**‡	**.30**‡	–
> others	.87	**.17**	.11
>= others	.96	**.48**	.41

Table 30: Ranking scores for entries in the English-Czech task (system combination track).

	REF	BBN-COMBO	CMU-HEAFIELD-COMBO	JHU-COMBO	KOC-COMBO	QUAERO-COMBO	RWTH-LEUSCH-COMBO	UPV-PRHLT-COMBO	UZH-COMBO
REF	–	.11‡	.09‡	.04‡	.09‡	.10‡	.14‡	.05‡	.09‡
BBN-COMBO	**.79‡**	–	**.45‡**	.32	.21‡	.28†	**.39**	.31⋆	**.36**
CMU-HEAFIELD-COMBO	**.84‡**	.23‡	–	.21‡	.17‡	.19‡	.25⋆	.19‡	.31
JHU-COMBO	**.85‡**	**.42**	**.55‡**	–	.25†	.28†	**.40†**	.28⋆	**.47⋆**
KOC-COMBO	**.83‡**	**.56‡**	**.62‡**	**.45†**	–	**.41**	**.54‡**	**.40⋆**	**.51†**
QUAERO-COMBO	**.86‡**	**.52†**	**.64‡**	**.45†**	.36	–	**.54‡**	**.49†**	**.48**
RWTH-LEUSCH-COMBO	**.83‡**	.28	**.41⋆**	.22†	.20‡	.22‡	–	.22‡	.38
UPV-PRHLT-COMBO	**.85‡**	**.47⋆**	**.57‡**	**.42⋆**	.25⋆	.26†	**.48‡**	–	**.49†**
UZH-COMBO	**.86‡**	.34	**.38**	.31⋆	.29†	.32	**.41**	.30†	–
> others	.84	.36	**.46**	.30	.22	.26	.39	.27	.39
>= others	.91	.61	**.70**	.56	.45	.46	.65	.52	.60

Table 31: Ranking scores for entries in the German-English task (system combination track).

	REF	CMU-HEAFIELD-COMBO	KOC-COMBO	UPV-PRHLT-COMBO	UZH-COMBO
REF	–	.11‡	.09‡	.10‡	.11‡
CMU-HEAFIELD-COMBO	**.81‡**	–	.19‡	.23‡	.32
KOC-COMBO	**.84‡**	**.48‡**	–	**.38‡**	**.47‡**
UPV-PRHLT-COMBO	**.81‡**	**.36‡**	.23‡	–	**.37⋆**
UZH-COMBO	**.80‡**	**.34**	.24‡	.31⋆	–
> others	.81	**.320**	.19	.25	**.318**
>= others	.90	**.61**	.46	.56	.58

Table 32: Ranking scores for entries in the English-German task (system combination track).

	REF	BBN-COMBO	CMU-HEAFIELD-COMBO	JHU-COMBO	KOC-COMBO	RWTH-LEUSCH-COMBO	UPV-PRHLT-COMBO
REF	–	.05‡	.09‡	.05‡	.07‡	.06‡	.08‡
BBN-COMBO	**.81‡**	–	**.34**	**.27**	.21‡	**.27**	.26
CMU-HEAFIELD-COMBO	**.84‡**	.31	–	.18‡	.15‡	**.29**	.20
JHU-COMBO	**.83‡**	.25	**.32‡**	–	.27	**.35‡**	.25
KOC-COMBO	**.84‡**	**.39‡**	**.39‡**	**.32**	–	**.39‡**	**.31⋆**
RWTH-LEUSCH-COMBO	**.81‡**	.24	.23	.16‡	.17‡	–	.14‡
UPV-PRHLT-COMBO	**.77‡**	**.30**	**.26**	**.27**	.22⋆	**.35‡**	–
> others	.82	.25	.27	.21	.18	**.28**	.21
>= others	.93	.64	.67	.62	.56	**.71**	.64

Table 33: Ranking scores for entries in the Spanish-English task (system combination track).

	REF	CMU-HEAFIELD-COMBO	KOC-COMBO	UOW-COMBO	UPV-PRHLT-COMBO
REF	–	.10‡	.07‡	.09‡	.08‡
CMU-HEAFIELD-COMBO	**.70**‡	–	.15‡	.21‡	.17‡
KOC-COMBO	**.76**‡	**.35**‡	–	**.36**‡	**.19**
UOW-COMBO	**.72**‡	**.29**‡	.22‡	–	.25‡
UPV-PRHLT-COMBO	**.76**‡	**.35**‡	.16	**.35**‡	–
> others	.73	**.27**	.15	.25	.17
>= others	.91	**.69**	.58	.63	.59

Table 34: Ranking scores for entries in the English-Spanish task (system combination track).

	REF	BBN-COMBO	CMU-HEAFIELD-COMBO	JHU-COMBO	LIUM-COMBO	RWTH-LEUSCH-COMBO	UPV-PRHLT-COMBO
REF	–	.04‡	.04‡	.06‡	.06‡	.06‡	.02‡
BBN-COMBO	**.82**‡	–	**.35**	.25	.18‡	.21⋆	.21‡
CMU-HEAFIELD-COMBO	**.90**‡	.29	–	.30	.20‡	.29	.25†
JHU-COMBO	**.83**‡	**.35**	**.40**	–	.31⋆	**.36**	.21†
LIUM-COMBO	**.83**‡	**.42**‡	**.40**‡	**.44**⋆	–	**.38**†	**.35**
RWTH-LEUSCH-COMBO	**.83**‡	**.34**⋆	.29	.30	.22†	–	.21‡
UPV-PRHLT-COMBO	**.91**‡	**.49**‡	**.40**†	**.34**†	.30	**.40**‡	–
> others	.85	**.32**	.31	.28	.21	.28	.21
>= others	.95	**.67**	.62	.59	.53	.63	.53

Table 35: Ranking scores for entries in the French-English task (system combination track).

	REF	CMU-HEAFIELD-COMBO	UPV-PRHLT-COMBO
REF	–	.11‡	.11‡
CMU-HEAFIELD-COMBO	**.74**‡	–	.23‡
UPV-PRHLT-COMBO	**.77**‡	**.38**‡	–
> others	.76	**.24**	.17
>= others	.89	**.51**	.43

Table 36: Ranking scores for entries in the English-French task (system combination track).

	REF	CMU-HEAFIELD-COMBO	KOC-COMBO	UPV-PRHLT-COMBO
REF	–	.01‡	.01‡	.01‡
CMU-HEAFIELD-COMBO	**.94**‡	–	.29‡	.21‡
KOC-COMBO	**.96**‡	**.48**‡	–	**.41**†
UPV-PRHLT-COMBO	**.94**‡	**.34**‡	.29†	–
> others	.95	**.28**	.20	.21
>= others	.99	**.52**	.38	.48

Table 37: Ranking scores for entries in the Haitian Creole (Clean)-English task (system combination track).

	REF	CMU-HEAFIELD-COMBO	UPV-PRHLT-COMBO
REF	–	.02‡	.02‡
CMU-HEAFIELD-COMBO	**.83**‡	–	.24
UPV-PRHLT-COMBO	**.86**‡	**.29**	–
> others	.84	**.16**	.13
>= others	.98	**.47**	.43

Table 38: Ranking scores for entries in the Haitian Creole (Raw)-English task (system combination track).

	AMBER	AMBER-NL	AMBER-TI	BLEU	F15	F15G3	MTERATER	MTERATER-PLUS	ROSE	TER	TINE-SRL-MATCH	METEOR-1.3-ADQ	METEOR-1.3-RANK	MP4IBM1	MPF	TESLA-B	TESLA-F	TESLA-M	WMPF
Czech-English News Task																			
BBN-COMBO	0.24	0.24	0.25	0.29	0.31	0.19	–9627	–10667	1.97	0.53	0.49	0.61	0.34	–65	44	0.48	0.03	0.51	43
CMU-HEAFIELD-COMBO	0.24	0.24	0.24	0.28	0.3	0.18	–9604	–10933	1.97	0.54	0.5	0.60	0.33	–65	43	0.48	0.03	0.52	42
CST	0.19	0.19	0.2	0.16	0.21	0.10	–27410	–27880	1.94	0.64	0.40	0.5	0.28	–65	34	0.38	0.02	0.42	33
CU-BOJAR	0.21	0.21	0.22	0.19	0.24	0.13	–23441	–22289	1.95	0.64	0.44	0.55	0.30	–65	37	0.42	0.02	0.46	36
CU-ZEMAN	0.20	0.2	0.21	0.14	0.21	0.11	–33520	–30938	1.93	0.66	0.38	0.52	0.29	–66	31	0.37	0.02	0.40	30
JHU	0.22	0.21	0.22	0.2	0.25	0.13	–21278	–20480	1.95	0.60	0.43	0.55	0.30	–65	37	0.42	0.02	0.46	36
JHU-COMBO	0.24	0.23	0.24	0.29	0.31	0.19	–12563	–12688	1.97	0.53	0.5	0.60	0.33	–65	44	0.48	0.03	0.52	43
ONLINE-B	0.24	0.23	0.24	0.29	0.31	0.19	–10673	–11506	1.97	0.52	0.50	0.60	0.33	–65	44	0.49	0.03	0.52	43
SYSTRAN	0.20	0.2	0.21	0.18	0.22	0.11	–23996	–24570	1.94	0.63	0.42	0.52	0.29	–65	36	0.4	0.02	0.45	34
UEDIN	0.22	0.22	0.23	0.22	0.26	0.14	–14958	–15342	1.96	0.59	0.45	0.57	0.31	–65	40	0.44	0.03	0.48	39
UPPSALA	0.21	0.20	0.21	0.20	0.23	0.12	–22233	–22509	1.95	0.62	0.43	0.53	0.29	–65	37	0.41	0.02	0.46	36
UPV-PRHLT-COMBO	0.24	0.23	0.24	0.29	0.31	0.19	–13904	–15260	1.97	0.54	0.49	0.60	0.33	–65	44	0.48	0.03	0.52	43

Table 39: Automatic evaluation metric scores for systems in the WMT11 Czech-English News Task (newssyscombtest2011)

	AMBER	AMBER-NL	AMBER-TI	BLEU	F15	F15G3	MTERATER	MTERATER-PLUS	ROSE	TER	TINE-SRL-MATCH	DFKI-PARSECONF	METEOR-1.3-ADQ	METEOR-1.3-RANK	MP4IBM1	MPF	TESLA-B	TESLA-F	TESLA-M	WMPF
German-English News Task																				
BBN-COMBO	0.23	0.22	0.23	0.25	0.28	0.16	–17103	–17837	1.97	0.56	0.46	0.06	0.59	0.32	–43	42	0.46	0.03	0.49	41
CMU-DYER	0.21	0.21	0.22	0.22	0.25	0.13	–26089	–29214	1.95	0.59	0.44	0.04	0.56	0.31	–45	39	0.43	0.03	0.47	38
CMU-HEAFIELD-COMBO	0.23	0.22	0.23	0.24	0.27	0.15	–12868	–16156	1.96	0.57	0.47	0.07	0.58	0.32	–44	41	0.46	0.03	0.51	40
CST	0.19	0.18	0.19	0.17	0.22	0.11	–61131	–60157	1.94	0.63	0.39	0.03	0.5	0.27	–46	34	0.37	0.02	0.41	33
CU-ZEMAN	0.2	0.19	0.20	0.14	0.22	0.11	–64860	–61329	1.93	0.65	0.37	0.06	0.51	0.28	–47	31	0.37	0.02	0.4	30
DFKI-XU	0.21	0.20	0.21	0.21	0.25	0.14	–40171	–39455	1.95	0.58	0.44	0.03	0.54	0.3	–45	38	0.42	0.02	0.46	37
JHU	0.19	0.19	0.2	0.17	0.22	0.11	–62997	–58673	1.94	0.64	0.39	0.03	0.51	0.28	–45	34	0.38	0.02	0.41	33
JHU-COMBO	0.22	0.22	0.23	0.24	0.27	0.15	–30492	–27016	1.96	0.57	0.46	0.04	0.57	0.31	–44	41	0.45	0.03	0.48	39
KIT	0.21	0.21	0.22	0.22	0.25	0.13	–31064	–31930	1.95	0.6	0.44	0.05	0.55	0.31	–44	39	0.43	0.02	0.47	37
KOC	0.2	0.2	0.20	0.18	0.23	0.12	–52337	–50231	1.94	0.63	0.41	0.05	0.52	0.29	–45	35	0.39	0.02	0.43	34
KOC-COMBO	0.21	0.21	0.21	0.22	0.26	0.14	–40002	–38374	1.96	0.59	0.44	0.03	0.54	0.3	–44	38	0.42	0.02	0.46	37
LIMSI	0.21	0.20	0.21	0.20	0.24	0.13	–39419	–38297	1.95	0.61	0.43	0.04	0.54	0.3	–44	38	0.42	0.02	0.46	36
LINGUATEC	0.19	0.19	0.2	0.16	0.22	0.11	–26064	–31116	1.94	0.68	0.42	0.15	0.53	0.29	–46	35	0.42	0.02	0.47	34
LIU	0.21	0.20	0.21	0.2	0.24	0.13	–40281	–40496	1.95	0.62	0.43	0.04	0.53	0.29	–44	37	0.41	0.02	0.45	36
ONLINE-A	0.22	0.21	0.22	0.21	0.26	0.14	–25411	–25675	1.95	0.6	0.45	0.06	0.57	0.31	–44	39	0.45	0.03	0.48	38
ONLINE-B	0.22	0.22	0.23	0.23	0.27	0.15	–15149	–19578	1.96	0.58	0.46	0.06	0.57	0.32	–44	41	0.46	0.03	0.5	39
QUAERO-COMBO	0.21	0.21	0.22	0.22	0.26	0.14	–34486	–33449	1.96	0.58	0.45	0.03	0.55	0.30	–44	39	0.43	0.03	0.47	38
RBMT-1	0.20	0.2	0.21	0.16	0.21	0.11	–32960	–34972	1.94	0.67	0.42	0.08	0.52	0.29	–45	36	0.42	0.02	0.46	34
RBMT-2	0.19	0.19	0.2	0.15	0.2	0.1	–40842	–43413	1.94	0.69	0.4	0.11	0.50	0.28	–45	34	0.4	0.02	0.44	33
RBMT-3	0.20	0.2	0.21	0.17	0.22	0.11	–32476	–33417	1.94	0.65	0.42	0.09	0.53	0.29	–44	36	0.42	0.02	0.47	35
RBMT-4	0.20	0.2	0.21	0.17	0.22	0.11	–34287	–34604	1.94	0.66	0.42	0.08	0.52	0.29	–45	36	0.42	0.02	0.47	35
RBMT-5	0.19	0.19	0.20	0.15	0.20	0.10	–49097	–46635	1.94	0.68	0.40	0.07	0.50	0.28	–46	34	0.4	0.02	0.44	33
RWTH-LEUSCH-COMBO	0.22	0.22	0.23	0.24	0.28	0.16	–22878	–22089	1.96	0.56	0.46	0.03	0.58	0.32	–44	41	0.45	0.03	0.49	40
RWTH-WUEBKER	0.21	0.20	0.21	0.21	0.24	0.13	–35973	–37140	1.95	0.60	0.44	0.04	0.54	0.3	–45	38	0.42	0.02	0.45	37
UEDIN	0.21	0.20	0.21	0.19	0.23	0.12	–32791	–34633	1.95	0.63	0.43	0.07	0.54	0.3	–45	37	0.42	0.02	0.46	36
UPPSALA	0.20	0.2	0.21	0.2	0.23	0.12	–40448	–41548	1.95	0.63	0.42	0.06	0.53	0.29	–45	37	0.41	0.02	0.44	36
UPV-PRHLT-COMBO	0.22	0.21	0.22	0.23	0.27	0.15	–33413	–31778	1.96	0.58	0.45	0.03	0.57	0.31	–44	40	0.44	0.03	0.48	39
UZH-COMBO	0.22	0.21	0.22	0.23	0.27	0.15	–16326	–20831	1.96	0.58	0.45	0.07	0.57	0.31	–44	40	0.45	0.03	0.48	39

Table 40: Automatic evaluation metric scores for systems in the WMT11 German-English News Task (newssyscombtest2011)

	AMBER	AMBER-NL	AMBER-TI	BLEU	F15	F15G3	MTERATER	MTERATER-PLUS	ROSE	TER	TINE-SRL-MATCH	METEOR-1.3-ADQ	METEOR-1.3-RANK	MP4IBM1	MPF	TESLA-B	TESLA-F	TESLA-M	WMPF
French-English News Task																			
BBN-COMBO	0.25	0.25	0.26	0.31	0.32	0.21	–19552	–22107	1.98	0.48	0.51	0.64	0.36	–43	47	0.49	0.03	0.54	46
CMU-DENKOWSKI	0.24	0.24	0.24	0.26	0.29	0.17	–34357	–37807	1.97	0.53	0.48	0.61	0.34	–45	43	0.46	0.03	0.50	42
CMU-HANNEMAN	0.24	0.23	0.24	0.27	0.29	0.17	–33662	–37698	1.97	0.52	0.49	0.60	0.33	–45	44	0.46	0.03	0.51	42
CMU-HEAFIELD-COMBO	0.25	0.25	0.25	0.30	0.31	0.2	–18365	–22937	1.98	0.5	0.51	0.63	0.35	–44	46	0.49	0.03	0.54	45
CU-ZEMAN	0.22	0.22	0.23	0.17	0.24	0.13	–67586	–64688	1.94	0.6	0.41	0.56	0.31	–47	34	0.39	0.02	0.42	33
JHU	0.24	0.24	0.24	0.25	0.29	0.17	–41567	–39578	1.96	0.53	0.47	0.61	0.34	–45	42	0.46	0.03	0.5	41
JHU-COMBO	0.25	0.25	0.25	0.31	0.32	0.20	–32785	–31712	1.98	0.49	0.50	0.63	0.35	–43	47	0.48	0.03	0.53	45
KIT	0.25	0.24	0.25	0.29	0.31	0.19	–22678	–28283	1.98	0.51	0.50	0.63	0.35	–44	46	0.49	0.03	0.53	44
LIA-LIG	0.25	0.24	0.25	0.29	0.3	0.18	–34063	–34716	1.97	0.52	0.49	0.62	0.34	–44	45	0.48	0.03	0.52	44
LIMSI	0.25	0.24	0.25	0.28	0.29	0.18	–26269	–29363	1.97	0.52	0.5	0.62	0.34	–44	45	0.48	0.03	0.52	44
LIUM	0.25	0.24	0.25	0.29	0.30	0.19	–29288	–36137	1.98	0.52	0.49	0.62	0.34	–44	45	0.48	0.03	0.53	44
LIUM-COMBO	0.25	0.24	0.25	0.31	0.31	0.2	–30678	–35365	1.98	0.50	0.5	0.62	0.34	–44	46	0.48	0.03	0.53	45
ONLINE-A	0.25	0.24	0.25	0.27	0.3	0.18	–38761	–34096	1.97	0.52	0.49	0.62	0.34	–44	44	0.48	0.03	0.52	43
ONLINE-B	0.25	0.24	0.25	0.29	0.31	0.19	–19157	–25284	1.98	0.50	0.51	0.62	0.35	–45	46	0.49	0.03	0.54	44
RBMT-1	0.24	0.23	0.24	0.23	0.26	0.15	–49115	–39153	1.96	0.59	0.46	0.60	0.33	–43	42	0.46	0.03	0.51	41
RBMT-2	0.23	0.22	0.23	0.21	0.24	0.13	–59549	–50466	1.95	0.63	0.44	0.57	0.32	–43	40	0.43	0.02	0.48	39
RBMT-3	0.23	0.23	0.23	0.22	0.25	0.14	–52047	–45073	1.96	0.59	0.46	0.58	0.32	–44	41	0.45	0.02	0.50	40
RBMT-4	0.23	0.22	0.24	0.22	0.25	0.14	–54507	–42933	1.96	0.63	0.45	0.59	0.33	–43	40	0.44	0.02	0.49	39
RBMT-5	0.23	0.22	0.23	0.21	0.24	0.13	–55545	–48332	1.95	0.62	0.45	0.57	0.32	–44	40	0.44	0.02	0.49	38
RWTH-HUCK	0.24	0.24	0.25	0.28	0.3	0.18	–44018	–42549	1.97	0.52	0.49	0.61	0.34	–44	44	0.47	0.03	0.51	43
RWTH-LEUSCH-COMBO	0.26	0.25	0.26	0.31	0.32	0.20	–21914	–21746	1.98	0.49	0.51	0.64	0.35	–43	47	0.50	0.03	0.54	46
SYSTRAN	0.24	0.23	0.24	0.25	0.27	0.16	–34321	–40119	1.96	0.54	0.48	0.59	0.33	–44	43	0.46	0.03	0.51	41
UEDIN	0.23	0.23	0.24	0.25	0.27	0.16	–47202	–47955	1.96	0.56	0.47	0.59	0.33	–45	42	0.45	0.03	0.49	40
UPV-PRHLT-COMBO	0.25	0.25	0.26	0.31	0.32	0.20	–26947	–28689	1.98	0.5	0.51	0.63	0.35	–43	47	0.49	0.03	0.54	46

Table 41: Automatic evaluation metric scores for systems in the WMT11 French-English News Task (newssyscombtest2011)

	AMBER	AMBER-NL	AMBER-TI	BLEU	F15	F15G3	MTERATER	MTERATER-PLUS	ROSE	TER	TINE-SRL-MATCH	METEOR-1.3-ADQ	METEOR-1.3-RANK	MP4IBM1	MPF	TESLA-B	TESLA-F	TESLA-M	WMPF
Spanish-English News Task																			
ALACANT	0.24	0.23	0.24	0.27	0.28	0.17	–30135	–29622	1.97	0.53	0.46	0.61	0.34	–45	43	0.46	0.03	0.50	42
BBN-COMBO	0.25	0.25	0.25	0.32	0.33	0.21	–15284	–16192	1.98	0.48	0.5	0.64	0.35	–44	47	0.49	0.03	0.53	46
CMU-HEAFIELD-COMBO	0.25	0.25	0.25	0.32	0.31	0.20	–13456	–16113	1.98	0.5	0.5	0.64	0.35	–44	47	0.5	0.03	0.54	46
CU-ZEMAN	0.20	0.20	0.21	0.16	0.22	0.12	–49428	–48440	1.93	0.61	0.36	0.51	0.28	–49	32	0.35	0.02	0.38	31
HYDERABAD	0.20	0.20	0.21	0.17	0.21	0.11	–47754	–47059	1.94	0.61	0.39	0.50	0.28	–47	34	0.36	0.02	0.41	33
JHU-COMBO	0.25	0.25	0.25	0.32	0.32	0.20	–23939	–22685	1.98	0.49	0.49	0.63	0.35	–44	47	0.48	0.03	0.52	46
KOC	0.24	0.24	0.24	0.26	0.29	0.17	–22724	–25857	1.96	0.53	0.46	0.61	0.34	–45	42	0.46	0.03	0.49	41
KOC-COMBO	0.25	0.24	0.25	0.28	0.30	0.19	–22678	–22267	1.97	0.52	0.48	0.62	0.34	–44	44	0.48	0.03	0.52	43
ONLINE-A	0.25	0.24	0.25	0.28	0.3	0.18	–19017	–20120	1.97	0.52	0.48	0.63	0.35	–44	45	0.48	0.03	0.52	43
ONLINE-B	0.24	0.24	0.24	0.29	0.30	0.19	–11980	–18589	1.97	0.50	0.49	0.62	0.34	–45	45	0.49	0.03	0.53	44
RBMT-1	0.24	0.24	0.25	0.28	0.28	0.17	–31202	–26151	1.97	0.57	0.46	0.61	0.34	–44	45	0.47	0.03	0.51	43
RBMT-2	0.23	0.23	0.24	0.24	0.25	0.15	–35157	–31405	1.96	0.6	0.44	0.59	0.33	–44	42	0.44	0.02	0.49	41
RBMT-3	0.23	0.23	0.24	0.25	0.26	0.15	–28289	–26082	1.97	0.59	0.45	0.6	0.33	–43	43	0.46	0.03	0.51	42
RBMT-4	0.24	0.23	0.24	0.25	0.26	0.16	–27892	–25546	1.97	0.59	0.46	0.60	0.33	–43	43	0.46	0.03	0.52	42
RBMT-5	0.24	0.23	0.24	0.27	0.26	0.16	–36770	–31613	1.96	0.58	0.45	0.6	0.33	–45	43	0.45	0.03	0.50	42
RWTH-LEUSCH-COMBO	0.25	0.25	0.26	0.32	0.32	0.21	–15172	–15261	1.98	0.49	0.5	0.64	0.35	–43	48	0.50	0.03	0.54	47
SYSTRAN	0.24	0.23	0.24	0.27	0.28	0.17	–20129	–26051	1.97	0.53	0.47	0.60	0.33	–46	44	0.46	0.03	0.51	42
UEDIN	0.22	0.22	0.23	0.22	0.25	0.14	–25462	–31678	1.96	0.58	0.45	0.57	0.32	–47	40	0.44	0.03	0.48	39
UFAL-UM	0.23	0.22	0.23	0.23	0.24	0.14	–42123	–37765	1.96	0.60	0.43	0.58	0.32	–43	41	0.43	0.02	0.48	40
UPM	0.22	0.22	0.23	0.22	0.24	0.14	–39748	–38433	1.95	0.58	0.43	0.57	0.32	–45	40	0.42	0.02	0.46	38
UPV-PRHLT-COMBO	0.25	0.25	0.26	0.32	0.32	0.20	–16094	–17723	1.98	0.50	0.49	0.64	0.35	–43	47	0.5	0.03	0.54	46

Table 42: Automatic evaluation metric scores for systems in the WMT11 Spanish-English News Task (newssyscombtest2011)

	AMBER	AMBER-NL	AMBER-TI	BLEU	F15	F15G3	ROSE	TER	METEOR-1.3-RANK	MP4IBM1	MPF	WMPF
English-Czech News Task												
CMU-HEAFIELD-COMBO	0.2	0.19	0.20	0.19	0.22	0.12	2.03	0.62	0.24	–62	29	27
COMMERCIAL1	0.16	0.15	0.16	0.11	0.16	0.08	2.01	0.70	0.19	–65	22	21
COMMERCIAL2	0.12	0.10	0.13	0.09	0.15	0.06	2.00	0.73	0.18	–65	21	19
CU-BOJAR	0.18	0.17	0.18	0.16	0.2	0.1	2.02	0.65	0.23	–63	26	24
CU-MARECEK	0.18	0.17	0.18	0.16	0.2	0.1	2.02	0.65	0.22	–63	26	24
CU-POPEL	0.17	0.16	0.18	0.14	0.19	0.1	2.02	0.66	0.21	–64	25	23
CU-TAMCHYNA	0.18	0.17	0.18	0.15	0.2	0.1	2.02	0.65	0.22	–63	26	24
CU-ZEMAN	0.17	0.16	0.17	0.13	0.18	0.09	2.02	0.66	0.21	–63	23	22
JHU	0.18	0.18	0.18	0.16	0.21	0.11	2.02	0.63	0.22	–63	26	24
ONLINE-B	0.2	0.19	0.20	0.2	0.22	0.12	2.03	0.62	0.24	–63	29	27
UEDIN	0.19	0.18	0.19	0.17	0.21	0.11	2.03	0.63	0.23	–63	27	26
UPV-PRHLT-COMBO	0.2	0.19	0.20	0.20	0.23	0.13	2.03	0.61	0.24	–63	29	28

Table 43: Automatic evaluation metric scores for systems in the WMT11 English-Czech News Task (newssyscombtest2011)

	AMBER	AMBER-NL	AMBER-TI	BLEU	F15	F15G3	ROSE	TER	METEOR-1.3-RANK	MP4IBM1	MPF	TESLA-B	TESLA-F	TESLA-M	WMPF
English-German News Task															
CMU-HEAFIELD-COMBO	0.19	0.18	0.19	0.17	0.21	0.11	1.96	0.66	0.39	–46	36	0.41	0.03	0.45	35
COPENHAGEN	0.17	0.17	0.18	0.14	0.18	0.09	1.95	0.69	0.36	–47	33	0.38	0.02	0.42	32
CU-TAMCHYNA	0.17	0.17	0.18	0.11	0.18	0.09	1.94	0.70	0.36	–48	31	0.36	0.02	0.4	30
CU-ZEMAN	0.16	0.15	0.16	0.05	0.17	0.08	1.92	0.71	0.34	–51	25	0.31	0.02	0.34	25
DFKI-FEDERMANN	0.17	0.16	0.17	0.13	0.17	0.08	1.95	0.71	0.34	–47	33	0.38	0.03	0.44	32
DFKI-XU	0.18	0.17	0.18	0.15	0.19	0.1	1.96	0.68	0.37	–47	35	0.39	0.03	0.43	34
ILLC-UVA	0.15	0.14	0.15	0.12	0.18	0.08	1.95	0.68	0.33	–49	32	0.36	0.02	0.4	31
JHU	0.17	0.17	0.18	0.14	0.18	0.09	1.95	0.68	0.35	–47	33	0.37	0.02	0.42	32
KIT	0.18	0.17	0.18	0.15	0.19	0.09	1.96	0.68	0.37	–47	35	0.39	0.03	0.43	34
KOC	0.17	0.16	0.17	0.12	0.17	0.08	1.95	0.69	0.35	–47	32	0.36	0.02	0.40	31
KOC-COMBO	0.18	0.17	0.18	0.15	0.2	0.1	1.95	0.67	0.37	–47	34	0.38	0.02	0.42	33
LIMSI	0.18	0.17	0.18	0.15	0.19	0.09	1.96	0.67	0.36	–47	35	0.39	0.03	0.44	33
LIU	0.17	0.17	0.18	0.15	0.19	0.09	1.95	0.68	0.36	–47	34	0.38	0.02	0.43	33
ONLINE-A	0.18	0.17	0.18	0.15	0.19	0.09	1.96	0.67	0.37	–47	35	0.40	0.03	0.45	33
ONLINE-B	0.19	0.18	0.19	0.17	0.21	0.11	1.96	0.65	0.38	–46	36	0.42	0.03	0.46	35
RBMT-1	0.17	0.17	0.18	0.13	0.18	0.08	1.95	0.7	0.35	–46	34	0.39	0.03	0.45	33
RBMT-2	0.16	0.16	0.17	0.12	0.16	0.08	1.94	0.73	0.33	–47	32	0.37	0.03	0.43	31
RBMT-3	0.18	0.17	0.18	0.14	0.18	0.09	1.95	0.69	0.36	–46	35	0.39	0.03	0.46	34
RBMT-4	0.17	0.16	0.17	0.13	0.17	0.08	1.95	0.70	0.34	–47	33	0.38	0.03	0.45	32
RBMT-5	0.17	0.16	0.17	0.12	0.17	0.08	1.95	0.71	0.34	–47	33	0.38	0.03	0.44	32
RWTH-FREITAG	0.17	0.17	0.17	0.15	0.19	0.09	1.95	0.68	0.36	–47	34	0.37	0.02	0.41	33
UEDIN	0.17	0.17	0.18	0.14	0.18	0.09	1.95	0.69	0.36	–47	34	0.38	0.02	0.42	33
UOW	0.17	0.16	0.17	0.13	0.17	0.08	1.95	0.7	0.35	–47	33	0.37	0.02	0.42	32
UPPSALA	0.17	0.16	0.17	0.14	0.18	0.09	1.95	0.68	0.35	–47	33	0.37	0.02	0.42	32
UPV-PRHLT-COMBO	0.18	0.18	0.19	0.17	0.20	0.10	1.96	0.66	0.38	–46	36	0.4	0.03	0.44	35
UZH-COMBO	0.19	0.18	0.19	0.17	0.21	0.11	1.96	0.66	0.38	–46	36	0.40	0.03	0.44	35

Table 44: Automatic evaluation metric scores for systems in the WMT11 English-German News Task (newssyscombtest2011)

	AMBER	AMBER-NL	AMBER-TI	BLEU	F15	F15G3	ROSE	TER	METEOR-1.3-RANK	MP4IBM1	MPF	TESLA-B	TESLA-F	TESLA-M	WMPF
English-French News Task															
CMU-HEAFIELD-COMBO	0.25	0.25	0.26	0.34	0.35	0.23	2.02	0.5	0.57	–41	52	0.54	–0.01	0.60	50
CU-ZEMAN	0.18	0.17	0.18	0.13	0.19	0.09	1.96	0.68	0.39	–46	35	0.34	–0.03	0.40	33
JHU	0.23	0.23	0.24	0.27	0.31	0.19	2.01	0.53	0.52	–43	47	0.49	–0.01	0.55	45
KIT	0.24	0.23	0.24	0.29	0.31	0.19	2.01	0.52	0.53	–42	49	0.51	–0.01	0.57	47
LATL-GENEVA	0.20	0.2	0.21	0.19	0.23	0.12	1.99	0.62	0.44	–43	41	0.44	–0.02	0.51	39
LIMSI	0.24	0.24	0.24	0.3	0.31	0.19	2.01	0.53	0.53	–41	49	0.51	–0.01	0.58	48
LIUM	0.24	0.23	0.24	0.29	0.31	0.19	2.01	0.53	0.53	–42	49	0.51	–0.01	0.57	47
ONLINE-A	0.24	0.23	0.24	0.27	0.3	0.18	2.01	0.53	0.52	–42	47	0.5	–0.01	0.56	46
ONLINE-B	0.25	0.25	0.25	0.33	0.35	0.23	2.02	0.5	0.56	–42	51	0.53	–0.01	0.59	50
RBMT-1	0.23	0.22	0.23	0.24	0.27	0.16	2.00	0.56	0.5	–41	45	0.48	–0.02	0.56	44
RBMT-2	0.22	0.21	0.22	0.22	0.25	0.14	1.99	0.58	0.47	–42	44	0.46	–0.02	0.53	42
RBMT-3	0.23	0.22	0.23	0.25	0.28	0.16	2.00	0.56	0.5	–41	46	0.48	–0.02	0.56	44
RBMT-4	0.22	0.21	0.22	0.23	0.26	0.15	1.99	0.58	0.47	–42	43	0.45	–0.02	0.51	42
RBMT-5	0.22	0.22	0.23	0.23	0.27	0.15	2	0.57	0.49	–41	45	0.47	–0.02	0.55	43
RWTH-HUCK	0.23	0.23	0.24	0.29	0.30	0.18	2.01	0.54	0.52	–42	48	0.5	–0.01	0.56	47
UEDIN	0.23	0.22	0.23	0.27	0.3	0.18	2.01	0.54	0.51	–42	47	0.49	–0.01	0.55	46
UPPSALA	0.23	0.22	0.23	0.27	0.29	0.17	2.00	0.55	0.51	–42	46	0.48	–0.01	0.55	45
UPPSALA-FBK	0.23	0.23	0.23	0.28	0.29	0.18	2.01	0.55	0.51	–42	47	0.49	–0.01	0.55	46
UPV-PRHLT-COMBO	0.25	0.24	0.25	0.32	0.34	0.22	2.02	0.50	0.55	–41	51	0.53	–0.01	0.59	49

Table 45: Automatic evaluation metric scores for systems in the WMT11 English-French News Task (newssyscombtest2011)

	AMBER	AMBER-NL	AMBER-TI	BLEU	F15	F15G3	ROSE	TER	METEOR-1.3-RANK	MP4IBM1	MPF	TESLA-B	TESLA-F	TESLA-M	WMPF
English-Spanish News Task															
CEU-UPV	0.24	0.24	0.24	0.29	0.3	0.18	2.01	0.51	0.55	–45	46	0.45	0.01	0.45	45
CMU-HEAFIELD-COMBO	0.26	0.25	0.26	0.35	0.34	0.22	2.02	0.47	0.58	–44	50	0.49	0.01	0.49	49
CU-ZEMAN	0.23	0.22	0.23	0.22	0.27	0.15	1.99	0.55	0.52	–48	39	0.41	0.00	0.41	38
KOC	0.23	0.23	0.23	0.25	0.27	0.16	2	0.54	0.52	–46	43	0.42	0.00	0.43	42
KOC-COMBO	0.25	0.24	0.25	0.31	0.32	0.2	2.01	0.5	0.56	–44	47	0.46	0.01	0.47	46
ONLINE-A	0.25	0.24	0.25	0.31	0.32	0.2	2.01	0.49	0.56	–44	48	0.46	0.01	0.47	46
ONLINE-B	0.25	0.25	0.25	0.33	0.32	0.2	2.02	0.50	0.57	–44	49	0.47	0.01	0.47	48
PROMT	0.24	0.23	0.24	0.28	0.28	0.17	2.00	0.53	0.52	–45	45	0.44	0.01	0.46	43
RBMT-1	0.23	0.23	0.23	0.25	0.27	0.16	2	0.55	0.51	–45	43	0.42	0.00	0.44	42
RBMT-2	0.23	0.22	0.23	0.25	0.26	0.15	1.99	0.55	0.5	–44	43	0.41	0.00	0.42	41
RBMT-3	0.24	0.23	0.24	0.28	0.28	0.17	2.00	0.53	0.52	–44	45	0.43	0.00	0.45	43
RBMT-4	0.23	0.22	0.23	0.26	0.26	0.16	1.99	0.54	0.51	–44	44	0.42	0.00	0.43	42
RBMT-5	0.23	0.22	0.23	0.24	0.26	0.15	1.99	0.57	0.49	–45	42	0.41	0.00	0.43	41
UEDIN	0.24	0.24	0.24	0.31	0.3	0.18	2.01	0.51	0.55	–45	47	0.45	0.01	0.45	46
UOW	0.23	0.23	0.24	0.28	0.28	0.16	2.00	0.53	0.53	–45	45	0.42	0.01	0.43	44
UOW-COMBO	0.25	0.25	0.25	0.33	0.32	0.2	2.01	0.50	0.56	–44	49	0.47	0.01	0.47	47
UPM	0.21	0.21	0.21	0.21	0.22	0.12	1.98	0.61	0.47	–47	39	0.37	0.00	0.37	38
UPPSALA	0.24	0.24	0.24	0.3	0.29	0.18	2.01	0.51	0.54	–45	46	0.44	0.01	0.44	45
UPV-PRHLT-COMBO	0.25	0.25	0.25	0.33	0.32	0.21	2.02	0.49	0.57	–44	49	0.47	0.01	0.48	48

Table 46: Automatic evaluation metric scores for systems in the WMT11 English-Spanish News Task (newssyscombtest2011)

	BLEU	MTeRater	MTeRater-Plus	ROSE	TER	METEOR-1.3-ADQ	METEOR-1.3-RANK	MPF	TESLA-B	TESLA-F	TESLA-M	WMPF
Haitian Creole (clean)-English Haitian Creole SMS Emergency Response Featured Translation Task												
BM-I2R	0.33	−6798	−4575	1.96	0.51	0.62	0.34	43	0.44	0.03	0.46	43
CMU-DENKOWSKI	0.29	−6849	−6172	1.95	0.53	0.58	0.32	40	0.39	0.02	0.40	39
CMU-HEAFIELD-COMBO	0.32	−6188	−4347	1.96	0.51	0.61	0.34	42	0.43	0.03	0.45	42
CMU-HEWAVITHARANA	0.28	−6523	−6341	1.95	0.57	0.57	0.32	39	0.38	0.02	0.40	38
HYDERABAD	0.14	−7548	−8502	1.92	0.66	0.50	0.28	26	0.3	0.02	0.30	26
KOC	0.23	−6490	−9020	1.94	0.67	0.49	0.27	36	0.32	0.02	0.34	35
KOC-COMBO	0.29	−4901	−5349	1.95	0.57	0.56	0.31	39	0.38	0.02	0.4	39
LIU	0.27	−6526	−6078	1.95	0.59	0.56	0.31	38	0.38	0.02	0.39	37
UMD-EIDELMAN	0.26	−4407	−6215	1.95	0.57	0.55	0.31	38	0.37	0.02	0.4	37
UMD-HU	0.22	−6379	−7460	1.94	0.59	0.51	0.28	35	0.36	0.02	0.39	34
UPPSALA	0.27	−5497	−6754	1.95	0.59	0.54	0.3	38	0.36	0.02	0.39	37
UPV-PRHLT-COMBO	0.32	−6896	−5968	1.96	0.53	0.6	0.33	42	0.41	0.02	0.43	41

Table 47: Automatic evaluation metric scores for systems in the WMT11 Haitian Creole (clean)-English Haitian Creole SMS Emergency Response Featured Translation Task (newssyscombtest2011)

	BLEU	MTeRater	MTeRater-Plus	ROSE	TER	METEOR-1.3-ADQ	METEOR-1.3-RANK	MPF	TESLA-B	TESLA-F	TESLA-M	WMPF
Haitian Creole (raw)-English Haitian Creole SMS Emergency Response Featured Translation Task												
BM-I2R	0.29	−3885	−3017	1.96	0.57	0.57	0.32	39	0.42	0.02	0.44	38
CMU-DENKOWSKI	0.25	−3965	−3905	1.95	0.60	0.53	0.3	35	0.38	0.02	0.4	35
CMU-HEAFIELD-COMBO	0.28	−3057	−2588	1.96	0.57	0.57	0.32	39	0.42	0.02	0.44	38
CMU-HEWAVITHARANA	0.25	−3701	−3824	1.95	0.61	0.53	0.3	35	0.37	0.02	0.39	35
JHU	0.14	−3207	−4279	1.92	0.74	0.43	0.24	26	0.30	0.02	0.32	26
LIU	0.25	−3447	−3445	1.95	0.60	0.54	0.30	36	0.38	0.02	0.4	35
UMD-EIDELMAN	0.24	−2826	−3754	1.94	0.64	0.52	0.29	34	0.36	0.02	0.39	34
UPV-PRHLT-COMBO	0.28	−3591	−3370	1.95	0.58	0.56	0.32	38	0.4	0.02	0.42	38

Table 48: Automatic evaluation metric scores for systems in the WMT11 Haitian Creole (raw)-English Haitian Creole SMS Emergency Response Featured Translation Task (newssyscombtest2011)

INTER-ANNOTATOR AGREEMENT (I.E. ACROSS ANNOTATORS)	ALL COMPARISONS			NO REF COMPARISONS		
	$P(A)$	$P(E)$	κ	$P(A)$	$P(E)$	κ
Czech-English, individual systems	0.591	0.354	0.367	0.535	0.343	0.293
English-Czech, individual systems	0.608	0.359	0.388	0.552	0.350	0.312
German-English, individual systems	0.562	0.377	0.298	0.536	0.370	0.264
English-German, individual systems	0.564	0.352	0.327	0.528	0.348	0.276
Spanish-English, individual systems	0.695	0.398	0.493	0.683	0.393	0.477
English-Spanish, individual systems	0.574	0.343	0.352	0.548	0.339	0.317
French-English, individual systems	0.616	0.367	0.393	0.584	0.361	0.349
English-French, individual systems	0.631	0.382	0.403	0.603	0.376	0.363
European languages, individual systems	0.601	0.362	0.375	0.561	0.355	0.320
Czech-English, system combinations	0.700	0.334	0.549	0.577	0.369	0.329
English-Czech, system combinations	0.812	0.348	0.711	0.696	0.392	0.500
German-English, system combinations	0.675	0.353	0.498	0.629	0.341	0.437
English-German, system combinations	0.608	0.346	0.401	0.547	0.334	0.320
Spanish-English, system combinations	0.638	0.335	0.456	0.604	0.359	0.382
English-Spanish, system combinations	0.657	0.335	0.485	0.603	0.371	0.369
French-English, system combinations	0.654	0.336	0.479	0.608	0.336	0.410
English-French, system combinations	0.678	0.352	0.503	0.595	0.339	0.388
European languages, system combinations	0.671	0.335	0.505	0.598	0.342	0.389
Haitian (Clean)-English, individual systems	0.693	0.364	0.517	0.640	0.353	0.443
Haitian (Raw)-English, individual systems	0.689	0.357	0.517	0.639	0.344	0.450
Haitian-English, individual systems	0.691	0.362	0.516	0.639	0.350	0.446
Haitian (Clean)-English, system combinations	0.770	0.367	0.636	0.645	0.333	0.468
Haitian (Raw)-English, system combinations	0.745	0.345	0.611	0.753	0.361	0.613
Haitian-English, system combinations	0.761	0.358	0.628	0.674	0.335	0.509
Tunable metrics task (Urdu-English)	0.692	0.337	0.535	0.641	0.363	0.437
WMT10 (European languages, individual vs. individual)	0.663	0.394	0.445	0.620	0.385	0.382
WMT10 (European languages, combo vs. combo)	0.728	0.344	0.586	0.629	0.334	0.443
WMT10 (European languages, individual vs. combo)	N/A	N/A	N/A	0.634	0.360	0.428
WMT10 (European languages, all systems)	0.658	0.374	0.454	0.626	0.367	0.409

Table 49: Inter-annotator agreement rates, for the various manual evaluation tracks of WMT11, broken down by language pair. The highlighted rows correspond to rows in the top half of Table 7. See Table 50 below for detailed *intra*-annotator agreement rates.

INTRA-ANNOTATOR AGREEMENT (I.E. SELF-CONSISTENCY)	ALL COMPARISONS			NO REF COMPARISONS		
	$P(A)$	$P(E)$	κ	$P(A)$	$P(E)$	κ
Czech-English, individual systems	0.762	0.354	0.632	0.713	0.343	0.564
English-Czech, individual systems	0.743	0.359	0.598	0.700	0.350	0.539
German-English, individual systems	0.675	0.377	0.478	0.670	0.370	0.475
English-German, individual systems	0.704	0.352	0.543	0.700	0.348	0.541
Spanish-English, individual systems	0.750	0.398	0.585	0.719	0.393	0.537
English-Spanish, individual systems	0.644	0.343	0.458	0.601	0.339	0.396
French-English, individual systems	0.829	0.367	0.730	0.816	0.361	0.712
English-French, individual systems	0.716	0.382	0.541	0.681	0.376	0.488
European languages, individual systems	0.722	0.362	0.564	0.685	0.355	0.512
Czech-English, system combinations	0.756	0.334	0.633	0.657	0.369	0.457
English-Czech, system combinations	0.923	0.348	0.882	0.842	0.392	0.740
German-English, system combinations	0.732	0.353	0.586	0.716	0.341	0.569
English-German, system combinations	0.722	0.346	0.575	0.676	0.334	0.513
Spanish-English, system combinations	0.783	0.335	0.673	0.720	0.359	0.562
English-Spanish, system combinations	0.741	0.335	0.610	0.711	0.371	0.540
French-English, system combinations	0.772	0.336	0.657	0.659	0.336	0.487
English-French, system combinations	0.841	0.352	0.755	0.714	0.339	0.568
European languages, system combinations	0.787	0.335	0.680	0.717	0.342	0.571
Haitian (Clean)-English, individual systems	0.758	0.364	0.619	0.686	0.353	0.515
Haitian (Raw)-English, individual systems	0.783	0.357	0.663	0.756	0.344	0.628
Haitian-English, individual systems	0.763	0.362	0.628	0.700	0.350	0.539
Haitian (Clean)-English, system combinations	0.882	0.367	0.813	0.778	0.333	0.667
Haitian (Raw)-English, system combinations	0.882	0.345	0.820	0.802	0.361	0.690
Haitian-English, system combinations	0.882	0.358	0.816	0.784	0.335	0.675
Tunable metrics task (Urdu-English)	0.857	0.337	0.784	0.856	0.363	0.774
WMT10 (European languages, individual vs. individual)	0.757	0.394	0.599	0.728	0.385	0.557
WMT10 (European languages, combo vs. combo)	0.783	0.344	0.670	0.719	0.334	0.578
WMT10 (European languages, individual vs. combo)	N/A	N/A	N/A	0.746	0.360	0.603
WMT10 (European languages, all systems)	0.755	0.374	0.609	0.734	0.367	0.580

Table 50: Intra-annotator agreement rates, for the various manual evaluation tracks of WMT11, broken down by language pair. The highlighted rows correspond to rows in the bottom half of Table 7. See Table 49 above for detailed *inter*-annotator agreement rates.

Evaluate with Confidence Estimation: Machine ranking of translation outputs using grammatical features

Eleftherios Avramidis, Maja Popovic, David Vilar, Aljoscha Burchardt
German Research Center for Artificial Intelligence (DFKI)
Language Technology (LT), Berlin, Germany
name.surname@dfki.de

Abstract

We present a pilot study on an evaluation method which is able to rank translation outputs with no reference translation, given only their source sentence. The system employs a statistical classifier trained upon existing human rankings, using several features derived from analysis of both the source and the target sentences. Development experiments on one language pair showed that the method has considerably good correlation with human ranking when using features obtained from a PCFG parser.

1 Introduction

Automatic evaluation metrics for Machine Translation (MT) have mainly relied on analyzing both the MT output against (one or more) reference translations. Though, several paradigms in Machine Translation Research pose the need to estimate the quality through many translation outputs, when no reference translation is given (n-best rescoring of SMT systems, system combination etc.). Such metrics have been known as *Confidence Estimation metrics* and quite a few projects have suggested solutions on this direction. With our submission to the Shared Task, we allow such a metric to be systematically compared with the state-of-the-art reference-aware MT metrics.

Our approach suggests building a Confidence Estimation metric using already existing human judgments. This has been motivated by the existence of human-annotated data containing comparisons of the outputs of several systems, as a result of the evaluation tasks run by the Workshops on Statistical Machine Translation (WMT) (Callison-Burch et al., 2008; Callison-Burch et al., 2009; Callison-Burch et al., 2010). This amount of data, which has been freely available for further research, gives an opportunity for applying machine learning techniques to model the human annotators' choices. Machine Learning methods over previously released evaluation data have been already used for tuning complex statistical evaluation metrics (e.g. SVM-Rank in Callison-Burch et al. (2010)). Our proposition is similar, but works without reference translations. We develop a solution of applying machine learning in order to build a statistical classifier that performs similar to the human ranking: it is trained to rank several MT outputs, given analysis of possible qualitative criteria on both the source and the target side of every given sentence. As qualitative criteria, we use statistical features indicating the quality and the grammaticality of the output.

2 Automatic ranking method

2.1 From Confidence Estimation to ranking

Confidence estimation has been seen from the Natural Language Processing (NLP) perspective as a problem of binary classification in order to assess the correctness of a NLP system output. Previous work focusing on Machine Translation includes statistical methods for estimating correctness scores or correctness probabilities, following a rich search over the spectrum of possible features (Blatz et al., 2004a; Ueffing and Ney, 2005; Specia et al., 2009; Raybaud and Caroline Lavecchia, 2009; Rosti et al.,

Proceedings of the 6th Workshop on Statistical Machine Translation, pages 65–70,
Edinburgh, Scotland, UK, July 30–31, 2011. ©2011 Association for Computational Linguistics

2007).

In this work we slightly transform the binary classification practice to fit the standard WMT human evaluation process. As human annotators have provided their evaluation in the form of ranking of five system outputs at a sentence level, we build our evaluation mechanism with similar functionality, aiming to training from and evaluating against this data. Evaluation scores and results can be then calculated based on comparative analysis of the performance of each system.

Whereas latest work, such as Specia et al. (2010), has focused on learning to assess segment performance independently for each system output, our contribution measures the performance by comparing the system outputs with each other and consequently ranking them. The exact method is described below.

2.2 Internal pairwise decomposition

We build one classifier over all input sentences. While the evaluation mechanism is trained and evaluated on a multi-class (ranking) basis as explained above, the classifier is expected to work on a binary level: we provide the features from the analysis of the two system outputs and the source, and the classifier should decide if the first system output is better than the second one or not.

In order to accomplish such training, the n systems' outputs for each sentence are broken down to $n \times (n-1)$ pairs, of all possible comparisons between two system outputs, in both directions (similar to the calculation of the Spearman correlation). For each pair, the classifier is trained with a class value c, for the pairwise comparison of system outputs t_i and t_j with respective ranks r_i and r_j, determined as:

$$c(r_i, r_j) = \begin{cases} 1 & r_i < r_j \\ -1 & r_i > r_j \end{cases}$$

At testing time, after the classifier has made all the pairwise decisions, those need to be converted back to ranks. System entries are ordered, according to how many times each of them won in the pairwise comparison, leading to rank lists similar to the ones provided by human annotators. Note that this kind of decomposition allows for *ties* when there are equal times of winnings.

2.3 Acquiring features

In order to obtain features indicating the quality of the MT output, automatic NLP analysis tools are applied on both the source and the two target (MT-generated) sentences of every pairwise comparison. Features considered can be seen in the following categories, according to their origin:

- **Sentence length:** Number of words of source and target sentences, source-length to target-length ratio.

- **Target language model:** Language models provide statistics concerning the correctness of the words' sequence on the target language. Such language model features include:
  - the smoothed n-gram probability of the entire target sentence for a language model of order 5, along with
  - uni-gram, bi-gram, tri-gram probabilities and a
  - count of unknown words

- **Parsing:** Processing features acquired from PCFG parsing (Petrov et al., 2006) for both source and target side include:
  - parse log likelihood,
  - number of n-best trees,
  - confidence for the best parse,
  - average confidence of all trees.

  Ratios of the above target features to their respective source features were included.

- **Shallow grammatical match:** The number of occurences of particular node tags on both the source and the target was counted on the PCFG parses. In particular, NPs, VPs, PPs, NNs and punctuation occurences were counted. Then the ratio of the occurences of each tag in the target sentence by its occurences on the source sentence was also calculated.

2.4 Classifiers

The machine learning core of the system was built supporting two classification approaches.

- **Naïve Bayes** allows prediction of a binary class, given the assumption that the features are statistically independent.

$$p(C, F_1, \ldots, F_n) = p(C) \prod_{n}^{i=1} p(F_i|C)$$

$p(C)$ is estimated by relative frequencies of the training pairwise examples, while $p(F_i|C)$ for our continuous features are estimated with LOESS (locally weighted linear regression similar to Cleveland (1979))

- **k-nearest neighbour** (knn) algorithm allows classifying based on the closest training examples in the feature space.

3 Experiment

3.1 Experiment setup

A basic experiment was designed in order to determine the exact setup and the feature set of the metric prior to the shared task submission. The classifiers for the task were learnt using the German-English testset of the WMT 2008 and 2010 (about 700 sentences)[1]. For testing, the classifiers were used to perform ranking on a test set of 184 sentences which had been kept apart from the 2010 data, with the criterion that they do not contain contradictions among human judgments.

In order to allow further comparison with other evaluation metrics, we performed an extended experiment: we trained the classifiers over the WMT 2008 and 2009 data and let them perform automatic ranking on the full WMT 2010 test set, this time without any restriction on human evaluation agreement.

In both experiments, tokenization was performed with the PUNKT tokenizer (Kiss et al., 2006; Garrette and Klein, 2009), while n-gram features were generated with the SRILM toolkit (Stolcke, 2002). The language model was relatively big and had been built upon all lowercased monolingual training sets for the WMT 2011 Shared Task, interpolated on the 2007 test set. As a PCFG parser, the Berkeley Parser (Petrov and Klein, 2007) was preferred, due to the possibility of easily obtaining complex internal statistics, including n-best trees. Unfortunately, the time required for parsing leads to significant delays at the overall processing. The machine learning algorithms were implemented with the Orange toolkit (Demšar et al., 2004).

[1]data acquired from http://www.statmt.org/wmt11

3.2 Feature selection

Although the automatic NLP tools provided a lot of features (section 2.3), the classification methods we used (and particularly naïve Bayes were the development was focused on) would be expected to perform better given a smaller group of statistically independent features. Since exhaustive training/testing of all possible feature subsets was not possible, we performed feature selection based on the Relieff method (Kononenko, 1994; Kira and Rendell, 1992). Automatic ranking was performed based on the most promising feature subsets. The results are examined below.

3.3 Results

The performance of the classifier is measured after the classifier output has been converted back to rank lists, similar to the WMT 2010 evaluation. We therefore calculated two types of rank coefficients: averaged Kendall's tau on a segment level, and Spearman's rho on a system level, based on the percentage that the each system's translations performed better than or equal to the translations of any other system.

The results for the various combinations of features and classifiers are depicted on Table 1. Naïve Bayes provides the best score on the test set, with $\rho = 0.81$ on a system level and $\tau = 0.26$ on a segment level, trained with features including the number of the unknown words, the source-length by target-length ratio, the VP count ratio and the source-target ratio of the parsing log-likelihood. The number of unknown words particularly appears to be a strong indicator for the quality of the sentence. On the first part of the table we can also observe that language model features do not perform as well as the features deriving from the processing information delivered by the parser. On the second part of the table we compare the use of various grammatical combinations. The third part contains the correlation obtained by various similar internal parsing-related features.

features	naïve Bayes		knn	
	rho	tau	rho	tau
basic experiment				
ngram	0.19	0.05	0.13	0.01
unk, len	0.67	0.20	0.73	0.24
unk, len, bigram	0.61	0.21	0.74	0.21
unk, len, ngram	0.63	0.19	0.59	0.21
unk, len, trigram	0.67	0.20	0.76	0.21
unk, len, $\log_{parse}$	0.75	0.21	0.74	0.25
unk, len, n_{parse}, VP	0.67	0.24	0.61	0.20
unk, len, n_{parse}, VP, $conf_{bestparse}$	0.78	0.25	0.75	0.24
unk, len, n_{parse}, NP, $conf_{bestparse}$	0.78	0.23	0.74	0.23
unk, len, n_{parse}, VP, $conf_{avg}$	0.75	0.21	0.78	0.23
unk, len, n_{parse}, VP, $conf_{bestparse}$	0.78	0.25	0.75	0.24
unk, len, n_{parse}, VP, $\log_{parse}$	**0.81**	**0.26**	0.75	0.23
extended experiment				
unk, len, n_{parse}, VP, $\log_{parse}$	**0.60**	**0.23**	0.28	0.02

Table 1: System-level Spearman's rho and segment-level Kendall's tau correlation coefficients achieved on automatic ranking (average absolute value)

The correlation coefficients of the extended experiment, allowing comparison with last year's shared task, are shown on the last line of the table. With coefficients $\rho = 0.60$ and $\tau = 0.23$, our metric performs relatively low compared to the other metrics of WMT10 (indicatively iBLEU: $\rho = 0.95$, $\tau = 0.39$ according to Callison-Burch et al. (2010). Though, it still has a position in the list, scoring better than several other reference-aware metrics (e.g. of $\rho = 0.47$ and $\tau = 0.12$ respectively) for the particular language pair.

4 Discussion

A concern on the use of Confidence Estimation for MT evaluation has to do with the possibility of a system "tricking" such metrics. This would for example be the case when a system offers a well-formed candidate translation and gets a good score, despite having no relation to the source sentence in terms of meaning. We should note that we are not capable of fully investigating this case based on the current set of experiments, because all of the systems in our data sets have shown acceptable scores (11-25 BLEU and 0.58-0.78 TERp according to Callison-Burch et al. (2010)), when evaluated against reference translations. Though, we would assume that we partially address this problem by using ratios of source to target features (length, syntactic constituents), which means that in order for a sentence to trick the metric, it would need a comparable sentence length and a grammatical structure that would allow it to achieve feature ratios similar to the other systems' outputs. Previous work (Blatz et al., 2004b; Ueffing and Ney, 2005) has used features based on word alignment, such as IBM Models, which would be a meaningful addition from this aspect.

Although *k-nearest-neighbour* is considered to be a superior classifier, best results are obtained by naïve Bayes. This may have been due of the fact that feature selection has led to small sets of uncorrelated features, where naïve Bayes is known to perform well. *K-nearest-neighbour* and other complex classification methods are expected to prove useful when more complex feature sets are employed.

5 Conclusion and Further work

The experiments presented in this article indicate that confidence metrics trained over human rankings can be possibly used for several tasks of evaluation, given particular conditions, where e.g. there is no reference translation given. Features obtained from a PCFG parser seem to be leading to better correlations, given our basic test set. Although correlation is not particularly high, compared to other reference-aware metrics in WMT 10, there is clearly a potential for further improvement.

Nevertheless this is still a small-scale experiment, given the restricted data size and the single translation direction. The performance of the system on broader training and test sets will be evaluated in the future. Feature selection is also subject to change if other language pairs are introduced, while more sophisticated machine learning algorithms, allowing richer feature sets, may also lead to better results.

Acknowledgments

This work was done with the support of the TaraXŰ Project[2], financed by TSB Technologiestiftung Berlin–Zukunftsfonds Berlin, co-financed by the European Union–European fund for regional development.

References

John Blatz, Erin Fitzgerald, George Foster, Simona Gandrabur, Cyril Goutte, Alex Kulesza, Alberto Sanchis, and Nicola Ueffing. 2004a. Confidence estimation for machine translation. In *Proceedings of the 20th international conference on Computational Linguistics*, COLING '04, Stroudsburg, PA, USA. Association for Computational Linguistics.

John Blatz, Erin Fitzgerald, George Foster, Simona Gandrabur, Cyril Goutte, Alex Kulesza, Alberto Sanchis, and Nicola Ueffing. 2004b. Confidence estimation for machine translation. In *M. Rollins (Ed.), Mental Imagery*. Yale University Press.

Chris Callison-Burch, Cameron Fordyce, Philipp Koehn, Christof Monz, and Josh Schroeder. 2008. Further meta-evaluation of machine translation. In *Proceedings of the Third Workshop on Statistical Machine Translation*, pages 70–106, Columbus, Ohio, June. Association for Computational Linguistics.

Chris Callison-Burch, Philipp Koehn, Christof Monz, and Josh Schroeder. 2009. Findings of the 2009 Workshop on Statistical Machine Translation. In *Proceedings of the Fourth Workshop on Statistical Machine Translation*, pages 1–28, Athens, Greece, March. Association for Computational Linguistics.

Chris Callison-Burch, Philipp Koehn, Christof Monz, Kay Peterson, Mark Przybocki, and Omar Zaidan. 2010. Findings of the 2010 joint workshop on statistical machine translation and metrics for machine translation. In *Proceedings of the Joint Fifth Workshop on Statistical Machine Translation and MetricsMATR*, pages 17–53, Uppsala, Sweden, July. Association for Computational Linguistics. Revised August 2010.

William S. Cleveland. 1979. Robust locally weighted regression and smoothing scatterplots. *Journal of the American statistical association*, 74(368):829–836.

Janez Demšar, Blaz Zupan, Gregor Leban, and Tomaz Curk. 2004. Orange: From experimental machine learning to interactive data mining. In *Principles of Data Mining and Knowledge Discovery*, pages 537–539.

Dan Garrette and Ewan Klein. 2009. An extensible toolkit for computational semantics. In *Proceedings of the Eighth International Conference on Computational Semantics*, IWCS-8 '09, pages 116–127, Stroudsburg, PA, USA. Association for Computational Linguistics.

Kenji Kira and Larry A. Rendell. 1992. The feature selection problem: traditional methods and a new algorithm. In *Proceedings of the tenth national conference on Artificial intelligence*, AAAI'92, pages 129–134. AAAI Press.

Tibor Kiss, Jan Strunk, Ruhr universität Bochum, and Ruhr universität Bochum. 2006. Unsupervised multilingual sentence boundary detection. In *Proceedings of IICS-04, Guadalajara, Mexico and Springer LNCS 3473*.

Igor Kononenko. 1994. Estimating attributes: analysis and extensions of relief. In *Proceedings of the European conference on machine learning on Machine Learning*, pages 171–182, Secaucus, NJ, USA. Springer-Verlag New York, Inc.

Slav Petrov and Dan Klein. 2007. Improved inference for unlexicalized parsing. In *In HLT-NAACL '07*.

Slav Petrov, Leon Barrett, Romain Thibaux, and Dan Klein. 2006. Learning accurate, compact, and interpretable tree annotation. In *In ACL '06*, pages 433–440.

Sylvain Raybaud and Kamel Smaili Caroline Lavecchia, David Langlois. 2009. Word-and sentence-level confidence measures for machine translation. In *European Association of Machine Translation 2009*.

Antti-Veikko Rosti, Necip Fazil Ayan, Bing Xiang, Spyros Matsoukas, Richard Schwartz, and Bonnie J. Dorr. 2007. Combining outputs from multiple machine translation systems. In *Proceedings of the North American Chapter of the Association for Computational Linguistics Human Language Technologies*, pages 228–235.

[2]http://taraxu.dfki.de

Lucia Specia, Marco Turchi, Zhuoran Wang, John Shawe-Taylor, and Craig Saunders. 2009. Improving the confidence of machine translation quality estimates. In *Machine Translation Summit XII*, Ottawa, Canada.

Lucia Specia, Dhwaj Raj, and Marco Turchi. 2010. Machine translation evaluation versus quality estimation. *Machine Translation*, 24:39–50, March.

Andreas Stolcke. 2002. Srilm—an extensible language modeling toolkit. In *Proceedings of the 7th International Conference on Spoken Language Processing (ICSLP 2002*, pages 901–904.

Nicola Ueffing and Hermann Ney. 2005. Word-level confidence estimation for machine translation using phrase-based translation models. *Computational Linguistics*, pages 763–770.

AMBER: A Modified BLEU, Enhanced Ranking Metric

Boxing Chen and Roland Kuhn
National Research Council of Canada, Gatineau, Québec, Canada
First.Last@nrc.gc.ca

Abstract

This paper proposes a new automatic machine translation evaluation metric: AMBER, which is based on the metric BLEU but incorporates recall, extra penalties, and some text processing variants. There is very little linguistic information in AMBER. We evaluate its system-level correlation and sentence-level consistency scores with human rankings from the WMT shared evaluation task; AMBER achieves state-of-the-art performance.

1 Introduction

Automatic evaluation metrics for machine translation (MT) quality play a critical role in the development of statistical MT systems. Several metrics have been proposed in recent years. Metrics such as BLEU (Papineni *et al.*, 2002), NIST (Doddington, 2002), WER, PER, and TER (Snover *et al.*, 2006) do not use any linguistic information - they only apply surface matching. METEOR (Banerjee and Lavie, 2005), METEOR-NEXT (Denkowski and Lavie 2010), TER-Plus (Snover *et al.*, 2009), MaxSim (Chan and Ng, 2008), and TESLA (Liu *et al.*, 2010) exploit some limited linguistic resources, such as synonym dictionaries, part-of-speech tagging or paraphrasing tables. More sophisticated metrics such as RTE (Pado *et al.*, 2009) and DCU-LFG (He *et al.*, 2010) use higher level syntactic or semantic analysis to score translations.

Though several of these metrics have shown better correlation with human judgment than BLEU, BLEU is still the *de facto* standard evaluation metric. This is probably due to the following facts:

1. BLEU is language independent (except for word segmentation decisions).
2. BLEU can be computed quickly. This is important when choosing a metric to tune an MT system.
3. BLEU seems to be the best tuning metric from a quality point of view - *i.e.*, models trained using BLEU obtain the highest scores from humans and even from other metrics (Cer *et al.*, 2010).

When we developed our own metric, we decided to make it a modified version of BLEU whose rankings of translations would (ideally) correlate even more highly with human rankings. Thus, our metric is called AMBER: "A Modified Bleu, Enhanced Ranking" metric. Some of the AMBER variants use an information source with a mild linguistic flavour – morphological knowledge about suffixes, roots and prefixes – but otherwise, the metric is based entirely on surface comparisons.

2 AMBER

Like BLEU, AMBER is composed of two parts: a score and a penalty.

$$AMBER = score \times penalty \quad (1)$$

To address weaknesses of BLEU described in the literature (Callison-Burch *et al.*, 2006; Lavie and Denkowski, 2009), we use more sophisticated formulae to compute the *score* and *penalty*.

2.1 Enhancing the *score*

First, we enrich the *score* part with geometric average of n-gram precisions (*AvgP*), F-measure derived from the arithmetic averages of precision and recall (*Fmean*), and arithmetic average of F-measure of precision and recall for each n-gram (*AvgF*). Let us define n-gram *precision* and *recall* as follows:

Proceedings of the 6th Workshop on Statistical Machine Translation, pages 71–77,
Edinburgh, Scotland, UK, July 30–31, 2011.

$$p(n) = \frac{\#ngrams(T \cap R)}{\#ngrams(T)} \quad (2)$$

$$r(n) = \frac{\#ngrams(T \cap R)}{\#ngrams(R)} \quad (3)$$

where T = translation, R = reference.

Then the geometric average of n-gram precisions *AvgP*, which is also the score part of the BLEU metric, is defined as:

$$AvgP(N) = \left(\prod_{n=1}^{N} p(n)\right)^{\frac{1}{N}} \quad (4)$$

The arithmetic averages for n-gram precision and recall are:

$$P(N) = \frac{1}{N}\sum_{n=1}^{N} p(n) \quad (5)$$

$$R(M) = \frac{1}{M}\sum_{n=1}^{M} r(n) \quad (6)$$

The F-measure that is derived from P(N) and R(M), (*Fmean*), is given by:

$$Fmean(N, M, \alpha) = \frac{P(N)R(M)}{\alpha P(N) + (1-\alpha)R(M)} \quad (7)$$

The arithmetic average of F-measure of precision and recall for each n-gram (*AvgF*) is given by:

$$AvgF(N, \alpha) = \frac{1}{N}\sum_{n=1}^{N} \frac{p(n)r(n)}{\alpha p(n) + (1-\alpha)r(n)} \quad (8)$$

The *score* is the weighted average of the three values: *AvgP, Fmean,* and *AvgF*.

$$\begin{aligned} score(N) &= \theta_1 \times AvgP(N) \\ &+ \theta_2 \times Fmean(N, M, \alpha) \\ &+ (1-\theta_1-\theta_2) \times AvgF(N, \alpha) \end{aligned} \quad (9)$$

The free parameters N, M, α, θ_1 and θ_2 were manually tuned on a dev set.

2.2 Various *penalties*

Instead of the original brevity penalty, we experimented with a product of various penalties:

$$penalty = \prod_{i=1}^{P} pen_i^{w_i} \quad (10)$$

where w_i is the weight of each penalty pen_i.

Strict brevity penalty (SBP): (Chiang *et al.*, 2008) proposed this penalty. Let t_i be the translation of input sentence i, and let r_i be its reference (or if there is more than one, the reference whose length in words $|r_i|$ is closest to length $|t_i|$). Set

$$SBP = \exp\left(1 - \frac{\sum_i |r_i|}{\sum_i \min\{|t_i|, |r_i|\}}\right) \quad (11)$$

Strict redundancy penalty (SRP): long sentences are preferred by recall. Since we rely on both recall and precision to compute the *score*, it is necessary to punish the sentences that are too long.

$$SRP = \exp\left(1 - \frac{\sum_i \max\{|t_i|, |r_i|\}}{\sum_i |r_i|}\right) \quad (12)$$

Character-based strict brevity penalty (CSBP) and **Character-based strict redundancy penalty (CSRP)** are defined similarly. The only difference with the above two penalties is that here, length is measured in characters.

Chunk penalty (CKP): the same penalty as in METEOR:

$$CKP = 1 - \gamma \times \left(\frac{\#chunks}{\#matches(word)}\right)^{\beta} \quad (13)$$

γ and β are free parameters. We do not compute the word alignment between the translation and reference; therefore, the number of chunks is computed as $\#chunks = \#matches(bigram) - \#matches(word)$. For example, in the following two-sentence translation (references not shown), let "m_i" stand for a matched word, "x" stand for zero, one or more unmatched words:

S1: $m_1\, m_2$ x $m_3\, m_4\, m_5$ x m_6

S2: m_7 x $m_8\, m_9$ x $m_{10}\, m_{11}\, m_{12}$ x m_{13}

If we consider only unigrams and bigrams, there are 13 matched words and 6 matched bigrams ($m_1\, m_2$, $m_3\, m_4$, $m_4\, m_5$, $m_8\, m_9$, $m_{10}\, m_{11}$, $m_{11}\, m_{12}$), so there are 13-6=7 chunks ($m_1\, m_2$, $m_3\, m_4\, m_5$, m_6, m_7, $m_8\, m_9$, $m_{10}\, m_{11}\, m_{12}$, m_{13}).

Continuity penalty (CTP): if all matched words are continuous, then $\frac{\#ngrams(T \cap R)}{\#(n-1)grams(T \cap R) - \#segment}$ equals 1.

Example:

S3: $m_1\, m_2\, m_3\, m_4\, m_5 m_6$

S4: $m_7\, m_8\, m_9 m_{10}\, m_{11}\, m_{12}\, m_{13}$

There are 13 matched unigrams, and 11 matched bi-grams; we get 11/(13-2)=1. Therefore, a continuity penalty is computed as:

$$CTP = \exp\left(-\frac{1}{N-1}\sum_{n=2}^{N}\frac{\#ngrams(T \cap R)}{\#(n-1)grams(T \cap R)\ \#segment}\right) \quad (14)$$

Short word difference penalty (SWDP): a good translation should have roughly the same number of stop words as the reference. To make AMBER more portable across all Indo-European languages, we use short words (those with fewer than 4 characters) to approximate the stop words.

$$SWDP = \exp\left(-\frac{|a-b|}{\#unigram(r)}\right) \quad (15)$$

where a and b are the number of short words in the translation and reference respectively.

Long word difference penalty (LWDP): is defined similarly to SWDP.

$$LWDP = \exp\left(-\frac{|c-d|}{\#unigram(r)}\right) \quad (15)$$

where c and d are the number of long words (those longer than 3 characters) in the translation and reference respectively.

Normalized Spearman's correlation penalty (NSCP): we adopt this from (Isozaki *et al.*, 2010). This penalty evaluates similarity in word order between the translation and reference. We first determine word correspondences between the translation and reference; then, we rank words by their position in the sentences. Finally, we compute Spearman's correlation between the ranks of the n words common to the translation and reference.

$$\rho = 1 - \frac{\sum_i d_i^2}{(n+1)n(n-1)} \quad (16)$$

where d_i indicates the distance between the ranks of the i-th element. For example:

T: *Bob reading book likes*

R: *Bob likes reading book*

The rank vector of the reference is [1, 2, 3, 4], while the translation rank vector is [1, 3, 4, 2]. The Spearman's correlation score between these two vectors is $1-\frac{0+(3-2)^2+(4-3)^2+(2-4)^2}{(4+1)\cdot 4\cdot (4-1)}$=0.90.

In order to avoid negative values, we normalized the correlation score, obtaining the penalty NSCP:

$$NSCP = (1+\rho)/2 \quad (17)$$

Normalized Kendall's correlation penalty (NKCP): this is adopted from (Birch and Osborne, 2010) and (Isozaki *et al.*, 2010). In the previous example, where the rank vector of the translation is [1, 3, 4, 2], there are $C_4^2 = 6$ pairs of integers. There are 4 increasing pairs: (1,3), (1,4), (1,2) and (3,4). Kendall's correlation is defined by:

$$\tau = 2 \times \frac{\#increasing\ pairs}{\#all\ \ pairs} - 1 \quad (18)$$

Therefore, Kendall's correlation for the translation "*Bob reading book likes*" is $2\times 4/6-1$=0.33.

Again, to avoid negative values, we normalized the coefficient score, obtaining the penalty NKCP:

$$NKCP = (1+\tau)/2 \quad (19)$$

2.3 Term weighting

The original BLEU metric weights all n-grams equally; however, different n-grams have different amounts of information. We experimented with applying *tf-idf* to weight each n-gram according to its information value.

2.4 Four matching strategies

In the original BLEU metric, there is only one matching strategy: n-gram matching. In AMBER, we provide four matching strategies (the best AMBER variant used three of these):

1. N-gram matching: involved in computing *precision* and *recall.*
2. Fixed-gap n-gram: the size of the gap between words "word1 [] word2" is fixed; involved in computing *precision* only.
3. Flexible-gap n-gram: the size of the gap between words "word1 * word2" is flexible; involved in computing *precision* only.
4. Skip n-gram: as used ROUGE (Lin, 2004); involved in computing *precision* only.

2.5 Input preprocessing

The AMBER score can be computed with different types of preprocessing. When using more than one type, we computed the final score as an average over runs, one run per type (our default AMBER variant used three of the preprocessing types):

$$Final\_AMBER = \frac{1}{T}\sum_{t=1}^{T} AMBER(t)$$

We provide 8 types of possible text input:

0. Original - true-cased and untokenized.

1. Normalized - tokenized and lower-cased. (All variants 2-7 below also tokenized and lower-cased.)
2. "Stemmed" - each word only keeps its first 4 letters.
3. "Suffixed" - each word only keeps its last 4 letters.
4. Split type 1 - each longer-than-4-letter word is segmented into two sub-words, with one being the first 4 letters and the other the last 2 letters. If the word has 5 letters, the 4th letter appears twice: e.g., "gangs" becomes "gang" + "gs". If the word has more than 6 letters, the middle part is thrown away
5. Split type 2 - each word is segmented into fixed-length (4-letter) sub-word sequences, starting from the left.
6. Split type 3 - each word is segmented into prefix, root, and suffix. The list of English prefixes, roots, and suffixes used to split the word is from the Internet[1]; it is used to split words from all languages. Linguistic knowledge is applied here (but not in any other aspect of AMBER).
7. Long words only - small words (those with fewer than 4 letters) are removed.

3 Experiments

3.1 Experimental data

We evaluated AMBER on WMT data, using WMT 2008 all-to-English submissions as the dev set. Test sets include WMT 2009 all-to-English, WMT 2010 all-to-English and 2010 English-to-all submissions. **Table 1** summarizes the dev and test set statistics.

Set	Dev	Test1	Test2	Test3
Year	2008	2009	2010	2010
Lang.	xx-en	xx-en	xx-en	en-xx
#system	43	39	53	32
#sent-pair	7,861	13,912	14,212	13,165

Table 1: statistics of the dev and test sets.

[1] http://en.wikipedia.org/wiki/List_of_Greek_and_Latin_roots_in_English

3.2 Default settings

Before evaluation, we manually tuned all free parameters on the dev set to maximize the system-level correlation with human judgments and decided on the following default settings for AMBER:

1. The parameters in the formula

$$score(N) = \theta_1 \times AvgP(N) + \theta_2 \times Fmean(N, M, \alpha) + (1 - \theta_1 - \theta_2) \times AvgF(N, \alpha)$$

are set as N=4, M=1, α=0.9, θ_1= 0.3 and θ_2= 0.5.
2. All penalties are applied; the manually set penalty weights are shown in **Table 2**.
3. We took the average of runs over input text types 1, 4, and 6 (*i.e.* normalized text, split type 1 and split type 3).
4. In Chunk penalty (CKP), $\beta = 3$, and γ=0.1.
5. By default, *tf-idf* is not applied.
6. We used three matching strategies: n-gram, fixed-gap n-gram, and flexible-gap n-gram; they are equally weighted.

Name of penalty	Weight value
SBP	0.30
SRP	0.10
CSBP	0.15
CSRP	0.05
SWDP	0.10
LWDP	0.20
CKP	1.00
CTP	0.80
NSCP	0.50
NKCP	2.00

Table 2: Weight of each penalty

3.3 Evaluation metrics

We used Spearman's rank correlation coefficient to measure the correlation of AMBER with the human judgments of translation at the system level. The human judgment score we used is based on the "Rank" only, *i.e.*, how often the translations of the system were rated as better than the translations from other systems (Callison-Burch *et al.*, 2008). Thus, AMBER and the other metrics were evaluated on how well their rankings correlated with the human ones. For the sentence level, we use consistency rate, *i.e.*, how consistent the ranking of sentence pairs is with the human judgments.

3.4 Results

All test results shown in this section are averaged over all three tests described in **3.1**. First, we compare AMBER with two of the most widely used metrics: original IBM BLEU and METEOR v1.0. **Table 3** gives the results; it shows both the version of AMBER with basic preprocessing, AMBER(1) (with tokenization and lowercasing) and the default version used as baseline for most of our experiments (AMBER(1,4,6)). Both versions of AMBER perform better than BLEU and METEOR on both system and sentence levels.

Metric		Dev	3 tests average	Δ tests
BLEU_ibm	sys	0.68	0.72	N/A
(baseline)	sent	0.37	0.40	N/A
METEOR	sys	0.80	0.80	+0.08
v1.0	sent	0.58	0.56	+0.17
AMBER(1)	sys	0.83	0.83	+0.11
(basic preproc.)	sent	0.61	0.58	+0.19
AMBER(1,4,6)	sys	0.84	**0.86**	**+0.14**
(default)	sent	0.62	**0.60**	**+0.20**

Table 3: Results of AMBER vs BLEU and METEOR

Second, as shown in **Table 4**, we evaluated the impact of different types of preprocessing, and some combinations of preprocessing (we do one run of evaluation for each type and average the results). From this table, we can see that splitting words into sub-words improves both system- and sentence-level correlation. Recall that input 6 preprocessing splits words according to a list of English prefixes, roots, and suffixes: AMBER(4,6) is the best variant. Although test 3 results, for target languages other than English, are not broken out separately in this table, they are as follows: input 1 yielded 0.8345 system-level correlation and 0.5848 sentence-level consistency, but input 6 yielded 0.8766 (+0.04 gain) and 0.5990 (+0.01) respectively. Thus, surprisingly, splitting non-English words up according to English morphology helps performance, perhaps because French, Spanish, German, and even Czech share some word roots with English. However, as indicated by the underlined results, if one wishes to avoid the use of any linguistic information, AMBER(4) performs almost as well as AMBER(4,6). The default setting, AMBER(1,4,6), doesn't perform quite as well as AMBER(4,6) or AMBER(4), but is quite reasonable.

Varying the preprocessing seems to have more impact than varying the other parameters we experimented with. In **Table 5**, "none+*tf-idf*" means we do one run without *tf-idf* and one run for "*tf-idf* only", and then average the scores. Here, applying *tf-idf* seems to benefit performance slightly.

Input		Dev	3 tests average	Δ tests
0	sys	0.84	0.79	N/A
(baseline)	sent	0.59	0.58	N/A
1	sys	0.83	0.83	+0.04
	sent	0.61	0.58	+0.00
2	sys	0.83	0.84	+0.05
	sent	0.61	0.59	+0.01
3	sys	0.83	0.84	+0.05
	sent	0.61	0.58	+0.00
4	sys	0.84	<u>0.87</u>	<u>+0.08</u>
	sent	0.62	<u>0.60</u>	<u>+0.01</u>
5	sys	0.82	0.86	+0.07
	sent	0.61	0.56	+0.01
6	sys	0.83	0.88	+0.09
	sent	0.62	0.60	+0.02
7	sys	0.34	0.56	-0.23
	sent	0.58	0.53	-0.05
1,4	sys	0.84	0.85	+0.07
	sent	0.62	0.60	+0.01
4,6	sys	0.83	**0.88**	**+0.09**
	sent	0.62	**0.60**	**+0.02**
1,4,6	sys	0.84	0.86	+0.07
	sent	0.62	0.60	+0.02

Table 4: Varying AMBER preprocessing (best linguistic = bold, best non-ling. = underline)

tf-idf		Dev	3 tests average	Δ tests
none	sys	0.84	0.86	N/A
(baseline)	sent	0.62	0.60	N/A
tf-idf	sys	0.81	**0.88**	**+0.02**
only	sent	0.62	0.61	+0.01
none+*tf-*	sys	0.82	0.87	+0.01
idf	sent	0.62	**0.61**	**+0.01**

Table 5: Effect of *tf-idf* on AMBER(1,4,6)

Table 6 shows what happens if you disable one penalty at a time (leaving the weights of the other penalties at their original values). The biggest system-level performance degradation occurs when LWDP is dropped, so this seems to be the most useful penalty. On the other hand, dropping CKP, CSRP, and SRP may actually improve performance. Firm conclusions would require retuning of weights each time a penalty is dropped; this is future work.

Penalties		Dev	3 tests average	Δ tests
All	sys	0.84	0.86	N/A
(baseline)	sent	0.62	0.60	N/A
-SBP	sys	0.82	0.84	-0.02
	sent	0.62	0.60	-0.00
-SRP	sys	0.83	0.88	+0.01
	sent	0.62	0.60	+0.00
-CSBP	sys	0.84	0.85	-0.01
	sent	0.62	0.60	+0.00
-CSRP	sys	0.83	0.87	+0.01
	sent	0.62	0.60	-0.00
-SWDP	sys	0.84	0.86	-0.00
	sent	0.62	0.60	+0.00
-LWDP	sys	0.83	**0.83**	**-0.03**
	sent	0.62	**0.60**	**-0.00**
-CTP	sys	0.82	0.84	-0.02
	sent	0.62	0.60	-0.00
-CKP	sys	0.83	0.87	+0.01
	sent	0.62	0.60	-0.00
-NSCP	sys	0.83	0.86	-0.00
	sent	0.62	0.60	+0.00
-NKCP	sys	0.82	0.85	-0.01
	sent	0.62	0.60	+0.00

Table 6: Dropping penalties from AMBER(1,4,6) – biggest drops on test in bold

Matching		Dev	3 tests avg	Δ tests
n-gram + fxd-gap+ flx-gap (default)	sys	0.84	**0.86**	N/A
	sent	0.62	**0.60**	N/A
n-gram	sys	0.84	0.86	-0.00
	sent	0.62	0.60	-0.00
fxd-gap+ n-gram	sys	0.84	0.86	-0.00
	sent	0.62	0.60	-0.00
flx-gap+ n-gram	sys	0.83	0.86	-0.00
	sent	0.62	0.60	-0.00
skip+ n-gram	sys	0.83	0.85	-0.01
	sent	0.62	0.60	-0.00
All four matchings	sys	0.83	0.86	-0.01
	sent	0.62	0.60	0.00

Table 7: Varying matching strategy for AMBER(1,4,6)

Finally, we evaluated the effect of the matching strategy. According to the results shown in **Table 7**, our default strategy, which uses three of the four types of matching (n-grams, fixed-gap n-grams, and flexible-gap n-grams) is close to optimal; the use of skip n-grams (either by itself or in combination) may hurt performance at both system and sentence levels.

4 Conclusion

This paper describes AMBER, a new machine translation metric that is a modification of the widely used BLEU metric. We used more sophisticated formulae to compute the *score*, we developed several new *penalties* to match the human judgment, we tried different preprocessing types, we tried *tf-idf*, and we tried four n-gram matching strategies. The choice of preprocessing type seemed to have the biggest impact on performance. AMBER(4,6) had the best performance of any variant we tried. However, it has the disadvantage of using some light linguistic knowledge about English morphology (which, oddly, seems to be helpful for other languages too). A purist may prefer AMBER(1,4) or AMBER(4), which use no linguistic information and still match human judgment much more closely than either BLEU or METEOR. These variants of AMBER share BLEU's virtues: they are language-independent and can be computed quickly.

Of course, AMBER could incorporate more linguistic information: *e.g.*, we could use linguistically defined stop word lists in the SWDP and LWDP penalties, or use synonyms or paraphrasing in the n-gram matching.

AMBER can be thought of as a weighted combination of dozens of computationally cheap features based on word surface forms for evaluating MT quality. This paper has shown that combining such features can be a very effective strategy for attaining better correlation with human judgment. Here, the weights on the features were manually tuned; in future work, we plan to learn weights on features automatically. We also plan to redesign AMBER so that it becomes a metric that is highly suitable for tuning SMT systems.

References

S. Banerjee and A. Lavie. 2005. METEOR: An automatic metric for MT evaluation with improved correlation with human judgments. In *Proceedings of ACL Workshop on Intrinsic & Extrinsic Evaluation Measures for Machine Translation and/or Summarization.*

A. Birch and M. Osborne. 2010. LRscore for evaluating lexical and reordering quality in MT. In *Proceedings of the Joint Fifth Workshop on Statistical Machine Translation and MetricsMATR*, pages 302–307.

C. Callison-Burch, C. Fordyce, P. Koehn, C. Monz and J. Schroeder. 2008. Further Meta-Evaluation of Machine Translation. In *Proceedings of WMT.*

C. Callison-Burch, M. Osborne, and P. Koehn. 2006. Re-evaluating the role of BLEU in machine translation research. In *Proceedings of EACL.*

D. Cer, D. Jurafsky and C. Manning. 2010. The Best Lexical Metric for Phrase-Based Statistical MT System Optimization. In *Proceedings of NAACL.*

Y. S. Chan and H. T. Ng. 2008. MAXSIM: A maximum similarity metric for machine translation evaluation. In *Proceedings of ACL.*

D. Chiang, S. DeNeefe, Y. S. Chan, and H. T. Ng. 2008. Decomposability of translation metrics for improved evaluation and efficient algorithms. In *Proceedings of EMNLP*, pages 610–619.

M. Denkowski and A. Lavie. 2010. Meteor-next and the meteor paraphrase tables: Improved evaluation support for five target languages. In *Proceedings of the Joint Fifth Workshop on Statistical Machine Translation and MetricsMATR*, pages 314–317.

George Doddington. 2002. Automatic evaluation of machine translation quality using n-gram co-occurrence statistics. In *Proceedings of HLT.*

Y. He, J. Du, A. Way, and J. van Genabith. 2010. The DCU dependency-based metric in WMT-MetricsMATR 2010. In *Proceedings of the Joint Fifth Workshop on Statistical Machine Translation and MetricsMATR*, pages 324–328.

H. Isozaki, T. Hirao, K. Duh, K. Sudoh, H. Tsukada. 2010. Automatic Evaluation of Translation Quality for Distant Language Pairs. In *Proceedings of EMNLP.*

A. Lavie and M. J. Denkowski. 2009. The METEOR metric for automatic evaluation of machine translation. *Machine Translation*, 23.

C.-Y. Lin. 2004. ROUGE: a Package for Automatic Evaluation of Summaries. In *Proceedings of the Workshop on Text Summarization Branches Out (WAS 2004)*, Barcelona, Spain.

C. Liu, D. Dahlmeier, and H. T. Ng. 2010. Tesla: Translation evaluation of sentences with linear-programming-based analysis. In *Proceedings of the Joint Fifth Workshop on Statistical Machine Translation and MetricsMATR*, pages 329–334.

S. Pado, M. Galley, D. Jurafsky, and C.D. Manning. 2009. Robust machine translation evaluation with entailment features. In *Proceedings of ACL-IJCNLP.*

K. Papineni, S. Roukos, T. Ward, and W.-J. Zhu. 2002. BLEU: a method for automatic evaluation of machine translation. In *Proceedings of ACL.*

M. Snover, B. Dorr, R. Schwartz, L. Micciulla, and J. Makhoul. 2006. A Study of Translation Edit Rate with Targeted Human Annotation. In *Proceedings of Association for Machine Translation in the Americas.*

M. Snover, N. Madnani, B. Dorr, and R. Schwartz. 2009. Fluency, Adequacy, or HTER? Exploring Different Human Judgments with a Tunable MT Metric. In *Proceedings of the Fourth Workshop on Statistical Machine Translation*, Athens, Greece.

TESLA at WMT 2011: Translation Evaluation and Tunable Metric

Daniel Dahlmeier[1] and **Chang Liu**[2] and **Hwee Tou Ng**[1,2]
[1]NUS Graduate School for Integrative Sciences and Engineering
[2]Department of Computer Science, National University of Singapore
{danielhe, liuchan1, nght}@comp.nus.edu.sg

Abstract

This paper describes the submission from the National University of Singapore to the WMT 2011 Shared Evaluation Task and the Tunable Metric Task. Our entry is TESLA in three different configurations: TESLA-M, TESLA-F, and the new TESLA-B.

1 Introduction

TESLA (Translation Evaluation of Sentences with Linear-programming-based Analysis) was first proposed in Liu et al. (2010). The simplest variant, TESLA-M (M stands for *minimal*), is based on N-gram matching, and utilizes light-weight linguistic analysis including lemmatization, part-of-speech tagging, and WordNet synonym relations. TESLA-B (B stands for *basic*) additionally takes advantage of bilingual phrase tables to model phrase synonyms. It is a new configuration proposed in this paper. The most sophisticated configuration TESLA-F (F stands for *full*) additionally uses language models and a ranking support vector machine instead of simple averaging. TESLA-F was called TESLA in Liu et al. (2010). In this paper, we rationalize the naming convention by using TESLA to refer to the whole family of metrics.

The rest of this paper is organized as follows. Sections 2 to 4 describe the TESLA variants TESLA-M, TESLA-B, and TESLA-F, respectively. Section 5 describes MT tuning with TESLA. Section 6 shows experimental results for the evaluation and the tunable metric task. The last section concludes the paper.

2 TESLA-M

The version of TESLA-M used in WMT 2011 is exactly the same as in Liu et al. (2010). The description is reproduced here for completeness.

We consider the task of evaluating machine translation systems in the direction of translating a *source language* to a *target language*. We are given a *reference translation* produced by a professional human translator and a machine-produced *system translation*. At the highest level, TESLA-M is the *arithmetic average* of F-measures between *bags of N-grams* (BNGs). A BNG is a multiset of weighted N-grams. Mathematically, a BNG B consists of tuples (b_i, b_i^W), where each b_i is an N-gram and b_i^W is a positive real number representing the weight of b_i. In the simplest case, a BNG contains every N-gram in a translated sentence, and the weights are just the counts of the respective N-grams. However, to emphasize the content words over the function words, we discount the weight of an N-gram by a factor of 0.1 for every function word in the N-gram. We decide whether a word is a function word based on its POS tag.

In TESLA-M, the BNGs are extracted in the target language, so we call them *bags of target language N-grams* (BTNGs).

2.1 Similarity functions

To match two BNGs, we first need a similarity measure between N-grams. In this section, we define the similarity measures used in our experiments. We adopt the similarity measure from MaxSim (Chan and Ng, 2008; Chan and Ng, 2009) as s_{ms}. For unigrams x and y,

Proceedings of the 6th Workshop on Statistical Machine Translation, pages 78–84,
Edinburgh, Scotland, UK, July 30–31, 2011. ©2011 Association for Computational Linguistics

- If $\text{lemma}(x) = \text{lemma}(y)$, then $s_{ms} = 1$.
- Otherwise, let

  $$a = I(\text{synsets}(x) \text{ overlap with synsets}(y))$$
  $$b = I(\text{POS}(x) = \text{POS}(y))$$

  where $I(\cdot)$ is the indicator function, then $s_{ms} = (a + b)/2$.

The synsets are obtained by querying WordNet (Fellbaum, 1998). For languages other than English, a synonym dictionary is used instead.

We define two other similarity functions between unigrams:

$$s_{lem}(x, y) = I(\text{lemma}(x) = \text{lemma}(y))$$
$$s_{pos}(x, y) = I(\text{POS}(x) = \text{POS}(y))$$

All the three unigram similarity functions generalize to N-grams in the same way. For two N-grams $x = x^{1,2,\ldots,n}$ and $y = y^{1,2,\ldots,n}$,

$$s(x, y) = \begin{cases} 0 & \text{if } \exists i,\ s(x^i, y^i) = 0 \\ \frac{1}{n}\sum_{i=1}^{n} s(x^i, y^i) & \text{otherwise} \end{cases}$$

2.2 Matching two BNGs

Now we describe the procedure of matching two BNGs. We take as input BNGs X and Y and a similarity measure s. The i-th entry in X is x_i and has weight x_i^W (analogously for y_j and y_j^W).

Intuitively, we wish to align the entries of the two BNGs in a way that maximizes the overall similarity. An example matching problem for bigrams is shown in Figure 1a, where the weight of each node is shown, along with the hypothetical similarity for each edge. Edges with a similarity of zero are not shown. Note that for each function word, we discount the weight by a factor of ten. The solution to the matching problem is shown in Figure 1b, and the overall similarity is $0.5 \times 0.01 + 0.8 \times 0.1 + 0.8 \times 0.1 = 0.165$.

Mathematically, we formulate this as a (real-valued) linear programming problem[1]. The variables are the allocated weights for the edges

$$w(x_i, y_j) \quad \forall i, j$$

[1] While integer linear programming is NP-complete, real-valued linear programming can be solved efficiently.

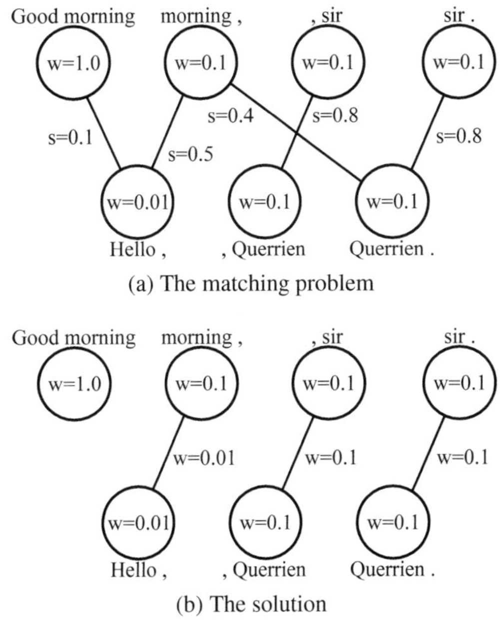

Figure 1: A BNG matching problem

We maximize

$$\sum_{i,j} s(x_i, y_j) w(x_i, y_j)$$

subject to

$$\begin{aligned} w(x_i, y_j) &\geq 0 & \forall i, j \\ \sum_j w(x_i, y_j) &\leq x_i^W & \forall i \\ \sum_i w(x_i, y_j) &\leq y_j^W & \forall j \end{aligned}$$

The value of the objective function is the overall similarity S. Assuming X is the reference and Y is the system translation, we have

$$\text{Precision} = \frac{S}{\sum_j y_j^W}$$
$$\text{Recall} = \frac{S}{\sum_i x_i^W}$$

The F-measure is derived from the precision and the recall:

$$F = \frac{\text{Precision} \times \text{Recall}}{\alpha \times \text{Precision} + (1 - \alpha) \times \text{Recall}}$$

In this work, we set $\alpha = 0.8$, following MaxSim. The value gives more importance to the recall than the precision.

If the similarity function is binary-valued and transitive, such as s_{lem} and s_{pos}, then we can use a much simpler and faster greedy matching procedure: the best match is simply $\sum_g \min(\sum_{x_i=g} x_i^W, \sum_{y_i=g} y_i^W)$.

2.3 Scoring

The TESLA-M sentence-level score for a reference and a system translation is the arithmetic average of the BTNG F-measures for unigrams, bigrams, and trigrams based on similarity functions s_{ms} and s_{pos}. We thus have $3 \times 2 = 6$ BTNG F-measures for TESLA-M.

We can compute a system-level score for a machine translation system by averaging its sentence-level scores over the complete test set.

3 TESLA-B

TESLA-B uses the average of two types of F-measures: (1) BTNG F-measures as in TESLA-M and (2) F-measures between bags of N-grams in one or more pivot languages, called *bags of pivot language N-grams* (BPNGs), The rest of this section focuses on the *generation* of the BPNGs. Their matching is done in the same way as described for BTNGs in the previous section.

3.1 Phrase level semantic representation

Given a sentence-aligned bitext between the target language and a pivot language, we can align the text at the word level using well known tools such as GIZA++ (Och and Ney, 2003) or the Berkeley aligner (Liang et al., 2006; Haghighi et al., 2009).

We observe that the distribution of aligned phrases in a pivot language can serve as a semantic representation of a target language phrase. That is, if two target language phrases are often aligned to the same pivot language phrase, then they can be inferred to be similar in meaning. Similar observations have been made by previous researchers (Bannard and Callison-Burch, 2005; Callison-Burch et al., 2006; Snover et al., 2009).

We note here two differences from WordNet synonyms: (1) the relationship is not restricted to the word level only, and (2) the relationship is not binary. The degree of similarity can be measured by the percentage of overlap between the semantic representations.

3.2 Segmenting a sentence into phrases

To extend the concept of this semantic representation of phrases to sentences, we segment a sentence in the target language into phrases. Given a phrase table, we can approximate the probability of a phrase p by:

$$Pr(p) = \frac{N(p)}{\sum_{p'} N(p')} \tag{1}$$

where $N(\cdot)$ is the count of a phrase in the phrase table. We then define the likelihood of segmenting a sentence S into a sequence of phrases $(p_1, p_2, \ldots, p_n)$ by:

$$Pr(p_1, p_2, \ldots, p_n|S) = \frac{1}{Z(S)} \prod_{i=1}^{n} Pr(p_i) \tag{2}$$

where $Z(S)$ is a normalizing constant. The segmentation of S that maximizes the probability can be determined efficiently using a dynamic programming algorithm. The formula has a strong preference for longer phrases, as every $Pr(p)$ is a small fraction. To deal with out-of-vocabulary (OOV) words, we allow any single word w to be considered a phrase, and if $N(w) = 0$, we set $N(w) = 0.5$ instead.

3.3 BPNGs as sentence level semantic representation

Simply merging the phrase-level semantic representation is insufficient to produce a sensible sentence-level semantic representation. As an example, we consider two target language (English) sentences segmented as follows:

1. ||| *Hello* , ||| *Querrien* ||| . |||
2. ||| *Good morning* , *sir* . |||

A naive comparison of the bags of aligned pivot language (French) phrases would likely conclude that the two sentences are completely unrelated, as the bags of aligned phrases are likely to be completely disjoint. We tackle this problem by constructing a confusion network representation of the aligned phrases, as shown in Figures 2 and 3. A confusion network is a compact representation of a potentially exponentially large number of weighted and likely malformed French sentences. We can collect the N-gram statistics of this ensemble of French sentences

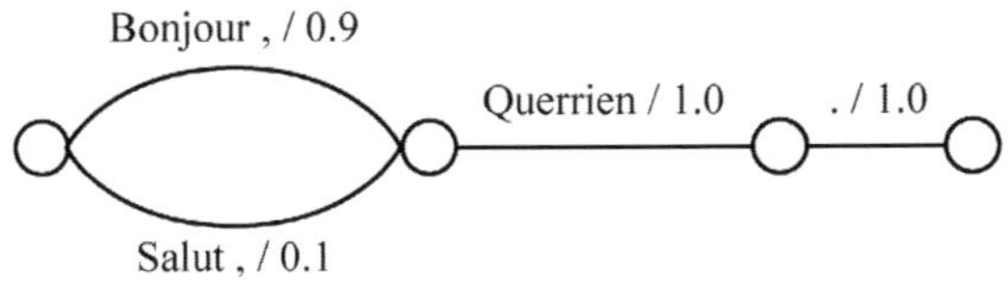

Figure 2: A confusion network as a semantic representation

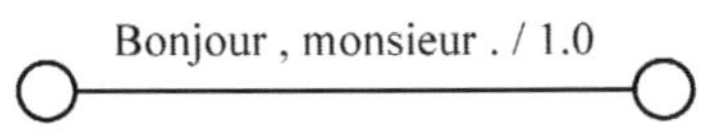

Figure 3: A degenerate confusion network as a semantic representation

efficiently from the confusion network representation. For example, the trigram *Bonjour , Querrien*[2] would receive a weight of $0.9 \times 1.0 = 0.9$ in Figure 2. As with BTNGs, we discount the weight of an N-gram by a factor of 0.1 for every function word in the N-gram, so as to place more emphasis on the content words.

The collection of all such N-grams and their corresponding weights forms the BPNG of a sentence. The reference and system BPNGs are then matched using the algorithm outlined in Section 2.2.

3.4 Scoring

The TESLA-B sentence-level score is a linear combination of (1) BTNG F-measures for unigrams, bigrams, and trigrams based on similarity functions s_{ms} and s_{pos}, and (2) BPNG F-measures for unigrams, bigrams, and trigrams based on similarity functions s_{lem} and s_{pos}. We thus have 3×2 F-measures from the BTNGs and $3 \times 2 \times$ *#pivot languages* F-measures from the BPNGs. We average the BTNG and BPNG scores to obtain s_{BTNG} and s_{BPNG}, respectively. The sentence-level TESLA-B score is then defined as $\frac{1}{2}(s_{\text{BTNG}} + s_{\text{BPNG}})$. The two-step averaging process prevents the BPNG scores from overwhelming the BTNG scores, especially when we have many pivot languages. The system-level TESLA-B score is the arithmetic average of the sentence-level TESLA-B scores.

[2]Note that an N-gram can span more than one segment.

4 TESLA-F

Unlike the simple arithmetic averages used in TESLA-M and TESLA-B, TESLA-F uses a general linear combination of three types of scores: (1) BTNG F-measures as in TESLA-M and TESLA-B, (2) BPNG F-measures as in TESLA-B, and (3) normalized language model scores of the system translation, defined as $\frac{1}{n}\log P$, where n is the length of the translation, and P the language model probability. The method of training the linear model depends on the development data. In the case of WMT, the development data is in the form of manual rankings, so we train SVM^{rank} (Joachims, 2006) on these instances to build the linear model. In other scenarios, some form of regression can be more appropriate.

The BTNG and BPNG scores are the same as used in TESLA-B. In the WMT campaigns, we use two language models, one generated from the Europarl dataset and one from the news-train dataset. We thus have 3×2 features from the BTNGs, $3 \times 2 \times$ *#pivot languages* features from the BPNGs, and 2 features from the language models. Again, we can compute system-level scores by averaging the sentence-level scores.

4.1 Scaling of TESLA-F Scores

While machine translation evaluation is concerned only with the relative order of the different translations but not with the absolute scores, there are practical advantages in normalizing the evaluation scores to a range between 0 and 1. For TESLA-M and TESLA-B, this is already the case, since every F-measure has a range of $[0, 1]$ and so do their averages. In contrast, the SVM^{rank}-produced model typically gives scores very close to zero.

To remedy that, we note that we have the freedom to scale and shift the linear SVM model without changing the metric. We observe that the F-measures have a range of $[0, 1]$, and studying the data reveals that $[-15, 0]$ is a good approximation of the range for normalized language model scores, for all languages involved in the WMT campaign. Since we know the range of values of an F-measure feature (between 0 and 1) and assuming that the range of the normalized LM score is between –15 and 0, we can find the maximum and minimum possible score given the weights. Then we linearly scale the range of scores from [min, max] to [0, 1]. We provide an option of scaling TESLA-F scores in the new release of TESLA.

5 MT tuning with TESLA

All variants of TESLA can be used for automatic MT tuning using Z-MERT (Zaidan, 2009). Z-MERT's modular design makes it easy to integrate a new metric. As TESLA already computes scores at the sentence level, integrating TESLA into Z-MERT was straightforward. First, we created a "streaming" version of each TESLA metric which reads translation candidates from standard input and prints the sentence-level scores to standard output. This allows Z-MERT to easily query the metric for sentence-level scores during MT tuning. Second, we wrote a Java wrapper that calls the TESLA code from Z-MERT. The resulting metric can be used for MERT tuning in the standard fashion. All that a user has to do is to change the metric in the Z-MERT configuration file to TESLA. All the necessary code for Z-MERT tuning is included in the new release of TESLA.

6 Experiments

6.1 Evaluation Task

We evaluate TESLA using the publicly available data from WMT 2009 for into-English and out-of-English translation. The pivot language phrase tables and language models are built using the WMT 2009 training data. The SVM^{rank} model for TESLA-F is trained on manual rankings from WMT 2008. The results for TESLA-M and TESLA-F have previously been reported in Liu et al. (2010)[3]. We add results for the new variant TESLA-B here.

Tables 1 and 2 show the sentence-level consistency and system-level Spearman's rank correlation, respectively for into-English translation. For comparison, we include results for some of the best performing metrics in WMT 2009. Tables 3 and 4 show the same results for out-of-English translation. We do not include the English-Czech language pair in our experiments, as we unfortunately do not have good linguistic resources for the Czech language.

[3]The English-Spanish system correlation differs from our previous result after fixing a minor mistake in the language model.

	cz-en	fr-en	de-en	es-en	hu-en	Overall
TESLA-M	0.60	0.61	0.61	0.59	0.63	0.61
TESLA-B	0.63	0.64	0.63	0.62	0.63	0.63
TESLA-F	0.63	0.65	0.64	0.62	0.66	0.63
ulc	0.63	0.64	0.64	0.61	0.60	0.63
maxsim	0.60	0.63	0.63	0.61	0.62	0.62
meteor-0.6	0.47	0.51	0.52	0.49	0.48	0.50

Table 1: Into-English sentence-level consistency on WMT 2009 data

	cz-en	fr-en	de-en	es-en	hu-en	Avg
TESLA-M	1.00	0.86	0.85	0.99	0.66	0.87
TESLA-B	1.00	0.92	0.67	0.95	0.83	0.87
TESLA-F	1.00	0.92	0.68	0.94	0.94	0.90
ulc	1.00	0.92	0.78	0.86	0.60	0.83
maxsim	0.70	0.91	0.76	0.98	0.66	0.80
meteor-0.6	0.70	0.93	0.56	0.87	0.54	0.72

Table 2: Into-English system-level Spearman's rank correlation on WMT 2009 data

The new TESLA-B metric proves to be competitive to its siblings and is often on par with the more sophisticated TESLA-F metric. The exception is the English-German language pair, where TESLA-B has very low system-level correlation. We have two possible explanations for this. First, the system-level correlation is computed on a very small sample size (the ranked list of MT systems). This makes the system-level correlation score more volatile compared to the sentence-level consistency score which is computed on thousands of sentence pairs. Second, German has a relatively free word order which potentially makes word alignment and phrase table extraction more noisy. Interestingly, all participating metrics in WMT 2009 had low system-level correlation for the English-German language pair.

	en-fr	en-de	en-es	Overall
TESLA-M	0.64	0.59	0.59	0.60
TESLA-B	0.65	0.59	0.60	0.61
TESLA-F	0.68	0.57	0.60	0.61
wpF	0.66	0.60	0.61	0.61
wpbleu	0.60	0.47	0.49	0.51

Table 3: Out-of-English sentence-level consistency on WMT 2009 data

	en-fr	en-de	en-es	Avg
TESLA-M	0.93	0.86	0.79	0.86
TESLA-B	0.91	0.05	0.63	0.53
TESLA-F	0.85	0.78	0.67	0.77
wpF	0.90	-0.06	0.58	0.47
wpbleu	0.92	0.07	0.63	0.54

Table 4: Out-of-English system-level Spearman's rank correlation on WMT 2009 data

Tune\Test	BLEU	TESLA-M	TESLA-B	TESLA-F
BLEU	**0.2715**	0.3756	0.3129	0.3920
TESLA-M	0.2279	0.4056	0.3279	0.3981
TESLA-B	0.2370	0.4001	0.3257	0.3977
TESLA-F	0.2432	**0.4076**	**0.3299**	**0.4007**

Table 5: Automatic evaluation scores on held out test portion for the tunable metric task. The best result in each column is printed in bold.

6.2 Tunable Metric Task

The goal of the new tunable metric task is to explore MT tuning with metrics other than BLEU (Papineni et al., 2002). To allow for a fair comparison, the WMT organizers provided participants with a complete Joshua MT system for an Urdu-English translation task. We tuned models for each variant of TESLA, using Z-MERT in the default configuration provided by the organizers. There are four reference translations for each Urdu source sentence. The size of the N-best list is set to 300.

For our own experiments, we randomly split the development set into a development portion (781 sentences) and a held-out test portion (200 sentences). We run the same Z-MERT tuning process for each TESLA variant on this reduced development set and evaluate the resulting models on the held out test set. We include a model trained with BLEU as an additional reference point. The results are shown in Table 5. We observe that the model trained with TESLA-F achieves the best results when evaluated with any of the TESLA metrics, although the differences between the scores are small. We found that TESLA produces slightly longer translations than BLEU: 22.4 words (TESLA-M), 21.7 words (TESLA-B), and 22.5 words (TESLA-F), versus 18.7 words (BLEU). The average reference length is 19.8 words.

The official evaluation for the tunable metric task is performed using manual rankings. The score of a system is calculated as the percentage of times the system is judged to be either better or equal (*score1*) or strictly better (*score2*) compared to each other system in pairwise comparisons. Although we submit results for all TESLA variants, only our primary submission TESLA-F is included in the manual evaluation. The results for TESLA-F are mixed. When evaluated with score1, TESLA-F is ranked 7th out of 8 participating systems, but when evaluated with score2, TESLA-F is ranked second best. These findings differ from previous results that we reported in Liu et al. (2011) where MT systems tuned with TESLA-M and TESLA-F consistently outperform two other systems tuned with BLEU and TER for translations from French, German, and Spanish into English on the WMT 2010 news data set. A manual inspection of the references in the tunable metric task shows that the translations are of lower quality compared to the news data sets used in WMT. As the SVM model in TESLA-F is trained with rankings from WMT 2008, it is possible that the model is less robust when applied to Urdu-English translations. This could explain the mixed performance of TESLA-F in the tunable metric task.

7 Conclusion

We introduce TESLA-B, a new variant of the TESLA machine translation metric and present experimental results for all TESLA variants in the setting of the WMT evaluation task and tunable metric task. All TESLA variants are integrated into Z-MERT for automatic machine translation tuning.

Acknowledgments

This research was done for CSIDM Project No. CSIDM-200804 partially funded by a grant from the National Research Foundation (NRF) administered by the Media Development Authority (MDA) of Singapore.

References

Colin Bannard and Chris Callison-Burch. 2005. Paraphrasing with bilingual parallel corpora. In *Proceedings of the 43rd Annual Meeting of the Association for Computational Linguistics*.

Chris Callison-Burch, Philipp Koehn, and Miles Osborne. 2006. Improved statistical machine translation using paraphrases. In *Proceedings of the Human Language Technology Conference of the North American Chapter of the Association for Computational Linguistics*.

Yee Seng Chan and Hwee Tou Ng. 2008. MaxSim: A maximum similarity metric for machine translation evaluation. In *Proceedings of the 46th Annual Meeting of the Association for Computational Linguistics*.

Yee Seng Chan and Hwee Tou Ng. 2009. MaxSim: Performance and effects of translation fluency. *Machine Translation*, 23(2–3):157–168.

Christiane Fellbaum. 1998. *WordNet: An Electronic Lexical Database*. The MIT Press.

Aria Haghighi, John Blitzer, John DeNero, and Dan Klein. 2009. Better word alignments with supervised ITG models. In *Proceedings of 47th Annual Meeting of the Association for Computational Linguistics and the 4th IJCNLP of the AFNLP*.

Thorsten Joachims. 2006. Training linear SVMs in linear time. In *Proceedings of the ACM Conference on Knowledge Discovery and Data Mining*.

Percy Liang, Ben Taskar, and Dan Klein. 2006. Alignment by agreement. In *Proceedings of the Human Language Technology Conference of the North American Chapter of the Association for Computational Linguistics*.

Chang Liu, Daniel Dahlmeier, and Hwee Tou Ng. 2010. TESLA: Translation evaluation of sentences with linear-programming-based analysis. In *Proceedings of the Joint Fifth Workshop on Statistical Machine Translation and MetricsMATR*.

Chang Liu, Daniel Dahlmeier, and Hwee Tou Ng. 2011. Better evaluation metrics lead to better machine translation. In *Proceedings of the 2011 Conference on Empirical Methods in Natural Language Processing*.

Franz Josef Och and Hermann Ney. 2003. A systematic comparison of various statistical alignment models. *Computational Linguistics*, 29(1).

Kishore Papineni, Salim Roukos, Todd Ward, and Wei-Jing Zhu. 2002. BLEU: a method for automatic evaluation of machine translation. In *Proceedings of the 40th Annual Meeting of the Association for Computational Linguistics*.

Matthew Snover, Nitin Madnani, Bonnie Dorr, and Richard Schwartz. 2009. Fluency, adequacy, or HTER? Exploring different human judgments with a tunable MT metric. In *Proceedings of of the Fourth Workshop on Statistical Machine Translation*.

Omar Zaidan. 2009. Z-MERT: A fully configurable open source tool for minimum error rate training of machine translation systems. *The Prague Bulletin of Mathematical Linguistics*, 91:79–88.

Meteor 1.3: Automatic Metric for Reliable Optimization and Evaluation of Machine Translation Systems

Michael Denkowski and **Alon Lavie**
Language Technologies Institute
School of Computer Science
Carnegie Mellon University
Pittsburgh, PA 15232, USA
{mdenkows,alavie}@cs.cmu.edu

Abstract

This paper describes Meteor 1.3, our submission to the 2011 EMNLP Workshop on Statistical Machine Translation automatic evaluation metric tasks. New metric features include improved text normalization, higher-precision paraphrase matching, and discrimination between content and function words. We include Ranking and Adequacy versions of the metric shown to have high correlation with human judgments of translation quality as well as a more balanced Tuning version shown to outperform BLEU in minimum error rate training for a phrase-based Urdu-English system.

1 Introduction

The Meteor[1] metric (Banerjee and Lavie, 2005; Denkowski and Lavie, 2010b) has been shown to have high correlation with human judgments in evaluations such as the 2010 ACL Workshop on Statistical Machine Translation and NIST Metrics MATR (Callison-Burch et al., 2010). However, previous versions of the metric are still limited by lack of punctuation handling, noise in paraphrase matching, and lack of discrimination between word types. We introduce new resources for all WMT languages including text normalizers, filtered paraphrase tables, and function word lists. We show that the addition of these resources to Meteor allows tuning versions of the metric that show higher correlation with human translation rankings and adequacy scores on unseen test data. The evaluation resources are modular, usable with any other evaluation metric or MT software.

We also conduct a MT system tuning experiment on Urdu-English data to compare the effectiveness of using multiple versions of Meteor in minimum error rate training. While versions tuned to various types of human judgments do not perform as well as the widely used BLEU metric (Papineni et al., 2002), a balanced Tuning version of Meteor consistently outperforms BLEU over multiple end-to-end tune-test runs on this data set.

The versions of Meteor corresponding to the translation evaluation task submissions, (Ranking and Adequacy), are described in Sections 3 through 5 while the submission to the tunable metrics task, (Tuning), is described in Section 6.

2 New Metric Resources

2.1 Meteor Normalizer

Whereas previous versions of Meteor simply strip punctuation characters prior to scoring, version 1.3 includes a new text normalizer intended specifically for translation evaluation. The normalizer first replicates the behavior of the tokenizer distributed with the Moses toolkit (Hoang et al., 2007), including handling of non-breaking prefixes. After tokenization, we add several rules for *normalization*, intended to reduce meaning-equivalent punctuation styles to common forms. The following two rules are particularly helpful:

- Remove dashes between hyphenated words. (Example: `far-off` → `far off`)

[1] The metric name has previously been stylized as "METEOR" or "METEOR". As of version 1.3, the official stylization is simply "Meteor".

Proceedings of the 6th Workshop on Statistical Machine Translation, pages 85–91,
Edinburgh, Scotland, UK, July 30–31, 2011. ©2011 Association for Computational Linguistics

- Remove full stops in acronyms/initials. (Example: `U.N.` → `UN`)

Consider the behavior of the Moses tokenizer and Meteor normalizers given a reference translation containing the phrase "`U.S.-based organization`":

Moses:	`U.S.-based organization`
Meteor ≤1.2:	`U S based organization`
Meteor 1.3:	`US based organization`

Of these, only the Meteor 1.3 normalization allows metrics to match all of the following stylizations:

```
U.S.-based organization
US-based organization
U.S. based organization
US based organization
```

While intended for Meteor evaluation, use of this normalizer is a suitable preprocessing step for other metrics to improve accuracy when reference sentences are stylistically different from hypotheses.

2.2 Filtered Paraphrase Tables

The original Meteor paraphrase tables (Denkowski and Lavie, 2010b) are constructed using the phrase table "pivoting" technique described by Bannard and Callison-Burch (2005). Many paraphrases suffer from word accumulation, the appending of unaligned words to one or both sides of a phrase rather than finding a true rewording from elsewhere in parallel data. To improve the precision of the paraphrase tables, we filter out all cases of word accumulation by removing paraphrases where one phrase is a substring of the other. Table 1 lists the number of phrase pairs found in each paraphrase table before and after filtering. In addition to improving accuracy, the reduction of phrase table sizes also reduces the load time and memory usage of the Meteor paraphrase matcher. The tables are a modular resource suitable for other MT or NLP software.

2.3 Function Word Lists

Commonly used metrics such as BLEU and earlier versions of Meteor make no distinction between content and function words. This can be problematic for ranking-based evaluations where two system outputs can differ by a single word, such as mistranslating either a main verb or a determiner. To improve Meteor's discriminative power in such cases, we introduce a function word list for each WMT language and a new δ parameter to adjust the relative weight given to content words (any word not on the list) versus function words (see Section 3). Function word lists are estimated according to relative frequency in large monolingual corpora. For each language, we pool freely available WMT 2011 data consisting of Europarl (Koehn, 2005), news (sentence-uniqued), and news commentary data. Any word with relative frequency of 10^{-3} or greater is added to the function word list. Table 2 lists corpus size and number of function words learned for each language. In addition to common words, punctuation symbols consistently rise to the tops of function word lists.

Language	Phrase Pairs	After Filtering
English	6.24M	5.27M
Czech	756K	684K
German	3.52M	3.00M
Spanish	6.35M	5.30M
French	3.38M	2.84M

Table 1: Sizes of paraphrase tables before and after filtering

Language	Corpus Size (sents)	FW Learned
English	836M	93
Czech	230M	68
French	374M	85
German	309M	92
Spanish	168M	66

Table 2: Monolingual corpus size (words) and number of function words learned for each language

3 Meteor Scoring

Meteor evaluates translation hypotheses by aligning them to reference translations and calculating sentence-level similarity scores. This section describes our extended version of the metric.

For a hypothesis-reference pair, the search space of possible alignments is constructed by identifying all possible matches between the two sentences according to the following matchers:

Exact: Match words if their surface forms are identical.

Stem: Stem words using a language-appropriate Snowball Stemmer (Porter, 2001) and match if the stems are identical.

Synonym: Match words if they share membership in any synonym set according to the WordNet (Miller and Fellbaum, 2007) database.

Paraphrase: Match phrases if they are listed as paraphrases in the paraphrase tables described in Section 2.2.

All matches are generalized to phrase matches with a start position and phrase length in each sentence. Any word occurring less than *length* positions after a match start is considered covered by the match. The exact and paraphrase matchers support all five WMT languages while the stem matcher is limited to English, French, German, and Spanish and the synonym matcher is limited to English.

Once matches are identified, the final alignment is resolved as the largest subset of all matches meeting the following criteria in order of importance:

1. Require each word in each sentence to be covered by zero or one matches.
2. Maximize the number of covered words across both sentences.
3. Minimize the number of *chunks*, where a *chunk* is defined as a series of matches that is contiguous and identically ordered in both sentences.
4. Minimize the sum of absolute distances between match start positions in the two sentences. (Break ties by preferring to align words and phrases that occur at similar positions in both sentences.)

Given an alignment, the metric score is calculated as follows. Content and function words are identified in the hypothesis (h_c, h_f) and reference (r_c, r_f) according to the function word lists described in Section 2.3. For each of the matchers (m_i), count the number of content and function words covered by matches of this type in the hypothesis ($m_i(h_c)$, $m_i(h_f)$) and reference ($m_i(r_c)$, $m_i(r_f)$). Calculate weighted precision and recall using matcher weights ($w_i...w_n$) and content-function word weight (δ):

$$P = \frac{\sum_i w_i \cdot (\delta \cdot m_i(h_c) + (1-\delta) \cdot m_i(h_f))}{\delta \cdot |h_c| + (1-\delta) \cdot |h_f|}$$

Target	WMT09	WMT10	Combined
English	20,357	24,915	45,272
Czech	11,242	9,613	20,855
French	2,967	5,904	7,062
German	6,563	10,892	17,455
Spanish	3,249	3,813	7,062

Table 3: Human ranking judgment data from 2009 and 2010 WMT evaluations

$$R = \frac{\sum_i w_i \cdot (\delta \cdot m_i(r_c) + (1-\delta) \cdot m_i(r_f))}{\delta \cdot |r_c| + (1-\delta) \cdot |r_f|}$$

The parameterized harmonic mean of P and R (van Rijsbergen, 1979) is then calculated:

$$F_{mean} = \frac{P \cdot R}{\alpha \cdot P + (1-\alpha) \cdot R}$$

To account for gaps and differences in word order, a fragmentation penalty is calculated using the total number of matched words (m, average over hypothesis and reference) and number of chunks (ch):

$$Pen = \gamma \cdot \left(\frac{ch}{m}\right)^{\beta}$$

The Meteor score is then calculated:

$$Score = (1 - Pen) \cdot F_{mean}$$

The parameters α, β, γ, δ, and $w_i...w_n$ are tuned to maximize correlation with human judgments.

4 Parameter Optimization

4.1 Development Data

The 2009 and 2010 WMT shared evaluation data sets are made available as development data for WMT 2011. Data sets include MT system outputs, reference translations, and human rankings of translation quality. Table 3 lists the number of judgments for each evaluation and combined totals.

4.2 Tuning Procedure

To evaluate a metric's performance on a data set, we count the number of pairwise translation rankings preserved when translations are re-ranked by metric score. We then compute Kendall's τ correlation coefficient as follows:

$$\tau = \frac{\text{concordant pairs} - \text{discordant pairs}}{\text{total pairs}}$$

	Tune τ (WMT09)		Test τ (WMT10)	
Lang	Met1.2	Met1.3	Met1.2	Met1.3
English	0.258	**0.276**	0.320	**0.343**
Czech	0.148	**0.162**	**0.220**	0.215
French	0.414	**0.437**	0.370	**0.384**
German	0.152	**0.180**	**0.170**	0.155
Spanish	0.216	**0.240**	0.310	**0.326**

Table 5: Meteor 1.2 and 1.3 correlation with ranking judgments on tune and test data

	Meteor-1.2 r		Meteor-1.3 r	
Tune / Test	MT08	MT09	MT08	MT09
MT08	0.620	0.625	0.650	0.636
MT09	0.612	0.630	0.642	0.648
Tune / Test	P2	P3	P2	P3
P2	-0.640	-0.596	-0.642	-0.594
P3	-0.638	-0.600	-0.625	-0.612

Table 6: Meteor 1.2 and 1.3 correlation with adequacy and H-TER scores on tune and test data

For each WMT language, we learn Meteor parameters that maximize τ over the combined 2009 and 2010 data sets using an exhaustive parametric sweep. The resulting parameters, listed in Table 4, are used in the default Ranking version of Meteor 1.3.

For each language, the δ parameter is above 0.5, indicating a preference for content words over function words. In addition, the fragmentation penalties are generally less severe across languages. The additional features in Meteor 1.3 allow for more balanced parameters that distribute responsibility for penalizing various types of erroneous translations.

5 Evaluation Experiments

To compare Meteor 1.3 against previous versions of the metric on the task of evaluating MT system outputs, we tune a version for each language on 2009 WMT data and evaluate on 2010 data. This replicates the 2010 WMT shared evaluation task, allowing comparison to Meteor 1.2. Table 5 lists correlation of each metric version with ranking judgments on tune and test data. Meteor 1.3 shows significantly higher correlation on both tune and test data for English, French, and Spanish while Czech and German demonstrate overfitting with higher correlation on tune data but lower on test data. This overfitting effect is likely due to the limited number of systems providing translations into these languages and the difficulty of these target languages leading to significantly noisier translations skewing the space of metric scores. We believe that tuning to combined 2009 and 2010 data will counter these issues for the official Ranking version.

5.1 Generalization to Other Tasks

To evaluate the impact of new features on other evaluation tasks, we follow Denkowski and Lavie (2010a), tuning versions of Meteor to maximize length-weighted sentence-level Pearson's r correlation coefficient with adequacy and H-TER (Snover et al., 2006) scores of translations. Data sets include 2008 and 2009 NIST Open Machine Translation Evaluation adequacy data (Przybocki, 2009) and GALE P2 and P3 H-TER data (Olive, 2005). For each type of judgment, metric versions are tuned and tested on each year and scores are compared. We compare Meteor 1.3 results with those from version 1.2 with results shown in Table 6. For both adequacy data sets, Meteor 1.3 significantly outperforms version 1.2 on both tune and test data. The version tuned on MT09 data is selected as the official Adequacy version of Meteor 1.3. H-TER versions either show no improvement or degradation due to overfitting. Examination of the optimal H-TER parameter sets reveals a mismatch between evaluation metric and human judgment type. As H-TER evaluation is ultimately limited by the TER aligner, there is no distinction between content and function words, and words sharing stems are considered nonmatches. As such, these features do not help Meteor improve correlation, but rather act as a source of additional possibility for overfitting.

6 MT System Tuning Experiments

The 2011 WMT Tunable Metrics task consists of using Z-MERT (Zaidan, 2009) to tune a pre-built Urdu-English Joshua (Li et al., 2009) system to a new evaluation metric on a tuning set with 4 reference translations and decoding a test set using the resulting parameter set. As this task does not provide a

Language	α	β	γ	δ	w_{exact}	w_{stem}	w_{syn}	w_{par}
English	0.85	0.20	0.60	0.75	1.00	0.60	0.80	0.60
Czech	0.95	0.20	0.60	0.80	1.00	–	–	0.40
French	0.90	1.40	0.60	0.65	1.00	0.20	–	0.40
German	0.95	1.00	0.55	0.55	1.00	0.80	–	0.20
Spanish	0.65	1.30	0.50	0.80	1.00	0.80	–	0.60

Table 4: Optimal Meteor parameters for WMT target languages on 2009 and 2010 data (Meteor 1.3 Ranking)

devtest set, we select a version of Meteor by exploring the effectiveness of using multiple versions of the metric to tune phrase-based translation systems for the same language pair.

We use the 2009 NIST Open Machine Translation Evaluation Urdu-English parallel data (Przybocki, 2009) plus 900M words of monolingual data from the English Gigaword corpus (Parker et al., 2009) to build a standard Moses system (Hoang et al., 2007) as follows. Parallel data is word aligned using the MGIZA++ toolkit (Gao and Vogel, 2008) and alignments are symmetrized using the "grow-diag-final-and" heuristic. Phrases are extracted using standard phrase-based heuristics (Koehn et al., 2003) and used to build a translation table and lexicalized reordering model. A standard SRI 5-gram language model (Stolke, 2002) is estimated from monolingual data. Using Z-MERT, we tune this system to baseline metrics as well as the versions of Meteor discussed in previous sections. We also tune to a balanced Tuning version of Meteor designed to minimize bias. This data set provides a single set of reference translations for MERT. To account for the variance of MERT, we run end-to-end tuning 3 times for each metric and report the average results on two unseen test sets: newswire and weblog. Test set translations are evaluated using BLEU, TER, and Meteor 1.2. The parameters for each Meteor version are listed in Table 7 while the results are listed in Table 8.

The results are fairly consistent across both test sets: the Tuning version of Meteor outperforms BLEU across all metrics while versions of Meteor that perform well on other tasks perform poorly in tuning. This illustrates the differences between evaluation and tuning tasks. In evaluation tasks, metrics are engineered to score 1-best translations from systems most often tuned to BLEU. As listed in Table 7, these parameters are often skewed to emphasize the differences between system outputs. In the tuning scenario, MERT optimizes translation quality with respect to the tuning metric. If a metric is biased (for example, assigning more weight to recall than precision), it will guide the MERT search toward pathological translations that receive lower scores across other metrics. Balanced between precision and recall, content and function words, and word choice versus fragmentation, the Tuning version of Meteor is significantly less susceptible to gaming. Chosen as the official submission for WMT 2011, we believe that this Tuning version of Meteor will further generalize to other tuning scenarios.

Newswire			
Tuning Metric	BLEU	TER	Met1.2
BLEU	23.67	72.48	50.45
TER	25.35	59.72	48.60
TER-BLEU/2	26.25	61.66	49.69
Meteor-tune	24.89	69.54	51.29
Meteor-rank	19.28	94.64	49.78
Meteor-adq	22.86	77.27	51.40
Meteor-hter	25.23	66.71	50.90

Weblog			
Tuning Metric	BLEU	TER	Met1.2
BLEU	17.10	76.28	41.86
TER	17.07	64.32	39.75
TER-BLEU/2	18.14	65.77	40.68
Meteor-tune	18.07	73.83	42.78
Meteor-rank	14.34	98.86	42.75
Meteor-adq	16.76	81.63	43.43
Meteor-hter	18.12	70.47	42.28

Table 8: Average metric scores for Urdu-English systems tuned to baseline metrics and versions of Meteor

Task	α	β	γ	δ	w_{exact}	w_{stem}	w_{syn}	w_{par}
Ranking	0.85	0.20	0.60	0.75	1.00	0.60	0.80	0.60
Adequacy	0.75	1.40	0.45	0.70	1.00	1.00	0.60	0.80
H-TER	0.40	1.50	0.35	0.55	1.00	0.20	0.60	0.80
Tuning	0.50	1.00	0.50	0.50	1.00	0.50	0.50	0.50

Table 7: Parameters for Meteor 1.3 tasks

7 Conclusions

We have presented Ranking, Adequacy, and Tuning versions of Meteor 1.3. The Ranking and Adequacy versions are shown to have high correlation with human judgments except in cases of overfitting due to skewed tuning data. We believe that these overfitting issues are lessened when tuning to combined 2009 and 2010 data due to increased variety in translation characteristics. The Tuning version of Meteor is shown to outperform BLEU in minimum error rate training of a phrase-based system on small Urdu-English data and we believe that it will generalize well to other tuning scenarios. The source code and all resources for Meteor 1.3 and the version of Z-MERT with Meteor integration will be available for download from the Meteor website.

References

Satanjeev Banerjee and Alon Lavie. 2005. METEOR: An Automatic Metric for MT Evaluation with Improved Correlation with Human Judgments. In *Proc. of ACL WIEEMMTS 2005.*

Colin Bannard and Chris Callison-Burch. 2005. Paraphrasing with bilingual parallel corpora. In *Proc. of ACL2005.*

Chris Callison-Burch, Philipp Koehn, Christof Monz, Kay Peterson, Mark Przybocki, and Omar Zaidan. 2010. Findings of the 2010 Joint Workshop on Statistical Machine Translation and Metrics for Machine Translation. In *Proc. of ACL WMT/MetricsMATR 2010.*

Michael Denkowski and Alon Lavie. 2010a. Choosing the Right Evaluation for Machine Translation: an Examination of Annotator and Automatic Metric Performance on Human Judgment Tasks. In *Proc. of AMTA 2010.*

Michael Denkowski and Alon Lavie. 2010b. METEOR-NEXT and the METEOR Paraphrase Tables: Improve Evaluation Support for Five Target Languages. In *Proc. of ACL WMT/MetricsMATR 2010.*

Qin Gao and Stephan Vogel. 2008. Parallel Implementations of Word Alignment Tool. In *Proc. of ACL WSETQANLP 2008.*

Hieu Hoang, Alexandra Birch, Chris Callison-burch, Richard Zens, Rwth Aachen, Alexandra Constantin, Marcello Federico, Nicola Bertoldi, Chris Dyer, Brooke Cowan, Wade Shen, Christine Moran, and Ondej Bojar. 2007. Moses: Open Source Toolkit for Statistical Machine Translation. In *Proc. of ACL 2007.*

Philipp Koehn, Franz Josef Och, and Daniel Marcu. 2003. Statistical Phrase-Based Translation. In *Proc. of NAACL/HLT 2003.*

Philipp Koehn. 2005. Europarl: A Parallel Corpus for Statistical Machine Translation. In *Proc. of MT Summit 2005.*

Zhifei Li, Chris Callison-Burch, Chris Dyer, Juri Ganitkevitch, Sanjeev Khudanpur, Lane Schwartz, Wren Thornton, Jonathan Weese, and Omar Zaidan. 2009. Joshua: An Open Source Toolkit for Parsing-based Machine Translation. In *Proc. of WMT 2009.*

George Miller and Christiane Fellbaum. 2007. WordNet. http://wordnet.princeton.edu/.

Joseph Olive. 2005. *Global Autonomous Language Exploitation (GALE).* DARPA/IPTO Proposer Information Pamphlet.

Kishore Papineni, Salim Roukos, Todd Ward, and Wei-Jing Zhu. 2002. BLEU: a Method for Automatic Evaluation of Machine Translation. In *Proc. of ACL 2002.*

Robert Parker, David Graff, Junbo Kong, Ke Chen, and Kazuaki Maeda. 2009. English Gigaword Fourth Edition. Linguistic Data Consortium, LDC2009T13.

Martin Porter. 2001. Snowball: A language for stemming algorithms. http://snowball.tartarus.org/texts/.

Mark Przybocki. 2009. NIST Open Machine Translation 2009 Evaluation. http://www.itl.nist.gov/iad/mig/tests/mt/2009/.

Matthew Snover, Bonnie Dorr, Richard Schwartz, Linnea Micciulla, and John Makhoul. 2006. A Study of Translation Edit Rate with Targeted Human Annotation. In *Proc. of AMTA 2006.*

Andreas Stolke. 2002. SRILM - an Extensible Language Modeling Toolkit. In *Proc. of ICSLP 2002.*

C. van Rijsbergen, 1979. *Information Retrieval*, chapter 7. 2nd edition.

Omar F. Zaidan. 2009. Z-MERT: A Fully Configurable Open Source Tool for Minimum Error Rate Training of Machine Translation Systems. *The Prague Bulletin of Mathematical Linguistics*.

Approximating a Deep-Syntactic Metric for MT Evaluation and Tuning*

Matouš Macháček and Ondřej Bojar
Charles University in Prague
Faculty of Mathematics and Physics
Institute of Formal and Applied Linguistics
Malostranské náměstí 25, Prague
{bojar,machacek}@ufal.mff.cuni.cz

Abstract

SemPOS is an automatic metric of machine translation quality for Czech and English focused on content words. It correlates well with human judgments but it is computationally costly and hard to adapt to other languages because it relies on a deep-syntactic analysis of the system output and the reference. To remedy this, we attempt at approximating SemPOS using only tagger output and a few heuristics. At a little expense in correlation to human judgments, we can evaluate MT systems much faster. Additionally, we describe our submission to the Tunable Metrics Task in WMT11.

1 Introduction

SemPOS metric for machine translation quality was introduced by Kos and Bojar (2009). It is inspired by a set of metrics relying on various linguistic features on syntactic and semantic level introduced by Giménez and Márquez (2007). One of their best performing metrics was Semantic role overlapping: the candidate and the reference translation are represented as bags of words and their semantic roles. The similarity between the candidate and the reference is calculated using a general similarity measure called Overlapping. The formal definition may be found in Section 4.

Instead of semantic role labels (not available for Czech), Kos and Bojar (2009) use TectoMT framework (Žabokrtský et al., 2008) to assign a semantic part of speech defined by Sgall et al. (1986). In addition they use t-lemmas (deep-syntactic lemmas) instead of surface word forms, which most importantly means that the metric considers *content words only*. In the following, we will use "sempos" to denote the semantic part of speech and "SemPOS" to denote the whole metric by Kos and Bojar (2009).

SemPOS correlates well with human judgments on system level, see Section 2 for a brief summary of how the correlation is computed. The main drawback of SemPOS is its computational cost because it requires full parsing up to the deep syntactic level to obtain t-lemmas and semposes. In Section 3 we propose four methods which approximate t-lemmas and semposes without the deep syntactic analysis. These methods require only part-of-speech tagging and therefore they are not only faster but also easier to adapt for other languages, not requiring more advanced linguistic tools.

Giménez and Márquez (2007) and Bojar et al. (2010) used different formulas to calculate the final overlapping.[1] In Section 4, we examine variations of the formula, adding one version of our own.

By combining one of the approximation techniques with one of the overlapping formulas, we ob-

* This work has been supported by the grants EuroMatrixPlus (FP7-ICT-2007-3-231720 of the EU and 7E09003 of the Czech Republic), P406/10/P259, P406/11/1499, and MSM 0021620838.

[1] In fact, Giménez and Márquez (2007) released two versions of the paper. Both of them are nearly identical except for the formula for overlapping, so we asked the authors which of the two versions is correct. It turns out that Bojar et al. (2010), unaware of the second version of the paper, used the wrong one but still obtained good results. We therefore (re-)examine both versions.

Proceedings of the 6th Workshop on Statistical Machine Translation, pages 92–98,
Edinburgh, Scotland, UK, July 30–31, 2011. ©2011 Association for Computational Linguistics

Workshop	Filename	Sentences	To English from	To Czech from
WMT08	test2008	2000	de, es, fr	–
WMT08	nc-test2008	2028	cs	en
WMT08	newstest2008	2051	cs, de, es, fr	en
WMT09	newstest2009	2525	cs, de, es, fr	en
WMT10	newssyscombtest2010	2034	cs, de, es, fr	en

Table 1: Datasets used to evaluate the correlation with human judgments. For example: the testset "test2008" was used for translation to English from German, Spanish and French and it was not used for any translation to Czech.

tain a variant of our metric. The performance of the individual variants is reported in Section 5.

Section 6 is devoted to our submission to the Tunable Metrics shared task of the Sixth Workshop on Statistical Machine Translation (WMT11).

2 Method of Evaluation

Our primary objective is to create a good metric for automatic MT evaluation and possibly also tuning. We are not interested much in how close is our proposed approximation to the (automatic or manual) semposes and t-lemmas. Therefore, we evaluate only how well do our metrics (the pair of a chosen approximation and a chosen formula for the overlapping) correlate with human judgments.

2.1 Test Data

We use the data collected during three Workshops on Statistical Machine Translation: WMT08 (Callison-Burch et al., 2008), WMT09 (Callison-Burch et al., 2009) and WMT10 (Callison-Burch et al., 2010). So far, we study only Czech and English as the target languages. Our test sets are summarized in Table 1: we have four sets with Czech as the target language and 16 sets with English as the target language.

Each testset in each translation direction gives us for each sentence one hypothesis for each participating MT system. Human judges (repeatedly) ranked subsets of these hypotheses comparing at most 5 hypotheses at once and indicating some ordering of the hypotheses. The ordering may include ties. In WMT, these 5-fold rankings are interpreted as "simulated pairwise comparisons": all pairwise comparisons are extracted from each ranking. The HUMAN SCORE for each system is then the percentage of pairs where the system was ranked better or equal to its competitor.

2.2 Correlation with Human Judgments

For each metric we examine, the correlation to human judgments is calculated as follows: given one of the test sets (the hypotheses and reference translations), the examined metric provides a single-figure score for each system. We use Spearman's rank correlation coefficient between the human scores and the scores of the given metric to see how well the metric matches human judgments. Because tied ranks do not exist, the correlation coefficient is given by:

$$\rho = 1 - \frac{6 \sum_i (p_i - q_i)^2}{n(n^2 - 1)} \quad (1)$$

Human scores across different test sets are not comparable, so we compute correlations for each test set separately and average them.

3 Approximations of SemPOS

We would like to obtain t-lemmas and semantic parts of speech without deep syntactic analysis, assuming only automatic tagging and lemmatization.

Except for one option (Section 3.4), we approximate t-lemmas simply by surface lemmas. For the majority of content words, this works perfectly, but there are several regular classes of words where the t-lemma differs. In such cases, the t-lemma usually consists of the lemma of the main content word and an auxiliary word that significantly changes the meaning of the content word. These are e.g. English phrasal verbs ("blow up" should have the t-lemma "blow_up") and Czech reflexive verbs ("smát_se").

The approximation of semantic part of speech deserves at least some minimal treatment. The following sections describe four variations of the approximation.

Morph. Tag	Sempos	Rel. Freq.
NN	n.denot	0.989
VBZ	v	0.766
VBN	v	0.953
JJ	adj.denot	0.975
NNP	n.denot	0.999
PRP	n.pron.def.pers	0.999
VB	v	0.875
VBP	v	0.663
VBD	v	0.810
WP	n.pron.indef	1.000
NNS	n.denot	0.996
JJR	adj.denot	0.813

Table 2: A sample of the mapping from English morphological tags to semposes, including the relative frequency, e.g. $\frac{\text{count(NN,n.denot)}}{\text{count(NN)}}$.

3.1 Sempos from Tag

We noticed that the morphological tag determines almost uniquely the semantic part of speech. We use the Czech-English sentence-parallel corpus CzEng (Bojar and Žabokrtský, 2009) to create a simple dictionary which maps morphological tags to most frequent semantic parts of speech. Some morphological tags belong almost always to auxiliary words which do not have a corresponding deep-syntactic node at all, so the t-lemma and sempos are not defined for them. We include these morphological tags in the dictionary and map them to a special sempos value "-". Ultimately, words with such sempos are not included in the overlapping at all.

Table 2 shows a sample of this dictionary. The high relative frequencies indicate that we are not losing too much of the accuracy: overall 93.6 % for English and 88.4 % for Czech on CzEng e-test.

The first approximation relies just on this (language-specific) dictionary. The input text is automatically tagged, the morphological tags are deterministically mapped to semposes using the dictionary and words where the mapping led to the special value of "-" are removed.

In the following, we label this method as APPROX.

3.2 Exclude Stop-Words

By definition, the deep syntactic layer we use represents more or less only content words. Most auxiliary words become only attributes of the deep-syntactic nodes and play no role in the overlapping between the hypothesis and the reference.

Our first approximation technique (Section 3.1) identifies auxiliary words only on the basis of the morphological tag. We attempt to refine the recall by excluding a certain number of most frequent words in each language. The frequency list was obtained from the Czech and English sides of the corpus CzEng. We choose the exact cut-off for stop-words in each language separately: 100 words in English and 220 words in Czech. See Section 5.1 below.

In the following, the method is called APPROX-STOPWORDS.

3.3 Restricting the Set of Examined Semposes

We noticed that the contribution of each sempos to the overall performance of the metric in terms of correlation to human judgments can differ a lot. One of the underlying reasons may be e.g. greater or lower tagging accuracy of certain word classes, another reason may be that translation errors in certain word classes may be more relevant for human judges of MT quality.

Tables 3 and 4 report the correlation to human judgments if only words in a given sempos are considered in the overlapping. Based on these observations, we assume that some sempos types raise the correlation of the overlapping with human judgments and some lower it. We therefore try one more variant of the approximation which considers only (language-specific) subset of semposes.

The approximation called APPROX-RESTR considers only these sempos tags in Czech: v, n.denot, adj.denot, n.pron.def.pers, n.pron.def.demon, adv.-denot.ngrad.nneg, adv.denot.grad.nneg. The considered sempos tags for English are: v, n.denot, adj.-denot, n.pron.indef.

3.4 T-lemma and Sempos Tagging

Our last approximation method differs a lot from the previous three approximations. We use the sequence labeling algorithm (Collins, 2002) as implemented in Featurama[2] to choose the t-lemma and sempos tag. The CzEng corpus (Bojar and Žabokrtský, 2009) serves to train two taggers: one for Czech and

[2] http://sourceforge.net/projects/featurama/

Tag	R. Fr.	Min.	Max.	Avg.
v	0.236	0.403	1.000	0.735
n.denot	0.506	0.189	1.000	0.728
adj.denot	0.124	0.264	0.964	0.720
n.pron.indef	0.019	0.224	1.000	0.639
n.quant.def	0.039	-0.084	0.893	0.495
n.pron.def.pers	0.068	-0.500	0.975	0.493
adv.pron.indef	0.005	-0.382	1.000	0.432
adv.denot.grad.neg	0.003	-1.000	0.904	0.413

Table 3: English semposes and their performance in terms of correlation with human judgments if only words of the given sempos in APPROX are checked for match with the reference. Averaged across all testsets. Overlapping CAP is used, see Section 4 below. Column R. Fr. reports relative frequency of each sempos in the testsets.

Tag	R. Fr.	Min.	Max.	Avg.
n.pron.def.pers	0.030	0.406	0.800	0.680
n.pron.def.demon	0.026	0.308	1.000	0.651
adj.denot	0.156	0.143	0.874	0.554
adv.denot.ngrad.nneg	0.047	0.291	0.800	0.451
adv.denot.grad.nneg	0.001	0.219	0.632	0.445
adj.quant.def	0.004	-0.029	0.800	0.393
n.denot.neg	0.037	0.029	0.736	0.391
adv.denot.grad.neg	0.018	-0.371	0.800	0.313
n.denot	0.432	-0.200	0.720	0.280
adv.pron.def	0.000	-0.185	0.894	0.262
adj.pron.def.demon	0.000	0.018	0.632	0.241
n.pron.indef	0.027	-0.200	0.423	0.112
adj.quant.grad	0.006	-0.225	0.316	0.079
v	0.180	-0.600	0.706	0.076
adj.quant.indef	0.002	-0.105	0.200	0.052
adv.denot.ngrad.neg	0.000	-0.883	0.775	0.000
n.quant.def	0.000	-0.800	0.713	-0.085

Table 4: Czech semposes. See Table 3 for explanation.

one for English. At each token, each of the taggers uses the word form, morphological tag and surface lemma (of the current and the previous two tokens) to choose one pair of t-lemma and sempos tag from a given set.

The set of possible t-lemma and sempos pairs is created as follows. At first the sempos set is obtained. We simply use all semposes being seen with the given morphological tag in the corpus. Then we find possible t-lemmas for each sempos. For most semposes we consider surface lemma as the only t-lemma. For the sempos tag "v" we also add t-lemmas composed of the surface lemma and some auxiliary word present in the sentence ("blow_up", "smát_se"). For some other sempos tags we add special t-lemmas for negation and personal pronouns ("#Neg", "#PersPron").

The overall accuracy of the tagger on the e-test is 97.9 % for English and 94.9 % for Czech, a better result on a harder task (t-lemmas also predicted) than the deterministic tagging in Section 3.1.

We call this approximation method TAGGER.

4 Variations of Overlapping

The original Overlapping defined by Giménez and Márquez (2007) is given in Equations 2 and 3:

$$\mathrm{O}(t) = \frac{\sum_{w \in r_i} \mathrm{cnt}(w,t,c_i)}{\sum_{w \in r_i \cup c_i} \max(\mathrm{cnt}(w,t,r_i), \mathrm{cnt}(w,t,c_i))} \tag{2}$$

where c_i and r_i denotes the candidate and reference translation of sentence i and $\mathrm{cnt}(w,t,s)$ denotes number of times t-lemma w of type (sempos) t appears in sentence s. For each sempos type t, Overlapping $\mathrm{O}(t)$ calculates the proportion of correctly translated items of type t. In this paper we will call this overlapping BOOST.

Equation 3 describes Overlapping of all types:

$$\mathrm{O}(*) = \frac{\sum_{t \in T} \sum_{w \in r_i} \mathrm{cnt}(w,t,c_i)}{\sum_{t \in T} \sum_{w \in r_i \cup c_i} \max(\mathrm{cnt}(w,t,r_i), \mathrm{cnt}(w,t,c_i))} \tag{3}$$

where T denotes the set of all sempos types. We will call this Overlapping BOOST-MICRO because it micro-averages the overlappings of individual sempos types.

Kos and Bojar (2009) used a slightly different Overlapping formula, denoted CAP in this paper:

$$\mathrm{O}(t) = \frac{\sum_{w \in r_i} \min(\mathrm{cnt}(w,t,r_i), \mathrm{cnt}(w,t,c_i))}{\sum_{w \in r_i} \mathrm{cnt}(w,t,r_i)} \tag{4}$$

To calculate Overlapping of all types, Kos and Bojar (2009) used ordinary macro-averaging. We call the method CAP-MACRO:

$$\mathrm{O}(*) = \frac{1}{|T|} \sum_{t \in T} \mathrm{O}(t) \tag{5}$$

The difference between micro- and macro-average is that in macro-average all types have

Reduction	Overlapping	Min.	Max.	Avg.
approx	cap-micro	0.409	1.000	0.804
orig	cap-macro	0.536	1.000	0.801
approx	cap-macro	0.420	1.000	0.799
approx-restr	cap-macro	0.476	1.000	0.798
tagger	cap-micro	0.409	1.000	0.790
orig	cap-micro	0.391	1.000	0.784
approx-restr	cap-micro	0.391	1.000	0.782
approx-stopwords	cap-micro	0.391	1.000	0.754
sempos-bleu		0.374	1.000	0.754
approx-stopwords	cap-macro	0.280	1.000	0.724
tagger	boost-micro	0.306	1.000	0.717
orig	boost-micro	0.324	1.000	0.711
approx-stopwords	boost-micro	0.133	1.000	0.697
approx-restr	boost-micro	0.126	1.000	0.688
approx	boost-micro	0.224	1.000	0.686
tagger	cap-macro	0.118	1.000	0.669
bleu		-0.143	1.000	0.628

Table 5: Metric correlations for English as a target language

Reduction	Overlapping	Min.	Max.	Avg.
approx-restr	cap-macro	0.400	0.800	0.608
tagger	cap-macro	0.143	0.800	0.428
orig	cap-macro	0.143	0.800	0.423
approx-restr	cap-micro	0.086	0.769	0.413
tagger	cap-micro	0.086	0.769	0.413
orig	cap-micro	0.086	0.741	0.406
approx-stopwords	cap-micro	0.086	0.790	0.368
approx	cap-micro	0.086	0.734	0.354
approx-stopwords	cap-macro	0.086	0.503	0.347
sempos-bleu		0.086	0.676	0.340
approx	cap-macro	0.086	0.469	0.338
tagger	boost-micro	0.086	0.664	0.337
bleu		0.029	0.490	0.279
orig	boost-micro	-0.200	0.692	0.273
approx-stopwords	boost-micro	-0.200	0.685	0.271
approx	boost-micro	-0.200	0.664	0.266
approx-restr	boost-micro	-0.200	0.664	0.266

Table 6: Metric correlations for Czech as a target language

the same weight regardless of count. For example O(n.denot) and O(adv.denot.grad.nneg) would have the same weight, however there are many more items of type n.denot than items of type adv.denot.grad.nneg (see Tables 3 and 4). We consider this unnatural and we suggest a new Overlapping formula CAP-MICRO:

$$O(*) = \frac{\sum\limits_{t \in T} \sum\limits_{w \in r_i} \min(\text{cnt}(w,t,r_i), \text{cnt}(w,t,c_i))}{\sum\limits_{t \in T} \sum\limits_{w \in r_i} \text{cnt}(w,t,r_i)} \tag{6}$$

In sum, we have three Overlappings which should be evaluated: BOOST-MICRO (Equation 3), CAP-MACRO (Equation 5), and CAP-MICRO (Equation 6).

5 Experiments

Table 5 shows the results for English as the target language. The first two columns denote the combination of an approximation method and an overlapping formula. For conciseness, we report only the minimum, maximum and average value among correlations of all test sets.

To compare metrics to original SemPOS, the table includes non-approximated variant ORIG where the t-lemmas and semposes are assigned by the TectoMT framework. For the purposes of comparison, we also report the correlations of BLEU (Papineni et al., 2002) and a linear combination of APPROX+CAP-MICRO and BLEU (even weights) under the name SEMPOS-BLEU since this metric was used in Tunable Metric Task (Section 6).

The best performing metric is the combination of approximation APPROX and overlapping CAP-MICRO. It actually slightly outperforms all non-approximated metrics. In general, the reductions APPROX and ORIG combined with CAP-MICRO or CAP-MACRO perform very well. Reductions APPROX-STOPWORDS and APPROX-RESTR do not improve on APPROX.

The TAGGER approximation correlates similarly to ORIG when micro-average is used.

Table 6 contains the results for Czech as the target language. The best performing metric for Czech is APPROX-RESTR together with CAP-MACRO. In general approximation APPROX-RESTR is better than APPROX-STOPWORDS which is slightly better than APPROX.

The success of overlapping CAP-MACRO in Czech is due to the higher contribution of less frequent semposes to the overall correlation. While in English the best correlating semposes are also very frequent (Table 3), this does not hold for Czech (Table 4). The underlying reasons have yet to be explained.

In both languages, the overlapping BOOST-MICRO has a very low correlation. We therefore consider this overlapping not suitable for any met-

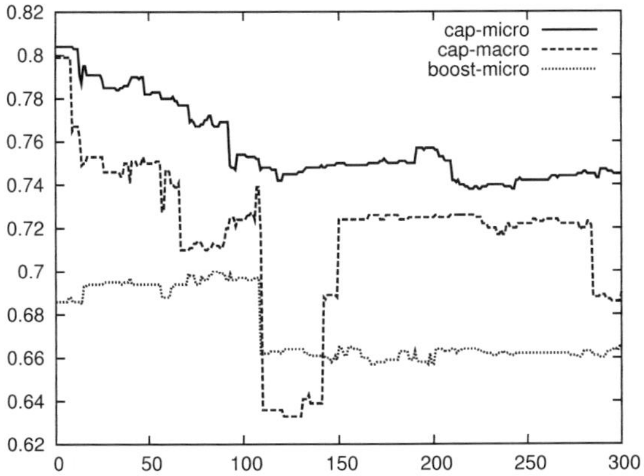

Figure 1: Correlation vs. the number of most frequent words which are thrown away for English. The big drop for lengths 109 and 110 is caused by the words 'who' and 'how'.

ric based on semposes.

On the other hand, most of the examined combinations are on average better than the baseline BLEU, sometimes by a very wide margin.

5.1 Dependency of Correlation on Stopwords List Length

We tried various stopwords list lengths for the approximation APPROX-STOPWORDS. Figure 5.1 shows the dependency of the correlation on stopwords list length for all overlappings in English. We see that the best correlation arises when no words are thrown away. One possible explanation is that auxiliary words are recognized by the morphological tag well enough anyway and stopwords lists remove also important content words, decreasing the overall accuracy of the overlapping.

6 Tunable Metric WMT11 Shared Task

The goal of the tunable metric task in WMT11 was to use the custom metric in MERT optimization (Och, 2003). The target language was English. We choose APPROX + CAP-MICRO since this combination correlates best with human judgments.

Based on the experience of Bojar and Kos (2010), we combine this metric with BLEU. In our opinion, the SemPOS metric and its variants alone are are good at comparing systems' outputs where sentence fluency has been already ensured. On the other hand, they fail in ranking sentences in n-best lists in MERT optimization because they observe only t-lemmas and don't penalize wrong morphological forms of words. We thus use BLEU to establish sentence fluency and our metrics to prefer sentences with correctly translated content words.

Weights		Devset scores	
BLEU	APPROX	BLEU	APPROX
1	0	0.246	0.546
0.75	0.25	0.242	0.584
0.5	0.5	0.229	0.594
0.25	0.75	0.215	0.602
0	1	0.025	0.631

Table 7: Results of MERT optimization. The last two columns contain metric scores of the last iteration of the MERT process with given combination weights.

We have tried several weights for the linear combination of BLEU and the chosen approximation. See Table 7 for details. We have submitted the variant with equal weights.

The preliminary results of manual evaluation (see the WMT11 overview paper) indicate that our system is fairly distinct from others: we won under the "> others" metric but we were the fifth of 8 systems in the official "$\geq$ others" (the percentage of pairs where the system was ranked better or equal to its competitor).

7 Conclusions

We have introduced and evaluated several approximations of a deep-syntactic MT evaluation metric SEMPOS. This allows us to reduce the computational load by far, use only shallow tagging and still reach reasonable correlation scores.

For English, our combination of APPROX and CAP-MICRO performs even marginally better than the original SEMPOS. For Czech, it is APPROX-RESTR and TAGGER approximations with CAP-MACRO that outperform the original SEMPOS.

The applicability of these metrics (in link with BLEU) in model optimization was confirmed by the manual judgments for the Tunable Metrics Task. Our submission was surprisingly different from others: the best one in the score excluding ties and mediocre in the score where ties are rewarded.

References

Ondrej Bojar and Kamil Kos. 2010. 2010 Failures in English-Czech Phrase-Based MT. In *Proceedings of the Joint Fifth Workshop on Statistical Machine Translation and MetricsMATR*, pages 60–66, Uppsala, Sweden, July. Association for Computational Linguistics.

Ondřej Bojar and Zdeněk Žabokrtský. 2009. CzEng0.9: Large Parallel Treebank with Rich Annotation. *Prague Bulletin of Mathematical Linguistics*, 92. in print.

Ondřej Bojar, Kamil Kos, and David Mareček. 2010. Tackling Sparse Data Issue in Machine Translation Evaluation. In *Proceedings of the ACL 2010 Conference Short Papers*, pages 86–91, Uppsala, Sweden, July. Association for Computational Linguistics.

Chris Callison-Burch, Cameron Fordyce, Philipp Koehn, Christof Monz, and Josh Schroeder. 2008. Further meta-evaluation of machine translation. In *Proceedings of the Third Workshop on Statistical Machine Translation*, pages 70–106, Columbus, Ohio, June. Association for Computational Linguistics.

Chris Callison-Burch, Philipp Koehn, Christof Monz, and Josh Schroeder. 2009. Findings of the 2009 Workshop on Statistical Machine Translation. In *Proceedings of the Fourth Workshop on Statistical Machine Translation*, pages 1–28, Athens, Greece, March. Association for Computational Linguistics.

Chris Callison-Burch, Philipp Koehn, Christof Monz, Kay Peterson, Mark Przybocki, and Omar Zaidan. 2010. Findings of the 2010 joint workshop on statistical machine translation and metrics for machine translation. In *Proceedings of the Joint Fifth Workshop on Statistical Machine Translation and MetricsMATR*, pages 17–53, Uppsala, Sweden, July. Association for Computational Linguistics. Revised August 2010.

Michael Collins. 2002. Discriminative training methods for hidden markov models: theory and experiments with perceptron algorithms. In *EMNLP '02: Proceedings of the ACL-02 conference on Empirical methods in natural language processing*, pages 1–8, Morristown, NJ, USA. Association for Computational Linguistics.

Jesús Giménez and Lluís Márquez. 2007. Linguistic Features for Automatic Evaluation of Heterogenous MT Systems. In *Proceedings of the Second Workshop on Statistical Machine Translation*, pages 256–264, Prague, June. Association for Computational Linguistics.

Kamil Kos and Ondřej Bojar. 2009. Evaluation of Machine Translation Metrics for Czech as the Target Language. *Prague Bulletin of Mathematical Linguistics*, 92.

Franz Josef Och. 2003. Minimum Error Rate Training in Statistical Machine Translation. In *Proc. of the Association for Computational Linguistics*, Sapporo, Japan, July 6-7.

Kishore Papineni, Salim Roukos, Todd Ward, and Wei-Jing Zhu. 2002. BLEU: a Method for Automatic Evaluation of Machine Translation. In *ACL 2002, Proceedings of the 40th Annual Meeting of the Association for Computational Linguistics*, pages 311–318, Philadelphia, Pennsylvania.

Petr Sgall, Eva Hajičová, and Jarmila Panevová. 1986. *The Meaning of the Sentence and Its Semantic and Pragmatic Aspects*. Academia/Reidel Publishing Company, Prague, Czech Republic/Dordrecht, Netherlands.

Zdeněk Žabokrtský, Jan Ptáček, and Petr Pajas. 2008. TectoMT: Highly modular MT system with tectogrammatics used as transfer layer. In *ACL 2008 WMT: Proceedings of the Third Workshop on Statistical Machine Translation*, pages 167–170, Columbus, OH, USA. Association for Computational Linguistics.

Evaluation without references: IBM1 scores as evaluation metrics

Maja Popović, David Vilar, Eleftherios Avramidis, Aljoscha Burchardt
German Research Center for Artificial Intelligence (DFKI)
Language Technology (LT), Berlin, Germany
name.surname@dfki.de

Abstract

Current metrics for evaluating machine translation quality have the huge drawback that they require human-quality reference translations. We propose a truly automatic evaluation metric based on IBM1 lexicon probabilities which does not need any reference translations. Several variants of IBM1 scores are systematically explored in order to find the most promising directions. Correlations between the new metrics and human judgments are calculated on the data of the third, fourth and fifth shared tasks of the Statistical Machine Translation Workshop. Five different European languages are taken into account: English, Spanish, French, German and Czech. The results show that the IBM1 scores are competitive with the classic evaluation metrics, the most promising being IBM1 scores calculated on morphemes and POS-4grams.

1 Introduction

Currently used evaluation metrics such as BLEU (Papineni et al., 2002), METEOR (Banerjee and Lavie, 2005), etc. are based on the comparison between human reference translations and the automatically generated hypotheses in the target language to be evaluated. While this scenario helps in the design of machine translation systems, it has two major drawbacks. The first one is the practical criticism that using reference translations is inefficient and expensive: in real-life situations, the quality of machine translation must be evaluated without having to pay humans for producing reference translations first. The second criticism is methodological: in using reference translation, the problem of evaluating translation quality (e.g., completeness, ordering, domain fit, etc.) is transformed into a kind of paraphrase evaluation in the target language, which is a very difficult problem itself. In addition, the set of selected references always represents only a small subset of all good translations. To remedy these drawbacks, we propose a truly automatic evaluation metric which is based on the IBM1 lexicon scores (Brown et al., 1993).

The inclusion of IBM1 scores in translation systems has shown experimentally to improve translation quality (Och et al., 2003). They also have been used for confidence estimation for machine translation (Blatz et al., 2003). To the best of our knowledge, these scores have not yet been used as an evaluation metric.

We carry out a systematic comparison between several variants of IBM1 scores. The Spearman's rank correlation coefficients on the document (system) level between the IBM1 metrics and the human ranking are computed on the English, French, Spanish, German and Czech texts generated by various translation systems in the framework of the third (Callison-Burch et al., 2008), fourth (Callison-Burch et al., 2009) and fifth (Callison-Burch et al., 2010) shared translation tasks.

2 IBM1 scores

The IBM1 model is a bag-of-word translation model which gives the sum of all possible alignment probabilities between the words in the source sentence and the words in the target sentence. Brown et al. (1993) defined the IBM1 probability score for a translation

Proceedings of the 6th Workshop on Statistical Machine Translation, pages 99–103,
Edinburgh, Scotland, UK, July 30–31, 2011.

pair f_1^J and e_1^I in the following way:

$$P(f_1^J|e_1^I) = \frac{1}{(I+1)^J}\prod_{j=1}^{J}\sum_{i=0}^{I} p(f_j|e_i) \quad (1)$$

where f_1^J is the source language sentence of length J and e_1^I is the target language sentence of length I.

As it is a conditional probability distribution, we investigated both directions as evaluation metrics. In order to avoid frequent confusions about what is the source and what the target language, we defined our scores in the following way:

- source-to-hypothesis (sh) IBM1 score:

$$\text{IBM1}_{sh} = \frac{1}{(H+1)^S}\prod_{j=1}^{S}\sum_{i=0}^{H} p(s_j|h_i) \quad (2)$$

- hypothesis-to-source (hs) IBM1 score:

$$\text{IBM1}_{hs} = \frac{1}{(S+1)^H}\prod_{i=1}^{H}\sum_{j=0}^{S} p(h_i|s_j) \quad (3)$$

where s_j are the words of the original source language sentence, S is the length of this sentence, h_i are the words of the target language hypothesis, and H is the length of this hypothesis.

In addition to the standard IBM1 scores calculated on words, we also investigated:

- MIBM1 scores – IBM1 scores of word morphemes in each direction;

- PnIBM1 scores – IBM1 scores of POS n-grams in each direction.

A parallel bilingual corpus for the desired language pair and a tool for training the IBM1 model are required in order to obtain IBM1 probabilities $p(f_j|e_i)$. For the POS n-gram scores, appropriate POS taggers for each of the languages are necessary. The POS tags cannot be only basic but must have all details (e.g. verb tenses, cases, number, gender, etc.). For the morpheme scores, a tool for splitting words into morphemes is necessary.

3 Experiments on WMT 2008, WMT 2009 and WMT 2010 test data

3.1 Experimental set-up

The IBM1 probabilities necessary for the IBM1 scores are learnt using the WMT 2010 News Commentary bilingual corpora consisting of the Spanish-English, French-English, German-English and Czech-English parallel texts. Spanish, French, German and English POS tags were produced using the TreeTagger[1], and the Czech texts are tagged using the COMPOST tagger (Spoustová et al., 2009). The morphemes for all languages are obtained using the Morfessor tool (Creutz and Lagus, 2005). The tool is corpus-based and language-independent: it takes a text as input and produces a segmentation of the word forms observed in the text. The obtained results are not strictly linguistic, however they often resemble a linguistic morpheme segmentation. Once a morpheme segmentation has been learnt from some text, it can be used for segmenting new texts. In our experiments, the splitting are learnt from the training corpus used for the IBM1 lexicon probabilities. The obtained segmentation is then used for splitting the corresponding source texts and hypotheses. Detailed corpus statistics are shown in Table 1.

Using the obtained IBM1 probabilities of words, morphemes and POS n-grams, the scores described in Section 2 are calculated for the Spanish-English, French-English, German-English and Czech-English translation outputs from each translation direction. For each of the IBM1 scores, the system level Spearman correlation coefficients ρ with the human ranking are calculated for each document. In total, 32 correlation coefficients are obtained for each score – four English outputs from the WMT 2010 task, four from the WMT 2009 and eight from the WMT 2008 task, together with sixteen outputs in other four target languages. The obtained correlation results were then summarised into the following three values:

- *mean*
  a correlation coefficient averaged over all translation outputs;

[1] http://www.ims.uni-stuttgart.de/projekte/corplex/TreeTagger/

	Spanish	English	French	English	German	English	Czech	English
sentences	97122		83967		100222		94693	
running words	2661344	2338495	2395141	2042085	2475359	2398780	2061422	2249365
vocabulary:								
words	69620	53527	56295	50082	107278	54270	125614	52081
morphemes	14178	13449	12004	12485	22211	13499	18789	12961
POS tags	69	44	33	44	54	44	611	44
POS-2grams	2459	1443	826	1443	1611	1454	27835	1457
POS-3grams	27350	20474	10409	19838	19928	20769	209481	20522
POS-4grams	135166	121182	62177	114555	114314	123550	637337	120646

Table 1: Statistics of the corpora for training IBM1 lexicon models.

- *rank>*
  percentage of documents where the particular score has better correlation than the other IBM1 scores;

- *rank≥*
  percentage of documents where the particular score has better or equal correlation than the other IBM1 scores.

3.2 Comparison of IBM1 scores

The first step towards deciding which IBM1 score to submit to the WMT 2011 evaluation task was a comparison of the average correlations i.e. *mean* values. These values for each of the IBM1 scores are presented in Table 2. The left column shows average correlations of the source-hypothesis (sh) scores, and the right one of the hypothesis-source (hs) scores.

mean	IBM1_{sh}	IBM1_{hs}
words	0.066	0.308
morphemes	0.227	0.445
POS tags	0.006	0.337
POS-2grams	0.058	0.337
POS-3grams	0.172	0.376
POS-4grams	0.196	0.442

Table 2: Average correlations of source-hypothesis (left column) and hypothesis-source (right column) IBM1 scores.

It can be seen that the morpheme, POS-3gram and POS-4gram scores have the best correlations in both directions. Apart from that, it can be observed that all the hs scores have better correlations than sh scores. Therefore, all the further experiments will deal only with the hs scores, and the subscript hs is omitted.

In the next step, all the hs scores are sorted according to each of the three values described in Section 3.1, i.e. average correlation *mean*, *rank>* and *rank≥*, and the results are shown in Table 3. The most promising scores according to each of the three values are morpheme score MIBM1, POS-3gram score P3IBM1 and POS-4gram score P4IBM1.

3.2.1 Combined IBM1 scores

The last experiment was to combine the most promising IBM1 scores in order to see if the correlation with human rankings can be further improved. In general, a combined IBM1 score is defined as arithmetic mean of various individual IBM1_{hs} scores described in Section 2:

$$\text{COMBIBM1} = \sum_{k=1}^{K} w_k \cdot \text{IBM1}_k \qquad (4)$$

The following combinations were investigated:

- P1234IBM1
  combination of all POS n-gram scores;

- MP1234IBM1
  combination of all POS n-gram scores and the morpheme score;

- MP34IBM1
  combination of the most promising individual scores, i.e. POS-3gram, POS-4gram and morpheme scores;

mean		*rank>*		*rank≥*	
0.445	morphemes	60.6	POS-4grams	71.3	POS-4grams
0.442	POS-4grams	54.4	morphemes	61.3	POS-3grams
0.376	POS-3grams	50.6	POS-3grams	56.3	morphemes
0.337	POS-2grams	39.4	POS tags	48.1	POS tags
0.337	POS tags	36.3	words	43.7	POS-2grams
0.308	words	35.6	POS-2grams	42.5	words

Table 3: IBM1$_{hs}$ scores sorted by average correlation (column 1), *rank>* value (column 2) and *rank≥* value (column 3). The most promising scores are those calculated on morphemes (MIBM1), POS-3grams (P3IBM1) and POS-4grams (P4IBM1).

- MP4IBM1
  combination of the two most promising individual scores, i.e. POS-4gram score and morpheme score.

For each of the scores, two variants were investigated, with and without (i.e. with uniform) weights w_k. The weigths were choosen proportionally to the average correlation of each individual score. Table 4 contains average correlations for all combined scores, together with the weight values.

combined score	*mean*
P1234IBM1	0.403
+weights (0.15, 0.15, 0.3, 0.4)	0.414
MP1234IBM1	0.466
+weights (0.2, 0.05, 0.05, 0.2, 0.5)	0.486
MP34IBM1	0.480
+weights (0.25, 0.25, 0.5)	**0.498**
MP4IBM1	0.494
+weights (0.4, 0.6)	**0.496**

Table 4: Average correlations of the investigated IBM1$_{hs}$ combinations. The weight values are choosen according to the average correlation of the particular individual IBM1 score.

The POS n-gram combination alone does not yield any improvement over the best individual scores. Introduction of the morpheme score increases the average correlation, especially when only the best n-gram scores are chosen. Apart from that, introducing weights improves the average correlation for each of the combined scores.

The final step in our experiments consists of ranking the weighted combined scores. The *rank>* and *rank≥* values for these scores are presented in Table 5. According to the *rank>* values, the MP4IBM1 score clearly outperforms all other scores. This score also has the highest *mean* value together with the MP34IBM1 score. As for *rank≥* values, all morpheme-POS scores have similar values significantly outperforming the P1234IBM1 score.

combined score	*rank>*	*rank≥*
P1234IBM1	25.0	36.4
MP1234IBM1	44.8	68.7
MP34IBM1	39.6	64.6
MP4IBM1	**55.2**	65.7

Table 5: *rank>* (column 1) and *rank≥* (column 2) values of the weighted IBM1$_{hs}$ combinations.

Following all these observations, we decided to submit the MP4IBM1 score to the WMT 2011 evaluation task.

4 Conclusions and outlook

The results presented in this article show that the IBM1 scores have the potential to be used as replacement of current evaluation metrics based on reference translations. Especially the scores abstracting away from word surface particularities (i.e. vocabulary, domain) based on morphemes, POS-3grams and 4grams show a high average correlation of about 0.5 (the average correlation of the BLEU score on the same data is 0.566).

An important point for future optimisation is to investigate effects of the selection of training data for the IBM1 models (and its similarity to the training data of the involved statistical translation systems). Furthermore, investigation of how to assign the weights for combining the corresponding individual scores, as well as of the possible impact of different morpheme splittings should be carried out. Other direction for future work is combination with other features (i.e. POS language models).

This method is currently being tested and further developed in the framework of the TARAXÜ project[2]. In this project, three industry and one research partners develop a hybrid machine translation architecture that satisfies current industry needs, which includes a number of large-scale evaluation rounds involving various languages: English, French, German, Czech, Spanish, Russian, Chinese and Japanese. By the time of writing this article, the first human evaluation round in TARAXÜ on a pilot set of about 7000 sentences is running. The metrics proposed in this paper will be tested on the TARAXÜ data as soon as they are available. First results will be reported in the presentation of this paper.

Acknowledgments

This work has been partly developed within the TARAXÜ project financed by TSB Technologiestiftung Berlin – Zukunftsfonds Berlin, co-financed by the European Union – European fund for regional development.

References

Satanjeev Banerjee and Alon Lavie. 2005. METEOR: An Automatic Metric for MT Evaluation with Improved Correlation with Human Judgements. In *Proceedings of the ACL 05 Workshop on Intrinsic and Extrinsic Evaluation Measures for MT and/or Summarization*, pages 65–72, Ann Arbor, MI, June.

John Blatz, Erin Fitzgerald, George Foster, Simona Gandrabur, Cyril Goutte, Alex Kulesza, Alberto Sanchis, and Nicola Ueffing. 2003. Confidence estimation for machine translation. Final report, JHU/CLSP Summer Workshop.

Peter F. Brown, Stephen A. Della Pietra, Vincent J. Della Pietra, and Robert L. Mercer. 1993. The mathematics of statistical machine translation: Parameter estimation. *Computational Linguistics*, 19(2):263–311, June.

Chris Callison-Burch, Cameron Fordyce, Philipp Koehn, Christof Monz, and Josh Schroeder. 2008. Further Meta-Evaluation of Machine Translation. In *Proceedings of the 3rd ACL 08 Workshop on Statistical Machine Translation (WMT 08)*, pages 70–106, Columbus, Ohio, June.

Chris Callison-Burch, Philipp Koehn, Christof Monz, and Josh Schroeder. 2009. Findings of the 2009 Workshop on Statistical Machine Translation. In *Proceedings of the Fourth Workshop on Statistical Machine Translation*, pages 1–28, Athens, Greece, March.

Chris Callison-Burch, Philipp Koehn, Christof Monz, Kay Peterson, Mark Przybocki, and Omar Zaidan. 2010. Findings of the 2010 joint workshop on statistical machine translation and metrics for machine translation. In *Proceedings of the Joint Fifth Workshop on Statistical Machine Translation and MetricsMATR (WMT 10)*, pages 17–53, Uppsala, Sweden, July.

Mathias Creutz and Krista Lagus. 2005. Unsupervised morpheme segmentation and morphology induction from text corpora using morfessor 1.0. Technical Report Report A81, Computer and Information Science, Helsinki University of Technology, Helsinki, Finland, March.

Franz Josef Och, Daniel Gildea, Sanjeev Khudanpur, Anoop Sarkar, Kenji Yamada, Alex Fraser, Shankar Kumar, Libin Shen, David Smith, Katherine Eng, Viren Jain, Zhen Jin, and Dragomir Radev. 2003. Syntax for statistical machine translation. Technical report, Johns Hopkins University 2003 Summer Workshop on Language Engineering, Center for Language and Speech Processing, Baltimore, MD, USA, August.

Kishore Papineni, Salim Roukos, Todd Ward, and Wie-Jing Zhu. 2002. BLEU: a method for automatic evaluation of machine translation. In *Proceedings of the 40th Annual Meeting of the Association for Computational Linguistics (ACL 02)*, pages 311–318, Philadelphia, PA, July.

Drahomíra "Johanka" Spoustová, Jan Hajič, Jan Raab, and Miroslav Spousta. 2009. Semi-supervised training for the averaged perceptron POS tagger. In *Proceedings of the 12th Conference of the European Chapter of the ACL (EACL 2009)*, pages 763–771, Athens, Greece, March.

[2]http://taraxu.dfki.de/

Morphemes and POS tags for n-gram based evaluation metrics

Maja Popović
German Research Center for Artificial Intelligence (DFKI)
Language Technology (LT), Berlin, Germany
maja.popovic@dfki.de

Abstract

We propose the use of morphemes for automatic evaluation of machine translation output, and systematically investigate a set of F score and BLEU score based metrics calculated on words, morphemes and POS tags along with all corresponding combinations. Correlations between the new metrics and human judgments are calculated on the data of the third, fourth and fifth shared tasks of the Statistical Machine Translation Workshop. Machine translation outputs in five different European languages are used: English, Spanish, French, German and Czech. The results show that the F scores which take into account morphemes and POS tags are the most promising metrics.

1 Introduction

Recent investigations have shown that the n-gram based evaluation metrics calculated on Part-of-Speech (POS) sequences correlate very well with human judgments (Callison-Burch et al., 2008; Callison-Burch et al., 2009; Popović and Ney, 2009) clearly outperforming the widely used metrics BLEU and TER. The BLEU score measured on morphemes is shown to be useful for evaluation of morphologically rich languages (Luong et al., 2010). We propose the use of morphemes for a set of n-gram based automatic evaluation metrics and investigate the correlation of the novel metrics with human judgments. We carry out a systematic comparison between the F and BLEU based metrics calculated on various combinations of words, morphemes and POS tags. The focus of this work is not a comparison of the morpheme and POS based metrics with the standard evaluation metrics[1] as in (Popović and Ney, 2009), but rather a comparison within the proposed set of metrics in order to decide which score(s) should be submitted to the WMT 2011 evaluation task. There are fifteen evaluation metrics in total, which can be divided in three groups: the metrics calculated on single units, i.e. words, morphemes or POS tags alone, the metrics calculated on pairs, i.e. words and POS tags, words and morphemes as well as morphemes and POS tags, and the metrics which take everything into account – lexical, morphological and syntactic information, i.e. words, morphemes and POS tags.

Spearman's rank correlation coefficients on the document (system) level between all the metrics and the human ranking are computed on the English, French, Spanish, German and Czech texts generated by various translation systems in the framework of the third (Callison-Burch et al., 2008), fourth (Callison-Burch et al., 2009) and fifth (Callison-Burch et al., 2010) shared translation tasks.

2 Evaluation metrics

We carried out a systematic comparison between the following metrics:

- single unit (word/morpheme/POS) metrics:
  - WORDF
    Standard F score: takes into account all word n-grams which have a counterpart

[1]Apart from the standard BLEU score which is tightly related.

Proceedings of the 6th Workshop on Statistical Machine Translation, pages 104–107,
Edinburgh, Scotland, UK, July 30–31, 2011.

both in the corresponding reference and in the hypothesis.

  - MORPHF
    Morpheme F score: takes into account all morpheme n-grams which have a counterpart both in the corresponding reference and in the hypothesis.
  - POSF
    POS F score: takes into account all POS n-grams which have a counterpart both in the corresponding reference and in the hypothesis.
  - BLEU
    The standard BLEU score (Papineni et al., 2002).
  - POSBLEU
    The standard BLEU score calculated on POS tags.
  - MORPHBLEU
    The standard BLEU score calculated on morphemes.

- pairwise metrics:
  - WPF
    F score of word and POS n-grams.
  - WMF
    F score of word and morpheme n-grams.
  - MPF
    F score of morpheme and POS n-grams.
  - WPBLEU
    Arithmetic mean of BLEU and POSBLEU scores.
  - WMBLEU
    Arithmetic mean of BLEU and MORPHBLEU scores.
  - MPBLEU
    Arithmetic mean of MORPHBLEU and POSBLEU scores.

- metrics taking everything into account:
  - WMPF
    F score on word, morpheme and POS n-grams.
  - WMPBLEU
    Arithmetic mean of BLEU, MORPHBLEU and POSBLEU scores.
  - WMPFBLEU
    Arithmetic mean of all F and BLEU scores.

The prerequisite for POS based metrics is availability of an appropriate POS tagger for the target language. It should be noted that the POS tags cannot be only basic but must have all details (e.g. verb tenses, cases, number, gender, etc.). For the morpheme based metrics, a tool for splitting words into morphemes is necessary.

All the F scores and the BLEU scores are based on four-grams (i.e. the value of maximal n is 4). Preliminary experiments on the morpheme based measures showed that there is no improvement by using six-grams, seven-grams or eight-grams. As for the n-gram averaging, BLEU scores use geometric mean. However, it is also argued not to be optimal because the score becomes equal to zero even if only one of the n-gram counts is equal to zero. In addition, previous experiments on the syntax-oriented n-gram metrics (Popović and Ney, 2009) showed that there is no significant difference between arithmetic and geometric mean in the terms of correlation coefficients. Therefore, arithmetic averaging without weights is used for all F-scores. For the WMPF score, an additional experiment with weights is carried out as well.

3 Experiments on WMT 2008, WMT 2009 and WMT 2010 test data

Experimental set-up

The evaluation metrics were compared with human rankings by means of Spearman correlation coefficients ρ. Spearman's rank correlation coefficient is equivalent to Pearson correlation on ranks, and its advantage is that it makes fewer assumptions about the data. The possible values of ρ range between 1 (if all systems are ranked in the same order) and -1 (if all systems are ranked in the reverse order). Thus the higher the value of ρ for an automatic metric, the more similar is to the human metric.

The scores were calculated for outputs of translations from Spanish, French, German and Czech into English and vice versa. Spanish, French, German and English POS tags were produced using the TreeTagger[2], and the Czech texts are tagged using the

[2] http://www.ims.uni-stuttgart.de/projekte/corplex/TreeTagger/

COMPOST tagger (Spoustová et al., 2009). In this way, all references and hypotheses were provided with detailed POS tags.

The words of all outputs were split into morphemes using the Morfessor tool (Creutz and Lagus, 2005). The tool is corpus-based and language-independent: it takes a text as input and produces a segmentation of the word forms observed in the text. The obtained results are not strictly linguistic, however they often resemble a linguistic morpheme segmentation. Once a morpheme segmentation has been learnt from some text, it can be used for segmenting new texts. In our experiments, for each document, first a corresponding reference translation has been split, and then this segmentation is used for splitting all translation hypotheses. In this way, possible discrepancies between reference and hypothesis segmentation of the same word are avoided. Effects of the training on the large(r) monolingual corpora have not been investigated yet.

In Table 1, an English reference sentence can be seen along with its morpheme and POS equivalents.

words	Another leading role in the film is played by Matt Damon .
morphemes	An other lead ing role in the film is play ed by Ma tt Da mon .
POS tags	DT VBG NN IN DT NN VBZ VBN IN NP NP SENT

Table 1: Example of an English sentence with its corresponding morpheme and POS sequences.

Comparison of metrics

For each evaluation metric described in Section 2, the system level Spearman correlation coefficients ρ were calculated for each document. In total, 33 correlation coefficients were obtained for each metric – four English outputs from the WMT 2010 task, five from the WMT 2009 and eight from the WMT 2008 task, together with sixteen outputs in other four target languages. The obtained correlation results were then summarised into the following three values:

- *mean*
  a correlation coefficient averaged over all translation outputs;
- *rank>*
  percentage of documents where the particular metric has better correlation than the other metrics investigated in this work;
- *rank≥*
  percentage of documents where the particular metric has better or equal correlation than the other metrics investigated in this work.

These values for each metric are presented in Table 2.

metric	*mean*	*rank>*	*rank≥*
WORDF	0.550	24.2	42.6
MORPHF	0.608	40.0	58.0
POSF	**0.673**	**63.4**	**78.0**
BLEU	0.566	20.6	38.6
MORPHBLEU	0.567	29.9	44.6
POSBLEU	**0.674**	**54.7**	**66.9**
WPF	0.627	44.0	66.9
WMF	0.587	37.0	53.9
MPF	**0.669**	**51.9**	**77.4**
WPBLEU	0.629	41.0	57.4
WMBLEU	0.557	23.6	41.0
MPBLEU	**0.634**	**44.6**	**66.6**
WMPF	0.645	46.3	71.1
WMPBLEU	0.610	32.7	54.7
WMPFBLEU	0.628	35.8	61.6
WMPF'	**0.668**	**51.9**	**78.8**

Table 2: Average correlation *mean* (column 1), *rank>* (column 2) and *rank≥* (column 3) for each evaluation metric. Bold represents the best value in the particular metric group. The most promising metrics are the F scores containing POS and morpheme information, namely WMPF', MPF and POSF, as well as the POSBLEU score. The standard BLEU score has very low values.

It can be observed that the morpheme based metrics outperform the word based metrics, however not the POS based metrics. As for pairwise metrics, the MPF score seems to be very promising. Adding the actual original words unfortunately deteriorates the system level correlations, nevertheless omitting the words can possibly lead to the poor sentence level correlations. Therefore an additional experiment is carried out with the most promising metric containing words, namely the WMPF score: a weighted

WMPF' score is introduced, with word weight of 0.2, morpheme weight of 0.3 and POS weight of 0.5. WMPF' clearly outperforms the simple WMPF score without weights, and it is comparable to the morpheme-POS F score MPF as well as POS-based metrics POSF and POSBLEU. Apart from that, it can be observed that, in general, the F scores are better than the BLEU scores. The combination of all F and all BLEU scores (WMPFBLEU) is better than the WMPBLEU score, but does not yield any improvements over the WMPF score.

The most promising metrics are the F scores containing POS and morpheme information, namely POSF, MPF and WMPF' together with the WMPF, as well as the POSBLEU score. The standard BLEU score has the third lowest average correlation and the lowest rank values.

4 Conclusions

The results presented in this article show that the use of morphemes improves n-gram based automatic evaluation metrics, particularly in combination with syntactic information in the form of detailed POS tags. Especially promising are the weighted WMPF and the MPF scores, which have been submitted to the WMT 2011 evaluation task. Weights for these two metrics should be further investigated in future work, as well as the possible impact of different morpheme splittings (such as training on larger texts).

Acknowledgments

This work has partly been developed within the TARAXÜ project[3] financed by TSB Technologiestiftung Berlin – Zukunftsfonds Berlin, co-financed by the European Union – European fund for regional development.

References

Chris Callison-Burch, Cameron Fordyce, Philipp Koehn, Christof Monz, and Josh Schroeder. 2008. Further Meta-Evaluation of Machine Translation. In *Proceedings of the 3rd ACL 08 Workshop on Statistical Machine Translation (WMT 08)*, pages 70–106, Columbus, Ohio, June.

Chris Callison-Burch, Philipp Koehn, Christof Monz, and Josh Schroeder. 2009. Findings of the 2009 Workshop on Statistical Machine Translation. In *Proceedings of the Fourth Workshop on Statistical Machine Translation*, pages 1–28, Athens, Greece, March.

Chris Callison-Burch, Philipp Koehn, Christof Monz, Kay Peterson, Mark Przybocki, and Omar Zaidan. 2010. Findings of the 2010 joint workshop on statistical machine translation and metrics for machine translation. In *Proceedings of the Joint Fifth Workshop on Statistical Machine Translation and MetricsMATR (WMT 10)*, pages 17–53, Uppsala, Sweden, July.

Mathias Creutz and Krista Lagus. 2005. Unsupervised morpheme segmentation and morphology induction from text corpora using morfessor 1.0. Technical Report Report A81, Computer and Information Science, Helsinki University of Technology, Helsinki, Finland, March.

Minh-Thang Luong, Preslav Nakov, and Min-Yen Kan. 2010. A Hybrid Morpheme-Word Representation for Machine Translation of Morphologically Rich Languages. In *Proceedings of the Conference on Empirical Methods in Natural Language Processing (EMNLP 10)*, pages 148–157, Cambridge, MA, October.

Kishore Papineni, Salim Roukos, Todd Ward, and Wie-Jing Zhu. 2002. BLEU: a method for automatic evaluation of machine translation. In *Proceedings of the 40th Annual Meeting of the Association for Computational Linguistics (ACL 02)*, pages 311–318, Philadelphia, PA, July.

Maja Popović and Hermann Ney. 2009. Syntax-oriented evaluation measures for machine translation output. In *Proceedings of the 4th EACL 09 Workshop on Statistical Machine Translation (WMT 09)*, pages 29–32, Athens, Greece, March.

Drahomíra "Johanka" Spoustová, Jan Hajič, Jan Raab, and Miroslav Spousta. 2009. Semi-supervised training for the averaged perceptron POS tagger. In *Proceedings of the 12th Conference of the European Chapter of the ACL (EACL 2009)*, pages 763–771, Athens, Greece, March.

[3] http://taraxu.dfki.de/

E-rating Machine Translation

Kristen Parton[1] **Joel Tetreault**[2] **Nitin Madnani**[2] **Martin Chodorow**[3]
[1]Columbia University, NY, USA
kristen@cs.columbia.edu
[2]Educational Testing Service, Princeton, NJ, USA
{jtetreault, nmadnani}@ets.org
[3]Hunter College of CUNY, New York, NY, USA
martin.chodorow@hunter.cuny.edu

Abstract

We describe our submissions to the WMT11 shared MT evaluation task: MTeRater and MTeRater-Plus. Both are machine-learned metrics that use features from e-rater®, an automated essay scoring engine designed to assess writing proficiency. Despite using only features from e-rater and without comparing to translations, MTeRater achieves a sentence-level correlation with human rankings equivalent to BLEU. Since MTeRater only assesses fluency, we build a meta-metric, MTeRater-Plus, that incorporates adequacy by combining MTeRater with other MT evaluation metrics and heuristics. This meta-metric has a higher correlation with human rankings than either MTeRater or individual MT metrics alone. However, we also find that e-rater features may not have significant impact on correlation in every case.

1 Introduction

The evaluation of machine translation (MT) systems has received significant interest over the last decade primarily because of the concurrent rising interest in statistical machine translation. The majority of research on evaluating translation quality has focused on metrics that compare translation hypotheses to a set of human-authored reference translations. However, there has also been some work on methods that are not dependent on human-authored translations.

One subset of such methods is task-based in that the methods determine the quality of a translation in terms of how well it serves the need of an extrinsic task. These tasks can either be downstream NLP tasks such as information extraction (Parton et al., 2009) and information retrieval (Fujii et al., 2009) or human tasks such as answering questions on a reading comprehension test (Jones et al., 2007).

Besides extrinsic evaluation, there is another set of methods that attempt to "learn" what makes a good translation and then predict the quality of new translations without comparing to reference translations. Corston-Oliver et al. (2001) proposed the idea of building a decision tree classifier to simply distinguish between machine and human translations using language model (LM) and syntactic features. Kulesza and Shieber (2004) attempt the same task using an support vector machine (SVM) classifier and features derived from reference-based MT metrics such as WER, PER, BLEU and NIST. They also claim that the confidence score for the classifier being used, if available, may be taken as an estimate of translation quality. Quirk (2004) took a different approach and examined whether it is possible to explicitly compute a confidence measure for each translated sentence by using features derived from both the source and target language sides. Albrecht and Hwa (2007a) expanded on this idea and conducted a larger scale study to show the viability of regression as a sentence-level metric of MT quality. They used features derived from several other reference-driven MT metrics. In other work (Albrecht and Hwa, 2007b), they showed that one could substitute translations from other MT systems for human-authored reference translations and derive the regression features from them.

Gamon et al. (2005) build a classifier to distinguish machine-generated translations from human

Proceedings of the 6th Workshop on Statistical Machine Translation, pages 108–115,
Edinburgh, Scotland, UK, July 30–31, 2011.

ones using *fluency-based* features and show that by combining the scores of this classifier with LM perplexities, they obtain an MT metric that has good correlation with human judgments but not better than the baseline BLEU metric.

The fundamental questions that inspired our proposed metrics are as follows:

- Can an operational English-proficiency measurement system, built with absolutely no forethought of using it for evaluation of translation quality, actually be used for this purpose?
- Obviously, such a system can only assess the fluency of a translation hypothesis and not the adequacy. Can the features derived from this system then be combined with metrics such as BLEU, METEOR or TERp—measures of adequacy—to yield a metric that performs better?

The first metric we propose (MTeRater) is an SVM ranking model that uses features derived from the ETS e-rater® system to assess fluency of translation hypotheses. Our second metric (MTeRater-Plus) is a meta-metric that combines MTeRater features with metrics such as BLEU, METEOR and TERp as well as features inspired by other MT metrics.

Although our work is intimately related to some of the work cited above in that it is a trained regression model predicting translation quality at the sentence level, there are two important differences:

1. We do not use *any* human translations – reference or otherwise – for MTeRater, not even when training the metric. The classifier is trained using human judgments of translation quality provided as part of the shared evaluation task.
2. Most of the previous approaches use feature sets that are designed to capture *both* translation adequacy and fluency. However, MTeRater uses only fluency-based features.

The next section provides some background on the e-rater system. Section 3 presents a discussion of the differences between MT errors and learner errors. Section 4 describes how we use e-rater to build our metrics. Section 5 outlines our experiments and Section 5 discusses the results of these experiments. Finally, we conclude in Section 6.

2 E-rater

E-rater is a proprietary automated essay scoring system developed by Educational Testing Service (ETS) to assess writing quality.[1] The system has been used operationally for over 10 years in high-stakes exams such as the GRE and TOEFL given its speed, reliability and high agreement with human raters.

E-rater combines 8 main features using linear regression to produce a numerical score for an essay. These features are grammar, usage, mechanics, style, organization, development, lexical complexity and vocabulary usage. The grammar feature covers errors such as sentence fragments, verb form errors and pronoun errors (Chodorow and Leacock, 2000). The usage feature detects errors related to articles (Han et al., 2006), prepositions (Tetreault and Chodorow, 2008) and collocations (Futagi et al., 2008). The mechanics feature checks for spelling, punctuation and capitalization errors. The style feature checks for passive constructions and word repetition, among others. Organization and development tabulate the presence or absence of discourse elements and the length of each element. Finally, the lexical complexity feature details how complex the writer's words are based on frequency indices and writing scales, and the vocabulary feature evaluates how appropriate the words are for the given topic). Since many of the features are essay-specific, there is certainly some mismatch between what e-rater was intended for and the genres we are using it for in this experiment (translated news articles).

In our work, we separate e-rater features into two classes: sentence level and document level. The sentence level features consist of all errors marked by the various features for each sentence alone. In contrast, the document level features are an aggregation of the sentence level features for the entire document.

[1] A detailed description of e-rater is outside the scope of this paper and the reader is referred to (Attali and Burstein, 2006).

3 Learner Errors vs. MT Errors

Since e-rater is trained on human-written text and designed to look for errors in usage that are common to humans, one research question is whether it is even useful for assessing the fluency of machine translated text. E-rater is unaware of the translation context, so it does not look for common MT errors, such as untranslated words, mistranslations and deleted content words. However, these may get flagged as other types of learner errors: spelling mistakes, confused words, and sentence fragments.

Machine translations do contain learner-like mistakes in verb conjugations and word order. In an error analysis of SMT output, Vilar et al. (2006) report that 9.9% - 11.7% of errors made by a Spanish-English SMT system were incorrect word forms, including incorrect tense, person or number. These error types are also account for roughly 14% of errors made by ESL (English as a Second Language) writers in the Cambridge Learner Corpus (Leacock et al., 2010).

On the other hand, some learner mistakes are unlikely to be made by MT systems. The Spanish-English SMT system made almost no mistakes in idioms (Vilar et al., 2006). Idiomatic expressions are strongly preferred by language models, but may be difficult for learners to memorize ("kicked *a* bucket"). Preposition usage is a common problem in non-native English text, accounting for 29% of errors made by intermediate to advanced ESL students (Bitchener et al., 2005) but language models are less likely to prefer local preposition errors e.g., "he went *to* outside". On the other hand, a language model will likely not prevent errors in prepositions (or in other error types) that rely on long-distance dependencies.

4 E-rating Machine Translation

The MTeRater metric uses only features from e-rater to score translations. The features are produced directly from the MT output, with no comparison to reference translations, unlike most MT evaluation metrics (such as BLEU, TERp and METEOR).

An obvious deficit of MTeRater is a measure of adequacy, or how much meaning in the source sentence is expressed in the translation. E-rater was not developed for assessing translations, and the MTeRater metric never compares the translation to the source sentence. To remedy this, we propose the MTeRater-Plus meta-metric that uses e-rater features plus all of the hybrid features described below. Both metrics were trained on the same data using the same machine learning model, and differ only in their feature sets.

4.1 E-rater Features

Each sentence is associated with an e-rater sentence-level vector and a document-level vector as previously described and each column in these vectors was used a feature.

4.2 Features for Hybrid Models

We used existing automatic MT metrics as baselines in our evaluation, and also as features in our hybrid metric. The metrics we used were:

1. **BLEU** (Papineni et al., 2002): Case-insensitive and case-sensitive BLEU scores were produced using mteval-v13a.pl, which calculates smoothed sentence-level scores.

2. **TERp** (Snover et al., 2009): Translation Edit Rate plus (TERp) scores were produced using terp v1. The scores were case-insensitive and edit costs from Snover et al. (2009) were used to produce scores tuned for fluency and adequacy.

3. **METEOR** (Lavie and Denkowski, 2009): Meteor scores were produced using Meteor-next v1.2. All types of matches were allowed (exact, stem, synonym and paraphrase) and scores tuned specifically to rank, HTER and adequacy were produced using the "-t" flag in the tool.

We also implemented features closely related to or inspired by other MT metrics. The set of these auxiliary features is referred to as "Aux".

1. **Character-level statistics**: Based on the success of the i-letter-BLEU and i-letter-recall metrics from WMT10 (Callison-Burch et al., 2010), we added the harmonic mean of precision (or recall) for character n-grams (from 1 to 10) as features.

2. **Raw n-gram matches**: We calculated the precision and precision for word n-grams (up to n=6) and added each as a separate feature (for a total of 12). Although these statistics are also calculated as part of the MT metrics above, breaking them into separate features gives the model more information.

3. **Length ratios**: The ratio between the lengths of the MT output and the reference translation was calculated on a character level and a word level. These ratios were also calculated between the MT output and the source sentence.

4. **OOV heuristic**: The percentage of tokens in the MT that match the source sentence. This is a low-precision heuristic for counting out of vocabulary (OOV) words, since it also counts named entities and words that happen to be the same in different languages.

4.3 Ranking Model

Following (Duh, 2008), we represent sentence-level MT evaluation as a ranking problem. For a particular source sentence, there are N machine translations and one reference translation. A feature vector is extracted from each {source, reference, MT} tuple. The training data consists of sets of translations that have been annotated with relative ranks. During training, all ranked sets are converted to sets of feature vectors, where the label for each feature vector is the rank. The ranking model is a linear SVM that predicts a relative score for each feature vector, and is implemented by SVM-rank (Joachims, 2006). When the trained classifier is applied to a set of N translations for a new source sentence, the translations can then be ranked by sorting the SVM scores.

5 Experiments

All experiments were run using data from three years of previous WMT shared tasks (WMT08, WMT09 and WMT10). In these evaluations, annotators were asked to rank 3-5 translation hypotheses (with ties allowed), given a source sentence and a reference translation, although they were only required to be fluent in the target language.

Since e-rater was developed to rate English sentences only, we only evaluated tasks with English as the target language. All years included source languages French, Spanish, German and Czech. WMT08 and WMT09 also included Hungarian and multisource English. The number of MT systems was different for each language pair and year, from as few as 2 systems (WMT08 Hungarian-English) to as many as 25 systems (WMT10 German-English). All years had a newswire testset, which was divided into stories. WMT08 had testsets in two additional genres, which were not split into documents.

All translations were pre-processed and run through e-rater. Each document was treated as an essay, although news articles are generally longer than essays. Testsets that were not already divided into documents were split into pseudo-documents of 20 contiguous sentences or less. Missing end of sentence markers were added so that e-rater would not merge neighboring sentences.

6 Results

For assessing our metrics prior to WMT11, we trained on WMT08 and WMT09 and tested on WMT10. The metrics we submitted to WMT11 were trained on all three years. One criticism of machine-learned evaluation metrics is that they may be too closely tuned to a few MT systems, and thus not generalize well as MT systems evolve or when judging new sets of systems. In this experiment, WMT08 has 59 MT systems, WMT09 has 70 different MT systems, and WMT10 has 75 different systems. Different systems participate each year, and those that participate for multiple years often improve from year to year. By training and testing across years rather than within years, we hope to avoid overfitting.

To evaluate, we measure correlation between each metric and the human annotated rankings according to (Callison-Burch et al., 2010): Kendall's tau is calculated for each language pair and the results are averaged across language pairs. This is preferable to averaging across all judgments because the number of systems and the number of judgments vary based on the language pair (e.g., there were 7,911 ranked pairs for 14 Spanish-English systems, and 3,575 ranked pairs for 12 Czech-English systems).

It is difficult to calculate the statistical significance of Kendall's tau on these data. Unlike the

Source language	cz	de	es	fr	avg
Individual Metrics & Baselines					
MTeRater	.32	.31	.19	.23	.26
bleu-case	.26	.27	.28	.22	.26
meteor-rank	.33	.36	.33	.27	.32
TERp-fluency	.30	.36	.28	.28	.30
Meta-Metric & Baseline					
BMT+Aux+MTeRater	.38	.42	.37	.38	.39
BMT	.35	.40	.35	.34	.36
Additional Meta-Metrics					
BMT+LM	.36	.41	.36	.36	.37
BMT+MTeRater	.38	.42	.36	.38	.38
BMT+Aux	.38	.41	.38	.37	.39
BMT+Aux+LM	.39	.42	.38	.36	.39

Table 1: Kendall's tau correlation with human rankings. BMT includes bleu, meteor and TERp; Aux includes auxiliary features. BMT+Aux+MTeRater is MTeRater-Plus.

Metrics MATR annotations (Przybocki et al., 2009), (Peterson and Przybocki, 2010), the WMT judgments do not give a full ranking over all systems for all judged sentences. Furthermore, the 95% confidence intervals of Kendall's tau are known to be very large (Carterette, 2009) – in Metrics MATR 2010, the top 7 metrics in the paired-preference single-reference into-English track were within the same confidence interval.

To compare metrics, we use McNemar's test of paired proportions (Siegel and Castellan, 1988) which is more powerful than tests of independent proportions, such as the chi-square test for independent samples.[2] As in Kendall's tau, each metric's relative ranking of a translation pair is compared to that of a human. Two metrics, A and B, are compared by counting the number of times both A and B agree with the human ranking, the number of times A disagrees but B agrees, the number of times A agrees but B disagrees, and the number of times both A and B disagree. These counts can be arranged in a 2 x 2 contingency table as shown below.

	A agrees	A disagrees
B agrees	a	b
B disagrees	c	d

McNemar's test determines if the cases of mismatch in agreement between the metrics (cells b and c) are symmetric or if there is a significant difference in favor of one of the metrics showing more agreement with the human than the other. The two-tailed probability for McNemar's test can be calculated using the binomial distribution over cells b and c.

6.1 Reference-Free Evaluation with MTeRater

The first group of rows in Table 1 shows the Kendall's tau correlation with human rankings of MTeRater and the best-performing version of the three standard MT metrics. Even though MTeRater is blind to the MT context and does not use the source or references at all, MTeRater's correlation with human judgments is the same as case-sensitive bleu (bleu-case). This indicates that a metric trained to assess English proficiency in non-native speakers is applicable to machine translated text.

6.2 Meta-Metrics

The second group in Table 1 shows the correlations of our second metric, MTeRater-Plus (BMT+Aux+MTeRater), and a baseline meta-metric (BMT) that combined BLEU, METEOR and TERp. MTeRater-Plus performs significantly better than BMT, according to McNemar's test.

We also wanted to determine whether the e-rater features have any significant impact when used as part of meta-metrics. To this end, we first created two variants of MTeRater-Plus: one that removed the MTeRater features (BMT+Aux) and another that replaced the MTeRater features with the LM likelihood and perplexity of the sentence (BMT+Aux+LM).[3] Both models perform as well as MTeRater-Plus, i.e., adding additional fluency features (either LM scores or MTeRater) to the BMT+Aux meta-metric has no significant impact.

To determine whether this was generally the case, we also created two variants of the BMT baseline meta-metric that added fluency features to it: one in the form of LM scores (BMT+LM) and another in the form of the MTeRater score (BMT+MTeRater). Based on McNemar's test, both models are significantly better than BMT, indicating that these reference-free fluency features indeed capture an aspect of translation quality that is absent from the standard MT metrics. However, there is no signficant difference between the two variants of BMT.

[2]See http://faculty.vassar.edu/lowry/propcorr.html for an excellent description.

[3]The LM was trained on English Gigaword 3.0, and was provided by WMT10 organizers.

1) Ref: Gordon Brown has discovered yet another hole to fall into; his way out of it remains the same MT+: Gordon Brown discovered a new hole in which to sink; even if it resigned, the position would not change. *Errors: None marked* MT-: Gordon Brown has discovered a new hole in which could, Even if it demissionnait, the situation does not change not. *Errors: Double negative, spelling, preposition*
2) Ref: Jancura announced this in the Twenty Minutes programme on Radiozurnal. MT+: Jancura said in twenty minutes Radiozurnal. *Errors: Spelling* MT-: He said that in twenty minutes. *Errors: none marked*

Table 2: Translation pairs ranked correctly by MTeRater but not bleu-case (1) and vice versa (2).

6.3 Discussion

Table 2 shows two pairs of ranked translations (MT+ is better than MT-), along with some of the errors detected by e-rater. In pair 1, the lower-ranked translation has major problems in fluency as detected by e-rater, but due to n-gram overlap with the reference, bleu-case ranks it higher. In pair 2, MT- is more fluent but missing two named entities and bleu-case correctly ranks it lower.

One disadvantage of machine-learned metrics is that it is not always clear which features caused one translation to be ranked higher than another. We did a feature ablation study for MTeRater which showed that document-level collocation features significantly improve the metric, as do features for sentence-level preposition errors. Discourse-level features were harmful to MT evaluation. This is unsurprising, since MT sentences are judged one at a time, so any discourse context is lost.

Overall, a metric with only document-level features does better than one with only sentence-level features due to data sparsity – many sentences have no errors, and we conjecture that the document-level features are a proxy for the quality of the MT system. Combining both document-level and sentence-level e-rater features does significantly better than either alone. Incorporating document-level features into sentence-level evaluation had one unforeseen effect: two identical translations can get different scores depending on how the rest of the document is translated. While using features that indicate the relative quality of MT systems can improve overall correlation, it fails when the sentence-level signal is not strong enough to overcome the prior belief.

7 Conclusion

We described our submissions to the WMT11 shared evaluation task: MTeRater and MTeRater-Plus. MTeRater is a fluency-based metric that uses features from ETS's operational English-proficiency measurement system (e-rater) to predict the quality of any translated sentence. MTeRater-Plus is a meta-metric that combines MTeRater's fluency-only features with standard MT evaluation metrics and heuristics. Both metrics are machine-learned models trained to rank new translations based on existing human judgments of translation.

Our experiments showed that MTeRater, by itself, achieves a sentence-level correlation as high as BLEU, despite not using reference translations. In addition, the meta-metric MTeRater-Plus achieves higher correlations than MTeRater, BLEU, METEOR, TERp as well as a baseline meta-metric combining BLEU, METEOR and TERp (BMT). However, further analysis showed that the MTeRater component of MTeRater-Plus does not contribute significantly to this improved correlation. However, when added to the BMT baseline meta-metric, MTeRater does make a significant contribution.

Our results, despite being a mixed bag, clearly show that a system trained to assess English-language proficiency can be useful in providing an indication of translation fluency even outside of the specific WMT11 evaluation task. We hope that this work will spur further cross-pollination between the fields of MT evaluation and grammatical error detection. For example, we would like to explore using MTeRater for confidence estimation in cases where reference translations are unavailable, such as task-oriented MT.

Acknowledgments

The authors wish to thank Slava Andreyev at ETS for his help in running e-rater. This research was supported by an NSF Graduate Research Fellowship for the first author.

References

Joshua Albrecht and Rebecca Hwa. 2007a. A Re-examination of Machine Learning Approaches for Sentence-Level MT Evaluation. In *Proceedings of ACL.*

Joshua Albrecht and Rebecca Hwa. 2007b. Regression for Sentence-Level MT Evaluation with Pseudo References. In *Proceedings of ACL.*

Yigal Attali and Jill Burstein. 2006. Automated essay scoring with e-rater v.2.0. *Journal of Technology, Learning, and Assessment*, 4(3).

John Bitchener, Stuart Young, and Denise Cameron. 2005. The effect of different types of corrective feedback on esl student writing. *Journal of Second Language Writing.*

Chris Callison-Burch, Philipp Koehn, Christof Monz, Kay Peterson, Mark Przybocki, and Omar F. Zaidan. 2010. Findings of the 2010 joint workshop on statistical machine translation and metrics for machine translation. In *Proceedings of the Joint Fifth Workshop on Statistical Machine Translation and MetricsMATR*, WMT '10, pages 17–53, Stroudsburg, PA, USA. Association for Computational Linguistics.

Ben Carterette. 2009. On rank correlation and the distance between rankings. In *Proceedings of the 32nd international ACM SIGIR conference on Research and development in information retrieval*, SIGIR '09, pages 436–443, New York, NY, USA. ACM.

Martin Chodorow and Claudia Leacock. 2000. An unsupervised method for detecting grammatical errors. In *Proceedings of the Conference of the North American Chapter of the Association of Computational Linguistics (NAACL)*, pages 140–147.

Simon Corston-Oliver, Michael Gamon, and Chris Brockett. 2001. A Machine Learning Approach to the Automatic Evaluation of Machine Translation. In *Proceedings of the 39th Annual Meeting on Association for Computational Linguistics*, pages 148–155.

Kevin Duh. 2008. Ranking vs. regression in machine translation evaluation. In *Proceedings of the Third Workshop on Statistical Machine Translation*, StatMT '08, pages 191–194, Stroudsburg, PA, USA. Association for Computational Linguistics.

Atsushi Fujii, Masao Utiyama, Mikio Yamamoto, and Takehito Utsuro. 2009. Evaluating Effects of Machine Translation Accuracy on Cross-lingual Patent Retrieval. In *Proceedings of SIGIR*, pages 674–675.

Yoko Futagi, Paul Deane, Martin Chodorow, and Joel Tetreault. 2008. A computational approach to detecting collocation errors in the writing of non-native speakers of English. *Computer Assisted Language Learning*, 21:353–367.

Michael Gamon, Anthony Aue, and Martine Smets. 2005. Sentence-level MT Evaluation Without Reference Translations: Beyond Language Modeling. In *Proceedings of the European Association for Machine Translation (EAMT).*

Na-Rae Han, Martin Chodorow, and Claudia Leacock. 2006. Detecting errors in English article usage by non-native speakers. *Natural Language Engineering*, 12(2):115–129.

Thorsten Joachims. 2006. Training linear SVMs in linear time. In *ACM SIGKDD International Conference On Knowledge Discovery and Data Mining (KDD)*, pages 217–226.

Douglas Jones, Martha Herzog, Hussny Ibrahim, Arvind Jairam, Wade Shen, Edward Gibson, and Michael Emonts. 2007. ILR-Based MT Comprehension Test with Multi-Level Questions. In *HLT-NAACL (Short Papers)*, pages 77–80.

Alex Kulesza and Stuart M. Shieber. 2004. A Learning Approach to Improving Sentence-level MT Evaluation. In *Proceedings of the 10th International Conference on Theoretical and Methodological Issues in Machine Translation (TMI).*

Alon Lavie and Michael J. Denkowski. 2009. The meteor metric for automatic evaluation of machine translation. *Machine Translation*, 23:105–115, September.

Claudia Leacock, Martin Chodorow, Michael Gamon, and Joel Tetreault. 2010. *Automated Grammatical Error Detection for Language Learners.* Morgan & Claypool Publishers.

Kishore Papineni, Salim Roukos, Todd Ward, and Wei-Jing Zhu. 2002. Bleu: a method for automatic evaluation of machine translation. In *Proceedings of the 40th Annual Meeting on Association for Computational Linguistics*, ACL '02, pages 311–318, Stroudsburg, PA, USA. Association for Computational Linguistics.

Kristen Parton, Kathleen R. McKeown, Bob Coyne, Mona T. Diab, Ralph Grishman, Dilek Hakkani-Tür, Mary Harper, Heng Ji, Wei Yun Ma, Adam Meyers, Sara Stolbach, Ang Sun, Gokhan Tur, Wei Xu, and Sibel Yaman. 2009. Who, What, When, Where, Why? Comparing Multiple Approaches to the Cross-Lingual 5W Task. In *Proceedings of the Joint Conference of the 47th Annual Meeting of the ACL and the 4th International Joint Conference on Natural Language Processing of the AFNLP*, pages 423–431.

Kay Peterson and Mark Przybocki. 2010. Nist 2010 metrics for machine translation evaluation (metricsmatr10) official release of results. `http://www.itl.nist.gov/iad/mig/tests/metricsmatr/2010/results.`

Mark Przybocki, Kay Peterson, Sébastien Bronsart, and Gregory Sanders. 2009. The nist 2008 metrics for machine translation challenge–overview, methodology, metrics, and results. *Machine Translation*, 23:71–103, September.

Christopher Quirk. 2004. Training a Sentence-level Machine Translation Confidence Measure. In *Proceedings of LREC*.

Sidney Siegel and N. John Castellan. 1988. *Nonparametric statistics for the behavioral sciences*. McGraw-Hill, 2 edition.

Matthew Snover, Nitin Madnani, Bonnie J. Dorr, and Richard Schwartz. 2009. Fluency, adequacy, or hter?: exploring different human judgments with a tunable mt metric. In *Proceedings of the Fourth Workshop on Statistical Machine Translation*, StatMT '09, pages 259–268, Stroudsburg, PA, USA. Association for Computational Linguistics.

Joel Tetreault and Martin Chodorow. 2008. The ups and downs of preposition error detection in ESL writing. In *Proceedings of the 22nd International Conference on Computational Linguistics (COLING)*, pages 865–872.

David Vilar, Jia Xu, Luis Fernando D'Haro, and Hermann Ney. 2006. Error analysis of machine translation output. In *International Conference on Language Resources and Evaluation*, pages 697–702, Genoa, Italy, May.

TINE: A Metric to Assess MT Adequacy

Miguel Rios, Wilker Aziz and **Lucia Specia**
Research Group in Computational Linguistics
University of Wolverhampton
Stafford Street, Wolverhampton, WV1 1SB, UK
{m.rios, w.aziz, l.specia}@wlv.ac.uk

Abstract

We describe TINE, a new automatic evaluation metric for Machine Translation that aims at assessing segment-level adequacy. Lexical similarity and shallow-semantics are used as indicators of adequacy between machine and reference translations. The metric is based on the combination of a lexical matching component and an adequacy component. Lexical matching is performed comparing bags-of-words without any linguistic annotation. The adequacy component consists in: i) using ontologies to align predicates (verbs), ii) using semantic roles to align predicate arguments (core arguments and modifiers), and iii) matching predicate arguments using distributional semantics. TINE's performance is comparable to that of previous metrics at segment level for several language pairs, with average Kendall's tau correlation from 0.26 to 0.29. We show that the addition of the shallow-semantic component improves the performance of simple lexical matching strategies and metrics such as BLEU.

1 Introduction

The automatic evaluation of Machine Translation (MT) is a long-standing problem. A number of metrics have been proposed in the last two decades, mostly measuring some form of matching between the MT output (hypothesis) and one or more human (reference) translations. However, most of these metrics focus on fluency aspects, as opposed to adequacy. Therefore, measuring whether the meaning of the hypothesis and reference translation are the same or similar is still an understudied problem.

The most commonly used metrics, BLEU (Papineni et al., 2002) and alike, perform simple exact matching of n-grams between hypothesis and reference translations. Such a simple matching procedure has well known limitations, including that the matching of non-content words counts as much as the matching of content words, that variations of words with the same meaning are disregarded, and that a perfect matching can happen even if the order of sequences of n-grams in the hypothesis and reference translation are very different, changing completely the meaning of the translation.

A number of other metrics have been proposed to address these limitations, for example, by allowing for the matching of synonyms or paraphrases of content words, such as in METEOR (Denkowski and Lavie, 2010). Other attempts have been made to capture whether the reference translation and hypothesis translations share the same meaning using shallow semantics, i.e., Semantic Role Labeling (Giménez and Márquez, 2007). However, these are limited to the exact matching of semantic roles and their fillers.

We propose TINE, a new metric that complements lexical matching with a shallow semantic component to better address adequacy. The main contribution of such a metric is to provide a more flexible way of measuring the overlap between shallow semantic representations that considers both the semantic structure of the sentence and the content of the semantic elements. The metric uses SRLs such as in (Giménez and Márquez, 2007). However, it analyses the content of predicates and arguments seeking for either exact or "similar" matches. The

Proceedings of the 6th Workshop on Statistical Machine Translation, pages 116–122,
Edinburgh, Scotland, UK, July 30–31, 2011. ©2011 Association for Computational Linguistics

inexact matching is based on the use of ontologies such as VerbNet (Schuler, 2006) and distributional semantics similarity metrics, such as Dekang Lin's thesaurus (Lin, 1998) .

In the remainder of this paper we describe some related work (Section 2), present our metric - TINE - (Section 3) and its performance compared to previous work (Section 4) as well as some further improvements. We then provide an analysis of these results and discuss the limitations of the metric (Section 5) and present conclusions and future work (Section 6).

2 Related Work

A few metrics have been proposed in recent years to address the problem of measuring whether a hypothesis and a reference translation share the same meaning. The most well-know metric is probably METEOR (Banerjee and Lavie, 2005; Denkowski and Lavie, 2010). METEOR is based on a generalized concept of unigram matching between the hypothesis and the reference translation. Alignments are based on exact, stem, synonym, and paraphrase matches between words and phrases. However, the structure of the sentences is not considered.

Wong and Kit (2010) measure word choice and word order by the matching of words based on surface forms, stems, senses and semantic similarity. The informativeness of matched and unmatched words is also weighted.

Liu et al. (2010) propose to match bags of unigrams, bigrams and trigrams considering both recall and precision and F-measure giving more importance to recall, but also using WordNet synonyms.

Tratz and Hovy (2008) use transformations in order to match short syntactic units defined as Basic Elements (BE). The BE are minimal-length syntactically well defined units. For example, nouns, verbs, adjectives and adverbs can be considered BE-Unigrams, while a BE-Bigram could be formed from a syntactic relation (e.g. subject+verb, verb+object). BEs can be lexically different, but semantically similar.

Padó et al. (2009) uses Textual Entailment features extracted from the Standford Entailment Recognizer (MacCartney et al., 2006). The Textual Entailment Recognizer computes matching and mismatching features over dependency parses. The metric then predicts the MT quality with a regression model. The alignment is improved using ontologies.

He et al. (2010) measure the similarity between hypothesis and reference translation in terms of the Lexical Functional Grammar (LFG) representation. The representation uses dependency graphs to generate unordered sets of dependency triples. Calculating precision, recall, and F-score on the sets of triples corresponding to the hypothesis and reference segments allows measuring similarity at the lexical and syntactic levels. The measure also matches WordNet synonyms.

The closest related metric to the one proposed in this paper is that by Giménez and Márquez (2007) and Giménez et al. (2010), which also uses shallow semantic representations. Such a metric combines a number of components, including lexical matching metrics like BLEU and METEOR, as well as components that compute the matching of constituent and dependency parses, named entities, discourse representations and semantic roles. However, the semantic role matching is based on exact matching of roles and role fillers. Moreover, it is not clear what the contribution of this specific information is for the overall performance of the metric.

We propose a metric that uses a lexical similarity component and a semantic component in order to deal with both word choice and semantic structure. The semantic component is based on semantic roles, but instead of simply matching the surface forms (i.e. arguments and predicates) it is able to match similar words.

3 Metric Description

The rationale behind TINE is that an adequacy-oriented metric should go beyond measuring the matching of lexical items to incorporate information about the semantic structure of the sentence, as in (Giménez et al., 2010). However, the metric should also be flexible to consider inexact matches of semantic components, similar to what is done with lexical metrics like METEOR (Denkowski and Lavie, 2010). We experiment with TINE having English as target language because of the availability of linguistic processing tools for this language. The metric is particularly dependent on semantic role labeling systems, which have reached satisfactory performance for English (Carreras and Márquez, 2005). TINE uses semantic role labels (SRL) and lexical semantics to fulfill two requirements by: (i) compare both the semantic structure and its content across matching arguments in the hypothesis and reference translations; and (ii) propose alternative ways of measuring inexact matches for both predicates and role fillers. Additionally, it uses an exact lexical matching component to reward hypotheses that present the same lexical choices as the reference translation. The overall score s is defined using the simple weighted average model in Equation (1):

$$s(H, \mathbf{R}) = max \left\{ \frac{\alpha L(H, R) + \beta A(H, R)}{\alpha + \beta} \right\}_{R \in \mathbf{R}} \quad (1)$$

where H represents the hypothesis translation, R represents a reference translation contained in the set of available references $\mathbf{R}$; L defines the (exact) lexical match component in Equation (2), A defines the adequacy component in Equation (3); and α and β are tunable weights for these two components. If multiple references are provided, the score of the segment is the maximum score achieved by comparing the segment to each available reference.

$$L(H, R) = \frac{|H \bigcap R|}{\sqrt{|H| * |R|}} \quad (2)$$

The lexical match component measures the overlap between the two representations in terms of the cosine similarity metric. A segment, either a hypothesis or a reference, is represented as a bag of tokens extracted from an unstructured representation, that is, bag of unigrams (words or stems). Cosine similarity was chosen, as opposed to simply checking the percentage of overlapping words (POW) because cosine does not penalize differences in the length of the hypothesis and reference translation as much as POW. Cosine similarity normalizes the cardinality of the intersection $|H \cap R|$ using the geometric mean $\sqrt{|H| * |R|}$ instead of the union $|H \cup R|$. This is particularly important for the matching of arguments - which is also based on cosine similarity. If an hypothesized argument has the same meaning as its reference translation, but differs from it in length, cosine will penalize less the matching than POW. That is specially interesting when core arguments get merged with modifiers due to bad semantic role labeling (e.g. *[A0 I] [T bought] [A1 something to eat yesterday]* instead of *[A0 I] [T bought] [A1 something to eat] [AM-TMP yesterday]*).

$$A(H, R) = \frac{\sum_{v \in V} verb\_score(H_v, R_v)}{|V_r|} \quad (3)$$

In the adequacy component, V is the set of verbs aligned between H and R, and $|V_r|$ is the number of verbs in R. Hereafter the indexes h and r stand for hypothesis and reference translations, respectively. Verbs are aligned using VerbNet (Schuler, 2006) and VerbOcean (Chklovski and Pantel, 2004). A verb in the hypothesis v_h is aligned to a verb in the reference v_r if they are related according to the following heuristics: (i) the pair of verbs share at least one class in VerbNet; or (ii) the pair of verbs holds a relation in VerbOcean.

For example, in VerbNet the verbs *spook* and *terrify* share the same class *amuse-31.1*, and in VerbOcean the verb *dress* is related to the verb *wear*.

$$verb\_score(H_v, R_v) = \frac{\sum_{a \in A_r \cap A_t} arg\_score(H_a, R_a)}{|A_r|} \quad (4)$$

The similarity between the arguments of a verb pair (v_h, v_r) in V is measured as defined in Equation (4), where A_h and A_t are the sets of labeled arguments of the hypothesis and the reference respectively and $|A_r|$ is the number of arguments of the verb in R. In other words, we only measure the similarity of arguments in a pair of sentences that are annotated with the same role. This ensures that the structure of the sentence is taken into account (for example, an argument in the role of *agent* would not be compared against an argument in a role of *experiencer*). Additionally, by restricting the comparison to arguments of a given verb pair, we avoid argument confusion in sentences with multiple verbs.

The *arg_score*(H_a, R_a) computation is based on the cosine similarity as in Equation (2). We treat the tokens in the argument as a bag-of-words. However, in this case we change the representation of the segments. If the two sets do not match exactly, we expand both of them by adding similar words. For every mismatch in a segment, we retrieve the

20-most similar words from Dekang Lin's distributional thesaurus (Lin, 1998), resulting in sets with richer lexical variety.

The following example shows how the computation of $A(H, R)$ is performed, considering the following hypothesis and reference translations:

H: The lack of snow discourages people from ordering ski stays in hotels and boarding houses.

R: The lack of snow is putting people off booking ski holidays in hotels and guest houses.

1. extract verbs from H: V_h = {discourages, ordering}
2. extract verbs from R: V_r = {putting, booking}
3. similar verbs aligned with VerbNet (shared class get-13.5.1): V = $\{(v_h = order, v_r = book)\}$
4. compare arguments of $(v_h = order, v_r = book)$:
   A_h = {A0, A1, AM-LOC}
   A_r = {A0, A1, AM-LOC}
5. $A_h \cap A_r$ = {A0, A1, AM-LOC}
6. exact matches:
   H_{A0} = {people} and R_{A0} = {people}
   argument_score = 1
7. different word forms: expand the representation:
   H_{A1} = {ski, stays} and R_{A1} = {ski, holidays}
   expand to:
   H_{A1} = {{ski},{stays, remain... journey...}}
   R_{A1} = {{ski},{holidays, vacations, trips... journey...}}
   argument_score = 0.5
8. similarly to H_{AM-LOC} and R_{AM-LOC}
   argument_score = 0.72
9. verb_score (*order*, *book*) = $\frac{1+0.5+0.72}{3}$ = 0.74
10. $A(H, R) = \frac{0.74}{2}$ = 0.37

Different from previous work, we have not used WordNet to measure lexical similarity for two main reasons: problems with lexical ambiguity and limited coverage in WordNet (instances of named entities are not in WordNet, e.g. *Barack Obama*). For example, in WordNet the aligned verbs (*order/book*) from the previous hypothesis and reference translations have: 9 senses - *order* (e.g. give instructions to or direct somebody to do something with authority, make a request for something, etc.) - and 4 senses - *book* (engage for a performance, arrange for and reserve (something for someone else) in advance, etc.). Thus, a WordNet-based similarity measure would require disambiguating segments, an additional step and a possible source of errors. Second, a thresholds would need to be set to determine when a pair of verbs is aligned. In contrast, the structure of VerbNet (i.e. clusters of verbs) allows a binary decision, although the VerbNet heuristic results in some errors, as we discuss in Section 5.

4 Results

We set the weights α and β by experimental testing to $\alpha = 1$ and $\beta = 0.25$. The lexical component weight is prioritized because it has shown a good average Kendall's tau correlation (0.23) on a development dataset (Callison-Burch et al., 2010). Table 1 shows the correlation of the lexical component with human judgments for a number of language pairs.

Table 1: Kendall's tau segment-level correlation of the lexical component with human judgments

Metric	cz-en	fr-en	de-en	es-en	avg
Lexical	0.27	0.21	0.26	0.19	0.23

We use the SENNA[1] SRL system to tag the dataset with semantic roles. SENNA has shown to have achieved an F-measure of 75.79% for tagging semantic roles over the CoNLL 2005 [2] benchmark.

We compare our metric against standard BLEU (Papineni et al., 2002), METEOR (Denkowski and Lavie, 2010) and other previous metrics reported in (Callison-Burch et al., 2010) which also claim to use some form of semantic information (see Section 2 for their description). The comparison is made in terms of Kendall's tau correlation against the human judgments at a segment-level. For our submission to the shared evaluation task, system-level scores are obtained by averaging the segment-level scores.

TINE achieves the same average correlation with BLUE, but outperforms it for some language pairs. Additionally, TINE outperforms some of the previous which use WordNet to deal with synonyms as part of the lexical matching.

The closest metric to TINE (Giménez et al., 2010), which also uses semantic roles as one of its

[1]http://ml.nec-labs.com/senna/

[2]http://www.lsi.upc.edu/ srlconll/

Table 2: Comparison with previous semantically-oriented metrics using segment-level Kendall's tau correlation with human judgments

Metric	cz-en	fr-en	de-en	es-en	avg
(Liu et al., 2010)	0.34	0.34	0.38	0.34	0.35
(Giménez et al., 2010)	0.34	0.33	0.34	0.33	0.33
(Wong and Kit, 2010)	0.33	0.27	0.37	0.32	0.32
METEOR	0.33	0.27	0.36	0.33	0.32
TINE	0.28	0.25	0.30	0.22	0.26
BLEU	0.26	0.22	0.27	0.28	0.26
(He et al., 2010)	0.15	0.14	0.17	0.21	0.17
(Tratz and Hovy, 2008)	0.05	0.0	0.12	0.05	0.05

components, achieves better performance. However, this metric is a rather complex combination of a number of other metrics to deal with different linguistic phenomena.

4.1 Further Improvements

As an additional experiment, we use BLEU as the lexical component $L(H, R)$ in order to test if the shallow-semantic component can contribute to the performance of this standard evaluation metric. Table 3 shows the results of the combination of BLEU and the shallow-semantic component using the same parameter configuration as in Section 4. The addition of the shallow-semantic component increased the average correlation of BLEU from 0.26 to 0.28.

Table 3: TINE-B: Combination of BLEU and the shallow-semantic component

Metric	cz-en	fr-en	de-en	es-en	avg
TINE-B	0.27	0.25	0.30	0.30	0.28

Finally, we improve the tuning of the weights of the components (α and β parameters) by using a simple genetic algorithm (Back et al., 1999) to select the weights that maximize the correlation with human scores on a development set (we use the development sets from WMT10 (Callison-Burch et al., 2010)). The configuration of the genetic algorithm is as follows:

- Fitness function: Kendall's tau correlation
- Chromosome: two real numbers, α and β
- Number of individuals: 80
- Number of generations: 100
- Selection method: roulette
- Crossover probability: 0.9
- Mutation probability: 0.01

Table 4 shows the parameter values obtaining from tuning for each language pair and the correlation achieved by the metric with such parameters. With such an optimization step the average correlation of the metric increases to 0.29.

Table 4: Optimized values of the parameters using a genetic algorithm and Kendall's tau and final correlation of the metric on the test sets

Language pair	Correlation	α	β
cz-en	0.28	0.62	0.02
fr-en	0.25	0.91	0.03
de-en	0.30	0.72	0.1
es-en	0.31	0.57	0.02
avg	0.29	–	–

5 Discussion

In what follows we discuss with a few examples some of the common errors made by TINE. Overall, we consider the following categories of errors:

1. Lack of coverage of the ontologies.

   R: This year, women were awarded the Nobel Prize in all fields except physics

   H: This year the women received the Nobel prizes in all categories less physical

   The lack of coverage in VerbNet prevented the detection of the similarity between *receive* and *award*.

2. Matching of unrelated verbs.

   R: If snow falls on the slopes this week, Christmas will sell out too, says Schiefert.

   H: If the roads remain snowfall during the week, the dates of Christmas will dry up, said Schiefert.

   In VerbOcean *remain* and *say* are incorrectly

said to be related. VerbOcean was created by a semi-automatic extraction algorithm (Chklovski and Pantel, 2004) with an average accuracy of 65.5%.

3. Incorrect tagging of the semantic roles by SENNA.

   R: Colder weather is forecast for Thursday, so if anything falls, it should be snow.

   H: On Thursday , must fall temperatures and, if there is rain, in the mountains should.

   The position of the predicates affects the SRL tagging. The predicate *fall* has the following roles (A1, V, and S-A1) in the reference, and the following roles (AM-ADV, A0, AM-MOD, and AM-DIS) in the hypothesis. As a consequence, the metric cannot attempt to match the fillers. Also, SRL systems do not detect phrasal verbs such as in the example of Section 3, where the action *putting people off* is similar to *discourages*.

6 Conclusions and Future Work

We have presented an MT evaluation metric based on the alignment of semantic roles and flexible matching of role fillers between hypothesis and reference translations. To deal with inexact matches, the metric uses ontologies and distributional semantics, as opposed to lexical databases like WordNet, in order to minimize ambiguity and lack of coverage. The metric also uses an exact lexical matching component to reward hypotheses that present lexical choices similar to those of the reference translation.

Given the simplicity of the metric, it has achieved competitive results. We have shown that the addition of the shallow-semantic component into a lexical component yields absolute improvements in the correlation of 3%-6% on average, depending on the lexical component used (cosine similarity or BLEU).

In future work, in order to improve the performance of the metric we plan to add components to address a few other linguistic phenomena such as in (Giménez and Márquez, 2007; Giménez et al., 2010). In order to deal with the coverage problem of an ontology, we plan to use distributional semantics (i.e. word space models) also to align the predicates. We consider using a backoff model for the shallow-semantic component to deal with the very frequent cases where there are no comparable predicates between the reference and hypothesis translations, which result in a 0 score from the semantic component. Finally, we plan to improve the lexical component to better tackle fluency, for example, by adding information about the word order.

References

Thomas Back, David B. Fogel, and Zbigniew Michalewicz, editors. 1999. *Evolutionary Computation 1, Basic Algorithms and Operators*. IOP Publishing Ltd., Bristol, UK, 1st edition.

Satanjeev Banerjee and Alon Lavie. 2005. METEOR: An automatic metric for MT evaluation with improved correlation with human judgments. In *Proceedings of the ACL Workshop on Intrinsic and Extrinsic Evaluation Measures for Machine Translation and/or Summarization*, pages 65–72, Ann Arbor, Michigan, June.

Chris Callison-Burch, Philipp Koehn, Christof Monz, Kay Peterson, Mark Przybocki, and Omar Zaidan. 2010. Findings of the 2010 joint workshop on statistical machine translation and metrics for machine translation. In *Proceedings of the Joint Fifth Workshop on Statistical Machine Translation and MetricsMATR*, pages 17–53, Uppsala, Sweden, July.

Xavier Carreras and Lluís Márquez. 2005. Introduction to the conll-2005 shared task: Semantic role labeling. In *Proceedings of the 9th Conference on Natural Language Learning, CoNLL-2005*, Ann Arbor, MI USA.

Timothy Chklovski and Patrick Pantel. 2004. VerbOcean: Mining the Web for Fine-Grained Semantic Verb Relations. In Dekang Lin and Dekai Wu, editors, *Proceedings of EMNLP 2004*, pages 33–40, Barcelona, Spain, July.

Michael Denkowski and Alon Lavie. 2010. Meteor-next and the meteor paraphrase tables: Improved evaluation support for five target languages. In *Proceedings of the Joint Fifth Workshop on Statistical Machine Translation and MetricsMATR*, pages 339–342, July.

Jesús Giménez and Lluís Márquez. 2007. Linguistic features for automatic evaluation of heterogenous mt systems. In *Proceedings of the Second Workshop on Statistical Machine Translation*, StatMT '07, pages 256–264, Stroudsburg, PA, USA.

Jesús Giménez, Lluís Márquez, Elisabet Comelles, Irene Castellón, and Victoria Arranz. 2010. Document-level automatic mt evaluation based on discourse representations. In *Proceedings of the Joint Fifth Workshop on Statistical Machine Translation and Metrics-MATR*, WMT '10, pages 333–338, Stroudsburg, PA, USA.

Yifan He, Jinhua Du, Andy Way, and Josef van Genabith. 2010. The dcu dependency-based metric in wmt-metricsmatr 2010. In *Proceedings of the Joint Fifth Workshop on Statistical Machine Translation and MetricsMATR*, WMT '10, pages 349–353, Stroudsburg, PA, USA.

Dekang Lin. 1998. Automatic retrieval and clustering of similar words. In *Proceedings of the 36th Annual Meeting of the Association for Computational Linguistics and 17th International Conference on Computational Linguistics - Volume 2*, ACL '98, pages 768–774, Stroudsburg, PA, USA.

Chang Liu, Daniel Dahlmeier, and Hwee Tou Ng. 2010. Tesla: translation evaluation of sentences with linear-programming-based analysis. In *Proceedings of the Joint Fifth Workshop on Statistical Machine Translation and MetricsMATR*, WMT '10, pages 354–359, Stroudsburg, PA, USA.

Bill MacCartney, Trond Grenager, Marie-Catherine de Marneffe, Daniel Cer, and Christopher D. Manning. 2006. Learning to recognize features of valid textual entailments. In *Proceedings of the Human Language Technology Conference of the NAACL*, pages 41–48, New York City, USA, June.

Sebastian Padó, Daniel Cer, Michel Galley, Dan Jurafsky, and Christopher D. Manning. 2009. Measuring machine translation quality as semantic equivalence: A metric based on entailment features. *Machine Translation*, 23:181–193, September.

Kishore Papineni, Salim Roukos, Todd Ward, and Wei-Jing Zhu. 2002. Bleu: a method for automatic evaluation of machine translation. In *Proceedings of the 40th Annual Meeting on Association for Computational Linguistics*, ACL '02, pages 311–318, Stroudsburg, PA, USA.

Karin Kipper Schuler. 2006. *VerbNet: A Broad-Coverage, Comprehensive Verb Lexicon*. Ph.D. thesis, University of Pennsylvania.

Stephen Tratz and Eduard Hovy. 2008. Summarisation evaluation using transformed basic elements. In *Proceedings TAC 2008*.

Billy T.-M. Wong and Chunyu Kit. 2010. The parameter-optimized atec metric for mt evaluation. In *Proceedings of the Joint Fifth Workshop on Statistical Machine Translation and MetricsMATR*, WMT '10, pages 360–364, Stroudsburg, PA, USA.

Regression and Ranking based Optimisation for Sentence Level Machine Translation Evaluation

Xingyi Song and **Trevor Cohn**
The Department of Computer Science
University of Sheffield
Sheffield, S1 4DP. UK
{xsong2,t.cohn}@shef.ac.uk

Abstract

Automatic evaluation metrics are fundamentally important for Machine Translation, allowing comparison of systems performance and efficient training. Current evaluation metrics fall into two classes: heuristic approaches, like BLEU, and those using supervised learning trained on human judgement data. While many trained metrics provide a better match against human judgements, this comes at the cost of including lots of features, leading to unwieldy, non-portable and slow metrics. In this paper, we introduce a new trained metric, ROSE, which only uses simple features that are easy portable and quick to compute. In addition, ROSE is sentence-based, as opposed to document-based, allowing it to be used in a wider range of settings. Results show that ROSE performs well on many tasks, such as ranking system and syntactic constituents, with results competitive to BLEU. Moreover, this still holds when ROSE is trained on human judgements of translations into a different language compared with that use in testing.

1 Introduction

Human judgements of translation quality are very expensive. For this reason automatic MT evaluation metrics are used to as an approximation by comparing predicted translations to human authored references. An early MT evaluation metric, BLEU (Papineni et al., 2002), is still the most commonly used metric in automatic machine translation evaluation. However, several drawbacks have been stated by many researchers (Chiang et al., 2008a; Callison-Burch et al., 2006; Banerjee and Lavie, 2005), most notably that it omits recall (substituting this with a penalty for overly short output) and not being easily applied at the sentence level. Later heuristic metrics such as METEOR (Banerjee and Lavie, 2005) and TER (Snover et al., 2006) account for both precision and recall, but their relative weights are difficult to determine manually.

In contrast to heuristic metrics, trained metrics use supervised learning to model directly human judgements. This allows the combination of different features and can better fit specific tasks, such as evaluation focusing more on fluency/adequacy/relative ranks or post editing effort. Previous work includes approaches using classification (Corston-Oliver et al., 2001), regression (Albercht and Hwa, 2008; Specia and Gimenez, 2010), and ranking (Duh, 2008). Most of which achieved good results and better correlations with human judgments than heuristic baseline methods.

Overall automatic metrics must find a balance between several key issues: a) applicability to different sized texts (documents vs sentences), b) easy of portability to different languages, c) runtime requirements and d) correlation with human judgement data. Previous work has typically ignored at least one of these issues, e.g., BLEU which applies only to documents (A), trained metrics (Albercht and Hwa, 2008; Specia and Gimenez, 2010) which tend to ignore B and C.

This paper presents ROSE, a trained metric which is loosely based on BLEU, but seeks to further simplify its components such that it can be used for sentence level evaluation. This contrasts with BLEU which is defined over large documents, and must

Proceedings of the 6th Workshop on Statistical Machine Translation, pages 123–129,
Edinburgh, Scotland, UK, July 30–31, 2011.

be coarsely approximated to allow sentence level application. The increased flexibility of ROSE allows the metric to be used in a wider range of situations, including during decoding. ROSE is a linear model with a small number of simple features, and is trained using regression or ranking against human judgement data. A benefit of using only simple features is that ROSE can be trivially ported between target languages, and that it can be run very quickly. Features include precision and recall over different sized n-grams, and the difference in word counts between the candidate and the reference sentences, which is further divided into content word, function word and punctuation. An extended versions also includes features over Part of Speech (POS) sequences.

The paper is structured as follows: Related work on metrics for statistical machine translation is described in Section 2. Four variations of ROSE and their features will be introduced in Section 3. In section 4 we presents the result, showing how ROSE correlates well with human judgments on both system and sentence levels. Conclusions are given at the end of the paper.

2 Related Work

The defacto standard metric in machine translation is BLEU (Papineni et al., 2002). This measures n-gram precision (n normally equal to 1,2,3,4) between a document of candidate sentences and a set of human authored reference documents. The idea is that high quality translations share many n-grams with the references. In order to reduce repeatedly generating the same word, BLEU clips the counts of each candidate N-gram to the maximum counts of that n-gram that in references, and with a brevity penalty to down-scale the score for output shorter than the reference. In BLEU, each n-gram precision is given equal weight in geometric mean, while NIST (Doddington and George, 2002) extended BLEU by assigning more informative n-grams higher weight.

However, BLEU and NIST have several drawbacks, the first being that BLEU uses a geometric mean over all n-grams which makes BLEU almost unusable for sentence level evaluations [1]. Secondly, BLEU and NIST both use the brevity penalty to replace recall, but Banerjee and Lavie (2005) in experiments show that the brevity penalty is a poor substitute for recall.

Banerjee and Lavie (2005) proposed a METEOR metric, which that uses recall instead of the BP. Callison-Burch et al. (2007; Callison-Burch et al. (2008) show that METEOR does not perform well in out of English task. This may because that Stemmer or WordNet may not available in some languages, which unable to model synonyms in these cases. In addition, the performance also varies when adjusting weights in precision and recall.

Supervised learning approaches have been proposed by many researchers (Corston-Oliver et al., 2001; Duh, 2008; Albercht and Hwa, 2008; Specia and Gimenez, 2010). Corston-Oliver et al. (2001) use a classification method to measure machine translation system quality at the sentence level as being human-like translation (good) or machine translated (bad). Features extracted from references and machine translation include heavy linguistic features (requires parser).

Quirk (2004) proposed a linear regression model which is trained to match translation quality. Albercht and Hwa (2008) introduced pseudo-references when data driven regression does not have enough training data. Most recently, Specia and Gimenez (2010) combined confidence estimation (without reference, just using the source) and reference-based metrics together in a regression framework to measure sentence-level machine translation quality.

Duh (2008) compared the ranking with the regression, with the results that with same feature set, ranking and regression have similar performance, while ranking can tolerate more training data noise.

3 Model

ROSE is a trained automatic MT evaluation metric that works on sentence level. It is defined as a linear model, and its weights will be trained by Support Vector Machine. It is formulated as

$$S = \overrightarrow{w} \cdot f(\overrightarrow{c}, \overrightarrow{r}) \quad (1)$$

where $\overrightarrow{w}$ is the feature weights vector, $f(\overrightarrow{c}, \overrightarrow{r})$ is the feature function which takes candidate transla-

[1] Note that various approximations exits (Lin and Och, 2004; Chiang et al., 2008b)

tion ($\vec{c}$) and reference ($\vec{c}$), and returns the feature vector. S is the response variable, measuring the 'goodness' of the candidate translation. A higher score means a better translation, although the magnitude is not always meaningful.

We present two different method for training: a linear regression approach ROSE-reg, trained to match human evaluation score, and a ranking approach ROSE-rank to match the relative ordering of pairs of translations assigned by human judge. Unlike ROSE-reg, ROSE-rank only gives relative score between sentences, such as A is better than B. The features that used in ROSE will be listed in section 3.1, and the regression and ranking training are described in section 3.2

ID	Description
1-4	n-gram precision, n=1...4
5-8	n-gram recall, n=1...4
9-12	n-gram f-measure, n=1...4
13	Average n-gram precision
14	Words count
15	Function words count
16	Punctuation count
17	Content words count
18-21	n-gram POS precision, n=1...4
22-25	n-gram POS recall, n=1...4
26-29	n-gram POS f-measure, n=1...4
30-33	n-gram POS string mixed precision, n=1...4

Table 1: ROSE Features. The first column is the feature number. The dashed line separates the core features from the POS extended features.

3.1 ROSE Features

Features used in ROSE listed in Table 1 include string n-gram matching, Word count and Part of Speech (POS). String N-gram matching features, are used for measure how closely of the candidate sentence resembles the reference. Both precision and recall are considered. Word count features measure length differences between the candidate and reference, which is further divided into function words, punctuation and content words. POS features are defined over POS n-gram matches between the candidate and reference.

3.1.1 String Matching Features

The string matching features include n-gram precision, n-gram recall and F1-measure. N-gram precision measures matches between sequence of words in the candidate sentence compared to the references,

$$P_n = \frac{\sum_{\text{n-gram} \in \vec{c}} Count(\text{n-gram})[\![\text{n-gram} \in \vec{r}]\!]}{\sum_{\text{n-gram} \in \vec{c}} Count(\text{ngram})} \quad (2)$$

where $Count$ are the occurrence counts of n-grams in the candidate sentence, the numerator measures the number of predicted n-grams that also occur in the reference.

Recall is also used in ROSE, so clipping was deemed unnecessary in precision calculation, where the repeating words will increasing precision but at the expense of recall. F-measure is also included, which is the harmonic mean of precision and recall. With there are multiple references, the n-gram precision error uses the same strategy as BLEU: n-grams in candidate can match any of the references. For recall, ROSE will match the n-grams in each reference separately, and then choose the recall for the reference with minimum error.

3.1.2 Word Count Features

The word count features measure the length difference between a candidate sentence and reference sentence. In a sentence, content words are more informative than function words (grammatical words) and punctuation. Therefore, the number of content word candidate is a important indicator in evaluation. In this case, besides measuring the length at whole sentences, we also measure difference in the number of *function words*, *punctuation* and *content words*. We normalise by the length of the reference which allows comparability between short versus long sentences. In multiple reference cases we choose the ratio that is closest to 1.

3.1.3 Part of Speech Features

The string matching features and word count features only measure similarities on the lexical level, but not over sentence structure or synonyms. To add this capability we also include Part of Speech (POS) features which work similar to the String Matching features, but using POS instead of words. The features measure precision, recall and F-measure over POS n-grams (n=1...4). In addition, we also include features that mixed string and POS.

The string/POS mixed feature is used for handling synonyms. One problem in string n-gram matching is not being able to deal with the synonyms between the candidate translation and the reference. One approach for doing so is to use an external resource such as WordNet (Banerjee and Lavie, 2005), however this would limit the portability of the metric. Instead we use POS as a proxy. In most of the cases, synonyms share the same POS, so this can be rewarded by forming n-grams over a mixture of tokens and POS. During the matching process, both words and its POS shall be considered, if either matches between reference and candidate, the n-gram matches will be counted.

Considering the example in table 2, candidate 1 has better translation than candidate 2 and 3. If only the string N-gram matching is used, that will give the same score to candidate 1, 2 and 3. The n-gram precision scores obtained by all candidate sentences in this example are: 2-gram = 1, 3-gram = 0. However, we can at least distinguish candidate 1 is better than candidate 3 if string POS mixed precision is used , n-gram precision for candidate 1 will be: 2-gram = 2, 3-gram = 1, which ranks candidate 1 better than candidate 3.

Example
reference: A/DT red/ADJ vehicle/NN
candidate 1: A/DT red/ADJ car/NN
candidate 2: A/DT red/ADJ rose/NN
candidate 3: A/DT red/ADJ red/ADJ

Table 2: Evaluation Example

3.2 Training

The model was trained on human evaluation data in two different ways, regression and ranking.These both used SVM-light (Joachims, 1999). In the ranking model, the training data are candidate translation and their relative rankings were ranked by human judge for a given input sentence. The SVM finds the minimum magnitude weights that are able to correctly rank training data which is framed as a series of constraints reflecting all pairwise comparisons. A soft-margin formulation is used to allow training errors with a penalty (Joachims, 2002). For regression, the training data is human annotation of post-edit effort (this will be further described in section 4.1). The Support vector Regression learns weights with minimum magnitude that limit prediction error to within an accepted range, again with a soft-margin formulation (Smola and Schlkopf, 2004).

A linear kernel function will be used, because non-linear kernels are much slower to use and are not decomposable. Our experiments showed that the linear kernel performed at similar accuracy to other kernel functions (see section 4.2).

4 Experimental Setup

Our experiments test ROSE performance on document level with three different Kernel functions: linear, polynomial and radial basis function. Then we compare four variants of ROSE with BLEU on both sentence and system (document) level.

The BLEU version we used here is NIST Open MT Evaluation tool mteval version 13a, smoothing was disabled and except for the sentence level evaluation experiment. The system level evaluation procedure follows WMT08 (Callison-Burch et al., 2008), which ranked each system submitted on WMT08 in three types of tasks:

- **Rank:** Human judges candidate sentence rank in order of quality. On the document level, documents are ranked according to the proportion of candidate sentences in a document that are better than all of the candidates.

- **Constituent:** The constituent task is the same as for ranking but operates over chosen syntactic constituents.

- **Yes/No:** WMT08 Yes/No task is to let human judge decide whether the particular part of a sentence is acceptable or not. Document level Yes/No ranks a document according to their number of YES sentences

Spearman's rho correlation was used to measure the quality of the metrics on system level. Four target languages (English, German, French and Spanish) were used in system level experiments. ROSE-reg and ROSE-rank were tested in all target language sets, but ROSE-regpos was only tested in the into-English set as it requires a POS tagger. On the sentence level, we compare sentences ranking that ranked by metrics against human ranking. The evaluation quality was examined by Kendall's tau correlation, and tied results from human judges were excluded.

Rank	**es-en**	**fr-en**	**de-en**	**avg**
Linear	0.57	0.97	0.69	0.74
Polynomial	**0.62**	0.97	**0.71**	**0.76**
RBF	0.60	**0.98**	0.62	0.73
Constituent				
Linear	0.79	0.90	0.39	0.69
Polynomial	0.80	0.89	**0.41**	**0.70**
RBF	**0.83**	**0.93**	0.34	**0.70**
Yes/No				
Linear	**0.92**	**0.93**	**0.67**	**0.84**
Polynomial	0.86	0.90	0.66	0.81
RBF	0.87	**0.93**	0.65	0.82

Table 3: ROSE-reg in with SVM kernel functions

Metric	**Kendall's tau**
BLEU-smoothed	**0.219**
ROSE-reg	0.120
ROSE-regpos	0.164
ROSE-rank	0.206
ROSE-rankpos	0.172

Table 4: Sentence Level Evaluation

4.1 Data

Training data used for ROSE is from WMT10 (Callison-Burch et al., 2010) human judged sentences. A regression model was trained by sentences with human annotation for post editing effort. The three levels used in WMT10 are 'OK', 'EDIT' and 'BAD', which we treat as response values of 3, 2 and 1. In total 2885 sentences were used in the regression training. The ranking model was trained by sentences with human annotating sentence ranking, and tied results are allowed in training. In this experiment, 1675 groups of sentences were used for training, and each group contains five sentences, which are manually ranked from 5 (best) to 1 (worst). In order to test the ROSE's ability to adapt the language without training data, ROSE was only trained with English data.

The testing data on sentence level used in this paper is human ranked sentences from WMT09 (Callison-Burch et al., 2009). Tied rankings were removed, leaving 1702 pairs. We only consider translations into English sentences. On system level, the testing data are the submissions for 'test2008' test set in WMT08 (Callison-Burch et al., 2008). ROSE, and BLEU were compared with human ranked submitted system in 'RANK', 'CONSTITUENT' and 'YES/NO' tasks.

English punctuation and 100 common function words list of four languages in this experiment were generated. English POS was tagged by NLTK (Bird and Loper, 2004).

4.2 Results and Discussion

Table 3 shows the results of ROSE-reg with three different SVM Kernel functions. Performance are similar among three different Kernel functions. However, the linear kernel is the fastest and simplest and there is no overall winner. Therefore, linear Kernel function was used in ROSE.

The results of Kendall's tau on sentence level evaluation are shown in Table 4. According to Table 4 ROSE-rank has the highest score in all versions of ROSE. The score is close to the smoothed version of BLEU. Results also showed adding POS feature helped in improving accuracy in the regression model, but not in ranking, The reason for this is not clear, but it may be due to over fitting.

Table 5 and Table 6 are the Spearman's rho in system ranking. Table 5 is the task evaluation for translation into English. ROSE-rank performed the best in the system ranking task. Also, ROSE-regpos is the best in the syntactic constituents task. This may because of ROSE-rank is a ranking based metric and ROSE-regpos incorporates POS that contains more linguistic information. Table 6 shows the results of evaluating translations from English. According to the table, ROSE performs less accurately than for the into-English tasks, but overall the ROSE scores are similar to those of BLEU.

Rank	**es-en**	**fr-en**	**de-en**	**avg**
BLEU	0.66	0.97	0.69	0.77
ROSE-reg	0.57	0.97	0.69	0.74
ROSE-rank	**0.85**	0.96	**0.76**	**0.86**
ROSE-regpos	0.59	**0.98**	0.71	0.76
ROSE-rankpos	0.83	0.96	0.69	0.82
Constituent				
BLEU	0.78	0.92	0.30	0.67
ROSE-reg	**0.79**	0.90	0.39	0.69
ROSE-rank	0.66	0.92	0.33	0.64
ROSE-regpos	**0.79**	0.90	**0.41**	**0.70**
ROSE-rankpos	0.64	**0.93**	0.31	0.63
Yes/No				
BLEU	**0.99**	**0.96**	0.66	**0.87**
ROSE-reg	0.92	0.93	**0.67**	0.84
ROSE-rank	0.78	**0.96**	0.61	0.78
ROSE-regpos	0.97	0.93	0.66	0.85
ROSE-rankpos	0.81	**0.96**	0.57	0.78

Table 5: System Level evaluation that translation into English

5 Conclusion

We presented the ROSE metric to make up for several drawbacks of BLEU and other trained metrics. Features including string matching, words ratio and POS were combined by the supervised learning approach. ROSE's overall performance was close to BLEU on system level and sentence level. However, it is better on tasks ROSE was specifically trained, such as ROSE-rank in the system level ranking task and ROSE-regpos in the syntactic constituents task. Results also showed that when training data is not available in the right language ROSE produces reasonable results.

Smoothed BLEU slightly outperformed ROSE in sentence evaluation. This might be due to the training data not being expert judgments, and consequently very noisy. In further work, we shall modify the training method to better tolerate noise. In addition, we will modify ROSE by substitute less informative features with more informative features in order to improve its performance and reduce over fitting.

Rank	**es-en**	**fr-en**	**de-en**	**avg**
BLEU	**0.85**	**0.98**	0.88	**0.90**
ROSE-reg	0.75	**0.98**	0.93	0.89
ROSE-rank	0.69	0.93	**0.94**	0.85
Constituent				
BLEU	**0.83**	**0.87**	0.35	**0.68**
ROSE-reg	0.73	**0.87**	**0.36**	0.65
ROSE-rank	0.72	0.78	0.32	0.61
Yes/No				
BLEU	0.75	**0.97**	0.89	0.87
ROSE-reg	0.72	**0.97**	**0.93**	0.87
ROSE-rank	**0.82**	0.96	0.87	**0.88**

Table 6: System Level evaluation that translation from English

References

Josha S. Albercht and Rebecca Hwa. 2008. Regression for machine translation evaluation at the sentence level. *Machine Translation*, 22:1–27.

Satanjeev Banerjee and Alon Lavie. 2005. Meteor: An automatic metric for mt evaluation with improved correlation with human judgments. *Proceedings of the ACL-05 Workshop*.

Steven Bird and Edward Loper. 2004. Nltk: The natural language toolkit. In *Proceedings of the ACL demonstration session*, pages 214–217, Barcelona, July.

Chris Callison-Burch, Miles Osborne, and Philipp Koehn. 2006. Re-evaluating the role of bleu in machine translation research. In *In EACL*, pages 249–256.

Chris Callison-Burch, Cameron Fordyce, Philipp Koehn, Christof Monz, and Josh Schroeder. 2007. (meta-) evaluation of machine translation. In *Proceedings of the Second Workshop on Statistical Machine Translation*, pages 136–158, Prague, Czech Republic, June. Association for Computational Linguistics.

Chris Callison-Burch, Cameron Fordyce, Philipp Koehn, Christof Monz, and Josh Schroeder. 2008. Further meta-evaluation of machine translation. In *Proceedings of the Third Workshop on Statistical Machine Translation*, pages 70–106, Columbus, Ohio, June. Association for Computational Linguistics.

Chris Callison-Burch, Philipp Koehn, Christof Monz, and Josh Schroeder. 2009. Findings of the 2009 Workshop on Statistical Machine Translation. In *Proceedings of the Fourth Workshop on Statistical Machine Translation*, pages 1–28, Athens, Greece, March. Association for Computational Linguistics.

Chris Callison-Burch, Philipp Koehn, Christof Monz, Kay Peterson, Mark Przybocki, and Omar Zaidan.

2010. Findings of the 2010 joint workshop on statistical machine translation and metrics for machine translation. In *Proceedings of the Joint Fifth Workshop on Statistical Machine Translation and MetricsMATR*, pages 17–53, Uppsala, Sweden, July. Association for Computational Linguistics. Revised August 2010.

David Chiang, Steve DeNeefe, Yee Seng Chan, and Hwee Tou Ng. 2008a. Decomposability of translation metrics for improved evaluation and efficient algorithms. In *Proceedings of the Conference on Empirical Methods in Natural Language Processing*, EMNLP '08, pages 610–619, Stroudsburg, PA, USA. Association for Computational Linguistics.

David Chiang, Yuval Marton, and Philip Resnik. 2008b. Online large-margin training of syntactic and structural translation features. In *Proceedings of the Conference on Empirical Methods in Natural Language Processing*, EMNLP '08, pages 224–233, Stroudsburg, PA, USA. Association for Computational Linguistics.

Simon Corston-Oliver, Michael Gamon, and Chris Brockett. 2001. A machine learning approach to the automatic evaluation of machine translation. In *proceedings of the Association for Computational Linguistics*.

Doddington and George. 2002. Automatic evaluation of machine translation quality using n-gram cooccurrence statistics. In *Proceedings of the second international conference on Human Language Technology Research*, HLT '02, pages 138–145, San Francisco, CA, USA. Morgan Kaufmann Publishers Inc.

Kevin Duh. 2008. Ranking vs. regression in machine translation evaluation. In *In Proceedings of the Third Workshop on Statistical Machine Translation*, pages 191–194, Columbus,Ohio,, June.

T. Joachims. 1999. Making large-scale svm learning practical. *Advances in Kernel Methods - Support Vector Learning,*.

T. Joachims. 2002. Optimizing search engines using clickthrough data. In *Proceedings of the ACM Conference on Knowledge Discovery and Data Mining (KDD)*.

Chin-Yew Lin and Franz Josef Och. 2004. Orange: a method for evaluating automatic evaluation metrics for machine translation. In *Proceedings of the 20th international conference on Computational Linguistics*, COLING '04, Stroudsburg, PA, USA. Association for Computational Linguistics.

Kishore Papineni, Salim Roukos, Todd Ward, and Wei-Jing Zhu. 2002. Bleu: a method for automatic evaluation of machine translation. In *Proceedings of the 40th Annual Meeting on Association for Computational Linguistics*, ACL '02, pages 311–318, Stroudsburg, PA, USA. Association for Computational Linguistics.

C Quirk. 2004. Training a sentence-level machine translation confidence measure. In *In: Proceedings of the international conference on language resources and evaluation*, pages 825–828, Lisbon, Portugal.

Alex J. Smola and Bernhard Schlkopf. 2004. A tutorial on support vector regression. *STATISTICS AND COMPUTING*, 14:199–222.

Matthew Snover, Bonnie Dorr, Richard Schwartz, Linnea Micciulla, and Ralph Weischedel. 2006. A study of translation error rate with targeted human annotation.

L. Specia and J. Gimenez. 2010. Combining confidence estimation and reference-based metrics for segment-level mt evaluation. In *The Ninth Conference of the Association for Machine Translation in the Americas*, Denver,Colorado.

MAISE: A Flexible, Configurable, Extensible Open Source Package for Mass AI System Evaluation

Omar F. Zaidan
Dept. of Computer Science
and
The Center for Language and Speech Processing
Johns Hopkins University
Baltimore, MD 21218, USA
ozaidan@cs.jhu.edu

Abstract

The past few years have seen an increasing interest in using Amazon's Mechanical Turk for purposes of collecting data and performing annotation tasks. One such task is the mass *evaluation* of system output in a variety of tasks. In this paper, we present MAISE, a package that allows researchers to evaluate the output of their AI system(s) using human judgments collected via Amazon's Mechanical Turk, greatly streamlining the process. MAISE is open source, easy to run, and platform-independent. The core of MAISE's codebase was used for the manual evaluation of WMT10, and the completed package is being used again in the current evaluation for WMT11. In this paper, we describe the main features, functionality, and usage of MAISE, which is now available for download and use.

1 Introduction

The ability to evaluate system output is one of the most important aspects of system development. A properly designed evaluation paradigm could help researchers test and illustrate the effectiveness, or lack thereof, of any changes made to their system. The use of an automatic metric, whether it is a simple one such as classification accuracy, or a more task-specific metric such as BLEU and TER for machine translation, has become a standard part of any evaluation of empricial methods. There is also extensive interest in exploring *manual* evaluation of system outputs, and in making such a process feasible and efficient, time- and cost-wise. Such human feedback would also be valuable because it would help identify systematic errors and guide future system development.

Amazon's Mechanical Turk (MTurk) is a virtual marketplace that allows anyone to create and post tasks to be completed by human workers around the globe. Each instance of those tasks, called a Human Intelligence Task (HIT) in MTurk lingo, typically requires human understanding and perception that machines are yet to achieve, hence making MTurk an example of "artificial artificial intelligence," as the developers of MTurk aptly put it. Arguably, the most attractive feature of MTurk is the low cost associated with completing HITs and the speed at which they are completed.

Having discovered this venue, many researchers in the fields of artificial intelligence and machine learning see MTurk as a valuable and effective source of annotations, labels, and data, namely the kind requiring human knowledge.

One such kind of data is indeed human evaluation of system outputs. For instance, if you construct several speech recognition systems, and would like to know how well each of the systems performs, you could create HITs on MTurk that 'showcase' the transcriptions obtained by the different systems, and ask annotators to indicate which systems are superior and which ones are inferior. The same can be applied to a variety of tasks, such as machine translation, object recognition, emotion detection, etc.

The aim of the MAISE package is to streamline the process of creating those evaluation tasks and uploading the relevant content to MTurk to be judged, without having to familiarize and involve oneself with the mechanics, if you will, of Mechanical Turk. This would allow you to spend more time worrying about improving your system rather than dealing with file input and output and MTurk's sometimes finicky interface.

Proceedings of the 6th Workshop on Statistical Machine Translation, pages 130–134,
Edinburgh, Scotland, UK, July 30–31, 2011.

2 Overview

MAISE is a collection of tools for Mass AI System Evaluation. MAISE allows you to evaluate the output of different systems (and/or different variations of a system) using the workforce of Amazon's Mechanical Turk (MTurk). MAISE can be used to compare two simple variants of the same system, working with a couple of variations of your task, or it can be used to perform complete evaluation campaigns involving tens of systems and many variations.

The core of MAISE's codebase was written to run the manual component of WMT10's evaluation campaign. In the manual evaluation, various MT systems are directly compared to each other, by annotators who indicate which systems produce better outputs (i.e. better translations). Starting in 2010, the evaluation moved from using a locally hosted web server, and onto MTurk, taking advantage of MTurk's existing infrastructure, and making available the option to collect data from a large pool of annotators, if desired, rather than relying solely on recruited volunteers. That evaluation campaign involved around 170 submissions over eight different language pairs. In 2011, the number increased to 190 submissions over ten language pairs.

We note here that although MAISE was written with MT in mind, it **can** be used for other ML/AI tasks as well. Some of the supported features are meant to make MT evaluation easier (e.g. MAISE is aware of which language is being translated to and from), but those could simply be ignored for other tasks. As long as the task has some concept of 'input' and some concept of 'output' (e.g. a foreign sentence and a machine translation), then MAISE is appropriate.

Given this paper's venue of publication, the remainder of the paper assumes the task at hand is machine translation.

3 The Mechanics of MAISE

The components of MAISE have been designed to completely eliminate the need to write any data processing code, and to minimize the need for the user to perform any manual tasks on MTurk's interface, since MAISE facilitates communication with MTurk. Whenever MAISE needs to communicate with MTurk, it will rely on MTurk's Java SDK, which is already included in the MAISE release (allowed under the SDK's license, Apache License V2.0).

Once you create your evaluation tasks and upload the necessary content to MTurk, workers will begin to complete the corresponding HITs. On a regular (e.g. daily) basis, you will tell MAISE to retrieve the new judgments that workers provided since the last time MAISE checked. The process continues until either all your tasks are completed, or you decide you have enough judgments.

You can use MAISE with any evaluation setup you like, as long as you design the user interface for it. Currently, MAISE comes with existing support for a particular evaluation setup that asks annotators to rank the outputs of different systems relative to each other. When we say "existing support" we mean the user interface is included, and so is an analysis tool that can make sense of the judgments. This way, you don't need to do anything extra to obtain rankings of the systems. You can read more about this evaluation setup in the overview papers of the Workshop on Statistical Machine Translation (WMT) for the past two years.

3.1 Requirements and Setup

MAISE is quite easy to use. Beyond compiling a few Java programs, there is no need to install anything, modify environment variables, etc. Furthermore, since it is Java-based, it is completely platform-independent.

To use MAISE, you will need:

- Java 6
- Apache Ant
- A hosting location (where you place certain HTML files)
- An MTurk Requester account

You will also need an active Internet connection whenever new tasks need to be uploaded to MTurk, and whenever judgments need to be collected from MTurk. The setup details are beyond the scope of this paper, but are straightforward, and can be found in MAISE's documentation, including guidance with all the MTurk-related administrative issues (e.g. the last point in the above list).

3.2 Essential Files

MAISE will assume that the user has a certain set of "essential files" that contain all the needed information to perform an evaluation. These files are:

1) **The system outputs** should be in plain text format, one file per system. The filenames should follow the pattern `PROJECT.xx-yy.sysname`, where `PROJECT` is any identifying string chosen by the user, `xx` is a short name for the source language, and `yy` is a short name for the the target language.

2) **The source files** should be in plain text as well, one file per language pair. The source filenames should follow the pattern `PROJECT.xx-yy.src`, where `PROJECT` matches the identifying string used in the submission filenames. (The contents of such a file are in the `xx` language.)

3) **The reference files**, also one per language pair, with filenames `PROJECT.xx-yy.ref`. (The contents of such a file are in the `yy` language.)

4) **A specification file** that contains values for various parameters about the project (e.g. the location of the above files).

5) **A batch details file** that contains information about the desired number of MTurk tasks and their particular properties.

As one could see, the user need only provide the bare minimum to get their evaluation started. More details about items (4) and (5) are provided in the documentation. Essentially, they are easily readable and editable files, and all the user needs to do to create them is to fill out the provided templates.

3.3 The Components of MAISE

There are three main steps necessary to perform an evaluation on MTurk: **create** the evaluation tasks, **upload** them to MTurk, and **retrieve** answers for them. Each of those three steps corresponds to a single component in MAISE.

3.3.1 The `BatchCreator`

The first step is to create some input files for MTurk: the files that contain actual instantiations of our tasks, with actual sentences. This will be the first step that requires you to make some real executive decisions regarding your tasks. Among other things, you will decide how many judgments to collect and who to allow to give you those judgments.

Each **batch** corresponds to a single task on MTurk. Typically, each batch corresponds to a single language pair. So, if you are performing a full evaluation campaign, you would be creating as many batches as there are language pairs. If you are merely comparing several variants of the same system, say, for Arabic-English, you would probably have just one batch.

That said, you may have more than one batch for the same language pair, that nonetheless differ in other properties. In fact, each batch has a number of settings that need to be specified, including:

1) what language pair does this batch involve?

2) how many HITs does this batch include?

3) how many times should each HIT be completed?

4) what is the reward per assignment?

5) what are the qualifications necessary for an annotator to be allowed to perform the task (e.g. location, approval rating)?

Those settings are all specified in a single file, the abovementioned **batch details file**. The user them simply runs the `BatchCreator` component, which processes all this information and creates the necessary files for each batch.

3.3.2 The `Uploader`

After the `BatchCreator` creates the different files for the different batches, those files must be uploaded to MTurk in order to create the various batches. There will be a single file, called the *upload info file*, that contains the locations of the files to be uploaded. The upload info file is created automatically, and all the user needs to do is pass it as a parameter to the next MAISE component, the `Uploader`.

The Uploader communicates with MTurk via a web connection. Once it has completed execution, HITs for your tasks will start to appear on the MTurk website, available for MTurk's workers to view and complete them.

3.3.3 The Retriever

At this point, you would be waiting for Turkers to find your task and start accepting HITs and completing them. You can retrieve those answers by using another MAISE component that communicates with MTurk called the Retriever. It can be instructed to retrieve all answers for your HITs or only a subset of them. It retrieves all the answers for those HITs, and appends those answers to an answer log file.

Note that the Retriever does not necessarily approve any of the newly submitted assignments. It can be instructed to explicitly retrieve those answers without approving them, giving you the chance to first review them for quality. Alternatively, it can be instructed to approve the assignments as it retrieves them, and also to reject certain assignments or certain annotators that you have identified as being of sub-par quality. All this information is placed in plain text files, easy to create and maintain.

When you use MAISE to perform an actual evaluation on MTurk, you should run the Retriever fairly regularly, perhaps once every day or two. Each time, review the retrieved results, and rerun the Retriever in "decision mode" enabled, to aprove/reject the pending submissions.

4 Analyzing the Results: An Example

Once the tasks have been completed, all the answers will have been written into an *answers log file*. The log file is in plain format, and contains extensive information about each HIT completed, including a worker ID, time required to complete, and, of course, the answers themselves. Naturally, analyzing the results of the evaluation depends on what the task was, and what the interface you designed looks like. You can write your own code to read the log file and make sense out of them.

MAISE already comes equipped with an analysis tool for one particular task: the *ranking task*. In this setup, the annotator evaluates system outputs by **ranking** them from best to worst. The rank labels are interpreted as pairwise comparisons (e.g. 5 rank labels correspond to $\binom{5}{2} = 10$ pairwise comparisons), and each system is assigned a score reflecting how often it wins those pairwise comparisons. This is the setup used in the evaluation campaigns of WMT10 and WMT11.

The analysis tool takes as input the answers log file as is, and extracts from it all the rank labels. Each system's score is computed, and the tool produces a table for each language pair displaying the participating systems, in descending order of their scores. It also creates an additional *head-to-head* table, that summarizes for a specific pair of systems how often each system outranked the other. The output is created in HTML format, for easy viewing in a browser.

Furthermore, the tool produces a detailed **worker profile table**. Each row in this table corresponds to one worker, identified by their Amazon worker ID, and includes certain measures that can help guide you identify bad workers, who are either clicking randomly, or perhaps simply not doing the task properly. Those measures include:

- **Average time required per HIT**: a suspiciously fast annotator might not be performing the task diligently.
- **The *reference preference rate* (RPR)**: how often did the annotator correctly prefer an embedded reference translation; a low RPR almost certainly indicates random clicking, with typical good values at 0.97 and up.
- **Prevalence of tied rank labels**: an overly high percentage of tied comparisons indicates an overly 'conservative' worker, hesitant to distinguish between outputs.
- **The annotator's intra-annotator agreement**: i.e. the annotator's consistency with themselves, based on how often they repeated the same judgment when comparing the same system pair.

To appreciate the tool's output, the reader is encouraged to view the results of a real-life evaluation campaign at http://bit.ly/jJYzkO. These are results of analyzing 85,000+ rank labels in an evaluation campaign of 40+ MT systems over six language pairs.

5 Download and Licensing

MAISE can be obtained from the author's webpage: `http://cs.jhu.edu/~ozaidan/maise/`. The release includes MAISE's source code, instructions, documentation, and a tutorial. MAISE is an open-source tool, licensed under the terms of the GNU Lesser General Public License (LGPL). Therefore, it is free for personal and scientific use by individuals and/or research groups. It may not be modified or redistributed, publicly or privately, unless the licensing terms are observed. If in doubt, contact the author for clarification and/or an explicit permission. The distribution also includes the MTurk Java SDK v1.2.2, which is licensed under the terms of the Apache License V2.0.

Acknowledgments

I developed MAISE while I was funded by DARPA's GALE Program, and in part by the EuroMatrixPlus Project. I would like to thank Chris Callison-Burch, Ondřej Bojar, and everybody who gave feedback during the WMT10 evaluation campaign. More importantly, much thanks goes to Josh Schroeder, the author of the previous implementation used pre-2010, who helped me navigate his code when I first started reimplementing the data processing components.

References

Chris Callison-Burch, Philipp Koehn, Christof Monz, Kay Peterson, Mark Przybocki, and Omar Zaidan. 2010. Findings of the 2010 joint workshop on statistical machine translation and metrics for machine translation. In *Proceedings of the Joint Fifth Workshop on Statistical Machine Translation and MetricsMATR*, pages 17–53, Uppsala, Sweden, July. Association for Computational Linguistics.

MANY improvements for WMT'11

Loïc Barrault
LIUM, University of Le Mans
Le Mans, France.
FirstName.LastName@lium.univ-lemans.fr

Abstract

This paper describes the development operated into MANY for the 2011 WMT system combination evaluation campaign. Hypotheses from French/English and English/French MT systems were combined with a new version of MANY, an open source system combination software based on confusion networks decoding currently developed at LIUM. MANY has been updated in order to optimize decoder parameters with MERT, which proves to find better weights. The system combination yielded significant improvements in BLEU score when applied on system combination data from two languages.

1 Introduction

This year, the LIUM computer science laboratory participated in the French-English system combination task at WMT'11 evaluation campaign. The system used for this task is MANY[1] (Barrault, 2010), an open source system combination software based on Confusion Networks (CN).

For this year evaluation, rather more technical than scientific improvements have been added to MANY. The tuning process has been improved by using MERT (Och, 2003) as a replacement of the numerical optimizer Condor (Berghen and Bersini, 2005). The impact of such change is detailed in section 3.

After the evaluation period, some experiments have been performed on the English-French system combination task. The results are presented in the section 5. Before that, a quick description of MANY, including recent developments, can be found in section 2.

[1]MANY is available at the following address http://www-lium.univ-lemans.fr/~barrault/MANY

2 System description

MANY is a system combination software (Barrault, 2010) based on the decoding of a lattice made of several Confusion Networks (CN). This is a widespread approach in MT system combination (Rosti et al., 2007; Shen et al., 2008; Karakos et al., 2008; Rosti et al., 2009). MANY can be decomposed in two main modules. The first one is the alignment module which actually is a modified version of TERp (Snover et al., 2009). Its role is to incrementally align the hypotheses against a backbone in order to create a confusion network. Those confusion networks are then connected together to create a lattice. This module uses different costs (which corresponds to a match, an insertion, a deletion, a substitution, a shift, a synonym and a stem) to compute the best alignment and incrementally build a confusion network. In the case of confusion network, the match (substitution, synonyms, and stems) costs are considered when the word in the hypothesis matches (is a substitution, a synonyms or a stems of) at least one word of the considered confusion sets in the CN.

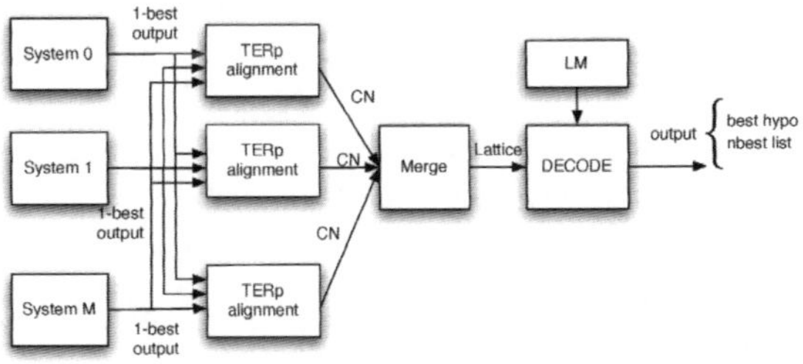

Figure 1: System combination based on confusion network decoding.

The second module is the decoder. This decoder is based on the token pass algorithm and it accepts as input the lattice previously created. The probabilities computed in the decoder can be expressed as follow :

Proceedings of the 6th Workshop on Statistical Machine Translation, pages 135–139,
Edinburgh, Scotland, UK, July 30–31, 2011. ©2011 Association for Computational Linguistics

$$log(P_W) = \sum_i \alpha_i \, log\Big(h_i(t)\Big) \quad (1)$$

where t is the hypothesis, the α_i are the weights of the feature functions h_i. The following features are considered for decoding:

- The language model probability: the probability given by a 4-gram language model.
- The word penalty: penalty depending on the size (in words) of the hypothesis.
- The null-arc penalty: penalty depending on the number of null-arcs crossed in the lattice to obtain the hypothesis.
- System weights: each word receive a weight corresponding to the sum of the weights of all systems which proposed it.

3 Tuning

As mentioned before, MANY is made of two main modules: the alignment module based on a modified version of TERp and the decoder. Considering a maximum of 24 systems for this year evaluation, 33 parameters in total have to be optimized. By default, TERp costs are set to 0.0 for match and 1.0 for everything else. These costs are not correct, since a shift in that case will hardly be possible. TERp costs are tuned with Condor (a numerical optimizer based on Powell's algorithm, (Berghen and Bersini, 2005)). Decoder feature functions weights are optimized with MERT (Och, 2003). The 300-best list created at each MERT iteration is appended to the n-best lists created at previous iterations. This proves to be a more reliable tuning as shown in the following experiments.

During experiments, data from WMT'09 evaluation campaign are used for testing the tuning approach. *news-dev2009a* is used as development set, and *news-dev2009b* as internal test, these corpora are described in Table 1.

NAME	#sent.	#words	#tok
news-dev2009a	1025	21583	24595
news-dev2009b	1026	21837	24940

Table 1: WMT'09 corpora : number of sentences, words and tokens calculated on the reference.

For the sake of simplicity, the five best systems (ranking given by score on dev) are considered only. Baseline systems performances on dev and test are presented in Table 2.

Corpus	Sys0	Sys1	Sys2	Sys3	Sys4
Dev	18.20	17.83	20.14	21.06	17.72
Test	18.53	18.33	20.43	21.35	18.15

Table 2: Baseline systems performance on WMT'09 data (%BLEU).

The 2-step tuning protocol applied on *news-dev2009a*, when using MERT to optimize decoder feature functions weights provides the set of parameters presented in Table 3.

Costs:	Del	Stem	Syn	Ins	Sub	Shift
	0.87	0.91	0.94	0.90	0.98	1.21
Dec.:	LM weight		Word pen.		Null pen.	
	0.056		0.146		0.042	
Wghts.:	Sys0	Sys1	Sys2	Sys3	Sys4	
	-0.03	-0.21	-0.23	-0.28	-0.02	

Table 3: Parameters obtained with tuning decoder parameters with MERT.

Results on development corpus of WMT'09 (used as test set) are presented in Table 4. We can observe that 2-step tuning provides almost +0.9 BLEU point improvement on development corpus which is well reflected on test set with a gain of more than 0.8 BLEU. By using MERT, this improvement is increased to reach almost +2 BLEU point on dev corpus and +1.7 BLEU on test.

System	Dev	Test
Best single	21.06	21.35
MANY (2010)	**22.08**	**22.28**
MANY-2steps (2010)	**21.94**	**22.09**
MANY-2steps/MERT (2011)	**23.05**	**23.07**

Table 4: System Combination results on WMT'09 data (%BLEU-cased).

There are two main reasons for this improvement. The first one is the use of MERT which make use of specific heuristics to better optimize toward BLEU score. The second one is the fully log-linear interpolation of features functions scores operated into the decoder (previously, the word and null penalties were applied linearly).

4 2011 evaluation campaign

A development corpus, *newssyscombtune2011*, and a test set, *newssyscombtest2011*, described in Table 5, were provided to participants.

NAME	#sent.	#words	#tok
newssyscombtune2011	1003	23108	26248
newssyscombtest2011	2000	42719	48502

Table 5: Description of WMT'11 corpora.

Language model: The English target language models has been trained on all monolingual data provided for the translation tasks. In addition, LDC's Gigaword collection was used for both languages. Data corresponding to the development and test periods were removed from the Gigaword collections.

Sys. #	BLEU	TER	Sys. #	BLEU	TER
Sys0	29.86	52.46	Sys11	27.23	53.48
Sys1	29.74	51.74	Sys12*	26.82	54.23
Sys2	29.73	52.90	Sys13	26.25	55.60
Sys3	29.58	52.73	Sys14*	26.13	55.65
Sys4*	29.39	52.91	Sys15	25.90	55.69
Sys5	28.89	53.74	Sys16	25.45	56.92
Sys6	28.53	53.27	Sys17	25.23	56.09
Sys7*	28.31	54.22	Sys18	23.63	60.25
Sys8*	28.08	54.47	Sys19	21.90	63.65
Sys9*	27.98	53.92	Sys20	21.77	60.78
Sys10	27.46	54.60	Sys21	20.97	64.00
			Sys22	16.63	65.83
MANY-5sys				**31.83**	**51.27**
MANY-10sys				**31.75**	51.91
MANY-allsys				**30.75**	54.33

Table 6: Systems performance on *newssyscombtune2011* development data (%BLEU-cased). (* indicate a contrastive run)

Choosing the right number of systems to combine: Table 6 shows the performance of the input systems (ordered by BLEU score computed on *newssyscombtune2011*) and the result of 3 system combination setups. The difference in these setups only reside on the number of inputs to use for combination (5, 10 and all system outputs). Notice that the contrastive runs have not been used when combining 5 and 10 systems. The motivation for this is to benefit from the multi-site systems development which more likely provide varied outputs (*i.e.* different ngrams and word choice). The results show that combining 5 systems is slightly better than 10, but give more than 1 BLEU point improvement compared to combining all systems. Still, the combination always provide an improvement, which was not the case in last year evaluation.

The results obtained by combining 5 and 10 systems are presented in Table 7.

Sys. #	BLEU	TER	Sys. #	BLEU	TER
Sys0	29.43	52.01	Sys6	28.08	53.19
Sys1	29.15	51.30	Sys11	27.24	53.74
Sys2	28.87	52.82	Sys13	26.74	52.92
Sys3	28.82	52.57	Sys15	26.31	54.61
Sys5	28.08	53.19	Sys16	25.23	55.38
MANY (5sys)				**30.74**	**51.17**
MANY (10sys)				30.60	51.39

Table 7: Baseline systems performance on WMT'11 syscomb test data (%BLEU-cased).

Optimizing MANY on *newssyscombtune2011* corpus produced the parameter set presented in Table 8. We can see that the weights of all system are not proportional to the BLEU score obtained on the development corpus. This suggest that a better system selection could be found. This is even more probable since the weight of system Sys2 is positive (which imply a negative impact on each word proposed by this system), which means that when an hypothesis contains a word coming from this system, then its score is decreased.

Costs:	Del	Stem	Syn	Ins	Sub	Shift
	0.90	0.88	0.96	0.97	1.01	1.19
Dec.:	LM weight		Null pen.		Len pen.	
	0.0204		0.26		0.005	
Wghts.:	Sys0	Sys1	Sys2	Sys3	Sys5	
	-0.16	-0.30	0.008	-0.16	-0.09	

Table 8: Parameters obtained after tuning the system parameter using 5 hypotheses.

Table 9 contains the BLEU scores computed between the outputs of the five systems used during combination. An interesting observation is that the system which receive the bigger weight is the one which "distance"[2] against all other system outputs

[2]This "distance" is expressed in terms of ngrams agreement

	Sys0	Sys1	Sys2	Sys3	Sys5	mean
Sys0	-	53.59	62.67	64.60	62.50	60.84
Sys1	53.51	-	54.19	52.42	51.69	**52.95**
Sys2	62.72	54.28	-	65.49	63.09	***61.40***
Sys3	64.63	52.51	65.47	-	61.35	60.99
Sys5	62.55	51.78	63.10	61.37	-	59.70
mean	60.85	**53.04**	***61.36***	60.97	59.66	

Table 9: Cross-system BLEU scores computed on WMT'11 French-English test corpus outputs (%BLEU-cased).

Corpus	syscombtune2011		syscombtest2011	
	BLEU	TER	BLEU	TER
Sys0	35.99	**49.16**	34.36	**49.78**
Sys1	32.99	51.90	30.73	52.52
Sys2	32.41	52.77	29.85	53.61
Sys3	32.40	51.26	30.48	52.20
Sys4	32.30	52.21	31.02	52.49
MANY	**36.81**	49.74	**34.51**	50.54

Table 11: Systems and combination performance on WMT'11 french data (%BLEU-cased).

is the highest, whereas the "closest" system get the smallest weight. This suggests that systems closer to other systems tends to be less useful for system combination. This is an interesting behaviour which has to be explored deeper and validated on other tasks and corpora.

5 MANY for french outputs

After the evaluation period, some experiments have been conducted in order to combine french outputs. The main difference lie in the fact that linguistic resources are not easily or freely available for that kind of language. Therefore, instead of using TERp with *relax*[3] shift constraint, the *strict* constraint was used (shifts occur only when a match is found).

The available data are detailed in the Table 10.

NAME	#sent.	#words	#tok
syscombtune	1003	24659	29171
syscombtest	2000	45372	53970

Table 10: Description of WMT'11 corpora for system combination in french.

The results obtained are presented in Table 11. The BLEU score increase by more than 0.8 point but the TER score decrease by 0.58. The metric targeted during tuning is BLEU, which can explain the improvement in that metric. When dealing with english text, the only case where such behaviour is observed is when combining all systems (see Table 6.

6 MANY technical news

Several improvements have been performed on MANY. The decoder is now based on a fully log-linear model (whereas before, the word and null penalties were applied linearly). Using MERT to tune the decoder parameters is therefore possible and allows to reach bigger improvement compared to using Condor. This is probably due to the fact that MERT uses several heuristics useful for tuning on BLEU score.

In order to facilitate the use of MANY, it has been integrated in the Experiment Management System, EMS - (Koehn, 2010). An experiment can now be setup/modified/re-run easily by modifying a single configuration file. The default behavior of this framework is to perform 3 runs of MERT in parallel (using torque) and take the best optimization run. Apart from avoiding local maximum, the procedure allows to see the variability of the optimization process and report more realistic results (for example, by taking the average).

7 Conclusion and future work

For WMT'11 system combination evaluation campaign, several rather technical improvements have been performed into MANY. By homogenizing the log-linear model used by the decoder and utilizing MERT for tuning, MANY achieves improvements of more than 2 BLEU points on WMT'09 data and about 1.3 BLEU point on *newssyscombtest2011* relatively to the best single system. Moreover, a dry-run operated on french data shows a promising result with an improvement of more than 0.8 BLEU points. This will be further explored in the future.

MANY can benefit from various information. At the moment, the decision taken by the decoder mainly depends on a target language model. This is clearly not enough to achieve greater performances. The next issues which will be addressed within the MANY framework is to estimate good confidence measure to use in place of the systems

[3]Shifts can occur when a match, a stem, a synonym or a paraphrase is found.

priors. These confidences measures have to be related to the system performances, but also to the complementarity of the systems considered.

8 Acknowledgement

This work has been partially funded by the European Union under the EuroMatrix Plus project (http://www.euromatrixplus.net, IST-2007.2.2-FP7-231720)

References

[Barrault, 2010] Barrault, L. (2010). MANY : Open source machine translation system combination. *Prague Bulletin of Mathematical Linguistics, Special Issue on Open Source Tools for Machine Translation*, 93:147–155.

[Berghen and Bersini, 2005] Berghen, F. V. and Bersini, H. (2005). CONDOR, a new parallel, constrained extension of Powell's UOBYQA algorithm: Experimental results and comparison with the DFO algorithm. *Journal of Computational and Applied Mathematics*, 181:157–175.

[Karakos et al., 2008] Karakos, D., Eisner, J., Khudanpur, S., and Dreyer, M. (2008). Machine translation system combination using ITG-based alignments. In *46th Annual Meeting of the Association for Computational Linguistics: Human Language Technologies.*, pages 81–84, Columbus, Ohio, USA.

[Koehn, 2010] Koehn, P. (2010). An experimental management system. *The Prague Bulletin of Mathematical Linguistics*, 94:87–96.

[Och, 2003] Och, F. (2003). Minimum error rate training in statistical machine translation. In *ACL*, Sapporo, Japan.

[Rosti et al., 2007] Rosti, A.-V., Matsoukas, S., and Schwartz, R. (2007). Improved word-level system combination for machine translation. In *Association for Computational Linguistics*, pages 312–319.

[Rosti et al., 2009] Rosti, A.-V., Zhang, B., Matsoukas, S., , and Schwartz, R. (2009). Incremental hypothesis alignment with flexible matching for building confusion networks: BBN system description for WMT09 system combination task. In *EACL/WMT*, pages 61–65.

[Shen et al., 2008] Shen, W., Delaney, B., Anderson, T., and Slyh, R. (2008). The MIT-LL/AFRL IWSLT-2008 MT System. In *International Workshop on Spoken Language Translation*, Hawaii, U.S.A.

[Snover et al., 2009] Snover, M., Madnani, N., Dorr, B., and Schwartz, R. (2009). TER-Plus: Paraphrase, semantic, and alignment enhancements to translation edit rate. *Machine Translation Journal*.

The UPV-PRHLT combination system for WMT 2011

Jesús González-Rubio and **Francisco Casacuberta**
Instituto Tecnológico de Informática
Departamento de Sistemas Informáticos y Computación
Universitat Politècnica de València
{jegonzalez|fcn}@dsic.upv.es

Abstract

This paper presents the submissions of the pattern recognition and human language technology (PRHLT) group to the system combination task of the sixth workshop on statistical machine translation (WMT 2011). Each submissions is generated by a multi-system minimum Bayes risk (MBR) technique. Our technique uses the MBR decision rule and a linear combination of the component systems' probability distributions to search for the minimum risk translation among all the sentences in the target language.

1 Introduction

The UPV-PHRLT approach to machine translation (MT) system combination is based on the minimum Bayes risk system combination (MBRSC) algorithm (Gonzlez-Rubio et al., 2011). A multi-system MBR technique that computes consensus translations over multiple component systems.

MBRSC operates directly on the outputs of the component models. We perform an MBR decoding using a linear combination of the component models' probability distributions. Instead of reranking the translations provided by the component systems, we search for the hypothesis with the minimum expected translation error among all the possible finite-length strings in the target language. By using a loss function based on BLEU (Papineni et al., 2002), we avoid the hypothesis alignment problem that is central to standard system combination approaches (Rosti et al., 2007). MBRSC assumes only that each translation model can produce expectations of n-gram counts; the latent derivation structures of the component systems can differ arbitrary. This flexibility allows us to combine a great variety of MT systems.

2 Minimum Bayes risk Decoding

SMT can be described as a mapping of a word sequence $\mathbf{f}$ in a source language to a word sequence $\mathbf{e}$ in a target language; this mapping is produced by the MT decoder $\mathcal{D}(\mathbf{f})$. If the reference translation $\mathbf{e}$ is known, the decoder performance can be measured by the loss function $\mathcal{L}(\mathbf{e}, \mathcal{D}(\mathbf{f}))$. Given such a loss function $\mathcal{L}(\mathbf{e}, \mathbf{e}')$ between an automatic translation $\mathbf{e}'$ and a reference $\mathbf{e}$, and an underlying probability model $P(\mathbf{e}|\mathbf{f})$, MBR decoding has the following form (Goel and Byrne, 2000; Kumar and Byrne, 2004):

$$\hat{\mathbf{e}} = \arg\min_{\mathbf{e}' \in E} \mathcal{R}(\mathbf{e}') \tag{1}$$

$$= \arg\min_{\mathbf{e}' \in E} \sum_{\mathbf{e} \in E} P(\mathbf{e}|\mathbf{f}) \cdot \mathcal{L}(\mathbf{e}, \mathbf{e}') , \tag{2}$$

where $\mathcal{R}(\mathbf{e}')$ denotes the Bayes risk of candidate translation $\mathbf{e}'$ under loss function $\mathcal{L}$, and E represents the space of translations.

If the loss function between any two hypotheses can be bounded: $\mathcal{L}(\mathbf{e}, \mathbf{e}') \leq \mathcal{L}_{max}$, the MBR decoder can be rewritten in term of a similarity function $\mathcal{S}(\mathbf{e}, \mathbf{e}') = \mathcal{L}_{max} - \mathcal{L}(\mathbf{e}, \mathbf{e}')$. In this case, instead of minimizing the Bayes risk, we maximize the Bayes gain $\mathcal{G}(\mathbf{e}')$:

$$\hat{\mathbf{e}} = \arg\max_{\mathbf{e}' \in E} \mathcal{G}(\mathbf{e}') \tag{3}$$

$$= \arg\max_{\mathbf{e}' \in E} \sum_{\mathbf{e} \in E} P(\mathbf{e}|\mathbf{f}) \cdot \mathcal{S}(\mathbf{e}, \mathbf{e}') . \tag{4}$$

MBR decoding can use different spaces for hypothesis selection and gain computation (arg max and sum in Eq. (4)). Therefore, the MBR decoder can be more generally written as follows:

$$\hat{\mathbf{e}} = \arg\max_{\mathbf{e}' \in E_h} \sum_{\mathbf{e} \in E_e} P(\mathbf{e}|\mathbf{f}) \cdot \mathcal{S}(\mathbf{e}, \mathbf{e}') , \tag{5}$$

Proceedings of the 6th Workshop on Statistical Machine Translation, pages 140–144,
Edinburgh, Scotland, UK, July 30–31, 2011.

where E_h refers to the hypotheses space form where the translations are chosen and E_e refers to the evidences space that is used to compute the Bayes gain. We will investigate the expansion of the hypotheses space while keeping the evidences space as provided by the decoder.

3 MBR System Combination

MBRSC is a multi-system generalization of MBR decoding. It uses the MBR decision rule on a linear combination of the probability distributions of the component systems. Unlike existing MBR decoding methods that re-rank translation outputs, MBRSC search for the minimum risk hypotheses on the complete set of finite-length hypotheses over the output vocabulary. We assume the component systems to be statistically independent and define the Bayes gain as a linear combination of the Bayes gains of the components. Each system provides its own space of evidences $\mathcal{D}_n(\mathbf{f})$ and its posterior distribution over translations $P_n(\mathbf{e}|\mathbf{f})$. Given a sentence $\mathbf{f}$ in the source language, MBRSC is written as follows:

$$\hat{\mathbf{e}} = \arg\max_{\mathbf{e}' \in E_h} \mathcal{G}(\mathbf{e}') \tag{6}$$

$$\approx \arg\max_{\mathbf{e}' \in E_h} \sum_{n=1}^{N} \alpha_n \cdot \mathcal{G}_n(\mathbf{e}') \tag{7}$$

$$= \arg\max_{\mathbf{e}' \in E_h} \sum_{n=1}^{N} \alpha_n \cdot \sum_{\mathbf{e} \in \mathcal{D}_n(\mathbf{f})} P_n(\mathbf{e}|\mathbf{f}) \cdot \mathcal{S}(\mathbf{e}, \mathbf{e}') \,, \tag{8}$$

where N is the total number of component systems, E_h represents the hypotheses space where the search is performed, $\mathcal{G}_n(\mathbf{e}')$ is the Bayes gain of hypothesis $\mathbf{e}'$ given by the nth component system and α_n is a scaling factor introduced to take into account the differences in quality of the component models. It is worth mentioning that by using a linear combination instead of a mixture model, we avoid the problem of component systems not sharing the same search space (Duan et al., 2010).

3.1 Computing BLEU-based Gain

We are interested in performing MBRSC under BLEU. Therefore, we rewrite the gain function $\mathcal{G}(\cdot)$ using single evidence (or reference) BLEU (Papineni et al., 2002) as the similarity function:

$$\mathcal{G}_n(\mathbf{e}') = \sum_{\mathbf{e} \in \mathcal{D}_n(\mathbf{f})} P_n(\mathbf{e}|\mathbf{f}) \cdot \mathrm{BLEU}(\mathbf{e}, \mathbf{e}') \tag{9}$$

$$\mathrm{BLEU} = \prod_{k=1}^{4} \left(\frac{m_k}{c_k}\right)^{\frac{1}{4}} \cdot \min\left(e^{1-\frac{r}{c}}, 1.0\right) \,, \tag{10}$$

where r is the length of the evidence, c the length of the hypothesis, m_k the number of n-gram matches of size k, and c_k the count of n-grams of size k in the hypothesis.

The evidences space $\mathcal{D}_n(\mathbf{f})$ may contain a huge number of hypotheses[1] which often make impractical to compute Eq. (9) directly. To avoid this problem, Tromble et al. (2008) propose *linear BLEU*, an approximation to the BLEU score to efficiently perform MBR decoding on the lattices provided by the component systems. However, we want to explore a hypotheses space not restricted to the evidences provided by the systems.

In Eq. (9), we have one hypothesis $\mathbf{e}'$ that is to be compared to a set of evidences $\mathbf{e} \in \mathcal{D}_n(\mathbf{f})$ which follow a probability distribution $P_n(\mathbf{e}|\mathbf{f})$. Instead of computing the expected BLEU score by calculating the BLEU score with respect to each of the evidences, our approach will be to use the expected n-gram counts and sentence length of the evidences to compute a single-reference BLEU score. We replace the reference statistics (r and m_n in Eq. (10)) by the expected statistics (r' and m'_n) given the posterior distribution $P_n(\mathbf{e}|\mathbf{f})$ over the evidences:

$$\mathcal{G}_n(\mathbf{e}') = \prod_{k=1}^{4} \left(\frac{m'_k}{c_k}\right)^{\frac{1}{4}} \cdot \min\left(e^{1-\frac{r'}{c}}, 1.0\right) \tag{11}$$

$$r' = \sum_{\mathbf{e} \in \mathcal{D}_n(\mathbf{f})} |\mathbf{e}| \cdot P_n(\mathbf{e}|\mathbf{f}) \tag{12}$$

$$m'_k = \sum_{ng \in \mathcal{N}_k(\mathbf{e}')} \min(C_{\mathbf{e}'}(ng), C'(ng)) \tag{13}$$

$$C'(ng) = \sum_{\mathbf{e} \in \mathcal{D}_n(\mathbf{f})} C_{\mathbf{e}}(ng) \cdot P_n(\mathbf{e}|\mathbf{f}) \,, \tag{14}$$

where $\mathcal{N}_k(\mathbf{e}')$ is the set of n-grams of size k in the hypothesis, $C_{\mathbf{e}'}(ng)$ is the count of the n-gram ng in

[1] For example, in a lattice the number of hypotheses may be exponential in the size of its state set.

the hypothesis and $C'(ng)$ is the expected count of ng in the evidences. To compute the n-gram matchings m'_k, the count of each n-gram is truncated, if necessary, to not exceed the expected count for that n-gram in the evidences.

We have replaced a summation over a possibly exponential number of items ($\mathbf{e}' \in \mathcal{D}_n(\mathbf{f})$ in Eq. (9)) with a summation over a polynomial number of n-grams that occur in the evidences[2]. Both, the expected length of the evidences r' and their expected n-gram counts m'_k can be pre-computed efficiently from N-best lists and translation lattices (Kumar et al., 2009; DeNero et al., 2010).

3.2 Model Training

The scaling factors in Eq. (8) denote the "quality" of each system with respect to the rest of them, i.e. the relative importance of each system in the Bayes gain computation. This scaling factors must be carefully tuned to obtain good translations.

We compute the scaling factor of each system as the number of times the hypothesis of the system is the best TER-scoring translation in the tuning corpora. Previous works show that this measure obtains the best translation results among other heuristic measures (González-Rubio et al., 2010) and even as good results as more complex methods such as MERT (Och, 2003). A normalization is performed to transform these counts into the range $[0.0, 1.0]$. After the normalization, a weight value of 0.0 is assigned to the lowest-scoring system, i.e. the lowest-scoring system is discarded and not taken into account in the computation of the Bayes gain.

3.3 Model Decoding

In most MBR algorithms, the hypotheses space is equal to the evidences space. However, we are interested in extend the hypotheses space by including new sentences created using fragments of the hypotheses in the evidences spaces of the component models. We perform the search ($argmax$ operation in Eq. (8)) using the approximate median string (AMS) algorithm (Martínez et al., 2000). AMS algorithm perform a hill-climbing search on a hypotheses space equal to the free monoid Σ^* of the vocabulary of the evidences $\Sigma = Voc(E_e)$.

Algorithm 1 MBRSC decoding algorithm.

Require: Initial hypothesis $\mathbf{e}$
Require: Vocabulary the evidences Σ
1: $\hat{\mathbf{e}} \leftarrow \mathbf{e}$
2: **repeat**
3: $\quad \mathbf{e}_{cur} \leftarrow \hat{\mathbf{e}}$
4: $\quad$ **for** $j = 1$ **to** $|\mathbf{e}_{cur}|$ **do**
5: $\quad\quad \hat{\mathbf{e}}_s \leftarrow \mathbf{e}_{cur}$
6: $\quad\quad$ **for** $a \in \Sigma$ **do**
7: $\quad\quad\quad \mathbf{e}'_s \leftarrow Substitute(\mathbf{e}_{cur}, a, j)$
8: $\quad\quad\quad$ **if** $\mathcal{G}(\mathbf{e}'_s) > \mathcal{G}(\hat{\mathbf{e}}_s)$ **then**
9: $\quad\quad\quad\quad \hat{\mathbf{e}}_s \leftarrow \mathbf{e}'_s$
10: $\quad\quad \hat{\mathbf{e}}_d \leftarrow Delete(\mathbf{e}_{cur}, j)$
11: $\quad\quad \hat{\mathbf{e}}_i \leftarrow \mathbf{e}_{cur}$
12: $\quad\quad$ **for** $a \in \Sigma$ **do**
13: $\quad\quad\quad \mathbf{e}'_i \leftarrow Insert(\mathbf{e}_{cur}, a, j)$
14: $\quad\quad\quad$ **if** $\mathcal{G}(\mathbf{e}'_i) > \mathcal{G}(\hat{\mathbf{e}}_i)$ **then**
15: $\quad\quad\quad\quad \hat{\mathbf{e}}_i \leftarrow \mathbf{e}'_i$
16: $\quad\quad \hat{\mathbf{e}} \leftarrow \arg\max_{\mathbf{e}' \in \{\mathbf{e}_{cur}, \hat{\mathbf{e}}_s, \hat{\mathbf{e}}_d, \hat{\mathbf{e}}_i\}} \mathcal{G}(\mathbf{e}')$
17: **until** $\mathcal{G}(\hat{\mathbf{e}}) \not> \mathcal{G}(\mathbf{e}_{cur})$
18: **return** $\mathbf{e}_{cur}$
Ensure: $\mathcal{G}(\mathbf{e}_{cur}) \geq \mathcal{G}(\mathbf{e})$

The AMS algorithm is shown in Algorithm 1. AMS starts with an initial hypothesis $\mathbf{e}$[3] that is modified using edit operations until there is no improvement in the Bayes gain (Lines 3–16). On each position j of the current solution $\mathbf{e}_{cur}$, we apply all the possible single edit operations: substitution of the jth word of $\mathbf{e}_{cur}$ by each word a in the vocabulary (Lines 5–9), deletion of the jth word of $\mathbf{e}_{cur}$ (Line 10) and insertion of each word a in the vocabulary in the jth position of $\mathbf{e}_{cur}$ (Lines 11–15). If the Bayes gain of any of the new edited hypotheses is higher than the Bayes gain of the current hypothesis (Line 17), we repeat the loop with this new hypotheses $\hat{\mathbf{e}}$, in other case, we return the current hypothesis.

AMS algorithm takes as input an initial hypothesis $\mathbf{e}$ and the combined vocabulary of the evidences spaces Σ. Its output is a possibly new hypothesis whose Bayes gain is assured to be higher or equal than the Bayes gain of the initial hypothesis.

The complexity of the main loop (lines 2-17) is $O(|\mathbf{e}_{cur}| \cdot |\Sigma| \cdot C_{\mathcal{G}})$, where $C_{\mathcal{G}}$ is the cost of com-

[2] If $\mathcal{D}_n(\mathbf{f})$ is represented by a lattice, the number of n-grams is polynomial in the number of edges in the lattice.

[3] In the experimentation we use the evidence with minimum Bayes' risk as the initial hypothesis of the algorithm.

		cz→en	en→cz	de→en	en→de	es→en	en→es	fr→en	en→fr
#systems		12	14	25	34	15	22	23	21
dev	Worst	15.6	8.8	12.8	4.5	15.1	20.3	15.8	13.9
	Best	25.9	**16.9**	**22.2**	16.3	27.8	32.7	28.6	**35.5**
	MBRSC	**26.7**	15.9	**22.2**	**17.1**	**30.5**	**33.3**	**30.2**	34.7
test	Worst	13.3	9.1	12.9	5.1	14.7	20.7	16.1	13.0
	Best	27.2	**18.6**	21.9	**16.7**	27.4	32.5	28.1	**33.5**
	MBRSC	**27.9**	17.7	**22.1**	16.5	**30.4**	**32.9**	**29.6**	32.7

Table 1: BLEU scores (case-sensitive) on the shared translation task development and test corpora of the best and worst single systems and MBRSC. For each translation direction, we show the number of systems being combined. Best translation results are in bold.

puting the gain of a hypothesis, and usually only a moderate number of iterations (< 10) is needed to converge (Martínez et al., 2000).

4 Results

Experiments were conducted on all the 8 translation directions of the shared translation task Czech–English (cz↔en), German–English (de↔en), Spanish–English (es↔en) and French–English (fr↔en) and also on the raw and clean versions of the Haitian creole–English featured translation task (ht→en). All the experiments were carried out with the true-cased, detokenized version of the tuning and test corpora, following the WMT 2011 submission guidelines.

4.1 Shared translation task

Table 1 shows the BLEU scores of MBRSC on the development and test corpora in comparison with the score of the best and worst individual systems. In most of the translation directions, MBRSC improved the results of the best individual system, e.g. +2.7/+3.0 BLEU point in es→en. However, in en→cz and en→fr, MBRSC performs worse than the best individual system. One thing we noticed is that for these translation directions, the translations from one provided single system (online-B) were much better in terms of BLEU than those of all other systems (in the former case by more than 14% relative in development). In our experience, MBRSC requires "comparably good" systems to be able to achieve significant improvements (particularly if using heuristic scaling factors). On the other hand, we would have achieved improvements over all remaining systems leaving out online-B.

4.2 Featured translation task

Regarding the ht→en featured translation task, MBRSC is not able to improve the results of the best individual system in any case. As in the en→cz and en→fr translation directions, one of the systems (bm-i2r) perform much much better than all other systems. We can notice the surprisingly low score of one of the systems (umd-hu) in the clean task. The translations of this system are all equal ("N / A") so we suppose that some error occurred during the translation or submission processes.

	ht→en	
	raw	clean
#systems	8	16
worst	15.4	2.9
best	**29.6**	**33.1**
MBRSC	28.6	32.2

Table 2: BLEU scores (case-sensitive) on the featured translation task development corpora of the best and worst single systems and MBRSC. Best translation results are in bold.

5 summary

The UPV-PRHLT submissions for WMT 2011 system combination task were described in this paper. The combination was based on a multi-system MBR technique that uses the MBR decision rule and a linear combination of the component systems' probability distributions to search for the minimum risk translation among all the finite-length strings in the output vocabulary. We introduced expected BLEU, an approximation to the BLEU score that allows to efficiently apply MBR in these conditions. In most of the translation directions we were able to obtain BLEU gains over the best individual systems.

Acknowledgements

This paper is based upon work supported by the EC (FEDER/FSE) and the Spanish MEC/MICINN under the MIPRCV "Consolider Ingenio 2010" program (CSD2007-00018), the iTrans2 (TIN2009-14511) project and the UPV under grant 20091027. Also supported by the Spanish MITyC under the erudito.com (TSI-020110-2009-439) project and by the Generalitat Valenciana under grant Prometeo/2009/014.

References

John DeNero, Shankar Kumar, Ciprian Chelba, and Franz Och. 2010. Model combination for machine translation. In *Human Language Technologies: The 2010 Annual Conference of the North American Chapter of the Association for Computational Linguistics*, pages 975–983, Morristown, NJ, USA. Association for Computational Linguistics.

Nan Duan, Mu Li, Dongdong Zhang, and Ming Zhou. 2010. Mixture model-based minimum bayes risk decoding using multiple machine translation systems. In *Proceedings of the 23rd International Conference on Computational Linguistics (Coling 2010)*, pages 313–321, Beijing, China, August. Coling 2010 Organizing Committee.

Vaibhava Goel and William J. Byrne. 2000. Minimum bayes-risk automatic speech recognition. *Computer Speech & Language*, 14(2):115–135.

Jesús González-Rubio, Germán Sanchis-Trilles, Joan-Andreu Sánchez, Jesús Andrés-Ferrer, Guillem Gascó, Pascual Martínez-Gómez, Martha-Alicia Rocha, and Francisco Casacuberta. 2010. The upv-prhlt combination system for wmt 2010. In *Proceedings of the Joint Fifth Workshop on Statistical Machine Translation and MetricsMATR*, pages 296–300, Uppsala, Sweden, July. Association for Computational Linguistics.

Jess Gonzlez-Rubio, Alfons Juan, and Francisco Casacuberta. 2011. Minimum bayes-risk system combination. In *Proceedings of the 49th Annual Meeting of the Association for Computational Linguistics: Human Language Technologies*, pages 1268–1277, Portland, Oregon, USA, June. Association for Computational Linguistics.

Shankar Kumar and William J. Byrne. 2004. Minimum bayes-risk decoding for statistical machine translation. In *HLT-NAACL*, pages 169–176.

Shankar Kumar, Wolfgang Macherey, Chris Dyer, and Franz Och. 2009. Efficient minimum error rate training and minimum bayes-risk decoding for translation hypergraphs and lattices. In *Proceedings of the Joint Conference of the 47th Annual Meeting of the ACL and the 4th International Joint Conference on Natural Language Processing of the AFNLP: Volume 1 - Volume 1*, pages 163–171, Morristown, NJ, USA. Association for Computational Linguistics.

C. D. Martínez, A. Juan, and F. Casacuberta. 2000. Use of Median String for Classification. In *Proceedings of the 15th International Conference on Pattern Recognition*, volume 2, pages 907–910, Barcelona (Spain), September.

Franz J. Och. 2003. Minimum error rate training in statistical machine translation. In *Proceedings of the 41st Annual Meeting on Association for Computational Linguistics - Volume 1*, pages 160–167, Morristown, NJ, USA. Association for Computational Linguistics.

Kishore Papineni, Salim Roukos, Todd Ward, and Wei-Jing Zhu. 2002. BLEU: a method for automatic evaluation of machine translation. In *Proceedings of the 40th Annual Meeting on Association for Computational Linguistics*, pages 311–318, Morristown, NJ, USA. Association for Computational Linguistics.

Antti-Veikko Rosti, Necip Fazil Ayan, Bing Xiang, Spyros Matsoukas, Richard Schwartz, and Bonnie Dorr. 2007. Combining outputs from multiple machine translation systems. In *Human Language Technologies 2007: The Conference of the North American Chapter of the Association for Computational Linguistics; Proceedings of the Main Conference*, pages 228–235, Rochester, New York, April. Association for Computational Linguistics.

Roy W. Tromble, Shankar Kumar, Franz Och, and Wolfgang Macherey. 2008. Lattice minimum bayes-risk decoding for statistical machine translation. In *Proceedings of the Conference on Empirical Methods in Natural Language Processing*, pages 620–629, Morristown, NJ, USA. Association for Computational Linguistics.

CMU System Combination in WMT 2011

Kenneth Heafield and Alon Lavie
Carnegie Mellon University
5000 Forbes Ave
Pittsburgh, PA, USA
{heafield,alavie}@cs.cmu.edu

Abstract

This paper describes our submissions, cmu-heafield-combo, to the ten tracks of the 2011 Workshop on Machine Translation's system combination task. We show how the combination scheme operates by flexibly aligning system outputs then searching a space constructed from the alignments. Humans judged our combination the best on eight of ten tracks.

1 Introduction

We participated in all ten tracks of the 2011 Workshop on Machine Translation system combination task as cmu-heafield-combo. This uses a system combination scheme that builds on our prior work (Heafield and Lavie, 2010), especially with respect to language modeling and handling non-English languages. We present a summary of the system, describe improvements, list the data used (all of the constrained monolingual data), and present automatic results in anticipation of human evaluation by the workshop.

2 Our Combination Scheme

Given single-best outputs from each system, the scheme aligns system outputs then searches a space based on these alignments. The scheme is a continuation of our previous system (Heafield and Lavie, 2010) so we describe unchanged parts of the system in less detail, preferring instead to focus on new components.

2.1 Alignment

We run the METEOR matcher (Denkowski and Lavie, 2010) on every pair of system outputs for a given sentence. It identifies exact matches, identical stems (Porter, 2001) except for Czech, WordNet synonym matches for English (Fellbaum, 1998), and automatically extracted matches for all five target languages. The automatic matches come from pivoting (Bannard and Callison-Burch, 2005) on constrained data. An example METEOR alignment is shown in Figure 1, though it need not be monotone.

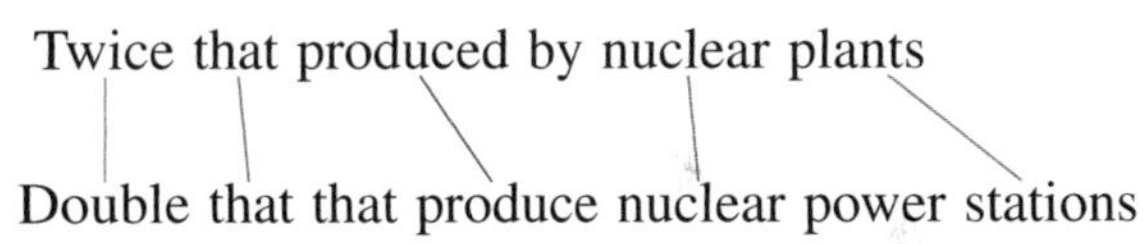

Figure 1: Alignment generated by METEOR showing exact (that–that and nuclear–nuclear), stem (produced–produce), synonym (twice–double), and unigram paraphrase (plants–stations) alignments.

2.2 Search

The search space is unchanged from Heafield and Lavie (2010), so we give a summary here. The general idea is to generate a combined sentence one word at a time, going from left to right. As the scheme creates an output, it also steps through the system outputs from left to right. Stepping through systems is synchronized with the partial output, so that words to the left are already captured in the hypothesis and the next word from any of the systems represents a meaningful extension of the partial output. All of these options are considered by hypothesis branching.

Proceedings of the 6th Workshop on Statistical Machine Translation, pages 145–151,
Edinburgh, Scotland, UK, July 30–31, 2011. ©2011 Association for Computational Linguistics

Thus far, we have assumed that system outputs are monotone: they agree on word order, so it is possible to step through all of them simultaneously. On the left are words captured in the partial output and on the right are the words whose meaning remains to be captured in the output. When systems disagree on word order, the partial output corresponds to disjoint pieces of a system's output. We still retain that notion that a word is either captured in the partial output or not captured, but do not have a single dividing line between them. In this case, we still proceed from left to right, considering the first uncaptured word for extension. Then, we skip over parts of a system's output that have already been captured.

Here, we have used the informal notion of words whose meaning is "captured" or "uncaptured" by the partial output. The system interprets words aligned to the partial output as captured while those not aligned to the hypothesis are considered uncaptured. A heuristic also cleans up excess words in order to keep the stepping process loosely synchronized across system outputs.

2.3 Features

We use three feature categories to guide search:

Length The length of the hypothesis in tokens.

Language Model Log probability and OOV count from an N-gram language model. Details are in Section 4.1.

Match Counts Counts of n-gram matches between systems outputs and the hypothesis.

The match count features report n-gram matches between each system and the hypothesis. Specifically, feature $m_{s,n}$ reports n-gram overlap between the hypothesis and system s. We track n-gram counts up to length N, typically 2 or 3, finding that tracking longer lengths adds little. An example is shown in Figure 2.

These match counts may be exact, in which case every word of the n-gram must be the same (up to case) or approximate, in which case any aligned word found by METEOR may be substituted. Because exact matches handle lexical choice and inexact matches collect more votes that better handle word order, we use both sets of features. However, the limit N may be different i.e. $N_e = 2$ counts exact matches up to length 2 and $N_a = 3$ counts inexact matches up to length 3.

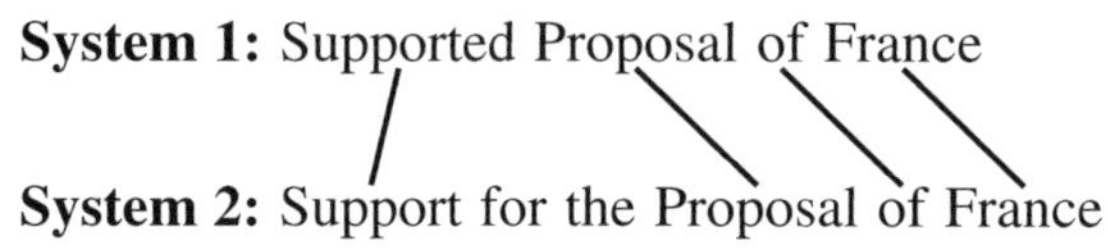

Candidate: Support for Proposal of France

	Unigram	Bigram	Trigram
System 1	4	2	1
System 2	5	3	1

Figure 2: Example match feature values with two systems and matches up to length three. Here, "Supported" counts because it aligns with "Support".

3 Related Work

Hypothesis selection (Hildebrand and Vogel, 2009) selects an entire sentence at a time instead of picking and merging words. This makes the approach less flexible, in that it cannot synthesize new sentences, but also less risky by avoiding matching and related problems entirely.

While our alignment is based on METEOR, other techniques are based on TER (Snover et al., 2006), Inversion Transduction Grammars (Narsale, 2010), and other alignment methods. These use exact alignments and positional information to infer alignments, ignoring the content-based method used by METEOR. This means they might align content words to function words, while we never do. In practice, using both signals would likely work better.

Confusion networks (Rosti et al., 2010; Narsale, 2010) are the dominant method for system combination. These base their word order on one system, dubbed the backbone, and have all systems vote on editing the backbone. Word order is largely fixed to that of one system; by contrast, ours can piece together word orders taken from multiple systems. In a loose sense, our approach is a confusion network where the backbone is permitted to switch after each word.

Interestingly, BBN (Rosti et al., 2010) this year added a novel-bigram penalty that penalizes bigrams in the output if they do not appear in one of the system outputs. This is the complement of our bigram match count features (and, since, we have a length feature, the same up to rearranging weights). However, they threshold it to indicate whether the bigram appears at all instead of how many systems support the bigram.

4 Resources

The resources we use are constrained to those provided for the shared task.

For the paraphrase matches described in Section 2.1, METEOR (Denkowski and Lavie, 2010) trains its paraphrase tables via pivoting (Bannard and Callison-Burch, 2005). The phrase tables are trained using parallel data from Europarl v6 (Koehn, 2005) (fr-en, es-en, de-en, and es-de), news commentary (fr-en, es-en, de-en, and cz-en), United Nations (fr-en and es-en), and CzEng (cz-en) (Bojar and Žabokrtský, 2009) sections 0–8.

4.1 Language Modeling

As with previous versions of the system, we use language model log probability as a feature to bias translations towards fluency. We add a second feature per language model that counts OOVs, allowing MERT to independently tune the OOV penalty. Language models often have poor OOV estimates for translation because they come not from new text in the same language but from new text in a different language. The distribution is even more biased in system combination, where most systems have already applied a language model. The new OOV feature replaces a previous feature that reported the average n-gram length matched by the model.

We added support for multiple language models so that their probabilities, OOV penalties, and all other features are dynamically interpolated using MERT. This we use for the Haitian Creole-English tasks, where the first language model is a large model built on the monolingual data except SMS messages and the second small language model is built on the SMS messages. The OOV features play an important role here because frequent anonymization markers such as "[firstname]" do not appear in the large language model.

To scale to larger language models, we use BigFatLM[1], an open-source builder of large unpruned models with modified Kneser-Ney smoothing. Then, we filter the models to the system outputs. In order for an n-gram to be queried, all of the words must appear in system outputs for the same sentence. This enables a filtering constraint stronger than normal vocabulary filtering, which permits n-grams supported only by words in different sentences. Finally, we use KenLM (Heafield, 2011) for inference at runtime.

Our primary use of data is for language modeling. We used essientially every constrained resource available and appended them together to build one large model. For every language, we used the provided Europarl v6 (Koehn, 2005), News Crawl, and News Commentary corpora. In addition, we used:

English Gigaword Fourth Edition (Parker et al., 2009) and the English parts of United Nations documents, Giga-FrEn, and CzEng (Bojar and Žabokrtský, 2009) sections 0–7. For the Haitian Creole-English tasks, we built a separate language model on the SMS messages and used it alongside the large English model.

Czech CzEng (Bojar and Žabokrtský, 2009) sections 0–7

French Gigaword Second Edition (Mendonça et al., 2009a) and the French parts of Giga-FrEn and United Nations documents.

German There were no additional corpora available.

Spanish Gigaword Second Edition (Mendonça et al., 2009b) and the Spanish parts of United Nations documents.

4.2 Preprocessing

Many corpora contained excessive duplicate text. We wrote a deduplicator that removes all but the first instance of each line. Clean corpora generally reduced line count by 10-25% when deduplicated, resulting from naturally-occuring duplicates such as "yes ." We left the duplicate lines in these corpora. The News Crawl corpus showed a 72.6% reduction in line count due mainly to boilerplace, such as the

[1] https://github.com/jhclark/bigfatlm

Reuters comment section header and Fark headlines that appear in a box on many pages. We deduplicated the News Crawl corpus, United Nations documents, and New York Times and LA Times portions of English Gigaword.

The Giga-FrEn corpus is noisy. We removed lines from Giga-FrEn if any of the following conditions held:

- Invalid UTF8 or control characters.
- Less than 90% of characters are in the Latin alphabet (including diacritics) or punctuation. We did not count "<" and ">" as punctuation to limit the amount of HTML code.
- Less than half the characters are Latin letters.

System outputs and language model training data were normalized using the provided punctuation normalization script, Unicode codepoint collapsing, the provided Moses (Koehn et al., 2007) tokenizer, and several custom rules. These remove formatting-related tokens from Gigaword, rejoin some French words with internal apostrophes, and threshold repetitive punctuation. In addition, German words were segmented as explained in Section 4.3. Text normalization is more difficult for system combination because the system outputs, while theoretically detokenized, contain errors that result from different preprocessing at each site.

4.3 German Segmentation

German makes extensive use of compounding, creating words that do not cleanly align to English and have less reliable statistics. German-English translation systems therefore typically segment German compounds as a preprocessing step. In our case, we are concerned with combining translations into German that may be segmented differently. These can be due to stylistic choices; for example both "jahrzehnte lang" and "jahrzehntelang" appear with approximately equal frequency as shown in Table 1. Translation systems add additional biases due to the various preprocessing approaches taken by individual sites and inherent biases in models such as word alignment.

In order to properly align differently segmented words, we normalize by segmenting all system outputs and our language model training data using the single-best segmentation from cdec (Dyer et al., 2010). Running our system therefore produces segmented German output. Internally, we tuned towards segmented references but for final output it is desirable to rejoin compound words. Since the cdec segmentation was designed for German-English translation, no corresponding desegmenter was provided.

Words	Separate	Compounded
jahrzehnte lang	554	542
klar gemacht	840	802
unter anderem	49538	4
wieder herzustellen	513	1532

Table 1: Counts of separate or compounded versions of select words in the lowercased German monolingual data. Compounding can be optional or biased in either way.

We created a German desegmenter in the natural way: segment German words then invert the mapping to identify words that should be rejoined. To do so, we ran every word from the German monolingual data and system outputs through the cdec segmenter, counted both the compounded and segmented versions in the monolingual data, and removed those that appear segmented more often. Desegmenting is a mildly ambiguous process because n-grams to rejoin may overlap. When an n-gram compounded to one word, we gave that a score of n^2. The total score is a sum of these squares, favoring compounds that cover more words. Maximizing the score is a fast and exact dynamic programming algorithm. Casing of unchanged words comes from equally-weighted system votes at the character level while casing of rejoined words is based on the majority appearance in the corpus; this is almost always initial capital. We ran our desegmenter followed by the workshop's provided detokenizer to produce the submitted output.

5 Results

We tried many variations on the scheme, such as selecting different systems, tuning to BLEU (Papineni et al., 2002) or METEOR (Denkowski and Lavie, 2010), and changing the structure of the match count features from Section 2.3. To try these, we ran MERT 242 times, or about 24 times for each of the ten tasks in which we participated. Then we selected the best performing systems on the tuning set and submitted them, with the secondary system chosen to meaningfully differ from the primary while still scoring well. Once the evaluation released references, we scored against them to generate Table 2.

On the featured Haitian Creole task, we show no and sometimes even negative improvement. This we attribute to the gap between the top system, bm-i2r, and the second place system. For htraw-en, where training data is noisy, the bm-i2r is 3.65 BLEU higher than the second place system at 28.53 BLEU. On htclean-en, the gap is 4.44 points to the second place cmu-denkowski-contrastive.

The main tasks were quite competitive and many systems were within a BLEU point of the top. This is an ideal scenario for system combination, and we show corresponding improvements. The English-Czech task is difficult for our scheme because we do not properly handle Czech morpology in alignment. On Czech-English, online-B beat other systems by a substantial (6.21 BLEU) margin, so we see little gain. On English-German, the gain is small but this is consistent with a general observation that more improvement is seen on higher-quality systems. Further, strength in this year's submission comes from language modeling, but only limited German data was available; segmenting German improved our scores. Translations into Spanish and French show the impact of Gigaword in those languages.

The evaluation's official metric is human ranking judgments. On this metric, our submissions score highest on eight of ten tracks: Czech-English, German-English, English-Czech, English-German, English-Spanish, English-French, the clean Haitian Creole-English task, and the raw Haitian Creole-English task. For Spanish-English, humans preferred RWTH's submission. For French-English, humans preferred RWTH and BBN. However, system combinations were ranked against other system combinations, but not against underlying systems, so we suspect that the bm-i2r submission still performs better than combinations on the Haitian Creole tasks. The human judges also preferred our translations more than BLEU (where we lead on three language pairs: English to German, Spanish, and French). We attribute this to the tendency of confusion networks to drop words supported by many systems due to position-based alignment er-

Track	Entry	BLEU	TER	MET
htraw-en	primary	32.30	56.57	61.05
	contrast	31.76	56.69	60.81
	bm-i2r	32.18	57.01	60.85
htclean-en	primary	36.39	51.16	63.72
	contrast	36.49	51.15	63.78
	bm-i2r	36.97	51.06	64.01
cz-en	primary	29.85	53.20	62.50
	contrast	29.88	53.19	62.40
	online-B	29.59	52.15	61.77
de-en	primary	26.21	56.19	60.56
	contrast	26.11	56.42	60.54
	online-B	24.30	57.95	59.63
es-en	primary	33.90	48.88	65.72
	contrast	33.47	49.41	66.41
	online-A	30.26	51.56	63.83
fr-en	primary	32.41	48.93	65.72
	contrast	32.15	49.12	65.71
	kit	30.36	50.74	64.32
en-cz	primary	20.80	61.17	41.68
	contrast	20.74	61.29	41.69
	online-B	20.37	61.38	41.40
en-de	primary	18.45	64.15	22.91
	contrast	18.27	64.48	22.75
	online-B	17.92	64.01	22.95
en-es	primary	36.47	47.08	34.96
	contrast	35.82	47.52	34.64
	online-B	33.85	50.09	33.96
en-fr	primary	36.42	48.28	24.29
	contrast	36.31	48.56	24.12
	online-B	35.34	48.68	23.53

Table 2: Automatic scores for our submissions. For comparison, the top individual system by BLEU is shown in the third row of each track. Test data and references were preprocessed prior to scoring. Metrics are uncased and METEOR 1.0 uses adequacy-fluency parameters. We show improvement on all tasks except Haitian Creole-English.

rors; our content-based alignment method avoids many of these errors. BLEU penalizes the missing word the same as missing punctuation while human judges will penalize heavily for missing content. For full results, we refer to the simultaneously published Workshop on Machine Translation findings paper.

6 Conclusion

We participated in the all ten tracks of the system combination, prioritizing participation and language support over optimizing for one particular language pair. Nonetheless, we show improvement on several tasks, including wins by BLEU on three tracks. The Haitian Creole and Czech-English tasks proved challenging due to the gap between top systems. However, other tracks show a variety of high-performing systems that make our scheme perform well. Unlike most other system combination schemes, our code is open source[2] so that these results may be replicated and brought to bear on similar problems.

Acknowledgements

Jon Clark assisted with language model construction and wrote BigFatLM. This material is based upon work supported by the National Science Foundation Graduate Research Fellowship under Grant No. 0750271 and by the DARPA GALE program.

References

Colin Bannard and Chris Callison-Burch. 2005. Paraphrasing with bilingual parallel corpora. In *Proceedings ACL*.

Ondřej Bojar and Zdeněk Žabokrtský. 2009. CzEng 0.9, building a large Czech-English automatic parallel treebank. *The Prague Bulletin of Mathematical Linguistics*, (92):63–83.

Michael Denkowski and Alon Lavie. 2010. Meteor-next and the meteor paraphrase tables: Improved evaluation support for five target languages. In *Proceedings of the Joint Fifth Workshop on Statistical Machine Translation and MetricsMATR*, pages 339–342, Uppsala, Sweden, July. Association for Computational Linguistics.

Chris Dyer, Adam Lopez, Juri Ganitkevitch, Johnathan Weese, Ferhan Ture, Phil Blunsom, Hendra Setiawan, Vladimir Eidelman, and Philip Resnik. 2010. cdec: A decoder, alignment, and learning framework for finite-state and context-free translation models. In *Proceedings of the ACL 2010 System Demonstrations*, ACLDemos '10, pages 7–12.

Christiane Fellbaum. 1998. *WordNet: An Electronic Lexical Database*. MIT Press.

Kenneth Heafield and Alon Lavie. 2010. CMU multi-engine machine translation for WMT 2010. In *Proceedings of the Joint Fifth Workshop on Statistical Machine Translation and MetricsMATR*. Association for Computational Linguistics.

Kenneth Heafield. 2011. KenLM: Faster and smaller language model queries. In *Proceedings of the Sixth Workshop on Statistical Machine Translation*, Edinburgh, UK, July. Association for Computational Linguistics.

Almut Silja Hildebrand and Stephan Vogel. 2009. CMU system combination for WMT'09. In *Proceedings of the Fourth Workshop on Statistical Machine Translation*, pages 47–50, Athens, Greece, March. Association for Computational Linguistics.

Philipp Koehn, Hieu Hoang, Alexandra Birch, Chris Callison-Burch, Marcello Federico, Nicola Bertoldi, Brooke Cowan, Wade Shen, Christine Moran, Richard Zens, Chris Dyer, Ondrej Bojar, Alexandra Constantin, and Evan Herbst. 2007. Moses: Open source toolkit for statistical machine translation. In *Annual Meeting of the Association for Computational Linguistics (ACL)*, Prague, Czech Republic, June.

Philipp Koehn. 2005. Europarl: A parallel corpus for statistical machine translation. In *Proceedings of MT Summit*.

Ângelo Mendonça, David Graff, and Denise DiPersio. 2009a. French gigaword second edition. LDC2009T28.

Ângelo Mendonça, David Graff, and Denise DiPersio. 2009b. Spanish gigaword second edition. LDC2009T21.

Sushant Narsale. 2010. JHU system combination scheme for wmt 2010. In *Proceedings of the Joint Fifth Workshop on Statistical Machine Translation and MetricsMATR*, pages 311–314, Uppsala, Sweden, July. Association for Computational Linguistics.

Kishore Papineni, Salim Roukos, Todd Ward, and Wei-Jing Zhu. 2002. BLEU: a method for automatic evaluation of machine translation. In *Proceedings of 40th Annual Meeting of the Association for Computational Linguistics (ACL)*, pages 311–318, Philadelphia, PA, July.

Robert Parker, David Graff, Junbo Kong, Ke Chen, and Kazuaki Maeda. 2009. English gigaword fourth edition. LDC2009T13.

[2] `http://kheafield.com/code/mt`

Martin Porter. 2001. Snowball: A language for stemming algorithms. http://snowball.tartarus.org/.

Antti-Veikko Rosti, Bing Zhang, Spyros Matsoukas, and Richard Schwartz. 2010. BBN system description for wmt10 system combination task. In *Proceedings of the Joint Fifth Workshop on Statistical Machine Translation and MetricsMATR*, pages 321–326, Uppsala, Sweden, July. Association for Computational Linguistics.

Matthew Snover, Bonnie Dorr, Richard Schwartz, Linnea Micciulla, and John Makhoul. 2006. A Study of Translation Edit Rate with Targeted Human Annotation. In *Proceedings of the 7th Conference of the Association for Machine Translation in the Americas (AMTA-2006)*, pages 223–231, Cambridge, MA, August.

The RWTH System Combination System for WMT 2011

Gregor Leusch, Markus Freitag, and Hermann Ney
RWTH Aachen University
Aachen, Germany
{leusch,freitag,ney}@cs.rwth-aachen.de

Abstract

RWTH participated in the System Combination task of the Sixth Workshop on Statistical Machine Translation (WMT 2011).

For three language pairs, we combined 6 to 14 systems into a single consensus translation. A three-level meta-combination scheme combining six different system combination setups with three different engines was applied on the French–English language pair. Depending on the language pair, improvements versus the best single system are in the range of $+1.9\%$ and $+2.5\%$ abs. on BLEU, and between -1.8% and -2.4% abs. on TER. Novel techniques compared with RWTH's submission to WMT 2010 include two additional system combination engines, an additional word alignment technique, meta combination, and additional optimization techniques.

1 Introduction

RWTH's main approach to System Combination (SC) for Machine Translation (MT) is a refined version of the ROVER approach in Automatic Speech Recognition (ASR) (Fiscus, 1997), with additional steps to cope with reordering between different hypotheses, and to use true casing information from the input hypotheses. The basic concept of the approach has been described by Matusov et al. (2006). Several improvements have been added later (Matusov et al., 2008). This approach includes an enhanced alignment and reordering framework. In contrast to existing approaches (Jayaraman and Lavie, 2005; Rosti et al., 2007b), the context of the whole corpus rather than a single sentence is considered in this iterative, unsupervised procedure, yielding a more reliable alignment. Majority voting on the generated lattice is performed using prior weights for each system as well as other statistical models such as a special n-gram language model. True casing is considered a separate step in RWTH's approach, which also takes the input hypotheses into account. The pipeline, and consequently the description of the main pipeline given in this paper, is based on our pipeline for WMT 2010 (Leusch and Ney, 2010), with extensions as described. When necessary, we denote this pipeline as *Align-to-Lattice*, or *A2L* .

For the French–English task, we used two additional system combination engines for the first time: The first one uses the same alignments as A2L, but generates lattices in the OpenFST framework (Allauzen et al., 2007). The OpenFST decoder (`fstshortestpath`) is then used to find the best path (consensus translation) in this lattice. Analogously, we call this engine *A2FST* . The second additional engine, which we call *SCUNC,* uses a TER-based alignment, similar to the approach by Rosti et al. (2007b). Instead of a lattice rescoring, finding the consensus translation is considered a per-node classification problem: For each slot, which one is the "correct" one (i.e. will give the "best" output)? This approach is inspired by iROVER (Hillard et al., 2007). Consensus translations from different settings of these approaches could then be combined again by an additional application of system combination – which we refer to as *meta combination* (Rosti et al., 2007a). These three approaches are described in more detail in Section 2. In Section 3 we describe how we tuned the parameters and decisions of our system combination approaches for WMT 2011. Section 4 then lists our experimental setup as well as the experimental results we obtained on the WMT 2011 system combination track. We conclude this paper in Section 5.

2 System Combination Algorithm (A2L)

In this section we present the details of our main system combination method, A2L. The upper part of Figure 1 gives an overview of the system combination architecture described in this section. After preprocessing the MT hypotheses, pairwise align-

Proceedings of the 6th Workshop on Statistical Machine Translation, pages 152–158,
Edinburgh, Scotland, UK, July 30–31, 2011. ©2011 Association for Computational Linguistics

ments between the hypotheses are calculated. The hypotheses are then reordered to match the word order of a selected *primary* (*skeleton*) hypothesis. From this, we create a confusion network (CN) which we then rescore using system prior weights and a language model (LM). The single best path in this CN then constitutes the consensus translation. The consensus translation is then true cased and post processed.

2.1 Word Alignment

The main proposed alignment approach is a statistical one. It takes advantage of multiple translations for a whole corpus to compute a consensus translation for each sentence in this corpus. It also takes advantage of the fact that the sentences to be aligned are in the same language.

For each of the K source sentences in the test corpus, we select one of its N translations from different MT systems $E_m m = 1, \ldots, N$, as the *primary* hypothesis. Then we align the *secondary* hypotheses $E_n (n = 1, \ldots, ; n \neq m)$ with E_n to match the word order in E_n. Since it is not clear which hypothesis should be primary, i. e. has the "best" word order, we let several or all hypothesis play the role of the primary translation, and align all pairs of hypotheses (E_n, E_m); $n \neq m$.

The word alignment is *trained* in analogy to the alignment training procedure in statistical MT. The difference is that the two sentences that have to be aligned are in the same language. We use the IBM Model 1 (Brown et al., 1993) and the Hidden Markov Model (HMM, (Vogel et al., 1996)) to estimate the alignment model.

The alignment training corpus is created from a test corpus of effectively $N \cdot (N-1) \cdot K$ sentences translated by the involved MT engines. Model parameters are trained iteratively using the GIZA++ toolkit (Och and Ney, 2003). The training is performed in the directions $E_m \rightarrow E_n$ and $E_n \rightarrow E_m$. The final alignments are determined using a cost matrix C for each sentence pair (E_m, E_n). Elements of this matrix are the local costs $C(j, i)$ of aligning a word $e_{m,j}$ from E_m to a word $e_{n,i}$ from E_n. Following Matusov et al. (2004), we compute these local costs by interpolating the negated logarithms of the state occupation probabilities from the "source-to-target" and "target-to-source" training of the HMM model.

A different approach that has e.g. been proposed by Rosti et al. (2007b) is the utilization of a TER alignment (Snover et al., 2006) for this purpose. Because the original TER is insensitive to small changes in spellings, synonyms etc., it has been proposed to use more complex variants, e.g. TERp. For our purposes, we utilized "poor-man's-stemming", i.e. shortening each word to its first four characters when calculating the TER alignment. Since a TER alignment already implies a reordering between the primary and the secondary hypothesis, an explicit reordering step is not necessary.

2.2 Word Reordering and Confusion Network Generation

After reordering each secondary hypothesis E_m and the rows of the corresponding alignment cost matrix, we determine $N-1$ monotone *one-to-one* alignments between E_n as the primary translation and $E_m, m = 1, \ldots, N; m \neq n$. We then construct the confusion network.

We consider words without a correspondence to the primary translation (and vice versa) to have a null alignment with the empty word ε, which will be transformed to an ε-arc in the corresponding confusion network.

The $N-1$ monotone one-to-one alignments can then be transformed into a confusion network, as described by Matusov et al. (2008).

2.3 Voting in the Confusion Network (A2L, A2FST)

Instead of choosing a fixed sentence to define the word order for the consensus translation, we generate confusion networks for N possible hypotheses as primary, and unite them into a single lattice. In our experience, this approach is advantageous in terms of translation quality compared to a minimum Bayes risk primary (Rosti et al., 2007b).

Weighted majority voting on a single confusion network is straightforward and analogous to ROVER (Fiscus, 1997). We sum up the probabilities of the arcs which are labeled with the same word and have the same start state and the same end state.

Compared to A2L, our new A2FST engine allows for a higher number of features for each arc. Consequently, we add a binary system feature for each system in addition to the logarithm of the sum of system weights, as before. The advantage of these features is that the weights are linear within a log-linear model, as opposed to be part of a logarithmic sum. Consequently they can later be optimized using techniques designed for linear feature weights, such as MERT, or MIRA.

2.4 Language Models

The lattice representing a union of several confusion networks can then be directly rescored with an n-gram language model (LM). When regarding

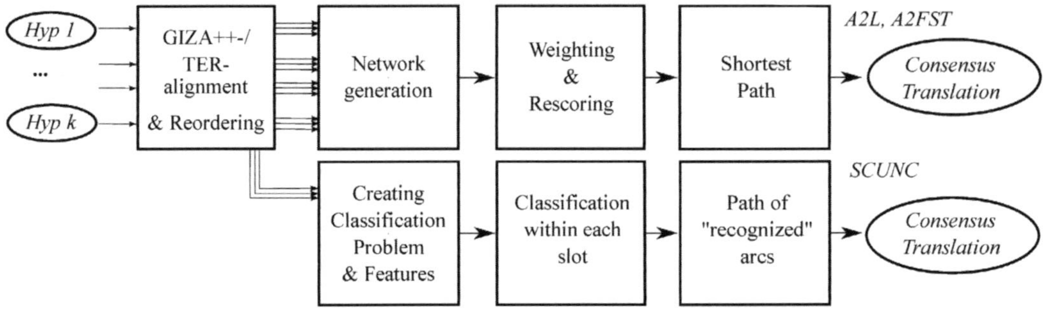

Figure 1: The system combination architecture.

the lattice as a weighted Finite State Transducer (FST), this can be regarded (and implemented) as composition with a LM FST.

In our approach, we train a trigram LM on the outputs of the systems involved in system combination. For LM training, we take the system hypotheses for the same test corpus for which the consensus translations are to be produced. Using this "adapted" LM for lattice rescoring thus gives bonus to n-grams from the original system hypotheses, in most cases from the original phrases. Presumably, many of these phrases have a correct word order. Previous experimental results show that using this LM in rescoring together with a word penalty notably improves translation quality. This even results in better translations than using a "classical" LM trained on a monolingual training corpus. We attribute this to the fact that most of the systems we combine already include such general LMs. Nevertheless, one of the SC systems we use for the French–English task (`IV` in Section 4.1) uses a filtered fourgram LM trained on GigaWord and other constrained training data sets for this WMT tasks as an additional LM.

2.5 Extracting Consensus Translations

To generate our consensus translation, we extract the single-best path from the rescored lattice, using "classical" decoding as in MT. In A2L, this is implemented as shortest-path decoder on a pruned lattice. In A2FST, we use the OpenFST `fstshortestpath` decoder, which does not require a pruning step for lattices of the size and density produced here.

2.6 Classification in the Confusion Network (SCUNC)

Instead of considering the selection of the consensus problem as a shortest-path problem in a rescored confusion network, we can treat it instead as a classification problem: For each slot (set of outgoing arcs from one node in a CN), we consider one or more arcs to be "correct", and train a classifier to identify these certain arcs. This is the idea of the iROVER approach in ASR (Hillard et al., 2007). We call our implementation *System Combination Using N-gram Classifiers*, or *SCUNC*.

For the WMT evaluation, we used the ICSI-Boost framework (Favre et al., 2007) as classifier (in binary mode, i.e. giving a yes/no-decision for each single arc). We generated 109 features from 8 families: Pairwise equality of words from different systems, Number of votes for a word, word that would win a simple majority voting, empty word (also in previous two arcs), position at beginning or end of sentence, cross-BLEU-S score of hypothesis, equality of system with system of last slot, and SRILM uni- to trigram scores. As this approach requires strict CN instead of lattices, a union of CNs for different primary hypotheses was no longer possible. We decided to select a fixed single primary system; other approaches would have been to train an additional classifier for this purpose, or to select a minimum-Bayes-risk (MBR) skeleton.

2.7 Consensus True Casing

Previous approaches to achieve true cased output in system combination operated on true-cased lattices, used a separate input-independent true caser, or used a general true-cased LM to differentiate between alternative arcs in the lattice, as described by Leusch et al. (2009). For WMT 2011, we use per-sentence information from the input systems to determine the consensus case of each output word. Lattice generation, rescoring, and reranking are performed on lower-cased input, with a lower-cased consensus hypothesis as their result. For each word in this hypothesis, we count how often each casing variant occurs in the input hypotheses for this sentence. We then use the variant with the highest support for the final consensus output.

Table 1: Corpus and Task statistics.

	avg. # words			#sys
	TUNE	DEV	TEST	
FR–EN	15670	11410	49832	25
DE–EN	15508	10878	49395	24
ES–EN	15989	11234	50612	15
# sent	609	394	2000	

3 Tuning

3.1 Feature weights

For lattice rescoring, we selected a linear combination of BLEU (Papineni et al., 2002) and TER (Snover et al., 2006) as optimization criterion, $\hat{\Theta} := \mathrm{argmax}_{\Theta}\{BLEU - TER\}$ for the A2L engine, based on previous experience (Mauser et al., 2008). To achieve more stable results, we use the case-insensitive variants for both measures, despite the explicit use of case information in the pipeline. System weights were tuned to this criterion using the Downhill Simplex method.

In the A2FST setup, we were able to generate full lattices, with separate costs for each individual feature on all arcs (Power Semiring). This allowed us to run Lattice MERT (Macherey et al., 2008) on the full lattice, with no need for pruning (and thus additional outer iterations for re-generating lattices). We tried different strategies – random lines vs axis-parallel lines, regularization, random restarts, etc, and selected the most stable results on TUNE and DEV for this engine. Optimization criterion here was BLEU.

3.2 Training a classifier for SCUNC

In MT system combination, even with given reference translations, there is no simple way to identify the "correct" arc in a slot. This renders a classifier-based approach even more difficult than iROVER in ASR. The problem is even aggravated because both the alignment of words, and their order, can be incorrect already in the CN. We thus consider an arc to be "correct" within this task exactly if it gives us the best possible total BLEU-S score.[1] These "correct" arcs, which lie on such an "oracle path" for BLEU-S, were therefore used as reference classes when training the classifier.

3.3 System Selection

With the large numbers of input systems – e.g., 25 for FR–EN – and their large spread in translation quality – e.g. from 22.2 to 31.4% in BLEU – not all systems should participate in the system combination process. This is especially the case since several of these e.g. 25 systems are often only small variants of each other (contrastive vs. primary submissions), which leads to a low variability of these translations. We considered several variants of the set of input systems, often starting from the top, and either replacing some of the systems very similar to others with systems further down the list, or not considering those as primary, adding further systems as additional secondaries. Depending on the engine we were using, we selected between 6 and 14 different systems as input.

4 Experimental Results

Each language pair in WMT 2011 had its own set of systems, so we selected and tuned separately for each language pair . Due to time constraints, we only participated in tasks with English as the target language. In preliminary experiments, it turned out that System Combination was not able to get a better result than the best single system on the Czech–English task. Consequently, we focused on the language pairs French–English, German–English, and Spanish–English.

We split the available tuning data document-wise into a 609-line TUNE set (for tuning), and a 394-line DEV set (to verify tuning results). More statistics on these sets can be found in Table 1.

Unfortunately, late in the evaluation campaign it turned out that the quality of several reference sentences used in TUNE and DEV was rather low: Many reference sentences contained spelling errors, a few dozen lines even contained French phrases or sentences within or after the English text. We corrected many of these errors manually in the references. In total 101 of 690 lines (16.6%) in TUNE and 58 of 394 lines (14.7%) in DEV were affected by this. While it was too late to rerun all of the optimization runs, we re-optimized at least a few final systems. All scores within this section were calculated on the corrected reference translations.

4.1 FR–EN

For French–English, we built in total seven different system combination setups to generate a single consensus translation and two contrastive translations. Figure 2 shows the structure and the data flow of our setup for FR–EN. Table 2 lists more details about the individual engines.

Our primary submission was focused on our experience that while rule-based MT systems (such as `RBMT-1..5` and `systran`) tend to have lower BLEU scores than statistical (SMT) systems, they usually give considerable improve-

[1]We are looking at the sentence level, so we use BLEU-S (Lin and Och, 2004) instead of BLEU

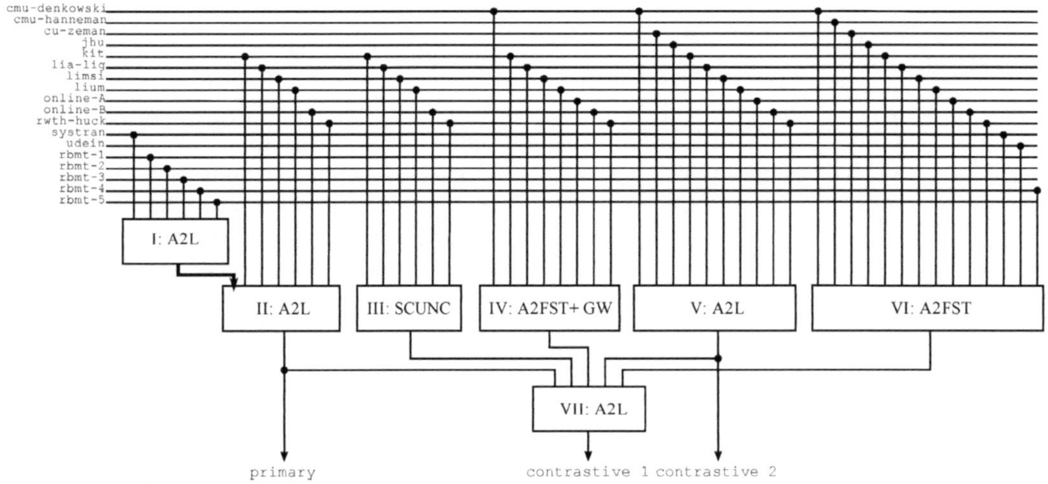

Bold arrows denote a system that is always considered as skeleton.
Note that there are two variants of setup `II`*, see text.*

Figure 2: System combination pipelines for FR–EN

Table 2: Engines and input systems for FR–EN.

	Engine	# Input	submitted?
I	A2L	6 RBMT	
II	A2L	I + 6	`primary`
II'	A2L	fix I + 6	*for VII*
III	SCUNC	6	
IV	A2FST	GW, 8	
V	A2L	10	`contrastive-2`
VI	A2FST	14	
VII	A2L	II'–VI	`contrastive-1`

"GW" means a 4-gram LM trained on GigaWord.
`II` *uses all skeletons,* `II'` *uses* `I` *as fixed skeleton.*

Table 3: Results for FR–EN.

	TUNE		DEV	
	BLEU	TER	BLEU	TER
`kit`	31.56	50.15	30.25	52.88
`systran`	28.18	53.32	26.50	56.07
I	27.37	54.73	26.72	57.73
II	33.69	48.47	32.45	51.09
II'	33.39	48.77	31.81	51.57
III	32.74	48.06	31.88	50.87
IV	34.16	48.31	31.95	51.64
V	33.17	48.95	32.60	51.14
VI	33.86	48.69	31.56	52.25
VII	34.41	48.20	32.15	51.49

`kit` *is the best single system.*
`systran` *is the best single rule-based system.*
All scores are case insensitive, and were calculated on the corrected reference translations.

ments to the latter in a SC setup. Here, though, the number of such systems was too high to simply add them to a reasonable set of SMT systems. Consequently, we first built a SC system (`I`) combining all RBMT/Systran systems, and then a second SC system (`II`) which combines the output of `I`, and 6 SMT systems. As further experiments showed, allowing all hypotheses as primary (or skeleton) gave significantly better scores than forcing SC to use the output of `I` as primary only. But vice versa, when looking at the meta combination scheme, `VII`, using `I` as primary only (a setup which we will now denote as `II'`) gave measurable improvements in the overall translation quality. We assume this is due to the similarity of the output of `II` with that of the other setups.

Setup `III` is a SCUNC setup, that is, we built a single CN for each sentence using poor-man's-stemming-TER, with `rwth-huck` as primary hypothesis. We then generated a large number of features for each arc, and trained an ICSIBoost classifier to recognize the arc (or system) that gave the best BLEU-S score. This then gave us the consensus translation.

For `IV`, we built an OpenFST lattice out of eight systems, and rescored it with both the Hypothesis LM (3-gram), and a 4-gram LM trained on GigaWord and other WMT constrained training data for this task. The log-linear weights were trained using lattice MERT for BLEU. Setup `V` is a classical A2L setup, using ten different input systems. This setup was tuned on BLEU – TER using the Downhill-Simplex algorithm. In setup `VI`, again the A2FST engine was used, this time using the Hyp LM only, without an additional LM. Tuning

Table 4: Results for DE–EN.

	TUNE		DEV	
	BLEU	TER	BLEU	TER
online-B	23.13	60.15	26.20	57.20
Primary	24.57	58.51	28.11	54.83
4 best sys	23.85	58.22	27.47	54.96
6 best sys	24.46	57.74	27.82	54.50

online-B *is the best single system.*

Table 5: Results for ES–EN.

	TUNE		DEV	
	BLEU	TER	BLEU	TER
online-A	30.58	51.69	30.77	51.95
Primary	34.29	48.47	33.41	49.71
Contrastive	34.23	48.27	33.30	49.51

online-A *is the best single system.*

was also performed using lattice MERT towards BLEU. And finally, setup VII combines the output of II′ to IV using the A2L engine again.

All the results of system combination on TUNE and DEV are listed in Table 3. It turns out that with the exception of I, all system combination approaches were able to achieve a significant improvement of at least $+1.8\%$ abs. in BLEU compared to the best input system. For I, we need to keep in mind that all other systems were several BLEU points worse than the best one – a scenario where we can expect system combination, which is based on the *consensus* translation after all, to underperform. We also see that both A2FST and SCUNC, with their large number of features, show a tendency to overfitting – we see large improvements on TUNE, but significantly smaller improvements on DEV. This tendency is, unfortunately, also the case for meta combination: While we see an additional $+0.3\%$ abs. in BLEU over the best first-level system combination on TUNE, this improvement does not reflect in the scores on DEV: While we still see a $+0.2\%$ abs. improvement in BLEU over the setup that performed best on TUNE, there is even a small deterioration of -0.4% in BLEU over the setup that performed best on DEV. Because of this effect, we decided to submit our meta combination output only as first contrastive, and the output that performed well both on TUNE and DEV as our primary submission for WMT. As second contrastive submission, we selected the setup that performed best on DEV.

4.2 DE–EN

24 systems were available in the German–English language pair, but incorporating only 7 of them turned out to deliver optimal results on DEV. We ran experiments on several settings of systems, but only in our tried and tested A2L framework. We settled for a combination of seven systems (online-B, cmu-dyer, dfki-xu, limsi, online-A, rwth-wuebker, kit) as primary submission. Table 4 also lists two different settings. One setting consists of the four best systems (online-B, cmu-dyer, rwth-wuebker, kit) and the other setting contains the six best systems (online-B, cmu-dyer, dfki-xu, rwth-wuebker, online-A, kit). When we added more systems to system combination, we lost performance in both TUNE and DEV.

4.3 ES–EN

For Spanish–English, we tried several settings of systems. We sticked to our tried and tested A2L framework. We settled for a combination of six systems (alacant, koc, online-A, online-B, rbmt-1, systran) as contrastive submission, and a combination of ten systems (+rbmt-2, rbmt-3, rbmt-4, udein) as primary submission. Table 5 lists the results for this task. The difference between our primary setup (10 systems) and our contrastive setup (6 systems) is rather small, less than 0.1% abs. in BLEU. Nevertheless, we see significant improvements over the best single system of $+2.4\%$ abs. in BLEU, and -2.2% in TER.

5 Conclusions

We have shown that our system combination approach leads to significant improvements over single best MT output where a significant number of comparably good translations is available on a single language pair. A meta combination can give additional improvement, but can be sensitive to overfitting; so in some cases, using one of its input system combination hypothesis may be a better choice. In any way, both of our new engines have shown that they can compete with our present approach, so we hope to make good use of the new possibilities they may offer.

Acknowledgments

This work was partly realized as part of the Quaero Programme, funded by OSEO, French State agency for innovation. This work was partly supported by the Defense Advanced Research Projects Agency (DARPA) under Contract No. HR0011-06-C-0023.

References

C. Allauzen, M. Riley, J. Schalkwyk, W. Skut, and M. Mohri. 2007. OpenFst: A general and efficient weighted finite-state transducer library. In *Proc. of the Twelfth International Conference on Implementation and Application of Automata (CIAA)*, volume 4783 of *Lecture Notes in Computer Science*, pages 11–23. Springer.

P. F. Brown, S. A. Della Pietra, V. J. Della Pietra, and R. L. Mercer. 1993. The mathematics of statistical machine translation: parameter estimation. *Computational Linguistics*, 19(2):263–311, June.

B. Favre, D. Hakkani-Tür, and S. Cuendet. 2007. Icsiboost. `http://code.google.come/p/icsiboost`.

J. Fiscus. 1997. A post-processing system to yield reduced word error rates: Recognizer output voting error reduction (ROVER). In *IEEE Workshop on Automatic Speech Recognition and Understanding*.

D. Hillard, B. Hoffmeister, M. Ostendorf, R. Schlüter, and H. Ney. 2007. iROVER: improving system combination with classification. In *Human Language Technologies 2007: The Conference of the North American Chapter of the Association for Computational Linguistics; Companion Volume, Short Papers*, NAACL-Short '07, pages 65–68. Association for Computational Linguistics.

S. Jayaraman and A. Lavie. 2005. Multi-engine machine translation guided by explicit word matching. In *Proc. of the 10th Annual Conf. of the European Association for Machine Translation (EAMT)*, pages 143–152, Budapest, Hungary, May.

G. Leusch and H. Ney. 2010. The rwth system combination system for wmt 2010. In *ACL 2010 Joint Fifth Workshop on Statistical Machine Translation and Metrics MATR*, pages 315–320, Uppsala, Sweden, July.

G. Leusch, E. Matusov, and H. Ney. 2009. The RWTH system combination system for WMT 2009. In *Fourth Workshop on Statistical Machine Translation*, pages 56–60, Athens, Greece, March. Association for Computational Linguistics.

C. Y. Lin and F. J. Och. 2004. Orange: a method for evaluation automatic evaluation metrics for machine translation. In *Proc. COLING 2004*, pages 501–507, Geneva, Switzerland, August.

W. Macherey, F. Och, I. Thayer, and J. Uszkoreit. 2008. Lattice-based minimum error rate training for statistical machine translation. In *Proc. of the 2008 Conference on Empirical Methods in Natural Language Processing (EMNLP)*, pages 725–734. Association for Computational Linguistics.

E. Matusov, R. Zens, and H. Ney. 2004. Symmetric word alignments for statistical machine translation. In *COLING '04: The 20th Int. Conf. on Computational Linguistics*, pages 219–225, Geneva, Switzerland, August.

E. Matusov, N. Ueffing, and H. Ney. 2006. Computing consensus translation from multiple machine translation systems using enhanced hypotheses alignment. In *Conference of the European Chapter of the Association for Computational Linguistics (EACL)*, pages 33–40, Trento, Italy, April.

E. Matusov, G. Leusch, R. E. Banchs, N. Bertoldi, D. Dechelotte, M. Federico, M. Kolss, Y. S. Lee, J. B. Marino, M. Paulik, S. Roukos, H. Schwenk, and H. Ney. 2008. System combination for machine translation of spoken and written language. *IEEE Transactions on Audio, Speech and Language Processing*, 16(7):1222–1237, September.

A. Mauser, S. Hasan, and H. Ney. 2008. Automatic evaluation measures for statistical machine translation system optimization. In *International Conference on Language Resources and Evaluation*, Marrakech, Morocco, May.

F. J. Och and H. Ney. 2003. A systematic comparison of various statistical alignment models. *Computational Linguistics*, 29(1):19–51, March.

K. Papineni, S. Roukos, T. Ward, and W. J. Zhu. 2002. BLEU: a Method for Automatic Evaluation of Machine Translation. In *Proc. of the 40th Annual Meeting of the Association for Computational Linguistics (ACL)*, pages 311–318, Philadelphia, PA, July.

A. V. Rosti, N. F. Ayan, B. Xiang, S. Matsoukas, R. M. Schwartz, and B. J. Dorr. 2007a. Combining outputs from multiple machine translation systems. In *HLT-NAACL'07*, pages 228–235.

A. V. Rosti, S. Matsoukas, and R. Schwartz. 2007b. Improved word-level system combination for machine translation. In *Proc. of the 45th Annual Meeting of the Association of Computational Linguistics (ACL)*, pages 312–319, Prague, Czech Republic, June.

M. Snover, B. Dorr, R. Schwartz, L. Micciulla, and J. Makhoul. 2006. A Study of Translation Error Rate with Targeted Human Annotation. In *Proc. of the 7th Conf. of the Association for Machine Translation in the Americas (AMTA)*, pages 223–231, Boston, MA, August.

S. Vogel, H. Ney, and C. Tillmann. 1996. HMM-based word alignment in statistical translation. In *COLING '96: The 16th Int. Conf. on Computational Linguistics*, pages 836–841, Copenhagen, Denmark, August.

Expected BLEU Training for Graphs: BBN System Description for WMT11 System Combination Task

Antti-Veikko I. Rosti* and **Bing Zhang** and **Spyros Matsoukas** and **Richard Schwartz**
Raytheon BBN Technologies, 10 Moulton Street, Cambridge, MA 02138, USA
{arosti,bzhang,smatsouk,schwartz}@bbn.com

Abstract

BBN submitted system combination outputs for Czech-English, German-English, Spanish-English, and French-English language pairs. All combinations were based on confusion network decoding. The confusion networks were built using incremental hypothesis alignment algorithm with flexible matching. A novel bi-gram count feature, which can penalize bi-grams not present in the input hypotheses corresponding to a source sentence, was introduced in addition to the usual decoder features. The system combination weights were tuned using a graph based expected BLEU as the objective function while incrementally expanding the networks to bi-gram and 5-gram contexts. The expected BLEU tuning described in this paper naturally generalizes to hypergraphs and can be used to optimize thousands of weights. The combination gained about 0.5-4.0 BLEU points over the best individual systems on the official WMT11 language pairs. A 39 system multi-source combination achieved an 11.1 BLEU point gain.

1 Introduction

The confusion networks for the BBN submissions to the WMT11 system combination task were built using incremental hypothesis alignment algorithm with flexible matching (Rosti et al., 2009). A novel bi-gram count feature was used in addition to the standard decoder features. The N-best list based expected BLEU tuning (Rosti et al., 2010), similar to the one proposed by Smith and Eisner (2006), was extended to operate on word lattices. This method is closely related to the consensus BLEU (CoBLEU) proposed by Pauls et al. (2009). The minimum operation used to compute the clipped counts (matches) in the BLEU score (Papineni et al., 2002) was replaced by a differentiable function, so there was no need to use sub-gradient ascent as in CoBLEU. The expected BLEU (xBLEU) naturally generalizes to hypergraphs by simply replacing the forward-backward algorithm with inside-outside algorithm when computing the expected n-gram counts and sufficient statistics for the gradient.

The gradient ascent optimization of the xBLEU appears to be more stable than the gradient-free direct 1-best BLEU tuning or N-best list based minimum error rate training (Och, 2003), especially when tuning a large number of weights. On the official WMT11 language pairs with up to 30 weights, there was no significant benefit from maximizing xBLEU. However, on a 39 system multi-source combination (43 weights total), it yielded a significant gain over gradient-free BLEU tuning and N-best list based expected BLEU tuning.

2 Hypothesis Alignment and Features

The incremental hypothesis alignment with flexible matching (Rosti et al., 2009) produces a confusion network for each system output acting as a skeleton hypothesis for the ith source sentence. A confusion network is a graph where all paths visit all

*This work was supported by DARPA/I2O Contract No. HR0011-06-C-0022 under the GALE program (Approved for Public Release, Distribution Unlimited). The views, opinions, and/or findings contained in this article/presentation are those of the author/presenter and should not be interpreted as representing the official views or policies, either expressed or implied, of the Defense Advanced Research Projects Agency or the Department of Defense.

Proceedings of the 6th Workshop on Statistical Machine Translation, pages 159–165,
Edinburgh, Scotland, UK, July 30–31, 2011. ©2011 Association for Computational Linguistics

vertices. Consecutive vertices are connected by one or more edges representing alternatives. Each edge l is associated with a token and a set of scores. A token may be a word, punctuation symbol, or special NULL token indicating a deletion in the alignment. The set of scores includes a vector of N_s system specific confidences, s_{iln}, indicating whether the token was aligned from the output of the system n.[1] Other scores may include a language model (LM) score as well as non-NULL and NULL token indicators (Rosti et al., 2007). As Rosti et al. (2010) described, the networks for all skeletons are connected to a start and end vertex with NULL tokens in order to form a joint lattice with multiple parallel networks. The edges connecting the start vertex to the initial vertices in each network have a heuristic prior estimated from the alignment statistics at the confidence corresponding to the skeleton system. The edges connecting the final vertices of each network to the end vertex have all system confidences set to one, so the final edge does not change the score of any path.

A single word confidence is produced from the confidence vector by taking an inner product with the system weights σ_n which are constrained to sum to one,[2] $\sum_n \sigma_n = 1$. The total edge score is produced by a log-linear interpolation of the word confidence with other features f_{ilm}:

$$s_{il} = \log\Big(\sum_{n=1}^{N_s} \sigma_n s_{iln}\Big) + \sum_m \lambda_m f_{ilm} \quad (1)$$

The usual features f_{ilm} include the LM score as well as non-NULL and NULL token indicators. Based on an analysis of the system combination outputs, a large number of bi-grams not present in any input hypothesis are often produced, some of which are clearly ungrammatical despite the LM. These novel bi-grams are due to errors in hypothesis alignment and the confusion network structure where any word from the incoming edges of a vertex can be followed by any word from the outgoing edges. After expanding and re-scoring the joint lattice with a bi-gram, a new feature indicating the presence of a novel bi-gram may be added on the edges. A negative weight for this feature discourages novel bi-grams in the output during decoding.

3 Weight Optimization

The most common objective function used in machine translation is the BLEU-N score (Papineni et al., 2002) defined as follows:[3]

$$\text{BLEU} = \prod_{n=1}^{N} \left(\frac{\sum_i m_i^n}{\sum_i h_i^n}\right)^{\frac{1}{N}} \phi\Big(1 - \frac{\sum_i r_i}{\sum_i h_i^1}\Big) \quad (2)$$

where N is the maximum n-gram order (typically $N = 4$), m_i^n is the number of n-gram matches (clipped counts) between the hypothesis e_i and reference $\hat{e}_i$ for segment i, h_i^n is the number of n-grams in the hypothesis, r_i is the reference length,[4] and $\phi(x) = \min(1.0, e^x)$ is the brevity penalty. Using g^n to represent an arbitrary n-gram, c_{ig^n} to represent the count of g^n in hypothesis e_i, and $\hat{c}_{ig^n}$ to represent the count of g^n in reference $\hat{e}_i$, the BLEU statistics can be defined as follows:

$$m_i^n = \sum_{g^n} \min(c_{ig^n}, \hat{c}_{ig^n}) \quad (3)$$

$$h_i^n = \sum_{g^n} c_{ig^n} \quad (4)$$

The unigram count h_i^1 is simply the hypothesis length and higher order n-gram counts can be obtained by $h_i^n = h_i^{n-1} - 1$. The reference n-gram counts for each sentence can be stored in an n-gram trie for efficient scoring.[5]

The BLEU score is not differentiable due to the minimum operations on the matches m_i^n and brevity penalty $\phi(x)$. Therefore gradient-free optimization algorithms, such as Powell's method or downhill simplex (Press et al., 2007), are often employed in weight tuning (Och, 2003). System combination weights tuned using the downhill simplex method to directly optimize 1-best BLEU score of the decoder outputs served as the first baseline in the experiments. The distributed optimization approach used here was first described in (Rosti et al., 2010).

[1]The confidences are binary when aligning 1-best outputs. More elaborate confidences may be estimated from N-best lists; see for example Rosti et al. (2007).

[2]See (Rosti et al., 2010) for a differentiable constraint.

[3]Superscripts indicate the n-gram order in all variables in this paper. They are used as exponents only for the constant e.

[4]If multiple references are available, r_i is the reference length closest to the hypothesis length, h_i^1.

[5]If multiple references are available, the maximum n-gram counts are stored.

A set of system combination weights was first tuned for unpruned lattices re-scored with a bi-gram LM. Another set of re-scoring weights was tuned for 300-best lists re-scored with a 5-gram LM.

3.1 Graph expected BLEU

Gradient-free optimization algorithms work well with a relatively small number of weights. Weight optimization for a 44 system combination in Rosti et al. (2010) was shown to be unstable with downhill simplex algorithm. Instead, an N-best list based expected BLEU tuning with gradient ascent yielded better results. This served as the second baseline in the experiments. The objective function is defined by replacing the n-gram statistics with expected n-gram counts and matches as in (Smith and Eisner, 2006), and brevity penalty with a differentiable approximation:

$$\varphi(x) = \frac{e^x - 1}{1 + e^{1000x}} + 1 \tag{5}$$

An N-best list represents a subset of the search space and multiple decoding iterations with N-best list merging is required to improve convergence. In this work, expected BLEU tuning is extended for lattices by replacing the minimum operation in n-gram matches with another differentiable approximation. The expected n-gram statistics for path j, which correspond to the standard statistics in Equations 3 and 4, are defined as follows:

$$\bar{m}_i^n = \sum_{g^n} \mu\Big(\sum_{j \in \mathcal{J}_i} P_{ij} c_{ijg^n}, \hat{c}_{ig^n}\Big) \tag{6}$$

$$\bar{h}_i^n = \sum_{g^n} \sum_{j \in \mathcal{J}_i} P_{ij} c_{ijg^n} \tag{7}$$

where $\mathcal{J}_i$ is the set of all paths in a lattice or all derivations in a hypergraph for the ith source sentence, P_{ij} is the posterior of path j, and c_{ijg^n} is the count of n-grams g^n in hypothesis e_{ij} on path j. The path posterior and approximate minimum are defined by:

$$P_{ij} = \frac{\prod_{l \in j} e^{\gamma s_{il}}}{\sum_{j' \in \mathcal{J}_i} \prod_{l \in j'} e^{\gamma s_{il}}} \tag{8}$$

$$\mu(x, c) = \frac{x - c}{1 + e^{1000(x-c)}} + c \tag{9}$$

where s_{il} is the total score on edge l defined in Equation 1 and γ is an edge score scaling factor. The scaling factor affects the shape of the edge posterior distribution; $\gamma > 1.0$ makes the edge posteriors on the 1-best path higher than edge posteriors on other paths and $\gamma < 1.0$ makes the posteriors on all paths more uniform.

The graph expected BLEU can be factored as $\text{xBLEU} = e^P B$ where:

$$P = \frac{1}{N} \sum_{n=1}^{N} \Big(\log \sum_i \bar{m}_i^n - \log \sum_i \bar{h}_i^n\Big) \tag{10}$$

$$B = \varphi\Big(1 - \frac{\sum_i r_i}{\sum_i \bar{h}_i^1}\Big) \tag{11}$$

and r_i is the reference length.[6] This objective function is closely related to CoBLEU (Pauls et al., 2009). Unlike CoBLEU, xBLEU is differentiable and standard gradient ascent algorithms can be used to find weights that maximize the objective.

Note, the expected counts can be expressed in terms of edge posteriors as:

$$\sum_{j \in \mathcal{J}_i} P_{ij} c_{ijg^n} = \sum_{l \in \mathcal{L}_i} p_{il} \delta(c_{il}^n, g^n) \tag{12}$$

where $\mathcal{L}_i$ is the set of all edges for the ith sentence, p_{il} is the edge posterior, $\delta(x, c)$ is the Kronecker delta function which is 1 if $x = c$ and 0 if $x \neq c$, and c_{il}^n is the n-gram context of edge l. The edge posteriors can be computed via standard forward-backward algorithm for lattices or inside-outside algorithm for hypergraphs. As with the BLEU statistics, only expected unigram counts $\bar{h}_i^1$ need to be accumulated for the hypothesis n-gram counts in Equation 7 as $\bar{h}_i^n = \bar{h}_i^{n-1} - 1$ for $n > 1$. Also, the expected n-gram counts for each graph can be stored in an n-gram trie for efficient gradient computation.

3.2 Gradient of graph expected BLEU

The gradient of the xBLEU with respect to weight λ can be factored as:

$$\frac{\partial \text{xBLEU}}{\partial \lambda} = \sum_i \sum_{l \in \mathcal{L}_i} \frac{\partial s_{il}}{\partial \lambda} \sum_{j \in \mathcal{J}_i} \frac{\partial \text{xBLEU}}{\partial \log P_{ij}} \frac{\partial \log P_{ij}}{\partial s_{il}} \tag{13}$$

where the gradient of the log-path-posterior with respect to the edge score is given by:

$$\frac{\partial \log P_{ij}}{\partial s_{il}} = \gamma\Big(\delta(l \in j) - p_{il}\Big) \tag{14}$$

[6]If multiple reference are available, r_i is the reference length closest to the expected hypothesis length $\bar{h}_i^1$.

$$\frac{\partial \text{xBLEU}}{\partial \lambda} = \gamma e^P \left(\frac{B}{N} \sum_{n=1}^{N} \sum_i \left(\frac{\hat{m}^n_{ik} - m^n_{ik}}{m^n} - \frac{\hat{h}^n_{ik} - h^n_{ik}}{h^n} \right) \right) + C\varphi'(1-C) \sum_i \frac{\hat{h}^1_{ik} - h^1_{ik}}{h^1} \tag{15}$$

and $\delta(l \in j)$ is one if edge l is on path j, and zero otherwise. Using the factorization $\text{xBLEU} = e^P B$, Equation 13 can be expressed using sufficient statistics as shown in Equation 15, where $\varphi'(x)$ is the derivative of $\varphi(x)$ with respect to x, $m^n = \sum_i \bar{m}^n_i$, $h^n = \sum_i \bar{h}^n_i$, $C = \sum r_i / \sum_i \bar{h}^1_i$, and the remaining sufficient statistics are given by:

$$\mu'_{ig^n} = \mu'\Big(\sum_{j \in \mathcal{J}_i} P_{ij} c_{ijg^n}, \hat{c}_{ig^n}\Big)$$

$$m^n_{ik} = \Big(\sum_{l \in \mathcal{L}_i} p_{il} \frac{\partial s_{il}}{\partial \lambda}\Big)\Big(\sum_{j \in \mathcal{J}_i} P_{ij} \sum_{g^n} \mu'_{ig^n} c_{ijg^n}\Big)$$

$$\hat{m}^n_{ik} = \sum_{l \in \mathcal{L}_i} \frac{\partial s_{il}}{\partial \lambda} \sum_{j: l \in \mathcal{J}_i} P_{ij} \sum_{g^n} \mu'_{ig^n} c_{ijg^n}$$

$$h^n_{ik} = \Big(\sum_{l \in \mathcal{L}_i} p_{il} \frac{\partial s_{il}}{\partial \lambda}\Big)\Big(\sum_{j \in \mathcal{J}_i} P_{ij} \sum_{g^n} c_{ijg^n}\Big)$$

$$\hat{h}^n_{ik} = \sum_{l \in \mathcal{L}_i} \frac{\partial s_{il}}{\partial \lambda} \sum_{j: l \in \mathcal{J}_i} P_{ij} \sum_{g^n} c_{ijg^n}$$

where $\mu'(x, c)$ is the derivative of $\mu(x, c)$ with respect to x, and the parentheses in the equations for m^n_{ik} and h^n_{ik} signify that the second terms do not depend on the edge l.

3.3 Forward-backward algorithm under expectation semiring

The sufficient statistics for graph expected BLEU can be computed using expectation semirings (Li and Eisner, 2009). Instead of computing single forward/backward or inside/outside scores, additional n-gram elements are tracked for matches and counts. For example in a bi-gram graph, the elements for edge l are represented by a 5-tuple[7] $s_l = \langle p_l, r^1_{lh}, r^2_{lh}, r^1_{lm}, r^2_{lm} \rangle$ where $p_l = e^{\gamma s_{il}}$ and:

$$r^n_{lh} = \sum_{g^n} \delta(c^n_{il}, g^n) e^{\gamma s_{il}} \tag{16}$$

$$r^n_{lm} = \sum_{g^n} \mu'_{ig^n} e^{\gamma s_{il}} \tag{17}$$

Assuming the lattice is topologically sorted, the forward algorithm[8] under expectation semiring for a 3-tuple[9] $s_l = \langle p_l, r^1_{lh}, r^1_{lm} \rangle$ is defined by:

$$\alpha_0 = \langle 1, 0, 0 \rangle \tag{18}$$

$$\alpha_v = \bigoplus_{l \in \mathcal{I}_v} \alpha_{u(l)} \otimes s_l \tag{19}$$

where $\mathcal{I}_v$ is the set of all edges with target vertex v and $u(l)$ is the source vertex for edge l, and the operations are defined by:

$$s_1 \oplus s_2 = \langle p_1 + p_2, r^1_{1h} + r^1_{2h}, r^1_{1m} + r^1_{2m} \rangle$$

$$s_1 \otimes s_2 = \langle p_1 p_2, p_1 r^1_{2h} + p_2 r^1_{1h}, p_1 r^1_{2m} + p_2 r^1_{1m} \rangle$$

The backward algorithm for β_u can be implemented via the forward algorithm in reverse through the graph. The sufficient statistics for the gradient can be accumulated during the backward pass noting that:

$$\sum_{j \in \mathcal{J}_i} P_{ij} \sum_{g^n} \mu'_{ig^n} c_{ijg^n} = \frac{r^n_m(\beta_0)}{p(\beta_0)} \tag{20}$$

$$\sum_{j \in \mathcal{J}_i} P_{ij} \sum_{g^n} c_{ijg^n} = \frac{r^n_h(\beta_0)}{p(\beta_0)} \tag{21}$$

where $r^n_m(\cdot)$ and $r^n_h(\cdot)$ extract the nth order r elements from the tuple for matches and counts, respectively, and $p(\cdot)$ extracts the p element. The statistics for the paths traveling via edge l can be computed by:

$$\sum_{j: l \in \mathcal{J}_i} P_{ij} \sum_{g^n} \mu'_{ig^n} c_{ijg^n} = \frac{r^n_m(\alpha_u \otimes s_l \otimes \beta_v)}{p(\beta_0)} \tag{22}$$

$$\sum_{j: l \in \mathcal{J}_i} P_{ij} \sum_{g^n} c_{ijg^n} = \frac{r^n_h(\alpha_u \otimes s_l \otimes \beta_v)}{p(\beta_0)} \tag{23}$$

where the u and v subscripts in α_u and β_v are the start and end vertices for edge l. To avoid underflow, all the computations can be carried out in log domain.

[7] The sentence index i is dropped for brevity.

[8] For inside-outside algorithm, see (Li and Eisner, 2009).

[9] A 3-tuple for uni-gram counts is used as an example in order to save space. In a 5-tuple for bi-gram counts, all r elements are computed independently of other r elements with the same operations. Similarly, tri-gram counts require 7-tuples and four-gram counts require 9-tuples.

tune	cz-en		de-en		es-en		fr-en	
System	TER	BLEU	TER	BLEU	TER	BLEU	TER	BLEU
worst	66.03	18.09	69.03	16.28	60.56	21.02	62.75	21.83
best	53.75	28.36	58.39	24.28	50.26	30.55	50.48	30.87
latBLEU	53.99	29.25	56.70	26.49	48.34	34.55	48.90	33.90
nbExpBLEU	54.43	29.04	56.36	27.33	48.44	34.73	48.58	34.23
latExpBLEU	53.89	29.37	56.24	27.36	48.27	34.93	48.53	34.24

test	cz-en		de-en		es-en		fr-en	
System	TER	BLEU	TER	BLEU	TER	BLEU	TER	BLEU
worst	65.35	17.69	69.03	15.83	61.22	19.79	62.36	21.36
best	52.21	29.54	58.00	24.16	50.15	30.14	50.15	30.32
latBLEU	52.80	29.89	55.87	26.22	48.29	33.91	48.51	32.93
nbExpBLEU	52.97	29.93	55.77	26.52	48.39	33.86	48.25	32.94
latExpBLEU	52.68	29.99	55.74	26.62	48.30	34.10	48.17	32.91

Table 1: Case insensitive TER and BLEU scores on newssyscombtune (tune) and newssyscombtest (test) for combinations of outputs from four source languages. Three tuning methods were used: lattice BLEU (latBLEU), N-best list based expected BLEU (nbExpBLEU), and lattice expected BLEU (latExpBLEU).

3.4 Entropy on a graph

Expanding the joint lattice to n-gram orders above $n = 2$ is often impractical without pruning. If the edge posteriors are not reliable, which is usually the case for unoptimized weights, pruning might remove good quality paths from the graph. As a compromise, an incremental expansion strategy may be adopted by first expanding and re-scoring the lattice with a bi-gram, optimizing weights for xBLEU-2, and then expanding and re-scoring the lattice with a 5-gram. Pruning should be more reliable with the edge posteriors computed using the tuned bi-gram weights. A second set of weights may be tuned with the 5-gram graph to maximize xBLEU-4.

When the bi-gram weights are tuned, it may be beneficial to increase the edge score scaling factor to focus the edge posteriors to the 1-best path. On the other hand, a lower scaling factor may be beneficial when tuning the 5-gram weights. Rosti et al. (2010) determined the scaling factor automatically by fixing the perplexity of the merged N-best lists used in tuning. Similar strategy may be adopted in incremental n-gram expansion of the lattices.

Entropy on a graph can also be computed using the expectation semiring formalism (Li and Eisner, 2009) by defining $s_l = \langle p_l, r_l \rangle$ where $p_l = e^{\gamma s_{il}}$ and $r_l = \log p_l$. The entropy is given by:

$$H_i = \log p(\beta_0) - \frac{r(\beta_0)}{p(\beta_0)} \qquad (24)$$

where $p(\beta_0)$ and $r(\beta_0)$ extract the p and r elements from the 2-tuple β_0, respectively. The average target entropy over all sentences was set manually to 3.0 in the experiments based on the tuning convergence and size of the pruned 5-gram lattices.

4 Experimental Evaluation

System outputs for all language pairs with English as the target were combined (cz-en, de-en, es-en, and fr-en). Unpruned English bi-gram and 5-gram language model components were trained using the WMT11 corpora: EuroParl, GigaFrEn, UNDoc_Es, UNDoc_Fr, NewsCommentary, News2007, News2008, News2009, News2010, and News2011. Additional six Gigaword v4 components included: AFP, APW, XIN+CNA, LTW, NYT, and Headlines+Datelines. The total number of words used to train the LMs was about 6.4 billion. Interpolation weights for the sixteen components were tuned to minimize perplexity on the newstest2010-ref.en development set. The modified Kneser-Ney smoothing (Chen and

Goodman, 1998) was used in training. Experiments using a LM trained on the system outputs and interpolated with the general LM were also conducted. The interpolation weights between 0.1 and 0.9 were tried, and the weight yielding the highest BLEU score on the tuning set was selected. A tri-gram true casing model was trained on all the LM training data. This model was used to restore the case of the lower-case system combination output.

All twelve 1-best system outputs on `cz-en`, 26 outputs on `de-en`, 16 outputs on `es-en`, and 24 outputs on `fr-en` were combined. Three different weight optimization methods were tried. First, lattice based 1-best BLEU optimization of the bi-gram decoding weights followed by N-best list based BLEU optimization of 5-gram re-scoring weights using 300-best lists, both using downhill simplex. Second, N-best list based expected BLEU optimization of the bi-gram and 5-gram weights using 300-best lists with merging between bi-gram decoding iterations. Third, lattice based expected BLEU optimization of bi-gram and 5-gram decoding weights. The L-BFGS (Liu and Nocedal, 1989) algorithm was used in gradient ascent. Results for all four single source experiments are shown in Table 1, including case insensitive TER (Snover et al., 2006) and BLEU scores for the worst and best systems, and the system combination outputs for the three tuning methods. The gains on tuning and test sets were consistent, though relatively smaller on `cz-en` due to a single system (`online-B`) dominating the other systems by about 5-6 BLEU points. The tuning method had very little influence on the test set scores apart from `de-en` where the lattice BLEU optimization yields slightly lower BLEU scores. This seems to suggest that the gradient free optimization is not as stable with a larger number of weights.[10] The novel bi-gram feature did not have significant influence on the TER or BLEU scores, but the number of novel bi-grams was reduced by up to 100%.

Finally, experiments combining 39 system outputs by taking the top half of the outputs from each language pair were performed. The selection was based on case insensitive BLEU scores on the tuning set. Table 2 shows the scores for seven combinations using the three tuning methods with or without the system output biased LM, and finally without the novel bi-gram count feature. There is a clear advantage from the expected BLEU tuning on the tuning set, and lattice tuning yields better scores than N-best list based tuning. The difference between `latBLEU` and `nbExpBLEU` without `biasLM` is not quite as large on the test set but `latExpBLEU` yields significant gains over both. The `biasLM` also yields significant gains on all but `latBLEU` tuning. Finally, removing the novel bi-gram count feature results in a significant loss, probably due to the large number of input hypotheses. The number of novel bi-grams in the test set output was reduced to zero when using this feature.

`xx-en`	**tune**		**test**	
System	TER	BLEU	TER	BLEU
worst	62.81	21.19	62.92	20.29
best	51.11	30.87	50.80	30.32
latBLEU	40.95	40.75	41.06	39.81
+biasLM	41.18	40.90	41.16	39.90
nbExpBLEU	40.81	41.36	41.05	40.15
+biasLM	40.72	41.99	40.65	40.89
latExpBLEU	40.57	41.68	40.62	40.60
+biasLM	40.42	42.23	40.52	41.38
-nBgF	40.85	41.41	40.88	40.55

Table 2: Case insensitive TER and BLEU scores on `newssyscombtune` (tune) and `newssyscombtest` (test) for `xx-en` combination. Combinations using lattice BLEU tuning (latBLEU), N-best list based expected BLEU tuning (nbExpBLEU), and lattice expected BLEU tuning (latExpBLEU) with and without the system output biased LM (`biasLM`) are shown. Final row, marked `nBgF`, corresponds to the above tuning without the novel bi-gram feature.

5 Conclusions

The BBN submissions for WMT11 system combination task were described in this paper together with a differentiable objective function, graph expected BLEU, which scales well for a large number of weights and can be generalized to hypergraphs. System output biased language model and a novel bi-gram count feature also gave significant gains on a 39 system multi-source combination.

[10] A total number of 30 weights, 26 system and 4 feature weights, were tuned for `de-en`.

References

Stanley F. Chen and Joshua Goodman. 1998. An empirical study of smoothing techniques for language modeling. Technical Report TR-10-98, Computer Science Group Harvard University.

Zhifei Li and Jason Eisner. 2009. First- and second-order expectation semirings with applications to minimum-risk training on translation forests. In *Proceedings of the 2009 Conference on Empirical Methods in Natural Language Processing*, pages 40–51.

Dong C. Liu and Jorge Nocedal. 1989. On the limited memory BFGS method for large scale optimization. *Mathematical Programming*, 45(3):503–528.

Franz J. Och. 2003. Minimum error rate training in statistical machine translation. In *Proceedings of the 41st Annual Meeting of the Association for Computational Linguistics*, pages 160–167.

Kishore Papineni, Salim Roukos, Todd Ward, and Wei-Jing Zhu. 2002. BLEU: a method for automatic evaluation of machine translation. In *Proceedings of the 40th Annual Meeting of the Association for Computational Linguistics*, pages 311–318.

Adam Pauls, John DeNero, and Dan Klein. 2009. Consensus training for consensus decoding in machine translation. In *Proceedings of the 2009 Conference on Empirical Methods in Natural Language Processing*, pages 1418–1427.

William H. Press, Saul A. Teukolsky, William T. Vetterling, and Brian P. Flannery. 2007. *Numerical recipes: the art of scientific computing*. Cambridge University Press, 3rd edition.

Antti-Veikko I. Rosti, Spyros Matsoukas, and Richard Schwartz. 2007. Improved word-level system combination for machine translation. In *Proceedings of the 45th Annual Meeting of the Association of Computational Linguistics*, pages 312–319.

Antti-Veikko I. Rosti, Bing Zhang, Spyros Matsoukas, and Richard Schwartz. 2009. Incremental hypothesis alignment with flexible matching for building confusion networks: BBN system description for WMT09 system combination task. In *Proceedings of the Fourth Workshop on Statistical Machine Translation*, pages 61–65.

Antti-Veikko I. Rosti, Bing Zhang, Spyros Matsoukas, and Richard Schwartz. 2010. BBN system description for WMT10 system combination task. In *Proceedings of the Fifth Workshop on Statistical Machine Translation*, pages 321–326.

David A. Smith and Jason Eisner. 2006. Minimum risk annealing for training log-linear models. In *Proceedings of the 21st International Conference on Computational Linguistics and 44th Annual Meeting of the Association for Computational Linguistics*, pages 787–794.

Matthew Snover, Bonnie Dorr, Richard Schwartz, Linnea Micciula, and John Makhoul. 2006. A study of translation edit rate with targeted human annotation. In *Proceedings of the 7th Conference of the Association for Machine Translation in the Americas*, pages 223–231.

The UZH System Combination System for WMT 2011

Rico Sennrich
Institute of Computational Linguistics
University of Zurich
Binzmühlestr. 14
CH-8050 Zürich
sennrich@cl.uzh.ch

Abstract

This paper describes the UZH system that was used for the WMT 2011 system combination shared task submission. We participated in the system combination task for the translation directions DE–EN and EN–DE. The system uses Moses as a backbone, with the outputs of the 2–3 best individual systems being integrated through additional phrase tables. The system compares well to other system combination submissions, with no other submission being significantly better. A BLEU-based comparison to the individual systems, however, indicates that it achieves no significant gains over the best individual system.

1 Introduction

For our submission to the WMT 2011 shared task, we built a system with the multi-engine MT approach described in (Sennrich, 2011), which builds on the idea by (Chen et al., 2007). A Moses SMT system (Koehn et al., 2007) is used as a backbone, trained on the WMT 2011 training data. Translation hypotheses by other systems are integrated through a second phrase table. In this second phrase table, the phrase translation probabilities and lexical weights are computed based on the word and phrase frequencies in both the translation hypotheses and a parallel training corpus. On the evaluation data in (Sennrich, 2011), this system significantly outperformed MEMT (Heafield and Lavie, 2010), which was among the best-performing system combination tools at WMT 2010 (Callison-Burch et al., 2010).

In this paper, we apply the same approach to a different translation scenario, namely the WMT 2011 shared task. We fail to significantly outperform the best individual system in terms of BLEU score. In section 2, we describe our system combination approach. In section 3, we present the results, and discuss possible reasons why the system fails to show the same performance gains as in the translation task on which it was evaluated initially.

2 System Description

We participated in the system combination task DE–EN and EN–DE. Since the combination is achieved by integrating translation hypotheses into an existing Moses system, which we will call the primary system, we first describe the methods and data used for training this primary system. Then, we describe how the translation hypotheses are selected out of the individual system submissions and integrated into the Moses system.

2.1 Primary System

For the training of the primary systems, we mostly followed the baseline instructions for the translation task[1]. We use *news-commentary* and *Europarl* as parallel training data. The language models are a linear interpolation of the *news-commentary*, *Europarl* and *news* corpora, optimized for minimal cross-entropy on the *newstest2008* data sets in the respective target language.

Additionally, we prune the primary phrase table using statistical significance tests, as described by (Johnson et al., 2007). For the translation direction DE–EN, the German source text is reordered based

[1]described at http://www.statmt.org/wmt11/baseline.html

Proceedings of the 6th Workshop on Statistical Machine Translation, pages 166–170,
Edinburgh, Scotland, UK, July 30–31, 2011.

on syntactic parsing with Pro3GresDE (Sennrich et al., 2009), and reordering rules similar to those described by (Collins et al., 2005).

The Moses phrase table consists of five features: phrase translation probabilities in both translation directions ($p(\bar{t}|\bar{s})$ and $p(\bar{s}|\bar{t})$), lexical weights ($lex(\bar{t}|\bar{s})$ and $lex(\bar{s}|\bar{t})$), and a constant phrase penalty (Koehn et al., 2003). The computation of the phrase translation probabilities and lexical weights is based on the word, phrase and word/phrase pair frequencies that are extracted from the parallel corpus. We modified the Moses training scripts to collect and store these frequencies for later re-use.

We did not submit the primary system outputs to the Machine Translation shared task, since we did not experiment with new techniques. Instead, the primary system forms the backbone of the system combination system.

2.2 Integrating Secondary Phrase Tables

To combine the output of several systems, we train a second phrase table on the translation hypotheses of these systems. For this, we create a parallel corpus consisting of n translation hypotheses and n copies of the corresponding source text, both lowercased and detokenized.[2]

We compute the word alignment with MGIZA++ (Gao and Vogel, 2008), based on the word alignment model from the primary corpus that we have previously saved to disk.

After training a phrase table from the word-aligned corpus with Moses, the lexical weights and translation probabilities are rescored, using the sufficient statistics (i.e. the word, phrase and word/phrase pair counts) of both the primary and the secondary corpus. This rescoring step has been shown to markedly improve performance in (Sennrich, 2011). We will discuss its effects in section 3.1. The rescored phrase table is integrated into the primary Moses system as an alternative decoding path, and tuned for maximal BLEU score on *newssyscombtune2011* with MERT.

[2]For convenience and speed, we combined the translation hypotheses for *newssyscombtune2011* and *newssyscombtest2011* into a single corpus. In principle, we could train separate phrase tables for each data set, or even for arbitrarily low numbers of sentences, without significant loss in performance (see (Sennrich, 2011)).

System	BLEU
Primary	21.11
Best individual	24.16
Submission	24.44
Vanilla scoring	24.42

Table 1: DE–EN results. Case-insensitive BLEU scores.

2.3 Hypothesis Selection

For the secondary phrase table, we chose to select the n best individual systems according to their BLEU score on the tuning set. We determined the optimal n empirically by trying different n, measuring each system's BLEU score on the tuning set and selecting the highest-scoring one. For the DE–EN translation task, $n = 2$ turned out to be optimal, for EN–DE, $n = 3$.

Chen et al. (2009) propose additional, tunable features in the phrase table to indicate the origin of phrase translations. For better comparability with the results described in (Sennrich, 2011), we did not add such features. This means that there are no *a priori* weights that bias the phrase selection for or against certain systems, but that decoding is purely driven by the usual Moses features: two phrase tables – the primary one and the re-scored, secondary one – the language model, the primary reordering model, and the corresponding parameters established through MERT.

3 Results

In the manual evaluation, the system combination submissions are only compared to each other, not to the individual systems. According to the manual evaluation, no other system combination submission outperforms ours by a statistically significant margin. In a comparison to individual systems, however, BLEU scores indicate that our system fails to yield a significant performance gain over the best individual system in this translation scenario.

In tables 1 and 2, we present case-insensitive BLEU scores (Papineni et al., 2002). As statistical significance test, we applied bootstrap resampling (Riezler and Maxwell, 2005). Tables 1 and 2 show the BLEU scores for the translation directions DE–EN and EN–DE, respectively. Systems included are the primary translation system described

System	BLEU
Primary	14.99
Best individual	17.44
Submission	17.51
Vanilla scoring	17.32

Table 2: EN–DE results. Case insensitive BLEU scores.

in section 2.1, the best individual system (online-B in both cases) and the submitted combination system. In terms of BLEU score, we achieved no statistically significant improvement over the best individual system.

As contrastive systems, we trained systems without the rescoring step described in section 2.2; we found no statistically significant difference from the submission system. In this translation task, the statistics from the parallel corpus seem to be ineffective at improving decoding, contrary to our findings in (Sennrich, 2011), where rescoring the phrase table improved BLEU scores by 0.7 points. We will address possible reasons for this discrepancy in the following section.

3.1 Interpretation

The main characteristic that sets our approach apart from other system combination software such as MANY (Barrault, 2010) and MEMT (Heafield and Lavie, 2010) is its reliance on word and phrase frequencies in a parallel corpus to guide decoding, whereas MANY and MEMT operate purely on the target side, without requiring/exploiting the source text or parallel data. We integrate the information from a parallel corpus into the decoding process by extracting phrase translations from the translation hypotheses and scoring these phrase translations on the basis of the frequencies from the parallel corpus.

The properties of this re-scored phrase table proved attractive for the translation task in (Sennrich, 2011), but less so for the WMT 2011 translation task. To explain why, let us look at $p(\overline{t}|\overline{s})$, i.e. the probability of a target phrase given a source phrase, as an example. It is computed as follows, c_{prim} and c_{sec} being the phrase count in the primary and secondary corpus, respectively.

$$p(\overline{t}|\overline{s}) = \frac{c_{prim}(\overline{s},\overline{t}) + c_{sec}(\overline{s},\overline{t})}{c_{prim}(\overline{s}) + c_{sec}(\overline{s})} \quad (1)$$

We can assume that $c_{sec}(\overline{s})$ and $c_{sec}(\overline{s},\overline{t})$ are mostly fixed, having values between 1 and the number of translation hypotheses.[3] If $c_{prim}(\overline{s})$ is high, the phrase translation probabilities in the secondary phrase table will only be marginally different from those in the primary phrase table (e.g. $\frac{500}{1000} = 0.5$ vs. $\frac{500+2}{1000+2} = 0.501$), whereas the secondary corpus has a stronger effect for phrases that are rare or unseen in the primary corpus (e.g. $\frac{1}{3} = 0.333$ vs. $\frac{1+2}{3+2} = 0.6$). Analogously, the same reasoning applies to $p(\overline{s}|\overline{t})$, $lex(\overline{t}|\overline{s})$ and $lex(\overline{s}|\overline{t})$.[4][5]

In short: the more frequent the phrases and phrase pairs in the primary corpus, the less effect does the secondary corpus have on the final feature values. This is a desirable behaviour if we can "trust" the phrase pairs extracted from the primary corpus. In (Sennrich, 2011), the primary corpus consisted of in-domain texts, whereas the translation hypotheses came from an out-of-domain SMT system and a rule-based one. There, it proved an effective strategy to only consider those translation hypotheses that either agreed with the data from the primary corpus, or for which the primary corpus had insufficient data, i.e. unknown or rare source words. With a primary system achieving a BLEU score of 17.18 and two translation hypotheses, scoring 13.29 and 12.94, we obtained a BLEU score of 20.06 for the combined system.

In the WMT 2011 system combination task, the statistics from the primary corpus failed to effectively improve translation quality. We offer these explanations based on an analysis of the results.

First, the 2–3 systems whose translation hypotheses we combine obtain higher scores than the primary system. This casts doubt on whether we should trust the scores from the primary system more than the translation hypotheses. And in fact, the results in table 1 and 2 show that the submission system

[3] Strictly speaking, this is only true if we build separate phrase tables for each sentence that is translated, and if there are no repeated phrases. This slight simplification serves illustrative purposes.

[4] For long phrases, phrase counts are typically low. Still, the primary corpus plays an important role in the computation of the lexical weights, which are computed from word frequencies, and thus typically less sparse than phrase frequencies.

[5] Rare target words may obtain a undesirably high probability, but are penalized in the language model. We set the LM log-probability of unknown words to -100.

(whose phrase table features take into account the primary corpus) is not better than a contrastive combination system with vanilla scoring, i.e. one that is solely based on the secondary corpus. We can also show why the primary corpus does not improve decoding by way of example. The German phrase *Bei der Wahl [der Matratze]* (English: *In the choice [of a mattress]*), is translated by the three systems as *in the selection*, *when choosing* and *in the election*. In this context, the last translation hypothesis is the least correct, but since the political domain is strongly represented in the training data, it is the most frequent one in the primary corpus, and the one being chosen by both the primary and the combined system.

Second, there seems to be a significant overlap in training data between the systems that we combine and our primary system[6]. We only saw few cases in which a system produced a translation against which there was evidence in our primary corpus. One instance is the German word *Kindergarten* (English: *kindergarten; nursery*), which is translated as *children's garden* by one system. In the combined system, this translation is dispreferred. (Chen et al., 2009) argue that a combination of dissimilar systems might yield better results. Rule-based systems could fulfill this role; they are also an attractive choice given their high quality (as judged by human evaluators) in earlier evaluations (e.g. WMT 2009 (Callison-Burch et al., 2009)). We did not pursue this idea, since we optimized for highest BLEU score, both during MERT and for the selection of the submission system, a scoring method that has been shown to undervalue rule-based systems (Callison-Burch et al., 2006).

The failure to outperform the individual best system in this translation task does not invalidate our approach. It merely highlights that different conditions call for different tools. Our approach relies strongly on parallel training data, in contrast to system combination tools such as MANY (Barrault, 2010) and MEMT (Heafield and Lavie, 2010). In this setting, this brought no benefit. However, when developing a SMT system for a specific domain and when combining an in-domain primary system with out-of-domain translation hypotheses, we expect that this strong dependence on the primary SMT system becomes an advantage. It allows the system to discriminate between source phrases that are well-documented in the primary training data, which will give other systems' hypotheses little effect, and those that occur rarely or not at all in the primary data, for which other systems may still produce a useful translation.

[6]This is especially true for all shared task participants building constrained systems. The amount of overlap between the anonymous online systems is unknown.

4 Conclusion

We described the UZH system combination submission to the Workshop of Machine Translation 2011. It uses the Moses architecture and includes translation hypotheses through a second phrase table. Its central characteristic is the extraction of phrase pairs from translations hypotheses and the scoring thereof on the basis of another parallel corpus. We find that, in the WMT 2011 system combination shared task, this approach fails to result in a significant improvement over the best individual system in terms of BLEU score. However, we argue that it is well suited for other translation tasks, such as the one described in (Sennrich, 2011).

Acknowledgments

This research was funded by the Swiss National Science Foundation under grant 105215_126999.

References

Loïc Barrault. 2010. MANY: Open source MT system combination at WMT'10. In *Proceedings of the Joint Fifth Workshop on Statistical Machine Translation and MetricsMATR*, pages 277–281, Uppsala, Sweden, July. Association for Computational Linguistics.

C. Callison-Burch, M. Osborne, and P. Koehn. 2006. Re-evaluating the role of BLEU in machine translation research. In *Proceedings the Eleventh Conference of the European Chapter of the Association for Computational Linguistics*, pages 249–256, Trento, Italy.

Chris Callison-Burch, Philipp Koehn, Christof Monz, and Josh Schroeder. 2009. Findings of the 2009 workshop on statistical machine translation. In *Proceedings of the Fourth Workshop on Statistical Machine Translation*, pages 1–28, Athens, Greece, March. Association for Computational Linguistics.

Chris Callison-Burch, Philipp Koehn, Christof Monz, Kay Peterson, Mark Przybocki, and Omar Zaidan. 2010. Findings of the 2010 joint workshop on statistical machine translation and metrics for machine translation. In *Proceedings of the Joint Fifth Workshop on Statistical Machine Translation and MetricsMATR*, pages 17–53, Uppsala, Sweden, July. Association for Computational Linguistics. Revised August 2010.

Yu Chen, Andreas Eisele, Christian Federmann, Eva Hasler, Michael Jellinghaus, and Silke Theison. 2007. Multi-engine machine translation with an open-source decoder for statistical machine translation. In *Proceedings of the Second Workshop on Statistical Machine Translation*, StatMT '07, pages 193–196, Morristown, NJ, USA. Association for Computational Linguistics.

Yu Chen, Michael Jellinghaus, Andreas Eisele, Yi Zhang, Sabine Hunsicker, Silke Theison, Christian Federmann, and Hans Uszkoreit. 2009. Combining multi-engine translations with Moses. In *Proceedings of the Fourth Workshop on Statistical Machine Translation*, StatMT '09, pages 42–46, Morristown, NJ, USA. Association for Computational Linguistics.

Michael Collins, Philipp Koehn, and Ivona Kučerová. 2005. Clause restructuring for statistical machine translation. In *ACL '05: Proceedings of the 43rd Annual Meeting on Association for Computational Linguistics*, pages 531–540, Morristown, NJ, USA. Association for Computational Linguistics.

Qin Gao and Stephan Vogel. 2008. Parallel implementations of word alignment tool. In *Software Engineering, Testing, and Quality Assurance for Natural Language Processing*, pages 49–57, Columbus, Ohio, June. Association for Computational Linguistics.

Kenneth Heafield and Alon Lavie. 2010. CMU multi-engine machine translation for WMT 2010. In *Proceedings of the Joint Fifth Workshop on Statistical Machine Translation and MetricsMATR*, WMT '10, pages 301–306, Stroudsburg, PA, USA. Association for Computational Linguistics.

Howard Johnson, Joel Martin, George Foster, and Roland Kuhn. 2007. Improving translation quality by discarding most of the phrasetable. In *Proceedings of the 2007 Joint Conference on Empirical Methods in Natural Language Processing and Computational Natural Language Learning (EMNLP-CoNLL)*, pages 967–975, Prague, Czech Republic, June. Association for Computational Linguistics.

Philipp Koehn, Franz Josef Och, and Daniel Marcu. 2003. Statistical phrase-based translation. In *NAACL '03: Proceedings of the 2003 Conference of the North American Chapter of the Association for Computational Linguistics on Human Language Technology*, pages 48–54, Morristown, NJ, USA. Association for Computational Linguistics.

Philipp Koehn, Hieu Hoang, Alexandra Birch, Chris Callison-Burch, Marcello Federico, Nicola Bertoldi, Brooke Cowan, Wade Shen, Christine Moran, Richard Zens, Chris Dyer, Ondřej Bojar, Alexandra Constantin, and Evan Herbst. 2007. Moses: Open Source Toolkit for Statistical Machine Translation. In *Proceedings of ACL 2007*, pages 177–180, Prague, Czech Republic, June.

Kishore Papineni, Salim Roukos, Todd Ward, and Wei-Jing Zhu. 2002. BLEU: A method for automatic evaluation of machine translation. In *ACL '02: Proceedings of the 40th Annual Meeting on Association for Computational Linguistics*, pages 311–318, Morristown, NJ, USA. Association for Computational Linguistics.

Stefan Riezler and John T. Maxwell. 2005. On some pitfalls in automatic evaluation and significance testing for MT. In *Proceedings of the ACL Workshop on Intrinsic and Extrinsic Evaluation Measures for Machine Translation and/or Summarization*, pages 57–64, Ann Arbor, Michigan, June. Association for Computational Linguistics.

Rico Sennrich, Gerold Schneider, Martin Volk, and Martin Warin. 2009. A New Hybrid Dependency Parser for German. In *Proceedings of the German Society for Computational Linguistics and Language Technology 2009 (GSCL 2009)*, Potsdam, Germany.

Rico Sennrich. 2011. Combining multi-engine machine translation and online learning through dynamic phrase tables. In *15th Annual Conference of the European Association for Machine Translation (EAMT 2011)*, Leuven, Belgium.

Description of the JHU System Combination Scheme for WMT 2011

Daguang Xu
Johns Hopkins University
Baltimore, USA
dxu5@jhu.edu

Yuan Cao
Johns Hopkins University
Baltimore, USA
yuan.cao@jhu.edu

Damianos Karakos
Johns Hopkins University
Baltimore, USA
damianos@jhu.edu

Abstract

This paper describes the JHU system combination scheme used in WMT-11. The JHU system combination is based on confusion network alignment, and inherited the framework developed by (Karakos et al., 2008). We improved our core system combination algorithm by making use of TER-plus, which was originally designed for string alignment, for alignment of confusion networks. Experimental results on French-English, German-English, Czech-English and Spanish-English combination tasks show significant improvements on BLEU and TER by up to 2 points on average, compared to the best individual system output, and improvements compared with the results produced by ITG which we used in WMT-10.

1 Introduction

System combination aims to improve the translation quality by combining the outputs from multiple individual MT systems. The state-of-the-art system combination methodologies can be roughly categorized as follows (Karakos et al., 2010):

1. *Confusion network based:* confusion network is a form of lattice with the constraint that all paths need to pass through all nodes. An example of a confusion network is shown in Figure 1.

   Here, the set of arcs between two consecutive nodes represents a bin, the number following a word is the count of this word in its bin, and each bin has the same size. The basic methodology of system combination based on confusion network includes the following steps: (a) Choose one system output as the "skeleton", which roughly decides the word order. (b) Align further system outputs to the skeleton, thus forming a confusion network. (c) Rescore the final confusion network using a language model, then pick the best path as the output of combination.

   A textual representation (where each line contains the words and counts of each bin) is usually the most convenient for machine processing.

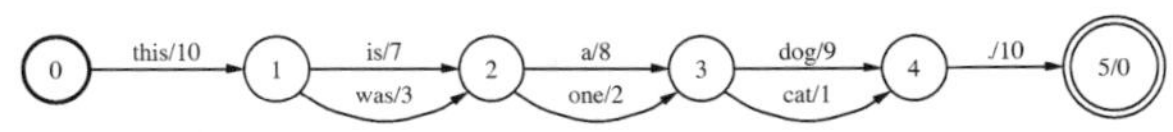

Figure 1: *Example confusion network. The total count in each bin is 10.*

2. *Joint optimization based:* unlike building confusion network, this method considers all system outputs at once instead of incrementally. Then a log-linear model is used to derive costs, followed by a search algorithm to explore the combination space (Jayaraman et al., 2005; Heafield et al., 2009; He et al., 2009).

3. *Hypothesis selection based:* this method only includes algorithms that output one of the input translations, and no word selection from multiple systems is performed. Typical algorithms can be found in (Rosti et al., 2007).

Proceedings of the 6th Workshop on Statistical Machine Translation, pages 171–176,
Edinburgh, Scotland, UK, July 30–31, 2011.

This paper describes the JHU system combination submitted to the Sixth Workshop on Statistical Machine Translation (WMT-11) (http://statmt.org/wmt11/index.html). The JHU system combination is confusion network based as described above, following the basic system combination framework described in (Karakos et al., 2008). However, instead of ITG alignments that were used in (Karakos et al., 2008), alignments based on TER-plus (Snover et al., 2009) were used now as the core system alignment algorithm.

The rest of the paper is organized as follows: Section 2 introduces the application of TER-plus in system combination. Section 3 introduces the JHU system combination pipeline. Section 4 presents the combination results and concluding remarks appear in Section 5.

2 Word Reordering for Hypothesis Alignment

Given the outputs of multiple MT systems, we would like to reorder and align the words of different hypothesis in a way such that an objective function is optimized, thus reaching better translations by making use of more information. In our system combination scheme, the objective function was based on Translation-Edit-Rate Plus (TER-plus).

2.1 Introduction to TER-plus

TER-plus is an extension of Translation Error Rate (TER) (Snover et al., 2006). TER is an evaluation metric for machine translation; it generalizes Word Error Rate (WER) by allowing block shifts in addition to the edit distance operations. However, one problem with TER is that only exact match of word blocks are allowed for shifting; this constraint might be too strict as it sometimes prevents reasonable shifts if two blocks have similar meanings.

TER-plus remedies this problem by introducing new flexible matches between words, thus allowing word substitutions and block shifts with costs much lower than that of TER. Specifically, substitution costs are now dependent on whether the words have the same stem (stem matches) or are synonyms (synonym matches). These operations relax the shifting constraints of TER; shifts are now allowed if the words of one string are synonyms or share the same stem as the words of the string they are compared to (Snover et al., 2009).

TER-plus identifies words with the same stem using the Porter stemming algorithm (Porter et al., 1980), and identifies synonyms using the WordNet database (Miller et al., 1995).

2.2 TER-plus for system combination

Originally, TER-plus was designed for aligning together word strings. However, similar to the work of (Karakos et al., 2010), who extended ITG to allow bilingual parsing of two *confusion networks* (by treating each confusion network bin as a multi-word entity), we converted the basic TER-plus code to take into account multiple words present in confusion network bins. Specifically, we define the cost of aligning two confusion network bins as (Karakos et al., 2010)

$$cost(b_1, b_2) = \frac{1}{|b_1||b_2|} \sum_{w_1 \in b_1} \sum_{w_2 \in b_2} \mathcal{C}(w_1, w_2)$$

in which b_1,b_2 are the confusion network bins which are candidates for alignment, $|\cdot|$ is the size of a bin, w_1, w_2 are words in b_1 and b_2 respectively, and $\mathcal{C}(w_1, w_2)$ is defined as follows:

$$\mathcal{C}(w_1, w_2) = \begin{cases} 0 & w_1 \text{ matches } w_2 \\ 0.5 & w_2 \text{ is deleted} \\ 0.6 & w_2 \text{ is inserted} \\ 0.2 & w_1 \text{ and } w_2 \text{ are synonyms} \\ 0.2 & w_1 \text{ and } w_2 \text{ share stems} \\ 1 & \text{none of the above} \end{cases}$$

Furthermore, the bin shift cost is set to 1.5. These numbers are empirically determined based on experimental results.

Similar to (Karakos et al., 2010), when a bin gets "deleted", it gets replaced with a *NULL* arc, which simply encodes the empty string, and is otherwise treated as a regular token in the alignments.

3 The JHU System Combination Pipeline

We now describe the JHU system combination pipeline in which TER-plus is used as the core confusion network alignment algorithm as introduced in the previous section.

3.1 Combination procedure overview

The JHU system combination scheme is based on confusion network as introduced in section 1. The confusion networks are built in two stages:

1. **Within-system combination:** (optional, only applicable in the case where per-system n-best lists are available.) the within-system combination generates system-specific confusion networks based on the alignment of the n-best translations.

2. **Between-system combination:** incremental alignment of the confusion networks of different systems generated in step 1, starting from 2-system combination up to the combination of all systems. The order with which the systems are selected is based on the individual BLEU scores (i.e., the best two systems are first combined, then the 3rd best is aligned to the resulting confusion network, etc.)

For the between-system combination we made use of TER-plus as described in section 2.2.

3.2 Language model Rescoring with Finite-State Transducer Operations

Once the between-system confusion networks are ready (one confusion network per sentence), a path through each of them has to be selected as the combination output. In order to pick out the the most fluent word sequence as the final translation, we need to rescore the confusion networks using a language model. This task can be performed efficiently via finite state transducer (FST) operations (Allauzen et al., 2002). First, we build an FST for each confusion network, called CN-FST. Since the confusion network is just a sequence of bins and each bin is a superposition of single words, the CN-FST can be built as a linear FST in a straightforward way (see Figure 1).

A 5-gram language model FST (LM-FST) is then built for each sentence. To build the LM-FST, we refer to the methodology described in (Allauzen et al., 2003). In brief, the LM-FST is constructed in the following way:

1. Extract the vocabulary of each segment.

2. Each state of the FST encodes an n-gram history ($n - 1$ words). Each (non-null) arc that originates from that state corresponds uniquely to a word type (i.e., word that follows that history in the training data).

3. The cost of each word arc is the corresponding language model score (negative log-probability, based on the modified Kneser-Ney formula (Kneser, 1995) for that n-gram).

4. Extra arcs are added for backing-off to lower-order histories, thus allowing all possible word strings to receive a non-zero probability.

In order to deal with the situation where a word in the confusion network is not in the vocabulary of the language model, we need to build another simple transducer, namely, the "unknown word" FST (UNK-FST), to map this word to the symbol *<unk>* that encodes the out-of-vocabulary (OOV) words. Note that this is useful only if one builds *open-vocabulary language models* which always give a non-zero probability to OOV words; e.g., check out the option *-unk* of the SRILM toolkit (Stolcke, 2002). (Obviously, the UNK-FST leaves all other words unmodified.)

After all these three transducers have been built, they are composed in the following manner (for each sentence):

CN-FST .o. UNK-FST .o. LM-FST

Note that a possible *re-weighting* of the arc costs of the CN-FST can be done in order to better account for the different dynamic ranges between the CN costs and the LM-FST costs. Furthermore, to avoid too many word deletions (especially in regions of the confusion network where the words disagree most) an additive *word deletion penalty* can be added to all *NULL* arcs. The best (minimum-cost) path from this resulting FST is selected as the output translation of the system combination for that sentence.

3.3 System combination pipeline summary

We now summarize the JHU system combination end-to-end pipeline as follows(since BLEU score is a key metric in the WMT11 translation evaluation, we use BLEU score as the system ranking criteria. The BLEU score we computed for the experiments below are all case-insensitive):

1. Process and re-format (lowercase, tokenize, romanize, etc.) all individual system outputs. Note that we compute the case-insensitive BLEU score in our experiments.

2. Build LM-FST and UNK-FST for each sentence.

3. Decide the between-system combination order according to the 1-best output BLEU score of individual systems.

4. Do between-system combination based on the order decided in step 3 using TER-plus.

5. Rescore the confusion network and start tuning on the parameters: convert the between-system confusion network into FST, compose it with the UNK-FST and with the LM-FST. When composing with LM-FST, try different CN arc coefficients (we tried the range $\{5, \ldots, 21\}$), and unknown word insertion penalties (we tried the values $\{0.3, 0.5, 0.7, 1\}$).

6. Compute the BLEU score for all *m*-syst_*x*_*y* outputs, where *m* is the number of systems for combination, *x* is the weight and *y* is the insertion penalty.

7. Among all the scores computed in step 6, find the best BLEU score, and keep the corresponding parameter setting(*m*, *x*, *y*).

8. Apply the best parameter setting to the test dataset for evaluation.

Obviously, if n-best outputs from systems are available, an extra step of producing within-system combinations (and searching for the best n-best size) will also be executed.

4 Results

In WMT11, we participated in French-English, German-English, Czech-English and Spanish-English system combination tasks. Although we followed the general system combination pipeline introduced in 3.3, we did not do the within-system combination since we received only 1-best outputs from all systems.

We built both primary and contrastive systems, and they differ in the way the 5-gram language models were trained. The language model for the primary system was trained with the monolingual Europarl, news commentary and news crawl corpus provided by WMT11. The language model for the contrastive system was trained using only the 1-best outputs from all individual systems (sentence-specific language model).

The number of systems used for combination tuning in each language pair was: 24 for French-English, 26 for German-English, 12 for Czech-English, and 16 for Spanish-English. The best results for the combination in the primary system made use of 23 systems for French-English, 5 systems for German-English, 10 systems for Czech-English, 10 systems for Spanish-English. In the contrastive system, the number of systems were 20, 5, 6, 10 respectively.

The TER and BLEU scores on the development set for the best individual system, the primary and contrastive combinations are given in Table 1, and the scores for test set are given in Table 2. From the results we see that, compared with the best individual system outputs, system combination results in significantly improved BLEU scores and remarkable reductions on TER, for all language pairs. Moreover, we observe that the primary system performs slightly better than the contrastive system in most cases.

We also did the experiment of xx-English which made combinations of all English outputs available across different source languages. We used 35 systems in this experiment for both primary and contrastive combination, and best result made use of 15 and 16 systems respectively. The development and test set results are shown in the "xx-en" column in table 1 and 2 respectively. From the results we see the improvements on TER and BLEU scores of both development and test sets almost doubled compared with the best results of single language pairs.

To make a comparison with the old technique we used in WMT10 system combination task, we ran the WMT11 system combination task using ITG with surface matching. The detailed implementation is described in (Narsale, 2010). Table 3 and 4 show the WMT11 results using ITG for alignment respectively. It can be seen that TER-plus outperforms ITG

System	fr-en		de-en		cz-en		es-en		xx-en	
	TER	BLEU	TER	BLEU	TER	BLEU	TER	BLEU	TER	BLEU
Best single system	56.2	28.1	60.1	23.6	**54.9**	27.9	51.8	30.2	51.8	30.2
Primary combination	**49.2**	**32.6**	**58.1**	**25.7**	55.1	28.7	**48.3**	**33.7**	**44.9**	35.5
Contrastive combination	49.8	32.3	58.2	25.6	**54.9**	**28.9**	49.1	33.3	45.0	**37.2**

Table 1: Results for all language pairs on development set. The best number in each column is shown in **bold**.

System	fr-en		de-en		cz-en		es-en		xx-en	
	TER	BLEU	TER	BLEU	TER	BLEU	TER	BLEU	TER	BLEU
Best single system	58.2	30.5	65.1	23.5	**59.7**	29.1	60.0	28.9	58.2	30.5
Primary combination	**55.9**	**31.9**	**64.4**	**25.0**	60.1	29.6	**55.4**	**33.5**	**51.7**	36.3
Contrastive combination	56.5	31.6	65.7	24.4	59.9	**29.8**	56.5	33.4	52.5	**36.5**

Table 2: Results for all language pairs on test set. The best number in each column is shown in **bold**.

System	fr-en		de-en		cz-en		es-en		xx-en	
	TER	BLEU	TER	BLEU	TER	BLEU	TER	BLEU	TER	BLEU
Best single system	56.2	28.1	60.1	23.6	54.9	27.9	51.8	30.2	51.8	30.2
Primary combination	**49.0**	**32.5**	**57.6**	**25.0**	**54.6**	**28.1**	**48.8**	**33.1**	**45.3**	35.7
Contrastive combination	56.1	31.7	58.0	24.9	55.0	28.0	49.4	33.0	45.6	**35.9**

Table 3: Results for all language pairs on development set using ITG. The best number in each column is shown in **bold**.

System	fr-en		de-en		cz-en		es-en		xx-en	
	TER	BLEU	TER	BLEU	TER	BLEU	TER	BLEU	TER	BLEU
Best single system	58.2	30.5	65.1	23.5	**59.7**	29.1	60.0	28.9	58.2	30.5
Primary combination	**55.9**	**31.9**	**64.5**	**24.7**	60.1	29.4	**55.8**	**33.0**	**52.2**	35.0
Contrastive combination	56.6	31.4	64.7	24.4	60.7	**29.6**	56.6	**33.0**	52.9	**35.3**

Table 4: Results for all language pairs on test set using ITG. The best number in each column is shown in **bold**.

almost in all results. We will experiment with ITG and *flexible match costs* and will report results in a subsequent publication.

5 Conclusion

We described the JHU system combination scheme that was used in WMT-11. The JHU system combination system is confusion network based, and we demonstrated the successful application of TER-plus (which was originally designed for string alignment) to confusion network alignment. The WMT-11 submission results show that significant improvements on the TER and BLEU scores (over the best individual system) were achieved.

Acknowledgments

This work was supported by the DARPA GALE program Grant No HR0022-06-2-0001. We would also like to thank the IBM Rosetta team for their strong support in the system combination evaluation tasks.

References

D. Karakos, J. Smith, and S. Khudanpur. 2010. *Hypothesis ranking and two-pass approaches for machine translation system combination.* Acoustics Speech and Signal Processing (ICASSP), IEEE International Conference on.

S. Jayaraman and A. Lavie. 2005. *Multi-engine machine translation guided by explicit word matching.* Proc. EAMT:143–152.

K. Heafield, G. Hanneman, and A. Lavie. 2009. *Machinetranslation system combination with flexible word ordering.* Proc. EACL 2009, WSMT.

X. He and K. Toutanova. 2009. *Joint optimization for machine translation system combination.* Proc. EMNLP.

A.-V.I. Rosti, S. Matsoukas, and R. Schwartz. 2007. *Improved word-level system combination for machine translation.* Proceedings of Association for Computational Linguistics(ACL)

D. Karakos, J. Eisner, S. Khudanpur, M. Dreyer. 2008. *Machine translation system combination using ITG-based alignments.* Proceedings of Association for Computational Linguistics(ACL) HLT, Short Papers (Companion Volume):81-84.

M. Snover, B. Dorr, R. Schwartz, L. Micciulla, J. Makhoul. 2006 *A Study of Translation Edit Rate with Targeted Human Annotation.* Proceedings of Association for Machine Translation in the Americas.

G.Miller. 1995 *WordNet: A Lexical Database for English.* . Communications of the ACM Vol. 38, No. 11.

M. Snover, N. Madnani, B. Dorr, R. Schwartz. 2009 *Fluency, adequacy, or HTER? Exploring different human judgments with a tunable MT metric.* Proceedings of the Fourth Workshop on Statistical Machine Translation at the 12th Meeting of the European Chapter of the Association for Computational Linguistics (EACL-2009), Athens, Greece.

M.F.Porter. 1980 *An algorithm for suffix stripping.* Program 14(3):130-137

C. Allauzen, M. Mohri, B. Roark 1980 *Generalized Algorithms for Constructing Statistical Language Models.* Proceedings of the 41st Annual Meeting of the Association for Computational Linguistics, July 2003, pp. 40-47.

Sushant Narsale. 2010 *JHU system combination scheme for WMT 2010.* Proceedings of Fifth Workshop on Machine Translation, ACL.

R. Kneser, Ney. H. 2010 *Improved backing-off for m-gram language modeling.* Proceedings of the IEEE International Conference on Acoustics, Speech, and Signal Processing, ICASSP.

A. Stolcke 2002 *SRILM - An Extensible Language Modeling Toolkit.* Proceedings of International Conference on Spoken Language Processing.

C. Allauzen, M. Riley, J. Schalkwyk, W. Skut, Mehryar Mohri. 2002 OpenFst: A General and Efficient Weighted Finite-State Transducer Library Proceedings of the Ninth International Conference on Implementation and Application of Automata, (CIAA 2007), vol. 4783, Lecture Notes in Computer Science, pages 11-23, 2007

WMT11 official webpage. *http://statmt.org/wmt11 /index.html*

Multiple-stream Language Models for Statistical Machine Translation

Abby Levenberg
Dept. of Computer Science
University of Oxford
ablev@cs.ox.ac.uk

Miles Osborne
School of Informatics
University of Edinburgh
miles@inf.ed.ac.uk

David Matthews
School of Informatics
University of Edinburgh
dave.matthews@ed.ac.uk

Abstract

We consider using online language models for translating multiple streams which naturally arise on the Web. After establishing that using just one stream can degrade translations on different domains, we present a series of simple approaches which tackle the problem of maintaining translation performance on all streams in small space. By exploiting the differing throughputs of each stream and how the decoder translates prior test points from each stream, we show how translation performance can equal specialised, per-stream language models, but do this in a single language model using far less space. Our results hold even when adding three billion tokens of additional text as a background language model.

1 Introduction

There is more natural language data available today than there has ever been and the scale of its production is increasing quickly. While this phenomenon provides the Statistic Machine Translation (SMT) community with a potentially extremely useful resource to learn from, it also brings with it nontrivial computational challenges of scalability.

Text streams arise naturally on the Web where millions of new documents are published each day in many different languages. Examples in the streaming domain include the thousands of multilingual websites that continuously publish newswire stories, the official proceedings of governments and other bureaucratic organisations, as well as the millions of "bloggers" and host of users on social network services such as Facebook and Twitter.

Recent work has shown good results using an incoming text stream as training data for either a static or online language model (LM) in an SMT setting (Goyal et al., 2009; Levenberg and Osborne, 2009). A drawback of prior work is the oversimplified scenario that all training and test data is drawn from the same distribution using a single, in-domain stream. In a real world scenario multiple incoming streams are readily available and test sets from dissimilar domains will be translated continuously. As we show, using stream data from one domain to translate another results in poor average performance for both streams. However, combining streams naively together hurts performance further still.

In this paper we consider this problem of multiple stream translation. Since monolingual data is very abundant, we focus on the subtask of updating an online LM using multiple incoming streams. The challenges in multiple stream translation include dealing with domain differences, variable throughput rates (the size of each stream per epoch), and the need to maintain constant space. Importantly, we impose the key requirement that our model match translation performance reached using the single stream approach on all test domains.

We accomplish this using the n-gram history of prior translations plus subsampling to maintain a constant bound on memory required for language modelling throughout all stream adaptation. In particular, when considering two test streams, we are able to improve performance on both streams from an average (per stream) BLEU score of 39.71 and 37.09 using a single stream approach (Tables 2 and 3) to an average BLEU score of 41.28 and 42.73 using multiple streams within a single LM using equal memory (Tables 6 and 7). We also show additive im-

Proceedings of the 6th Workshop on Statistical Machine Translation, pages 177–186,
Edinburgh, Scotland, UK, July 30–31, 2011. ©2011 Association for Computational Linguistics

provements using this approach when using a large background LM consisting of over one billion n-grams. To our knowledge our approach is the first in the literature to deal with adapting an online LM to multiple streams in small space.

2 Previous Work

2.1 Randomised LMs

Randomised techniques for LMs from Talbot and Osborne (2007) and Talbot and Brants (2008) are currently industry state-of-the-art for fitting very large datasets into much smaller amounts of memory than lossless representations for the data. Instead of representing the n-grams exactly, the randomised representation exchanges a small, one-sided error of false positives for massive space savings.

2.2 Stream-based LMs

An unbounded text stream is an input source of natural language documents that is received sequentially and so has an implicit timeline attached. In Levenberg and Osborne (2009) a text stream was used to initially train and subsequently adapt an online, randomised LM (ORLM) with good results. However, a weakness of Levenberg and Osborne (2009) is that the experiments were all conducted over a single input stream. It is an oversimplification to assume that all test material for a SMT system will be from a single domain. No work was done on the multi-stream case where we have more than one incoming stream from arbitrary domains.

2.3 Domain Adaptation for SMT

Within MT there has been a variety of approaches dealing with domain adaptation (for example (Wu et al., 2008; Koehn and Schroeder, 2007)). Our work is related to domain adaptation but differs in that we are not skewing the distribution of an out-of-domain LM to accommodate some test data for which we have little or no training data for. Rather, we have varying amounts of training data from all the domains via the incoming streams and the LM must account for each domain appropriately. However, known domain adaptation techniques are potentially applicable to multi-stream translation as well.

3 Multiple Streams and their Properties

Any source that provides a continuous sequence of natural language documents over time can be thought of as an *unbounded stream* which is time-stamped and access to it is given in strict chronological order. The ubiquity of technology and the Internet means there are many such text streams available already and their number is increasing quickly. For SMT, multiple text streams provide a potentially abundant source of new training data that may be useful for combating model sparsity.

Of primary concern is building models whose space complexity is independent of the size of the incoming stream. Allowing unbounded memory to handle unbounded streams is unsatisfactory. When dealing with more than one stream we must also consider how the properties of single streams interact in a multiple stream setting.

Every text stream is associated with a particular domain. For example, we may draw a stream from a newswire source, a daily web crawl of new blogs, or the output of a company or organisation. Obviously the distribution over the text contained in these streams will be very different from each other. As is well-known from the work on domain adaptation throughout the SMT literature, using a model from one domain to translate a test document from another domain would likely produce poor results.

Each stream source will also have a different rate of production, or *throughput*, which may vary greatly between sources. Blog data may be received in abundance but the newswire data may have a significantly lower throughput. This means that the text stream with higher throughput may dominate and overwhelm the more nuanced translation options of the stream with less data in the LM during decoding. This is bad if we want to translate well for all domains in small space using a single model.

4 Multi-Stream Retraining

In a stream-based translation setting we can expect to translate test points from various domains on any number of incoming streams. Our goal is a single unified LM that obtains equal performance in less space than when using a separate LM per stream. The underlying LMs could be exact, but here we use randomised versions based on the ORLM.

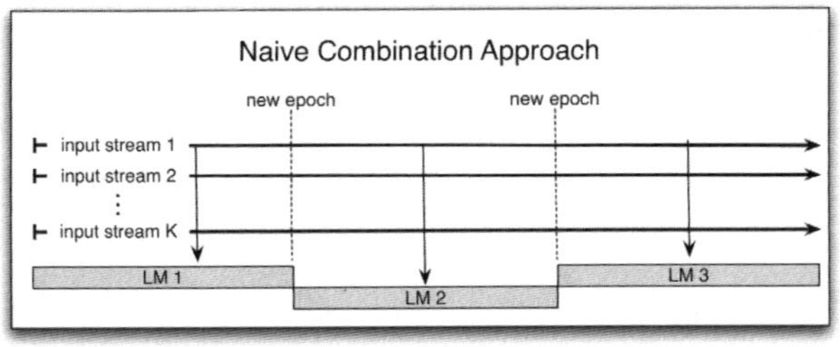

Figure 1: In the naive approach all K streams are simply combined into a single LM for each new epoch encountered.

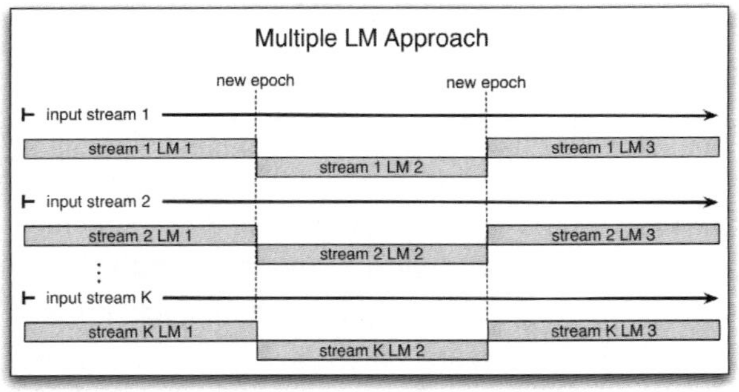

Figure 2: Each stream $1 \dots K$ gets its own stream-based LM using the multiple LM approach.

Given an incoming number K of unbounded streams over a potentially infinite timeline T, with $t \subset T$ an *epoch* or windowed subset of the timeline, the full set of n-grams in all K streams over all T is denoted with S. By S_t we denote n-grams from all K streams and S_{kt}, $k \in [1, K]$, as the n-grams in the kth stream over epoch t. Since the streams are unbounded, we do not have access to all the n-grams in S at once. Instead we select n-grams from each stream $S_{kt} \subset S$. We define the collection of n-grams encoded in the LM at time t over all K streams as C_t. Initially, at time $t = 0$ the LM is composed of the n-grams in the stream so $C_0 = S_0$.

Since it is unsatisfactory to allow unbounded memory usage for the model and more bits are needed as we see more novel n-grams from the streams, we enforce a memory constraint and use an adaptation scheme to delete n-grams from the LM C_{t-1} before adding any new n-grams from the streams to get the current n-gram set C_t. Below we describe various approaches of updating the LM with data from the streams.

4.1 Naive Combinations

Approach The first obvious approach for an online LM using multiple input streams is to simply store all the streams in one LM. That is, n-grams from all the streams are only inserted into the LM once and their stream specific counts are combined into a single value in the composite LM.

Modelling the Stream In the naive case we retrain the LM C_t in full at epoch t using all the new data from the streams. We have simply

$$C_t = \bigcup_{k=1}^{K} S_{kt} \tag{1}$$

where each of the K streams is combined into a single model and the n-grams counts are merged linearly. Here we carry no n-grams over from the LM C_{t-1} from the previous epoch. The space needed is the number of unique n-grams present in the combined streams for each epoch.

Resulting LM To query the resulting LM C_t during decoding with a test n-gram $w_i^n = (w_i, \dots, w_n)$ we use a simple smoothing algorithm called Stupid Backoff (Brants et al., 2007). This returns the probability of an n-gram as

$$P(w_i|w_{i-n+1}^{i-1}) :=$$

$$\begin{cases} \frac{C_t(w_{i-n+1}^{i})}{C_t(w_{i-n+1}^{i-1})} & \text{if } C_t(w_{i-n+1}^{i}) > 0 \\ \alpha P(w_i|w_{i-n+2}^{i-1}) & \text{otherwise} \end{cases} \tag{2}$$

where $C_t(.)$ denotes the frequency count returned by the LM for an n-gram and α is a backoff parameter. The recursion ends once the unigram is reached in which case the probability is $P(w_i) := w_i/N$ where N is the size of the current training corpus.

Each stream provides a distribution over the n-grams contained in it and, for SMT, if a *separate* LM was constructed for each domain it would most likely cause the decoder to derive different 1-best hypotheses than using a LM built from all the stream data. Using the naive approach blurs the distribution distinctions between streams and negates any stream specific differences when the decoder produces a 1-best hypothesis. It has been shown that doing linear combinations of this type produces poor performance in theory (Mansour et al., 2008).

4.2 Weighted Interpolation

Approach An improved approach to using multiple streams is to build a separate LM for each stream and using a weighted combination of each during decoding. Each stream is stored in isolation and we interpolate the information contained within each during decoding using a weighting on each stream.

Modelling the Stream Here we model the streams by simply storing each stream at time t in its own LM so $C_{kt} = S_{kt}$ for each stream S_k. Then the LM after epoch t is

$$C_t = \{C_{1t}, \ldots, C_{Kt}\}.$$

We use more space here than all other approaches since we must store each n-gram/count occurring in each stream separately as well as the overhead incurred for each separate LM in memory.

Resulting LM During decoding, the probability of a test n-gram w_i^n is a weighted combination of all the individual stream LMs. We can write

$$P(w_i^n) := \sum_{k=1}^{K} f_k P_{C_{kt}}(w_i^n) \tag{3}$$

where we query each of the individual LMs C_{kt} to get a score from each LM using Equation 2 and combine them together using a weighting f_k specific to each LM. Here we impose the restriction on the weights that $\sum_{k=1}^{K} f_k = 1$. (We discuss specific weight selections in the next section.)

By maintaining multiple stream specific LMs we maintain the particular distribution of the individual streams. This keeps the more nuanced translations from the lower throughput streams available during decoding without translations being dominated by a stream with higher throughput. However using multiple distinct LMs is wasteful of memory.

4.3 Combining Models via History

Approach We want to combine the streams into a single LM using less memory than when storing each stream separately but still achieve at least as good a translation for each test point. Naively combining the streams removes stream specific translations but using the history of n-grams selected by the decoder during the previous test point in the stream was done in Levenberg and Osborne (2009) for the single stream case with good results. This is applicable to the multi-stream case as well.

Modelling the Stream For multiple streams and epoch $t > 0$ we model the stream combination as

$$C_t = f_T(C_{t-1}) \cup \bigcup_{k=1}^{K} (S_{kt}). \tag{4}$$

where for each epoch a selected subset of the previous n-grams in the LM C_{t-1} is merged with all the newly arrived stream data to create the new LM set C_t. The parameter f_T denotes a function that filters over the previous set of n-grams in the model. It represents the specific adaptation scheme employed and stays constant throughout the timeline T. In this work we consider any n-grams queried by the decoder in the last test point as potentially useful to the next point. Since all of the n-grams S_t in the stream at time t are used the space required is of the same order of complexity as the naive approach.

Resulting LM Since all the n-grams from the streams are now encoded in a single LM C_t we can query it using Equation 2 during decoding. The goal of retraining using decoding history is to keep useful n-grams in the current model so a better model is obtained and performance for the next translation point is improved. Note that making use of the history for hypothesis combination is theoretically well-founded and is the same approach used here for history based combination. (Mansour et al., 2008)

4.4 Subsampling

Approach The problem of multiple streams with highly varying throughput rates can be seen as a type of class imbalance problem in the machine learning literature. Given a binary prediction problem with two classes, for instance, the imbalance problem occurs when the bulk of the examples in the training data are instances of one class and only a much smaller proportion of examples are available from the other class. A frequently used approach to balancing the distribution for the statistical model is to use *random under sampling* and select only a subset of the dominant class examples during training (Japkowicz and Stephen, 2002).

This approach is applicable to the multiple stream translation problem with imbalanced throughput rates between streams. Instead of storing the n-grams from each stream separately, we can apply a

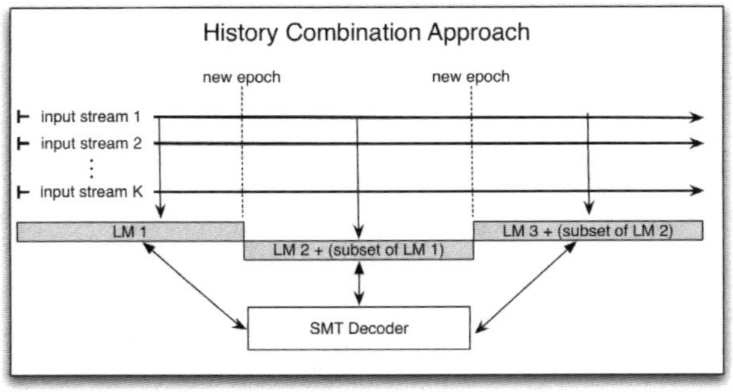

Figure 3: Using decoding history all the streams are combined into a unified LM.

subsampling selection scheme directly to the incoming streams to balance each stream's contribution in the final LM. Note that subsampling is also related to weighting interpolation. Since all returned LM scores are based on frequency counts of the n-grams and their prefixes, taking a weighting on a full probability of an n-gram is akin to having fewer counts of the n-grams in the LM to begin with.

Modelling the Stream To this end we use the weighted function parameter f_k from Equation 3 to serve as the sampling probability rate for accepting an n-gram from a given stream k. The sampling rate serves to limit the amount of stream data from a stream that ends up in the model. For $K > 1$ we have

$$C_t = f_T(C_{t-1}) \cup \bigcup_{k=1}^{K} f_k(S_{kt}) \quad (5)$$

where f_k is the probability a particular n-gram from stream S_k at epoch t will be included in C_t. The adaptation function f_T remains the same as in Equation 4. The space used in this approach is now dependent on the rate f_k used for each stream.

Resulting LM Again, since we obtain a single LM from all the streams, we use Equation 2 to get the probability of an n-gram during decoding.

The subsampling method is applicable to all of the approaches discussed in this section. However, since we are essentially limiting the amount of data that we store in the final LM we can expect to take a performance hit based on the rate of acceptance given by the parameters f_k. By using subsampling with the history combination approach we obtain good performance for all streams in small space.

Stream	1-grams	3-grams	5-grams
EP	19K	520K	760K
GW (xie)	120K	3M	5M
RCV1	630K	21M	42M

Table 1: Sample statistics of unique n-gram counts from the streams from epoch 2 of our timeline. The *throughput* rate varies a lot between streams.

5 Experiments

Here we report on our SMT experiments with multiple streams for translation using the approaches outlined in the previous section.

5.1 Experimental Setup

The SMT setup we employ is standard and all resources used are publicly available. We translate from Spanish into English using phrase-based decoding with Moses (Koehn and Hoang, 2007) as our decoder. Our parallel data came from Europarl.

We use three streams (all are timestamped): RCV1 (Rose et al., 2002), Europarl (EP) (Koehn, 2003), and Gigaword (GW) (Graff et al., 2007). GW is taken from six distinct newswire sources but in our initial experiments we limit the incoming stream from Gigaword to one of the sources (xie). GW and RCV1 are both newswire domain streams with high rates of incoming data whereas EP is a more nuanced, smaller throughput domain of spoken transcripts taken from sessions of the European Parliament. The RCV1 corpus only spans one calender year from October, 1996 through September, 1997 so we selected only data in this time frame from the other two streams so our timeline consists of the same full calendar year for all streams.

For this work we use the ORLM. The crux of the ORLM is an online perfect hash function that provides the ability to insert and delete from the data structure. Consequently the ORLM has the ability to adapt to an unbounded input stream whilst maintaining both constant memory usage and error rate. All the ORLMs were 5-gram models built with training data from the streams discussed above and used Stupid Backoff smoothing for n-gram scoring (Brants et al., 2007). All results are reported using the BLEU metric (Papineni et al., 2001).

For testing we held-out three random test points

LM Type	Test 1	Test 2	Test 3
RCV1 (Static)	39.30	38.28	33.06
RCV1 (Online)	39.30	40.64	39.19
EP (Online)	30.22	30.31	26.66
RCV1+EP (Online)	39.00	40.15	39.46
RCV1+EP+GW (Online)	**41.29**	**41.73**	**40.41**

Table 2: Results for the RCV1 test points. RCV1 and GW streams are in-domain and EP is out-of-domain. Translation results are improved using more stream data since most n-grams are in-domain to the test points.

LM Type	Test 1	Test 2	Test 3
EP (Static)	**42.09**	44.15	36.42
EP (Online)	**42.09**	**45.94**	**37.22**
RCV1 (Online)	36.46	42.10	32.73
EP+RCV1 (Online)	40.82	44.07	35.01
EP+RCV1+GW (Online)	40.91	44.05	35.56

Table 3: EP results using in and out-of-domain streams. The last two rows show that naive combination gets poor results compared to single stream approaches.

from both the RCV1 and EP stream's timeline for a total of six test points. This divided the streams into three *epochs*, and we updated the online LM using the data encountered in the epoch prior to each translation point. The n-grams and their counts from the streams are combined in the LM using one of the approaches from the previous section.

Using the notation from Section 4 we have the RCV1, EP, and GW streams described above and $K = 3$ as the number of incoming streams from two distinct domains (newswire and spoken dialogue). Our timeline T is one year's worth of data split into three epochs, $t \in \{1, 2, 3\}$, with test points at the end of each epoch t. Since we have no test points from the GW stream it acts as a background stream for these experiments. [1]

5.2 Baselines and Naive Combinations

In this section we report on our translation experiments using a single stream and the naive linear combination approach with multiple incoming data streams from Section 4.1.

Using the RCV1 corpus as our input stream we tested single stream translation first. Here we are replicating the experiments from Levenberg and Osborne (2009) so both training and test data comes from a single in-domain stream. Results are in Table 2 where each row represents a different LM type. *RCV1 (Static)* is the traditional baseline with no adaptation where we use the training data for the first epoch of the stream. *RCV1 (Online)* is the online LM adapted with data from the in-domain stream. Confirming the previous work we get improvements when using an online LM that incorporates recent data against a static baseline.

We then ran the same experiments using a stream generated from the EP corpus. EP consists of the proceedings of the European Parliament and is a significantly different domain than the RCV1 newswire stream. We updated the online LM using n-grams from the latest stream epoch before translating each in-domain EP test set. Results are in Table 3 and follow the same naming convention as Table 2 (except now in-domain is EP and out-of-domain is RCV1).

Using a single stream we also cross tested and translated each test point using the online LM adapted on the out-of-domain stream. As expected, translation performance decreases (sometimes drastically) in this case since the data of the out-of-domain stream are not suited to the domain of the current test point being translated.

We then tested the naive approach and combined both streams into a single LM by taking the union of the n-grams and adding their counts together. This is the *RCV1+EP (Online)* row in Tables 2 and 3 and clearly, though it contains more data compared to each single stream LM, the naively combined LM does not help the RCV1 test points much and degrades the performance of the EP translation results. This translation hit occurs as the throughput of each stream is significantly different. The EP stream contains far less data per epoch than the RCV1 counterpart (see Table 1) hence using a naive combination means that the more abundant newswire data from the RCV1 stream overrides the probabilities of the more domain specific EP n-grams during decoding.

When we added a third newswire stream from a portion of GW, shown in the last row of Tables 2 and 3, improvements are obtained for the RCV1 test

[1] A background stream is one that only serves as training data for all other test domains.

Weighting	Test 1	Test 2	Test 3
$.33_R + .33_E + .33_G$	38.97	39.78	35.66
$.50_R + .25_E + .25_G$	39.59	40.40	37.22
$.25_R + .50_E + .25_G$	36.57	38.03	34.23
$.70_R + 0.0_E + .30_G$	**40.54**	**41.46**	**39.23**

Table 4: Weighted LM interpolation results for the RCV1 test points where E = Europarl, R = RCV1, and G = Gigaword (xie).

Weighting	Test 1	Test 2	Test 3
$.33_E + .33_R + .33_G$	40.75	45.65	35.77
$.50_E + .25_R + .25_G$	41.46	46.37	36.94
$.25_E + .50_R + .25_G$	40.57	44.90	35.77
$.70_E + .20_R + .10_G$	**42.47**	**46.83**	**38.08**

Table 5: EP results in BLEU for the interpolated LMs.

points due to the addition of in-domain data but the EP test performance still suffers.

This highlights why naive combination is unsatisfactory. While using more in-domain data aids in the translation of the newswire tests, for the EP test sets, naively combining the n-grams from all streams means the hypotheses the decoder selects are weighted heavily in favor of the out-of-domain data. As the out-of-domain stream's throughput is significantly larger it swamps the model.

5.3 Interpolating Weighted Streams

Straightforward linear stream combination into a single LM results in degradation of translations for test points whose in-domain training data is drawn from a stream with lower throughput than the other data streams. We could maintain a separate MT system for each streaming domain but intuitively some combination of the streams may benefit average performance since using all the data available should benefit test points from streams with low throughput. To test this we used an alternative approach described in Section 4.2 and used a weighted combination of the single stream LMs during decoding.

We tested this approach using our three streams: RCV1, EP and GW (xie). We used a separate ORLM for each stream and then, during testing, the result returned for an n-gram queried by the decoder was a value obtained from some weighted interpolation of each individual LM's score for that n-gram. To get the interpolation weights for each streaming LM we minimised the perplexity of all the models on held-out development data from the streams. [2] Then we used the corresponding stream specific weights to decode the test points from that domain.

Results are shown in Tables 4 and 5 using the weighting scheme described above plus a selection of random parameter settings for comparison. Using the notation from Section 4.2, a caption of "$.5_R + .25_E + .25_G$", for example, denotes a weighting of $f_{RCV1} = 0.5$ for the scores returned from the RCV1 stream LM while f_{EP} and $f_{GW} = 0.25$ for the EP and GW stream LMs.

The weighted interpolation results suggest that while naive combination of the streams may be misguided, average translation performance can be improved upon when using more than a single in-domain stream. Comparing the best results in Tables 2 and 3 to the single stream baselines in Tables 4 and 5 we achieve comparable, if not improved, translation performance for *both* domains. This is especially true for test domains such as EP which have low training data throughput from the stream. Here adding some information from the out-of-domain stream that contains a lot more data aids significantly in the translation of in-domain test points.

However, the optimal weighting differs between each test domain. For instance, the weighting that gives the best results for the EP tests results in much poorer translation performance for the RCV1 test points requiring us to track which stream we are decoding and then select the appropriate weighting. This adds unnecessary complexity to the SMT system. And, since we store each stream separately, memory usage is not optimal using this scheme.

5.4 History and Subsampling

For space efficiency we want to represent multiple streams non-redundantly instead of storing each stream/domain in its own LM. Here we report on experiments using both the history combination and subsampling approaches from Sections 4.3 and 4.4.

Results are in Tables 6 and 7 for the RCV1 and

[2] Due to the lossy nature of the encoding of the ORLM means that the perplexity measures were approximations. Nonetheless the weighting from this approach had the best performance.

LM Type	Test 1	Test 2	Test 3
Multi-f_k	41.19	41.73	39.23
Multi-f_T	**41.29**	42.23	**40.51**
Multi-$f_k + f_T$	41.19	**42.52**	40.12

Table 6: RCV1 test results using history and subsampling approaches.

LM Type	Test 1	Test 2	Test 3
Multi-f_k	**40.91**	43.50	36.11
Multi-f_T	**40.91**	47.84	**39.29**
Multi-$f_k + f_T$	**40.91**	**48.05**	39.23

Table 7: Europarl test results with history and subsampling approaches.

EP test sets respectively with the column headers denoting the test point. The row *Multi-f_k* shows results using only the random subsampling parameter f_k and the rows *Multi-f_T* show results with just the time-based adaptation parameter without subsampling. The final row *Multi-$f_k + f_T$* uses both the f parameters with random subsampling as well as taking decoding history into account.

Multi-f_k uses the random subsampling parameter f_k to filter out higher order n-grams from the streams. All n-grams that are sampled from the streams are then combined into the joint LM. The counts of n-grams sampled from more than one stream are added together in the composite LM. The parameter f_k is set dependent on a stream's throughput rate, we only subsample from the streams with high throughput, and the rate was chosen based on the weighted interpolation results described previously. In Tables 6 and 7 the subsampling rate $f_k = 0.3$ for the combined newswire streams RCV1 and GW and we kept all of the EP data. We experimented with various other values for the f_k sampling rates and found translation results only minorly impacted. Note that the subsampling is truly random so two adaptation runs with equal subsampling rates may produce different final translations. Nonetheless, in our experiments we saw expected performance, observing slight variation in performance for all test points that correlated to the percentage of in-domain data residing in the model.

The next row, *Multi-f_T*, uses recency criteria to keep potentially useful n-grams but uses no subsampling and accepts all n-grams from all streams into the LM. Here we get better results than naive combination or plain subsampling at the expense of more memory for the same error rate for the ORLM.

The final row, *Multi-$f_k + f_T$* uses both the subsampling function f_k and f_T so maintains a history of the n-grams queried by the decoder for the prior test points. This approach achieves significantly better results than naive adaptation and compares to using all the data in the stream. Combining translation history as well as doing random subsampling over the stream means we match the performance of but use far less memory than when using multiple online LMs whilst maintaining the same error rate.

5.5 Experiments Summary

We have shown that using data from multiple streams benefits SMT performance. Our best approach, using history based combination along with subsampling, combines all incoming streams into a single, succinct LM and obtains translation performance equal to single stream, domain specific LMs on all test domains. Crucially we do this in bounded space, require less memory than storing each stream separately, and do not incur translation degradations on any single domain.

A note on memory usage. The multiple LM approach uses the most memory since this requires all overlapping n-grams in the streams to be stored separately. The naive and history combination approaches use less memory since they store all n-grams from all the streams in a unified LM. For the sampling the exact amount of memory is of course dependent on the sampling rate used. For the results in Tables 6 and 7 we used significantly less memory (300MB) but still achieved comparable performance to approaches that used more memory by storing the full streams (600MB).

6 Scaling Up

The experiments described in the preceding section used combinations of relatively small (compared to current industry standards) input streams. The question remains if using such approaches aids in the performance of translation if used in conjunction with large static LMs trained on large corpora. In this section we describe scaling up the previous stream-

Order	Count
1-grams	3.7M
2-grams	46.6M
3-grams	195.5M
4-grams	366.8M
5-grams	454.2M
Total	1067M

Table 8: Singleton-pruned n-gram counts (in millions) for the GW3 background LM.

LM Type	Test 1	Test 2	Test 3
GW (static)	41.69	42.40	35.48
+ RCV1 (online)	42.44	43.83	**40.55**
+ EP (online)	**42.80**	**43.94**	38.82

Table 9: Test results for the RCV1 stream using the large background LM. Using stream data benefits translation.

based translation experiments using a large background LM trained on a billion n-grams.

We used the same setup described in Section 5.1. However, instead of using only a subset of the GW corpus as one of our incoming streams, we trained a static LM using the *full* GW3 corpus of over three billion tokens and used it as a background LM. As the n-gram statistics for this background LM show in Table 8, it contains far more data than each of the stream specific LMs (Table 1). We tested whether using streams atop this large background LM had a positive effect on translation for a given domain.

Baseline results for all test points using only the GW background LM are shown in the top row in Tables 9 and 10. We then interpolated the ORLMs with this LM. For each stream test point we interpolated with the big GW LM an online LM built with the most recent epoch's data. Here we used separate models per stream so the RCV1 test points used the GW LM along with a RCV1 specific ORLM. We used the same mechanism to obtain the interpolation weights as described in Section 5.3 and minimised the perplexity of the static LM along with the stream specific ORLM. Interestingly, the tuned weights returned gave approximately a 50-50 weighting between LMs and we found that simply using a 50-50 weighting for all test points resulted had no negative effect on BLEU. In the third row of the Tables 9 and 10 we show the results of interpolating the big background LM with ORLMs built using the approach described in Section 4.4. In this case all streams were combined into a single LM using a subsampling rate for higher order n-grams. As before our sampling rate for the newswire streams was 30% chosen by the perplexity reduction weights.

LM Type	Test 1	Test 2	Test 3
GW (static)	40.78	44.26	34.36
+ EP (online)	**43.94**	**47.82**	38.71
+ RCV1 (online)	43.07	47.72	**39.15**

Table 10: EP test results using the background GW LM.

The results show that even with a large amount of static data adding small amounts of stream specific data relevant to a given test point has an impact on translation quality. Compared to only using the large background model we obtain significantly better results when using a streaming ORLM to compliment it for all test domains. However the large amount of data available to the decoder in the background LM positively impacts translation performance compared to single-stream approaches (Tables 2 and 3). Further, when we combine the streams into a single LM using the subsampling approach we get, on average, comparable scores for all test points. Thus we see that the patterns for multiple stream adaptation seen in previous sections hold in spite of big amounts of static data.

7 Conclusions and Future Work

We have shown how multiple streams can be efficiently incorporated into a translation system. Performance need not degrade on any of the streams. As well, these results can be additive. Even when using large amounts of additional background data, adding stream specific data continues to improve translation. Further, we achieve all results in bounded space. Future work includes investigating more sophisticated adaptation for multiple streams. We also plan to explore alternative ways of sampling the stream when incorporating data.

Acknowledgements

Special thanks to Adam Lopez and Conrad Hughes and Phil Blunosm for helpful discussion and advice. This work was sponsored in part by the GALE program, DARPA Contract No. HR0011-06-C-0022 and by ESPRC Grant No. EP/I010858/1bb.

References

Thorsten Brants, Ashok C. Popat, Peng Xu, Franz J. Och, and Jeffrey Dean. 2007. Large language models in machine translation. In *Proceedings of the 2007 Joint Conference on Empirical Methods in Natural Language Processing and Computational Natural Language Learning (EMNLP-CoNLL)*, pages 858–867.

Amit Goyal, Hal Daumé III, and Suresh Venkatasubramanian. 2009. Streaming for large scale NLP: Language modeling. In *North American Chapter of the Association for Computational Linguistics (NAACL)*, Boulder, CO.

David Graff, Junbo Kong, Ke Chen, and Kazuaki Maeda. 2007. English Gigaword Third Edition. Linguistic Data Consortium (LDC-2007T07).

Nathalie Japkowicz and Shaju Stephen. 2002. The class imbalance problem: A systematic study. *Intell. Data Anal.*, 6:429–449, October.

Philipp Koehn and Hieu Hoang. 2007. Factored translation models. In *Proceedings of the 2007 Joint Conference on Empirical Methods in Natural Language Processing and Computational Natural Language Learning (EMNLP-CoNLL)*, pages 868–876.

Philipp Koehn and Josh Schroeder. 2007. Experiments in domain adaptation for statistical machine translation. In *Proceedings of the Second Workshop on Statistical Machine Translation*, pages 224–227, Prague, Czech Republic, June. Association for Computational Linguistics.

Philipp Koehn. 2003. Europarl: A multilingual corpus for evaluation of machine translation. Available at: `http://www.statmt.org/europarl/`.

Abby Levenberg and Miles Osborne. 2009. Stream-based randomised language models for SMT. In *Proceedings of the Conference on Empirical Methods in Natural Language Processing (EMNLP)*.

Yishay Mansour, Mehryar Mohri, and Afshin Rostamizadeh. 2008. Domain adaptation with multiple sources. In *NIPS*, pages 1041–1048.

Kishore Papineni, Salim Roukos, Todd Ward, and Wei-Jing Zhu. 2001. Bleu: a method for automatic evaluation of machine translation. In *ACL '02: Proceedings of the 40th Annual Meeting on Association for Computational Linguistics*, pages 311–318, Morristown, NJ, USA. Association for Computational Linguistics.

Tony Rose, Mark Stevenson, and Miles Whitehead. 2002. The reuters corpus volume 1 - from yesterdays news to tomorrows language resources. In *In Proceedings of the Third International Conference on Language Resources and Evaluation*, pages 29–31.

David Talbot and Thorsten Brants. 2008. Randomized language models via perfect hash functions. In *Proceedings of ACL-08: HLT*, pages 505–513, Columbus, Ohio, June. Association for Computational Linguistics.

David Talbot and Miles Osborne. 2007. Smoothed Bloom filter language models: Tera-scale LMs on the cheap. In *Proceedings of the 2007 Joint Conference on Empirical Methods in Natural Language Processing and Computational Natural Language Learning (EMNLP-CoNLL)*, pages 468–476.

Hua Wu, Haifeng Wang, and Chengqing Zong. 2008. Domain adaptation for statistical machine translation with domain dictionary and monolingual corpora. In *Proceedings of the 22nd International Conference on Computational Linguistics (Coling 2008)*, pages 993–1000. Coling 2008 Organizing Committee, August.

KenLM: Faster and Smaller Language Model Queries

Kenneth Heafield
Carnegie Mellon University
5000 Forbes Ave
Pittsburgh, PA 15213 USA
heafield@cs.cmu.edu

Abstract

We present KenLM, a library that implements two data structures for efficient language model queries, reducing both time and memory costs. The PROBING data structure uses linear probing hash tables and is designed for speed. Compared with the widely-used SRILM, our PROBING model is 2.4 times as fast while using 57% of the memory. The TRIE data structure is a trie with bit-level packing, sorted records, interpolation search, and optional quantization aimed at lower memory consumption. TRIE simultaneously uses less memory than the smallest lossless baseline and less CPU than the fastest baseline. Our code is open-source[1], thread-safe, and integrated into the Moses, cdec, and Joshua translation systems. This paper describes the several performance techniques used and presents benchmarks against alternative implementations.

1 Introduction

Language models are widely applied in natural language processing, and applications such as machine translation make very frequent queries. This paper presents methods to query N-gram language models, minimizing time and space costs. Queries take the form $p(w_n|w_1^{n-1})$ where w_1^n is an n-gram. Backoff-smoothed models estimate this probability based on the observed entry with longest matching history w_f^n, returning

$$p(w_n|w_1^{n-1}) = p(w_n|w_f^{n-1}) \prod_{i=1}^{f-1} b(w_i^{n-1}). \quad (1)$$

where the probability $p(w_n|w_f^{n-1})$ and backoff penalties $b(w_i^{n-1})$ are given by an already-estimated model. The problem is to store these two values for a large and sparse set of n-grams in a way that makes queries efficient.

Many packages perform language model queries. Throughout this paper we compare with several packages:

SRILM 1.5.12 (Stolcke, 2002) is a popular toolkit based on tries used in several decoders.

IRSTLM 5.60.02 (Federico et al., 2008) is a sorted trie implementation designed for lower memory consumption.

MITLM 0.4 (Hsu and Glass, 2008) is mostly designed for accurate model estimation, but can also compute perplexity.

RandLM 0.2 (Talbot and Osborne, 2007) stores large-scale models in less memory using randomized data structures.

BerkeleyLM revision 152 (Pauls and Klein, 2011) implements tries based on hash tables and sorted arrays in Java with lossy quantization.

Sheffield Guthrie and Hepple (2010) explore several randomized compression techniques, but did not release code.

TPT Germann et al. (2009) describe tries with better locality properties, but did not release code.

These packages are further described in Section 3. We substantially outperform all of them on query

[1] http://kheafield.com/code/kenlm

Proceedings of the 6th Workshop on Statistical Machine Translation, pages 187–197,
Edinburgh, Scotland, UK, July 30–31, 2011.

speed and offer lower memory consumption than lossless alternatives. Performance improvements transfer to the Moses (Koehn et al., 2007), cdec (Dyer et al., 2010), and Joshua (Li et al., 2009) translation systems where our code has been integrated. Our open-source (LGPL) implementation is also available for download as a standalone package with minimal (POSIX and g++) dependencies.

2 Data Structures

We implement two data structures: PROBING, designed for speed, and TRIE, optimized for memory. The set of n-grams appearing in a model is sparse, and we want to efficiently find their associated probabilities and backoff penalties. An important subproblem of language model storage is therefore sparse mapping: storing values for sparse keys using little memory then retrieving values given keys using little time. We use two common techniques, hash tables and sorted arrays, describing each before the model that uses the technique.

2.1 Hash Tables and PROBING

Hash tables are a common sparse mapping technique used by SRILM's default and BerkeleyLM's hashed variant. Keys to the table are hashed, using for example Austin Appleby's MurmurHash[2], to integers evenly distributed over a large range. This range is collapsed to a number of buckets, typically by taking the hash modulo the number of buckets. Entries landing in the same bucket are said to collide.

Several methods exist to handle collisions; we use linear probing because it has less memory overhead when entries are small. Linear probing places at most one entry in each bucket. When a collision occurs, linear probing places the entry to be inserted in the next (higher index) empty bucket, wrapping around as necessary. Therefore, a populated probing hash table consists of an array of buckets that contain either one entry or are empty. Non-empty buckets contain an entry belonging to them or to a preceding bucket where a conflict occurred. Searching a probing hash table consists of hashing the key, indexing the corresponding bucket, and scanning buckets until a matching key is found or an empty bucket is encountered, in which case the key does not exist in the table.

Linear probing hash tables must have more buckets than entries, or else an empty bucket will never be found. The ratio of buckets to entries is controlled by space multiplier $m > 1$. As the name implies, space is $O(m)$ and linear in the number of entries. The fraction of buckets that are empty is $\frac{m-1}{m}$, so average lookup time is $O\left(\frac{m}{m-1}\right)$ and, crucially, constant in the number of entries.

When keys are longer than 64 bits, we conserve space by replacing the keys with their 64-bit hashes. With a good hash function, collisions of the full 64-bit hash are exceedingly rare: one in 266 billion queries for our baseline model will falsely find a key not present. Collisions between two keys in the table can be identified at model building time. Further, the special hash 0 suffices to flag empty buckets.

The PROBING data structure is a rather straightforward application of these hash tables to store N-gram language models. Unigram lookup is dense so we use an array of probability and backoff values. For $2 \leq n \leq N$, we use a hash table mapping from the n-gram to the probability and backoff[3]. Vocabulary lookup is a hash table mapping from word to vocabulary index. In all cases, the key is collapsed to its 64-bit hash. Given counts c_1^n where e.g. c_1 is the vocabulary size, total memory consumption, in bits, is

$$(96m + 64)c_1 + 128m \sum_{n=2}^{N-1} c_n + 96mc_N.$$

Our PROBING data structure places all n-grams of the same order into a single giant hash table. This differs from other implementations (Stolcke, 2002; Pauls and Klein, 2011) that use hash tables as nodes in a trie, as explained in the next section. Our implementation permits jumping to any n-gram of any length with a single lookup; this appears to be unique among language model implementations.

2.2 Sorted Arrays and TRIE

Sorted arrays store key-value pairs in an array sorted by key, incurring no space overhead. SRILM's compact variant, IRSTLM, MITLM, and BerkeleyLM's

[2] http://sites.google.com/site/murmurhash/

[3] N-grams do not have backoff so none is stored.

sorted variant are all based on this technique. Given a sorted array A, these other packages use binary search to find keys in $O(\log |A|)$ time. We reduce this to $O(\log \log |A|)$ time by evenly distributing keys over their range then using interpolation search[4] (Perl et al., 1978). Interpolation search formalizes the notion that one opens a dictionary near the end to find the word "zebra." Initially, the algorithm knows the array begins at $b \leftarrow 0$ and ends at $e \leftarrow |A| - 1$. Given a key k, it estimates the position

$$pivot \leftarrow \frac{k - A[b]}{A[e] - A[b]}(e - b).$$

If the estimate is exact ($A[pivot] = k$), then the algorithm terminates succesfully. If $e < b$ then the key is not found. Otherwise, the scope of the search problem shrinks recursively: if $A[pivot] < k$ then this becomes the new lower bound: $l \leftarrow pivot$; if $A[pivot] > k$ then $u \leftarrow pivot$. Interpolation search is therefore a form of binary search with better estimates informed by the uniform key distribution.

If the key distribution's range is also known (i.e. vocabulary identifiers range from 0 to the number of words), then interpolation search can use this information instead of reading $A[0]$ and $A[|A| - 1]$ to estimate pivots; this optimization alone led to a 24% speed improvement. The improvement is due to the cost of bit-level reads and avoiding reads that may fall in different virtual memory pages.

Vocabulary lookup is a sorted array of 64-bit word hashes. The index in this array is the vocabulary identifier. This has the effect of randomly permuting vocabulary identifiers, meeting the requirements of interpolation search when vocabulary identifiers are used as keys.

While sorted arrays could be used to implement the same data structure as PROBING, effectively making $m = 1$, we abandoned this implementation because it is slower and larger than a trie implementation. The trie data structure is commonly used for language modeling. Our TRIE implements the popular reverse trie, in which the last word of an n-gram is looked up first, as do SRILM, IRSTLM's inverted variant, and BerkeleyLM except for the scrolling variant. Figure 1 shows an example. Nodes in the trie are based on arrays sorted by vocabulary identifier.

[4]Not to be confused with interpolating probabilities, which is outside the scope of this paper.

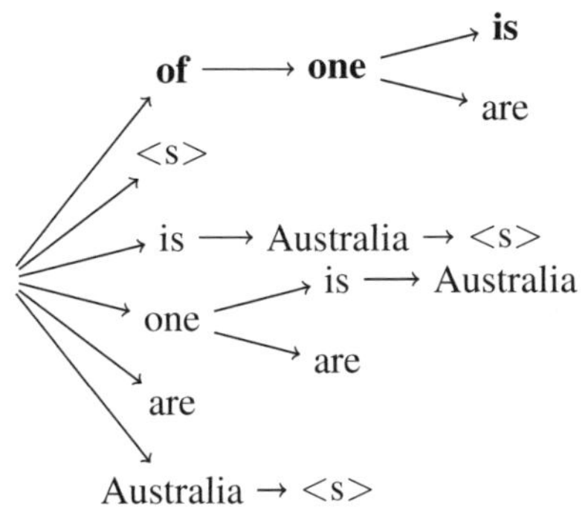

Figure 1: Lookup of "is one of" in a reverse trie. Children of each node are sorted by vocabulary identifier so order is consistent but not alphabetical: "is" always appears before "are". Nodes are stored in column-major order. For example, nodes corresponding to these n-grams appear in this order: "are one", "<s> Australia", "is one of", "are one of", "<s> Australia is", and "Australia is one".

We maintain a separate array for each length n containing all n-gram entries sorted in suffix order. Therefore, for n-gram w_1^n, all leftward extensions w_0^n are an adjacent block in the $n + 1$-gram array. The record for w_1^n stores the offset at which its extensions begin. Reading the following record's offset indicates where the block ends. This technique was introduced by Clarkson and Rosenfeld (1997) and is also implemented by IRSTLM and BerkeleyLM's compressed option. SRILM inefficiently stores 64-bit pointers.

Unigram records store probability, backoff, and an index in the bigram table. Entries for $2 \leq n < N$ store a vocabulary identifier, probability, backoff, and an index into the $n+1$-gram table. The highest-order N-gram array omits backoff and the index, since these are not applicable. Values in the trie are minimally sized at the bit level, improving memory consumption over trie implementations in SRILM, IRSTLM, and BerkeleyLM. Given n-gram counts $\{c_n\}_{n=1}^N$, we use $\lceil \log_2 c_1 \rceil$ bits per vocabulary identifier and $\lceil \log_2 c_n \rceil$ per index into the table of n-grams.

When SRILM estimates a model, it sometimes removes n-grams but not $n + 1$-grams that extend it to the left. In a model we built with default settings, 1.2% of $n + 1$-grams were missing their n-

gram suffix. This causes a problem for reverse trie implementations, including SRILM itself, because it leaves $n+1$-grams without an n-gram node pointing to them. We resolve this problem by inserting an entry with probability set to an otherwise-invalid value ($-\infty$). Queries detect the invalid probability, using the node only if it leads to a longer match. By contrast, BerkeleyLM's hash and compressed variants will return incorrect results based on an $n-1$-gram.

2.2.1 Quantization

Floating point values may be stored in the trie exactly, using 31 bits for non-positive log probability and 32 bits for backoff[5]. To conserve memory at the expense of accuracy, values may be quantized using q bits per probability and r bits per backoff[6]. We allow any number of bits from 2 to 25, unlike IRSTLM (8 bits) and BerkeleyLM ($17-20$ bits). To quantize, we use the binning method (Federico and Bertoldi, 2006) that sorts values, divides into equally sized bins, and averages within each bin. The cost of storing these averages, in bits, is

$$[32(N-1)2^q + 32(N-2)2^r$$

Because there are comparatively few unigrams, we elected to store them byte-aligned and unquantized, making every query faster. Unigrams also have 64-bit overhead for vocabulary lookup. Using c_n to denote the number of n-grams, total memory consumption of TRIE, in bits, is

$$(32+32+64+64)c_1 + \sum_{n=2}^{N-1}(\lceil \log_2 c_1 \rceil + q + r + \lceil \log_2 c_{n+1} \rceil)c_n + (\lceil \log_2 c_1 \rceil + q)c_N$$

plus quantization tables, if used. The size of TRIE is particularly sensitive to $\lceil \log_2 c_1 \rceil$, so vocabulary filtering is quite effective at reducing model size.

3 Related Work

SRILM (Stolcke, 2002) is widely used within academia. It is generally considered to be fast (Pauls and Klein, 2011), with a default implementation based on hash tables within each trie node. Each trie node is individually allocated and full 64-bit pointers are used to find them, wasting memory. The compact variant uses sorted arrays instead of hash tables within each node, saving some memory, but still stores full 64-bit pointers. With some minor API changes, namely returning the length of the n-gram matched, it could also be faster—though this would be at the expense of an optimization we explain in Section 4.1. The PROBING model was designed to improve upon SRILM by using linear probing hash tables (though not arranged in a trie), allocating memory all at once (eliminating the need for full pointers), and being easy to compile.

IRSTLM (Federico et al., 2008) is an open-source toolkit for building and querying language models. The developers aimed to reduce memory consumption at the expense of time. Their default variant implements a forward trie, in which words are looked up in their natural left-to-right order. However, their inverted variant implements a reverse trie using less CPU and the same amount of memory[7]. Each trie node contains a sorted array of entries and they use binary search. Compared with SRILM, IRSTLM adds several features: lower memory consumption, a binary file format with memory mapping, caching to increase speed, and quantization. Our TRIE implementation is designed to improve upon IRSTLM using a reverse trie with improved search, bit level packing, and stateful queries. IRSTLM's quantized variant is the inspiration for our quantized variant. Unfortunately, we were unable to correctly run the IRSTLM quantized variant. The developers suggested some changes, such as building the model from scratch with IRSTLM, but these did not resolve the problem.

Our code has been publicly available and intergrated into Moses since October 2010. Later, BerkeleyLM (Pauls and Klein, 2011) described ideas similar to ours. Most similar is *scrolling queries*, wherein left-to-right queries that add one word at a time are optimized. Both implementations employ a state object, opaque to the application, that carries information from one query to the next; we

[5]Backoff "penalties" are occasionally positive in log space.

[6]One probability is reserved to mark entries that SRILM pruned. Two backoffs are reserved for Section 4.1. That leaves 2^q-1 probabilities and 2^r-2 non-zero backoffs.

[7]Forward tries are faster to build with IRSTLM and can efficiently return a list of rightward extensions, but this is not used by the decoders we consider.

discuss both further in Section 4.2. State is implemented in their scrolling variant, which is a trie annotated with forward and backward pointers. The hash variant is a reverse trie with hash tables, a more memory-efficient version of SRILM's default. While the paper mentioned a sorted variant, code was never released. The compressed variant uses block compression and is rather slow as a result. A direct-mapped cache makes BerkeleyLM faster on repeated queries, but their fastest (scrolling) cached version is still slower than uncached PROBING, even on cache-friendly queries. For all variants, we found that BerkeleyLM always rounds the floating-point mantissa to 12 bits then stores indices to unique rounded floats. The 1-bit sign is almost always negative and the 8-bit exponent is not fully used on the range of values, so in practice this corresponds to quantization ranging from 17 to 20 total bits.

Lossy compressed models RandLM (Talbot and Osborne, 2007) and Sheffield (Guthrie and Hepple, 2010) offer better memory consumption at the expense of CPU and accuracy. These enable much larger models in memory, compensating for lost accuracy. Typical data structures are generalized Bloom filters that guarantee a customizable probability of returning the correct answer. Minimal perfect hashing is used to find the index at which a quantized probability and possibly backoff are stored. These models generally outperform our memory consumption but are much slower, even when cached.

4 Optimizations

In addition to the optimizations specific to each data-structure described in Section 2, we implement several general optimizations for language modeling.

4.1 Minimizing State

Applications such as machine translation use language model probability as a feature to assist in choosing between hypotheses. Dynamic programming efficiently scores many hypotheses by exploiting the fact that an N-gram language model conditions on at most $N-1$ preceding words. We call these $N-1$ words *state*. When two partial hypotheses have equal state (including that of other features), they can be recombined and thereafter efficiently handled as a single packed hypothesis. If there are too many distinct states, the decoder prunes low-scoring partial hypotheses, possibly leading to a search error. Therefore, we want state to encode the minimum amount of information necessary to properly compute language model scores, so that the decoder will be faster and make fewer search errors.

We offer a state function $s(w_1^n) = w_m^n$ where substring w_m^n is guaranteed to extend (to the right) in the same way that w_1^n does for purposes of language modeling. The state function is integrated into the query process so that, in lieu of the query $p(w_n|w_1^{n-1})$, the application issues query $p(w_n|s(w_1^{n-1}))$ which also returns $s(w_1^n)$. The returned state $s(w_1^n)$ may then be used in a follow-on query $p(w_{n+1}|s(w_1^n))$ that extends the previous query by one word. These make left-to-right query patterns convenient, as the application need only provide a state and the word to append, then use the returned state to append another word, etc. We have modified Moses (Koehn et al., 2007) to keep our state with hypotheses; to conserve memory, phrases do not keep state. Syntactic decoders, such as cdec (Dyer et al., 2010), build state from null context then store it in the hypergraph node for later extension.

Language models that contain w_1^k must also contain prefixes w_1^i for $1 \leq i \leq k$. Therefore, when the model is queried for $p(w_n|w_1^{n-1})$ but the longest matching suffix is w_f^n, it may return state $s(w_1^n) = w_f^n$ since no longer context will be found. IRSTLM and BerkeleyLM use this state function (and a limit of $N-1$ words), but it is more strict than necessary, so decoders using these packages will miss some recombination opportunities.

State will ultimately be used as context in a subsequent query. If the context w_f^n will never extend to the right (i.e. $w_f^n v$ is not present in the model for all words v) then no subsequent query will match the full context. If the log backoff of w_f^n is also zero (it may not be in filtered models), then w_f should be omitted from the state. This logic applies recursively: if w_{f+1}^n similarly does not extend and has zero log backoff, it too should be omitted, terminating with a possibly empty context. We indicate whether a context with zero log backoff will extend using the sign bit: $+0.0$ for contexts that extend and -0.0 for contexts that do not extend. RandLM and SRILM also remove context that will not extend, but

SRILM performs a second lookup in its trie whereas our approach has minimal additional cost.

4.2 Storing Backoff in State

Section 4.1 explained that state s is stored by applications with partial hypotheses to determine when they can be recombined. In this section, we extend state to optimize left-to-right queries. All language model queries issued by machine translation decoders follow a left-to-right pattern, starting with either the begin of sentence token or null context for mid-sentence fragments. Storing state therefore becomes a time-space tradeoff; for example, we store state with partial hypotheses in Moses but not with each phrase.

To optimize left-to-right queries, we extend state to store backoff information:

$$s(w_1^{n-1}) = \left(w_m^{n-1}, \{b(w_i^{n-1})\}_{i=m}^{n-1}\right)$$

where m is the minimal context from Section 4.1 and b is the backoff penalty. Because b is a function, no additional hypothesis splitting happens.

As noted in Section 1, our code finds the longest matching entry w_f^n for query $p(w_n|s(w_1^{n-1}))$ then computes

$$p(w_n|w_1^{n-1}) = p(w_n|w_f^{n-1}) \prod_{i=1}^{f-1} b(w_i^{n-1}).$$

The probability $p(w_n|w_f^{n-1})$ is stored with w_f^n and the backoffs are immediately accessible in the provided state $s(w_1^{n-1})$.

When our code walks the data structure to find w_f^n, it visits $w_n^n, w_{n-1}^n, \ldots, w_f^n$. Each visited entry w_i^n stores backoff $b(w_i^n)$. These are written to the state $s(w_1^n)$ and returned so that they can be used for the following query.

Saving state allows our code to walk the data structure exactly once per query. Other packages walk their respective data structures once to find w_f^n and again to find $\{b(w_i^{n-1})\}_{i=1}^{f-1}$ if necessary. In both cases, SRILM walks its trie an additional time to minimize context as mentioned in Section 4.1.

BerkeleyLM uses states to optimistically search for longer n-gram matches first and must perform twice as many random accesses to retrieve backoff information. Further, it needs extra pointers in the trie, increasing model size by 40%. This makes memory usage comparable to our PROBING model. The PROBING model can perform optimistic searches by jumping to any n-gram without needing state and without any additional memory. However, this optimistic search would not visit the entries necessary to store backoff information in the outgoing state. Though we do not directly compare state implementations, performance metrics in Table 1 indicate our overall method is faster.

4.3 Threading

Only IRSTLM does not support threading. In our case multi-threading is trivial because our data structures are read-only and uncached. Memory mapping also allows the same model to be shared across processes on the same machine.

4.4 Memory Mapping

Along with IRSTLM and TPT, our binary format is memory mapped, meaning the file and in-memory representation are the same. This is especially effective at reducing load time, since raw bytes are read directly to memory—or, as happens with repeatedly used models, are already in the disk cache.

Lazy mapping reduces memory requirements by loading pages from disk only as necessary. However, lazy mapping is generally slow because queries against uncached pages must wait for the disk. This is especially bad with PROBING because it is based on hashing and performs random lookups, but it is not intended to be used in low-memory scenarios. TRIE uses less memory and has better locality. However, TRIE partitions storage by n-gram length, so walking the trie reads N disjoint pages. TPT has theoretically better locality because it stores n-grams near their suffixes, thereby placing reads for a single query in the same or adjacent pages.

We do not experiment with models larger than physical memory in this paper because TPT is unreleased, factors such as disk speed are hard to replicate, and in such situations we recommend switching to a more compact representation, such as RandLM. In all of our experiments, the binary file (whether mapped or, in the case of most other packages, interpreted) is loaded into the disk cache in advance so that lazy mapping will never fault to disk. This is similar to using the Linux `MAP_POPULATE`

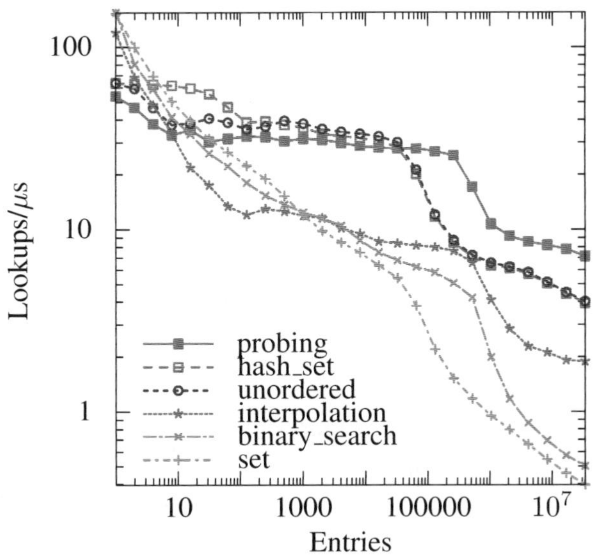

Figure 2: Speed in lookups per microsecond by data structure and number of 64-bit entries. Performance dips as each data structure outgrows the processor's 12 MB L2 cache. Among hash tables, indicated by shapes, probing is initially slower but converges to 43% faster than unordered or hash_set. Interpolation search has a more expensive pivot function but does less reads and iterations, so it is initially slower than binary_search and set, but becomes faster above 4096 entries.

flag that is our default loading mechanism.

5 Benchmarks

This section measures performance on shared tasks in order of increasing complexity: sparse lookups, evaluating perplexity of a large file, and translation with Moses. Our test machine has two Intel Xeon E5410 processors totaling eight cores, 32 GB RAM, and four Seagate Barracuda disks in software RAID 0 running Linux 2.6.18.

5.1 Sparse Lookup

Sparse lookup is a key subproblem of language model queries. We compare three hash tables: our probing implementation, GCC's hash_set, and Boost's[8] unordered. For sorted lookup, we compare interpolation search, standard C++ binary_search, and standard C++ set based on red-black trees. The data structure was populated with 64-bit integers sampled uniformly without replacement. For queries, we uniformly sampled 10 million hits and 10 million misses. The same numbers were used for each data structure. Time includes all queries but excludes random number generation and data structure population. Figure 2 shows timing results.

For the PROBING implementation, hash table sizes are in the millions, so the most relevant values are on the right size of the graph, where linear probing wins. It also uses less memory, with 8 bytes of overhead per entry (we store 16-byte entries with $m = 1.5$); linked list implementations hash_set and unordered require at least 8 bytes per entry for pointers. Further, the probing hash table does only one random lookup per query, explaining why it is faster on large data.

Interpolation search has a more expensive pivot but performs less pivoting and reads, so it is slow on small data and faster on large data. This suggests a strategy: run interpolation search until the range narrows to 4096 or fewer entries, then switch to binary_search. However, reads in the TRIE data structure are more expensive due to bit-level packing, so we found that it is faster to use interpolation search the entire time. Memory usage is the same as with binary_search and lower than with set.

5.2 Perplexity

For the perplexity and translation tasks, we used SRILM to build a 5-gram English language model on 834 million tokens from Europarl v6 (Koehn, 2005) and the 2011 Workshop on Machine Translation News Crawl corpus with duplicate lines removed. The model was built with open vocabulary, modified Kneser-Ney smoothing, and default pruning settings that remove singletons of order 3 and higher. Unlike Germann et al. (2009), we chose a model size so that all benchmarks fit comfortably in main memory. Benchmarks use the package's binary format; our code is also the fastest at building a binary file. As noted in Section 4.4, disk cache state is controlled by reading the entire binary file before each test begins. For RandLM, we used the settings in the documentation: 8 bits per value and false positive probability $\frac{1}{256}$.

We evaluate the time and memory consumption of each data structure by computing perplexity on 4 billion tokens from the English Gigaword corpus (Parker et al., 2009). Tokens were converted to vocabulary identifiers in advance and state was carried

[8] http://boost.org

from each query to the next. Table 1 shows results of the benchmark. Compared to decoding, this task is cache-unfriendly in that repeated queries happen only as they naturally occur in text. Therefore, performance is more closely tied to the underlying data structure than to the cache. In fact, we found that enabling IRSTLM's cache made it slightly slower, so results in Table 1 use IRSTLM without caching. Moses sets the cache size parameter to 50 so we did as well; the resulting cache size is 2.82 GB.

The results in Table 1 show PROBING is 81% faster than TRIE, which is in turn 31% faster than the fastest baseline. Memory usage in PROBING is high, though SRILM is even larger, so where memory is of concern we recommend using TRIE, if it fits in memory. For even larger models, we recommend RandLM; the memory consumption of the cache is not expected to grow with model size, and it has been reported to scale well. Another option is the closed-source data structures from Sheffield (Guthrie and Hepple, 2010). Though we are not able to calculate their memory usage on our model, results reported in their paper suggest lower memory consumption than TRIE on large-scale models, at the expense of CPU time.

Package	Variant	Queries/ms	RAM (GB)
Ken	PROBING	1818	5.28
	TRIE	1139	2.72
	TRIE 8 bits[a]	1127	1.59
SRI	Default	750	9.19
	Compact	238	7.27
IRST[b]	Invert	426	2.91
	Default	368	2.91
MIT	Default	410	7.72+1.34[c]
Rand	Backoff 8 bits[a]	56	1.30+2.82[c]
Berkeley	Hash+Scroll[a]	913	5.28+2.32[d]
	Hash[a]	767	3.71+1.72[d]
	Compressed[a]	126	1.73+0.71[d]
Estimates for unreleased packages			
Sheffield	C-MPHR[a]	607[e]	
TPT	Default	357[f]	

Table 1: Single-threaded speed and memory use on the perplexity task. The PROBING model is fastest by a substantial margin but generally uses more memory. TRIE is faster than competing packages and uses less memory than non-lossy competitors. The timing basis for Queries/ms includes kernel and user time but excludes loading time; we also subtracted time to run a program that just reads the query file. Peak virtual memory is reported; final resident memory is similar except for BerkeleyLM. We tried both aggressive reading and lazy memory mapping where applicable, but results were much the same.

[a]Uses lossy compression.

[b]The 8-bit quantized variant returned incorrect probabilities as explained in Section 3. It did 402 queries/ms using 1.80 GB.

[c]Memory use increased during scoring due to batch processing (MIT) or caching (Rand). The first value reports use immediately after loading while the second reports the increase during scoring.

[d]BerkeleyLM is written in Java which requires memory be specified in advance. Timing is based on plentiful memory. Then we ran binary search to determine the least amount of memory with which it would run. The first value reports resident size after loading; the second is the gap between post-loading resident memory and peak virtual memory. The developer explained that the loading process requires extra memory that it then frees.

[e]Based on the ratio to SRI's speed reported in Guthrie and Hepple (2010) under different conditions. Memory usage is likely much lower than ours.

[f]The original paper (Germann et al., 2009) provided only 2s of query timing and compared with SRI when it exceeded available RAM. The authors provided us with a ratio between TPT and SRI under different conditions.

5.3 Translation

This task measures how well each package performs in machine translation. We run the baseline Moses system for the French-English track of the 2011 Workshop on Machine Translation,[9] translating the 3003-sentence test set. Based on revision 4041, we modified Moses to print process statistics before terminating. Process statistics are already collected by the kernel (and printing them has no meaningful impact on performance). SRILM's compact variant has an incredibly expensive destructor, dwarfing the time it takes to perform translation, and so we also modified Moses to avoiding the destructor by calling `_exit` instead of returning normally. Since our destructor is an efficient call to `munmap`, bypassing the destructor favors only other packages. The binary language model from Section 5.2 and text phrase table were forced into disk cache before each run. Time starts when Moses is launched and therefore includes model loading time. These con-

[9]http://statmt.org/wmt11/baseline.html

Package	Variant	Time (m) CPU	Time (m) Wall	RAM (GB) Res	RAM (GB) Virt
Ken	PROBING-L	72.3	72.4	7.83	7.92
	PROBING-P	73.6	74.7	7.83	7.92
	TRIE-L	80.4	80.6	4.95	5.24
	TRIE-P	80.1	80.1	4.95	5.24
	TRIE-L 8[a]	79.5	79.5	3.97	4.10
	TRIE-P 8[a]	79.9	79.9	3.97	4.10
SRI	Default	85.9	86.1	11.90	11.94
	Compact	155.5	155.7	9.98	10.02
IRST	Cache-Invert-L	106.4	106.5	5.36	5.84
	Cache-Invert-R	106.7	106.9	5.73	5.84
	Invert-L	117.2	117.3	5.27	5.67
	Invert-R	117.7	118.0	5.64	5.67
	Default-L	126.3	126.4	5.26	5.67
	Default-R	127.1	127.3	5.64	5.67
Rand	Backoff[a]	277.9	278.0	4.05	4.18
	Backoff[b]	247.6	247.8	4.06	4.18

Table 2: Single-threaded time and memory consumption of Moses translating 3003 sentences. Where applicable, models were loaded with lazy memory mapping (-L), prefaulting (-P), and normal reading (-R); results differ by at most than 0.6 minute.

[a]Lossy compression with the same weights.
[b]Lossy compression with retuned weights.

Package	Variant	Time (m) CPU	Time (m) Wall	RAM (GB) Res	RAM (GB) Virt
Ken	PROBING-L	130.4	20.2	7.91	8.53
	PROBING-P	132.6	21.7	7.91	8.41
	TRIE-L	132.1	20.6	5.03	5.85
	TRIE-P	132.2	20.5	5.02	5.84
	TRIE-L 8[a]	137.1	21.2	4.03	4.60
	TRIE-P 8[a]	134.6	20.8	4.03	4.72
SRI	Default	153.2	26.0	11.97	12.56
	Compact	243.3	36.9	10.05	10.55
Rand	Backoff[a]	346.8	49.4	5.41	6.78
	Backoff[b]	308.7	44.4	5.26	6.81

Table 3: Multi-threaded time and memory consumption of Moses translating 3003 sentences on eight cores. Our code supports lazy memory mapping (-L) and prefaulting (-P) with `MAP_POPULATE`, the default. IRST is not threadsafe. Time for Moses itself to load, including loading the language model and phrase table, is included. Along with locking and background kernel operations such as prefaulting, this explains why wall time is not one-eighth that of the single-threaded case.

[a]Lossy compression with the same weights.
[b]Lossy compression with retuned weights.

ditions make the value appropriate for estimating repeated run times, such as in parameter tuning. Table 2 shows single-threaded results, mostly for comparison to IRSTLM, and Table 3 shows multi-threaded results.

Part of the gap between resident and virtual memory is due to the time at which data was collected. Statistics are printed before Moses exits and after parts of the decoder have been destroyed. Moses keeps language models and many other resources in static variables, so these are still resident in memory. Further, we report current resident memory and peak virtual memory because these are the most applicable statistics provided by the kernel.

Overall, language modeling significantly impacts decoder performance. In line with perplexity results from Table 1, the PROBING model is the fastest followed by TRIE, and subsequently other packages. We incur some additional memory cost due to storing state in each hypothesis, though this is minimal compared with the size of the model itself. The TRIE model continues to use the least memory of the non-lossy options. For RandLM and IRSTLM, the effect of caching can be seen on speed and memory usage. This is most severe with RandLM in the multi-threaded case, where each thread keeps a separate cache, exceeding the original model size. As noted for the perplexity task, we do not expect cache to grow substantially with model size, so RandLM remains a low-memory option. Caching for IRSTLM is smaller at 0.09 GB resident memory, though it supports only a single thread. The BerkeleyLM direct-mapped cache is in principle faster than caches implemented by RandLM and by IRSTLM, so we may write a C++ equivalent implementation as future work.

5.4 Comparison with RandLM

RandLM's stupid backoff variant stores counts instead of probabilities and backoffs. It also does not prune, so comparing to our pruned model would be unfair. Using RandLM and the documented settings (8-bit values and $\frac{1}{256}$ false-positive probability), we built a stupid backoff model on the same data as in Section 5.2. We used this data to build an unpruned ARPA file with IRSTLM's

Pack	Variant	Time (m)	RAM (GB) Res	Virt	BLEU
Ken	TRIE	82.9	12.16	14.39	27.24
	TRIE 8 bits	82.7	8.41	9.41	27.22
	TRIE 4 bits	83.2	7.74	8.55	27.09
Rand	Stupid 8 bits	218.7	5.07	5.18	25.54
	Backoff 8 bits	337.4	7.17	7.28	25.45

Table 4: CPU time, memory usage, and uncased BLEU (Papineni et al., 2002) score for single-threaded Moses translating the same test set. We ran each lossy model twice: once with specially-tuned weights and once with weights tuned using an exact model. The difference in BLEU was minor and we report the better result.

`improved-kneser-ney` option and the default three pieces. Table 4 shows the results. We elected run Moses single-threaded to minimize the impact of RandLM's cache on memory use. RandLM is the clear winner in RAM utilization, but is also slower and lower quality. However, the point of RandLM is to scale to even larger data, compensating for this loss in quality.

6 Future Work

There any many techniques for improving language model speed and reducing memory consumption. For speed, we plan to implement the direct-mapped cache from BerkeleyLM. Much could be done to further reduce memory consumption. Raj and Whittaker (2003) show that integers in a trie implementation can be compressed substantially. Quantization can be improved by jointly encoding probability and backoff. For even larger models, storing counts (Talbot and Osborne, 2007; Pauls and Klein, 2011; Guthrie and Hepple, 2010) is a possibility. Beyond optimizing the memory size of TRIE, there are alternative data structures such as those in Guthrie and Hepple (2010). Finally, other packages implement language model estimation while we are currently dependent on them to generate an ARPA file.

While we have minimized forward-looking state in Section 4.1, machine translation systems could also benefit by minimizing backward-looking state. For example, syntactic decoders (Koehn et al., 2007; Dyer et al., 2010; Li et al., 2009) perform dynamic programming parametrized by both backward- and forward-looking state. If they knew that the first four words in a hypergraph node would never extend to the left and form a 5-gram, then three or even fewer words could be kept in the backward state. This information is readily available in TRIE where adjacent records with equal pointers indicate no further extension of context is possible. Exposing this information to the decoder will lead to better hypothesis recombination. Generalizing state minimization, the model could also provide explicit bounds on probability for both backward and forward extension. This would result in better rest cost estimation and better pruning.[10] In general, tighter, but well factored, integration between the decoder and language model should produce a significant speed improvement.

7 Conclusion

We have described two data structures for language modeling that achieve substantial reductions in time and memory cost. The PROBING model is 2.4 times as fast as the fastest alternative, SRILM, and uses less memory too. The TRIE model uses less memory than the smallest lossless alternative and is still faster than SRILM. These performance gains transfer to improved system runtime performance; though we focused on Moses, our code is the best lossless option with cdec and Joshua. We attain these results using several optimizations: hashing, custom lookup tables, bit-level packing, and state for left-to-right query patterns. The code is open-source, has minimal dependencies, and offers both C++ and Java interfaces for integration.

Acknowledgments

Alon Lavie advised on this work. Hieu Hoang named the code "KenLM" and assisted with Moses along with Barry Haddow. Adam Pauls provided a pre-release comparison to BerkeleyLM and an initial Java interface. Nicola Bertoldi and Marcello Federico assisted with IRSTLM. Chris Dyer integrated the code into cdec. Juri Ganitkevitch answered questions about Joshua. This material is based upon work supported by the National Science Foundation Graduate Research Fellowship under Grant No. 0750271 and by the DARPA GALE program.

[10]One issue is efficient retrieval of bounds, though these could be quantized, rounded in the safe direction, and stored with each record.

References

Philip Clarkson and Ronald Rosenfeld. 1997. Statistical language modeling using the CMU-Cambridge toolkit. In *Proceedings of Eurospeech*.

Chris Dyer, Adam Lopez, Juri Ganitkevitch, Johnathan Weese, Ferhan Ture, Phil Blunsom, Hendra Setiawan, Vladimir Eidelman, and Philip Resnik. 2010. cdec: A decoder, alignment, and learning framework for finite-state and context-free translation models. In *Proceedings of the ACL 2010 System Demonstrations*, pages 7–12.

Marcello Federico and Nicola Bertoldi. 2006. How many bits are needed to store probabilities for phrase-based translation? In *Proceedings of the Workshop on Statistical Machine Translation*, pages 94–101, New York City, June.

Marcello Federico, Nicola Bertoldi, and Mauro Cettolo. 2008. IRSTLM: an open source toolkit for handling large scale language models. In *Proceedings of Interspeech*, Brisbane, Australia.

Ulrich Germann, Eric Joanis, and Samuel Larkin. 2009. Tightly packed tries: How to fit large models into memory, and make them load fast, too. In *Proceedings of the NAACL HLT Workshop on Software Engineering, Testing, and Quality Assurance for Natural Language Processing*, pages 31–39, Boulder, Colorado.

David Guthrie and Mark Hepple. 2010. Storing the web in memory: Space efficient language models with constant time retrieval. In *Proceedings of EMNLP 2010*, Los Angeles, CA.

Bo-June Hsu and James Glass. 2008. Iterative language model estimation: Efficient data structure & algorithms. In *Proceedings of Interspeech*, Brisbane, Australia.

Philipp Koehn, Hieu Hoang, Alexandra Birch, Chris Callison-Burch, Marcello Federico, Nicola Bertoldi, Brooke Cowan, Wade Shen, Christine Moran, Richard Zens, Chris Dyer, Ondrej Bojar, Alexandra Constantin, and Evan Herbst. 2007. Moses: Open source toolkit for statistical machine translation. In *Annual Meeting of the Association for Computational Linguistics (ACL)*, Prague, Czech Republic, June.

Philipp Koehn. 2005. Europarl: A parallel corpus for statistical machine translation. In *Proceedings of MT Summit*.

Zhifei Li, Chris Callison-Burch, Chris Dyer, Sanjeev Khudanpur, Lane Schwartz, Wren Thornton, Jonathan Weese, and Omar Zaidan. 2009. Joshua: An open source toolkit for parsing-based machine translation. In *Proceedings of the Fourth Workshop on Statistical Machine Translation*, pages 135–139, Athens, Greece, March. Association for Computational Linguistics.

Kishore Papineni, Salim Roukos, Todd Ward, and Wei-Jing Zhu. 2002. BLEU: A method for automatic evalution of machine translation. In *Proceedings 40th Annual Meeting of the Association for Computational Linguistics*, pages 311–318, Philadelphia, PA, July.

Robert Parker, David Graff, Junbo Kong, Ke Chen, and Kazuaki Maeda. 2009. English gigaword fourth edition. LDC2009T13.

Adam Pauls and Dan Klein. 2011. Faster and smaller n-gram language models. In *Proceedings of ACL*, Portland, Oregon.

Yehoshua Perl, Alon Itai, and Haim Avni. 1978. Interpolation search—a log log N search. *Commun. ACM*, 21:550–553, July.

Bhiksha Raj and Ed Whittaker. 2003. Lossless compression of language model structure and word identifiers. In *Proceedings of IEEE International Conference on Acoustics, Speech and Signal Processing*, pages 388–391.

Andreas Stolcke. 2002. SRILM - an extensible language modeling toolkit. In *Proceedings of the Seventh International Conference on Spoken Language Processing*, pages 901–904.

David Talbot and Miles Osborne. 2007. Randomised language modelling for statistical machine translation. In *Proceedings of ACL*, pages 512–519, Prague, Czech Republic.

Wider Context by Using Bilingual Language Models in Machine Translation

Jan Niehues[1], **Teresa Herrmann**[1], **Stephan Vogel**[2] **and Alex Waibel**[1,2]
[1]Institute for Anthropomatics, KIT - Karlsruhe Institute of Technology, Germany
[2] Language Techonolgies Institute, Carnegie Mellon University, USA
[1]`firstname.lastname@kit.edu` [2]`lastname@cs.cmu.edu`

Abstract

In past Evaluations for Machine Translation of European Languages, it could be shown that the translation performance of SMT systems can be increased by integrating a bilingual language model into a phrase-based SMT system. In the bilingual language model, target words with their aligned source words build the tokens of an n-gram based language model. We analyzed the effect of bilingual language models and show where they could help to better model the translation process. We could show improvements of translation quality on German-to-English and Arabic-to-English. In addition, for the Arabic-to-English task, training an extra bilingual language model on the POS tags instead of the surface word forms led to further improvements.

1 Introduction

In many state-of-the art SMT systems, the phrase-based (Koehn et al., 2003) approach is used. In this approach, instead of building the translation by translating word by word, sequences of source and target words, so-called phrase pairs, are used as the basic translation unit. A table of correspondences between source and target phrases forms the translation model in this approach. Target language fluency is modeled by a language model storing monolingual n-gram occurrences. A log-linear combination of these main models as well as additional features is used to score the different translation hypotheses. Then the decoder searches for the translation with the highest score.

A different approach to SMT is to use a stochastic finite state transducer based on bilingual n-grams (Casacuberta and Vidal, 2004). This approach was for example successfully applied by Allauzen et al. (2010) on the French-English translation task. In this so-called n-gram approach the translation model is trained by using an n-gram language model of pairs of source and target words, called tuples. While the phrase-based approach captures only bilingual context within the phrase pairs, in the n-gram approach the n-gram model trained on the tuples is used to capture bilingual context between the tuples. As in the phrase-based approach, the translation model can also be combined with additional models like, for example, language models using log-linear combination.

Inspired by the n-gram-based approach, we introduce a bilingual language model that extends the translation model of the phrase-based SMT approach by providing bilingual word context. In addition to the bilingual word context, this approach enables us also to integrate a bilingual context based on part of speech (POS) into the translation model. When using phrase pairs it is complicated to use different kinds of bilingual contexts, since the context of the POS-based phrase pairs should be bigger than the word-based ones to make the most use of them. But there is no straightforward way to integrate phrase pairs of different lengths into the translation model in the phrase-based approach, while it is quite easy to use n-gram models with different context lengths on the tuples. We show how we can use bilingual POS-based language models to capture longer bilingual context in phrase-based translation

Proceedings of the 6th Workshop on Statistical Machine Translation, pages 198–206,
Edinburgh, Scotland, UK, July 30–31, 2011.

systems.

This paper is structured in the following way: In the next section, we will present some related work. Afterwards, in Section 3, a motivation for using the bilingual language model will be given. In the following section the bilingual language model is described in detail. In Section 5, the results and an analysis of the translation results is given, followed by a conclusion.

2 Related Work

The n-gram approach presented in Mariño et al. (2006) has been derived from the work of Casacuberta and Vidal (2004), which used finite state transducers for statistical machine translation. In this approach, units of source and target words are used as basic translation units. Then the translation model is implemented as an n-gram model over the tuples. As it is also done in phrase-based translations, the different translations are scored by a log-linear combination of the translation model and additional models.

Crego and Yvon (2010) extended the approach to be able to handle different word factors. They used factored language models introduced by Bilmes and Kirchhoff (2003) to integrate different word factors into the translation process. In contrast, we use a log-linear combination of language models on different factors in our approach.

A first approach of integrating the idea presented in the n-gram approach into phrase-based machine translation was described in Matusov et al. (2006). In contrast to our work, they used the bilingual units as defined in the original approach and they did not use additional word factors.

Hasan et al. (2008) used lexicalized triplets to introduce bilingual context into the translation process. These triplets include source words from outside the phrase and form and additional probability $p(f|e, e')$ that modifies the conventional word probability of f given e depending on trigger words e' in the sentence enabling a context-based translation of ambiguous phrases.

Other approaches address this problem by integrating word sense disambiguation engines into a phrase-based SMT system. In Chan and Ng (2007) a classifier exploits information such as local collocations, parts-of-speech or surrounding words to determine the lexical choice of target words, while Carpuat and Wu (2007) use rich context features based on position, syntax and local collocations to dynamically adapt the lexicons for each sentence and facilitate the choice of longer phrases.

In this work we present a method to extend the locally limited context of phrase pairs and n-grams by using bilingual language models. We keep the phrase-based approach as the main SMT framework and introduce an n-gram language model trained in a similar way as the one used in the finite state transducer approach as an additional feature in the log-linear model.

3 Motivation

To motivate the introduction of the bilingual language model, we will analyze the bilingual context that is used when selecting the target words. In a phrase-based system, this context is limited by the phrase boundaries. No bilingual information outside the phrase pair is used for selecting the target word. The effect can be shown in the following example sentence:

> *Ein gemeinsames Merkmal aller extremen Rechten in Europa ist ihr Rassismus und die Tatsache, dass sie das Einwanderungsproblem als politischen Hebel benutzen.*

Using our phrase-based SMT system, we get the following segmentation into phrases on the source side: *ein gemeinsames*, *Merkmal*, *aller*, *extremen Rechten*. That means, that the translation of *Merkmal* is not influenced by the source words *gemeinsames* or *aller*.

However, apart from this segmentation, other phrases could have been conceivable for building a translation:
ein, *ein gemeinsames*, *ein gemeinsames Merkmal*, *gemeinsames*, *gemeinsames Merkmal*, *Merkmal aller*, *aller*, *extremen*, *extremen Rechten* and *Rechten*.

As shown in Figure 1 the translation for the first three words *ein gemeinsames Merkmal* into *a common feature* can be created by segmenting it into *ein gemeinsames* and *Merkmal* as done by the

Figure 1: Alternative Segmentations

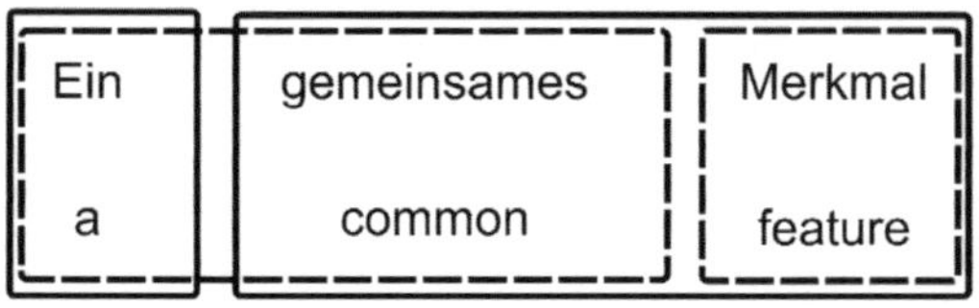

phrase-based system or by segmenting it into *ein* and *gemeinsames Merkmal*. In the phrase-based system, the decoder cannot make use of the fact that both segmentation variants lead to the same translation, but has to select one and use only this information for scoring the hypothesis.

Consequently, if the first segmentation is chosen, the fact that *gemeinsames* is translated to *common* does effect the translation of *Merkmal* only by means of the language model, but no bilingual context can be carried over the segmentation boundaries.

To overcome this drawback of the phrase-based approach, we introduce a bilingual language model into the phrase-based SMT system. Table 1 shows the source and target words and demonstrates how the bilingual phrases are constructed and how the source context stays available over segment boundaries in the calculation of the language model score for the sentence. For example, when calculating the language model score for the word *feature* *P(feature_Merkmal | common_gemeinsames*) we can see that through the bilingual tokens not only the previous target word but also the previous source word is known and can influence the translation even though it is in a different segment.

4 Bilingual Language Model

The bilingual language model is a standard n-gram-based language model trained on bilingual tokens instead of simple words. These bilingual tokens are motivated by the tuples used in n-gram approaches to machine translation. We use different basic units for the n-gram model compared to the n-gram approach, in order to be able to integrate them into a phrase-based translation system.

In this context, a bilingual token consists of a target word and all source words that it is aligned to. More formally, given a sentence pair $e_1^I = e_1...e_I$ and $f_1^J = f_1...f_J$ and the corresponding word alignment $A = \{(i,j)\}$ the following tokens are created:

$$t_j = \{f_j\} \cup \{e_i | (i,j) \in A\} \quad (1)$$

Therefore, the number of bilingual tokens in a sentence equals the number of target words. If a source word is aligned to two target words like the word *aller* in the example sentence, two bilingual tokens are created: *all_aller* and *the_aller*. If, in contrast, a target word is aligned to two source words, only one bilingual token is created consisting of the target word and both source words.

The existence of unaligned words is handled in the following way. If a target word is not aligned to any source word, the corresponding bilingual token consists only of the target word. In contrast, if a source word is not aligned to any word in the target language sentence, this word is ignored in the bilingual language model.

Using this definition of bilingual tokens the translation probability of source and target sentence and the word alignment is then defined by:

$$p(e_1^I, f_1^J, A) = \prod_{j=1}^{J} P(t_j | t_{j-1}...t_{j-n}) \quad (2)$$

This probability is then used in the log-linear combination of a phrase-based translation system as an additional feature. It is worth mentioning that although it is modeled like a conventional language model, the bilingual language model is an extension to the translation model, since the translation for the source words is modeled and not the fluency of the target text.

To train the model a corpus of bilingual tokens can be created in a straightforward way. In the generation of this corpus the order of the target words defines the order of the bilingual tokens. Then we can use the common language modeling tools to train the bilingual language model. As it was done for the normal language model, we used Kneser-Ney smoothing.

4.1 Comparison to Tuples

While the bilingual tokens are motivated by the tuples in the n-gram approach, there are quite some differences. They are mainly due to the fact that the

Source	Target	Bi-word	LM Prob
ein	a	a_ein	P(a_ein | <s>)
gemeinsames	common	common_gemeinsames	P(common_gemeinsames | a_ein, <s>)
Merkmal	feature	feature_Merkmal	P(feature_Merkmal | common_gemeinsames)
	of	of_	P(of_ | feature_Merkmal)
aller	all	all_aller	P(all_aller | of_)
aller	the	the_aller	P(the_aller | all_aller, of_)
extremen	extreme	extreme_extremen	P(extreme_extremen)
Rechten	right	right_Rechten	P(right_Rechten | extreme_extremen)

Table 1: Example Sentence: Segmentation and Bilingual Tokens

tuples are also used to guide the search in the n-gram approach, while the search in the phrase-based approach is guided by the phrase pairs and the bilingual tokens are only used as an additional feature in scoring.

While no word inside a tuple can be aligned to a word outside the tuple, the bilingual tokens are created based on the target words. Consequently, source words of one bilingual token can also be aligned to target words inside another bilingual token. Therefore, we do not have the problems of embedded words, where there is no independent translation probability.

Since we do not create a a monotonic segmentation of the bilingual sentence, but only use the segmentation according to the target word order, it is not clear where to put source words, which have no correspondence on the target side. As mentioned before, they are ignored in the model.

But an advantage of this approach is that we have no problem handling unaligned target words. We just create bilingual tokens with an empty source side. Here, the placing order of the unaligned target words is guided by the segmentation into phrase pairs.

Furthermore, we need no additional pruning of the vocabulary due to computation cost, since this is already done by the pruning of the phrase pairs. In our phrase-based system, we allow only for twenty translations of one source phrase.

4.2 Comparison to Phrase Pairs

Using the definition of the bilingual language model, we can again have a look at the introductory example sentence. We saw that when translating the phrase *ein gemeinsames Merkmal* using a phrase-based system, the translation of *gemeinsames* into *common* can only be influenced by either the preceeding *ein # a* or by the succeeding *Merkmal # feature*, but not by both of them at the same time, since either the phrase *ein gemeinsames* or the phrase *gemeinsames Merkmal* has to be chosen when segmenting the source sentence for translation. If we now look at the context that can be used when translating this segment applying the bilingual language model, we see that the translation of *gemeinsames* into *common* is on the one hand influenced by the translation of the token *ein # a* within the bilingual language model probability $P(common\_gemeinsames \mid a\_ein, <s>)$.

On the other hand, it is also influenced by the translation of the word *Merkmal* into *feature* encoded into the probability $P(feature\_Merkmal \mid common\_gemeinsames)$. In contrast to the phrase-based translation model, this additional model is capable of using context information from both sides to score the translation hypothesis. In this way, when building the target sentence, the information of aligned source words can be considered even beyond phrase boundaries.

4.3 POS-based Bilingual Language Models

When translating with the phrase-based approach, the decoder evaluates different hypotheses with different segmentations of the source sentence into phrases. The segmentation depends on available phrase pair combinations but for one hypothesis translation the segmentation into phrases is fixed. This leads to problems, when integrating parallel POS-based information. Since the amount of different POS tags in a language is very small compared to the number of words in a language, we could manage much longer phrase pairs based on POS tags compared to the possible length of phrase pairs on the word level.

In a phrase-based translation system the average phrase length is often around two words. For POS sequences, in contrast, sequences of 4 tokens can often be matched. Consequently, this information can only help, if a different segmentation could be chosen for POS-based phrases and for word-based phrases. Unfortunately, there is no straightforward way to integrate this into the decoder.

If we now look at how the bilingual language model is applied, it is much easier to integrate the POS-based information. In addition to the bilingual token for every target word we can generate a bilingual token based on the POS information of the source and target words. Using this bilingual POS token, we can train an additional bilingual POS-based language model and apply it during translation. In this case it is no longer problematic if the context of the POS-based bilingual language model is longer than the one based on the word information, because word and POS sequences are scored separately by two different language models which cover different n-gram lengths.

The training of the bilingual POS language model is straightforward. We can build the corpus of bilingual POS tokens based on the parallel corpus of POS tags generated by running a POS tagger over both source and target side of the initial parallel corpus and the alignment information for the respective words in the text corpora.

During decoding, we then also need to know the POS tag for every source and target word. Since we build the sentence incrementally, we cannot use the tagger directly. Instead, we store also the POS source and target sequences during the phrase extraction. When creating the bilingual phrase pair with POS information, there might be different possibilities of POS sequences for the source and target phrases. But we keep only the most probable one for each phrase pair. For the Arabic-to-English translation task, we compared the generated target tags with the tags created by the tagger on the automatic translations. They are different on less than 5% of the words.

Using the alignment information as well as the source and target POS sequences we can then create the POS-based bilingual tokens for every phrase pair and store it in addition to the normal phrase pairs. At decoding time, the most frequent POS tags in the bilingual phrases are used as tags for the input sentence and the translation is done based on the bilingual POS tokens built from these tags together with their alignment information.

5 Results

We evaluated and analyzed the influence of the bilingual language model on different languages. On the one hand, we measured the performance of the bilingual language model on German-to-English on the News translation task. On the other hand, we evaluated the approach on the Arabic-to-English direction on News and Web data. Additionally, we present the impact of the bilingual language model on the English-to-German, German-to-English and French-to-English systems with which we participated in the WMT 2011.

5.1 System Description

The German-to-English translation system was trained on the European Parliament corpus, News Commentary corpus and small amounts of additional Web data. The data was preprocessed and compound splitting was applied. Afterwards the discriminative word alignment approach as described in (Niehues and Vogel, 2008) was applied to generate the alignments between source and target words. The phrase table was built using the scripts from the Moses package (Koehn et al., 2007). The language model was trained on the target side of the parallel data as well as on additional monolingual News data. The translation model as well as the language model was adapted towards the target domain in a log-linear way.

The Arabic-to-English system was trained using GALE Arabic data, which contains 6.1M sentences. The word alignment is generated using EMDC, which is a combination of a discriminative approach and the IBM Models as described in Gao et al. (2010). The phrase table is generated using Chaski as described in Gao and Vogel (2010). The language model data we trained on the GIGAWord

V3 data plus BBN English data. After splitting the corpus according to sources, individual models were trained. Then the individual models were interpolated to minimize the perplexity on the MT03/MT04 data.

For both tasks the reordering was performed as a preprocessing step using POS information from the TreeTagger (Schmid, 1994) for German and using the Amira Tagger (Diab, 2009) for Arabic. For Arabic the approach described in Rottmann and Vogel (2007) was used covering short-range reorderings. For the German-to-English translation task the extended approach described in Niehues et al. (2009) was used to cover also the long-range reorderings typical when translating between German and English.

For both directions an in-house phrase-based decoder (Vogel, 2003) was used to generate the translation hypotheses and the optimization was performed using MER training. The performance on the testsets were measured in case-insensitive BLEU and TER scores.

5.2 German to English

We evaluated the approach on two different test sets from the News Commentary domain. The first consists of 2000 sentences with one reference. It will be referred to as Test 1. The second test set consists of 1000 sentences with two references and will be called Test 2.

5.2.1 Translation Quality

In Tables 2 and 3 the results for translation performance on the German-to-English translation task are summarized.

As it can been seen, the improvements of translation quality vary considerably between the two different test sets. While using the bilingual language model improves the translation by only 0.15 BLEU and 0.21 TER points on Test 1, the improvement on Test 2 is nearly 1 BLEU point and 0.5 TER points.

5.2.2 Context Length

One intention of using the bilingual language model is its capability to capture the bilingual contexts in a different way. To see, whether additional bilingual context is used during decoding, we analyzed the context used by the phrase pairs and by the n-gram bilingual language model.

However, a comparison of the different context lengths is not straightforward. The context of an n-gram language model is normally described by the average length of applied n-grams. For phrase pairs, normally the average target phrase pair length (avg. Target PL) is used as an indicator for the size of the context. And these two numbers cannot be compared directly.

To be able to compare the context used by the phrase pairs to the context used in the n-gram language model, we calculated the average left context that is used for every target word where the word itself is included, i.e. the context of a single word is 1. In case of the bilingual language model the score for the average left context is exactly the average length of applied n-grams in a given translation. For phrase pairs the average left context can be calculated in the following way: A phrase pair of length 1 gets a left context score of 1. In a phrase pair of length 2, the first word has a left context score of 1, since it is not influenced by any target word to the left. The second word in that phrase pair gets a left context count of 2, because it is influenced by the first word in the phrase. Correspondingly, the left context score of a phrase pair of length 3 is 6 (composed of the score 1 for the first word, score 2 for the second word and score 3 for the third word). To get the average left context for the whole translation, the context scores of all phrases are summed up and divided by the number of words in the translation.

The scores for the average left contexts for the two test sets are shown in Tables 2 and 3. They are called avg. PP Left Context. As it can be seen, the context used by the bilingual n-gram language model is longer than the one by the phrase pairs. The average n-gram length increases from 1.58 and 1.57, respectively to 2.21 and 2.18 for the two given test sets.

If we compare the average n-gram length of the bilingual language model to the one of the target language model, the n-gram length of the first is of course smaller, since the number of possible bilingual tokens is higher than the number of possible monolingual words. This can also be seen when looking at the perplexities of the two language models on the generated translations. While the perplexity of the target language model is 99 and 101 on Test 1 and 2, respectively, the perplexity of the bilingual language model is 512 and 538.

Metric	No BiLM	BiLM
BLEU	30.37	30.52
TER	50.27	50.06
avg. Target PL	1.66	1.66
avg. PP Left Context	1.57	1.58
avg. Target LM N-Gram	3.28	3.27
avg. BiLM N-Gram		2.21

Table 2: German-to-English results (Test 1)

Metric	No BiLM	BiLM
BLEU	44.16	45.09
TER	41.02	40.52
avg. Target PL	1.65	1.65
avg. PP Left Context	1.56	1.57
avg. Target LM N-Gram	3.25	3.23
avg. BiLM N-Gram		2.18

Table 3: German-to-English results (Test 2)

5.2.3 Overlapping Context

An additional advantage of the n-gram-based approach is the possibility to have overlapping context. If we would always use phrase pairs of length 2 only half of the adjacent words would influence each other in the translation. The others are only influenced by the other target words through the language model. If we in contrast would have a bilingual language model which uses an n-gram length of 2, this means that every choice of word influences the previous and the following word.

To analyze this influence, we counted how many borders of phrase pairs are covered by a bilingual n-gram. For Test 1, 16783 of the 27785 borders between phrase pairs are covered by a bilingual n-gram. For Test 2, 9995 of 16735 borders are covered. Consequently, in both cases at around 60 percent of the borders additional information can be used by the bilingual n-gram language model.

5.2.4 Bilingual N-Gram Length

For the German-to-English translation task we performed an additional experiment comparing different n-gram lengths of the bilingual language model. To ensure comparability between the experiments and avoid additional noise due to different optimization results, we did not perform separate optimization runs for for each of the system variants with different n-gram length, but used the same scaling factors for all of them. Of course, the system using no bilingual language model was trained independently. In Tables 4 and 5 we can see that the length of the actually applied n-grams as well as the BLEU score increased until the bilingual language model reaches an order of 4. For higher order bilingual language models, nearly no additional n-grams can be found in the language models. Also the translation quality does not increase further when using longer n-grams.

BiLM Length	aNGL	BLEU	TER
No		30.37	50.27
1	1	29.67	49.73
2	1.78	30.36	50.05
3	2.11	30.47	50.08
4	2.21	30.52	50.06
5	2.23	30.52	50.07
6	2.24	30.52	50.07

Table 4: Different N-Gram Lengths (Test 1)

BiLM Length	aNGL	BLEU	TER
No		44.16	41.02
1	1	44.22	40.53
2	1.78	45.11	40.38
3	2.09	45.18	40.51
4	2.18	45.09	40.52
5	2.21	45.10	40.52
6	2.21	45.10	40.52

Table 5: Different N-Gram Lengths (Test 2)

5.3 Arabic to English

The Arabic-to-English system was optimized on the MT06 data. As test set the Rosetta in-house test set DEV07-nw (News) and wb (Web Data) was used.

The results for the Arabic-to-English translation task are summarized in Tables 6 and 7. The performance was tested on two different domains, translation of News and Web documents. On both tasks, the translation could be improved by more than 1

BLEU point. Measuring the performance in TER also shows an improvement by 0.7 and 0.5 points.

By adding a POS-based bilingual language model, the performance could be improved further. An additional gain of 0.2 BLEU points and decrease of 0.3 points in TER could be reached. Consequently, an overall improvement of up to 1.7 BLEU points could be achieved by integrating two bilingual language models, one based on surface word forms and one based on parts-of-speech.

System	Dev	Test	
	BLEU	TER	BLEU
NoBiLM	48.42	40.77	52.05
+ BiLM	49.29	40.04	53.51
+ POS BiLM	49.56	39.85	53.71

Table 6: Results on Arabic to English: Translation of News

System	Dev	Test	
	BLEU	TER	BLEU
NoBiLM	48.42	47.14	41.90
+ BiLM	49.29	46.66	43.12
+ POS BiLM	49.56	46.40	43.28

Table 7: Results on Arabic to English: Translation of Web documents

As it was done for the German-to-English system, we also compared the context used by the different models for this translation direction. The results are summarized in Table 8 for the News test set and in Table 9 for the translation of Web data. It can be seen like it was for the other language pair that the context used in the bilingual language model is bigger than the one used by the phrase-based translation model.

Furthermore, it is worth mentioning that shorter phrase pairs are used, when using the POS-based bilingual language model. Both bilingual language models seem to model the context quite good, so that less long phrase pairs are needed to build the translation. Instead, the more frequent short phrases can be used to generate the translation.

5.4 Shared Translation Task @ WMT2011

The bilingual language model was included in 3 systems built for the WMT2011 Shared Translation Task evaluation. A phrase-based system similar to the one described before for the German-to-English results was used. A detailed system description can be found in Herrmann et al. (2011). The results are summarized in Table 10. The performance of competitive systems could be improved in all three languages by up to 0.4 BLEU points.

Metric	No	BiLM	POS BiLM
BLEU	52.05	53.51	53.71
avg. Target PL	2.12	2.03	1.79
avg. PP Left Context	1.92	1.85	1.69
avg. BiLM N-Gram		2.66	2.65
avg. POS BiLM			4.91

Table 8: Bilingual Context in Arabic-to-English results (News)

Metric	No	BiLM	POS BiLM
BLEU	41.90	43.12	43.28
avg. Target PL	1.82	1.80	1.57
avg. PP Left Context	1.72	1.69	1.53
avg. BiLM N-Gram		2.33	2.31
avg. POS BiLM			4.49

Table 9: Bilingual Context in Arabic-to-English results (Web data)

Language Pair	No BiLM	BiLM
German-English	24.12	24.52
English-German	16.89	17.01
French-English	28.17	28.34

Table 10: Preformance of Bilingual language model at WMT2011

6 Conclusion

In this work we showed how a feature of the n-gram-based approach can be integrated into a phrase-based statistical translation system. We performed a detailed analysis on how this influences the scoring of the translation system. We could show improvements on a variety of translation tasks covering different languages and domains. Furthermore, we could show that additional bilingual context information is used.

Furthermore, the additional feature can easily be

extended to additional word factors such as part-of-speech, which showed improvements for the Arabic-to-English translation task.

Acknowledgments

This work was realized as part of the Quaero Programme, funded by OSEO, French State agency for innovation.

References

Alexandre Allauzen, Josep M. Crego, İlknur Durgar El-Kahlout, and François Yvon. 2010. LIMSI's Statistical Translation Systems for WMT'10. In *Fifth Workshop on Statistical Machine Translation (WMT 2010)*, Uppsala, Sweden.

Jeff A. Bilmes and Katrin Kirchhoff. 2003. Factored language models and generalized parallel backoff. In *Proceedings of the 2003 Conference of the North American Chapter of the Association for Computational Linguistics on Human Language Technology*, pages 4–6, Stroudsburg, PA, USA.

Marine Carpuat and Dekai Wu. 2007. Improving Statistical Machine Translation using Word Sense Disambiguation. In *In The 2007 Joint Conference on Empirical Methods in Natural Language Processing and Computational Natural Language Learning*.

Francisco Casacuberta and Enrique Vidal. 2004. Machine Translation with Inferred Stochastic Finite-State Transducers. *Comput. Linguist.*, 30:205–225, June.

Yee Seng Chan and Hwee Tou Ng. 2007. Word Sense Disambiguation improves Statistical Machine Translation. In *In 45th Annual Meeting of the Association for Computational Linguistics (ACL-07*, pages 33–40.

Josep M. Crego and François Yvon. 2010. Factored bilingual n-gram language models for statistical machine translation. *Machine Translation*, 24, June.

Mona Diab. 2009. Second Generation Tools (AMIRA 2.0): Fast and Robust Tokenization, POS tagging, and Base Phrase Chunking. In *Proc. of the Second International Conference on Arabic Language Resources and Tools*, Cairo, Egypt, April.

Qin Gao and Stephan Vogel. 2010. Training Phrase-Based Machine Translation Models on the Cloud: Open Source Machine Translation Toolkit Chaski. In *The Prague Bulletin of Mathematical Linguistics No. 93*.

Qin Gao, Francisco Guzman, and Stephan Vogel. 2010. EMDC: A Semi-supervised Approach for Word Alignment. In *Proc. of the 23rd International Conference on Computational Linguistics*, Beijing, China.

Saša Hasan, Juri Ganitkevitch, Hermann Ney, and Jesús Andrés-Ferrer. 2008. Triplet Lexicon Models for Statistical Machine Translation. In *Proc. of Conference on Empirical Methods in NLP*, Honolulu, USA.

Teresa Herrmann, Mohammed Mediani, Jan Niehues, and Alex Waibel. 2011. The Karlsruhe Institute of Technology Translation Systems for the WMT 2011. In *Sixth Workshop on Statistical Machine Translation (WMT 2011)*, Edinbugh, U.K.

Philipp Koehn, Franz Josef Och, and Daniel Marcu. 2003. Statistical Phrase-Based Translation. In *Proceedings of the 2003 Conference of the North American Chapter of the Association for Computational Linguistics on Human Language Technology*, pages 48–54, Edmonton, Canada.

Philipp Koehn, Hieu Hoang, Alexandra Birch, Chris Callison-Burch, Marcello Federico, Nicola Bertoldi, Brooke Cowan, Wade Shen, Christine Moran, Richard Zens, Chris Dyer, Ondrej Bojar, Alexandra Constantin, and Evan Herbst. 2007. Moses: Open Source Toolkit for Statistical Machine Translation. In *ACL 2007, Demonstration Session*, Prague, Czech Republic, June 23.

José B. Mariño, Rafael E. Banchs, Josep M. Crego, Adrià de Gispert, Patrik Lambert, José A. R. Fonollosa, and Marta R. Costa-jussà. 2006. N-gram-based machine translation. *Comput. Linguist.*, 32, December.

Evgeny Matusov, Richard Zens, David Vilar, Arne Mauser, Maja Popović, Saša Hasan, and Hermann Ney. 2006. The rwth machine translation system. In *TC-STAR Workshop on Speech-to-Speech Translation*, pages 31–36, Barcelona, Spain, June.

Jan Niehues and Stephan Vogel. 2008. Discriminative Word Alignment via Alignment Matrix Modeling. In *Proc. of Third ACL Workshop on Statistical Machine Translation*, Columbus, USA.

Jan Niehues, Teresa Herrmann, Muntsin Kolss, and Alex Waibel. 2009. The Universität Karlsruhe Translation System for the EACL-WMT 2009. In *Fourth Workshop on Statistical Machine Translation (WMT 2009)*, Athens, Greece.

Kay Rottmann and Stephan Vogel. 2007. Word Reordering in Statistical Machine Translation with a POS-Based Distortion Model. In *TMI*, Skövde, Sweden.

Helmut Schmid. 1994. Probabilistic Part-of-Speech Tagging Using Decision Trees. In *International Conference on New Methods in Language Processing*, Manchester, UK.

Stephan Vogel. 2003. SMT Decoder Dissected: Word Reordering. In *Int. Conf. on Natural Language Processing and Knowledge Engineering*, Beijing, China.

A Minimally Supervised Approach for Detecting and Ranking Document Translation Pairs

Kriste Krstovski
Department of Computer Science
University of Massachusetts Amherst
Amherst, MA 01003, USA
kriste@cs.umass.edu

David A. Smith
Department of Computer Science
University of Massachusetts Amherst
Amherst, MA 01003, USA
dasmith@cs.umass.edu

Abstract

We describe an approach for generating a ranked list of candidate document translation pairs without the use of bilingual dictionary or machine translation system. We developed this approach as an initial, filtering step, for extracting parallel text from large, multilingual—but non-parallel—corpora. We represent bilingual documents in a vector space whose basis vectors are the overlapping tokens found in both languages of the collection. Using this representation, weighted by tf·idf, we compute cosine document similarity to create a ranked list of candidate document translation pairs. Unlike cross-language information retrieval, where a ranked list in the target language is evaluated for each source query, we are interested in, and evaluate, the more difficult task of finding translated document pairs. We first perform a feasibility study of our approach on parallel collections in multiple languages, representing multiple language families and scripts. The approach is then applied to a large bilingual collection of around 800k books. To avoid the computational cost of $O(n^2)$ document pair comparisons, we employ locality sensitive hashing (LSH) approximation algorithm for cosine similarity, which reduces our time complexity to $O(n \log n)$.

1 Introduction

A dearth of parallel data has been, and still is, a major problem for developing highly reliable statistical machine translation systems in many languages and domains. There have been many proposed approaches for alleviating this problem by utilizing techniques for creating and extracting parallel documents, sentences or phrases from comparable bilingual data available on the open web (Resnik and Smith, 2003), such as Wikipedia articles (Smith et. al, 2010), to name a few, or through digitized archives from various sources (Zhao and Vogel, 2002), (Munteanu and Marcu, 2005).

In general, in the process of utilizing comparable corpora to obtain sentence-aligned bilingual text, the first step involves performing initial filtering where text entities from both language collections are compared to each other and based on comparison score they are matched and grouped as potential translation candidate pairs. After this initial step, text entity pairs or tuples are further analyzed in order to extract parallel sentence pairs. In this paper we only focus on this initial step. We present a novel exploration of approaches that retrieve actual document translation pairs without the use of any bilingual resources such as lexicons or sentence aligned bitext.

Rather than solving separate retrieval or translation problems for each source language document, we retrieve translation pairs from the space of all possible bilingual document pairs. Most machine

Proceedings of the 6th Workshop on Statistical Machine Translation, pages 207–216,
Edinburgh, Scotland, UK, July 30–31, 2011.

translation (MT) and information retrieval (IR) systems rely on conditional probabilities; in contrast, we require comparable scores or probabilities over all document pairs. To avoid directly computing the similarity of all pairs, we use a randomized approximation algorithm based on locality sensitive hashing (LSH).

For this joint approach, we represent each document in both languages using an n-dimensional feature vector template which consists of the set of intersecting words which are found across all documents in both language collections. For each dimension i.e. word, in the feature vector template we calculate tf·idf score for the given document. Unlike other approaches, where documents or their word representations are first translated from foreign language to English using bilingual dictionary (Fung and Cheung, 2004), (Munteanu and Marcu, 2005) and (Uszkoreit et. al., 2010) in our approach we don't utilize any existing MT type artifact. In other words, for a given language pair we don't use translation lexicon by training an existing statistical machine translation system using sentence aligned parallel bilingual data in the same language or existing translation lexicon. Earlier work done by Enright and Kondrak (2007) uses only hapax words to represent and rank (based on the overlap number) translation documents pair in a parallel bilingual collection which is an easier task to evaluation due to the presence of a one-to-one matching among the bilingual documents. Most recently, Patry and Langlais (2011) show an improvement over this method by using an IR system to first retrieve translation document candidates and then identify translation document pairs by training a classifier.

We start off by giving detailed explanation of the above mentioned data representation. We then test the feasibility of our approach using aligned parallel document data from three different bilingual collections in several languages and writing systems. Results from these tests are given in section 3. The goal of developing our approach was to utilize it as an initial filtering step in developing parallel corpora from large, multilingual collections, such as the collection of more than 800K English and German books we describe in section 4. Since we start with no information on the possible translation pairs in our large collection and in order to verify the potential of our method, we first show results on retrieving 17 known parallel book pairs embedded in a small randomly selected subset of 1K books (section 4.1). Since performing cosine similarity across all document pairs is computationally expensive with time complexity of $O(n^2)$ we utilize the LSH based approximation algorithm for the cosine similarity measurement based on the work by Ravichandran et. al (2005). A brief overview of this approach is given in Section 5, which is followed by our implementation results explained and analyzed in section 6. To conclude the paper, we give a brief outlook on future work.

2 Document Representation

In Figure 1, we depict the process that we use to represent documents from bilingual collections in vector space and perform similarity measurements. We start by computing a word frequency count for each of the documents in our collection and creating a word frequency list. For each language, we take a union of the words in each document's frequency list to construct a global word list for the given language. The two global word lists are then intersected, and a list of overlapping words is created. From the initial list of overlapping words in both languages, we remove stop words by using stop word lists (words with high document frequency). The space-separated tokens extracted in this process are not necessarily words in the linguistic sense; therefore, we further refine the overlapping word list by removing tokens that contain non-alphanumeric characters. We make one exception for tokens (such as might appear in a time/date format) that contain hyphens, backslashes, apostrophes, and periods so long as these characters do not occur at the beginning or at the end of the token.

We call this list of overlapping tokens a feature vector template, where each token in the list is one feature. Using this feature vector template we go back and represent each document in the bilingual collection using the template vector by computing the tf·idf value for each token in the template vector over each particular document. Now that we have the original documents from both languages represented in a language-independent space, we compute vector similarity across all document pairs in order to come up with a single ranked list. We talk more in detail about the similarity metrics that we have considered and decided to use in the following section.

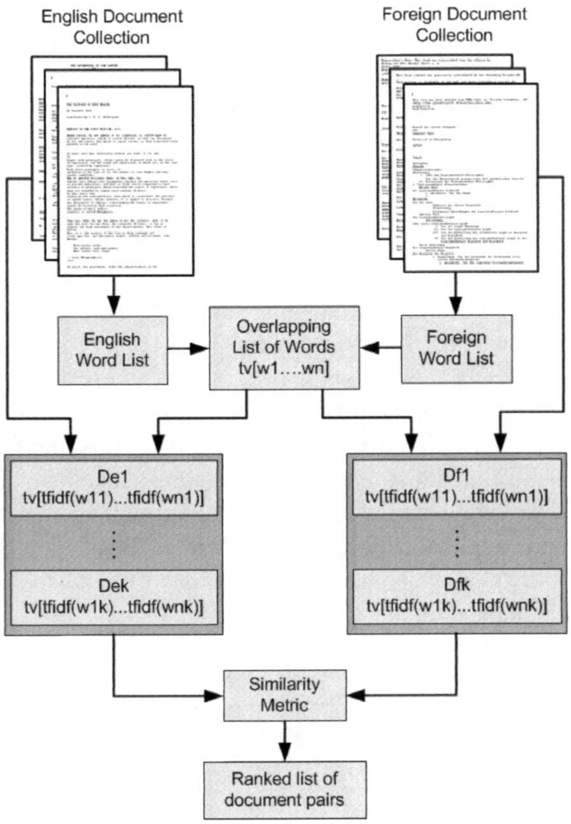

Figure 1. Process of creating and representing each document of a bilingual collection in an independent vector space.

3 Motivational Experiments

3.1 Evaluation Collections

We start off by evaluating the above proposed approach of determining candidate document translation pairs using three different parallel collections: Europarl, created by Koehn (2005), UN Arabic English Parallel Text (LDC2004E13) and the Arabic News Translation Part 1 (LDC2004T17). The purposes of first testing our approach using the Europarl corpus were twofold: This collection contains parallel documents (sessions of the European Parliament) that are further aligned at the speech and sentence level, which allows us to test alignment accuracy at several levels of granularity. Second, this collection contains parallel data from different groups of languages (Germanic, Romance, Slavic, Hellenic, etc.) and therefore is useful to observe the performance of our approach across different language families, which in turn are important to observe the difference in the cognate rates and the size of the overlapping words. In addition to the Europarl corpus we use the two English-Arabic parallel collections to test our approach across various alphabets (Arabic in addition to the Latin, Greek and Cyrillic found in the Europarl collection). Shown in Table 1 are basic statistics for all 3 corpora on the language pairs considered. We give min, max and median values over the number of words in each document.

Collection	# doc. Pairs	Lang.	Min	Max	Median
Europarl en-de	654	En	92	109030	46800.5
		De	95	99753	43161.0
Europarl en-bg	430	En	4872	59284	10706.5
		Bg	4771	56907	10167.0
Europarl en-es	642	En	92	109793	46790.5
		Es	104	114770	48989.0
Europarl en-gr	412	En	92	93886	21290.0
		Gr	103	93304	21122.0
Newswire en-ar	230	En	66	47784	691.5
		Ar	62	34272	560.0
UN en-ar	430	En	17672	71594	23027.0
		Ar	15478	62448	19682.0

Table 1. Document length statistics over 6 Parallel Collections.

From the Europarl collection we sentence aligned sessions in the following four language pairs where the English language is the source language: English-German, English-Spanish, English-Bulgarian and English-Greek. The foreign language in all four language pairs is selected from a different language group (Germanic, Romanic, Slavic), with Greek being a more isolated branch. For the Arabic language we used two parallel document collections in different domains – newswire and documents published by the United Nations. The Newswire parallel collection consisted of 1526 news stories which we combined based on the news story publication date and obtained 230 parallel documents. The purpose of combining the news articles is to increase the number of words present in each document since the original size of the news articles was not at a level to be treated as a document as in the case of the remaining two collections. The UN parallel collection consists of 34,575 document pairs.

3.2 Similarity Metrics

We considered five similarity metrics proposed at one time or another for vector space models in IR: Cosine (shown below), Dice, Product, Jaccard and Euclidean.

$$\frac{\sum x_i y_i}{\sqrt{\sum x_i^2 \sum y_i^2}} \quad (1)$$

Document similarity using the cosine metric relies on the angle between the vector representations and it is length invariant. The Dice metric relies on the number of common tokens between the two documents. Euclidean computes the similarity as a point distance between the two vector representations and is not normalized by the vector length which does not make it vector invariant. Jaccard distance is the ratio of the intersection and the union of the two vector representations while the product coefficient is simply the inner product of the two vectors. While there is no clear evidence across the literature whether one similarity metric is more useful across a range of tasks compared to another, the cosine similarity metric is mostly preferred. Shown in Figure 2 are the precision vs. recall plots of the above similarity measurements when used with our method. Tests were done on our set of 654 English-German sessions from the Europarl collections. To test the impact of the document length on the performance of the metric we performed two types of tests across all 5 metrics. In the first type we performed similarity analysis on the full document length (marked as 100%) and on the final 10% of each document (marked as 10%). We deliberately omitted the top part of the document to avoid any inadvertent inclusion of session date, topic, title, etc. (As it turned out, this was not a problem in our data.) We perform similarity measurements across all document pairs, and we generate a single ranked list. As can be seen from the plot, all five metrics yield better performance when all words in documents are considered compared to only considering 10%. The performance ranking of all five metrics was identical on both versions of the document set. Even though depicted in the above plot, the Jaccard distance performed pretty much the same as the Dice distance and therefore there is no visible difference between the two. While on the 10% version of the collection, the Euclidean distance has the worst precision, it could still be explored as a metric to obtain document translation pairs with the original collection with a modest to moderate recall range for P=1. The Jaccard distance along with the Dice distance yield the highest precision values across all recall values but they achieve the same recall range for P=1 as the Cosine metric. Since we are only interested in top-N document pairs that have P=1 and furthermore there are approximate algorithms for the Cosine similarity metrics we decided to further utilize this metric. The same metric has been previously used in determining potential translation candidates on sentence level by Munteanu and Marcu (2005) and in our case we are extending it to perform pair-wise document similarity.

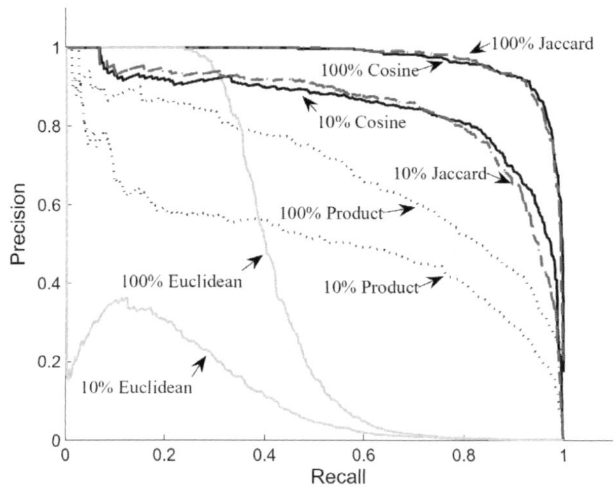

Figure 2. Precision vs. recall plot using various similarity measurements on the Europarl English-German collection.

When run on the same English-German collection, Enright's and Kondrak's (2007) approach achieves mean reciprocal rank (MRR) of 0.989 when using document specific hapax words and MRR=0.795 when using collection specific hapax words. With the above explained approach we obtain MRR=0.995.

3.3 Post Filtering Approaches

To further improve the precision of our approach we tested out two types of filtering the initial results. Since we threat documents as "bag of words" and since the Cosine metric uses the angle between the vector representations and is length invariant there may be instances of source documents that would yield high cosine coefficients over all target documents. In these instances, multiple document pairs with the same source document may be ranked high. To alleviate this problem, we consider two types of filtering the initial results. We go over the single ranked list and we only keep the top five document pairs for a given source document, thus introducing "diversity" in the ranked list. The second filter is motivated by the basic assumption used in the machine translation field that the length of the target sentence is in a given length range of the source sentence. We extend this assumption on a document level and we filter out all document pairs from the ranked list that are not in the ±20% range of the source document length. Both of the above values were selected based on empirical evidence without detailed explanation. Shown in Figure 3 are the effects of these two simple filtering techniques.

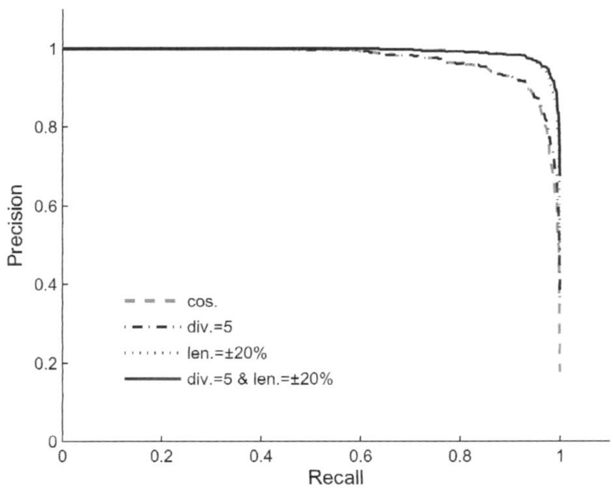

Figure 3. Diversity and length based filtering effects on the English-German Europarl collection.

Compared to the diversity filter, the length based filter yields better gain in precision while a combination of both methods achieves the highest recall range for P=1.

3.4 Target Languages and Writing Systems

Shown in Figure 4 are the precision/recall results on all six collections explained in Section 3.1. Post-filtering steps explained in the previous section were not utilized on these results. Our approach yields best precision on the Arabic News Translation Part 1 collection while the worst performance is on the UN Arabic English Parallel Text. While the performance on the English-German and English-Spanish collections is somewhat the same, out of all 4 Europarl collections we achieve best results on the Greek collection and worst results on the Bulgarian target language.

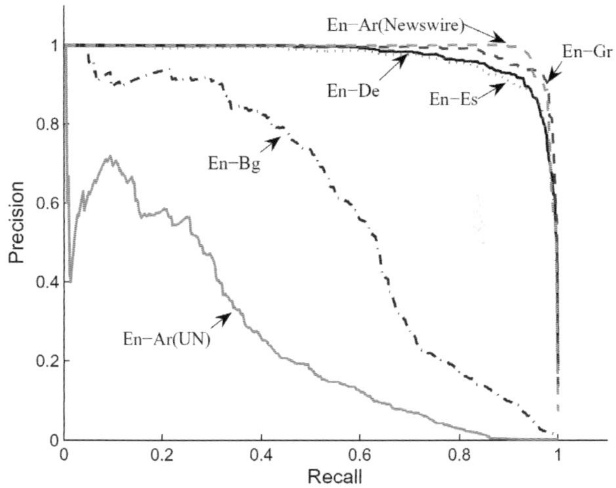

Figure 4. Precision vs. recall on 5 different language pairs using cosine similarity distance metric.

In Table 2, we give the vector template length for each collection.

Collection	# of overlapping tokens
Europarl en-de	37785
Europarl en-es	36476
Europarl en-bg	29360
Europarl en-gr	17220
UN en-ar	3945
Newswire en-ar	1262

Table 2. Number of overlapping words (vector template length) in the six parallel collections.

Unsurprisingly, due to the difference in script and language family, the feature vector templates for the English-Arabic collections have the smallest lengths.

Shown in Figure 5 are effects of the trivial diversity and length based filtering on the above precision vs. recall results. Bulgarian has improve substantially and so has the UN Arabic, but recall on the Arabic newswire is truncated on reaching P=0.4.

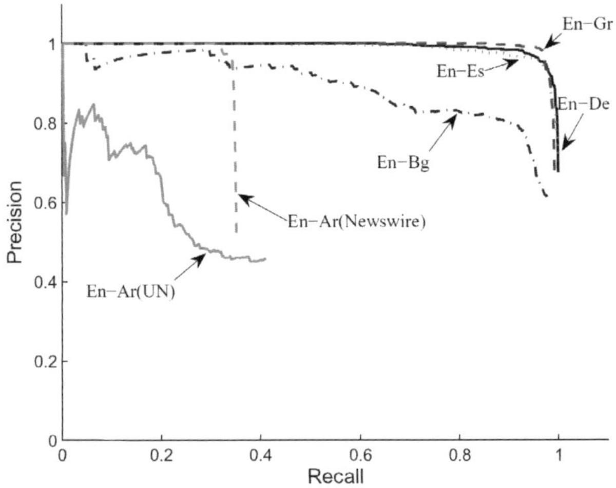

Figure 5. Precision vs. recall on 6 collections using div=5 and length filtering with ±20%.

3.5 Randomly Selected Documents

While useful to evaluate the feasibility of our approach, the previous parallel bilingual collections are unrealistic because there is, by the corpus' design, a translation for each document. To observe the performance on a bilingual document collection where there is no a priori information on translation pairs we created ten random subsets from the Europarl English-German collection. These subsets were created by randomly selecting 50% (328 documents) of the English and 5% (33 documents) of the German documents for each subset collection. Shown in is interpolated average precision over the ten subsets. The Mean Average Precision (MAP) obtained was 0.986.

4 Multilingual Book Collection

Our multilingual book collection consists of around 800k books in German and English languages. It is a subset of a larger Internet Archive[1] collection of books in over 200 languages. The whole collection consists of OCRed books incorporating a small number of human transcribed books from Project Gutenberg[2]. The collection was initially annotated with author and language information using the existing database obtained from the Internet Archive. This database originally contained incorrect language metadata. Using the freely available language identifier TextCat (Cavnar and Trenkle, 2005) we tagged the whole book collection and extracted 705692 English and 96752 German books. This process had the additional benefit of cleaning the German book collection of books written in the Fraktur script due to the bad OCR output. (Incredibly noisy OCR was simply recognized as "not German" by the character n-gram models.) Shown in Table 3 are word length statistics over the books in the collection.

Language	# of books	# of uniq. words	Min	Max	Median
German	96752	5030095	33	2372278	109820
English	705692	20001702	37	5155032	75016

Table 3. Bilingual book collection statistics.

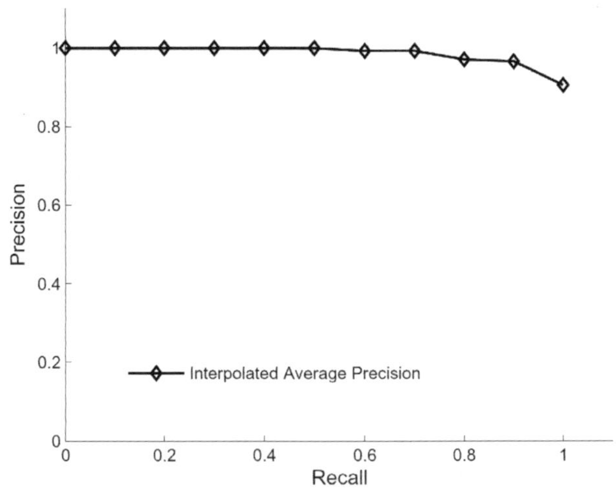

Figure 6. Average precision interpolated at 11 points over ten randomly created subsets consisting of 50% English and 10% German documents from the English-German Europarl collection.

4.1 Development Set

Moving onto our book collection, we start off by evaluating the method on a smaller randomly selected subset of 1000 books in both languages. Since it is not feasible to perform a full recall

[1] http://www.archive.org/details/texts/

[2] http://www.gutenberg.org

evaluation on the whole book set we include 17 known book translation pairs in the 1000 random bilingual book collection. The 17 book translation pairs were constructed by hand by running a prevision version of our full algorithm and indentifying translation pairs. Shown in Figure 7 is the precision vs. recall plot on the 17 book pairs. As in the case of the 10 randomly selected Europarl subsets, we also performed diversity and length based filtering of the initial results prior to computing precision vs. recall.

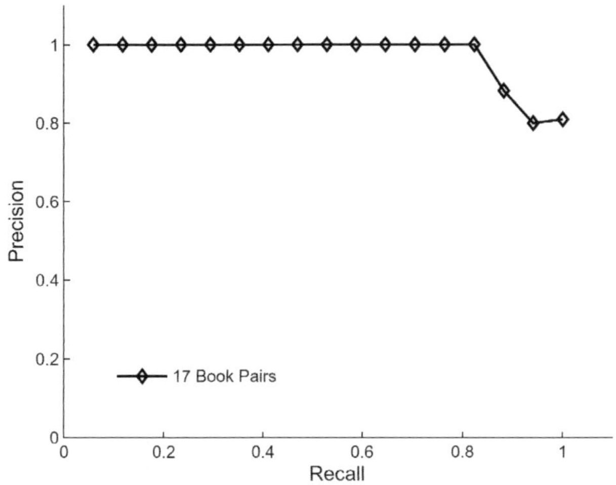

Figure 7. Precision vs. recall running our method on a 1000 randomly selected bilingual book subset with 17 book translation pairs inserted.

5 LSH Based Approximate Algorithm for Cosine Similarity

Due to the collection size and length of each book it is infeasible to perform cosine similarity over all possible book pairs, i.e. approximately 68.2B comparisons. This brute force approach has time complexity of $O(n^2k)$ where n is the number of books in the collection and k is the vector template length. We therefore employ a fast cosine similarity calculation approach developed by Charikar (2002) and utilized by Ravichandran et. al (2005) for creating similarity lists of nouns in large collection. In this section we give a summary of this approach and explain how it was applied for our task.

Locality Sensitive Hashing (LSH), initially introduced by Idyik and Motwani (1998), is used for finding approximate nearest neighbors in high dimensional spaces. In general, their approach hashes query vectors into bins where the probability of collision is higher due to the fact that vectors in the same bin share the same locality. Their approach reduces the approximate nearest neighbor problem on the Hamming space.

Charikar expanded this approach and showed that the probability of collision of hashed vectors for appropriately chosen hash function h is related to the angle between the vectors as:

$$\Pr[h(x) = h(y)] = 1 - \frac{\theta(x, y)}{\pi} \qquad (2)$$

This is closely related to the cosine function. From the above equation we thus have:

$$\cos(\theta(x, y)) = \cos\{(1 - \Pr[h(x) = h(y)])\pi\} \qquad (3)$$

Charikar uses a hash function based on random hyperplanes and creates a fingerprint for each original vector using the following approach:

Generate d, k-dimensional random vectors from a standard normal (Gaussian) distribution: $\{r_1, r_2, \ldots. r_d\}$. For each original vector x use the following hash function to generate a fingerprint of d bits:

$$h_r(x) = \begin{cases} 0 & if \sum x_i r_i < 0 \\ 1 & if \sum x_i r_i \geq 0 \end{cases} \qquad (4)$$

By doing this we represent each vector in our original vector set into a bit stream that reduces our vector space representation from k to d dimensions, where $d << k$. Having bit stream as our data representation, the probability of hash collision, i.e. the probability of two vectors being equal $\Pr[h(x) = h(y)]$, is equivalent to the Hamming distance between the two bit streams:

$$\Pr[h(x) = h(y)] = \frac{HD}{d} \qquad (5)$$

Therefore, performing fast cosine similarity boils down to finding the Hamming distance between the two bit streams.

Now that we have an approximate method of finding the cosine similarity between two vectors, we use Ravichandran's (2005) formulation of the fast search algorithm developed by Charikar, which in turn used Indyk and Motwani's orginal PLEB (Point Location in Equal Balls) algorithm as a starting point. The steps of this algorithm are outlined in the next subsection. For more detailed explanation of this algorithm the reader is referred to Section 5 of Charikar's work (2002).

5.1 Nearest Neighbor Search Algorithm

We now outline the steps of the fast search algorithm. For more detailed explanation of the algorithmic implementation users are referred to Section 3 of Ravichandran's work (2005):

- For all m documents represented in the vector space using the template vector, compute LSH d-bit signature using the formula given in (4).
- Generate q permutations of length d.
- For each of the q permutations, generate m permuted LSH signatures.
- For each of the q permutation bins, lexicographically sort the m permutated bit vectors.
- For each lexicographically sorted bin, go over the m bit streams and compute the Hamming distance between the current bit stream and the subsequent b bit streams in the sorted list starting from the top.
- If the Hamming distance is above a previously set threshold, output the book pair along with the Hamming distance result.

Compared to Ravichandran's algorithm for creating noun similarity lists, in our approach we deal with two distinct groups of documents: those in each language. We start off by creating a single list of documents and we represent each document in this list using the LSH based fingerprint. We then generate q permutation vector bins, and we lexicographically sort each bin. In our beam search approach, since we have documents in two different languages, we only consider documents that have a different language. The results of the beam search for each bin are then combined. Since in each beam the same permutation is performed over all fingerprints, the Hamming distance across all bins for a given document pair would be the same. Therefore after combining the results we remove duplicate document pairs and sort by the Hamming distance to obtain the final ranked list. The run-time of this algorithm is dominated by the $O(qn \log n)$ step of sorting the permuted bit vectors in each of the bins.

6 Detecting and Ranking Book Translation Pairs in a Large Book Collection

Using the previously explained method we processed the large book collection by first computing the vector template. For the large book collection, the vector template size k, i.e. the number of overlapping tokens obtained, was 638,005. After removing stop words and unwanted tokens (explained in Section 2) the template vector length was reduced to 563,053. Shown in Table 4 are statistics over the number of vector template tokens whose tf·idf values are greater than zero across the two languages.

Language	Min	Max	Median
German	7	7212	229
English	11	6637	585

Table 4. Statistics over the number of tokens in the vector representation of each book whose tf·idf are greater than zero.

Once processed and represented in vector space, we proceed with computing the approximate cosine similarity across the bilingual collection. We precompute the Hamming distance based on a cosine similarity threshold of 0.18 which is equivalent to different Hamming distance values depending on the length of the LSH based fingerprint. For the book collection we experimented with 4 different sets of values for the number of hyperplane based hash functions, the number of permutations and the length of the beam search. For each of these parameters in our setup we created ranked lists as explained in Section 5.1. We then went over the top 300 book pairs in each list and annotated the correct book translations. Based on the human annotation we then computed average precision over the ranked list. Shown in Table 5 are the results for LSH based fingerprint of size d=500. Due to the randomness introduced by the permutations, there is not a monotonic increase in accuracy, but in general more permutations and wider beams show substantial improvements.

q\b		AP	Time [hrs]
q=25	b=25	0.307	24.9
	b=50	0.213	41.1
	b=100	0.280	67.2
q=100	b=25	0.488	99.6
	b=50	0.388	164.4
	b=100	0.461	269.1
q=200	b=25	0.357	199.2
	b=50	0.412	328.8
	b=100	0.455	538.2
q=500	b=25	0.489	498.1
	b=50	0.490	822.0
	b=100	0.493	1345.5

Table 5. Average precision on the large English-German book collection across various parameters of the LSH based search algorithm.

For the above given results for d=500, we calculated an estimated time that it would take to perform the fast cosine similarity if the algorithm were to be run in serial fashion. Shown in Figure 8 is a scatter plot of the time vs. the average precision obtained.

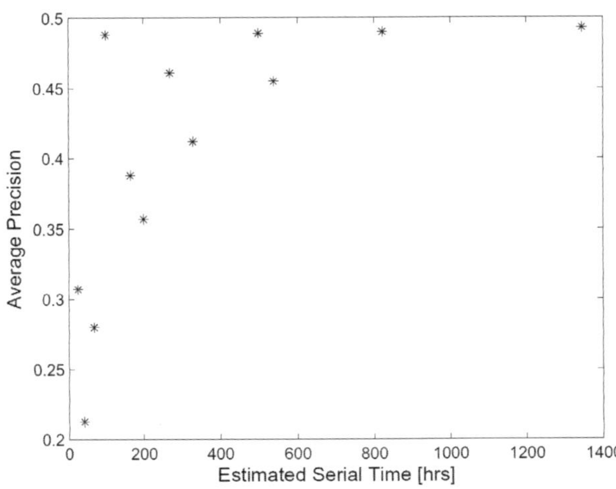

Figure 8. Estimated serial time vs. average precision with d=500 dimensional LSH based fingerprints.

In summary, while increasing the number of permutations and the beam search over different values increases the average precision the time cost required is significantly larger especially for increasing the number of permutations.

7 Future Work

In the future we plan on experimenting with larger dimensionality d for the LSH fingerprint, the number of random permutations q i.e. bins and the beam search parameter b. In order to further improve the average precision we would also like to experiment with different longest common subsequence (LCS) based approaches for re-ranking the cosine based ranked lists. Furthermore, we plan on exploring more accurate joint models of translation. It would also be interesting to observe the performance of our system on other language pairs, such as English-Chinese and languages with resource-poor bilingual collections.

8 Conclusion

This paper presents and evaluates a new approach to detecting and ranking document translation pairs. We showed that this simple method achieves high precision vs. recall on parallel bilingual collections where there is one document translation for each source document. We also showed that the method is capable of detecting document translations in random subsets where no known document translation information is available. Using an approximation algorithm for cosine similarity, we showed that this method is useful for detecting and ranking document translation pairs in a large bilingual collection with hundreds of thousands of books and billions of possible book pairs. This method is conceivable to be used for other languages and collection genres and also on other types of translation methods such as transliteration. While in some instances other simple methods of aligning the dictionaries might be needed, as in the case of the Chinese language.

Acknowledgments

This work was supported in part by the Center for Intelligent Information Retrieval and in part by NSF grant #IIS-0910884. Any opinions, findings and conclusions or recommendations expressed in this material are the authors' and do not necessarily reflect those of the sponsor.

References

Alexandre Patry and Philippe Langlais, 2011. Identifying Parallel Documents from a Large Bilingual Collection of Texts: Application to Parallel Article

Extraction in Wikipedia. Proceedings of the 4th Workshop on Building and Using Comparable Corpora, pages 87-95, Portland, OR.

Bing Zhao and Stephan Vogel. 2002. Adaptive Parallel Sentences Mining from Web Bilingual News Collection. Proceedings of IEEE International Conference on Data Mining, pages 745-750. Maebashi City, Japan.

Deepak Ravichandran, Patrick Pantel, and Eduard Hovy. 2005. Randomized Algorithms and NLP: Using Locality Sensitive Hash Function for High Speed Noun Clustering. Proceedings of the 43rd Annual Meeting on Association for Computational Linguistics, pages 622–629, Morristown, NJ.

Dragos Stefan Munteanu and Daniel Marcu. 2005. Improving Machine Translation Performance by Exploiting Non-Parallel Corpora. Computational Linguistics, 31(4): 477-504.

Jacob Uszkoreit, Jay Ponte, Ashok Popat and Moshe Dubiner, 2010. Large Scale Parallel Document Mining for Machine Translation. Proceedings of the 23rd International Conference on Computational Linguistics (Coling 2010), pp. 1101-1109. Beijing, China.

Jason R. Smith, Chris Quirk, and Kristina Toutanova, 2010. Extracting Parallel Sentences from Comparable Corpora using Document Level Alignment, Proceedings of Human Language Technologies: The 2010 Annual Conference of the North American Chapter of the ACL (HLT NAACL'10), Los Angeles, California.

Jessica Enright and Grzegorz Kondrak 2007. A Fast Method for Parallel Document Identification, Proceedings of Human Language Technologies: The Conference of the North American Chapter of the Association for Computational Linguistics (HLT-NAACL'07) companion volume, pages 29-32, Rochester, NY.

Matthew Snover, Bonnie Dorr, and Richard Schwartz. 2008. Language and Translation Model Adaptation using Comparable Corpora. Proceedings of Conference on Empirical Methods in Natural Language Processing (EMNLP'08), pages 856–865, Honolulu, HI.

Moses S. Charikar. 2002. Similarity estimation techniques from rounding algorithms. In Proceedings of the thiry-fourth annual ACM symposium on Theory of computing (STOC'02), pages 380–388, New York, NY.

Pascale Fung and Percy Cheung. 2004. Mining Very-Non-Parallel Corpora: Parallel Sentence and Lexicon Extraction via Bootstrapping and EM. In Proceedings of Conference on Empirical Methods in Natural Language Processing (EMNLP'04), Barcelona, Spain.

Philip Resnik and Noah Smith. 2003. The Web as a Parallel Corpus. Computational Linguistics, 29(3): 349-380.

Philipp Koehn, 2005. Europarl: A Parallel Corpus for Statistical Machine Translation. MT Summit 2005. Phuket, Thailand.

Piotr Indyk and Rajeev Motwani. 1998. Approximate nearest neighbors: towards removing the curse of dimensionality. In Proceedings of the thirtieth annual ACM symposium on Theory of computing (STOC '98), pages 604–613, New York, NY.

William B. Cavnar and John M. Trenkle. 1994. N-Gram-Based Text Categorization. Proceedings of the Third Annual Symposium on Document Analysis and Information Retrieval, pages 161-175, Las Vegas, NV.

Agreement Constraints for Statistical Machine Translation into German

Philip Williams and **Philipp Koehn**
School of Informatics
University of Edinburgh
10 Crichton Street
EH8 9AB, UK
p.j.williams-2@sms.ed.ac.uk
pkoehn@inf.ed.ac.uk

Abstract

Languages with rich inflectional morphology pose a difficult challenge for statistical machine translation. To address the problem of morphologically inconsistent output, we add unification-based constraints to the target-side of a string-to-tree model. By integrating constraint evaluation into the decoding process, implausible hypotheses can be penalised or filtered out during search. We use a simple heuristic process to extract agreement constraints for German and test our approach on an English-German system trained on WMT data, achieving a small improvement in translation accuracy as measured by BLEU.

1 Introduction

Historically, most work in statistical machine translation (SMT) has focused on translation into English. Languages with richer inflectional morphologies pose additional challenges for translation and conventional SMT approaches tend to perform poorly when either source or target language has rich morphology (Koehn, 2005).

For complex source inflection, a successful approach has been to cluster inflectional variants into equivalence classes. This removes information that is redundant for translation and can be performed as a preprocessing step for input to a conventional surface form based translation model (Nießen and Ney, 2001; Goldwater and McClosky, 2005; Talbot and Osborne, 2006).

For complex target inflection, Minkov et al. (2007) investigate how post-processing can be used to generate inflection for a system that produces uninflected output. Their approach is successfully applied to English-Arabic and English-Russian systems by Toutanova et al. (2008).

Another promising line of research involves the direct integration of linguistic information into SMT models. Koehn and Hoang (2007) generalise the phrase-based model's representation of the word from a string to a vector, allowing additional features such as part-of-speech and morphology to be associated with, or even to replace, surface forms during search. Luong et al. (2010) decompose words into morphemes and use this extended representation throughout the training, tuning, and testing pipeline.

Departing further from traditional SMT models, the transfer-based systems of Riezler and Maxwell (2006), Bojar and Hajič (2008), and Graham et al. (2009) employ rich feature structure representations for linguistic attributes, but have so far been limited by their dependence on non-stochastic parsers with limited coverage. The Stat-XFER transfer-based framework (Lavie, 2008) is neutral with regard to the rule acquisition method and the author describes a manually developed Hebrew-English transfer grammar, which includes a small number of constraints between agreement features. In Hanneman et al. (2009) the framework is used with a large automatically-extracted grammar, though this does not use feature constraints.

In this paper we propose a model that retains the use of surface forms during decoding whilst also checking linguistic constraints defined over associated feature structures. Specifically, we extend a string-to-tree model by adding unification-based

Proceedings of the 6th Workshop on Statistical Machine Translation, pages 217–226,
Edinburgh, Scotland, UK, July 30–31, 2011.

constraints to the target-side of the synchronous grammar. We suggest that such a constraint system can:

- improve the model by enforcing inflectional consistency in combinations unseen by the language model
- improve search by allowing the early elimination of morphologically-inconsistent hypotheses

To evaluate the approach, we develop a system for English-German with constraints to enforce intra-NP/PP and subject-verb agreement, and with a simple probabilistic model for NP case.

2 Preliminaries

There is an extensive literature on constraint-based approaches to grammar, employing a rich variety of terminology and linguistic devices. We use only a few of the core ideas, which we briefly describe in this section. We borrow the terminology and notation of PATR-II (Shieber, 1984), a minimal constraint-based formalism that extends context-free grammar.

Central to our model are the concepts of *feature structures* and *unification*. Feature structures are of two kinds:

- *atomic* feature structures are untyped, indivisible values, such as `NP`, `nom`, or `sg`
- *complex* feature structures are partial functions mapping features to values, the values themselves being feature structures.

Complex feature structures are conventionally written as attribute-value matrices. For example, the following might represent lexical entries for the German definite article, *die*, and the German noun, *Katze*, meaning *cat*:

$$\textit{die} \longrightarrow \begin{bmatrix} \text{POS} & \texttt{ART} \\ \text{AGR} & \begin{bmatrix} \text{CASE} & \texttt{acc} \\ \text{DECL} & \texttt{weak} \\ \text{GENDER} & \texttt{fem} \\ \text{NUMBER} & \texttt{sg} \end{bmatrix} \end{bmatrix}$$

$$\textit{Katze} \longrightarrow \begin{bmatrix} \text{POS} & \texttt{NN} \\ \text{AGR} & \begin{bmatrix} \text{CASE} & \texttt{acc} \\ \text{GENDER} & \texttt{fem} \\ \text{NUMBER} & \texttt{sg} \end{bmatrix} \end{bmatrix}$$

An equivalent representation, and the one we use for implementation, is that of a rooted, labelled, directed acyclic graph.

A value belonging to a complex feature structure can be specified using a path notation that describes the chain of features in enclosing feature structures. In the examples above, the path $\langle$ AGR GENDER $\rangle$ specifies the atomic value `fem`.

Informally, *unification* is a merging operation that given two feature structures, yields the minimal feature structure containing all information from both inputs. A unification failure results if the input feature structures have mutually-conflicting values. The subject of unification, both in the context of natural language processing and more generally, is surveyed in Knight (1989). In this work, we use destructive graph-based unification, which results in the source feature structures sharing values upon unification.

For example, the result of unifying the agreement values for the feature structures above would be:

$$\textit{die} \longrightarrow \begin{bmatrix} \text{POS} & \texttt{ART} \\ \text{AGR} & \boxed{1} \begin{bmatrix} \text{CASE} & \texttt{acc} \\ \text{DECL} & \texttt{weak} \\ \text{GENDER} & \texttt{fem} \\ \text{NUMBER} & \texttt{sg} \end{bmatrix} \end{bmatrix}$$

$$\textit{Katze} \longrightarrow \begin{bmatrix} \text{POS} & \texttt{NN} \\ \text{AGR} & \boxed{1} \end{bmatrix}$$

The index boxes are used to indicate that a value is shared.

3 Grammar

In this section we describe the synchronous grammar used in our string-to-tree model. Rule extraction is similar to the syntax-augmented model of Zollmann and Venugopal (2006), though we do not use extended categories in this work. We then describe how we extend the grammar with target-side constraints.

3.1 Synchronous Grammar

Our translation model is based on a synchronous context-free grammar (SCFG) learned from a parallel corpus. Rule extraction follows the hierarchical phrase-based algorithm of Chiang (2005; 2007). Source non-terminals are given the undistinguished label X, whereas the target non-terminals are given part-of-speech and constituent labels obtained from a parse of the target-side of the parallel corpus. Rules in which the target span is not covered by a parse tree constituent are discarded.

Compared with the hierarchical phrase-based model, the restriction to constituent target phrases reduces the total grammar size and the addition of linguistic labels reduces the problem of spurious ambiguity. We therefore relax Chiang's (2007) rule filtering in the following ways:

1. Up to seven source-side terminal / non-terminal elements are allowed.

2. Rules with scope greater than three are filtered out (Hopkins and Langmead, 2010).

3. Consecutive source non-terminals are permitted.

4. Single-word lexical phrases are allowed for hierarchical subphrase subtraction.

3.2 Constraint Grammar

We extend the synchronous grammar by adding constraints to the target-side. A constraint is an identity between either:

i) feature structure values belonging to two rule elements,

ii) a feature structure value belonging to a rule element and a constant value, or

iii) a feature structure value belonging to a rule element and a random variable with an associated probability function

For example, the following synchronous rule:

$$\text{NP-SB} \rightarrow \textit{the}\ \text{X}_1\ \textit{cat} \mid \textit{die}\ \text{AP}_1\ \textit{Katze}$$

might have the target constraint rule shown in Figure 1.

$$\begin{aligned}
&\text{NP-SB} \rightarrow \textit{die}\ \text{AP}\ \textit{Katze}\\
&\quad\langle\ \text{NP-SB}\ \text{AGR}\rangle = \langle\ \textit{die}\ \text{AGR}\rangle\\
&\quad\langle\ \text{NP-SB}\ \text{AGR}\rangle = \langle\ \text{AP}\ \text{AGR}\rangle\\
&\quad\langle\ \text{NP-SB}\ \text{AGR}\rangle = \langle\ \textit{Katze}\ \text{AGR}\rangle\\
&\quad\langle\ \text{NP-SB}\ \text{AGR CASE}\rangle = C\\
&\quad\langle\ \textit{die}\ \text{POS}\rangle = \text{ART}\\
&\quad\langle\ \textit{Katze}\ \text{POS}\rangle = \text{NN}
\end{aligned}$$

$$P(C=c) = \begin{cases} 0.990, c = \text{NOM} \\ 0.005, c = \text{DAT} \\ 0.004, c = \text{GEN} \\ 0.001, c = \text{ACC} \end{cases}$$

Figure 1: Example target constraint rule

The first three constraints ensure that any AP has agreement values consistent with the lexical items *die* and *Katze*. The next provides a probability based on the resulting case value. The final two are used to disambiguate between possible parts-of-speech.

Constraints are evaluated by attempting to unify the specified feature structures. A rule element may have more than one associated feature structure, so unification is attempted between all combinations. If no combination can be successfully unified then the constraint fails.

Ultimately, all feature structures originate in the *lexicon*, which maps a surface form word to a set of zero or more complex feature structures.

3.3 Some Constraints for German

We now describe the German constraints that we use in this paper. Whilst the constraint model described above is language-independent, the actual form of the constraints will largely be language- and corpus-specific.

In this work, the linguistic annotation is obtained from a statistical parser and a morphological analyser. We use the BitPar parser (Schmid, 2004) trained on the TIGER treebank (Brants et al., 2002) and the Morphisto morphological analyser (Zielinski and Simon, 2009). We find that we can extract useful constraints for German based on a minimal set of simple manually-developed heuristics.

Base NP/PP Agreement

German determiners and adjectives are inflected to agree in gender and number with the nouns that they modify. As in English, a distinction is made between singular and plural number, with most nouns having separate forms for each. Grammatical gender has three values: masculine, feminine, and neuter.

A noun phrase's case is usually determined by its

$$\begin{array}{rcl}
\left\{\begin{array}{l}\texttt{ADJA, ART, NN, PDAT,} \\ \texttt{PIAT, PPOSAT, PWAT}\end{array}\right\} & \rightarrow & \{\texttt{NP, PP}\} \\
\{\texttt{APPR, APPRART}\} & \rightarrow & \{\texttt{PP}\} \\
\{\texttt{ADJA}\} & \rightarrow & \{\texttt{AP, CAP}\} \\
\{\texttt{AP}\} & \rightarrow & \{\texttt{CAP}\} \\
\{\texttt{AP, CAP}\} & \rightarrow & \{\texttt{NP, PP}\}
\end{array}$$

Figure 2: Propagation rules used to capture NP/PP agreement relations

role in the clause. For example, nominative case usually indicates the subject of a verb. The case of a prepositional phrase is usually determined by the choice of preposition.

We model these grammatical properties by i) associating, via the lexicon, a set of possible agreement values with each preposition, determiner, adjective, and noun, and ii) enforcing *agreement relations* through pairwise identities between rule elements (as in the example in Figure 1).

For constraint extraction, we first group parse tree nodes into agreement relations. We use the parse tree labels to determine whether a parent shares agreement information with a child. Figure 2 shows the rules that we used in experiments. These should be read as saying that if a child node has a label that appears on the left-hand side of a rule, r, and its parent node has a label that appears on the right-hand side of r then the parent and child share agreement information.

These rules are applied bottom-up from the preterminal nodes of the training data trees. Agreement relations are merged if they share a common parent. Finally, relations are extended to include child words. Figure 3 shows a sentence pair in which the target-side tree has been annotated to show two NP agreement relations found according to the rules of Figure 2.

Of course, this process is not perfect and finds many spurious relations. We guard against the most frequent errors by:

i) Filtering out relations based on label-patterns found during error analysis (for example, relations containing multiple NN nodes)

ii) Attempting to unify the agreement feature structures of the words and rejecting relations for which this fails

Having annotated the training data trees with agreement relations, rule extraction is extended to accept annotated trees and to generate constraint rules of the form shown in Figure 1. Constraints are produced where any two target-side rule elements belong to a common agreement relation. The resulting constraints are grouped by relation into distinct *constraint sets.*

Subject-Verb Agreement

We add limited subject-verb agreement in a similar manner. The additional propagation rules are given in Figure 4. To determine the subject we rely upon the TIGER treebank's grammatical function labels, which the parser affixes to constituent labels. These are otherwise ignored in all propagation rules.

Probabilistic Constraints for NP Case

We make further use of the treebank's grammatical function labels in order to define probabilistic constraints for noun phrase case. Many of the function labels are strongly biased towards a particular case (NP-TOP uses nominative case in 91.5% of unambiguous occurrences, for example). We estimate probabilities by evaluating NP agreement relations in the training data and counting case-label co-occurrences. Ambiguous case values are ignored. The training data uses only 23 distinct NP labels, most of which occur very frequently, so no smoothing is applied. Table 1 shows the 10 most common labels and their case frequencies.

4 Model

As is standard, we frame the decoding problem as a search for the most probable target language tree $\hat{\mathbf{t}}$ given a source language string s:

$$\hat{\mathbf{t}} = \arg\max_{\mathbf{t}} p(\mathbf{t}|\mathbf{s})$$

The function $p(\mathbf{t}|\mathbf{s})$ is modelled by a log-linear sum of weighted feature functions:

$$p(\mathbf{t}|\mathbf{s}) = \frac{1}{Z}\sum_{i=1}^{n} \lambda_i h_i(s,t)$$

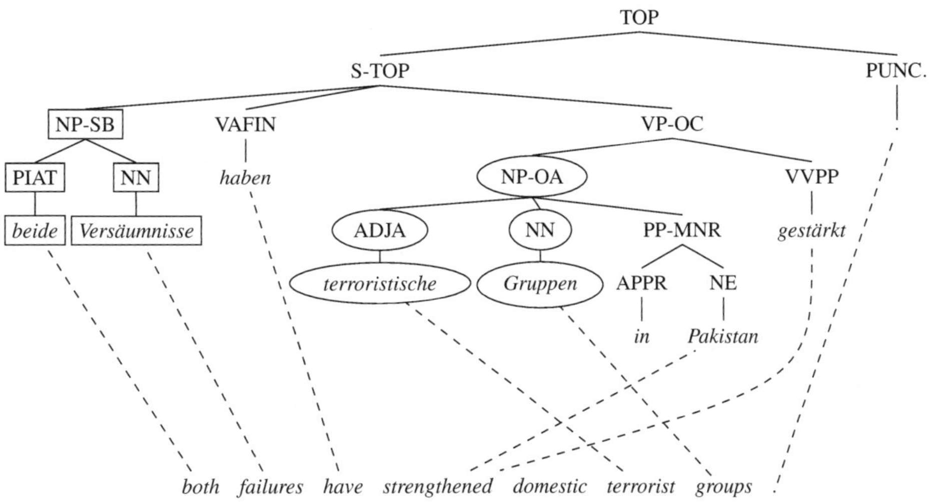

Figure 3: Sentence pair from training data. The two NP agreement relations used for constraint extraction are indicated by the rectangular and elliptical node borders.

$$\{\texttt{VAFIN}, \texttt{VMFIN}, \texttt{VVFIN}\} \rightarrow \{\texttt{S}\}$$
$$\{\texttt{NP-SB}\} \rightarrow \{\texttt{S}\}$$

Figure 4: Propagation rules used to capture subject-verb agreement relations

Label	Nom	Acc	Gen	Dat	Freq
AG	0.1	0.0	99.9	0.0	308156
CJ	10.9	10.3	32.4	46.4	77198
OA	1.6	91.5	0.7	6.2	67686
SB	99.0	0.1	0.4	0.5	60245
DA	1.9	0.2	1.4	96.5	41624
PD	98.2	0.2	1.4	0.3	19736
APP	39.4	7.3	8.7	44.6	7739
MO	18.6	17.3	56.9	7.2	7591
PNC	30.6	0.0	47.4	22.0	4888
OG	0.1	0.0	97.9	2.0	2060

Table 1: The 10 most freqently occurring NP labels with their case frequencies (shown as percentages)

4.1 String-to-Tree Features

Our feature functions include the n-gram language model probability of $\mathbf{t}$'s yield, a count of the words in $\mathbf{t}$'s yield, and various scores for the synchronous derivation. We score grammar rules according to the following functions:

- $p(\text{RHS}_s|\text{RHS}_t, \text{LHS})$, the noisy-channel translation probability.
- $p(\text{RHS}_t|\text{RHS}_s, \text{LHS})$, the direct translation probability, which we further condition on the root label of the target tree fragment.
- $p_{lex}(\text{RHS}_t|\text{RHS}_s)$ and $p_{lex}(\text{RHS}_s|\text{RHS}_t)$, the direct and indirect lexical weights (Koehn et al., 2003).
- $p_{pcfg}(\text{FRAG}_t)$, the monolingual PCFG probability of the tree fragment from which the rule was extracted. This is defined as $\prod_{i=1}^{n} p(r_i)$, where $r_1 \ldots r_n$ are the constituent CFG rules of the fragment. The PCFG parameters are estimated from the parse of the target-side training data. All lexical rules are given the probability 1. This is similar to the p_{cfg} feature used in Marcu et al. (2006) and is intended to encourage the production of syntactically well-formed derivations.
- $exp(1)$, a rule penalty.

4.2 Constraint Model Features

In addition to the string-to-tree features, we add two features related to constraint evaluation:

- $exp(f)$, where f is the derivation's constraint set failure count. This serves as a penalty feature in a soft constraint variant of the model: for each constraint set in which a unification failure occurs, this count is increased and an empty feature structure is produced, permitting decoding to continue.

- $\prod_n p_{case}(c_n)$, the product of the derivation's case model probabilities. Where the case value is ambiguous we take the highest possible probability.

5 Decoding

We use the Moses (Koehn et al., 2007) decoder, a bottom-up synchronous parser that implements the CYK+ algorithm (Chappelier and Rajman, 1998) with cube pruning (Chiang, 2007).

The constraint model requires some changes to decoding, which we briefly describe here:

5.1 Hypothesis State

Bottom-up constraint evaluation requires a feature structure set for every rule element that participates in a constraint. For lexical rule elements these are obtained from the lexicon. For non-lexical rule elements these are obtained from predecessor hypotheses. After constraint evaluation, each hypothesis therefore stores the resulting, possibly empty, set of feature structures corresponding to its root rule element.

Hypothesis recombination must take these feature structure states into account. We take the simplest approach of requiring sets to be equal for recombination.

5.2 Cube Pruning

At each chart cell, the decoder determines which rules can be applied to the span and which combinations of subspans they can cover (the application contexts). An n-dimensional cube is created for each application context of a rule, where $n-1$ is the rank of the rule. Each cube has one dimension per subspan and one for target-side translation options. Cube pruning begins with these cubes being placed into a priority queue ordered according to the model score of their corner hypotheses.

With the introduction of the constraint model, the cube pruning algorithm must also allow for constraint failure. For the hard constraint model, we make the following modifications:

1. Since the corner hypothesis might fail the constraint check, rule cube ordering is based on the score of the nearest hypothesis to the corner that satisifies its constraints (if any exists). This hypothesis is found by exploring neighbours in order of estimated score (that is, without calculating the full language model score) starting at the corner.

2. When a hypothesis is popped from a cube and its neighbours created, constraint-failing neighbours are added to a 'bad neighbours' queue.

3. If a cube cannot produce a new hypothesis because all of the neighbours fail constraints, it starts exploring neighbours of the bad neighbours.

We place an arbitrary limit of 10 on the number of consecutive constraint-failing hypotheses to consider before discarding the cube.

We anticipate that decoding for a highly inflected target language will result in a less monotonic search space due to the increased formation of inflectionally-inconsistent combinations.

6 Experiments

6.1 Baseline Setup

We trained a baseline system using the English-German Europarl and News Commentary data from the ACL 2010 Joint Fifth Workshop on Statistical Machine Translation and Metrics MATR[1].

The German-side of the parallel corpus was parsed using the BitPar[2] parser. Where a parse failed the pair was discarded, leaving a total of 1,516,961 sentence pairs. These were aligned using GIZA++

[1] http://www.statmt.org/wmt10/translation-task.html

[2] http://www.ims.uni-stuttgart.de/tcl/SOFTWARE/BitPar.html

and SCFG rules were extracted as described in section 3.1 using the Moses toolkit. The resulting grammar contained just under 140 million synchronous rules.

We used all of the available monolingual German data to train three 5-gram language models (one each for the Europarl, News Commentary, and News data sets). These were interpolated using weights optimised against the development set and the resulting language model was used in experiments. We used the SRILM toolkit (Stolcke, 2002) with Kneser-Ney smoothing (Chen and Goodman, 1998).

The baseline system's feature weights were tuned on the *news-test2008* dev set (2,051 sentence pairs) using minimum error rate training (Och, 2003).

6.2 Constraint Model Setup

A feature structure lexicon was generated by running the Morphisto[3] morphological analyser over the training vocabulary and then extracting feature values from the output.

The constraint rules were extracted using the agreement relation identification and filtering methods described in section 3.3.

We tested two constraint model systems, one using the rules as hard constraints and the other as soft constraints. The former discarded all hypotheses that failed constraints and used the modified cube pruning search algorithm. The latter allowed constraint failure but used the failure count feature as a penalty. Both systems used the NP case probability feature. The weights for these two features were optimised using MERT (with all baseline weights fixed). The systems were otherwise identical to the baseline.

6.3 Evaluation

The systems were evaluated against constrained versions of the *newstest2009*, *newstest2010*, and *newstest2011* test sets. We used a maximum rule span of 20 tokens for decoding. In order that the input could be covered without the use of glue rules (except for unknown words), we used sentences of 20 or fewer tokens, giving test sets of 1,025, 1,054, and 1,317 sentences, respectively. We evaluated translation quality using case-sensitive BLEU-4 (Papineni et al., 2002) with a single reference.

[3]http://code.google.com/p/morphisto/

(NP-AG der (ADJA regelmäßigen) (ADJA täglichen) (NN Handel))

(PP-MO nach Angaben der (ADJA örtlichen) (NN Index))

(NP-CJ die (ADJA amerikanischen) (NN Blutbad))

(PP-MNR für die (ADJA asiatischen) (NN Handel))

(TOP (NP-SB der (NN Vorsprung) des (NN razor))
    (VVFIN kämpfen)
    (CNP-OA : (NN MP3-Player) (KON und) (NN Mobiltelefone))
    .)

Figure 5: Tree fragments containing the first five constraint failures found on the baseline 1-best output

Table 2 shows the results for the three constrained test tests. The p-values were calculated using paired bootstrap resampling (Koehn, 2004). We suspect that the substantially lower baseline scores on the *newstest2011* test set are largely due to recency effects (since we use 2010 data for training).

To gauge the frequency of agreement violations in the baseline output we matched constraint rules to the 1-best baseline derivations and performed a bottom-up evaluation for each target-side tree. For the three constrained test sets, *newstest2009*, *newstest2010*, and *newstest2011*, we found that 15.5%, 14.4%, and 15.6% of sentences, respectively, contained one or more constraint failures. Figure 5 shows the tree fragments for the first five failures found in *newstest2009*.

In order to explore the interaction of the constraint model with search we then repeated the experiments for varying cube pruning pop limits. Figure 6 shows how the mean test set BLEU score varies against pop limit. Except at very low pop limits, the soft constraint system outperforms the hard constraint system. Together with the high p-values for the hard constraint system, this suggests that, despite filtering, our simple constraint extraction heuristics may be introducing significant numbers of spurious constraints. Alternatively, enforcing the hard constraint may eliminate too many hypotheses that cannot be satisifactorily substituted — constraint-satisfying alternatives frequently differ in more than just inflection. Either way, the soft constraint model is able to overcome some of these deficiencies by permitting some constraint failures in the 1-best output.

Experiment	newstest2009-20 BLEU	p-value	newstest2010-20 BLEU	p-value	newstest2011-20 BLEU	p-value
baseline	15.34	-	15.65	-	12.90	-
hard constraint	15.49	0.164	15.95	0.065	12.87	0.318
soft constraint	15.67	0.006	15.98	0.009	13.11	0.053

Table 2: BLEU scores and p-values for the three test sets

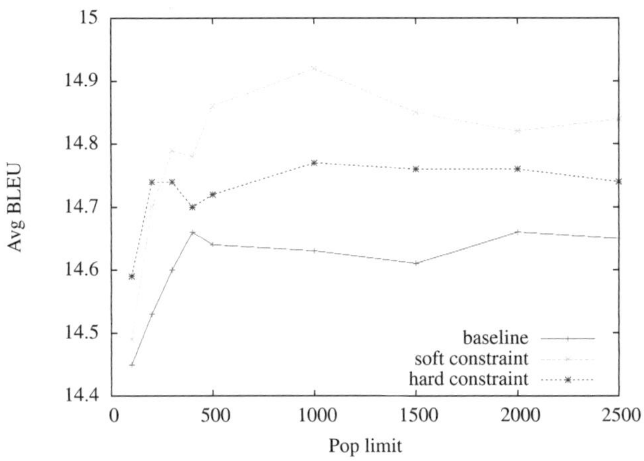

Figure 6: Cube pruning pop limit vs average BLEU score

7 Conclusion

In this paper we have presented an SMT model that allows the addition of linguistic constraints to the target-side of a conventional string-to-tree model. We have developed a simple heuristic method to extract constraints for German and demonstrated the approach on a constrained translation task, achieving a small improvement in translation accuracy.

In future work we intend to investigate the development of constraint models for target languages with more complex inflection. Besides the requirement for suitable language processing tools, this requires the development of reliable language-specific constraint extraction techniques.

We also plan to investigate how the model could be extended to generate inflection during decoding: a complementary constraint system could curb the overgeneration of surface form combinations that has limited previous approaches.

Acknowledgements

We would like to thank the anonymous reviewers for their helpful feedback and suggestions. This work was supported by the EuroMatrixPlus project funded by the European Commission (7th Framework Programme) and made use of the resources provided by the Edinburgh Compute and Data Facility.[4] The ECDF is partially supported by the eDIKT initiative.[5] This work was also supported in part under the GALE program of the Defense Advanced Research Projects Agency, Contract No. HR0011-06-C-0022. The first author was supported by an EPSRC Studentship.

References

Ondřej Bojar and Jan Hajič. 2008. Phrase-based and deep syntactic english-to-czech statistical machine translation. In *StatMT '08: Proceedings of the Third Workshop on Statistical Machine Translation*, pages 143–146, Morristown, NJ, USA. Association for Computational Linguistics.

Sabine Brants, Stefanie Dipper, Silvia Hansen, Wolfgang Lezius, and George Smith. 2002. The TIGER treebank. In *Proceedings of the workshop on treebanks and linguistic theories*, pages 24–41.

J.-C. Chappelier and M. Rajman. 1998. A generalized cyk algorithm for parsing stochastic cfg. In *Proceedings of the First Workshop on Tabulation in Parsing and Deduction*, pages 133–137.

Stanley F. Chen and Joshua Goodman. 1998. An empirical study of smoothing techniques for language modeling. Technical report, Harvard University.

David Chiang. 2005. A hierarchical phrase-based model for statistical machine translation. In *ACL '05: Proceedings of the 43rd Annual Meeting on Association for Computational Linguistics*, pages 263–270, Morristown, NJ, USA. Association for Computational Linguistics.

[4] http://www.ecdf.ed.ac.uk

[5] http://www.edikt.org.uk

David Chiang. 2007. Hierarchical phrase-based translation. *Comput. Linguist.*, 33(2):201–228.

Sharon Goldwater and David McClosky. 2005. Improving statistical mt through morphological analysis. In *HLT '05: Proceedings of the conference on Human Language Technology and Empirical Methods in Natural Language Processing*, pages 676–683, Morristown, NJ, USA. Association for Computational Linguistics.

Yvette Graham, Anton Bryl, and Josef van Genabith. 2009. F-structure transfer-based statistical machine translation. In *In Proceedings of Lexical Functional Grammar Conference 2009*.

Greg Hanneman, Vamshi Ambati, Jonathan H. Clark, Alok Parlikar, and Alon Lavie. 2009. An improved statistical transfer system for french–english machine translation. In *Proceedings of the Fourth Workshop on Statistical Machine Translation*, StatMT '09, pages 140–144, Stroudsburg, PA, USA. Association for Computational Linguistics.

Mark Hopkins and Greg Langmead. 2010. SCFG decoding without binarization. In *Proceedings of the 2010 Conference on Empirical Methods in Natural Language Processing*, pages 646–655, Cambridge, MA, October. Association for Computational Linguistics.

Kevin Knight. 1989. Unification: a multidisciplinary survey. *ACM Comput. Surv.*, 21(1):93–124.

Philipp Koehn and Hieu Hoang. 2007. Factored translation models. In *In Proceedings of EMNLP, 2007.*

Philipp Koehn, Franz Josef Och, and Daniel Marcu. 2003. Statistical phrase-based translation. In *NAACL '03: Proceedings of the 2003 Conference of the North American Chapter of the Association for Computational Linguistics on Human Language Technology*, pages 48–54, Morristown, NJ, USA. Association for Computational Linguistics.

Philipp Koehn, Hieu Hoang, Alexandra Birch, Chris Callison-Burch, Marcello Federico, Nicola Bertoldi, Brooke Cowan, Wade Shen, Christine Moran, Richard Zens, Chris Dyer, Ondřej Bojar, Alexandra Constantin, and Evan Herbst. 2007. Moses: open source toolkit for statistical machine translation. In *Proceedings of the 45th Annual Meeting of the ACL on Interactive Poster and Demonstration Sessions*, ACL '07, pages 177–180, Morristown, NJ, USA. Association for Computational Linguistics.

Philipp Koehn. 2004. Statistical significance tests for machine translation evaluation. In Dekang Lin and Dekai Wu, editors, *Proceedings of EMNLP 2004*, pages 388–395, Barcelona, Spain, July. Association for Computational Linguistics.

Philipp Koehn. 2005. Europarl: A parallel corpus for statistical machine translation. In *MT Summit 2005.*

Alon Lavie. 2008. Stat-xfer: a general search-based syntax-driven framework for machine translation. In *Proceedings of the 9th international conference on Computational linguistics and intelligent text processing*, CICLing'08, pages 362–375, Berlin, Heidelberg. Springer-Verlag.

Minh-Thang Luong, Preslav Nakov, and Min-Yen Kan. 2010. A hybrid morpheme-word representation for machine translation of morphologically rich languages. In *Proceedings of the 2010 Conference on Empirical Methods in Natural Language Processing*, pages 148–157, Cambridge, MA, October. Association for Computational Linguistics.

Daniel Marcu, Wei Wang, Abdessamad Echihabi, and Kevin Knight. 2006. Spmt: statistical machine translation with syntactified target language phrases. In *EMNLP '06: Proceedings of the 2006 Conference on Empirical Methods in Natural Language Processing*, pages 44–52, Morristown, NJ, USA. Association for Computational Linguistics.

Einat Minkov, Kristina Toutanova, and Suzuki Hisami. 2007. Generating complex morphology for machine translation. In *Proceedings of the ACL.*

Sonja Nießen and Hermann Ney. 2001. Toward hierarchical models for statistical machine translation of inflected languages. In *Proceedings of the workshop on Data-driven methods in machine translation*, pages 1–8, Morristown, NJ, USA. Association for Computational Linguistics.

Franz Josef Och. 2003. Minimum error rate training in statistical machine translation. In *Proceedings of the 41st Annual Meeting on Association for Computational Linguistics - Volume 1*, ACL '03, pages 160–167, Morristown, NJ, USA. Association for Computational Linguistics.

Kishore Papineni, Salim Roukos, Todd Ward, and Wei-Jing Zhu. 2002. Bleu: a method for automatic evaluation of machine translation. In *Proceedings of the 40th Annual Meeting on Association for Computational Linguistics*, ACL '02, pages 311–318, Stroudsburg, PA, USA. Association for Computational Linguistics.

Stefan Riezler and John T. Maxwell, III. 2006. Grammatical machine translation. In *Proceedings of the main conference on Human Language Technology Conference of the North American Chapter of the Association of Computational Linguistics*, pages 248–255, Morristown, NJ, USA. Association for Computational Linguistics.

Helmut Schmid. 2004. Efficient parsing of highly ambiguous context-free grammars with bit vectors. In *Proceedings of the 20th international conference on Computational Linguistics*, COLING '04, Stroudsburg, PA, USA. Association for Computational Linguistics.

Stuart M. Shieber. 1984. The design of a computer language for linguistic information. In *Proceedings of the 10th international conference on Computational linguistics*, COLING '84, pages 362–366, Stroudsburg, PA, USA. Association for Computational Linguistics.

Andreas Stolcke. 2002. Srilm - an extensible language modeling toolkit. In *Intl. Conf. Spoken Language Processing, Denver, Colorado, September 2002.*

David Talbot and Miles Osborne. 2006. Modelling lexical redundancy for machine translation. In *ACL-44: Proceedings of the 21st International Conference on Computational Linguistics and the 44th annual meeting of the Association for Computational Linguistics*, pages 969–976, Morristown, NJ, USA. Association for Computational Linguistics.

Kristina Toutanova, Hisami Suzuki, and Achim Ruopp. 2008. Applying morphology generation models to machine translation. In *Proceedings of ACL, Association for Computational Linguistics, June 2008.*

Andrea Zielinski and Christian Simon. 2009. Morphisto –an open source morphological analyzer for german. In *Proceeding of the 2009 conference on Finite-State Methods and Natural Language Processing: Post-proceedings of the 7th International Workshop FSMNLP 2008*, pages 224–231, Amsterdam, The Netherlands, The Netherlands. IOS Press.

Andreas Zollmann and Ashish Venugopal. 2006. Syntax augmented machine translation via chart parsing. In *StatMT '06: Proceedings of the Workshop on Statistical Machine Translation*, pages 138–141, Morristown, NJ, USA. Association for Computational Linguistics.

Fuzzy Syntactic Reordering for Phrase-based Statistical Machine Translation

Jacob Andreas and **Nizar Habash** and **Owen Rambow**
Center for Computational Learning Systems
Columbia University
jda2129@columbia.edu
{habash, rambow}@ccls.columbia.edu

Abstract

The quality of Arabic-English statistical machine translation often suffers as a result of standard phrase-based SMT systems' inability to perform long-range re-orderings, specifically those needed to translate VSO-ordered Arabic sentences. This problem is further exacerbated by the low performance of Arabic parsers on subject and subject span detection. In this paper, we present two parse "fuzzification" techniques which allow the translation system to select among a range of possible S–V re-orderings. With this approach, we demonstrate a 0.3-point improvement in BLEU score (69% of the maximum possible using gold parses), and a corresponding improvement in the percentage of syntactically well-formed subjects under a manual evaluation.

1 Introduction

The question of how to effectively use phrase-based statistical machine translation (PSMT) to translate between language pairs which require long-range reordering has attracted a great deal of interest in recent years. The inability to capture long-range reordering behaviors is a weakness inherent in PSMT systems, which typically have only two mechanisms to control the reordering between source and target language: (1) distortion penalties, which penalize or forbid long-distance re-orderings in order to reduce the search space explored by the decoder, and (2) lexicalized reordering models, which capture the preferences of individual phrases to orient themselves monotonically, reversed with their preceding phrases or discontinuously. Because both of these mechanisms work at the phrase level, they have proven very effective at capturing short-range reordering behaviors, but unable to describe long range movements; in fact, the distortion penalty effectively causes the translation system to not prefer long-range re-orderings, even when they are assigned significantly higher probability by the language model.

The problem is particularly acute in translating from Arabic to English: Arabic sentences frequently exhibit a VSO ordering (both VSO and SVO are permitted in Arabic), while English permits only an SVO order. Past research has shown that verb anticipation and subject-span detection is a major source of error when translating from Arabic to English (Green et al., 2009; Bisazza and Federico, 2010). Unable to perform long-range reordering, PSMT frequently produces English sentences in which verbs precede their subjects (sometimes with "hallucinated" pronouns in front of them) or do not appear at all. Intuitively, better handling of these reorderings has the potential to improve both accuracy and fluency of translation.

In this paper, we present two parse fuzzification techniques which allow the translation system to select among a range of possible S–V re-orderings. With this approach, we demonstrate a 0.3-point improvement in BLEU score (69% of the maximum possible using gold parses), and a corresponding improvement in the percentage of syntactically well-formed subjects under a manual evaluation.

The rest of the paper is structured as follows. Section 2 gives a review of research on this topic. Section 3 motivates the approach discussed in Section 4.

Proceedings of the 6th Workshop on Statistical Machine Translation, pages 227–236,
Edinburgh, Scotland, UK, July 30–31, 2011.

Section 5 presents the results of a set of machine translation experiments using the automatic metrics BLEU (Papineni et al., 2002) and METEOR (Banerjee and Lavie, 2005), and a manual-evaluation of subject integrity. Section 6 discusses our conclusions and future plans.

2 Related Work

The general approach pursued in this paper—that of using pre-ordering to improve translation output–has been explored by many researchers. Most work has focused on automatically learning reordering rules (Xia and McCord, 2004; Habash, 2007b; Elming, 2008; Elming and Habash, 2009; Dyer and Resnik, 2010). Xia and McCord (2004) describe an approach for translation from French to English, where context-free constituency reordering rules are acquired automatically using source and target parses and word alignment. Elming (2008) and Elming and Habash (2009) use a large set of linguistic features to automatically learn reordering rules for English-Danish and English-Arabic; the rules are used to pre-order the input into a lattice of variant orders. Habash (2007b) learns syntactic reordering rules targeting Arabic-English word order differences and integrated them as deterministic preprocessing. He reports improvements in BLEU compared to phrase-based SMT limited to monotonic decoding, but these improvements do not hold with distortion. He hypothesizes that parse errors are responsible for lack of improvement. Dyer and Resnik (2010) use an input forest structure to represent word-order alternatives and learn models for long-range source reordering that maximize translation quality. Their results for Arabic-English are negative.

In contrast to these approaches, Collins et al. (2005) apply six *manually* defined transformations to German parse trees which yield an improvement on a German-English translation task. In this paper, we follow Collins et al. (2005) and restrict ourselves to handcrafted rules (in our case, actually a single over-generating rule) motivated by linguistic understanding.

One major concern not addressed in any of the aforementioned research on syntax-based reordering is the fact that the quality of parsers for many languages is still quite poor. Collins et al. (2005), for example, assume that the parse trees they use are correct. While the state-of-the-art in English parsing is fairly good (though far from perfect), this is not the case in other languages, where parsing shows substantial error rates. Moreover, when attempting to reorder so as to bring the source text more grammatically in line with the target language, a bad parse can be disastrous: moving parts of the sentence that shouldn't be moved, and introducing more distortion error than it is able to correct. To address the problem of noisy parse data, Bisazza and Federico (2010) identify the subject using a chunker, then *fuzzify* it, creating a lattice in which the translation system has a choice of several different paths, corresponding to re-orderings of different subject spans.

In investigating syntax-based reordering for Arabic specifically, Carpuat et al. (2010) show that a syntax-driven reordering of the training data only for the purpose of alignment improvement leads to a substantial improvement in translation quality, but do not report a corresponding improvement when reordering test data in a similar fashion. Interestingly, Bisazza and Federico (2010) report that fuzzy reordering the test data improves MT output, suggesting that fuzzification may be the mechanism necessary to render reordering on test data useful. To the best of our knowledge, nobody has yet used fuzzification to correct the identified subject span of complete Arabic dependency parses. Green et al. (2009) use a conditional random field sequence classifier to detect Arabic noun phrase subjects in verb-initial clauses achieving an F-score of 61.3%. They integrate their classifier's decisions as additional features in the Moses decoder (Koehn et al., 2007), but do not show any gains.

The present work may be thought of as extending the fuzzification explored by Bisazza and Federico (2010) to the domain of full parsing—a combination, in some sense, of their approach with the work of Carpuat et al. (2010). The approach examined in this paper differs from Collins et al. (2005) in its use of fuzzification, from Bisazza and Federico (2010) in its use of a complete dependency parse, and from Carpuat et al. (2010) in its use of a reordered test set.

Figure 1: An example of a dependency tree of a Verb-Object-Subject Arabic sentence: هز الرياض مساء اليوم هجومان ب+ سيارتين مفخختين *hz AlryAD msA' Alywm hjwmAn b+ syArtyn mfxxtyn* 'Two car bombs shook Riyadh this evening'. The predicted tree (on the left) shows an incorrect subject span (words 5-8).

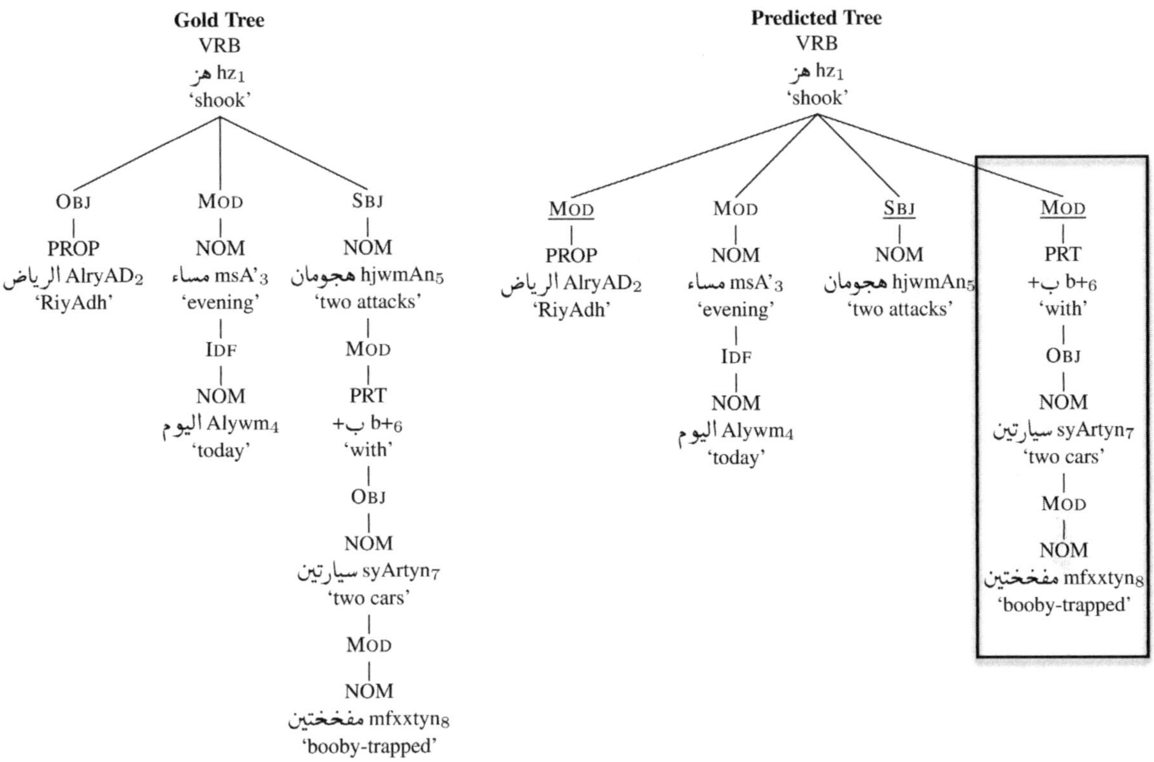

3 Motivation

While the VSO order is common at both the matrix and non-matrix level in Arabic newswire text, matrix VSO constructions are almost always reordered in translation, while non-matrix VSO constructions are frequently translated monotonically (they are instead passivized or otherwise transformed in a fashion that leaves them parallel to the source Arabic text) (Carpuat et al., 2010). This reordering, as noted in the introduction, is notoriously difficult for phrase-based statistical machine translation systems to capture. It is further exacerbated by the low quality of Arabic parsing especially for subject span identification (Green et al., 2009).

3.1 Reordering

We began by performing a series of reordering experiments using gold-standard parses of the NIST MT05 data set:[1] (a) a baseline experiment with no reordering, (b) an experiment which forced reordering on all matrix subjects, and (c) an experiment in which the translation system was presented with a lattice, in which one path contained the original sentence and the other path contained the sentence with the matrix subject reordered. The baseline system produced a BLEU score of 47.13, forced reordering produced a BLEU score of 47.43, and optional reordering produced a BLEU score of 47.55. These results indicate that, given correct reordering boundaries, the translation quality can indeed be improved with reordered test data. Furthermore, the improvement noted above between the forced reordering and optional reordering experiments, while small, indicates that even with correct parses it is sometimes preferable to leave the input sentence un-reordered. This is consistent with Carpuat et al. (2010)'s ob-

[1]The gold parses for NIST MT05 are part of the Columbia Arabic Treeebank (CATiB) (Habash and Roth, 2009).

servation that even VS-ordered matrix verbs in Arabic are sometimes translated monotonically into English (as, for example, in passive constructions). An alternative explanation may be that since the training data itself is not re-ordered, it is plausible that some re-ordering may cause otherwise good possible matches in the phrase table to not match any more.

3.2 Parser Error

The problem of finding correct subject span boundaries for reordering, however, is a particularly difficult one. Both Habash (2007b) and Green et al. (2009) have noted previously that even state-of-the-art Arabic dependency parsers tend to perform poorly, and we would expect that incorrect boundaries would do more harm than good for translation. In order to determine how to "fix" these spans, it is first necessary to understand the kinds of errors that the parser makes. A set of predicted parses of the NIST MT05 data was compared to the gold parses of the same data set.

There are three categories of error the parser can make in identifying subjects: labeling errors, attachment errors and span errors. In labeling errors, the parser either incorrectly marks a node `SBJ` when no such label appears in the gold tree, or fails to identify one of the gold-labeled `SBJ`s. In attachment error, the identified subject is marked as depending on the wrong node. Finally, in span error, the descendants assigned to a labeled SBJ are wrong. The distribution of parser errors in the NIST MT05 data is as follows:

- Label errors: 19.8% of predicted subjects are not gold subjects, and 19.1% of gold subjects are not identified as predicted subjects.
- Attachment errors: 16.92% of gold subjects are incorrectly attached in the predicted tree.
- Span errors: 26.4% of predicted subject spans are incorrect.

In this paper, we focus on correcting the largest sources of error: incorrect span and false-positive subjects. We now provide further analysis of the span errors.

In principle, spans can be marked incorrectly both on their front and back ends; however, because left-dependency is fairly uncommon in Arabic and happens in a limited number of predictable cases, the parser made so few errors in identifying the left boundary of spans (1.8%) that it is not worth trying to correct them.[2]

The question is thus how to correct the right edge of spans assuming that label and attachment have been predicted correctly. Span classifications can be broken into three categories: those that are too long (i.e. that have too many right descendants), too short (i.e. that have too few right descendants), or correct (so that the predicted tree has all the same descendants as the gold tree, without regard to their syntactic structure). A comparison of gold and predicted trees for MT05 was conducted, revealing the distribution shown in Table 1. We see that the 26.4% of subjects with incorrect spans are roughly equally divided between subjects that are too short and subjects that are too long.

Type	#	%
Long	260	12.4%
Short	293	14.0%
Correct	1538	73.6%
Total	2091	100%

Table 1: Distribution of span errors in NIST MT05

To gain further insight into the nature of the subject span errors, we examined more closely the 26.4% of cases where the span is incorrectly labeled, looking specifically at the "difference box": the set of contiguous nodes that must be added to or removed from the predicted span to bring it into agreement with the gold span (see Fig. 1).[3] Specifically, we wished to know how many top-level constituents required addition or removal to cover the entire difference. The smaller the number of top-level constituents that needs to be added, the fewer reordering variations possible, and the better the expected performance of the system.

Roughly 2% of these difference boxes are what we might call "pathological" cases: due to some se-

[2] A note on terminology: "left" and "right" are used throughout this paper with reference to word order when using the Latin alphabet. "Left" should be understood to mean "towards the beginning of the sentence", and "right" to mean "towards the end of the sentence."

[3] Arabic transliteration is presented in the Habash-Soudi-Buckwalter scheme (Habash et al., 2007).

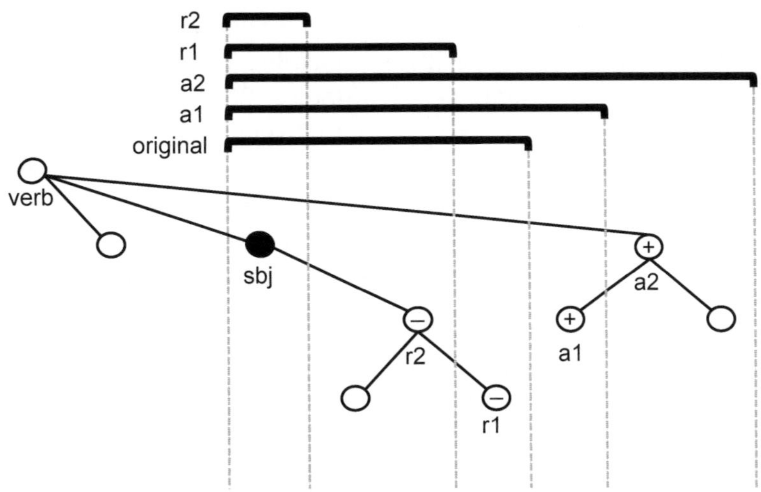

Figure 2: A schematic representation of the fuzzification algorithm. The black node is the matrix subject, + indicates that a node (and its descendants) can be added, − indicates that a node (and its descendants) can be removed, and the black brackets denote the boundaries of the candidate spans.

rious error in parsing, there is a constituent inside the difference box with descendants outside the box. These are algorithmically very difficult to correct as they require us to either add a constituent and then prune it, or remove a constituent and then reattach some of its children; attempting to correct for this possibility in all sentences will lead to a combinatorial explosion of possible parses. Fortunately, these pathological cases make up a small enough portion of the data set that they can be safely disregarded.

More promisingly, 66.5% of incorrect spans can be corrected with the addition or removal of a single constituent; in other words, the recall of span identification can be improved from 73.6% to 91.2% by adding or removing at most one constituent at the end of the parser's identified span.

4 Approach

To improve translation of matrix subjects, we implement fuzzy reordering by using a lattice-based approach similar to Bisazza and Federico (2010) to correct the matrix subject spans identified by a state-of-the-art dependency parser (Marton et al., 2010). Specifically, we take a twofold approach to fuzzy reordering. First, we present the translation system with both un-reordered and reordered options. This is motivated by the observation that on gold parses, optional reordering outperformed forced reordering (Section 3.1). Second, we apply a fuzzification algorithm to the reordered subject span, adding yet more options to the lattice. This is motivated by the observation that the greatest source of parsing errors in subjects is span errors (Section 3.2). We discuss these two techniques in turn.

4.1 Optional Reordering

In keeping with results from the initial gold experiments, we decided to generate a lattice identical to that used for the optional-reordering experiment, in which the translation system was presented with the input sentence both un-reordered and reordered, using a predicted parse to perform the reordering.

4.2 Subject Span Fuzzification

The observation that 91.2% of spans can be recalled with single-constituent modifications led very naturally to the following fuzzification algorithm, which is illustrated in Fig. 2:

1. For each matrix subject in the parse tree[4], create an empty list to hold fuzzified boundaries.
2. Original span: Add to the list the tuple (l, r, v), where l is the index of the predicted span's left-most descendant, r is the index of the predicted span's rightmost descendant and v is the verb

[4]Allowance must be made for parsers which incorrectly identify multiple subjects for the matrix verb.

that the predicted span attaches to. (This step produces the span labeled "original" in Fig. 2.)

3. Expansion: Add to the list all tuples of the form (l, r^+, v), where r^+ is the index of the rightmost descendant of a node whose leftmost descendant has index $r + 1$. (This step produces the spans labeled "a1" and "a2" in Fig. 2.)
4. Contraction: Add to the list all tuples of the form $(l, r^- - 1, v)$, where r^- is the index of the leftmost descendant of a node whose rightmost descendant has index r. (This step produces the spans labeled "r1" and "r2" in Fig. 2.)
5. Create the list of all valid combinations of spans by taking the Cartesian product of all the per-subject span lists, and rejecting all entries in which two spans overlap. (This step accounts for multiple subject cases.)

The result of this algorithm is a list of lists of tuples, where each tuple defines a single reordering, and each list of tuples defines a set of spans that must be moved to the left of the matrix verb for one reordering. These re-orderings are then joined together to form the final lattice. If a single-constituent correction to the span exists (except in the aforementioned pathological and left-attachment cases), it is guaranteed to appear as one path through the lattice.

5 Evaluation

5.1 Experimental Setup

We used the open-source Moses PSMT toolkit (Koehn et al., 2007). Training data was a newswire (MSA-English) parallel text with 12M words on the Arabic side (LDC2007E103)[5] Sentences were reordered only for alignment, following the approach of Carpuat et al. (2010). Parses were obtained using a publicly available parser for Arabic (Marton et al., 2010). GIZA++ was used for word alignment (Och and Ney, 2003) and phrase translations of up to 10 words are extracted in the Moses phrase table. The same baseline phrase table was used in all experiments.

The system's language model was trained both on the English portion of the training corpus and English Gigaword (Graff and Cieri, 2003). We used a 5-gram language model with modified Kneser-Ney smoothing implemented using the SRILM toolkit (Stolcke, 2002). Feature weights were tuned with MERT (Och, 2003) to maximize BLEU on the NIST MT06 corpus. MERT was done only for the baseline system; these same weights were used for all experiments to control for the effect of MERT instability. In the future, we plan to experiment with approach-specific optimization and to use recent published suggestions on controlling for optimizer instability (Clark et al., 2011).

English data was tokenized using simple punctuation-based rules. Arabic data was segmented with to the Arabic Treebank tokenization scheme (Maamouri et al., 2004) using the MADA+TOKAN morphological disambiguator and tokenizer (Habash and Rambow, 2005; Habash, 2007a; Roth et al., 2008). The Arabic text was also Alif/Ya normalized (Habash, 2010). MADA-produced Arabic lemmas were used for word alignment.

We compare four settings with predicted parses (as opposed to the gold parse experiments discussed in Section 3):

- **BASE** An un-reordered test set;
- **FORCE** A test set which forced reordering on matrix verbs;
- **OPT** A test set with fuzzification through optional reordering on matrix verbs; and
- **SPAN** A test set with fuzzification through optional reordering on matrix verbs and through fuzzification of the subject span according to the algorithm shown in Section 4.2.

Each reordering corpus used Moses' lattice input format (Dyer et al., 2008) (including the baselines, which had only one path). Results are presented in terms of the standard BLEU metric (Papineni et al., 2002), METEOR metric (Banerjee and Lavie, 2005) and a manual evaluation targeting subject span translation correctness.

5.2 Automatic Evaluation Results

Table 2 presents the results for the experiments discussed above. Columns three and Four (Prec-1g and Prec-4g) indicate the corresponding 1-gram and 4-gram (sub-BLEU) precision scores, respectively.

[5] All data is available from the Linguistic Data Consortium: http://www.ldc.upenn.edu.

System	BLEU	Prec-1g	Prec-4g	METEOR
BASE	47.13	81.91	29.52	53.09
FORCE	47.03	81.78	29.52	53.11
OPT	47.42	81.88	30.04	53.22
SPAN	47.41	81.92	30.03	53.21

Table 2: Automatic evaluation results

Both OPT and SPAN showed a statistically significant improvement in BLEU score over BASE and FORCE above the 95% level. Statistical significance is computed using paired bootstrap resampling (Koehn, 2004). The difference between OPT and SPAN, however, was not statistically significant.

The relatively small difference in BLEU score between the baseline and *gold* reordering (Section 3: baseline 47.13 and optional reordering 47.55) suggests that we should expect at most a modest increase in BLEU from improving the predicted trees.

The first key observation in these results is that with a noisy parser, translation quality actually goes down with forced reordering—the opposite of what was observed in the gold experiment. By introducing either optional reordering or complete fuzzification, however, BLEU score increases .3 past the baseline to achieve nearly three quarters of the gain obtained by optional reordering using the gold parse (Section 3: baseline 47.13 and optional reordering 47.55). In other words, it is possible to compensate for the parser noisiness without actually attempting to correct spans: simply allowing the translation system to fall back on an un-reordered input leads to a significant gain in BLEU.

One possible explanation for this fact is that we only ever correct for parses on the right-hand side—the left sides are virtually always correct. Thus, when we perform any reordering, even if the subject span is not entirely perfect, we guarantee that we bring at least one word from the sentence (and usually more) into alignment where it was out of alignment before; this obviously leads to better BLEU n-gram scores along that boundary.

The general trend in these results is confirmed by the results of a METEOR analysis, also provided in Tab. 2. Again, both the OPT and SPAN systems result exhibit comparable performance, and demonstrate an improvement over the baseline.

The second observation is that introducing span fuzzification did not improve over simple optional reordering. There are a several reasons this could be happening:

- The increased fluency and introduction of unseen phrases cancel each other out.
- All the gains that come from reordering occur at the left; the presence or absence of correct words at the right end is less important.
- Better sentences are proposed during the translation process, but they are not selected during the final filtering stage.
- The sentences being output are actually better, but the improvement is not captured by the automatic evaluation.

Further experiments will be necessary to determine whether any of the first three possibilities is the case. We next consider the fourth possibility in more detail.

5.3 Manual Evaluation

We additionally conducted a manual evaluation to examine how subject quality differed in fuzzified vs. unfuzzified parses. Each sentence examined was assigned one of the six labels below. Examples are with respect to the reference sentence *"Recep Tayyip Erdogan announced that Turkey is strong."*

- **MM**: both verb and subject missing. *"Turkey is strong."*
- **MV**: verb missing. *"Recep Tayyip Erdogan Turkey is strong."*
- **MS**: subject missing. *"announced that Turkey is strong."*
- **SO**: subject overlaps with verb. *"Recep announced Tayyip Erdogan Turkey is strong."*
- **SI**: verb precedes subject (as in Arabic). *"announced Recep Tayyip Erdogan that Turkey is strong."*
- **C**: verb follows subject (as in English), i.e. the correct ordering. *"Recep Tayyip Erdogan announced that Turkey is strong."* We also include in this category sentences where the English reference contains no verb (e.g. in newspaper headlines).

System	MM	MS	MV	SI	SO	C	M*	S*	C
BASE	8	13	11	9	3	53	33	12	53
OPT	7	11	10	5	5	61	28	10	61
SPAN	8	10	09	5	2	64	27	7	64

Table 3: Subject integrity analysis results. All numbers are %s.

By grouping some of these categories together, we obtained the following label scheme:

- **M***: MM, MV or MS, i.e. verb or subject is missing.
- **S***: SO or SI, i.e. word order is incorrect.
- **C**: as above.

280 sentences selected randomly from our test set were evaluated, generating 461 unique output sentences. Annotation was performed by two English speakers, with 40 input sentences (68 unique outputs) annotated by both authors to collect agreement statistics. For the complete label scheme, the annotators agreed on 86.8% of labels, with Cohen's $\kappa = 0.811$. For the simple label scheme, the annotators agreed on 92.6% of labels, with $\kappa = .883$. Results for the BASE, OPT and SPAN systems are shown in Table 3. Each annotator's labels were assigned a weight of .5 in the section that was jointly annotated.

Again, both the OPT and SPAN systems display statistically significant improvements over the baseline system ($p < 0.001$). While the SPAN system consistently displays better results than the OPT system, the significance is low ($p < .3$). Statistical significance was measured using the McNemar test of statistical significance (McNemar, 1947).

These results thus agree with the BLEU score in indicating that the OPT and SPAN systems are substantially better than the baseline, but statistically indistinguishable from each other. They further indicate that most of the improvements in the OPT system come from preventing dropped subjects or verbs, while the improvements in the SPAN system result in roughly equal proportion from preventing word-dropping and ensuring correct ordering.

6 Conclusion & Future Work

We presented an approach for improving Arabic-English PSMT using syntactic information from a noisy parser. We demonstrated that translation quality goes down with forced reordering, but improves with the introduction of either optional reordering and subject span fuzzification. The BLEU score increases by 0.3% absolute past the baseline achieve nearly three quarters of the maximum possible gain starting with gold parses. A detailed manual evaluation produces results generally consistent with BLEU, but highlights the small improvements that can be gained by subject span fuzzification.

In the future, we plan to explore a more sophisticated approach to the lattice of re-orderings presented here. We would take into account the fact that it is possible to suggest to the system that certain re-orderings are less likely than others without removing them from the search space completely. The same can be done for the fuzzification task: while we might wish to add additional fuzzification options, we also don't want the correct choice to be crowded out by too many alternatives.

Acknowledgements

We would like to thank Marine Carpuat, Yuval Marton, Amit Abbi and Ahmed El Kholy for helpful discussions and feedback. The second and third authors were supported by the Defense Advanced Research Projects Agency (DARPA) under GALE Contract No HR0011-08-C-0110. Any opinions, findings and conclusions or recommendations expressed in this material are those of the authors and do not necessarily reflect the views of DARPA.

References

Satanjeev Banerjee and Alon Lavie. 2005. METEOR: An Automatic Metric for MT Evaluation with Improved Correlation with Human Judgments. In *Proceedings of the ACL Workshop on Intrinsic and Extrinsic Evaluation Measures for Machine Translation and/or Summarization*, pages 65–72, Ann Arbor, Michigan.

Arianna Bisazza and Marcello Federico. 2010. Chunk-based verb reordering in VSO sentences for Arabic-English statistical machine translation. In *Proceedings of ACL 2010: Joint Fifth Workshop on Statistical Machine Translation and MetricsMATR*, Uppsala, Sweden.

Marine Carpuat, Yuval Marton, and Nizar Habash. 2010. Improving Arabic-to-English Statistical Machine Translation by Reordering Post-Verbal Subjects for Alignment. In *Proceedings of the ACL 2010 Conference Short Papers*, pages 178–183, Uppsala, Sweden, July.

Jonathan H. Clark, Chris Dyer, Alon Lavie, and Noah A. Smith. 2011. Better hypothesis testing for statistical machine translation: Controlling for optimizer instability. In *Proceedings of the 49th Annual Meeting of the Association for Computational Linguistics: Human Language Technologies*, pages 176–181, Portland, Oregon, USA.

Michael Collins, Philipp Koehn, and Ivona Kucerova. 2005. Clause Restructuring for Statistical Machine Translation. In *Proceedings of the 43rd Annual Meeting of the Association for Computational Linguistics (ACL'05)*, pages 531–540, Ann Arbor, Michigan.

Chris Dyer and Philip Resnik. 2010. Context-free reordering, finite-state translation. In *Human Language Technologies: The 2010 Annual Conference of the North American Chapter of the Association for Computational Linguistics*, pages 858–866, Los Angeles, California.

Christopher Dyer, Smaranda Muresan, and Philip Resnik. 2008. Generalizing word lattice translation. In *Proceedings of ACL-08: HLT*, Columbus, Ohio.

Jakob Elming and Nizar Habash. 2009. Syntactic Reordering for English-Arabic Phrase-Based Machine Translation. In *Proceedings of the EACL 2009 Workshop on Computational Approaches to Semitic Languages*, pages 69–77, Athens, Greece, March.

J. Elming. 2008. Syntactic reordering integrated with phrase-based smt. In *Proceedings of the ACL Workshop on Syntax and Structure in Statistical Translation (SSST-2)*.

David Graff and Christopher Cieri. 2003. English Gigaword, LDC Catalog No.: LDC2003T05. Linguistic Data Consortium, University of Pennsylvania.

Spence Green, Conal Sathi, and Christopher D. Manning. 2009. NP Subject Detection in Verb-initial Arabic Clauses. In *Proceedings of the Third Workshop on Computational Approaches to Arabic Script-based Languages (CAASL3)*.

Nizar Habash and Owen Rambow. 2005. Arabic Tokenization, Part-of-Speech Tagging and Morphological Disambiguation in One Fell Swoop. In *Proceedings of the 43rd Annual Meeting of the Association for Computational Linguistics (ACL'05)*, pages 573–580, Ann Arbor, Michigan.

Nizar Habash and Ryan Roth. 2009. CATiB: The Columbia Arabic Treebank. In *Proceedings of the ACL-IJCNLP 2009 Conference Short Papers*, pages 221–224, Suntec, Singapore.

Nizar Habash, Abdelhadi Soudi, and Tim Buckwalter. 2007. On Arabic Transliteration. In A. van den Bosch and A. Soudi, editors, *Arabic Computational Morphology: Knowledge-based and Empirical Methods*. Springer.

Nizar Habash. 2007a. Arabic Morphological Representations for Machine Translation. In A. van den Bosch and A. Soudi, editors, *Arabic Computational Morphology: Knowledge-based and Empirical Methods*. Springer.

Nizar Habash. 2007b. Syntactic preprocessing for statistical machine translation. In *Proceedings of the 11th MT Summit*.

Nizar Habash. 2010. *Introduction to Arabic Natural Language Processing*. Morgan & Claypool Publishers.

Philipp Koehn, Hieu Hoang, Alexandra Birch, Christopher Callison-Burch, Marcello Federico, Nicola Bertoldi, Brooke Cowan, Wade Shen, Christine Moran, Richard Zens, Christopher Dyer, Ondrej Bojar, Alexandra Constantin, and Evan Herbst. 2007. Moses: open source toolkit for statistical machine translation. In *Proceedings of the 45th Annual Meeting of the Association for Computational Linguistics Companion Volume Proceedings of the Demo and Poster Sessions*, pages 177–180, Prague, Czech Republic.

Philipp Koehn. 2004. Statistical significance tests for machine translation evaluation. In *Proceedings of the Empirical Methods in Natural Language Processing Conference (EMNLP'04)*, Barcelona, Spain.

Mohamed Maamouri, Ann Bies, Tim Buckwalter, and Wigdan Mekki. 2004. The Penn Arabic Treebank: Building a Large-Scale Annotated Arabic Corpus. In *NEMLAR Conference on Arabic Language Resources and Tools*, pages 102–109, Cairo, Egypt.

Yuval Marton, Nizar Habash, and Owen Rambow. 2010. Improving Arabic Dependency Parsing with Lexical and Inflectional Morphological Features. In *Proceedings of the NAACL HLT 2010 First Workshop on Statistical Parsing of Morphologically-Rich Languages*, pages 13–21, Los Angeles, CA, USA, June.

Quinn McNemar. 1947. Note on the sampling error of the difference between correlated proportions or percentages. *Psychometrika*, 12(2):153–157.

F. J. Och and H. Ney. 2003. A systematic comparison of various statistical alignment models. *Computational Linguistics*, 29(1):19–51.

Franz Josef Och. 2003. Minimum Error Rate Training for Statistical Machine Translation. In *Proceedings of the 41st Annual Conference of the Association for Computational Linguistics*, pages 160–167, Sapporo, Japan.

Kishore Papineni, Salim Roukos, Todd Ward, and Wei-Jing Zhu. 2002. BLEU: a Method for Automatic Evaluation of Machine Translation. In *Proceedings of the 40th Annual Meeting of the Association for Computational Linguistics*, pages 311–318, Philadelphia, PA.

Ryan Roth, Owen Rambow, Nizar Habash, Mona Diab, and Cynthia Rudin. 2008. Arabic Morphological Tagging, Diacritization, and Lemmatization Using Lexeme Models and Feature Ranking. In *Proceedings of ACL-08: HLT, Short Papers*, pages 117–120, Columbus, Ohio.

Andreas Stolcke. 2002. SRILM - an Extensible Language Modeling Toolkit. In *Proceedings of the International Conference on Spoken Language Processing (ICSLP)*, volume 2, pages 901–904, Denver, CO.

Fei Xia and Michael McCord. 2004. Improving a statistical mt system with automatically learned rewrite patterns. In *Proceedings of the 20th International Conference on Computational Linguistics (COLING 2004)*, pages 508–514, Geneva, Switzerland.

Filtering Antonymous, Trend-Contrasting, and Polarity-Dissimilar Distributional Paraphrases for Improving Statistical Machine Translation

Yuval Marton
T.J. Watson Research Center
IBM
yymarton@us.ibm.com

Ahmed El Kholy and **Nizar Habash**
Center for Computational Learning Systems
Columbia University
{akholy,habash}@ccls.columbia.edu

Abstract

Paraphrases are useful for statistical machine translation (SMT) and natural language processing tasks. Distributional paraphrase generation is independent of parallel texts and syntactic parses, and hence is suitable also for resource-poor languages, but tends to erroneously rank antonyms, trend-contrasting, and polarity-dissimilar candidates as good paraphrases. We present here a novel method for improving distributional paraphrasing by filtering out such candidates. We evaluate it in simulated low and mid-resourced SMT tasks, translating from English to two quite different languages. We show statistically significant gains in English-to-Chinese translation quality, up to 1 BLEU from non-filtered paraphrase-augmented models (1.6 BLEU from baseline). We also show that yielding gains in translation to Arabic, a morphologically rich language, is not straightforward.

1 Introduction

Paraphrase recognition and generation has proven useful for various natural language processing (NLP) tasks, including statistical machine translation (SMT), information retrieval, query expansion, document summarization, and natural language generation. We concentrate here on phrase-level (as opposed to sentence-level) paraphrasing for SMT. Paraphrasing is useful for SMT as it increases translation coverage – a persistent problem, even in large-scale systems. Two common approaches are "pivot" and distributional paraphrasing. Pivot paraphrasing translates phrases of interest to other languages and back (Callison-Burch et al., 2006; Callison-Burch, 2008). It relies on parallel texts (or translation phrase tables) in various languages, which are typically scarce, and hence limit its applicability. Distributional paraphrasing (Marton et al., 2009) generates paraphrases using a distributional semantic distance measure computed over a large monolingual corpus.[1] Monolingual corpora are relatively easy and inexpensive to collect, but distributional semantic distance measures are known to rank antonymous and polarity-dissimilar phrasal candidates high. We therefore attempt to identify and filter out such ill-suited paraphrase candidates.

A phrase pair may have a varying degree of antonymy, beyond the better-known complete opposites (*hot / cold*) and contradictions (*did / did not*), e.g., weaker contrasts (*hot / cool*), contrasting trends (*covered / reduced coverage*), or sentiment polarity (*happy / sad*). Information extraction, opinion mining and sentiment analysis literature has been grappling with identifying such pairs (Pang and Lee, 2008), e.g., in order to distinguish positive and negative reviews or comments, or to detect contradictions (Marneffe et al., 2008; Voorhees, 2008). We transfer some of the insights, data and techniques to the area of paraphrasing and SMT. We distributionally expand a small seed set of antonyms in an unsupervised manner, following Mohammad et al. (2008). We then present a method for filtering antonymous and polarity-dissimilar distributional paraphrases using the expanded antonymous list and a list of negators (e.g., *cannot*) and trend-decreasing words (*reduced*). We evaluate the impact of our approach in a SMT setting, where non-

[1] Other variants use a lexical resource in conjunction with the monolingual corpus (Mirkin et al., 2009; Marton, 2010).

Proceedings of the 6th Workshop on Statistical Machine Translation, pages 237–249,
Edinburgh, Scotland, UK, July 30–31, 2011.

baseline translation models are augmented with distributional paraphrases. We show gains of up to 1 BLEU relative to non-filtered models (1.6 BLEU from non-augmented baselines) in English-Chinese models trained on small and medium-large size data, but lower to no gains in English-Arabic. The small training size simulates resource-poor languages.

The rest of this paper is organized as follows: We describe distributional paraphrase generation in Section 2, antonym discovery in Section 3, and paraphrase-augmented SMT in Section 4. We then report experimental results in Section 5, and discuss the implications in Section 6. We survey related work in Section 7, and conclude with future work in Section 8.

2 Distributional Paraphrases

Our method improves on the method presented in Marton et al. (2009). Using a non-annotated monolingual corpus, our method constructs distributional profiles (DP; a.k.a. context vectors) of focal words or phrases. Each DP_{phr} is a vector containing log-likelihood ratios of the focal phrase phr and each word w in the corpus. Given a paraphrase candidate phrase $cand$, the semantic distance between phr and $cand$ is calculated using the cosine of their respective DPs (McDonald, 2000). For details on DPs and distributional measures, see Weeds et al. (2004) and Turney and Pantel (2010).

The search of the corpus for paraphrase candidates is performed in the following manner:

1. For each focal phrase phr, build distributional profile DP_{phr}.
2. Gather contexts: for each occurrence of phr, keep surrounding (left and right) context $L\_\_R$.
3. For each such context, gather paraphrase candidates $cand$ which occur between L and R in other locations in the training corpus, i.e., all $cand$ such that L $cand$ R occur in the corpus.
4. For each candidate $cand$, build a profile DP_{cand} and measure profile similarity between DP_{cand} and DP_{phr}.
5. Rank all $cand$ according to the profile similarity score.
6. Filter out every candidate $cand$ that textually entails phr: This is approximated by filtering $cand$ if its words all appear in phr in the same order. For example, if *phr* is *spoken softly*, then *spoken very softly* would be filtered out.
7. Filter out every candidate $cand$ that is antonymous to phr (See Algorithm 1 below).
8. Output k-best remaining candidates above a certain similarity score threshold t.

Most of the steps above are similar to, and have been elaborated in, Marton et al. (2009). Due to space limitations, we concentrate on the main novel element here, which is the antonym filtering step, detailed below. Antonyms (largely speaking) are opposites, terms that contrast in meaning, such as *hot / cold*. Negators are terms such as *not* and *lost*, which often flip the meaning of the word or phrase that follows or contains them, e.g., *confidence / lost confidence*. Details on obtaining their definitions and on obtaining the antonymous pair list and the negator list are given in Section 3.

Algorithm 1 Antonymous candidate filtering

Given an antonymous pair list, a negator list, and a phrase-paraphrase candidate (phr-$cand$) pair list,
for all phr-$cand$ pairs **do**
  for all words w in phr **do**
    if w is also in $cand$, and there is a negator up to two words before it in either phr or $cand$ (but not both!) **then**
      filter out this pair
    if w, ant is an antonymous pair, and ant is in $cand$, and there is no negator up to two words before w and ant, or there is such a negator before both **then**
      filter out this pair

3 Antonyms, Trends, Sentiment Polarity

Native speakers of a language are good at determining whether two words are antonyms (*hot–cold, ascend–descend, friend–foe*) or not (*penguin–clown, cold–chilly, boat–rudder*) (Cruse, 1986; Lehrer and Lehrer, 1982; Deese, 1965). Strict antonyms apart, there are also many word pairs that exhibit some degree of contrast in meaning, for example, *lukewarm–cold, ascend–slip,* and *fan–enemy* (Mohammad et al., 2008). Automatically identifying such contrasting word pairs has many uses including detecting and generating paraphrases (*The lion* ***caught*** *the gazel / The gazel could* ***not escape*** *the lion*) and detecting contradictions (Marneffe et al., 2008; Voorhees, 2008) (*The inhabitants of Peru are **well off** / the inhabitants of Peru are **poor***). Of course, such "contradictions" may be a result of differing sentiment, new information, non-coreferent mentions, or genuinely contradictory statements. Identifying paraphrases and contradictions are in turn useful in effectively re-ranking target language hypotheses in machine translation, and for re-ranking query responses in information retrieval. Identifying contrasting word pairs (or short phrase pairs) is also useful for detecting humor (Mihalcea and Strapparava, 2005), as satire and jokes tend to have contradictions and oxymorons. Lastly, it is useful to know which words contrast a focal word, even if only to filter them out. For example, in the automatic creation of a thesaurus it is necessary to distinguish near-synonyms from contrasting word pairs. Distributional similarity measures typically fail to do so.

Instances of strong contrast are recorded to some extent in manually created dictionaries, but hundreds of thousands of other contrasting pairs are not. Further, antonyms can be of many kinds such as those described in Section 3.1 below. We use the Mohammad et al. (2008) method to automatically generate a large list of contrasting word pairs, which are used to identify false paraphrases. Their method is briefly described in Section 3.2.

3.1 Kinds of antonyms

Antonyms can be classified into different kinds. A detailed description of one such classification can be found in Cruse (1986) (Chapters 9, 10, and 11), where the author describes complementaries (*open–shut, dead–alive*), gradable adjective pairs (*long–short, slow–fast*) (further classified into polar, overlapping, and equipollent antonyms), directional opposites (*up–down, north–south*), (further classified into antipodals, counterparts, and reversives), relational opposites (*husband–wife, predator–prey*), indirect converses (*give–receive, buy–pay*), congruence variants (*huge–little, doctor–patient*), and pseudo opposites (*black–white*). It should be noted, however, that even though contrasting word pairs and antonyms have long been studied by linguists, lexicographers, and others, experts do not always agree on the scope of antonymy and the kinds of contrasting word pairs. Some lexical relations have also received attention at the Educational Testing Services (ETS). They classify antonyms into contradictories (*alive–dead, masculine–feminine*), contraries (*old–young, happy-sad*), reverses (*attack–defend, buy–sell*), directionals (*front–back, left–right*), incompatibles (*happy–morbid, frank–hypocritical*), asymmetric contraries (*hot–cool, dry–moist*), pseudoantonyms (*popular–shy, right–bad*), and defectives (*default–payment, limp–walk*) (Bejar et al., 1991).

As mentioned earlier, in addition to antonyms, there are other meaning-contrasting phenomena, or other ways to classify them, such as contrasting trends and sentiment polarity. They all may have varying degrees of contrast in meaning. Hereafter we sometime broadly refer to all of these as *antonymous phrases*. The antonymous phrase pair generation algorithm that we use here does not employ any antonym-subclass-specific techniques.

3.2 Detecting antonyms

Mohammad et al. (2008) used a Roget-like thesaurus, co-occurrence statistics, and a seed set of antonyms to identify the degree of antonymy between two words, and generate a list of antonymous words. The thesaurus divides the vocabulary into about a thousand coarse categories. Each category has, on average, about a hundred closely related words. (A word with more than one sense, is listed in more than one category.) Mohammad et al. first determine pairs of thesaurus categories that are contrasting in meaning. A category pair is said to be contrasting if it has a seed antonym pair. A list of seed antonyms is compiled using 16 affix patterns such as X and unX (*clear–unclear*) and X and disX (*honest–dishonest*). Once a contrasting category pair is identified, all the word pairs across the two categories are considered to have contrasting meaning. The strength of co-occurrence (as measured by pointwise mutual information) between two contrasting word pairs is taken to be the degree of antonymy. This is based on the *distributional hypothesis of antonyms*, which states that antonymous pairs tend to co-occur in text more often than chance. Co-occurrence counts are made from the *British National Corpus (BNC)* (Burnard, 2000). The approach attains more than 80% accuracy on GRE-style closest opposite questions.

3.3 Detecting negators

The General Inquirer (GI) (Stone et al., 1966) has 11,788 words labeled with 182 categories of word tags, such as positive and negative semantic orientation, pleasure, pain, and so on.[2] Two of the GI categories, NOTLW and DECREAS, contain terms that negate the meaning of what follows (Choi and Cardie, 2008; Kennedy and Inkpen, 2005). These terms (with limited added inflection variation) form our list of negators.

4 Paraphrase-Augmented SMT

Augmenting the source side of SMT phrase tables with paraphrases of out-of-vocabulary (OOV) items was introduced by Callison-Burch et al. (2006), and was adopted practically 'as-is' in consequent work (Callison-Burch, 2008; Marton et al., 2009; Marton, 2010). Given an OOV source-side phrase f, if the translation model has a rule $\langle f', e \rangle$ whose source side is a paraphrase f' of f, then a new rule $\langle f, e \rangle$ is added, with an extra weighted log-linear feature, whose value for the new rule is the similarity score between f and f' (computed as a function of the pivot translation probabilities or the distributional semantic distance of the respective DPs). We follow the same line here:

$$h(e,f) = \begin{cases} asim(DP_{f'}, DP_f) & \text{If phrase table entry } (e,f) \text{ is generated from } (e,f') \text{ using monolingually-derived paraphrases.} \\ 1 & \text{Otherwise.} \end{cases} \quad (1)$$

where the definition of $asim$ is repeated below. As noted in that previous work, it is possible to construct a new translation rule from f to e via more than one pair of source-side phrase and its paraphrase; e.g., if f_1 is a paraphrase of f, and so is f_2, and both f_1, f_2 translate to the same e, then both lead to the construction of the new rule translating f to e, but with potentially different feature scores. In order to leverage on these paths and resolve feature value conflicts, an aggregated similarity measure was applied: For each paraphrase f of source-side phrases f_i with similarity scores $sim(f_i, f)$,

$$asim_i = asim_{i-1} + (1 - asim_{i-1})\, sim(f_i, f) \quad (2)$$

where $asim_0 = 0$. We only augment the phrase table with a single rule from f to e, and in it are the feature values of the phrase f_i for which $sim(f_i, f)$ was the highest.

5 Experiment

5.1 System and Parameters

We augmented translation models with paraphrases based on distributional semantic distance measures, with our novel antonym-filtering, and without it. We tested all models in English-to-Chinese and English-to-Arabic translation, augmenting the models with translation rules for unknown English phrases. We also contrasted these models with non-augmented baseline models.

For baseline we used the phrase-based SMT system Moses (Koehn et al., 2007), with the default model features: 1. phrase translation probability, 2. reverse phrase translation probability, 3. lexical translation probability, 4. reverse lexical translation probability, 5. word penalty, 6. phrase penalty, 7. six lexicalized reordering features, 8. distortion cost, and 9. language model (LM) probability. We used Giza++ (Och and Ney, 2000) for word alignment. All features were weighted in a log-linear framework (Och and Ney, 2002). Feature weights were set with minimum error rate training (Och, 2003) on a tuning set using BLEU (Papineni et al., 2002) as the objective function. Test results were evaluated using BLEU and TER (Snover et al., 2006): The higher the BLEU score, the better the result; the *lower* the TER score, the better the result. This is denoted with BLEU$\uparrow$ and TER$\downarrow$ in Table 1. Statistical significance of model output differences was determined using Koehn (2004)'s test on the objective function (BLEU).

The paraphrase-augmented models were created as described in Section 4. We used the same data and parameter settings as in Marton (2010).[3] We used cosine distance over DPs of log-likelihood ratios (McDonald, 2000), built with a sliding win-

[2] http://www.wjh.harvard.edu/~inquirer

[3] Data preprocessing and paraphrasing code slightly differ from those used in Marton et al. (2009) and Marton (2010), and hence scores are not exactly the same across these publications.

dow of size ± 6, a sampling threshold of 10000 occurrences, and a maximal paraphrase length of 6 tokens. We applied a paraphrase score threshold $t = 0.05$; a dynamic context length (the shortest non-stoplisted left context L occurring less than 512 times in the corpus, and similarly for R); paraphrasing of OOV unigrams; filtering paraphrase candidates occurring less than 25 times in the corpus (inspired by McDonald, 2000); and allowing up to $k = 100$ best paraphrases per phrase. We tuned the weights of each model (non-augmented baseline, unigram-augmented, and unigram-augmented-filtered) with a separate minimum error rate training.

We explored here augmenting OOV unigrams, although our paraphrasing and antonym filtering methods can be applied to longer n-grams with no further modifications. However, preliminary experiments showed that longer n-grams require additional provisions in order to yield gains.

5.2 Data

In order to take advantage of the English antonym resource, we chose English as the source language for the translation task. We chose Chinese as the translation target language in order to compare with Marton (2010), and for the same reasons it was chosen there: It is quite different from English (e.g., in word order), and four reference translation were available from NIST. We chose Arabic as another target language, because it is different from both English and Chinese, and richer morphologically, which introduces additional challenges.

English-Chinese: For training we used the LDC Sinorama and FBIS tests (LDC2005T10 and LDC2003E14), and segmented the Chinese side with the Stanford Segmenter (Tseng et al., 2005). After tokenization and filtering, this bitext contained 231,586 lines (6.4M + 5.1M tokens). We trained a trigram language model on the Chinese side, with the SRILM toolkit (Stolcke, 2002), using the modified Kneser-Ney smoothing option. We followed the split in Marton (2010), and constructed the reduced set of about 29,000 sentence pairs. The purpose of creating this subset model was to simulate a resource-poor language. We trained separate translation models, using either the subset or the full-size training dataset.

For weight tuning we used the Chinese-English NIST MT 2005 evaluation set. In order to use it for the reverse translation direction (English-Chinese), we arbitrarily chose the first English reference set as the tuning "source", and the Chinese source as a single "reference translation". For testing we used the English-Chinese NIST MT evaluation 2008 test set with its four reference translations.

English-Arabic: We use an English-Arabic parallel corpus of about 135k sentences (4 million words) and a subset of 30K sentences (one million words) for the translation models' training data. The sentences were extracted from Arabic News (LDC2004T17), eTIRR (LDC2004E72), English translation of Arabic Treebank (LDC2005E46), and Ummah (LDC2004T18).[4] For Arabic preprocessing, we follow previously reported best tokenization scheme (TB)[5] and orthographic word normalization condition (Reduced) when translating from English to Arabic (El Kholy and Habash, 2010b). MADA (Habash and Rambow, 2005) is used to pre-process the Arabic text for the translation model and 5-gram language model (LM). As a post-processing step, we jointly denormalize and detokenize the text to produce the final Arabic output. Following El Kholy and Habash (2010a), we use their best detokenization technique, T+R+LM. The technique crucially utilizes a lookup table (T), mapping tokenized forms to detokenized forms, based on our MADA-fied LM. Alternatives are given conditional probabilities, $P(detokenized|tokenized)$. Tokenized words absent from the tables are detokenized using deterministic rules (R), as a backoff strategy. We use a 5-gram untokenized LM and the `disambig` utility in the SRILM toolkit to decide among different alternatives. Word alignment is done using GIZA++, as in English-Chinese system. We use lemma-based alignment which consistently yields superior results to surface-based alignment (El Kholy and Habash, 2010b). For LM, we use 200M words from the Arabic Gigaword Corpus (LDC2007T40) together with the Arabic side of our training data.

All experiments were conducted using Moses here as well. We used a maximum phrase length

[4] All are available from the Linguistic Data Consortium (LDC) `http://www.ldc.upenn.edu`

[5] TB: Penn Arabic Tree Bank tokenization scheme

of size 8 tokens. Weight optimization was done using a set of 300 sentences from the NIST MT 2004 Arabic-English evaluation test set (MT04). The tuning was based on tokenized Arabic without detokenization. Testing was done on the NIST Arabic-English MT05 and MEDAR 2010 English-Arabic four-reference evaluation sets. For both tuning on MT04 and testing on MT05, since we need the reverse English-Arabic direction, we chose one English reference translation as the "source", and the Arabic as a single "reference". We evaluated using BLEU and TER here too.

English paraphrases: We augmented the baseline models with paraphrases generated as described above, using a monolingual text of over 516M tokens, consisting of the BNC and English Gigaword documents from 2004 and 2008 (LDC2009T13), pre-processed to remove punctuation and to conflate numbers, dates, months, days of week, and alphanumeric tokens to their respective classes.

5.3 Results

English-Chinese: Results are given in Table 1. Augmenting SMT phrase tables with paraphrases of OOV unigrams resulted in gains of 0.6-0.7 BLEU points for both subset and full models, but TER scores were worse (higher) for the full model. Augmenting same models with same paraphrases filtered for antonyms resulted in further gains of 1.6 and 1 BLEU points for both subset and full models, respectively, relative to the respective baselines. The TER scores of the antonym filtered models were also as good or better (lower) than those of the baselines.

	reduced size		*large size*	
model	**BLEU↑**	**TER↓**	**BLEU↑**	**TER↓**
baseline	15.8	69.2	21.8	63.8
aug-1gram	16.4^{B}	68.9	22.5^{B}	64.4
aug-1gram-ant-filt	$\mathbf{17.4}^{BD}$	**68.7**	$\mathbf{22.8}^{BD}$	**63.7**

Table 1: English-Chinese scores. B/D = statistically significant w.r.t. (B)aseline or (D)istributional 1gram model, using Koehn (2004)'s statistical significance.

English-Arabic: Results are given in columns 1-7 of Table 2. On the MT05 test set, the 135k-sentence aug-1gram model outperformed its baseline in both BLEU and TER scores. The lemmatized variants of the scores showed higher or same gains. Since only one entry was antonym-filtered here, we do not provide separate scores for aug-1gram-ant-filt. Surprisingly, for the reduced 30k models, all scores (BLEU, TER, and even their lemmatized variants) of the augmented 1gram model were somewhat worse than the baseline's, and those of the antonym-filtered model were the worst. we also ran a 4-reference test (Medar) to see whether the single MT05 reference was problematic, but results were similar. We examine possible reasons for this in the next section.

6 Discussion

Filtering quality: Our filtering technique is based on antonymous pair and negator lists that were expanded distributionally from seed sets. Therefore, they are noisy. From a small random sample (Table 3) it seems that only about 10% of filtered cases should not have been filtered; of the rest, 50% were strongly antonymous, 25% mildly so, and 15% were siblings (*co-hypernyms*) in a natural categorical hierarchy or otherwise noisy paraphrases filtered due to a noisy antonym pair. Negators in the unigrams' paraphrase candidates were rare.

English-Chinese: Our paraphrase filtering technique yielded an additional 1 BLEU point gain over the non-filtered paraphrase-augmented reduced model (totaling 1.6 BLEU over baseline). The reduced and large augmented models' phrase table size increased by about 27% and 4%, respectively – and antonym filtering did not change these numbers by much (see left side of Table 4). Therefore, the difference in performance between the filtered and non-filtered systems is unlikely to be quantitative (phrase table size). The out of vocabulary (OOV) rate of the 29k subset model is somewhat high (see Table 4), especially for the test set; but only after these experiments were completed did we peek at the test set for calculating these statistics, and in any case, we should not be guided by such information in choosing the test set. At first glance it may seem surprising that only 0.4% of the paraphrase candidates of the English OOV unigrams (248 candidates) were filtered by our procedure, and that it accounted for as much as 1 BLEU in the reduced set. (For English-Arabic only 0.6%, or 23 candidates, were filtered). Leaving the estimation of antonymous phrase detection recall for the future, we note that these num-

	BLEU ↑	Lemm. BLEU	Brev. penal.	Ref/Sys ratio	TER ↓	Lemm. TER	Unigram Lemma Match Analysis: Exact Match	Lemma-only	Unmatchable	Total
30k-sentence (1M word) training dataset models										
MT05 baseline	**23.6**	**31.3**	99.2	1.008	**57.6**	**47.3**	15614 55.4%	4055 14.4%	8550 30.3%	28219
aug-1gram	23.2	30.8	99.9	1.001	58.8	48.4	15387 54.2%	**4195** 14.8%	8831 31.1%	28413
aug-1gram-ant-filt	23.2	30.8	99.9	1.001	58.8	48.3	15387 54.2%	**4195** 14.8%	8831 31.1%	28413
MEDAR baseline	**13.6**	**18.7**	93.6	1.066	**67.6**	**61.3**	4924 53.0%	1563 16.8%	2800 30.1%	9287
aug-1gram	12.9	18.3	94.2	1.060	68.9	62.3	4894 52.0%	1710 18.2%	2815 29.9%	9419
aug-1gram-ant-filt	12.9	18.3	94.2	1.060	69.0	62.3	4891 51.9%	**1715** 18.2%	2815 29.9%	9421
135k-sentence (4M word) training dataset models										
MT05 baseline	25.8	33.5	99.2	1.008	55.7	45.3	16115 57.1%	3999 14.2%	8128 28.8%	28242
aug-1gram	**26.4**	**34.3**^{B}	99.5	1.005	**55.1**	**44.7**	16156 57.1%	4068 14.4%	8089 28.6%	28313
aug-1gram-ant-filt	**26.4**	**34.3**^{B}	99.5	1.005	**55.0**	**44.6**	16153 57.1%	**4090** 14.5%	8068 28.5%	28311
MEDAR baseline	17.1	23.1	94.7	1.054	65.1	58.6	5483 57.7%	1577 16.6%	2438 25.7%	9498
aug-1gram	**17.2**	**23.5**	95.3	1.048	65.1	58.6	5586 58.1%	**1606** 16.7%	2424 25.2%	9616
aug-1gram-ant-filt	**17.2**	**23.5**	95.3	1.048	65.1	58.6	5586 58.1%	**1606** 16.7%	2424 25.2%	9616

Table 2: English-Arabic translation scores and analysis for NIST MT05 and MEDAR test sets. B = statistically significant w.r.t. (B)aseline using Koehn (2004)'s statistical significance test.

bers from English are not directly comparable to the Chinese side: they relate to paraphrase candidates and not phrase table entries; they relate to types and not tokens; each OOV English word may translate to one or more Chinese words, each of which may comprise of one or more characters; and last but not least, the BLEU score we use is character-based.

phrase	||| paraphrase	||| score	comments
absence	||| occupation	||| 0.06	mild
absence	||| presence	||| 0.33	good
backwards	||| forwards	||| 0.21	good
wooden	||| plastic lawn	||| 0.12	sibling
dump	||| dispose of	||| 0.41	bad
cooler	||| warm	||| 0.45	mild
diminished	||| increased	||| 0.23	good
minor	||| serious	||| 0.42	good
relic	||| youth activist in the	||| 0.12	harmless
dive	||| rise	||| 0.15	good
argue	||| also recognize	||| 0.05	mild
bother	||| waste time	||| 0.79	bad
dive	||| climb	||| 0.17	good
moonlight	||| spring	||| 0.05	harmless
sharply	||| slightly	||| 0.60	good
substantial	||| meager	||| 0.14	good
warmer	||| cooler	||| 0.72	good
tough	||| delicate	||| 0.07	good
tiny	||| mostly muslim	||| 0.06	mild
softly	||| deep	||| 0.06	mild

Table 3: Random filtering examples

While individual unigram to 4gram scores for the augmented models were lower than the baseline's, filtered model's unigram and bigram scores were lower or similar to the baseline's, and their trigram and 4gram scores were higher than the baseline's. We intend to further investigate the cause for this pattern, and its effect on translation quality, with the help of a native Chinese speaker – and on BLEU, together with the brevity penalty – in the future.

English-Arabic: The most striking fact is the set of differences between the language pairs: In English-Chinese, we see gains with distributional paraphrase augmentation, and further gains when antonymous and contrasting paraphrase candidates are filtered out. But in the 30k-sentence English-Arabic models, paraphrase augmentation actually degrades performance, even in lemma scores. It has been observed before that BLEU (and similarly TER) is not ideal for evaluation of contributions of this sort (Callison-Burch et al., 2006). Therefore we conducted both manual and focused automatic analysis, including OOV statistics and unigram lemma match analysis[6]

[6]Unigram lemma match analysis is a classification of all the words in the translation hypothesis (against the translation reference) into: (a) exact match, which is equal to simple unigram precision, (b) lemma-only match, which counts words that can only be matched at the lemma level, and (c) unmatchable.

between the system output and the reference translation.

Table 4 shows that the OOV rates for English-Arabic are lower than English-Chinese. But if they were negligible, we would not expect to see gains (or in fact any change) in either model size, contrary to fact. It is interesting to point out that our translation model augmentation technique handles about 50% of the (non-digit, non-punctuation) OOV words in all models (except for only half that in the 135k model, which still showed gains).

Another concern is that the current maximal paraphrase length (6 tokens) may be too far from the paraphrasee's length (unigram), resulting in lower quality. However, a closer examination of the length difference evident through the BLEU brevity penalty and the reference:system-output length ratio (columns 4-5 of Table 2), reveals that the differences are small and inconsistent; on average, the brevity penalty difference accounts for roughly 0.1 absolute BLEU points and 0.2 absolute lemmatized BLEU points of the respective differences.[7]

Last, Modern Standard Arabic is a morphologically rich language: It has many inflected forms for most verbs, and several inflected forms for nouns, adjectives and other parts of speech – and complex syntactic agreement patterns showing these inflections. It might be the case that the inflected Arabic LM model might not serve well the augmented models, since they include translation rules that are more likely to be "off" inflection-wise (e.g., showing ungrammatical syntactic agreement or simply an acceptable choice that differs from the reference). Presumably, the smaller the training set, the larger this problem, since there would be fewer rules and hence smaller variety of inflected forms per similar core meaning. The unigram lemma match analysis and lemma scores' statistics (Table 2) support this concern. In the 30k model, lemma-only match seems to even further increase, at the expense of the exact word-form match. Possible solutions include using a lemma-based LM, or another LM that is adjusted to this sort of inflection-wise "off" text.

[7]These values are computed by subtracting the difference between two BLEU scores from the difference between the same two BLEU scores without the effect of brevity penalty (i.e., each divided by its brevity penalty).

Error Analysis We conducted an error analysis of our Arabic 30k system using part of the MT05 test set. That set had 571 OOV types, out of which, we were able to augment phrases for 196 OOV types. The majority of OOV words were proper nouns (67.8%), with the rest being mostly nouns, adjectives and verbs (in the order of their frequency). Among the OOVs for which we augmented phrases, the proper noun ratio was smaller than the full set (45.4% relative). We selected a random sample of 50 OOV words, and examined their translations in the MT05 test set. The analysis considered all the OOV word occurrences (96 sentences). We classified each OOV translation in the augmented system and the augmented-filtered system as follows:

- **a1** correct (and in reference)
- **a2** correct (morphological variation)
- **a3** acceptable translation into a synonym
- **a4** acceptable translation into a hypernym
- **b1** wrong translation into a hypernym
- **b2** co-hypernym: a sibling in a psychologically natural category hierarchy
- **b3** antonymous, trend-contrasting, or polarity dissimilar meaning
- **c1** wrong proper-noun translation (sibling)
- **c2** wrong proper-noun translation (other)
- **d** wrong translation for other reasons

Both the augmented and augmented-filtered system had 27.1% correct cases (category **a**). Only one-quarter of these were exact matches with the reference (category **a1**) that can be captured by BLEU. Incorrect proper-noun translation (category **c**) was the biggest error (augmented model: 33.3%, filtered model: 37.5%); within this category, sibling mistranslations (category **c1**), e.g., *Buddhism* is translated as *Islam*, were the majority (over half in augmented model, and about two-thirds in the filtered model). Proper nouns seem to be a much bigger problem for translation into Arabic than into Chinese in our sets. Category **b** mis-translations appeared in 20.8% of the time (equally in augmented and filtered). Almost half of these were sibling mistranslations (category **b2**), e.g., *diamond* translated as *gold*. Only two OOV translations in our sample were antonymous (category **b3**). It is possible, therefore, that our Arabic sets do not give room for our filtering method to be effective. In one case, the verb *deepen* (reference translation تعمق) is mistranslated as *summit* (قمة). In the other case, the adjective *cool (political relations)*, whose reference translation uses a figure of speech *periods of tension* (فترات من التوتر), is mistranslated as *good* (جيدة), which carries the opposite sentiment. The rest of category **b** involve hypernyms (**b1**), such as translating the OOV word *telecom* into *company* (الشركة).

Overall, the filtered model did not behave significantly differently from its augmented counterpart.

Chinese-Arabic score difference: We conjecture that another possible reason for the different score gain patterns between the two language pairs is the fact that in Chinese, many words that are siblings-in-meaning share a character, which doesn't necessarily have a stand-alone meaning; therefore, character-based BLEU was able to give credit to such paraphrases on the Chinese side, which was not case for the word-based BLEU on the Arabic side.

7 Related Work

This paper brings together several sub-areas: SMT, paraphrase generation, distributional semantic distance measures, and antonym-related work. Therefore we can only briefly survey the most relevant work here. Our work can be viewed as an extension of the line of research that seeks to augment translation tables with automatically generated paraphrases of OOV words or phrases in a fashion similar to Section 4: Callison-Burch et al. (2006) use pivoting technique (translating to other languages and back) in order to generate paraphrases, and the pivot translation probability as their similarity score; Callison-Burch (2008) filters such paraphrases using syntactic parsing information; Marton et al. (2009) use distributional paraphrasing technique that applies distributional semantic distance measure for the paraphrase score; Marton (2010) applies a lexical resource / corpus-based hybrid semantic distance measure for the paraphrase score instead, approximating word senses; here, we apply a distributional semantic distance measure that is similar to Marton et al. (2009), with the main difference being the filtering of the resulting paraphrases for antonymity.

Other work on augmentating SMT: Habash and Hu (2009) show, pivoting via a trilingual parallel text, that using English as a pivot language between Chinese and Arabic outperforms translation using a direct Chinese-Arabic bilingual parallel text. Other attempts to reduce the OOV rate by augmenting the phrase table's source side include Habash (2009), providing an online tool for paraphrasing OOV phrases by lexical and morphological expansion of known phrases and dictionary terms – and transliteration of proper names.

Bond et al. (2008) also pivot for paraphrasing. They improve SMT coverage by using a manually crafted monolingual HPSG grammar for generating meaning and grammar-preserving paraphrases. This grammar allows for certain word reordering, lexical substitutions, contractions, and "typo" corrections.

Onishi et al. (2010), Du et al. (2010), and others, pivot-paraphrase the input, and represent the paraphrases in a lattice format, decoding it with Moses.

Work on paraphrase generation: Barzilay and McKeown (2001) extract paraphrases from a monolingual parallel corpus, containing multiple translations of the same source. However, monolingual parallel corpora are extremely rare and small. Dolan et al. (2004) use edit distance for paraphrasing. Max (2009) and others take the context of the paraphrased word's occurrence into account. Zhao et al. (2008) apply SMT-style decoding for paraphrasing, using several log linear weighted resources while Zhao et al. (2009) filter out paraphrase candidates and weight paraphrase features according to the desired NLP task. Chevelu et al. (2009) introduce a new paraphrase generation tool based on Monte-Carlo sampling. Mirkin et al. (2009), *inter alia*, frame paraphrasing as a special, symmetrical case of (WordNet-based) textual entailment. See Madnani and Dorr (2010) for a good paraphrasing survey.

Work on measuring distributional semantic distance: For one survey of this rich topic, see Weeds et al. (2004) and Turney and Pantel (2010). We use here cosine of log-likelihood ratios (McDonald, 2000). A recent paper (Kazama et al., 2010) advocates a Bayesian approach, making rare terms have lower strength of association, as a by-product of relying on their probabilistic Expectation.

Work on detecting antonyms: Our work with antonyms can be thought of as an application-based extension of the (Mohammad et al., 2008) method. Some of the earliest computational work in this area is by Lin et al. (2003) who used patterns

model	e2z:29k		e2z:232k		e2a:30k		e2a:135k	
phrase table baseline vocab. (# source-side types)	13916		34825		24371		49854	
phrase table entries: baseline	1996k		13045k		2606k		12344k	
phrase table entries: aug-1gram	2543k	127.38%	13615k	104.37%	2635k	101.09%	*12373k	100.23%
phrase table entries: aug-1gram-ant-filt	2542k	127.35%	13615k	104.37%	2635k	101.09%	*12373k	100.23%
OOV types in tune (% tune types)	1097	21.58%	451	8.87%	141	7.31%	84	4.35%
OOV tokens in tune (% tune tokens)	2138	6.10%	917	2.62%	193	2.18%	115	1.30%
OOV types in test (% test types)	2473	33.59%	1227	16.66%	574	12.42%	339	7.34%
OOV tokens in test (% test tokens)	4844	10.40%	2075	4.46%	992	2.83%	544	1.55%
tune OOV token decrease in aug-1gram/ant-filt	1343	27.73%	510	24.58%	79	7.96%	28	5.15%
tune OOV type decrease in aug-1gram/ant-filt	646	58.89%	203	45.01%	60	42.55%	22	26.19%
test OOV token decrease in aug-1gram /ant-filt	2776	57.31%	996	48.00%	460	46.37%	127	23.35%
test OOV type decrease in aug-1gram/ant-filt	1394	56.37%	585	47.68%	246	42.86%	76	22.42%

Table 4: Out-of-vocabulary (OOV) word rates and phrase table sizes for all model sizes and language pairs. e2z = English-Chinese; e2a = English-Arabic. The statistics marked with * in the top-right cell are identical, see §5.3.

such as "from *X* to *Y*" and "either *X* or *Y*" to distinguish between antonymous and similar word pairs. Harabagiu et al. (2006) detected antonyms by determining if their WordNet synsets are connected by the hypernymy–hyponymy links and exactly one antonymy link. Turney (2008) proposed a supervised method to solve word analogy questions that require identifying synonyms, antonyms, hypernyms, and other lexical-semantic relations between word pairs.

8 Conclusions and Future Work

We presented here a novel method for filtering out antonymous phrasal paraphrase candidates, adapted from sentiment analysis literature, and tested in simulated low- and mid-resourced SMT tasks from English to two quite different languages. We used an antonymous word pair list extracted distributionally by extending a seed list. Then, the extended list, together with a negator list and a novel heuristic, were used to filter out antonymous paraphrase candidates. Finally, SMT models were augmented with the filtered paraphrases, yielding English-Chinese translation improvements of up to 1 BLEU from the corresponding non-filtered paraphrase-augmented model (up to 1.6 BLEU from the corresponding baseline model). Our method proved effective for models trained on both reduced and mid-large English-Chinese parallel texts. The reduced models simulated "low density" languages by limiting the amount of the training text.

We also showed for the first time translation gains for English-Arabic with paraphrase-augmented (non-filtered) models. However, Arabic, and presumably other morphologically rich languages, may require more complex models in order to benefit from our filtering method.

Our antonym detection and filtering method is distributional and heuristic-based; hence it is noisy. We suspect that OOV terms in larger models tend to be harder to paraphrase (judging by the difference from the reduced models, and the lower OOV rate), and also harder to filter paraphrase candidates of (due to the lower paraphrase quality, which might not even include sufficiently distributionally similar candidates, antonymous or otherwise). In the future, we intend to improve our method, so that it can be used to improve also the quality of models trained on even larger parallel texts.

Last, we intend to extend our method beyond unigrams, limit paraphrase length to the vicinity of the paraphrasee's length, and improve our inflected Arabic generation technique, so it can handle this novel type of augmented data well.

Acknowledgments

Part of this work was done while the first author was at Columbia University. The second author was funded through a Google research award. The authors wish to thank Saif Mohammad for providing his data and for useful discussion, and also thank the anonymous reviewers for their useful feedback.

References

Regina Barzilay and Kathleen McKeown. 2001. Extracting paraphrases from a parallel corpus. In *Proceedings of the Association for Computational Linguistics (ACL)*.

Isaac I. Bejar, Roger Chaffin, and Susan Embretson. 1991. *Cognitive and Psychometric Analysis of Analogical Problem Solving*. Springer-Verlag, New York, NY.

Francis Bond, Eric Nichols, Darren Scott Appling, and Michael Paul. 2008. Improving statistical machine translation by paraphrasing the training data. In *Proceedings of IWSLT*, Hawai'i, USA.

Lou Burnard. 2000. *Reference Guide for the British National Corpus (World Edition)*. Oxford University Computing Services.

Chris Callison-Burch, Philipp Koehn, and Miles Osborne. 2006. Improved statistical machine translation using paraphrases. In *Proceedings of the North American Chapter of the Association for Computational Linguistics (NAACL)*.

Chris Callison-Burch. 2008. Syntactic constraints on paraphrases extracted from parallel corpora. In *Proceedings of the Conference on Empirical Methods in Natural Language Processing (EMNLP)*, Waikiki, Hawai'i.

Jonathan Chevelu, Thomas Lavergne, Yves Lepage, and Thierry Moudenc. 2009. Introduction of a new paraphrase generation tool based on monte-carlo sampling. In *Proceedings of the 47th Annual Meeting of the Association for Computational Linguistics (ACL) - the 4th International Joint Conference on Natural Language Processing of the Asian Federation of Natural Language Processing (IJCNLP) Short Papers*, pages 249–252, Suntec, Singapore.

Yejin Choi and Claire Cardie. 2008. Learning with compositional semantics as structural inference for subsentential sentiment analysis. In *Proceedings of Empirical Methods in Natural Language Processing (EMNLP)*, Waikiki, Hawaii.

David A. Cruse. 1986. *Lexical semantics*. Cambridge University Press.

James Deese. 1965. *The structure of associations in language and thought*. The Johns Hopkins Press.

Bill Dolan, Chris Quirk, and Chris Brockett. 2004. Unsupervised construction of large paraphrase corpora: exploiting massively parallel news sources. In *Proceedings of the 20th Annual Meeting of the Association for Computational Linguistics (ACL)*, Geneva, Switzerland.

Jinhua Du, Jie Jiang, and Andy Way. 2010. Facilitating translation using source language paraphrase lattices. In *Proceedings of the Conference on Empirical Methods in Natural Language Processing (EMNLP)*, pages 420–429, MIT, Massachusetts, USA.

Ahmed El Kholy and Nizar Habash. 2010a. Techniques for Arabic Morphological Detokenization and Orthographic Denormalization. In *Proceedings of the seventh International Conference on Language Resources and Evaluation (LREC)*, Valletta, Malta.

Ahmed El Kholy and Nizar Habash. 2010b. Orthographic and Morphological Processing for English-Arabic Statistical Machine Translation. In *In Actes de Traitement Automatique des Langues Naturelles (TALN)*, Montreal, Canada.

Nizar Habash and Jun Hu. 2009. Improving Arabic-Chinese statistical machine translation using English as pivot language. In *Proceedings of the 4th EACL Workshop on Statistical Machine Translation*, pages 173–181, Athens, Greece.

Nizar Habash and Owen Rambow. 2005. Arabic Tokenization, Part-of-Speech Tagging and Morphological Disambiguation in One Fell Swoop. In *Proceedings of the 43rd Annual Meeting of the Association for Computational Linguistics (ACL)*, pages 573–580, Ann Arbor, Michigan, June. Association for Computational Linguistics.

Nizar Habash. 2009. REMOOV: A tool for online handling of out-of-vocabulary words in machine translation. In *Proceedings of the 2nd International Conference on Arabic Language Resources and Tools (MEDAR)*, Cairo, Egypt.

Sanda M. Harabagiu, Andrew Hickl, and Finley Lacatusu. 2006. Lacatusu: Negation, contrast and contradiction in text processing. In *Proceedings of the 23rd National Conference on Artificial Intelligence (AAAI)*, Boston, MA.

Junichi Kazama, Stijn De Saeger, Kow Kuroda, Masaki Murata, and Kentaro Torisawa. 2010. A Bayesian method for robust estimation of distributional similarities. In *Proceedings of the 48th Annual Meeting of the Association for Computational Linguistics (ACL)*, pages 247–256, Uppsala, Sweden.

Alistair Kennedy and Diana Inkpen. 2005. Sentiment classification of movie and product reviews using contextual valence shifters. *COMPUTATIONAL INTELLIGENCE*, pages 110–125.

Philipp Koehn, Hieu Hoang, Alexandra Birch, Chris Callison-Burch, Marcello Federico, Nicola Bertoldi, Brooke Cowan, Wade Shen, Christine Moran Richard Zens, Chris Dyer, Ondrej Bojar, Alexandra Constantin, and Evan Herbst. 2007. Moses: Open source toolkit for statistical machine translation. In *the Annual Meeting of the Association for Computational Linguistics (ACL) demonstration session*, Prague, Czech Republic.

Philipp Koehn. 2004. Statistical significance tests for

machine translation evaluation. In *Proceedings of the Conference on Empirical Methods in Natural Language Processing (EMNLP)*.

Adrienne Lehrer and K. Lehrer. 1982. Antonymy. *Linguistics and Philosophy*, 5:483–501.

Dekang Lin, Shaojun Zhao, Lijuan Qin, and Ming Zhou. 2003. Identifying synonyms among distributionally similar words. In *Proceedings of the 18th International Joint Conference on Artificial Intelligence (IJCAI)*, pages 1492–1493, Acapulco, Mexico.

Nitin Madnani and Bonnie Dorr. 2010. Generating phrasal and sentential paraphrases: A survey of data-driven methods. *Computational Linguistics*, 36(3).

Marie-Catherine de Marneffe, Anna Rafferty, and Christopher D. Manning. 2008. Finding contradictions in text. In *Proceedings of the 46th Annual Meeting of the Association for Computational Linguistics (ACL)*, Columbus, OH.

Yuval Marton, Chris Callison-Burch, and Philip Resnik. 2009. Improved statistical machine translation using monolingually-derived paraphrases. In *Proceedings of the Conference on Empirical Methods in Natural Language Processing (EMNLP)*, Singapore.

Yuval Marton. 2010. Improved statistical machine translation using monolingual text and a shallow lexical resource for hybrid phrasal paraphrase generation. In *Proceedings of the Ninth Conference of the Association for Machine Translation in the Americas (AMTA)*, Denver, Colorado.

Aurelien Max. 2009. Sub-sentential paraphrasing by contextual pivot translation. In *Proceedings of the 47th Annual Meeting of the Association for Computational Linguistics (ACL) - the 4th International Joint Conference on Natural Language Processing of the Asian Federation of Natural Language Processing (IJCNLP) - Workshop on Applied Textual Inference*, pages 18–26, Singapore. Suntec.

Scott McDonald. 2000. *Environmental determinants of lexical processing effort*. Ph.D. thesis, University of Edinburgh.

Rada Mihalcea and Carlo Strapparava. 2005. Making computers laugh: Investigations in automatic humor recognition. In *Proceedings of the Conference on Human Language Technology and Empirical Methods in Natural Language Processing*, pages 531–538, Vancouver, Canada.

Shachar Mirkin, Lucia Specia, Nicola Cancedda, Ido Dagan, Marc Dymetman, and Idan Szpektor . 2009. Source-language entailment modeling for translating unknown terms. In *Proceedings of the 47th Annual Meeting of the Association for Computational Linguistics (ACL) - the 4th International Joint Conference on Natural Language Processing of the Asian Federation of Natural Language Processing (IJCNLP)*, pages 791–799, Suntec, Singapore.

Saif Mohammad, Bonnie Dorr, and Codie Dunn. 2008. Computing word-pair antonymy. In *Proceedings of the Conference on Empirical Methods in Natural Language Processing (EMNLP)*, pages 982–991, Waikiki, Hawaii.

Franz Josef Och and Hermann Ney. 2000. Improved statistical alignment models. In *Proceedings of the 38th Annual Meeting of the Association for Computational Linguistics (ACL)*, pages 440–447.

Franz Josef Och and Hermann Ney. 2002. Discriminative training and maximum entropy models for statistical machine translation. In *Proceedings of ACL*.

Franz Josef Och. 2003. Minimum error rate training in statistical machine translation. In *Proceedings of the 41st Annual Meeting of the ACL*, pages 160–167.

Takashi Onishi, Masao Utiyama, and Eiichiro Sumita. 2010. Paraphrase lattice for statistical machine translation. In *Proceedings of the Association for Computational Linguistics (ACL) Short Papers*, pages 1–5, Uppsala, Sweden.

Bo Pang and Lillian Lee. 2008. Opinion mining and sentiment analysis. *Foundations and Trends in Information Retrieval*, 2(1–2):1–135.

Kishore Papineni, Salim Roukos, Todd Ward, John Henderson, and Florence Reeder. 2002. Corpus-based comprehensive and diagnostic MT evaluation: Initial Arabic, Chinese, French, and Spanish results. In *Proceedings of the ACL Human Language Technology Conference*, pages 124–127, San Diego, CA.

Matthew Snover, Bonnie Dorr, Richard Schwartz, Linnea Micciulla, and John Makhoul. 2006. A study of translation edit rate with targeted human annotation. In *Proceedings of Association for Machine Translation in the Americas*, pages 223–231, Cambridge, MA.

Andreas Stolcke. 2002. SRILM – an extensible language modeling toolkit. In *Proceedings of the International Conference on Spoken Language Processing*, volume 2, pages 901–904.

Philip Stone, Dexter C. Dunphy, Marshall S. Smith, Daniel M. Ogilvie, and associates. 1966. *The General Inquirer: A Computer Approach to Content Analysis*. The MIT Press.

Huihsin Tseng, Pichuan Chang, Galen Andrew, Daniel Jurafsky, and Christopher Manning. 2005. A conditional random field word segmenter. In *Fourth SIGHAN Workshop on Chinese Language Processing*.

Peter D. Turney and Patrick Pantel. 2010. From frequency to meaning: Vector space models of semantics. *Journal of Articial Intelligence Research*, 37:141–188.

Peter Turney. 2008. A uniform approach to analogies, synonyms, antonyms, and associations. In *Proceedings of the 22nd International Conference on Computational Linguistics (COLING)*, pages 905–912, Manchester, UK.

Ellen M Voorhees. 2008. Contradictions and justifications: Extensions to the textual entailment task. In *Proceedings of the 46th Annual Meeting of the Association for Computational Linguistics (ACL)*, Columbus, OH.

Julie Weeds, David Weir, and Diana McCarthy. 2004. Characterising measures of lexical distributional similarity. In *Proceedings of the 20th International Conference on Computational Linguistics (COLING)*, pages 1015–1021, Geneva, Switzerland.

Shiqi Zhao, Cheng Niu, Ming Zhou, Ting Liu, and Sheng Li. 2008. Combining multiple resources to improve smt-based paraphrasing model. In *Proceedings of the Association for Computational Linguistics (ACL)Human Language Technology (HLT)*, pages 1021–1029, Columbus, Ohio, USA.

Shiqi Zhao, Xiang Lan, Ting Liu, and Sheng Li. 2009. Application-driven statistical paraphrase generation. In *Proceedings of the 47th Annual Meeting of the Association for Computational Linguistics (ACL) - the 4th International Joint Conference on Natural Language Processing of the Asian Federation of Natural Language Processing (IJCNLP)*, pages 834–842, Suntec, Singapore.

Productive Generation of Compound Words in Statistical Machine Translation

Sara Stymne
Linköping University
Linköping, Sweden
sara.stymne@liu.se

Nicola Cancedda
Xerox Research Centre Europe
Meylan, France
nicola.cancedda@xrce.xerox.com

Abstract

In many languages the use of compound words is very productive. A common practice to reduce sparsity consists in splitting compounds in the training data. When this is done, the system incurs the risk of translating components in non-consecutive positions, or in the wrong order. Furthermore, a post-processing step of *compound merging* is required to reconstruct compound words in the output. We present a method for increasing the chances that components that should be merged are translated into contiguous positions and in the right order. We also propose new heuristic methods for merging components that outperform all known methods, and a learning-based method that has similar accuracy as the heuristic method, is better at producing novel compounds, and can operate with no background linguistic resources.

1 Introduction

In many languages including most of the Germanic (German, Swedish etc.) and Uralic (Finnish, Hungarian etc.) language families so-called closed compounds are used productively. Closed compounds are written as single words without spaces or other word boundaries, as the Swedish:

gatstenshuggare	*gata + sten + huggare*
paving stone cutter	*street stone cutter*

To cope with the productivity of the phenomenon, any effective strategy should be able to correctly process compounds that have never been seen in the training data as such, although possibly their components have, either in isolation or within a different compound.

The extended use of compounds make them problematic for machine translation. For translation into a compounding language, often fewer compounds than in normal texts are produced. This can be due to the fact that the desired compounds are missing in the training data, or that they have not been aligned correctly. When a compound is the idiomatic word choice in the translation, a MT system can often produce separate words, genitive or other alternative constructions, or translate only one part of the compound.

Most research on compound translation in combination with SMT has been focused on translation *from* a compounding language, into a non-compounding one, typically into English. A common strategy then consists in splitting compounds into their components prior to training and translation.

Only few have investigated translation into a compounding language. For translation into a compounding language, the process becomes:

- Splitting compounds on the target (compounding language) side of the training corpus;
- Learn a translation model from this split training corpus from source (e.g. English) into decomposed-target (e.g. decomposed-German)
- At translation time, translate using the learned model from source into decomposed-target.
- Apply a post-processing "merge" step to reconstruct compounds.

The merging step must solve two problems: identify which words should be merged into compounds, and choose the correct form of the compound parts.

Proceedings of the 6th Workshop on Statistical Machine Translation, pages 250–260,
Edinburgh, Scotland, UK, July 30–31, 2011. ©2011 Association for Computational Linguistics

The former problem can become hopelessly difficult if the translation did not put components nicely side by side and in the correct order. Preliminary to merging, then, the problem of promoting translations where compound elements are correctly positioned needs to be addressed. We call this promoting compound *coalescence*.

2 Related work

The first suggestion of a compound merging method for MT that we are aware of was described by Popović et al. (2006). Each word in the translation output is looked up in a list of compound parts, and merged with the next word if it results in a known compound. This method led to improved overall translation results from English to German. Stymne (2008) suggested a merging method based on part-of-speech matching, in a factored translation system, where compound parts had a special part-of-speech tag, and compound parts are only merged with the next word if the part-of-speech tags match. This resulted in improved translation quality from English to German, and from English to Swedish (Stymne and Holmqvist, 2008). Another method, based on several decoding runs, was investigated by Fraser (2009).

Stymne (2009a) investigated and compared merging methods inspired by Popović et al. (2006), Stymne (2008) and a method inspired by morphology merging (El-Kahlout and Oflazer, 2006; Virpioja et al., 2007), where compound parts were annotated with symbols, and parts with symbols in the translation output were merged with the next word.

3 Promoting coalescence of compounds

If compounds are split in the training set, then there is no guarantee that translations of components will end up in contiguous positions and in the correct order. This is primarily a language model problem, and we will model it as such by applying POS language models on specially designed part-of-speech sets, and by applying language model inspired count features.

The approach proposed in Stymne (2008) consists in running a POS tagger on the target side of the corpus, decompose only tokens with some predefined POS (e.g. Nouns), and then marking with special POS-tags whether an element is a head or a modifier. As an example, the German compound "Fremdsprachenkenntnisse", originally tagged as N(oun), would be decomposed and re-tagged before training as:

fremd	sprachen	kenntnisse
N-Modif	N-Modif	N

A POS n-gram language model using these extended tagset, then, naturally steers the decoder towards translations with good relative placement of these components

We modify this approach by blurring distinctions among POS not relevant to the formation of compounds, thus further reducing the tagset to only three tags:

- N-p – all parts of a split compound except the last
- N – the last part of the compound (its head) and all other nouns
- X – all other tokens

The above scheme assumes that only noun compounds are treated but it could easily be extended to other types of compounds. Alternatively, splitting can be attempted irrespective of POS on all tokens longer than a fixed threshold, removing the need of a POS tagger.

3.1 Sequence models as count features

We expect a POS-based n-gram language model on our reduced tagset to learn to discourage sequences unseen in the training data, such as the sequence of compound parts not followed by a suitable head. Such a generative LM, however, might also have a tendency to bias lexical selection towards translations with fewer compounds, since the corresponding tag sequences might be more common in text. To compensate for this bias, we experiment with injecting a little dose of a-priori knowledge, and add a count feature, which explicitly counts the number of occurrences of POS-sequences which we deem good and bad in the translation output.

Table 1 gives an overview of the possible bigram combinations, using the three symbol tagset, plus sentence beginning and end markers, and their judgment as good, bad or neutral.

Combination	Judgment
N-p N-p	Good
N-p N	Good
N-p $< \backslash s >$	Bad
N-p X	Bad
all other combinations	Neutral

Table 1: Tag combinations in the translation output

We define two new feature functions: one counting the number of occurrences of Good sequences (the *Boost model*) and the other counting the occurrences of Bad sequences (the *Punish model*). The two models can be used either in isolation or combined, with or without a further POS n-gram language model.

4 Merging compounds

Once a translation is generated using a system trained on split compounds, a post-processing step is required to merge components back into compounds. For all pairs of consecutive tokens we have to decide whether to combine them or not. Depending on the language and on preprocessing choices, we might also have to decide whether to apply any boundary transformation like e.g. inserting an 's' between components.

The method proposed in Popović et al. (2006) maintains a list of known compounds and compound modifiers. For any pair of consecutive tokens, if the first is in the list of known modifiers and the combination of the two is in the list of compounds, than the two tokens are merged.

A somewhat orthogonal approach is the one proposed in Stymne (2008): tokens are labeled with POS-tags; compound modifiers are marked with special POS-tags based on the POS of the head. If a word with a modifier POS-tag is followed by either another modifier POS-tag of the same type, or the corresponding head POS-tag, then the two tokens are merged.

In the following sections we describe how we modify and combine these two heuristics, and how we alternatively formulate the problem as a sequence labelling problem suitable for a machine learning approach.

4.1 Improving and combining heuristics

We empirically verified that the simple heuristics in Popović et al. (2006) tends to misfire quite often, leading to too many compounds. We modify it by adding an additional check: tokens are merged if they appear combined in the list of compounds, but only if their observed frequency as a compound is larger than their frequency as a bigram. This blocks the merging of many consecutive words, which just happen to form a, often unrelated, compound when merged, such as *för små* (*too small*) into *försmå* (*spurn*) in Swedish. Compound and bigram frequencies can be computed on any available monolingual corpus in the domain of interest.

We furthermore observed that the (improved) list-based heuristic and the method based on POS patterns lead to complementary sets of false negatives. We thus propose to combine the two heuristics in this way: we merge two consecutive tokens if they would be combined by either the list-based heuristic or the POS-based heuristic. We empirically verified improved performance when combining heuristics in this way (Section 5.2).

4.2 Compound merging as sequence labelling

Besides extending and combining existing heuristics, we propose a novel formulation of compound merging as a sequence labelling problem. The opposite problem, compound splitting, has successfully been cast as a sequence labelling problem before (Dyer, 2010), but here we apply this formulation in the opposite direction.

Depending on choices made at compound splitting time, this task can be either a binary or multiclass classification task. If compound parts were kept as-is, the merging task is a simple concatenation of two words, and each separation point must receive a binary label encoding whether the two tokens should be merged. An option at splitting time is to normalize compound parts, which often have a morphological form specific to compounds, to a canonical form (Stymne, 2009b). In this case the compound form has to be restored before concatenating the parts. This can be modeled as a multiclass classifier that have the possible boundary transformations as its classes.

Consider for instance translating into German the

English sentence:

> Europe should promote the knowledge of foreign languages

Assuming that the training corpus did not contain occurrences of the pair ("knowledge of foreign languages","fremdsprachenkenntnisse") but contained occurrences of ("knowledge","kenntnisse"), ("foreign","fremd") and ("languages","sprachen"), then the translation model from English into decomposed-German could be able to produce:

> Europa sollte fremd sprachen kenntnisse fördern

We cast the problem of merging compounds as one of making a series of correlated binary decisions, one for each pair of consecutive words, each deciding whether the whitespace between the two words should be suppressed (label "1") or not (label "0"). In the case above, the correct labelling for the sentence would be $\{0,0,1,1,0\}$, reconstructing the correct German:

> Europa sollte fremdsprachenkenntnisse fördern[1]

If conversely, components are normalized upon splitting, then labels are no longer binary, but come from a set describing all local orthographic transformations possible for the language under consideration. In this work we limited our attention to the case when compounds are not normalized upon splitting, and labels are hence binary.

While in principle one could address each atomic merging decision independently, it seems intuitive that a decision taken at one point should influence merging decisions in neighboring separation points. For this reason, instead of a simple (binary or n-ary) classification problem, we prefer a sequence labelling formulation.

The array of sequence labelling algorithms potentially suitable to our problem is fairly broad, including Hidden Markov Models (HMMs) (Rabiner, 1989), Conditional Random Fields (CRFs) (Lafferty et al., 2001), structured perceptrons (Collins, 2002), and more. Since the focus of this work is on the application rather than on a comparison among alternative structured learning approaches, we limited ourselves to a single implementation. Considering its good scaling capabilities, appropriateness in presence of strongly redundant and overlapping features, and widespread recognition in the NLP community, we chose to use Conditional Random Fields.

4.2.1 Features

Each sequence item (i.e. each separation point between words) is represented by means of a sparse vector of features. We used:

- Surface words: word-1, word+1
- Part-of-speech: POS-1, POS+1
- Character n-grams around the merge point
  - 3 character suffix of word-1
  - 3 character prefix of word+1
  - Combinations crossing the merge points: 1+3, 3+1, 3+3 characters
- Normalized character n-grams around the merge point, where characters are replaced by phonetic approximations, and grouped according to phonetic distribution, see Figure 1 (only for Swedish)
- Frequencies from the training corpus, binned by the following method:

$$\bar{f} = \begin{cases} 10\lfloor \log_{10}(f) \rfloor & \text{if } f > 1 \\ f & \text{otherwise} \end{cases}$$

  for the following items:
  - bigram, word-1,word+1
  - Compound resulting from merging word-1,word+1
  - Word-1 as a true prefix of words in the corpus
  - Word+1 as a true suffix of words in the corpus
- Frequency comparisons of two different frequencies in the training corpus, classified into four categories: freq1 = freq2 = 0, freq1 < freq2, freq1 = freq2, freq1 > freq2

[1] Nouns in German are capitalized. This is normally dealt as a further "truecasing" postprocessing, and is an orthogonal problem from the one we deal with here.

```
# vowels (soft versus hard)
$word =  s/[aouå]/a/g;
$word =  s/[eiyäöé]/e/g;

# consonant combinations and
# spelling alternations
$word =  s/ng/N/g;
$word =  s/gn/G/g;
$word =  s/ck/K/g;
$word =  s/[lhgd]j/J/g;
$word =  s/^ge/Je/g;
$word =  s/^ske/Se/g;
$word =  s/^s[kt]?j/S/g;
$word =  s/^s?ch/S/g;
$word =  s/^tj/T/g;
$word =  s/^ke/Te/g;

#consonants grouping
$word =  s/[ptk]/p/g;
$word =  s/[bdg]/b/g;
$word =  s/[lvw]/l/g;
$word =  s/[cqxz]/q/g;
```

Figure 1: Transformations performed for normalizing Swedish consonants (Perl notation).

- word-1,word+1 as bigram vs compound
- word-1 as true prefix vs single word
- word+1 as true suffix vs single word

where -1 refers to the word before the merge point, and +1 to the word after.

We aimed to include features representing the knowledge available to the list and POS heuristics, by including part-of-speech tags and frequencies for compounds and bigrams, as well as a comparison between them. Features were also inspired by previous work on compound splitting, based on the intuition that features that are useful for splitting compounds, could also be useful for merging. Character n-grams has successfully been used for splitting Swedish compounds, as the only knowledge source by Brodda (1979), and as one of several knowledge sources by Sjöbergh and Kann (2004). Friberg (2007) tried to normalize letters, beside using the original letters. While she was not successful, we still believe in the potential of this feature. Larson et al. (2000), used frequencies of prefixes and suffixes from a corpus, as a basis of their method for splitting German compounds.

4.2.2 Training data for the sequence labeler

Since features are strongly lexicalized, a suitably large training dataset is required to prevent overfitting, ruling out the possibility of manual labelling.

We created our training data automatically, using the two heuristics described earlier, plus a third one enabled by the availability, when estimating parameters for the CRF, of a reference translation: merge if two tokens are observed combined in the reference translation (possibly as a sub-sequence of a longer word). We compared multiple alternative combinations of heuristics on a validation dataset. The validation and test data were created by applying all heuristics, and then manually check all positive annotations.

A first possibility to automatically generate a training dataset consists in applying the compound splitting preprocessing of choice to the target side of the parallel training corpus for the SMT system: separation points where merges should occur are thus trivially identified. In practice, however, merging decisions will need be taken on the noisy output of the SMT system, and not on the clean training data. To acquire training data that is similar to the test data, we could have held out from SMT training a large fraction of the training data, used the trained SMT to translate the source side of it, and then label decision points according to the heuristics. This would, however, imply making a large fraction of the data unavailable to training of the SMT. We thus settled for a compromise: we trained the SMT system on the whole training data, translated the whole source, then labeled decision points according to the heuristics. The translations we obtain are thus biased, of higher quality than those we should expect to obtain on unseen data. Nevertheless they are substantially more similar to what will be observed in operations than the reference translations.

5 Experiments

We performed experiments on translation from English into Swedish and Danish on two different corpora, an automotive corpus collected from a proprietary translation memory, and on Europarl (Koehn, 2005) for the merging experiments. We used factored translation (Koehn and Hoang, 2007), with both surface words and part-of-speech tags on the

	EU-Sv	Auto-Sv	Auto-Da
Corpus	Europarl	Automotive	Automotive
Languages	English→Swedish	English→Swedish	English→Danish
Compounds split	N, V, Adj	N, V, Adj	N
POS tag-sets	POS	POS,RPOS	RPOS
Decoder	Moses	in-house	in-house
Training sentences SMT	1,520,549	329,090	168,047
Training words SMT (target)	34,282,247	3,061,282	1,553,382
Training sentences CRF	248,808	317,398	164,702
Extra training sentences CRF	3,000	3,000	163,201

Table 2: Overview of the experimental settings

target side, with a sequence model on part-of-speech. We used two decoders, Matrax (Simard et al., 2005) and Moses (Koehn et al., 2007), both standard statistical phrase based decoders. For parameter optimization we used minimum error rate training (Och, 2003) with Moses and gradient ascent on smoothed NIST for the in-house decoder. In the merging experiments we used the CRF++ toolkit.[2]

Compounds were split before training using a corpus-based method (Koehn and Knight, 2003; Stymne, 2008). For each word we explored all possible segmentations into parts that had at least 3 characters, and choose the segmentation which had the highest arithmetic mean of frequencies for each part in the training corpus. We constrained the splitting based on part-of-speech by only allowing splitting options where the compound head had the same tag as the full word. The split compound parts kept their form, which can be special to compounds, and no symbols or other markup were added.

The experiment setup is summarized in Table 2. The extra training sentences for CRF are sentences that were not also used to train the SMT system. For tuning, test and validation data we used 1,000 sentence sets, except for Swedish auto, where we used 2,000 sentences for tuning. In the Swedish experiments we split nouns, adjectives and verbs, and used the full POS-set, except in the coalescence experiments where we compared the full and restricted POS-sets. For Danish we only split nouns, and used the restricted POS-set. For frequency calculations of compounds and compound parts that were needed for compound splitting and some of the compound merging strategies, we used the respective training data in all cases. Significance testing was performed using approximate randomization (Riezler and Maxwell, 2005), with 10,000 iterations, and $\alpha < 0.05$.

[2]Available at `http://crfpp.sourceforge.net/`

5.1 Experiments: Promoting compound coalescence

We performed experiments with factored translation models with the restricted part-of-speech set on the Danish and Swedish automotive corpus. In these experiments we compared the restricted part-of-speech set we suggest in this work to several baseline systems without any compound processing and with factored models using the extended part-of-speech set suggested by Stymne (2008). Compound parts were merged using the POS-based heuristic. Results are reported on two standard metrics, NIST (Doddington, 2002) and Bleu (Papineni et al., 2002), on lower-cased data. For all sequence models we use 3-grams.

Results on the two Automotive corpora are summarized in Table 3. The scores are very high, which is due to the fact that it is an easy domain with many repetitive sentence types. On the Danish dataset, we observe significant improvements in BLEU and NIST over the baseline for all methods where compounds were split before translation and merged afterwards. Some of the gain is already obtained using a language model on the extended part-of-speech set. Additional gains can however be obtained using instead a language model on a reduced set of POS-tags (RPOS), and with a count feature explicitly boosting desirable RPOS sequences. The count feature on undesirable sequences did not bring any improvements over any of the systems with compound splitting.

Results on the Swedish automotive corpus are less clear-cut than for Danish, with mostly insignificant differences between systems. The system with decomposition and a restricted part-of-speech model is significantly better on Bleu than all other systems, except the system with decomposition and a standard part-of-speech model. Not splitting actually gives the highest NIST score, even though the difference to the other systems is not significant, except for the system with a combination of a trained RPOS model and a boost model, which also has significantly lower Bleu score than the other systems with compound splitting.

5.2 Experiments: Compound merging

We compared alternative combinations of heuristics on our three validation datasets, see Figure 2. In order to estimate the amount of false negatives for all three heuristics, we inspected the first 100 sentences of each validation set, looking for words that should be merged, but were not marked by any of the heuristics. In no case we could find any such words, so we thus assume that between them, the heuristics can find the overwhelming majority of all compounds to be merged.

We conducted a round of preliminary experiments to identify the best combination of the heuristics available at training time (modified list-based, POS-based, and reference-based) to use to create automatically the training data for the CRF. Best results on the validation data are obtained by different combination of heuristics for the three datasets, as could be expected by the different distribution of errors in Figure 2. In the experiments below we trained the CRF using for each dataset the combination of heuristics corresponding to leaving out the grey portions of the Venn diagrams. This sort of preliminary optimization requires hand-labelling a certain amount of data. Based on our experiments, skipping this optimization and just using ref$\vee$(list$\wedge$POS) (the optimal configuration for the Swedish-English Europarl corpus) seems to be a reasonable alternative.

The validation data was also used to set a frequency cut-off for feature occurrences (set at 3 in the following experiments) and to tune the regularization parameter in the CRF objective function.

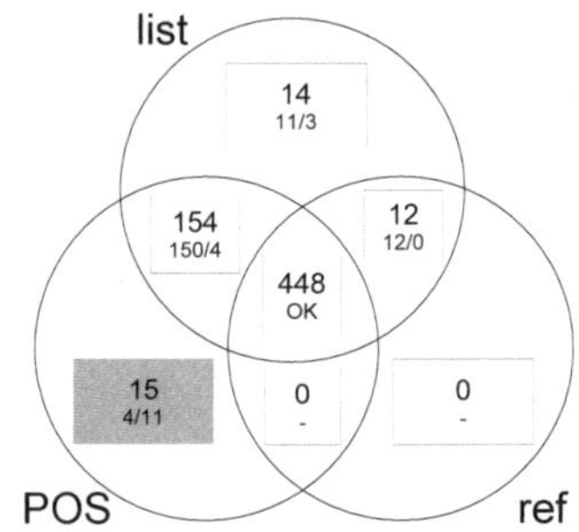

Automotive, Swedish

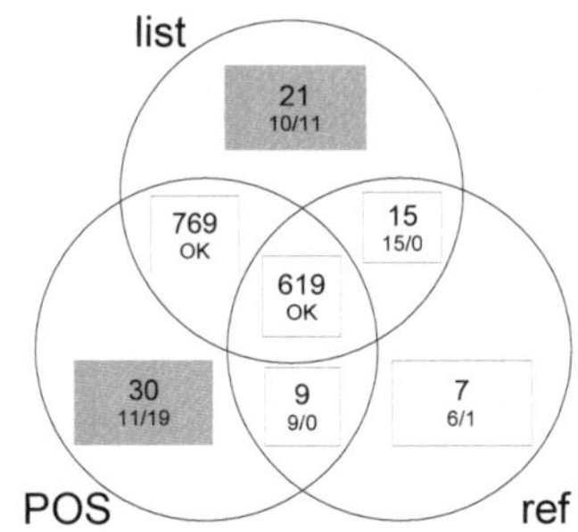

Europarl, Swedish

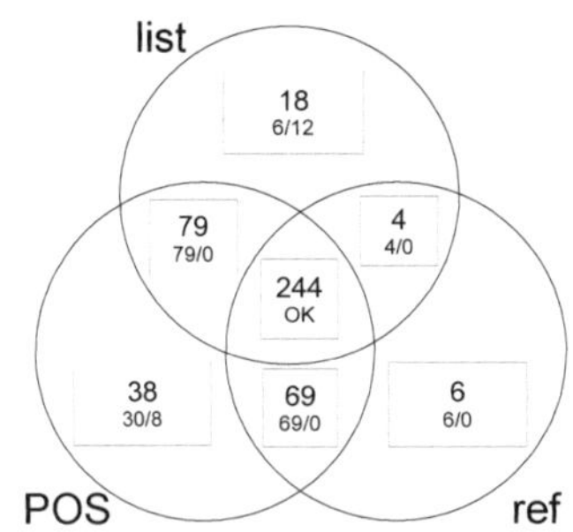

Automotive, Danish

Figure 2: Evaluation of the different heuristics on validation files from the three corpora. The number in each region of the Venn diagrams indicates the number of times a certain combination of heuristics fired (i.e. the number of positives for that combination). The two smaller numbers below indicate the number of true and false positive, respectively. Venn diagram regions corresponding to unreliable combinations of heuristics have corresponding figures on a grey background. OK means that a large fraction of the Venn cell was inspected, and no error was found.

		Danish auto		Swedish auto	
		BLEU	NIST	BLEU	NIST
No compound	Base	70.91	8.8816		
splitting	Base+POSLM	72.08	8.9338	56.79	**9.2674**
	POSLM	74.11*	9.2341*	57.28	9.1717
With	RPOSLM	74.26*	9.2767*	**58.12***	9.1694
compound	punish model	73.34*	9.1543*		
splitting	boost model	**74.96****	9.3028**	57.31	9.1736
	RPOSLM + boost	74.76**	**9.3368****	55.82	9.1088

Table 3: Results of experiments with methods for promoting coalescence. Compounds are merged based on the POS heuristic. Scores that are significantly better than Base+POSLM, are marked '*', and scores that are also better than POSLM with '**'.

Results are largely insensitive to variations in these hyper-parameters, especially to the CRF regularization parameter.

For the Danish auto corpus we had access to training data that were not also used to train the SMT system, that we used to compare the performance with that on the possibly biased training data that was also used to train the SMT system. There were no significant differences between the two types of training data on validation data, which confirmed that reusing the SMT training data for CRF training was a reasonable strategy.

The overall merging results of the heuristics, the best sequence labeler, and the sequence labeler without POS are shown in Table 4. Notice how the (modified) list and POS heuristics have complementary sets of false negatives: when merging on the OR of the two heuristics, the number of false negatives decreases drastically, in general compensating for the inevitable increase in false positives.

Among the heuristics, the combination of the improved list heuristic and the POS-based heuristic has a significantly higher recall and F-score than the POS-based heuristic alone in all cases except on the validation data for Swedish Auto, and than the list-based strategy in several cases. The list heuristic alone performs reasonably well on the two Swedish data sets, but has a very low recall on the Danish dataset. In all three cases the SMT training data has been used for the list used by the heuristic, so this is unexpected, especially considering the fact that the Danish dataset is in the same domain as one of the Swedish datasets. The Danish training data is smaller than the Swedish data though, which might be an influencing factor. It is possible that this heuristic could perform better also for Danish given more data for frequency calculations.

The sequence labeler is competitive with the heuristics; on F-score it is only significantly worse than any of the heuristics once, for Danish auto test data, and in several cases it has a significantly higher F-score than some of the heuristics. The sequence labeler has a higher precision, significantly so in three cases, than the best heuristic, the combination heuristic, which is positive, since erroneously merged compounds are usually more disturbing for a reader or post-editor than non-merged compounds.

The sequence-labelling approach can be used also in the absence of a POS tagger, which can be important if no such tool of suitable quality is available for the target language and the domain of interest. We thus also trained a CRF-based compound merger without using POS features, and without using the POS-based heuristic when constructing the training data. Compared to the CRF with access to POS-tags, on validation data F-score is significantly worse on the Europarl Swedish condition and the Automotive Danish condition, and are unchanged on Automotive Swedish. On test data there are no significant differences of the two sequence labelers on the two Automotive corpora. On Swedish Europarl, the CRF without POS has a higher recall at the cost of a lower precision. Compared to the list heuristic, which is the only other alternative strategy that works in the absence of a POS tagger, the CRF without POS performs significantly better on recall and F-score for Danish automotive, and mostly comparative on the two Swedish corpora.

	Validation data			Test data		
	Precision	Recall	F-score	Precision	Recall	F-score
			Swedish auto			
list	.9889^{p,lp}	.9936^{p}	.9912^{p}	.9900	.9770	.9835
POS	.9757	.9632	.9694	.9916^{lp}	.9737	.9826
list∨POS	.9720	1^{p}	.9858^{p}	.9822	.9984^{l,p,c,cp}	.9902^{l,p,cp}
CRF (ref∨list)	.9873^{p,lp}	.9984^{p}	.9928^{p,lp}	.9869	.9869	.9869
CRF without POS	.9873^{p,lp}	.9968^{p}	.9920^{p,lp}	.9836	.9852	.9844
			Swedish Europarl			
list	.9923^{lp,c,cp}	.9819	.9871	.9882^{lp,cp}	.9849	.9865
POS	.9867^{lp}	.9785	.9825	.9893^{lp}	.9751	.9822
list∨POS	.9795	.9958^{l,p,c,cp}	.9876^{p,cp}	.9782	.9993^{l,p,c,cp}	.9886^{p,cp}
CRF (ref∨(list∧POS))	.9841^{cp}	.9916^{l,p}	.9879^{p,cp}	.9953^{l,p,lp,cp}	.9790	.9871^{p}
CRF without POS	.9780	.9882^{p}	.9831	.9805	.9882^{p,c}	.9843
			Danish auto			
list	.9250	.7603	.8346	.9905^{lp}	.7640	.8626
POS	.9814^{l,lp}	.9635^{l,cp}	.9724^{l,lp,cp}	.9779	.9294^{l}	.9538^{l}
list∨POS	.9251	.9863^{l,p,cp}	.9547^{l}	.9760	.9878^{l,p,c}	.9819^{l,p,c}
CRF (ref∨list∨POS)	.9775^{l,lp}	.9932^{l,p,cp}	.9853^{l,p,lp,cp}	.9778	.9659^{l,p}	.9718^{l,p}
CRF without POS	.9924^{l,lp,c}	.8973^{l}	.9424^{l}	.9826	.9635^{l,p}	.9729^{l,p}

Table 4: Precision, Recall, and F-score for compound merging methods based on heuristics or sequence labelling on validation data and on held-out test data. The superscripts marks the systems that are significantly worse than the system in question (l-list, p-POS, lp-list∨POS, c-best CRF configuration, cp-CRF without POS).

The sequence labeler has the advantage over the heuristics that it is able to merge completely novel compounds, whereas the list strategy can only merge compounds that it has seen, and the POS-based strategy can create novel compounds, but only with known modifiers. An inspection of the test data showed that there were a few novel compounds merged by the sequence labeler that were not identified with either of the heuristics. In the test data we found *knap+start* (*button start*) and *vand+nedsænkning* (*water submersion*) in Danish Auto, and *kvarts sekel* (*quarter century*) and *bostad(s)+ersättning* (*housing grant*) in Swedish Europarl. This confirms that the sequence labeler, from automatically labeled data based on heuristics, can learn to merge new compounds that the heuristics themselves cannot find.

6 Discussion and conclusions

In this article, we described several methods for promoting coalescence and deciding if and how to merge word compounds that are either competitive with, or superior to, any currently known method.

For promoting compound coalescence we experimented with introducing additional LMs based on a restricted set of POS-tags, and with dedicated SMT model features counting the number of sequences known a priori to be desirable and undesirable. Experiments showed that this method can lead to large improvements over systems using no compound processing, and over previously known compound processing methods.

For merging, we improved an existing list-based heuristic, consisting in checking whether the first of two consecutive words has been observed in a corpus as a compound modifier and their combination has been observed as a compound, introducing the additional constraint that words are merged only if their corpus frequency as a compound is larger than their frequency as a bigram.

We observed that the false negatives of this improved list-based heuristic and of another, known, heuristic based on part-of-speech tags were complementary, and proposed a logical OR of them that generally improves over both.

We furthermore cast the compound merging problem as a sequence labelling problem, opening it to solutions based on a broad array of models and algorithms. We experimented with one model, Conditional Random Fields, designed a set of easily computed features reaching beyond the information accessed by the heuristics, and showed that it gives very competitive results.

Depending on the choice of the features, the sequence labelling approach has the potential to be truly productive, i.e. to form new compounds in an unrestricted way. This is for instance the case with the feature set we experimented with. The list-based heuristic is not productive: it can only form a compound if this was already observed as such. The POS-based heuristic presents some limited productivity. Since it uses special POS-tags for compound modifiers, it can form a compound provided its head has been seen alone or as a head, and its modifier(s) have been seen elsewhere, possibly separately, as modifier(s) of compounds. The sequence labelling approach can decide to merge two consecutive words even if neither was ever seen before in a compound.

In this paper we presented results on Swedish and Danish. We believe that the methods would work well also for other compounding languages such as German and Finnish. If the linguistic resources required to extract some of the features, e.g. a POS tagger, are unavailable (or are available only at training time but not in operations) for some language, the sequence-labelling method can still be applied. It is competitive or better than the list heuristic, which is the only heuristic available in that scenario.

Experiments on three datasets show that the improved and combined heuristics perform generally better than any already known method, and that, besides being fully productive, the sequence-labelling version is highly competitive, tends to generate fewer false positives than the combination heuristic, and can be used flexibly with limited or no linguistic resources.

References

Benny Brodda. 1979. Något om de svenska ordens fonotax och morfotax: Iakttagelse med utgångspunkt från experiment med automatisk morfologisk analys. In *PILUS nr 38*. Inst. för lingvistik, Stockholms universitet, Sweden.

Michael Collins. 2002. Discriminative training methods for hidden markov models: Theory and experiments with perceptron algorithms. In *Proceedings of the 2002 Conference on Empirical Methods in Natural Language Processing*, Philadelphia, PA.

George Doddington. 2002. Automatic evaluation of machine translation quality using n-gram co-occurence statistics. In *Proceedings of the Second International Conference on Human Language Technology*, pages 228–231, San Diego, California, USA.

Chris Dyer. 2010. *A Formal Model of Ambiguity and its Applications in Machine Translation*. Ph.D. thesis, University of Maryland, USA.

İlknur Durgar El-Kahlout and Kemal Oflazer. 2006. Initial explorations in English to Turkish statistical machine translation. In *Proceedings of the Workshop on Statistical Machine Translation*, pages 7–14, New York City, New York, USA.

Alexander Fraser. 2009. Experiments in morphosyntactic processing for translating to and from German. In *Proceedings of the Fourth Workshop on Statistical Machine Translation*, pages 115–119, Athens, Greece.

Karin Friberg. 2007. Decomposing Swedish compounds using memory-based learning. In *Proceedings of the 16th Nordic Conference on Computational Linguistics (Nodalida'07)*, pages 224–230, Tartu, Estonia.

Philipp Koehn and Hieu Hoang. 2007. Factored translation models. In *Proceedings of the 2007 Joint Conference on Empirical Methods in Natural Language Processing and Computational Natural Language Learning*, pages 868–876, Prague, Czech Republic.

Philipp Koehn and Kevin Knight. 2003. Empirical methods for compound splitting. In *Proceedings of the 10th Conference of the EACL*, pages 187–193, Budapest, Hungary.

Philipp Koehn, Hieu Hoang, Alexandra Birch, Chris Callison-Burch, Marcello Federico, Nicola Bertoldi, Brooke Cowan, Wade Shen, Christine Moran, Richard Zens, Chris Dyer, Ondrej Bojar, Alexandra Constantin, and Evan Herbst. 2007. Moses: Open source toolkit for statistical machine translation. In *Proceedings of the 45th Annual Meeting of the ACL, demonstration session*, pages 177–180, Prague, Czech Republic.

Philipp Koehn. 2005. Europarl: A parallel corpus for statistical machine translation. In *Proceedings of MT Summit X*, pages 79–86, Phuket, Thailand.

John Lafferty, Andrew McCallum, and Fernando Pereira. 2001. Conditional random fields: Probabilistic models for segmenting and labeling sequence data. In *Proceedings of the Eighteenth International Conference on Machine Learning*, Williamstown, MA.

Martha Larson, Daniel Willett, Joachim Köhler, and Gerhard Rigoll. 2000. Compound splitting and lexical unit recombination for improved performance of a speech recognition system for German parliamentary speeches. In *Proceedings of the Sixth International Conference on Spoken Language Processing*, volume 3, pages 945–948, Beijing, China, October.

Franz Josef Och. 2003. Minimum error rate training in statistical machine translation. In *Proceedings of the 42nd Annual Meeting of the ACL*, pages 160–167, Sapporo, Japan.

Kishore Papineni, Salim Roukos, Todd Ward, and Wei-Jing Zhu. 2002. BLEU: A method for automatic evaluation of machine translation. In *Proceedings of the 40th Annual Meeting of the ACL*, pages 311–318, Philadelphia, Pennsylvania, USA.

Maja Popović, Daniel Stein, and Hermann Ney. 2006. Statistical machine translation of German compound words. In *Proceedings of FinTAL – 5th International Conference on Natural Language Processing*, pages 616–624, Turku, Finland. Springer Verlag, LNCS.

Lawrence R. Rabiner. 1989. A tutorial on hidden markov models and selected applications in speech recognition. *Proceedings of IEEE*, 77(2):257–286.

Stefan Riezler and John T. Maxwell. 2005. On some pitfalls in automatic evaluation and significance testing for MT. In *Proceedings of the Workshop on Intrinsic and Extrinsic Evaluation Measures for MT and/or Summarization at ACL'05*, pages 57–64, Ann Arbor, Michigan, USA.

Michel Simard, Nicola Cancedda, Bruno Cavestro, Marc Dymetman, Eric Gaussier, Cyril Goutte, Kenji Yamada, Philippe Langlais, and Arne Mauser. 2005. Translating with non-contiguous phrases. In *Proceedings of the Human Language Technology Conference and the conference on Empirical Methods in Natural Language Processing*, pages 755–762, Vancouver, British Columbia, Canada.

Jonas Sjöbergh and Viggo Kann. 2004. Finding the correct interpretation of Swedish compounds, a statistical approach. In *Proceedings of the 4th International Conference on Language Resources and Evaluation (LREC'04)*, Lisbon, Portugal.

Sara Stymne and Maria Holmqvist. 2008. Processing of Swedish compounds for phrase-based statistical machine translation. In *Proceedings of the 12th Annual Conference of the European Association for Machine Translation*, pages 180–189, Hamburg, Germany.

Sara Stymne. 2008. German compounds in factored statistical machine translation. In *Proceedings of GoTAL – 6th International Conference on Natural Language Processing*, pages 464–475, Gothenburg, Sweden. Springer Verlag, LNCS/LNAI.

Sara Stymne. 2009a. A comparison of merging strategies for translation of German compounds. In *Proceedings of the EACL 2009 Student Research Workshop*, pages 61–69, Athens, Greece.

Sara Stymne. 2009b. *Compound processing for phrase-based statistical machine translation*. Licentiate thesis, Linköping University, Sweden.

Sami Virpioja, Jaako J. Väyrynen, Mathias Creutz, and Markus Sadeniemi. 2007. Morphology-aware statistical machine translation based on morphs induced in an unsupervised manner. In *Proceedings of MT Summit XI*, pages 491–498, Copenhagen, Denmark.

SampleRank Training for Phrase-Based Machine Translation

Barry Haddow
School of Informatics
University of Edinburgh
bhaddow@inf.ed.ac.uk

Abhishek Arun
Microsoft UK
abarun@microsoft.com

Philipp Koehn
School of Informatics
University of Edinburgh
pkoehn@inf.ed.ac.uk

Abstract

Statistical machine translation systems are normally optimised for a chosen gain function (metric) by using MERT to find the best model weights. This algorithm suffers from stability problems and cannot scale beyond 20-30 features. We present an alternative algorithm for discriminative training of phrase-based MT systems, SampleRank, which scales to hundreds of features, equals or beats MERT on both small and medium sized systems, and permits the use of sentence or document level features. SampleRank proceeds by repeatedly updating the model weights to ensure that the ranking of output sentences induced by the model is the same as that induced by the gain function.

1 Introduction

In phrase-based machine translation (PBMT), the standard approach is to express the probability distribution $p(a, e|f)$ (where f is the source sentence and (a, e) is the aligned target sentence) in terms of a linear model based on a small set of feature functions

$$p(a, e|f) \propto \exp\left(\sum_{i=1}^{n} w_i h_i(a, e, f)\right) \tag{1}$$

The feature functions $\{h_i\}$ typically include log probabilities of generative models such as translation, language and reordering, as well as non-probabilistic features such as word, phrase and distortion penalties. The feature weights $\mathbf{w} = \{w_i\}$ are normally trained using MERT (minimum error rate training) (Och, 2003), to maximise performance as measured by an automated metric such as BLEU (Papineni et al., 2002). MERT training uses a parallel data set (known as the tuning set) consisting of about 1000-2000 sentences, distinct from the data set used to build the generative models. Optimising the weights in Equation (1) is often referred to as *tuning* the MT system, to differentiate it from the process of training the generative models.

MERT's inability to scale beyond 20-30 features, as well as its instability (Foster and Kuhn, 2009) have led to investigation into alternative ways of tuning MT systems. The development of tuning methods is complicated, however by, the use of BLEU as an objective function. This objective in its usual form is not differentiable, and has a highly non-convex error surface (Och, 2003). Furthermore BLEU is evaluated at the corpus level rather than at the sentence level, so tuning methods either have to consider the entire corpus, or resort to a sentence-level approximation of BLEU. It is unlikely, however, that the difficulties in discriminative MT tuning are due solely to the use of BLEU as a metric – because evaluation of translation is so difficult, any reasonable gain function is likely to have a complex relationship with the model parameters.

Gradient-based tuning methods, such as minimum risk training, have been investigated as possible alternatives to MERT. Expected BLEU is normally adopted as the objective since it is differentiable and so can be optimised by a form of stochastic gradient ascent. The feature expectations required for the gradient calculation can be obtained from n-best lists or lattices (Smith and Eisner, 2006; Li and Eisner, 2009), or using sampling (Arun et al., 2010), both of which can be computationally expensive.

Proceedings of the 6th Workshop on Statistical Machine Translation, pages 261–271,
Edinburgh, Scotland, UK, July 30–31, 2011.

Margin-based techniques such as perceptron training (Liang et al., 2006) and MIRA (Chiang et al., 2008; Watanabe et al., 2007) have also been shown to be able to tune MT systems and scale to large numbers of features, but these generally involve repeatedly decoding the tuning set (and so are expensive) and require sentence-level approximations to the BLEU objective.

In this paper we present an alternative method of tuning MT systems known as *SampleRank*, which has certain advantages over other methods in use today. SampleRank operates by repeatedly sampling pairs of translation hypotheses (for a given source sentence) and updating the feature weights if the ranking induced by the MT model (1) is different from the ranking induced by the gain function (i.e. BLEU). By considering the translation hypotheses in batches, it is possible to directly optimise corpus level metrics like BLEU without resorting to sentence level approximations.

Tuning using SampleRank does not limit the size of the feature set in the same way as MERT does, and indeed it will be shown that SampleRank can successfully train a model with several hundred features. Using just the core PBMT features and training using SampleRank will be shown to achieve BLEU scores which equal or exceed those produced by MERT trained models.

Since SampleRank does not require repeated decoding of the tuning set, and is easily parallelisable, it can run at an acceptable speed, and since it always maintains a complete translation hypothesis, it opens up the possibility of sentence or document level features[1].

2 Method

2.1 SampleRank Training

SampleRank (Culotta, 2008; Wick et al., 2009) is an online training algorithm that was introduced for parameter learning in weighted logics, and has been applied to complex graphical models (Wick et al., 2011). Assume a probabilistic model $p(y|x)$ admitting a log-linear parametrisation

$$p(y|x) \propto \exp \sum_i (w_i \phi_i(x, y)) \qquad (2)$$

where $\{\phi_i\}$ are a set of feature functions and $\{w_i\}$ are corresponding feature weights. SampleRank can be used to optimise the feature weights to maximise a given gain function.

SampleRank is a supervised training algorithm, requiring a set of labelled training data $D = \{(x^1, y^1\}, \ldots, (x^n, y^n)\}$, where the x^i are the inputs and the y^i the outputs. The algorithm works by considering each training example (x^i, y^i) in turn, and repeatedly sampling pairs of outputs from a neighbourhood defined in the space of all possible outputs, updating the weights when the ranking of the pair due to the model scores is different from the ranking due to the gain function. So if the sampled pair of outputs for x^i is (y, y'), where $p(y'|x^i) > p(y|x^i)$, the weights are updated iff $gain(y', y^i) < gain(y, y^i)$.

The sampled pairs are drawn from a chain which can be constructed in a similar way to an MCMC (Markov Chain Monte Carlo) chain.

In (Culotta, 2008) different strategies are explored for building the chain, choosing the neighbourhood and updating the weights.

2.2 SampleRank Training for Machine Translation

We adapted SampleRank for the tuning of PBMT systems, as summarised in Algorithm 1. The definitions of the functions in the algorithm (described in the following subsections) draw inspiration from work on MIRA training for MT (Watanabe et al., 2007; Chiang et al., 2008). SampleRank is used to optimise the parameter weights in (1) using the tuning set.

2.2.1 Gain Function

The first thing that needs to be defined in Algorithm 1 is the gain function. For this we use BLEU, the most popular gain function for automated MT evaluation, although the procedure described here will work with any gain function that can be evaluated quickly. Using BLEU, however, creates a problem, as BLEU is defined at the corpus level rather than the sentence level, and in previous work on SampleRank, the training data is processed one example at a time. In other work on online training for SMT, (Liang et al., 2006; Chiang et al., 2008), sentence-level approximations to BLEU were

[1] As long as the batches described in Section 2.2.1 respect document boundaries.

Algorithm 1 The SampleRank algorithm for tuning phrase-based MT systems.

Require: Tuning data:
$D = \{(f^1, e^1), \ldots, (f^n, e^n)\}$

Require: $gain(y, y')$: A function which scores a set of hypotheses (y') against a set of references (y).

Require: $score(x, y)$: A function which computes a model score for a set of hypotheses y and source sentences x.

1: **for** $epoch = 1$ to number of epochs **do**
2:   $A \leftarrow D$
3:   **while** A is non-empty **do**
4:     Pick (x, y), a batch of sentence pairs, randomly from A, and remove.
5:     Initialise y_0, a set of translation hypotheses for x.
6:     **for** $s = 1$ to number of samples **do**
7:       $N \leftarrow ChooseNeighbourhood(y_{s-1})$
8:       $y' \leftarrow ChooseSample(N)$
9:       $y^+ \leftarrow ChooseOracle(N)$
10:       **if** $\frac{gain(y,y') - gain(y,y^+)}{score(x,y') - score(x,y^+)} < 0$ **then**
11:         $UpdateWeights()$
12:       **end if**
13:       $y_s \leftarrow y'$
14:     **end for**
15:   **end while**
16: **end for**

---

employed, however in this work we directly optimise corpus BLEU by processing the data in small batches. Using batches was found to work better than processing the data sentence by sentence.

So the while loop in Algorithm 1 iterates through the tuning data in batches of parallel sentences, rather than single sentences. One complete pass through the tuning data is known as an *epoch*, and normally SampleRank training is run for several epochs. The gain on a particular batch is calculated by scoring the current set of hypotheses for the whole batch against the references for that batch. When calculating BLEU, a smoothing constant of 0.01 is added to all counts in order to avoid zero counts.

2.2.2 Sample Generation

For each iteration of the while loop in Algorithm 1, a new batch of parallel sentences is chosen from the tuning set, and a corresponding new set of translation hypotheses must be generated (the y_0 in line 5 of Algorithm 1). These initial hypotheses are generated by glossing. For each word in the source, the most likely translation option (according to the weighted phrase-internal score) is selected, and these translations are joined together monotonically. This method of initialisation was chosen because it was simple and fast, and experiments with an alternative method of initialisation (where the decoder was run with random scores assigned to hypotheses) showed very little difference in performance.

Once the initial set of hypotheses for the new batch is created, the SampleRank innermost loop (lines 6-14 in Algorithm 1) proceeds by repeatedly choosing a sample hypothesis set (y') and an oracle hypothesis set (y^+), corresponding to the source side of the batch (x).

Given the current hypothesis set $y_{s-1} = (e_1, \ldots, e_k)$, the sample and oracle are chosen as follows. Firstly, a hypothesis e_j is selected randomly from y_{s-1} , and a neighbourhood of alternate hypotheses $N \ni e_j$ generated using operators from Arun et al. (2009) (explained shortly). Model scores are calculated for all the hypotheses in N, converted to probabilities using Equation (1), and a sample e'_j taken from N using these probabilities. The sample hypothesis set (y') is then the current hypothesis set (y_{s-1}) with e_j replaced by e'_j. The oracle is created, analogously Chiang et al. (2008), by choosing $e^+_j \in N$ to maximise the sum of gain (calculated on the batch) and model score. The oracle hypothesis set (y^+) is then y_{s-1} with e_j replaced by e^+_j.

We now describe how the neighbourhood is chosen. Given a single hypothesis e_j, a neighbourhood is generated by first randomly choosing one of the two operators MERGE-SPLIT or REORDER, then randomly choosing a point of application for the operator, then applying it to generate the neighbourhood. The MERGE-SPLIT operator can be applied at any inter-word position, and generates its neighbourhood by listing all hypotheses obtained by optionally merging or splitting the phrases(s) touching that position, and retranslating them. The REORDER operator applies at a pair of target phrases (subject to distortion limits) and generates a neighbourhood containing two hypotheses, one with the original order and one with the chosen phrases swapped. The distortion limits and translation option pruning used by the operators matches those used in decoding, so together they are able to explore the same hypothesis space as the decoder. A fuller explanation of the two operators is give in Arun et al. (2009).

2.2.3 Weight Updates

After choosing the sample and oracle hypothesis set (y' and y^+), the weight update may be performed. The weights of the model are updated if the relative ranking of the sample hypothesis set and the oracle hypothesis set provided by the model score is different from that provided by the gain. The model score function $score(x, y)$ is defined for a hypothesis set $y = e_1, \ldots e_k$ as follows:

$$score(x, y) = \sum_{j=1}^{k} \left(\sum_{i=1}^{n} w_i h_i(a_j, e_j, f_j) \right) \quad (3)$$

where $x = f_1, \ldots f_k$ are the corresponding source sentences. The weight update is performed iff $score(x, y') \neq score(x, y^+)$ and the following condition is satisfied:

$$\frac{gain(y, y') - gain(y, y^+)}{score(x, y') - score(x, y^+)} < 0 \quad (4)$$

where the $gain()$ function is just the BLEU score.

The weight update used in this work is a MIRA-like update from $\mathbf{w}_{s-1}$ to $\mathbf{w}_s$ defined as follows:

$$\mathbf{w}_s = \arg\min_{\mathbf{w}} \left(\|\mathbf{w} - \mathbf{w}_{s-1}\| + C\xi \right) \quad (5)$$

subject to

$$score_{\mathbf{w}}(x, y^+) - score_{\mathbf{w}}(x, y') + \xi \geq M \cdot (gain(y, y^+) - gain(y, y')) \quad (6)$$

The margin scaling M is set to be $gain(y, y^+)$, so that ranking violations of low BLEU solutions are assigned a lower importance than ranking violations of high BLEU solutions. The ξ in (5) is a slack variable, whose influence is controlled by C (set to 0.01), and which has the effect of "clipping" the magnitude of the weight updates. Since there is only one constraint, there is no need to use an iterative method such as Hildreth's, because it is straightforward to solve the optimisation in (5) and (6) exactly using its Lagrangian dual, following (Crammer et al., 2006). The weight update is then given by

$$\mathbf{w}_s = \mathbf{w}_{s-1} + \min\left(\frac{b}{\|\mathbf{a}\|^2}, C \right) \mathbf{a}$$

$$\text{where} \quad \mathbf{a} = \mathbf{h}(a_j^+, e_j^+, f_j) - \mathbf{h}(a'_j, e'_j, f_j)$$

$$\text{and} \quad b = M\left(gain(y, y^+) - gain(y, y')\right) - \left(score(x, y^+) - gain(y, y')\right)$$

After updating the weights, the current hypothesis set (y_s) is updated to be the sample hypothesis set (y'), as in line 13 of Algorithm 1, and then the next sample is generated.

2.2.4 Implementation Considerations

After each iteration of the inner loop of Algorithm 1, the weights are collected, and the overall weights output by the tuning algorithm are the average of all these collected weights. When each new batch is loaded at the start of the inner loop, a period of burn-in is run, analogous to the burn-in used in MCMC sampling, where no weight updates are performed and weights are not collected.

In order to help the stability of the tuning algorithm, and to enable it to process the tuning data more quickly, several chains are run in parallel, each with their own set of current weights, and each processing a distinct subset of the tuning data. The weights are mixed (averaged) after each epoch. The same technique is frequently adopted for the averaged perceptron (McDonald et al., 2010).

3 Experiments

3.1 Corpora and Baselines

The experiments in this section were conducted with French-English and German-English sections of the WMT2011[2] shared task data. In particular, we used News-Commentary data (`nc11`), and Europarl data (`ep11`) for training the generative models. Phrase tables were built from lowercased versions of the

[2] `http://www.statmt.org/wmt11/`

parallel texts using the standard Moses[3] training pipeline, with the target side of the texts used to build Kneser-Ney smoothed language models using the SRILM toolkit[4]. These data sets were used to build two phrase-based translation systems: WMT-SMALL and WMT-LARGE.

The WMT-SMALL translation system uses a translation model built from just the `nc11` data (about 115,000 sentences), and a 3-gram language model built from the target side of this data set. The features used in the WMT-SMALL translation system were the five Moses translation features, a language model feature, a word penalty feature and a distortion distance feature.

To build the WMT-LARGE translation system, both the `ep11` data set and the `nc11` data set were concatenated together before building the translation model out of the resulting corpus of about 2 million sentences. Separate 5-gram language models were built from the target side of the two data sets and then they were interpolated using weights chosen to minimise the perplexity on the tuning set (Koehn and Schroeder, 2007). In the WMT-LARGE system, the eight core features were supplemented with the six features of the lexicalised reordering model, which was trained on the same data as was used to build the translation model. Whilst a training set size of 2 million sentences would not normally be sufficient to build a competitive system for an MT shared task, it is sufficient to show that how SampleRank training performs on a realistic sized system, whilst still allowing for plenty of experimenation with the algorithm's parameters.

For tuning, the `nc-devtest2007` was used, with the first half of `nc-test2007` corpus used for heldout testing and `nc-test2008` and `newstest2010` reserved for final testing. The tuning and heldout sets are about 1000 sentences in size, whereas the final test sets are approximately 2000 sentences each.

In Table 1, the performance (in BLEU[5]) of untrained and MERT-tuned models on the heldout set is shown[6]. The untuned models use the default weights output by the Moses `train-model.perl` script, whereas the performance of the tuned models is the mean across five different MERT runs.

All decoding in this paper is with Moses, using default settings.

Pair	System	untuned	MERT-tuned
fr-en	WMT-SMALL	28.0	29.2 (0.2)
	WMT-LARGE	29.4	32.5 (0.1)
de-en	WMT-SMALL	25.0	25.3 (0.1)
	WMT-LARGE	26.6	26.8 (0.2)

Table 1: Untrained and MERT-trained performance on heldout. MERT training is repeated five times, with the table showing the mean BLEU, and standard deviation in brackets.

3.2 SampleRank Training For Small Models

First we look at how SampleRank training compares to MERT training using the WMT-SMALL models. Using the smaller models allows reasonably quick experimentation with a large range of different parameter settings.

For these experiments, the epoch size is set at 1024, and we vary both the number of cores and the number of samples used in training. The number of cores n is set to either 1,2,4,8 or 16, meaning that each epoch we split the tuning data into n different, non-overlapping shards, passing a different shard to each process, so the shard size k is set to $1024/n$. In each process, a burn of $100 * k$ samples is run (without updating the weights), followed by either $100 * k$ or $500 * k$ samples with weight updates, using the algorithm described in Section 2.2. After an epoch is completed, the current weights are averaged across all processes to give the new current weights in each process. At intervals of 50000 samples in each core, weights are averaged across all samples so far, and across all cores, and used to decode the heldout set to measure performance.

In Figure 1, learning curves are shown for the 100 sample-per-sentence case, for 1, 4 and 16 cores, for French-English. The training is repeated five times and the error bars in the graph indicate the

[3] `http://www.statmt.org/moses/`

[4] `http://www-speech.sri.com/projects/srilm/`

[5] Calculated with `multi-bleu.perl`

[6] All BLEU scores and standard deviations are rounded to one decimal place.

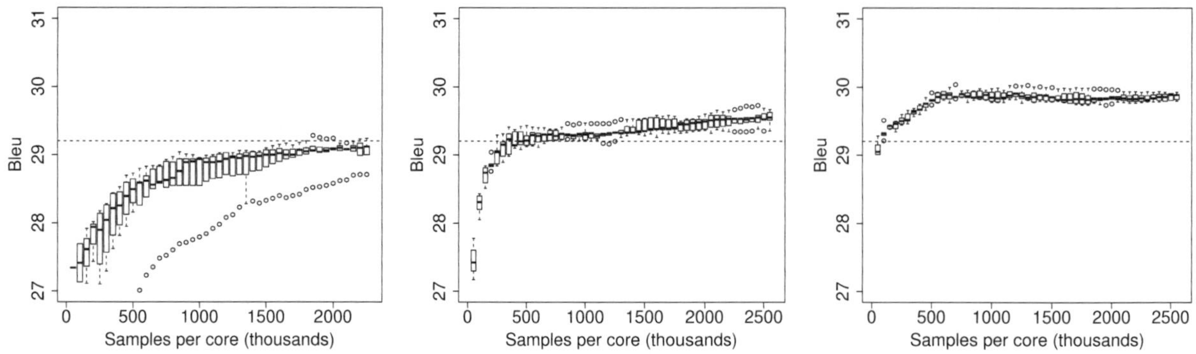

(a) 1 core (b) 4 cores (c) 16 cores

Figure 1: SampleRank learning curves for the WMT-SMALL French-English system, for 1, 4 and 16 cores. The dashed line shows the mean MERT performance, which has a standard deviation of 0.2.

spread across the different training runs. Increasing the number of cores makes a clear difference to the training, with the single core training run failing to reach the the level of MERT, and the 16 core training run exceeding the mean MERT performance by more than 0.5 BLEU. Using a single core also results in a much bigger training variance, which makes sense as using more cores and averaging weights reduces the adverse effect of a single chain going astray. The higher BLEU score achieved when using the larger number of cores is probably because a larger portion of the parameter space is being explored.

In one sense, the x axes of the graphs in Figure 1 are not comparable, since increasing the number of cores and keeping the number of samples per core increases the total computing time. However even if the single core training was run for much longer, it did not reach the level of performance obtained by multi-core training. Limited experimentation with increasing the core count to 32 did not show any appreciable gain, despite greatly increasing the computing resources required.

The training runs shown in Figure 1 take between 21 hours (for 16 cores) and 35 hours (for a single core)[7]. In the 16 core runs each core is doing the same amount of work as in the single core runs, so the difference in time is due to the extra effort involved in dealing with larger batches. These times are for the 100 samples-per-sentence condition, and increasing to 500 samples-per-sentence provides a speed-up of about 25%, since proportionally less time is spent on burn-in. Most of the time is spent in BLEU evaluation, so improved memoisation and incremental evaluation would reduce training time.

In Table 2 the mean maximum BLEU achieved on the heldout set at each parameter setting is shown. By this it is meant that for each of the five training runs at each (samples,cores) setting, the maximum BLEU on heldout data is observed, and these maxima are averaged across the five runs. It can be seen that changing the samples-per-sentence makes little difference, but there is a definite effect of increasing the core count.

Cores	100 Samples	500 Samples
1	29.1 (0.2)	29.2 (0.1)
2	29.3 (0.1)	29.3 (0.1)
4	29.6 (0.1)	29.5 (0.1)
8	30.0 (0.0)	29.9 (0.1)
16	30.0 (0.1)	29.8 (0.1)

Table 2: Mean maximum heldout performance for SampleRank training of the French-English WMT-SMALL model. Standard deviations are shown in brackets.

The learning curves for the equivalent German-English model are shown in Figure 2 and show a fairly different behaviour to their French-English counterparts. Again, using more cores helps to im-

[7]The processors are Intel Xeon 5450 (3GHz)

prove and stabilise the performance, but there is little if any improvement throughout training. As with MERT training, SampleRank training of the model weights makes little difference to the BLEU score, suggesting a fairly flat error surface.

Table 3 shows the mean maximum BLEU score on heldout data, the equivalent of Table 2, but for German-English. The results show very little variation as the samples-per-sentence and core counts are changed.

Cores	100 Samples	500 Samples
1	25.2 (0.0)	25.3 (0.1)
2	25.4 (0.1)	25.4 (0.1)
4	25.4 (0.1)	25.4 (0.1)
8	25.4 (0.1)	25.4 (0.1)
16	25.3 (0.1)	25.4 (0.1)

Table 3: Mean maximum heldout performance for SampleRank training of the German-English WMT-SMALL model. Standard deviations are shown in brackets

3.3 SampleRank Training for Larger Models

For the training of the WMT-LARGE systems with SampleRank, similar experiments to those in Section 3.2 were run, although only for 8 and 16 cores. The learning curves for the two language pairs (Figure 3) show roughly similar patterns to those in the previous section, in that the French-English system gradually increases performance through training to reach a maximum, as opposed to the German-English system with its fairly flat learning curve. Training times are around 27 hours for the 500 sample curve shown in Figure 3, increasing to 64 hours for 100 samples-per-sentence.

In Table 4, the mean maximum BLEU scores are shown for each configuration. of each language pair, calculated in the manner described in the previous section. For the larger system, SampleRank shows a smaller advantage over MERT for French-English, and little if any gain for German-English. For both large and small German-English models, neither of the parameter tuning algorithms are able to lift BLEU scores very far above the scores obtained from the untuned weights set by the Moses training script.

Pair	Cores	100 Samples	500 Samples
fr-en	8	32.6 (0.1)	32.7 (0.1)
	16	32.8 (0.1)	32.9 (0.1)
de-en	8	26.9 (0.0)	27.0 (0.1)
	16	26.8 (0.1)	26.9 (0.1)

Table 4: Mean (and standard deviation) of maximum heldout performance for SampleRank training of the WMT-LARGE model.

3.4 SampleRank Training for Larger Feature Sets

The final set of experiments are concerned with using SampleRank training for larger feature sets than the 10-20 typically used in MERT-trained models. The models considered in this section are based on the WMT-SMALL systems, but also include a family of part-of-speech tag based phrase boundary features.

The phrase boundary features are defined by considering the target-side part-of-speech tag bigrams spanning each phrase boundary in the hypothesis, and allowing a separate feature to fire for each bigram. Dummy phrases with parts-of-speech <s> and </s> are inserted at the start and end of the sentence, and also used to construct phrase boundary features. The example in Figure 4 shows the phrase-boundary features from a typical hypothesis. The idea is similar to a part-of-speech language model, but discriminatively trained, and targeted at how phrases are joined together in the hypothesis.

The target-side part-of-speech tags are added using the Brill tagger, and incorporated into the phrase table using the factored translation modelling capabilities of Moses (Koehn and Hoang, 2007).

Adding the phrase boundary features to the WMT-SMALL system increased the feature count from 8 to around 800. Training experiments were run for both the French-English and German-English models, using the same configuration as in Section 3.2, varying the number of cores (8 or 16) and the number of samples per sentence (100 or 500). Training times were similar to those for the WMT-SMALL system. The mean maximum scores on heldout are shown in Table 5. We suspect that these features are fixing some short range reordering problems which

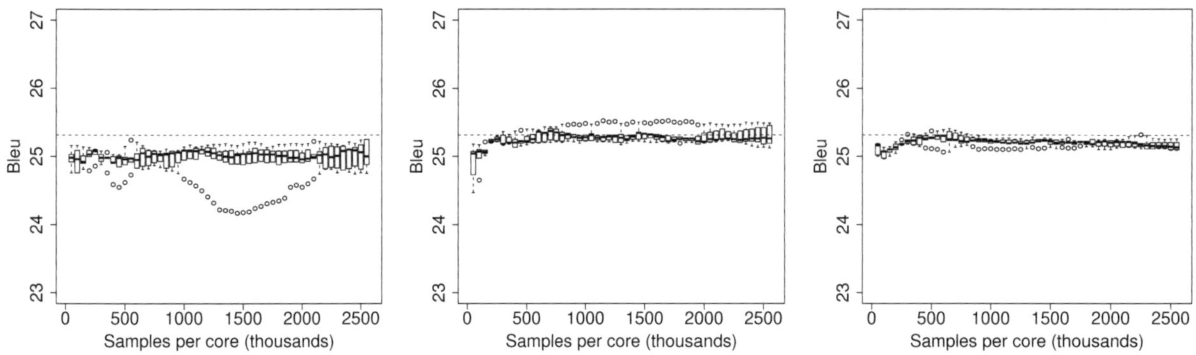

(a) 1 core (b) 4 cores (c) 16 cores

Figure 2: SampleRank learning curves for the WMT-SMALL German-English system, for 1, 4 and 16 cores. The dashed line shows the mean MERT performance, which has a standard deviation of 0.1.

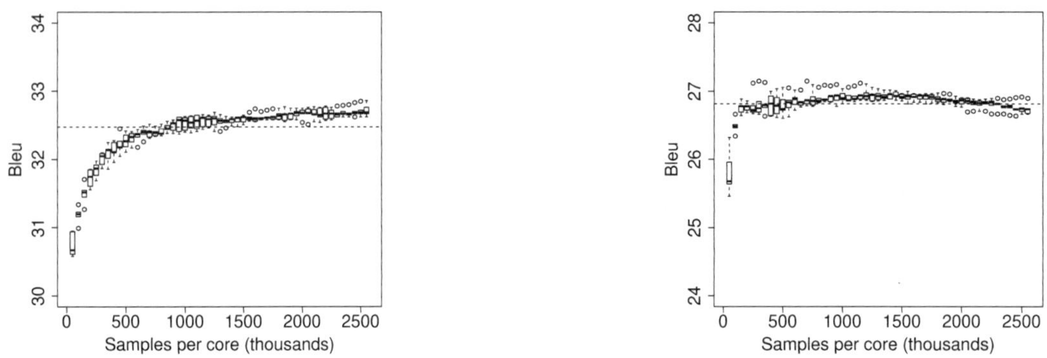

(a) French-English (b) German-English

Figure 3: SampleRank learning curves for the WMT-LARGE French-English and German-English systems, using 8 cores and 500 samples per sentence. The dashed line shows the mean MERT performance, which has a standard deviation of 0.07 (fr-en) and 0.2 (de-en).

occur in the former language pair, but since the reordering problems in the latter language pair tend to be longer range, adding these extra features just tend to add extra noise to the model.

3.5 Comparison of MERT and SampleRank on Test Data

Final testing was performed on the `nc-test2008` and `newstest2010` data sets. The former is quite similar to the tuning and heldout data, whilst the latter can be considered to be "out-of-domain", so provides a check to see whether the model weights are being tuned too heavily towards the domain.

For the SampleRank experiments on the test set, the best training configurations were chosen from the results in Tables 2, 3, 4 and 5, and the best performing weight sets for each of the five runs for this configuration. For the MERT trained models, the same five models from Table 1 were used. The test set results are shown in Table 6.

The patterns observed on the heldout data carry over, to a large extent, to the test data. This is especially true for the WMT-SMALL system, where similar improvements (for French-English) over the MERT trained system are observed on the SampleRank trained system. For the WMT-LARGE system, the slightly improved performance that SampleRank offered on the in-domain data is no longer there, al-

Hypothesis		[europe	's]	[after]	[racial]	[house	divided	against	itself]	
Tags	<S>	NNP	POS	IN	JJ	NN	VBN	IN	PRP	</S>

This produces five phrase boundary features: <S>:NNP, POS:IN, IN:JJ, JJ:NN and PRP:</S>.

Figure 4: The definition of the phrase boundary feature from part-of-speech tags

		fr-en		de-en	
Training	System	nc-test2008	newstest2010	nc-test2008	newstest2010
MERT	WMT-SMALL	28.1 (0.1)	19.6 (0.1)	25.9 (0.1)	16.4 (0.2)
SampleRank	WMT-SMALL	28.7 (0.0)	20.1 (0.1)	25.9 (0.1)	16.6 (0.1)
SampleRank	WMT-SMALL+pb	28.8 (0.1)	19.8 (0.1)	25.9 (0.1)	16.7 (0.1)
MERT	WMT-LARGE	30.1 (0.1)	22.9 (0.1)	28.0 (0.2)	19.1 (0.2)
SampleRank	WMT-LARGE	30.0 (0.1)	23.6 (0.3)	28.1 (0.1)	19.5 (0.2)

Table 6: Comparison of MERT trained and SampleRank trained models on the test sets. The WMT-SMALL+pb model is the model with phrase boundary features, as described in Section 3.4

Pair	Cores	100 Samples	500 Samples
fr-en	8	30.2 (0.0)	30.2 (0.0)
	16	30.3 (0.0)	30.3 (0.00)
de-en	8	25.1 (0.1)	25.1 (0.0)
	16	25.0 (0.1)	25.0 (0.0)

Table 5: Mean (and standard deviation) of maximum heldout performance for SampleRank training of the WMT-SMALL model, with the phrase boundary feature.

though interestingly there is a reasonable improvement on out-of-domain, over the MERT trained model, similar to the effect observed in (Arun et al., 2010). Finally, the improvements offered by the phrase boundary feature are reduced, perhaps an indication of some over-fitting.

4 Related Work

Whilst MERT (Och, 2003) is still the dominant algorithm used for discriminative training (tuning) of SMT systems, research into improving on MERT's line search has tended to focus either on gradient-based or margin-based techniques.

Gradient-based techniques require a differentiable objective, and expected sentence BLEU is the most popular choice, beginning with Smith and Eisner (2006). They used n-best lists to calculate the feature expectations required for the gradient, optimising a second order Taylor approximation of expected sentence BLEU. They also introduced the idea of deterministic annealing to the SMT community, where an entropy term is added to the objective in training, and has its temperature progressively lowered in order to sharpen the model probability distribution. The work of Smith and Eisner was extended by Li and Eisner (2009) who were able to obtain much better estimates of feature expectations by using a packed chart instead of an n-best list. They also demonstrated that their method could extend to large feature sets, although their experiments were only run on small data sets.

An alternative method of calculating the feature expectations for expected BLEU training is Monte-Carlo Markov Chain (MCMC) approximation, and this was explored in (Arun et al., 2009) and (Arun et al., 2010). The sampling methods introduced in this earlier work form the basis of the current work, although in using the sampler for expected BLEU training, many samples must be collected before making a parameter weight update, as opposed to the current work where weights may be updated after every sample. One novel feature of Arun et al. (2010) is that they were able to train to directly maximise corpus BLEU, instead of its sentence-based approximation, although this only made a small difference to the results. The training methods in (Arun et al.,

2010) are very resource intensive, with the experiments running for 48 hours on around 40 cores, on a pruned phrase table derived from Europarl, and a 3-gram language model.

Instead of using expected BLEU as a training objective, Blunsom et al. (2008) trained their model to directly maximise the log-likelihood of the discriminative model, estimating feature expectations from a packed chart. Their model treats derivations as a latent variable, directly modelling the translation probability.

Margin-based techniques have the advantage that they do not have to employ expensive and complex algorithms to calculate the feature expectations. Typically, either perceptron ((Liang et al., 2006), (Arun and Koehn, 2007)) or MIRA ((Watanabe et al., 2007), (Chiang et al., 2008)) is employed, but in both cases the idea is to repeatedly decode sentences from the tuning set, and update the parameter weights if the best hypothesis according to the model differs from some "oracle" sentence. The approaches differ in the way they compute the oracle sentence, as well as the way the weights are updated. Normally sentences are processed one-by-one, with a weight update after considering each sentence, and sentence BLEU is used as the objective. However Chiang et al. (2008) introduced an approximation to corpus BLEU by using a rolling history. Both papers on MIRA demonstrated its ability to extend to large numbers of features.

In the only known application of SampleRank to SMT, Roth et al. (2010) deploys quite a different translation model to the usual phrase-based model, allowing overlapping phrases and implemented as a factor graph. Decoding is with a rather slow stochastic search and performance is quite poor, but this model, in common with the training algorithm presented in the current work, permits features which depend on the whole sentence.

5 Discussion and Conclusions

The results presented in Table 6 show that SampleRank is a viable method of parameter tuning for phrase-based MT systems, beating MERT in many cases, and equalling it in others. It is also able to do what MERT cannot do, and scale to a large number of features, with the phrase boundary feature of Section 3.4 providing a "proof-of-concept".

A further potential advantage of SampleRank is that it allows training with features which depend on the whole sentence, or even the whole document, since a full set of hypotheses is retained throughout training. Of course adding these features precludes decoding with the usual dynamic programming based decoders, and would require an alternative method, such as MCMC (Arun et al., 2009).

As with the other alternatives to MERT mentioned in this paper, SampleRank training presents the problem of determining convergence. With MERT this is straightforward, since training (normally) comes to a halt when the estimated tuning BLEU stops increasing and the weights stop changing. With methods such as minimum risk training, MIRA and SampleRank, some kind of early stopping criterion is usually employed, which lengthens training unnecessarily, and adds costly decodes to the training process. Building up sufficient practical experience with each of these methods will offset these problems somewhat.

Another important item for future work is to compare SampleRank training with MIRA training, in terms of performance, speed and ability to handle large feature sets.

The code used for the experiments in this paper is available under an open source license[8].

Acknowledgements

This research was supported by the EuroMatrixPlus project funded by the European Commission (7th Framework Programme) and by the GALE program of the Defense Advanced Research Projects Agency, Contract No. HR0011-06-2-001. The project made use of the resources provided by the Edinburgh Compute and Data Facility (http://www.ecdf.ed.ac.uk/). The ECDF is partially supported by the eDIKT initiative (http://www.edikt.org.uk/).

The authors would like to thank Sebastian Riedel for helpful discussions related to this work.

References

Abhishek Arun and Philipp Koehn. 2007. Online Learning Methods For Discriminative Training of Phrase

[8] https://mosesdecoder.svn.sourceforge.net/svnroot/mosesdecoder/branches/samplerank

Based Statistical Machine Translation. In *Proceedings of MT Summit*.

Abhishek Arun, Chris Dyer, Barry Haddow, Phil Blunsom, Adam Lopez, and Philipp Koehn. 2009. Monte Carlo inference and maximization for phrase-based translation. In *Proceedings of the Thirteenth Conference on Computational Natural Language Learning (CoNLL-2009)*, pages 102–110, Boulder, Colorado, June. Association for Computational Linguistics.

Abhishek Arun, Barry Haddow, and Philipp Koehn. 2010. A Unified Approach to Minimum Risk Training and Decoding. In *Proceedings of the Joint Fifth Workshop on Statistical Machine Translation and Metrics-MATR*, pages 365–374, Uppsala, Sweden, July. Association for Computational Linguistics.

Phil Blunsom, Trevor Cohn, and Miles Osborne. 2008. A Discriminative Latent Variable Model for Statistical Machine Translation. In *Proceedings of ACL*.

David Chiang, Yuval Marton, and Philip Resnik. 2008. Online Large-Margin Training of Syntactic and Structural Translation Features. In *Proceedings of EMNLP*.

Koby Crammer, Ofer Dekel, Joseph Keshet, Shai Shalev-Shwartz, and Yoram Singer. 2006. Online Passive-Aggressive Algorithms. *Journal of Machine Learning Research*, 7:551–585, March.

Aron Culotta. 2008. *Learning and inference in weighted logic with application to natural language processing*. Ph.D. thesis, University of Massachusetts, May.

George Foster and Roland Kuhn. 2009. Stabilizing Minimum Error Rate Training. In *Proceedings of the Fourth Workshop on Statistical Machine Translation*, pages 242–249, Athens, Greece, March. Association for Computational Linguistics.

Philipp Koehn and Hieu Hoang. 2007. Factored Translation Models. In *Proceedings of the 2007 Joint Conference on Empirical Methods in Natural Language Processing and Computational Natural Language Learning (EMNLP-CoNLL)*, pages 868–876.

Philipp Koehn and Josh Schroeder. 2007. Experiments in Domain Adaptation for Statistical Machine Translation. In *Proceedings of the Second Workshop on Statistical Machine Translation*, pages 224–227, Prague, Czech Republic, June. Association for Computational Linguistics.

Zhifei Li and Jason Eisner. 2009. First- and Second-order Expectation Semirings with Applications to Minimum-Risk Training on Translation Forests. In *Proceedings of EMNLP*.

Percy Liang, Alexandre Bouchard-Côté, Dan Klein, and Ben Taskar. 2006. An End-to-End Discriminative Approach to Machine Translation. In *Proceedings of the 21st International Conference on Computational Linguistics and 44th Annual Meeting of the Association for Computational Linguistics*, pages 761–768, Sydney, Australia, July. Association for Computational Linguistics.

Ryan McDonald, Keith Hall, and Gideon Mann. 2010. Distributed Training Strategies for the Structured Perceptron. In *Human Language Technologies: The 2010 Annual Conference of the North American Chapter of the Association for Computational Linguistics*, pages 456–464, Los Angeles, California, June. Association for Computational Linguistics.

Franz J. Och. 2003. Minimum Error Rate Training in Statistical Machine Translation. In *Proceedings of ACL*.

Kishore Papineni, Salim Roukos, Todd Ward, and Wei-Jing Zhu. 2002. Bleu: a Method for Automatic Evaluation of Machine Translation. In *Proceedings of 40th Annual Meeting of the Association for Computational Linguistics*, pages 311–318, Philadelphia, Pennsylvania, USA, July. Association for Computational Linguistics.

Benjamin Roth, Andrew McCallum, Marc Dymetman, and Nicola Cancedda. 2010. Machine Translation Using Overlapping Alignments and SampleRank. In *Proceedings of AMTA*.

David A. Smith and Jason Eisner. 2006. Minimum risk annealing for training log-linear models. In *Proceedings of COLING/ACL*, pages 787–794, Morristown, NJ, USA. Association for Computational Linguistics.

Taro Watanabe, Jun Suzuki, Hajime Tsukada, and Hideki Isozaki. 2007. Online Large-Margin Training for Statistical Machine Translation. In *Proceedings of the 2007 Joint Conference on Empirical Methods in Natural Language Processing and Computational Natural Language Learning (EMNLP-CoNLL)*, pages 764–773, Prague, Czech Republic, June. Association for Computational Linguistics.

Michael Wick, Khashayar Rohanimanesh, Aron Culotta, and Andrew McCallum. 2009. SampleRank: Learning Preferences from Atomic Gradients. In *Proceedings of NIPS Workshop on Advances in Ranking*.

Michael Wick, Khashayar Rohanimanesh, Kedare Bellare, Aron Culotta, and Andrew McCallum. 2011. SampleRank: training factor graphs with atomic gradients. In *Proceedings of ICML*.

Instance Selection for Machine Translation using Feature Decay Algorithms

Ergun Biçici
Koç University
34450 Sariyer, Istanbul, Turkey
ebicici@ku.edu.tr

Deniz Yuret
Koç University
34450 Sariyer, Istanbul, Turkey
dyuret@ku.edu.tr

Abstract

We present an empirical study of instance selection techniques for machine translation. In an active learning setting, instance selection minimizes the human effort by identifying the most informative sentences for translation. In a transductive learning setting, selection of training instances relevant to the test set improves the final translation quality. After reviewing the state of the art in the field, we generalize the main ideas in a class of instance selection algorithms that use feature decay. Feature decay algorithms increase diversity of the training set by devaluing features that are already included. We show that the feature decay rate has a very strong effect on the final translation quality whereas the initial feature values, inclusion of higher order features, or sentence length normalizations do not. We evaluate the best instance selection methods using a standard Moses baseline using the whole 1.6 million sentence English-German section of the Europarl corpus. We show that selecting the best 3000 training sentences for a specific test sentence is sufficient to obtain a score within 1 BLEU of the baseline, using 5% of the training data is sufficient to exceed the baseline, and a $\sim$ 2 BLEU improvement over the baseline is possible by optimally selected subset of the training data. In out-of-domain translation, we are able to reduce the training set size to about 7% and achieve a similar performance with the baseline.

1 Introduction

Statistical machine translation (SMT) makes use of a large number of parallel sentences, sentences whose translations are known in the target language, to derive translation tables, estimate parameters, and generate the actual translation. Not all of the parallel corpus nor the translation table that is generated is used during decoding a given set of test sentences and filtering is usually performed for computational advantage (Koehn et al., 2007). Some recent regression-based statistical machine translation systems rely on a small sized training data to learn the mappings between source and target features (Wang and Shawe-Taylor, 2008; Serrano et al., 2009; Bicici and Yuret, 2010). Regression has some computational disadvantages when scaling to large number of training instances.

Previous work shows that the more the training data, the better the translations become (Koehn, 2006). However, with the increased size of the parallel corpus there is also the added noise, making relevant instance selection important. Phrase-based SMT systems rely heavily on accurately learning word alignments from the given parallel corpus. Proper instance selection plays an important role in obtaining a small sized training set with which correct alignments can be learned. Word-level translation accuracy is also affected by the number of times a word occurs in the parallel corpus (Koehn and Knight, 2001). Koehn and Knight find that about 50 examples per word are required to achieve a performance close to using a bilingual lexicon in their experiments. Translation performance can improve as we include multiple possible translations for a given word, which increases

Proceedings of the 6th Workshop on Statistical Machine Translation, pages 272–283,
Edinburgh, Scotland, UK, July 30–31, 2011.

the diversity of the training set.

Transduction uses test instances, which can sometimes be accessible at training time, to learn specific models tailored towards the test set which also reduces computation by not using the full training set. Transductive retrieval selects training data close to the test set given a parallel corpus and a test set. This work shows that *transductive retrieval* of the training set for statistical machine translation allows us to achieve a performance better than using all of the parallel corpus. When selecting training data, we seek to maximize the coverage or the percentage of test source and target features (i.e. n-grams) found in the training set using minimal number of target training features and a fixed number of training instances. Diversifying the set of training sentences can help us increase the coverage. We show that target coverage bounds the achievable BLEU score with a given training set and small increases can result in large increases on this BLEU bound.

We develop the feature decay algorithms (FDA) that aim to maximize the coverage of the target language features and achieve significant gains in translation performance. We find that decaying feature weights has significant effect on the performance. We achieve improvements of $\sim$2 BLEU points using about 20% of the available training data in terms of target words and $\sim$1 BLEU points with only about 5%. We show that selecting 3000 instances for a test sentence is sufficient to obtain a score within 1 BLEU of the baseline. In the out-of-domain translation task, we are able to reduce the training set size to its 7% to achieve a similar performance with the baseline.

The next section reviews related previous work. We discuss the FDA in section 3. Section 4 presents our coverage and translation results both in and out-of-domain and includes an instance selection method also designed for improving word alignment results. We list our contributions in the last section.

2 Related Work

Transductive learning makes use of test instances, which can sometimes be accessible at training time, to learn specific models tailored towards the test set. Selection of training instances relevant to the test set improves the final translation quality as in transductive learning and decreases human effort by identifying the most informative sentences for translation as in active learning. Instance selection in a transductive learning framework selects the best instances for a given test set (Lü et al., 2007). *Active learning* selects training samples that will benefit the learning algorithm the most over the unlabeled dataset $\mathcal{U}$ from a labeled training set $\mathcal{L}$ or from $\mathcal{U}$ itself after labeling (Banko and Brill, 2001). Active learning in SMT selects which instances to add to the training set to improve the performance of a baseline system (Haffari et al., 2009; Ananthakrishnan et al., 2010). Recent work involves selecting sentence or phrase translation tasks for external human effort (Bloodgood and Callison-Burch, 2010). Below we present examples of both with a label indicating whether they follow an approach close to active learning [AL] or transductive learning [TL] and in our experiments we use the transductive framework.

TF-IDF [TL]: Lü et al. (2007) use tf-idf information retrieval technique based cosine score to select a subset of the parallel corpus close to the test set for SMT training. They outperform the baseline system when the top 500 training instances per test sentence are selected. The terms used in their tf-idf measure correspond to words where this work focuses on bigram feature coverage. When the combination of the top N selected sentences are used as the training set, they show increase in the performance at the beginning and decrease when 2000 sentences are selected for each test sentence.

N-gram coverage [AL]: Eck et al. (2005) use n-gram feature coverage to sort and select training instances using the following score:

$$\phi_{NGRAM}(S) = \frac{\sum_{i=1}^{n} \sum_{\text{unseen } x \in X_i(S)} C(x)}{|S|}, \quad (1)$$

for sentence S with $X_i(S)$ storing the i-grams found in S and $C(x)$ returning the count of x in the parallel corpus. ϕ_{NGRAM} score sums over unseen n-grams to increase the coverage of the training set. The denominator involving the length of the sentence takes the translation cost of the sentence into account. Eck et al. (2005) also note that longer sentences are more difficult for training SMT models. In their experiments, they are not able to reach a performance above the baseline system's BLEU score, which is using all of the parallel corpus, but they achieve close performance by using about 15% of the parallel corpus.

DWDS [AL]: Density weighted diversity sampling (*DWDS*) (Ambati et al., 2010) score tries to select sentences containing the n-gram features in the unlabeled dataset $\mathcal{U}$ while increasing the diversity among the sentences selected, $\mathcal{L}$ (labeled). *DWDS* increases the score of a sentence with increasing frequency of its n-grams found in $\mathcal{U}$ and decreases with increasing frequency in the already selected set of sentences, $\mathcal{L}$, in favor of diversity. Let $P_{\mathcal{U}}(x)$ denote the probability of feature x in $\mathcal{U}$ and $C_{\mathcal{L}}(x)$ denote its count in $\mathcal{L}$. Then:

$$d(S) = \frac{\sum_{x \in X(S)} P_{\mathcal{U}}(x) e^{-\lambda C_{\mathcal{L}}(x)}}{|X(S)|} \quad (2)$$

$$u(S) = \frac{\sum_{x \in X(S)} I(x \notin X(\mathcal{L}))}{|X(S)|} \quad (3)$$

$$\phi_{DWDS}(S) = \frac{2 d(S) u(S)}{d(S) + u(S)}, \quad (4)$$

where $X(S)$ stores the features of S and λ is a decay parameter. $d(S)$ denotes the density of S proportional to the probability of its features in $\mathcal{U}$ and inversely proportional to their counts in $\mathcal{L}$ and $u(S)$ its uncertainty, measuring the percentage of new features in S. These two scores are combined using harmonic mean. *DWDS* tries to select sentences containing similar features in $\mathcal{U}$ with high diversity. In their active learning experiments, they selected 1000 training instances in each iteration and retrained the SMT system.

Log-probability ratios [AL]: Haffari et al. (2009) develop sentence selection scores using feature counts in $\mathcal{L}$ and $\mathcal{U}$, increasing for frequent features in $\mathcal{U}$ and decreasing for frequent features in $\mathcal{L}$. They use geometric and arithmetic averages of log-probability ratios in an active learning setting where 200 sentences from $\mathcal{U}$ are selected and added to $\mathcal{L}$ with their translations for 25 iterations (Haffari et al., 2009). Later, Haffari et al. (2009) distinguish between features found in the phrase table, x_{reg}, and features not found, x_{oov}. OOV features are segmented into subfeatures (i.e. feature "go to school" is segmented as: (go to school), (go)(to school), (go to)(school), (go)(to)(school)). *Expected log probability ratio (ELPR)* score is used:

$$\phi_{ELPR}(S) = \frac{0.4}{|X_{reg}(S)|} \sum_{x \in X_{reg}(S)} \log \frac{P_{\mathcal{U}}(x)}{P_{\mathcal{L}}(x)} + \frac{0.6}{|X_{oov}(S)|} \sum_{x \in X_{oov}(S)} \sum_{h \in H(x)} \frac{1}{|H(x)|} \sum_{y \in Y_h(x)} \log \frac{P_{\mathcal{U}}(y)}{P_{\mathcal{L}}(y)}, \quad (5)$$

where $H(x)$ return the segmentations of x and $Y_h(x)$ return the features found in segment h. ϕ_{ELPR} performs better than geometric average in their experiments (Haffari and Sarkar, 2009).

Perplexity [AL & TL]: Perplexity of the training instance as well as inter-SMT-system disagreement are also used to select training data for translation models (Mandal et al., 2008). The increased difficulty in translating a parallel sentence or its novelty as found by the perplexity adds to its importance for improving the SMT model's performance. A sentence having high perplexity (a rare sentence) in $\mathcal{L}$ and low perplexity (a common sentence) in $\mathcal{U}$ is considered as a candidate for addition. They are able to improve the performance of a baseline system trained on some initial corpus together with additional parallel corpora using the initial corpus and part of the additional data.

Alignment [TL]: Uszkoreit et al. (2010) mine parallel text to improve the performance of a baseline translation model on some initial document translation tasks. They retrieve similar documents using inverse document frequency weighted cosine similarity. Then, they filter nonparallel sentences using their word alignment performance, which is estimated using the following score:

$$\text{score}(A) = \sum_{(s,t) \in A} \ln \frac{p(s,t)}{p(s)p(t)}, \quad (6)$$

where A stands for an alignment between source and target words and the probabilities are estimated using a word aligned corpus. The produced parallel data is used to expand a baseline parallel corpus and shown to improve the translation performance of machine translation systems.

3 Instance Selection with Feature Decay

In this section we will describe a class of instance selection algorithms for machine translation that use feature decay, i.e. increase the diversity of the training set by devaluing features that have already been included. Our abstraction makes three components of such algorithms explicit permitting experimentation with their alternatives:

- The value of a candidate training sentence as a function of its features.
- The initial value of a feature.
- The update of the feature value as instances are added to the training set.

A feature decay algorithm (FDA) aims to maximize the coverage of the target language features (such as words, bigrams, and phrases) for the test set. A target language feature that does not appear in the selected training instances will be difficult to produce regardless of the decoding algorithm (impossible for unigram features). In general we do not know the target language features, only the source language side of the test set is available. Unfortunately, selecting a training instance with a particular source language feature does not guarantee the coverage of the desired target language feature. There may be multiple translations of a feature appropriate for different senses or different contexts. For each source language feature in the test set, FDA tries to find as many training instances as possible to increase the chances of covering the appropriate target language feature. It does this by reducing the value of the features that are already included after picking each training instance. Algorithm 1 gives the pseudo-code for FDA.

Algorithm 1: The Feature Decay Algorithm

Input: Bilingual corpus $\mathcal{U}$, test set features $\mathcal{F}$, and desired number of training instances N.
Data: A priority queue $\mathcal{Q}$, sentence scores `score`, feature values `fvalue`.
Output: Subset of the corpus to be used as the training data $\mathcal{L} \subseteq \mathcal{U}$.

foreach $f \in \mathcal{F}$ **do**
  $\texttt{fvalue}(f) \leftarrow \texttt{init}(f, \mathcal{U})$
foreach $S \in \mathcal{U}$ **do**
  $\texttt{score}(S) \leftarrow \sum_{f \in \texttt{features}(S)} \texttt{fvalue}(f)$
  $\texttt{push}(\mathcal{Q}, S, \texttt{score}(S))$
while $|\mathcal{L}| < N$ **do**
  $S \leftarrow \texttt{pop}(\mathcal{Q})$
  $\texttt{score}(S) \leftarrow \sum_{f \in \texttt{features}(S)} \texttt{fvalue}(f)$
  if $\texttt{score}(S) \geq \texttt{topval}(\mathcal{Q})$ **then**
    $\mathcal{L} \leftarrow \mathcal{L} \cup \{S\}$
    foreach $f \in \texttt{features}(S)$ **do**
      $\texttt{fvalue}(f) \leftarrow \texttt{decay}(f, \mathcal{U}, \mathcal{L})$
  else
    $\texttt{push}(\mathcal{Q}, S, \texttt{score}(S))$

The input to the algorithm is a parallel corpus, the number of desired training instances, and the source language features of the test set. We use unigram and bigram features; adding trigram features does not seem to significantly affect the results. The user has the option of running the algorithm for each test sentence separately, then possibly combining the resulting training sets. We will present results with these variations in Section 4.

The first foreach loop initializes the value of each test set feature. We experimented with initial feature values that are constant, proportional to the length of the n-gram, or log-inverse of the corpus frequency. We have observed that the initial value does not have a significant effect on the quality of training instances selected. The feature decay rule dominates the behavior of the algorithm after the first few iterations. However, we prefer the log-inverse values because they lead to fewer score ties among candidate instances and result in faster running times.

The second foreach loop initializes the score for each candidate training sentence and pushes them onto a priority queue. The score is calculated as the sum of the feature values. Note that as we change the feature values, the sentence scores in the priority queue will no longer be correct. However they will still be valid upper bounds because the feature values only get smaller. Features that do not appear in the test set are considered to have zero value. This observation can be used to speed up the initialization by using a feature index and only iterating over the sentences that have features in common with the test set.

Finally the while loop populates the training set by picking candidate sentences with the highest scores. This is done by popping the top scoring candidate S from the priority queue at each iteration. We recalculate its score because the values of its features may have changed. We compare the recalculated score of S with the score of the next best candidate. If the score of S is equal or better we are sure that it is the top candidate because the scores in the priority queue are upper bounds. In this case we place S in our training set and decay the values of its features. Otherwise we push S back on the priority queue with its updated score.

The feature decay function on Line 12 is the heart of the algorithm. Unlike the choice of features (bigram vs trigram) or their initial values (constant vs log–inverse–frequency) the rate of decay has a significant effect on the performance. We found it is optimal to reduce feature values at a rate of $1/n$ where n is the current training set count of the feature. The results get significantly worse with no feature decay. They also get worse with faster, exponential feature decay, e.g. $1/2^n$. Table 1 presents the experimental results that support these conclusions. We use the following settings for the experiments in Section 4:

$$\texttt{init}(f,\mathcal{U}) = 1 \text{ or } \log(|\mathcal{U}|/\texttt{cnt}(f,\mathcal{U}))$$
$$\texttt{decay}(f,\mathcal{U},\mathcal{L}) = \frac{\texttt{init}(f,\mathcal{U})}{1+\texttt{cnt}(f,\mathcal{L})} \text{ or } \frac{\texttt{init}(f,\mathcal{U})}{1+2^{\texttt{cnt}(f,\mathcal{L})}}$$

init	decay	en→de		de→en	
1	none	.761	.484	.698	.556
$\log(1/f)$	none	.855	.516	.801	.604
1	$1/n$	**.967**	**.575**	**.928**	**.664**
$\log(1/f)$	$1/n$	.967	.570	.928	.656
1	$1/2^n$	.967	.553	.928	.653
$\log(1/f)$	$1/2^n$	.967	.557	.928	.651

Table 1: FDA experiments. The first two columns give the initial value and decay formula used for features. f is the corpus frequency of a feature and n is its count in selected instances. The next four columns give the expected coverage of the source and target language bigrams of a test sentence when 100 training sentences are selected.

4 Experiments

We perform translation experiments on the English-German language pair using the parallel corpus provided in WMT'10 (Callison-Burch et al., 2010). The English-German section of the Europarl corpus contains about 1.6 million sentences. We perform *in-domain* experiments to discriminate among different instance selection techniques better in a setting with low out-of-vocabulary rate. We randomly select the test set *test* with $2,588$ target words and separate development set *dev* with $26,178$ target words. We use the language model corpus provided in WMT'10 (Callison-Burch et al., 2010) to build a 5-gram model.

We use target language *bigram* coverage, $tcov$, as a quality measure for a given training set, which measures the percentage of the target bigram features of the test sentence found in a given training set. We compare $tcov$ and the translation performance of FDA with related work. We also perform small scale SMT experiments where only a couple of thousand training instances are used for each test sentence.

4.1 The Effect of Coverage on Translation

BLEU (Papineni et al., 2001) is a precision based measure and uses n-gram match counts up to order n to determine the quality of a given translation. The absence of a given word or translating it as another word interrupts the continuity of the translation and decreases the BLEU score even if the order among the words is determined correctly. Therefore, the target coverage of an out-of-domain test set whose translation features are not found in the training set bounds the translation performance of an SMT system.

We estimate this translation performance bound from target coverage by assuming that the missing tokens can appear randomly at any location of a given sentence where sentence lengths are normally distributed with mean 25.6 and standard deviation 14.1. This is close to the sentence length statistics of the German side Europarl corpus used in WMT'10 (WMT, 2010). We replace all unknown words found with an UNK token and calculate the BLEU score. We perform this experiment for $10,000$ instances and repeat for 10 times.

The obtained BLEU scores for target coverage values is plotted in Figure 1 with label *estimate*. We also fit a third order polynomial function of target coverage 0.025 BLEU scores above the *estimate* values to show the similarity with the

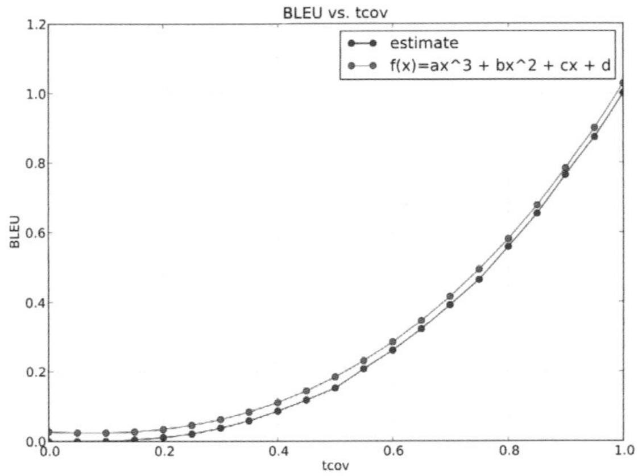

Figure 1: Effect of coverage on translation performance. BLEU bound is a third-order function of target coverage. High coverage → High BLEU.

BLEU scores bound estimated, whose parameters are found to be $[0.56, 0.53, -0.09, 0.003]$ with a least-squares fit. Figure 1 shows that the BLEU score bound obtained has a third-order polynomial relationship with target coverage and small increases in the target coverage can result in large increases on this BLEU bound.

4.2 Coverage Results

We select N training instances per test sentence using FDA (Algorithm 1), *TF-IDF* with bigram features, *NGRAM* scoring (Equation 1), *DWDS* (Equation 4), and *ELPR* (Equation 5) techniques from previous work. For the active learning algorithms, source side test corpus becomes $\mathcal{U}$ and the selected training set $\mathcal{L}$. For all the techniques, we compute 1-grams and 2-grams as the features used in calculating the scores and add only one sentence to the training set at each iteration except for *TF-IDF*. We set λ parameter of *DWDS* to 1 as given in their paper. We adaptively select the top scoring instance at each step from the set of possible sentences $\mathcal{U}$ with a given scorer $\phi(.)$ and add the instance to the training set, $\mathcal{L}$, until the size of $\mathcal{L}$ reaches N for the related work other than *TF-IDF*. We test all algorithms in this transductive setting.

We measure the *bigram* coverage when all of the training sentences selected for each test sentence are combined. The results are presented in Figure 2 where the x-axis is the number of words of the training set and y-axis is the target coverage obtained. FDA has a steep slope in its increase and it is able to reach target coverage of ~ 0.84. *DWDS* performs worse initially but its target coverage improve after a number of instances are selected due to its exponential feature decay procedure. *TF-IDF* performs worse than *DWDS* and it provides a fast alternative to FDA instance selection but with some decrease in coverage. *ELPR* and *NGRAM* instance selection techniques perform worse. *NGRAM* achieves better coverage than *ELPR*, although it lacks a decay procedure.

When we compare the sentences selected, we observe that FDA prefers longer sentences due to summing feature weights and it achieves larger target coverage value. *NGRAM* is not able to discriminate between sentences well and a lot of sentences of the same length get the same score when the unseen n-grams belong to the same frequency class. The statistics of $\mathcal{L}$ obtained with the instance selection techniques differ from each other as given in Table 2, where $N = 1000$ training instances selected per test sentence. We observe that *DWDS* has fewer unique target bigram features than *TF-IDF* although it selects longer target sentences. *NGRAM* obtains a large number of unique target bigrams although its selected target sentences have similar lengths with *DWDS* and *ELPR* prefers short sentences.

Technique	Unique bigrams	Words per sent	*tcov*
FDA	827,928	35.8	.74
DWDS	412,719	16.7	.67
TF-IDF	475,247	16.2	.65
NGRAM	626,136	16.6	.55
ELPR	172,703	10.9	.35

Table 2: Statistics of the obtained target $\mathcal{L}$ for $N = 1000$.

4.3 Translation Results

We develop separate phrase-based SMT models using Moses (Koehn et al., 2007) using default settings with maximum sentence length set to 80 and obtained baseline system score as 0.3577 BLEU. We use the training instances selected by FDA in

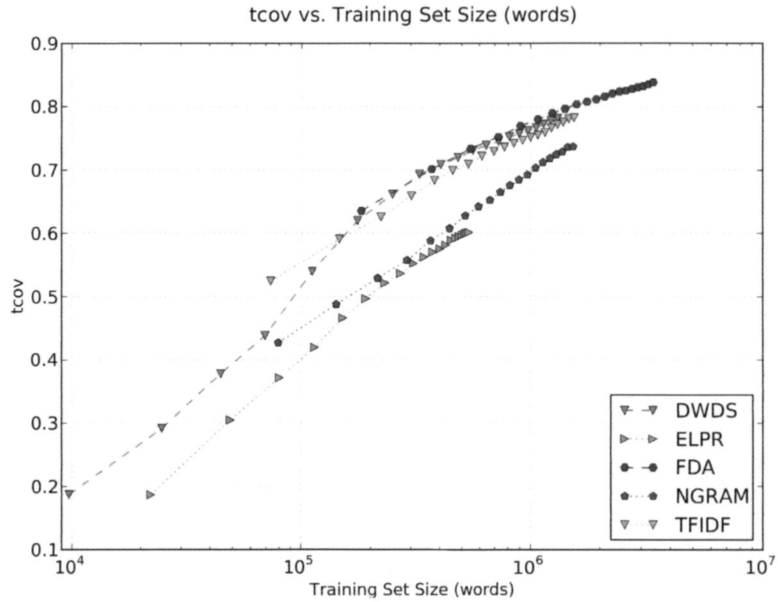

Figure 2: Target coverage curve comparison with previous work. Figure shows the rate of increase in $tcov$ as the size of $\mathcal{L}$ increase.

three learning settings:

- $\mathcal{L}_{\cup}$ $\mathcal{L}$ is the union of the instances selected for each test sentence.
- $\mathcal{L}_{\cup_{\mathcal{F}}}$ $\mathcal{L}$ is selected using all of the features found in the test set.
- $\mathcal{L}_{\mathcal{I}}$ $\mathcal{L}$ is the set of instances selected for each test sentence.

We develop separate Moses systems with each training set and $\mathcal{L}_{\mathcal{I}}$ corresponds to developing a Moses system for each test sentence. $\mathcal{L}_{\cup}$ results are plot in Figure 3 where we increasingly select $N \in \{100, 200, 500, 1000, 2000, 3000, 5000, 10000\}$ instances for each test sentence for training. The improvements over the baseline are statistically significant with paired bootstrap resampling using 1000 samples (Koehn, 2004). As we select more instances, the performance of the SMT system increases as expected and we start to see a decrease in the performance after selecting $\sim 10^7$ target words. We obtain comparable results for the *de-en* direction. The performance increase is likely to be due to the reduction in the number of noisy or irrelevant training instances and the increased precision in the probability estimates in the generated phrase tables.

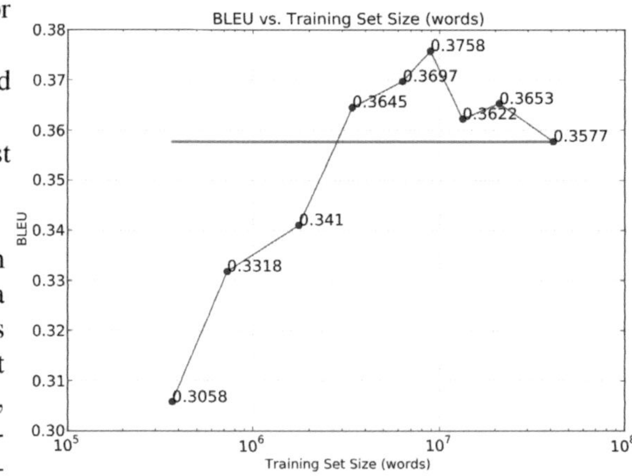

Figure 3: BLEU vs. the number of target words in $\mathcal{L}_{\cup}$.

$\mathcal{L}_{\cup_{\mathcal{F}}}$ results given in Table 3 show that we can achieve within 1 BLEU performance using about 3% of the parallel corpus target words (30,000 instances) and better performance using only about 5% (50,000 instances).

The results with $\mathcal{L}_{\mathcal{I}}$ when building an individ-

# sent	# target words	BLEU	NIST
10,000	449,116	0.3197	5.7788
20,000	869,908	0.3417	6.0053
30,000	1,285,096	0.3492	6.0246
50,000	**2,089,403**	**0.3711**	**6.1561**
100,000	**4,016,124**	**0.3648**	**6.1331**
ALL	41,135,754	0.3577	6.0653

Table 3: Performance for *en-de* using $\mathcal{L}_{\cup\mathcal{F}}$. ALL corresponds to the baseline system using all of the parallel corpus. **bold** correspond to statistically significant improvement over the baseline result.

ual Moses model for each test sentence are given in Table 4. Individual SMT training and translation can be preferable due to smaller computational costs and high parallelizability. As we translate a single sentence with each SMT system, tuning weights becomes important. We experiment three settings: (1) using 100 sentences for tuning, which are randomly selected from *dev.1000*, (2) using the mean of the weights obtained in (1), and (3) using the weights obtained in the union learning setting ($\mathcal{L}_{\cup}$). We observe that we can obtain a performance within 2 BLEU difference to the baseline system by training on 3000 instances per sentence (underlined) using the mean weights and 1 BLEU difference using the union weights. We also experimented with increasing the N-best list size used during MERT optimization (Hasan et al., 2007), with increased computational cost, and observed some increase in the performance.

N	100 dev sents	Mean	Union
1000	0.3149	0.3242	0.3354
2000	0.3258	0.3352	0.3395
3000	0.3270	<u>0.3374</u>	<u>0.3501</u>
5000	0.3217	0.3303	<u>0.3458</u>

Table 4: $\mathcal{L}_{\mathcal{I}}$ performance for *en-de* using 100 sentences for tuning or mean of the weights or dev weights obtained with the union setting.

Comparison with related work: Table 5 presents the translation results compared with previous work selecting 1000 instances per test sentence. We observe that coverage and translation performance are correlated. Although the coverage increase of *DWDS* and FDA appear similar, due to the third-order polynomial growth of BLEU with respect to coverage, we achieve large BLEU gains in translation. We observe increased BLEU gains when compared with the results of *TF-IDF*, *NGRAM*, and *ELPR* in order.

FDA	*DWDS*	*TF-IDF*	*NGRAM*	*ELPR*
0.3645	0.3547	0.3405	0.2572	0.2268

Table 5: BLEU results using different techniques with $N = 1000$. High coverage $\rightarrow$ High BLEU.

We note that *DWDS* originally selects instances using the whole test corpus to estimate $P_{\mathcal{U}}(x)$ and selects 1000 instances at each iteration. We experimented with both of these settings and obtained 0.3058 and 0.3029 BLEU respectively. Lower performance suggest the importance of updating weights after each instance selection step.

4.4 Instance Selection for Alignment

We have shown that high coverage is an integral part of training sets for achieving high BLEU performance. SMT systems also heavily rely on the word alignment of the parallel corpus to derive a phrase table that can be used for translation. GIZA++ (Och and Ney, 2003) is commonly used for word alignment and phrase table generation, which is prone to making more errors as the length of the training sentence increase (Ravi and Knight, 2010). Therefore, we analyze instance selection techniques that optimize coverage and word alignment performance and at the same time do not produce very long sentences. Too few words per sentence may miss the phrasal structure, whereas too many words per sentence may miss the actual word alignment for the features we are interested. We are also trying to retrieve relevant training sentences for a given test sentence to increase the feature alignment performance.

Shortest: A baseline strategy that can minimize the training feature set's size involves selecting the shortest translations containing each feature.

Co-occurrence: We use *co-occurrence* of words in the parallel corpus to retrieve sentences containing co-occurring items. Dice's coefficient (Dice, 1945) is used as a heuristic word alignment technique giving an association score for each pair of word positions (Och and Ney, 2003).

We define Dice's coefficient score as:

$$dice(x, y) = \frac{2C(x, y)}{C(x)C(y)}, \quad (7)$$

where $C(x, y)$ is the number of times x and y co-occur and $C(x)$ is the count of observing x in the selected training set. Given a test source sentence, $S_{\mathcal{U}}$, we can estimate the goodness of a training sentence pair, (S, T), by the sum of the alignment scores:

$$\phi_{dice}(S_{\mathcal{U}}, S, T) = \frac{\sum_{x \in X(S_{\mathcal{U}})} \sum_{j=1}^{|T|} \sum_{y \in Y(x)} dice(y, T_j)}{|T| \log |S|}, \quad (8)$$

where $X(S_{\mathcal{U}})$ stores the features of $S_{\mathcal{U}}$ and $Y(x)$ lists the tokens in feature x. The difficulty of word aligning a pair of training sentences, (S, T), can be approximated by $|S|^{|T|}$. We use a normalization factor proportional to $|T| \log |S|$.

The average target words per sentence using ϕ_{dice} drops to 26.2 compared to 36.3 of FDA. We still obtain a better performance than the baseline *en-de* system with the union of 1000 training instances per sentence with 0.3635 BLEU and 6.1676 NIST scores. Coverage comparison with FDA shows slight improvement with lower number of target bigrams and similar trend for others (Figure 4). We note that shortest strategy achieves better performance than both *ELPR* and *NGRAM*. We obtain 0.3144 BLEU and 5.5 NIST scores in the individual translation task with 1000 training instances per sentence and 0.3171 BLEU and 5.4662 NIST scores when the mean of the weights is used.

4.5 Out-of-domain Translation Results

We have used FDA and *dice* algorithms to select training sets for the out-of-domain challenge test sets used in (Callison-Burch et al., 2011). The parallel corpus contains about 1.9 million training sentences and the test set contain 3003 sentences. We built separate Moses systems using all of the parallel corpus for the language pairs *en-de*, *de-en*, *en-es*, and *es-en*. We created training sets using all of the features of the test set to select training instances. The results given in Table 6 show that we can achieve similar BLEU performance using about 7% of the parallel corpus target words (200,000 instances) using *dice* and about 16% using FDA. In the out-of-domain translation task, we are able to reduce the training set size to achieve a performance close to the baseline. The sample points presented in the table is chosen proportional to the relative sizes of the parallel corpus sizes of WMT'10 and WMT'11 datasets and the training set size of the peak in Figure 3. We may be able to achieve better performance in the out-of-domain task as well. The sample points in Table 6 may be on either side of the peak.

5 Contributions

We have introduced the feature decay algorithms (FDA), a class of instance selection algorithms that use feature decay, which achieves better target coverage than previous work and achieves significant gains in translation performance. We find that decaying feature weights has significant effect on the performance. We demonstrate that target coverage and translation performance are correlated, showing that target coverage is also a good indicator of BLEU performance. We have shown that target coverage provides an upper bound on the translation performance with a given training set.

We achieve improvements of $\sim$2 BLEU points using about 20% of the available training data in terms of target words with FDA and ~ 1 BLEU points with only about 5%. We have also shown that by training on only 3000 instances per sentence we can reach within 1 BLEU difference to the baseline system. In the out-of-domain translation task, we are able to reduce the training set size to achieve a similar performance with the baseline.

Our results demonstrate that SMT systems can improve their performance by transductive training set selection. We have shown how to select instances and achieved significant performance improvements.

References

Vamshi Ambati, Stephan Vogel, and Jaime Carbonell. 2010. Active learning and crowd-sourcing for machine translation. In Nicoletta Calzolari (Conference Chair), Khalid Choukri, Bente Maegaard, Joseph Mariani, Jan Odijk, Stelios Piperidis, Mike Rosner, and Daniel Tapias, editors, *Proceedings of the Seventh conference on International Language Resources and Evaluation (LREC'10)*, Valletta, Malta, May. European Language Resources Association (ELRA).

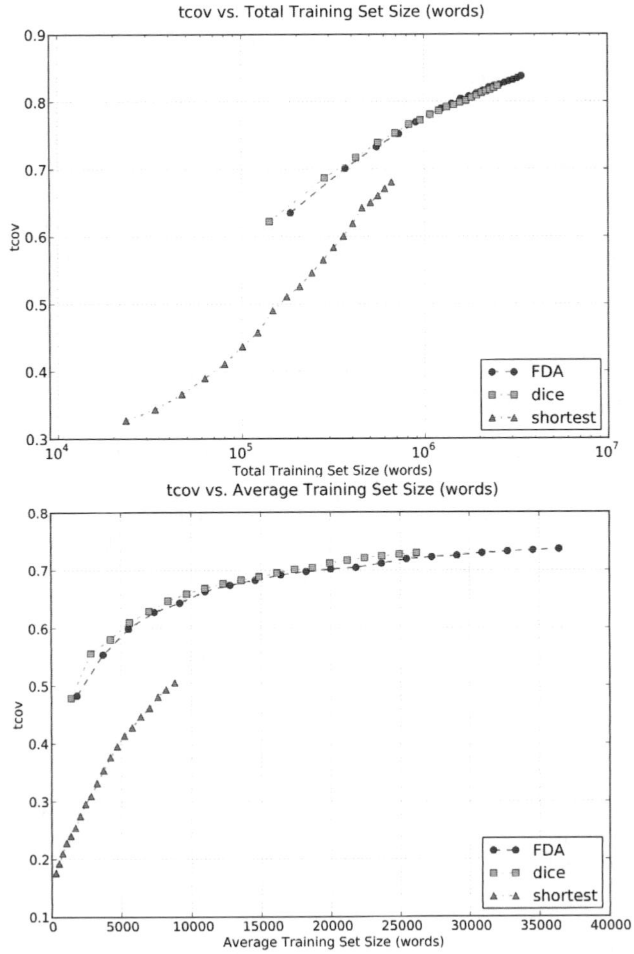

Figure 4: Target coverage per target words comparison. Figure shows the rate of increase in $tcov$ as the size of $\mathcal{L}$ increase. Target coverage curves for total training set size is given on the left plot and for average training set size per test sentence on the right plot.

		en-de	*de-en*	*en-es*	*es-en*
BLEU	ALL	0.1376	0.2074	0.2829	0.2919
	FDA	0.1363	0.2055	0.2824	0.2892
	dice	0.1374	0.2061	0.2834	0.2857
# target words $\times 10^6$	ALL	47.4	49.6	52.8	50.4
	FDA	7.9	8.0	8.7	8.2
	dice	6.9	7.0	3.9	3.6
% of ALL	FDA	17	16	16	16
	dice	14	14	7.4	7.1

Table 6: Performance for the out-of-domain task of (Callison-Burch et al., 2011). ALL corresponds to the baseline system using all of the parallel corpus.

Sankaranarayanan Ananthakrishnan, Rohit Prasad, David Stallard, and Prem Natarajan. 2010. Discriminative sample selection for statistical machine translation. In *Proceedings of the 2010 Conference on Empirical Methods in Natural Language Processing*, pages 626–635, Cambridge, MA, October. Association for Computational Linguistics.

Michele Banko and Eric Brill. 2001. Scaling to very very large corpora for natural language disambiguation. In *Proceedings of 39th Annual Meeting of the Association for Computational Linguistics*, pages 26–33, Toulouse, France, July. Association for Computational Linguistics.

Ergun Bicici and Deniz Yuret. 2010. L_1 regularized regression for reranking and system combination in machine translation. In *Proceedings of the ACL 2010 Joint Fifth Workshop on Statistical Machine Translation and Metrics MATR*, Uppsala, Sweden, July. Association for Computational Linguistics.

Michael Bloodgood and Chris Callison-Burch. 2010. Bucking the trend: Large-scale cost-focused active learning for statistical machine translation. In *Proceedings of the 48th Annual Meeting of the Association for Computational Linguistics*, pages 854–864, Uppsala, Sweden, July. Association for Computational Linguistics.

Chris Callison-Burch, Philipp Koehn, Christof Monz, Kay Peterson, and Omar Zaidan, editors. 2010. *Proceedings of the Joint Fifth Workshop on Statistical Machine Translation and MetricsMATR*. Association for Computational Linguistics, Uppsala, Sweden, July.

Chris Callison-Burch, Philipp Koehn, Christof Monz, Kay Peterson, and Omar Zaidan, editors. 2011. *Proceedings of the Sixth Workshop on Statistical Machine Translation*. Edinburgh, England, July.

Lee R. Dice. 1945. Measures of the amount of ecologic association between species. *Ecology*, 26(3):297–302.

Matthias Eck, Stephan Vogel, and Alex Waibel. 2005. Low cost portability for statistical machine translation based on n-gram coverage. In *Proceedings of the 10th Machine Translation Summit, MT Summit X*, pages 227–234, Phuket, Thailand, September.

Gholamreza Haffari and Anoop Sarkar. 2009. Active learning for multilingual statistical machine translation. In *Proceedings of the Joint Conference of the 47th Annual Meeting of the ACL and the 4th International Joint Conference on Natural Language Processing of the AFNLP*, pages 181–189, Suntec, Singapore, August. Association for Computational Linguistics.

Gholamreza Haffari, Maxim Roy, and Anoop Sarkar. 2009. Active learning for statistical phrase-based machine translation. In *Proceedings of Human Language Technologies: The 2009 Annual Conference of the North American Chapter of the Association for Computational Linguistics*, pages 415–423, Boulder, Colorado, June. Association for Computational Linguistics.

Saša Hasan, Richard Zens, and Hermann Ney. 2007. Are very large N-best lists useful for SMT? In *Human Language Technologies 2007: The Conference of the North American Chapter of the Association for Computational Linguistics; Companion Volume, Short Papers*, pages 57–60, Rochester, New York, April. Association for Computational Linguistics.

Philipp Koehn and Kevin Knight. 2001. Knowledge sources for word-level translation models. In *Proceedings of the 2001 Conference on Empirical Methods in Natural Language Processing*.

Philipp Koehn, Hieu Hoang, Alexandra Birch, Chris Callison-Burch, Marcello Federico, Nicola Bertoldi, Brooke Cowan, Wade Shen, Christine Moran, Richard Zens, Chris Dyer, Ondrej Bojar, Alexandra Constantin, and Evan Herbst. 2007. Moses: Open source toolkit for statistical machine translation. In *Annual Meeting of the Assoc. for Computational Linguistics*, pages 177–180, Prague, Czech Republic, June.

Philipp Koehn. 2004. Statistical significance tests for machine translation evaluation. In Dekang Lin and Dekai Wu, editors, *Proceedings of EMNLP 2004*, pages 388–395, Barcelona, Spain, July. Association for Computational Linguistics.

Philipp Koehn. 2006. Statistical machine translation: the basic, the novel, and the speculative. Tutorial at EACL 2006.

Yajuan Lü, Jin Huang, and Qun Liu. 2007. Improving statistical machine translation performance by training data selection and optimization. In *Proceedings of the 2007 Joint Conference on Empirical Methods in Natural Language Processing and Computational Natural Language Learning (EMNLP-CoNLL)*, pages 343–350, Prague, Czech Republic, June. Association for Computational Linguistics.

A. Mandal, D. Vergyri, W. Wang, J. Zheng, A. Stolcke, G. Tur, D. Hakkani-Tur, and N.F. Ayan. 2008. Efficient data selection for machine translation. In *Spoken Language Technology Workshop, 2008. SLT 2008. IEEE*, pages 261 –264.

Franz Josef Och and Hermann Ney. 2003. A systematic comparison of various statistical alignment models. *Computational Linguistics*, 29(1):19–51.

Kishore Papineni, Salim Roukos, Todd Ward, and Wei-Jing Zhu. 2001. BLEU: a method for automatic evaluation of machine translation. In *ACL '02: Proceedings of the 40th Annual Meeting on Association for*

Computational Linguistics, pages 311–318, Morristown, NJ, USA. Association for Computational Linguistics.

Sujith Ravi and Kevin Knight. 2010. Does giza++ make search errors? *Computational Linguistics*, 36(3):295–302.

Nicolas Serrano, Jesus Andres-Ferrer, and Francisco Casacuberta. 2009. On a kernel regression approach to machine translation. In *Iberian Conference on Pattern Recognition and Image Analysis*, pages 394–401.

Jakob Uszkoreit, Jay Ponte, Ashok Popat, and Moshe Dubiner. 2010. Large scale parallel document mining for machine translation. In *Proceedings of the 23rd International Conference on Computational Linguistics (Coling 2010)*, pages 1101–1109, Beijing, China, August. Coling 2010 Organizing Committee.

Zhuoran Wang and John Shawe-Taylor. 2008. Kernel regression framework for machine translation: UCL system description for WMT 2008 shared translation task. In *Proceedings of the Third Workshop on Statistical Machine Translation*, pages 155–158, Columbus, Ohio, June. Association for Computational Linguistics.

WMT. 2010. ACL Workshop: Joint Fifth Workshop on Statistical Machine Translation and Metrics MATR, July.

Investigations on Translation Model Adaptation Using Monolingual Data

Patrik Lambert, Holger Schwenk, Christophe Servan and Sadaf Abdul-Rauf
LIUM, University of Le Mans
72085 Le Mans, France
FirstName.LastName@lium.univ-lemans.fr

Abstract

Most of the freely available parallel data to train the translation model of a statistical machine translation system comes from very specific sources (European parliament, United Nations, etc). Therefore, there is increasing interest in methods to perform an adaptation of the translation model. A popular approach is based on unsupervised training, also called self-enhancing. Both only use monolingual data to adapt the translation model. In this paper we extend the previous work and provide new insight in the existing methods. We report results on the translation between French and English. Improvements of up to 0.5 BLEU were observed with respect to a very competitive baseline trained on more than 280M words of human translated parallel data.

1 Introduction

Adaptation of a statistical machine translation system (SMT) is a topic of increasing interest during the last years. Statistical (n-gram) language models are used in many domains and several approaches to adapt such models were proposed in the literature, for instance in the framework of automatic speech recognition. Many of these approaches were successfully used to adapt the language model of an SMT system. On the other hand, it seems more challenging to adapt the other components of an SMT system, namely the translation and reordering models. In this work we consider the adaptation of the translation model of a phrase-based SMT system.

While rule-based machine translation rely on rules and linguistic resources built for that purpose, SMT systems can be developed without the need of any language-specific expertise and are only based on bilingual sentence-aligned data ("*bitexts*") and large monolingual texts. However, while monolingual data are usually available in large amounts and for a variety of tasks, bilingual texts are a sparse resource for most language pairs.

Current parallel corpora mostly come from one domain (proceedings of the Canadian or European Parliament, or of the United Nations). This is problematic when SMT systems trained on such corpora are used for general translations, as the language jargon heavily used in these corpora is not appropriate for everyday life translations or translations in some other domain. This problem could be attacked by either searching for more in-domain training data, e.g. by exploring comparable corpora or the WEB, or by adapting the translation model to the task. In this work we consider translation model adaptation without using additional *bilingual data*. One can distinguish two types of translation model adaptation: first, adding new source words or/and new translations to the model; and second, modifying the probabilities of the existing model to better fit the topic of the task. These two directions are complementary and could be simultaneously applied. In this work we focus on the second type of adaptation.

In this work, we focus on statistical phrase-based machine translations systems (PBSMT), but the methods could be also applied to hierarchical systems. In PBSMT, the translation model is represented by a large list of all known source phrases and their translations. Each entry is weighted using several probabilities, e.g. the popular Moses

Proceedings of the 6th Workshop on Statistical Machine Translation, pages 284–293,
Edinburgh, Scotland, UK, July 30–31, 2011. ©2011 Association for Computational Linguistics

system uses phrase translation probabilities in the forward and backward direction, as well as lexical probabilities in both directions. The entries of the phrase-table are automatically extracted from sentence aligned parallel data and they are usually quite noisy. It is not uncommon to encounter several hundreds, or even thousands of possible translations of frequent source phrases. Many of these automatically extracted translations are probably wrong and are never used since their probabilities are (fortunately) small in comparison to better translations. Therefore, several approaches were proposed to filter these phrase-tables, reducing considerably their size without any loss of the quality, or even achieving improved performance (Johnson et al., 2007).

Given these observations, adaptation of the translation model of PBSMT systems could be performed by modifying the probability distribution of the existing phrases without necessarily modifying the entries. The idea is of course to increase the probabilities of translations that are appropriate to the task and to decrease the probabilities of the other ones. Ideally, we should also add new translations or source phrase, but this seems to be more challenging without any additional parallel data.

A common way to modify a statistical model is to use a mixture model and to optimize the coefficients to the adaptation domain. This was investigated in the framework of SMT by several authors, for instance for word alignment (Civera and Juan, 2007), for language modeling (Zhao et al., 2004; Koehn and Schroeder, 2007) and to a lesser extent for the translation model (Foster and Kuhn, 2007; Chen et al., 2008). This mixture approach has the advantage that only few parameters need to be modified, the mixture coefficients. On the other hand, many translation probabilities are modified at once and it is not possible to selectively modify the probabilities of particular phrases.

Another direction of research is self-enhancing of the translation model. This was first proposed by Ueffing (2006). The idea is to translate the test data, to filter the translations with help of a confidence score and to use the most reliable ones to train an additional small phrase table that is jointly used with the generic phrase table. This could be also seen as a mixture model with the in-domain component being build on-the-fly for each test set. In practice, such an approach is probably only feasible when large amounts of test data are collected and processed at once, e.g. a typical evaluation set up with a test set of about 50k words. This method of self-enhancing the translation model seems to be more difficult to apply for on-line SMT, e.g. a WEB service, since often the translation of some sentences only is requested. In follow up work, this approach was refined (Ueffing et al., 2007). Domain adaptation was also performed simultaneously for the translation, language and reordering model (Chen et al., 2008).

A somehow related approach was named lightly-supervised training (Schwenk, 2008). In that work an SMT system is used to translate large amounts of monolingual texts, to filter them and to add them to the translation model training data. This approach was reported to obtain interesting improvements in the translations quality (Schwenk and Senellart, 2009; Bertoldi and Federico, 2009). In comparison to *self enhancing* as proposed by Ueffing (2006), lightly-supervised training does not adapt itself to the test data, but large amounts of monolingual training data are translated and a completely new model is built. This model can be applied to any test data, including a WEB service.

In this paper we propose to extend this approach in several ways. First, we argue that the automatic translations should not be performed from the source to the target language, but in the opposite direction. Second, we propose to use the segmentation obtained during translation instead of performing word alignments with GIZA++ (Och and Ney, 2003) of the automatic translations. Finally, we propose to enrich the vocabulary of the adapted system by detecting untranslated words and automatically inferring possible translations from the stemmed form and the existing translations in the phrase table.

This paper is organized as follows. In the next section we first describe our approach in detail. Section 3 describes the considered task, the available resources and the baseline PBSMT system. Results are summarized in section 4 and the paper concludes with a discussion and perspectives of this work.

2 Architecture of the approach

In this paper we propose to extend in several ways the translation model adaptation by unsupervised training as proposed by Schwenk (2008). In that paper the authors propose to first build a PBSMT system using all available human translated bitexts. This system is then used to translate large amounts of monolingual data in the source language. These automatic translations are filtered using the sentence-length normalized log score of Moses, i.e. the sum of the log-scores of all feature functions. Putting a threshold on this score, only the most reliable translations are kept. This threshold was determined experimentally. The automatic translations were added to the parallel training data and a new PBSMT model was build, performing the complete pipeline of word alignment with GIZA++, phrase extraction and scoring and tuning the system on development data with MERT. In Schwenk (2009) significant improvement were obtained by this approach when translating from Arabic to French.

2.1 Choice of the translation direction

First, we argue that it should be better to translate monolingual data in the opposite translation direction of the system that we want to improve, i.e. from the target into the source language. When translating large amounts of monolingual data, the system will of course produce some wrong translations with respect to choice of the vocabulary, to word order, to morphology, etc. If we translate from the source to the target language, these wrong translations are added to the phrase table and may be used in future translations performed by the adapted system. When we add the automatic translations performed in the opposite direction to the training data, the possibly wrong translations will appear on the source side of the entries in the adapted phrase table. PBSMT systems segment the source sentence according to the available entries in the phrase table. Since the source sentence is usually grammatically and semantically correct, with the eventual exception of speech translation, it is unlikely that the wrong entries in the phrase table will be ever used, e.g. phrases with bad word choice or wrong morphology.

The question of the choice of the translation direction was already raised by Bertoldi and Federico (2009). However, when data in the source language is available they adapt only the translation model (TM), while they adapt the TM *and the language model* (LM) when data in the target language is given. Of course the system with adapted LM is much better, but this doesn't prove that target monolingual data are better than source monolingual data for TM adaptation. In our paper, we use the same, best, LM for all systems and we adapt the baseline system with bitexts synthesized from source or target monolingual data.

2.2 Word alignment

In the work of Schwenk (2008), the filtered automatic translation were added to the parallel training data and the full pipeline to build a PBSMT system was performed again, including word alignment with GIZA++. Word alignment of bitexts of several hundreds of millions of words is a very time consuming step. Therefore we propose to use the segmentation into phrases and words obtained implicitly during the translation of the monolingual data with the moses toolkit. These alignments are simply added to the previously calculated alignments of the human translated bitexts and a new phrase table is built.

This new procedure does not only speed-up the overall processing, but there are also investigations that these alignments obtained by decoding are more suitable to extract phrases than the symmetrized word alignments produced by GIZA++. For instance, Wuebker et al. (2010) proposed to translate the *training data*, using forced alignment and a leave-one-out technique, and to use the induced alignments to extract phrases. They have observed improvements with respect to word alignment obtained by GIZA++. On the other hand, Bertoldi and Federico (2009) adapted an SMT system with automatic translations and trained the translation and reordering models on the word alignment used by moses. They reported a very small drop in performance with respect to training word alignments with GIZA++. Similar ideas were also used in pivot translation. Bertoldi et al. (2008) translated from the pivot language to the source language to create parallel training data for the direct translation.

2.3 Treatment of unknown words

Statistical machine translation systems have some trouble dealing with morphologically rich languages. It can happen, in function of the available training data, that translations of words are only

Source language French	Source language stemmed form	Target language English
finies	fini	finished
effacés	effacé	erased
hawaienne	hawaien	Hawaiian
...	...	...

Table 1: Example of translations from French to English which are automatically extracted from the phrase-table with the stemmed form.

known in some forms and not in others. For instance, for a user of MT technology it is quite difficult to understand why the system can translate the French word "je pense"[1], but not "tu penses"[2]. There have been attempts in the literature to address this problem, for instance by Habash (2008) to deal with the Arabic language. It is actually possible to automatically infer possible translations when translating from a morphologically rich language, to a simpler language. In our case we use this approach to translate from French to English.

Several of the unknown words are actually adjectives, nouns or verbs in a particular form that itself is not known, but the phrase table would contain the translation of a different form. As an example we can mention the French adjective *finies* which is in the female plural form. After stemming we may be able to find the translation in a dictionary which is automatically extracted from the phrase-table (see Table 1). This idea was already outlined by (Bojar and Tamchyna, 2011) to translate from Czech to English.

First, we automatically extract a dictionary from the phrase table. This is done, be detecting all 1-to-1 entries in the phrase table. When there are multiple entries, all are kept with their lexical translations probabilities. Our dictionary has about 680k unique source words with a total of almost 1M translations.

source segment	les travaux sont **finis**
stemmed	les travaux sont **fini**
segment proposed	les travaux sont <n translation="finished||ended" prob="0.008||0.0001">**finis**</n>

Table 2: Example of the treatment of an unknown French word and its automatically inferred translation.

The detection of unknown words is performed by comparing the n-grams contained in the phrase table and the source segment in order to detect identical words. Once the unknown word is selected, we are looking for its stemmed form in the dictionary and propose some translations for the unknown word based on lexical score of the phrase table (see Table 2 for some examples). The stemmer used is the snowball stemmer[3]. Then the different hypothesis are evaluated with the target language model.

This kind of processing could be done either before running the Moses decoder, *i.e.* using the XML mark-up of Moses, or after decoding by post-processing the untranslated words. In both cases, we are unable to differentiate the possible translations of the same source phrase with meaningful translation probabilities, and they won't be added to the phrase-table, nor put into a context with other words that may trigger their use.

Therefore, we propose to use this technique to replace unknown words during the translation of the monolingual data that we use to adapt the translation model. By these means, the automatically induced translations of previously unknown morphological forms will be put into a context and actually appear in the new adapted phrase-table. The corresponding translation probabilities will be those corresponding to their frequency in the monolingual in-domain data.

This procedure has been implemented, but we were not able to obtain improvements in the BLEU score. However, one can ask if automatic metrics, evaluated on a test corpus of limited size, are the best choice to judge this technique. In fact, in our setting we have observed that less than 0.2% of the words in the test set are unknown. We argue that the ability to complement the phrase-table with many morphological forms of other wise known words, can only improve the usability of SMT systems.

3 Task Description and resources

In this paper, we consider the translation of news texts between French and English, in both directions. In order to allow comparisons, we used exactly the same data as those allowed for the international evaluation organized in the framework of the sixth workshop on SMT, to be held in Edinburgh

[1] I think

[2] you think

[3] `http://snowball.tartarus.org/`

Parallel data	Size [M words]	English/French Dev	English/French Test	French/English Dev	French/English Test
Eparl + nc	54	26.20 (0.06)	28.06 (0.2)	26.70 (0.06)	27.41 (0.2)
Eparl + nc + crawled1	168	26.84 (0.09)	29.08 (0.1)	27.96 (0.09)	28.20 (0.04)
Eparl + nc + crawled2	**286**	**26.95 (0.04)**	**29.29 (0.03)**	**28.20 (0.03)**	**28.57 (0.1)**
Eparl + nc + un	379	26.57	28.52	-	-
Eparl + nc + crawled1 + un	514	26.87	28.99	-	-
Eparl + nc + crawled2 + un	631	26.99	29.26	-	-

Table 4: Case sensitive BLEU scores as a function of the amount of parallel training data. (Eparl=Europarl, nc=News Commentary, crawled1/2=sub-sampled crawled bitexts, un=sub-sampled United Nations bitexts).

Corpus	English	French
Bitexts:		
Europarl	50.5M	54.4M
News Commentary	2.9M	3.3M
United Nations	344M	393M
Crawled (10^9 bitexts)	667M	794M
Development data:		
newstest2009	65k	73k
newstest2010	62k	71k
Monolingual data:		
LDC Gigaword	4.1G	920M
Crawled news	2.6G	612M

Table 3: Available training data for the translation between French and English for the translation evaluation at WMT'11 (number of words after tokenisation).

in July 2011. Preliminary results of this evaluation are available on the Internet.[4] Table 3 summarizes the available training and development data. We optimized our systems on `newstest2009` and used `newstest2010` as internal test set. For both corpora, only one reference translations is available. Scoring was performed with NIST's implementation of the BLEU score ('mt-eval' version 13).

3.1 Baseline system

The baseline system is a standard phrase-based SMT system based on the the Moses SMT toolkit (Koehn et al., 2007). It uses fourteen features functions for translation, namely phrase and lexical translation probabilities in both directions, seven features for the lexicalized distortion model, a word and a phrase penalty, and a target language model. It is constructed as follows. First, word alignments in both directions are calculated. We used a multi-threaded version of the GIZA++ tool (Gao and Vogel, 2008). Phrases and lexical reorderings are extracted using the default settings of the Moses toolkit. All the bitexts were concatenated. The parameters of Moses are tuned on the development data using the MERT tool. For most of the runs, we performed three optimizations using different starting points and report average results. English and French texts were tokenised using a modified version of the tools of the Moses suite. Punctuation and case were preserved.

The language models were trained on all the available data, i.e. the target side of the bitexts, the whole Gigaword corpus and the crawled monolingual data. We build 4-gram back-off LMs with the SRI LM toolkit using Modified Kneser-Ney and no cut-off on all the n-grams. Past experience has shown that keeping all n-grams slightly improves the performance although this produces quite huge models (10G and 30G of disk space for French and English respectively).

Table 4 gives the baseline results using various amounts of bitexts. Starting with the Europarl and the News Commentary corpora, various amounts of human translated data were added. The organizers of the evaluation provide the so called 10^9 French-English parallel corpus which contains almost 800 million words of data crawled from Canadian and European Internet pages. Following works from the 2010 WMT evaluation (Lambert et al., 2010), we filtered this data using IBM-1 probabilities and language model scores to keep only the most reliable translations. Two subsets were built with 115M and 232M English words respectively (using two differ-

[4]http://matrix.statmt.org

alignment	Dev	Test	
	BLEU	BLEU	TER
giza	27.34 (0.01)	29.80 (0.06)	55.34 (0.06)
reused giza	27.40 (0.05)	29.82 (0.10)	55.30 (0.02)
reused moses	27.42 (0.02)	29.77 (0.06)	55.27 (0.03)

Table 5: Results for systems trained via different word alignment configurations. The values are the average over 3 MERT runs performed with different seeds. The numbers in parentheses are the standard deviation of these three values. Translation was performed from English to French, adding 45M words of automatic translations (translated from French to English) to the baseline system "eparl+nc+crawled2".

ent settings of the filter thresholds). They are referred to as "crawled1" and "crawled2" respectively. Adding this data improved the BLEU score of almost 1 BLEU point (28.30 → 29.27). This is our baseline system to be improved by translation model adaptation. Using the UN data gave no significant improvement despite its huge size. This is probably a typical example that it is not necessarily useful to use all available parallel training data, in particular when a very specific (out-of domain) jargon is used. Consequently, the UN data was not used in the subsequent experiments.

We were mainly working on the translation from English to French. Therefore only one baseline system was build for the reverse translation direction.

Corpus	French (fe)		English (ef)	
	available	filtered	available	filtered
2009	92	31	121	45
2010	43	12	112	49
2011	8	2	15	6
total	219	45	177	100

Table 6: Monolingual data used to adapt the systems, given in millions of English words. Under "French (fe)", we indicated the number of translated English words from French, and under "English (ef)" we reported the number of source English words translated into French. Thus "fe" and "ef" refer respectively to French–English and English–French translation direction of monolingual data. In the experiments we used the 100M English–French (ef) filtered monolingual data, as well as a 45M-word subset (in order to have the same amount of data as for French–English) and a 65M-word subset.

4 Experimental Evaluation

The system trained on Europarl, News Commentary and the sub-sampled version of the 10^9 bitexts ("eparl+nc+crawled2", in the third line of Table 3), was used to translate parts of the crawled news in French and English. Statistics on the translated data are given in Table 6.

We focused on the most recent data since the time period of our development and test data was end of 2008 and 2009 respectively. In the future we will translate all the available monolingual data and make it available to the community in order to ease the widespread use of this kind of translation model adaptation methods. These automatic translations were filtered using the sentence normalized log-score of the decoder, as proposed by (Schwenk, 2008). However, we did not perform systematic experiments to find the optimal threshold on this score, but simply used a value which seems to be a good compromise of quality and quantity of the translations. This gave us about 45M English words of automatic translations from French, as well as the translations into French of 100M English words, to be used to adapt the baseline systems.

4.1 Word alignment

In order to build a phrase table with the translated data, we re-used the word alignment obtained during the translation with the moses toolkit. We compared the system trained via these alignments to the systems built by running GIZA++ on all the data. When word alignments of the baseline corpus (not adapted) are trained together with the translated data, they could be affected by phrase pairs coming from incorrect translations. To measure this effect, we trained an additional system, for which the alignments of the baseline corpus are those trained without the translated data. For the translated data, we re-use the GIZA++ alignments trained on all the data. Results for these three alignment configura-

baseline	translated bitexts	Dev	Test	
		BLEU	BLEU	TER
Eparl + nc	-	26.20 (0.06)	28.06 (0.22)	56.85 (0.09)
	news fe 45M	**27.18 (0.09)**	**29.03 (0.07)**	**55.97 (0.07)**
	news ef 45M	26.15 (0.04)	28.44 (0.09)	56.56 (0.11)
Eparl + nc + crawled2	-	26.95 (0.04)	29.29 (0.03)	55.77 (0.19)
	news fe 45M	**27.42 (0.02)**	**29.77 (0.06)**	**55.27 (0.03)**
	news ef 45M	26.75 (0.04)	28.88 (0.10)	56.06 (0.05)

Table 7: Translation results of the English–French systems augmented with a bitext obtained by translating news data from English to French (ef) and French to English (fe). 45M refers to the number of English running words.

baseline	translated bitexts	Dev	Test	
		BLEU	BLEU	TER
Eparl + nc	-	26.70 (0.06)	27.41 (0.24)	55.07 (0.17)
	news fe 45M	27.47 (0.08)	27.77 (0.23)	54.84 (0.13)
	news ef 45M	27.55 (0.05)	28.51 (0.10)	54.12 (0.09)
	news ef 65M	27.58 (0.03)	28.70 (0.09)	54.06 (0.17)
	news ef 100M	**27.63 (0.06)**	**28.68 (0.06)**	**54.02 (0.06)**
Eparl + nc + crawled2	-	28.20 (0.03)	28.54 (0.12)	54.17 (0.15)
	news fe 45M	28.02 (0.11)	28.40 (0.10)	54.45 (0.06)
	news ef 45M	28.24 (0.06)	28.93 (0.22)	53.90 (0.08)
	news ef 65M	28.16 (0.19)	28.75 (0.06)	54.03 (0.14)
	news ef 100M	**28.28 (0.09)**	**28.96 (0.03)**	**53.79 (0.09)**

Table 8: Translation results of the French–English systems augmented with a bitext obtained by translating news data from English to French (ef) and French to English (fe). 45M/65M/100M refers to the number of English running words.

tions are presented in Table 5. In these systems French sources and English translations (45 million words) were added to the "eparl+nc+crawled2" baseline corpus. According to BLEU and TER metrics, reusing Moses alignments to build the adapted phrase table has no significant impact on the system performance. We repeated the experiment without the 10^9 corpus and with the smaller selection of 10^9 (`crawled1`) and arrived to the same conclusion. However, the re-use of Moses alignments saves time and resources. On the larger baseline corpus, the mGiza process lasted 46 hours with two jobs of 4 thread running and a machine with two Intel X5650 quad-core processors.

4.2 Choice of the translation direction

A second point under study in this work is the effect of the translation direction of the monolingual data used to adapt the translation model. Tables 7 and 8 present results for, respectively, English–French and French–English systems adapted with news data translated from English to French (ef) and French to English (fe). The experiment was repeated with two baseline corpora. The results show clearly that target to source translated data are more useful than source to target translated data. The improvement in terms of BLEU score due to the use of target-to-source translated data instead of source-to-target translated data ranges from 0.5 to 0.9 for the French–English and English–French systems. For instance, when translating from English to French (Table 7), the baseline system "eparl+nc" achieves a BLEU score of 28.06 on the test set. This could be improved to 29.03 using automatic translations in the reverse direction (French to English), while we only achieve a BLEU score of 28.44 when using automatic translation performed in the same direction as the system to be adapted. The effect is even clearer when we try to adapt the large system "eparl+nc+crawled2". Adding automatic translations translated from English-to-French did actually lead to a lower BLEU score (29.29 → 28.88) while we observe an improvement of nearly 0.5 BLEU in the other case.

With target-to-source translated news data, the gain with respect to the baseline corpus for English-French systems (Table 7) is nearly 1 BLEU for "Eparl+nc" and 0.5 BLEU for "Eparl+nc+crawled2". With the same amount of translated data (45 million English words), approximately the same gains are observed in French–English systems. Due to the larger availability of English news data, we were able to use larger sets of target-to-source translated data for French-English systems, as can be seen in Table 8. With a bitext containing additionally 20 million English words, we get a further improvement of 0.2 BLEU for "Eparl+nc" (28.51 → 28.70), but no improvement for "Eparl+nc+crawled2" (the BLEU score is even lower, but the scores lie within the error interval). No further gain on the test data is achieved if we add again 35 million English words (total of 100M words) to the system "Eparl+nc". With the "Eparl+nc+crawle2" baseline, no significant improvement is observed if we adapt the system with 100M words instead of only 45M.

4.3 Result analysis

To get more insight into what happens to the model when we add the automatic translations, we calculated some statistics of the phrase table, presented in Table 9. Namely, we calculated the number of entries in the phrase table, the average number of translation options of each source phrase, the average entropy for each source phrase, the average source phrase length (in words) and the average target phrase length. The entropy is calculated over the probabilities of all translation options for each source phrase. Comparing the baseline with "Eparl+nc" and the baseline with "Eparl+nc+crawl2", we can observe that the average number of translation options was nearly multiplied by 3 with the addition of 230 million words of human translated bitexts. As a consequence the average entropy was increased from 1.84 to 2.08. On the contrary, adding 100 million words of in-domain automatic translations, the average number of translation options increased by only 5% for the "Eparl+nc" baseline, and decreased for the "Eparl+nc+crawl2" baseline. A decrease may occur if new source phrases with less translation options than the average are added. Furthermore, with the addition of 45 million words of in-domain data, the average entropy dropped from 1.84 to 1.33 or 1.60 for the "Eparl+nc" baseline, and from 2.08 to 1.81 or 1.96 for the "Eparl+nc+crawl2" baseline. With both baselines, the more translations are added to the system, the lower the entropy, although in some case the number of translation options increases (this is the case when we pass from 65M to 100M words of synthetic data). These results illustrate the fact that the automatic translations only reinforce some probabilities in the model, with the subsequent decrease in entropy, while human translations add new vocabulary. Note also that in the corpus using automatic translations, new words can only occur in the source side. Thus when translating from French to English, automatic translations from English to French are expected to yield more translation options and a higher entropy than the automatic translations from French to English. This is what is effectively observed in Table 9.

5 Conclusion

Unsupervised training is widely used in other areas, in particular large vocabulary speech recognition. The statistical models in speech recognition use a *generative approach* based on small units, usually triphones. Each triphone is modeled by a hidden Markov model and Gaussian mixture probability distributions (plus many improvements like parameter tying etc). Many methods were developed to adapt such models. The corresponding model in statistical machine translation is the phrase table, a long list of known words with their translations and probabilities. It seems much more challenging to adapt this kind of statistical model with unsupervised training, i.e. monolingual data. Nevertheless, we believe that unsupervised training can be also very useful in SMT. To the best of our knowledge, work in this area is very recent and only in its beginnings. This paper tries to give additional insights in this promising method.

Our work is based on the approach initially pro-

baseline	translated bitexts	entries (M)	translations	entropy	src size	trg size
Eparl + nc	-	7.16	83.83	1.84	1.80	2.81
	news fe 45M	7.42	70.00	1.33	1.83	2.80
	news ef 45M	8.24	81.58	1.60	1.86	2.79
	news ef 65M	8.42	81.58	1.55	1.88	2.79
	news ef 100M	9.21	85.93	1.54	1.90	2.79
Eparl + nc + crawl2	-	25.42	235.16	2.08	1.76	2.93
	news fe 45M	25.54	217.21	1.81	1.77	2.93
	news ef 45M	26.09	228.07	1.96	1.78	2.93
	news ef 65M	26.21	226.45	1.91	1.78	2.93
	news ef 100M	26.79	227.08	1.89	1.79	2.93

Table 9: Phrase table statistics for French–English systems augmented with bitexts built via automatic translations. Only the entries useful to translate the development set were present in the considered phrase table.

posed in (Schwenk, 2008): build a first SMT system, use it to translate large amounts of monolingual data, filter the obtained translations, add them to the bitexts and build a new system from scratch.

We proposed several extensions to this technique which seem to improve the translations quality in our experiments. First of all, we have observed that it is clearly better to add automatically translated texts to the translations model training data which were translated from the target to the source language. This seems to ensure that potentially wrong translations are not used in the new model.

Second, we were able to skip the process of performing word alignment of this additional parallel data without any significant loss in the BLEU score. Performing word alignments with GIZA++ can easily take several days when several hundred millions of bitexts are available. Instead, we directly used the word alignments produced by Moses when translating the monolingual data. This resulted in an appreciable speed-up of the procedure, but has also interesting theoretical aspects. Reusing the word alignment from the translation process is expected to result in a phrase extraction process that is more consistent with the use of the phrases.

Finally, we outlined a method to automatically add new translations without any additional parallel training data. In fact, when translating from a morphologically rich language to an easier one, in our case from French to English, it is often possible to infer the translations of unobserved morphological forms of nouns, verbs or adjectives. This is obtained by looking up the stemmed form in an automatically constructed dictionary. This kind of approach could be also applied to a classical PBSMT system, by adding various forms to the phrase table, but it is not obvious to come up with reasonable translations probabilities for these new entries. In our approach, the unknown word forms are processed in large amounts of monolingual data and the induced translations will appear in the context of complete sentences. Wrong translations can be blocked by the language model and the new translations can appear in phrases of various lengths.

This paper provided a detailed experimental evaluation of these methods. We considered the translation between French and English using the same data than was made available for the 2011 WMT evaluation. Improvement of up to 0.5 BLEU were observed with respect to an already competitive system trained on more than 280M words of human translated parallel data.

Acknowledgments

This work has been partially funded by the French Government under the project COSMAT (ANR ANR-09-CORD-004.) and the European Commission under the project EUROMATRIXPLUS (ICT-2007.2.2-FP7-231720).

References

Nicola Bertoldi and Marcello Federico. 2009. Domain adaptation for statistical machine translation. In *Forth Workshop on SMT*, pages 182–189.

Nicola Bertoldi, Madalina Barbaiani, Marcello Federico, and Roldano Cattoni. 2008. Phrase-based statistical machine translation with pivot languages. In *IWSLT*, pages 143–149.

Ondřej Bojar and Aleš Tamchyna. 2011. Forms Wanted: Training SMT on Monolingual Data. Abstract at Machine Translation and Morphologically-Rich Languages. Research Workshop of the Israel Science Foundation University of Haifa, Israel, January.

Boxing Chen, Min Zhang, Aiti Aw, and Haizhou Li. 2008. Exploiting n-best hypotheses for SMT self-enhancement. In *ACL*, pages 157–160.

Jorge Civera and Alfons Juan. 2007. Domain adaptation in statistical machine translation with mixture modelling. In *Second Workshop on SMT*, pages 177–180, June.

George Foster and Roland Kuhn. 2007. Mixture-model adaptation for SMT. In *EMNLP*, pages 128–135.

Qin Gao and Stephan Vogel. 2008. Parallel implementations of word alignment tool. In *Software Engineering, Testing, and Quality Assurance for Natural Language Processing*, pages 49–57, Columbus, Ohio, June. Association for Computational Linguistics.

Nizar Habash. 2008. Four techniques for online handling of out-of-vocabulary words in arabic-english statistical machine translation. In *ACL 08*.

Howard Johnson, Joel Martin, George Foster, and Roland Kuhn. 2007. Improving translation quality by discarding most of the phrasetable. In *EMNLP*, pages 967–975, Prague, Czech Republic.

Philipp Koehn and Josh Schroeder. 2007. Experiments in domain adaptation for statistical machine translation. In *Second Workshop on SMT*, pages 224–227, June.

Philipp Koehn, Hieu Hoang, Alexandra Birch, Chris Callison-Burch, Marcello Federico, Nicola Bertoldi, Brooke Cowan, Wade Shen, Christine Moran, Richard Zens, Chris Dyer, Ondrej Bojar, Alexandra Constantin, and Evan Herbst. 2007. Moses: Open source toolkit for statistical machine translation. In *ACL, demonstration session*.

Patrik Lambert, Sadaf Abdul-Rauf, and Holger Schwenk. 2010. LIUM SMT machine translation system for WMT 2010. In *Workshop on SMT*, pages 121–126.

Franz Josef Och and Hermann Ney. 2003. A systematic comparison of various statistical alignement models. *Computational Linguistics*, 29(1):19–51.

Holger Schwenk and Jean Senellart. 2009. Translation model adaptation for an Arabic/French news translation system by lightly-supervised training. In *MT Summit*.

Holger Schwenk. 2008. Investigations on large-scale lightly-supervised training for statistical machine translation. In *IWSLT*, pages 182–189.

Nicola Ueffing, Gholamreza Haffari, and Anoop Sarkar. 2007. Transductive learning for statistical machine translation. In *ACL*, pages 25–32.

Nicola Ueffing. 2006. Using monolingual source-language data to improve MT performance. In *IWSLT*, pages 174–181.

Joern Wuebker, Arne Mauser, and Hermann Ney. 2010. Training phrase translation models with leaving-one-out. In *ACL*, pages 475–484, Uppsala, Sweden, July. Association for Computational Linguistics.

Bing Zhao, Matthias Eck, and Stephan Vogel. 2004. Language model adaptation for statistical machine translation with structured query models. In *Coling*.

Topic Adaptation for Lecture Translation through Bilingual Latent Semantic Models

Nick Ruiz*
Free University of Bozen-Bolzano
Bolzano, Italy
nicruiz@fbk.eu

Marcello Federico
FBK-irst
Fondazione Bruno Kessler
Trento, Italy
federico@fbk.eu

Abstract

This work presents a simplified approach to bilingual topic modeling for language model adaptation by combining text in the source and target language into very short documents and performing Probabilistic Latent Semantic Analysis (PLSA) during model training. During inference, documents containing only the source language can be used to infer a full topic-word distribution on all words in the target language's vocabulary, from which we perform Minimum Discrimination Information (MDI) adaptation on a background language model (LM). We apply our approach on the English-French IWSLT 2010 TED Talk exercise, and report a 15% reduction in perplexity and relative BLEU and NIST improvements of 3% and 2.4%, respectively over a baseline only using a 5-gram background LM over the entire translation task. Our topic modeling approach is simpler to construct than its counterparts.

1 Introduction

Adaptation is usually applied to reduce the performance drop of Statistical Machine Translation (SMT) systems when translating documents that deviate from training and tuning conditions. In this paper, we focus primarily on language model (LM) adaptation. In SMT, LMs are used to promote fluent translations. As probabilistic models of sequences of words, language models guide the selection and ordering of phrases in translation. With respect to LM training, LM adaptation for SMT tries to improve an existing LM by using smaller amounts of texts. When adaptation data represents the translation task domain one generally refers to *domain adaptation*, while when they just represent the content of the single document to be translated one typically refers to *topic adaptation*.

We propose a cross-language topic adaptation method, enabling the adaptation of a LM based on the topic distribution of the source document during translation. We train a latent semantic topic model on a collection of bilingual documents, in which each document contains both the source and target language. During inference, a latent topic distribution of words across both the source and target languages is inferred from a source document to be translated. After inference, we remove all source language words from the topic-word distributions and construct a unigram language model which is used to adapt our background LM via Minimum Discrimination Information (MDI) estimation (Federico, 1999, 2002; Kneser et al., 1997).

We organize the paper as follows: In Section 2, we discuss relevant previous work. In Section 3, we review topic modeling. In Section 4, we review MDI adaptation. In Section 5, we describe our new bilingual topic modeling based adaptation technique. In Section 6, we report adaptation experiments, followed by conclusions and future work in Section 7.

2 Previous work

Zhao et al. (2004) construct a baseline SMT system using a large background language model and use it to retrieve relevant documents from large monolin-

*This work was carried out during an internship period at Fondazione Bruno Kessler.

Proceedings of the 6th Workshop on Statistical Machine Translation, pages 294–302,
Edinburgh, Scotland, UK, July 30–31, 2011.

gual corpora and subsequently interpolate the resulting small domain-specific language model with the background language model. In Sethy et al. (2006), domain-specific language models are obtained by including only the sentences that are similar to the ones in the target domain via a relative entropy based criterion.

Researchers such as Foster and Kuhn (2007) and Koehn and Schroeder (2007) have investigated mixture model approaches to adaptation. Foster and Kuhn (2007) use a mixture model approach that involves splitting a training corpus into different components, training separate models on each component, and applying mixture weights as a function of the distances of each component to the source text. Koehn and Schroeder (2007) learn mixture weights for language models trained with in-domain and out-of-domain data respectively by minimizing the perplexity of a tuning (development) set and interpolating the models. Although the application of mixture models yields significant results, the number of mixture weights to learn grows linearly with the number of independent language models applied.

Most works focus on monolingual language model adaptation in the context of automatic speech recognition. Federico (2002) combines Probabilistic Latent Semantic Analysis (PLSA) (Hofmann, 1999) for topic modeling with the minimum discrimination information (MDI) estimation criterion for speech recognition and notes an improvement in terms of perplexity and word error rate (WER). Latent Dirichlet Allocation (LDA) techniques have been proposed as an alternative to PLSA to construct purely generative models. LDA techniques include variational Bayes (Blei et al., 2003) and HMM-LDA (Hsu and Glass, 2006).

Recently, bilingual approaches to topic modeling have also been proposed. A Hidden Markov Bilingual Topic AdMixture (HM-BiTAM) model is proposed by Zhao and Xing (2008), which constructs a generative model in which words from a target language are sampled from a mixture of topics drawn from a Dirichlet distribution. Foreign words are sampled via alignment links from a first-order Markov process and a topic specific translation lexicon. While HM-BiTAM has been used for bilingual topic extraction and topic-specific lexicon mapping in the context of SMT, Zhao and Xing (2008) note that HM-BiTAM can generate unigram language models for both the source and target language and thus can be used for language model adaptation through MDI in a similar manner as outlined in Federico (2002). Another bilingual LSA approach is proposed by Tam et al. (2007), which consists of two hierarchical LDA models, constructed from parallel document corpora. A one-to-one correspondence between LDA models is enforced by learning the hyperparameters of the variational Dirichlet posteriors in one LDA model and bootstrapping the second model by fixing the hyperparameters. The technique is based on the assumption that the topic distributions of the source and target documents are identical. It is shown by Tam et al. (2007) that the bilingual LSA framework is also capable of adapting the translation model. Their work is extended in Tam and Schultz (2009) by constructing parallel document clusters formed by monolingual documents using M parallel seed documents.

Additionally, Gong et al. (2010) propose translation model adaptation via a monolingual LDA training. A monolingual LDA model is trained from either the source or target side of the training corpus and each phrase pair is assigned a phrase-topic distribution based on:

$$\hat{M_i^j} = \frac{w_k^j \cdot M_i^j}{\sum_{k=1}^{m} w_k^j}, \tag{1}$$

where M^j is the topic distribution of document j and w_k is the number of occurrences of phrase pair X_k in document j.

Mimno et al. (2009) extend the original concept of LDA to support polylingual topic models (PLTM), both on parallel (such as EuroParl) and partly comparable documents (such as Wikipedia articles). Documents are grouped into tuples $\mathbf{w} = (\mathbf{w}^1, ..., \mathbf{w}^L)$ for each language $l = 1, ..., L$. Each document $\mathbf{w}^l$ in tuple $\mathbf{w}$ is assumed to have the same topic distribution, drawn from an asymmetric Dirichlet prior. Tuple-specific topic distributions are learned using LDA with distinct topic-word concentration parameters β^l. Mimno et al. (2009) show that PLTM sufficiently aligns topics in parallel corpora.

3 Topic Modeling

3.1 PLSA

The original idea of LSA is to map documents to a *latent semantic space*, which reduces the dimensionality by means of singular value decomposition (Deerwester et al., 1990). A word-document matrix A is decomposed by the formula $A = U\Sigma V^t$, where U and V are orthogonal matrices with unit-length columns and Σ is a diagonal matrix containing the singular values of A. LSA approximates Σ by casting all but the largest k singular values in Σ to zero.

PLSA is a statistical model based on the likelihood principle that incorporates mixing proportions of latent class variables (or topics) for each observation. In the context of topic modeling, the latent class variables $z \in Z = \{z_1, ..., z_k\}$ correspond to topics, from which we can derive probabilistic distributions of words $w \in W = \{w_1, ..., w_m\}$ in a document $d \in D = \{d_1, ..., d_n\}$ with $k << n$. Thus, the goal is to learn $P(z \mid d)$ and $P(w|z)$ by maximizing the log-likelihood function:

$$L(W, D) = \sum_{d \in D} \sum_{w \in W} n(w, d) \log P(w \mid d), \quad (2)$$

where $n(w, d)$ is the term frequency of w in d. Using Bayes' formula, the conditional probability $P(w \mid d)$ is defined as:

$$P(w \mid d) = \sum_{z \in Z} P(w \mid z) P(z \mid d). \quad (3)$$

Using the Expectation Maximization (EM) algorithm (Dempster et al., 1977), we estimate the parameters $P(z|d)$ and $P(w|z)$ via an iterative process that alternates two steps: (i) an expectation step (E) in which posterior probabilities are computed for each latent topic z; and (ii) a maximization (M) step, in which the parameters are updated for the posterior probabilities computed in the previous E-step. Details of how to efficiently implement the re-estimation formulas can be found in Federico (2002).

Iterating the E- and M-steps will lead to a convergence that approximates the maximum likelihood equation in (2).

A document-topic distribution $\hat{\theta}$ can be inferred on a new document d' by maximizing the following equation:

$$\hat{\theta} = \arg\max_{\theta} \sum_{w} n(w, d') \log \sum_{z} P(w \mid z) \theta_{z,d'}, \quad (4)$$

where $\theta_{z,d'} = P(z \mid d')$. (4) can be maximized by performing Expectation Maximization on document d' by keeping fixed the word-topic distributions already estimated on the training data. Consequently, a word-document distribution can be inferred by applying the mixture model (3) (see Federico, 2002 for details).

4 MDI Adaptation

An n-gram language model approximates the probability of a sequence of words in a text $W_1^T = w_1, ..., w_T$ drawn from a vocabulary V by the following equation:

$$P(W_1^T) = \prod_{i=1}^{T} P(w_i | h_i), \quad (5)$$

where $h_i = w_{i-n+1}, ..., w_{i-1}$ is the history of $n-1$ words preceding w_i. Given a training corpus B, we can compute the probability of a n-gram from a smoothed model via interpolation as:

$$P_B(w|h) = f_B^*(w|h) + \lambda_B(h) P_B(w|h'), \quad (6)$$

where $f_B^*(w|h)$ is the discounted frequency of sequence hw, h' is the lower order history, where $|h| - 1 = |h'|$, and $\lambda_B(h)$ is the zero-frequency probability of h, defined as:

$$\lambda_B(h) = 1.0 - \sum_{w \in V} f_B^*(w|h).$$

Federico (1999) has shown that MDI Adaptation is useful to adapt a background language model with a small adaptation text sample A, by assuming to have only sufficient statistics on unigrams. Thus, we can reliably estimate $\hat{P}_A(w)$ constraints on the marginal distribution of an adapted language model $P_A(h, w)$ which minimizes the Kullback-Leibler distance from B, i.e.:

$$P_A(\cdot) = \arg\min_{Q(\cdot)} \sum_{hw \in V^n} Q(h, w) \log \frac{Q(h, w)}{P_B(h, w)}. \quad (7)$$

The joint distribution in (7) can be computed using Generalized Iterative Scaling (Darroch and Ratcliff, 1972). Under the unigram constraints, the GIS algorithm reduces to the closed form:

$$P_A(h, w) = P_B(h, w)\alpha(w), \tag{8}$$

where

$$\alpha(w) = \frac{\hat{P}_A(w)}{P_B(w)}. \tag{9}$$

In order to estimate the conditional distribution of the adapted LM, we rewrite (8) and simplify the equation to:

$$P_A(w|h) = \frac{P_B(w|h)\alpha(w)}{\sum_{\hat{w}\in V} P_B(\hat{w}|h)\alpha(\hat{w})}. \tag{10}$$

The adaptation model can be improved by smoothing the scaling factor in (9) by an exponential term γ (Kneser et al., 1997):

$$\alpha(w) = \left(\frac{\hat{P}_A(w)}{P_B(w)}\right)^{\gamma}, \tag{11}$$

where $0 < \gamma \leq 1$. Empirically, γ values less than one decrease the effect of the adaptation ratio to reduce the bias.

As outlined in Federico (2002), the adapted language model can also be written in an interpolation form:

$$f_A^*(w|h) = \frac{f_B^*(w|h)\alpha(w)}{z(h)}, \tag{12}$$

$$\lambda_A(h) = \frac{\lambda_B(h)z(h')}{z(h)}, \tag{13}$$

$$z(h) = (\sum_{w:N_B(h,w)>0} f_B^*(w|h)\alpha(w)) + \lambda_B(h)z(h'), \tag{14}$$

which permits to efficiently compute the normalization term for high order n-grams recursively and by just summing over observed n-grams. The recursion ends with the following initial values for the empty history ϵ:

$$z(\epsilon) = \sum_w P_B(w)\alpha(w), \tag{15}$$

$$P_A(w|\epsilon) = P_B(w)\alpha(w)z(\epsilon)^{-1}. \tag{16}$$

MDI adaptation is one of the adaptation methods provided by the IRSTLM toolkit and was applied as explained in the following section.

5 Bilingual Latent Semantic Models

Similar to the treatment of documents in HM-BiTAM (Zhao and Xing, 2008), we combine parallel texts into a document-pair $(\mathbf{E}, \mathbf{F})$ containing n parallel sentence pairs $(e_i, f_i), 1 < i \leq n$, corresponding to the source and target languages, respectively. Based on the assumption that the topics in a parallel text share the same semantic meanings across languages, the topics are sampled from the same topic-document distribution. We make the additional assumption that stop-words and punctuation, although having high word frequencies in documents, will generally have a uniform topic distribution across documents; therefore, it is not necessary to remove them prior to model training, as they will not adversely affect the overall topic distribution in each document. In order to ensure the uniqueness between word tokens between languages, we annotate $\mathbf{E}$ with special characters. We perform PLSA training, as described in Section 3.1 and receive word-topic distributions $P(w|z), w \in V_E \cup V_F$

Given an untranslated text $\hat{\mathbf{E}}$, we split $\hat{\mathbf{E}}$ into a sequence of documents D. For each document $d_i \in D$, we infer a full word-document distribution by learning $\hat{\theta}$ via (4). Via (3), we can generate the full word-document distribution $P(w \mid d)$ for $w \in V_F$.

We then convert the word-document probabilities into pseudo-counts via a scaling function:

$$n(w \mid d) = \frac{P(w \mid d)}{\max_{w'} P(w' \mid d)} \cdot \Delta, \tag{17}$$

where Δ is a scaling factor to raise the probability ratios above 1. Since our goal is to generate a unigram language model on the target language for adaptation, we remove the source words generated in (17) prior to building the language model.

From our newly generated unigram language model, we perform MDI adaptation on the background LM to yield an adapted LM for translating the source document used for the PLSA inference step.

6 Experiments

Our experiments were done using the TED Talks collection, used in the IWSLT 2010 evaluation task[1].

[1]http://iwslt2010.fbk.eu/

In IWSLT 2010, the challenge was to translate talks from the TED website[2] from English to French. The talks include a variety of topics, including photography and pyschology and thus do not adhere to a single genre. All talks were given in English and were manually transcribed and translated into French. The TED training data consists of 329 parallel talk transcripts with approximately 84k sentences. The TED test data consists of transcriptions created via 1-best ASR outputs from the KIT Quaero Evaluation System. It consists of 758 sentences and 27,432 and 27,307 English and French words, respectively. The TED talk data is segmented at the clause level, rather than at the level of sentences.

Our SMT systems are built upon the Moses open-source SMT toolkit (Koehn et al., 2007)[3]. The translation and lexicalized reordering models have been trained on parallel data. One 5-gram background LM was constructed from the French side of the TED training data (740k words), smoothed with the improved Kneser-Ney technique (Chen and Goodman, 1999) and computed with the IRSTLM toolkit (Federico et al., 2008). The weights of the log-linear interpolation model were optimized via minimum error rate training (MERT) (Och, 2003) on the TED development set, using 200 best translations at each tuning iteration.

This paper investigates the effects of language model adaptation via bilingual latent semantic modeling on the TED background LM against a baseline model that uses only the TED LM.

6.1 Bilingual Latent Semantic Model

Using the technique outlined in Section 5, we construct bilingual documents by splitting the parallel TED training corpus into 41,847 documents of 5 lines each. While each individual TED lecture could be used as a document, our experimental goal is to simulate near-time translation of speeches; thus, we prefer to construct small documents to simulate topic modeling on a spoken language scenario in which the length of a talk is not known a priori. We annotate the English source text for removal after inference. Figure 1 contains a sample document constructed for PLSA training. (In fact, we distinguish English words from French words by attaching to the former a special suffix.) By using our in-house implementation, training of the PLSA model on the bilingual collection converged after 20 EM iterations.

> robert lang is a pioneer of the newest kind of origami – using math and engineering principles to fold mind-blowingly intricate designs that are beautiful and , sometimes , very useful . my talk is " flapping birds and space telescopes . " and you would think that should have nothing to do with one another , but i hope by the end of these 18 minutes , you 'll see a little bit of a relation . robert lang est un pionnier des nouvelles techniques d' origami - basées sur des principes mathématiques et d' ingénierie permettant de créer des modèles complexes et époustouflants , qui sont beaux et parfois , très utiles . ma conférence s' intitule " oiseaux en papier et télescopes spatiaux " . et vous pensez probablement que les uns et les autres n' ont rien en commun , mais j' espère qu' à l' issue de ces 18 minutes , vous comprendrez ce qui les relie .

Figure 1: A sample bilingual document used for PLSA training.

Using our PLSA model, we run inference on each of the 476 test documents from the TED lectures, constructed by splitting the test set into 5-line documents. Since our goal is to translate and evaluate the test set, we construct monolingual (English) documents. Figure 2 provides an example of a document to be inferred. We collect the bilingual unigram pseudocounts after 10 iterations of inference and remove the English words. The TED lecture data is transcribed by clauses, rather than full sentences, so we do not add sentence splitting tags before training our unigram language models.

As a result of PLSA inference, the probabilities of target words increase with respect to the background language model. Table 1 demonstrates this phenomenon by outlining several of the top ranked words that have similar semantic meaning to non-stop words on the source side. In every case, the probability $P_A(w)$ increases fairly substantially with respect to the $P_B(w)$. As a result, we expect that the adapted language model will favor both fluent and semantically correct translations as the adaptation is suggesting better lexical choices of words.

[2]http://www.ted.com/talks/

[3]http://www.statmt.org/moses/

we didn 't have money , so we had a cheap , little ad , but we wanted college students for a study of prison life . 75 people volunteered , took personality tests . we did interviews . picked two dozen : the most normal , the most healthy .

Figure 2: A sample English-only document (#230) used for PLSA inference. A full unigram word distribution will be inferred for both English and French.

Rank	Word	$P_A(w)$	$P_B(w)$	$P_A(w)/P_B(w)$
20	gens	8.41E-03	4.55E-05	184.84
22	vie	8.30E-03	1.09E-04	76.15
51	prix	2.59E-03	8.70E-05	29.77
80	école	1.70E-03	6.13E-05	27.73
83	argent	1.60E-03	3.96E-05	40.04
86	personnes	1.52E-03	2.75E-04	5.23
94	aide	1.27E-03	7.71E-05	16.47
98	étudiants	1.20E-03	7.12E-05	16.85
119	marché	9.22E-04	9.10E-05	10.13
133	étude	7.63E-04	4.55E-05	16.77
173	éducation	5.04E-04	2.97E-05	16.97
315	prison	2.65E-04	1.98E-05	13.38
323	université	2.60E-04	2.97E-05	8.75

Table 1: Sample unigram probabilities of the adaptation model for document #230, compared to the baseline unigram probabilities. The French words selected are semantically related to the English words in the adapted document. The PLSA adaptation infers higher unigram probabilities for words with latent topics related to the source document.

6.2 MDI Adaptation

We perform MDI adaptation with each of the unigram language models to update the background TED language model. We configure the adaptation rate parameter γ to 0.3, as recommended in Federico (2002). The baseline LM is replaced with each adapted LM, corresponding to the document to be translated. We then calculate the mean perplexity of the adapted LMs and the baseline, respectively. The perplexity scores are shown in Table 2. We observe a 15.3% relative improvement in perplexity score over the baseline.

6.3 Results

We perform MT experiments on the IWSLT 2010 evaluation set to compare the baseline and adapted LMs. In the evaluation, we notice a 0.85 improvement in BLEU (%), yielding a 3% improvement over the baseline. The same performance trend in NIST is observed with a 2.4% relative improvement compared to the unadapted baseline. Our PLSA and MDI-based adaptation method not only improves fluency but also improves adequacy: the topic-based adaptation approach is attempting to suggest more appropriate words based on increased unigram probabilities than that of the baseline LM. Table 3 demonstrates a large improvement in unigram selection for the adapted TED model in terms of the individual contribution to the NIST score, with diminishing effects on larger n-grams. The majority of the overall improvements are on individual word selection.

Examples of improved fluency and adequacy are shown in Figure 3. Line 285 shows an example of a translation that doesn't provide much of an n-gram improvement, but demonstrates more fluent output, due to the deletion of the first comma and the movement of the second comma to the end of the clause. While "installation" remains an inadequate noun in this clause, the adapted model reorders the root words "rehab" and "installation" (in comparison with the baseline) and improves the grammaticality of the sentence; however, the number does not match between the determiner and the noun phrase. Line 597 demonstrates a perfect phrase translation with respect to the reference translation using semantic paraphrasing. The baseline phrase "d'origine" is transformed and attributed to the noun. Instead of translating "original" as a phrase for "home", the adapted model captures the original meaning of the word in the translation. Line 752 demonstrates an improvement in adequacy through the replacement of the word "quelque" with "autre." Additionally, extra words are removed.

These lexical changes result in the improvement in translation quality due to topic-based adaptation via PLSA.

LM	Perplexity	BLEU (%)	NIST
Adapt TED	162.44	**28.49**	**6.5956**
Base TED	191.76	27.64	6.4405

Table 2: Perplexity, BLEU, and NIST scores for the baseline and adapted models. The perplexity scores are averaged across each document-specific LM adaptation.

NIST	1-gram	2-gram	3-gram
Adapt TED	4.8077	1.3925	0.3229
Base TED	4.6980	1.3527	0.3173
Difference	0.1097	0.0398	0.0056

Table 3: Individual unigram NIST scores for n-grams 1-3 of the baseline and adapted models. The improvement of the adapted model over the baseline is listed below.

(Line 285)

, j' ai eu la chance de travailler dans les *installations , rehab*

j' ai eu la chance de travailler dans les *rehab installation* ,

j' ai la chance de travailler dans un centre de désintoxication ,

(Line 597)

d' origine , les idées qui ont de la valeur –

d' avoir des idées originales qui ont de la valeur –

d' avoir des idées originales qui ont de la valeur –

(Line 752)

un nom qui appartient à *quelque* chose *d' autre* , le soleil .

un nom qui appartient à *autre* chose , le soleil .

le nom d' une *autre* chose , le soleil .

Figure 3: Three examples of improvement in MT results: the first sentence in each collection corresponds to the baseline, the second utilizes the adapted TED LMs, and the third is the reference translation.

7 Conclusions

An alternative approach to bilingual topic modeling has been presented that integrates the PLSA framework with MDI adaptation that can effectively adapt a background language model when given a document in the source language. Rather than training two topic models and enforcing a one-to-one correspondence for translation, we use the assumption that parallel texts refer to the same topics and have a very similar topic distribution. Preliminary experiments show a reduction in perplexity and an overall improvement in BLEU and NIST scores on speech translation. We also note that, unlike previous works involving topic modeling, we did not remove stop words and punctuation, but rather assumed that these features would have a relatively uniform topic distribution.

One downside to the MDI adaptation approach is that the computation of the normalization term $z(h)$ is expensive and potentially prohibitive during continuous speech translation tasks. Further investigation is needed to determine if there is a suitable approximation that avoids computing probabilities across all n-grams.

Acknowledgments

This work was supported by the T4ME network of excellence (IST-249119), funded by the DG INFSO of the European Commission through the Seventh Framework Programme. The first author received a grant under the Erasmus Mundus Language & Communication Technologies programme.

References

David M. Blei, Andrew Ng, and Michael Jordan. Latent Dirichlet Allocation. *JMLR*, 3:993–1022, 2003.

Stanley F. Chen and Joshua Goodman. An empirical study of smoothing techniques for language modeling. *Computer Speech and Language*, 4(13): 359–393, 1999.

J. N. Darroch and D. Ratcliff. Generalized iterative scaling for log-linear models. *The Annals of Mathematical Statistics*, 43(5):1470–1480, 1972.

Scott Deerwester, Susan T. Dumais, George W. Furnas, Thomas K. Landauer, and Richard Harshman. Indexing by Latent Semantic Analysis. *Journal of the American Society for Information Science*, 41:391–407, 1990.

A. P. Dempster, N. M. Laird, and D. B. Rubin. Maximum-likelihood from incomplete data via the EM algorithm. *Journal of the Royal Statistical Society, B*, 39:1–38, 1977.

Marcello Federico. Efficient language model adaptation through MDI estimation. In *Proceedings of the 6th European Conference on Speech Communication and Technology*, volume 4, pages 1583–1586, Budapest, Hungary, 1999.

Marcello Federico. Language Model Adaptation through Topic Decomposition and MDI Estimation. In *Proceedings of the IEEE International Conference on Acoustics, Speech and Signal Processing*, volume I, pages 703–706, Orlando, FL, 2002.

Marcello Federico, Nicola Bertoldi, and Mauro Cettolo. IRSTLM: an Open Source Toolkit for Handling Large Scale Language Models. In *Proceedings of Interspeech*, pages 1618–1621, Melbourne, Australia, 2008.

George Foster and Roland Kuhn. Mixture-model adaptation for SMT. In *Proceedings of the Second Workshop on Statistical Machine Translation*, pages 128–135, Prague, Czech Republic, June 2007. Association for Computational Linguistics. URL `http://www.aclweb.org/anthology/W/W07/W07-0217`.

Zhengxian Gong, Yu Zhang, and Guodong Zhou. Statistical Machine Translation based on LDA. In *Universal Communication Symposium (IUCS), 2010 4th International*, pages 286 –290, oct. 2010. doi: 10.1109/IUCS.2010.5666182.

Thomas Hofmann. Probabilistic Latent Semantic Analysis. In *Proceedings of the 15th Conference on Uncertainty in AI*, pages 289–296, Stockholm, Sweden, 1999.

Bo-June (Paul) Hsu and James Glass. Style & topic language model adaptation using HMM-LDA. In *in Proc. ACL Conf. on Empirical Methods in Natural Language Processing – EMNLP*, pages 373–381, 2006.

Reinhard Kneser, Jochen Peters, and Dietrich Klakow. Language Model Adaptation Using Dynamic Marginals. In *Proceedings of the 5th European Conference on Speech Communication and Technology*, pages 1971–1974, Rhodes, Greece, 1997.

P. Koehn, H. Hoang, A. Birch, C. Callison-Burch, M. Federico, N. Bertoldi, B. Cowan, W. Shen, C. Moran, R. Zens, C. Dyer, O. Bojar, A. Constantin, and E. Herbst. Moses: Open Source Toolkit for Statistical Machine Translation. In *Proceedings of the 45th Annual Meeting of the Association for Computational Linguistics Companion Volume Proceedings of the Demo and Poster Sessions*, pages 177–180, Prague, Czech Republic, 2007. URL `http://aclweb.org/anthology-new/P/P07/P07-2045.pdf`.

Philipp Koehn and Josh Schroeder. Experiments in Domain Adaptation for Statistical Machine Translation. In *Proceedings of the Second Workshop on Statistical Machine Translation*, pages 224–227, Prague, Czech Republic, June 2007. Association for Computational Linguistics. URL `http://www.aclweb.org/anthology/W/W07/W07-0233`.

David Mimno, Hanna M. Wallach, Jason Naradowsky, David A. Smith, and Andrew McCallum. Polylingual Topic Models. In *Proceedings of the 2009 Conference on Empirical Methods in Natural Language Processing*. Association for Computational Linguistics, August 2009. URL `http://www.cs.umass.edu/~mimno/papers/mimno2009polylingual.pdf`.

Franz Josef Och. Minimum Error Rate Training in Statistical Machine Translation. In Erhard Hinrichs and Dan Roth, editors, *Proceedings of the 41st Annual Meeting of the Association for Computational Linguistics*, pages 160–167, 2003. URL `http://www.aclweb.org/anthology/P03-1021.pdf`.

Abhinav Sethy, Panayiotis Georgiou, and Shrikanth Narayanan. Selecting relevant text subsets from web-data for building topic specific language models. In *Proceedings of the Human Language Technology Conference of the NAACL, Companion Volume: Short Papers*, pages 145–148, New York City, USA, June 2006. Association for Computational Linguistics. URL `http://www.aclweb.org/anthology/N/N06/N06-2037`.

Yik-Cheung Tam and Tanja Schultz. Incorporating monolingual corpora into bilingual latent semantic analysis for crosslingual lm adaptation. In *Acoustics, Speech and Signal Processing, 2009. ICASSP 2009. IEEE International Conference on*, pages 4821 –4824, april 2009. doi: 10.1109/ICASSP.2009.4960710.

Yik-Cheung Tam, Ian Lane, and Tanja Schultz. Bilingual LSA-based adaptation for statistical machine translation. *Machine Translation*, 21:187–207, December 2007. ISSN 0922-6567. doi: 10.1007/s10590-008-9045-2. URL `http://portal.acm.org/citation.cfm?id=1466799.1466803`.

Bing Zhao and Eric P. Xing. HM-BiTAM: Bilingual topic exploration, word alignment, and translation. In J.C. Platt, D. Koller, Y. Singer, and S. Roweis, editors, *Advances in Neural Information Processing Systems 20*, pages 1689–1696. MIT Press, Cambridge, MA, 2008.

Bing Zhao, Matthias Eck, and Stephan Vogel. Language Model Adaptation for Statistical Machine Translation via Structured Query Models. In *Proceedings of Coling 2004*, pages 411–417, Geneva, Switzerland, Aug 23–Aug 27 2004. COLING.

Personal Translator at WMT2011

- A rule-based MTsystem with hybrid components -

Vera Aleksić
Linguatec Gmbh
Gottfried-Keller-Str. 12
Munich, Germany
v.aleksic@linguatec.de

Gregor Thurmair
Linguatec Gmbh
Gottfried-Keller-Str. 12
Munich, Germany
g.thurmair@linguatec.de

Abstract

This paper presents the Linguatec submission to the WMT 2011 sixth workshop on statistical machine translation. It describes the architecture of our machine translation system 'Personal Translator' (hereinafter also referred to as PT), developed by Linguatec, which is a rule-based translation system, enriched by statistical approaches.

We participate for the German-English translation direction. For the current submission we have chosen the latest commercial version of the system, PT14. The translation quality improvement for the submission was done mainly by lexicon tuning: detection of unknown words, extracting of possible translations, partly from the wmt11 training corpora, and enlarging the lexicon by manually coding the chosen transfer candidates.

1 Introduction

The origin of the PT technology dates back to the 80's when a translation system based on logic programming and slot grammars was developed by Michael McCord at IBM T.J. Watson Research Center. In many years of development the translation engine has been driven forward and enhanced. Most recently we have added statistical approaches for tasks such as erroneous input correction, subject area recognition and word disambiguation. Today 'Personal Translator' is one of the leading programs in the translation technology field. It is a commercial MT system whose product range includes 7 language pairs, i.e. 14 translation directions, for single users and networks. Linguatec is a leading provider of language-technology software for office use in Germany. In addition to machine translation, we develop and provide commercial products in the fields of speech recognition and speech synthesis. Linguatec is the only company to have won the European Information Technology Prize three times.

2 System fundamentals

Personal Translator is implemented as a modular system which basically consists of the following components:

- the grammar, written in Prolog, based on the concept of slot grammar
- the lexicon, administrated in the data base internally called TransLexis
- additional morphological analysers written partly in C and C++
- hybrid (rule-based and statistical) methods for word disambiguation, subject area recognition and spell-checking
- a range of pre- and post-processing components such as format converters for

Proceedings of the 6th Workshop on Statistical Machine Translation, pages 303–308,
Edinburgh, Scotland, UK, July 30–31, 2011.

html, pdf, doc, txt and rtf formats, sentence splitter, tokeniser, lemmatizer.

As Personal Translator is a commercial system, aiming at providing a complete translator work bench and creating added value for users, it integrates a wide range of advanced features such as:

- Translation memory system for management, creation, analysis and maintenance of TMs, as well as large system modules, containing tens of thousands of sentence pairs
- Translation project management tool, enabling the user to save and administer all important translation settings and project relevant options
- Text to speech functionality to support editing and learning processes such as text revision/correction in the language(s) mastered by the user, or getting a feeling for the correct pronunciation in a foreign language, to name just a few.

2.1 LMT and Slot Grammar

Personal Translator is based on the LMT (Logic programming based Machine Translation). The core of LMT uses the principles of **slot grammar**, a grammatical description system developed originally by Michael McCord[1] at IBM.

Slot grammar is based on the concept of word valence. It is dependency oriented, i.e. each phrase has a head word. Each (head) word is characterised by **slots** which represent empty places in its grammatical surroundings such as subject, object, modifier etc. which can be realised in text or not. The slots represent either **complements** of the head word which have to be defined in the lexicon or **adjuncts** which are rather associated with the part of speech and defined more generally in the grammar rules. The possible **slot fillers** are typified by their morphological, syntactic or semantic properties. The analysis of a word is finished and the phrase is considered as satisfied if the appropriate fillers are found in the text and all (obligatory) slots of the word are filled

[1] McCord (1989); McCord, Vernth (1992)

3 Advanced translation features

There are some well-known restrictions concerning the automatic translation process. One of them is the ability of most MT systems to operate on only one sentence at a time. The same is also true for the PT but only to a limited degree. PT integrates several methods for semantic and context analysis on multi-sentence level and for the identification of concepts which are repeated throughout the text. This applies in particular to the recognition of pronoun references and coreference analysis of proper names, as well as subject area recognition and neural transfer which are described further below.

3.1 Recognition of pronoun reference

Pronouns can refer to other words (their antecedents) which had occurred in the previous text. When translating from German into English and vice versa the fact that e.g. the English personal pronouns *he/she* apply only to humans and *it* to all other things, whereas in German *er/sie/es* can refer to any noun, has to be considered when searching for appropriate translation:

This is a desk. It is new.
Dies ist ein Schreibtisch. Er ist neu.

versus:

This is a bag. It is new.
Dies ist eine Tasche. Sie ist neu.

The user can either select the translation option „Automatic recognition of pronoun reference", when translating a continuous text, or deselect it in case of translating lists of independent sentences (as we did for the current submission). If this option is deselected, the PT output for the sentences above reads as follows:

Dies ist ein Schreibtisch. Es ist neu.
Dies ist eine Tasche. Es ist neu.

Also the translation of other words in the context can benefit from correct pronoun reference recognition:

The dogs found biscuits. They ate them.
Die Hunde fanden Kekse. Sie fraßen sie.

versus:

The children found biscuits. They ate them.
Die Kinder fanden Kekse. Sie aßen sie.

The last example demonstrates an improvement in the translation of the verb *eat* which is to be translated into German with *fressen* if its subject is an animal or with *essen* if the subject is a human. The pronoun *they* in the first sentence refers to dogs (animals), in the second to children (humans) respectively.

3.2 Named entity recognition

The treatment of proper names is a real challenge for machine translation. There is a huge number of proper names, even growing constantly if e.g. the companies and product names are considered. Furthermore, person names are constantly changing in their degree of topicality, so it is not of much use to have Kohl and Fischer in the lexicon when the texts to be translated speak about Merkel and Rösler. As such, the proper names are unsuitable to be primarily stored in the lexicon. The second problem is homography: If a proper name is spelled in the same way as a common word, it is very likely to be translated by an MT system (Brown => Braun; Metzger => Butcher).

Personal Translator integrates a named entity recognition component which runs both:

- as a pre-processing tool: It puts mark-ups on the proper names to exclude them of other pre-processing components such as e.g. spell checker
- as part of the translation process, integrated into the lexicon and the complete analysis-transfer-generation process: Morphological and syntactic analysis/generation bases among other things on semantic roles (person, place…), as the proper names have special inflection patterns and specific syntactic behaviour (preposition slots, appositions etc.).

By this, we could achieve an increase in translation quality of about 30% for sentences containing proper names.[2]

3.3 Word sense disambiguation

Another important issue is the treatment of ambiguous words. Most glossaries contain several million translations, among them large amounts of words with multiple meanings. Traditionally, 'Personal Translator' uses several ways to disambiguate ambiguous words and select the most proper translation:

- Interpretion of gender/number and other morphosyntactic information:
  der Kiefer (m) = jaw
  die Kiefer (f) = pine
  minute (sg) = Minute
  minutes (pl) = Protokoll
- Analysis of slot fillers:
  anmachen (Licht) = turn on (light)
  anmachen (Salat) = prepare (salad)
  anmachen (jmd.) = chat (s.o.) up
  bestehen (auf) = insist (on)
  bestehen (aus) = be made (of)
- Use of orthographic information:
  fest (lower case) = stable, firm
  Fest (capitalised) = celebration
- Definition of different subject area codes for the translations:
  die Mutter (general) = mother
  die Mutter (techn.) = nut

4 Hybrid technology

All these disambiguation methods are labour-intensive in terms of manual coding efforts, and they require, to a certain extent, user interaction (e.g. selecting appropriate options such as subject area) that in turn needs reliable knowledge of the contents to be translated which is often not the case. And not at least, manual setting of the disambiguation contexts is not only inefficient but also prone to errors.

For these reasons Linguatec continually tests new, innovative solutions to reduce manual coding efforts and increase translation quality. Therefore it seemed obvious to try to draw statistical significant, reliable, and empirically-sound information from the immense Linguatec corpus and enrich the RMT with this knowledge. Thus an innovative hybrid component, which has been filed as patent[3], has been developed.

4.1 Neural transfer

We as humans rarely have problems to distinguish between two or more different meanings of a word. The decision happens automatically, supported by accessing the world knowledge stored in our brains. Many efforts have been made to artificially imitate these processes. In linguistics, traditionally ontologies have been created which aim at

[2] cf. Thurmair (2005)

[3] cf. Linguatec Patent „Hybrid transfer selection in Machine Translation" US: 11/885.688, EPA: Nr. 05715789.3

reflecting the relations and the hierarchy in the nature. In information technology, artificial neural networks try to approximate the operation of the human brain. Linguatec's hybrid disambiguation model tries to single out the best translation for a word by identifying its semantic network. We call it 'neural transfer'.

The disambiguation model for the neural transfer has been trained on a significant amount of different contexts for each lexicon entry with multiple translations, where this method could be considered as appropriate. Clusters of different meanings of words were built manually and statistical methods were applied on them in order to identify the most distinctive terms in their surroundings and represent the results in neural networks. The neural transfer technology has been integrated into the PT by modifying the affected lexicon entries, and by adding a pre-processing component which assigns a semantic net to the affected text passage.

The neural transfer enables the PT to 'understand' the context beyond sentence boundaries. Thus it is possible to deliver two different translations for the word *Gericht* (court, dish) in absolutely identical sentences, depending on the textual context:

*Ich kann mich noch an dieses **Gericht** erinnern. Es hat die Klage meiner Firma auf Entschädigung abgewiesen.*

*I can still remember this **court**. It has rejected the complaint of my company on reimbursement.*

versus:

*Ich kann mich noch an dieses **Gericht** erinnern. Es war eines dieser Gerichte aus der Küche der Balkanländer, mit Gemüse und Knoblauch.*

*I can still remember this **dish**. It was one of these dishes from the kitchen of the Balkan States with vegetables and garlic.*

The test results showed an improvement of the translation quality by about 40% for texts containing the affected concepts.

4.2 Automatic subject area recognition

In order to overcome the problems mentioned above (manual coding effort, required user interaction), a component for automatic topic identification has been developed and integrated into the PT. Its principle works in a similar way to neural transfer. The most important difference is that the automatic topic identifier assigns the recognised subject area to the whole text to be translated, whereas the neural transfer can operate on the single paragraph level.

4.3 SmartCorrect

Regarding the enormous amount of texts to be translated, most of which are from internet or other unscanned sources, it is not reasonable to expect from MT users to keep control of correct spelling. Nevertheless, a MT system is only able to translate correctly spelled words. For these reasons most MT systems, as well as text processing programmes, include a spellchecker. The problem is that they mostly just identify the typos/spelling errors and leave it up to the user to choose the correct form from a list of suggestions. This is process which requires intensive user interaction and experience has taught us, that users are not always ready to invest their time. In addition, this can only be expected if the text to be corrected belongs to the language mastered by the user.

Therefore Linguatec developed SmartCorrect which not only recognises spelling errors in the text but also corrects them automatically. Trained on very large corpora, the model is likely to detect the best variant in nearly all cases. Clever enough, it cooperates with the named entities recogniser and thus does not identify unknown proper names as spelling errors. Entries from the user lexicons are also save from SmartCorrect intervention.

However, a major part of the misspelling corrections is already performed in a pre-processing step, which adopts some proven methods[4] to identify and correct frequent errors, such as letter deletion, insertion, substitution, inversion and duplication.

5 WMT2011 Submission

We participate for the German-English translation direction. Linguatec has not used the training corpus because we wanted to submit the results of our general purpose MT system.

The only system tuning consisted of lexicon coding. Unknown words were detected automatically by analysing the test set. Appropriate translations were found, some of them from the training corpus. About 200 terms were manually coded or imported into the PT lexicon.

---

[4] cf. Habash (2008)

Furthermore, we have observed that the test set contained some spelling errors which have been corrected by SmartCorrect (ca. 150 misspelling corrections were done), for example:

offiziel	=>	*offiziell*
Sympatie	=>	*Sympathie*
enhüllten	=>	*enthüllten*
bessseren	=>	*besseren*
unbwohnbar	=>	*unbewohnbar*
zwiwchen	=>	*zwischen*

Thus, for comparison purposes we translated the test set three times:

- Out-of-the-box PT, without SmartCorrect
- Out-of-the-box PT, with SmartCorrect
- Out-of-the-box PT, with SmartCorrect plus lexicon adaptation

The BLEU score in the first run was 17,0. Interestingly, the BLEU score of the second run did not reflect any improvements caused by correction of typos; on the contrary, it declined by 0,2 from 17,0 to 16,8. However, by manual evaluation of sample sentences we gained a more positive impression of the results. With the third run, after the lexicon coding, a BLEU of 17,1, i.e. a minimal increase compared with the firs run, was achieved. Here again, the manual inspection of random sentences, containing the coded terms, left an impression of some more significant improvements than measured by BLEU.

5.1 Conclusion

Automatic metrics have shown a minimal improvement of translation quality. However, the manual inspection suggested much more significant influences of spelling correction and lexicon coding on the translation adequacy and sentence structure and consequently on the readability of the output than the BLEU score did.

5.2 Combined system submission by DFKI

At WMT 2011 our PT will also participate in the combined translation task in a combination of rule-based and SMT systems submitted by the DFKI[5].

[5] Xu et al.(2011)

6 Outlook

Simultaneously with the current submission a 'hybrid experiment' was performed: An attempt at using SMT methods to improve the transfer selection for coding new entries in PT.

An existing (crawled) parallel corpus in the automotive domain was cleaned, segmented by Liguatec sentence splitter, sentence-aligned by Hunalign (supported by using the Linguatec dictionary), word-aligned by GIZA++ and finally phrase tables were produced by using Moses. The objective was to extract meaningful phrases and their translations which are particularly suitable for import into the PT lexicon and thus generate a glossary.

First a phrase table filter, based on frequency, was applied. Then part of speech information was added to both source and target entries as a basis for filtering linguistically motivated phrases. A glossary was generated. For testing purposes a very small set of about 250 terms, namely those which were unknown in the PT lexicon, was chosen to be imported. On a test corpus of about 320 sentences from the automotive domain the translation quality improvement, measured by BLEU, turned out to be about 3.1% (before coding: 14.87, after coding: 17.97).

We will continue researching in that field.

References

Bogdan Babych, Anthony Hartley. 2003. Improving Machine Translation Quality with Automatic Named Entity Recognition. Proc. EACL-EAMT, Budapest.

Arendse Bernth. 1992. The LMT Book. IBM Deutschland Informationssysteme GmbH Scientific Center Institute for Logic and Linguistics.

Nazar Habash. 2008. Four techniqes for Online Handling of Out-of-Vocabulary Words in Arabic-English Statistical Machine Translation. Proceedings of ACL-08: HLT, Short Papers (Companion Volume), pages 57-60, Columbus, Ohio, USA.

Roland Kaplan and Joan Bresnan. 1982. Lexical functional grammar: A formal system for grammatical representation. In Joan Bresnan (Ed.) The mental representation of Grammatical Relations. MIT Press.

Michael McCord. 1989. A new version of slot grammar. Research report RC 14506, IBM research division, Yorktown Heights.

Michael McCord and Arendse Bernth. 1992. Using Slot Grammar. IBM Deutschland Informationssysteme GmbH Scientific Center Institute for Logic and Linguistics.

Gregor Thurmair. 2004. Using corpus information to improve MT quality. In Yuste Rodrigo, Elia (ed) Paris: ELRA (European Language Resources Association): Proceedings of the Third International Workshop on Language Resources for Translation Work, Reseach & Training (LR4Trans-III)

Gregor Thurmair. 2005. Improving MT Quality: Towards a Hybrid MT Architecture in the Linguatec 'Personal Translator'. International MT Summit X, Phuket. Invited paper.

Gregor Thurmair. 2009. Comparing different architectures of hybrid Machine Translation systems. Proceedings of the Twelft Machine Translation Summit. Ottawa, Canada. p.340-348

Jia Xu, Xiaojun Zhang, David Vilar, Casey Kennington and Hans Uszkoreit. 2011. The DFKI Hybrid Machine Translation System for WMT 2011 - On the Integration of SMT and RBMT. Submission paper for WMT 2011 sixth workshop on statistical machine translation. Edinburgh.

LIMSI @ WMT11

Alexandre Allauzen
Hélène Bonneau-Maynard
Hai-Son Le
Aurélien Max
Guillaume Wisniewski
François Yvon
Univ. Paris-Sud and LIMSI-CNRS
B.P. 133, 91403 Orsay cedex, France

Gilles Adda
Josep M. Crego
Adrien Lardilleux
Thomas Lavergne
Artem Sokolov
LIMSI-CNRS
B.P. 133, 91403 Orsay cedex, France

Abstract

This paper describes LIMSI's submissions to the Sixth Workshop on Statistical Machine Translation. We report results for the French-English and German-English shared translation tasks in both directions. Our systems use *n*-code, an open source Statistical Machine Translation system based on bilingual *n*-grams. For the French-English task, we focussed on finding efficient ways to take advantage of the large and heterogeneous training parallel data. In particular, using a simple filtering strategy helped to improve both processing time and translation quality. To translate from English to French and German, we also investigated the use of the SOUL language model in Machine Translation and showed significant improvements with a 10-gram SOUL model. We also briefly report experiments with several alternatives to the standard *n*-best MERT procedure, leading to a significant speed-up.

1 Introduction

This paper describes LIMSI's submissions to the Sixth Workshop on Statistical Machine Translation, where LIMSI participated in the French-English and German-English tasks in both directions. For this evaluation, we used *n*-code, our in-house Statistical Machine Translation (SMT) system which is open-source and based on bilingual *n*-grams.

This paper is organized as follows. Section 2 provides an overview of *n*-code, while the data pre-processing and filtering steps are described in Section 3. Given the large amount of parallel data available, we proposed a method to filter the French-English *GigaWord* corpus (Section 3.2). As in our previous participations, data cleaning and filtering constitute a non-negligible part of our work. This includes detecting and discarding sentences in other languages; removing sentences which are also included in the provided development sets, as well as parts that are repeated (for the monolingual news data, this can reduce the amount of data by a factor 3 or 4, depending on the language and the year); normalizing the character set (non-utf8 characters which are aberrant in context, or in the case of the *GigaWord* corpus, a lot of non-printable and thus invisible control characters such as *EOT (end of transmission)*[1]).

For target language modeling (Section 4), a standard back-off *n*-gram model is estimated and tuned as described in Section 4.1. Moreover, we also introduce in Section 4.2 the use of the SOUL language model (LM) (Le et al., 2011) in SMT. Based on neural networks, the SOUL LM can handle an arbitrary large vocabulary and a high order markovian assumption (up to 10-gram in this work). Finally, experimental results are reported in Section 5 both in terms of BLEU scores and translation edit rates (TER) measured on the provided *newstest2010* dataset.

2 System Overview

Our in-house *n*-code SMT system implements the bilingual *n*-gram approach to Statistical Machine Translation (Casacuberta and Vidal, 2004). Given a

[1]This kind of characters was used for Teletype up to the seventies or early eighties.

Proceedings of the 6th Workshop on Statistical Machine Translation, pages 309–315,
Edinburgh, Scotland, UK, July 30–31, 2011.

source sentence s_1^J, a translation hypothesis $\hat{t}_1^I$ is defined as the sentence which maximizes a linear combination of feature functions:

$$\hat{t}_1^I = \arg\max_{t_1^I} \left\{ \sum_{m=1}^{M} \lambda_m h_m(s_1^J, t_1^I) \right\} \quad (1)$$

where s_1^J and t_1^I respectively denote the source and the target sentences, and λ_m is the weight associated with the feature function h_m. The translation feature is the log-score of the translation model based on bilingual units called *tuples*. The probability assigned to a sentence pair by the translation model is estimated by using the n-gram assumption:

$$p(s_1^J, t_1^I) = \prod_{k=1}^{K} p((s,t)_k | (s,t)_{k-1} \ldots (s,t)_{k-n+1})$$

where s refers to a source symbol (t for target) and $(s,t)_k$ to the kth tuple of the given bilingual sentence pair. It is worth noticing that, since both languages are linked up in tuples, the context information provided by this translation model is bilingual. In addition to the translation model, *eleven* feature functions are combined: a *target-language model* (see Section 4 for details); four *lexicon models*; two *lexicalized reordering models* (Tillmann, 2004) aiming at predicting the orientation of the next translation unit; a "weak" distance-based *distortion model*; and finally a *word-bonus model* and a *tuple-bonus model* which compensate for the system preference for short translations. The four *lexicon models* are similar to the ones used in a standard phrase-based system: two scores correspond to the relative frequencies of the tuples and two lexical weights are estimated from the automatically generated word alignments. The weights associated to feature functions are optimally combined using a discriminative training framework (Och, 2003) (Minimum Error Rate Training (MERT), see details in Section 5.4), using the provided *newstest2009* data as development set.

2.1 Training

Our translation model is estimated over a training corpus composed of tuple sequences using classical smoothing techniques. Tuples are extracted from a word-aligned corpus (using MGIZA++[2] with default settings) in such a way that a unique segmentation of the bilingual corpus is achieved, allowing to estimate the n-gram model. Figure 1 presents a simple example illustrating the unique tuple segmentation for a given word-aligned pair of sentences (top).

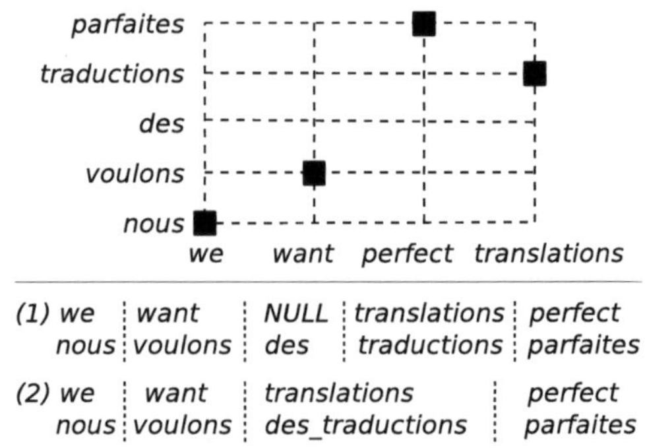

Figure 1: Tuple extraction from a sentence pair.

The resulting sequence of tuples *(1)* is further refined to avoid *NULL* words in the source side of the tuples *(2)*. Once the whole bilingual training data is segmented into tuples, n-gram language model probabilities can be estimated. In this example, note that the English source words *perfect* and *translations* have been reordered in the final tuple segmentation, while the French target words are kept in their original order.

2.2 Inference

During decoding, source sentences are encoded in the form of word lattices containing the most promising reordering hypotheses, so as to reproduce the word order modifications introduced during the tuple extraction process. Hence, at decoding time, only those encoded reordering hypotheses are translated. Reordering hypotheses are introduced using a set of reordering rules automatically learned from the word alignments.

In the previous example, the rule [*perfect translations* $\rightsquigarrow$ *translations perfect*] produces the swap of the English words that is observed for the French and English pair. Typically, part-of-speech (POS) information is used to increase the generalization power of such rules. Hence, rewriting rules are built using POS rather than surface word forms. Refer

[2] `http://geek.kyloo.net/software`

to (Crego and Mariño, 2007) for details on tuple extraction and reordering rules.

3 Data Pre-processing and Selection

We used all the available parallel data allowed in the constrained task to compute the word alignments, except for the French-English tasks where the United Nation corpus was not used to train our translation models. To train the target language models, we also used all provided data and monolingual corpora released by the LDC for French and English. Moreover, all parallel corpora were POS-tagged with the TreeTagger (Schmid, 1994). For German, the fine-grained POS information used for pre-processing was computed by the RFTagger (Schmid and Laws, 2008).

3.1 Tokenization

We took advantage of our in-house text processing tools for the tokenization and detokenization steps (Déchelotte et al., 2008). Previous experiments have demonstrated that better normalization tools provide better BLEU scores (Papineni et al., 2002). Thus all systems are built in "true-case."

As German is morphologically more complex than English, the default policy which consists in treating each word form independently is plagued with data sparsity, which poses a number of difficulties both at training and decoding time. Thus, to translate from German to English, the German side was normalized using a specific pre-processing scheme (described in (Allauzen et al., 2010)), which aims at reducing the lexical redundancy and splitting complex compounds.

Using the same pre-processing scheme to translate from English to German would require to post-process the output to undo the pre-processing. As in our last year's experiments (Allauzen et al., 2010), this pre-processing step could be achieved with a two-step decoding. However, by stacking two decoding steps, we may stack errors as well. Thus, for this direction, we used the German tokenizer provided by the organizers.

3.2 Filtering the *GigaWord* Corpus

The available parallel data for English-French includes a large Web corpus, referred to as the *GigaWord* parallel corpus. This corpus is very noisy, and contains large portions that are not useful for translating news text. The first filter aimed at detecting foreign languages based on perplexity and lexical coverage. Then, to select a subset of parallel sentences, trigram LMs were trained for both French and English languages on a subset of the available News data: the French (resp. English) LM was used to rank the French (resp. English) side of the corpus, and only those sentences with perplexity above a given threshold were selected. Finally, the two selected sets were intersected. In the following experiments, the threshold was set to the median or upper quartile value of the perplexity. Therefore, half (or 75%) of this corpus was discarded.

4 Target Language Modeling

Neural networks, working on top of conventional n-gram models, have been introduced in (Bengio et al., 2003; Schwenk, 2007) as a potential means to improve conventional n-gram language models (LMs). However, probably the major bottleneck with standard NNLMs is the computation of posterior probabilities in the output layer. This layer must contain one unit for each vocabulary word. Such a design makes handling of large vocabularies, consisting of hundreds thousand words, infeasible due to a prohibitive growth in computation time. While recent work proposed to estimate the n-gram distributions only for the most frequent words (short-list) (Schwenk, 2007), we explored the use of the SOUL (Structured OUtput Layer Neural Network) language model for SMT in order to handle vocabularies of arbitrary sizes.

Moreover, in our setting, increasing the order of standard n-gram LM did not show any significant improvement. This is mainly due to the data sparsity issue and to the drastic increase in the number of parameters that need to be estimated. With NNLM however, the increase in context length at the input layer results in only a linear growth in complexity in the worst case (Schwenk, 2007). Thus, training longer-context neural network models is still feasible, and was found to be very effective in our system.

4.1 Standard n-gram Back-off Language Models

To train our language models, we assumed that the test set consisted in a selection of news texts dating from the end of 2010 to the beginning of 2011. This assumption was based on what was done for the 2010 evaluation. Thus, for each language, we built a development corpus in order to optimize the vocabulary and the target language model.

Development set and vocabulary In order to cover different periods, two development sets were used. The first one is *newstest2008*. This corpus is two years older than the targeted time period; therefore, a second development corpus named *dev2010-2011* was collected by randomly sampling bunches of 5 consecutive sentences from the provided news data of 2010 and 2011.

To estimate such large LMs, a vocabulary was first defined for each language by including all tokens observed in the Europarl and News-Commentary corpora. For French and English, this vocabulary was then expanded with all words that occur more than 5 times in the French-English *GigaWord* corpus, and with the most frequent proper names taken from the monolingual news data of 2010 and 2011. As for German, since the amount of training data was smaller, the vocabulary was expanded with the most frequent words observed in the monolingual news data of 2010 and 2011. This procedure resulted in a vocabulary containing around 500k words in each language.

Language model training All the training data allowed in the constrained task were divided into several sets based on dates or genres (resp. 9 and 7 sets for English and French). On each set, a standard 4-gram LM was estimated from the 500k words vocabulary using absolute discounting interpolated with lower order models (Kneser and Ney, 1995; Chen and Goodman, 1998).

All LMs except the one trained on the news corpora from 2010-2011 were first linearly interpolated. The associated coefficients were estimated so as to minimize the perplexity evaluated on *dev2010-2011*. The resulting LM and the 2010-2011 LM were finaly interpolated with *newstest2008* as development data. This procedure aims to avoid overestimating the weight associated to the 2010-2011 LM.

4.2 The SOUL Model

We give here a brief overview of the SOUL LM; refer to (Le et al., 2011) for the complete training procedure. Following the classical work on distributed word representation (Brown et al., 1992), we assume that the output vocabulary is structured by a clustering tree, where each word belongs to only one class and its associated sub-classes. If w_i denotes the i-th word in a sentence, the sequence $c_{1:D}(w_i) = c_1, \dots, c_D$ encodes the path for the word w_i in the clustering tree, with D the depth of the tree, $c_d(w_i)$ a class or sub-class assigned to w_i, and $c_D(w_i)$ the leaf associated with w_i (the word itself). The n-gram probability of w_i given its history h can then be estimated as follows using the chain rule:

$$P(w_i|h) = P(c_1(w_i)|h) \prod_{d=2}^{D} P(c_d(w_i)|h, c_{1:d-1})$$

Figure 2 represents the architecture of the NNLM to estimate this distribution, for a tree of depth $D = 3$. The SOUL architecture is the same as for the standard model up to the output layer. The main difference lies in the output structure which involves several layers with a softmax activation function. The first softmax layer *(class layer)* estimates the class probability $P(c_1(w_i)|h)$, while other output *sub-class layers* estimate the sub-class probabilities $P(c_d(w_i)|h, c_{1:d-1})$. Finally, the *word layers* estimate the word probabilities $P(c_D(w_i)|h, c_{1:D-1})$. Words in the short-list are a special case since each of them represents its own class without any sub-classes ($D = 1$ in this case).

5 Experimental Results

The experimental results are reported in terms of BLEU and translation edit rate (TER) using the *newstest2010* corpus as evaluation set. These automatic metrics are computed using the scripts provided by the NIST after a detokenization step.

5.1 English-French

Compared with last year evaluation, the amount of available parallel data has drastically increased with about 33M of sentence pairs. It is worth noticing

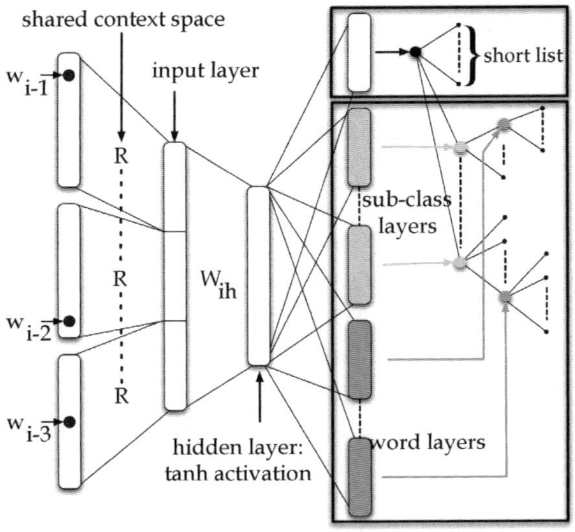

Figure 2: Architecture of the Structured Output Layer Neural Network language model.

that the provided corpora are not homogeneous, neither in terms of genre nor in terms of topics. Nevertheless, the most salient difference is the noise carried by the *GigaWord* and the *United Nation* corpora. The former is an automatically collected corpus drawn from different websites, and while some parts are indeed relevant to translate news texts, using the whole *GigaWord* corpus seems to be harmful. The latter *(United Nation)* is obviously more homogeneous, but clearly out of domain. As an illustration, discarding the *United Nation* corpus improves performance slightly.

Table 1 summarizes some of our attempts at dealing with such a large amount of parallel data. As stated above, translation models are trained with the *news-commentary*, *Europarl*, and *GigaWord* corpora. For this last data set, results show the reward of sentence pair selection as described in Section 3.2. Indeed, filtering out 75% of the corpus yields to a significant BLEU improvement when translating from English to French and of 1 point in the other direction (line *upper quartile* in Table 1). Moreover, a larger selection (50% in the *median* line) still increases the overall performance. This shows the room left for improvement by a more accurate data selection process such as a well optimized threshold in our approach, or a more sophisticated filtering strategy (see for example (Foster et al., 2010)).

Another issue when using such a large amount

System	en2fr		fr2en	
	BLEU	*TER*	BLEU	*TER*
All	27.4	56.6	26.8	55.0
Upper quartile	27.8	56.3	28.4	53.8
Median	28.1	56.0	28.6	53.5

Table 1: **English-French** translation results in terms of BLEU score and TER estimated on *newstest2010* with the NIST script. *All* means that the translation model is trained on *news-commentary*, *Europarl*, and the whole *GigaWord*. The rows *upper quartile* and *median* correspond to the use of a filtered version of the *GigaWord*.

of data is the mismatch between the target vocabulary derived from the translation model and that of the LM. The translation model may generate words which are unknown to the LM, and their probabilities could be overestimated. To avoid this behaviour, the probability of unknown words for the target LM is penalized during the decoding step.

5.2 English-German

For this translation task, we compare the impact of two different POS-taggers to process the German part of the parallel data. The results are reported in Table 2. Results show that to translate from English to German, the use of a fine-grained POS information (RFTagger) leads to a slight improvement, whereas it harms the source reordering model in the other direction. It is worth noticing that to translate from German to English, the RFTagger is always used during the data pre-processing step, while a different POS tagger may be involved for the source reordering model training.

System	en2de		de2en	
	BLEU	*TER*	BLEU	*TER*
RFTagger	22.8	60.1	16.3	66.0
TreeTagger	23.1	59.4	16.2	66.0

Table 2: Translation results in terms of BLEU score and translation edit rate (TER) estimated on *newstest2010* with the NIST scoring script.

5.3 The SOUL Model

As mentioned in Section 4.2, the order of a continuous n-gram model such as the SOUL LM can be raised without a prohibitive increase in complexity. We summarize in Table 3 our experiments with

SOUL LMs of orders 4, 6, and 10. The SOUL LM is introduced in the SMT pipeline by rescoring the n-best list generated by the decoder, and the associated weight is tuned with MERT. We observe for the English-French task: a BLEU improvement of 0.3, as well as a similar trend in TER, when introducing a 4-gram SOUL LM; an additional BLEU improvement of 0.3 when increasing the order from 4 to 6; and a less important gain with the 10-gram SOUL LM. In the end, the use of a 10-gram SOUL LM achieves a 0.7 BLEU improvement and a TER decrease of 0.8. The results on the English-German task show the same trend with a 0.5 BLEU point improvement.

SOUL LM	en2fr		en2de	
	BLEU	*TER*	BLEU	*TER*
without	28.1	56.0	16.3	66.0
4-gram	28.4	55.5	16.5	64.9
6-gram	28.7	55.3	16.7	64.9
10-gram	28.8	55.2	16.8	64.6

Table 3: Translation results from English to French and English to German measured on *newstest2010* using a 100-best rescoring with SOUL LMs of different orders.

5.4 Optimization Issues

Along with MIRA (Margin Infused Relaxed Algorithm) (Watanabe et al., 2007), MERT is the most widely used algorithm for system optimization. However, standard MERT procedure is known to suffer from instability of results and very slow training cycle with approximate estimates of one decoding cycle for each training parameter. For this year's evaluation, we experimented with several alternatives to the standard n-best MERT procedure, namely, MERT on word lattices (Macherey et al., 2008) and two differentiable variants to the BLEU objective function optimized during the MERT cycle. We have recast the former in terms of a specific semiring and implemented it using a general-purpose finite state automata framework (Sokolov and Yvon, 2011). The last two approaches, hereafter referred to as ZHN and BBN, replace the BLEU objective function, with the usual BLEU score on *expected n-gram counts* (Rosti et al., 2010) and with an *expected BLEU score* for normal n-gram counts (Zens et al., 2007), respectively. All expectations (of the n-gram counts in the first case and the BLEU score in the second) are taken over all hypotheses from n-best lists for each source sentence.

Experiments with the alternative optimization methods achieved virtually the same performance in terms of BLEU score, but 2 to 4 times faster. Neither approach, however, showed any consistent and significant improvement for the majority of setups tried (with the exception of the BBN approach, that had almost always improved over n-best MERT, but for the sole French to English translation direction). Additional experiments with 9 complementary translation models as additional features were performed with lattice-MERT, but neither showed any substantial improvement. In the view of these rather inconclusive experiments, we chose to stick to the classical MERT for the submitted results.

6 Conclusion

In this paper, we described our submissions to WMT'11 in the French-English and German-English shared translation tasks, in both directions. For this year's participation, we only used n-code, our open source Statistical Machine Translation system based on bilingual n-grams. Our contributions are threefold. First, we have shown that n-gram based systems can achieve state-of-the-art performance on large scale tasks in terms of automatic metrics such as BLEU. Then, as already shown by several sites in the past evaluations, there is a significant reward for using data selection algorithms when dealing with large heterogeneous data sources such as the *GigaWord*. Finally, the use of a large vocabulary continuous space language model such as the SOUL model has enabled to achieve significant and consistent improvements. For the upcoming evaluation(s), we would like to suggest that the important work of data cleaning and pre-processing could be shared among all the participants instead of being done independently several times by each site. Reducing these differences could indeed help improve the reliability of SMT systems evaluation.

Acknowledgment

This work was achieved as part of the Quaero Programme, funded by OSEO, French State agency for innovation.

References

Alexandre Allauzen, Josep M. Crego, İlknur Durgar El-Kahlout, and Francois Yvon. 2010. LIMSI's statistical translation systems for WMT'10. In *Proc. of the Joint Workshop on Statistical Machine Translation and MetricsMATR*, pages 54–59, Uppsala, Sweden.

Yoshua Bengio, Réjean Ducharme, Pascal Vincent, and Christian Janvin. 2003. A neural probabilistic language model. *JMLR*, 3:1137–1155.

P.F. Brown, P.V. de Souza, R.L. Mercer, V.J. Della Pietra, and J.C. Lai. 1992. Class-based n-gram models of natural language. *Computational Linguistics*, 18(4):467–479.

Francesco Casacuberta and Enrique Vidal. 2004. Machine translation with inferred stochastic finite-state transducers. *Computational Linguistics*, 30(3):205–225.

Stanley F. Chen and Joshua T. Goodman. 1998. An empirical study of smoothing techniques for language modeling. Technical Report TR-10-98, Computer Science Group, Harvard University.

Josep Maria Crego and José Bernardo Mariño. 2007. Improving statistical MT by coupling reordering and decoding. *Machine Translation*, 20(3):199–215.

Daniel Déchelotte, Gilles Adda, Alexandre Allauzen, Olivier Galibert, Jean-Luc Gauvain, Hélène Meynard, and François Yvon. 2008. LIMSI's statistical translation systems for WMT'08. In *Proc. of the NAACL-HTL Statistical Machine Translation Workshop*, Columbus, Ohio.

George Foster, Cyril Goutte, and Roland Kuhn. 2010. Discriminative instance weighting for domain adaptation in statistical machine translation. In *Proceedings of the 2010 Conference on Empirical Methods in Natural Language Processing*, pages 451–459, Cambridge, MA, October.

Reinhard Kneser and Herman Ney. 1995. Improved backing-off for m-gram language modeling. In *Proceedings of the International Conference on Acoustics, Speech, and Signal Processing, ICASSP'95*, pages 181–184, Detroit, MI.

Hai-Son Le, Ilya Oparin, Alexandre Allauzen, Jean-Luc Gauvain, and François Yvon. 2011. Structured output layer neural network language model. In *IEEE International Conference on Acoustics, Speech and Signal Processing (ICASSP 2011)*, Prague (Czech Republic), 22-27 May.

Wolfgang Macherey, Franz Josef Och, Ignacio Thayer, and Jakob Uszkoreit. 2008. Lattice-based minimum error rate training for statistical machine translation. In *Proc. of the Conf. on EMNLP*, pages 725–734.

Franz Josef Och. 2003. Minimum error rate training in statistical machine translation. In *ACL '03: Proc. of the 41st Annual Meeting on Association for Computational Linguistics*, pages 160–167.

Kishore Papineni, Salim Roukos, Todd Ward, and Wei-Jing Zhu. 2002. BLEU: a method for automatic evaluation of machine translation. In *ACL '02: Proc. of the 40th Annual Meeting on Association for Computational Linguistics*, pages 311–318. Association for Computational Linguistics.

Antti-Veikko I. Rosti, Bing Zhang, Spyros Matsoukas, and Richard Schwartz. 2010. BBN system description for wmt10 system combination task. In *Proceedings of the Joint Fifth Workshop on Statistical Machine Translation and MetricsMATR*, WMT '10, pages 321–326, Stroudsburg, PA, USA. Association for Computational Linguistics.

Helmut Schmid and Florian Laws. 2008. Estimation of conditional probabilities with decision trees and an application to fine-grained POS tagging. In *Proceedings of the 22nd International Conference on Computational Linguistics (Coling 2008)*, pages 777–784, Manchester, UK, August.

Helmut Schmid. 1994. Probabilistic part-of-speech tagging using decision trees. In *Proc. of International Conference on New Methods in Language Processing*, pages 44–49, Manchester, UK.

Holger Schwenk. 2007. Continuous space language models. *Computer, Speech & Language*, 21(3):492–518.

Artem Sokolov and François Yvon. 2011. Minimum error rate training semiring. In *Proceedings of the 15th Annual Conference of the European Association for Machine Translation*, EAMT'2011, May.

Christoph Tillmann. 2004. A unigram orientation model for statistical machine translation. In *Proceedings of HLT-NAACL 2004*, pages 101–104. Association for Computational Linguistics.

Taro Watanabe, Jun Suzuki, Hajime Tsukada, and Hideki Isozaki. 2007. Online large-margin training for statistical machine translation. In *Proceedings of the 2007 Joint Conference on Empirical Methods in Natural Language Processing and Computational Natural Language Learning (EMNLP-CoNLL)*, pages 764–773, Prague, Czech Republic.

Richard Zens, Sasa Hasan, and Hermann Ney. 2007. A systematic comparison of training criteria for statistical machine translation. In *Proceedings of the 2007 Joint Conference on Empirical Methods in Natural Language Processing and Computational Natural Language Learning (EMNLP-CoNLL)*, pages 524–532.

Shallow Semantic Trees for SMT

Wilker Aziz, Miguel Rios and **Lucia Specia**
Research Group in Computational Linguistics
University of Wolverhampton
Stafford Street, Wolverhampton, WV1 1SB, UK
{w.aziz, m.rios, l.specia}@wlv.ac.uk

Abstract

We present a translation model enriched with shallow syntactic and semantic information about the source language. Base-phrase labels and semantic role labels are incorporated into an hierarchical model by creating shallow semantic "trees". Results show an increase in performance of up to 6% in BLEU scores for English-Spanish translation over a standard phrase-based SMT baseline.

1 Introduction

The use of semantic information to improve Statistical Machine Translation (SMT) is a very recent research topic that has been attracting significant attention. In this paper we describe our participation in the shared translation task of the 6th Workshop on Statistical Machine Translation (WMT) with a system that incorporates shallow syntactic and semantic information into hierarchical SMT models.

The system is based on the Moses toolkit (Hoang et al., 2009; Koehn et al., 2007) using hierarchical models informed with shallow syntactic (chunks) and semantic (semantic role labels) information for the source language. The toolkit SENNA (Collobert et al., 2011) is used to provide base-phrases (chunks) and semantic role labels.

Experiments with English-Spanish and English-German news datasets show promising results and highlight important issues about the use of semantic information in hierarchical models as well as a number of possible directions for further research.

The remaining of the paper is organized as follows: Section 2 presents related work; Section 3 describes the method; Section 4 presents the results obtained for the English-Spanish and English-German translation tasks; and Section 5 brings some conclusions and directions for further research.

2 Related Work

In hierarchical SMT (Chiang, 2005), a Synchronous Context Free Grammar (SCFG) is learned from a parallel corpus.The model capitalizes on the recursive nature of language replacing sub-phrases by an unlabeled nonterminal. Hierarchical models are known to produce high coverage rules, once they are only constrained by the word alignment. Nevertheless the lack of specialized vocabulary also leads to spurious ambiguity (Chiang, 2005).

Syntax-based models are hierarchical models whose rules are constrained by syntactic information.The syntactic constraints have an impact in the rule extraction process, reducing drastically the number of rules available to the system. While this may be helpful to reduce ambiguity, it can lead to poorer performance (Ambati and Lavie, 2008).

Motivated by the fact that syntactically constraining a hierarchical model can decrease translation quality, some attempts to overcome the problems at rule extraction time have been made. Venugopal and Zollmann (2006) propose a heuristic method to relax parse trees known as Syntax Augmented Machine Translation (SAMT). Significant gains are obtained by grouping nonterminals under categories when they do not span across syntactic constituents.

Hoang and Koehn (2010) propose a soft syntax-based model which combines the precision of a syntax-constrained model with the coverage of an

Proceedings of the 6th Workshop on Statistical Machine Translation, pages 316–322,
Edinburgh, Scotland, UK, July 30–31, 2011.

unconstrained hierarchical model. Instead of having heuristic strategies to combine nonterminals in a parse tree, whenever a rule cannot be retrieved because it does not span a constituent, the extraction procedure falls back to the hierarchical approach, retrieving a rule with unlabeled nonterminals. Performance gains are reported over standard hierarchical models using both full parse trees and shallow syntax.

Moving beyond syntactic information, some attempts have recently been made to add semantic annotations to SMT. Wu and Fung (2009) present a two-pass model to incorporate semantic information to the phrase-based SMT pipeline. The method performs conventional translation in a first step, followed by a constituent reordering step seeking to maximize the cross-lingual match of the semantic role labels of the translation and source sentences.

Liu and Gildea (2010) add features extracted from the source sentences annotated with semantic role labels in a tree-to-string SMT model. They modify a syntax-based SMT system in order to penalize/reward role reordering and role deletion. The input sentence is parsed for semantic roles and the roles are then projected onto the target side using word alignment information at decoding time. They assume that a one-to-one mapping between source and target roles is desirable.

Baker et al. (2010) propose to graft semantic information, namely named entities and modalities, to syntactic tags in a syntax-based model. The vocabulary of nonterminals is specialized using the semantic categories, for instance, a noun phrase (NP) whose head is a geopolitical entity (GPE) will be tagged as NPGPE, making the rule table less ambiguous.

Similar to (Baker et al., 2010) we specialize a vocabulary of syntactic nonterminals with semantic information, however we use shallow syntax (base-phrases) and semantic role labels instead of constituent parse and named entities. The resulting shallow trees are relaxed following SAMT (Venugopal and Zollmann, 2006). Different from previous work we add the semantic knowledge at the level of the corpus annotation. As a consequence, instead of biasing deletion and reordering through additional features (Liu and Gildea, 2010), we learn hierarchical rules that encode those phenomena, taking also into account the semantic role of base-phrases.

3 Proposed Method

The proposed method is based on an extension of the hierarchical models in Moses using source language information. Our submission included systems for two language pairs: English-Spanish (en-es) and English-German (en-de) and was constrained to using data provided by WMT11. Phrase and rule extraction were performed using the entire en-es and en-de portions of Europarl. Model parameters were tuned using the *news-test2008* dataset. Three 5-gram Spanish and German language models were trained using SRILM[1] with the News Commentaries ($\sim$ 160K sentences), Europarl ($\sim$ 2M sentences) and News ($\sim$ 5M sentences) corpora. These models were interpolated using scripts provided in Moses (Koehn and Schroeder, 2007).

At pre-processing stage, sentences longer than 80 tokens were filtered from the training/development corpus. The parallel corpus was then tokenized and truecased. Additionally, for en-de, compound splitting of the German side of the corpus was performed using a frequency based method described in (Koehn and Knight, 2003). This method helps alleviate sparsity, reducing the size of the vocabulary by decomposing compounds into their base words. Recasing and detokenization, along with compound merging of the translations into German, were handled at post-processing stage. Compound merging was performed by finding the most likely sequences of words to be merged into previously seen compounds (Stymne, 2009).

3.1 Source Language Annotation

For rule extraction, training and test, the English side of the corpus was annotated with Semantic Role Labels (SRL) using the toolkit SENNA[2], which also outputs POS and base-phrase (without prepositional attachment) tags. The resulting source language annotation was used to produce trees in order to build a tree-to-string model in Moses.

[1] http://www.speech.sri.com/projects/srilm/

[2] http://ml.nec-labs.com/senna/

S															
NP	VP			NP		PP	NP	O	O	NP	VP			NP	ADVP
PRP	VBZ	TO	VB	DT	NN	TO	NN	PUNC	CC	PRP	VBZ	RB	VBD	WDT	RB
he	intends	to	donate	this	money	to	charity	,	but	he	has	not	decided	which	yet

Figure 1: Example of POS tags and base-phrase annotation. Base-phrases: noun-phrase (NP), verb-phrase (VP), prepositional-phrase (PP), adverbial-phrase (ADVP), outside-of-a-phrase (O)

In order to derive trees for the source side of the corpus from this annotation, a new level is created to add the POS tags for each word form. Syntactic tags are then added by grouping words and POS tags into base phrases using linguistic information as given by SENNA. Figure 1 shows an example of an input sentence annotated with POS and base-phrase information. Additionally, SRLs are used to enrich the POS and base-phrase annotation levels. Semantic roles are assigned to each predicate independently. As a consequence, the resulting annotation cannot be considered a tree and there is not an obvious hierarchy of predicates in a sentence. For example, Figure 2 shows the SRL annotation for the example in Figure 1.

[A0 He] [T intends] [A1 to donate this money to charity], but he has not decided which yet
[A0 He] intends to [T donate] [A1 this money] [A2 to charity], but he has not decided which yet
He intends to donate this money to charity, but [A0 he] has [AM-NEG not] [T decided] [A1 which] [AM-TMP yet]

Figure 2: SRL for sentence in Figure 1

Arguments of a single predicate never overlap, however in longer sentences, the occurrence of multiple verbs increases the chances that arguments of different predicates overlap, that is, the argument of a verb might contain or even coincide with the argument of another verb and depending on the verb the argument role might change. For example, in Figure 2: i) *He* is both the agent of *intend* and *donate*; ii) *this money* is the donated thing and also part of the chunk which express the intention (*to donate this money to charity*). In a different example we can see that arguments might overlap and their roles change completely depending on their target predicates (e.g in *I gave you something to eat*, *you* is the recipient of the verb *give* and the agent of the verb *eat*). For this reason, why semantic role labels are usually annotated individually in different structures, as shown in Figure 2, each annotation focusing on a single target verb. In order to convert the predicates and arguments of a sentence into a single tree, we enrich the POS-tags and base-phrase annotation as follows:

- Semantic labels are directly grafted to the base-phrase annotation whenever possible, that is, if a predicate argument coincides with a single base-phrase, the base-phrase type is specialized with the argument role. In Figure 3, the noun-phrase (NP) *the money* is specialized into *NP:A1:donate*, since that single NP is the argument A1 of *donate*.

- If a predicate argument groups multiple base-phrases, the semantic label applies to a node in a new level of the tree subsuming all these base-phrases. In Figure 3, the base-phrases *to* (PP) and *charity* (NP) are grouped by *A2:donate*.

- We add the labels sequentially from the shortest chunks to the largest ones. If two labels spanning the same number of tokens: i) overlap completely, we merge them so that no hierarchy is imposed between their targets (e.g. in Figure 3, the noun-phrase *He* is specialized into *NP:A0:donate,intend*); ii) overlap partially, we merge them so that the resulting label will compete against other labels in a different length category. If a label spanning a larger chunk overlaps partially with a label spanning a shorter chunk, or contains it, we stack them in a way that the first subsumes the second (e.g in Figure 3, *A1:intend* subsumes *VP:T:donate*, *NP:A1:donate,intend* and *A2:donate*).

- Verb phrases might get split if they contain multiple target predicates (e.g. in Figure 3, the VP *intends to donate* is split into two verb-phrases, each specialized with its own role label).

- Finally, tags are lexicalized, that is, semantic labels are composed by their type (e.g. *A0*) and target predicate lemma (verb).

Figure 3 shows and example of how semantic labels are combined with shallow syntax in order to produce the input tree for the sentence in Figure 1. The argument *A1* of *intend* subsumes the target verb *donate* and its arguments *A1* and *A2*; *A2:donate* groups base-phrases so as to attach the preposition to the noun phrase.

Finally, following the method for syntactic trees by Venugopal and Zollmann (2006), the input trees are relaxed in order to alleviate the impact of the linguistic constraints on rule extraction. We relax trees[3] by combining any pairs of neighboring nodes. For example, *NP:A0:donate,intend+VP:T:intend* and *NP:A1:donate+A2:donate* are created for the tree in Figure 3.

4 Results

As a baseline to compare against our proposed approach (**srl**), we took a phrase-based SMT system (**pb**) built using the Moses toolkit with the same datasets and training conditions described in Section 3. The results are reported in terms of standard BLEU (Papineni et al., 2002) (and its case sensitive version, BLEU-c) and tested for statistical significance using an approximate randomization test (Riezler and Maxwell, 2005) with 100 iterations.

In addition, we included an intermediate model between these two: a hierarchical model informed with source-language base-phrase information (**chunk**). For the English-Spanish task we also built a purely hierarchical model (**hier**) using Moses and the same datasets and training conditions. For the English-German task, hierarchical models have not been shown to outperform standard phrase-based models in previous work (Koehn et al., 2010).

Table 1 shows the performance achieved for the English-Spanish translation task test set, where (**srl**) is our official submission. One can notice a significant gain in performance (up to 6% BLEU) in using tree-based models (with or without source language annotation) as opposed to using standard phrase-based models.

Model	BLEU	BLEU-c
pb	0.2429	0.2340
srl	0.2901	0.2805
hier	0.3029	0.2933
chunk	0.3034	0.2935

Table 1: English-Spanish experiments - differences between all pairs of models are statistically significant with 99% confidence, except for the pair (**hier**, **chunk**)

The purely hierarchical approach performs as well as our linguistically informed tree-based models (**chunk** and **srl**). On the one hand this finding is somewhat disappointing as we expected that tree-based models would benefit from linguistic annotation. On the other hand it shows that the linguistic annotation yields a significant reduction in the number of unnecessary productions: the linguistically informed models are much smaller than **hier** (Table 5), but perform just as well. Whether the linguistic annotation significantly helps make the productions less ambiguous or not is still a question to be addressed in further experimentation.

Table 2 shows the performance achieved for the English-German translation task test set. These results indicate that the linguistic information did not lead to any significant gains in terms of automatic metrics. An in-depth comparative analysis based on a manual inspection of the translations remains to be done.

Model	BLEU	BLEU-c
pb	0.1398	0.1360
srl	0.1381	0.1344
chunk	0.1403	0.1367

Table 2: English-German experiments - differences between pairs of models are not statistically significant

In Table 3 we also show the impact of three compound merging strategies as post-processing for en-de: i) no compound merging (**nm**), ii) frequency-based compound merging (**fb**), and iii) frequency-

[3]Using the Moses implementation *relax-parse* for SAMT 2

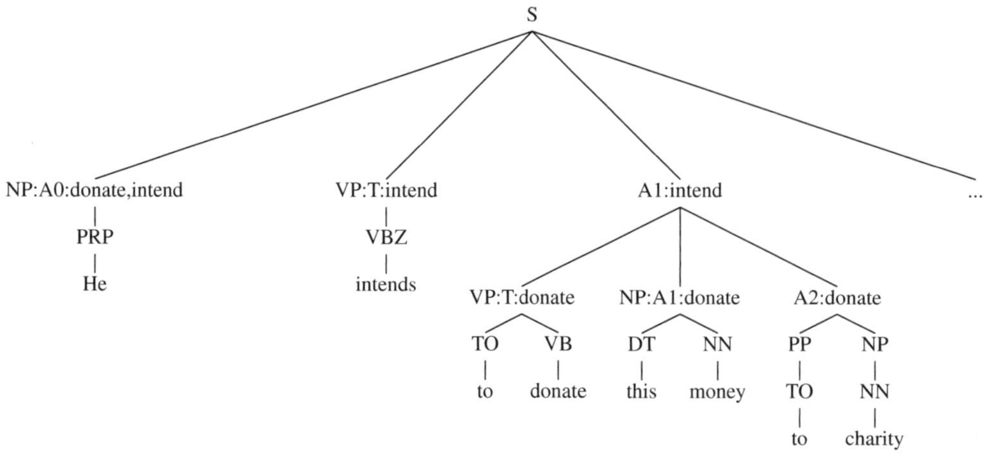

Figure 3: Tree for example in Figure 1

based compound merging constrained by POS[4] (**cfb**). Applying both frequency-based compound merging strategies (Stymne, 2009) resulted in significant improvements of nearly 0.5% in BLEU.

Model	BLEU	BLEU-c
nm	0.1334	0.1298
fb	0.1369	0.1332
cfb	0.1381	0.1344

Table 3: English-German compound merging - differences between all pairs of models are statistically significant with 99% confidence

Another somewhat disappoint result is the performance of **srl** when compared to **chunk**. We believe the main reason why the **chunk** models outperform the **srl** models is data sparsity. The semantic information, and particularly the way it was used in this paper, with lexicalized roles, led to a very sparse model. As an attempt to make the **srl** model less sparse, we tested a version of this model without lexicalizing the semantic tags, in other words, using the semantic role labels only, for example, *A1* instead of *A1:intend* in Figure 3. Table 4 shows that models with lexicalized semantic roles (*lex*) consistently outperform the alternative version (*non lex*), although the differences were only statistically significant for the en-de dataset. One reason for that may be that non-lexicalized rules do not help making the **chunk** rules less ambiguous.

Model	BLEU	BLEU-c
en-es$_{non\ lex}$	0.2891	0.2795
en-es$_{lex}$	0.2901	0.2805
en-de$_{non\ lex}$	0.1319	0.1284
en-de$_{lex}$	0.1381	0.1344

Table 4: Alternative model with non-lexicalized tags - differences are statistically significant with 99% confidence for en-de only

Table 5 shows how the additional annotation constrains the rule extraction (for the en-es dataset). The unconstrained model **hier** presents the largest rule table, followed by the **chunk** model, which is only constrained by syntactic information. The models enriched with semantic labels, both the lexicalized or non-lexicalized versions, contain a comparable number of rules. They are at least half the size of the **chunk** model and about 9 times smaller than the **hier** model. However, the number of nonterminals in the lexicalized models highlights the sparsity of such models.

Model	Rules	Nonterminals
hier	962,996,167	1
chunk	235,910,731	3,390
srl$_{non\ lex}$	92,512,493	44,095
srl$_{lex}$	117,563,878	3,350,145

Table 5: Statistics from the rule table

In order to exemplify the importance of having

[4]POS tagging was performed using the TreeTagger toolkit: `http://www.ims.uni-stuttgart.de/projekte/corplex/TreeTagger/`

some form of lexicalized information as part of the semantic models, Figure 4 shows two predicates which present different semantic roles, even though they have nearly the same shallow syntactic structure. In this case, unless lexicalized, rules mapping semantic roles into base-phrases become ambiguous. Besides, the same role might appear several times in the same sentence (Figure 2). In this case, if the semantic roles are not annotated with their target lemma, they bring additional confusion. Therefore, the model needs the lexical information to distinguish role deletion and reordering phenomena across predicates.

Figure 4: Different SRL for similar chunks

[NP:A0 I] [VP:T gave] [NP:A2 you] [NP:A1 a car]
[NP:A0 I] [VP:T dropped] [NP:A1 the glass] [AM-LOC [PP on] [NP the floor]]

In WMT11's official manual evaluation, our system submissions (**srl**) were ranked 10th out of 15 systems in the English-Spanish task, and 18th out of 22 systems participating in the English-German task. For detailed results refer to the overview paper of the Shared Translation Task of the Sixth Workshop on Machine Translation (WMT11).

5 Conclusions

We have presented an effort towards using shallow syntactic and semantic information for SMT. The model based on shallow syntactic information (chunk annotation) has significantly outperformed a baseline phrase-based model and performed as well as a hierarchical phrase-based model with a significantly smaller number of translation rules.

While annotating base-phrases with semantic labels is intuitively a promising research direction, the current model suffers from sparsity and representation issues resulting from the fact that multiple predicates share arguments within a given sentence. As a consequence, shallow semantics has not yet shown improvements with respect to the chunk-based models.

In future work, we will address the sparsity issues in the lexicalized semantic models by clustering predicates in a way that semantic roles can be specialized with semantic categories, instead of the verb lemmas.

References

Vamshi Ambati and Alon Lavie. 2008. Improving syntax driven translation models by re-structuring divergent and non-isomorphic parse tree structures. In *The Eight Conference of the Association for Machine Translation in the Americas (AMTA)*.

Kathryn Baker, Michael Bloodgood, Chris Callison-burch, Bonnie J. Dorr, Nathaniel W. Filardo, Lori Levin, Scott Miller, and Christine Piatko. 2010. Semantically-informed syntactic machine translation: A tree-grafting approach.

David Chiang. 2005. A hierarchical phrase-based model for statistical machine translation. In *Proceeding of the 43rd Annual Meeting of the Association for Computational Linguistics*, pages 263–270.

Ronan Collobert, Jason Weston, Leon Bottou, Michael Karlen, Koray Kavukcuoglu, and Pavel Kuksa. 2011. Natural language processing (almost) from scratch. *arXiv:1103.0398v1*.

Hieu Hoang and Philipp Koehn. 2010. Improved translation with source syntax labels. In *Proceedings of the Joint Fifth Workshop on Statistical Machine Translation and MetricsMATR*, pages 409–417.

Hieu Hoang, Philipp Koehn, and Adam Lopez. 2009. A unified framework for phrase-based, hierarchical, and syntax-based statistical machine translation. In *Proceedings of International Workshop on Spoken Language Translation*, pages 152 – 159.

Philipp Koehn and Kevin Knight. 2003. Empirical methods for compound splitting. In *Proceedings of the tenth conference on European chapter of the Association for Computational Linguistics - Volume 1*, pages 187–193.

Philipp Koehn and Josh Schroeder. 2007. Experiments in domain adaptation for statistical machine translation. In *Proceedings of the Second Workshop on Statistical Machine Translation*, pages 224–227.

Philipp Koehn, Hieu Hoang, Alexandra Birch, Chris Callison Burch, Marcello Federico, Nicola Bertoldi, Brooke Cowan, Wade Shen, Christine Moran, Richard Zens, Chris Dyer, Ondrej Bojar, Alexandra Constantin, and Evan Herbst. 2007. Moses: Open source toolkit for statistical machine translation. In *45th Annual Meeting of the Association for Computational Linguistics*.

Philipp Koehn, Barry Haddow, Philip Williams, and Hieu Hoang. 2010. More linguistic annotation for statistical machine translation. In *Proceedings of the Joint Fifth Workshop on Statistical Machine Translation and MetricsMATR*, pages 115–120.

Ding Liu and Daniel Gildea. 2010. Semantic role features for machine translation. In *Proceedings of the 23rd International Conference on Computational Linguistics*, pages 716–724.

Kishore Papineni, Salim Roukos, Todd Ward, and Wei-Jing Zhu. 2002. Bleu: a method for automatic evaluation of machine translation. In *Proceedings of the 40th Annual Meeting on Association for Computational Linguistics*, pages 311–318.

Stefan Riezler and John Maxwell. 2005. On some pitfalls in automatic evaluation and significance testing for mt. In *Proceedings of the 43rd Annual Meeting of the Association for Computational Linguistics, Workshop in Intrinsic and Extrinsic Evaluation Measures for MT and Summarization.*

Sara Stymne. 2009. A comparison of merging strategies for translation of german compounds. In *Proceedings of the 12th Conference of the European Chapter of the Association for Computational Linguistics: Student Research Workshop*, pages 61–69.

Ashish Venugopal and Andreas Zollmann. 2006. Syntax augmented machine translation via chart parsing. In *Proceedings on the Workshop on Statistical Machine Translation*, pages 138–141.

Dekai Wu and Pascale Fung. 2009. Semantic roles for smt: a hybrid two-pass model. In *Proceedings of Human Language Technologies: The 2009 Annual Conference of the North American Chapter of the Association for Computational Linguistics, Companion Volume: Short Papers*, pages 13–16.

RegMT System for Machine Translation, System Combination, and Evaluation

Ergun Biçici
Koç University
34450 Sariyer, Istanbul, Turkey
ebicici@ku.edu.tr

Deniz Yuret
Koç University
34450 Sariyer, Istanbul, Turkey
dyuret@ku.edu.tr

Abstract

We present the results we obtain using our RegMT system, which uses transductive regression techniques to learn mappings between source and target features of given parallel corpora and use these mappings to generate machine translation outputs. Our training instance selection methods perform feature decay for proper selection of training instances, which plays an important role to learn correct feature mappings. RegMT uses L_2 regularized regression as well as L_1 regularized regression for sparse regression estimation of target features. We present translation results using our training instance selection methods, translation results using graph decoding, system combination results with RegMT, and performance evaluation with the F_1 measure over target features as a metric for evaluating translation quality.

1 Introduction

Regression can be used to find mappings between the source and target feature sets derived from given parallel corpora. Transduction learning uses a subset of the training examples that are closely related to the test set without using the model induced by the full training set. In the context of statistical machine translation, translations are performed at the sentence level and this enables us to select a small number of training instances for each test instance to guide the translation process. This also gives us a computational advantage when considering the high dimensionality of the problem as each sentence can be mapped to many features.

The goal in transductive regression based machine translation (RegMT) is both reducing the computational burden of the regression approach by reducing the dimensionality of the training set and the feature set and also improving the translation quality by using transduction.

We present translation results using our training instance selection methods, translation results using graph decoding, system combination results with RegMT, and performance evaluation with the F_1 measure over target features as a metric for evaluating translation quality. RegMT work builds on our previous regression-based machine translation results (Bicici and Yuret, 2010) especially with instance selection and additional graph decoding capability. We present our results to this year's challenges.

Outline: Section 2 gives an overview of the RegMT model. In section 3, we present our training instance selection techniques and WMT'11 results. In section 4, we present the graph decoding results on the Haitian Creole-English translation task. Section 5 presents our system combination results using reranking with the RegMT score. Section 6 evaluates the F_1 measure that we use for the automatic evaluation metrics challenge. The last section present our contributions.

2 Machine Translation Using Regression

Let X and Y correspond to the sets of tokens that can be used in the source and target strings, then, m training instances are represented as $(\mathbf{x}_1, \mathbf{y}_1), \ldots, (\mathbf{x}_m, \mathbf{y}_m) \in X^* \times Y^*$, where $(\mathbf{x}_i, \mathbf{y}_i)$ corresponds to a pair of source and target language

Proceedings of the 6th Workshop on Statistical Machine Translation, pages 323–329,
Edinburgh, Scotland, UK, July 30–31, 2011. ©2011 Association for Computational Linguistics

token sequences for $1 \leq i \leq m$. Our goal is to find a mapping $f : X^* \rightarrow Y^*$ that can convert a source sentence to a target sentence sharing the same meaning in the target language (Figure 1).

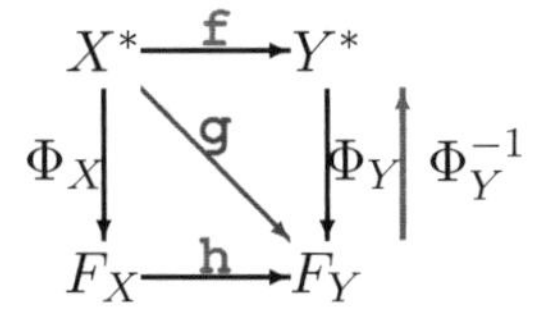

Figure 1: String-to-string mapping.

We define feature mappers $\Phi_X : X^* \rightarrow F_X = \mathbb{R}^{N_X}$ and $\Phi_Y : Y^* \rightarrow F_Y = \mathbb{R}^{N_Y}$ that map each string sequence to a point in high dimensional real number space. Let $\mathbf{M}_X \in \mathbb{R}^{N_X \times m}$ and $\mathbf{M}_Y \in \mathbb{R}^{N_Y \times m}$ such that $\mathbf{M}_X = [\Phi_X(\mathbf{x}_1), \ldots, \Phi_X(\mathbf{x}_m)]$ and $\mathbf{M}_Y = [\Phi_Y(\mathbf{y}_1), \ldots, \Phi_Y(\mathbf{y}_m)]$. The ridge regression solution using L_2 regularization is found by minimizing the following cost:

$$\mathbf{W}_{L_2} = \underset{\mathbf{W} \in \mathbb{R}^{N_Y \times N_X}}{\arg\min} \parallel \mathbf{M}_Y - \mathbf{W}\mathbf{M}_X \parallel_F^2 + \lambda \parallel \mathbf{W} \parallel_F^2 . \quad (1)$$

Two main challenges of the regression based machine translation (RegMT) approach are learning the regression function, $h : F_X \rightarrow F_Y$, and solving the *pre-image problem*, which, given the features of the estimated target string sequence, $h(\Phi_X(\mathbf{x})) = \Phi_Y(\hat{\mathbf{y}})$, attempts to find $\mathbf{y} \in Y^*$: $\mathbf{y} = \arg\min_{\mathbf{y} \in Y^*} ||h(\Phi_X(\mathbf{x})) - \Phi_Y(\mathbf{y})||^2$. Pre-image calculation involves a search over possible translations minimizing the cost function:

$$f(\mathbf{x}) = \underset{\mathbf{y} \in Y^*}{\arg\min} \parallel \Phi_Y(\mathbf{y}) - \mathbf{W}\Phi_X(\mathbf{x}) \parallel^2 . \quad (2)$$

2.1 L_1 Regularized Regression

String kernels lead to sparse feature representations and L_1 regularized regression is effective to find the mappings between sparsely observed features.We would like to observe only a few nonzero target coefficients corresponding to a source feature in the coefficient matrix. L_1 regularization helps us achieve solutions close to permutation matrices by increasing sparsity (Bishop, 2006) (page 145). In contrast, L_2 regularized solutions give us dense matrices.

$\mathbf{W}_{L_2}$ is not a sparse solution and most of the coefficients remain non-zero. We are interested in penalizing the coefficients better; zeroing the irrelevant ones leading to sparsification to obtain a solution that is closer to a permutation matrix. L_1 norm behaves both as a feature selection technique and a method for reducing coefficient values.

$$\mathbf{W}_{L_1} = \underset{\mathbf{W} \in \mathbb{R}^{N_Y \times N_X}}{\arg\min} \parallel \mathbf{M}_Y - \mathbf{W}\mathbf{M}_X \parallel_F^2 + \lambda \parallel \mathbf{W} \parallel_1 . \quad (3)$$

Equation 3 presents the *lasso* (Tibshirani, 1996) solution where the regularization term is now the L_1 matrix norm defined as $\|\mathbf{W}\|_1 = \sum_{i,j} |W_{i,j}|$. $\mathbf{W}_{L_2}$ can be found by taking the derivative but since L_1 regularization cost is not differentiable, $\mathbf{W}_{L_1}$ is found by optimization or approximation techniques. We use forward stagewise regression (FSR) (Hastie et al., 2006), which approximates *lasso* for L_1 regularized regression.

2.2 Related Work:

Regression techniques can be used to model the relationship between strings (Cortes et al., 2007). Wang et al. (2007) applies a string-to-string mapping approach to machine translation by using ordinary least squares regression and n-gram string kernels to a small dataset. Later they use L_2 regularized least squares regression (Wang and Shawe-Taylor, 2008). Although the translation quality they achieve is not better than Moses (Koehn et al., 2007), which is accepted to be the state-of-the-art, they show the feasibility of the approach. Serrano et al. (2009) use kernel regression to find translation mappings from source to target feature vectors and experiment with translating hotel front desk requests. Locally weighted regression solves separate weighted least squares problems for each instance (Hastie et al., 2009), weighted by a kernel similarity function.

3 Instance Selection for Machine Translation

Proper selection of training instances plays an important role for accurately learning feature mappings with limited computational resources. Coverage of the features is important since if we do not have the correct features in the training matrices, we will not be able to translate them. Coverage is measured by the percentage of target features of the test set found in the training set. For each test sentence, we pick a limited number of training instances designed to improve the coverage of correct features to build a regression model.

We use two techniques for this purpose: (1) Feature Decay Algorithm (FDA), which optimizes source languge bigram coverage to maximize the target coverage, (2) *dice*. Feature decay algorithms (FDA) aim to maximize the coverage of the target language features (such as words, bigrams, and phrases) for the test sentences. FDA selects training instances one by one updating the coverage of the features already added to the training set in contrast to the features found in the test sentence.

We also use a technique that we call *dice*, which optimizes source language bigram coverage such that the difficulty of aligning source and target features is minimized. We define Dice's coefficient score as:

$$dice(x, y) = \frac{2C(x, y)}{C(x)C(y)}, \tag{4}$$

where $C(x, y)$ is the number of times x and y co-occurr and $C(x)$ is the count of observing x in the selected training set. Given a test source sentence, $S_{\mathcal{U}}$, we can estimate the goodness of a training sentence pair, (S, T), by the sum of the alignment scores:

$$\phi_{dice}(S_{\mathcal{U}}, S, T) = \frac{\sum_{x \in X(S_{\mathcal{U}})} \sum_{j=1}^{|T|} \sum_{y \in Y(x)} dice(y, T_j)}{|T| \log |S|}, \tag{5}$$

where $X(S_{\mathcal{U}})$ stores the features of $S_{\mathcal{U}}$ and $Y(x)$ lists the tokens in feature x. The difficulty of word aligning a pair of training sentences, (S, T), can be approximated by $|S|^{|T|}$. We use a normalization factor proportional to $|T| \log |S|$.

The details of both of these techniques and further results can be found in (Bicici and Yuret, 2011).

3.1 Moses Experiments on the Translation Task

We have used FDA and *dice* algorithms to select training sets for the out-of-domain challenge test sets used in (Callison-Burch et al., 2011). The parallel corpus contains about 1.9 million training sentences and the test set contain 3003 sentences. We built separate Moses systems using all of the parallel corpus for the language pairs *en-de*, *de-en*, *en-es*, and *es-en*. We created training sets using all of the features of the test set to select training instances. The results given in Table 1 show that we can achieve similar BLEU performance using about 7% of the parallel corpus target words (200,000 instances) using *dice* and about 16% using FDA. In the out-of-domain translation task, we are able to reduce the training set size to achieve a performance close to the baseline. We may be able to achieve better performance in this out-of-domain task as well as explained in (Bicici and Yuret, 2011).

		en-de	*de-en*	*en-es*	*es-en*
BLEU	ALL	.1376	.2074	.2829	.2919
	FDA	.1363	.2055	.2824	.2892
	dice	.1374	.2061	.2834	.2857
words	ALL	47.4	49.6	52.8	50.4
	FDA	7.9	8.0	8.7	8.2
	dice	6.9	7.0	3.9	3.6
% ALL	FDA	17	16	16	16
	dice	14	14	7.4	7.1

Table 1: Performance for the out-of-domain task of (Callison-Burch et al., 2011). ALL corresponds to the baseline system using all of the parallel corpus. words list the size of the target words used in millions.

4 Graph Decoding for RegMT

We perform graph-based decoding by first generating a De Bruijn graph from the estimated $\hat{\mathbf{y}}$ (Cortes et al., 2007) and then finding Eulerian paths with maximum path weight. We use four features when scoring paths: (1) estimation weight from regression, (2) language model score, (3) brevity penalty as found by $e^{\alpha(l_R - |s|/|path|)}$ for l_R representing the length ratio from the parallel corpus and $|path|$ representing the length of the current path, (4) future cost as in Moses (Koehn et al., 2007) and weights are tuned using MERT (Och, 2003) on the *de-en dev* set.

We demonstrate that sparse L_1 regularized regression performs better than L_2 regularized regression. Graph based decoding can provide an alternative to state of the art phrase-based decoding system Moses in translation domains with small vocabulary and training set size.

4.1 Haitian Creole to English Translation Task with RegMT

We have trained a Moses system for the Haitian Creole to English translation task, cleaned corpus, using the options as described in section 3.1. Moses achieves 0.3186 BLEU on this task. We observed that graph decoding performs better where target coverage is high such that the bigrams used lead to a connected graph. To increase the connectivity, we have included Moses translations in the training set and performed graph decoding with RegMT. RegMT with L_2 regularized regression achieves 0.2708 BLEU with graph decoding and *lasso* achieves 0.26 BLEU.

Moses makes use of a number of distortion parameters and lexical weights, which are estimated using all of the parallel corpus. Thus, our Moses translation achieves a better performance than graph decoding with RegMT using 100 training instances for translating each source test sentence.

5 System Combination with RegMT

We perform experiments on the system combination task for the English-German, German-English, English-Spanish, and Spanish-English language pairs using the training corpus provided in WMT'11 (Callison-Burch et al., 2011). We have tokenized and lowercased each of the system outputs and combined these in a single N-best file per language pair. We use these N-best lists for reranking by RegMT to select the best translation model. Feature mappers used are 2-spectrum counting word kernels (Taylor and Cristianini, 2004).

We rerank N-best lists by a linear combination of the following scoring functions:

1. RegMT: Regression based machine translation scores as found by Equation 2.

2. CBLEU: Comparative BLEU scores we obtain by measuring the average BLEU performance of each translation relative to the other systems' translations in the N-best list.

3. LM: We calculate 5-gram language model scores for each translation using the language model trained over the target corpus provided in the translation task.

Since we do not have access to the reference translations nor to the translation model scores each system obtained for each sentence, we estimate translation model performance (CBLEU) by measuring the average BLEU performance of each translation relative to the other translations in the N-best list. Thus, each possible translation in the N-best list is BLEU scored against other translations and the average of these scores is selected as the CBLEU score for the sentence. Sentence level BLEU score calculation avoids singularities in n-gram precisions by taking the maximum of the match count and $\frac{1}{2|s_i|}$ for $|s_i|$ denoting the length of the source sentence s_i as used in (Macherey and Och, 2007).

Table 2 presents reranking results on all of the language pairs we considered, using RegMT, CBLEU, and LM scores with the same combination weights as above. We also list the performance of the best model (Max) as well as the worst (Min). We are able to achieve close or better BLEU scores in all of the listed systems when compared with the performance of the best translation system except for the *ht-en* language pair. The lower performance in the *ht-en* language pair may be due to having a single best translation system that outperforms others significantly. This happens for instance when an unconstrained model use external resources to achieve a significantly better performance than the second best model. 2nd best in Table 2 lists the second best model's performance to estimate how much the best model's performance is better than the rest.

BLEU	*en-de*	*de-en*	*en-es*	*es-en*	*ht-en*
Min	.1064	.1572	.2174	.1976	.2281
Max	.1727	.2413	.3375	.3009	.3708
2nd best	.1572	.2302	.3301	.2973	.3288
Average	.1416	.1997	.292	.2579	.2993
Oracle	.2529	.3305	.4265	.4233	.4336
RegMT	.1631	.2322	.3311	.3052	.3234

Table 2: System combination results.

RegMT model may prefer sentences with lower BLEU, which can sometimes cause it to achieve a lower BLEU performance than the best model. This is clearly the case for *en-de* with 1.6 BLEU points difference with the second best model performance and for *de-en* task with 1.11 BLEU points difference. Also this observation holds for *en-es* with 0.74 BLEU points difference and for *ht-en* with 4.2 BLEU points difference. For *es-en* task, there is 0.36 BLEU points difference with the second best model and these models likely to complement each other.

The existence of complementing SMT models is important for the reranking approach to achieve a performance better than the best model, as there is a need for the existence of a model performing better than the best model on some test sentences. We can use the competitive SMT model to achieve the performance of the best with a guarantee even when a single model is dominating the rest (Bicici and Kozat, 2010). For competing translation systems in an on-line machine translation setting adaptively learning of model weights can be performed based on the previous transaltion performance (Bicici and Kozat, 2010).

6 Target F_1 as a Performance Evaluation Metric

We use target sentence F_1 measure over the target features as a translation performance evaluation metric. We optimize the parameters of the RegMT model with the F_1 measure comparing the target vector with the estimate we get from the RegMT model. F_1 measure uses the 0/1-class predictions over the target feature with the estimate vector, $\Phi_Y(\hat{\mathbf{y}})$. Let TP be the true positive, TN the true negative, FP the false positive, and FN the false negative rates, we use the following measures for evaluation:

$$\text{prec} = \frac{\text{TP}}{\text{TP}+\text{FP}}, \quad \text{BER} = \left(\frac{\text{FP}}{\text{TN+FP}} + \frac{\text{FN}}{\text{TP+FN}}\right)/2 \quad (6)$$

$$\text{rec} = \frac{\text{TP}}{\text{TP}+\text{FN}}, \quad F_1 = \frac{2\times\text{prec}\times\text{rec}}{\text{prec+rec}} \quad (7)$$

where BER is the balanced error rate, prec is precision, and rec is recall. The evaluation techniques measure the effectiveness of the learning models in identifying the features of the target sentence making minimal error to increase the performance of the decoder and its translation quality.

We use gapped word sequence kernels (Taylor and Cristianini, 2004) when using F_1 for evaluating translations since a given translation system may not be able to translate a given word but can correctly identify the surrounding phrase. For instance, let the reference translation be the following sentence:

```
a sound compromise has been reached
```

Some possible translations for the reference are given in Table 3 together with their BLEU (Papineni et al., 2001) and F_1 scores for comparison. F_1 score does not have a brevity penalty but a brief translation is penalized by a low recall value. We use up to 3 tokens as gaps. F_1 measure is able to increase the ranking of Trans_4 by using a gapped sequence kernel, which can be preferrable to Trans_3.

We note that a missing token corresponds to varying decreases in the n-gram precision used in the BLEU score. A sentence containing m tokens has m 1-grams, $m-1$ 2-grams, and $m-n+1$ n-grams. A missing token degrades the performance more in higher order n-gram precision values. A missing token decreases n-gram precision by $\frac{1}{m}$ for 1-grams and by $\frac{n}{m-n+1}$ for n-grams. Based on this observation, we use F_1 measure with gapped word sequence kernels to evaluate translations. Gapped features allows us to consider the surrounding phrase for a missing token as present in the translation.

Let the reference sentence be represented with `a b c d e f` where a-f, x, y, z correspond to tokens in the sentence. Then, Trans_3 has the form `a b x y f`, and Trans_4 has the form `a c y f`. Then, F_1 ranks Trans_4 higher than Trans_3 for orders greater than 3 as there are two consecutive word errors in Trans_3. F_1 can also prefer a missing token rather than a word error as we see by comparing Trans_4 and Trans_5 and it can still prefer contiguity over a gapped sequence as we see by comparing Trans_5 and Trans_6 in Table 3.

We calculate the correlation of F_1 with BLEU on the *en-de* development set. We use 5-grams with the F_1 measure as this increases the correlation with 4-gram BLEU. Table 4 gives the correlation results using both Pearson's correlation score and Spearman's correlation score. Spearman's correlation score is a better metric for comparing the relative orderings.

Metric	No gaps	Gaps
Pearson	.8793	.7879
Spearman	.9068	.8144

Table 4: F_1 correlation with 4-gram BLEU using blended 5-gram gapped word sequence features on the development set.

7 Contributions

We present the results we obtain using our RegMT system, which uses transductive regression techniques to learn mappings between source and tar-

Ref: `a sound compromise has been reached`	Format a b c d e f	BLEU 4-grams	F_1 3-grams	F_1 4-grams	F_1 5-grams
Trans_1: `a sound agreement has been reached`	a b x d e f	.2427	.6111	.5417	.5
Trans_2: `a compromise has reached`	a c d f	.137	.44	.3492	.3188
Trans_3: `a sound agreement is reached`	a b x y f	.1029	.2	.1558	.1429
Trans_4: `a compromise is reached`	a c y f	.0758	.2	.1587	.1449
Trans_5: `a good compromise is reached`	a z c y f	.0579	.1667	.1299	.119
Trans_6: `a good compromise is been`	a z c y e	.0579	.2	.1558	.1429

Table 3: BLEU vs. F_1 on sample sentence translation task.

get features of given parallel corpora and use these mappings to generate machine translation outputs. We also present translation results using our training instance selection methods, translation results using graph decoding, system combination results with RegMT, and performance evaluation with F_1 measure over target features. RegMT work builds on our previous regression-based machine translation results (Bicici and Yuret, 2010) especially with instance selection and additional graph decoding capability.

References

Ergun Bicici and S. Serdar Kozat. 2010. Adaptive model weighting and transductive regression for predicting best system combinations. In *Proceedings of the ACL 2010 Joint Fifth Workshop on Statistical Machine Translation and Metrics MATR*, Uppsala, Sweden, July. Association for Computational Linguistics.

Ergun Bicici and Deniz Yuret. 2010. L_1 regularized regression for reranking and system combination in machine translation. In *Proceedings of the ACL 2010 Joint Fifth Workshop on Statistical Machine Translation and Metrics MATR*, Uppsala, Sweden, July. Association for Computational Linguistics.

Ergun Bicici and Deniz Yuret. 2011. Instance selection for machine translation using feature decay algorithms. In *Proceedings of the EMNLP 2011 Sixth Workshop on Statistical Machine Translation*, Edinburgh, England, July.

Christopher M. Bishop. 2006. *Pattern Recognition and Machine Learning*. Springer.

Chris Callison-Burch, Philipp Koehn, Christof Monz, Kay Peterson, and Omar Zaidan, editors. 2011. *Proceedings of the Sixth Workshop on Statistical Machine Translation*. Edinburgh, England, July.

Corinna Cortes, Mehryar Mohri, and Jason Weston. 2007. A general regression framework for learning string-to-string mappings. In Gokhan H. Bakir, Thomas Hofmann, and Bernhard Sch editors, *Predicting Structured Data*, pages 143–168. The MIT Press, September.

Trevor Hastie, Jonathan Taylor, Robert Tibshirani, and Guenther Walther. 2006. Forward stagewise regression and the monotone lasso. *Electronic Journal of Statistics*, 1.

Trevor Hastie, Robert Tibshirani, and Jerome Friedman. 2009. *The Elements of Statistical Learning: Data Mining, Inference and Prediction*. Springer-Verlag, 2nd edition.

Philipp Koehn, Hieu Hoang, Alexandra Birch, Chris Callison-Burch, Marcello Federico, Nicola Bertoldi, Brooke Cowan, Wade Shen, Christine Moran, Richard Zens, Chris Dyer, Ondrej Bojar, Alexandra Constantin, and Evan Herbst. 2007. Moses: Open source toolkit for statistical machine translation. In *Annual Meeting of the Assoc. for Computational Linguistics*, pages 177–180, Prague, Czech Republic, June.

Wolfgang Macherey and Franz Josef Och. 2007. An empirical study on computing consensus translations from multiple machine translation systems. In *Proceedings of the 2007 Joint Conference on Empirical Methods in Natural Language Processing and Computational Natural Language Learning (EMNLP-CoNLL)*, pages 986–995, Prague, Czech Republic, June. Association for Computational Linguistics.

Franz Josef Och. 2003. Minimum error rate training in statistical machine translation. *Association for Computational Linguistics*, 1:160–167.

Kishore Papineni, Salim Roukos, Todd Ward, and Wei-Jing Zhu. 2001. BLEU: a method for automatic evaluation of machine translation. In *ACL '02: Proceedings of the 40th Annual Meeting on Association for Computational Linguistics*, pages 311–318, Morristown, NJ, USA. Association for Computational Linguistics.

Nicolas Serrano, Jesus Andres-Ferrer, and Francisco Casacuberta. 2009. On a kernel regression approach to machine translation. In *Iberian Conference on Pattern Recognition and Image Analysis*, pages 394–401.

J. Shawe Taylor and N. Cristianini. 2004. *Kernel Methods for Pattern Analysis*. Cambridge University Press.

Robert J. Tibshirani. 1996. Regression shrinkage and selection via the lasso. *Journal of the Royal Statistical Society, Series B*, 58(1):267–288.

Zhuoran Wang and John Shawe-Taylor. 2008. Kernel regression framework for machine translation: UCL system description for WMT 2008 shared translation task. In *Proceedings of the Third Workshop on Statistical Machine Translation*, pages 155–158, Columbus, Ohio, June. Association for Computational Linguistics.

Zhuoran Wang, John Shawe-Taylor, and Sandor Szedmak. 2007. Kernel regression based machine translation. In *Human Language Technologies 2007: The Conference of the North American Chapter of the Association for Computational Linguistics; Companion Volume, Short Papers*, pages 185–188, Rochester, New York, April. Association for Computational Linguistics.

Improving Translation Model by Monolingual Data*

Ondřej Bojar and Aleš Tamchyna
`bojar@ufal.mff.cuni.cz, a.tamchyna@gmail.com`
Institute of Formal and Applied Linguistics,
Faculty of Mathematics and Physics, Charles University in Prague

Abstract

We use target-side monolingual data to extend the vocabulary of the translation model in statistical machine translation. This method called "reverse self-training" improves the decoder's ability to produce grammatically correct translations into languages with morphology richer than the source language esp. in small-data setting. We empirically evaluate the gains for several pairs of European languages and discuss some approaches of the underlying back-off techniques needed to translate unseen forms of known words. We also provide a description of the systems we submitted to WMT11 Shared Task.

1 Introduction

Like any other statistical NLP task, SMT relies on sizable language data for training. However the parallel data required for MT are a very scarce resource, making it difficult to train MT systems of decent quality. On the other hand, it is usually possible to obtain large amounts of monolingual data.

In this paper, we attempt to make use of the monolingual data to reduce the sparseness of surface forms, an issue typical for morphologically rich languages. When MT systems translate into such languages, the limited size of parallel data often causes the situation where the output should include a word form never observed in the training data. Even though the parallel data do contain the desired word in other forms, a standard phrase-based decoder has no way of using it to generate the correct translation.

Reverse self-training addresses this problem by incorporating the available monolingual data in the translation model. This paper builds upon the idea outlined in Bojar and Tamchyna (2011), describing how this technique was incorporated in the WMT Shared Task and extending the experimental evaluation of reverse self-training in several directions – the examined language pairs (Section 4.2), data size (Section 4.3) and back-off techniques (Section 4.4).

2 Related Work

The idea of using monolingual data for improving the translation model has been explored in several previous works. Bertoldi and Federico (2009) used monolingual data for adapting existing translation models to translation of data from different domains. In their experiments, the most effective approach was to train a new translation model from "fake" parallel data consisting of target-side monolingual data and their machine translation into the source language by a baseline system.

Ueffing et al. (2007) used a boot-strapping technique to extend translation models using monolingual data. They gradually translated additional source-side sentences and selectively incorporated them and their translations in the model.

Our technique also bears a similarity to de Gispert et al. (2005), in that we try to use a back-off for surface forms to generalize our model and produce translations with word forms never seen in the original parallel data. However, instead of a rule-based approach, we take advantage of the available

* This work has been supported by the grants EuroMatrixPlus (FP7-ICT-2007-3-231720 of the EU and 7E09003 of the Czech Republic), P406/10/P259, and MSM 0021620838.

Proceedings of the 6th Workshop on Statistical Machine Translation, pages 330–336,
Edinburgh, Scotland, UK, July 30–31, 2011. ©2011 Association for Computational Linguistics

	Source English		Target Czech	Czech Lemmatized
Parallel (small)	a cat chased...	=	**kočka** honila...	*kočka honit...*
	I saw a cat	=	viděl jsem **kočku**	*vidět být kočka*
	I read about a dog	=	četl jsem o psovi	*číst být o pes*
Monolingual (large)	?		četl jsem o **kočce**	*číst být o kočka*
	I read about a cat	←	Use reverse translation backed-off by lemmas.	

Figure 1: The essence of reverse self-training: a new phrase pair ("about a cat" = "o **kočce**") is learned based on a small parallel corpus and large target-side monolingual texts.

data and learn these forms statistically. We are therefore not limited to verbs, but our system is only able to generate surface forms observed in the target-side monolingual data.

3 Reverse Self-Training

Figure 1 illustrates the core of the method. Using available parallel data, we first train an MT system to translate from the target to the source language. Since we want to gather new word forms from the monolingual data, this reverse model needs the ability to translate them. For that purpose we use a factored translation model (Koehn and Hoang, 2007) with two alternative decoding paths: form→form and back-off→form. We experimented with several options for the back-off (simple stemming by truncation or full lemmatization), see Section 4.4. The decoder can thus use a less sparse representation of words if their exact forms are not available in the parallel data.

We use this reverse model to translate (much larger) target-side monolingual data into the source language. We preserve the word alignments of the phrases as used in the decoding so we directly obtain the word alignment in the new "parallel" corpus. This gives us enough information to proceed with the standard MT system training – we extract and score the phrases consistent with the constructed word alignment and create the phrase table.

We combine this enlarged translation model with a model trained on the true parallel data and use Minimum Error Rate Training (Och, 2003) to find the balance between the two models. The final model has four separate components – two language models (one trained on parallel and one on monolingual data) and the two translation models.

We do not expect the translation quality to improve simply because more data is included in training – by adding translations generated using known data, the model could gain only new combinations of known words. However, by using a back-off to less sparse units (e.g. lemmas) in the factored target→source translation, we enable the decoder to produce previously unseen surface forms. These translations are then included in the model, reducing the data sparseness of the target-side surface forms.

4 Experiments

We used common tools for phrase-based translation – Moses (Koehn et al., 2007) decoder and tools, SRILM (Stolcke, 2002) and KenLM (Heafield, 2011) for language modelling and GIZA++ (Och and Ney, 2000) for word alignments.

For reverse self-training, we needed Moses to also output word alignments between source sentences and their translations. As we were not able to make the existing version of this feature work, we added a new option and re-implemented this funcionality.

We rely on automatic translation quality evaluation throughout our paper, namely the well-established BLEU metric (Papineni et al., 2002). We estimate 95% confidence bounds for the scores as described in Koehn (2004). We evaluated our translations on lower-cased sentences.

4.1 Data Sources

Aside from the WMT 2011 Translation Task data, we also used several additional data sources for the experiments aimed at evaluating various aspects of reverse self-training.

JRC-Acquis

We used the JRC-Acquis 3.0 corpus (Steinberger et al., 2006) mainly because of the number of available languages. This corpus contains a large amount

Source	Target	Corpus Size (k sents) Para	Mono	Vocabulary Size Ratio	Baseline	+Mono LM	+Mono TM
English	Czech	94	662	1.67	40.9±1.9	43.5±2.0	*44.3±2.0
English	Finnish	123	863	2.81	27.0±1.9	27.6±1.8	28.3±1.7
English	German	127	889	1.83	34.8±1.8	36.4±1.8	37.6±1.8
English	Slovak	109	763	2.03	35.3±1.6	37.3±1.7	37.7±1.8
French	Czech	95	665	1.43	39.9±1.9	42.5±1.8	43.1±1.8
French	Finnish	125	875	2.45	26.7±1.8	27.8±1.7	28.3±1.8
French	German	128	896	1.58	38.5±1.8	40.2±1.8	*40.5±1.8
German	Czech	95	665	0.91	35.2±1.8	37.0±1.9	*37.3±1.9

Table 1: BLEU scores of European language pairs on JRC data. Asterisks in the last column mark experiments for which MERT had to be re-run.

of legislative texts of the European Union. The fact that all data in the corpus come from a single, very narrow domain has two effects – models trained on this corpus perform mostly very well in that domain (as documented e.g. in Koehn et al. (2009)), but fail when translating ordinary texts such as news or fiction. Sentences in this corpus also tend to be rather long (e.g. 30 words on average for English).

CzEng

CzEng 0.9 (Bojar and Žabokrtský, 2009) is a parallel richly annotated Czech-English corpus. It contains roughly 8 million parallel sentences from a variety of domains, including European regulations (about 34% of tokens), fiction (15%), news (3%), technical texts (10%) and unofficial movie subtitles (27%). We do not make much use of the rich annotation in this paper, however we did experiment with using Czech lemmas (included in the annotation) as the back-off factor for reverse self-training.

4.2 Comparison Across Languages

In order to determine how successful our approach is across languages, we experimented with Czech, Finnish, German and Slovak as target languages. All of them have a rich morphology in some sense. We limited our selection of source languages to English, French and German because our method focuses on the target language anyway. We did however combine the languages with respect to the richness of their vocabulary – the source language has less word forms in almost all cases.

Czech and Slovak are very close languages, sharing a large portion of vocabulary and having a very similar grammar. There are many inflectional rules for verbs, nouns, adjectives, pronouns and numerals. Sentence structure is exhibited by various agreement rules which often apply over long distance. Most of the issues commonly associated with rich morphology are clearly observable in these languages.

German also has some inflection, albeit much less complex. The main source of German vocabulary size are the compound words. Finnish serves as an example of agglutinative languages well-known for the abundance of word forms.

Table 1 contains the summary of our experimental results. Here, only the JRC-Acquis corpus was used for training, development and evaluation. For every language pair, we extracted the first 10 percent of the parallel corpus and used them as the parallel data. The last 70 percent of the same corpus were our "monolingual" data. We used a separate set of 1000 sentences for the development and another 1000 for testing.

Sentence counts of the corpora are shown in the columns Corpus Size Para and Mono. The table also shows the ratio between observed vocabulary size of the target and source language. Except for the German→Czech language pair, the ratios are higher than 1. The Baseline column contains the BLEU score of a system trained solely on the parallel data (i.e. the first 10 percent). A 5-gram language model was used. The "+Mono LM" scores were achieved by adding a 5-gram language model trained on the monolingual data as a separate component (its weight was determined by MERT). The last column contains the scores after adding the translation model self-trained on target monolingual data. This model was also added as another component and the weights associated with it were found by MERT.

For the back-off in the reverse self-training, we used a simple suffix-trimming heuristic suitable for fusional languages: cut off the last three characters of each word always keeping at least the first three characters. This heuristic reduces the vocabulary size to a half for Czech and Slovak but it is much less effective for Finish and German (Table 2), as can be expected from their linguistic properties.

Language	Vocabulary reduced to (%)
Czech	52
Finnish	64
German	73
Slovak	51

Table 2: Reduction of vocabulary size by suffix trimming

Figure 2: Vocabulary ratio and BLEU score

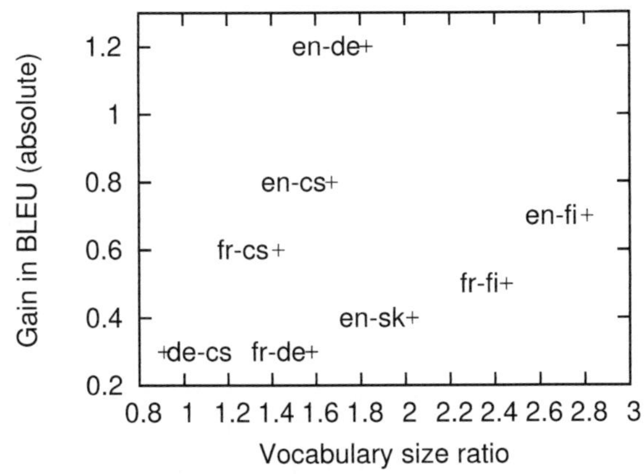

We did not use any linguistic tools, such as morphological analyzers, in this set of experiments. We see the main point of this section in illustrating the applicability of our technique on a wide range of languages, including languages for which such tools are not available.

We encountered problems when using MERT to balance the weights of the four model components. Our model consisted of 14 features – one for each language model, five for each translation model (phrase probability and lexical weight for both directions and phrase penalty), word penalty and distortion penalty. The extra 5 weights of the reversely trained translation model caused MERT to diverge in some cases. Since we used the `mert-moses.pl` script for tuning and kept the default parameters, MERT ran for 25 iterations and stopped. As a result, even though our method seemed to improve translation performance in most language pairs, several experiments contradicted this observation. We simply reran the final tuning procedure in these cases and were able to achieve an improvement in BLEU as well. These language pairs are marked with a '*' sign in Table 1.

A possible explanation for this behaviour of MERT is that the alternative decoding paths add a lot of possible derivations that generate the same string. To validate our hypothesis we examined a diverging run of MERT for English→Czech translation with two translation models. Our n-best lists contained the best 100 derivations for each translated sentence from the development data. On average (over all 1000 sentences and over all runs), the n-best list only contained 6.13 different translations of a sentence. The result of the same calculation applied on the baseline run of MERT (which converged in 9 iterations) was 34.85 hypotheses. This clear disproportion shows that MERT had much less information when optimizing our model.

Overall, reverse self-training seems helpful for translating into morphologically rich languages. We achieved promising gains in BLEU, even over the baseline including a language model trained on the monolingual data. The improvement ranges from roughly 0.3 (e.g. German→Czech) to over 1 point (English→German) absolute. This result also indicates that suffix trimming is a quite robust heuristic, useful for a variety of language types.

Figure 2 illustrates the relationship between vocabulary size ratio of the language pair and the improvement in translation quality. Although the points are distributed quite irregularly, a certain tendency towards higher gains with higher ratios is observable. We assume that reverse self-training is most useful in cases where a single word form in the source language can be translated as several forms in the target language. A higher ratio between vocabulary sizes suggests that these cases happen more often, thus providing more space for improvement using our method.

4.3 Data Sizes

We conducted a series of English-to-Czech experiments with fixed parallel data and a varying size of monolingual data. We used the CzEng corpus, 500 thousand parallel sentences and from 500 thousand up to 5 million monolingual sentences. We used two separate sets of 1000 sentences from CzEng for development and evaluation. Our results are summarized in Figure 3. The gains in BLEU become more significant as the size of included monolingual data increases. The highest improvement can be observed when the data are largest – over 3 points absolute. Figure 4 shows an example of the impact on translation quality – the "Mono" data are 5 million sentences.

When evaluated from this point of view, our method can also be seen as a way of considerably improving translation quality for languages with little available parallel data.

We also experimented with varying size of parallel data (500 thousand to 5 million sentences) and its effect on reverse self-training contribution. The size of monolingual data was always 5 million sentences. We first measured the percentage of test data word forms covered by the training data. We calculated the value for parallel data and for the combination of parallel and monolingual data. For word forms that appeared only in the monolingual data, a different form of the word had to be contained in the parallel data (so that the model can learn it through the back-off heuristic) in order to be counted in. The difference between the first and second value can simply be thought of as the upper-bound estimation of reverse self-training contribution. Figure 5 shows the results along with BLEU scores achieved in translation experiments following this scenario.

Our technique has much greater effect for small parallel data sizes; the amount of newly learned word forms declines rapidly as the size grows. Similarly, improvement in BLEU score decreases quickly and becomes negligible around 2 million parallel sentences.

4.4 Back-off Techniques

We experimented with several options for the back-off factor in English→Czech translation. Data from training section of CzEng were used, 1 million parallel sentences and another 5 million sentences as target-side monolingual data. As in the previous section, the sizes of our development and evaluation sets were a thousand sentences.

Figure 3: Relation between monolingual data size and gains in BLEU score

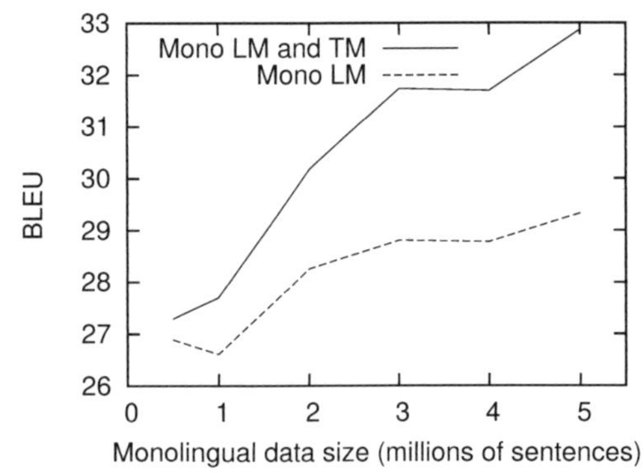

Figure 5: Varying parallel data size, surface form coverage ("Parallel", "Parallel and Mono") and BLEU score ("Mono LM", "Mono LM and TM")

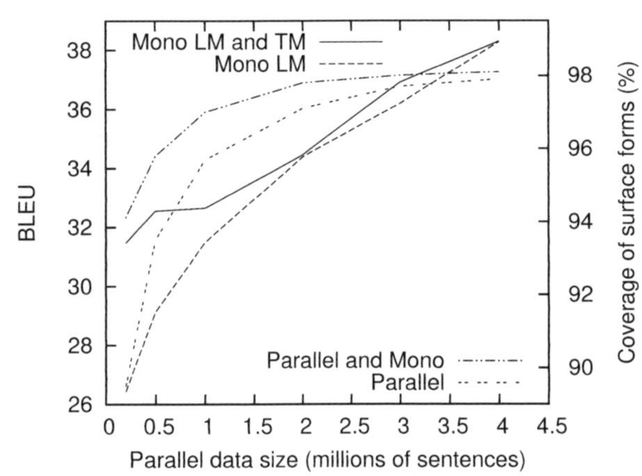

CzEng annotation contains lexically disambiguated word lemmas, an appealing option for our purposes. We also tried trimming the last 3 characters of each word, keeping at least the first 3 characters intact. Stemming of each word to four characters was also evaluated (Stem-4).

Table 3 summarizes our results. The last column shows the vocabulary size compared to original vocabulary size, estimated on lower-cased words.

We are not surprised by stemming performing the

System	Translation	Gloss
Baseline	Jsi tak zrcadla?	Are you$_{SG}$ so mirrors? (ungrammatical)
+Mono LM	Jsi neobjednávejte zrcadla?	Did you$_{SG}$ don't order$_{PL}$ mirrors? (ungrammatical)
+Mono TM	Už sis objednal zrcadla?	Have you$_{SG}$ ordered$_{SG}$ the mirrors (for yourself) yet?

Figure 4: Translation of the sentence "Did you order the mirrors?" by baseline systems and a reversely-trained system. Only the last one is able to generate the correct form of the word "order".

worst – the equivalence classes generated by this simple heuristic are too broad. Using lemmas seems optimal from the linguistic point of view, however suffix trimming outperformed this approach in our experiments. We feel that finding well-performing back-off techniques for other languages merits further research.

Back-off	BLEU	Vocabulary Size (%)
Baseline	31.82±3.24	100
Stem-4	32.73±3.19	19
Lemma	33.05±3.40	54
Trimmed Suffix	**33.28±3.32**	47

Table 3: Back-off BLEU scores comparison

4.5 WMT Systems

We submitted systems that used reverse self-training (`cu-tamchyna`) for English→Czech and English→German language pairs.

Our parallel data for German were constrained to the provided set (1.9 million sentences). For Czech, we used the training sections of CzEng and the supplied WMT11 News Commentary data (7.3 million sentences in total).

In case of German, we only used the supplied monolingual data, for Czech we used a large collection of texts for language modelling (i.e. unconstrained). The reverse self-training used only the constrained data – 2.3 million sentences in German and 2.2 in Czech. In case of Czech, we only used the News monolingual data from 2010 and 2011 for reverse self-training – we expected that recent data from the same domain as the test set would improve translation performance the most.

We achieved mixed results with these systems – for translation into German, reverse self-training did not improve translation performance. For Czech, we were able to achieve a small gain, even though the reversely translated data contained less sentences than the parallel data. Our BLEU scores were also affected by submitting translation outputs without normalized punctuation and with a slightly different tokenization.

In this scenario, a lot of parallel data were available and we did not manage to prepare a reversely trained model from larger monolingual data. Both of these factors contributed to the inconclusive results.

Table 4 shows case-insensitive BLEU scores as calculated in the official evaluation.

Target Language	Mono LM	+Mono TM
German	14.8	14.8
Czech	15.7	15.9

Table 4: Case-insensitive BLEU of WMT systems

5 Conclusion

We introduced a technique for exploiting monolingual data to improve the quality of translation into morphologically rich languages.

We carried out experiments showing improvements in BLEU when using our method for translating into Czech, Finnish, German and Slovak with small parallel data. We discussed the issues of including similar translation models as separate components in MERT.

We showed that gains in BLEU score increase with growing size of monolingual data. On the other hand, growing parallel data size diminishes the effect of our method quite rapidly. We also documented our experiments with several back-off techniques for English to Czech translation.

Finally, we described our primary submissions to the WMT 2011 Shared Translation Task.

References

Nicola Bertoldi and Marcello Federico. 2009. Domain adaptation for statistical machine translation with monolingual resources. In *Proceedings of the Fourth Workshop on Statistical Machine Translation*, pages 182–189, Athens, Greece, March. Association for Computational Linguistics.

Ondřej Bojar and Aleš Tamchyna. 2011. Forms Wanted: Training SMT on Monolingual Data. Abstract at Machine Translation and Morphologically-Rich Languages. Research Workshop of the Israel Science Foundation University of Haifa, Israel, January.

Ondřej Bojar and Zdeněk Žabokrtský. 2009. CzEng 0.9: Large Parallel Treebank with Rich Annotation. *Prague Bulletin of Mathematical Linguistics*, 92:63–83.

Adrià de Gispert, José B. Mariño, and Josep M. Crego. 2005. Improving statistical machine translation by classifying and generalizing inflected verb forms. In *Eurospeech 2005*, pages 3185–3188, Lisbon, Portugal.

Kenneth Heafield. 2011. Kenlm: Faster and smaller language model queries. In *Proceedings of the Sixth Workshop on Statistical Machine Translation*, Edinburgh, UK, July. Association for Computational Linguistics.

Philipp Koehn and Hieu Hoang. 2007. Factored Translation Models. In *Proc. of EMNLP*.

Philipp Koehn, Hieu Hoang, Alexandra Birch, Chris Callison-Burch, Marcello Federico, Nicola Bertoldi, Brooke Cowan, Wade Shen, Christine Moran, Richard Zens, Chris Dyer, Ondrej Bojar, Alexandra Constantin, and Evan Herbst. 2007. Moses: Open source toolkit for statistical machine translation. In *ACL*. The Association for Computer Linguistics.

Philipp Koehn, Alexandra Birch, and Ralf Steinberger. 2009. 462 machine translation systems for europe. In *MT Summit XII*.

Philipp Koehn. 2004. Statistical significance tests for machine translation evaluation. In *EMNLP*, pages 388–395. ACL.

Franz Josef Och and Hermann Ney. 2000. Improved statistical alignment models. pages 440–447, Hongkong, China, October.

Franz Josef Och. 2003. Minimum error rate training in statistical machine translation. In *ACL*, pages 160–167.

Kishore Papineni, Salim Roukos, Todd Ward, and Wei-Jing Zhu. 2002. Bleu: a method for automatic evaluation of machine translation. In *ACL*, pages 311–318.

Ralf Steinberger, Bruno Pouliquen, Anna Widiger, Camelia Ignat, Tomaz Erjavec, Dan Tufis, and Daniel Varga. 2006. The JRC-acquis: A multilingual aligned parallel corpus with 20+ languages. *CoRR*, abs/cs/0609058. informal publication.

Andreas Stolcke. 2002. Srilm — an extensible language modeling toolkit, June 06.

Nicola Ueffing, Gholamreza Haffari, and Anoop Sarkar. 2007. Semi-supervised model adaptation for statistical machine translation. *Machine Translation*, 21(2):77–94.

The CMU-ARK German-English Translation System

Chris Dyer   Kevin Gimpel   Jonathan H. Clark   Noah A. Smith
Language Technologies Institute
Carnegie Mellon University
Pittsburgh, PA, 15213, USA
{cdyer,kgimpel,jhclark,nasmith}@cs.cmu.edu

Abstract

This paper describes the German-English translation system developed by the ARK research group at Carnegie Mellon University for the Sixth Workshop on Machine Translation (WMT11). We present the results of several modeling and training improvements to our core hierarchical phrase-based translation system, including: feature engineering to improve modeling of the derivation structure of translations; better handing of OOVs; and using development set translations into other languages to create additional pseudo-references for training.

1 Introduction

We describe the German-English translation system submitted to the shared translation task in the Sixth Workshop on Machine Translation (WMT11) by the ARK research group at Carnegie Mellon University.[1] The core translation system is a hierarchical phrase-based machine translation system (Chiang, 2007) that has been extended in several ways described in this paper.

Some of our innovations focus on modeling. Since German and English word orders can diverge considerably, particularly in non-matrix clauses, we focused on feature engineering to improve the modeling of long-distance relationships, which are poorly captured in standard hierarchical phrase-based translation models. To do so, we developed features that assess the goodness of the source language parse tree under the translation grammar (rather than of a "linguistic" grammar). To train the feature weights, we made use of a novel two-phase training algorithm that incorporates a probabilistic training objective and standard minimum error training (Och, 2003). These segmentation features were supplemented with a 7-gram class-based language model, which more directly models long-distance relationships. Together, these features provide a modest improvement over the baseline and suggest interesting directions for future work. While our work on parse modeling was involved and required substantial changes to the training pipeline, some other modeling enhancements were quite simple: for example, improving how out-of-vocabulary words are handled. We propose a very simple change, and show that it provides a small, consistent gain.

On the training side, we had two improvements over our baseline system. First, we were inspired by the work of Madnani (2010), who showed that when training to optimize BLEU (Papineni et al., 2002), overfitting is reduced by supplementing a single human-generated reference translation with additional computer-generated references. We generated supplementary pseudo-references for our development set (which is translated into many languages, but once) by using MT output from a secondary Spanish-English translation system. Second, following Foster and Kuhn (2009), we used a secondary development set to select from among many optimization runs, which further improved generalization.

We largely sought techniques that did not require language-specific resources (e.g., treebanks, POS

[1] http://www.ark.cs.cmu.edu

Proceedings of the 6th Workshop on Statistical Machine Translation, pages 337–343,
Edinburgh, Scotland, UK, July 30–31, 2011.

annotations, morphological analyzers). An exception is a compound segmentation model used for preprocessing that was trained on a corpus of manually segmented German. Aside from this, no further manually annotated data was used, and we suspect many of the improvements described here can be had in other language pairs. Despite avoiding language-specific resources and using only the training data provided by the workshop, an extensive manual evaluation determined that the outputs produced were of significantly higher quality than both statistical and rule-based systems that made use of language-specific resources (Callison-Burch et al., 2011).

2 Baseline system and data

Our translation system is based on a hierarchical phrase-based translation model (Chiang, 2007), as implemented in the `cdec` decoder (Dyer et al., 2010). Since German is a language that makes productive use of "closed" compounds (compound words written as a single orthographic token), we use a CRF segmentation model of to evaluate the probability of all possible segmentations, encoding the most probable ones compactly in a lattice (Dyer, 2009). For the purposes of grammar induction, the single most probable segmentation of each word in the source side of the parallel training data under the model was inferred.

The parallel data were aligned using the Giza++ implementation of IBM Model 4 run in both directions and then symmetrized using the `grow-diag-final-and` heuristic (Och and Ney, 2002; Brown et al., 1993; Koehn et al., 2003). The aligned corpus was encoded as a suffix array (Lopez, 2008) and lattice-specific grammars (containing just the rules that are capable of matching spans in the input lattice) were extracted for each sentence in the test and development sets, using the heuristics recommended by Chiang (2007).

A 4-gram modified Kneser-Ney language model (Chen and Goodman, 1996) was constructed using the SRI language modeling toolkit (Stolcke, 2002) from the English side of the parallel text, the monolingual English data, and the English version 4 Gigaword corpus (Parker et al., 2009). Since there were many duplicate segments in the training data (much of which was crawled from the web), duplicate segments and segments longer than 100 words were removed. Inference was carried out using the language modeling library described by Heafield (2011).

The `newstest-2009` set (with the 500 longest segments removed) was used for development,[2] and `newstest-2010` was used as a development test set. Results in this paper are reported on the dev-test set using uncased BLEU_4 with a single reference translation. Minimum error rate training (Och, 2003) was used to optimize the parameters of the system to maximize BLEU on the development data, and inference was performed over a pruned hypergraph representation of the translation hypothesis space (Kumar et al., 2009).

For the experiments reported in this paper, Viterbi (max-derivation) decoding was used. The system submitted for manual evaluation used segment-level MBR decoding with $1 - \text{BLEU}$ as the loss function, approximated over a 500-best list for each sentence. This reliably results in a small but consistent improvement in translation quality, but is much more time consuming to compute (Kumar and Byrne, 2004).

3 Source parse structure modeling

Improving phrase-based translation systems is challenging in part because our intuitions about what makes a "good" phrase or translation derivation are often poor. For example, restricting phrases and rules to be consistent with syntactic constituents consistently harms performance (Chiang, 2007; Galley et al., 2006; Koehn et al., 2003), although our intuitions might suggest this is a reasonable thing to do. On the other hand, it has been shown that incorporating syntactic information in the form of features *can* lead to improved performance (Chiang, 2010; Gimpel and Smith, 2009; Marton and Resnik, 2008). Syntactic features that are computed by assessing the overlap of the translation parse with a linguistic parse can be understood to improve translation because they lead to a better model of what a "correct" parse of the source sentence is *under the translation grammar*.

Like the "soft syntactic features" used in pre-

[2]Removing long segments substantially reduces training time and does not appear to negatively affect performance.

vious work (Marton and Resnik, 2008; Chiang et al., 2008), we propose features to assess the tree structure induced during translation. However, unlike that work, we do not rely on linguistic source parses, but instead only make use of features that are directly computable from the source sentence and the parse structure being considered in the decoder. In particular, we take inspiration from the model of Klein and Manning (2002), which models constituency in terms of the *contexts* that rule productions occur in. Additionally, we make use of salient aspects of the spans being dominated by a nonterminal, such as the words at the beginning and end of the span, and the length of the span. Importantly, the features do not rely on the target words being predicted, but only look at the structure of the translation derivation. As such, they can be understood as *monolingual parse features*.[3]

Table 1 lists the feature templates that were used.

Template	Description
CTX:f_{i-1}, f_j	context bigram
CTX:f_{i-1}, f_j, x	context bigram + NT
CTX:$f_{i-1}, f_j, x, (j-i)$	context bigram + NT + len
LU:f_{i-1}	left unigram
LB:f_{i-1}, f_i	left bigram (overlapping)
RU:f_j	right unigram
RB:f_{j-1}, f_j	right bigram (overlapping)

Table 1: Context feature templates for features extracted from every translation rule used; i and j indicate hypothesized constituent span, x is its nonterminal category label (in our grammar, X or S), and f_k is the kth word of the source sentence, with $f_{<1} = \langle \text{s} \rangle$ and $f_{>|\mathbf{f}|} = \langle /\text{s} \rangle$. If a word f_k is not among the 1000 most frequent words in the training corpus, it is replaced by a special unknown token. The SMALLCAPS prefixes prevent accidental feature collisions.

3.1 Two-phase discriminative learning

The parse features just introduced are numerous and sparse, which means that MERT can not be used to infer their weights. Instead, we require a learning algorithm that can cope with millions of features and avoid overfitting, perhaps by eliminating most of the features and keeping only the most valuable (which would also keep the model compact). Furthermore, we would like to be able to still target the BLEU measure of translation quality during learning. While large-scale discriminative training for machine translation is a widely studied problem (Hopkins and May, 2011; Li and Eisner, 2009; Devlin, 2009; Blunsom et al., 2008; Watanabe et al., 2007; Arun and Koehn, 2007; Liang et al., 2006), no tractable algorithm exists for learning a large number of feature weights while directly optimizing a corpus-level metric like BLEU. Rather than resorting to a decomposable approximation, we have explored a new two-phase training algorithm in development of this system.

The two-phase algorithm works as follows. In phase 1, we use a non-BLEU objective to train a translation model that includes the large feature set. Then, we use this model to compute a small number of coarse "summary features," which summarize the "opinion" of the first model about a translation hypothesis in a low dimensional space. Then, in the second training pass, MERT is used to determine how much weight to give these summary features together with the other standard coarse translation features. At test time, translation becomes a multi-step process as well. The hypothesis space is first scored using the phase-1 model, then summary features are computed, then the hypothesis space is rescored with the phase-2 model. As long as the features used factor with the edges in the translation space (which ours do), this can be carried out in linear time in the size of the translation forest.

3.1.1 Phase 1 training

For the first model, which includes the sparse parse features, we learn weights in order to optimize penalized conditional log likelihood (Blunsom et al., 2008). We are specifically interested in modeling an *unobserved* variable (i.e., the parse tree underlying a translation derivation), this objective is quite natural, since probabilistic models offer a principled account of unobserved data. Furthermore, because our features factor according to edges in the translation forest (they are "stateless" in standard MT terminology), there are efficient dynamic programming algorithms that can be used to exactly compute the expected values of the features (Lari and Young, 1990), which are necessary for computing the gradients used in optimization.

[3]Similar features have been proposed for use in discriminative monolingual parsing models (Taskar et al., 2004).

We are therefore optimizing the following objective, given a set $\mathcal{T}$ of parallel training sentences:

$$\mathcal{L} = \lambda R(\theta) - \sum_{\langle \mathbf{f},\mathbf{e}\rangle \in \mathcal{T}} \log \sum_{\mathbf{d}} p_\theta(\mathbf{e}, \mathbf{d} \mid \mathbf{f})$$

$$\text{where } p_\theta(\mathbf{e}, \mathbf{d} \mid \mathbf{f}) = \frac{\exp \theta^\top \mathbf{h}(\mathbf{f}, \mathbf{e}, \mathbf{d})}{Z(\mathbf{f})} \quad ,$$

where **d** is a variable representing the *unobserved* synchronous parses giving rise to the pair of sentences $\langle \mathbf{f}, \mathbf{e} \rangle$, and where $R(\theta)$ is a penalty that favors less complex models. Since we not only want to prevent over fitting but also want a small model, we use $R(\theta) = \sum_k |\theta_k|$, the ℓ_1 norm, which forces many parameters to be exactly 0.

Although $\mathcal{L}$ is not convex in θ (on account of the latent derivation variable), we make use of an online stochastic gradient descent algorithm that imposes an ℓ_1 penalty on the objective (Tsuruoka et al., 2009). Online algorithms are often effective for non-convex objectives (Liang and Klein, 2009).

We selected 12,500 sentences randomly from the news-commentary portion of the training data to use to train the latent variable model. Using the standard rule extraction heuristics (Chiang, 2007), 9,967 of the sentence pairs could be derived.[4] In addition to the parse features describe above, the standard phrase features (relative frequency and lexical translation probabilities), and a rule count feature were included. Training was run for 48 hours on a single machine, which resulted in 8 passes through the training data, instantiating over 8M unique features. The regularization strength λ was chosen so that approximately $10,000$ (of the 8M) features would be non-zero.[5]

3.1.2 Summary features

As outlined above, the phase 1 model will be incorporated into the final translation model using a low dimensional "summary" of its opinion. Because we are using a probabilistic model, posterior probabilities (given the source sentence **f**) under the parsing model are easily defined and straightforward to compute with dynamic programming. We made use of four summary features: the posterior log probability $\log p_\theta(\mathbf{e}, \mathbf{d}|\mathbf{f})$; for every rule $r \in \mathbf{d}$, the probability of its span being a constituent under the parse model; the probabilities that *some* span starts at the r's starting index, or that some rule ends at r's ending index.

Once these summary features have been computed, the sparse features are discarded, and the summary features are reweighted using coefficients learned by MERT, together with the standard MT features (language model, word penalty, etc.). This provides a small improvement over our already very strong baseline, as the first two rows in Table 2 show.

Condition	BLEU
baseline	25.0
+ parse features	25.2
+ parse features + 7-gram LM	25.4

Table 2: Additional features designed to improve model of long-range reordering.

3.2 7-gram class-based LM

The parsing features above were intended to improve long range reordering quality. To further support the modeling of larger spans, we incorporated a 7-gram class-based language model. Automatic word clusters are attractive because they can be learned for any language without supervised data, and, unlike part-of-speech annotations, each word is in only a single class, which simplifies inference. We performed Brown clustering (Brown et al., 1992) on 900k sentences from our language modeling data (including the news commentary corpus and a subset of Gigaword). We obtained 1,000 clusters using an implementation provided by Liang (2005),[6] as Turian et al. (2010) found that relatively large numbers clusters gave better performance for information extraction tasks. We then replaced words with their clusters in our language modeling data and built a 7-gram LM with Witten-Bell smoothing (Witten and Bell, 1991).[7] The last two rows of Ta-

[4]When optimizing conditional log likeligood, it is necessary to be able to exactly derive the training pair. See Blunsom et al. (2008) for more information.

[5]Ideally, λ would have been tuned to optimize held-out likelihood or BLEU; however, the evaluation deadline prevented us from doing this.

[6]`http://www.cs.berkeley.edu/~pliang/software`

[7]The distributional assumptions made by the more commonly used Kneser-Ney estimator do not hold in the word-

ble 2 shows that in conjunction with the source parse features, a slight improvement comes from including the 7-gram LM.

4 Non-translating tokens

When two languages share a common alphabet (as German and English largely do), it is often appropriate to leave some tokens untranslated when translating. Named entities, numbers, and graphical elements such as emoticons are a few common examples of such "non-translating" elements. To ensure that such elements are well-modeled, we augment our translation grammar so that every token in the input can translate as itself and add a feature that counts the number of times such self-translation rules are used in a translation hypothesis. This is in contrast to the behavior of most other decoders, such as Moses, which only permit a token to translate as itself if it is learned from the training data, or if there is no translation in the phrase table at all.

Since many non-translating tokens are out-of-vocabulary (OOV) in the target LM, we also add a feature that fires each time the LM encounters a word that is OOV.[8] This behavior be understood as discriminatively learning the unknown word penalty that is part of the LM. Again, this is in contrast to the behavior of other decoders, which typically add a fixed (and very large) cost to the LM feature for every OOV. Our multi-feature parameterization permits the training algorithm to decide that, e.g., some OOVs are acceptable if they occur in a "good" context rather than forcing the decoder to avoid them at all costs. Table 3 shows that always providing a non-translating translation option together with a discriminative learned OOV feature improves the quality of German-English translation.[9]

Condition	BLEU
−OOV (baseline)	24.6
+OOV and non-translating rules	25.0

Table 3: Effect of discriminatively learned penalties for OOV words.

classified corpus.

[8]When multiple LMs are used, there is an extra OOV feature for each LM.

[9]Both systems were trained using the human+ES-EN reference set described below (§5).

5 Computer-generated references

Madnani (2010) shows that models learned by optimizing BLEU are liable to overfit if only a single reference is used, but that this overfitting can be mitigated by supplementing the single reference with supplemental computer-generated references produced by paraphrasing the human reference using a whole-sentence statistical paraphrase system. These computer-generated paraphrases are just used to compute "better" BLEU scores, but not directly as examples of target translations.

Although we did not have access to a paraphrase generator, we took advantage of the fact that our development set (`newstest-2009`) was translated into several languages other than English. By translating these back into English, we hypothesized we would get suitable pseudo-references that could be used in place of computer-generated paraphrases. Table 4 shows the results obtained on our held-out test set simply by altering the reference translations used to score the development data. These systems all contain the OOV features described above.

Condition	BLEU
1 human	24.7
1 human + ES-EN	**25.0**
1 human + FR-EN	24.0
1 human + ES-EN + FR-EN	24.2

Table 4: Effect of different sets of reference translations used during tuning.

While the effect is somewhat smaller than Madnani (2010) reports using a sentential paraphraser, the extremely simple technique of adding the output of a Spanish-English (ES-EN) system was found to consistently improve the quality of the translations of the held-out data. However, a comparable effect was not found when using references generated from a French-English (FR-EN) translation system, indicating that the utility of this technique must be assessed empirically and depends on several factors.

6 Case restoration

Our translation system generates lowercased output, so we must restore case as a post-processing step. We do so using a probabilistic transducer as implemented in SRILM's `disambig` tool. Each lowercase token in the input can be mapped to a cased variant that was observed in the target language training data. Ambiguities are resolved using a language model that predicts true-cased sentences.[10] We used the same data sources to construct this model as were used above. During development, it was observed that many named entities that did not require translation required some case change, from simple uppercasing of the first letter, to more idiosyncratic casings (e.g., *iPod*). To ensure that these were properly restored, even when they did not occur in the target language training data, we supplement the true-cased LM training data and case transducer training data with the German *source* test set.

Condition	BLEU (Cased)
English-only	24.1
English+test-set	24.3

Table 5: Effect of supplementing recasing model training data with the test set *source*.

7 Model selection

Minimum error rate training (Och, 2003) is a stochastic optimization algorithm that typically finds a different weight vector each time it is run. Foster and Kuhn (2009) showed that while the variance on the development set objective may be narrow, the held-out test set variance is typically much greater, but that a secondary development set can be used to select a system that will have better generalization. We therefore replicated MERT 6 times and selected the output that performed best on NEWSTEST-2010. Since we had no additional blind test set, we cannot measure what the impact is. However, the BLEU scores we selected on varied from 25.4 to 26.1.

8 Summary

We have presented a summary of the enhancements made to a hierarchical phrase-based translation system for the WMT11 shared translation task. Some of our results are still preliminary (the source parse model), but a number of changes we made were quite simple (OOV handling, using MT output to provide additional references for training) and also led to improved results.

[10] The model used is $p(\mathbf{y} \mid \mathbf{x})p(\mathbf{y})$. While this model is somewhat unusual (the conditional probability is backwards from a noisy channel model), it is a standard and effective technique for case restoration.

Acknowledgments

This research was supported in part by the NSF through grant IIS-0844507, the U. S. Army Research Laboratory and the U. S. Army Research Office under contract/grant number W911NF-10-1-0533, and Sandia National Laboratories (fellowship to K. Gimpel). We thank the anonymous reviewers for their thorough feedback.

References

A. Arun and P. Koehn. 2007. Online learning methods for discriminative training of phrase based statistical machine translation. In *Proc. of MT Summit XI*.

P. Blunsom, T. Cohn, and M. Osborne. 2008. A discriminative latent variable model for statistical machine translation. In *Proc. of ACL-HLT*.

P. F. Brown, P. V. de Souza, R. L. Mercer, V. J. Della Pietra, and J. C. Lai. 1992. Class-based n-gram models of natural language. *Computational Linguistics*, 18:467–479.

P. F. Brown, V. J. Della Pietra, S. A. Della Pietra, and R. L. Mercer. 1993. The mathematics of statistical machine translation: parameter estimation. *Computational Linguistics*, 19(2):263–311.

C. Callison-Burch, P. Koehn, C. Monz, and O. F. Zaidan. 2011. Findings of the 2011 workshop on statistical machine translation. In *Proc. of the Sixth Workshop on Statistical Machine Translation*.

S. F. Chen and J. Goodman. 1996. An empirical study of smoothing techniques for language modeling. In *Proc. of ACL*, pages 310–318.

D. Chiang, Y. Marton, and P. Resnik. 2008. Online large-margin training of syntactic and structural translation features. In *Proc. EMNLP*, pages 224–233.

D. Chiang. 2007. Hierarchical phrase-based translation. *Computational Linguistics*, 33(2):201–228.

D. Chiang. 2010. Learning to translate with source and target syntax. In *Proc. of ACL*, pages 1443–1452.

J. Devlin. 2009. Lexical features for statistical machine translation. Master's thesis, University of Maryland.

C. Dyer, A. Lopez, J. Ganitkevitch, J. Weese, F. Ture, P. Blunsom, H. Setiawan, V. Eidelman, and P. Resnik. 2010. cdec: A decoder, alignment, and learning framework for finite-state and context-free translation models. In *Proc. of ACL (demonstration session)*.

C. Dyer. 2009. Using a maximum entropy model to build segmentation lattices for MT. In *Proc. of NAACL*.

G. Foster and R. Kuhn. 2009. Stabilizing minimum error rate training. *Proc. of WMT*.

M. Galley, J. Graehl, K. Knight, D. Marcu, S. DeNeefe, W. Wang, and I. Thayer. 2006. Scalable inference and training of context-rich syntactic translation models. In *Proc. of ACL*, pages 961–968.

K. Gimpel and N. A. Smith. 2009. Feature-rich translation by quasi-synchronous lattice parsing. In *Proc. of EMNLP*, pages 219–228.

K. Heafield. 2011. KenLM: Faster and smaller language model queries. In *Proc. of the Sixth Workshop on Statistical Machine Translation*.

M. Hopkins and J. May. 2011. Tuning as ranking. In *Proc. of EMNLP*.

D. Klein and C. D. Manning. 2002. A generative constituent-context model for improved grammar induction. In *Proc. of ACL*, pages 128–135.

P. Koehn, F. J. Och, and D. Marcu. 2003. Statistical phrase-based translation. In *Proc. of NAACL*.

S. Kumar and W. Byrne. 2004. Minimum Bayes-risk decoding for statistical machine translation. In *Processings of HLT-NAACL*.

S. Kumar, W. Macherey, C. Dyer, and F. Och. 2009. Efficient minimum error rate training and minimum bayes-risk decoding for translation hypergraphs and lattices. In *Proc. of ACL-IJCNLP*.

K. Lari and S. Young. 1990. The estimation of stochastic context-free grammars using the inside-outside algorithm. *Computer Speech and Language*.

Z. Li and J. Eisner. 2009. First- and second-order expectation semirings with applications to minimum-risk training on translation forests. In *Proc. of EMNLP*, pages 40–51.

P. Liang and D. Klein. 2009. Online EM for unsupervised models. In *Proc. of NAACL*.

P. Liang, A. Bouchard-Côté, D. Klein, and B. Taskar. 2006. An end-to-end discriminative approach to machine translation. In *Proc. of ACL*.

P. Liang. 2005. Semi-supervised learning for natural language. Master's thesis, Massachusetts Institute of Technology.

A. Lopez. 2008. Tera-scale translation models via pattern matching. In *Proc. of COLING*.

N. Madnani. 2010. *The Circle of Meaning: From Translation to Paraphrasing and Back*. Ph.D. thesis, Department of Computer Science, University of Maryland College Park.

Y. Marton and P. Resnik. 2008. Soft syntactic constraints for hierarchical phrased-based translation. In *Proc. of ACL*, pages 1003–1011, Columbus, Ohio.

F. J. Och and H. Ney. 2002. Discriminative training and maximum entropy models for statistical machine translation. In *Proceedings of ACL*, pages 295–302.

F. J. Och. 2003. Minimum error rate training in statistical machine translation. In *Proc. of ACL*, pages 160–167.

K. Papineni, S. Roukos, T. Ward, and W.-J. Zhu. 2002. BLEU: a method for automatic evaluation of machine translation. In *Proc. of ACL*.

R. Parker, D. Graff, J. Kong, K. Chen, and K. Maeda. 2009. English gigaword fourth edition.

A. Stolcke. 2002. SRILM – an extensible language modeling toolkit. In *Intl. Conf. on Spoken Language Processing*.

B. Taskar, D. Klein, M. Collins, D. Koller, and C. Manning. 2004. Max-margin parsing. In *Proc. of EMNLP*.

Y. Tsuruoka, J. Tsujii, and S. Ananiadou. 2009. Stochastic gradient descent training for l_1-regularized log-linear models with cumulative penalty. In *Proc. of ACL-IJCNLP*.

J. Turian, L. Ratinov, and Y. Bengio. 2010. Word representations: a simple and general method for semi-supervised learning. In *Proc. of ACL*, pages 384–394.

T. Watanabe, J. Suzuki, H. Tsukuda, and H. Isozaki. 2007. Online large-margin training for statistical machine translation. In *Proc. of EMNLP*.

I. H. Witten and T. C. Bell. 1991. The zero-frequency problem: Estimating the probabilities of novel events in adaptive text compression. *IEEE Trans. Information Theory*, 37(4).

Noisy SMS Machine Translation in Low-Density Languages

Vladimir Eidelman[†], **Kristy Hollingshead**[†], and **Philip Resnik**[†‡]
[†]UMIACS Laboratory for Computational Linguistics and Information Processing
[‡]Department of Linguistics
University of Maryland, College Park
{vlad,hollingk,resnik}@umiacs.umd.edu

Abstract

This paper presents the system we developed for the 2011 WMT Haitian Creole–English SMS featured translation task. Applying standard statistical machine translation methods to noisy real-world SMS data in a low-density language setting such as Haitian Creole poses a unique set of challenges, which we attempt to address in this work. Along with techniques to better exploit the limited available training data, we explore the benefits of several methods for alleviating the additional noise inherent in the SMS and transforming it to better suite the assumptions of our hierarchical phrase-based model system. We show that these methods lead to significant improvements in BLEU score over the baseline.

1 Introduction

For the featured translation task of the Sixth Workshop on Statistical Machine Translation, we developed a system for translating Haitian Creole Emergency SMS messages. Given the nature of the task, translating text messages that were sent during the January 2010 earthquake in Haiti to an emergency response service called Mission 4636, we were not only faced with the problem of dealing with a low-density language, but additionally, with noisy, real-world data in a domain which has thus far received relatively little attention in statistical machine translation. We were especially interested in this task because of the unique set of challenges that it poses for existing translation systems. We focused our research effort on techniques to better utilize the limited available training resources, as well as ways in which we could automatically alleviate and transform the noisy data to our advantage through the use of automatic punctuation prediction, finite-state raw-to-clean transduction, and grammar extraction. All these techniques contributed to improving translation quality as measured by BLEU score over our baseline system.

The rest of this paper is structured as follows. First, we provide a brief overview of our baseline system in Section 2, followed by an examination of issues posed by this task and the steps we have taken to address them in Section 3, and finally we conclude with experimental results and additional analysis.

2 System Overview

Our baseline system is based on a hierarchical phrase-based translation model, which can formally be described as a synchronous context-free grammar (SCFG) (Chiang, 2007). Our system is implemented in cdec, an open source framework for aligning, training, and decoding with a number of different translation models, including SCFGs. (Dyer et al., 2010). [1] SCFG grammars contain pairs of CFG rules with aligned nonterminals, where by introducing these nonterminals into the grammar, such a system is able to utilize both word and phrase level reordering to capture the hierarchical structure of language. SCFG translation models have been shown to produce state-of-the-art translation for most language pairs, as they are capable of both exploiting lexical information for and efficiently computing all possible reorderings using a CKY-based decoder (Dyer et al., 2009).

[1] http://cdec-decoder.org

Proceedings of the 6th Workshop on Statistical Machine Translation, pages 344–350,
Edinburgh, Scotland, UK, July 30–31, 2011. ©2011 Association for Computational Linguistics

One benefit of cdec is the flexibility allowed with regard to the input format, as it expects either a string, lattice, or context-free forest, and subsequently generates a hypergraph representing the full translation forest without any pruning. This forest can now be rescored, by intersecting it with a language model for instance, to obtain output translations. These capabilities of cdec allow us to perform the experiments described below, which may have otherwise proven to be quite impractical to carry out in another system.

The set of features used in our model were the rule translation relative frequency $P(e|f)$, a target n-gram language model $P(e)$, lexical translation probabilities $P_{lex}(\overline{e}|\overline{f})$ and $P_{lex}(\overline{f}|\overline{e})$, a count of the total number of rules used, a target word penalty, and a count of the number of times the glue rule is used. The number of non-terminals allowed in a synchronous grammar rule was restricted to two, and the non-terminal span limit was 12 for non-glue grammars. The hierarchical phrase-based translation grammar was extracted using a suffix array rule extractor (Lopez, 2007).

To optimize the feature weights for our model, we used an implementation of the hypergraph minimum error rate training (MERT) algorithm (Dyer et al., 2010; Och, 2003) for training with an arbitrary loss function. The error function we used was BLEU (Papineni et al., 2002), and the decoder was configured to use cube pruning (Huang and Chiang, 2007) with a limit of 100 candidates at each node.

2.1 Data Preparation

The SMS messages were originally translated by English speaking volunteers for the purpose of providing first responders with information and locations requiring their assistance. As such, in order to create a suitable parallel training corpus from which to extract a translation grammar, a number of steps had to be taken in addition to lowercasing and tokenizing both sides of training data. Many of the English translations had additional notes sections that were added by the translator to the messages with either personal notes or further informative remarks. As these sections do not correspond to any text on the source side, and would therefore degrade the alignment process, these had to be identified and removed. Furthermore, the anonymization of the data resulted in tokens such as *firstname* and *phonenumber* which were prevalent and had to be preserved as they were. Since the total amount of Haitian-English parallel data provided is quite limited, we found additional data and augmented the available set with data gathered by the CrisisCommons group and made it available to other WMT participants. The combined training corpus from which we extracted our grammar consisted of 123,609 sentence pairs, which was then filtered for length and aligned using the GIZA++ implementation of IBM Model 4 (Och and Ney, 2003) to obtain one-to-many alignments in either direction and symmetrized using the grow-diag-final-and method (Koehn et al., 2003).

We trained a 5-gram language model using the SRI language modeling toolkit (Stolcke, 2002) from the English monolingual News Commentary and News Crawl language modeling training data provided for the shared task and the English portion of the parallel data with modified Kneser-Ney smoothing (Chen and Goodman, 1996). We have previously found that since the beginnings and ends of sentences often display unique characteristics that are not easily captured within the context of the model, explicitly annotating beginning and end of sentence markers as part of our translation process leads to significantly improved performance (Dyer et al., 2009).

A further difficulty of the task stems from the fact that there are two versions of the SMS test set, a raw version, which contains the original messages, and a clean version which was post-edited by humans. As the evaluation of the task will consist of translating these two versions of the test set, our baseline system consisted of two systems, one built on the clean data using the 900 sentences in SMS dev clean to tune our feature weights, and evaluated using SMS devtest clean, and one built analogously for the raw data tuned on the 900 sentences in SMS dev raw and evaluated on SMS devtest raw. We report results on these sets as well as the 1274 sentences in the SMS test set.

3 Experimental Variation

The results produced by the baseline systems are presented in Table 1. As can be seen, the clean version performs on par with the French-English trans-

Baseline			
Version	Set	BLEU	TER
clean	dev	30.36	56.04
	devtest	28.15	57.45
	test	27.97	59.19
raw	dev	25.62	63.27
	devtest	24.09	63.82
	test	23.33	65.93

Table 1: Baseline system BLEU and TER scores

lation quality in the 2011 WMT shared translation task,[2] and significantly outperforms the raw version, despite the content of the messages being identical. This serves to underscore the importance of proper post-processing of the raw data in order to attempt to close the performance gap between the two versions. Through analysis of the raw and clean data we identified several factors which we believe greatly contribute to the difference in translation output. We examine punctuation in Section 3.2, grammar post-processing in Section 3.3, and morphological differences in Sections 3.4 and 3.5.

3.1 Automatic Resource Confidence Weighting

A practical technique when working with a low-density language with limited resources is to duplicate the same trusted resource multiple times in the parallel training corpus in order for the translation probabilities of the duplicated items to be augmented. For instance, if we have confidence in the entries of the glossary and dictionary, we can duplicate them 10 times in our training data to increase the associated probabilities. The aim of this strategy is to take advantage of the limited resources and exploit the reliable ones.

However, what happens if some resources are more reliable than others? Looking at the provided resources, we saw that in the Haitisurf dictionary, the entry for *paske* is matched with *for*, while in glossary-all-fix, *paske* is matched with *because*. If we then consider the training data, we see that in most cases, *paske* is in fact translated as *because*. Motivated by this type of phenomenon, we employed an alternative strategy to simple duplication which allows us to further exploit our prior knowledge.

[2] http://matrix.statmt.org/matrix

First, we take the previously word-aligned baseline training corpus and for each sentence pair and word e_i compute the alignment link count $c(e_i, f_j)$ over the positions j that e_i is aligned with, repeating for $c(f_i, e_j)$ in the other direction. Then, we process each resource we are considering duplicating, and augment its score by $c(e_i, f_j)$ for every pair of words which was observed in the training data and is present in the resource. This score is then normalized by the size of the resource, and averaged over both directions. The outcome of this process is a score for each resource. Taking these scores on a log scale and pinning the top score to associate with 20 duplications, the result is a decreasing number of duplications for each subsequent resources, based on our confidence in its entries. Thus, every entry in the resource receives credit, as long as there is evidence that the entries we have observed are reliable. On our set of resources, the process produces a score of 17 for the Haitisurf dictionary and 183 for the glossary, which is in line with what we would expect. It may be that the resources may have entries which occur in the test set but not in the training data, and thus we may inadvertently skew our distribution in a way which negatively impacts our performance, however, overall we believe it is a sound assumption that we should bias ourselves toward the more common occurrences based on the training data, as this should provide us with a higher translation probability from the *good* resources since the entries are repeated more often. Once we obtain a proper weighting scheme for the resources, we construct a new training corpus, and proceed forward from the alignment process.

Table 2 presents the BLEU and TER results of the standard strategy of duplication against the confidence weighting scheme outlined above. As can be

Version	Set	Conf. Wt.		x10	
		BLEU	TER	BLEU	TER
clean	dev	30.79	55.71	30.61	55.31
	devtest	27.92	57.66	28.22	57.06
	test	27.97	59.65	27.74	59.34
raw	dev	26.11	62.64	25.72	62.99
	devtest	24.16	63.71	24.18	63.71
	test	23.66	65.69	23.06	66.78

Table 2: Confidence weighting versus x10 duplication

seen, the confidence weighting scheme substantially outperforms the duplication for the dev set of both versions, but these improvements do not carry over to the clean devtest set. Therefore, for the rest of the experiments presented in the paper, we will use the confidence weighting scheme for the raw version, and the standard duplication for the clean version.

3.2 Automatic Punctuation Prediction

Punctuation does not usually cause a problem in text-based machine translation, but this changes when venturing into the domain of SMS. Punctuation is very informative to the translation process, providing essential contextual information, much as the aforementioned sentence boundary markers. When this information is lacking, mistakes which would have otherwise been avoided can be made. Examining the data, we see there is substantially more punctuation in the clean set than in the raw. For example, there are 50% more comma's in the clean dev set than in the raw. A problem of lack of punctuation has been studied in the context of spoken language translation, where punctuation prediction on the source language prior to translation has been shown to improve performance (Dyer, 2007). We take an analogous approach here, and train a hidden 5-gram model using SRILM on the punctuated portion of the Haitian side of the parallel data. We then applied the model to punctuate the raw dev set, and tuned a system on this punctuated set. However, the translation performance did not improve. This may have been do to several factors, including the limited size of the training set, and the lack of in-domain punctuated training data. Thus, we applied a self-training approach. We applied the punctuation model to the SMS training data, which is only available in the raw format. Once punctuated, we re-trained our punctuation prediction model, now including the automatically punctuated SMS data as part of the punctuation language model training data. We use this second punctuation prediction model to predict punctuation for the tuning and evaluation sets. We continue by creating a new parallel training corpus which substitutes the original SMS training data with the punctuated version, and build a new translation system from it. The results from using the self-trained punctuation method are presented in Table 3. Future experiments on the raw version are performed using this punctuation.

AUTO-PUNC			
Version	Set	BLEU	TER
raw	dev	26.09	62.84
	devtest	24.38	64.26
	test	23.59	65.91

Table 3: Automatic punctuation prediction results

3.3 Grammar Filtering

Although the grammars of a SCFG model permit high-quality translation, the grammar extraction procedure extracts many rules which are formally licensed by the model, but are otherwise incapable of helping us produce a good translation. For example, in this task we know that the token *firstname* must always translate as *firstname*, and never as *phonenumber*. This refreshing lack of ambiguity allows us to filter the grammar after extracting it from the training corpus, removing any grammar rule where these conditions are not met, prior to decoding. Filtering removed approximately 5% of the grammar rules.[3] Table 4 shows the results of applying grammar filtering to the raw and clean version.

GRAMMAR			
Version	Set	BLEU	TER
clean	dev	30.88	54.53
	devtest	28.69	56.21
	test	28.29	58.78
raw	dev	26.41	62.47
	devtest	24.47	63.26
	test	23.96	65.82

Table 4: Results of filtering the grammar in a post-processing step before decoding

3.4 Raw-Clean Segmentation Lattice

As noted above, a major cause of the performance degradation from the clean to the raw version is related to the morphological errors in the messages. Figure 1 presents a segmentation lattice with two versions of the same sentence; the first being from

[3]We experimented with more aggressive filtering based on punctuation and numbers, but translation quality degraded rapidly.

the raw version, and the second from the clean. We can see that that *Ilavach* has been broken into two segments, while *ki sou* has been combined into one.

Since we do not necessarily know in advance which segmentation is the correct one for a better quality translation, it may be of use to be able to utilize both segmentations and allow the decoder to learn the appropriate one. In previous work, word segmentation lattices have been used to address the problem of productive compounding in morphologically rich languages, such as German, where morphemes are combined to make words but the orthography does not delineate the morpheme boundaries. These lattices encode alternative ways of segmenting compound words, and allow the decoder to automatically choose which segmentation is best for translation, leading to significantly improved results (Dyer, 2009). As opposed to building word segmentation lattices from a linguistic morphological analysis of a compound word, we propose to utilize the lattice to encode all alternative ways of segmenting a word as presented to us in either the clean or raw versions of a sentence. As the task requires us to produce separate clean and raw output on the test set, we tune one system on a lattice built from the clean and raw dev set, and use the single system to decode both the clean and raw test set separately. Table 5 presents the results of using segmentation lattices.

3.5 Raw-to-Clean Transformation Lattice

As can be seen in Tables 1, 2, and 3, system performance on clean text greatly outperforms system performance on raw text, with a difference of almost 5 BLEU points. Thus, we explored the possibility of automatically transforming raw text into clean text, based on the "parallel" raw and clean texts that were provided as part of the task.

One standard approach might have been to train a Haitian-to-Haitian MT system to "translate" from raw text to clean text. However, since the training set was only available as raw text, and only the dev and devtest datasets had been cleaned, we clearly did not have enough data to train a raw-to-clean translation system. Thus, we created a finite-state transducer (FST) by aligning the raw dev text to the clean dev text, on a sentence-by-sentence basis. These raw-to-clean alignments were created using a simple minimum edit distance algorithm; substitution costs were calculated according to orthographic match.

SEG-LATTICE			
Version	Set	BLEU	TER
raw	dev	26.17	61.88
	devtest	24.64	62.53
	test	23.89	65.27

Table 5: Raw-Clean segmentation lattice tuning results

FST-LATTICE			
Version	Set	BLEU	TER
raw	dev	26.20	62.15
	devtest	24.21	63.45
	test	22.56	67.79

Table 6: Raw-to-clean transformation lattice results

One option would be to use the resulting raw-to-clean transducer to greedily replace each word (or phrase) in the raw input with the predicted transformation into clean text. However, such a destructive replacement method could easily introduce cascading errors by removing text that might have been translated correctly. Fortunately, as mentioned in Section 2, and utilized in the previous section, the cdec decoder accepts lattices as input. Rather than replacing raw text with the predicted transformation into "clean" text, we add a path to the input lattice for each possible transform, for each word and phrase in the input. We tune a system on a lattice built from this approach on the dev set, and use the FST developed from the dev set in order to create lattices for decoding the devtest and test sets. An example is shown in Figure 3.4. Note that in this example, the transformation technique correctly inserted new paths for *ilavach* and *ki sou*, correctly retained the single path for *zile*, but overgenerated many (incorrect) options for *nan*. Note, though, that the original path for *nan* remains in the lattice, delaying the ambiguity resolution until later in the decoding process. Results from creating raw-to-clean transformation lattices are presented in Table 6.

By comparing the results in Table 6 to those in Table 5, we can see that the noise introduced by the finite-state transformation process outweighed the

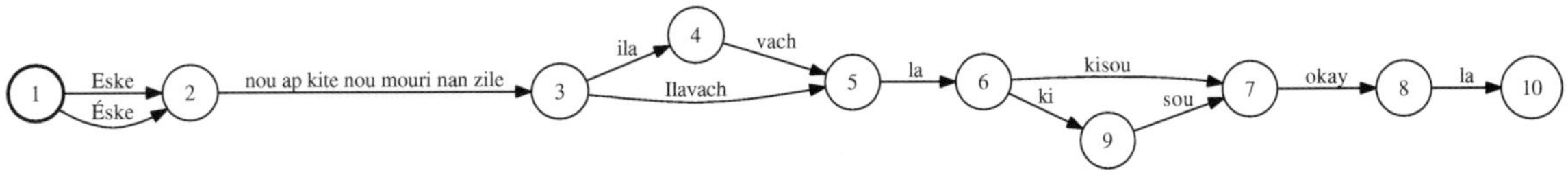

Figure 1: Partial segmentation lattice combining the raw and clean versions of the sentence:
Are you going to let us die on Ile à Vaches which is located close the city of Les Cayes.

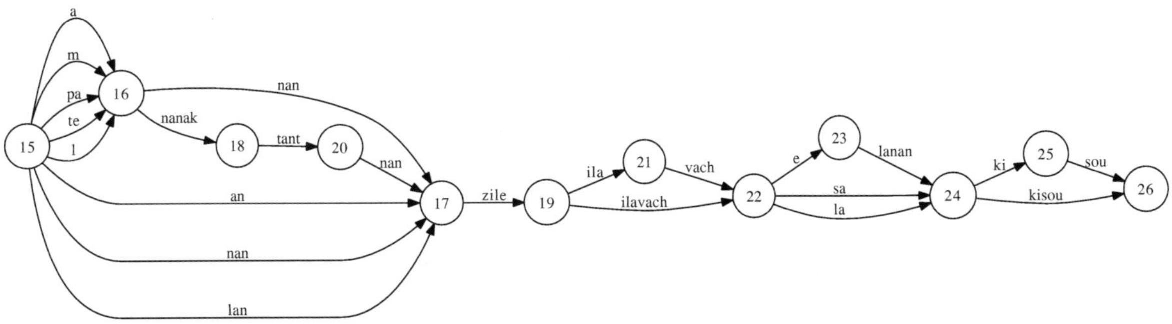

Figure 2: Partial input lattice for sentence in Figure 3.4, generated using the raw-to-clean transform technique described in Section 3.5.

gains of adding new phrases for tuning.

4 System Comparison

Table 7 shows the performance on the devtest set of each of the system variations that we have presented in this paper. From this table, we can see that our best-performing system on clean data was the GRAMMAR system, where the training data was multiplied by ten as described in Section 3.1, then the grammar was filtered as described in Section 3.3. Our performance on clean test data, using this system, was 28.29 BLEU and 58.78 TER. Table 7 also demonstrates that our best-performing system on raw data was the SEG-LATTICE system, where the training data was confidence-weighted (Section 3.1), the grammar was filtered (Section 3.3), punctuation was automatically added to the raw data as described in Section 3.2, and the system was tuned on a lattice created from the raw and clean dev dataset. Our performance on raw test data, using this system, was 23.89 BLEU and 65.27 TER.

System	clean		raw	
	BLEU	TER	BLEU	TER
BASELINE	28.15	57.45	24.09	63.82
CONF. WT.	27.92	57.66	24.16	63.71
x10	28.22	57.06	24.18	63.71
GRAMMAR	**28.69**	**56.21**	24.47	63.26
AUTO-PUNC	–	–	24.38	64.26
SEG-LATTICE	–	–	**24.64**	**62.53**
FST-LATTICE	–	–	24.21	63.45

Table 7: Comparison of all systems' performance on devtest set

5 Conclusion

In this paper we presented our system for the 2011 WMT featured Haitian Creole–English translation task. In order to improve translation quality of low-density noisy SMS data, we experimented with a number of methods that improve performance on both the clean and raw versions of the data, and help close the gap between the post-edited and real-world data according to BLEU and TER evaluation. The methods employed were developed to specifically address shortcomings we observed in the data, such as segmentation lattices for morphological ambiguity, confidence weighting for resource utilization, and punctuation prediction for lack thereof. Overall, this work emphasizes the feasibility of adapting existing translation technology to as-yet underexplored domains, as well as the shortcomings that need to be addressed in future work in real-world data.

6 Acknowledgments

The authors gratefully acknowledge partial support from the DARPA GALE program, No. HR0011-06-2-001. In addition, the first author was supported by the NDSEG Fellowship. Any opinions or findings do not necessarily reflect the view of the sponsors.

References

Stanley F. Chen and Joshua Goodman. 1996. An empirical study of smoothing techniques for language modeling. In *Proceedings of the 34th Annual Meeting of the Association for Computational Linguistics*, pages 310–318.

David Chiang. 2007. Hierarchical phrase-based translation. In *Computational Linguistics*, volume 33(2), pages 201–228.

Chris Dyer, Hendra Setiawan, Yuval Marton, and Philip Resnik. 2009. The University of Maryland statistical machine translation system for the Fourth Workshop on Machine Translation. In *Proceedings of the EACL-2009 Workshop on Statistical Machine Translation*.

Chris Dyer, Adam Lopez, Juri Ganitkevitch, Jonathan Weese, Ferhan Ture, Phil Blunsom, Hendra Setiawan, Vladimir Eidelman, and Philip Resnik. 2010. cdec: A decoder, alignment, and learning framework for finite-state and context-free translation models. In *Proceedings of ACL System Demonstrations*.

Chris Dyer. 2007. The University of Maryland Translation system for IWSLT 2007. In *Proceedings of IWSLT*.

Chris Dyer. 2009. Using a maximum entropy model to build segmentation lattices for MT. In *Proceedings of NAACL-HLT*.

Liang Huang and David Chiang. 2007. Forest rescoring: Faster decoding with integrated language models. In *Proceedings of the 45th Annual Meeting of the Association of Computational Linguistics*, pages 144–151.

Philipp Koehn, Franz Josef Och, and Daniel Marcu. 2003. Statistical phrase-based translation. In *NAACL '03: Proceedings of the 2003 Conference of the North American Chapter of the Association for Computational Linguistics on Human Language Technology*, pages 48–54.

Adam Lopez. 2007. Hierarchical phrase-based translation with suffix arrays. In *Proceedings of EMNLP*, pages 976–985.

Franz Och and Hermann Ney. 2003. A systematic comparison of various statistical alignment models. In *Computational Linguistics*, volume 29(21), pages 19–51.

Franz Josef Och. 2003. Minimum error rate training in statistical machine translation. In *Proceedings of the 41st Annual Meeting of the Association for Computational Linguistics*, pages 160–167.

Kishore Papineni, Salim Roukos, Todd Ward, and Wei-Jing Zhu. 2002. BLEU: a method for automatic evaluation of machine translation. In *Proceedings of 40th Annual Meeting of the Association for Computational Linguistics*, pages 311–318.

Andreas Stolcke. 2002. SRILM - an extensible language modeling toolkit. In *Intl. Conf. on Spoken Language Processing*.

Stochastic Parse Tree Selection for an Existing RBMT System

Christian Federmann
DFKI GmbH
Language Technology Lab
Saarbrücken, Germany
cfedermann@dfki.de

Sabine Hunsicker
DFKI GmbH
Language Technology Lab
Saarbrücken, Germany
sabine.hunsicker@dfki.de

Abstract

In this paper we describe our hybrid machine translation system with which we participated in the WMT11 shared translation task for the English→German language pair. Our system was able to outperform its RBMT baseline and turned out to be the best-scored participating system in the manual evaluation. To achieve this, we extended an existing, rule-based MT system with a module for stochastic selection of analysis parse trees that allowed to better cope with parsing errors during the system's analysis phase. Due to the integration into the analysis phase of the RBMT engine, we are able to preserve the benefits of a rule-based translation system such as proper generation of target language text. Additionally, we used a statistical tool for terminology extraction to improve the lexicon of the RBMT system. We report results from both automated metrics and human evaluation efforts, including examples which show how the proposed approach can improve machine translation quality.

1 Introduction

Rule-based machine translation (RBMT) systems that employ a transfer-based translation approach, highly depend on the quality of their analysis phase as it provides the basis for its later processing phases, namely transfer and generation. Any parse failures encountered in the initial analysis phase will proliferate and cause further errors in the following phases. Very often, bad translation results can be traced back to incorrect analysis trees that have been computed for the respective input sentences. Henceforth, any improvements that can be achieved for the analysis phase of a given RBMT system directly lead to improved translation output which makes this an interesting topic in the context of hybrid MT.

In this paper we present a study how the rule-based analysis phase of a commercial RBMT system can be supplemented by a stochastic parser. The system under investigation is the rule-based engine Lucy LT. This software uses a sophisticated RBMT transfer approach with a long research history; it is explained in more detail in (Alonso and Thurmair, 2003).

The output of its analysis phase is a parse forest containing a small number of tree structures. For our hybrid system we investigated if the existing rule base of the Lucy LT system chooses the best tree from the analysis forest and how the selection of this best tree out of the set of candidates can be improved by adding stochastic knowledge to the rule-based system.

The remainder of this paper is structured in the following way: in Section 2 we first describe the transfer-based architecture of the rule-based Lucy LT engine, giving special focus to its analysis phase which we are trying to optimize. Afterwards, we provide details on the implementation of the stochastic selection component, the so-called "tree selector" which allows to integrate knowledge from a stochastic parser into the analysis phase of the rule-based system. Section 3 reports on the results of both automated metrics and manual evaluation efforts, including examples which show how the proposed approach has improved or degraded MT quality. Finally, we conclude and provide an outlook on future work in this area.

Proceedings of the 6th Workshop on Statistical Machine Translation, pages 351–357,
Edinburgh, Scotland, UK, July 30–31, 2011. ©2011 Association for Computational Linguistics

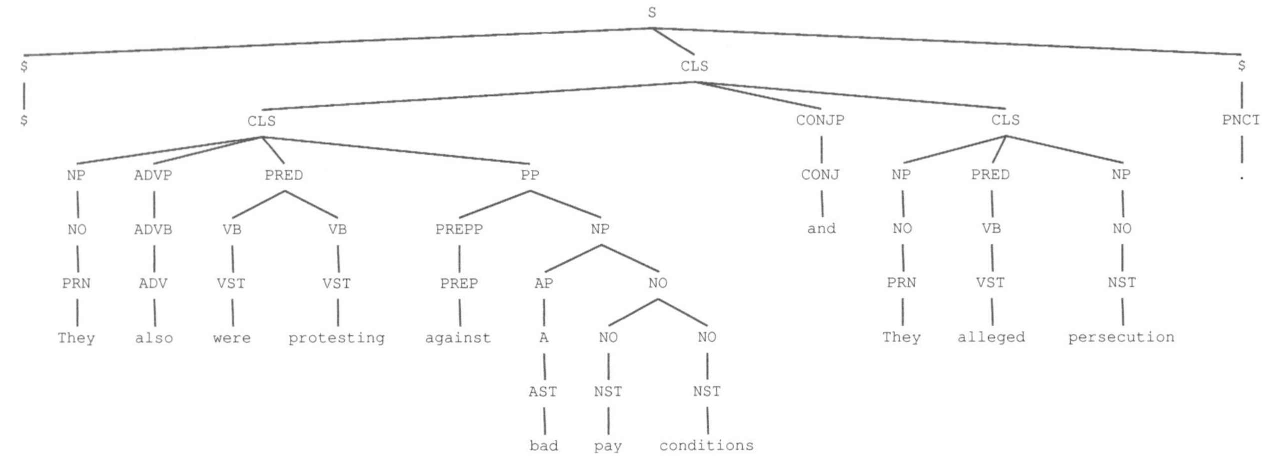

Figure 1: Original analysis tree from the rule-based MT system

2 System Architecture

2.1 Lucy LT Architecture

The Lucy LT engine is a renowned RMBT system which follows a "classical", transfer-based machine translation approach. The system first *analyses* the given source sentence creating a forest of several analysis parse trees. One of these parse trees is then selected (as "best" analysis) and transformed in the *transfer* phase into a tree structure from which the target text (i.e. the translation) can be *generated.*

It is clear that any errors that occur during the initial analysis phase proliferate and cause negative side effects on the outcome of the final translation result. As the analysis phase is thus of very special importance, we have investigated it in more detail. The Lucy LT analysis consists of several phases:

1. The input is tokenised with regards to the system's source language lexicon.
2. The resulting tokens undergo a morphological analysis, which is able to identify possible combinations of allomorphs for a token.
3. This leads to a chart which forms the basis for the actual parsing, using a head-driven strategy[1]. Special handling is performed for the analysis of *multi-word expressions* and also for *verbal framing*.

At the end of the analysis, there is an extra phase named *phrasal analysis* which is called whenever the grammar was not able to construct a legal constituent from all the elements of the input. This happens in several different scenarios:

- The input is ungrammatical according to the LT analysis grammar.
- The category of the derived constituent is not one of the allowed categories.
- A grammatical phenomenon in the source sentence is not covered.
- There are missing lexical entries for the input sentence.

During the phrasal analysis, the LT engine collects all partial trees and greedily constructs an overall interpretation of the chart. Based on our findings from many experiments with the Lucy LT engine, phrasal analyses are performed for more than 40% of the sentences from our test sets and very often result in bad translations.

Each resulting analysis parse tree, independent of whether it is a grammatical or a result from the phrasal analysis, is also assigned an integer score by the grammar. The tree with the highest score is then handed over to the transfer phase, thus pre-defining the final translation output.

2.2 The "Tree Selector"

An initial evaluation of the translation quality based on the tree selection of the analysis phase showed that there is potential for improvement. The integer score assigned by the analysis grammar provides a

[1] grammar formalism + number of rules

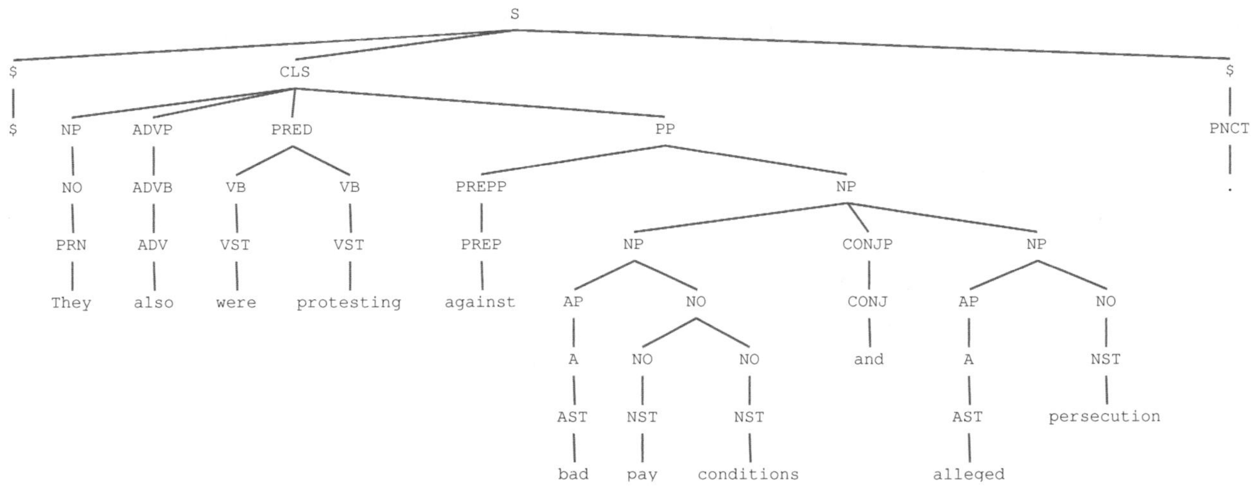

Figure 2: Improved analysis tree resulting from stochastic parse selection

good indication of which trees lead to good translations, as is depicted in Table 1. Still, in many cases an alternative tree would have lead to a better translation.

As additional feature, we chose to use the tree edit distance of each analysis candidate to a stochastic parse tree. An advantage of stochastic parsing lies in the fact that parsers from this class can deal very well even with ungrammatical or unknown output, which we have seen is problematic for a rule-base parser. We decided to make use of the Stanford Parser as described in (Klein and Manning, 2003), which uses an unlexicalised probabilistic context-free grammar that was trained on the Penn Treebank[2]. We parse the original source sentence with this PCFG grammar to get a stochastic parse tree that can be compared to the trees from the Lucy analysis forest.

In our experiments, we compare the stochastic parse tree with the alternatives given by Lucy LT. Tree comparison is implemented based on the *Tree Edit Distance*, as originally defined in (Zhang and Shasha, 1989). In analogy to the *Word Edit* or *Levenshtein Distance*, the distance between two trees is the number of editing actions that are required to transform the first tree into the second tree. The Tree Edit Distance knows three actions:

- Insertion
- Deletion
- Renaming (substitution in Levenshtein Distance)

Since the Lucy LT engine uses its own tag set, a mapping between this proprietary and the Penn Treebank tag set was created. Our implementation, called "Tree Selector" uses a normalised version of the Tree Edit Distance to estimate the quality of the trees from the Lucy analysis forest, possibly overriding the analysis decision taken by the unmodified RBMT engine. The integration of the Tree Selector has been possible by using an adapted version of the rule-based MT system which allowed to communicate the selection result from our external process to the Lucy LT kernel which would then load the respective parse tree for all further processing steps.

[2]Further experiments with different grammars are currently on-going.

Best Analysis Tree	Percentage
Default (id=1)	42 (61.76%)
Alternative (id=2-7)	26 (38.24%)

Table 1: Evaluation of Analysis Forests

2.3 LiSTEX Terminology Extraction

The LiSTEX extension of the Lucy RBMT engine allows to improve the system's lexicon; the approach is described in more detail in (Federmann et al., 2011). To extend the lexicon, terminology lists are extracted from parallel corpora. These lists are then enriched with linguistic information, such as part-of-speech tag, internal structure of multi-word expressions and frequency. For English and German, about 26,000 terms were imported using this procedure.

2.4 Named Entity Handling

Named entities are often handled incorrectly and wrongly translated, such as *George Bush* → *George Busch*. To reduce the frequency of such errors, we added a pre- and post-processing modules to deal with named entities. Before translation, the input text is scanned for named entities. We use both HeiNER (Wolodja Wentland and Hartung (2008)) and the OpenNLP toolkit[3]. HeiNER is a dictionary containing named entities extracted from Wikipedia. This provides us with a wide range of well-translated entities. To increase the coverage, we also use the named entity recogniser in OpenNLP. These entities have to be translated using the RBMT engine. We save the named entity translations and insert placeholders for all NEs. The modified text is translated using the hybrid set-up described above. After the translation is finished, the placeholders are replaced by their respective translations.

3 Evaluation

3.1 Shared Task Setup

For the WMT11 shared translation task, we submitted three different runs of our hybrid MT system:

1. Hybrid Transfer (without the Tree Selector, but with the extended lexicon)
2. Full Hybrid (with both the Tree Selector and the extended lexicon)
3. Full Hybrid+Named Entities (full hybrid and named entity handling)

Our primary submission was run #3. All three runs were evaluated using BLEU (Papineni et al. (2001)) and TER (Snover et al. (2006)). The results from these automated metrics are reported in Table 2.

Table 2: Automatic metric scores for WMT11

System	BLEU	TER
Hybrid Transfer	13.4	0.792
Full Hybrid	13.1	0.796
Full Hybrid+Named Entities	12.8	0.800

[3] http://incubator.apache.org/opennlp/

Table 3 shows that we were able to outperform the original Lucy version. Furthermore, it turned out that our hybrid system was the best-scoring system from all shared task participants.

Table 3: Manual evaluation scores for WMT11

System	Normalized Score
Full Hybrid+Named Entities	0.6805
Original Lucy	0.6599

3.2 Error Analysis

The selection process following the decision factors as explained in Section 2.2 may fail due to wrong assumptions in two areas:

1. The tree with the lowest distance does not result in the best translation.
2. There are several trees associated with the lowest distance, but the tree with the highest score does not result in the best translation.

To calculate the error rate of the Tree Selector, we ran experiments on the test set of the WMT10 shared task and evaluated a sample of 100 sentences with regards to translation quality. To do so, we created all seven possible translations for each of the phrasal analyses and checked whether the Tree Selector returned a tree that led to exactly this translation. In case it did not, we investigated the reasons for this. Sentences for which all trees created the same translation were skipped. This sample contains both examples in which the translation changed and in which the translation stayed the same.

Table 4 shows the error rate of the Tree Selector while Table 5 contains the error analysis. As one can see, the optimal tree was chosen for 56% of the sentences. We also see that the minimal tree edit distance seems to be a good feature to use for comparisons, as it holds for 71% of the trees, including those examples where the best tree was not scored highest by the LT engine. This also means that additional features for choosing the tree out of the group of trees with the minimal edit distance are required. Even for the 29% of sentences, in which the optimal tree was not chosen, little quality was lost: in 75.86% of those cases, the translations didn't change

Best Translation Returned	56%
Other Translation Returned	44%
Best Tree has Minimal Edit Distance	71%
Best Tree has Higher Distance	29%

Table 4: Error Rate of the Tree Selector

at all (obviously the trees resulted in equal translation output). In the remaining cases the translations were divided evenly between slight degradations and and equal quality.

Other Translation: Selected Tree	
Tree 1 (Default)	31
Tree 2-7 (Alternatives)	13
Reasons for Selection	
Source contained more than 50 tokens	16
Time-out before best tree is reached	13
Chosen tree had minimal distance	15

Table 5: Evaluation of Tree Selector Errors

In the cases when the best tree was not chosen, the first tree (which is the default tree) was selected in 70.45% . This is due to a combinations of robustness factors that are implemented in the RBMT system and have been beyond our control in the experiments. The LT engine has several different indicators which may throw a time-out exception, if, for example, the analysis phase takes too long to produce a result. To avoid getting time-out errors, only sentences with up to 50 tokens are treated with the Tree Selector. Additionally the Tree Selector itself checks the processing time and returns intermediate results, if this limit is reached. This ensures that we receive a proper translation for all sentences.[4]

3.3 Examples

Using our stochastic selection component, we are able to fix errors which can be found in translation output generated by the original Lucy engine.

Table 6 shows several examples including *source* text, *reference* text, and *translations* from both the original Lucy engine (*A*) and our hybrid system (*B*). We will briefly discuss our observations for these examples in the following section.

[4]We are currently working on eliminating this time-out issue as it prevents us from driving our approach to its full potential.

1. Translation A is the default translation. The parse tree for this translation can be seen in Figure 1. Here the adjective *alleged* is wrongly parsed as a verb. By contrast, Figure 2 shows the tree selected by our hybrid implementation, which contains the correct analysis of *alleged* and results in a correct translation.

2. Word order is improved in the Example 2.

3. Lexical items are associated with a domain area in the lexicon of the rule-based system. Items that are contained within a different domain than the input text are still accessible, but items in the same domain are preferred. In Example 3, this may lead to the incorrect disambiguation of multi-word expressions: the translation of *to blow up* as *in die Luft fliegen* was not preferred in Translation A due to the chosen domain and a more superficial translation was chosen. This problem is fixed in Translation B. Our system chose a tree leading to the correct idiomatic translation.

4. Something similar happens in Example 4 where the choice of preposition is improved.

5. These changes remain at a rather local scope, but we also have instances where the sentence improves globally: Example 5 illustrates this well. In translation A, the name of the book, *"After the Ice"*, has been moved to an entirely different place in the sentence, removing it from its original context.

6. The same process can be observed in Example 6, where the translation of *device* was moved from the main clause to the sub clause in Translation A.

7. An even more impressive example is Example 7. Here, translation A was not even a grammatically correct sentence. This is due to the heuristics of the Lucy engine, although they could also create a correct translation B.

These examples show that our initial goal of improving the given RMBT system has been reached and that a hybrid MT system with an architecture similar to what we have described in this paper does in fact perform quite well.

Table 6: Translation Examples for Original (A) and Improved (B) Lucy

1	**Source:**	They were also protesting against bad pay conditions and alleged persecution.
	Reference:	Sie protestierten auch gegen die schlechten Zahlungsbedingungen und angebliche Schikanen.
	Translation A:	Sie protestierten auch gegen schlechte Soldbedingungen und *behaupteten Verfolgung*.
	Translation B:	Sie protestierten auch gegen schlechte Soldbedingungen und *angebliche Verfolgung*.
2	**Source:**	If the finance minister can't find the money elsewhere, the project will have to be aborted and sanctions will be imposed, warns Janota.
	Reference:	Sollte der Finanzminister das Geld nicht anderswo finden, müsste das Projekt gestoppt werden und in diesem Falle kommen Sanktionen, warnte Janota.
	Translation A:	Wenn der Finanzminister das Geld nicht anderswo finden kann, das Projekt abgebrochen *werden müssen wird* und Sanktionen auferlegt werden werden, warnt Janota.
	Translation B:	Wenn der Finanzminister das Geld nicht anderswo finden kann, *wird* das Projekt abgebrochen *werden müssen* und Sanktionen werden auferlegt werden, warnt Janota.
3	**Source:**	Apparently the engine blew up in the rocket's third phase.
	Reference:	Vermutlich explodierte der Motor in der dritten Raketenstufe.
	Translation A:	Offenbar *blies* der Motor *hinauf* die dritte Phase der Rakete in.
	Translation B:	Offenbar *flog* der Motor in der dritten Phase der Rakete *in die Luft*.
4	**Source:**	As of January, they should be paid for by the insurance companies and not compulsory.
	Reference:	Ab Januar soll diese von den Versicherungen bezahlt und freiwillig sein.
	Translation A:	Ab Januar sollten sie *für von* den Versicherungsgesellschaften und nicht obligatorisch bezahlt werden.
	Translation B:	Ab Januar sollten sie *von* den Versicherungsgesellschaften und nicht obligatorisch gezahlt werden.
5	**Source:**	In his new book, "After the Ice", Alun Anderson, a former editor of New Scientist, offers a clear and chilling account of the science of the Arctic and a gripping glimpse of how the future may turn out there.
	Reference:	In seinem neuen Buch "Nach dem Eis" (Originaltitel "After the Ice") bietet Alun Anderson, ein ehemaliger Herausgeber des Wissenschaftsmagazins "New Scientist", eine klare und beunruhigende Beschreibung der Wissenschaft der Arktis und einen packenden Einblick, wie die Zukunft sich entwickeln könnte.
	Translation A:	In seinem neuen Buch bietet Alun Anderson, ein früherer Redakteur von Neuem Wissenschaftler, *"Nach dem Eis"* einen klaren und kalten Bericht über die Wissenschaft der Arktis und einen spannenden Blick davon an, wie die Zukunft sich hinaus dort drehen kann.
	Translation B:	*In seinem neuen Buch, "Nach dem Eis"*, bietet Alun Anderson, ein früherer Redakteur von Neuem Wissenschaftler, einen klaren und kalten Bericht über die Wissenschaft der Arktis und einen spannenden Blick davon an, wie die Zukunft sich hinaus dort drehen kann.
6	**Source:**	If he does not react, and even though the collision is unavoidable, the device exerts the maximum force to the brakes to minimize damage.
	Reference:	Falls der Fahrer nicht auf die Warnung reagiert und sogar wenn der Zusammenstoss schon unvermeidlich ist, übt der Bremsassistent den maximalen Druck auf die Bremsen aus, um auf diese Weise die Schäden so gering wie möglich zu halten.
	Translation A:	Wenn er nicht reagiert, und *das Gerät* auch wenn der Zusammenstoß unvermeidlich ist, die größtmögliche Kraft zu den Bremsen ausübt, um Schaden zu bagatellisieren.
	Translation B:	Wenn er nicht reagiert, und auch wenn der Zusammenstoß unvermeidlich ist, übt *das Gerät* die größtmögliche Kraft zu den Bremsen aus, um Schaden zu bagatellisieren.
7	**Source:**	For the second year, the Walmart Foundation donated more than $150,000 to purchase, and transport the wreaths.
	Reference:	Die Walmart-Stiftung spendete zum zweiten Mal mehr als 150.000 Dollar für Kauf und Transport der Kränze.
	Translation A:	Für das zweite Jahr, *die Walmart-Gründung, mehr gespendet* als $150,000, um die Kränze zu kaufen, und zu transportieren.
	Translation B:	Für das zweite Jahr *spendete die Walmart-Gründung* mehr als $150,000, um die Kränze zu kaufen, und zu transportieren.

4 Conclusion and Outlook

The analysis phase proves to be crucial for the overall quality of the translation in rule-based machine translation systems. Our hybrid approach indicates that it is possible to improve the analysis results of such a rule-based engine by a better selection method of the trees created by the grammar. Our evaluation shows that the selection itself is no trivial task, as our initial experiments deliver results of varying quality. The degradations we have observed in our own manual evaluation can be fixed by a more fine-grained selection mechanism, as we already know that better trees exist, i.e. the default translations.

While the work reported on in this paper is a dedicated extension of a specific rule-based machine translation system, the overall approach can be used with any transfer-based RBMT system. Future work will concentrate on the circumvention of e.g. the time-out errors that prevented a better performance of the stochastic selection module. Also, we will more closely investigate the issue of decreased translation quality and experiment with other decision factors that may help to alleviate the negative effects.

The LiSTEX module provides us with high quality entries for the lexicon, increasing the coverage of the lexicon and fluency of the translation. As a side-effect, the new terms also help to reduce parsing errors, as formerly unknown multiword expressions are now properly recognised and treated. Further work is being carried out to increase the precision of the extracted terminology lists.

The addition of stochastic knowledge into an existing rule-based machine translation system is an example of a successful, hybrid combination of different MT paradigms into a joint system. Our system turned out to be the winning system for the English→German language pair of the WMT11 shared task.

Acknowledgements

The work described in this paper was supported by the EuroMatrixPlus project (IST-231720) which is funded by the European Community under the Seventh Framework Programme for Research and Technological Development.

References

Juan A. Alonso and Gregor Thurmair. 2003. The Comprendium Translator system. In *Proceedings of the Ninth Machine Translation Summit*.

Christian Federmann, Sabine Hunsicker, Petra Wolf, and Ulrike Bernardi. 2011. From statistical term extraction to hybrid machine translation. In *Proceedings of the 15th Annual Conference of the European Association for Machine Translation*.

Dan Klein and Christopher D. Manning. 2003. Accurate unlexicalized parsing. In *Proceedings of the 41st Annual Meeting of the ACL*, pages 423–430.

Kishore Papineni, Salim Roukos, Todd Ward, and Wei-Jing Zhu. 2001. Bleu: a method for automatic evaluation of machine translation. IBM Research Report RC22176(W0109-022), IBM.

Matthew Snover, Bonnie Dorr, Richard Schwartz, Linnea Micciulla, and John Makhoul. 2006. A study of translation edit rate with targeted human annotation. In *In Proceedings of Association for Machine Translation in the Americas*, pages 223–231.

Carina Silberer Wolodja Wentland, Johannes Knopp and Matthias Hartung. 2008. Building a multilingual lexical resource for named entity disambiguation, translation and transliteration. In European Language Resources Association (ELRA), editor, *Proceedings of the Sixth International Language Resources and Evaluation (LREC'08)*, Marrakech, Morocco, may.

K. Zhang and D. Shasha. 1989. Simple fast algorithms for the editing distance between trees and related problems. *SIAM J. Comput.*, 18:1245–1262, December.

Joint WMT Submission of the QUAERO Project

*Markus Freitag, *Gregor Leusch, *Joern Wuebker, *Stephan Peitz, *Hermann Ney,
†Teresa Herrmann, †Jan Niehues, †Alex Waibel,
‡Alexandre Allauzen, ‡Gilles Adda,‡Josep Maria Crego,
§Bianka Buschbeck, §Tonio Wandmacher, §Jean Senellart
*RWTH Aachen University, Aachen, Germany
†Karlsruhe Institute of Technology, Karlsruhe, Germany
‡LIMSI-CNRS, Orsay, France
§SYSTRAN Software, Inc.
*surname@cs.rwth-aachen.de
†firstname.surname@kit.edu
‡firstname.lastname@limsi.fr §surname@systran.fr

Abstract

This paper describes the joint QUAERO submission to the WMT 2011 machine translation evaluation. Four groups (RWTH Aachen University, Karlsruhe Institute of Technology, LIMSI-CNRS, and SYSTRAN) of the QUAERO project submitted a joint translation for the WMT German→English task. Each group translated the data sets with their own systems. Then RWTH system combination combines these translations to a better one. In this paper, we describe the single systems of each group. Before we present the results of the system combination, we give a short description of the RWTH Aachen system combination approach.

1 Overview

QUAERO is a European research and development program with the goal of developing multimedia and multilingual indexing and management tools for professional and general public applications (http://www.quaero.org). Research in machine translation is mainly assigned to the four groups participating in this joint submission. The aim of this WMT submission was to show the quality of a joint translation by combining the knowledge of the four project partners. Each group develop and maintain their own different machine translation system. These single systems differ not only in their general approach, but also in the preprocessing of training and test data. To take the advantage of these differences of each translation system, we combined all hypotheses of the different systems, using the RWTH system combination approach.

1.1 Data Sets

For WMT 2011 each QUAERO partner trained their systems on the parallel Europarl and News Commentary corpora. All single systems were tuned on the newstest2009 dev set. The newstest2008 dev set was used to train the system combination parameters. Finally the newstest2010 dev set was used to compare the results of the different system combination approaches and settings.

2 Translation Systems

2.1 RWTH Aachen Single Systems

For the WMT 2011 evaluation the RWTH utilized RWTH's state-of-the-art phrase-based and hierarchical translation systems. GIZA++ (Och and Ney, 2003) was employed to train word alignments, language models have been created with the SRILM toolkit (Stolcke, 2002).

2.1.1 Phrase-Based System

The phrase-based translation (PBT) system is similar to the one described in Zens and Ney (2008). After phrase pair extraction from the word-aligned bilingual corpus, the translation probabilities are estimated by relative frequencies. The standard feature set also includes an n-gram language model, phrase-level IBM-1 and word-, phrase- and distortion-penalties, which are combined in log-linear fashion. Parameters are optimized with the Downhill-Simplex algorithm (Nelder and Mead, 1965) on the word graph.

Proceedings of the 6th Workshop on Statistical Machine Translation, pages 358–364,
Edinburgh, Scotland, UK, July 30–31, 2011. ©2011 Association for Computational Linguistics

2.1.2 Hierarchical System

For the hierarchical setups described in this paper, the open source Jane toolkit (Vilar et al., 2010) is employed. Jane has been developed at RWTH and implements the hierarchical approach as introduced by Chiang (2007) with some state-of-the-art extensions. In hierarchical phrase-based translation, a weighted synchronous context-free grammar is induced from parallel text. In addition to contiguous *lexical* phrases, *hierarchical* phrases with up to two gaps are extracted. The search is typically carried out using the cube pruning algorithm (Huang and Chiang, 2007). The model weights are optimized with standard MERT (Och, 2003) on 100-best lists.

2.1.3 Phrase Model Training

For some PBT systems a forced alignment procedure was applied to train the phrase translation model as described in Wuebker et al. (2010). A modified version of the translation decoder is used to produce a phrase alignment on the bilingual training data. The phrase translation probabilities are estimated from their relative frequencies in the phrase-aligned training data. In addition to providing a statistically well-founded phrase model, this has the benefit of producing smaller phrase tables and thus allowing more rapid and less memory consuming experiments with a better translation quality.

2.1.4 Final Systems

For the German→English task, RWTH conducted experiments comparing the standard phrase extraction with the phrase training technique described in Section 2.1.3. Further experiments included the use of additional language model training data, reranking of n-best lists generated by the phrase-based system, and different optimization criteria.

A considerable increase in translation quality can be achieved by application of German compound splitting (Koehn and Knight, 2003). In comparison to standard heuristic phrase extraction techniques, performing force alignment phrase training (FA) gives an improvement in BLEU on newstest2008 and newstest2009, but a degradation in TER. The addition of LDC Gigaword corpora (+GW) to the language model training data shows improvements in both BLEU and TER. Reranking was done on 1000-best lists generated by the the best available system (PBT (FA)+GW). Following models were applied: n-gram posteriors (Zens and Ney, 2006), sentence length model, a 6-gram LM and IBM-1 lexicon models in both normal and inverse direction. These models are combined in a log-linear fashion and the scaling factors are tuned in the same manner as the baseline system (using TER−4BLEU on newstest2009).

The final table includes two identical Jane systems which are optimized on different criteria. The one optimized on TER−BLEU yields a much lower TER.

2.2 Karlsruhe Institute of Technology Single System

2.2.1 Preprocessing

We preprocess the training data prior to training the system, first by normalizing symbols such as quotes, dashes and apostrophes. Then smart-casing of the first words of each sentence is performed. For the German part of the training corpus we use the hunspell[1] lexicon to learn a mapping from old German spelling to new German spelling to obtain a corpus with homogeneous spelling. In addition, we perform compound splitting as described in (Koehn and Knight, 2003). Finally, we remove very long sentences, empty lines, and sentences that probably are not parallel due to length mismatch.

2.2.2 System Overview

The KIT system uses an in-house phrase-based decoder (Vogel, 2003) to perform translation. Optimization with regard to the BLEU score is done using Minimum Error Rate Training as described by Venugopal et al. (2005). The translation model is trained on the Europarl and News Commentary Corpus and the phrase table is based on a GIZA++ Word Alignment. We use two 4-gram SRI language models, one trained on the News Shuffle corpus and one trained on the Gigaword corpus. Reordering is performed based on continuous and non-continuous POS rules to cover short and long-range reorderings. The long-range reordering rules were also applied to the training corpus and phrase extraction was performed on the resulting reordering lattices. Part-of-speech tags are obtained using the TreeTag-

[1] http://hunspell.sourceforge.net/

ger (Schmid, 1994). In addition, the system applies a bilingual language model to extend the context of source language words available for translation. The individual models are described briefly in the following.

2.2.3 POS-based Reordering Model

We use a reordering model that is based on parts-of-speech (POS) and learn probabilistic rules from the POS tags of the words in the training corpus and the alignment information. In addition to continuous reordering rules that model short-range reordering (Rottmann and Vogel, 2007), we apply non-continuous rules to address long-range reorderings as typical for German-English translation (Niehues and Kolss, 2009). The reordering rules are applied to the source sentences and the reordered sentence variants as well as the original sequence are encoded in a word lattice which is used as input to the decoder.

2.2.4 Lattice Phrase Extraction

For the test sentences, the POS-based reordering allows us to change the word order in the source sentence so that the sentence can be translated more easily. If we apply this also to the training sentences, we would be able to extract also phrase pairs for originally discontinuous phrases and could apply them during translation of reordered test sentences.

Therefore, we build reordering lattices for all training sentences and then extract phrase pairs from the monotone source path as well as from the reordered paths. To limit the number of extracted phrase pairs, we extract a source phrase only once per sentence, even if it is found in different paths and we only use long-range reordering rules to generate the lattices for the training corpus.

2.2.5 Bilingual Language Model

In phrase-based systems the source sentence is segmented by the decoder during the search process. This segmentation into phrases leads to the loss of context information at the phrase boundaries. The language model can make use of more target side context. To make also source language context available we use a bilingual language model, an additional language model in the phrase-based system in which each token consist of a target word and all source words it is aligned to. The bilingual tokens enter the translation process as an additional target factor.

2.3 LIMSI-CNRS Single System

2.3.1 System overview

The LIMSI system is built with n-code[2], an open source statistical machine translation system based on bilingual n-grams.

2.3.2 n-code Overview

In a nutshell, the translation model is implemented as a stochastic finite-state transducer trained using a n-gram model of (source,target) pairs (Casacuberta and Vidal, 2004). Training this model requires to reorder source sentences so as to match the target word order. This is performed by a stochastic finite-state reordering model, which uses part-of-speech information[3] to generalize reordering patterns beyond lexical regularities.

In addition to the translation model, eleven feature functions are combined: a *target-language model;* four *lexicon models;* two *lexicalized reordering models* (Tillmann, 2004) aiming at predicting the orientation of the next translation unit; a weak distance-based *distortion model*; and finally a *word-bonus model* and a *tuple-bonus model* which compensate for the system preference for short translations. The four *lexicon models* are similar to the ones use in a standard phrase based system: two scores correspond to the relative frequencies of the tuples and two lexical weights estimated from the automatically generated word alignments. The weights associated to feature functions are optimally combined using a discriminative training framework (Och, 2003), using the *newstest2009* data as development set.

The overall search is based on a beam-search strategy on top of a dynamic programming algorithm. Reordering hypotheses are computed in a preprocessing step, making use of reordering rules built from the word reorderings introduced in the tuple extraction process. The resulting reordering hypotheses are passed to the decoder in the form of word lattices (Crego and Mariño, 2007).

[2] `http://www.limsi.fr/Individu/jmcrego/n-code`

[3] Part-of-speech information for English and German is computed using the TreeTagger.

2.3.3 Data Preprocessing

Based on previous experiments which have demonstrated that better normalization tools provide better *BLEU* scores (K. Papineni and Zhu, 2002), all the English texts are tokenized and detokenized with in-house text processing tools (Déchelotte et al., 2008). For German, the standard tokenizer supplied by evaluation organizers is used.

2.3.4 Target n-gram Language Models

The English language model is trained assuming that the test set consists in a selection of news texts dating from the end of 2010 to the beginning of 2011. This assumption is based on what was done for the 2010 evaluation. Thus, a development corpus is built in order to create a vocabulary and to optimize the target language model.

Development Set and Vocabulary In order to cover different period, two development sets are used. The first one is *newstest2008*. However, this corpus is two years older than the targeted time period. Thus a second development corpus is gathered by randomly sampling bunches of 5 consecutive sentences from the provided news data of 2010 and 2011.

To estimate a LM, the English vocabulary is first defined by including all tokens observed in the Europarl and news-commentary corpora. This vocabulary is then expanded with all words that occur more that 5 times in the French-English giga-corpus, and with the most frequent proper names taken from the monolingual news data of 2010 and 2011. This procedure results in a vocabulary around 500k words.

Language Model Training All the training data allowed in the constrained task are divided into 9 sets based on dates on genres. On each set, a standard 4-gram LM is estimated from the 500k word vocabulary with in-house tools using absolute discounting interpolated with lower order models (Kneser and Ney, 1995; Chen and Goodman, 1998).

All LMs except the one trained on the news corpora from 2010-2011 are first linearly interpolated. The associated coefficients are estimated so as to minimize the perplexity evaluated on the *dev2010-2011*. The resulting LM and the 2010-2011 LM are finally interpolated with *newstest2008* as development data. This two steps interpolation aims to avoid an overestimate of the weight associated to the 2010-2011 LM.

2.4 SYSTRAN Software, Inc. Single System

The data submitted by SYSTRAN were obtained by the SYSTRAN baseline system in combination with a *statistical post editing* (SPE) component.

The SYSTRAN system is traditionally classified as a rule-based system. However, over the decades, its development has always been driven by pragmatic considerations, progressively integrating many of the most efficient MT approaches and techniques. Nowadays, the baseline engine can be considered as a linguistic-oriented system making use of dependency analysis, general transfer rules as well as of large manually encoded dictionaries (100k – 800k entries per language pair).

The basic setup of the SPE component is identical to the one described in (L. Dugast and Koehn, 2007). A statistical translation model is trained on the rule-based translation of the source and the target side of the parallel corpus. This is done separately for each parallel corpus. Language models are trained on each target half of the parallel corpora and also on additional in-domain corpora. Moreover, the following measures – limiting unwanted statistical effects – were applied:

- Named entities are replaced by special tokens on both sides. This usually improves word alignment, since the vocabulary size is significantly reduced. In addition, entity translation is handled more reliably by the rule-based engine.
- The intersection of both vocabularies (i.e. vocabularies of the rule-based output and the reference translation) is used to produce an additional parallel corpus (whose target is identical to the source). This was added to the parallel text in order to improve word alignment.
- Singleton phrase pairs are deleted from the phrase table to avoid overfitting.
- Phrase pairs not containing the same number of entities on the source and the target side are also discarded.

- Phrase pairs appearing less than 2 times were pruned.

The SPE language model was trained 15M phrases from the news/europarl corpora, provided as training data for *WMT 2011*. Weights for these separate models were tuned by the MERT algorithm provided in the Moses toolkit (P. Koehn et al., 2007), using the provided news development set.

3 RWTH Aachen System Combination

System combination is used to produce consensus translations from multiple hypotheses produced with different translation engines that are better in terms of translation quality than any of the individual hypotheses. The basic concept of RWTH's approach to machine translation system combination has been described by Matusov et al. (2006; 2008). This approach includes an enhanced alignment and reordering framework. A lattice is built from the input hypotheses. The translation with the best score within the lattice according to a couple of statistical models is selected as consensus translation. A deeper description will be also given in the WMT11 system combination paper of RWTH Aachen University. For this task only the A2L framework has been used.

4 Experiments

We tried different system combinations with different sets of single systems and different optimization criteria. As RWTH has two different translation systems, we put the output of both systems into system combination. Although both systems have the same preprocessing, their hypotheses differ. Finally, we added for both RWTH systems two additional hypotheses to the system combination. The two hypotheses of Jane were optimized on different criteria. The first hypothesis was optimized on BLEU and the second one on TER−BLEU. The first RWTH phrase-based hypothesis was generated with force alignment, the second RWTH phrase-based hypothesis is a reranked version of the first one as described in 2.1.4. Compared to the other systems, the system by SYSTRAN has a completely different approach (see section 2.4). It is mainly based on a rule-based system. For the German→English pair, SYSTRAN achieves a lower BLEU score in each test set compared to the other groups. But since the SYSTRAN system is very different to the others, we still obtain an improvement when we add it also to system combination.

We obtain the best result from system combination of all seven systems, optimizing the parameters on BLEU. This system was the system we submitted to the WMT 2011 evaluation.

For each dev set we obtain an improvement compared to the best single systems. For newstest2008 and newstest2009 we get an improvement of 0.5 points in BLEU and 1.8 points in TER compared to the best single system of Karlsruhe Institute of Technology. For newstest2010 we get an improvement of 1.8 points in BLEU and 2.7 points in TER compared to the best single system of RWTH. The system combination weights optimized for the best run are listed in Table 2. We see that although the single system of SYSTRAN has the lowest BLEU scores, it gets the second highest system weight. This high value shows the influence of a completely different system. On the other hand, all RWTH systems are very similar, because of their same preprocessing and their small variations. Therefor the system combination parameter of all four systems by themselves are relatively small. The summarized "RWTH approach" system weight, though, is again on par with the other systems.

5 Conclusion

The four statistical machine translation systems of Karlsruhe Institute of Technology, RWTH Aachen and LIMSI and the very structural approach of SYSTRAN produce hypotheses with a huge variability compared to the others. Finally the RWTH Aachen system combination combined all single system hypotheses to one hypothesis with a higher BLEU compared to each single system. If the system combination implementation can handle enough single systems we would recommend to add all single systems to the system combination. Although the single system of SYSTRAN has the lowest BLEU scores and the RWTH single systems are similar we achieved the best result in using all single systems.

newstest2008		newstest2009		newstest2010		description
BLEU	TER	BLEU	TER	BLEU	TER	
22.73	60.73	22.50	59.82	25.26	57.37	sc (all systems) BLEU opt
22.61	60.60	22.28	59.39	25.07	56.95	sc (all systems - (1)) TER−BLEU opt
22.50	60.41	22.52	59.61	25.23	57.40	sc (all systems) TER−BLEU opt
22.19	60.09	22.05	59.31	24.74	56.89	sc (all systems - (4)) TER−BLEU opt
22.21	60.71	21.89	59.95	24.72	57.58	sc (all systems - (4,7)) TER−BLEU opt
22.22	60.45	21.79	59.72	24.32	57.59	sc (all systems - (3,4)) TER−BLEU opt
22.27	60.60	21.75	59.92	24.35	57.64	sc (all systems - (3,4)) BLEU opt
22.10	62.59	22.01	61.64	23.34	60.35	(1) Karlsruhe Institute of Technology
21.41	62.77	21.12	61.91	23.44	60.06	(2) RWTH PBT (FA) rerank +GW
21.11	62.96	21.06	62.16	23.29	60.26	(3) RWTH PBT (FA)
21.47	63.89	21.00	63.33	22.93	61.71	(4) RWTH jane + GW BLEU opt
20.89	61.05	20.36	60.47	23.42	58.31	(5) RWTH jane + GW TER−BLEU opt
20.33	64.50	19.79	64.91	21.97	61.44	(6) Limsi-CNRS
17.06	69.48	17.52	67.34	18.68	66.37	(7) SYSTRAN Software

Table 1: All systems for the WMT 2011 German→English translation task (truecase). BLEU and TER results are in percentage. FA denotes systems with phrase training, +GW the use of LDC data for the language model. sc denotes system combination.

system	weight
Karlsruhe Institute of Technology	0.350
RWTH PBT (FA) rerank +GW	0.001
RWTH PBT (FA)	0.046
RWTH jane + GW BLEU opt	0.023
RWTH jane + GW TER−BLEU opt	0.034
Limsi-CNRS	0.219
SYSTRAN Software	0.328

Table 2: Optimized systems weights for each system of the best system combination result.

Acknowledgments

This work was achieved as part of the QUAERO Programme, funded by OSEO, French State agency for innovation.

References

F. Casacuberta and E. Vidal. 2004. Machine translation with inferred stochastic finite-state transducers. *Computational Linguistics*, 30(3):205–225.

S.F. Chen and J.T. Goodman. 1998. An empirical study of smoothing techniques for language modeling. Technical Report TR-10-98, Computer Science Group, Harvard University.

D. Chiang. 2007. Hierarchical Phrase-Based Translation. *Computational Linguistics*, 33(2):201–228.

J.M. Crego and J.B. Mariño. 2007. Improving statistical MT by coupling reordering and decoding. *Machine Translation*, 20(3):199–215.

D. Déchelotte, O. Galibert G. Adda, A. Allauzen, J. Gauvain, H. Meynard, and F. Yvon. 2008. LIMSI's statistical translation systems for WMT'08. In *Proc. of the NAACL-HTL Statistical Machine Translation Workshop*, Columbus, Ohio.

L. Huang and D. Chiang. 2007. Forest Rescoring: Faster Decoding with Integrated Language Models. In *Proc. Annual Meeting of the Association for Computational Linguistics*, pages 144–151, Prague, Czech Republic, June.

T. Ward K. Papineni, S. Roukos and W. Zhu. 2002. Bleu:

a method for automatic evaluation of machine translation. In *ACL '02: Proc. of the 40th Annual Meeting on Association for Computational Linguistics*, pages 311–318. Association for Computational Linguistics.

R. Kneser and H. Ney. 1995. Improved backing-off for m-gram language modeling. In *Proceedings of the International Conference on Acoustics, Speech, and Signal Processing, ICASSP'95*, pages 181–184, Detroit, MI.

P. Koehn and K. Knight. 2003. Empirical Methods for Compound Splitting. In *Proceedings of European Chapter of the ACL (EACL 2009)*, pages 187–194.

J. Senellart L. Dugast and P. Koehn. 2007. Statistical post-editing on systran's rule-based translation system. In *Proceedings of the Second Workshop on Statistical Machine Translation*, StatMT '07, pages 220–223, Stroudsburg, PA, USA. Association for Computational Linguistics.

E. Matusov, N. Ueffing, and H. Ney. 2006. Computing Consensus Translation from Multiple Machine Translation Systems Using Enhanced Hypotheses Alignment. In *Conference of the European Chapter of the Association for Computational Linguistics (EACL)*, pages 33–40.

E. Matusov, G. Leusch, R.E. Banchs, N. Bertoldi, D. Dechelotte, M. Federico, M. Kolss, Y.-S. Lee, J.B. Mari no, M. Paulik, S. Roukos, H. Schwenk, and H. Ney. 2008. System Combination for Machine Translation of Spoken and Written Language. *IEEE Transactions on Audio, Speech and Language Processing*, 16(7):1222–1237.

J.A. Nelder and R. Mead. 1965. The Downhill Simplex Method. *Computer Journal*, 7:308.

J. Niehues and M. Kolss. 2009. A POS-Based Model for Long-Range Reorderings in SMT. In *Fourth Workshop on Statistical Machine Translation (WMT 2009)*, Athens, Greece.

F.J. Och and H. Ney. 2003. A Systematic Comparison of Various Statistical Alignment Models. *Computational Linguistics*, 29(1):19–51.

F.J. Och. 2003. Minimum Error Rate Training for Statistical Machine Translation. In *Proc. Annual Meeting of the Association for Computational Linguistics*, pages 160–167, Sapporo, Japan, July.

A. Birch P. Koehn, H. Hoang, C. Callison-Burch, M. Federico, N. Bertoldi, B. Cowan, W. Shen, C. Moran, R. Zens, C. Dyer, O. Bojar, A. Constantin, and E. Herbst. 2007. Moses: open source toolkit for statistical machine translation. In *Proceedings of the 45th Annual Meeting of the ACL on Interactive Poster and Demonstration Sessions*, ACL '07, pages 177–180, Stroudsburg, PA, USA. Association for Computational Linguistics.

K. Rottmann and S. Vogel. 2007. Word Reordering in Statistical Machine Translation with a POS-Based Distortion Model. In *TMI*, Skövde, Sweden.

H. Schmid. 1994. Probabilistic Part-of-Speech Tagging Using Decision Trees. In *International Conference on New Methods in Language Processing*, Manchester, UK.

A. Stolcke. 2002. SRILM - an extensible language modeling toolkit. In *Proc. Int. Conf. on Spoken Language Processing*, volume 2, pages 901–904, Denver, Colorado, USA, September.

C. Tillmann. 2004. A unigram orientation model for statistical machine translation. In *Proceedings of HLT-NAACL 2004*, pages 101–104. Association for Computational Linguistics.

A. Venugopal, A. Zollman, and A. Waibel. 2005. Training and Evaluation Error Minimization Rules for Statistical Machine Translation. In *Workshop on Data-drive Machine Translation and Beyond (WPT-05)*, Ann Arbor, MI.

D. Vilar, S. Stein, M. Huck, and H. Ney. 2010. Jane: Open Source Hierarchical Translation, Extended with Reordering and Lexicon Models. In *ACL 2010 Joint Fifth Workshop on Statistical Machine Translation and Metrics MATR*, pages 262–270, Uppsala, Sweden, July.

S. Vogel. 2003. SMT Decoder Dissected: Word Reordering. In *Int. Conf. on Natural Language Processing and Knowledge Engineering*, Beijing, China.

J. Wuebker, A. Mauser, and H. Ney. 2010. Training Phrase Translation Models with Leaving-One-Out. In *Proceedings of the 48th Annual Meeting of the Assoc. for Computational Linguistics*, pages 475–484, Uppsala, Sweden, July.

R. Zens and H. Ney. 2006. N-gram Posterior Probabilities for Statistical Machine Translation. In *Human Language Technology Conf. / North American Chapter of the Assoc. for Computational Linguistics Annual Meeting (HLT-NAACL), Workshop on Statistical Machine Translation*, pages 72–77, New York City, June.

R. Zens and H. Ney. 2008. Improvements in Dynamic Programming Beam Search for Phrase-based Statistical Machine Translation. In *Proc. of the Int. Workshop on Spoken Language Translation (IWSLT)*, Honolulu, Hawaii, October.

CMU Syntax-Based Machine Translation at WMT 2011

Greg Hanneman and **Alon Lavie**
Language Technologies Institute
Carnegie Mellon University
Pittsburgh, PA 15213 USA
{ghannema, alavie}@cs.cmu.edu

Abstract

We present the Carnegie Mellon University Stat-XFER group submission to the WMT 2011 shared translation task. We built a hybrid syntactic MT system for French–English using the Joshua decoder and an automatically acquired SCFG. New work for this year includes training data selection and grammar filtering. Expanded training data selection significantly increased translation scores and lowered OOV rates, while results on grammar filtering were mixed.

1 Introduction

During the past year, the statistical transfer machine translation group at Carnegie Mellon University has continued its work on large-scale syntactic MT systems based on automatically acquired synchronous context-free grammars (SCFGs). For the 2011 Workshop on Machine Translation, we built a hybrid MT system, including both syntactic and non-syntactic rules, and submitted it as a constrained entry to the French–English translation task. This is our fourth yearly submission to the WMT shared translation task.

In design and construction, the system is similar to our submission from last year's workshop (Hanneman et al., 2010), with changes in the methods we employed for training data selection and SCFG filtering. Continuing WMT's general trend, we worked with more data than in previous years, basing our 2011 system on 13.9 million sentences of parallel French–English training data and an English language model of 1.8 billion words. Decoding was carried out in Joshua (Li et al., 2009), an open-source framework for parsing-based MT. We managed our experiments with LoonyBin (Clark and Lavie, 2010), an open-source tool for defining, modifying, and running complex experimental pipelines.

We describe our system-building process in more detail in Section 2. In Section 3, we evaluate the system's performance on WMT development sets and examine the aftermath of training data selection and grammar filtering. Section 4 concludes with possible directions for future work.

2 System Construction

2.1 Training Data Selection

WMT 2011's provided French–English training data consisted of 36.8 million sentence pairs from the Europarl, news commentary, UN documents, and Giga-FrEn corpora (Table 1). The first three of these are, for the most part, clean data resources that have been successfully employed as MT corpora for a number of years. The Giga-FrEn corpus, though the largest, is also the least precise, as its Web-crawled data sources are less homogeneous and less structured than the other corpora. Nevertheless, Pino et al. (2010) found significant improvements in French–English MT output quality by including it. Our goal for this year was to strike a middle ground: to avoid computational difficulties in using the entire 36.8 million sentence pairs of training data, but to mine the Giga-FrEn corpus for sentences to increase our system's vocabulary coverage.

Our method of training data selection proceeded as follows. We first tokenized all the parallel training

Proceedings of the 6th Workshop on Statistical Machine Translation, pages 365–371,
Edinburgh, Scotland, UK, July 30–31, 2011.

Corpus	Released	Used
Europarl	1,825,077	1,614,111
News commentary	115,562	95,138
UN documents	12,317,600	9,352,232
Giga-FrEn	22,520,400	2,839,466
Total	**36,778,639**	**13,900,947**

Table 1: Total number of training sentence pairs released, by corpus, and the number used in building our system.

data using the Stanford parser's tokenizer (Klein and Manning, 2003) for English and our own in-house script for French. We then passed the Europarl, news commentary, and UN data through a filtering script that removed lines longer than 95 tokens in either language, empty lines, lines with excessively imbalanced length ratios, and lines containing tokens of more than 25 characters in either language. From the filtered data, we computed a list of the source-side vocabulary words along with their frequency counts. Next, we searched the Giga-FrEn corpus for relatively short lines on the source side (up to 50 tokens long) that contained either a new vocabulary word or a word that had been previously seen fewer than 20 times. Such lines were added to the filtered training data to make up our system's final parallel training corpus.

The number of sentences retained from each data source is listed in Table 1; in the end, we trained our system from 13.9 million parallel sentences. With the Giga-FrEn data included, the source side of our parallel corpus had a vocabulary of just over 1.9 million unique words, compared with a coverage of 545,000 words without using Giga-FrEn.

We made the decision to leave the training data in mixed case for our entire system-building process. At the cost of slightly sparser estimates for word alignments and translation probabilities, a mixed-case system avoids the extra step of building a statistical recaser to treat our system's output.

2.2 Grammar Extraction and Scoring

Once we had assembled the final training corpus, we annotated it with statistical word alignments and constituent parse trees on both sides. Unidirectional word alignments were provided by MGIZA++ (Gao and Vogel, 2008), then symmetrized with the grow-diag-final-and heuristic (Koehn et al., 2005). For generating parse trees, we used the French and English grammars of the Berkeley statistical parser (Petrov and Klein, 2007).

Except for minor bug fixes, our method for extracting and scoring a translation grammar remains the same as in our WMT 2010 submission. We extracted both syntactic and non-syntactic portions of the translation grammar. The non-syntactic grammar was extracted from the parallel corpus and word alignments following the standard heuristics of phrase-based SMT (Koehn et al., 2003). The syntactic grammar was produced using the method of Lavie et al. (2008), which decomposes each pair of word-aligned parse trees into a series of minimal SCFG rules. The word alignments are first generalized to node alignments, where nodes s and t are aligned between the source and target parse trees if all word alignments in the yield of s land within the yield of t and vice versa. Minimal SCFG rules are derived from adjacent levels of node alignments: the labels from each pair of aligned nodes forms a rule's left-hand side, and the right-hand side is made up of the labels from the frontier of aligned nodes encountered when walking the left-hand side's subtrees. Within a phrase length limit, each aligned node pair generate an all-terminal phrase pair rule as well.

Since both grammars are extracted from the same Viterbi word alignments using similar alignment consistency constraints, the phrase pair rules from the syntactic grammar make up a subset of the rules extracted according to phrase-based SMT heuristics. We thus share instance counts between identical phrases extracted in both grammars, then delete the non-syntactic versions. Remaining non-syntactic phrase pairs are converted to SCFG rules, with the phrase pair forming the right-hand side and the dummy label PHR::PHR as the left-hand side. Except for the dummy label, all nonterminals in the final SCFG are made up of a syntactic category label from French joined with a syntactic category label from English, as extracted in the syntactic grammar. A sampling of extracted SCFG rules is shown in Figure 1.

The combined grammar was scored according to the 22 translation model features we used last year. For a generic SCFG rule of the form $\ell_s :: \ell_t \rightarrow$

$$\text{PHR} :: \text{PHR} \rightarrow [\text{, ainsi qu'}] :: [\text{as well as}]$$

$$\text{V} :: \text{VBN} \rightarrow [\text{modifiées}] :: [\text{modified}]$$

$$\text{NP} :: \text{NP} \rightarrow [\text{les conflits armés}] :: [\text{armed conflict}]$$

$$\text{AP} :: \text{SBAR} \rightarrow [\text{tel qu' VPpart}^1] :: [\text{as VP}^1]$$

$$\text{NP} :: \text{NP} \rightarrow [\text{D}^1\ \text{N}^2\ \text{A}^3] :: [\text{CD}^1\ \text{JJ}^3\ \text{NNS}^2]$$

Figure 1: Sample extracted SCFG rules. They include non-syntactic phrase pairs, single-word and multi-word syntactic phrase pairs, partially lexicalized hierarchical rules, and fully abstract hierarchical rules.

$[r_s] :: [r_t]$, we computed 11 maximum-likelihood features as follows:

- Phrase translation scores $P(r_s \mid r_t)$ and $P(r_t \mid r_s)$ for phrase pair rules, using the larger non-syntactic instance counts for rules that were also extracted syntactically.
- Hierarchical translation scores $P(r_s \mid r_t)$ and $P(r_t \mid r_s)$ for syntactic rules with nonterminals on the right-hand side.
- Labeling scores $P(\ell_s :: \ell_t \mid r_s)$, $P(\ell_s :: \ell_t \mid r_t)$, and $P(\ell_s :: \ell_t \mid r_s, r_t)$ for syntactic rules.
- "Not syntactically labelable" scores $P(\ell_s :: \ell_t = \text{PHR} :: \text{PHR} \mid r_s)$ and $P(\ell_s :: \ell_t = \text{PHR} :: \text{PHR} \mid r_t)$, with additive smoothing ($n = 1$), for all rules.
- Bidirectional lexical scores for all rules with lexical items, calculated from a unigram lexicon over Viterbi-aligned word pairs as in the Moses decoder (Koehn et al., 2007).

We also included the following 10 binary indicator features using statistics local to each rule:

- Three low-count features that equal 1 when the extracted frequency of the rule is exactly equal to 1, 2, or 3.
- A syntactic feature that equals 1 when the rule's label is syntactic, and a corresponding non-syntactic feature that equals 1 when the rule's label is PHR::PHR.
- Five rule format features that equal 1 when the rule's right-hand side has a certain composition. If a_s and a_t are true when the source and target sides contain only nonterminals, respectively, our rule format features are equal to a_s, a_t, $a_s \wedge \bar{a}_t$, $\bar{a}_s \wedge a_t$, and $\bar{a}_s \wedge \bar{a}_t$.

Finally, our model includes a glue rule indicator feature that equals 1 when the rule is a generic glue rule. In the Joshua decoder, glue rules monotonically stitch together adjacent parsed translation fragments at no model cost.

2.3 Language Modeling

This year, our constrained-track system made use of part of the English Gigaword data, along with other provided text, in its target-side language model. From among the data released directly for WMT 2011, we used the English side of the Europarl, news commentary, French–English UN document, and English monolingual news corpora. From the English Gigaword corpus, we included the entire Xinhua portion and the most recent 13 million sentences of the AP Wire portion. Some of these corpora contain many lines that are repeated a disproportionate number of times — the monolingual news corpus in particular, when filtered to only one occurrence of each sentence, reaches only 27% of its original line count. As part of preparing our language modeling data, we deduplicated both the English news and the UN documents, the corpora with the highest percentages of repeated sentences. We also removed lines containing more than 750 characters (about 125 average English words) before tokenization.

The final prepared corpus was made up of approximately 1.8 billion words of running text. We built a 5-gram language model from it with the SRI language modeling toolkit (Stolcke, 2002). To match the treatment given to the training data, the language model was also built in mixed case.

2.4 Grammar Filtering for Decoding

As is to be expected from a training corpus of 13.9 million sentence pairs, the grammars we extract according to the procedure of Section 2.2 are quite large: approximately 2.53 billion non-syntactic and 440 million syntactic rule instances, for a combined grammar of 1.26 billion unique rules. In preparation for tuning or decoding, we are faced with the engineering challenge of selecting a subset of the grammar that contains useful rules and fits in a reasonable amount of memory.

Before even extracting a syntactic grammar, we passed the automatically generated parse trees on the training corpus through a small tag-correction script as a pre-step. In previous experimentation, we noticed that a surprising proportion of cardinal numbers in English had been tagged with labels other than CD, their correct tag. We also found errors in labeling marks of punctuation in both English and French, when again the canonical labels are unambiguous. To fix these errors, we forcibly overwrote the labels of English tokens made up of only digits with CD, and we overwrote the labels of 25 English and 24 French marks of punctuation or other symbols with the appropriate tag as defined by the relevant treebank tagging guidelines.

After grammar extraction and combination of syntactic and non-syntactic rules, we ran an additional filtering step to reduce derivational ambiguity in the case where the same SCFG right-hand side appeared with more than one left-hand-side label. For each right-hand side, we sorted its possible labels by extracted frequency, then threw out the labels in the bottom 10% of the left-hand-side distribution.

Finally, we ran a main grammar filtering step prior to tuning or decoding, experimenting with two different filtering methods. In both cases, the phrase pair rules in the grammar were split off and filtered so that only those whose source sides completely matched the tuning or test set were retained.

The first, more naive grammar filtering method sorted all hierarchical rules by extracted frequency, then retained the most frequent 10,000 rules to join all matching phrase pair rules in the final translation grammar. This is similar to the basic grammar filtering we performed for our WMT 2010 submission. It is based on the rationale that the most frequently extracted rules in the parallel training data are likely to be the most reliably estimated and also frequently used in translating a new data set. However, it also passes through a disproportionate number of fully abstract rules — that is, rules whose right-hand sides are made up entirely of nonterminals — which can apply more recklessly on the test set because they are not lexically grounded.

Our second, more advanced method of filtering made two improvements over the naive approach. First, it controlled for the imbalance of hierarchical rules by splitting the grammar's partially lexicalized rules into a separate group that can be filtered independently. Second, it applied a lexical-match filter such that a partially lexicalized rule was retained only if all its lexicalized source phrases up to bigrams matched the intended tuning or testing set. The final translation grammar in this case was made up of three parts: all phrase pair rules matching the test set (as before), the 100,000 most frequently extracted partially lexicalized rules whose bigrams match the test set, and the 2000 most frequently extracted fully abstract rules.

3 Experimental Results and Analysis

We tuned each system variant on the newstest2008 data set, using the Z-MERT package (Zaidan, 2009) for minimum error-rate training to the BLEU metric. We ran development tests on the newstest2009 and newstest2010 data sets; Table 2 reports the results obtained according to various automatic metrics. The evaluation consists of case-insensitive scoring according to METEOR 1.0 (Lavie and Denkowski, 2009) tuned to HTER with the exact, stemming, and synonymy modules enabled, case-insensitive BLEU (Papineni et al., 2002) as implemented by the NIST `mteval-v13` script, and case-insensitive TER 0.7.25 (Snover et al., 2006).

Table 2 gives comparative results for two major systems: one based on our WMT 2011 data selection as outlined in Section 2.1, and one based on the smaller WMT 2010 training data that we used last year (8.6 million sentence pairs). Each system was run with the two grammar filtering variants described in Section 2.4: the 10,000 most frequently extracted hierarchical rules of any type ("10k"), and a combination of the 2000 most frequently extracted abstract rules and the 100,000 most frequently extracted partially lexicalized rules that matched the test set ("2k+100k"). Our primary submission to the WMT 2011 shared task was the fourth line of Table 2 ("WMT 2011 2k+100k"); we also made a constrastive submission with the system from the second line ("WMT 2010 2k+100k").

Using part of the Giga-FrEn data — along with the additions to the Europarl, news commentary, and UN document courses released since last year

System	newstest2009 METEOR	BLEU	TER	newstest2010 METEOR	BLEU	TER
WMT 2010 10k	54.94	24.77	56.53	56.66	25.78	55.06
WMT 2010 2k+100k	55.16	24.88	56.19	56.89	26.05	54.66
WMT 2011 10k	55.82	26.02	54.77	58.13	27.71	52.96
WMT 2011 2k+100k	55.77	26.01	54.70	57.88	27.38	53.04

Table 2: Development test results for systems based on WMT 2010 data (without the Giga-FrEn corpus) and WMT 2011 data (with some Giga-FrEn). The fourth line is our primary shared-task submission.

Applications	10k	2k+100k
Unique rules	1,305	1,994
Rule instances	14,539	12,130

Table 3: Summary of 2011 system syntactic rule applications on both test sets.

— is beneficial to translation quality, as there is a clear improvement in metric scores between the 2010 and 2011 systems. Our BLEU score improvements of 1.2 to 1.9 points are statistically significant according to the paired bootstrap resampling method (Koehn, 2004) with $n = 1000$ and $p < 0.01$. They are also larger than the 0.7- to 1.1-point gains reported by Pino et al. (2010) when the full Giga-FrEn was added. The 2011 system also shows a significant reduction in the out-of-vocabulary (OOV) rate on both test sets: 38% and 47% fewer OOV types, and 44% and 45% fewer OOV tokens, when compared to the 2010 system.

Differences between grammar filtering techniques, on the other hand, are much less significant according to all three metrics. Under paired bootstrap resampling on the newstest2009 set, the grammar variants in both the 2010 and 2011 systems are statistically equivalent according to BLEU score. On newstest2010, the 2k+100k grammar improves over the 10k version ($p < 0.01$) in the 2010 system, but the situation is reversed in the 2011 system.

We investigated differences in grammar use with an analysis of rule applications in the two variants of the 2011 system, the results of which are summarized in Table 3. Though the configuration with the 2k+100k grammar does apply syntactic rules 20% more frequently than its 10k counterpart, the 10k system uses overall 53% more unique rules. One contributing factor to this situation could be that the fully abtract rule cutoff is set too low compared to the increase in partially lexicalized rules. The effect of the 2k+100k filtering is to reduce the number of abstract rules from 4000 to 2000 while increasing the number of partially lexicalized rules from 6000 to 100,000. However, we find that the 10k system makes heavy use of some short, meaningful abstract rules that were excluded from the 2k+100k system. The 2k+100k grammar, by contrast, includes a long tail of less frequently used partially lexicalized grammar rules.

In practice, there is a balance between the use of syntactic and non-syntactic grammar rules during decoding. We highlight an example of how both types of rules work together in Figure 2, which shows our primary system's translation of part of newstest2009 sentence 2271. The French source text is given in italics and segmented into phrases. The SCFG rules used in translation are shown above each phrase, where numerical superscripts on the nonterminal labels indicate those constituents' relative ordering in the original French sentence. (Monotonic glue rules are not shown.) While non-syntactic rules can be used for short-distance reordering and fixed phrases, such as *téléphones mobiles* ↔ *mobile phones*, the model prefers syntactic translations for more complicated patterns, such as the head–children reversal in *appareils musicaux portables* ↔ *portable music devices*.

4 Conclusions and Future Work

Compared to last year, the two main differences in our current WMT submission are: (1) a new training data selection strategy aimed at increasing system vocabulary without hugely increasing corpus size, and (2) a new method of grammar filtering that emphasizes partially lexicalized rules over fully ab-

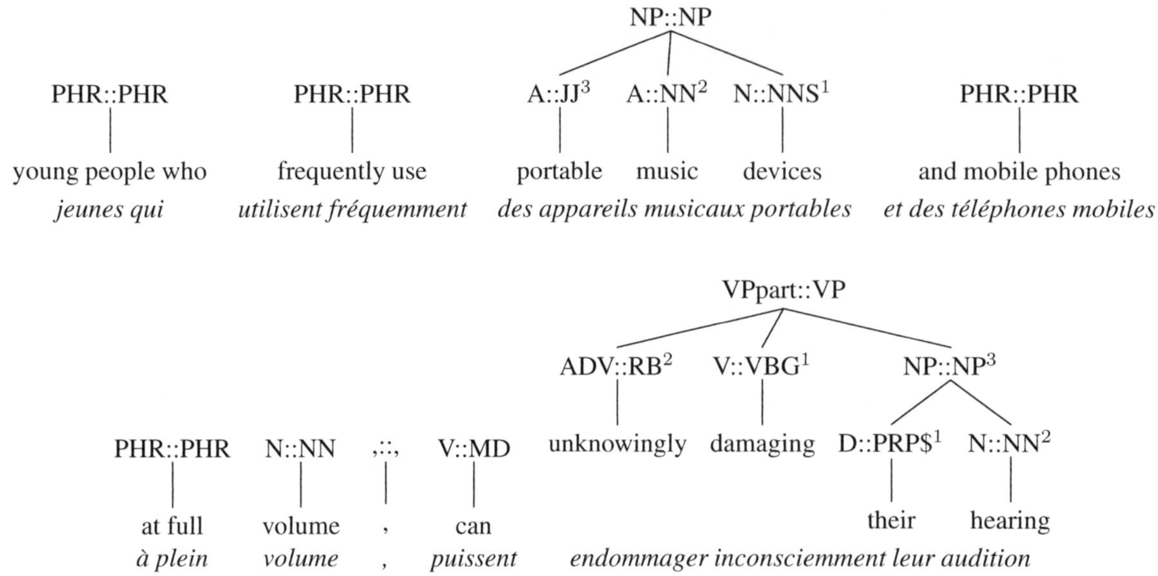

Figure 2: Our primary submission's translation of a partial sentence from the newstest2009 set, showing a combination of syntactic and non-syntactic rules.

stract ones.

Based on the results presented in Section 3, we feel confident in declaring vocabulary-based filtering of the Giga-FrEn corpus a success. By increasing the size of our parallel corpus by 26%, we more than tripled the number of unique words appearing in the source text. In conjunction with supplements to the Europarl, news commentary, and UN document corpora, this improvement led to 44% fewer OOV tokens at decoding time on two different test sets, as well as a boost in automatic metric scores of 0.6 METEOR, 1.2 BLEU, and 1.5 TER points compared to last year's system. We expect to employ similar data selection techniques when building future systems, especially as the amount of parallel data available continues to increase.

We did not, however, find significant improvements in translation quality by changing the grammar filtering method. As discussed in Section 3, limiting the grammar to only 2000 fully abstract rules may not have been enough, since additional abstract rules applied fairly frequently in test data if they were available. We plan to experiment with larger filtering cutoffs in future work. A complementary solution could be to increase the number of partially lexicalized rules. Although we found mixed results in their application within our current system, the success of Hiero-derived MT systems (Chiang, 2005; Chiang, 2010) shows that high translation quality can be achieved with rules that are only partially abstract. A major difference between such systems and our current implementation is that ours, at 102,000 rules, has a much smaller grammar.

Acknowledgments

This research was supported in part by U.S. National Science Foundation grants IIS-0713402 and IIS-0915327, as well as by the DARPA GALE program. Thanks to Kenneth Heafield for processing the English monolingual data and building the language model file, and to Jonathan Clark for LoonyBin support and bug fixes. We also thank Yahoo! for the use of the M45 research computing cluster, where we ran many steps of our experimental pipeline.

References

David Chiang. 2005. A hierarchical phrase-based model for statistical machine translation. In *Proceedings of the 43rd Annual Meeting of the ACL*, pages 263–270, Ann Arbor, MI, June.

David Chiang. 2010. Learning to translate with source and target syntax. In *Proceedings of the 48th Annual Meeting of the Association for Computational Linguistics*, pages 1443–1452, Uppsala, Sweden, July.

Jonathan Clark and Alon Lavie. 2010. LoonyBin: Keeping language technologists sane through automated management of experimental (hyper)workflows. In *Proceedings of the Seventh International Conference on Language Resources and Evaluation*, pages 1301–1308, Valletta, Malta, May.

Qin Gao and Stephan Vogel. 2008. Parallel implementations of word alignment tool. In *Software Engineering, Testing, and Quality Assurance for Natural Language Processing*, pages 49–57, Columbus, OH, June.

Greg Hanneman, Jonathan Clark, and Alon Lavie. 2010. Improved features and grammar selection for syntax-based MT. In *Proceedings of the Joint Fifth Workshop on Statistical Machine Translation and MetricsMATR*, pages 82–87, Uppsala, Sweden, July.

Dan Klein and Christopher D. Manning. 2003. Fast exact inference with a factored model for natural language parsing. In *Advances in Neural Information Processing Systems 15*, pages 3–10. MIT Press, Cambridge, MA.

Philipp Koehn, Franz Josef Och, and Daniel Marcu. 2003. Statistical phrase-based translation. In *Proceedings of HLT-NAACL 2003*, pages 48–54, Edmonton, Alberta, May–June.

Philipp Koehn, Amittai Axelrod, Alexandra Birch Mayne, Chris Callison-Burch, Miles Osborne, and David Talbot. 2005. Edinburgh system description for the 2005 IWSLT speech translation evaluation. In *Proceedings of IWSLT 2005*, Pittsburgh, PA, October.

Philipp Koehn, Hieu Hoang, Alexandra Birch, Chris Callison-Burch, Marcello Federico, Nicola Bertoldi, Brooke Cowan, Wade Shen, Christine Moran, Richard Zens, Chris Dyer, Ondrej Bojar, Alexandra Constantin, and Evan Herbst. 2007. Moses: Open source toolkit for statistical machine translation. In *Proceedings of the ACL 2007 Demo and Poster Sessions*, pages 177–180, Prague, Czech Republic, June.

Philipp Koehn. 2004. Statistical significance tests for machine translation evaluation. In *Proceedings of EMNLP 2004*, pages 388–395, Barcelona, Spain, July.

Alon Lavie and Michael J. Denkowski. 2009. The METEOR metric for automatic evaluation of machine translation. *Machine Translation*, 23(2–3):105–115.

Alon Lavie, Alok Parlikar, and Vamshi Ambati. 2008. Syntax-driven learning of sub-sentential translation equivalents and translation rules from parsed parallel corpora. In *Proceedings of the Second ACL Workshop on Syntax and Structure in Statistical Translation*, pages 87–95, Columbus, OH, June.

Zhifei Li, Chris Callison-Burch, Chris Dyer, Juri Ganitkevitch, Sanjeev Khudanpur, Lane Schwartz, Wren N.G. Thornton, Jonathan Weese, and Omar F. Zaidan. 2009. Joshua: An open source toolkit for parsing-based machine translation. In *Proceedings of the Fourth Workshop on Statistical Machine Translation*, pages 135–139, Athens, Greece, March.

Kishore Papineni, Salim Roukos, Todd Ward, and Wei-Jing Zhu. 2002. BLEU: A method for automatic evalution of machine translation. In *Proceedings of the 40th Annual Meeting of the Association for Computational Linguistics*, pages 311–318, Philadelphia, PA, July.

Slav Petrov and Dan Klein. 2007. Improved inference for unlexicalized parsing. In *Proceedings of NAACL HLT 2007*, pages 404–411, Rochester, NY, April.

Juan Pino, Gonzalo Iglesias, Adrià de Gispert, Graeme Blackwood, Jaime Brunning, and William Byrne. 2010. The CUED HiFST system for the WMT10 translation shared task. In *Proceedings of the Joint Fifth Workshop on Statistical Machine Translation and MetricsMATR*, pages 155–160, Uppsala, Sweden, July.

Matthew Snover, Bonnie Dorr, Richard Schwartz, Linnea Micciulla, and John Makhoul. 2006. A study of translation edit rate with targeted human annotation. In *Proceedings of the Seventh Conference of the Association for Machine Translation in the Americas*, pages 223–231, Cambridge, MA, August.

Andreas Stolcke. 2002. SRILM — an extensible language modeling toolkit. In *Proceedings of the Seventh International Conference on Spoken Language Processing*, pages 901–904, Denver, CO, September.

Omar F. Zaidan. 2009. Z-MERT: A fully configurable open source tool for minimum error rate training of machine translation systems. *The Prague Bulletin of Mathematical Linguistics*, 91:79–88.

The Uppsala-FBK systems at WMT 2011

Christian Hardmeier
Jörg Tiedemann
Uppsala universitet
Inst. för lingvistik och filologi
Uppsala, Sweden
first.last@lingfil.uu.se

Markus Saers
Human Language
Technology Center
Hong Kong Univ. of
Science & Technology
masaers@cs.ust.hk

Marcello Federico
Mathur Prashant
Fondazione Bruno Kessler
Human Language Technologies
Trento, Italy
lastname@fbk.eu

Abstract

This paper presents our submissions to the shared translation task at WMT 2011. We created two largely independent systems for English-to-French and Haitian Creole-to-English translation to evaluate different features and components from our ongoing research on these language pairs. Key features of our systems include anaphora resolution, hierarchical lexical reordering, data selection for language modelling, linear transduction grammars for word alignment and syntax-based decoding with monolingual dependency information.

1 English to French

Our submission to the English-French task was a phrase-based Statistical Machine Translation based on the Moses decoder (Koehn et al., 2007). Phrase tables were separately trained on Europarl, news commentary and UN data and then linearly interpolated with uniform weights. For language modelling, we used 5-gram models trained with the IRSTLM toolkit (Federico et al., 2008) on the monolingual News corpus and parts of the English-French 10^9 corpus. More unusual features of our system included a special component to handle pronominal anaphora and the hierarchical lexical reordering model by Galley and Manning (2008). Selected features of our system will be discussed in depth in the following sections.

1.1 Handling pronominal anaphora

Pronominal anaphora is the use of pronominal expressions to refer to "something previously mentioned in the discourse" (Strube, 2006). It is a very common phenomenon found in almost all kinds of texts. Anaphora can be local to a sentence, or it can cross sentence boundaries. Standard SMT methods do not handle this phenomenon in a satisfactory way at present: For sentence-internal anaphora, they depend on the n-gram language model with its limited history, while cross-sentence anaphora is left to chance. We therefore added a word-dependency model (Hardmeier and Federico, 2010) to our system to handle anaphora explicitly.

Our processing of anaphoric pronouns follows the procedure outlined by Hardmeier and Federico (2010). We use the open-source coreference resolution system BART (Broscheit et al., 2010) to link pronouns to their antecedents in the text. Coreference links are handled differently depending on whether or not they cross sentence boundaries. If a coreference link points to a previous sentence, we process the sentence containing the antecedent with the SMT system and look up the translation of the antecedent in the translated output. If the coreference link is sentence-internal, the translation lookup is done dynamically by the decoder during search. In either case, the word-dependency model adds a feature function to the decoder score representing the probability of a particular pronoun choice given the translation of the antecedent.

In our English-French system, this model was only applied to the inanimate pronouns *it* and *they*, which seemed to be the most promising candidates for improvement since their French equivalents require gender marking. It was trained on data automatically annotated for anaphora taken from the news-commentary corpus, and the vocabulary of the predicted pronouns was limited to words recognised as pronouns by the POS tagger.

Proceedings of the 6th Workshop on Statistical Machine Translation, pages 372–378,
Edinburgh, Scotland, UK, July 30–31, 2011. ©2011 Association for Computational Linguistics

1.2 Hierarchical lexical reordering

The basic word order model of SMT penalises any divergence between the order of the words in the input sentence and the order of their translation equivalents in the MT output. All reordering must thus be driven by the language model when no other reordering model is present. Lexical reordering models making certain word order choices in the MT output conditional on the identity of the words involved have been a standard component in SMT for some years. The lexical reordering model usually employed in the Moses decoder was implemented by Koehn et al. (2005). Adopting the perspective of the SMT decoder, which produces the target sentence from left to right while covering source phrases in free order, the model distinguishes between three ordering classes, *monotone*, *swap* and *discontinuous*, depending on whether the source phrases giving rise to the two last target phrases emitted were adjacent in the same order, adjacent in swapped order or separated by other source words. Probabilities for each ordering class given source and target phrase are estimated from a word-aligned training corpus and integrated into MT decoding as extra feature functions.

In our submission, we used the hierarchical lexical reordering model proposed by Galley and Manning (2008) and recently implemented in the Moses decoder.[1] This model uses the same approach of classifying movements as *monotone*, *swap* or *discontinuous*, but unlike the phrase-based model, it does not require the source language phrases to be strictly adjacent in order to be counted as *monotone* or *swap*. Instead, a phrase can be recognised as adjacent to, or swapped with, a contiguous block of source words that has been segmented into multiple phrases. Contiguous phrase blocks are recognised by the decoder with a shift-reduce parsing algorithm. As a result, fewer jumps are labelled with the uninformative *discontinuous* class.

1.3 Data selection from the WMT Giga corpus

One of the supplied language resources for this evaluation is the French-English WMT Giga corpus,

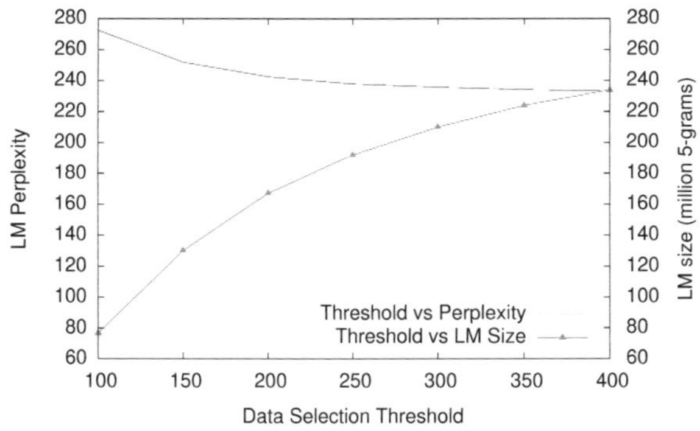

Figure 1: Perplexity and size of language models trained on data of the WMT Giga corpus that were selected using different perplexity thresholds.

aka 10^9 corpus, a large collection of parallel sentences crawled from Canadian and European Union sources. While this corpus was too large to be used for model training with the means at our disposal, we exploited it as a source of parallel data for translation model training as well as monolingual French data for the language model by filtering it down to a manageable size. In order to extract sentences close to the news translation task, we applied a simple data selection procedure based on perplexity. Sentence pairs were selected from the WMT Giga corpus if the perplexity of their French part with respect to a language model (LM) trained on French news data was below a given threshold. The rationale is that text sentences which are better predictable by the LM should be closer to the news domain. The threshold was set in a way to capture enough novel n-grams, from one side, but also to avoid adding too many irrelevant n-grams. It was tuned by training a 5-gram LM on the selected data and checking its size and its perplexity on a development set. In figure 1 we plot perplexity and size of the WMT Giga LM for different values of the data-selection threshold. Perplexities are computed on the newstest2009 set. As a good perplexity-size trade-off, the threshold 250 was chosen to estimate an additional 5-gram LM (WMT Giga 250) that was interpolated with the original News LM. The resulting improvement in perplexity is reported in table 1. For translation model data, a perplexity threshold of 159 was applied.

[1]The hierarchical lexical reordering model was implemented in Moses during MT Marathon 2010 by Christian Hardmeier, Gabriele Musillo, Nadi Tomeh, Ankit Srivastava, Sara Stymne and Marcello Federico.

LM	*Perplexity*	*OOV rate*
News	*146.84*	*0.82*
News + WMT Giga 250	*130.23*	*0.71*

Table 1: Perplexity reduction after interpolating the News LM with data selected from the 10^9 corpus.

	newstest 2009	2010	2011
Primary submission	0.246	0.286	0.284
w/o Anaphora handling	0.246	0.286	0.284
WMT Giga data			
w/o LM	0.244	0.289	0.280
w/o TM	0.247	0.286	0.282
w/o LM and TM	0.247	0.289	0.278
Lexical reordering			
phrase-based reo	0.239	0.281	0.275
no lexical reo	0.239	0.281	0.275
with LDC data	0.254	0.293	0.291

Table 2: Ablation test results (case-sensitive BLEU)

1.4 Results and Ablation tests

Owing to time constraints, we were not able to run thorough tests on our system before submitting it to the evaluation campaign. We therefore evaluated the various components included in a *post hoc* fashion by running ablation tests. In each test, we left out one of the system components to identify its effect on the overall performance. The results of these tests are reported in table 2.

Performance-wise, the most important particularity of our SMT system was the hierarchical lexical reordering model, which led to a sizeable improvement of 0.7, 0.5 and 0.9 BLEU points for the 2009, 2010 and 2011 test sets, respectively. We had previously seen negative results when trying to apply the same model to English-German SMT, so its performance seems to be strongly dependent on the language pair it is used with.

Compared to the scores obtained using the full system, the anaphora handling system did not have any effect on the BLEU scores. This result is similar to our result for English-German translation (Hardmeier and Federico, 2010). Unfortunately, for English-French, the negative results extends to the pronoun translation scores (not reported here), where slightly higher recall with the word-dependency model was overcompensated by degraded precision, so the outcome of the experiments clearly suggests that the anaphora handling procedure is in need of improvement.

The effect of the WMT Giga language model differs among the test sets. For the 2009 and 2011 test sets, it results in an improvement of 0.2 and 0.4 BLEU points, respectively, while the 2010 test set fares better without this additional language model. However, it should be noted that there may be a problem with the 2010 test set and the News language model, which was used as a component in all our systems. In particular, upgrading the News LM data from last year's to this year's release led to an improvement of 4 BLEU points on the 2010 test set and an unrealistically low perplexity of 73 as compared to 130 for the 2009 test set, which makes us suspect that the latest News LM data may be tainted with data from the 2010 test corpus. If this is the case, the 2010 test set should be considered unreliable for LM evaluation. The benefit of adding WMT Giga data to the translation model is less clear. For the 2009 and 2010 test sets, this leads to a slight degradation, but for the 2011 corpus, we obtained a small improvement.

Our shared task submission did not use the French Gigaword corpus from the Linguistic Data Consortium (LDC2009T28), which is not freely available to sites without LDC membership. After the submission, we ran a contrastive experiment including a 5-gram model trained on this corpus, which led to a sizeable improvement of 0.7–0.8 BLEU points across all test sets.

2 Haitian Creole to English

Our experiments with the Haitian Creole-English data are independent of the system presented for the English to French task above. We experimented with both phrase-based SMT and syntax-based SMT. The main questions we investigated were i) whether we can improve word alignment and phrase extraction for phrase-based SMT and ii) whether we can integrate dependency parsing into a syntax-based approach. All our experiments were conducted on the *clean* data set using Moses for training and decoding. In the following we will first describe the experiments with phrase-based models and linear transduction grammars for word alignment and, thereafter, our findings from integrating English dependency parses into a syntax-based approach.

2.1 Phrase-based SMT

The phrase-based system that we used in this series of experiments uses a rather traditional setup. For the translations into English we used the news data provided for the other translations tasks in WMT 2011 to build a large scale-background language model. The English data from the Haitian Creole task were used as a separate domain-specific language model. For the other translation direction we only used the in-domain data provided. We used standard 5-gram models with Witten-Bell discounting and backoff interpolation for all language models. For the translation model we applied standard techniques and settings for phrase extraction and score estimations. However, we applied two different systems for word alignment: One is the standard GIZA++ toolbox implementing the IBM alignment models (Och and Ney, 2003) and extensions and the other is based on transduction grammars which will briefly be introduced in the next section.

2.1.1 Alignment with PLITGs

By making the assumption that the parallel corpus constitutes a *linear transduction* (Saers, 2011)[2] we can induce a grammar that is the most likely to have generated the observed corpus. The grammar induced will generate a parse forest for each sentence pair in the corpus, and each parse tree in that forest will correspond to an alignment between the two sentences. Following Saers et al. (2010), the alignment corresponding to the best parse can be extracted and used instead of other word alignment approaches such as GIZA++. There are several grammar types that generate linear transductions, and in this work, *stochastic bracketing preterminalized linear inversion transduction grammars* (PLITG) were used (Saers and Wu, 2011). Since we were mainly interested in the word alignments, we did not induce phrasal grammars.

Although alignments from PLITGs may not reach the same level of translation quality as GIZA++, they make different mistakes, so both complement each other. By duplicating the training corpus and aligning each copy of the corpus with a different alignment tool, the phrase extractor seems to be able to pick the best of both worlds, producing a phrase table that is superior to one produced with either of the alignments tools used in isolation.

2.1.2 Results

In the following we present our results on the provided test set[3] for translating into both languages with phrase-based systems trained on different word alignments. Table 3 summarises the BLEU scores obtained.

English-Haitian	BLEU	phrase-table
GIZA++	0.2567	3,060,486
PLITG	0.2407	5,007,254
GIZA++ & PLITG	**0.2572**	7,521,754
Haitian-English	BLEU	phrase-table
GIZA++	0.3045	3,060,486
PLITG	0.2922	5,049,280
GIZA++ & PLITG	**0.3105**	7,561,043

Table 3: Phrase-based SMT (*pbsmt*) on the Haitian Creole-English test set with different word alignments.

From the table we can see that phrase-based systems trained on PLITG alignments performs slightly worse than the ones trained on GIZA++. However combining both alignments with the simple data duplication technique mentioned earlier produces the overall best scores in both translation directions. The fact that both alignments lead to complementary information can be seen in the size of the phrase tables extracted (see table 3).

2.2 Syntax-based SMT

We used Moses and its syntax-mode for our experiments with hierarchical phrase-based and syntax-augmented models. Our main interest was to investigate the influence of monolingual parsing on the translation performance. In particular, we tried to integrate English dependency parses created by MaltParser (Nivre et al., 2007) trained on the Wall Street Journal section of the Penn Treebank (Marcus et al., 1993) extended with about 4000 questions

[2]A transduction is a set of pairs of strings, and thus represents a relation between two languages.

[3]We actually swapped the development set and the test set by mistake. But, of course, we never mixed development and test data in any result reported.

from the Question Bank (Judge et al., 2006). The conversion to dependency trees was done using the Stanford Parser (de Marneffe et al., 2006). Again, we ran both translation directions to test our settings in more than just one task. Interesting here is also the question whether there are significant differences when integrating monolingual parses on the source or on the target side.

The motivation for applying dependency parsing in our experiments is to use the specific information carried by dependency relations. Dependency structures encode functional relations between words that can be seen as an interface to the semantics of a sentence. This information is usually not available in phrase-structure representations. We believe that this type of information can be beneficial for machine translation. For example, knowing that a noun acts as the subject of a sentence is more informative than just marking it as part of a noun phrase. Whether or not this information can be explored by current syntax-based machine translation approaches that are optimised for phrase-structure representations is a question that we liked to investigate. For comparison we also trained hierarchical phrase-based models without any additional annotation.

2.2.1 Converting projective dependency trees

First we needed to convert dependency parses to a tree representation in order to use our data in the standard models of syntax-based models implemented in Moses. In our experiments, we used a parser model that creates projective dependency graphs that can be converted into tree structures of nested segments. We used the yield of each word (referring to that word and its transitive dependents) to define spans of phrases and their dependency relations are used as span labels. Furthermore, we also defined pre-terminal nodes that encode the part-of-speech information of each word. These tags were obtained using the HunPos tagger (Halácsy et al., 2007) trained on the Wall Street Journal section of the Penn Treebank. Figure 2 illustrates the conversion process. Tagging and parsing is done for all English data without any manual corrections or optimisation of parameters. After the conversion, we were able to use the standard training procedures implemented in Moses.

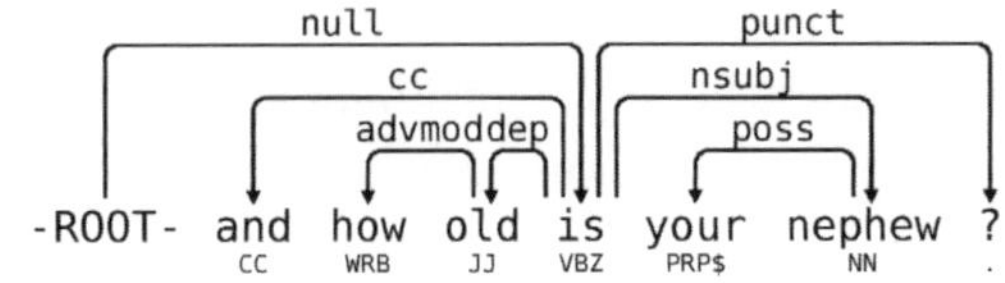


```
<tree label="null">
  <tree label="cc">
    <tree label="CC">and</tree>
  </tree>
  <tree label="dep">
    <tree label="advmod">
      <tree label="WRB">how</tree>
    </tree>
    <tree label="JJ">old</tree>
  </tree>
  <tree label="VBZ">is</tree>
  <tree label="nsubj">
    <tree label="poss">
      <tree label="PRP$">your</tree>
    </tree>
    <tree label="NN">nephew</tree>
  </tree>
  <tree label="punct">
    <tree label=".">?</tree>
  </tree>
</tree>
```

Figure 2: A dependency graph from the training corpus and its conversion to a nested tree structure. The yield of each word in the sentence defines a span with the label taken from the relation of that word to its head. Part-of-speech tags are used as additional pre-terminal nodes.

2.2.2 Experimental Results

We ran several experiments with slightly different settings. We used the same basic setup for all of them including the same language models and GIZA++ word alignments that we have used for the phrase-based models already. Further, we used Moses for extracting rules of the syntax-based translation model. We use standard settings for the baseline system (=hiero) that does not employ any linguistic markup. For the models that include dependency-based trees we changed the maximum span threshold to a high value of 999 (default: 15) in order to extract as many rules as possible. This large degree of freedom is possible due to the otherwise strong constraints on rule flexibility imposed by the monolingual syntactic markup. Rule tables are dramatically smaller than for the unrestricted hierarchical models (see table 4).

However, rule restriction by linguistic constraints usually hurts performance due to the decreased coverage of the rule set. One common way of improving

reference	Are you going to let us die on Ile à Vaches which is located close the city of Les Cayes. I am ...
pbsmt	Do you are letting us die in Ilavach island's on in Les Cayes. I am ...
hiero	do you will let us die in the island Ilavach on the in Les Cayes . I am ...
samt2	Are you going to let us die in the island Ilavach the which is on the Les. My name is ...
reference	I'm begging you please help me my situation is very critical.
pbsmt	Please help me please. Because my critical situation very much.
hiero	please , please help me because my critical situation very much .
samt2	Please help me because my situation very critical.
reference	I don't have money to go and give blood in Port au Prince from La Gonave.
pbsmt	I don't have money, so that I go to give blood Port-au-Prince since lagonave.
hiero	I don 't have any money , for me to go to give blood Port-au-Prince since lagonave .
samt2	I don't have any money, to be able to go to give blood Port-au-Prince since Gonâve Island.

Figure 3: Example translations for various models.

English-Haitian	BLEU	number of rules
hiero	**0.2549**	34,118,622
malt (source)	0.2180	1,628,496
- binarised	0.2327	9,063,933
- samt1	0.2311	11,691,279
- samt2	0.2366	29,783,694
Haitian-English	BLEU	number of rules
hiero	**0.3034**	33,231,535
malt (target)	0.2739	1,922,688
- binarised	0.2857	8,922,343
- samt1	0.2952	11,073,764
- samt2	*0.2954*	*24,554,317*

Table 4: Syntax-based SMT on the Haitian Creole-English test set with (=malt) or without (=hiero) English parse trees and various parse relaxation strategies. The final system submitted to WMT11 is *malt(target)-samt2*.

rule extraction is based on tree manipulation and relaxed extraction algorithms. Moses implements several algorithms that have been proposed in the literature. Tree binarisation is one of them. This can be done in a left-branching and in a right-branching mode. We used a combination of both in the settings denoted as *binarised*. The other relaxation algorithms are based on methods proposed for syntax-augmented machine translation (Zollmann et al., 2008). We used two of them: *samt1* combines pairs of neighbouring children nodes into combined complex nodes and creates additional complex nodes of all children nodes except the first child and similar complex nodes for all but the last child. *samt2* combines any pair of neighbouring nodes even if they are not children of the same parent. All of these relaxation algorithms lead to increased rule sets (table 4). In terms of translation performance there seems to be a strong correlation between rule table size and translation quality as measured by BLEU. None of the dependency-based models beats the unrestricted hierarchical model. Both translation directions behave similar with slightly worse performances of the dependency-based models (relative to the baseline) when syntax is used on the source language side. Note also that all syntax-based models (including hiero) are below the corresponding phrase-based SMT systems. Of course, automatic evaluation has its limits and interesting qualitative differences may be more visible in manual assessments. The use of linguistic information certainly has an impact on the translation hypotheses produced as we can see in the examples in figure 3. In the future, we plan to investigate the effect of dependency information on grammaticality of translated sentences in more detail.

3 Conclusions

In our English-French and Haitian Creole-English shared task submissions, we investigated the use of anaphora resolution, hierarchical lexical reordering and data selection for language modelling (English-French) as well as LTG word alignment and syntax-based decoding with dependency information (Haitian Creole-English). While the results for the systems with anaphora handling were somewhat disappointing and the effect of data filtering was inconsistent, hierarchical lexical reordering brought substantial improvements. We also obtained consistent gains by combining information from different word aligners, and we presented a simple way of including dependency parses in standard tree-based decoding.

Acknowledgements

Most of the features used in our English-French system were originally developed while Christian Hardmeier was at FBK. Activities at FBK were supported by the EuroMatrixPlus project (IST-231720) and the T4ME network of excellence (IST-249119), both funded by the DG INFSO of the European Commission through the Seventh Framework Programme.

References

Samuel Broscheit, Massimo Poesio, Simone Paolo Ponzetto, Kepa Joseba Rodriguez, Lorenza Romano, Olga Uryupina, Yannick Versley, and Roberto Zanoli. 2010. BART: A multilingual anaphora resolution system. In *Proceedings of the 5th International Workshop on Semantic Evaluations (SemEval-2010)*, Uppsala.

Marie-Catherine de Marneffe, Bill MacCartney, and Christopher D. Manning. 2006. Generating typed dependency parses from phrase structure parses. In *Proceedings of LREC*.

Marcello Federico, Nicola Bertoldi, and Mauro Cettolo. 2008. IRSTLM: an open source toolkit for handling large scale language models. In *Interspeech 2008*, pages 1618–1621. ISCA.

Michel Galley and Christopher D. Manning. 2008. A simple and effective hierarchical phrase reordering model. In *Proceedings of the 2008 Conference on Empirical Methods in Natural Language Processing*, pages 847–855, Honolulu, Hawaii, October. Association for Computational Linguistics.

Péter Halácsy, András Kornai, and Csaba Oravecz. 2007. Hunpos: an open source trigram tagger. In *Proceedings of the 45th Annual Meeting of the ACL on Interactive Poster and Demonstration Sessions*, pages 209–212.

Christian Hardmeier and Marcello Federico. 2010. Modelling Pronominal Anaphora in Statistical Machine Translation. In Marcello Federico, Ian Lane, Michael Paul, and François Yvon, editors, *Proceedings of the seventh International Workshop on Spoken Language Translation (IWSLT)*, pages 283–289.

John Judge, Aoife Cahill, and Josef van Genabith. 2006. Questionbank: creating a corpus of parse-annotated questions. In *Proceedings of the 21st International Conference on Computational Linguistics and the 44th annual meeting of the Association for Computational Linguistics*, pages 497–504.

Philipp Koehn, Amittai Axelrod, Alexandra Birch Mayne, et al. 2005. Edinburgh system description for the 2005 iwslt speech translation evaluation. In *International workshop on spoken language translation*, Pittsburgh.

Philipp Koehn, Hieu Hoang, Alexandra Birch, et al. 2007. Moses: open source toolkit for Statistical Machine Translation. In *Annual meeting of the Association for Computational Linguistics: Demonstration session*, pages 177–180, Prague.

Mitchell P. Marcus, Mary Ann Marcinkiewicz, and Beatrice Santorini. 1993. Building a large annotated corpus of english: The Penn Treebank. *Computational Linguistics*, 19:313–330, June.

Joakim Nivre, Johan Hall, Jens Nilsson, Atanas Chanev, Gülsen Eryigit, Sandra Kübler, Svetoslav Marinov, and Erwin Marsi. 2007. MaltParser: A language-independent system for data-driven dependency parsing. *Natural Language Engineering*, 13(2):95–135.

Franz Josef Och and Hermann Ney. 2003. A systematic comparison of various statistical alignment models. *Computational linguistics*, 29:19–51.

Markus Saers and Dekai Wu. 2011. Principled induction of phrasal bilexica. In *Proceedings of the 15th Annual Conference of the European Association for Machine Translation*, Leuven, Belgium, May.

Markus Saers, Joakim Nivre, and Dekai Wu. 2010. Word alignment with stochastic bracketing linear inversion transduction grammar. In *Human Language Technologies: The 2010 Annual Conference of the North American Chapter of the Association for Computational Linguistics*, pages 341–344, Los Angeles, California, June.

Markus Saers. 2011. *Translation as Linear Transduction: Models and Algorithms for Efficient Learning in Statistical Machine Translation*. Ph.D. thesis, Uppsala University, Department of Linguistics and Philology.

M. Strube. 2006. Anaphora and coreference resolution, Statistical. In *Encyclopedia of language and linguistics*, pages 216–222. Elsevier.

Andreas Zollmann, Ashish Venugopal, Franz Och, and Jay Ponte. 2008. A systematic comparison of phrase-based, hierarchical and syntax-augmented statistical mt. In *Proceedings of the 22nd International Conference on Computational Linguistics - Volume 1*, pages 1145–1152.

The Karlsruhe Institute of Technology Translation Systems for the WMT 2011

Teresa Herrmann, Mohammed Mediani, Jan Niehues and Alex Waibel
Karlsruhe Institute of Technology
Karlsruhe, Germany
firstname.lastname@kit.edu

Abstract

This paper describes the phrase-based SMT systems developed for our participation in the WMT11 Shared Translation Task. Translations for English↔German and English↔French were generated using a phrase-based translation system which is extended by additional models such as bilingual and fine-grained POS language models, POS-based reordering, lattice phrase extraction and discriminative word alignment. Furthermore, we present a special filtering method for the English-French Giga corpus and the phrase scoring step in the training is parallelized.

1 Introduction

In this paper we describe our systems for the EMNLP 2011 Sixth Workshop on Statistical Machine Translation. We participated in the Shared Translation Task and submitted translations for English↔German and English↔French. We use a phrase-based decoder that can use lattices as input and developed several models that extend the standard log-linear model combination of phrase-based MT. These include advanced reordering models and corresponding adaptations to the phrase extraction process as well as extension to the translation and language model in form of discriminative word alignment and a bilingual language model to extend source word context. For English-German, language models based on fine-grained part-of-speech tags were used to address the difficult target language generation due to the rich morphology of German.

We also present a filtering method directly addressing the problems of web-crawled corpora, which enabled us to make use of the French-English Giga corpus. Another novelty in our systems this year is the parallel phrase scoring method that reduces the time needed for training which is especially convenient for such big corpora as the Giga corpus.

2 System Description

The baseline systems for all languages use a translation model that is trained on EPPS and the News Commentary corpus and the phrase table is based on a GIZA++ word alignment. The language model was trained on the monolingual parts of the same corpora by the SRILM Toolkit (Stolcke, 2002). It is a 4-gram SRI language model using Kneser-Ney smoothing.

The problem of word reordering is addressed using the POS-based reordering model as described in Section 2.4. The part-of-speech tags for the reordering model are obtained using the TreeTagger (Schmid, 1994).

An in-house phrase-based decoder (Vogel, 2003) is used to perform translation and optimization with regard to the BLEU score is done using Minimum Error Rate Training as described in Venugopal et al. (2005). During decoding only the top 20 translation options for every source phrase were considered.

2.1 Data

We trained all systems using the parallel EPPS and News Commentary corpora. In addition, the UN corpus and the Giga corpus were used for training

Proceedings of the 6th Workshop on Statistical Machine Translation, pages 379–385,
Edinburgh, Scotland, UK, July 30–31, 2011. ©2011 Association for Computational Linguistics

the French-English systems.

Optimization was done for most languages using the news-test2008 data set and news-test2010 was used as test set. The only exception is German-English, where news-test2009 was used for optimization due to system combination arrangements. The language models for the baseline systems were trained on the monolingual versions of the training corpora. Later on, we used the News Shuffle and the Gigaword corpus to train bigger language models. For training a discriminative word alignment model, a small amount of hand-aligned data was used.

2.2 Preprocessing

The training data is preprocessed prior to training the system. This includes normalizing special symbols, smart-casing the first words of each sentence and removing long sentences and sentences with length mismatch.

For the German parts of the training corpus we use the hunspell[1] lexicon to map words written according to old German spelling to new German spelling, to obtain a corpus with homogenous spelling.

Compound splitting as described in Koehn and Knight (2003) is applied to the German part of the corpus for the German-to-English system to reduce the out-of-vocabulary problem for German compound words.

2.3 Special filtering of the Giga parallel Corpus

The Giga corpus incorporates non-neglegible amounts of noise even after our usual preprocessing. This noise may be due to different causes. For instance: non-standard HTML characters, meaningless parts composed of only hypertext codes, sentences which are only partial translation of the source, or eventually not a correct translation at all.

Such noisy pairs potentially degrade the translation model quality, therefore it seemed more convenient to eliminate them.

Given the size of the corpus, this task could not be performed manually. Consequently, we used an automatic classifier inspired by the work of Munteanu and Marcu (2005) on comparable corpora. This classifier should be able to filter out the pairs which likely are not beneficial for the translation model.

In order to reliably decide about the classifier to use, we evaluated several techniques. The training and test sets for this evaluation were built respectively from nc-dev2007 and nc-devtest2007. In each set, about 30% randomly selected source sentences switch positions with the immediate following so that they form negative examples. We also used lexical dictionaries in both directions based on EPPS and UN corpora.

We relied on seven features in our classifiers: IBM1 score in both directions, number of unaligned source words, the difference in number of words between source and target, the maximum source word fertility, number of unaligned target words, and the maximum target word fertility. It is noteworthy that all the features requiring alignment information (such as the unaligned source words) were computed on the basis of the Viterbi path of the IBM1 alignment. The following classifiers were used:

Regression Choose either class based on a weighted linear combination of the features and a fixed threshold of 0.5.

Logistic regression The probability of the class is expressed as a sigmoid of a linear combination of the different features. Then the class with the highest probability is picked.

Maximum entropy classifier We used the same set of features to train a maximum entropy classifier using the Megam package[2].

Support vector machines classifier An SVM classifier was trained using the SVM-light package[3].

Results of these experiments are summarized in Table 1.

The regression weights were estimated so that to minimize the squared error. This gave us a pretty poor F-measure score of 90.42%. Given that the logistic regression is more suited for binary classification in our case than the normal regression, it led to significant increase in the performance. The training

[1] `http://hunspell.sourceforge.net/`

[2] `http://www.cs.utah.edu/~hal/megam/`

[3] `http://svmlight.joachims.org/`

Approach	Precision	Recall	F-measure
Regression	93.81	87.27	90.42
LogReg	93.43	94.84	94.13
MaxEnt	93.69	94.54	94.11
SVM	98.20	96.87	97.53

Table 1: Results of the filtering experiments

was held by maximizing the likelihood to the data with L_2 regularization (with $\alpha = 0.1$). This gave an F-measure score of 94.78%.

The maximum entropy classifier performed better than the logistic regression in terms of precision but however it had worse F-measure.

Significant improvements could be noticed using the SVM classifier in both precision and recall: 98.20% precision, 96.87% recall, and thus 97.53% F-measure.

As a result, we used the SVM classifier to filter the Giga parallel corpus. The corpus contained originally around 22.52 million pairs. After preprocessing and filtering it was reduced to 16.7 million pairs. Thus throwing around 6 million pairs.

2.4 Word Reordering

In contrast to modeling the reordering by a distance-based reordering model and/or a lexicalized distortion model, we use a different approach that relies on part-of-speech (POS) sequences. By abstracting from surface words to parts-of-speech, we expect to model the reordering more accurately.

2.4.1 POS-based Reordering Model

To model reordering we first learn probabilistic rules from the POS tags of the words in the training corpus and the alignment information. Continuous reordering rules are extracted as described in Rottmann and Vogel (2007) to model short-range reorderings. When translating between German and English, we apply a modified reordering model with non-continuous rules to cover also long-range reorderings (Niehues and Kolss, 2009). The reordering rules are applied to the source text and the original order of words and the reordered sentence variants generated by the rules are encoded in a word lattice which is used as input to the decoder.

2.4.2 Lattice Phrase Extraction

For the test sentences, the POS-based reordering allows us to change the word order in the source sentence so that the sentence can be translated more easily. If we apply this also to the training sentences, we would be able to extract the phrase pairs for originally discontinuous phrases and could apply them during translation of reordered test sentences.

Therefore, we build reordering lattices for all training sentences and then extract phrase pairs from the monotone source path as well as from the reordered paths.

To limit the number of extracted phrase pairs, we extract a source phrase only once per sentence even if it is found in different paths.

2.5 Translation and Language Models

In addition to the models used in the baseline system described above we conducted experiments including additional models that enhance translation quality by introducing alternative or additional information into the translation or language modelling process.

2.5.1 Discriminative Word Alignment

In most of our systems we use the PGIZA++ Toolkit[4] to generate alignments between words in the training corpora. The word alignments are generated in both directions and the grow-diag-final-and heuristic is used to combine them. The phrase extraction is then done based on this word alignment.

In the English-German system we applied the Discriminative Word Alignment approach as described in Niehues and Vogel (2008) instead. This alignment model is trained on a small corpus of hand-aligned data and uses the lexical probability as well as the fertilities generated by the PGIZA++ Toolkit and POS information.

2.5.2 Bilingual Language Model

In phrase-based systems the source sentence is segmented by the decoder according to the best combination of phrases that maximize the translation and language model scores. This segmentation into phrases leads to the loss of context information at the phrase boundaries. Although more target side context is available to the language model, source

[4] http://www.cs.cmu.edu/~qing/

side context would also be valuable for the decoder when searching for the best translation hypothesis. To make also source language context available we use a bilingual language model, an additional language model in the phrase-based system in which each token consist of a target word and all source words it is aligned to. The bilingual tokens enter the translation process as an additional target factor and the bilingual language model is applied to the additional factor like a normal language model. For more details see (Niehues et al., 2011).

2.5.3 Parallel phrase scoring

The process of phrase scoring is held in two runs. The objective of the first run is to compute the necessary counts and to estimate the scores, all based on the source phrases; while the second run is similarly held based on the target phrases. Thus, the extracted phrases have to be sorted twice: once by source phrase and once by target phrase. These two sorting operations are almost always done on an external storage device and hence consume most of the time spent in this step.

The phrase scoring step was reimplemented in order to exploit the available computation resources more efficiently and therefore reduce the processing time. It uses optimized sorting algorithms for large data volumes which cannot fit into memory (Vitter, 2008). In its core, our implementation relies on STXXL: an extension of the STL library for external memory (Kettner, 2005) and on OpenMP for shared memory parallelization (Chapman et al., 2007).

Table 2 shows a comparison between Moses and our phrase scoring tools. The comparison was held using sixteen-core 64-bit machines with 128 Gb RAM, where the files are accessed through NFS on a RAID disk. The experiments show that the gain grows linearly with the size of input with an average of 40% of speed up.

#pairs(G)	Moses $*10^3$(s)	KIT $*10^3$(s)
0.203	25.99	17.58
1.444	184.19	103.41
1.693	230.97	132.79

Table 2: Comparison of Moses and KIT phrase extraction systems

2.5.4 POS Language Models

In addition to surface word language models, we did experiments with language models based on part-of-speech for English-German. We expect that having additional information in form of probabilities of part-of-speech sequences should help especially in case of the rich morphology of German and therefore the more difficult target language generation.

The part-of-speeches were generated using the TreeTagger and the RFTagger (Schmid and Laws, 2008), which produces more fine-grained tags that include also person, gender and case information. While the TreeTagger assigns 54 different POS tags to the 357K German words in the corpus, the RFTagger produces 756 different fine-grained tags on the same corpus.

We tried n-gram lengths of 4 and 7. While no improvement in translation quality could be achieved using the POS language models based on the normal POS tags, the 4-gram POS language model based on fine-grained tags could improve the translation system by 0.2 BLEU points as shown in Table 3. Surprisingly, increasing the n-gram length to 7 decreased the translation quality again.

To investigate the impact of context length, we performed an analysis on the outputs of two different systems, one without a POS language model and one with the 4-gram fine-grained POS language model. For each of the translations we calculated the average length of the n-grams in the translation when applying one of the two language models using 4-grams of surface words or parts-of-speech. The results are also shown in Table 3.

The average n-gram length of surface words on the translation generated by the system without POS language model and the one using the 4-gram POS language model stays practically the same. When measuring the n-gram length using the 4-gram POS language model, the context increases to 3.4. This increase of context is not surprising, since with the more general POS tags longer contexts can be matched. Comparing the POS context length for the two translations, we can see that the context increases from 3.18 to 3.40 due to longer matching POS sequences. This means that the system using the POS language model actually generates translations with more probable POS sequences so that longer matches are possible. Also the perplexity drops by half since the POS language model helps constructing sentences that have a better structure.

System	BLEU	avg. ngram length		PPL
		Word	POS	POS
no POS LM	16.64	2.77	3.18	66.78
POS LM	16.88	2.81	3.40	33.36

Table 3: Analysis of context length

3 Results

Using the models described above we performed several experiments leading finally to the systems used for generating the translations submitted to the workshop. The following sections describe the experiments for the individual language pairs and show the translation results. The results are reported as case-sensitive BLEU scores (Papineni et al., 2002) on one reference translation.

3.1 German-English

The German-to-English baseline system applies short-range reordering rules and uses a language model trained on the EPPS and News Commentary. By exchanging the baseline language model by one trained on the News Shuffle corpus we improve the translation quality considerably, by more than 3 BLEU points. When we expand the coverage of the reordering rules to enable long-range reordering we can improve even further by 0.4 and adding a second language model trained on the English Gigaword corpus we gain another 0.3 BLEU points. To ensure that the phrase table also includes reordered phrases, we use lattice phrase extraction and can achieve a small improvement. Finally, a bilingual language model is added to extend the context of source language words available for translation, reaching the best score of 23.35 BLEU points. This system was used for generating the translation submitted to the German-English Translation Task.

System	Dev	Test
Baseline	18.49	19.10
+ NewsShuffle LM	20.63	22.24
+ LongRange Reordering	21.00	22.68
+ Additional Giga LM	21.80	22.92
+ Lattice Phrase Extraction	21.87	22.96
+ Bilingual LM	**22.05**	**23.35**

Table 4: Translation results for German-English

3.2 English-German

The English-to-German baseline system also includes short-range reordering and uses translation and language model based on EPPS and News Commentary. Exchanging the language model by the News Shuffle language model again yields a big improvement by 2.3 BLEU points. Adding long-range reordering improves a lot on the development set while the score on the test set remains practically the same. Replacing the GIZA++ alignments by alignments generated using the Discriminative Word Alignment Model again only leads to a small improvement. By using the bilingual language model to increase context we can gain 0.1 BLEU points and by adding the part-of-speech language model with rich parts-of-speech including case, number and gender information for German we achieve the best score of 16.88. This system was used to generate the translation used for submission.

System	Dev	Test
Baseline	13.55	14.19
+ NewsShuffle LM	15.10	16.46
+ LongRange Reordering	15.79	16.46
+ DWA	15.81	16.52
+ Bilingual LM	15.85	16.64
+ POS LM	**15.88**	**16.88**

Table 5: Translation results for English-German

3.3 English-French

Table 6 summarizes how our system for English-French evolved. The baseline system for this direction was trained on the EPPS and News Commentary corpora, while the language model was trained on the French part of the EPPS, News Commentary and UN parallel corpora. Some improvement could be already seen by introducing the short-range reorderings trained on the baseline parallel corpus.

Apparently, the UN data brought only slight improvement to the overall performance. On the other hand, adding bigger language models trained on the monolingual French version of EPPS, News Commentary and the News Shuffle together with the French Gigaword corpus introduces an improvement of 3.7 on test. Using a system trained only on the Giga corpus data with the same last configuration shows a significant gain. It showed an improvement of around 1.0. We were able to obtain some further improvements by merging the translation models of the last two systems. i.e. the one system based on EPPS, UN, and News Commentary and the other on the Giga corpus. This merging increased our score by 0.2. Finally, our submitted system for this direction was obtained by using a single language model trained on the union of all the French corpora instead of using multiple models. This resulted in an improvement of 0.1 leading to our best score: 28.28.

System	Dev	Test
Baseline	20.62	22.36
+ Reordering	21.29	23.11
+ UN	21.27	23.24
+ Big LMs	23.77	26.90
Giga data	24.53	27.94
Merge	24.74	28.14
+ Merged LMs	**25.07**	**28.28**

Table 6: Translation results for English-French

3.4 French-English

The development of our system for the French-English direction is summarized in Table 7. Our system for this direction evolved quite similarly to the opposite direction. The largest improvement accompanied the integration of the bigger language models (trained on the English version of EPPS, News Commentary, News Shuffle and the Gigaword corpus): 3.3 BLEU points, whereas smaller improvements could be gained by applying the short reordering rules and almost no change by including the UN data. Further gains were obtained by training the system on the Giga corpus added to the previous parallel data. This increased our performance by 0.6. The submitted system was obtained by augmenting the last system with a bilingual language model adding around 0.2 to the previous score and thus giving 28.34 as final score.

System	Dev	Test
Baseline	20.76	23.78
+ Reordering	21.42	24.28
+ UN	21.55	24.21
+ Big LMs	24.16	27.55
+ Giga data	24.86	28.17
+ BiLM	**25.01**	**28.34**

Table 7: Translation results for French-English

4 Conclusions

We have presented the systems for our participation in the WMT 2011 Evaluation for English↔German and English↔French. For English↔French, a special filtering method for web-crawled data was developed. In addition, a parallel phrase scoring technique was implemented that could speed up the MT training process tremendously. Using these two features, we were able to integrate the huge amounts of data available in the Giga corpus into our systems translating between English and French.

We applied POS-based reordering to improve our translations in all directions, using short-range reordering for English↔French and long-range reordering for English↔German. For German-English, reordering also the training corpus lead to further improvements of the translation quality.

A Discriminative Word Alignment Model led to an increase in BLEU for English-German. For this direction we also tried fine-grained POS language models of different n-gram lengths. The best translations could be obtained by using 4-grams.

For nearly all experiments, a bilingual language model was applied that expands the context of source words that can be considered during decoding. The improvements range from 0.1 to 0.4 in BLEU score.

Acknowledgments

This work was realized as part of the Quaero Programme, funded by OSEO, French State agency for innovation.

References

Barbara Chapman, Gabriele Jost, and Ruud van der Pas. 2007. *Using OpenMP: Portable Shared Memory Parallel Programming (Scientific and Engineering Computation)*. The MIT Press.

Roman Dementiev Lutz Kettner. 2005. Stxxl: Standard template library for xxl data sets. In *Proceedings of ESA 2005. Volume 3669 of LNCS*, pages 640–651. Springer.

Philipp Koehn and Kevin Knight. 2003. Empirical Methods for Compound Splitting. In *EACL*, Budapest, Hungary.

Dragos Stefan Munteanu and Daniel Marcu. 2005. Improving machine translation performance by exploiting non-parallel corpora. *Computational Linguistics*, 31:477–504.

Jan Niehues and Muntsin Kolss. 2009. A POS-Based Model for Long-Range Reorderings in SMT. In *Fourth Workshop on Statistical Machine Translation (WMT 2009)*, Athens, Greece.

Jan Niehues and Stephan Vogel. 2008. Discriminative Word Alignment via Alignment Matrix Modeling. In *Proc. of Third ACL Workshop on Statistical Machine Translation*, Columbus, USA.

Jan Niehues, Teresa Herrmann, Stephan Vogel, and Alex Waibel. 2011. Wider Context by Using Bilingual Language Models in Machine Translation. In *Sixth Workshop on Statistical Machine Translation (WMT 2011)*, Edinburgh, UK.

Kishore Papineni, Salim Roukos, Todd Ward, and Wei-Jing Zhu. 2002. Bleu: a Method for Automatic Evaluation of Machine Translation. Technical Report RC22176 (W0109-022), IBM Research Division, T. J. Watson Research Center.

Kay Rottmann and Stephan Vogel. 2007. Word Reordering in Statistical Machine Translation with a POS-Based Distortion Model. In *TMI*, Skövde, Sweden.

Helmut Schmid and Florian Laws. 2008. Estimation of Conditional Probabilities with Decision Trees and an Application to Fine-Grained POS Tagging. In *COLING 2008*, Manchester, Great Britain.

Helmut Schmid. 1994. Probabilistic Part-of-Speech Tagging Using Decision Trees. In *International Conference on New Methods in Language Processing*, Manchester, UK.

Andreas Stolcke. 2002. SRILM – An Extensible Language Modeling Toolkit. In *Proc. of ICSLP*, Denver, Colorado, USA.

Ashish Venugopal, Andreas Zollman, and Alex Waibel. 2005. Training and Evaluation Error Minimization Rules for Statistical Machine Translation. In *Workshop on Data-drive Machine Translation and Beyond (WPT-05)*, Ann Arbor, MI.

Jeffrey Scott Vitter. 2008. *Algorithms and Data Structures for External Memory*. now Publishers Inc.

Stephan Vogel. 2003. SMT Decoder Dissected: Word Reordering. In *Int. Conf. on Natural Language Processing and Knowledge Engineering*, Beijing, China.

CMU Haitian Creole-English Translation System for WMT 2011

Sanjika Hewavitharana, Nguyen Bach, Qin Gao, Vamshi Ambati, Stephan Vogel
Language Technologies Institute
Carnegie Mellon University
Pittsburgh, PA 15213, USA
{sanjika,nbach,qing,vamshi,vogel+}@cs.cmu.edu

Abstract

This paper describes the statistical machine translation system submitted to the WMT11 Featured Translation Task, which involves translating Haitian Creole SMS messages into English. In our experiments we try to address the issue of noise in the training data, as well as the lack of parallel training data. Spelling normalization is applied to reduce out-of-vocabulary words in the corpus. Using Semantic Role Labeling rules we expand the available training corpus. Additionally we investigate extracting parallel sentences from comparable data to enhance the available parallel data.

1 Introduction

In this paper we describe the CMU-SMT Haitian Creole-English translation system that was built as part of the Featured Translation Task of the WMT11. The task involved translating text (SMS) messages that were collected during the humanitarian operations in the aftermath of the earthquake in Haiti in 2010.

Due to the circumstances of this situation, the SMS messages were often noisy, and contained incomplete information. Additionally they sometimes contained text from other languages (e.g. French). As is typical in SMS messages, abbreviated text (as well as misspelled words) were present. Further, since the Haitian Creole orthography is not fully standardized (Allen, 1998), the text inherently contained several different spelling variants.

These messages were translated into English by a group of volunteers during the disaster response. The background and the details of this crowdsourcing translation effort is discussed in Munro (2010). Some translations contain additional annotations which are not part of the original SMS, possibly added by the translators to clarify certain issues with the original message. Along with the noise, spelling variants, and fragmented nature of the SMS messages, the annotations contribute to the overall difficulty in building a machine translation system with this type of data. We aim to address some of these issues in out effort.

Another challenge with building a Haitian Creole-English translation system is the lack of parallel data. As Haitian Creole is a less commonly spoken language, the available resources are limited. Other than the manually translated SMS messages, the available Haitian Creole-English parallel data is about 2 million tokens, which is considerably smaller than the parallel data available for the Standard Translation Task of the WMT11.

Lewis (2010) details the effort quickly put forth by the Microsoft Translator team in building a Haitian Creole-English translation system from scratch, as part of the relief effort in Haiti. We took a similar approach to this shared task: rapidly building a translation system to a new language pair utilizing available resources. Within a short span (of about one week), we built a baseline translation system, identified the problems with the system, and exploited several approaches to rectify them and improve its overall performance. We addressed the issues above (namely: noise in the data and sparsity of parallel data) when building our translation system for Haitian Creole-English task. We also normalized

Proceedings of the 6th Workshop on Statistical Machine Translation, pages 386–392,
Edinburgh, Scotland, UK, July 30–31, 2011. ©2011 Association for Computational Linguistics

different spelling variations to reduce the number of out-of-vocabulary (OOV) tokens in the corpus. We used Semantic Role Labeling to expand the available training corpus. Additionally we exploited other resources, such as comparable corpora, to extract parallel data to enhance the limited amount of available parallel data.

The paper is organized as follows: Section 2 presents the baseline system used, along with a description of training and testing data used. Section 3 explains different preprocessing schemes that were tested for SMS data, and their effect on the translation performance. Corpus expansion approach is given in Section 4. Parallel data extraction from comparable corpora is presented in section 5. We present our concluding remarks in Section 6.

2 System Architecture

The WMT11 has provided a collection of Haitian Creole-English parallel data from a variety of sources, including data from CMU[1]. A summary of the data is given in Table 1. The primary in-domain data comprises the translated (noisy) SMS messages. The additional data contains newswire text, medical dialogs, the Bible, several bilingual dictionaries, and parallel sentences from Wikipedia.

Corpus	Sentences	Tokens (HT/EN)
SMS messages	16,676	351K / 324K
Newswire text	13,517	336K / 292K
Medical dialog	1,619	10K / 10K
Dictionaries	42,178	97K / 92K
Other	41,872	939K / 865K
Wikipedia	8,476	77K / 90K
Total	124,338	1.81M / 1.67M

Table 1: Haitian Creole (HT) and English (EN) parallel data provide by WMT11

We preprocessed the data by separating the punctuations, and converting both sides into lower case. SMS data was further processed to normalize quotations and other punctuation marks, and to remove all markups.

To build a baseline translation system we followed the recommended steps: generate word alignments using GIZA++ (Och and Ney, 2003) and phrase extraction using Moses (Koehn et al., 2007). We built a 4-gram language model with the SRI LM toolkit (Stolcke, 2002) using English side of the training corpus. Model parameters for the language model, phrase table, and lexicalized reordering model were optimized via minimum error-rate (MER) training (Och, 2003).

The SMS test sets were provided in two formats: raw (r) and cleaned (cl), where the latter had been manually cleaned. We used the *SMS dev clean* to optimize the decoder parameters and the *SMS devtest clean* and *SMS devtest raw* as held-out evaluation sets. Each set contains 900 sentences. A separate *SMS test*, with 1274 sentences, was used as the unseen test set in the final evaluation. For each experiment we report the case-insensitive BLEU (Papineni et al., 2002) score.

Using the available training data we built several baseline systems: The first system (Parallel-OOD), uses all the out-of-domain parallel data except the Wikipedia sentences. The second system, in addition, includes Wikipedia data. The third system uses all available parallel training data (including both the out-of-domain data as well as in-domain SMS data). We used the third system as the baseline for later experiments.

	dev (cl)	devtest (cl)	devtest (r)
Parallel-OOD	23.84	22.28	17.32
+Wikipedia	23.89	22.42	17.37
+SMS	32.28	33.49	29.95

Table 2: Translation results in BLEU for different corpora

Translation results for different test sets using the three systems are presented in Table 2. No significant difference in BLEU was observed with the addition of Wikipedia data. However, a significant improvement in performance can be seen when in-domain SMS data is added, despite the fact that this is noisy data. Because of this, we paid special attention to clean the noisy SMS data.

3 Preprocessing of SMS Data

In this section we explain two approaches that we explored to reduce the noise in the SMS data.

[1] www.speech.cs.cmu.edu/haitian/

3.1 Lexicon-based Collapsing of OOV Words

We observed that a number of words in the raw SMS data consisted of asterisks or special character symbols. This seems to occur because either users had to type with a phone-based keyboard or simply due to processing errors in the pipeline. Our aim, therefore, was to collapse these incorrectly spelled words to their closest vocabulary entires from the rest of the data.

We first built a lexicon of words using the entire data provided for the Featured Task. We then built a second probabilistic lexicon by cross-referencing *SMS dev raw* with the cleaned-up *SMS dev clean*. The first resource can be treated as a dictionary while the second is a look-up table. We processed incoming text by first selecting all the words with special characters in the text, and then computing an edit distance with each of the words in the first lexicon. We return the most frequent word that is the closest match as a substitute. For all words that don't have a closest match, we looked them up in the probabilistic dictionary and return a potential substitution if it exists. As the probabilistic dictionary is constructed using a very small amount of data, the two-level lookup helps to place less trust in it and use it only as a back-off option for a missing match in the larger lexicon.

This approach only collapses words with special characters to their closest in-vocabulary words. It does not make a significant difference to the OOV ratios, but reduces the number of tokens in the dataset. Using this approach we were able to collapse about 80% of the words with special characters to existing vocabulary entries.

3.2 Spelling Normalization

One of the most problematic issues in Haitian Creole SMS translation system is misspelled words. When training data contains misspelled words, the translation system performance will be affected at several levels, such as word alignment, phrase/rule extractions, and tuning parameters (Bertoldi et al., 2010). Therefore, it is desirable to perform spelling correction on the data. Spelling correction based on the noisy channel model has been explored in (Kernighan et al., 1990; Brill and Moore, 2000; Toutanova and Moore, 2002). The model is generally presented in the following form:

$$p(\hat{c}|h) = \arg\max_{\forall c} p(h|c)p(c) \qquad (1)$$

where h is the Haitian Creole word, and c is a possible correction. $p(c)$ is a source model which is a prior of word probabilities. $p(h|c)$ is an error model or noisy channel model that accounts for spelling transformations on letter sequences.

Unfortunately, in the case of Haitian Creole SMS we do not have sufficient data to estimate $p(h|c)$ and $p(c)$. However, we can assume $p(c|h) \approx p(c)$ and c is in the French vocabulary and is not an English word. The rationale for this, from linguistic point of view, is that Haitian Creole developed from the 18th century French. As a result, an important part of the Haitian Creole lexicon is directly derived from French. Furthermore, SMS messages sometimes were mixed with English words. Therefore, we ignore c if it appears in an English dictionary.

Given h, how do we get a list of possible normalization c and estimate $p(c)$? We use edit distance of 1 between h and c. An edit can be a deletion, transposition, substitution, or insertion. If a word has l characters, there will be $66l$+31 possible corrections[2]. It may result in a large list. However, we only keep possible normalizations which appear in a French dictionary and do not appear in an English dictionary[3]. To approximate $p(c)$, we use the French parallel Giga training data from the Shared Task of the WMT11. $p(c)$ is estimated by MLE. Finally, our system chooses the French word with the highest probability.

	dev (cl)	devtest (cl)	test (cl)
Before	2.6 ; 16	2.7 ; 16	2.6 ; 16
After	2.2 ; 13.63	2.3 ; 13.95	2.2 ; 14.3

Table 3: Percentage of OOV tokens and types in test sets before and after performing spelling normalization.

Table 3 shows that spelling normalization helps to bring down the percentage of OOV tokens and types by 0.4% and 2% respectively on the three test

[2] l deletions, l-1 transpositions, 32l substitutions, and 32(l+1) insertions; Haitian Creole orthography has 32 forms.

[3] The English dictionary was created from the English Gigaword corpus.

sets. Some examples of Haitian Creole words and their French normalization are (*tropikal:tropical*), (*economiques:economique*), (*irjan:iran*), (*idantifie:identifie*).

	dev (cl)	devtest (cl)	devtest (r)
Baseline	32.28	33.49	29.95
S1	32.18	30.22	25.45
S2	28.9	31.06	27.69

Table 4: Translation results in BLEU with/without spelling correction

Given the encouraging OOV reductions, we applied the spelling normalization for the full corpus, and built new translation systems. Our baseline system has no spelling correction (for the training corpus or the test sets); in S1, the spelling corrections is applied to all words; in S2, the spelling correction is only applied to Haitian Creole words that occur only once or twice in the data. In S1, 11.5% of Haitian Creole words had been mapped to French, including high frequency words. Meanwhile, 4.5% Haitian Creole words on training data were mapped to French words in S2. Table 4 presents a comparison of translation performance of the baseline, S1 and S2 for the SMS test sets. Unfortunately, none of systems with spelling normalization outperformed the system trained on the original data. Restricting the spelling correction only to infrequent words (S2) performed better for the devtest sets, but not for the dev set, although all the test sets come from the same domain.

4 Corpus Expansion using Semantic Role Labeling

To address the problem of limited resources, we tried to expand the training corpus by applying the corpus expansion method described in (Gao and Vogel, 2011). First, we parsed and labeled the semantic roles of the English side of the corpus, using the ASSERT labeler (Pradhan et al., 2004). Next, using the word alignment models of the parallel corpus, we extracted Semantic Role Label (SRL) substitution rules. SRL rules consist of source and target phrases that cover whole constituents of semantic roles, the verb frames they belong to, and the role labels of the constituents. The source and target phrases must comply with the restrictions detailed in (Gao and Vogel, 2011). Third, for each sentence, we replaced one of embedded SRL substitution rules with equivalent rules that have the same verb frame and the same role label.

The original method includes an additional but crucial step of filtering out the grammatically incorrect sentences using an SVM classifier, trained with labeled samples. However, we were unable to find Haitian Creole speakers who could manually label training data for the filtering step. Therefore, we were forced to skip this filtering step. We expanded the full training corpus which contained 124K sentence pairs, resulting in an expanded corpus with 505K sentences. The expanded corpus was force-aligned using the word alignment models trained on the original unexpanded corpus. A new translation system was built using the original plus the expanded corpus. As seen in Table 5, we observed a small improvement with the expanded corpus for the raw devtest. This method did not improve performance for the other two test sets.

	dev (cl)	devtest (cl)	devtest (r)
Baseline	32.28	33.49	29.95
+Expanded	31.79	32.98	30.1

Table 5: Translation results in BLEU with/without corpus expansion

A possible explanation for this, in addition to the missing component of filtering, is the low quality of SRL parsing on the SMS corpus. We observed a very small ratio of expansions in the Haitian Creole-English data, when compared to the Chinese-English experiment shown in (Gao and Vogel, 2011). The latter used a high quality corpus for the expansion and the expanded corpus was 20 times larger than the original one. Due to the noisy nature of the available parallel data, only 61K of the 124K sentences were successfully parsed and SRL-labeled by the labeler.

5 Extracting Parallel Data from Comparable Data

As we only have a limited amount of parallel data, we focused on automatically extracting additional parallel data from other available resources, such as comparable corpora. We were not able to find comparable news articles in Haitian Creole and English. However, we found several hundred Haitian Creole medical articles on the Web which were linked to comparable English articles[4]. Although some of the medical articles seemed to be direct translations of each other, converting the original pdf formats into text did not produce sentence aligned parallel articles. Rather, it produced sentence fragments (sometimes in different orders) due to the structural differences in the article pair. Hence a parallel sentence detection technique was necessary to process the data. Because the SMS messages are related to the disaster relief effort, which may include many words in the medical domain, we believe the newly extracted data may help improve translation performance.

Following Munteanu and Marcu (2005), we used a Maximum Entropy classifier to identify comparable sentence. To avoid the problem of having different sentence orderings in the article pair, we take every source-target sentence pair in the two articles, and apply the classifier to detect if they are parallel. The classifier approach is appealing to a low-resource language such as Haitian Creole, because the features for the classifier can be generated with minimal translation resources (i.e. a translation lexicon).

5.1 Maximum Entropy Classifier

The classifier probability can be defined as:

$$Pr(c_i|S,T) = \frac{exp\left(\sum_{j=1}^{n} \lambda_j f_{ij}(c_i,S,T)\right)}{Z(S,T)} \quad (2)$$

where (S,T) is a sentence pair, c_i is the class, f_{ij} are feature functions and $Z(S)$ is a normalizing factor. The parameters λ_i are the weights for the feature functions and are estimated by optimizing on a training data set. For the task of classifying a sentence pair, there are two classes, $c_0 = non-parallel$ and $c_1 = parallel$. A value closer to one for $Pr(c_1|S,T)$ indicates that (S,T) are parallel.

The features are defined primarily based on translation lexicon probabilities. Rather than computing word alignment between the two sentences, we use lexical probabilities to determine alignment points as follows: a source word s is aligned to a target word t if $p(s|t) > 0.5$. Target word alignment is computed similarly. We defined a feature set which includes: length ratio and length difference between source and target sentences, lexical probability scores similar to IBM model 1 (Brown et al., 1993), number of aligned/unaligned words and the length of the longest aligned word sequence. Lexical probability score, and alignment features generate two sets of features based on translation lexica obtained by training in both directions. Features are normalized with respect to the sentence length.

5.2 Training and Testing the Classifier

To train the model we need training examples that belong to each of the two classes: parallel and non-parallel. Initially we used a subset of the available parallel data as training examples for the classifier. This data was primarily sourced from medical conversations and newswire text, whereas the comparable data was found in medical articles. This mismatch in domain resulted in poor classification performance. Therefore we manually aligned a set of 250 Haitian Creole-English sentence pairs from the medical articles and divided them in to a training set (175 sentences) and a test set (100 sentences).

The parallel sentence pairs were directly used as positive examples. In selecting negative examples, we followed the same approach as in (Munteanu and Marcu, 2005): pairing all source phrases with all target phrases, but filter out the parallel pairs and those that have high length difference or a low lexical overlap, and then randomly select a subset of phrase pairs as the negative training set. The test set was generated in a similar manner. The model parameters were estimated using the GIS algorithm. We used the trained ME model to classify the sentences in the test set into the two classes, and notice how many instances are classified correctly.

Classification results are as given in Table 6. We notice that even with a smaller training set, the classifier produces results with high precision. Using

[4] Two main sources were: www.rhin.org and www.nlm.nih.gov

	Precision	Recall	F-1 Score
Training Set	93.90	77.00	84.61
Test Set	85.53	74.29	79.52

Table 6: Performance of the Classifier

the trained classifier, we processed 220 article pairs which contained a total of 20K source sentences and 18K target sentences. The classifier selected about 10K sentences as parallel. From these, we selected sentences where $pr(c_1|S,T) > 0.7$ for translation experiments. The extracted data expanded the source vocabulary by about 5%.

We built a second translation system by combining the baseline parallel corpus and the extracted corpus. Table 7 shows the translation results for this system.

	dev (cl)	devtest (cl)	devtest (r)
Baseline	32.28	33.49	29.95
+Extracted	32.29	33.29	29.89

Table 7: Translation results in BLEU with/without extracted data

The results indicate that there is no significant performance difference in using the extracted data. This may be due to the relatively small size of the comparable corpus we used when extract the data.

6 Conclusion

Building an MT system to translate Haitian Creole SMS messages involved several challenges. There was only a limited amount of parallel data to train the models. The SMS messages tend to be quite noisy. After building a baseline MT system, we investigated several approaches to improve its performance. In particular, we tried collapsing OOV words using a lexicon generated with clean data, and normalize different variations in spelling. However, these methods did not results in improved translation performance.

We tried to address the data sparseness problem with two approaches: expanding the corpus using SRL rules, and extracting parallel sentences from a collection of comparable documents. Corpus expansion showed a small improvement for the raw devtest. Both corpus expansion and parallel data extraction did not have a positive impact on other test sets. Both these methods have shown significant performance improvement in the past in large data scenarios (for Chinese-English and Arabic-English), but failed to show improvements in the current low-data scenario. Thus, we need further investigations in handling noisy data, especially in low-resource scenarios.

Acknowledgment

We thank Julianne Mentzer for assisting with editing and proofreading the final version of the paper. We also thank the anonymous reviewers for their valuable comments.

References

Jeff Allen. 1998. Lexical variation in haitian creole and orthographic issues for machine translation (MT) and optical character recognition (OCR) applications. In *Proceedings of the First Workshop on Embedded Machine Translation systems of AMTA conference*, Philadelphia, Pennsylvania, USA, October.

Nicola Bertoldi, Mauro Cettolo, and Marcello Federico. 2010. Statistical machine translation of texts with misspelled words. In *Human Language Technologies: The 2010 Annual Conference of the North American Chapter of the Association for Computational Linguistics*, Los Angeles, California, June.

Eric Brill and Robert C. Moore. 2000. An improved error model for noisy channel spelling correction. In *Proceedings of the 38th Annual Meeting on Association for Computational Linguistics (ACL 2000)*, pages 286–293.

Peter F. Brown, Stephen A. Della Pietra, Vincent J. Della Pietra, and Robert L. Mercer. 1993. The mathematics of statistical machine translation: Parameter estimation. *Computational Linguistics*, 19(2):263–311.

Qin Gao and Stephan Vogel. 2011. Corpus expansion for statistical machine translation with semantic role label substitution rules. In *Proceedings of the 49th Annual Meeting of the Association for Computational Linguistics: Human Language Technologies*, Portland, Oregon, USA, June.

Mark D. Kernighan, Kenneth W. Church, and William A. Gale. 1990. A spelling correction program based on a noisy channel model. In *Proceedings of the 13th conference on Computational linguistics - Volume 2*, COLING '90, pages 205–210.

Philipp Koehn, Hieu Hoang, Alexandra Birch, Chris Callison-Burch, Marcello Federico, Nicola Bertoldi, Brooke Cowan, Wade Shen, Christine Moran, Richard Zens, Chris Dyer, Ondrej Bojar, Alexandra Constantin, and Evan Herbst. 2007. Moses: Open source toolkit for statistical machine translation. In *Proceedings of the 45th Annual Meeting of the Association for Computational Linguistics*, Prague, Czech Republic, June.

William Lewis. 2010. Haitian Creole: How to build and ship an mt engine from scratch in 4 days, 17 hours, & 30 minutes. In *Proceedings of the 14th Annual conference of the European Association for Machine Translation (EAMT)*, Saint-Raphaël, France, May.

Robert Munro. 2010. Crowdsourced translation for emergency response in haiti: the global collaboration of local knowledge. In *AMTA Workshop on Collaborative Crowdsourcing for Translation*, Denver, Colorado, USA, October-November.

Dragos Stefan Munteanu and Daniel Marcu. 2005. Improving machine translation performance by exploiting non-parallel corpora. *Computational Linguistics*, 31(4):477–504.

Franz Josef Och and Hermann Ney. 2003. A systematic comparison of various statistical alignment models. *Computational Linguistics*, 29(1):19–51.

Franz Josef Och. 2003. Minimum error rate training in statistical machine translation. In *Proceedings of the 41st Annual Meeting of the Association for Computational Linguistics*, pages 160–167, Sapporo, Japan.

Kishore Papineni, Salim Roukos, Todd Ward, and Wei-Jing Zhu. 2002. Bleu: a method for automatic evaluation of machine translation. In *Proceedings of the 40th Annual Meeting of the Association for Computational Linguistics*, pages 311–318, Philadelphia, Pennsylvania, USA, July.

Sameer S. Pradhan, Wayne Ward, Kadri Hacioglu, James H. Martin, and Daniel Jurafsky. 2004. Shallow semantic parsing using support vector machines. In *Proceedings of the Human Language Technology Conference/North American chapter of the Association for Computational Linguistics annual meeting (HLT/NAACL-2004)*.

Andreas Stolcke. 2002. An extensible language modeling toolkit. In *Proc. of International Conference on Spoken Language Processing*, volume 2, pages 901–904, Denver, CO, September.

Kristina Toutanova and Robert Moore. 2002. Pronunciation modeling for improved spelling correction. In *40th Annual Meeting of the Association for Computational Linguistics (ACL 2002)*.

Experiments with word alignment, normalization and clause reordering for SMT between English and German

Maria Holmqvist, Sara Stymne and Lars Ahrenberg
Department of Computer and Information Science
Linköping University, Sweden
firstname.lastname@liu.se

Abstract

This paper presents the LIU system for the WMT 2011 shared task for translation between German and English. For English–German we attempted to improve the translation tables with a combination of standard statistical word alignments and phrase-based word alignments. For German–English translation we tried to make the German text more similar to the English text by normalizing German morphology and performing rule-based clause reordering of the German text. This resulted in small improvements for both translation directions.

1 Introduction

In this paper we present the LIU system for the WMT11 shared task, for translation between English and German in both directions. We added a number of features that address problems for translation between German and English such as word order differences, incorrect alignment of certain words such as verbs, and the morphological complexity of German compared to English, as well as dealing with previously unseen words.

In both translation directions our systems include compound processing, morphological sequence models, and a hierarchical reordering model. For German–English translation we also added morphological normalization, source side reordering, and processing of out-of-vocabulary words (OOVs). For English–German translation, we extracted word alignments with a supervised method and combined these alignments with Giza++ alignments in various ways to improve the phrase table. We experimented with different ways of combining the two alignments such as using heuristic symmetrization and interpolating phrase tables.

Results are reported on three metrics, BLEU (Papineni et al., 2002), NIST (Doddington, 2002) and Meteor ranking scores (Agarwal and Lavie, 2008) based on truecased output.

2 Baseline System

This years improvements were added to the LIU baseline system (Stymne et al., 2010). Our baseline is a factored phrase based SMT system that uses the Moses toolkit (Koehn et al., 2007) for translation model training and decoding, GIZA++ (Och and Ney, 2003) for word alignment, SRILM (Stolcke, 2002) an KenLM (Heafield, 2011) for language modelling and minimum error rate training (Och, 2003) to tune model feature weights. In addition, the LIU baseline contains:

- Compound processing, including compound splitting and for translation into German also compound merging
- Part-of-speech and morphological sequence models

All models were trained on truecased data. Translation and reordering models were trained using the bilingual Europarl and News Commentary corpora that were concatenated before training. We created two language models. The first model is a 5-gram model that we created by interpolating two language

Proceedings of the 6th Workshop on Statistical Machine Translation, pages 393–398,
Edinburgh, Scotland, UK, July 30–31, 2011.

models from bilingual News Commentary and Europarl with more weight on the News Commentary model. The second model is a 4-gram model trained on monolingual News only. All models were created using entropy-based pruning with 10^{-8} as the threshold.

Due to time constraints, all tuning and evaluation were performed on half of the provided shared task data. Systems were tuned on 1262 sentences from newstest2009 and all results reported in Tables 1 and 2 are based on a devtest set of 1244 sentences from newstest2010.

2.1 Sequence models with part-of-speech and morphology

To improve target word order and agreement in the translation output, we added an extra output factor in our translation models consisting of tags with POS and morphological features. For English we used tags that were obtained by enriching POS tags from TreeTagger (Schmid, 1994) with additional morphological features such as number for determiners. For German, the POS and morphological tags were obtained from RFTagger (Schmid and Laws, 2008) which provides morphological information such as case, number and gender for nouns and tense for verbs. We trained two sequence models for each system over this output factor and added them as features in our baseline system. The first sequence model is a 7-gram model interpolated from models of bilingual Europarl and News Commentary. The second model is a 6-gram model trained on monolingual News only.

2.2 Compound processing

In both translation directions we split compounds, using a modified version of the corpus-based splitting method of Koehn and Knight (2003). We split nouns, verb, and adjective compounds into known parts that were content words or cardinal numbers, based on the arithmetic mean of the frequency of the parts in the training corpus. We allowed 10 common letter changes (Langer, 1998) and hyphens at split points. Compound parts were kept in their surface form and compound modifiers received a part-of-speech tag based on that of the tag of the full compound.

For translation into German, compounds were merged using the POS-merging strategy of Stymne (2009). A compound part in the translation output, identified by the special part-of-speech tags, was merged with the next word if that word had a matching part-of-speech tag. If the compound part was followed by the conjunction *und* (*and*), we added a hyphen to the part, to account for coordinated compounds.

2.3 Hierarchical reordering

In our baseline system we experimented with two lexicalized reordering models. The standard model in Moses (Koehn et al., 2005), and the hierarchical model of Galley and Manning (2008). In both models the placement of a phrase is compared to that of the previous and/or next phrase. In the standard model up to three reorderings are distinguished, monotone, swap, and discontinuous. In the hierarchical model the discontinuous class can be further subdivided into two classes, left and right discontinuous. The hierarchical model further differs from the standard model in that it compares the order of the phrase with the next or previous block of phrases, not only with the next or previous single phrase.

We investigated one configuration of each model. For the standard model we used the *msd-bidirectional-fe* setting, which uses three orientations, is conditioned on both the source and target language, and considers both the previous and next phrase. For the hierarchical model we used all four orientations, and again it is conditioned on both the source and target language, and considers both the previous and next phrase.

The result of replacing the standard reordering model with an hierarchical model is shown in Table 1 and 2. For translation into German adding the hierarchical model led to small improvements as measured by NIST and Meteor. For translation in the other direction, the differences on automatic metrics were very small. Still, we decided to use the hierarchical model in all our systems.

3 German–English

For translation from German into English we focused on making the German source text more similar to English by removing redundant morphology and changing word order before training translation models.

3.1 Normalization

We performed normalization of German words to remove distinctions that do not exist in English, such as case distinctions on nouns. This strategy is similar to that of El-Kahlout and Yvon (2010), but we used a slightly different set of transformations, that we thought better mirrored the English structure. For morphological tags we used RFTagger and for lemmas we used TreeTagger. The morphological transformations we performed were the following:

- Nouns:
  - Replace with *lemma+s* if plural number
  - Replace with *lemma* otherwise
- Verbs:
  - Replace with *lemma* if present tense, not third person singular
  - Replace with *lemma+p* if past tense
- Adjectives:
  - Replace with *lemma+c* if comparative
  - Replace with *lemma+sup* if superlative
  - Replace with *lemma* otherwise
- Articles:
  - Definite articles:
    * Replace with *des* if genitive
    * Replace with *der* otherwise
  - Indefinite articles:
    * Replace with *eines* if genitive
    * Replace with *ein* otherwise
- Pronouns:
  - Replace with *RELPRO* if relative
  - Replace with *lemma* if indefinite, interrogative, or possessive pronouns
  - Add *+g* to all pronouns which are genitive, unless they are possessive

For all word types that are not mentioned in the list, surface forms were kept.

	BLEU	NIST	Meteor
Baseline	21.01	6.2742	41.32
+hier reo	20.94	6.2800	41.24
+normalization	20.85	6.2370	41.04
+source reordering	21.06	6.3082	41.40
+ OOV proc.	21.22	6.3692	41.51

Table 1: German–English translation results. Results are cumulative.

We also performed those tokenization and spelling normalizations suggested by El-Kahlout and Yvon (2010), that we judged could safely be done for translation from German without collecting corpus statistics. We split words with numbers and letters, such as *40-jährigen* or *40jährigen* (*40 year-old*), unless the suffix indicates that it is a ordinal, such as *70sten* (*70th*). We also did some spelling normalization by exchanging *ß* with *ss* and replacing tripled consonants with doubled consonants. These changes would have been harmful for translation into German, since they change the language into a normalized variant, but for translation from German we considered them safe.

3.2 Source side reordering

To make the word order of German input sentences more English-like a version of the rules of (Collins et al., 2005) were partially implemented using tagged output from the RFTagger. Basically, beginnings of subordinate clauses, their subjects (if present) and final verb clusters were identified based on tag sequences, and the clusters were moved to the beginning of the clause, and reordered so that the finite verb ended up in the second clause position. Also, some common adverbs were moved with the verb cluster and placed between finite and non-finite verbs. After testing, we decided to apply these rules only to subordinate clauses at the end of sentences, since these were the only ones that could be identified with good precision. Still, some 750,000 clauses were reordered.

3.3 OOV Processing

We also added limited processing of OOVs. In a preprocessing step we replaced unknown words with known cased variants if available, removed markup from normalized words if that resulted in an unknown token, and split hyphened words. We also split suspected names in cases where we had a pattern with a single upper-case letter in the middle of a word, such as *ConocoPhillips* into *Conoco Phillips*. In a post-processing step we changed the number formatting of unknown numbers by changing decimal points and thousand separators, to agree with English orthography. This processing only affects a small number of words, and cannot be expected to make a large impact on the final results. Out of 884 OOVs in the devtest, 39 had known cased options, 126 hyphened words were split, 147 cases had markup from the normalization removed, and 13 suspected names were split.

3.4 Results

The results of these experiments can be seen in Table 1 where each new addition is added to the previous system. When we compare the new additions with the baseline with hierarchical reordering, we see that while the normalization did not seem to have a positive effect on any metric, both source reordering and OOV processing led to small increases on all scores.

4 English–German

For translation from English into German we attempted to improve the quality of the phrase table by adding new word alignments to the standard Giza++ alignments.

4.1 Phrase-based word alignment

We experimented with different ways of combining word alignments from Giza++ with alignments created using phrase-based word alignment (PAL) which previously has been shown to improve alignment quality for English–Swedish (Holmqvist, 2010). The idea of phrase-based word alignment is to use word and part-of-speech sequence patterns from manual word alignments to align new texts. First, parallel phrases containing a source segment, a target segment and links between source and target words are extracted from word aligned texts (Figure 1). In the second step, these phrases are matched against new parallel text and if a matching phrase is found, word links from the phrase are added to the corresponding words in the new text. In order to increase the number of matching phrases and improve word alignment recall, words in the parallel

```
En:    a typical example
De:    ein typisches Beispiel
Links: 0-0 1-1 2-2

En:    a JJ example
De:    ein ADJA Beispiel
Links: 0-0 1-1 2-2

En:    DT JJ NN
De:    ART ADJA N
Links: 0-0 1-1 2-2
```

Figure 1: Examples of parallel phrases used in word alignment.

	BLEU	NIST	Meteor
Baseline	16.16	6.2742	50.89
+hier reo	16.06	6.2800	51.25
+pal-gdfa	16.14	5.6527	51.10
+pal-dual	15.71	5.5735	50.43
+pal-inter	15.92	5.6230	50.73

Table 2: English–German translation results, results are cumulative except for the three alternative *PAL*-configurations.

segments were replaced by POS/morphological tags from RFTagger.

Alignment patterns were extracted from 1000 sentences in the manually word aligned sample of English–German Europarl texts from Pado and Lapata (2006). All parallel phrases were extracted from the word aligned texts, as when extracting a translation model. Parallel phrases that contain at least 3 words were generalized with POS tags to form word/POS patterns for alignment. A subset of these patterns, with high alignment precision (> 0.80) on the 1000 sentences, were used to align the entire training corpus.

We combined the new word alignments with the Giza++ alignments in two ways. In the first method, we used a symmetrization heuristic similar to grow-diag-final-and to combine three word alignments into one, the phrase-based alignment and two Giza++ alignments in different directions. In the second method we extracted a separate phrase table from the sparser phrase-based alignment using a constrained method of phrase extraction that limited the number of unaligned words in each phrase pair. The reason for constraining the phrase table extraction was that the standard extraction method does not work well for the sparse word alignments that PAL produces, but we think it could still be useful for extracting highly reliable phrases. After some experimentation we decided to allow an unlimited number of internal unaligned words, that is unaligned words that are surrounded by aligned words, but limit the number of external unaligned words, i.e., unaligned words at the beginning or end of the phrase, to either one each in the source and target phrase, or to zero.

We used two ways to include the sparse phrase-table into the translation process:

- Have two separate phrase-tables, the sparse table, and the standard GIZA++ based phrase-table, and use Moses' dual decoding paths.

- Interpolate the sparse phrase-table with the standard phrase-table, using the mixture model formulation of Ueffing et al. (2007), with equal weights, in order to boost the probabilities of highly reliable phrases.

4.2 Results

We evaluated our systems on devtest data and found that the added phrase-based alignments did not produce large differences in translation quality compared to the baseline system with hierarchical reordering as shown in Table 2. The system created with a heuristic combination of PAL and Giza++ (pal-gdfa) had a small increase in BLEU, but no improvement on the other metrics. Systems using a phrase table extracted from the sparse alignments did not produce better results than baseline. The system using dual decoding paths (pal-dual) produced worse results than the system using an interpolated phrase table (pal-inter).

5 Submitted systems

The LIU system participated in German–English and English–German translation in the WMT 2011 shared task. The new additions were a combination of unsupervised and supervised word alignments, spelling normalization, clause reordering and OOV processing. Our submitted systems contain all additions described in this paper. For English-German we used the best performing method of word alignment combination which was the method that uses heuristic combination similar to grow-diag-final-and.

		BLEU	
	System	Devtest	Test
en-de	baseline +hier	16.1	14.5
	submitted	16.1	14.8
de-en	baseline +hier	20.9	19.3
	submitted	21.2	19.9

Table 3: Summary of devtest results and shared task test results for submitted systems and LIU baseline with hierarchical reordering.

The results of our submitted systems are shown in Table 3 where we compare them to the LIU baseline system with hierarchical reordering models. We report modest improvements on the devtest set for both translation directions. We also found small improvements of our submitted systems in the official shared task evaluation on the test set newstest2011.

References

Abhaya Agarwal and Alon Lavie. 2008. Meteor, M-BLEU and M-TER: Evaluation metrics for high-correlation with human rankings of machine translation output. In *Proceedings of the Third Workshop on Statistical Machine Translation*, pages 115–118, Columbus, Ohio.

Michael Collins, Philipp Koehn, and Ivona Kucerová. 2005. Clause restructuring for statistical machine translation. In *Proceedings of the 43rd Annual Meeting of the ACL*, pages 531–540, Ann Arbor, Michigan.

George Doddington. 2002. Automatic evaluation of machine translation quality using n-gram co-occurence statistics. In *Proceedings of the Second International Conference on Human Language Technology*, pages 228–231, San Diego, California.

İlknur Durgar El-Kahlout and François Yvon. 2010. The pay-offs of preprocessing for German-English statistical machine translation. In *Proceedings of the International Workshop on Spoken Language Translation*, pages 251–258, Paris, France.

Michel Galley and Christopher D. Manning. 2008. A simple and effective hierarchical phrase reordering model. In *Proceedings of the Conference on Empirical Methods in Natural Language Processing*, pages 848–856, Honolulu, Hawaii.

Kenneth Heafield. 2011. KenLM: Faster and Smaller Language Model Queries. In *Proceedings of the Sixth*

Workshop on Statistical Machine Translation, Edinburgh, UK.

Maria Holmqvist. 2010. Heuristic word alignment with parallel phrases. In *Proceedings of the Seventh Conference on International Language Resources and Evaluation*, pages 744-748, Valletta, Malta.

Philipp Koehn and Kevin Knight. 2003. Empirical methods for compound splitting. In *Proceedings of the Tenth Conference of EACL*, pages 187–193, Budapest, Hungary.

Philipp Koehn, Amittai Axelrod, Alexandra Birch Mayne, Chris Callison-Burch, Miles Osborne, and David Talbot. 2005. Edinburgh system description for the 2005 IWSLT speech translation evaluation. In *Proceedings of the International Workshop on Spoken Language Translation*, Pittsburgh, Pennsylvania.

Philipp Koehn, Hieu Hoang, Alexandra Birch, Chris Callison-Burch, Marcello Federico, Nicola Bertoldi, Brooke Cowan, Wade Shen, Christine Moran, Richard Zens, Chris Dyer, Ondrej Bojar, Alexandra Constantin, and Evan Herbst. 2007. Moses: Open source toolkit for statistical machine translation. In *Proceedings of the 45th Annual Meeting of the ACL, Demonstration Session*, 177–180, Prague, Czech Republic.

Stefan Langer. 1998. Zur Morphologie und Semantik von Nominalkomposita. In *Tagungsband der 4. Konferenz zur Verarbeitung natürlicher Sprache*, pages 83–97, Bonn, Germany.

Franz Josef Och and Hermann Ney. 2003. A systematic comparison of various statistical alignment models. *Computational Linguistics*, 29(1):19–51.

Franz Josef Och. 2003. Minimum error rate training in statistical machine translation. In *Proceedings of the 41st Annual Meeting of the ACL*, pages 160–167, Sapporo, Japan.

Sebastian Pado and Mirella Lapata. 2006. Optimal constituent alignment with edge covers for semantic projection. In *Proceedings of the 21st International Conference on Computational Linguistics and 44th Annual Meeting of the ACL*, pages 1161–1168, Sydney, Australia.

Kishore Papineni, Salim Roukos, Todd Ward, and Wei-Jing Zhu. 2002. BLEU: a method for automatic evaluation of machine translation. In *Proceedings of the 40th Annual Meeting of ACL*, pages 311–318, Philadelphia, Pennsylvania.

Helmut Schmid and Florian Laws. 2008. Estimation of conditional probabilities with decision trees and an application to fine-grained POS tagging. In *Proceedings of the 20th International Conference on Computational Linguistics*, pages 777–784, Manchester, UK.

Helmut Schmid. 1994. Probabilistic part-of-speech tagging using decision trees. In *International Conference on New Methods in Language Processing*, pages 44–49, Manchester, UK.

Andreas Stolcke. 2002. SRILM - an extensible language modeling toolkit. In *Proceedings of the Seventh International Conference on Spoken Language Processing*, pages 901–904, Denver, Colorado.

Sara Stymne, Maria Holmqvist, and Lars Ahrenberg. 2010. Vs and OOVs: Two problems for translation between German and English. In *Proceedings of the Joint Fifth Workshop on Statistical Machine Translation and MetricsMATR*, pages 189–194, Uppsala, Sweden.

Sara Stymne. 2009. A comparison of merging strategies for translation of German compounds. In *Proceedings of the EACL Student Research Workshop*, pages 61–69, Athens, Greece.

Nicola Ueffing, Gholamreza Haffari, and Anoop Sarkar. 2007. Semi-supervised model adaptation for statistical machine translation. *Machine Translation*, 21(2):77–94.

The Value of Monolingual Crowdsourcing in a Real-World Translation Scenario: Simulation using Haitian Creole Emergency SMS Messages

Chang Hu[‡], **Philip Resnik**[†‡], **Yakov Kronrod**[†]
Vladimir Eidelman[‡], **Olivia Buzek**[†‡], **Benjamin B. Bederson**[‡]
[†]UMIACS and Department of Linguistics
[‡]UMIACS and Department of Computer Science
University of Maryland, College Park
{changhu,bederson}@cs.umd.edu
{resnik,vlad,buzek}@umiacs.umd.edu
yakov@umd.edu

Abstract

MonoTrans2 is a translation system that combines machine translation (MT) with human computation using two *crowds* of monolingual source (Haitian Creole) and target (English) speakers. We report on its use in the WMT 2011 Haitian Creole to English translation task, showing that MonoTrans2 translated 38% of the sentences well compared to Google Translate's 25%.

1 Introduction

One of the most remarkable success stories to come out of the January 2010 earthquake in Haiti involved translation (Munro, 2010). While other forms of emergency response and communication channels were failing, text messages were still getting through, so a number of people came together to create a free phone number for emergency text messages, which allowed earthquake victims to report those who were trapped or in need of medical attention. The problem, of course, was that most people were texting in Haitian Creole (Kreyol), a language not many of the emergency responders understood, and few, if any, professional translators were available. The availability of usable translations literally became a matter of life and death.

In response to this need, Stanford University graduate student Rob Munro coordinated the rapid creation of a crowdsourcing framework, which allowed volunteers – including, for example, Haitian expatriates and French speakers – to translate messages, providing responders with usable information in as little as ten minutes. Translations may not have been perfect, but to a woman in labor, it had to have made a big difference for English-speaking responders to see *Undergoing children delivery Delmas 31* instead of *Fanm gen tranche pou fè yon pitit nan Delmas 31*.

What about a scenario, though, in which even amateur bilingual volunteers are hard to find, or too few in number? What about a scenario, e.g. the March 2011 earthquake and tsunami in Japan, in which there are many people worldwide who wish to help but are not fluent in both the source and target languages?

For the last few years, we have been exploring the idea of *monolingual* crowdsourcing for translation – that is, technology-assisted collaborative translation involving crowds of participants who know only the source or target language (Buzek et al., 2010; Hu, 2009; Hu et al., 2010; Hu et al., 2011; Resnik et al., 2010). Our MonoTrans2 framework has previously shown very promising results on children's books: on a test set where Google Translate produced correct translations for only 10% of the input sentences, monolingual German and Spanish speakers using our framework produced translations that were fully correct (as judged by two independent bilinguals) nearly 70% of the time (Hu et al., 2011).

We used the same framework in the WMT 2011 Haitian-English translation task. For this experiment, we hired Haitian Creole speakers located in Haiti, and recruited English speakers located in the U.S., to serve as the monolingual crowds.

2 System

MonoTrans2 is a translation system that combines machine translation (MT) with human computation (Quinn et al., 2011) using two "crowds" of monolingual source (Haitian Creole) and target (English)

Proceedings of the 6th Workshop on Statistical Machine Translation, pages 399–404,
Edinburgh, Scotland, UK, July 30–31, 2011.

speakers.[1] We summarize its operation here; see Hu et al. (2011) for details.

The Haitian Creole sentence is first automatically translated into English and presented to the English speakers. The English speakers then can take any of the following actions for candidate translations:

- Mark a phrase in the candidate as an error
- Suggest a new translation candidate
- Vote candidates up or down

Identifying likely errors and voting for candidates are things monolinguals can do reasonably well: even without knowing the intended interpretation, you can often identify when some part of a sentence doesn't make sense, or when one sentence seems more fluent or plausible than another. Sometimes rather than identifying errors, it is easier to suggest an entirely new translation candidate based on the information available on the target side, a variant of monolingual post-editing (Callison-Burch et al., 2004).

Any new translation candidates are then back-translated into Haitian Creole, and any spans marked as translation errors are projected back to identify the corresponding spans in the source sentence, using word alignments as the bridge (cf. Hwa et al. (2002), Yarowsky et al. (2001)).[2] The Haitian Creole speakers can then:

- Rephrase the entire source sentence (cf. (Morita and Ishida, 2009))
- "Explain" spans marked as errors
- Vote candidates up or down (based on the back-translation)

Source speakers can "explain" error spans by offering a different way of phrasing that piece of the source sentence (Resnik et al., 2010), in order to produce a new source sentence, or by annotating the spans with images (e.g. via Google image search) or Web links (e.g. to Wikipedia). The protocol then continues: new source sentences created via partial- or full-sentence paraphrase pass back through MT to the English side, and any explanatory annotations are projected back to the corresponding spans in the English candidate translations (where the error spans had been identified). The process is asynchronous: participants on the Haitian Creole and English sides can work independently on whatever is available to them at any time. At any point, the voting-based scores can be used to extract a 1-best translation.

In summary, the MonoTrans2 framework uses noisy MT to cross the language barrier, and supports monolingual participants in doing small tasks that gain leverage from redundant information, the human capacity for linguistic and real-world inference, and the wisdom of the crowd.

3 Experiment

We recruited 26 English speakers and 4 Haitian Creole speakers. The Haitian Creole speakers were recruited from Haiti and do not speak English. Five of the 26 English speakers were paid UMD undergraduates; the other 21 were volunteer researchers, graduate students, and staff unrelated to this research. [3] Over a 13 day period, Haitian Creole and English speaker efforts totaled 15 and 29 hours, respectively.

4 Data Sets

Our original goal of fully processing the entire SMS clean test and devtest sets could not be realized in the available time, owing to unanticipated reshuffling of the data by the shared task organizers and logistical challenges working with participants in Haiti. Table 1 summarizes the data set sizes before and after reshuffling. We put 1,224 sentences from the pre-reshuffling test set, interspersed with 123 of the 925 sentences from the pre-reshuffling devtest set, into the system — 1,347 sentences in total. We report

	before	after
test	1,224	1,274
devtest	925	900

Table 1: SMS clean data sets before and after reshuffling

[1]For the work reported here, we used Google Translate as the MT component via the Google Translate Research API.

[2]The Google Translate Research API provides alignments with its hypotheses.

[3]These, obviously, did not include any of the authors.

results on the union of pre- and post-reshuffling devtest sentences (Set A, $|A| = 1516$), and the post-reshuffling test set (Set B, $|B| = 1274$).

5 Evaluation

Of the 1,347 sentences available for processing in MonoTrans2, we define three subsets:

- $Touched$: Sentences that were processed by at least one person (657 sentences)
- *Each-side*: Sentences that were processed by at least one English speaker followed by at least one Haitian Creole speaker (431 sentences)
- $Full$: Sentences that have at least three translation candidates, of which the most voted-for one received at least three votes (207 sentences)

We intersect these three sets with sets A and B in order to evaluate MonoTrans2 output against the provided references (Table 2).[4]

Set S	$\|S\|$	$\|S \cap A\|$	$\|S \cap B\|$
$Touched$	657	162	168
Each-side	431	127	97
$Full$	207	76	60

Table 2: Data sets for evaluation and their sizes

Tables 3 and 4 report two automatic scoring metrics, uncased BLEU and TER, comparing MonoTrans2 (M2) against Google Translate (GT) as a baseline.

Set	Condition	BLEU	TER
$Touched \cap A$	GT	21.75	56.99
	M2	23.25	57.27
Each-side $\cap A$	GT	21.44	57.51
	M2	21.47	58.98
$Full \cap A$	GT	25.05	54.15
	M2	27.59	52.78

Table 3: BLEU and TER results for different levels of completion on the devtest set A

Since the number of sentences in each evaluated set is different (Table 2), we cannot directly compare

Set	Condition	BLEU	TER
$Touched \cap B$	GT	19.78	59.88
	M2	24.09	58.15
Each-side $\cap B$	GT	21.15	56.88
	M2	23.80	57.19
$Full \cap B$	GT	22.51	54.51
	M2	28.90	52.22

Table 4: BLEU and TER results for different levels of completion on the test set B

scores between the sets. However, Table 4 shows that when the MonoTrans2 process is run on test items "to completion", in the sense defined by "Full" (i.e. $Full \cap B$), we see a dramatic BLEU gain of 6.39, and a drop in TER of 2.29 points. Moreover, even when only target-side or only source-side monolingual participation is available we see a gain of 4.31 BLEU and a drop of 1.73 TER points ($Touched \cap B$).

By contrast, the results on the devtest data are encouraging, but arguably mixed (Table 3). In order to step away from the vagaries of single-reference automatic evaluations, therefore, we also conducted an evaluation based on human judgments. Two native English speakers unfamiliar with the project were recruited and paid for fluency and adequacy judgments: for each target translation paired with its corresponding reference, each evaluator rated the target sentence's fluency and adequacy on a 5-point scale, where fluency of 5 indicates complete fluency and adequacy of 5 indicates complete preservation of meaning (Dabbadie et al., 2002).[5]

Sentences	N	Google		MonoTrans2	
$Full \cap A$	76	18	(24%)	30	(39%)
$Full \cap B$	60	15	(25%)	23	(38%)

Table 5: Number of sentences with maximum possible adequacy (5) in $Full \cap A$ and $Full \cap B$, respectively.

Similar to Hu et al. (2011), we adopt the very conservative criterion that a translation output is considered correct only if *both* evaluators independently give it a rating of 5. Unlike Hu et al. (2011), for whom children's book translation requires both fluency and adequacy, we make this a requirement only

[4]Note that according to these definitions, $Touched$ contains both *Each-side* and $Full$, but *Each-side* does not contain $Full$.

[5]Presentation order was randomized.

for adequacy, since in this scenario what matters to aid organizations is not whether a translation is fully fluent, but whether it is correct. On this criterion, the Google Translate baseline of around 25% correct improves to around 40% for Monotrans, consistently for both the devtest and test data (Table 5). Nonetheless, Figures 1 and 2 make it clear that the improvements in fluency are if anything more striking.

5.1 Statistical Analysis

Variable	Adequacy	Fluency
Positive		
mostSingleCandidateVote	**	***
candidateCount	**	**
numOfAnswers	*	NS
Negative		
roundTrips	***	***
voteCount	*	.

Table 6: Effects of independent variables in linear regression for 330 touched sentences
(Signif. codes: '***' 0.001, '**' 0.01, '*' 0.05, '.' 0.1)

In addition to the main evaluation, we investigated the relationship between tasks performed in the MonoTrans2 system and human judgments using linear regression and an analysis of variance. We evaluate the set of all 330 touched sentences in $Touched \cap A$ and $Touched \cap B$ in order to understand which properties of the MonoTrans2 process correlate with better translation outcomes.

Our analysis focused on improvement over the Google Translate baseline, looking specifically at the improvement based on the human evaluators' averaged fluency and adequacy scores.

Table 6 summarizes the positive and negative effects for five of six variables we considered that came out significant for at least one of the measures. 6

The positive results were as expected. Having more votes for the winning candidate (*mostSingleCandidateVote*) made it more successful, since this means that more people felt it was a good representative translation. Having more candidates to choose from (*candidateCount*) meant that more people had taken the time to generate alternatives, reflecting attention paid to the sentence. Also, the amount of attention paid to target speakers' requests for clarification (*numOfAnswers*) is as expected related to the adequacy of the final translation, and perhaps as expected does not correlate with fluency of the output since it helps with meaning and not actual target-side wording.

We were, however, confused at first by the negative influence of the *roundTrips* measure and *voteCount* measures. We conjecture that the first effect arises due to a correlation between roundTrips and translation difficulty; much harder sentences would have led to many more paraphrase requests, and hence to more round trips. We attempted to investigate this hypothesis by testing correlation with a naive measure of sentence difficulty, length, but this was not fruitful. We suspect that inspecting use of abbreviations, proper nouns, source-side mistakes, and syntactic complexity would give us more insight into this issue.

As for *voteCount*, the negative correlation is understandable when considered side by side with the other vote-based measure, *mostSingleCandidateVote*. Having a higher number of votes for the winning candidate leads to improvement (strongly significant for both adequacy and fluency), so a higher general vote count means that people were also voting more times for other candidates. Hence, once the positive winning vote count is taken into account, the remaining votes actually represent disagreement on the candidates, hence correlating negatively with overall improvement over baseline.

It is important to note that when these measures are all considered together, they show that there is a clear correlation between the MonoTrans2 system's human processing and the eventual increase in both quality and fluency of the sentences. As people give more attention to sentences, these sentences show better performance, as judged by increase over baseline.

6 Discussion

Our experiment did not address acquisition of, and incentives for, monolingual participants. In fact, getting time from Haitian Creole speakers, even for pay,

[6] A sixth, *numOfVoters*, was not significant in the linear regression for either adequacy or fluency.

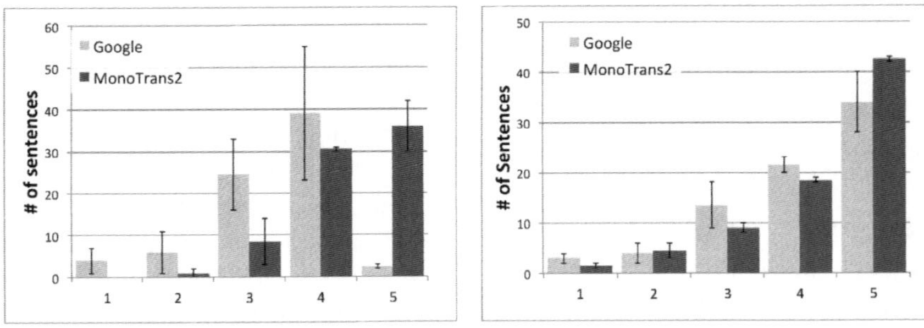

(a) Fluency Distribution (b) Adequacy Distribution

Figure 1: Human judgments for fluency and adequacy in fully processed devtest items ($Full \cap A$)

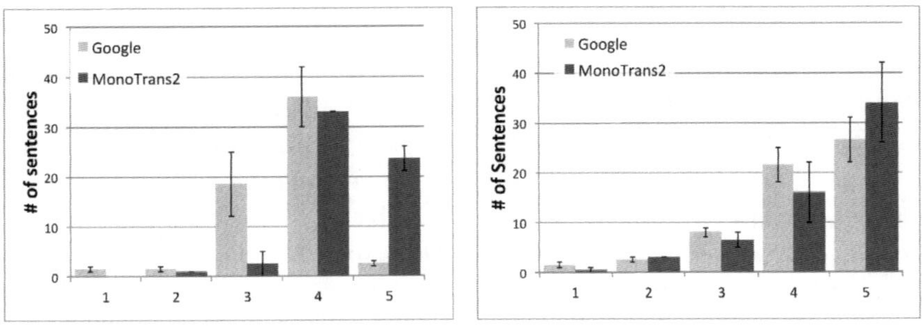

(a) Fluency Distribution (b) Adequacy Distribution

Figure 2: Human judgments for fluency and adequacy in fully processed test items ($Full \cap B$)

created a large number of logistical challenges, and was a contributing factor as to why we did not obtain translations for the entire test set. However, availability of monolingual participants is not the issue being addressed in this experiment: we are confident that in a real-world scenario like the Haitian or Japanese earthquakes, large numbers of monolingual volunteers would be eager to help, certainly in larger total numbers than *bilingual* volunteers. What matters here, therefore, is not how much of the test set was translated in total, but how much the translations improved for the sentences where monolingual crowdsourcing was involved, compared to the MT baseline, and what throughput might be like in a real-world scenario.

We also were interested in throughput, particularly in comparison to bilingual translators. In previous experimentation (Hu et al., 2011), throughput in MonoTrans2 extrapolated to roughly 800 words per day, a factor of 2.5 slower than professional translators' typical speed of 2000 words per day. In this experiment, overall translation speed averaged about 300 words per day, a factor of more than 6 times slower. However, this is an extremely pessimistic estimate, for several reasons. First, our previous experiment had more than 20 users per side, while here our Haitian crowd consisted of only four people. Second, we discovered after beginning the experiment that the translation of our instructions into Haitian Creole had been done somewhat sloppily. And, third, we encountered a range of technical and logistical problems with our Haitian participants, ranging from finding a location with Internet access to do the work (ultimately an Internet Café turned out to be the best option), to slow and sporadic connections (even in an Internet Café), to relative lack of motivation for part-time rather than full-time work. It is fair to assume that in a real-world scenario, some unanticipated problems like these might crop up, but it also seems fair to assume that many would not; for example, most people from the Haitian Creole and French-speaking communities who volunteered using Munro et al.'s system in January 2010 were not themselves located in the third world.

Finally, regarding quality, the results here are promising, albeit not as striking as those Hu et al. (2011) obtained for Spanish-German translation of children's books. The nature of SMS messages themselves may have been a contributing factor to the lower translation adequacy: even in clean form, these are sometimes written using shorthand (e.g. "SVP"), and are sometimes not syntactically correct. The text messages are seldom related to each other, unlike sentences in larger bodies of text where even partially translated sentences can be related to each other to provide context, as is the case for children's books. One should also keep in mind that the underlying machine translation engine, Google Translate between Haitian Creole and English, is still in an alpha phase.

Those considerations notwithstanding, it is encouraging to see a set of machine translations get better without the use of any human bilingual expertise. We are optimistic that with further refinements and research, monolingual translation crowdsourcing will make it possible to harness the vast number of technologically connected people who want to help in some way when disaster strikes.

7 Acknowledgments

This research is supported by NSF contract #BCS0941455 and by a Google Research Award.

References

Olivia Buzek, Philip Resnik, and Benjamin B. Bederson. 2010. Error driven paraphrase annotation using mechanical turk. In *NAACL 2010 Workshop on Creating Speech and Text Language Data With Amazon's Mechanical Turk*.

Chris Callison-Burch, Colin Bannard, , and Josh Schroeder. 2004. Improving statistical translation through editing. In *Workshop of the European Association for Machine Translation*.

Marianne Dabbadie, Anthony Hartley, Margaret King, Keith J. Miller, Widad Mustafa El Hadi, Andrei Popescu-Belis, Florence Reeder, and Michelle Vanni. 2002. A hands-on study of the reliability and coherence of evaluation metrics. In *Workshop at the LREC 2002 Conference*, page 8. Citeseer.

Chang Hu, Benjamin B. Bederson, and Philip Resnik. 2010. Translation by iterative collaboration between monolingual users. In *Proceedings of Graphics Interface 2010 on Proceedings of Graphics Interface 2010*, pages 39–46, Ottawa, Ontario, Canada. Canadian Information Processing Society.

Chang Hu, Ben Bederson, Philip Resnik, and Yakov Kronrod. 2011. Monotrans2: A new human computation system to support monolingual translation. In *Human Factors in Computing Systems (CHI 2011)*, Vancouver, Canada, May. ACM, ACM.

Chang Hu. 2009. Collaborative translation by monolingual users. In *Proceedings of the 27th international conference extended abstracts on Human factors in computing systems*, pages 3105–3108, Boston, MA, USA. ACM.

Rebecca Hwa, Philip Resnik, Amy Weinberg, and Okan Kolak. 2002. Evaluating translational correspondence using annotation projection. In *Proceedings of the 40th Annual Meeting on Association for Computational Linguistics*, pages 392–399, Philadelphia, Pennsylvania. Association for Computational Linguistics.

Daisuke Morita and Toru Ishida. 2009. Designing protocols for collaborative translation. In *PRIMA '09: Proceedings of the 12th International Conference on Principles of Practice in Multi-Agent Systems*, pages 17–32, Berlin, Heidelberg. Springer-Verlag.

Robert Munro. 2010. Crowdsourced translation for emergency response in haiti: the global collaboration of local knowledge. In *AMTA Workshop on Collaborative Crowdsourcing for Translation*. Keynote.

Alexander J. Quinn, Bederson, and Benjamin B. Bederson. 2011. Human computation: A survey and taxonomy of a growing field. In *Human Factors in Computing Systems (CHI 2011)*, Vancouver, Canada, May. ACM, ACM.

Philip Resnik, Olivia Buzek, Chang Hu, Yakov Kronrod, Alexander J. Quinn, and Benjamin B. Bederson. 2010. Improving translation via targeted paraphrasing. In *EMNLP*.

David Yarowsky, Grace Ngai, and Richard Wicentowski. 2001. Inducing multilingual text analysis tools via robust projection across aligned corpora. In *HLT '01: Proceedings of the first international conference on Human language technology research*, pages 1–8, Morristown, NJ, USA. Association for Computational Linguistics.

The RWTH Aachen Machine Translation System for WMT 2011

Matthias Huck, Joern Wuebker, Christoph Schmidt, Markus Freitag, Stephan Peitz, Daniel Stein, Arnaud Dagnelies, Saab Mansour, Gregor Leusch and Hermann Ney
RWTH Aachen University
Aachen, Germany
surname@cs.rwth-aachen.de

Abstract

This paper describes the statistical machine translation (SMT) systems developed by RWTH Aachen University for the translation task of the EMNLP 2011 Sixth Workshop on Statistical Machine Translation. Both phrase-based and hierarchical SMT systems were trained for the constrained German-English and French-English tasks in all directions. Experiments were conducted to compare different training data sets, training methods and optimization criteria, as well as additional models on dependency structure and phrase reordering. Further, we applied a system combination technique to create a consensus hypothesis from several different systems.

1 Overview

We sketch the baseline architecture of RWTH's setups for the WMT 2011 shared translation task by providing an overview of our translation systems in Section 2. In addition to the baseline features, we adopted several novel methods, which will be presented in Section 3. Details on the respective setups and translation results for the French-English and German-English language pairs (in both translation directions) are given in Sections 4 and 5. We finally conclude the paper in Section 6.

2 Translation Systems

For the WMT 2011 evaluation we utilized RWTH's state-of-the-art phrase-based and hierarchical translation systems as well as our in-house system combination framework. GIZA++ (Och and Ney, 2003) was employed to train word alignments, language models have been created with the SRILM toolkit (Stolcke, 2002).

2.1 Phrase-Based System

We applied a phrase-based translation (PBT) system similar to the one described in (Zens and Ney, 2008). Phrase pairs are extracted from a word-aligned bilingual corpus and their translation probability in both directions is estimated by relative frequencies. The standard feature set moreover includes an n-gram language model, phrase-level single-word lexicons and word-, phrase- and distortion-penalties. To lexicalize reordering, a discriminative reordering model (Zens and Ney, 2006a) is used. Parameters are optimized with the Downhill-Simplex algorithm (Nelder and Mead, 1965) on the word graph.

2.2 Hierarchical System

For the hierarchical setups described in this paper, the open source Jane toolkit (Vilar et al., 2010) was employed. Jane has been developed at RWTH and implements the hierarchical approach as introduced by Chiang (2007) with some state-of-the-art extensions. In hierarchical phrase-based translation, a weighted synchronous context-free grammar is induced from parallel text. In addition to contiguous *lexical* phrases, *hierarchical* phrases with up to two gaps are extracted. The search is typically carried out using the cube pruning algorithm (Huang and Chiang, 2007). The standard models integrated into our Jane systems are: phrase translation probabilities and lexical translation probabilities on phrase level, each for both translation directions, length

Proceedings of the 6th Workshop on Statistical Machine Translation, pages 405–412,
Edinburgh, Scotland, UK, July 30–31, 2011. ©2011 Association for Computational Linguistics

penalties on word and phrase level, three binary features marking hierarchical phrases, glue rule, and rules with non-terminals at the boundaries, source-to-target and target-to-source phrase length ratios, four binary count features and an n-gram language model. The model weights are optimized with standard MERT (Och, 2003) on 100-best lists.

2.3 System Combination

System combination is used to produce consensus translations from multiple hypotheses produced with different translation engines that are better in terms of translation quality than any of the individual hypotheses. The basic concept of RWTH's approach to machine translation system combination has been described by Matusov et al. (Matusov et al., 2006; Matusov et al., 2008). This approach includes an enhanced alignment and reordering framework. A lattice is built from the input hypotheses. The translation with the best score within the lattice according to a couple of statistical models is selected as consensus translation.

3 Translation Modeling

We incorporated several novel methods into our systems for the WMT 2011 evaluation. This section provides a short survey of three of the methods which we suppose to be of particular interest.

3.1 Language Model Data Selection

For the English and German language models, we applied the data selection method proposed in (Moore and Lewis, 2010). Each sentence is scored by the difference in cross-entropy between a language model trained from in-domain data and a language model trained from a similar-sized sample of the out-of-domain data. As in-domain data we used the news-commentary corpus. The out-of-domain data from which the data was selected are the news crawl corpus for both languages and for English the 10^9 corpus and the LDC Gigaword data. We used a 3-gram trained with the SRI toolkit to compute the cross-entropy. For the news crawl corpus, only $1/8$ of the sentences were discarded. Of the 10^9 corpus we retained $1/2$ and of the LDC Gigaword data we retained $1/4$ of the sentences to train the language models.

3.2 Phrase Model Training

For the German→English and French→English translation tasks we applied a forced alignment procedure to train the phrase translation model with the EM algorithm, similar to the one described in (DeNero et al., 2006). Here, the phrase translation probabilities are estimated from their relative frequencies in the phrase-aligned training data. The phrase alignment is produced by a modified version of the translation decoder. In addition to providing a statistically well-founded phrase model, this has the benefit of producing smaller phrase tables and thus allowing more rapid experiments. A detailed description of the training procedure is given in (Wuebker et al., 2010).

3.3 Soft String-to-Dependency

Given a dependency tree of the target language, we are able to introduce language models that span over longer distances than the usual n-grams, as in (Shen et al., 2008). To obtain dependency structures, we apply the Stanford parser (Klein and Manning, 2003) on the target side of the training material. RWTH's open source hierarchical translation toolkit Jane has been extended to include dependency information in the phrase table and to build dependency trees on the output hypotheses at decoding time from this information.

Shen et al. (2008) use only phrases that meet certain restrictions. The first possibility is what the authors call a *fixed* dependency structure. With the exception of one word within this phrase, called the *head*, no outside word may have a dependency within this phrase. Also, all inner words may only depend on each other or on the head. For a second structure, called a *floating* dependency structure, the head dependency word may also exist outside the phrase. If the dependency structure of a phrase conforms to these restrictions, it is denoted as *valid*.

In our phrase table, we mark those phrases that possess a valid dependency structure with a binary feature, but all phrases are retained as translation options. In addition to storing the dependency information, we also memorize for all hierarchical phrases if the content of gaps has been dependent on the left or on the right side. We utilize the dependency information during the search process by adding three

	French	English
Sentences	3 710 985	
Running Words	98 352 916	87 689 253
Vocabulary	179 548	216 765

Table 1: Corpus statistics of the preprocessed high-quality training data (Europarl, news-commentary, and selected parts of the 10^9 and UN corpora) for the RWTH systems for the WMT 2011 French→English and English→French translation tasks. Numerical quantities are replaced by a single category symbol.

	French	English
Sentences	29 996 228	
Running Words	916 347 538	778 544 843
Vocabulary	1 568 089	1 585 093

Table 2: Corpus statistics of the preprocessed full training data for the RWTH primary system for the WMT 2011 English→French translation task. Numerical quantities are replaced by a single category symbol.

features to the log-linear model: merging errors to the left, merging errors to the right, and the ratio of valid vs. non-valid dependency structures. The decoder computes the corresponding costs when it tries to construct a dependency tree of a (partial) hypothesis on-the-fly by merging the dependency structures of the used phrase pairs.

In an n-best reranking step, we compute dependency language model scores on the dependencies which were assembled on the hypotheses by the search procedure. We apply one language model for left-side dependencies and one for right-side dependencies. For head structures, we also compute their scores by exploiting a simple unigram language model. We furthermore include a language count feature that is incremented each time we compute a dependency language model score. As trees with few dependencies have less individual costs to be computed, they tend to obtain lower overall costs than trees with more complex structures in other sentences. The intention behind this feature is thus comparable to the word penalty in combination with a normal n-gram language model.

4 French-English Setups

We set up both hierarchical and standard phrase-based systems for the constrained condition of the WMT 2011 French→English and English→French translation tasks. The English→French RWTH primary submission was produced with a single hierarchical system, while a system combination of three systems was used to generate a final hypothesis for the French→English primary submission.

Besides the Europarl and news-commentary corpora, the provided parallel data also comprehends the large French-English 10^9 corpus and the French-English UN corpus. Since model training with such a huge amount of data requires a considerable computational effort, RWTH decided to select a high-quality part of altogether about 2 Mio. sentence pairs from the latter two corpora. The selection of parallel sentences was carried out according to three criteria: (1) Only sentences of minimum length of 4 tokens are considered, (2) at least 92% of the vocabulary of each sentence occurs in newstest2008, and (3) the ratio of the vocabulary size of a sentence and the number of its tokens is minimum 80%. Word alignments in both directions were trained with GIZA++ and symmetrized according to the refined method that was proposed in (Och and Ney, 2003). The phrase tables of the translation systems are extracted from the Europarl and news-commentary parallel training data as well as the selected high-quality parts the 10^9 and UN corpora only. The only exception is the hierarchical system used for the English→French RWTH primary submission which comprehends a second phrase table with lexical (i.e. non-hierarchical) phrases extracted from the full parallel data (approximately 30 Mio. sentence pairs).

Detailed statistics of the high-quality parallel training data (Europarl, news-commentary, and the selected parts of the 10^9 and UN corpora) are given in Table 1, the corpus statistics of the full parallel data from which the second phrase table with lexical phrases for the English→French RWTH primary system was created are presented in Table 2.

The translation systems use large 4-gram language models with modified Kneser-Ney smoothing. The French language model was trained on most of the provided French data including the monolingual LDC Gigaword corpora, the English

French→English	newstest2009 BLEU	newstest2009 TER	newstest2010 BLEU	newstest2010 TER
System combination of † systems (primary)	26.7	56.0	27.4	54.9
PBT with triplet lexicon, no forced alignment (contrastive) †	26.2	56.7	27.2	55.3
Jane as below + improved LM (contrastive)	26.3	57.4	26.7	56.2
Jane with parse match + syntactic labels + dependency †	26.2	57.5	26.5	56.4
PBT with forced alignment phrase training †	26.0	57.1	26.3	56.0

Table 3: RWTH systems for the WMT 2011 French→English translation task (truecase). BLEU and TER results are in percentage.

English→French	newstest2009 BLEU	newstest2009 TER	newstest2010 BLEU	newstest2010 TER
Jane shallow + in-domain TM + lexical phrases from full data	25.3	60.1	27.1	57.2
Jane shallow + in-domain TM + triplets + DWL + parse match	24.8	60.5	26.6	57.5
PBT with triplets, DWL, sentence-level word lexicon, discrim. reord.	24.8	60.1	26.5	57.3

Table 4: RWTH systems for the WMT 2011 English→French translation task (truecase). BLEU and TER results are in percentage.

language model was trained on automatically selected English data (cf. Section 3.1) from the provided resources including the 10^9 corpus and LDC Gigaword.

The scaling factors of the log-linear model combination are optimized towards BLEU on newstest2009, newstest2010 is used as an unseen test set.

4.1 Experimental Results French→English

The results for the French→English task are given in Table 3. RWTH's three submissions – one primary and two contrastive – are labeled accordingly in the table. The first contrastive submission is a phrase-based system with a standard feature set plus an additional triplet lexicon model (Mauser et al., 2009). The triplet lexicon model was trained on in-domain news commentary data only. The second contrastive submission is a hierarchical Jane system with three syntax-based extensions: A parse match model (Vilar et al., 2008), soft syntactic labels (Stein et al., 2010), and the soft string-to-dependency extension as described in Section 3.3. The primary submission combines the phrase-based contrastive system, a hierarchical system that is very similar to the Jane contrastive submission but with a slightly worse language model, and an additional PBT system that has been trained with forced alignment (Wuebker et al., 2010) on WMT 2010 data only.

4.2 Experimental Results English→French

The results for the English→French task are given in Table 4. We likewise submitted two contrastive systems for this translation direction. The first contrastive submission is a phrase-based system, enhanced with a triplet lexicon model and a discriminative word lexicon model (Mauser et al., 2009) – both trained on in-domain news commentary data only – as well as a sentence-level single-word lexicon model and a discriminative reordering model (Zens and Ney, 2006a). The second contrastive submission is a hierarchical Jane system with shallow rules (Iglesias et al., 2009), a triplet lexicon model, a discriminative word lexicon, the parse match model, and a second phrase table extracted from in-domain data only. Our primary submission is very similar to the latter Jane setup. It does not comprise the extended lexicon models and the parse match extension, but instead includes lexical phrases from the full 30 Mio. sentence corpus as described above.

5 German-English Setups

We trained phrase-based and hierarchical translation systems for both translation directions of the German-English language pair. The corpus statis-

	German	English
Sentences	1 857 745	
Running Words	48 449 977	50 559 217
Vocabulary	387 593	123 470

Table 5: Corpus statistics of the preprocessed training data for the WMT 2011 German→English and English→German translation tasks. Numerical quantities are replaced by a single category symbol.

tics can be found in Table 5. Word alignments were generated with GIZA++ and symmetrized as for the French-English setups.

The language models are 4-grams trained on the bilingual data as well as the provided News crawl corpus. For the English language model the 10^9 French-English and LDC Gigaword corpora were used additionally. For the 10^9 French-English and LDC Gigaword corpora RWTH applied the data selection technique described in Section 3.1. We examined two different language models, one with LDC data and one without.

Systems were optimized on the newstest2009 data set, newstest2008 was used as test set. The scores for newstest2010 are included for completeness.

5.1 Morpho-Syntactic Analysis

In order to reduce the source vocabulary size for the German→English translation, the source side was preprocessed by splitting German compound words with the frequency-based method described in (Koehn and Knight, 2003). To further reduce translation complexity, we performed the long-range part-of-speech based reordering rules proposed by (Popović et al., 2006). For additional experiments we used the TreeTagger (Schmid, 1995) to produce a lemmatized version of the German source.

5.2 Optimization Criterion

We studied the impact of different optimization criteria on tranlsation performance. The usual practice is to optimize the scaling factors to maximize BLEU. We also experimented with two different combinations of BLEU and Translation Edit Rate (TER): TER−BLEU and TER−4BLEU. The first denotes the equally weighted combination, while for the latter BLEU is weighted 4 times as strong as TER.

5.3 Experimental Results German→English

For the German→English task we conducted experiments comparing the standard phrase extraction with the phrase training technique described in Section 3.2. For the latter we applied log-linear phrase-table interpolation as proposed in (Wuebker et al., 2010). Further experiments included the use of additional language model training data, reranking of n-best lists generated by the phrase-based system, and different optimization criteria. We also carried out a system combination of several systems, including phrase-based systems on lemmatized German and on source data without compound splitting and two hierarchical systems optimized for different criteria. The results are given in Table 6.

A considerable increase in translation quality can be achieved by application of German compound splitting. The system that operates on German surface forms without compound splitting (SUR) clearly underperforms the baseline system with morphological preprocessing. The system on lemmatized German (LEM) is at about the same level as the system on surface forms.

In comparison to the standard heuristic phrase extraction technique, performing phrase training (FA) gives an improvement in BLEU on newstest2008 and newstest2009, but a degradation in TER. The addition of LDC Gigaword corpora (+GW) to the language model training data shows improvements in both BLEU and TER. Reranking was done on 1000-best lists generated by the the best available system (PBT (FA)+GW). Following models were applied: n-gram posteriors (Zens and Ney, 2006b), sentence length model, a 6-gram LM and single-word lexicon models in both normal and inverse direction. These models are combined in a log-linear fashion and the scaling factors are tuned in the same manner as the baseline system (using TER−4BLEU on newstest2009).

The table includes three identical Jane systems which are optimized for different criteria. The one optimized for TER−4BLEU offers the best balance between BLEU and TER, but was not finished in time for submission. As primary submission we chose the reranked PBT system, as secondary the system combination.

German→English	opt criterion	newstest2008 BLEU	newstest2008 TER	newstest2009 BLEU	newstest2009 TER	newstest2010 BLEU	newstest2010 TER
Syscombi of † (secondary)	TER−BLEU	21.1	62.1	20.8	61.2	23.7	59.2
Jane +GW †	BLEU	21.5	63.9	21.0	63.3	22.9	61.7
Jane +GW	TER−4BLEU	21.4	62.6	21.1	62.0	23.5	60.3
PBT (FA) rerank +GW (primary) †	TER−4BLEU	21.4	62.8	21.1	61.9	23.4	60.1
PBT (FA) +GW †	TER−4BLEU	21.1	63.0	21.1	62.2	23.3	60.3
Jane +GW †	TER−BLEU	20.9	61.1	20.4	60.5	23.4	58.3
PBT (FA)	TER−4BLEU	21.1	63.2	20.6	62.4	23.2	60.4
PBT	TER−4BLEU	20.6	62.7	20.3	61.9	23.3	59.7
PBT (SUR) †	TER−4BLEU	19.5	66.5	18.9	65.8	21.0	64.9
PBT (LEM) †	TER−4BLEU	19.2	66.1	18.9	65.4	21.0	63.5

Table 6: RWTH systems for the WMT 2011 German→English translation task (truecase). BLEU and TER results are in percentage. FA denotes systems with phrase training, +GW the use of LDC data for the language model. SUR and LEM denote the systems without compound splitting and on the lemmatized source, respectively. The three hierarchical Jane systems are identical, but used different parameter optimization criterea.

English→German	opt criterion	newstest2008 BLEU	newstest2008 TER	newstest2009 BLEU	newstest2009 TER	newstest2010 BLEU	newstest2010 TER
PBT + discrim. reord. (primary)	TER−4BLEU	15.3	70.2	15.1	69.8	16.2	65.6
PBT + discrim. reord.	BLEU	15.2	70.6	15.2	70.1	16.2	66.0
PBT	TER−4BLEU	15.2	70.7	15.2	70.2	16.2	66.1
Jane	BLEU	15.1	72.1	15.4	71.2	16.4	67.4
Jane	TER−4BLEU	15.1	68.4	14.6	69.5	14.6	65.9

Table 7: RWTH systems for the WMT 2011 English→German translation task (truecase). BLEU and TER results are in percentage.

5.4 Experimental Results English→German

We likewise studied the effect of using BLEU only versus using TER−4BLEU as optimization criterion in the English→German translation direction. Moreover, we tested the impact of the discriminative reordering model (Zens and Ney, 2006a). The results can be found in Table 7. For the phrase-based system, optimizing towards TER−4BLEU leads to slightly better results both in BLEU and TER than optimizing towards BLEU. Using the discriminative reordering model yields some improvements both on newstest2008 and newstest2010. In the case of the hierarchical system, the effect of the optimization criterion is more pronounced than for the phrase-based system. However, in this case it clearly leads to a tradeoff between BLEU and TER, as the choice of TER−4BLEU harms the translation results of test2010 with respect to BLEU.

6 Conclusion

For the participation in the WMT 2011 shared translation task, RWTH experimented with both phrase-based and hierarchical translation systems. We used all bilingual and monolingual data provided for the constrained track. To limit the size of the language model, a data selection technique was applied. Several techniques yielded improvements over the baseline, including three syntactic models, extended lexicon models, a discriminative reordering model, forced alignment training, reranking methods and different optimization criteria.

Acknowledgments

This work was achieved as part of the Quaero Programme, funded by OSEO, French State agency for innovation.

References

D. Chiang. 2007. Hierarchical Phrase-Based Translation. *Computational Linguistics*, 33(2):201–228.

J. DeNero, D. Gillick, J. Zhang, and D. Klein. 2006. Why Generative Phrase Models Underperform Surface Heuristics. In *Proceedings of the Workshop on Statistical Machine Translation*, pages 31–38.

L. Huang and D. Chiang. 2007. Forest Rescoring: Faster Decoding with Integrated Language Models. In *Proc. Annual Meeting of the Association for Computational Linguistics*, pages 144–151, Prague, Czech Republic, June.

G. Iglesias, A. de Gispert, E.R. Banga, and W. Byrne. 2009. Rule Filtering by Pattern for Efficient Hierarchical Translation. In *Proceedings of the 12th Conference of the European Chapter of the ACL (EACL 2009)*, pages 380–388.

D. Klein and C.D. Manning. 2003. Accurate Unlexicalized Parsing. In *Proceedings of the 41st Annual Meeting on Association for Computational Linguistics - Volume 1*, ACL '03, pages 423–430.

P. Koehn and K. Knight. 2003. Empirical Methods for Compound Splitting. In *Proceedings of European Chapter of the ACL (EACL 2009)*, pages 187–194.

E. Matusov, N. Ueffing, and H. Ney. 2006. Computing Consensus Translation from Multiple Machine Translation Systems Using Enhanced Hypotheses Alignment. In *Conference of the European Chapter of the Association for Computational Linguistics (EACL)*, pages 33–40.

E. Matusov, G. Leusch, R.E. Banchs, N. Bertoldi, D. Dechelotte, M. Federico, M. Kolss, Y.-S. Lee, J.B. Marino, M. Paulik, S. Roukos, H. Schwenk, and H. Ney. 2008. System Combination for Machine Translation of Spoken and Written Language. *IEEE Transactions on Audio, Speech and Language Processing*, 16(7):1222–1237.

A. Mauser, S. Hasan, and H. Ney. 2009. Extending Statistical Machine Translation with Discriminative and Trigger-Based Lexicon Models. In *Conference on Empirical Methods in Natural Language Processing*, pages 210–217.

R.C. Moore and W. Lewis. 2010. Intelligent Selection of Language Model Training Data. In *ACL (Short Papers)*, pages 220–224, Uppsala, Sweden, July.

J.A. Nelder and R. Mead. 1965. The Downhill Simplex Method. *Computer Journal*, 7:308.

F.J. Och and H. Ney. 2003. A Systematic Comparison of Various Statistical Alignment Models. *Computational Linguistics*, 29(1):19–51.

F.J. Och. 2003. Minimum Error Rate Training for Statistical Machine Translation. In *Proc. Annual Meeting of the Association for Computational Linguistics*, pages 160–167, Sapporo, Japan, July.

M. Popović, D. Stein, and H. Ney. 2006. Statistical Machine Translation of German Compound Words. In *FinTAL - 5th International Conference on Natural Language Processing, Springer Verlag, LNCS*, pages 616–624.

H. Schmid. 1995. Improvements in Part-of-Speech Tagging with an Application to German. In *Proceedings of the ACL SIGDAT-Workshop*, pages 47–50, Dublin, Ireland, March.

L. Shen, J. Xu, and R. Weischedel. 2008. A New String-to-Dependency Machine Translation Algorithm with a Target Dependency Language Model. In *Proceedings of ACL-08: HLT. Association for Computational Linguistics*, pages 577–585, June.

D. Stein, S. Peitz, D. Vilar, and H. Ney. 2010. A Cocktail of Deep Syntactic Features for Hierarchical Machine Translation. In *Conference of the Association for Machine Translation in the Americas 2010*, page 9, Denver, USA, October.

A. Stolcke. 2002. SRILM - an extensible language modeling toolkit. In *Proc. Int. Conf. on Spoken Language Processing*, volume 2, pages 901 – 904, Denver, Colorado, USA, September.

D. Vilar, D. Stein, and H. Ney. 2008. Analysing Soft Syntax Features and Heuristics for Hierarchical Phrase Based Machine Translation. In *Proc. of the Int. Workshop on Spoken Language Translation (IWSLT)*, pages 190–197, Waikiki, Hawaii, October.

D. Vilar, S. Stein, M. Huck, and H. Ney. 2010. Jane: Open Source Hierarchical Translation, Extended with Reordering and Lexicon Models. In *ACL 2010 Joint Fifth Workshop on Statistical Machine Translation and Metrics MATR*, pages 262–270, Uppsala, Sweden, July.

J. Wuebker, A. Mauser, and H. Ney. 2010. Training Phrase Translation Models with Leaving-One-Out. In *Proceedings of the 48th Annual Meeting of the Assoc. for Computational Linguistics*, pages 475–484, Uppsala, Sweden, July.

R. Zens and H. Ney. 2006a. Discriminative Reordering Models for Statistical Machine Translation. In *Human Language Technology Conf. / North American Chapter of the Assoc. for Computational Linguistics Annual Meeting (HLT-NAACL), Workshop on Statistical Machine Translation*, pages 55–63, New York City, June.

R. Zens and H. Ney. 2006b. N-gram Posterior Probabilities for Statistical Machine Translation. In *Human Language Technology Conf. / North American Chapter of the Assoc. for Computational Linguistics Annual Meeting (HLT-NAACL), Workshop on Statistical Machine Translation*, pages 72–77, New York City, June.

R. Zens and H. Ney. 2008. Improvements in Dynamic Programming Beam Search for Phrase-based Statistical Machine Translation. In *Proc. of the Int. Workshop on Spoken Language Translation (IWSLT)*, Honolulu, Hawaii, October.

ILLC-UvA translation system for EMNLP-WMT 2011

Maxim Khalilov and **Khalil Sima'an**
Institute for Logic, Language and Computation
University of Amsterdam
P.O. Box 94242
1090 GE Amsterdam, The Netherlands
{m.khalilov,k.simaan}@uva.nl

Abstract

In this paper we describe the Institute for Logic, Language and Computation (University of Amsterdam) phrase-based statistical machine translation system for English-to-German translation proposed within the EMNLP-WMT 2011 shared task. The main novelty of the submitted system is a syntax-driven pre-translation reordering algorithm implemented as source string permutation via transfer of the source-side syntax tree.

1 Introduction

For the WMT 2011 shared task, ILLC-UvA submitted two translations (primary and secondary) for the English-to-German translation task. This year, we directed our research toward addressing the word order problem for statistical machine translation (SMT) and discover its impact on output translation quality. We reorder the words of a sentence of the source language with respect to the word order of the target language and a given source-side parse tree. The difference from the baseline Moses-based translation system lies in the pre-translation step, in which we introduce a discriminative source string permutation model based on probabilistic parse tree transduction.

The idea here is to permute the order of the source words in such a way that the resulting permutation allows as monotone a translation process as possible is not new. This approach to enhance SMT by using a reordering step prior to translation has proved to be successful in improving translation quality for many translation tasks, see (Genzel, 2010; Costa-jussà and Fonollosa, 2006; Collins et al., 2005), for example.

The general problem of source-side reordering is that the number of permutations is factorial in n, and learning a sequence of transductions for explaining a source permutation can be computationally rather challenging. We propose to address this problem by defining the source-side permutation process as the learning problem of how to transfer a given source parse tree into a parse tree that minimizes the divergence from target word order.

Our reordering system is inspired by the direction taken in (Tromble and Eisner, 2009), but differs in defining the space of permutations, using local probabilistic tree transductions, as well as in the learning objective aiming at scoring permutations based on a log-linear interpolation of a local syntax-based model with a global string-based (language) model.

The reordering (novel) and translation (standard) components are described in the following sections. The rest of this paper is structured as follows. After a brief description of the phrase-based translation system in Section 2, we present the architecture and details of our reordering system (Section 3), Section 4 reviews related work, Section 5 reports the experimental setup, details the submissions and discusses the results, while Section 6 concludes the article.

2 Baseline system

2.1 Statistical machine translation

In SMT the translation problem is formulated as selecting the target translation t with the highest probability from a set of target hypothesis sentences for

Proceedings of the 6th Workshop on Statistical Machine Translation, pages 413–419,
Edinburgh, Scotland, UK, July 30–31, 2011.

the source sentence s: $\hat{t} = \arg\max_{t} \{ p(t|s) \} = \arg\max_{t} \{ p(s|t) \cdot p(t) \}$.

2.2 Phrase-based translation

While first systems following this approach performed translation on the word level, modern state-of-the-art phrase-based SMT systems (Och and Ney, 2002; Koehn et al., 2003) start-out from a word-aligned parallel corpus working with (in principle) arbitrarily large phrase pairs (also called blocks) acquired from word-aligned parallel data under a simple definition of translational equivalence (Zens et al., 2002).

The conditional probabilities of one phrase given its counterpart is estimated as the relative frequency ratio of the phrases in the multiset of phrase-pairs extracted from the parallel corpus and are interpolated log-linearly together with a set of other model estimates:

$$\hat{e}_1^I = \arg\max_{e_1^I} \left\{ \sum_{m=1}^{M} \lambda_m h_m(e_1^I, f_1^J) \right\} \qquad (1)$$

where a feature function h_m refer to a system model, and the corresponding λ_m refers to the relative weight given to this model.

A phrase-based system employs feature functions for a phrase pair translation model, a language model, a reordering model, and a model to score translation hypothesis according to length. The weights λ_m are optimized for system performance (Och, 2003) as measured by BLEU (Papineni et al., 2002).

Apart from the novel syntax-based reordering model, we consider two reordering methods that are widely used in phrase-based systems: a simple distance-based reordering and a lexicalized block-oriented data-driven reordering model (Tillman, 2004).

3 Architecture of the reordering system

We approach the word order challenge by including syntactic information in a pre-translation reordering framework. This section details the general idea of our approach and details the reordering model that was used in English-to-German experiments.

3.1 Pre-translation reordering framework

Given a word-aligned parallel corpus, we define the source string permutation as the task of learning to unfold the crossing alignments between sentence pairs in the parallel corpus. Let be given a source-target sentence pair $s \rightarrow t$ with word alignment set a between their words. Unfolding the crossing instances in a should lead to as monotone an alignment $a^{'}$ as possible between a permutation $s^{'}$ of s and the target string t. Conducting such a "monotonization" on the parallel corpus gives two parallel corpora: (1) a source-to-permutation parallel corpus ($s \rightarrow s^{'}$) and (2) a source permutation-to-target parallel corpus ($s^{'} \rightarrow t$). The latter corpus is word-aligned automatically again and used for training a phrase-based translation system, while the former corpus is used for training our model for pre-translation source permutation via parse tree transductions.

In itself, the problem of permuting the source string to unfold the crossing alignments is computationally intractable (see (Tromble and Eisner, 2009)). However, different kinds of constraints can be made on unfolding the crossing alignments in a. A common approach in hierarchical SMT is to assume that the source string has a binary parse tree, and the set of eligible permutations is defined by binary ITG transductions on this tree. This defines permutations that can be obtained only by at most inverting pairs of children under nodes of the source tree.

3.2 Conditional tree reordering model

Given a parallel corpus with string pairs $s \rightarrow t$ with word alignment a, the source strings s are parsed, leading to a single parse tree τ_s per source string. We create a *source permuted* parallel corpus $s \rightarrow s^{'}$ by unfolding the crossing alignments in a without/with syntactic tree to provide constraints on the unfolding.

Our model aims at learning from the source permuted parallel corpus $s \rightarrow s^{'}$ a probabilistic optimization $\arg\max_{\pi(s)} P(\pi(s) \mid s, \tau_s)$. We assume that the set of permutations $\{\pi(s)\}$ is defined through a finite set of local transductions over the tree τ_s. Hence, we view the permutations leading from s to $s^{'}$ as a sequence of local tree transductions $\tau_{s'_0} \to \ldots \to \tau_{s'_n}$, where $s'_0 = s$ and $s'_n = s'$, and each transduction $\tau_{s'_{i-1}} \to \tau_{s'_i}$ is defined using a tree transduction operation that *at most permutes the children of a single node in* $\tau_{s'_{i-1}}$ *as defined next.*

A local transduction $\tau_{s'_{i-1}} \to \tau_{s'_i}$ is modelled by an operation that applies to a single node with address x in $\tau_{s'_{i-1}}$, labeled N_x, and may permute the ordered sequence of children α_x dominated by node x. This constitutes a direct generalization of the ITG binary inversion transduction operation. We assign a conditional probability to each such local transduction:

$$P(\tau_{s'_i} \mid \tau_{s'_{i-1}}) \approx P(\pi(\alpha_x) \mid N_x \to \alpha_x, C_x) \quad (2)$$

where $\pi(\alpha_x)$ is a permutation of α_x (the ordered sequence of node labels under x) and C_x is a local tree context of node x in tree $\tau_{s'_{i-1}}$. One wrinkle in this definition is that the number of possible permutations of α_x is factorial in the length of α_x. Fortunately, the source permuted training data exhibits only a fraction of possible permutations even for longer α_x sequences. Furthermore, by conditioning the probability on local context, the general applicability of the permutation is restrained.

In principle, if we would disregard the computational cost, we could define the probability of the sequence of local tree transductions $\tau_{s'_0} \to \ldots \to \tau_{s'_n}$ as

$$P(\tau_{s'_0} \to \ldots \to \tau_{s'_n}) = \prod_{i=1}^{n} P(\tau_{s'_i} \mid \tau_{s'_{i-1}}) \quad (3)$$

The problem of calculating the most likely permutation under this kind of transduction probability is intractable because every local transduction conditions on local context of an intermediate tree[1]. Hence, we disregard this formulation and in practice we take a pragmatic approach and greedily select at every intermediate point $\tau_{s'_{i-1}} \to \tau_{s'_i}$ the single most likely local transduction that can be conducted on any node of the current intermediate tree $\tau_{s'_{i-1}}$. The individual steps are made more effective by interpolating the term in Equation 2 with string probability ratios:

$$P(\pi(\alpha_x) \mid N_x \to \alpha_x, C_x) \times \left(\frac{P(s'_{i-1})}{P(s'_i)} \right) \quad (4)$$

The rationale behind this interpolation is that our source permutation approach aims at finding the optimal permutation s' of s that can serve as input for a subsequent translation model. Hence, we aim at tree transductions that are syntactically motivated that also lead to improved string permutations. In this sense, the tree transduction definitions can be seen as an efficient and syntactically informed way to define the space of possible permutations.

We estimate the string probabilities $P(s'_i)$ using 5-gram language models trained on the s' side of the source permuted parallel corpus $s \to s'$. We estimate the conditional probability $P(\pi(\alpha_x) \mid N_x \to \alpha_x, C_x)$ using a Maximum-Entropy framework, where feature functions are defined to capture the permutation as a class, the node label N_x and its head POS tag, the child sequence α_x together with the corresponding sequence of head POS tags and other features corresponding to different contextual information.

We were particularly interested in those linguistic features that motivate reordering phenomena from the syntactic and linguistic perspective. The features that were used for training the permutation system are extracted for every internal node of the source tree that has more than one child:

- *Local tree topology.* Sub-tree instances that include parent node and the ordered sequence of child node labels.

- *Dependency features.* Features that determine the POS tag of the head word of the current node, together with the sequence of POS tags of the head words of its child nodes.

- *Syntactic features.* Two binary features from this class describe: (1) whether the parent node is a child of the node annotated with the same syntactic category, (2) whether the parent node is a descendant of a node annotated with the same syntactic category.

[1] Note that a single transduction step on the current tree $\tau_{s'_{i-1}}$ leads to a forest of trees $\tau_{s'_i}$ because there can be multiple alternative transduction rules. Hence, this kind of a model demands optimization over many possible sequences of trees, which can be packed into a sequence of parse-forests with transduction links between them.

4 Related work

The integration of linguistic syntax into SMT systems offers a potential solution to reordering problem. For example, syntax is successfully integrated into hierarchical SMT (Zollmann and Venugopal, 2006). In (Yamada and Knight, 2001), a set of tree-string channel operations is defined over the parse tree nodes, while reordering is modeled by permutations of children nodes. Similarly, the tree-to-string syntax-based transduction approach offers a complete translation framework (Galley et al., 2006).

The idea of augmenting SMT by a reordering step prior to translation has often been shown to improve translation quality. Clause restructuring performed with hand-crafted reordering rules for German-to-English and Chinese-to-English tasks are presented in (Collins et al., 2005) and (Wang et al., 2007), respectively. In (Xia and McCord, 2004; Khalilov, 2009) word reordering is addressed by exploiting syntactic representations of source and target texts.

In (Costa-jussà and Fonollosa, 2006) source and target word order harmonization is done using well-established SMT techniques and without the use of syntactic knowledge. Other reordering models operate provide the decoder with multiple word orders. For example, the MaxEnt reordering model described in (Xiong et al., 2006) provides a hierarchical phrasal reordering system integrated within a CKY-style decoder. In (Galley and Manning, 2008) the authors present an extension of the famous MSD model (Tillman, 2004) able to handle long-distance word-block permutations. Coming up-to-date, in (PVS, 2010) an effective application of data mining techniques to syntax-driven source reordering for MT is presented.

Different syntax-based reordering systems can be found in (Genzel, 2010). In this system, reordering rules capable to capture many important word order transformations are automatically learned and applied in the preprocessing step.

Recently, Tromble and Eisner (Tromble and Eisner, 2009) define source permutation as the word-ordering learning problem; the model works with a preference matrix for word pairs, expressing preference for their two alternative orders, and a corresponding weight matrix that is fit to the parallel data. The huge space of permutations is then structured using a binary synchronous context-free grammar (Binary ITG) with $O(n^3)$ parsing complexity, and the permutation score is calculated recursively over the tree at every node as the accumulation of the relative differences between the word-pair scores taken from the preference matrix. Application to German-to-English translation exhibits some performance improvement.

5 Experiments and submissions

Design, architecture and configuration of the translation system that we used in experimentation coincides with the Moses-based translation system (Baseline system) described in details on the WMT 2011 web page[2].

This section details the experiments carried out to evaluate the proposed reordering model, experimental set-up and data.

5.1 Data

In our experiments we used EuroParl v6.0 German-English parallel corpus provided by the organizers of the evaluation campaign.

A detailed statistics of the training, development, internal (*test int.*) and official (*test of.*) test datasets can be found in Table 1. The development corpus coincides with the 2009 test set and for internal testing we used the test data proposed to the participants of WMT 2010.

"ASL" stands for average sentence length. All the sets were provided with one reference translation.

Data		Sent.	Words	Voc.	ASL
train	En	1.7M	46.0M	121.3K	27.0
train	Ge	1.7M	43.7M	368.5K	25.7
dev	En	2.5K	57.6K	13.2K	22.8
test int.	En	2.5K	53.2K	15.9K	21.4
test of.	En	3.0K	74.8K	11.1K	24.9

Table 1: *German-English EuroParl corpus (version 6.0).*

Apart from the German portion of the EuroParl parallel corpus, two additional monolingual corpora from news domain (the News Commentary corpus (NC) and the News Crawl Corpus 2011 (NS)) were

[2] http://www.statmt.org/wmt11/baseline.html

used to train a language model for German. The characteristics of these datasets can be found in Table 2. Notice that the data were not de-duplicated.

Data		Sent.	Words	Voc.	ASL
NC	Ge	161.8M	3.9G	136.7M	23.9
NS	Ge	45.3M	799.4M	3.0M	17.7

Table 2: *Monolingual German corpora used for target-side language modeling.*

5.2 Experimental setup

Moses toolkit (Koehn et al., 2007) in its standard setting was used to build the SMT systems:

- GIZA++/mkcls (Och, 2003; Och, 1999) for word alignment.
- SRI LM (Stolcke, 2002) for language modeling. A 3-gram target language model was estimated and smoothed with modified Kneser-Ney discounting.
- MOSES (Koehn et al., 2007) to build an unfactored translation system.
- the Stanford parser (Klein and Manning, 2003) was used as a source-side parsing engine[3].
- For maximum entropy modeling we used the maxent toolkit[4].

The discriminative syntactic reordering model is applied to reorder training, development, and test corpora. A Moses-based translation system (corpus realignment included[5]) is then trained using the reordered input.

5.3 Internal results and submissions

The outputs of two translation system were submitted. First, we piled up all feature functions into a single model as described in Section 3. It was our "secondary" submission. However, our experience tells that the system performance can increase if the set of patterns is split into partial classes conditioned on the current node label (Khalilov and Sima'an, 2010). Hence, we trained three separate MaxEnt models for the categories with potentially high reordering requirements, namely NP, $SENT$ and $SBAR(Q)$. It was defines as our "primary" submission.

The ranking of submission was done according to the results shown on internal testing, shown in Table 3.

System	BLEU dev	BLEU test	NIST test
Baseline	11.03	9.78	3.78
Primary	11.07	10.00	3.79
Secondary	10.92	9.91	3.78

Table 3: *Internal testing results.*

5.4 Official results and discussion

Unfortunately, the results of our participation this year were discouraging. The primary submission was ranked 30th (12.6 uncased BLEU-4) and the secondary 31th (11.2) out of 32 submitted systems.

It turned out that our preliminary idea to extrapolate the positive results of English-to-Dutch translation reported in (Khalilov and Sima'an, 2010) to the WMT English-to-German translation task was not right.

Analyzing the reasons of negative results during the post-evaluation period, we discovered that translation into German differs from English-to-Dutch task in many cases. In contrast to English-to-Dutch translation, the difference in terms of automatic scores between the internal baseline system (without external reordering) and the system enhanced with the pre-translation reordering is minimal. It turns out that translating into German is more complex in general and discriminative reordering is more advantageous for English-to-Dutch than for English-to-German translation.

A negative aspect influencing is the way how the rules are extracted and applied according to our approach. Syntax-driven reordering, as described in this paper, involves large contextual information applied cumulatively. Under conditions of scarce data, alignment and parsing errors, it introduces noise to the reordering system and distorts the feature prob-

[3]The parser was trained on the English treebank set provided with 14 syntactic categories and 48 POS tags.

[4]http://homepages.inf.ed.ac.uk/lzhang10/maxent_toolkit.html

[5]Some studies show that word re-alignment of a monotonized corpus gives better results than unfolding of alignment crossings (Costa-jussà and Fonollosa, 2006).

ability space. At the same time, many reorderings can be performed more efficiently based on fixed (hand-crafted) rules (as it is done in (Collins et al., 2005)). A possible remedy to this problem is to combine automatically extracted features with fixed (hand-crafted) rules. Our last claims are supported by the observations described in (Visweswariah et al., 2010).

During post-evaluation period we analyzed the reasons why the system performance has slightly improved when separate MaxEnt models are applied. The outline of reordered nodes for each of syntactic categories considered ($SENT$, $SBAR(Q)$ and NP) can be found in Table 4 (the size of the corpus is 1.7 M of sentences).

Category	# of applications
NP	497,186
SBAR(Q)	106,243
SENT	221,568

Table 4: *Application of reorderings for separate syntactic categories.*

It is seen that the reorderings for NP nodes is higher than for $SENT$ and $SBAR(Q)$ categories. While SENT and SBAR(Q) reorderings work analogously for Dutch and German, our intuition is that German has more features that play a role in reordering of NP structures than Dutch and there is a need of more specific features to model NP permutations in an accurate way.

6 Conclusions

This paper presents the ILLC-UvA translation system for English-to-German translation task proposed to the participants of the EMNLP-WMT 2011 evaluation campaign. The novel feature that we present this year is a source reordering model in which the reordering decisions are conditioned on the features from the source parse tree.

Our system has not managed to outperform the majority of the participating systems, possibly due to its generic approach to reordering. We plan to investigate why our approach works well for English-to-Dutch and less well for the English-to-German translation in order to discover more generic ways for learning discriminative reordering rules. One possible explanation of the bad results is a high sparseness of automatically extracted rules that does not allow for sufficient generalization of reordering instances.

In the future, we plan (1) to perform deeper analysis of the dissimilarity between English-to-Dutch and English-to-German translations from SMT perspective, and (2) to investigate linguistically-motivated ideas to extend our model such that we can bring about some improvement to English-to-German translation.

7 Acknowledgements

Both authors are supported by a VIDI grant (nr. 639.022.604) from The Netherlands Organization for Scientific Research (NWO).

References

M. Collins, P. Koehn, and I. Kučerová. 2005. Clause restructuring for statistical machine translation. In *Proceedings of ACL'05*, pages 531–540.

M. R. Costa-jussà and J. A. R. Fonollosa. 2006. Statistical machine reordering. In *Proceedings of HLT/EMNLP'06*, pages 70–76.

M. Galley and Ch. D. Manning. 2008. A simple and effective hierarchical phrase reordering model. In *Proceedings of EMNLP'08*, pages 848–856.

M. Galley, J. Graehl, K. Knight, D. Marcu, S. DeNeefe, W. Wang, and I. Thaye. 2006. Scalable inference and training of context-rich syntactic translation models. In *Proc. of COLING/ACL'06*, pages 961–968.

D. Genzel. 2010. Aumotatically learning source-side reordering rules for large scale machine translation. In *Proc. of COLING'10*, pages 376–384, Beijing, China.

M. Khalilov and K. Sima'an. 2010. A discriminative syntactic model for source permutation via tree transduction. In *Proc. of the Fourth Workshop on Syntax and Structure in Statistical Translation (SSST-4) at COLING'10*, pages 92–100, Beijing (China), August.

M. Khalilov. 2009. *New statistical and syntactic models for machine translation.* Ph.D. thesis, Universitat Politècnica de Catalunya, October.

D. Klein and C. Manning. 2003. Accurate unlexicalized parsing. In *Proceedings of the 41st Annual Meeting of the ACL'03*, pages 423–430.

Ph. Koehn, F. Och, and D. Marcu. 2003. Statistical phrase-based machine translation. In *Proceedings of the HLT-NAACL 2003*, pages 48–54.

Ph. Koehn, H. Hoang, A. Birch, C. Callison-Burch, M. Federico, N. Bertoldi, B. Cowan, W. Shen,

C. Moran, R. Zens, C. Dyer, O. Bojar, A. Constantin, and E. Herbst. 2007. Moses: open-source toolkit for statistical machine translation. In *Proceedings of ACL 2007*, pages 177–180.

F. Och and H. Ney. 2002. Discriminative training and maximum entropy models for statistical machine translation. In *Proceedings of ACL'02*, pages 295–302.

F. Och. 1999. An efficient method for determining bilingual word classes. In *Proceedings of ACL 1999*, pages 71–76.

F. Och. 2003. Minimum error rate training in statistical machine translation. In *Proceedings of ACL'03*, pages 160–167.

K. Papineni, S. Roukos, T. Ward, and W. Zhu. 2002. Bleu: a method for automatic evaluation of machine translation. In *Proceedings of ACL'02*, pages 311–318.

A. PVS. 2010. A data mining approach to learn reorder rules for SMT. In *Proceedings of NAACL/HLT'10*, pages 52–57.

A. Stolcke. 2002. SRILM: an extensible language modeling toolkit. In *Proceedings of SLP'02*, pages 901–904.

C. Tillman. 2004. A unigram orientation model for statistical machine translation. In *Proceedings of HLT-NAACL'04*, pages 101–104.

R. Tromble and J. Eisner. 2009. Learning linear ordering problems for better translation. In *Proceedings of EMNLP'09*, pages 1007–1016.

K. Visweswariah, J. Navratil, J. Sorensen, V. Chenthamarakshan, and N. Kambhatla. 2010. Syntax based reordering with automatically derived rules for improved statistical machine translation. In *Proc. of COLING'10*, pages 1119–1127, Beijing, China.

C. Wang, M. Collins, and Ph. Koehn. 2007. Chinese syntactic reordering for statistical machine translation. In *Proceedings of EMNLP-CoNLL'07*, pages 737–745.

F. Xia and M. McCord. 2004. Improving a statistical MT system with automatically learned rewrite patterns. In *Proceedings of COLING'04*, pages 508–514.

D. Xiong, Q. Liu, and S. Lin. 2006. Maximum entropy based phrase reordering model for statistical machine translation. In *Proceedings of ACL'06*, pages 521–528.

K. Yamada and K. Knight. 2001. A syntax-based statistical translation model. In *Proceedings of ACL'01*, pages 523–530.

R. Zens, F. Och, and H. Ney. 2002. Phrase-based statistical machine translation. In *Proceedings of KI: Advances in Artificial Intelligence*, pages 18–32.

A. Zollmann and A. Venugopal. 2006. Syntax augmented machine translation via chart parsing. In *Proceedings of NAACL'06*, pages 138–141.

UPM system for the translation task

Verónica López-Ludeña
Grupo de Tecnología del Habla
Universidad Politécnica de Madrid
veronicalopez@die.upm.es

Rubén San-Segundo
Grupo de Tecnología del Habla
Universidad Politécnica de Madrid
lapiz@die.upm.es

Abstract

This paper describes the UPM system for translation task at the EMNLP 2011 workshop on statistical machine translation (http://www.statmt.org/wmt11/), and it has been used for both directions: Spanish-English and English-Spanish. This system is based on Moses with two new modules for pre and post processing the sentences. The main contribution is the method proposed (based on the similarity with the source language test set) for selecting the sentences for training the models and adjusting the weights. With system, we have obtained a 23.2 BLEU for Spanish-English and 21.7 BLEU for English-Spanish.

1 Introduction

The Speech Technology Group of the Universidad Politécnica de Madrid has participated in the sixth workshop on statistical machine translation in the Spanish-English and English-Spanish translation task.

Our submission is based on the state-of-the-art SMT toolkit Moses (Koehn, 2010) adding a pre-processing and a post-processing module. The main contribution is a corpus selection method for training the translation models based on the similarity of each source corpus sentence with the language model of the source language test set.

There are several related works on filtering the training corpus by using a similarity measure based on the alignment score or based on sentences length (Khadivi and Ney, 2005; Sanchis-Trilles et al, 2010). However, these techniques are focused on removing noisy data, i.e., their idea is to eliminate possible errors in the databases.

The difference between these techniques and the method that we propose is that we do not search "bad" pairs of sentences, but we search those sentences in source training corpus that are more similar with the language model generated with the source test sentences and we select them for training.

Other interesting technique of corpus selection is based on transductive learning (Ueffing, 2007). In this work, authors use of transductive semi-supervised methods for the effective use of monolingual data from the source language in order to improve translation quality.

The method proposed in this paper is also applied to the validation corpus. There are other works related to select development set (Hui, 2010) that they combine different development sets in order to find the more similar one with test set.

2 Overall description of the system

The translation system used is based on Moses, the software released to support the translation task (http://www.statmt.org/wmt11/) at the EMNLP 2011 workshop on statistical machine translation.

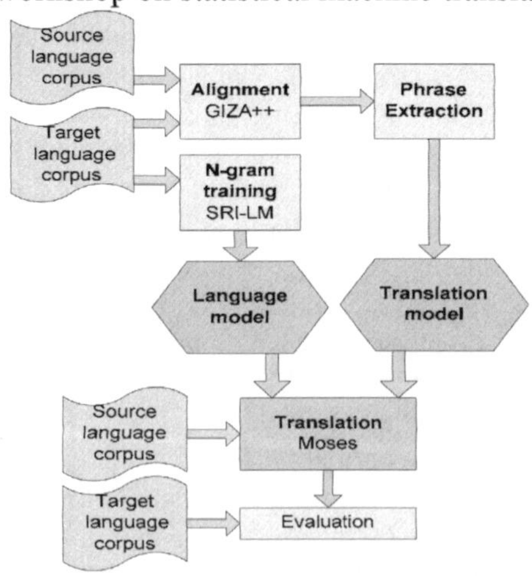

Figure 1: Moses translation system

Proceedings of the 6th Workshop on Statistical Machine Translation, pages 420–425,
Edinburgh, Scotland, UK, July 30–31, 2011.

The phrase model has been trained following these steps (Figure 1):

- Word alignment computation. GIZA++ (Och and Ney, 2003) is a statistical machine translation toolkit that is used to calculate the alignments between Spanish and English words in both direction (Spanish-English and English-Spanish). To generate the translation model, the parameter "alignment" was fixed to "grow-diag-final" (default value), and the parameter "reordering" was fixed to "msd-bidirectional-fe" as the best option, based on experiments on the development set.
- Phrase extraction (Koehn et al 2003). All phrase pairs that are consistent with the word alignment (grow-diag-final alignment in our case) are collected. To extract the phrases, the parameter "max-phrase-length" was fixed to "7" (default value), based on experiments on the development set.
- Phrase scoring. In this step, the translation probabilities are computed for all phrase pairs. Both translation probabilities are calculated: forward and backward.

The Moses decoder is used for the translation process (Koehn, 2010). This program is a beam search decoder for phrase-based statistical machine translation models. In order to obtain a 3-gram language model, the SRI language modeling toolkit has been used (Stolcke, 2002).

In addition, a pre-processing module was developed for adapting the format of the corpus before training (pre-processing of training, development and test corpora). And a post-processing for ordering punctuations, recasing, etc. is also applied to Moses output.

3 Corpora used in these experiments

For the system development, we have only used the free corpora distributed in the EMNLP 2011 translation task.

In particular, we have considered the union of the Europarl corpus, the United Nations Organization (UNO) Corpus, the News Commentary Corpus and the test sets of 2000, 2006, 2007 and 2008.

For developing the system, we have developed and evaluated the system considering the union of 2009 and 2010 test sets.

All these files can be free downloaded from http://www.statmt.org/wmt11/.

A pre-processing of these databases is necessary for adapting the original format to our system.

We have not used the complete union of all corpora, but a corpus selection by filtering the union of the training set and also filtering the union of the development set. This selection will be explained in section 5.

The main characteristics of the corpus are shown in Table 1: the previous corpora and the filtered corpora.

		Original sentences	**Filtered sentences**
Training (Translation Model (TM) /Language Model (LM))	**Europarl Training Corpus**	1,650,152	150,000 (TM) 3,000,000 (LM)
	UNO Corpus	6,222,450	
	News commentary	98,598	
	Previous test sets	15,150	
Development	**news-test2009**	2,525	1,000
	news-test2010	2,489	
Test	**news-test2011**	3,003	3,003

Table 1: Main characteristics of the corpus

4 Preparing the corpora

In order to use the corpus described in section 3 with the mentioned translation systems, it is necessary a pre-processing. This pre-processing, for training files, consists of:

- UTF-8 to Windows format conversion, because our software adapted to Windows had several problems with the UTF-8 format: it does not know accent marks, ñ letter, etc.
- Deletion of blank lines and sentences that are comments (for instance: "<CHAPTER ID=1>")
- Deletion of special characters (.,;:¿?¡!-/\, etc.), except those that are next to numbers (for instance: "1.4", "2,000", "1/3"). We decided to remove these special characters to avoid including them in the translation model. During translation, these characters will be considered as phrase limits.

- Words were kept in their natural case, but the first letter of each sentence was lowercased, because first words of sentences are used to be lowercased as their most common form.
- Contracted words were separated for training each word separately. For instance, "it's" becomes "it is". For the ambiguous cases, like "he's" that can be "he is" or "he has", we have not done any further processing: we have considered the most frequent situation. For the case of Saxon genitive, when proper names are used (instead of pronouns), "'s" is a Saxon genitive most of the times. But, when using a pronoun, it is a contracted word.

For development and test sets, the same actions were carried out, but now, special characters were not deleted, but separated in tokens, i.e., a blank space was introduced between special characters and adjacent words. For instance, "*la bolsa de Praga , al principio del martes comercial , reaccionó inmediatamente a la caída del lunes cuando descendió aproximadamente a un 6 % .*"

So, special characters are considered as independent tokens in translation. The main idea was to force the system to consider special characters as phrase limits during the translation process.

5 Selecting the training corpus

Scattering of training data is a problem when integrating training material from different sources for developing a statistical system. In this case, we want to use a big training corpus joining all available corpora obtaining about 8 millions sentences.

But an excessive amount of data can produce an important scattering that the statistical model cannot learn properly.

The technique proposed by the Speech Technology Group at UPM in the translation task (Spanish-English and English-Spanish) consists of a filtering of the training data in order to obtain better results, without having memory problems.

The first step is to compute a language model of the source language considering sentences to translate (sentences from the 2011 source test set).

Secondly, the system computes the similarity of each source sentence in the training to the language model obtained in the first step. This similarity is computed with the following formula:

$$sim = \frac{1}{n}\sum_{i=0}^{n} \log(P_n) \quad (1)$$

For example, if one sentence is "A B C D" (where each letter is a word of the sentence):

$$sim = \frac{1}{4}(P_A + P_{AB} + P_{ABC} + P_{BCD}) \quad (2)$$

Each probability is extracted from the language model calculated in the first step. This similarity is the negative of the source sentence perplexity given the language model.

With all the similarities, the mean and the standard deviation values are computed and used to define a threshold. For example, calculating the similarity of all sentences in our train corpus (about 8,000,000 of sentences) a similarity histogram is obtained (Figure 2).

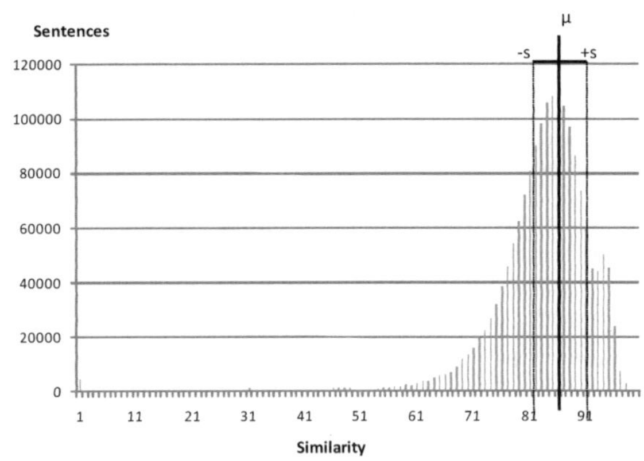

Figure 2: Similarity histogram of Spanish-English system

This histogram indicates the number of sentences inside each interval. There are 100 different intervals: the minimum similarity is mapped into 0 and the maximum one into 100.

Finally, source training sentences with a similarity lower than the threshold are eliminated from the training set (the corresponding target sentences are also removed).

The whole process is shown in Figure 3. This process takes 20 hours approximately for filtering more than 8 million sentences in an Intel core 2 quad computer.

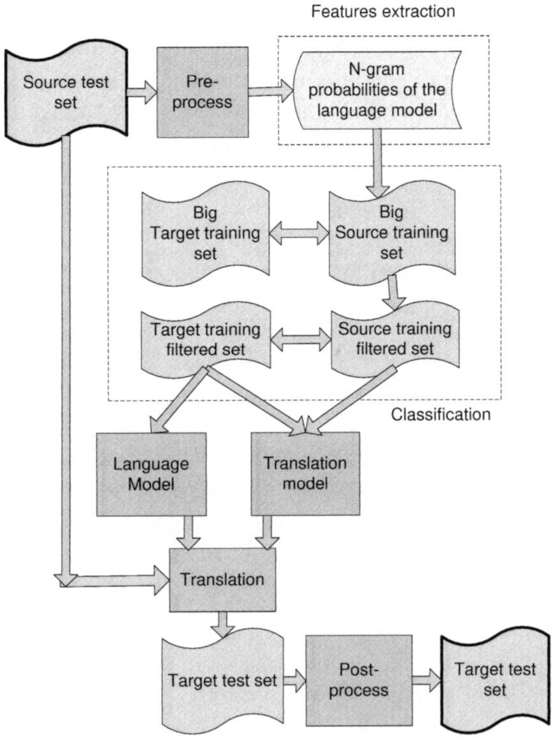

Figure 3: Diagram of complete process

Figure 4 shows the results of the experiments in Spanish-English system selecting the training corpus with different similarity thresholds. These results were obtained before filtering the development corpus, with the same filtered training corpus for translation and language models and before post-processing.

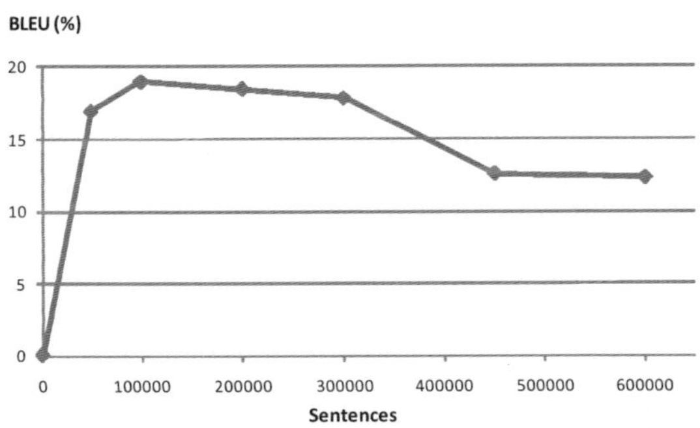

Figure 4: Translation results of baseline Spanish-English system with different number of training sentences

As can be observed, with more than 400,000 sentences there is a 12% BLEU (with an asymptotic tendency), but there is an important improvement filtering up to 100,000 (there is already not scattering). But results start to fall off when there are insufficient sentences (problem of sparseness of data with less than 100,000 sentences).

6 Post processing

After performing the statistical translation, we have incorporated a post-processing module with the following functions:

- To check the date format, detecting possible order errors and correcting them.
- To check the format of the numbers, numerical and ordinal ones: 1° into 1st and so on.
- Detokenization and ordering the punctuations marks when there are several ones consecutively (i.e. '“.' or ').'), trying to follow, always, the same order.
- To put the first letter of the sentences in capital letters.
- To use a backup dictionary for translating isolated words. This aspect has improved 2% (BLEU) but it has also introduced some errors. For example in the case of English-Spanish, there was a checking process for translating English words into Spanish. But there were several English words that also are Spanish words. For example, “un” is an article in Spanish but in English means “United Nations” (Naciones Unidas) so some “un” were translated as “Naciones Unidas” by error.

7 Selecting the development corpus

The development corpus is used to adapt the different weights used in the translation process for combining the different sources of information. Weight computation is a sensible task. In order to better adapt these weights, the development corpus is also filtered considering the same strategy commented in section 5.

Our solution consists of using two different corpora (2009 and 2010 test sets) and “choosing” the best sentences to use in development task with the same filtering technique explained in section 5. Finally, we select the 1,000 sentences with the greater similarity respect to the source language model of the test set.

Other action carried out in final experiments is using different corpora for training translation and language models. In order to generate the language model it is better to use a big corpus; so, we use 3,000,000 sentences that it is the biggest model that we can generate without memory problems.

But in order to generate the translation model, the final one is trained with 150,000 sentences.

The final results are shown in Table 2.

Spanish-English	BLEU	BLEU cased
Baseline	12.57	12.15
Best result	**23.20**	**21.90**
English-Spanish	**BLEU**	**BLEU cased**
Baseline	10.73	10.30
Best result	**21.70**	**20.90**

Table 2: Final results of the translation system

With this work, we have demonstrated that filtering the corpus for training the translation module, can improve the translation results. But there are still important problems that must be addressed like the high number of out of vocabulary words (OOVs) (more than 40% of the test corpus vocabulary) that they have to be improved in the selecting method.

About the selection, it is important to comment that this method more likely filters long sentences out: the average number of words in the selected corpus is 14 while in the whole training set and in the test set is higher than 25.

Other interesting aspect to comment is that in the selected training corpus, more than 70% of the sentences come from the Europarl or the News Commentary corpus, being the UNO corpus the biggest one.

Anyway, although the improvement is interesting, the system can not compete with other well-known translation systems until we incorporate additional modules for reordering or n-best post processing.

8 Conclusions

This paper has presented and described the UPM statistical machine translation system for Spanish-English and English-Spanish. This system is based on Moses with pre-processing and post-processing modules. The main contribution has been the proposed method for selecting the sentences used for training and developing the system. This selection is based on the similarity with the source language test set. The results have been 23.2 BLEU for Spanish into English and 21.7 for English into Spanish.

9 Future work

One of the main problems we have observed in the selection proposed method has been the high number of OOVs during translation. This problem has been addressed by incorporating a backup vocabulary in the post-processing module. This solution has solved some cases but it has not able to deal with order problems. Because of this, in the near future, we will try to improve the corpus selection method for reducing the number of OOVs.

Acknowledgments

The authors would like to thank discussions and suggestions from the colleagues at GTH-UPM. This work has been supported by Plan Avanza Exp Nº: TSI-020100-2010-489), INAPRA (MEC ref: DPI2010-21247-C02-02), and SD-TEAM (MEC ref: TIN2008-06856-C05-03) projects and FEDER program.

References

Hui, C., Zhao, H., Song, Y., Lu, B., 2010 "An Empirical Study on Development Set Selection Strategy for Machine Translation Learning" on Fifth Workshop on Statistical Machine Translation.

Koehn P., F.J. Och D. Marcu. 2003. "Statistical Phrase-based translation". Human Language Technology Conference 2003 (HLT-NAACL 2003), Edmonton, Canada, pp. 127-133, May 2003.

Koehn, Philipp. 2010. "Statistical Machine Translation". Cambridge University Press.

Khadivi, S., Ney, H., 2005. "Automatic filtering of bilingual corpora for statistical machine translation." In Natural Language Processing and Information Systems, 10th Int. Conf. on Applications of Natural Language to Information Systems, volume 3513 of Lecture Notes in Computer Science, pages 263–274, Alicante, Spain, June. Springer.

Och J., Ney. H., 2003. "A systematic comparison of various alignment models". Computational Linguistics, Vol. 29, No. 1 pp. 19-51, 2003.

Sanchis-Trilles, G., Andrés-Ferrer, J., Gascó, G., González-Rubio, J., Martínez-Gómez, P., Rocha, M., Sánchez, J., Casacuberta, F., 2010. "UPV-PRHLT English–Spanish System for WMT10". On ACL Fifth Workshop on Statistical Machine Translation.

Stolcke A., 2002. "SRILM – An Extensible Language Modelling Toolkit". Proc. Intl. Conf. on Spoken Language Processing, vol. 2, pp. 901-904, Denver.

Ueffing, N., Haffari, G., Sarkar, A., 2007. "Transductive learning for statistical machine translation". On ACL Second Workshop on Statistical Machine Translation.

Two-step translation with grammatical post-processing*

David Mareček, Rudolf Rosa, Petra Galuščáková and Ondřej Bojar
Charles University in Prague, Faculty of Mathematics and Physics
Institute of Formal and Applied Linguistics
Malostranské náměstí 25, Prague
{marecek,rosa,galuscakova,bojar}@ufal.mff.cuni.cz

Abstract

This paper describes an experiment in which we try to automatically correct mistakes in grammatical agreement in English to Czech MT outputs. We perform several rule-based corrections on sentences parsed to dependency trees. We prove that it is possible to improve the MT quality of majority of the systems participating in WMT shared task. We made both automatic (BLEU) and manual evaluations.

1 Introduction

This paper is a joint report on two English-to-Czech submissions to the WMT11 shared translation task. The main contribution is however the proposal and evaluation of a rule-based post-processing system DEPFIX aimed at correcting errors in Czech grammar applicable to any MT system. This is somewhat the converse of other approaches (e.g. Simard et al. (2007)) where a statistical system was applied for the post-processing of a rule-based one.

2 Our phrase-based systems

This section briefly describes our underlying phrase-based systems. One of them (CU-BOJAR) was submitted directly to the WMT11 manual evaluation, the other one (CU-TWOSTEP) was first corrected by the proposed method (Section 3 below) and then submitted under the name CU-MARECEK.

*This research has been supported by the European Union Seventh Framework Programme (FP7) under grant agreement n° 247762 (Faust), n° 231720 (EuroMatrix Plus), and by the grants GAUK 116310 and GA201/09/H057.

2.1 Data for statistical systems

Our training parallel data consists of CzEng 0.9 (Bojar and Žabokrtský, 2009), the News Commentary corpus v.6 as released by the WMT11 organizers, the EMEA corpus, a corpus collected from the transcripts of TED talks (http://www.ted.com), the parallel news and separately some of the parallel web pages of the European Commission (http://ec.europa.eu), and the Official Journal of the European Union as released by the Apertium consortium (http://apertium.eu/data).

A custom web crawler was used for the European Commission website. English and Czech websites were matched according to their URLs. Unfortunately, Czech websites very often contain untranslated parts of English texts. Because of this, we aimed especially at the news articles, which are very often translated correctly and also more relevant for the shared task. Texts were segmented using trainable tokenizer (Klyueva and Bojar, 2008) and deduplicated. Processed texts were automatically aligned by Hunalign (Varga and others, 2005).

The data from the Official Journal were first converted from XML to plain text. The documents were paired according to their filenames. To better handle the nature of these data, we decided to divide the documents into two classes based on the average number of words per sentence: "lists" are documents with less than 2.8 words per sentence, other documents are called "texts". The corresponding "lists" were aligned line by line. The corresponding "texts" were automatically segmented by trainable tokenizer and aligned automatically by Hunalign.

We use the following two Czech language mod-

Proceedings of the 6th Workshop on Statistical Machine Translation, pages 426–432,
Edinburgh, Scotland, UK, July 30–31, 2011. ©2011 Association for Computational Linguistics

els, their weights are optimized in MERT:

- 5-gram LM from the Czech side of CzEng (excluding the Navajo section). The LM was constructed by interpolating LMs of the individual domains (news, EU legislation, technical documentation, etc.) to achieve the lowest perplexity on the WMT08 news test set.
- 6-gram LM from the monolingual data supplied by WMT11 organizers (news of the individual years and News Commentary), the Czech National Corpus and a web collection of Czech texts. Again, the final LM is constructed by interpolating the smaller LMs[1] for the WMT08 news test set.

2.2 Baseline Moses (CU-BOJAR)

The system denoted CU-BOJAR for English-to-Czech is simple phrase-based translation, i.e. Moses without factors. We tokenized, lemmatized and tagged all texts using the tools wrapped in TectoMT (Popel and Žabokrtský, 2010). We further tokenize e.g. dashed words ("23-year") after all the processing is finished. Phrase-based MT is then able to handle such expressions both at once, or decompose them as needed to cover unseen variations. We use lexicalized reordering (orientation-bidirectional-fe). The translation runs in "supervised truecase", which means that we use the output of our lemmatizers to decide whether the word should be lowercased or should preserve uppercasing. After the translation, the first letter in the output is simply uppercased. The model is optimized using Moses' standard MERT on the WMT09 test set.

The organizers of WMT11 encouraged participants to apply simple normalization to their data (both for training and testing).[2] The main purpose of the normalization is to improve the consistency of typographical rules. Unfortunately, some of the automatic changes may accidentally damage the meaning of the expression.[3] We therefore opted to submit the output based on *non-normalized* test sets as our primary English-to-Czech submission.

We invested much less effort into the submission called CU-BOJAR for Czech-to-English. The only interesting feature there is the use of alternative decoding paths to translate either from the Czech form or from the Czech lemma equipped with meaning-bearing morphological properties, e.g. the number of nouns. Bojar and Kos (2010) used the same setup with simple lemmas in the fallback decoding path. The enriched lemmas perform marginally better.

2.3 Two-step translation

Our two-step translation is essentially the same setup as detailed by Bojar and Kos (2010): (1) the English source is translated to simplified Czech, and (2) the simplified Czech is monotonically translated to fully inflected Czech. Both steps are simple phrase-based models. Instead of word forms, the simplified Czech uses lemmas enriched by a subset of morphological features selected manually to encode only properties overt both in English and Czech such as the tense of verbs or number of nouns. Czech-specific morphological properties indicating various agreements (e.g. number and gender of adjectives, gender of verbs) are imposed in the second step solely on the basis of the language model.

The first step uses the same parallel and monolingual corpora as CU-BOJAR, except the LMs being trained on the enriched lemmas, not on word forms. The second step uses exactly the same LM as CU-BOJAR but the phrase-table is extracted from all our Czech monolingual data (phrase length limit of 1.)

3 Grammatical post-processing

Phrase-based machine translation systems often have problems with grammatical agreement, especially on longer dependencies. Sometimes, there is a mistake in agreement even between adjacent words because each one belongs to a different phrase. The goal of our post-processing is to correct forms of some words so that they do not violate grammatical rules (eg. grammatical agreement).

The problem is how to find the correct syntactic relations in the output of an MT system. Parsers trained on correct sentences can rely on grammatical agreement, according to which they determine

[1] The interpolated LM file (gzipped ARPA format) is 5.1 GB so we applied LM pruning as implemented in SRI toolkit with the threshold 10^{-14} to reduce the file size to 2.3 GB.

[2] http://www.statmt.org/wmt11/normalize-punctuation.perl

[3] Fixing the ordering of the full stop and the quote is wrong because the order (at least in Czech typesetting) depends on whether it is the full sentence or a final phrase that is captured in the quotes. Even riskier are rules handling decimal and thousand separators in numbers. While there are language-specific conventions, they are not always followed and the normalization can in such cases confuse the order of magnitude by 3.

the dependencies between words. Unfortunately, the agreement in MT outputs is often wrong and the parser fails to produce a correct parse tree. Therefore, we would need a parser trained on a manually annotated treebank consisting of specific outputs of machine translation systems. Such a treebank does not exist and we do not even want to create one, because the MT systems are changing constantly and also because manual annotation of texts that are often not even understandable would be almost a superhuman task.

The DEPFIX system was implemented in TectoMT framework (Popel and Žabokrtský, 2010). MT outputs were tagged by Morče tagger (Spoustová et al., 2007) and then parsed with MST parser (McDonald et al., 2005) that was trained on the Prague Dependency Treebank (Hajič and others, 2006), i.e. on correct Czech sentences. We used an improved implementation with some additional features especially tuned for Czech (Novák and Žabokrtský, 2007). The parser accuracy is much lower on the "noisy" MT output sentences, but a lot of dependencies in which we are to correct grammatical agreement are determined correctly. Adapting the parser for outputs of MT systems will be addressed in the coming months.

A typical example of a correction is the agreement between the subject and the predicate: they should share the morphological number and gender. If they do not, we simply change the number and gender of the predicate in agreement with the subject.[4] An example of such a changed predicate is in Figure 1.

Apart from the dependency tree of the target sentence, we can also use the dependency tree of the source sentence. Source sentences are grammatically correct and the accuracy of the tagger and the parser is accordingly higher there. Words in the source and target sentences are aligned using GIZA++[5] (Och and Ney, 2003) but verbose outputs of the original MT systems would be possibly a better option. The rules for fixing grammatical agreement between words can thus consider also the dependency relations and morphological caregories of their English counterparts in the input sentence.

[4]In this case, we suppose that the number of the subject has a much higher chance to be correct.

[5]GIZA++ was run on lemmatized texts in both directions and intersection symmetrization was used.

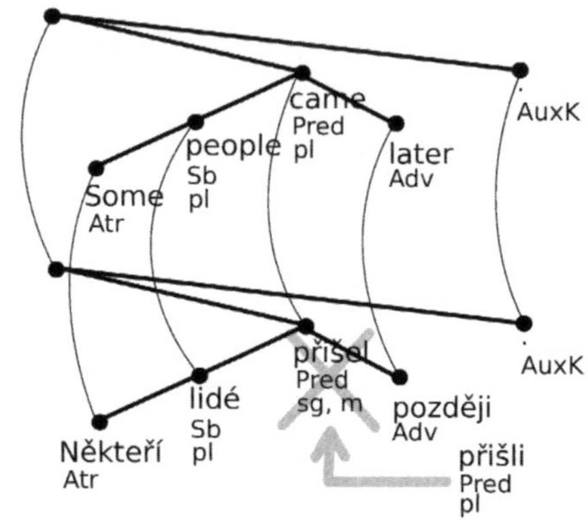

Figure 1: Example of fixing subject-predicate agreement. The Czech word *přišel [he came]* has a wrong morphological number and gender.

3.1 Grammatical rules

We have manually devised a set of the following rules. Their input is the dependency tree of a Czech sentence (MT output) and its English source sentence (MT input) with the nodes aligned where possible. Each of the rules fires if the specified conditions ("IF") are matched, executes the command ("DO") , usually changing one or more morphological categories of the word, and generates a new word form for any word which was changed.

The rules make use of several morphological categories of the word (`node:number`, `node:gender`...), its syntactic relation to its parent in the dependency tree (`node:afun`) and the same information for its English counterpart (`node:en`) and other nodes in the dependency trees.

The order of the rules in this paper follows the order in which they are applied; this is important, as often a rule changes a morphological category of a word which is then used by a subsequent rule.

3.1.1 Noun number (NounNum)

In Czech, a word in singular sometimes has the same form as in plural. Because the tagger often fails to tag the word correctly, we try to correct the tag of a noun tagged as singular if its English counterpart is in plural, so that the subsequent rules can work correctly.

We trust the form of the word but changing the number may also require to change the morphological case (i.e. the tagger was wrong with both number and case). In such cases we choose the first (linearly from nominative to instrumentative) case matching the form. The rule is:

IF: `node:pos = noun &`
`node:number = singular &`
`node:en:number = plural`
DO: `node:number := plural;`
`node:case := find_case(node:form, plural);`

3.1.2 Subject case (SubjCase)

The subject of a Czech sentence must be in the nominative case. Since the parser often fails in marking the correct word as a subject, we use the English source sentence and presuppose that the Czech counterpart of the English subject is also a subject in the Czech sentence.

IF: `node:en:afun = subject`
DO: `node:case := nominative;`

3.1.3 Subject-predicate agreement (SubjPred)

Subject and predicate in Czech agree in their morphological number. To identify a Czech Subject, we trust the subject in the English sentence. Then we copy the number from the (Czech) Subject to the Czech Predicate.

IF: `node:en:afun = subject &`
`parent:afun = predicate`
DO: `parent:number := node:number;`

3.1.4 Subject-past participle agreement (SubjPP)

Czech past participles agree with subject in morphological gender.

IF: `node:pos = noun|pronoun &`
`node:en:afun = subject &`
`parent:pos = verb_past_participle`
DO: `parent:number := node:number;`
`parent:gender := node:gender;`

3.1.5 Preposition without children (PrepNoCh)

In our dependency trees, the preposition is the parent of the words it belongs to (usually a noun). A preposition without children is incorrect so we find nodes aligned to its English counterpart's children and rehang them under the preposition.

IF: `node:afun = preposition &`
`!node:has_children &`
`node:en:has_children`
DO: `foreach node:en:child;`
`node:en:child:cs:parent := node;`

3.1.6 Preposition-noun agreement (PrepNoun)

Every prepositions gets a morphological case assigned to it by the tagger, with which the dependent noun should agree.

IF: `parent:pos = preposition &`
`node:pos = noun`
DO: `node:case := parent:case;`

3.1.7 Noun-adjective agreement (NounAdj)

Czech adjectives and nouns agree in morphological gender, number and case. We assume that the noun is correct and change the adjective accordingly.

IF: `node:pos = adjective &`
`parent:pos = noun`
DO: `node:gender := parent:gender;`
`node:number := parent:number;`
`node:case := parent:case;`

3.1.8 Reflexive particle deletion (ReflTant)

Czech reflexive verbs are accompanied by reflexive particles ('se' and 'si'). We delete particles not beloning to any verb (or adjective derived from a verb).

IF: `node:form = 'se'|'si' &`
`node:pos = pronoun &`
`parent:pos != verb|verbal_adjective`
DO: `remove node;`

4 Experiments and results

We tested our CU-TWOSTEP system with DEPFIX post-processing on both WMT10 and WMT11 testing data. This combined system was submitted to shared translation task as CU-MARECEK. We also ran the DEPFIX post-processing on all other participating systems.

4.1 Automatic evaluation

The achieved BLEU scores are shown in Tables 1 and 2. They show the scores before and after the DEPFIX post-processing. It is interesting that the improvements are quite different between the years 2010 and 2011 in terms of their BLEU score. While the average improvement on WMT10 test set was 0.21 BLEU points, it was only 0.05 BLEU points on the WMT11 test set. Even the results of the same TWOSTEP system differ in a similar way, so it must have been caused by the different data.

system	before	after	improvement
cu-twostep	*15.98*	*16.13*	*0.15 (0.05 - 0.26)*
cmu-heaf.	16.95	17.04	0.09 (-0.01 - 0.20)
cu-bojar	15.85	16.09	0.24 (0.14 - 0.36)
cu-zeman	12.33	12.55	0.22 (0.12 - 0.32)
dcu	13.36	13.59	0.23 (0.13 - 0.37)
dcu-combo	18.79	18.90	0.11 (0.02 - 0.23)
eurotrans	10.10	10.11	0.01 (-0.04 - 0.07)
koc	11.74	11.91	0.17 (0.08 - 0.26)
koc-combo	16.60	16.86	0.26 (0.16 - 0.37)
onlineA	11.81	12.08	0.27 (0.17 - 0.38)
onlineB	16.57	16.79	0.22 (0.11 - 0.33)
potsdam	12.34	12.57	0.23 (0.14 - 0.35)
rwth-combo	17.54	17.79	0.25 (0.15 - 0.35)
sfu	11.43	11.83	0.40 (0.29 - 0.52)
uedin	15.91	16.19	0.28 (0.18 - 0.40)
upv-combo	17.51	17.73	0.22 (0.10 - 0.34)

Table 1: Depfix improvements on the WMT10 systems in BLEU score. Confidence intervals, which were computed on 1000 bootstrap samples, are in brackets.

system	before	after	improvement
cu-twostep	16.57	16.60	0.03 (-0.07 - 0.13)
cmu-heaf.	20.24	20.32	0.08 (-0.03 - 0.19)
commerc2	09.32	09.32	0.00 (-0.04 - 0.04)
cu-bojar	16.88	16.85	-0.03 (-0.12 - 0.07)
cu-popel	14.12	14.11	-0.01 (-0.06 - 0.03)
cu-tamch.	16.32	16.28	-0.04 (-0.14 - 0.06)
cu-zeman	14.61	14.80	0.19 (0.09 - 0.29)
jhu	17.36	17.42	0.06 (-0.03 - 0.16)
online-B	20.26	20.31	0.05 (-0.06 - 0.16)
udein	17.80	17.88	0.08 (-0.02 - 0.17)
upv-prhlt.	20.68	20.69	0.01 (-0.08 - 0.11)

Table 2: Depfix improvements on the WMT11 systems in BLEU score. Confidence intervals are in brackets.

4.2 Manual evaluation

Two independent annotators evaluated DEPFIX manually on the outputs of CU-TWOSTEP and ONLINE-B. We randomly selected 1000 sentences from the `newssyscombtest2011` data set and the appropriate translations made by these two systems. The annotators got the outputs before and after DEPFIX post-processing and their task was to decide which translation[6] from these two is better and label it by the letter *'a'*. If it was not possible to determine which is better, they labeled both by *'n'*.

[6]They were also provided with the source English sentence and the reference translation. The options were shuffled and indentical candidate sentences were collapsed.

A / B	improved	worsened	indefinite	total
improved	273	20	15	308
worsened	12	59	7	78
indefinite	53	35	42	130
total	338	114	64	516

Table 5: Matrix of the inter-annotator agreement

rule	fired	impr.	wors.	% impr.
SubjCase	51	46	5	90.2
SubjPP	193	165	28	85.5
NounAdj	434	354	80	81.6
NounNum	156	122	34	78.2
PrepNoun	135	99	36	73.3
SubjPred	68	48	20	70.6
ReflTant	15	10	5	66.7
PrepNoCh	45	29	16	64.4

Table 6: Rules and their utility.

Table 3 below shows that about 60% of sentences fixed by DEPFIX were improved and only about 20% were worsened. DEPFIX worked a little better on the ONLINE-B, making fewer changes but also fewer wrong changes. It is probably connected with the fact that overall better translations by ONLINE-B are easier to parse.

The matrix of inter-annotator agreement is in Table 5. Our two annotators agreed in 374 sentences (out of 516), that is 72.5%. On the other hand, if we consider only cases where both annotators chose different translation as better (no indefinite marks), we get only 8.8% disagreement (32 out of 364).

Using the manual evaluation, we can also measure performance of the individual rules. Table 6 shows the number of all, improved or worsened sentences where a particular rule was applied. Definitely, the most useful rule (used often and quite reliable) was the one correcting noun-adjective agreement, followed by the subject-pastparticiple agreement rule.

In each changed sentence, two rules (not necessarily related ones) were applied on average.

4.3 Manual evaluation across data sets

The fact that the improvements in BLEU scores on WMT10 test set are much higher has led us to one more experiment: we compare manual annotations of 330 sentences from each of the WMT10 and

system	annotator	changed	improved		worsened		indefinite	
			count	%	count	%	count	%
cu-bojar-twostep	A	269	152	56.5	39	14.5	78	29.0
cu-bojar-twostep	B	269	173	64.3	50	18.6	46	17.1
online-B	A	247	156	63.1	39	15.9	52	21.1
online-B	B	247	165	66.8	64	25.9	18	7.3

Table 3: Manual evaluation of the DEPFIX post-processing on 1000 randomly chosen sentences from WMT11 test set.

test set	changed	improved		worsened		indefinite		BLEU		
		count	%	count	%	count	%	before	after	diff
newssyscombtest2010	104	52	50.0	20	19.2	32	30.8	16.99	17.38	0.39
newssyscombtest2011	101	66	65.3	19	18.8	16	15.8	13.99	13.87	-0.12

Table 4: Manual and automatic evaluation of the DEPFIX post-processing on CU-TWOSTEP system across different datasets. 330 sentences were randomly selected from each of the WMT10 and WMT11 test sets. Both manual scores and BLEU are computed only on the sentences that were changed by the DEPFIX post-processing.

WMT11 sets as translated by CU-TWOSTEP and corrected by DEPFIX. Table 4 shows that WMT10 and WMT11 are comparable in manually estimated improvement (50–65%). BLEU does not indicate that and even estimates a drop in quality on this subset WMT11. (The absolute BLEU scores differ from BLEUs on the whole test sets but we are interested only in the change of the scores.) BLEU is thus not very suitable for the evaluation of DEPFIX.

5 Conclusions and future work

Manual evaluation shows that our DEPFIX approach to improving MT output quality is sensible. Although it is unable to correct many serious MT errors, such as wrong lexical choices, it can improve the grammaticality of the output in a way that the language model often cannot, which leads to output that is considered to be better by humans. We also suggest that BLEU is not appropriate metric for measuring changes in grammatical correctness of sentences, especially with inflective languages.

An advantage of our method is that it is possible to apply it on output of any MT system (although it works better for phrase-based MT systems). While DEPFIX has been developed using the output of CU-BOJAR, the rules we devised are not specific to any MT system. They simply describe several grammatical rules of Czech language that can be machine-checked and if errors are found, the output can be corrected. Moreover, our method only requires the source sentence and the translation output for its operation – i.e. it is not necessary to modify the MT system itself.

We are now considering modifications of the parser so that it is able to parse the incorrect sentences produced by MT. Theoretically it would be possible to train the parser on annotated ungrammatical sentences, but we do not want to invest such annotation labour. Instead, when parsing the Czech sentence we will make the parser utilize the information contained in the parse tree of the English sentence, which is usually correct. We will probably also have to make the parser put less weight to the often incorrect tagger output. An alternative is to avoid parsing of the target and project the source parse to the target side using word alignments, if provided by the MT system.

Because some of our rules are able to work using only the tagger output, we will also try to apply them before the parsing as they might help the parser by correcting some of the tags.

We will also try several modifications of the tagger, but the English sentence does not help us so much here, because it does not contain any information regarding the most common errors – incorrect assignment of morphological gender and case. However, it could help with part of speech and morphological number disambiguation. Moreover, it would be probably helpful for us if the tagger included several most probable hypotheses, as the single-output-only disambiguation is often erroneous on ungrammatical sentences.

References

Ondrej Bojar and Kamil Kos. 2010. 2010 Failures in English-Czech Phrase-Based MT. In *Proceedings of the Joint Fifth Workshop on Statistical Machine Translation and MetricsMATR*, pages 60–66, Uppsala, Sweden, July. Association for Computational Linguistics.

Ondřej Bojar and Zdeněk Žabokrtský. 2009. CzEng0.9: Large Parallel Treebank with Rich Annotation. *Prague Bulletin of Mathematical Linguistics*, 92.

Jan Hajič et al. 2006. Prague Dependency Treebank 2.0. CD-ROM, Linguistic Data Consortium, LDC Catalog No.: LDC2006T0 1, Philadelphia.

Natalia Klyueva and Ondřej Bojar. 2008. UMC 0.1: Czech-Russian-English Multilingual Corpus. In *Proceedings of International Conference Corpus Linguistics*, pages 188–195, Saint-Petersburg.

Ryan McDonald, Fernando Pereira, Kiril Ribarov, and Jan Hajič. 2005. Non-projective dependency parsing using spanning tree algorithms. In *HLT '05: Proceedings of the conference on Human Language Technology and Empirical Methods in Natural Language Processing*, pages 523–530, Vancouver, British Columbia, Canada.

Václav Novák and Zdeněk Žabokrtský. 2007. Feature engineering in maximum spanning tree dependency parser. In Václav Matoušek and Pavel Mautner, editors, *Lecture Notes in Artificial Intelligence, Proceedings of the 10th I nternational Conference on Text, Speech and Dialogue*, Lecture Notes in Computer Science, pages 92–98, Pilsen, Czech Republic. Springer Science+Business Media Deutschland GmbH.

Franz Josef Och and Hermann Ney. 2003. A Systematic Comparison of Various Statistical Alignment Models. *Computational Linguistics*, 29(1):19–51.

Martin Popel and Zdeněk Žabokrtský. 2010. TectoMT: modular NLP framework. In *Proceedings of the 7th international conference on Advances in natural language processing*, IceTAL'10, pages 293–304, Berlin, Heidelberg. Springer-Verlag.

Michel Simard, Cyril Goutte, and Pierre Isabelle. 2007. Statistical phrase-based post-editing. In *Human Language Technologies 2007: The Conference of the North American Chapter of the Association for Computational Linguistics; Proceedings of the Main Conference*, pages 508–515, Rochester, New York, April. Association for Computational Linguistics.

Drahomíra Spoustová, Jan Hajič, Jan Votrubec, Pavel Krbec, and Pavel Květoň. 2007. The best of two worlds: Cooperation of statistical and rule-based taggers for czech. In *Proceedings of the Workshop on Balto-Slavonic Natural Language Processing, ACL 2007*, pages 67–74, Praha.

Dániel Varga et al. 2005. Parallel corpora for medium density languages. In *Proceedings of the Recent Advances in Natural Language Processing*, pages 590–596, Borovets, Bulgaria.

Influence of Parser Choice on Dependency-Based MT

Martin Popel, David Mareček, Nathan Green and Zdeněk Žabokrtský
Charles University in Prague
Faculty of Mathematics and Physics
Institute of Formal and Applied Linguistics
{popel,marecek,green,zabokrtsky}@ufal.mff.cuni.cz

Abstract

Accuracy of dependency parsers is one of the key factors limiting the quality of dependency-based machine translation. This paper deals with the influence of various dependency parsing approaches (and also different training data size) on the overall performance of an English-to-Czech dependency-based statistical translation system implemented in the Treex framework. We also study the relationship between parsing accuracy in terms of unlabeled attachment score and machine translation quality in terms of BLEU.

1 Introduction

In the last years, statistical n-gram models dominated the field of Machine Translation (MT). However, their results are still far from perfect. Therefore we believe it makes sense to investigate alternative statistical approaches. This paper is focused on an analysis-transfer-synthesis translation system called TectoMT whose transfer representation has a shape of a deep-syntactic dependency tree. The system has been introduced by Žabokrtský et al. (2008). The translation direction under consideration is English-to-Czech.

It has been shown by Popel (2009) that the current accuracy of the dependency parser employed in this translation system is one of the limiting factors from the viewpoint of its output quality. In other words, the parsing phase is responsible for a large portion of translation errors. The biggest source of translation errors in the referred study was (and probably still is) the transfer phase, however the proportion has changed since and the relative importance of the parsing phase has grown, because the tranfer phase errors have already been addressed by improvements based on Hidden Markov Tree Models for lexical and syntactic choice as shown by Žabokrtský and Popel (2009), and by context sensitive translation models based on maximum entropy as described by Mareček et al. (2010).

Our study proceeds along two directions. First, we train two state-of-the-art dependency parsers on training sets with varying size. Second, we use five parsers based on different parsing techniques. In both cases we document the relation between parsing accuracy (in terms of Unlabeled Attachment Score, UAS) and translation quality (estimated by the well known BLEU metric).

The motivation behind the first set of experiments is that we can extrapolate the learning curve and try to predict how new advances in dependency parsing can affect MT quality in the future.

The second experiment series is motivated by the hypothesis that parsers based on different approaches are likely to have a different distribution of errors, even if they can have competitive performance in parsing accuracy. In dependency parsing metrics, all types of incorrect edges typically have the same weight,[1] but some incorrect edges can be more harmful than others from the MT viewpoint. For instance, an incorrect attachment of an adverbial node is usually harmless, while incorrect attachment of a subject node might have several negative conse-

[1]This issue has been tackled already in the parsing literature; for example, some authors disregard placement of punctuation nodes within trees in the evaluation (Zeman, 2004).

Proceedings of the 6th Workshop on Statistical Machine Translation, pages 433–439,
Edinburgh, Scotland, UK, July 30–31, 2011.

quences such as:

- unrecognized finiteness of the governing verb, which can lead to a wrong syntactization on the target side (an infinitive verb phrase instead of a finite clause),
- wrong choice of the target-side verb form (because of unrecognized subject-predicate agreement),
- missing punctuation (because of wrongly recognized finite clause boundaries),
- wrong placement of clitics (because of wrongly recognized finite clause boundaries),
- wrong form of pronouns (personal and possessive pronouns referring to the clause's subject should have reflexive forms in Czech).

Thus it is obvious that the parser choice is important and that it might not be enough to choose a parser, for machine translation, only according to its UAS.

Due to growing popularity of dependency syntax in the last years, there are a number of dependency parsers available. The present paper deals with five parsers evaluated within the translation framework: three genuine dependency parsers, namely the parsers described in (McDonald et al., 2005), (Nivre et al., 2007), and (Zhang and Nivre, 2011), and two constituency parsers (Charniak and Johnson, 2005) and (Klein and Manning, 2003), whose outputs were converted to dependency structures by Penn Converter (Johansson and Nugues, 2007).

As for the related literature, there is no published study measuring the influence of dependency parsers on dependency-based MT to our knowledge.[2]

The remainder of this paper is structured as follows. The overall translation pipeline, within which the parsers are tested, is described in Section 2. Section 3 lists the parsers under consideration and their main features. Section 4 summarizes the influence of the selected parsers on the MT quality in terms of BLEU. Section 5 concludes.

[2]However, the parser bottleneck of the dependency-based MT approach was observed also by other researchers (Robert Moore, personal communication).

2 Dependency-based Translation in Treex

We have implemented our experiments in the Treex software framework (formerly TectoMT, introduced by Žabokrtský et al. (2008)), which already offers tool chains for analysis and synthesis of Czech and English sentences.

We use the tectogrammatical (deep-syntactic) layer of language representation as the transfer layer in the presented MT experiments. Tectogrammatics was introduced by Sgall (1967) and further elaborated within the Prague Dependency Treebank project (Hajič et al., 2006). On this layer, each sentence is represented as a tectogrammatical tree, whose main properties (from the MT viewpoint) are the following:

1. nodes represent autosemantic words,
2. edges represent semantic dependencies (a node is an argument or a modifier of its parent),
3. there are no functional words (prepositions, auxiliary words) in the tree, and the autosemantic words appear only in their base forms (lemmas). Morphologically indispensable categories (such as number with nouns or tense with verbs, but not number with verbs as it is only imposed by agreement) are stored in separate node attributes (grammatemes).

The intuitions behind the decision to use tectogrammatics for MT are the following: we believe that (1) tectogrammatics largely abstracts from language-specific means (inflection, agglutination, functional words etc.) of expressing non-lexical meanings and thus tectogrammatical trees are supposed to be highly similar across languages, (2) it enables a natural transfer factorization,[3] (3) and local tree contexts in tectogrammatical trees carry more information (especially for lexical choice) than local linear contexts in the original sentences.

The translation scenario is outlined in the rest of this section.

[3]Morphological categories can be translated almost independently from lemmas, which makes parallel training data 'denser', especially when translating from/to a language with rich inflection such as Czech.

2.1 Analysis

The input English text is segmented into sentences and tokens. The tokens are lemmatized and tagged with Penn Treebank tags using the Morce tagger (Spoustová et al., 2007). Then one of the studied dependency parsers is applied and a surface-syntax dependency tree (analytical tree in the PDT terminology) is created for each sentence.

This tree is converted to a tectogrammatical tree. Each autosemantic word with its associated functional words is collapsed into a single tectogrammatical node, labeled with a lemma, formeme,[4] and semantically indispensable morphologically categories; coreference is also resolved.

2.2 Transfer

The transfer phase follows, whose most difficult part consists especially in labeling the tree with target-side lemmas and formemes. There are also other types of changes, such as node addition and deletion. However, as shown by Popel (2009), changes of tree topology are required relatively infrequently due to the language abstractions on the tectogrammatical layer.

Currently, translation models based on Maximum Entropy classifiers are used both for lemmas and formemes (Mareček et al., 2010). Tree labeling is optimized using Hidden Tree Markov Models (Žabokrtský and Popel, 2009), which makes use of target-language dependency tree probabilistic model.

All models used in the transfer phase are trained using training sections of the Czech-English parallel corpus CzEng 0.9 (Bojar and Žabokrtský, 2009).

2.3 Synthesis

Finally, surface sentence shape is synthesized from the tectogrammatical tree, which is basically the reverse operation of the tectogrammatical analysis. It consists of adding punctuation and functional words, spreading morphological categories according to grammatical agreement, performing inflection (using Czech morphology database (Hajič, 2004)), arranging word order etc.

The difference from the analysis phase is that there is not very much space for optimization in the synthesis phase. In other words, final sentence shape is determined almost uniquely by the tectogrammatical tree (enriched with formemes) resulting from the transfer phase. However, if there are not enough constraints for a unique choice of a surface form of a lemma, then a unigram language model is used for the final decision. The model was trained using 500 million words from the Czech National Corpus.[5]

3 Involved Parsers

We performed experiments with parsers from three families: graph-based parsers, transition-based parsers, and phrase-structure parsers (with constituency-to-dependency postprocessing).

3.1 Graph-based Parser

In graph-based parsing, we learn a model for scoring graph edges, and we search for the highest-scoring tree composed of the graph's edges. We used Maximum Spanning Tree parser (Mcdonald and Pereira, 2006) which is capable of incorporating second order features (`MST` for short).

3.2 Transition-based Parsers

Transition-based parsers utilize the shift-reduce algorithm. Input words are put into a queue and consumed by shift-reduce actions, while the output parser is gradually built. Unlike graph-based parsers, transition-based parsers have linear time complexity and allow straightforward application of non-local features.

We included two transition-based parsers into our experiments:

- `Malt` – Malt parser introduced by Nivre et al. (2007) [6]

[4]Formeme captures the morphosyntactic means which are used for expressing the tectogrammatical node in the surface sentence shape. Examples of formeme values: `v:that+fin` – finite verb in a subordinated clause introduced with conjunction *that*, `n:sb` – semantic noun in a subject position, `n:for+X` – semantic noun in a prepositional group introduced with preposition *for*, `adj:attr` – semantic adjective in an attributive position.

[5]http://ucnk.ff.cuni.cz

[6]We used *stackeager* algorithm, *liblinear* learner, and the enriched feature set for English (the same configuration as in pretrained English models downloadable at http://maltparser.org.

- ZPar – Zpar parser[7] which is basically an alternative implementation of the Malt parser, employing a richer set of non-local features as described by Zhang and Nivre (2011).

3.3 CFG-based Tree Parsers

Another option how to obtain dependency trees is to apply a constituency parser, recognize heads in the resulting phrase structures and apply a recursive algorithm for converting phrase-structure trees into constituency trees (the convertibility of the two types of syntactic structures was studied already by Gaifman (1965)).

We used two constituency parsers:

- Stanford – The Stanford parser (Klein and Manning, 2003),[8]
- CJ – a MaxEnt-based parser combined with discriminative reranking (Charniak and Johnson, 2005).[9]

Before applying the parsers on the text, the system removes all spaces within tokens. For instance U. S. becomes U.S. to restrict the parsers from creating two new tokens. Tokenization built into both parsers is bypassed and the default tokenization in Treex is used.

After parsing, Penn Converter introduced by Johansson and Nugues (2007) is applied, with the -conll2007 option, to change the constituent structure output, of the two parsers, into CoNLL dependency structure. This allows us to keep the formats consistent with the output of both MST and MaltParser within the Treex framework.

There is an implemented procedure for creating tectogrammatical trees from the English phrase structure trees described by Kučerová and Žabokrtský (2002). Using the procedure is more straightforward, as it does not go through the CoNLL-style trees; English CoNLL-style trees differ slightly from the PDT conventions (e.g. in attaching auxiliary verbs) and thus needs additional postprocessing for our purposes. However, we decided to stick to Penn Converter, so that the similarity of the translation scenarios is maximized for all parsers.

3.4 Common Preprocessing: Shallow Sentence Chunking

According to our experience, many dependency parsers have troubles with analyzing sentences that contain parenthesed or quoted phrases, especially if they are long.

We use the assumption that in most cases the content of parentheses or quotes should correspond to a connected subgraph (subtree) of the syntactic tree. We implemented a very shallow sentence chunker (SentChunk) which recognizes parenthesed word sequences. These sequences can be passed to a parser first, and be parsed independently of the rest of the sentence. This was shown to improve not only parsing accuracy of the parenthesed word sequence (which is forced to remain in one subtree), but also the rest of the sentence.[10]

In our experiments, SentChunk is used only in combination with the three genuine dependency parsers.

4 Experiments and Evaluation

4.1 Data for Parsers' Training and Evaluation

The dependency trees needed for training the parsers and evaluating their UAS were created from the Penn Treebank data (enriched first with internal noun phrase structure applied via scripts provided by Vadas and Curran (2007)) by Penn Converter (Johansson and Nugues, 2007) with the -conll2007 option (PennConv for short).

All the parsers were evaluated on the same data – section 23.

All the parsers were trained on sections 02–21, except for the Stanford parser which was trained on sections 01–21. We were able to retrain the parser models only for MST and Malt. For the other parsers we used pretrained models available on the Internet: CJ's default model ec50spfinal, Stanford's wsjPCFG.ser.gz model, and

[7] http://sourceforge.net/projects/zpar/ (version 0.4)

[8] Only the constituent, phrase based, parsed output is used in these experiments.

[9] We are using the default settings from the August 2006 version of the software.

[10] Edge length is a common feature in dependency parsers, so "deleting" parenthesed words may give higher scores to correct dependency links that happened to span over the parentheses.

ZPar's english.tar.gz. The model of ZPar is trained on data converted to dependencies using Penn2Malt tool,[11] which selects the last member of a coordination as the head. To be able to compare ZPar's output with the other parsers, we postprocessed it by a simple ConjAsHead code that converts this style of coordinations to the one used in CoNLL2007, where the conjuction is the head.

4.2 Reference Translations Used for Evaluation

Translation experiments were evaluated using reference translations from the new-dev2009 data set, provided by the organizors of shared translation task with the Workshop on Statistical Machine Translation.

4.3 Influence of Parser Training Data Size

We trained a sequence of parser models for MST and Malt, using a roughly exponentially growing sequence of Penn Treebank subsets. The subsets are contiguous and start from the beginning of section 02. The results are collected in Tables 1 and 2.[12]

#tokens	UAS	BLEU	NIST
100	0.362	0.0579	3.6375
300	0.509	0.0859	4.3853
1000	0.591	0.0995	4.6548
3000	0.623	0.1054	4.7972
10000	0.680	0.1130	4.9695
30000	0.719	0.1215	5.0705
100000	0.749	0.1232	5.1193
300000	0.776	0.1257	5.1571
990180	0.793	0.1280	5.1915

Table 1: The effect of training data size on parsing accuracy and on translation performance with MST.

The trend of the relation between the training data size and BLEU is visible also in Figure 1. It is obvious that increasing the training data has a positive effect on the translation quality. However, the pace of growth of BLEU is sublogarithmic, and becomes unconvincing above 100,000 training tokens. It indicates that given one of the two parsers integrated into our translation framework, increasing the parser training data alone would probably not lead to a substantial improvement of the translation performance.

#tokens	UAS	BLEU	NIST
100	0.454	0.0763	4.0555
300	0.518	0.0932	4.4698
1000	0.591	0.1042	4.6769
3000	0.616	0.1068	4.7472
10000	0.665	0.1140	4.9100
30000	0.695	0.1176	4.9744
100000	0.723	0.1226	5.0504
300000	0.740	0.1238	5.1005
990180	0.759	0.1253	5.1296

Table 2: The effect of training data size on parsing accuracy and on translation performance with Malt.

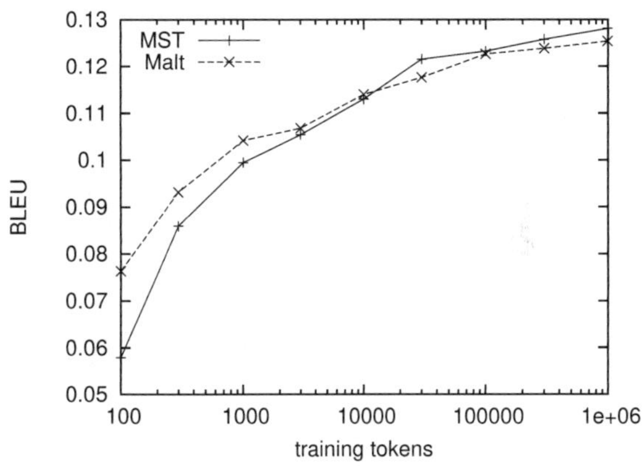

Figure 1: The effect of parser training data size of BLEU with Malt and MST parsers.

4.4 Influence of Parser Choice

Table 3 summarizes our experiments with the five parsers integrated into the tectogrammatical translation pipeline. Two configurations (with and without SentChunk) are listed for the genuine dependency parsers. The relationship between UAS and BLEU for (the best configurations of) all five parsers is depicted also in Figure 2.

Additionally, we used paired bootstrap 95% confidence interval testing (Zhang et al., 2004), to check which BLEU differences are significant. For the five compared parser (with SentChunk if applicable), only four comparisons are not significant: MST-CJ, MST-Stanford, Malt-Stanford, and CJ-Stanford.

[11] http://w3.msi.vxu.se/~nivre/research/Penn2Malt.html

[12] To our knowledge, the best system participating in the shared task reaches BLEU 17.8 for this translation direction.

Parser	Training data	Preprocessing	Postprocessing	UAS	BLEU	NIST	TER
MST	PennTB + PennConv	SentChunk	–	0.793	0.1280	5.192	0.735
MST	PennTB + PennConv	–	–	0.794	0.1236	5.149	0.739
Malt	PennTB + PennConv	SentChunk	–	0.760	0.1253	5.130	0.740
Malt	PennTB + PennConv	–	–	0.761	0.1214	5.088	0.744
Zpar	PennTB + Penn2Malt	SentChunk	ConjAsHead	0.793	0.1176	5.039	0.749
Zpar	PennTB + Penn2Malt	–	ConjAsHead	0.792	0.1127	4.984	0.754
CJ	PennTB	–	PennConv	0.904	0.1284	5.189	0.737
Stanford	PennTB	–	PennConv	0.825	0.1277	5.137	0.740

Table 3: Dependency parsers tested in the translation pipeline.

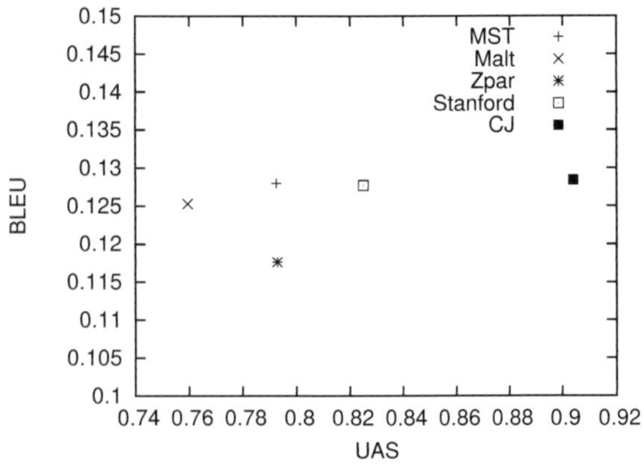

Figure 2: Unlabeled Attachment Score versus BLEU.

Even if BLEU grows relatively smoothly with UAS for different parsing models of the same parser, one can see that there is no obvious relation between UAS and BLEU accross all parsers. MST and Zpar have the same UAS but quite different BLEU, whereas MST and CJ have very similar BLEU but distant UAS. It confirms the original hypothesis that it is not only the overall UAS, but also the parser-specific distribution of errors what matters.

4.5 Influence of Shallow Sentence Chunking

Table 3 confirms that parsing the contents parentheses separately from the rest of the sentence (SentChunk) has a positive effect with all three dependency parsers. Surprisingly, even if the effect on UAS is negligible, the improvement is almost half of BLEU point which is significant for all the three parsers.

4.6 Discussion on Result Comparability

We tried to isolate the effects of the properties of selected parsers, however, the separation from other influencing factors is not perfect due to several technical issues:

- So far, we were not able to retrain the models for all parsers ourselves and therefore their pretrained models (one of them based on slightly different Penn Treebank division) must have been used.
- Some parsers make their own choice of POS tags within the parsed sentences, while other parsers require the sentences to be tagged already on their input.
- The trees in the CzEng 0.9 parallel treebank were created using MST. CzEng 0.9 was used for training translation models used in the transfer phase of the translation scenario; thus these translation models might compensate for some MST's errors, which might handicap other parsers. So far we were not able to reparse 8 million sentence pairs in CzEng 0.9 by all studied parsers.

5 Conclusions

This paper is a study of how the choice of a dependency parsing technique influences the quality of English-Czech dependency-based translation. Our main observations are the following. First, BLEU grows with the increasing amount of training dependency trees, but only in a sublogarithmic pace. Second, what seems to be quite effective for translation is to facilitate the parsers' task by dividing the sentences into smaller chunks using parenthesis boundaries. Third, if the parsers are based on different approaches, their UAS does not correlate well with their effect on the translation quality.

Acknowledgments

This research was supported by the grants MSM0021620838, GAUK 116310, GA201/09/H057, and by the European Commission's 7th Framework Program (FP7) under grant agreements n° 238405 (CLARA), n° 247762 (FAUST), and n° 231720 (EuroMatrix Plus).

References

Ondřej Bojar and Zdeněk Žabokrtský. 2009. CzEng 0.9, Building a Large Czech-English Automatic Parallel Treebank. *The Prague Bulletin of Mathematical Linguistics*, 92:63–83.

Eugene Charniak and Mark Johnson. 2005. Coarse-to-fine n-best parsing and maxent discriminative reranking. In *Proceedings of the 43rd Annual Meeting of Association for Computational Linguistics*, ACL '05, pages 173–180, Stroudsburg, PA, USA. Association for Computational Linguistics.

Haim Gaifman. 1965. Dependency systems and phrase-structure systems. *Information and Control*, pages 304–337.

Jan Hajič et al. 2006. Prague Dependency Treebank 2.0. CD-ROM, Linguistic Data Consortium, LDC Catalog No.: LDC2006T01, Philadelphia.

Jan Hajič. 2004. *Disambiguation of Rich Inflection – Computational Morphology of Czech*. Charles University – The Karolinum Press, Prague.

Richard Johansson and Pierre Nugues. 2007. Extended constituent-to-dependency conversion for English. In *Proceedings of NODALIDA 2007*, pages 105–112, Tartu, Estonia, May 25-26.

Dan Klein and Christopher D. Manning. 2003. Accurate unlexicalized parsing. In *Proceedings of the 41st Annual Meeting of Association for Computational Linguistics*, pages 423–430.

Ivona Kučerová and Zdeněk Žabokrtský. 2002. Transforming Penn Treebank Phrase Trees into (Praguian) Tectogrammatical Dependency Trees. *The Prague Bulletin of Mathematical Linguistics*, (78):77–94.

David Mareček, Martin Popel, and Zdeněk Žabokrtský. 2010. Maximum entropy translation model in dependency-based MT framework. In *Proceedings of the Joint Fifth Workshop on Statistical Machine Translation and MetricsMATR*, pages 201–201, Uppsala, Sweden. Association for Computational Linguistics.

Ryan Mcdonald and Fernando Pereira. 2006. Online learning of approximate dependency parsing algorithms. In *Proceedings of EACL*, pages 81–88.

Ryan McDonald, Fernando Pereira, Kiril Ribarov, and Jan Hajič. 2005. Non-projective dependency parsing using spanning tree algorithms. In *Proceedings of HLT / EMNLP*, pages 523–530, Vancouver, Canada.

Joakim Nivre, Johan Hall, Jens Nilsson, Atanas Chanev, Gulsen Eryigit, Sandra Kübler, Svetoslav Marinov, and Erwin Marsi. 2007. MaltParser: A language-independent system for data-driven dependency parsing. *Natural Language Engineering*, 13(2):95–135.

Martin Popel. 2009. Ways to Improve the Quality of English-Czech Machine Translation. Master's thesis, Institute of Formal and Applied Linguistics, Charles University, Prague, Czech Republic.

Petr Sgall. 1967. *Generativní popis jazyka a česká deklinace*. Academia, Prague.

Drahomíra Spoustová, Jan Hajič, Jan Votrubec, Pavel Krbec, and Pavel Květoň. 2007. The Best of Two Worlds: Cooperation of Statistical and Rule-Based Taggers for Czech. In *Proceedings of the Workshop on Balto-Slavonic Natural Language Processing, ACL 2007*, pages 67–74, Praha.

David Vadas and James Curran. 2007. Adding Noun Phrase Structure to the Penn Treebank. In *Proceedings of the 45th Annual Meeting of the Association of Computational Linguistics*, pages 240–247, Prague, Czech Republic, June. Association for Computational Linguistics.

Zdeněk Žabokrtský and Martin Popel. 2009. Hidden Markov Tree Model in Dependency-based Machine Translation. In *Proceedings of the ACL-IJCNLP 2009 Conference Short Papers*, pages 145–148, Suntec, Singapore.

Zdeněk Žabokrtský, Jan Ptáček, and Petr Pajas. 2008. TectoMT: Highly Modular MT System with Tectogrammatics Used as Transfer Layer. In *Proceedings of the 3rd Workshop on Statistical Machine Translation, ACL*, pages 167–170.

Daniel Zeman. 2004. *Parsing with a Statistical Dependency Model*. Ph.D. thesis, Faculty of Mathematics and Physics, Charles University in Prague.

Yue Zhang and Joakim Nivre. 2011. Transition-based dependency parsing with rich non-local features. In *To appear in the Proceedings of the 49th Annual Meeting of the Association of Computational Linguistics*.

Ying Zhang, Stephan Vogel, and Alex Waibel. 2004. Interpreting bleu/nist scores: How much improvement do we need to have a better system. In *Proceedings of LREC*, volume 4, pages 2051–2054.

The LIGA (LIG/LIA) Machine Translation System for WMT 2011

Marion Potet[1], **Raphaël Rubino**[2], **Benjamin Lecouteux**[1], **Stéphane Huet**[2], **Hervé Blanchon**[1], **Laurent Besacier**[1] and **Fabrice Lefèvre**[2]

[1]UJF-Grenoble1, UPMF-Grenoble2
LIG UMR 5217
Grenoble, F-38041, France
FirstName.LastName@imag.fr

[2]Université d'Avignon
LIA-CERI
Avignon, F-84911, France
FirstName.LastName@univ-avignon.fr

Abstract

We describe our system for the news commentary translation task of WMT 2011. The submitted run for the French-English direction is a combination of two MOSES-based systems developed at LIG and LIA laboratories. We report experiments to improve over the standard phrase-based model using statistical post-edition, information retrieval methods to subsample out-of-domain parallel corpora and ROVER to combine n-best list of hypotheses output by different systems.

1 Introduction

This year, LIG and LIA have combined their efforts to produce a joint submission to WMT 2011 for the French-English translation task. Each group started by developing its own solution whilst sharing resources (corpora as provided by the organizers but also aligned data etc) and acquired knowledge (current parameters, effect of the size of n-grams, etc.) with the other. Both LIG and LIA systems are standard phrase-based translation systems based on the MOSES toolkit with appropriate carefully-tuned setups. The final LIGA submission is a combination of the two systems.

We summarize in Section 2 the resources used and the main characteristics of the systems. Sections 3 and 4 describe the specificities and report experiments of resp. the LIG and the LIA system. Section 5 presents the combination of n-best lists hypotheses generated by both systems. Finally, we conclude in Section 6.

2 System overview

2.1 Used data

Globally, our system[1] was built using all the French and English data supplied for the workshop's shared translation task, apart from the Gigaword monolingual corpora released by the LDC. Table 1 sums up the used data and introduces designations that we follow in the remainder of this paper to refer to corpora. Four corpora were used to build translation models: *news-c*, *euro*, *UN* and *giga*, while three others are employed to train monolingual language models (LMs). Three bilingual corpora were devoted to model tuning: *test09* was used for the development of the two seed systems (LIG and LIA), whereas *test08* and *testcomb08* were used to tune the weights for system combination. *test10* was finally put aside to compare internally our methods.

2.2 LIG and LIA system characteristics

Both LIG and LIA systems are phrase-based translation models. All the data were first tokenized with the tokenizer provided for the workshop. Kneser-Ney discounted LMs were built from monolingual corpora using the SRILM toolkit (Stolcke, 2002), while bilingual corpora were aligned at the word-level using GIZA++ (Och and Ney, 2003) or its multi-threaded version MGIZA++ (Gao and Vogel, 2008) for the large corpora *UN* and *giga*. Phrase table and lexicalized reordering models were built with MOSES (Koehn et al., 2007). Finally, 14 features were used in the phrase-based models:

[1]When not specified otherwise "our" system refers to the LIGA system.

Proceedings of the 6th Workshop on Statistical Machine Translation, pages 440–446,
Edinburgh, Scotland, UK, July 30–31, 2011.

CORPORA	DESIGNATION	SIZE (SENTENCES)
English-French Bilingual training		
News Commentary v6	*news-c*	116 k
Europarl v6	*euro*	1.8 M
United Nation corpus	*UN*	12 M
10^9 corpus	*giga*	23 M
English Monolingual training		
News Commentary v6	*mono-news-c*	181 k
Shuffled News Crawl corpus (from 2007 to 2011)	*news-s*	25 M
Europarl v6	*mono-euro*	1.8 M
Development		
newstest2008	*test08*	2,051
newssyscomb2009	*testcomb09*	502
newstest2009	*test09*	2,525
Test		
newstest2010	*test10*	2,489

Table 1: Used corpora

- 5 translation model scores,
- 1 distance-based reordering score,
- 6 lexicalized reordering score,
- 1 LM score and
- 1 word penalty score.

The score weights were optimized on the *test09* corpus according to the BLEU score with the MERT method (Och, 2003). The experiments led specifically with either LIG or LIA system are respectively described in Sections 3 and 4. Unless otherwise indicated, all the evaluations were performed using case-insensitive BLEU and were computed with the `mteval-v13a.pl` script provided by NIST. Table 2 summarizes the differences between the final configuration of the systems.

3 The LIG machine translation system

LIG participated for the second time to the WMT shared news translation task for the French-English language pair.

3.1 Pre-processing

Training data were first lowercased with the PERL script provided for the campaign. They were also processed in order to normalize a special French form (named euphonious "t") as described in (Potet et al., 2010).

The baseline system was built using a 4-gram LM trained on the monolingual corpora provided last year and translation models trained on *news-c* and *euro* (Table 3, System 1). A significant improvement in terms of BLEU is obtained when taking into account a third corpus, *UN*, to build translation models (System 2). The next section describes the LMs that were trained using the monolingual data provided this year.

3.2 Language model training

Target LMs are standard 4-gram models trained on the provided monolingual corpus (*mono-news-c*, *mono-euro* and *news-s*). We decided to test two different n-gram cut-off settings. The fist set has low cut-offs: 1-2-3-3 (respectively for 1-gram, 2-gram, 3-gram and 4-gram counts), whereas the second one (LM_2) is more aggressive: 1-5-7-7. Experiment results (Table 3, Systems 3 and 4) show that resorting to LM_2 leads to an improvement of BLEU with respect to LM_1. LM_2 was therefore used in the subsequent experiments.

FEATURES	LIG SYSTEM	LIA SYSTEM
Pre-processing	Text lowercased Normalization of French euphonious 't'	Text truecased Reaccentuation of French words starting with a capital letter
LM	Training on *mono-news-c*, *news-s* and *mono-euro* 4-gram models	Training on *mono-news-c* and *news-s* 5-gram models
Translation model	Training on *news-c*, *euro* and *UN* Phrase table filtering Use of *-monotone-at-punctuation* option	Training on 10 M sentence pairs selected in *news-c*, *euro*, *UN* and *giga*

Table 2: Distinct features between final configurations retained for the LIG and LIA systems

3.3 Translation model training

Translation models were trained from the parallel corpora *news-c*, *euro* and *UN*. Data were aligned at the word-level and then used to build standard phrase-based translation models. We filtered the obtained phrase table using the method described in (Johnson et al., 2007). Since this technique drastically reduces the size of the phrase table, while not degrading (and even slightly improving) the results on the development and test corpora (System 6), we decided to employ filtered phrase tables in the final configuration of the LIG system.

3.4 Tuning

For decoding, the system uses a log-linear combination of translation model scores with the LM log-probability. We prevent phrase reordering over punctuation using the MOSES option *-monotone-at-punctuation*. As the system can be beforehand tuned by adjusting the log-linear combination weights on a development corpus, we used the MERT method (System 5). Optimizing weights according to BLEU leads to an improvement with respect to the system with MOSES default value weights (System 5 *vs* System 4).

3.5 Post-processing

We also investigated the interest of a statistical post-editor (SPE) to improve translation hypotheses. About 9,000 sentences extracted from the news domain test corpora of the 2007–2009 WMT translation tasks were automatically translated by a system very similar to that described in (Potet et al., 2010), then manually post-edited. Manual corrections of translations were performed by means of the crowd-sourcing platform AMAZON MECHANICAL TURK[2] ($0.15/sent.). These collected data make a parallel corpus whose source part is MT output and target part is the human post-edited version of MT output. This are used to train a phrase-based SMT (with Moses without the tuning step) that automatically post-edit the MT output. That aims at learning how to correct translation hypotheses. System 7 obtained when post-processing MT 1-best output shows a slight improvement. However, SPE was not used in the final LIG system since we lacked time to apply SPE on the N-best hypotheses for the development and test corpora (the N-best being necessary for combination of LIG and LIA systems). Ths LIGA submission is thus a constrained one.

3.6 Recasing

We trained a phrase-based recaser model on the *news-s* corpus using the provided MOSES scripts and applied it to uppercase translation outputs. A common and expected loss of around 1.5 case-sensitive BLEU points was observed on the test corpus (*news10*) after applying this recaser (System 7) with respect to the score case-insensitive BLEU previously measured.

[2]http://www.mturk.com/mturk/welcome

♯	SYSTEM DESCRIPTION	BLEU SCORE *test09*	*test10*
1	Training: *euro+news-c*	24.89	26.01
2	**Training:** *euro+news-c+UN*	25.44	26.43
3	2 + LM_1	24.81	27.19
4	2 + $\mathbf{LM_2}$	25.37	27.25
5	4 + **MERT** on *test09*	26.83	27.53
6	5 + **phrase-table filtering**	27.09	**27.64**
7	6 + SPE	27.53	27.74
8	6 + recaser	24.95	26.07

Table 3: Incremental improvement of the LIG system in terms of case-insensitive BLEU (%), except for line 8 where case-sensitive BLEU (%) are reported

4 The LIA machine translation system

This section describes the particularities of the MT system which was built at the LIA for its first participation to WMT.

4.1 System description

The available corpora were pre-processed using an in-house script that normalizes quotes, dashes, spaces and ligatures. We also reaccentuated French words starting with a capital letter. We significantly cleaned up the crawled parallel *giga* corpus, keeping 19.3 M of the original 22.5 M sentence pairs. For example, sentence pairs with numerous numbers, non-alphanumeric characters or words starting with capital letters were removed. The whole training material is truecased, meaning that the words occuring after a strong punctuation mark were lowercased when they belonged to a dictionary of common all-lowercased forms; the others were left unchanged.

The training of a 5-gram English LM was restrained to the news corpora *mono-news-c* and *news-s* that we consider large enough to ignore other data. In order to reduce the size of the LM, we first limited the vocabulary of our model to a 1 M word vocabulary taking the most frequent words in the news corpora. We also resorted to cut-offs to discard infrequent n-grams (2-2-3-5 thresholds on 2- to 5-gram counts) and uses the SRILM option `prune`, which allowed us to train the LM on large data with 32 Gb RAM.

Our translation models are phrase-based models (PBMs) built with MOSES with the following non-default settings:

- maximum sentence length of 80 words,
- limit on the number of phrase translations loaded for each phrase fixed to 30.

Weights of LM, phrase table and lexicalized reordering model scores were optimized on the development corpus thanks to the MERT algorithm.

Besides the size of used data, we experimented with two advanced features made available for MOSES. Firstly, we filtered phrase tables using the default setting `-l a+e -n 30`. This dramatically reduced phrase tables by dividing their size by a factor of 5 but did not improve our best configuration from the BLEU score perspective (Table 4, line 1); the method was therefore not kept in the LIA system. Secondly, we introduced reordering constraints in order to consider quoted material as a block. This method is particularly useful when citations included in sentences have to be translated. Two configurations were tested: *zone* markups inclusion around quotes and *wall* markups inclusion within *zone* markups. However, the measured gains were finally too marginal to include the method in the final system.

4.2 Parallel corpus subsampling

As the only news parallel corpus provided for the workshop contains 116 k sentence pairs, we must resort to parallel out-of-domain corpora in order to build reliable translation models. Information retrieval (IR) methods have been used in the past to subsample parallel corpora. For example, Hildebrand et al. (2005) used sentences belonging to the development and test corpora as queries to select the k most similar source sentences in an indexed parallel corpus. The retrieved sentence pairs constituted a training corpus for the translation models.

The RALI submission for WMT10 proposed a similar approach that builds queries from the monolingual news corpus in order to select sentence pairs stylistically close to the news domain (Huet et al., 2010). This method has the major interest that it does not require to build a new training parallel corpus for each news data set to translate. Following the best configuration tested in (Huet et al.,

2010), we index the three out-of-domain corpora using LEMUR[3], and build queries from English *news-s* sentences where stop words are removed. The 10 top sentence pairs retrieved per query are selected and added to the new training corpus if they are not redundant with a sentence pair already collected. The process is repeated until the training parallel corpus reaches a threshold over the number of retrieved pairs.

Table 4 reports BLEU scores obtained with the LIA system using the in-domain corpus *news-c* and various amounts of out-of-domain data. MERT was re-run for each set of training data. The first four lines display results obtained with the same number of sentence pairs, which corresponds to the size of *news-c* appended to *euro*. The experiments show that using *euro* instead of the first sentences of *UN* and *giga* significantly improves BLEU scores, which indicates the better adequacy of *euro* with respect to the *test10* corpus. The use of the IR method to select sentences from *euro*, *UN* and *giga* leads to a similar BLEU score to the one obtained with *euro*. The increase of the collected pairs up to 3 M pairs generates a significant improvement of 0.9 BLEU point. A further rise of the amount of collected pairs does not introduce a major gain since retrieving 10 M sentence pairs only augments BLEU from 29.1 to 29.3. This last configuration which leads to the best BLEU was used to build the final LIA system. Let us note that 2 M, 3 M and 15 M queries were required to respectively obtain 3 M, 5 M and 10 M sentence pairs because of the removal of redundant sentences in the increased corpus.

For a matter of comparison, a system was also built taking into account all the training material, i.e. 37 M sentence pairs[4]. This last system is outperformed by our best system built with IR and has finally close performance to the one obtained with *news-c+euro* relatively to the quantity of used data.

5 The system combination

System combination is based on the 500-best outputs generated by the LIA and the LIG systems.

USED PARALLEL CORPORA	FILTERING without	FILTERING with
news-c + *euro* (1.77 M)	28.1	28.0
news-c + 1.77 M of *UN*	27.2	-
news-c + 1.77 M of *giga*	27.1	-
news-c + 1.77 M with IR	28.2	-
news-c + 3 M with IR	29.1	29.0
news-c + 5 M with IR	28.8	-
***news-c* + 10 M with IR**	**29.3**	29.2
All data	28.9	29.0

Table 4: BLEU (%) on test10 measured with the LIA system using different training parallel corpora

They both used the MOSES option `distinct`, ensuring that the hypotheses produced for a given sentence are different inside an N-best list. Each N-best list is associated with a set of 14 scores and combined in several steps.

The first step takes as input lowercased 500-best lists, since preliminary experiments have shown a better behavior using only lowercased output (with cased output, combination presents some degradations). The score combination weights are optimized on the development corpus, in order to maximize the BLEU score at the sentence level when N-best lists are reordered according to the 14 available scores. To this end, we resorted to the SRILM `nbest-optimize` tool to do a simplex-based Amoeba search (Press et al., 1988) on the error function with multiple restarts to avoid local minima.

Once the optimized feature weights are computed independently for each system, N-best lists are turned into confusion networks (Mangu et al., 2000). The 14 features are used to compute posteriors relatively to all the hypotheses in the N-best list. Confusion networks are computed for each sentence and for each system. In Table 5 we present the ROVER (Fiscus, 1997) results for the LIA and LIG confusion networks (LIA CNC and LIG CNC). Then, both confusion networks computed for each sentence are merged into a single one. A ROVER is applied on the combined confusion network and generates a lowercased 1-best.

The final step aims at producing cased hypotheses. The LIA system built from truecased corpora achieved significantly higher performance than the

[3] `www.lemurproject.org`

[4] For this experiment, the data were split into three parts to build independent alignment models: *news-c+euro*, *UN* and *giga*, and they were joined afterwards to build translation models.

		LIG	LIA	LIG CNC	LIA CNC	LIG+LIA
case-insensitive	*test10*	27.6	29.3	28.1	29.4	29.7
BLEU	*test11*	28.5	29.4	28.5	29.3	29.9
case-sensitive	*test10*	26.1	28.4	27.0	28.4	28.7
BLEU	*test11*	26.9	28.4	27.5	28.4	28.8

Table 5: Performance measured before and after combining systems

LIG system trained on lowercased corpora (Table 5, two last lines). In order to get an improvement when combining the outputs, we had to adopt the following strategy. The 500-best truecased outputs of the LIA system are first merged in a word graph (and not a mesh lattice). Then, the lowercased 1-best previously obtained with ROVER is aligned with the graph in order to find the closest existing path, which is equivalent to matching an oracle with the graph. This method allows for several benefits. The new hypothesis is based on a "true" decoding pass generated by a truecased system and discarded marginal hypotheses. Moreover, the selected path offers a better BLEU score than the initial hypothesis with and without case. This method is better than the one which consists of applying the LIG recaser (section 3.6) on the combined (un-cased) hypothesis.

The new recased one-best hypothesis is then used as the final submission for WMT. Our combination approach improves on *test11* the best single system by 0.5 case-insensitive BLEU point and by 0.4 case-sensitive BLEU (Table 5). However, it also introduces some mistakes by duplicating in particular some segments. We plan to apply rules at the segment level in order to reduce these artifacts.

6 Conclusion

This paper presented two statistical machine translation systems developed at different sites using MOSES and the combination of these systems. The LIGA submission presented this year was ranked among the best MT system for the French-English direction. This campaign was the first shot for LIA and the second for LIG. Beside following the traditional pipeline for building a phrase-based translation system, each individual system led to specific works: LIG worked on using SPE as post-treatment, LIA focused on extracting useful data from large-sized corpora. And their combination implied to address the interesting issue of matching results from systems with different casing approaches.

WMT is a great opportunity to chase after performance and joining our efforts has allowed to save considerable amount of time for data preparation and tuning choices (even when final decisions were different among systems), yet obtaining very competitive results. This year, our goal was to develop state-of-the-art systems so as to investigate new approaches for related topics such as translation with human-in-the-loop or multilingual interaction systems (e.g. vocal telephone information-query dialogue systems in multiple languages or language portability of such systems).

References

Jonathan G. Fiscus. 1997. A post-processing system to yield reduced word error rates:recognizer output voting error reduction (ROVER). In *Proceedings of the IEEE Workshop on Automatic Speech Recognition and Understanding*, pages 347–354, Santa Barbara, CA, USA.

Qin Gao and Stephan Vogel. 2008. Parallel implementations of word alignment tool. In *Proceedings of the ACL Workshop: Software Engineering, Testing, and Quality Assurance for Natural Language Processing*, pages 49–57, Columbus, OH, USA.

Almut Silja Hildebrand, Matthias Eck, Stephan Vogel, and Alex Waibel. 2005. Adaptation of the translation model for statistical machine translation based on information retrieval. In *Proceedings of the 10th conference of the European Association for Machine Translation (EAMT)*, Budapest, Hungary.

Stéphane Huet, Julien Bourdaillet, Alexandre Patry, and Philippe Langlais. 2010. The RALI machine translation system for WMT 2010. In *Proceedings of the ACL Joint 5th Workshop on Statistical Machine Translation and Metrics (WMT)*, Uppsala, Sweden.

Howard Johnson, Joel Martin, George Foster, and Roland

Kuhn. 2007. Improving translation quality by discarding most of the phrasetable. In *Proceedings of the Joint Conference on Empirical Methods in Natural Language Processing and Computational Natural Language Learning (EMNLP-CoNLL)*, pages 967–975, Prague, Czech Republic, jun.

Philipp Koehn, Hieu Hoang, Alexandra Birch, Chris Callison-Burch, Marcello Federico, Nicola Bertoldi, Brooke Cowan, Wade Shen, Christine Moran, Richard Zens, Chris Dyer, Ondrej Bojar, Alexandra Constantin, and Evan Herbst. 2007. Moses: Open source toolkit for statistical machine translation. In *Proceedings of the 45th Annual Meeting of the Association for Computational Linguistics (ACL), Companion Volume*, pages 177–180, Prague, Czech Republic, June.

Lidia Mangu, Eric Brill, and Andreas Stolcke. 2000. Finding consensus in speech recognition: Word error minimization and other applications of confusion networks. *Computer Speech and Language*, 14(4):373–400.

Franz Josef Och and Hermann Ney. 2003. A systematic comparison of various statistical alignment models. *Computational Linguistics*, 29(1):19–51.

Franz Josef Och. 2003. Minimum error rate training in statistical machine translation. In *Proceedings of the 41st Annual Meeting on Association for Computational Linguistics (ACL)*, Sapporo, Japan.

Marion Potet, Laurent Besacier, and Hervé Blanchon. 2010. The LIG machine translation for WMT 2010. In *Proceedings of the ACL Joint 5th Workshop on Statistical Machine Translation and Metrics (WMT)*, Uppsala, Sweden.

William H. Press, Brian P. Flannery, Saul A. Teukolsky, and William T. Vetterling. 1988. *Numerical Recipes in C: The Art of Scientific Computing*. Cambridge University Press.

Andreas Stolcke. 2002. SRILM — an extensible language modeling toolkit. In *Proceedings of the 7th International Conference on Spoken Language Processing (ICSLP)*, Denver, CO, USA.

Factored Translation with Unsupervised Word Clusters

Christian Rishøj
Center for Language Technology
University of Copenhagen
crjensen@hum.ku.dk

Anders Søgaard
Center for Language Technology
University of Copenhagen
soegaard@hum.ku.dk

Abstract

Unsupervised word clustering algorithms — which form word clusters based on a measure of distributional similarity — have proven to be useful in providing beneficial features for various natural language processing tasks involving supervised learning. This work explores the utility of such word clusters as factors in statistical machine translation.

Although some of the language pairs in this work clearly benefit from the factor augmentation, there is no consistent improvement in translation accuracy across the board. For all language pairs, the word clusters clearly improve translation for some proportion of the sentences in the test set, but has a weak or even detrimental effect on the rest.

It is shown that if one could determine whether or not to use a factor when translating a given sentence, rather substantial improvements in precision could be achieved for all of the language pairs evaluated. While such an "oracle" method is not identified, evaluations indicate that unsupervised word cluster are most beneficial in sentences *without* unknown words.

1 Factored translation

One can go far in terms of translation quality with plenty of bilingual text and a translation model that maps small chunks of tokens as they appear in the surface form, that is, the usual phrase-based statistical machine translation model. Yet even with a large parallel corpus, data sparsity is still an issue. Factored translation models are an extension of phrase-based models which allow integration of additional word-level annotation into the model. Operating on more general representations, such as lemmas or some kind of stems, translation model can draw on richer statistics and to some degree offset the data sparsity problem.

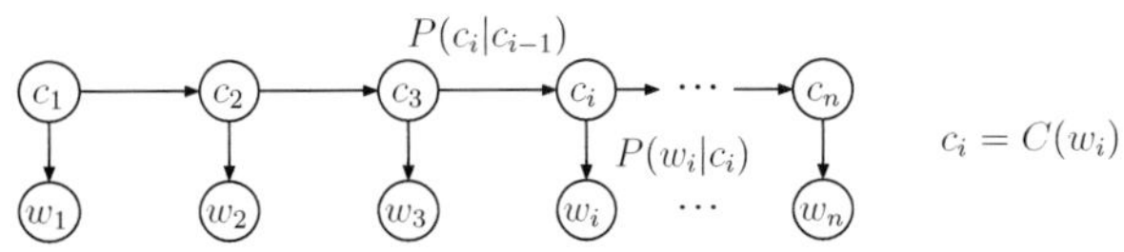

Figure 1: Bayesian network illustrating the class-based language model that is used to define the quality of a clustering in the Brown algorithm [Liang, 2005]

2 Unsupervised word clusters

Unsupervised word clusters owe their appeal perhaps mostly to the relative ease of obtaining them. Obtaining regular morphological, syntactic or semantic analyses for tokens in a text relies on some sort of tagger, either based on manually crafted rules or trainable on an annotated corpus. Both rule-crafting and corpus annotation are time-consuming and expensive processes, and might not be feasible for a small or resource-scarce language.

For unsupervised word clusters, on the other hand, one merely needs a large amount of raw (unannotated) text and some processing power. Such clustering is thus particularly interesting for resource-scarce languages, and especially so if the clusters enable the training of more generalized translation models without more bilingual text.

The independence of annotated corpora or hand-crafted rules make unsupervised clusters interesting for languages rich in NLP resources too. They offer a way to exploit vast amounts of raw, unannotated, monolingual text, in a manner akin to the way language models profitably may be trained on vast amounts of raw monolingual text.

With the broad coverage achievable from vast amounts of monolingual text, word clusters might help alleviate the problem of unknown words in translation. It is imaginable that a word form otherwise unknown to the translation model belongs to

Proceedings of the 6th Workshop on Statistical Machine Translation, pages 447–451,
Edinburgh, Scotland, UK, July 30–31, 2011. ©2011 Association for Computational Linguistics

a known cluster. Appropriate use of word clusters, coupled with a broad-coverage language model, could make it be possible for the translation model to arrive at the intended translation.

In this work we use two unsupervised clustering algorithms: Brown and Unsupos. Other clustering algorithms were on the drawing board as well, namely embeddings from the Neural Language Model of Collobert and Weston [2008] and word representations from random indexing (RI)[1]. These, however, were abandoned due to time constraints.

2.1 The Brown algorithm

The bottom-up agglomerative algorithm of Brown et al. [1992] processes a sequence of tokens and produces a binary tree with tokens as leaf nodes. Each internal node in the tree can be interpreted as a cluster containing the tokens on the leaf nodes of that subtree. The clustering produced is thus a *hierarchical* clustering.

Very briefly, the algorithm proceeds by first assigning every token to its own cluster, and then iteratively merges the two clusters that maximises the quality of the resulting clustering, where the *quality* of a clustering is defined in terms of a *class-based language model* (figure 1).

Note that this algorithm produces a *hard clustering*, in the sense that it assigns each token to a single cluster. From a semantic perspective, there are homographic words whose underlying senses are conceptually and possibly syntactically distinct, and whose cluster-tag intuitively should depend on their use in running text. The clustering obtained from the Brown algorithm does not accommodate this wish.

We use the implementation[2] of Liang [2005].

2.2 jUnsupos

Contrary to the hard clustering of the Brown algorithm, the jUnsupos algorithm of Biemann [2006] emits a Viterbi tagger which is sensitive to the context of a token in running text. Thus, word forms can belong to more than a single cluster, and such word forms — which are considered ambiguous by the algorithm — will be assigned to a cluster depending on their context.

In a coarse outline, the algorithm works by first inducing a distributional clustering for unambiguous high-frequency tokens, as well as a co-occurrence-based clustering for less common tokens. The two partly overlapping clusterings are then combined to produce a lexicon with derived syntactic categories and word forms.

[1] https://github.com/turian/random-indexing-wordrepresentations

[2] Available at http://www.cs.berkeley.edu/~pliang/software/

100001001 immediate urgent ongoing absolute extraordinary exceptional ideological unprecedented appalling overwhelming alleged automatic [...]

11111100111111110 worried concerned skeptical unhappy uneasy reticent unsure perplexed excited apprehensive legion unconcerned [...]

111111100010001 cover include involve exclude confuse encompass designate preclude transcend duplicate defy precede [...]

1111111000000 encourage promote protect defend safeguard restore assist preserve coordinate convince destroy integrate [...]

0111000 china russia iran israel turkey ukraine india japan pakistan georgia serbia europol [...]

1000110010 waste water drugs land fish material meat profit alcohol forest blood chemicals [...]

Figure 2: Exemplars of word clusters obtained using the Brown algorithm (C=1000), showing the 12 most frequent tokens per cluster

2.3 Cluster count and complexion

A reasonable question when faced with the task of inducing word clusters in an unsupervised manner is: How many clusters to produce? This question is presumably closely intertwined with the question of what sort of beast a cluster obtained in this manner can be expected to be. Would a clustering with around 30-90 clusters correspond somewhat closely to an ordinary part-of-speech tag-set for the given language?

Looking at the handful of exemplar clusters shown in figure 2, which were obtained with the Brown algorithm (using a cluster count of 1000), we cautiously note some apparent patterns.

- The clusters appear to be subsets of the clustering implied by conventional part-of-speech tags: The first two consist of adjectives (including the rather ambiguous form *legion*), the next two (transitive) verbs and the final two nouns.

- Syntactically, members of the two apparent verb

clusters seem to consist of verbs in their infinitive (or plurally inflected) form.

- From a quasi-semantic perspective, the last cluster appears to consist of nouns for corporeal goods (as apposed to immaterial things).

- While most exemplars from the second-last cluster are countries, all of the shown forms can be said to be proper nouns.

Note that only the 12 most frequent forms from each cluster are displayed, the apparent patterns should be taken with a pinch of salt. Although the qualities suggested can be expected to relate to distributional properties that the clusters reflect, exceptional members are perhaps to be expected.

In the present work, we went with the pre-trained models for jUnsupos[3], which have the following characteristics[4]:

Lang	Corpus	# Sents	# Tags
cs	LCC	4 M	539
de	Wortschatz	40 M	396
en	Medline 2004	34 M	480
es	LCC	4.5 M	415
fr	LCC	3 M	359

For the Brown algorithm, we are contrasting cluster count choices of 320 and 1000, based on reports of other successful applications [Turian et al., 2010][5], with clustering models trained on monolingual data from the Europarl corpus and the News Commentary corpus.

3 Experimental setup

The baseline systems were set up in accordance with the guidelines on the shared task website. That is, they were trained with `grow-diag-final-and` word alignment heuristics and `msd-bidirectional-fe` reordering.

Translation models were trained on a concatenation of the Europarl and News Commentary corpora, which were first tokenized, then filtered to sentence lengths of up to 40 tokens, and finally lowercased.

5-gram language models were built using `ngram-count` on a concatenation of the Europarl corpora and the News Commentary corpora.

[3]As available at http://wortschatz.uni-leipzig.de/~cbiemann/software/unsupos.html

[4]LCC refers to the Leipzig Corpora, available at http://corpora.uni-leipzig.de/. Wortschatz refers to http://www.wortschatz.uni-leipzig.de/. Medline is available at http://www.nlm.nih.gov/mesh/filelist.html.

[5]A planned evaluation of a cluster count of 3200 was abandoned due to time constraints

For the unsupervised word clusters, 5-gram language models were used as well, built from tagged versions of the same corpora. All language models were binarised and loaded using KenLM [Heafield, 2011].

Minimum error rate training (MERT) was used to optimise parameters on both baseline and factored models against the 2008 news test set, as suggested on the shared task website[6].

All phrase tables were filtered and binarised for the development and testing corpora during tuning and testing, respectively.

Seeing that the preparation of the raw corpora, word clustering models, factored corpora, language models, as well as training, optimization and evaluation of the various models was a rather involved, yet repetitive process, we took a stab at making a GNU Makefile-based approach for automated handling (and parallelisation) of the whole dependency graph of subtasks. The ongoing effort, which shares some aspirations and abilities with the recently announced Experiment Management System (EMS), is publicly available[7].

4 Results

Table 1a lists BLEU scores for adding jUnsupos tags (*uPOS*), Brown clusters with 320 clusters (*C320*) or Brown clusters with 1000 clusters (*C1000*) as either an alignment factor, a two-sided translation factor or a source-sided translation factor.

Although using Brown clusters (C1000) as a two-sided translation factor improves BLEU scores for some language pairs, most notably *en-cs*, *en-de* and *cs-en*, no clear across-the-board benefit is seen.

4.1 Oracle scores

Based on the hypothesis that the factorisations are beneficial when translation some sentences, and not when translating others, we completed an oracle-based evaluation, in which we assume to know *a priori* whether to use the factored model for translating a given sentence, or just go with the baseline, unfactored model. In reality, we don't have such an oracle method for arbitrary sentences, but when dealing with the shared task test set (or other corpora for which we have reference translations), it was easy enough to check per-sentence BLEU scores for each model and make the decision based on a comparison.

Table 1b lists BLEU scores obtainable with each factor configuration given such an oracle method. In this scenario, most factored models beat the baseline, indicating that the factorisations are beneficial for certain sentences, and detrimental for others.

[6]http://www.statmt.org/wmt11/translation-task.html

[7]At https://gibhub.com/crishoj/factored

Pair	Baseline	Alignment factor			Two-sided translation			Source-sided transl.			Best	
		C1000	C320	uPOS	C1000	C320	uPOS	C1000	C320	uPOS	Δ	%
cs-en	18.18	17.77	17.19	13.54	**18.59**	18.36	17.50	18.19	18.19	17.59	*0.41*	2.3%
de-en	18.45	17.94	17.57	16.36	**18.56**	18.42	17.93	18.12	18.12	17.86	*0.11*	0.6%
en-cs	11.85	11.82	11.61	9.75	**12.73**	12.28	10.94	11.92	11.92	11.85	*0.88*	7.4%
en-de	13.27	12.90	12.83	11.98	13.81	**13.84**	13.19	12.94	12.94	12.92	*0.57*	4.3%
en-es	28.08	27.10	26.52	24.90	**28.40**	28.16	27.50	27.31	27.31	27.19	*0.32*	1.1%
en-fr	**25.90**	24.60	23.98	21.85	25.89	20.59	24.16	24.89	24.89	24.74	–	–
es-en	**26.70**	24.87	24.71	23.92	25.76	25.96	25.40	24.92	24.92	24.92	–	–
fr-en	**24.73**	23.18	23.13	21.76	24.01	22.86	23.23	23.37	23.37	23.04	–	–

(a) BLEU scores for factor configurations in comparison to the unfactored baseline

Pair	Baseline	Alignment factor			Two-sided translation			Source-sided transl.			Best	
		C1000	C320	uPOS	C1000	C320	uPOS	C1000	C320	uPOS	Δ	%
cs-en	18.18	19.93	19.81	19.19	**20.01**	20.00	19.83	19.58	19.58	19.63	1.83	10.1%
de-en	18.45	20.06	20.00	19.75	**20.28**	20.26	20.15	19.84	19.84	19.90	1.83	9.9%
en-cs	11.85	13.18	13.14	12.81	**13.77**	13.58	12.98	12.83	12.83	12.93	1.92	16.2%
en-de	13.27	14.56	14.60	14.36	14.98	**15.10**	14.81	14.21	14.21	14.28	1.83	13.8%
en-es	28.08	29.70	29.50	29.17	**30.33**	30.2	30.00	29.54	29.54	29.56	2.25	8.0%
en-fr	25.90	27.34	27.22	26.90	**27.84**	26.98	27.32	27.15	27.15	27.16	1.94	7.5%
es-en	26.70	27.83	27.81	27.74	28.16	**28.20**	28.06	27.64	27.64	27.73	1.50	5.6%
fr-en	24.73	25.86	25.95	25.83	26.16	**26.31**	26.05	25.66	25.66	25.69	1.58	6.4%

(b) BLEU scores with an *oracle*-directed, per-sentence selective usage of either the baseline or the factored model

Table 1: BLEU scores when using Brown Clusters with granularity 1000 (*C1000*), granularity 320 (*C320*) and unsupervised part-of-speech tags (*uPOS*) as either an added alignment factor, a two-sided translation factor or a source-sided translation factor

Pair	Baseline	Oracle	Abs. Δ	Rel. %
cs-en	18.18	22.60	4.42	24.3%
de-en	18.45	22.42	3.97	21.5%
en-cs	11.85	15.89	4.04	34.1%
en-de	13.27	17.16	3.89	29.3%
en-es	28.08	32.52	4.44	15.8%
en-fr	25.90	30.07	4.17	16.1%
es-en	26.70	30.22	3.52	13.2%
fr-en	24.73	28.67	3.94	15.9%

Table 2: BLEU scores under the assumption of an oracle function indicating the optimal factor configuration for each sentence

4.2 Combined oracle scores

Imagine another oracle function, which would not simply determine whether to prefer a given factored model over the baseline for a given sentence, but instead indicate which of several possible factored models to use when translating a given sentence.

BLEU scores obtainable under the assumption of such a combined oracle function are listed in table 2. As was the case for the individual factored models (table 1a), *en-cs*, *en-de* and *cs-en* see the largest benefits over the baselines.

These oracle scores are obviously an idealised case. They indicate an upper bound that one could seek to approximate by constructing an appropriate oracle function.

4.3 Unknown words

In section 2 it was hypothesised that word clusters are potentially beneficial in translating sentences with unknown words — that is, word forms which were not seen in any aligned sentences (but which may belong to a word cluster known by the translation model).

With this hypothesis in mind, we would like to

Pair	Sentences		Baseline	C1000	Rel. %
cs-en	1955	65%	17.63	**17.70**	0.4%
de-en	1925	64%	**17.84**	17.56	-1.6%
en-cs	1583	53%	11.85	**12.63**	6.6%
en-de	1395	46%	**13.65**	13.47	-1.3%
en-es	1327	44%	27.77	**27.97**	0.7%
en-fr	1369	46%	**25.43**	25.11	-1.3%
es-en	1316	44%	**26.43**	25.41	-3.9%
fr-en	1423	47%	**24.20**	23.56	-2.6%
Avg.	*1537*	*51%*	***20.60***	*20.43*	*-0.4%*

(a) BLEU scores for sentences *with* unknown words

Pair	Sentences		Baseline	C1000	Rel. %
cs-en	1048	35%	19.63	**20.77**	5.8%
de-en	1078	36%	20.03	**21.24**	6.0%
en-cs	1420	47%	11.85	**12.90**	8.9%
en-de	1608	54%	12.97	**14.22**	9.6%
en-es	1676	56%	28.41	**28.88**	1.7%
en-fr	1634	54%	26.46	**26.81**	1.3%
es-en	1687	56%	**27.01**	26.15	-3.2%
fr-en	1580	53%	**25.40**	24.58	-3.2%
Avg.	*1466*	*49%*	*21.47*	***21.94***	*3.4%*

(b) BLEU scores for sentences with *no* unknown words

Table 3: BLEU scores for the best overall factorisation, Brown clusters (C=1000) as a two-sided translation factor, on sentences *with* (table 3a) and *without* (table 3b) unknown words

see how the factored models fare in comparison to the unfactored baselines, specifically for those sentences containing unknown words, and for the rest (sentences *without* unknown words). This targeted evaluation was done using the best overall factor configuration: Brown clusters (C=1000) as a two-sided translation factor.

The results are shown in tables 3a and 3b. On average (across language paris), 51% test set sentences contain at least 1 unknown word. Contrary to what might be expected, the factorisation seems to be most beneficial for sentences with all *known* words (3.4% improvement in BLEU score on average). For sentences with unknown words, the effect is weak or detrimental (except for *en-cs*), averaging a slight decrease (-0.4%) in BLEU score across the language pairs.

The lack of benefit for sentences with unknown words is likely due to the fact that no additional monolingual data was used to make the Brown clusters for this experiment. In other words, there is no chance of knowing the Brown cluster for an unknown word. Furthermore, we assume that gains for sentences with unknown words are more likely with a factorisation that includes an alternative decoding path for word clusters[8].

5 Conclusions and future work

In this work we have explored the utility of three unsupervised word clusterings as either an alignment factor, a two-sided translation factor or a source-sided translation factor.

Although no across-the-board benefit was seen, it was evident that the factorisations help in translating some proportion of the test set sentences. Being able to determine for which sentences to use a factored model is clearly desirable.

Overall, the single most beneficial of the factor configurations explored was Brown clusters with a granularity of 1000, as a two-sided translation factor. A more detailed evaluation of the effects of different cluster sizes, as well as using clusters induced from more text, would be interesting in a follow-up study.

Using clusters in some more interesting factor configurations, particularly in alternative decoding paths, is still pending.

References

C. Biemann. Unsupervised part-of-speech tagging employing efficient graph clustering. In *Proceedings of the 21st International Conference on computational Linguistics and 44th Annual Meeting of the Association for Computational Linguistics: Student Research Workshop*, pages 7–12, 2006.

P. F Brown, V. J.D Pietra, P. V deSouza, J. C Lai, and R. L Mercer. Class-based n-gram models of natural language. *Computational linguistics*, 18(4):467–479, 1992.

R. Collobert and J. Weston. A unified architecture for natural language processing: Deep neural networks with multitask learning. In *Proceedings of the 25th international conference on Machine learning*, page 160–167, 2008.

K. Heafield. KenLM: faster and smaller language model queries. In *Proceedings of the Sixth Workshop on Statistical Machine Translation*, Edinburgh, UK, July 2011. Association for Computational Linguistics.

P. Liang. *Semi-supervised learning for natural language*. PhD thesis, Massachusetts Institute of Technology, 2005.

J. Turian, L. Ratinov, and Y. Bengio. Word representations: A simple and general method for semi-supervised learning. In *Proceedings of the 48th Annual Meeting of the Association for Computational Linguistics*, page 384–394, 2010.

[8]Evaluation of factor configurations with alternative decoding paths were abandoned due to limited computational resources and initially discouraging results

The BM-I2R Haitian-Créole-to-English translation system description for the WMT 2011 evaluation campaign

Marta R. Costa-jussà
Barcelona Media Innovation Center
Av Diagonal, 177, 9th floor
08018 Barcelona
marta.ruiz@barcelonamedia.org

Rafael E. Banchs
Institute for Infocomm Research
1 Fusionopolis Way 21-01
Singapore 138632
rembanchs@i2r.a-star.edu.sg

Abstract

This work describes the Haitian-Créole to English statistical machine translation system built by Barcelona Media Innovation Center (BM) and Institute for Infocomm Research (I2R) for the 6th Workshop on Statistical Machine Translation (WMT 2011). Our system carefully processes the available data and uses it in a standard phrase-based system enhanced with a source context semantic feature that helps conducting a better lexical selection and a feature orthogonalization procedure that helps making MERT optimization more reliable and stable. Our system was ranked first (among a total of 9 participant systems) by the conducted human evaluation.

1 Introduction

During years there has been a big effort to produce natural language processing tools that try to understand well written sentences, but the question is how well do these tools work to analyze the contents of SMS. For example, not even syntactic tools like stemming can bring to common stems words that have been shortened (like Xmas or Christmas).

This paper describes our participation on the 6th Workshop on Statistical Machine Translation (WMT 2011). The featured task from the workshop was to translate Haitian-Créole SMS messages into English. According to the WMT 2011 organizers, these text messages (SMS) were sent by people in Haiti in the aftermath of the January 2010 earthquake. Our objective in this featured task is to translate from Haitian-Créole into English either using raw or clean data.

We propose to build an SMT system which could be used for both raw and clean data. Our baseline system is an standard phrase-based SMT system built with Moses (Koehn et al., 2007). Starting from this system we propose to introduce a semantic feature function based on latent semantic indexing (Landauer et al., 1998). Additionally, as a total different approximation, we propose to orthogonalize the standard feature functions of the phrase-based table using the Gram-Schmidt methodology (Greub, 1975). Then, we experimentally combine both enhancements.

The only difference among the raw and clean SMT system were the training sentences. In order to translate the clean data, we propose to normalize the corpus of short messages given very scarce resources. We only count with a small set of parallel corpus at the level of sentence of chat and standard language. A nice normalization methodology can allow to make the task of communication easier. We propose a statistical normalization technique using the scarce resources we have based on a combination of statistical machine translation techniques.

The rest of this paper is organized as follows. Section 2 briefly describes the phrase-based SMT system which is used as a reference system. Next, section 3 describes our approximation to introduce semantics in the baseline system. Section 4 reports our idea of orthogonalizing the feature functions in the translation table. Section 5 details the data processing and the data conversion from raw to clean. As follows, section 6 shows the translation results. Finally, section 7 reports most relevant conclusions of this work.

Proceedings of the 6th Workshop on Statistical Machine Translation, pages 452–456,
Edinburgh, Scotland, UK, July 30–31, 2011. ©2011 Association for Computational Linguistics

2 Phrase-based SMT baseline system

The phrase-based approach to SMT performs the translation splitting the source sentence in segments and assigning to each segment a bilingual phrase from a phrase-table. Bilingual phrases are translation units that contain source words and target words, e.g. *unité de traduction — translation unit*, and have different scores associated to them. These bilingual phrases are then selected in order to maximize a linear combination of feature functions. Such strategy is known as the log-linear model (Och, 2003) and it is formally defined as:

$$\hat{e} = \arg\max_{e} \left[\sum_{m=1}^{M} \lambda_m h_m (e, f) \right] \tag{1}$$

where h_m are different feature functions with weights λ_m. The two main feature functions are the translation model (TM) and the target language model (LM). Additional models include lexical weights, phrase and word penalty and reordering.

3 Semantic feature function

Source context information is generally disregarded in phrase-based systems given that all training sentences contribute equally to the final translation. The main objective in this section is to motivate the use of a semantic feature function we have recently proposed (Banchs and Costa-jussà, 2011) for incorporating source context information into the phrase-based statistical machine translation framework. Such a feature is based on the use of a similarity metric for assessing the degree of similarity between the sentences to be translated and the sentences in the original training dataset.

The measured similarity is used to favour those translation units that have been extracted from training sentences that are similar to the current sentence to be translated and to penalize those translation units than have been extracted from unrelated or dissimilar training sentences. In the proposed feature, sentence similarity is measured by means of the cosine distance in a reduced dimension vector-space model, which is constructed by using Latent Semantic Indexing (Landauer et al., 1998), a well know dimensionality reduction technique that is based on the singular value decomposition of a matrix (Golub and Kahan, 1965).

The main motivation of this semantic feature is the fact that source context information is actually helpful for disambiguating the sense of a given word during the translation process. Consider for instance the Spanish word *banco* which can be translated into English as either *bank* or *bench* depending on the specific context it occurs. By comparing a given input sentence containing the Spanish word *banco* with all training sentences from which phrases including this word where extracted, we can figure out which is the most appropriated sense for this word in the given sentence. This is because for the sense *bank* the Spanish word *banco* will be more like to co-occur with words such as *dinero* (money), *cuenta* (account), *intereses* (interest), etc., while for the sense *bench* it would be more likely to co-occur with words such as *plaza* (square), *parque (park)*, *mesa (table)*, etc; and the chances are high for such disambiguating words to appear in one or more of the training sentences from which bilingual phrases containing banco has been extracted.

In the particular case of translation tasks where multi-domain corpora is used for training machine translation systems, such as the Haitian-Creole-to-English task considered here, the proposed semantic feature has proven to contribute to a better lexical selection during the decoding process. However, in tasks considering mono-domain corpora the semantic feature does not improves translation quality as the most frequent translation pairs learned by the system are actually the correct ones.

Another important issue related to the semantic feature discussed here is that it is a dynamic feature in the sense that it is computed for each potential translation unit according to the current input sentence being translated. This makes the implementation of this semantic feature very expensive from a computational point of view. At this moment, we do not have an efficient implementation, which makes it unfeasible in the practice to apply this methodology to large training corpora.

As the training corpus available for the Haitian-Creole-to-English is both small in size and multi-domain in nature, it constitutes the perfect scenario for experimenting with the recently proposed source context semantic feature. For more details about implementation and performance of this methodology in a different translation task, the reader should refer to (Banchs and Costa-jussà, 2011).

4 Heuristic enhacement

The phrase-based SMT baseline system contains, by default, 5 feature functions which are the conditional and posterior probabilities, the direct and indirect lexical scores and the phrase penalty. Usually, these feature functions are not statistical independent from each other. Based on the analogy between the statistical and geometrical concepts of independence and orthogonality, and given that, during MERT, the optimization of feature combination is conducted on log-probability space; we decided to explore the effect of using a set of orthogonal features during MERT optimization.

It is well know in both spectral analysis and vector space decomposition that orthogonal bases allow for optimal representations of signals and variables, as they allow for each individual natural component to be represented independently of the others. In linear lattice predictors, for instance, each filter coefficient can be optimized independently from the others while convergence to the optimal solution is guarantied (Haykin, 1996). In the case of statistical machine translation, the linear nature of feature combination in log-probability space suggested us that transforming the features into a set of orthogonal features could make MERT optimization more robust and efficient.

According to this, we used Gram-Schmidt (Greub, 1975) to transform all available feature functions into an orthogonal set of feature functions. This orthogonalization process was conducted directly over the log-probability space, i.e, given the five vectors representing the feature functions h_1, h_2, h_3, h_4, h_5, we used the Gram-Schmidt algorithm to construct an orthogonal basis v_1, v_2, v_3, v_4, v_5. The resulting set of features consisted of 5 vectors that form an orthogonal basis. This new orthogonal set of features was used for MERT optimization and decoding.

5 Experimental framework

In this section we report the details of the used data preprocessing and raw to clean data conversion.

5.1 Data preprocessing

The WMT evaluation provided a high variety of data. Our preprocessing consisted of the following:

- Lowercase and tokenize all files using the scripts from Moses.
- In the case of the haitian-Creole side of the data, replace all stressed vowels by their plain forms.
- Filter out those sentences which had no words or more than 120.

Table 1 shows the data statistics of the different sources before and after this preprocessing. The different sources of the table include: in-domain SMS data (SMS); medical domain (medical); newswire domain (newswire); united nations (un); state department (state depart.); guidelines for approapriate international disaster donations (guidelines); krengle senetences (krengle) and a glossary includes wikipedia name entities and haitisurf dictionary. The sources of this material are specified in the web page of the workshop.

All data from table 1 was concatenated and used as training corpus. The English part of this data was used to build the language model. As development and test corpus we used the data provided by the organization. Both development and test contained 900 sentences.

Finally, in the evaluation, we included development and tests as part of the training corpus, and then, we translated the evaluation set.

5.2 Raw to clean data conversion

This featured task contained two subtasks. One was to translate raw data and the other was to translate clean data. Therefore, we have to build two systems. Our raw data system was built using the training data from table 1. The clean data system was built using all training data from table 1 except in-domain SMS data. Particularly, a modified version of the in-domain SMS data was included in the clean data system. The modification consisted in cleaning the original in-domain SMS data using an standard Moses SMT system. We built an SMT system to translate from raw data to clean data. This SMT system was built with the development, test and evaluation data which in total were 2700 sentences. We

		Statistics	
		before	after
SMS	sentences	17,192	16,594
	words	386.0k	383.0k
medical	sentences	1,619	1,619
	words	10.4k	10.4k
newswire	sentences	13,517	13,508
	words	326.9k	326.7k
wikipedia	sentences	8,476	8,476
	words	113.9k	113.9k
un	sentences	91	91
	words	1,906	1,906
state depart.	sentences	56	14
	words	450	355
guidelines	sentences	60	9
	words	795	206
krengle	sentences	658	655
	words	4.2k	4.2k
bible	sentences	30,715	30,677
	words	946k	944k
glossary	sentences	49,990	49,980
	words	126.4k	126.3k

Table 1: Data Statistics before and after training preprocessing. Number of words are from the English side.

used 2500 sentences as training data and 200 sentences for development to adjust weights. The raw and clean systems were tuned with their respective developments and tested on their respective tests.

6 Experimental results

In this section we report the results of the approaches proposed in previous sections. Table 2 and 3 report the results on the development and test sets on the raw and clean subtask, respectively.

First row on both tables report the results of the baseline system briefly described in section 2. Second row and third row on both tables report the performance of the semantic feature function and on the heuristic approach of orthogonalization (orthofeatures) respectively. Finally, the last row on both tables report the performance of both semantic and heuristic features when combined.

Results shown in tables 2 and 3 do not show coherent improvements when introducing the new

System	Dev	Test
baseline	32.00	**31.01**
+semanticfeature	**32.34**	30.68
+orthofeatures	31.63	29.90
+semanticfeature+orthofeatures	32.21	30.34

Table 2: BLEU results for the raw data. Best results in bold.

System	Dev	Test
baseline	35.86	33.78
+semanticfeature	35.98	33.90
+orthofeatures	35.57	**34.10**
+semanticfeature+orthofeatures	**36.28**	33.53

Table 3: BLEU results for the clean data. Best results in bold.

methodologies proposed. The clean data seems to benefit from the semantic features and the orthofeatures separately. However, the raw data seems not to benefit from the orthofeatures and keep the similar performance to the baseline system when using the semantic feature. Although, this trend is clear, the results are not conclusive. Therefore, we decided to participate in the evaluation with the full system (including the semantic features and orthofeatures) in the clean track and with the system including the semantic feature in the raw track. Actually, we used those systems that performed best in the development set. Additionally, results with the semantic feature may not be significantly better than the baseline system, but we have seen it actually heps to improve lexical selection in practice in previous works (Banchs and Costa-jussà, 2011).

7 Conclusions

This paper reports the BM-I2R system description in the Haitian-Créole to English translation task. This system was ranked first in the WMT 2011 by the conducted human evaluation. The translation system uses a PBSMT system enhanced with two different methodologies. First, we experiment with the introduction of a semantic feature which is capable of introducing source context information. Second, we propose to transform the five standard feature functions used in the translation model of the PBSMT system into five orthogonal feature functions using the Gram-Schmidt methodology. Results show that the first methodology can be used for both raw and clean data. Whereas the second seems to only benefit clean data.

Acknowledgments

The research leading to these results has received funding from the Spanish Ministry of Science and Innovation through the Juan de la Cierva fellowship program. The authors would like to thank Barcelona Media Innovation Center and Institute for Infocomm Research for their support and permission to publish this research.

References

R. Banchs and M.R. Costa-jussà. 2011. A semantic feature for statistical machine translation. In *5th Workshop on Syntax, Semantics and Structure in Statistical Translation (at ACL HLT 2011)*, Portland.

G. H. Golub and W. Kahan. 1965. Calculating the singular values and pseudo-inverse of a matrix. journal of the society for industrial and applied mathematics. In *Numerical Analysis 2(2)*, pages 205–224.

W. Greub. 1975. *Linear Algebra*. Springer.

S. Haykin. 1996. *Adaptive Filter Theory*. Prentice Hall.

P. Koehn, H. Hoang, A. Birch, C. Callison-Burch, M. Federico, N. Bertoldi, B. Cowan, W. Shen, C. Moran, R. Zens, C. Dyer, O. Bojar, A. Constantin, and E. Herbst. 2007. Moses: Open source toolkit for statistical machine translation. In *Proc. of the 45th Annual Meeting of the Association for Computational Linguistics*, pages 177–180, Prague, Czech Republic, June.

T. K. Landauer, D. Laham, and P. Foltz. 1998. Learning human-like knowledge by singular value decomposition: A progress report. In *Conference on Advances in Neural Information Processing Systems*, pages 45–51, Denver.

F.J. Och. 2003. Minimum error rate training in statistical machine translation. In *Proc. of the 41th Annual Meeting of the Association for Computational Linguistics*, pages 160–167, Sapporo, July.

The Universitat d'Alacant hybrid machine translation system for WMT 2011

Víctor M. Sánchez-Cartagena, Felipe Sánchez-Martínez, Juan Antonio Pérez-Ortiz
Transducens Research Group
Departament de Llenguatges i Sistemes Informàtics
Universitat d'Alacant, E-03071, Alacant, Spain
{vmsanchez,fsanchez,japerez}@dlsi.ua.es

Abstract

This paper describes the machine translation (MT) system developed by the Transducens Research Group, from Universitat d'Alacant, Spain, for the WMT 2011 shared translation task. We submitted a hybrid system for the Spanish–English language pair consisting of a phrase-based statistical MT system whose phrase table was enriched with bilingual phrase pairs matching transfer rules and dictionary entries from the Apertium shallow-transfer rule-based MT platform. Our hybrid system outperforms, in terms of BLEU, GTM and METEOR, a standard phrase-based statistical MT system trained on the same corpus, and received the second best BLEU score in the automatic evaluation.

1 Introduction

This paper describes the system submitted by the Transducens Research Group (Universitat d'Alacant, Spain) to the shared translation task of the EMNLP 2011 Sixth Workshop on Statistical Machine Translation (WMT 2011). We participated in the Spanish–English task with a hybrid system that combines, in a phrase-based statistical machine translation (PBSMT) system, bilingual information obtained from parallel corpora in the usual way (Koehn, 2010, ch. 5), and bilingual information from the Spanish–English language pair in the Apertium (Forcada et al., 2011) rule-based machine translation (RMBT) platform.

A wide range of hybrid approaches (Thurmair, 2009) may be taken in order to build a machine translation system which takes advantage of a parallel corpus and explicit linguistic information from RBMT. In particular, our hybridisation approach directly enriches the phrase table of a PBSMT system with phrase pairs generated from the explicit linguistic resources from an Apertium-based shallow-transfer RBMT system. Apertium, which is described in detail below, does not perform a complete syntactic analysis of the input sentences, but rather works with simpler linear intermediate representations.

The rest of the paper is organised as follows. Next section overviews the two MT systems we combine in our submission. Section 3 outlines related hybrid approaches, whereas our approach is described in Section 4. Sections 5 and 6 describe, respectively, the resources we used to build our submission and the results achieved for the Spanish–English language pair. The paper ends with some concluding remarks.

2 Translation approaches

We briefly describe the rationale behind the PBSMT (section 2.1) and the shallow-transfer RBMT (section 2.2) systems we have used in our hybridisation approach.

2.1 Phrase-based statistical machine translation

Phrase-based statistical machine translation systems (Koehn et al., 2003) translate sentences by maximising the translation probability as defined by the log-linear combination of a number of feature functions, whose weights are chosen to opti-

Proceedings of the 6th Workshop on Statistical Machine Translation, pages 457–463,
Edinburgh, Scotland, UK, July 30–31, 2011.

mise translation quality (Och, 2003). A core component of every PBSMT system is the phrase table, which contains bilingual phrase pairs extracted from a bilingual corpus after word alignment (Och and Ney, 2003). The set of translations from which the most probable one is chosen is built by segmenting the source-language (SL) sentence in all possible ways and then combining the translation of the different source segments according to the phrase table. Common feature functions are: source-to-target and target-to-source phrase translation probabilities, source-to-target and target-to-source lexical weightings (calculated by using a probabilistic bilingual dictionary), reordering costs, number of words in the output (word penalty), number of phrase pairs used (phrase penalty), and likelihood of the output as given by a target-language (TL) model.

2.2 Shallow-transfer rule-based machine translation

The RBMT process (Hutchins and Somers, 1992) can be split into three different steps: i) analysis of the SL text to build a SL intermediate representation, ii) transfer from that SL intermediate representation to a TL intermediate representation, and iii) generation of the final translation from the TL intermediate representation.

Shallow-transfer RBMT systems use relatively simple intermediate representations, which are based on lexical forms consisting of lemma, part of speech and morphological inflection information of the words in the input sentence, and apply simple shallow-transfer rules that operate on sequences of lexical forms: this kind of systems do not perform a full parsing. Apertium (Forcada et al., 2011), the shallow-transfer RBMT platform we have used, splits the transfer step into structural and lexical transfer. The lexical transfer is done by using a bilingual dictionary which, for each SL lexical form, always provides the same TL lexical form; thus, no lexical selection is performed. Multi-word expressions (such as *on the other hand*, which acts as a single adverb) may be analysed by Apertium to (or generated from) a single lexical form.

Structural transfer in Apertium is done by applying a set of rules in a left-to-right, longest-match fashion to prevent the translation from being performed word for word in those cases in which this would result in an incorrect translation. Structural transfer rules process sequences of lexical forms by performing operations such as reorderings or gender and number agreements. For the translation between non-related language pairs, such as Spanish–English, the structural transfer may be split into three levels in order to facilitate the writing of rules by linguists. The first level performs short-distance operations, such as gender and number agreement between nouns and adjectives, and groups sequences of lexical forms into *chunks*; second-level rules perform inter *chunk* operations, such as agreements between more distant constituents (i.e. subject and main verb); and third-level ones de-encapsulate the chunks and generate a sequence of TL lexical forms from each *chunk*. Note that, although the multilevel shallow transfer allows performing operations between words which are distant in the source sentence, shallow-transfer RBMT systems are less powerful that the ones which perform full parsing. In addition, each lexical form is processed at most by one rule in the same level.

The following example illustrates how lexical and structural transfer are performed in Apertium. Suppose that the Spanish sentence *Por otra parte mis amigos americanos han decidido venir* is to be translated into English. First, it is analysed as:

```
por otra parte<adv>
mío<det><pos><mf><pl>
amigo<n><m><pl>
americano<adj><m><pl>
haber<vbhaver><pri><p3><pl>
decidir<vblex><pp><m><sg>
venir<vblex><inf>
```

which splits the sentence in seven lexical forms: a multi-word adverb (*por otra parte*), a plural possessive determiner (*mío*), a noun and an adjective in masculine plural (*amigo* and *americano*, respectively), the third-person plural form of the present tense of the verb *to be* (*haber*), the masculine singular past participle of the verb *decidir* and the verb *venir* in infinitive mood. Then, the transfer step is executed. It starts by performing the lexical transfer and applying the first-level rules of the structural transfer in parallel. The lexical transfer of each SL lexical form gives as a result:

```
on the other hand<adv>
my<det><pos><pl>
friend<n><pl>
american<adj>
```

```
have<vbhaver><pres>
decide<vblex><pp>
come<vblex><inf>
```

Four first-level structural transfer rules are triggered: the first one matches a single adverb (the first lexical form in the example); the second one matches a determiner followed by an adjective and a noun (the next three lexical forms); the third one matches a form of the verb *haber* plus the past participle form of another verb (the next two lexical forms); and the last one matches a verb in infinitive mood (last lexical form). Each of these first-level rules group the matched lexical forms in the same *chunk* and perform local operations within the chunk; for instance, the second rule reorders the adjective and the noun:

```
ADV{ on the other hand<adv> }
NOUN_PHRASE{ my<det><pos><pl>
american<adj> friend<n><pl> }
HABER_PP{ have<vbhaver><pres>
decide<vblex><pp> }
INF{ come<vblex><inf> }
```

After that, inter *chunk* operations are performed. The *chunk* sequence *HABER_PP* (verb in present perfect tense) *INF* (verb in infinitive mood) matches a second-level rule which adds the preposition *to* between them:

```
ADV{ on the other hand<adv> }
NOUN_PHRASE{ my<det><pos><pl>
friend<n><pl> american<adj> }
HABER_PP{ have<vbhaver><pres>
decide<vblex><pp> }
TO{ to<pr> }
INF{ come<vblex><inf> }
```

Third-level structural transfer removes *chunk* encapsulations so that a plain sequence of lexical forms is generated:

```
on the other hand<adv>
my<det><pos><pl>
american<adj>
friend<n><pl>
have<vbhaver><pres>
decide<vblex><pp>
to<pr> come<vblex><inf>
```

Finally, the translation into TL is generated from the TL lexical forms: *On the other hand my American friends have decided to come.*

3 Related work

Linguistic data from RBMT have already been used to enrich SMT systems in different ways. Bilingual dictionaries have been added to SMT systems since its early days (Brown et al., 1993); one of the simplest strategies involves adding the dictionary entries directly to the training parallel corpus (Tyers, 2009; Schwenk et al., 2009). Other approaches go beyond that. Eisele et al. (2008) first translate the sentences in the test set with an RBMT system, then apply the usual phrase-extraction algorithm over the resulting small parallel corpus, and finally add the obtained phrase pairs to the original phrase table. It is worth noting that neither of these two strategies guarantee that the multi-word expressions in the RBMT bilingual dictionary appearing in the sentences to translate will be translated as such because they may be split into smaller units by the phrase-extraction algorithm. Our approach overcomes this issue by adding the data obtained from the RBMT system directly to the phrase table. Preliminary experiments with Apertium data shows that our hybrid approach outperforms the one by Eisele et al. (2008) when translating Spanish texts into English.

4 Enhancing phrase-based SMT with shallow-transfer linguistic resources

As already mentioned, the Apertium structural transfer detects sequences of lexical forms which need to be translated together to prevent them from being translated word for word, which would result in an incorrect translation. Therefore, adding to the phrase table of a PBSMT system all the bilingual phrase pairs which either match one of these sequences of lexical forms in the structural transfer or an entry in the bilingual dictionary suffices to encode all the linguistic information provided by Apertium. We add these bilingual phrase pairs directly to the phrase table, instead of adding them to the training corpus and rely on the phrase extraction algorithm (Koehn, 2010, sec. 5.2.3), to avoid splitting the multi-word expressions provided by Apertium into smaller phrases (Schwenk et al., 2009, sec. 2).

4.1 Phrase pair generation

Generating the set of bilingual phrase pairs which match bilingual dictionary entries is straightforward. First, all the SL surface forms that are recognised by Apertium and their corresponding lexical forms are generated. Then, these SL lexical forms are translated using the bilingual dictionary, and finally their TL surface forms are generated.

Bilingual phrase pairs which match structural transfer rules are generated in a similar way. First, the SL sentences to be translated are analysed to get their SL lexical forms, and then the sequences of lexical forms that either match a first-level or a second-level structural transfer rule are passed through the Apertium pipeline to get their translations. If a sequence of SL lexical forms is matched by more than one structural transfer rule in the same level, it will be used to generate as many bilingual phrase pairs as different rules it matches. This differs from the way in which Apertium translates, since in those case only the longest rule would be applied.

The following example illustrates this procedure. Let the Spanish sentence *Por otra parte mis amigos americanos han decidido venir*, from the example in the previous section, be one of the sentences to be translated. The SL sequences *por otra parte*, *mis amigos americanos*, *amigos americanos*, *han decidido*, *venir* and *han decidido venir* would be used to generate bilingual phrase pairs because they match a first-level rule, a second-level rule, or both. The SL words *amigos americanos* are used twice because they are covered by two first-level rules: one that matches a determiner followed by a noun and an adjective, and another that matches a noun followed by an adjective. Note that when using Apertium in the regular way, outside this hybrid approach, only the first rule is applied as a consequence of the left-to-right, longest match policy. The SL words *han decidido* and *venir* are used because they match first-level rules, whereas *han decidido venir* matches a second-level rule.

It is worth noting that the generation of bilingual phrase pairs from the shallow-transfer rules is guided by the test corpus. We decided to do it in this way in order to avoid meaningless phrases and also to make our approach computationally feasible. Consider, for instance, the rule which is triggered every time a determiner followed by a noun and an adjective is detected. Generating all the possible phrase pairs matching this rule would involve combining all the determiners in the dictionary with all the nouns and all the adjectives, causing the generation of many meaningless phrases, such as *el niño inalámbrico – the wireless boy*. In addition, the number of combinations to deal with becomes unmanageable as the length of the rule grows.

4.2 Scoring the new phrase pairs

State-of-the-art PBSMT systems usually attach 5 scores to every phrase pair in the translation table: source-to-target and target-to-source phrase translation probabilities, source-to-target and target-to-source lexical weightings, and phrase penalty.

To calculate the phrase translation probabilities of the phrase pairs obtained from the shallow-transfer RBMT resources we simply add them once to the list of corpus-extracted phrase pairs, and then compute the probabilities by relative frequency as it is usually done (Koehn, 2010, sec. 5.2.5). In this regard, it is worth noting that, as RBMT-generated phrase pairs are added only once, if one of them happens to share its source side with many other corpus-extracted phrase pairs, or even with a single, very frequent one, the RBMT-generated phrase pair will receive lower scores, which penalises its use. To alleviate this without adding the same phrase pair an arbitrary amount of times, we introduce an additional boolean score to flag phrase pairs obtained from the RBMT resources.

The fact that the generation of bilingual phrase pairs from shallow transfer rules is guided by the test corpus may cause the translation of a sentence to be influenced by other sentences in the test set. This happens when the translation provided by Apertium for a subsegment of a test sentence matching an Apertium structural transfer rule is shared with one or more subsegments in the test corpus. In that case, the phrase translation probability $p(\text{source}|\text{target})$ of the resulting bilingual phrase pair is lower than if no subsegments with the same translation were found.

To calculate the lexical weightings (Koehn, 2010, sec. 5.3.3) of the RBMT-generated phrase pairs, the alignments between the words in the source side and those in the target side are needed. These word alignments are obtained by tracing back the operations carried out in the different steps of the shallow-transfer RBMT system. Only those words which are neither split nor joint with other words by the RBMT engine are included in the alignments; thus, multi-word expressions are left unaligned. This is done for convenience, since in this way multi-word

Figure 1: Example of word alignment obtained by tracing back the operations done by Apertium when translating from Spanish to English the sentence *Por otra parte mis amigos americanos han decidido venir*. Note that *por otra parte* is analysed by Apertium as a multi-word expression whose words are left unaligned for convenience (see section 4.2).

expressions are assigned a lexical weighting of 1.0. Figure 1 shows the alignment between the words in the running example.

5 System training

We submitted a hybrid system for the Spanish–English language pair built by following the strategy described above. The initial phrase table was built from all the parallel corpora distributed as part of the WMT 2011 shared translation task, namely Europarl (Koehn, 2005), News Commentary and United Nations. In a similar way, the language model was built from the the Europarl (Koehn, 2005) and the News Crawl monolingual English corpora. The weights of the different feature functions were optimised by means of minimum error rate training (Och, 2003) on the 2008 test set.[1] Table 1 summarises the data about the corpora used to build our submission. We also built a baseline PBSMT system trained on the same corpora and a reduced version of our system whose phrase table was enriched only with dictionary entries.

The Apertium (Forcada et al., 2011) engine and the linguistic resources for Spanish–English were downloaded from the Apertium Subversion repository.The linguistic data contains 326 228 entries in the bilingual dictionary, 106 first-level structural transfer rules, and 31 second-level rules. As entries in the bilingual dictionary contain mappings between SL and TL lemmas, when phrase pairs matching the bilingual dictionary are generated all the possible inflections of these lemmas are produced.

We used the free/open-source PBSMT system Moses (Koehn et al., 2007), together with the IRSTLM language modelling toolkit (Federico et al., 2008), which was used to train a 5-gram language model using interpolated Kneser-Ney discounting (Goodman and Chen, 1998). Word alignments from the training parallel corpus were computed by means of GIZA++ (Och and Ney, 2003). The cube pruning (Huang and Chiang, 2007) decoding algorithm was chosen in order to speed-up the tuning step and the translation of the test set.

Task	Corpus	Sentences
Language model	Europarl	2 015 440
	News Crawl	112 905 708
	Total	114 921 148
Training	Europarl	1 786 594
	News Commentary	132 571
	United Nations	10 662 993
	Total	12 582 158
	Total clean	8 992 751
Tuning	newstest2008	2 051
Test	newstest2011	3 003

Table 1: Size of the corpora used in the experiments. The bilingual training corpora has been cleaned to remove empty parallel sentences and those which contain more than 40 tokens.

6 Results and discussion

Table 2 reports the translation performance as measured by BLEU (Papineni et al., 2002), GTM (Melamed et al., 2003) and METEOR[2] (Banerjee and Lavie, 2005) for Apertium and the three systems presented in the previous section, as well as the size of the phrase table and the amount of unknown words in the test set. The hybrid approach outperforms the baseline PBSMT system in terms of the three evaluation metrics. The confidence interval of the difference between them, computed by doing 1 000 iterations of paired

[1]The corpora can be downloaded from `http://www.statmt.org/wmt11/translation-task.html`.

[2]Modules *exact*, *stem*, *synonym* and *paraphrase* (Denkowski and Lavie, 2010) were used.

system	BLEU	GTM	METEOR	# of unknown words	phrase table size
baseline	28.06	52.40	47.27	1 447	254 693 494
UA-dict	28.58	52.55	47.41	1 274	255 860 346
UA	**28.73**	**52.66**	**47.51**	1 274	255 872 094
Apertium	23.89	50.71	45.65	4 064	-

Table 2: Case-insensitive BLEU, GTM, and METEOR scores obtained by the hybrid approach submitted to the WMT 2011 shared translation task (*UA*), a reduced version of it whose phrase table is enriched using only bilingual dictionary entries (*UA-dict*), a baseline PBSMT system trained with the same corpus (*baseline*), and Apertium on the *newstest2011* test set. The number of unknown words and the phrase table size are also reported when applicable.

bootstrap resampling (Zhang et al., 2004) with a p-level of 0.05, does not overlap with zero for any evaluation metric,[3] which confirms that it is statistically significant. Our hybrid approach also outperforms Apertium in terms of the three evaluation metrics.[4] However, the difference between our complete hybrid system and the version which only takes advantage of bilingual dictionary is not statistically significant for any metric.[5]

The results show how the addition of RBMT-generated data leads to an improvement over the baseline PBMST system, even though it was trained with a very large parallel corpus and the proportion of entries from the Apertium data in the phrase table is very small (0.46%). 5.94% of the phrase pairs chosen by the decoder were generated from the Apertium data. The improvement may be explained by the fact that the sentences in the test set belong to the news domain and Apertium data has been developed bearing in mind the translation of general texts (mainly news), whereas most of the bilingual training corpus comes from specialised domains. In addition, the morphology of Spanish is quite rich, which makes it very difficult to find all possible inflections of the same lemma in a parallel corpus. Therefore, Apertium-generated phrases, which contain handcrafted knowledge from a general domain, cover some sequences of words in the input text which are not covered, or are sparsely found, in the original training corpora, as shown by the reduction in the amount of unknown words (1 447 unknown words versus 1 274). In other words, Apertium linguistic information does not completely overlap with the data learned from the parallel corpus. Regarding the small difference between the hybrid system enriched with all the Apertium resources and the one that only includes the bilingual dictionary, preliminary experiments shows that the impact of the shallow-transfer rules is higher when the TL is highly inflected and the SL is not, which is exactly the scenario opposite to the one described in this paper.

7 Concluding remarks

We have presented the MT system submitted by the Transducens Research Group from Universitat d'Alacant to the WMT2011 shared translation task. This is the first submission of our team to this shared task. We developed a hybrid system for the Spanish–English language pair which enriches the phrase table of a standard PBSMT system with phrase pairs generated from the RBMT linguistic resources provided by Apertium. Our system outperforms a baseline PBSMT in terms of BLEU, GTM and METEOR scores by a statistically significant margin.

Acknowledgements

Work funded by the Spanish Ministry of Science and Innovation through project TIN2009-14009-C02-01 and by Generalitat Valenciana through grant ACIF/2010/174 (VALi+d programme).

[3]The confidence interval of the difference between our system and the baseline PBSMT system for BLEU, GTM and METEOR is $[0.38, 0.93]$, $[0.06, 0.45]$, and $[0.06, 0.42]$, respectively.

[4]The confidence interval of the difference between our approach and Apertium for BLEU, GTM and METEOR is $[4.35, 5.35]$, $[1.55, 2.32]$, and $[1.50, 2.21]$, respectively.

[5]The confidence interval of the difference between our approach and the reduced version which does not use structural transfer rules for BLEU, GTM and METEOR is $[-0.07, 0.37]$, $[-0.06, 0.27]$, and $[-0.06, 0.26]$, respectively.

References

S. Banerjee and A. Lavie. 2005. METEOR: An automatic metric for MT evaluation with improved correlation with human judgments. In *Proceedings of the ACL Workshop on Intrinsic and Extrinsic Evaluation Measures for Machine Translation and/or Summarization*, pages 65–72, Ann Arbor, Michigan.

P. F. Brown, S. A. D. Pietra, V. J. D. Pietra, M. J. Goldsmith, J. Hajic, R. L. Mercer, and S. Mohanty. 1993. But dictionaries are data too. In *Proceedings of the workshop on Human Language Technology*, pages 202–205, Princeton, New Jersey.

M. Denkowski and A. Lavie. 2010. METEOR-NEXT and the METEOR paraphrase tables: Improved evaluation support for five target languages. In *Proceedings of the ACL 2010 Joint Workshop on Statistical Machine Translation and Metrics MATR*, pages 339–342, Uppsala, Sweden.

A. Eisele, C. Federmann, H. Saint-Amand, M. Jellinghaus, T. Herrmann, and Y. Chen. 2008. Using Moses to integrate multiple rule-based machine translation engines into a hybrid system. In *Proceedings of the Third Workshop on Statistical Machine Translation*, pages 179–182, Columbus, Ohio.

M. Federico, N. Bertoldi, and M. Cettolo. 2008. IRSTLM: an open source toolkit for handling large scale language models. In *INTERSPEECH-2008*, pages 1618–1621, Brisbane, Australia.

M.L. Forcada, M. Ginestí-Rosell, J. Nordfalk, J. O'Regan, S. Ortiz-Rojas, J.A. Pérez-Ortiz, F. Sánchez-Martínez, G. Ramírez-Sánchez, and F.M. Tyers. 2011. Apertium: a free/open-source platform for rule-based machine translation. *Machine Translation. Special Issue on Free/Open-Source Machine Translation*, In press.

J. Goodman and S. F. Chen. 1998. An empirical study of smoothing techniques for language modeling. Technical Report TR-10-98, Harvard University, August.

L. Huang and D. Chiang. 2007. Forest rescoring: Faster decoding with integrated language models. In *Proceedings of the 45th Annual Meeting of the Association of Computational Linguistics*, pages 144–151, Prague, Czech Republic.

W. J. Hutchins and H. L. Somers. 1992. *An introduction to machine translation*, volume 362. Academic Press New York.

P. Koehn, F. J. Och, and D. Marcu. 2003. Statistical phrase-based translation. In *Proceedings of the Human Language Technology and North American Association for Computational Linguistics Conference*, pages 48–54, Edmonton, Canada.

P. Koehn, H. Hoang, A. Birch, C. Callison-Burch, M. Federico, N. Bertoldi, B. Cowan, C. Shen, W.and Moran, R. Zens, C. Dyer, O. Bojar, A. Constantin, and E. Herbst. 2007. Moses: Open Source Toolkit for Statistical Machine Translation. In *Proceedings of the 45th Annual Meeting of the ACL on Interactive Poster and Demonstration Sessions*, pages 177–180, Prague, Czech Republic.

P. Koehn. 2005. Europarl: A parallel corpus for statistical machine translation. *MT summit*, 5:12–16.

P. Koehn. 2010. *Statistical Machine Translation*. Cambridge University Press.

I. D. Melamed, R. Green, and J. P. Turian. 2003. Precision and recall of machine translation. In *Proceedings of the 2003 Conference of the North American Chapter of the Association for Computational Linguistics on Human Language Technology*, pages 61–63, Edmonton, Canada.

F. J. Och and H. Ney. 2003. A systematic comparison of various statistical alignment models. *Computational Linguistics*, 29:19–51, March.

F. J. Och. 2003. Minimum error rate training in statistical machine translation. In *Proceedings of the 41st Annual Meeting on Association for Computational Linguistics*, pages 160–167, Sapporo, Japan.

K. Papineni, S. Roukos, T. Ward, and W. Zhu. 2002. BLEU: a method for automatic evaluation of machine translation. In *Proceedings of the 40th Annual Meeting on Association for Computational Linguistics*, pages 311–318, Philadelphia, Pennsylvania.

H. Schwenk, S. Abdul-Rauf, L. Barrault, and J. Senellart. 2009. SMT and SPE machine translation systems for WMT'09. In *Proceedings of the Fourth Workshop on Statistical Machine Translation*, pages 130–134, Athens, Greece.

G. Thurmair. 2009. Comparing different architectures of hybrid Machine Translation systems. In *Proceedings MT Summit XII*, Ottawa, Ontario, Canada.

F. M. Tyers. 2009. Rule-based augmentation of training data in Breton-French statistical machine translation. In *Proceedings of the 13th Annual Conference of the European Association for Machine Translation*, pages 213–217, Barcelona, Spain.

Y. Zhang, S. Vogel, and A. Waibel. 2004. Interpreting BLEU/NIST scores: How much improvement do we need to have a better system. In *Proceedings of the Fourth International Conference on Language Resources and Evaluation*, pages 2051–2054, Lisbon, Portugal.

LIUM's SMT Machine Translation Systems for WMT 2011

Holger Schwenk, Patrik Lambert, Loïc Barrault,
Christophe Servan, Haithem Afli, Sadaf Abdul-Rauf and Kashif Shah
LIUM, University of Le Mans
72085 Le Mans cedex 9, FRANCE
FirstName.LastName@lium.univ-lemans.fr

Abstract

This paper describes the development of French–English and English–French statistical machine translation systems for the 2011 WMT shared task evaluation. Our main systems were standard phrase-based statistical systems based on the Moses decoder, trained on the provided data only, but we also performed initial experiments with hierarchical systems. Additional, new features this year include improved translation model adaptation using monolingual data, a continuous space language model and the treatment of unknown words.

1 Introduction

This paper describes the statistical machine translation systems developed by the Computer Science laboratory at the University of Le Mans (LIUM) for the 2011 WMT shared task evaluation. We only considered the translation between French and English (in both directions). The main differences with respect to previous year's system (Lambert et al., 2010) are as follows: use of more training data as provided by the organizers, improved translation model adaptation by unsupervised training, a continuous space language model for the translation into French, some attempts to automatically induce translations of unknown words and first experiments with hierarchical systems. These different points are described in the rest of the paper, together with a summary of the experimental results showing the impact of each component.

2 Resources Used

The following sections describe how the resources provided or allowed in the shared task were used to train the translation and language models of the system.

2.1 Bilingual data

Our system was developed in two stages. First, a baseline system was built to generate automatic translations of some of the monolingual data available. These automatic translations were then used directly with the source texts to create additional bitexts. In a second stage, these additional bilingual data were incorporated into the system (see Section 5 and Tables 4 and 5).

The latest version of the News-Commentary (NC) corpus and of the Europarl (Eparl) corpus (version 6) were used. We also took as training data a subset of the French–English Gigaword (10^9) corpus. We applied the same filters as last year to select this subset. The first one is a lexical filter based on the IBM model 1 cost (Brown et al., 1993) of each side of a sentence pair given the other side, normalised with respect to both sentence lengths. This filter was trained on a corpus composed of Eparl, NC, and UN data. The other filter is an n-gram language model (LM) cost of the target sentence (see Section 3), normalised with respect to its length. This filter was trained with all monolingual resources available except the 10^9 data. We generated two subsets, both by selecting sentence pairs with a lexical cost inferior to 4, and an LM cost respectively inferior to 2.3 (10^9_1, 115 million English words) and 2.6 (10^9_2, 232 million English words).

Proceedings of the 6th Workshop on Statistical Machine Translation, pages 464–469,
Edinburgh, Scotland, UK, July 30–31, 2011. ©2011 Association for Computational Linguistics

2.2 Use of Automatic Translations

Available human translated bitexts such as the Europarl or 10^9 corpus seem to be out-of domain for this task. We used two types of automatically extracted resources to adapt our system to the task domain.

First, we generated automatic translations of the provided monolingual News corpus and selected the sentences with a normalised translation cost (returned by the decoder) inferior to a threshold. The resulting bitext contain no new translations, since all words of the translation output come from the translation model, but it contains new combinations (phrases) of known words, and reinforces the probability of some phrase pairs (Schwenk, 2008). This year, we improved this method in the following way. In the original approach, the automatic translations are added to the human translated bitexts and a complete new system is build, including time consuming word alignment with GIZA++. For WMT'11, we directly used the word-to-word alignments produced by the decoder at the output instead of GIZA's alignments. This speeds-up the procedure and yields the same results in our experiments. A detailed comparison is given in (Lambert et al., 2011).

Second, as in last year's evaluation, we automatically extracted and aligned parallel sentences from comparable in-domain corpora. We used the AFP and APW news texts since there are available in the French and English LDC Gigaword corpora. The general architecture of our parallel sentence extraction system is described in detail by Abdul-Rauf and Schwenk (2009). We first translated 91M words from French into English using our first stage SMT system. These English sentences were then used to search for translations in the English AFP and APW texts of the Gigaword corpus using information retrieval techniques. The Lemur toolkit (Ogilvie and Callan, 2001) was used for this purpose. Search was limited to a window of ± 5 days of the date of the French news text. The retrieved candidate sentences were then filtered using the Translation Error Rate (TER) with respect to the automatic translations. In this study, sentences with a TER below 75% were kept. Sentences with a large length difference (French versus English) or containing a large fraction of numbers were also discarded. By these means, about 27M words of additional bitexts were obtained.

2.3 Monolingual data

The French and English target language models were trained on all provided monolingual data. In addition, LDC's Gigaword collection was used for both languages. Data corresponding to the development and test periods were removed from the Gigaword collections.

2.4 Development data

All development was done on *newstest2009*, and *newstest2010* was used as internal test set. The default Moses tokenization was used. However, we added abbreviations for the French tokenizer. All our models are case sensitive and include punctuation. The BLEU scores reported in this paper were calculated with the tool multi-bleu.perl and are case sensitive.

3 Architecture of the SMT system

The goal of statistical machine translation (SMT) is to produce a target sentence e from a source sentence f. Our main system is a phrase-based system (Koehn et al., 2003; Och and Ney, 2003), but we have also performed some experiments with a hierarchical system (Chiang, 2007). Both use a log linear framework in order to introduce several models explaining the translation process:

$$\begin{aligned} e^* &= \arg\max p(e|f) \\ &= \arg\max_e \{exp(\sum_i \lambda_i h_i(e,f))\} \end{aligned} \quad (1)$$

The feature functions h_i are the system models and the λ_i weights are typically optimized to maximize a scoring function on a development set (Och and Ney, 2002). The phrase-based system uses fourteen features functions, namely phrase and lexical translation probabilities in both directions, seven features for the lexicalized distortion model, a word and a phrase penalty and a target language model (LM). The hierarchical system uses only 8 features: a LM weight, a word penalty and six weights for the translation model.

Both systems are based on the Moses SMT toolkit (Koehn et al., 2007) and constructed as follows.

First, word alignments in both directions are calculated. We used a multi-threaded version of the GIZA++ tool (Gao and Vogel, 2008).[1] This speeds up the process and corrects an error of GIZA++ that can appear with rare words.

Phrases, lexical reorderings or hierarchical rules are extracted using the default settings of the Moses toolkit. The parameters of Moses were tuned on *newstest2009*, using the 'new' MERT tool. We repeated the training process three times, each with a different seed value for the optimisation algorithm. In this way we have an rough idea of the error introduced by the tuning process.

4-gram back-off LMs were used. The word list contains all the words of the bitext used to train the translation model and all words that appear at least ten times in the monolingual corpora. Words of the monolingual corpora containing special characters or sequences of uppercase characters were not included in the word list. Separate LMs were build on each data source with the SRI LM toolkit (Stolcke, 2002) and then linearly interpolated, optimizing the coefficients with an EM procedure. The perplexities of these LMs were 99.4 for French and 129.7 for English. In addition, we build a 5-gram continuous space language model for French (Schwenk, 2007). This model was trained on all the available French texts using a resampling technique. The continuous space language model is interpolated with the 4-gram back-off model and used to rescore n-best lists. This reduces the perplexity by about 8% relative.

4 Treatment of unknown words

Finally, we propose a method to actually add new translations to the system inspired from (Habash, 2008). For this, we propose to identity unknown words and propose possible translations.

Moses has two options when encountering an unknown word in the source language: keep it as it is or drop it. The first option may be a good choice for languages that use the same writing system since the unknown word may be a proper name. The second option is usually used when translating between language based on different scripts, e.g. translating from Arabic to English. Alternatively, we propose to infer automatically possible translations when translating from a morphologically rich language, to a simpler language. In our case, we use this approach to translate from French to English.

[1]The source is available at `http://www.cs.cmu.edu/~qing/`

Source language French	Source language stemmed form	Target language English
finies	fini	finished
effacés	effacé	erased
hawaienne	hawaien	Hawaiian
...	...	...

Table 1: Example of translations from French to English which are automatically extracted from the phrase-table with the stemmed form.

Several of the unknown words are actually adjectives, nouns or verbs in a particular form that itself is not known, but the phrase table would contain the translation of a different form. As an example we can mention the French adjective *finies* which is in the female plural form. After stemming we may be able to find the translation in a dictionary which is automatically extracted from the phrase-table (see Table 1). This idea was already outlined by (Bojar and Tamchyna, 2011) to translate from Czech to English.

First, we automatically extract a dictionary from the phrase table. This is done, be detecting all 1-to-1 entries in the phrase table. When there are multiple entries, all are kept with their lexical translations probabilities. Our dictionary has about 680k unique source words with a total of almost 1M translations.

source segment	les travaux sont **finis**
target segment	works are **finis**
stemmed word found	**fini**
translations found	**finished, ended**
segment proposed	works are **finished** works are **ended**
segment kept	works are **finished**

Table 2: Example of the treatment of an unknown French word and its automatically inferred translation.

The detection of unknown words is performed by comparing the source and the target segment in order to detect identical words. Once the unknown word is selected, we are looking for its stemmed form in the dictionary and propose some translations for the unknown word based on lexical score of the phrase table (see Table 2 for some examples). The snowball

Bitext	#Fr Words (M)	PT size (M)	newstest2009 BLEU	newstest2010 BLEU	newstest2010 TER	newstest2010 METEOR
Eparl+NC	56	7.1	26.74	27.36 (0.19)	55.11 (0.14)	60.13 (0.05)
Eparl+NC+10_1^9	186	16.3	27.96	28.20 (0.04)	54.46 (0.10)	60.88 (0.05)
Eparl+NC+10_2^9	323	25.4	28.20	28.57 (0.10)	54.12 (0.13)	61.20 (0.05)
Eparl+NC+news	140	8.4	27.31	28.41 (0.13)	54.15 (0.14)	61.13 (0.04)
Eparl+NC+10_2^9+news	406	25.5	27.93	28.70 (0.24)	54.12 (0.16)	61.30 (0.20)
Eparl+NC+10_2^9+IR	351	25.3	28.07	28.51 (0.18)	54.07 (0.06)	61.18 (0.07)
Eparl+NC+10_2^9+news+IR	435	26.1	27.99	28.93 (0.02)	53.84 (0.07)	61.46 (0.07)
+larger beam+pruned PT	435	8.2	28.44	29.05 (0.14)	53.74 (0.16)	61.68 (0.09)

Table 4: French–English results: number of French words (in million), number of entries in the filtered phrase-table (in million) and BLEU scores in the development (newstest2009) and internal test (newstest2010) sets for the different systems developed. The BLEU scores and the number in parentheses are the average and standard deviation over 3 values (see Section 3)

corpus	newstest2010	subtest2010
number of sentences	2489	109
number of words	70522	3586
number of UNK detected	118	118
nbr of sentences containing UNK	109	109
BLEU Score without UNK process	29.43	24.31
BLEU Score with UNK process	29.43	24.33
TER Score without UNK process	53.08	58.54
TER Score with UNK process	53.08	58.59

Table 3: Statistics of the unknown word (UNK) processing algorithm on our internal test (newstest2010) and its sub-part containing only the processed sentences (subtest2010).

stemmer[2] was used. Then the different hypothesis are evaluated with the target language model.

We processed the produced translations with this method. It can happen that some words are translations of themselves, e.g. the French word "duel" can be translated by the English word "duel". If theses words are present into the extracted dictionary, we keep them. If we do not find any translation in our dictionary, we keep the translation. By these means we hope to keep named entities.

Several statistics made on our internal test (newstest2010) are shown in Table 3. Its shows that the influence of the detected unknown words is minimal. Only 0.16% of the words in the corpus are actually unknown. However, the main goal of this process is to increase the human readability and usefulness without degrading automatic metrics. We also expect a larger impact in other tasks for which we have smaller amounts of parallel training data. In future versions of this detection process, we will try to detect unknown words before the translation process and propose alternatives hypothesis to the Moses decoder.

[2]http://snowball.tartarus.org/

5 Results and Discussion

The results of our SMT system for the French–English and English–French tasks are summarized in Tables 4 and 5, respectively. The MT metric scores are the average of three optimisations performed with different seeds (see Section 3). The numbers in parentheses are the standard deviation of these three values. The standard deviation gives a lower bound of the significance of the difference between two systems. If the difference between two average scores is less than the sum of the standard deviations, we can say that this difference is not significant. The reverse is not true. Note that most of the improvements shown in the tables are small and not significant. However many of the gains are cumulative and the sum of several small gains makes a significant difference.

Baseline French–English System

The first section of Table 4 shows results of the development of the baseline SMT system, used to generate automatic translations.

Although no French translations were generated, we did similar experiments in the English–French direction (first section of Table 5).

Bitext	#En Words (M)	newstest2009 BLEU	newstest2010 BLEU	newstest2010 TER
Eparl+NC	52	26.20	28.06 (0.22)	56.85 (0.08)
Eparl+NC+10^9_1	167	26.84	29.08 (0.12)	55.83 (0.14)
Eparl+NC+10^9_2	284	26.95	29.29 (0.03)	55.77 (0.19)
Eparl+NC+10^9_2+news	299	27.34	29.56 (0.14)	55.44 (0.18)
Eparl+NC+10^9_2+IR	311	27.14	29.43 (0.12)	55.48 (0.06)
Eparl+NC+10^9_2+news+IR	371	27.32	29.73 (0.21)	55.16 (0.20)
+rescoring with CSLM	371	27.46	30.04	54.79

Table 5: English–French results: number of English words (in million) and BLEU scores in the development (newstest2009) and internal test (newstest2010) sets for the different systems developed. The BLEU scores and the number in parentheses are the average and standard deviation over 3 values (see Section 3.)

In both cases the best system is the one trained on the Europarl, News-commentary and 10^9_2 corpora. This system was used to generate the automatic translations. We did not observe any gain when adding the United Nations data, so we discarded this data.

Impact of the Additional Bitexts

With the baseline French–English SMT system (see above), we translated the French News corpus to generate an additional bitext (News). We also translated some parts of the French LDC Gigaword corpus, to serve as queries to our IR system (see section 2.2). The resulting additional bitext is referred to as IR. The second section of Tables 4 and 5 summarize the system development including the additional bitexts.

With the News additional bitext added to Eparl+NC, we obtain a system of similar performance as the baseline system used to generate the automatic translations, but with less than half of the data. Adding the News corpus to a larger corpus, such as Eparl+NC+10^9_2, has less impact but still yields some improvement: 0.1 BLEU point in French–English and 0.3 in English–French. Thus, the News bitext translated from French to English may have more impact when translating from English to French than in the opposite direction. This effect is studied in detail in a separate paper (Lambert et al., 2011). With the IR additional bitext added to Eparl+NC+10^9_2, we observe no improvement in French to English, and a very small improvement in English to French. However, added to the baseline system (Eparl+NC+10^9_2) adapted with the News data, the IR additional bitexts yield a small (0.2 BLEU) improvement in both translation directions.

Final System

In both translation directions our best system was the one trained on Eparl+NC+10^9_2+News+IR. We further achieved small improvements by pruning the phrase-table and by increasing the beam size. To prune the phrase-table, we used the 'sigtest-filter' available in Moses (Johnson et al., 2007), more precisely the $\alpha - \epsilon$ filter[3].

We also build hierarchical systems on the various human translated corpora, using up to 323M words (corpora Eparl+NC+10^9_2). The systems yielded similar results than the phrase-based approach, but required much more computational resources, in particular large amounts of main memory to perform the translations. Running the decoder was actually only possible with binarized rule-tables. Therefore, the hierarchical system was not used in the evaluation system.

[3]The p-value of two-by-two contingency tables (describing the degree of association between a source and a target phrase) is calculated with Fisher exact test. This probability is interpreted as the probability of observing by chance an association that is at least as strong as the given one, and hence as its significance. An important special case of a table occurs when a phrase pair occurs exactly once in the corpus, and each of the component phrases occurs exactly once in its side of the parallel corpus (1-1-1 phrase pairs). In this case the negative log of the p-value is $\alpha = logN$ (N is number of sentence pairs in the corpus). $\alpha - \epsilon$ is the largest threshold that results in all of the 1-1-1 phrase pairs being included.

6 Conclusions and Further Work

We presented the development of our statistical machine translation systems for the French–English and English–French 2011 WMT shared task. In the official evaluation the English–French system was ranked first according to the BLEU score and the French–English system second.

Acknowledgments

This work has been partially funded by the European Union under the EuroMatrixPlus project ICT-2007.2.2-FP7-231720 and the French government under the ANR project COSMAT ANR-09-CORD-004.

References

Sadaf Abdul-Rauf and Holger Schwenk. 2009. On the use of comparable corpora to improve SMT performance. In *Proceedings of the 12th Conference of the European Chapter of the ACL (EACL 2009)*, pages 16–23, Athens, Greece.

Ondřej Bojar and Aleš Tamchyna. 2011. Forms Wanted: Training SMT on Monolingual Data. Abstract at Machine Translation and Morphologically-Rich Languages. Research Workshop of the Israel Science Foundation University of Haifa, Israel, January.

Peter F. Brown, Stephen A. Della Pietra, Vincent J. Della Pietra, and Robert L. Mercer. 1993. The mathematics of statistical machine translation: Parameter estimation. *Computational Linguistics*, 19(2):263–311.

David Chiang. 2007. Hierarchical phrase-based translation. *Computational Linguistics*, 33(2):201–228.

Qin Gao and Stephan Vogel. 2008. Parallel implementations of word alignment tool. In *Software Engineering, Testing, and Quality Assurance for Natural Language Processing*, pages 49–57, Columbus, Ohio, June. Association for Computational Linguistics.

Nizar Habash. 2008. Four techniques for online handling of out-of-vocabulary words in arabic-english statistical machine translation. In *ACL 08*.

Howard Johnson, Joel Martin, George Foster, and Roland Kuhn. 2007. Improving translation quality by discarding most of the phrasetable. In *Proceedings of the 2007 Joint Conference on Empirical Methods in Natural Language Processing and Computational Natural Language Learning (EMNLP-CoNLL)*, pages 967–975, Prague, Czech Republic.

Philipp Koehn, Franz Josef Och, and Daniel Marcu. 2003. Statistical phrased-based machine translation. In *HLT/NACL*, pages 127–133.

Philipp Koehn, Hieu Hoang, Alexandra Birch, Chris Callison-Burch, Marcello Federico, Nicola Bertoldi, Brooke Cowan, Wade Shen, Christine Moran, Richard Zens, Chris Dyer, Ondrej Bojar, Alexandra Constantin, and Evan Herbst. 2007. Moses: Open source toolkit for statistical machine translation. In *ACL, demonstration session*.

Patrik Lambert, Sadaf Abdul-Rauf, and Holger Schwenk. 2010. LIUM SMT machine translation system for WMT 2010. In *Proceedings of the Joint Fifth Workshop on Statistical Machine Translation and Metrics-MATR*, pages 121–126, Uppsala, Sweden, July.

Patrik Lambert, Holger Schwenk, Christophe Servan, and Sadaf Abdul-Rauf. 2011. Investigations on translation model adaptation using monolingual data. In *Sixth Workshop on SMT*, page this volume.

Franz Josef Och and Hermann Ney. 2002. Discriminative training and maximum entropy models for statistical machine translation. In *Proc. of the Annual Meeting of the Association for Computational Linguistics*, pages 295–302.

Franz Josef Och and Hermann Ney. 2003. A systematic comparison of various statistical alignement models. *Computational Linguistics*, 29(1):19–51.

Paul Ogilvie and Jamie Callan. 2001. Experiments using the Lemur toolkit. In *In Proceedings of the Tenth Text Retrieval Conference (TREC-10)*, pages 103–108.

Holger Schwenk. 2007. Continuous space language models. *Computer Speech and Language*, 21:492–518.

Holger Schwenk. 2008. Investigations on large-scale lightly-supervised training for statistical machine translation. In *IWSLT*, pages 182–189.

A. Stolcke. 2002. SRILM: an extensible language modeling toolkit. In *Proc. of the Int. Conf. on Spoken Language Processing*, pages 901–904, Denver, CO.

Spell Checking Techniques for Replacement of Unknown Words and Data Cleaning for Haitian Creole SMS Translation

Sara Stymne
Department of Computer and Information Science
Linköping University, Sweden
sara.stymne@liu.se

Abstract

We report results on translation of SMS messages from Haitian Creole to English. We show improvements by applying spell checking techniques to unknown words and creating a lattice with the best known spelling equivalents. We also used a small cleaned corpus to train a cleaning model that we applied to the noisy corpora.

1 Introduction

In this paper we report results on the WMT 2011 featured shared task on translation of SMS messages from Haitian Creole into English, which featured a number of challenges. The in-domain data available is small and noisy, with a lot of non-standard language. Furthermore, Haitian Creole is a low resource language, for which there are few language technology tools and corpora available.

Our main focus has been to make the best possible use of the available training data through different ways of cleaning the data, and by replacing unknown words in the test data by plausible spelling equivalents. We have also investigated effects of different ways to combine the available data in translation and language models.

2 Baseline system

We performed all our experiments using a standard phrase-based statistical machine translation (PBSMT) system, trained using the Moses toolkit (Koehn et al., 2007), with SRILM (Stolcke, 2002) and KenLM (Heafield, 2011) for language modeling, and GIZA++ (Och and Ney, 2003) for word alignment. We also used a lexicalized reordering model (Koehn et al., 2005). We optimized each system separately using minimum error rate training (Och, 2003). The development and devtest data were available in two versions, as *raw*, noisy data, and in a *clean* version, where the raw data had been cleaned by human post-editors.

The different subcorpora had different tokenizations and casing conventions. We normalized punctuation by applying a tokenizer that separated most punctuation marks into separate tokens, excluding apostrophes that were suspected to belong to contracted words or Haitian short forms, periods for abbreviations, and periods in URLs. There were often many consecutive punctuation marks; these were replaced by only the first of the punctuation marks. In the English translations of the SMS data there were often translator's notes at the end of the translations. These were removed when introduced by two standard formulations: *Additional Notes* or *translator's note/interpretation*. In addition the translation marker *The SMS [. . .]* were removed.

Case information was inconsistent, especially for SMS data, and for this reason we lower-cased all Haitian source data. On the English target side we wanted to use true-cased data, since we wanted case distinctions in the translation output. We based the true-casing on Koehn and Haddow (2009), who changed the case of the first word in each sentence, to the most common case variant of that word in the corpus when it is not sentence initial. In the noisy SMS data, though, there were many sentences with all capital letters that would influence this truecasing method negatively. To address this, we modified the algorithm to exclude sentences with more than 40% capital letters when calculating corpus statistics, and to lowercase all unknown capitalized words.

Proceedings of the 6th Workshop on Statistical Machine Translation, pages 470–477,
Edinburgh, Scotland, UK, July 30–31, 2011. ©2011 Association for Computational Linguistics

Data	Sentences	Words	TM	LM	Reo	TC
In-domain SMS data	17,192	35k	SMS	SMS	yes	yes
Medical domain	1,619	10k	other	other	–	–
Newswire domain	13,517	30k	other	other	–	yes
Glossary	35,728	85k	other	other	–	–
Wikipedia parallel sentence	8,476	90k	other	other	–	yes
Wikipedia named entities	10,499	25k	other	other	–	–
Haitisurf dictionary	1,687	3k	other	other	–	yes
Krengle sentences	658	3k	other	other	–	yes
The Bible	30,715	850k	bible	bible	–	yes

Table 1: Corpora used for training translation models (TM), language models (LM), lexicalized reordering model (Reo), and true-casing model (TC). All corpora are bilingual English–Haitian Creole.

All translation results are reported for the devtest corpus, on truecased data. We report results on three metrics, Bleu (Papineni et al., 2002), NIST (Doddington, 2002), and Meteor optimized on fluency/adequacy (Lavie and Agarwal, 2007).

3 Corpus Usage

The corpora available for the task was a small bilingual in-domain corpus of SMT data, a limited amount of bilingual out-of-domain corpora, such as dictionaries and the Bible. This is different to the common situation of domain adaptation, as in the standard WMT shared tasks, where there is a small bilingual in-domain corpus, a larger in-domain monolingual corpus, and possibly several out-of-domain corpora that can be both monolingual and bilingual. In such a scenario it is often useful to use all available training data for both translation and language models, possibly in separate models (Koehn and Schroeder, 2007).

Table 1 summarizes how we used the available corpora, in our different models. For translation and language models we separated the bilingual data into three parts, the SMS data, the Bible, and everything else. For our lexicalized reordering model we only used SMS data, since we believe word order there is likely to differ from the other corpora. For the English true-casing model we concatenated the English side of all bilingual corpora that were not lower-cased.

Table 2 shows the results of the different model combinations on the clean devtest data. When we used only the SMS data in the translation model, the scores changed only slightly regardless of which combinations of language models we used. Using two translation models for the SMS data and the other bilingual data overall gave better results than when only using SMS data for the translation model. With double translation models it was best only to use the SMS data in the language model. Including the Bible data had a minor impact. Based on these experiments we will use all available training data in two translation models, one for SMS and one for everything else, but only use SMS data in one language model, which corresponds to the line marked in bold in Table 2, and which we will call the *dual* system.

We did not perform model combination experiments for the raw input data, since we believed the pattern would be similar as for the clean data. The results for the raw devtest as input are considerably lower than for the clean data. Using the best model combination, we got a Bleu score of only 26.25, which can be compared to 29.90 using the clean data.

4 Data Cleaning Model

While the training data is noisy, we had access to cleaned versions of dev, devtest and test data. We decided to use the dev data to build a model for cleaning the noisy SMS data. We did this by training a standard PBSMT model from raw to clean dev data. When inspecting this translation model we found that it very often changed the place holders for names and phone numbers, and thus we filtered out all entries in the phrase table that did not have matching place holders. We then used this model to perform monotone decoding of the raw SMS data, thus creating a cleaner version of it.

This approach is similar to that of Aw et al.

TMs	LMs	Bleu	NIST	Meteor
SMS	SMS	29.04	5.578	52.32
SMS	SMS, other	28.76	5.543	51.96
SMS	SMS, other+bible	29.18	5.696	51.77
SMS, other	SMS	29.78	5.808	52.86
SMS, other+bible	**SMS**	29.90	5.764	52.88
SMS, other+bible	SMS, other	29.59	5.742	52.28
SMS, other+bible	SMS, other+bible	28.75	5.587	52.52

Table 2: Translation results, with different combinations of translation and language models. Model names separated by a comma stands for separate models, and names separated with a plus for one model built from concatenated corpora.

Model	Testset	Bleu	NIST	Meteor
Dual	**clean**	29.90	5.764	52.88
Dual+CM	clean	29.78	5.740	52.95
Dual	raw	26.25	5.231	50.79
Dual	raw+CM	26.26	5.348	51.30
Dual+CM	raw	25.64	5.120	50.01
Dual+CM	**raw+CM**	26.24	5.362	51.64

Table 3: Translation results, with and without an additional cleaning model (+CM) on the clean and raw devtest data

(2006), who trained a model for translation from English SMS language to standard written English, with very good results both on this task itself, and on a task of translating English SMS messages into Chinese. For training they used up to 5000 sentences, but the results stabilized already when using 3000 training sentences. Our task is different, though, since we do not aim at standard written Haitian, but into cleaned up SMS language, and our training corpus is a lot smaller, only 900 sentences.

Table 3 shows the results of using the cleaning model on training data and raw translation input. For the clean data using the cleaning model on the training data had very little effect on any of the metrics used. For the raw data translation results are improved as measured by NIST and Meteor when we use the filter on the devtest data, compared to using the raw devtest data. Using the filter on the training data gives worse results for non-filtered devtest data, but the overall best results are had by filtering both training and devtest data for raw translation input. Based on these experiments we used the cleaning model both on test and training data for raw input, but not at all for clean input, marked in bold in Table 3.

5 Spell Checking-based Replacement of Unknown Words

The SMS data is noisy, and there are often many spelling variations of the same word. One example is the word *airport*, which occur in the training corpus in at least six spelling variants: the correct *ayeropò*, and *aeoport, ayeopò, aeroport, aeyopòt,* and *aewopo*, and in the devtest in a seventh variant *ayéoport*. The non-standardized spelling means that many unknown words (out-of-vocabulary words, OOVs) have a known spelling variant in the training corpus. We thus decided to treat OOVs using a method inspired by spell-checking techniques, and applied an approximate string matching technique to OOVs in the translation input in order to change them into known spelling variants.

OOV replacement has been proposed by several researchers, replacing OOVs e.g. by morphological variants (Arora et al., 2008) or synonyms (Mirkin et al., 2009). Habash (2008) used several techniques for expanding OOVs in order to extend the phrase-table. Yang and Kirchhoff (2006) trained a morphologically based back-off model for OOVs. Bertoldi et al. (2010) created confusion networks as input of translation input with artificially created misspelled words, not specifically targetting OOVs, however. The work most similar to ours is DeNeefe et al. (2008), who also created lattices with spelling alternatives for OOVs, which did not improve translation results, however. Contrary to us, they only considered one edit per word, and did not weigh edits or lattice arcs.

Many standard spell checkers are based on the noisy channel model, which use an error (channel) model and a source model, which is normally modeled by a language model. The error model normally use some type of approximate string matching, such as Levenshtein distance (Levenshtein, 1966), which measures the distance between two strings as the number of insertions, deletions, and substitutions of characters. It is often normalized based on the length of the strings (Yujian and Bo, 2007), and the distance calculation has also been improved by associating different costs to individual error operations. Church and Gale (1991) used a large training corpus to assign probabilities to each unique error operation, and also conditioned operations on one consecutive character. Brill and Moore (2000) introduced a model that worked on character sequences, not only on character level, and was conditioned on where in the word the sequences occurred. They trained weights on a corpus of misspelled words with corrections.

Treating OOVs in the SMS corpus as a spell checking problem differs from a standard spell checking scenario in that the goal is not necessarily to change an incorrectly spelled word into a correct word, but rather to change a word that is not in our corpus into a spelling variant that we have seen in the corpus, but which might not necessarily be correctly spelled. It is also the case that many of the OOVs are not wrong, but just happen to be unseen; for instance there are many place names. Thus we must make sure that our algorithm for finding spelling equivalents is bi-directional, so that it cannot only change incorrect spellings into correct spellings, but also go the other way, which could be needed in some cases. We also need to try not to suggest alternatives for words that does not have any plausible alternatives in the corpus, such as unknown place names.

5.1 Approximate String Matching Algorithm

The approximate string matching algorithm we suggest is essentially that of Brill and Moore (2000), a modified weighted Levenshtein distance, where we allow error operations on character sequences as well as on single characters. We based our weight estimations on the automatically created list of lexical variants that was built as a step in building the cleaning model, described in section 4. This list is very noisy, but does also contain some true spelling equivalents. We implemented two versions of the algorithm, first a simple version which used manually identified error operations, then a more complex variant where error operations and weights were found automatically.

Manually Assigned Weights

We went through the lexicon list manually to identify edits that could correct the misspellings that occurred in the list. We identified substitutions limited to three characters in length, and at the beginning and end of words we also identified letter insertions and deletions. The inspection showed that it was very common for letters to be replaced by the same letter but with a diacritic, or with a different diacritic, for instance to vary between [*e, é, è*]. Another common operation was between a single character and two consecutive occurrences of the same character. Table 4 shows the 46 identified operations. To account for the fact that we do not want our error model to have a directionality from wrong to correct, we allow operations in both directions.

Since the operations were found manually we did not have a reliable way to estimate weights, and used uniform weights for all operations. The operations in Table 4 have the weights given in the table, substitution of a letter with a diacritic variant 0, single to double letters 0.1, insertions and deletions 1 and substitutions other than those in the table, 1.6.

Automatically Assigned Weights

To automatically train weights from the very noisy list of lexical variants, we filtered it by applying the edit distance with the manual weights described above to phrase pair that did not differ in length by more than three characters. We used a cut-off threshold of 2.8 for words where both versions had at least six characters, and 1 for shorter words. This gave us a list of 587 plausible spelling variants, from the original list with 1635 word pairs.

To find good character substitutions and assign weights to them, we used standard PBSMT techniques as implemented in Moses, but on character level, with the filtered list of word pairs as training data. We inserted spaces between each character of the words, and also added beginning and end of word markers, e.g., the word *problém* was tokenized as '*B p r o b l é m E*'. Thus we could train a PBSMT system that aligned characters using GIZA++, and extracted and scored phrases, which in this case

Type	Manual Instances	Manual Weight	Automatic Examples+weights	Automatic Count
mid 1-1	e-i, a-o, i-y, a-e, i-u, s-c, r-w, c-k, j-g, s-z, n-m	.2	n-m .90, e-c .74, j-g .62	12
mid 1-2	z-sz, i-iy, m-nm, n-nm, y-il, i-ye, s-rs, t-th, o-an, x-ks, x-kz, e-a,	.2	x-ks .35, i-ue .83, w-rr .74	107
mid 1-3	–	–	e-ait .75 e-eur .66	29
mid 2-2	wa-oi, we-oi, en-un, xs-ks	.2	we-oi .67, wo-ro .20, ie-ye .54	103
mid 2-3	wa-oir, ye-ier, an-ent, eo-eyo	.2	iv-eve .79, ey-eyi .18	160
mid 3-3	syo-tio, syo-tyo	.2	ant-ent .81, dyo,dia .67	116
beg 0-1	ϵ-h, ϵ-l	.2	ϵ-n .95, ϵ-m .90, ϵ-h .50	9
beg 0-2	–	–	ϵ-te .95, ϵ-pa .82	6
beg 1-1	h-l	.2	a-e .89, w-r .67 i-u .33	5
beg 1-2,3	–	–	e-ai .68, a-za .74 k-pak .48	30
beg 2,3-2,3	–	–	wo-ro 0, ex-ekz .65, ens-ins .17	58
end 0-1	ϵ-e, ϵ-t, ϵ-n, ϵ-m, ϵ-r, ϵ-y	.2	ϵ-r .57 ϵ-e .85, ϵ-v .75	12
end 0-2	ϵ-te, ϵ-de, ϵ-ue, ϵ-le	1	ϵ-de .93, ϵ-le .75	7
end 1-1	–	–	e-o .74, n-m .86	5
end 1-2,3	–	–	i-li .81, c-se .62 n-nne .66	48
end 2,3-2,3	–	–	sm-me .67, ns-nce .38, wen-oin .36	70

Table 4: Error operations at the *mid*dle, *beg*inning and *end* of words. For manually defined operations all instances are shown, with their uniform score. For automaticcally identified operations examples are shown with their score, and the total count of each operation type.

amounts to creating a phrase-table with character sequences. The phrase probabilities are given in both translation directions, $P(S|T)$ and $P(T|S)$. Since we do not want our scores to have any direction, we used the arithmetic mean of these two probabilities to calculate the score for the pair, which is calculated as $1 - ((P(S|T) + P(T|S))/2)$, to also convert the probabilities to costs. To compensate for errors made in the extraction process, we filtered out phrase pairs where both probabilities were lower than 0.1.

To get fair scores for character sequences of different lengths we applied the phrase table construction four times, while increasing the limit of the maximum phrase length from one to four. From the first phrase table, with maximum length 1, we extracted 1-1 substitutions, from the second table 1-2 and 2-2 substitutions, and so on. We used the beginning and end of word markers both to extract substitutions that were only used at the beginning or end of sentences, and to extract deletions and insertions used at the beginning and end of words. Again, we only allowed substitutions up to three characters in length. The fourth phrase-table, with phrases of length four, were only used to allow us to extract substitutions of length three at the beginning and end of words, since the markers count as tokens. Table 4 shows the types of transformations extracted, some examples of each with their score, and the count of each transformation. A total of 777 operations were found, compared to only 46 manual operations. There were few substitutions with diacritic variants, so again we allowed them with a zero cost. The costs for deletions, additions, and substitutions not given any weights were the same as before, 1, 1, and 1.6. For the edit distance with the automatic weights, we used scores that were normalized by the length of the shortest string.

Application to OOVs

We applied the edit distance operation on all OOVs longer than 3 characters, and calculated the distance to all words in the training corpora that did not differ in length with more than two characters. We used the standard dynamic programming implementation of our edit distance, but extended to check the scores not only in directly neighbouring cells, but in cells up to a distance of 3 away, to account for the maximum length of the character sequence substitutions. It would have been possible to use a fast trie imple-

System	Clean devtest Bleu	NIST	Meteor	Raw devtest Bleu	NIST	Meteor
No OOV treatment	29.90	5.764	52.88	26.24	5.362	51.64
Manual 1-best	29.76	5.721	52.91	26.60	5.417	52.17
Automatic 1-best	29.90	5.746	52.83	26.26	5.351	51.60
Manual lattice	30.53	5.957	54.06	27.12	5.574	53.27
Automatic lattice	30.94	5.982	54.62	27.27	5.554	52.99
Automatic lattice + LM	30.33	5.912	54.07	27.79	5.555	52.98

Table 5: Translation results, using the approximate string matching algorithm for OOVs. The submitted system is marked with bold.

mentation (Brill and Moore, 2000), however.

We performed both 1-best substitution of OOVs, and lattice decoding where we kept the three best alternatives for each word. In both cases we only replaced OOVs if the edit distance scores were below a threshold of 1.2 for the manual weights, which were not normalized, and for the normalized automatic weights below 0.25, or below 0.33 for word pairs where both words had at least 6 characters. These thresholds were set by inspecting the results, but resulted in a different number of substitutions:

- clean (total 691)
  - manual: 251
  - automatic: 222
- raw (total 932)
  - manual: 601
  - automatic: 437

The lattice arcs were weighted with the edit distance score, normalized to fall between 0-1. We also tried to include a source language model score in the weights in the lattice, to account for the source model that has been shown to be useful for spelling correction, but which has not been found useful for OOV replacement. We trained a 3-gram language model on the Haitian SMS text, and applied this model for a five-word context around the replaced OOV. We used a single lattice weight where half the score came from the edit distance, and the other half represented the language model component. A better approach though, would probably have been to use two weights.

5.2 Results

Table 5 shows the results of the OOV treatment. When using 1-best substitutions there are small differences compared to the baseline on both test sets, except for the system with manual weights on raw data, which was improved on all metrics. All three ways of applying the lattice substitutions led to large improvements on all metrics on both test sets. On the clean test set it was better to use automatic than manual weights when not using the language model score, which made the results worse. On the raw test set the highest Meteor and NIST scores were had by using manual weights, whereas the highest Bleu score was had by using automatic weights with the language model. The system submitted to the workshop is the system with a lattice with manual weights, marked in bold in Table 5, since the automatic weights were not ready in time for the submission.

6 Conclusion

In this article we presented methods for translating noisy Haitian Creole SMS messages, which we believe are generally suitable for small and noisy corpora and under-resourced languages. We used an automatically trained cleaning model, trained on only 900 manually cleaned sentences, that led to improvements for noisy translation input. Our main contribution was to apply methods inspired by spell checking to suggest known spelling variants of unknown words, which we presented as a lattice to the decoder. Several versions of this method gave consistent improvements over the baseline system. There are still many questions left about which configuration that is best for weighting and pruning the lattice, however, which we intend to investigate in future work. In this work we only considered OOVs in the translation input, but it would also be interesting to address misspelled words in the training corpus.

References

Karunesh Arora, Michael Paul, and Eiichiro Sumita. 2008. Translation of unknown words in phrase-based statistical machine translation for languages of rich morphology. In *Proceedings of the First International Workshop on Spoken Languages Technologies for Under-resourced languages (SLTU-2008)*, pages 70–75, Hanoi, Vietnam.

AiTi Aw, Min Zhang, Juan Xiao, and Jian Su. 2006. A phrase-based statistical model for SMS text normalization. In *Proceedings of the 21st International Conference on Computational Linguistics and 44th Annual Meeting of the ACL, poster session*, pages 33–40, Sydney, Australia.

Nicola Bertoldi, Mauro Cettolo, and Marcello Federico. 2010. Statistical machine translation of texts with misspelled words. In *Proceedings of Human Language Technologies: The 2010 Annual Conference of the NAACL*, pages 412–419, Los Angeles, California, USA.

Eric Brill and Robert C. Moore. 2000. An improved error model for noisy channel spelling correction. In *Proceedings of the 38th Annual Meeting of the ACL*, pages 286–293, Hong Kong.

Kenneth W. Church and William A. Gale. 1991. Probability scoring for spelling correction. *Statistics and Computing*, 1:93–103.

Steve DeNeefe, Ulf Hermjakob, and Kevin Knight. 2008. Overcoming vocabulary sparsity in MT using lattices. In *Proceedings of the 8th Conference of the Association for Machine Translation in the Americas*, pages 89–96, Waikiki, Hawaii, USA.

George Doddington. 2002. Automatic evaluation of machine translation quality using n-gram co-occurence statistics. In *Proceedings of the Second International Conference on Human Language Technology*, pages 228–231, San Diego, California, USA.

Nizar Habash. 2008. Four techniques for online handling of out-of-vocabulary words in Arabic-English statistical machine translation. In *Proceedings of the 46th Annual Meeting of the ACL: Human Language Technologies, Short papers*, pages 57–60, Columbus, Ohio, USA.

Kenneth Heafield. 2011. KenLM: Faster and smaller language model queries. In *Proceedings of the Sixth Workshop on Statistical Machine Translation*, Edinburgh, UK.

Philipp Koehn and Barry Haddow. 2009. Edinburgh's submission to all tracks of the WMT 2009 shared task with reordering and speed improvements to Moses. In *Proceedings of the Fourth Workshop on Statistical Machine Translation*, pages 160–164, Athens, Greece.

Philipp Koehn and Josh Schroeder. 2007. Experiments in domain adaptation for statistical machine translation. In *Proceedings of the Second Workshop on Statistical Machine Translation*, pages 224–227, Prague, Czech Republic, June.

Philipp Koehn, Amittai Axelrod, Alexandra Birch Mayne, Chris Callison-Burch, Miles Osborne, and David Talbot. 2005. Edinburgh system description for the 2005 IWSLT speech translation evaluation. In *Proceedings of the International Workshop on Spoken Language Translation*, Pittsburgh, Pennsylvania, USA.

Philipp Koehn, Hieu Hoang, Alexandra Birch, Chris Callison-Burch, Marcello Federico, Nicola Bertoldi, Brooke Cowan, Wade Shen, Christine Moran, Richard Zens, Chris Dyer, Ondrej Bojar, Alexandra Constantin, and Evan Herbst. 2007. Moses: Open source toolkit for statistical machine translation. In *Proceedings of the 45th Annual Meeting of the ACL, demonstration session*, pages 177–180, Prague, Czech Republic.

Alon Lavie and Abhaya Agarwal. 2007. METEOR: An automatic metric for MT evaluation with high levels of correlation with human judgments. In *Proceedings of the Second Workshop on Statistical Machine Translation*, pages 228–231, Prague, Czech Republic.

Vladimir Iosifovich Levenshtein. 1966. Binary codes capable of correcting deletions, insertions and reversals. *Soviet Physics Doklady*, 10(8):707–710.

Shachar Mirkin, Lucia Specia, Nicola Cancedda, Ido Dagan, Marc Dymetman, and Idan Szpektor. 2009. Source-language entailment modeling for translating unknown terms. In *Proceedings of the Joint Conference of the 47th Annual Meeting of the ACL and the 4th International Joint Conference on Natural Language Processing of the AFNLP*, pages 791–799, Suntec, Singapore.

Franz Josef Och and Hermann Ney. 2003. A systematic comparison of various statistical alignment models. *Computational Linguistics*, 29(1):19–51.

Franz Josef Och. 2003. Minimum error rate training in statistical machine translation. In *Proceedings of the 42nd Annual Meeting of the ACL*, pages 160–167, Sapporo, Japan.

Kishore Papineni, Salim Roukos, Todd Ward, and Wei-Jing Zhu. 2002. BLEU: A method for automatic evaluation of machine translation. In *Proceedings of the 40th Annual Meeting of the ACL*, pages 311–318, Philadelphia, Pennsylvania, USA.

Andreas Stolcke. 2002. SRILM – an extensible language modeling toolkit. In *Proceedings of the Seventh International Conference on Spoken Language Processing*, pages 901–904, Denver, Colorado, USA.

Mei Yang and Katrin Kirchhoff. 2006. Phrase-based backoff models for machine translation of highly inflected languages. In *Proceedings of the 11th Conference of the EACL*, pages 41–48, Trento Italy.

Li Yujian and Liu Bo. 2007. A normalized Levenshtein distance metric. *IEEE Transactions on Pattern Analysis and Machine Intelligence*, 29(6):1091–1095.

Joshua 3.0: Syntax-based Machine Translation with the Thrax Grammar Extractor

Jonathan Weese[1], **Juri Ganitkevitch**[1], **Chris Callison-Burch**[1], **Matt Post**[2] and **Adam Lopez**[1,2]
[1]Center for Language and Speech Processing
[2]Human Language Technology Center of Excellence
Johns Hopkins University

Abstract

We present progress on Joshua, an open-source decoder for hierarchical and syntax-based machine translation. The main focus is describing Thrax, a flexible, open source synchronous context-free grammar extractor. Thrax extracts both hierarchical (Chiang, 2007) and syntax-augmented machine translation (Zollmann and Venugopal, 2006) grammars. It is built on Apache Hadoop for efficient distributed performance, and can easily be extended with support for new grammars, feature functions, and output formats.

1 Introduction

Joshua is an open-source[1] toolkit for hierarchical machine translation of human languages. The original version of Joshua (Li et al., 2009) was a reimplementation of the Python-based Hiero machine-translation system (Chiang, 2007); it was later extended (Li et al., 2010) to support richer formalisms, such as SAMT (Zollmann and Venugopal, 2006).

The main focus of this paper is to describe this past year's work in developing *Thrax* (Weese, 2011), an open-source grammar extractor for Hiero and SAMT grammars. Grammar extraction has shown itself to be something of a black art, with decoding performance depending crucially on a variety of features and options that are not always clearly described in papers. This hindered direct comparison both between and within grammatical formalisms. Thrax standardizes Joshua's grammar extraction procedures by providing a flexible and configurable means of specifying these settings. Section 3 presents a systematic comparison of the two grammars using identical feature sets.

In addition, Joshua now includes a single parameterized script that implements the entire MT pipeline, from data preparation to evaluation. This script is built on top of a module called *CachePipe*. CachePipe is a simple wrapper around shell commands that uses SHA-1 hashes and explicitly-provided lists of dependencies to determine whether a command needs to be run, saving time both in running and debugging machine translation pipelines.

[1]`http://github.com/joshua-decoder/joshua`

2 Thrax: grammar extraction

In modern machine translation systems such as Joshua (Li et al., 2009) and cdec (Dyer et al., 2010), a translation model is represented as a synchronous context-free grammar (SCFG). Formally, an SCFG may be considered as a tuple

$$(N, S, T_\sigma, T_\tau, G)$$

where N is a set of nonterminal symbols of the grammar, $S \in N$ is the goal symbol, T_σ and T_τ are the source- and target-side terminal symbol vocabularies, respectively, and G is a set of *production rules* of the grammar.

Each rule in G is of the form

$$X \rightarrow \langle \alpha, \gamma, \sim \rangle$$

where $X \in N$ is a nonterminal symbol, α is a sequence of symbols from $N \cup T_\sigma$, γ is a sequence of

Proceedings of the 6th Workshop on Statistical Machine Translation, pages 478–484,
Edinburgh, Scotland, UK, July 30–31, 2011.

symbols from $N \cup T_\tau$, and $\sim$ is a one-to-one correspondence between the nonterminal symbols of α and γ.

The language of an SCFG is a set of ordered pairs of strings. During decoding, the set of candidate translations of an input sentence f is the set of all e such that the pair (f, e) is licensed by the translation model SCFG. Each candidate e is generated by applying a sequence of production rules $(r_1 \dots r_n)$. The cost of applying each rule is:

$$w(X \to \langle \alpha, \gamma \rangle) = \prod_i \phi_i(X \to \langle \alpha, \gamma \rangle)^{\lambda_i} \quad (1)$$

where each ϕ_i is a *feature function* and λ_i is the weight for ϕ_i. The total *translation model score* of a candidate e is the product of the rules used in its derivation. This translation model score is then combined with other features (such as a language model score) to produce an overall score for each candidate translation.

2.1 Hiero and SAMT

Throughout this work, we will reference two particular SCFG types known as Hiero and Syntax-Augmented Machine Translation (SAMT).

A Hiero grammar (Chiang, 2007) is an SCFG with only one type of nonterminal symbol, traditionally labeled X. A Hiero grammar can be extracted from a parallel corpus of word-aligned sentence pairs as follows: If (f_i^j, e_k^l) is a sub-phrase of the sentence pair, we say it is *consistent* with the pair's alignment if none of the words in f_i^j are aligned to words outside of e_k^l, and vice-versa. The consistent sub-phrase may be extracted as an SCFG rule. Furthermore, if a consistent phrase is contained within another one, a hierarchical rule may be extracted by replacing the smaller piece with a nonterminal.

An SAMT grammar (Zollmann and Venugopal, 2006) is similar to a Hiero grammar, except that the nonterminal symbol set is much larger, and its labels are derived from a parse tree over either the source or target side in the following manner. For each rule, if the target side is spanned by one constituent of the parse tree, we assign that constituent's label as the nonterminal symbol for the rule. Otherwise, we assign an extended category of the form $C_1 + C_2$, C_1/C_2, or $C_2 \backslash C_1$ — indicating that the target side spans two adjacent constituents, is a C_1 missing a C_2 to the right, or is a C_1 missing a C_2 on the left, respectively. Table 1 contains a list of Hiero and SAMT rules extracted from the training sentence pair in Figure 1.

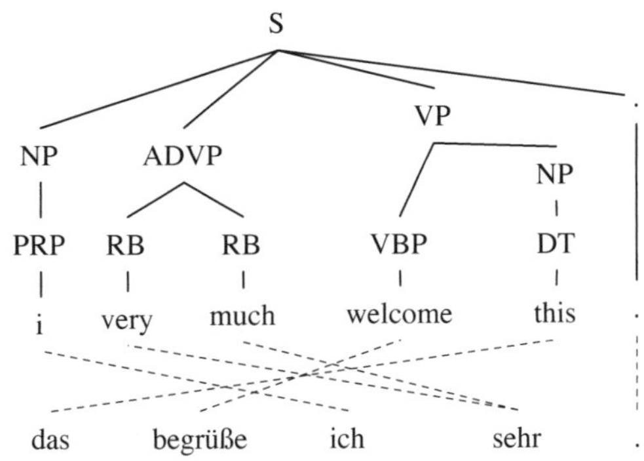

Figure 1: An aligned sentence pair.

2.2 System overview

The following were goals in the design of Thrax:

- the ability to extract different SCFGs (such as Hiero and SAMT), and to adjust various extraction parameters for the grammars;
- the ability to easily change and extend the feature sets for each rule
- scalability to arbitrarily large training corpora.

Thrax treats the grammar extraction and scoring as a series of dependent Hadoop jobs. Hadoop (Venugopal and Zollmann, 2009) is an implementation of Google's MapReduce (Dean and Ghemawat, 2004), a framework for distributed processing of large data sets. Hadoop jobs have two parts. In the *map* step, a set of key/value pairs is mapped to a set of intermediate key/value pairs. In the *reduce* step, all intermediate values associated with an intermediate key are merged.

The first step in the Thrax pipeline is to extract all the grammar rules. The map step in this job takes as input word-aligned sentence pairs and produces a set of ordered pairs (r, c) where r is a rule and c is the number of times it was extracted. During the reduce step, these rule counts are summed, so the result is a set of rules, along with the total number of times each rule was extracted from the entire corpus.

Span	Hiero	SAMT
$[1,3]$	$X \rightarrow \langle$sehr, very much$\rangle$	$ADVP \rightarrow \langle$sehr, very much$\rangle$
$[0,3]$	$X \rightarrow \langle X$ sehr, X very much$\rangle$	$PRP + ADVP \rightarrow \langle PRP$ sehr, PRP very much$\rangle$
$[3,4]$	$X \rightarrow \langle$begrüße, welcome$\rangle$	$VBP \rightarrow \langle$begrüße, welcome$\rangle$
$[0,6]$	$X \rightarrow \langle X$ ich sehr ., i very much X .$\rangle$	$S \rightarrow \langle VP$ ich sehr ., i very much VP .$\rangle$
$[0,6]$	$X \rightarrow \langle X$., X .$\rangle$	$S \rightarrow \langle S/.$., $S/.$.$\rangle$

Table 1: A subset of the Hiero and SAMT rules extracted from the sentence pair of Figure 1.

Given the rules and their counts, a separate Hadoop job is run for each feature. These jobs can all be submitted at once and run in parallel, avoiding the linear sort-and-score workflow. The output from each feature job is the same set of pairs (r, c) as the input, except each rule r has been annotated with some feature score f.

After the feature jobs have been completed, we have several copies of the grammar, each of which has been scored with one feature. A final Hadoop job combines all these scores to produce the final grammar.

Some users may not have access to a Hadoop cluster. Thrax can be run in standalone or pseudo-distributed mode on a single machine. It can also be used with Amazon Elastic MapReduce,[2] a web service that provides computation time on a Hadoop cluster on-demand.

2.3 Extraction

The first step in the Thrax workflow is the extraction of grammar rules from an input corpus. As mentioned above, Hiero and SAMT grammars both require a parallel corpus with word-level alignments. SAMT additionally requires that the target side of the corpus be parsed.

There are several parameters that can make a significant difference in a grammar's overall translation performance. Each of these parameters is easily adjustable in Thrax by changing its value in a configuration file.

- maximum rule span
- maximum span of consistent phrase pairs
- maximum number of nonterminals
- minimum number of aligned terminals in rule
- whether to allow adjacent nonterminals on source side
- whether to allow unaligned words at the edges of consistent phrase pairs

[2]http://aws.amazon.com/elasticmapreduce/

Chiang (2007) gives reasonable heuristic choices for these parameters when extracting a Hiero grammar, and Lopez (2008) confirms some of them (maximum rule span of 10, maximum number of source-side symbols at 5, and maximum number of nonterminals at 2 per rule). **?**) provided comparisons among phrase-based, hierarchical, and syntax-based models, but did not report extensive experimentation with the model parameterizations.

When extracting Hiero- or SAMT-style grammars, the first Hadoop job in the Thrax workflow takes in a parallel corpus and produces a set of rules. But in fact Thrax's extraction mechanism is more general than that; all it requires is a function that maps a string to a set of rules. This makes it easy to implement new grammars and extract them using Thrax.

2.4 Feature functions

Thrax considers feature functions of two types: first, there are features that can be calculated by looking at each rule in isolation. Such features do not require a Hadoop job to calculate their scores, since we may inspect the rules in any order. (In practice, we calculate the scores at the very last moment before outputting the final grammar.) We call these features *simple features*. Thrax implements the following simple features:

- a binary indicator functions denoting:
  - whether the rule is purely abstract (i.e., has no terminal symbols)

- the rule is purely lexical (i.e., has no nonterminals)
- the rule is monotonic or has reordering
- the rule has adjacent nonterminals on the source side

- counters for
  - the number of unaligned words in the rule
  - the number of terminals on the target side of the rule

- a constant phrase penalty

In addition to simple features, Thrax also implements *map-reduce features*. These are features that require comparing rules in a certain order. Thrax uses Hadoop to sort the rules efficiently and calculate these feature functions. Thrax implements the following map-reduce features:

- Phrasal translation probabilities $p(\alpha|\gamma)$ and $p(\gamma|\alpha)$, calculated with relative frequency:

$$p(\alpha|\gamma) = \frac{C(\alpha, \gamma)}{C(\gamma)} \tag{2}$$

(and vice versa), where $C(\cdot)$ is the number of times a given event was extracted.

- Lexical weighting $p_{lex}(\alpha|\gamma, A)$ and $p_{lex}(\gamma|\alpha, A)$. We calculate these weights as given in (Koehn et al., 2003): let A be the alignment between α and γ, so $(i, j) \in A$ if and only if the ith word of α is aligned to the jth word of γ. Then we can define $p_{lex}(\gamma|\alpha)$ as

$$\prod_{i=1}^{n} \frac{1}{|\{j : (i, j) \in A\}|} \sum_{(i,j)\in A} w(\gamma_j|\alpha_i) \tag{3}$$

where α_i is the ith word of α, γ_j is the jth word of γ, and $w(y|x)$ is the relative frequency of seeing word y given x.

- Rarity penalty, given by

$$\exp(1 - C(X \rightarrow \langle\alpha, \gamma\rangle)) \tag{4}$$

where again $C(\cdot)$ is a count of the number of times the rule was extracted.

The above features are all implemented and can be turned on or off with a keyword in the Thrax configuration file.

It is easy to extend Thrax with new feature functions. For simple features, all that is needed is to implement Thrax's SIMPLEFEATURE interface defining a method that takes in a rule and calculates a feature score. Map-reduce features are slightly more complex: to subclass MAPREDUCEFEATURE, one must define a mapper and reducer, but also a sort comparator to determine in what order the rules are compared during the reduce step.

2.5 Related work

Joshua includes a simple Hiero extractor (Schwartz and Callison-Burch, 2010). The extractor runs as a single Java process, which makes it difficult to extract larger grammars, since the host machine must have enough memory to hold all of the rules at once. Joshua's extractor scores each rule with three feature functions — lexical probabilities in two directions, and one phrasal probability score $p(\gamma|\alpha)$.

The SAMT implementation of Zollmann and Venugopal (2006) includes a several-thousand-line Perl script to extract their rules. In addition to phrasal and lexical probabilities, this extractor implements several other features that are also described in section 2.4.

Finally, the cdec decoder (Dyer et al., 2010) includes a grammar extractor that performs well only when all rules can be held in memory.

Memory usage is a limitation of both the Joshua and cdec extractors. Translation models can be very large, and many feature scores require accumulation of statistical data from the entire set of extracted rules. Since it is impractical to keep the entire grammar in memory, rules are usually sorted on disk and then read sequentially. Different feature calculations may require different sort orders, leading to a linear workflow that alternates between sorting the grammar and calculating a feature score. To calculate more feature scores, more sorts have to be performed. This discourages the implementation of new features. For example, Joshua's built-in rule extractor calculates the phrasal probability $p(\gamma|\alpha)$ for each rule but, to save time, does not calculate its obvious counterpart $p(\alpha|\gamma)$, which would require another sort.

Language pair	sentences (K)	words (M)
cs–en	332	4.7
de–en	279	5.5
en–cs	487	6.9
en–de	359	7.2
en–fr	682	12.5
fr–en	792	14.4

Table 2: Training data size after subsampling.

pair	hiero	SAMT	improvement
cz-en	21.1	21.7	+0.6
en-cz	16.8	16.9	+0.1
de-en	18.9	19.5	+0.6
en-de	14.3	14.9	+0.6
fr-en	28.0	-	-
en-fr	30.4	-	-

Table 3: Single-reference BLEU-4 scores.

The SAMT extractor does not have a problem with large data sets; SAMT can run on Hadoop, as Thrax does.

The Joshua and cdec extractors only extract Hiero grammars, and Zollmann and Venugopal's extractor can only extract SAMT-style grammars. They are not designed to score arbitrary feature sets, either. Since variation in translation models and feature sets can have a significant effect on translation performance, we have developed Thrax in order to make it easy to build and test new models.

3 Experiments

We built systems for six language pairs for the WMT 2011 shared task: cz-en, en-cz, de-en, en-de, fr-en, and en-fr.[3] For each language pair, we built both SAMT and hiero grammars.[4] Table 3 contains the results on the complete WMT 2011 test set.

To train the translation models, we used the provided Europarl and news commentary data. For cz-en and en-cz, we also used sections of the CzEng parallel corpus (Bojar and Žabokrtský, 2009). The parallel data was subsampled using Joshua's built-in subsampler to select sentences with n-grams relevant to the tuning and test set. We used SRILM to train a 5-gram language model with Kneser-Ney smoothing using the appropriate side of the parallel data. For the English LM, we also used English Gigaword Fourth Edition.[5]

Before extracting an SCFG with Thrax, we used the provided Perl scripts to tokenize and normalize the data. We also removed any sentences longer than 50 tokens (after tokenization). For SAMT grammar extraction, we parsed the English training data using the Berkeley Parser (Petrov et al., 2006) with the provided Treebank-trained grammar.

We tuned the model weights against the WMT08 test set (`news-test2008`) using Z-MERT (Zaidan, 2009), an implementation of minimum error-rate training included with Joshua. We decoded the test set to produce a 300-best list of unique translations, then chose the best candidate for each sentence using Minimum Bayes Risk reranking (Kumar and Byrne, 2004). Figure 2 shows an example derivation with an SAMT grammar. To re-case the 1-best test set output, we trained a true-case 5-gram language model using the same LM training data as before, and used an SCFG translation model to translate from the lowercased to true-case output. The translation model used rules limited to five tokens in length, and contained no hierarchical rules.

4 CachePipe: Cached pipeline runs

Machine translation pipelines involve the specification and execution of many different datasets, training procedures, and pre- and post-processing techniques that can have large effects on translation outcome, and which make direct comparisons between systems difficult. The complexity of managing these pipelines and experimental environments has led to a number of different experimental management systems, such as Experiment.perl,[6] Joshua 2.0's Makefile system (Li et al., 2010), and LoonyBin (Clark and Lavie, 2010). In addition to managing the pipeline, these scripts employ different techniques to avoid expensive recomputation by caching steps.

[3] fr=French, cz=Czech, de=German, en=English.

[4] Except for fr-en and en-fr. We were unable to decode with SAMT grammars for these language pairs due to their large size. We have since resolved this issue and will have scores for the final version of the paper.

[5] LDC2009T13

[6] `http://www.statmt.org/moses/?n=FactoredTraining.EMS`

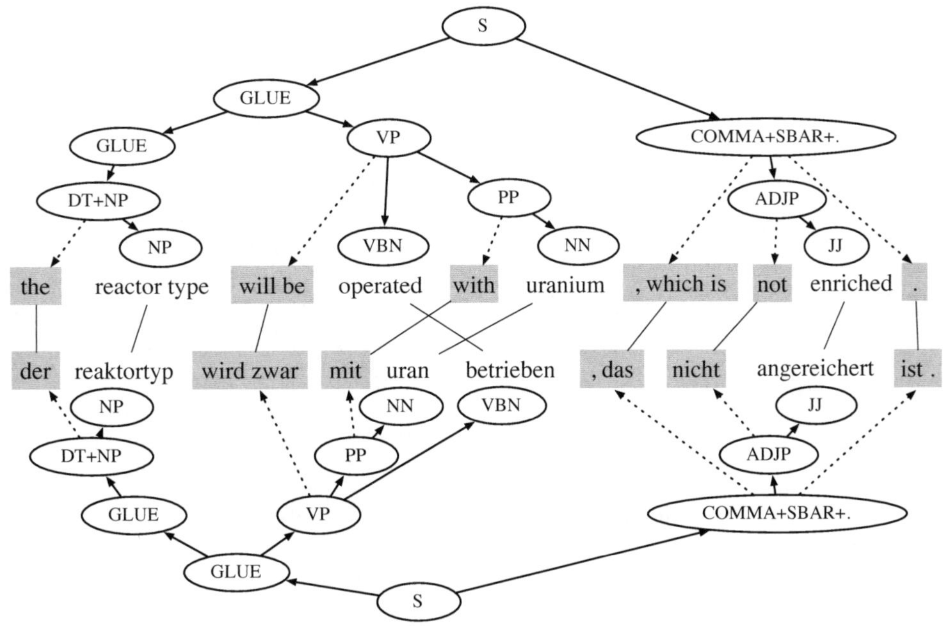

Figure 2: An SAMT derivation. The shaded terminal symbols are the lexicalized part of a rule with terminals and non-terminals. The unshaded terminals are directly dominated by a nonterminal symbol.

However, these approaches are based on simple but unreliable heuristics (such as timestamps or file existence) to make the caching determination.

Our solution to the caching dependency problem is CachePipe. CachePipe is designed with the following goals: (1) robust content-based dependency checking and (2) ease of use, including minimal editing of existing scripts. CachePipe is essentially a wrapper around command invocations. Presented with a command to run and a list of file dependencies, it computes SHA-1 hashes of the dependencies and of the command invocation and stores them; the command is executed only if any of those hashes are different from previous runs. A basic invocation involves specifying (1) a name or identifier associated with the command or step, (2) the command to run, and (3) a list of file dependencies. For example, to copy file `a` to `b` from a shell prompt, the following command could be used:

```
cachecmd copy "cp a b" a b
```

The first time the command is run, the file would be copied; afterwards, the command would be skipped after CachePipe verified that the contents of the dependencies `a` and `b` had not changed.

CachePipe is open-source software, distributed with Joshua or available separately.[7] It currently provides both a shell script interface and a programmatic API for Perl. It accepts a number of other arguments and dependency types. It also serves as the foundation of a new script in Joshua 3.0 that implements the complete Joshua pipeline, from data preparation to evaluation.

5 Future work

Thrax is currently limited to SCFG-based translation models. A natural development would be to extract GHKM grammars (Galley et al., 2004) or more recent tree-to-tree models (Zhang et al., 2008; Liu et al., 2009; Chiang, 2010). We also hope that Thrax will continue to be extended with more feature functions as researchers develop and contribute them.

Acknowledgements

This research was supported by in part by the EuroMatrixPlus project funded by the European Commission (7th Framework Programme), and by the NSF under grant IIS-0713448. Opinions, interpretations, and conclusions are the authors' alone.

[7] `https://github.com/joshua-decoder/cachepipe`

References

Ondřej Bojar and Zdeněk Žabokrtský. 2009. CzEng0.9: Large Parallel Treebank with Rich Annotation. *Prague Bulletin of Mathematical Linguistics*, 92. in print.

David Chiang. 2007. Hierarchical phrase-based translation. *Computational Linguistics*, 33(2):201–228.

David Chiang. 2010. Learning to translate with source and target syntax. In *Proc. ACL*, Uppsala, Sweden, July.

Jonathan H. Clark and Alon Lavie. 2010. Loonybin: Keeping language technologists sane through automated management of experimental (hyper) workflows. In *Proc. LREC*.

Jeffrey Dean and Sanjay Ghemawat. 2004. Mapreduce: Simplified data processing on large clusters. In *OSDI*.

Chris Dyer, Adam Lopez, Juri Ganitkevitch, Jonathan Weese, Ferhan Ture, Phil Blunsom, Hendra Setiawan, Vladimir Eidelman, and Philip Resnik. 2010. cdec: A decoder, alignment, and learning framework for finite-state and context-free translation models. In *Proc. ACL 2010 System Demonstrations*, pages 7–12.

Michel Galley, Mark Hopkins, Kevin Knight, and Daniel Marcu. 2004. What's in a translation rule? In *Proc. NAACL*, Boston, Massachusetts, USA, May.

Philipp Koehn, Franz Josef Och, and Daniel Marcu. 2003. Statistical phrase-based translation. In *Proc. NAACL*, Morristown, NJ, USA.

Shankar Kumar and William Byrne. 2004. Minimum bayes-risk decoding for statistical machine translation. In *Proc. NAACL*, Boston, Massachusetts, USA, May.

Zhifei Li, Chris Callison-Burch, Chris Dyer, Juri Ganitkevitch, Sanjeev Khudanpur, Lane Schwartz, Wren Thornton, Jonathan Weese, and Omar Zaidan. 2009. Joshua: An open source toolkit for parsing-based machine translation. In *Proc. WMT*, Athens, Greece, March.

Zhifei Li, Chris Callison-Burch, Chris Dyer, Juri Ganitkevitch, Ann Irvine, Sanjeev Khudanpur, Lane Schwartz, Wren N.G. Thornton, Ziyuan Wang, Jonathan Weese, and Omar F. Zaidan. 2010. Joshua 2.0: a toolkit for parsing-based machine translation with syntax, semirings, discriminative training and other goodies. In *Proc. WMT*.

Yang Liu, Yajuan Lü, and Qun Liu. 2009. Improving tree-to-tree translation with packed forests. In *Proc. ACL*, Suntec, Singapore, August.

Adam Lopez. 2008. Tera-scale translation models via pattern matching. In *Proc. COLING*, Manchester, UK, August.

Slav Petrov, Leon Barrett, Romain Thibaux, and Dan Klein. 2006. Learning accurate, compact, and interpretable tree annotation. In *Proc. ACL*, Sydney, Australia, July.

Lane Schwartz and Chris Callison-Burch. 2010. Hierarchical phrase-based grammar extraction in joshua: Suffix arrays and prefix trees. *The Prague Bulletin of Mathematical Linguistics*, 93:157–166, January.

Mark Steedman. 1999. Alternating quantifier scope in ccg. In *Proc. ACL*, Stroudsburg, PA, USA.

Ashish Venugopal and Andreas Zollmann. 2009. Grammar based statistical MT on Hadoop: An end-to-end toolkit for large scale PSCFG based MT. *The Prague Bulletin of Mathematical Linguistics*, 91:67–78.

Jonathan Weese. 2011. A systematic comparison of synchronous context-free grammars for machine translation. Master's thesis, Johns Hopkins University, May.

Omar F. Zaidan. 2009. Z-MERT: A fully configurable open source tool for minimum error rate training of machine translation systems. *The Prague Bulletin of Mathematical Linguistics*, 91:79–88.

Min Zhang, Hongfei Jiang, Aiti Aw, Haizhou Li, Chew Lim Tan, and Sheng Li. 2008. A tree sequence alignment-based tree-to-tree translation model. In *Proc. ACL*, Columbus, Ohio, June.

Andreas Zollmann and Ashish Venugopal. 2006. Syntax augmented machine translation via chart parsing. In *Proc. NAACL Workshop on Statistcal Machine Translation*, New York, New York.

DFKI Hybrid Machine Translation System for WMT 2011 - On the Integration of SMT and RBMT

Jia Xu and Hans Uszkoreit and Casey Kennington and David Vilar and Xiaojun Zhang
DFKI GmbH, Language Technology Lab
Stuhlsatzenhausweg 3
D-66123 Saarbrücken Germany
{Jia.Xu,uszkoreit,David.Vilar}@dfki.de, {bakuzen,xiaojun.zhang.iiken}@gmail.com

Abstract

We present the DFKI hybrid translation system at the WMT workshop 2011. Three SMT and two RBMT systems are combined at the level of the final translation output. The translation results show that our hybrid system significantly outperformed individual systems by exploring strengths of both rule-based and statistical translations.

1 Introduction

Machine translation (MT), in particular the statistical approach to it, has undergone incremental improvements in recent years. While rule-based machine translation (RBMT) maintains competitiveness in human evaluations. Combining the advantages of both approaches have been investigated by many researchers such as (Eisele et al., 2008). Nonetheless, significant improvements over statistical approaches still remain to be shown. In this paper, we present the DFKI hybrid system in the WMT workshop 2011. Our system is different from the system of the last year (Federmann et al., 2010), which is based on the shallow phrase substitution. In this work, two rule-based translation systems are applied. In addition, three statistical machine translation systems are built, including a phrase-based, a hierarchical phrase-based and a syntax-based system. Instead of combining with rules or post-editing, we perform system combination on the final translation hypotheses. We applied the CMU open toolkit (Heafield and Lavie, 2010) among numerous combination methods such as (Matusov, 2009), (Sim et al., 2007) and (He et al., 2008). The final translation output outperforms each individual output significantly.

2 Individual translation systems

2.1 Phrase-based system

We use the IBM model 1 and 4 (Brown et al., 1993) and Hidden-Markov model (HMM) (Vogel et al., 1996) to train the word alignment using the mgiza toolkit[1]. We applied the EMS in Moses (Koehn et al., 2007) to build up the phrase-based translation system. Features in the log-linear model include translation models in two directions, a language model, a distortion model and a sentence length penalty. A dynamic programming beam search algorithm is used to generate the translation hypothesis with maximum probability. We applied a 5-gram mixture language model with each sub-model trained on one fifth of the monolingual corpus with Kneser-Ney smoothing using SRILM toolkit (Stolcke, 2002). We did not perform any tuning, because it hurts the evaluation performance in our experiments.

2.2 Syntax-based system

To capture the syntactic structure, we also built a tree-based system using the same configuration of EMS in Moses (Koehn et al., 2007). Tree-based models operate on so-called grammar rules, which include variables in the mapping rules. To increase the diversity of models in combination, the language model in each individual translation system is trained differently. For the tree-based system, we applied a 4-gram language model with Kneser-Ney smoothing using SRILM toolkit (Stolcke, 2002) trained on the whole monolingual corpus. The test2007 news part is applied to tune the feature weights using mert, because the tuning on test2007

[1]http://geek.kyloo.net/software/doku.php/mgiza:overview

Proceedings of the 6th Workshop on Statistical Machine Translation, pages 485–489,
Edinburgh, Scotland, UK, July 30–31, 2011. ©2011 Association for Computational Linguistics

improves the translation performance more than the tuning on test2008 in a small-scale experiment for the tree-based system.

2.3 Hierarchical phrase-based system

For the hierarchical system, we used the open source hierarchical phrased-based system Jane, developed at RWTH and free for non-commercial use (Vilar et al., 2010). This approach is an extension of the phrase-based approach, where the phrases are allowed to have gaps (Chiang, 2007). In this way long-range dependencies and reorderings can be modeled in a consistent statistical framework.

The system uses a fairly standard setup, trained using the bilingual data provided by the organizers, word aligned using the mgiza. Two 5-gram language models were used during decoding: one trained on the monolingual part of the bilingual training data, and a larger one trained on the additional news data. Decoding was carried out using the cube pruning algorithm. The tuning is performed on test2008 without further experiments.

2.4 Rule-based systems

We applied two rule-based translation systems, the Lucy system (Lucy, 2011) and the Linguatec system (Aleksić and Thurmair, 2011). The Lucy system is a recent offspring of METAL. The Linguatec system is a modular system consisting of grammar, lexicon and morphological analyzers based on logic programming using slot grammar.

3 Hybrid translation

A hybrid approach combining rule-based and statistical machine translation is usually investigated with an in-box integration, such as multi-way translation (Eisele et al., 2008), post-editing (Ueffing et al., 2008) or noun phrase substitution (Federmann et al., 2010). However, significant improvements over state-of-the-art statistical machine translation are still expected. In the meanwhile system combination methods for instance described in (Matusov, 2009), (Sim et al., 2007) and (He et al., 2008) are mostly evaluated to combine statistical translation systems, rule-based systems are not considered. In this work, we integrate the rule-based and statistical machine translation system on the level of the final translation hypothesis and treat the rule-based system anonymously as an individual system. In this way an black-box integration is allowed using the current system combination techniques.

We applied the CMU open toolkit (Heafield and Lavie, 2010) MEMT, a package by Kenneth Heafield to combine the translation hypotheses. The language model is trained on the target side of the parallel training corpus using SRILM (Stolcke, 2002). We used only the Europarl part to train language models for tuning and all target side of parallel data to train language models for decoding. The beam size is set to 80, and 300 nbest is considered.

	PBT	Syntax
PBT-2010	18.32	
Max80words	20.65	21.10
Max100words	20.78	
+Compound	21.52	22.13
+Newparallel	21.77	

Table 1: Translation performance BLEU[%] on phrase/syntax-based system using various settings evaluated on test10.

4 Translation experiments

4.1 MT Setup

The parallel training corpus consists of 1.8 million German-English parallel sentences from Europarl-v6 (Koehn, MT Summit 2005) and news-commentary with 48 million tokenized German words and 54 million tokenized English words respectively. The monolingual training corpus contains the target side of the parallel training corpus and the additional monolingual language model training data downloaded from (SMT, 2011). We did not apply the large-scale Gigaword corpus, because it does not significantly reduce the perplexity of our language model but raises the computational requirement heavily.

4.2 Single systems

For each individual translation system, different configurations are experimented to achieve a higher translation quality. We take phrase- and syntax-based translation system as examples. Table 1 presents official submission result on DE-EN by

PBT+Syntax	20.37
PBT+Syntax+HPBT	20.78
PBT+HPBT+Linguatec+Lucy	20.27
PBT+Syntax+HPBT+Linguatec+Lucy	20.81

Table 2: Translation performance BLEU[%] on test2011 using hybrid system tuned on test10 with various settings (DE-EN).

DFKI in 2010. In 2010's translation system only Europarl parallel corpus was applied, and the translation output was evaluated as 18.32% in the BLEU score. In 2011, we added the News Commentary parallel corpus and trained the language model on all monolingual data provided by (SMT, 2011) except for Gigaword. As shown in Table 1, if we increase the maximum sentence length of the training corpus from 80 to 100, the BLEU score increases from 20.65% to 20.78%. In the error analysis, we found that many OOVs come from the compound words in German. Therefore, we applied the compound splitting for both German and English by activating the corrensponding settings in the EMS in Moses. This leads to a further improvement of nearly 1% in the BLEU score. As we add the new parallel corpus provided on the homepage of SMT workshop in 2011 (SMT, 2011) to the corpus in 2010, a slight improvement can be achieved. Within one year, the score for the DFKI PBT system DE-EN has improved by nearly 3.5% absolute and 20% relative BLEU score points, as shown in Table 1.

In the phrase-based translation, the tuning was not applied, because it improves the results on the held-out data but hurts the results on the evaluation set. In our observation, the decrease is in the range of 0.01% to 1% in the BLEU score. However tuning does help for the Tree-based system. Therefore we applied the test2007 to optimize the parameters, which enhanced the BLEU score from 17.52% to 21.10%. The compound splitting also improves the syntax system, with about 1% in the BLEU score. We did not add the new parallel corpus into the training for syntax system due to its larger computational requirement than that of the phrase-based system.

	Test10	Test08	Test11
Hybrid-2010	17.43		
PBT	21.77	20.70	20.40
Syntax	22.13	20.50	20.49
HPBT	19.21	18.26	17.06
Linguatec	16.59	16.07	15.97
Lucy	16.57	16.66	16.68
Hybrid-2011	23.88	21.13	21.25

Table 3: Translation performance BLEU[%] on three test sets using different translation systems in 2011 submission (DE-EN).

	Test10	Test11
Hybrid-2010	14.42	
PBT	15.46	14.05
Linguatec	14.92	12.92
Lucy	13.77	13.0
Hybrid-2011	15.55	15.83

Table 4: Translation performance BLEU[%] on two test sets using different translation systems in 2011 submission (EN-DE).

4.3 Hybrid system

We applied test10 as the held-out data to tune the German-English and English-German translation systems. For experiments, we applied a small-scaled 4-gram language model trained only on the target side of the Europarl parallel training data. As shown in Table 2, different combinations are performed on the hypotheses generated from single systems. We first combined the PBT with syntax system, then together with the HPBT system. The translation result in the BLEU score performs best when we combine all three statistical machine translation systems and two rule-based systems together.

4.4 Evaluation results

For the decoding during the WMT evaluation, we applied a larger 4-gram language model trained on the target side of all parallel training corpus. As shown in Table 3, in last year's evaluation the DFKI hybrid translation result was evaluated as 17.34% in the BLEU score. In 2011, among all the translation systems, the syntax system performs the best on test10 and test11, while the PBT performs the

SRC	Diese Verordnung wurde vom Gesundheitsministerium in diesem Jahr einigermassen gemildert - die Kühlschrankpflicht fiel weg.
REF	It was mitigated by the Ministry of Health this year - the obligation to have a refrigerator has been removed.
PBT	This regulation by the Ministry of Health in this year - somewhat mitigated the fridge duty fell away.
Syntax	This regulation was somewhat mitigated by the Ministry of Health this year - the refrigerator duty fell away.
HPBT	This regulation was by the Ministry of Health in reasonably Dokvadze this year - the Kühlschrankpflicht fell away.
Linguatec	This ordinance was soothed to some extent by the brazilian ministry of health this year, the refrigerator duty was discontinued.
Lucy	This regulation was quite moderated by the Department of Health, Education and Welfare this year - the refrigerator duty was omitted.
Hybrid	This regulation was somewhat mitigated by the Ministry of Health this year - the fridge duty fell away.
SRC	Die Deregulierung und Bakalas ehemalige Bergarbeiterwohnungen sind ein brisantes Thema.
REF	Deregulation and Bakala 's former mining flats are local hot topic.
PBT	The deregulation and Bakalas former miners' homes are a sensitive issue.
Syntax	The deregulation and Bakalas former miners' homes are a sensitive issue.
HPBT	The deregulation and Bakalas former Bergarbeiterwohnungen are a hot topic.
Linguatec	Former miner flats are an explosive topic the deregulation and Bakalas.
HPBT	The deregulation and Bakalas former miner apartments are an explosive topic.
Hybrid	The deregulation and Bakalas former miners' apartments are a sensitive issue.

Table 5: Examples of translation output by the different systems.

best on test08. The rule-based sytems, Linguatec and Lucy are expected to have a higher score in the human evaluation than in the automatic evaluation. Furthermore, as we can see from Table 3, there is still room to improve the Jane system, with better modeling, configurations or even higher-order language model. Using the hybrid system we successfully improved the translation result to 23.88% on test10. The hybrid system outperforms the best single system by 0.43% and 0.76% in the BLEU score on the test08 and test11, respectively.

For the translation from English to German, the translation result of last year's submission was evaluated as 14.42% in the BLEU score, as shown in Table 4. In this year, the phrase-based translation result is 15.46% in the BLEU score. We only set up one statistical translation system due to time limitation. With the respect of the BLEU score, phrase-based translation outperforms rule-based translations. Between rule-based translation systems, Linguatec performs better on the test10 (14.92%) and Lucy performs better on the test11 (13.0%). Combining three translation hypotheses leads to a smaller improvement (from 15.46% to 15.55%) on the test10 and a greater improvement (from 14.05% to 15.83%) on the test11 in the BLEU score over the single best translation system. Comparing to last year's translation output, the improvement is over one percent absolutely (from 14.42% to 15.55%) in the BLEU score on the test10.

4.5 Output examples

Table 5 shows two translation examples from the MT output of the test2011. We list the source sentence in German and its reference translation as well as the translation results generated by different translation systems. As can be seen from Table 5, the translation quality of source sentences is greatly improved using the hybrid system over the single individual systems. Translations of words and word orderings are more appropriate by the hybrid system.

5 Conclusion and future work

We presented the DFKI hybrid translation system submitted in the WMT workshop 2011. The hybrid translation is performed on the final translation output by individual systems, including a phrase-based system, a syntax-based system, a hierarchical phrase-based system and two rule-based systems. Combining the results from statistical and rule-based systems significantly improved the translation performance over the single-best system, which is shown by the automatic evaluation scores and the output examples. Despite of the encouraging results, there is still room to improve our system, such as the tuning in the phrase-based translation and a better language model in the combination.

References

Vera Aleksić and Gregor Thurmair. 2011. Personal translator at wmt2011 - a rule-based mt system with hybrid components. In *Proceedings of WMT workshop*.

Peter F. Brown, Stephen A. Della Pietra, Vincent J. Della Pietra, and R. L. Mercer. 1993. The mathematics of statistical machine translation: Parameter estimation. *Computational Linguistics*, 19(2):263–311, June.

David Chiang. 2007. Hierarchical phrase-based translation. *Computational Linguistics*, 33(2):201–228, June.

Andreas Eisele, Christian Federmann, Hans Uszkoreit, Hervé Saint-Amand, Martin Kay, Michael Jellinghaus, Sabine Hunsicker, Teresa Herrmann, and Yu Chen. 2008. Hybrid architectures for multi-engine machine translation. In *Proceedings of Translating and the Computer 30*, pages ASLIB, ASLIB/IMI, London, United Kingdom, November.

Christian Federmann, Andreas Eisele, Hans Uszkoreit, Yu Chen, Sabine Hunsicker, and Jia Xu. 2010. Further experiments with shallow hybrid mt systems. In *Proceedings of the Joint Fifth Workshop on Statistical Machine Translation and MetricsMATR*, pages 237–248, Uppsala, Sweden. John Benjamins.

Xiaodong He, Mei Yang, Jianfeng Gao, Patrick Nguyen, and Robert Moore. 2008. Indirect-hmm-based hypothesis alignment for combining outputs from machine translation systems. In *Proceedings of EMNLP*, October.

Kenneth Heafield and Alon Lavie. 2010. Voting on n-grams for machine translation system combination. In *Proc. Ninth Conference of the Association for Machine Translation in the Americas*, Denver, Colorado, October.

Philipp Koehn, Hieu Hoang, Alexandra Birch, Chris Callison-Burch, Marcello Federico, Nicola Bertoldi, Brooke Cowan, Wade Shen, Christine Moran, Richard Zens, Chris Dyer, Ondrej Bojar, Alexandra Constantin, and Evan Herbst. 2007. Moses: Open source toolkit for statistical machine translation. In *Proceedings of ACL*.

Philipp Koehn. MT Summit 2005. Europarl: A parallel corpus for statistical machine translation.

Lucy. 2011. Home page of software lucy and services. `http://www.lucysoftware.com`.

Evgeny Matusov. 2009. *Combining Natural Language Processing Systems to Improve Machine Translation of Speech*. Ph.D. thesis, Department of Electrical and Computer Engineering, Johns Hopkins University, Baltimore, MD.

K. C. Sim, W. J. Byrne, M. J. F. Gales, H. Sahbi, and P. C. Woodland. 2007. Consensus network decoding for statistical machine translation system combination. In *IN IEEE INT. CONF. ON ACOUSTICS, SPEECH, AND SIGNAL PROCESSING*.

SMT. 2011. Sixth workshop on statistical machine translation home page. http://www.statmt.org/wmt11/.

Andreas Stolcke. 2002. SRILM - an extensible language modeling toolkit. In *Proceedings of the International Conference On Spoken Language Processing*, pages 901–904, Denver, Colorado, September.

Nicola Ueffing, Jens Stephan, Evgeny Matusov, Lo ic Dugast, George F. Foster, Roland Kuhn, Jean Senellart, and Jin Yang. 2008. Tighter integration of rule-based and statistical mt in serial system combination. In *Proceedings of COLING 2008*, pages 913–920.

David Vilar, Daniel Stein, Matthias Huck, and Hermann Ney. 2010. Jane: Open Source Hierarchical Translation, Extended with Reordering and Lexicon Models. In *Proceedings of the Joint Fifth Workshop on Statistical Machine Translation and MetricsMATR*, pages 262–270, Uppsala, Sweden, July.

Stephan Vogel, Hermann Ney, and Christoph Tillmann. 1996. HMM-based word alignment in statistical translation. In *COLING '96: The 16th Int. Conf. on Computational Linguistics*, pages 836–841, Copenhagen, Denmark, August.

CEU-UPV English–Spanish system for WMT11

Francisco Zamora-Martínez
D. Física, Matemática, y Computación
Universidad CEU-Cardenal Herrera
Alfara del Patriarca (Valencia), Spain
fzamora@dsic.upv.es

M.J. Castro-Bleda
D. Sistemas Informáticos y Computación
Universitat Politècnica de València
Valencia, Spain
mcastro@dsic.upv.es

Abstract

This paper describes the system presented for the English-Spanish translation task by the collaboration between CEU-UCH and UPV for 2011 WMT. A comparison of independent phrase-based translation models interpolation for each available training corpora were tested, giving an improvement of 0.4 BLEU points over the baseline. Output N-best lists were rescored via a target Neural Network Language Model. An improvement of one BLEU point over the baseline was obtained adding the two features, giving 31.5 BLEU and 57.9 TER for the primary system, computed over lowercased and detokenized outputs. The system was positioned second in the final ranking.

1 Introduction

The goal of Statistical Machine Translation (SMT) is to translate a sentence between two languages. Giving the source language sentence $\mathbf{f}$, it would be translated to an equivalent target language sentence $\mathbf{e}$. The most extended formalization is done via log-linear models (Papineni et al., 1998; Och and Ney, 2002) as follows:

$$\hat{\mathbf{e}} = \arg\max_{\mathbf{e}} \sum_{k=1}^{K} \lambda_k h_k(\mathbf{f}, \mathbf{e}) \quad (1)$$

where $h_k(\mathbf{f}, \mathbf{e})$ is a score function representing an important feature for the translation of $\mathbf{f}$ into $\mathbf{e}$, K is the number of models (or features) and λ_k are the weights of the log-linear combination. Typically, the weights λ_k are optimized during the tuning stage with the use of a development set.

SMT systems rely on a bilingual sentence aligned training corpus. These sentences are aligned at the word level (Brown et al., 1993), and after that, different h_k feature functions are trained. In some practical cases, the out-of-domain training data is larger than the in-domain training data. In these cases the target Language Model (LM) is composed of a linear interpolation of independent LMs, one for each available training domain or corpus. Nevertheless, the training of phrase-based translation models is an open problem in these cases.

Some recent works (Resnik and Smith, 2003; Yasuda et al., ; Koehn and Schroeder, 2007; Matsoukas et al., 2009; Foster et al., 2010; Sanchis-Trilles and Casacuberta, 2010) related to corpus weighting, make use of data selection, data weighting, and translation model adaptation to overcome this problem. In this work, we explore a simple corpus weighting technique to interpolate any number of different phrase tables. Two different approaches are tested, obtaining similar performance. On the one hand, a count-based smoothing technique that applies a weight to the counting of phrases and lexical links depending on the relevance of each corpus. On the other hand, a linear interpolation of independent trained phrase tables.

Another important feature of this work is the use of Neural Network Language Models (NN LMs) (Bengio, 2008). This kind of LMs has been successfully applied in some connectionist approaches to language modeling (Bengio et al., 2003; Castro-Bleda and Prat, 2003; Schwenk et al., 2006;

Proceedings of the 6th Workshop on Statistical Machine Translation, pages 490–495,
Edinburgh, Scotland, UK, July 30–31, 2011. ©2011 Association for Computational Linguistics

Schwenk, 2010). The advantage of these NN LMs is the projection of words on a continuous space were the probabilities of n-grams are learned. A Neural Network (NN) is proposed to learn both the word projections and the n-gram probabilities.

The presented system combines a standard, state-of-the-art SMT system with a NN LM via log-linear combination and N-best output re-scoring. We chose to participate in the English-Spanish direction.

2 Translation models

A standard phrase-based translation model is composed of the following five h_k features:

- inverse phrase translation probability $p(\overline{f}|\overline{e})$
- inverse lexical weighting $l(\overline{f}|\overline{e})$
- direct phrase translation probability $p(\overline{e}|\overline{f})$
- direct lexical weighting $l(\overline{e}|\overline{f})$
- phrase penalty (always $e = 2.718$).

We rely only on the first four features. They are computed from word alignments at the sentence level, by counting over the alignments, and using the inverse and direct lexical dictionaries. Given a pair of phrases, $\overline{f}$ on the source language and $\overline{e}$ in the target language, the phrase translation probabilities are computed by relative frequency as:

$$p(\overline{f}|\overline{e}) = \frac{\text{count}(\overline{f},\overline{e})}{\sum_{e'} \text{count}(\overline{f},\overline{e}')}$$
$$p(\overline{e}|\overline{f}) = \frac{\text{count}(\overline{f},\overline{e})}{\sum_{f'} \text{count}(\overline{f}',\overline{e})}$$

Given a word f on the source language, and a word e in the target language, the lexical translation distribution is computed again by relative frequency as:

$$w(f|e) = \frac{\text{count}(f,e)}{\sum_{e'} \text{count}(f,e')}$$
$$w(e|f) = \frac{\text{count}(f,e)}{\sum_{f'} \text{count}(f',e)}$$

Given the previous lexical translation distribution, two phrase pairs $\overline{f}$ and $\overline{e}$, and a, the word alignment between the source word positions $i = 1, \ldots, n$ and the target word positions $j = 1, \ldots, m$, the inverse lexical weighting is computed as:

$$l(\overline{f}|\overline{e}) = \prod_{i=1}^{n} \frac{1}{|\{j|(i,j) \in a\}|} \sum_{(i,j)\in a} w(f_i|e_j)$$

and the direct lexical weighting is computed as:

$$l(\overline{e}|\overline{f}) = \prod_{j=1}^{m} \frac{1}{|\{i|(i,j) \in a\}|} \sum_{(i,j)\in a} w(e_j|f_i)$$

3 Weighting different translation models

The proposed modifications of the phrase-based translation models are similar to (Foster et al., 2010; Matsoukas et al., 2009), but in this case the weighting is simpler and focused at the corpus level. If we have T different training sets, we could define β_t as the weight of the set t, for $1 \leq t \leq T$. The word alignments are computed via Giza++ (Och and Ney, 2003) over the concatenation of all the training material available for the translation models (in this case, Europarl, News-Commentary, and United Nations). After that, we could recompute the lexical translation distribution using the weights information, and compute the phrase-based translation models taking into account these weights. The `count` function will be redefined to take into account only information of the corresponding training set.

3.1 Count smoothing

The weight β_t is applied to the `count` function, in order to modify the corpus effect on the probability of each phrase pair alignment, and each word pair alignment. First, we modify the lexical translation distribution in this way:

$$w(f|e) = \frac{\sum_t \beta_t \text{count}_t(f,e)}{\sum_t \beta_t \sum_{e'} \text{count}_t(f,e')}$$
$$w(e|f) = \frac{\sum_t \beta_t \text{count}_t(f,e)}{\sum_t \beta_t \sum_{f'} \text{count}_t(f',e)}$$

having a global lexical translation distribution for the alignment between words. Second, we modify the phrase translation probabilities for each direction, remaining without modification the lexical weightings:

$$p(\overline{f}|\overline{e}) = \frac{\sum_t \beta_t \text{count}_t(\overline{f},\overline{e})}{\sum_t \beta_t \sum_{\overline{e}'} \text{count}_t(\overline{f},\overline{e}')}$$
$$p(\overline{e}|\overline{f}) = \frac{\sum_t \beta_t \text{count}_t(\overline{f},\overline{e})}{\sum_t \beta_t \sum_{\overline{f}'} \text{count}_t(\overline{f}',\overline{e})}$$

When some phrase/word count is not found, count is set to zero.

3.2 Linear interpolation

In this case, we compute independently the translation models for each training set. We have T models, one for each set. The final translation models are obtained by means of a linear interpolation of each independent translation model. If some phrase pair is not found, the translation model is set to have zero probability.

First, we redefine the lexical translation distribution. In this case we have $w_1, w_2, \ldots, w_T$ lexical dictionaries:

$$w_t(f|e) = \frac{\text{count}_t(f,e)}{\sum_{e'} \text{count}_t(f,e')}$$
$$w_t(e|f) = \frac{\text{count}_t(f,e)}{\sum_{f'} \text{count}_t(f',e)}.$$

Then, we could compute the linear interpolation of phrase translation probabilities as follows:

$$p(\overline{f}|\overline{e}) = \sum_t \beta_t \frac{\text{count}_t(\overline{f},\overline{e})}{\sum_{\overline{e}'} \text{count}_t(\overline{f},\overline{e}')}$$
$$p(\overline{e}|\overline{f}) = \sum_t \beta_t \frac{\text{count}_t(\overline{f},\overline{e})}{\sum_{\overline{f}'} \text{count}_t(\overline{f}',\overline{e})}$$

And finally, the inverse lexical weighting is obtained as:

$$l(\overline{f}|\overline{e}) = \sum_t \beta_t \prod_{i=1}^{n} \frac{1}{|\{j|(i,j) \in a\}|} \sum_{(i,j)\in a} w_t(f_i|e_j)$$

and the direct lexical weighting:

$$l(\overline{e}|\overline{f}) = \sum_t \beta_t \prod_{j=1}^{m} \frac{1}{|\{i|(i,j) \in a\}|} \sum_{(i,j)\in a} w_t(e_j|f_i).$$

4 Neural Network Language Models

In SMT the most useful language models are n-grams (Bahl et al., 1983; Jelinek, 1997; Bahl et al., 1983). They compute the probability of each word given the context of the $n-1$ previous words:

$$p(s_1 \ldots s_{|S|}) \approx \prod_{i=1}^{|S|} p(s_i|s_{i-n+1} \ldots s_{i-1}) \quad (2)$$

where S is the sequence of words for which we want compute the probability, and $s_i \in S$, from a vocabulary Ω.

A NN LM is a statistical LM which follows equation (2) as n-grams do, but where the probabilities that appear in that expression are estimated with a NN (Bengio et al., 2003; Castro-Bleda and Prat, 2003; Schwenk, 2007; Bengio, 2008). The model naturally fits under the probabilistic interpretation of the outputs of the NNs: if a NN, in this case a MLP, is trained as a classifier, the outputs associated to each class are estimations of the posterior probabilities of the defined classes (Bishop, 1995).

The training set for a LM is a sequence $s_1 s_2 \ldots s_{|S|}$ of words from a vocabulary Ω. In order to train a NN to predict the next word given a history of length $n-1$, each input word must be encoded. A natural representation is a local encoding following a "1-of-$|\Omega|$" scheme. The problem of this encoding for tasks with large vocabularies (as is typically the case) is the huge size of the resulting NN. We have solved this problem following the ideas of (Bengio et al., 2003; Schwenk, 2007), learning a distributed representation for each word. Figure 1 illustrates the architecture of the feed-forward NN used to estimate the NN LM.

This n-gram NN LM predicts the posterior probability of each word of the vocabulary given the $n-1$ previous words. A single forward pass of the MLP gives $p(\omega|s_{i-n+1} \ldots s_{i-1})$ for every word $\omega \in \Omega$. After training the projection layer is replaced by a table look-up.

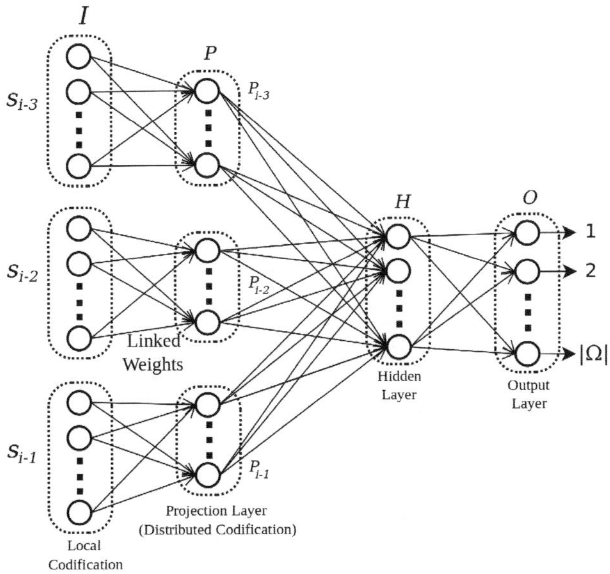

Figure 1: Architecture of the continuous space NN LM during training. The input words are $s_{i-n+1}, \ldots, s_{i-1}$ (in this example, the input words are s_{i-3}, s_{i-2}, and s_{i-1} for a 4-gram). I, P, H, and O are the input, projection, hidden, and output layer, respectively, of the MLP.

Table 1: Spanish corpora statistics. NC stands for News-Commentary and UN for United Nations, while $|\Omega|$ stands for vocabulary size, and M/K for millions/thousands of elements. All numbers are computed with tokenized and lowercased data.

Set	# Lines	# Words	$\|\Omega\|$
NC v6	$159K$	$4.44M$	$80K$
News-Shuffled	$9.17M$	$269M$	$596K$
Europarl v6	$1.94M$	$55M$	$177K$
UN	$6.22M$	$214M$	$579K$
Total	$21.93M$	$678M$	$1.03M$

Table 2: Weights of different combination of phrase-based translation models.

System	Europarl	NC	UN
Smooth1	0.35	0.35	0.30
Smooth2	0.40	0.40	0.20
Smooth3	0.15	0.80	0.05
Linear	0.35	0.35	0.30

The major advantage of the connectionist approach is the automatic smoothing performed by the neural network estimators. This smoothing is done via a continuous space representation of the input words. Learning the probability of n-grams, together with their representation in a continuous space (Bengio et al., 2003), is an appropriate approximation for large vocabulary tasks. However, one of the drawbacks of such approach is the high computational cost entailed whenever the NN LM is computed directly, with no simplification whatsoever. For this reason, the vocabulary size will be restricted in the experiments presented in this work.

5 Experiments

The baseline SMT system is built with the open-source SMT toolkit Moses (Koehn et al., 2007), in its standard setup. The decoder includes a log-linear model comprising a phrase-based translation model, a language model, a lexicalized distortion model and word and phrase penalties. The weights of the log-linear interpolation were optimized by means of MERT (Och, 2003), using the News-Commentary test set of the 2008 shared task as a development set. The phrase-based translation model uses the concatenation of News-Commentary, United Nations, and Europarl corpora, to estimate the four translation model features.

The baseline LM was a regular n-gram LM with Kneser-Ney smoothing (Kneser and Ney, 1995) and interpolation by means of the SRILM toolkit (Stolcke, 2002). Specifically, we trained a 6-gram LM on United Nations, a 5-gram on Europarl and News-Shuffled, and a 4-gram on News-Commentary. Once these LMs had been built, they were interpolated so as to maximize the perplexity of the News-Commentary test set of the 2009 shared task. The final model was pruned out using a threshold of 10^{-8}. This was done so according to preliminary research.

Three different weights for the count smoothing technique described in section 3.1 were tested. For the interpolation model of section 3.2, we select the weights minimizing the perplexity of the corresponding three LMs (Europarl, NC, and UN) over the News2008 set. Table 2 summarizes these weights.

NN LM was trained with all the corpora described in Table 1, using a weighted replacement algorithm to modify the impact of each corpus in the training algorithm. The weights were the same that for the standard LM. In order to reduce the complexity of the model, the input vocabulary of the NN LM was restricted using only words that appears more than 10 times in the corpora. The vocabulary is formed by the 107 607 more frequent words, with two additional inputs: one to represent the words out of this vocabulary, and another for the begin-of-sentence cue. The output of the NN LM was restricted much more, using only a shortlist (Schwenk, 2007) of the $10K$ more frequent words, plus the end-of-sentence cue. The rest of words are collected by an additional output in the neural network. When the probability of an out-of-shortlist word is required, its probability is computed multiplying this additional output activation by the unigram probability distribution of every out-of-shortlist word. This implies that 10.7% of the running words of the News2009 set, and 11.1% of the running words of the News2011 official test set, will be considered as out-of-shortlist words for the NN LM.

A 6-gram NN LM was trained for this task, based in previous works (Zamora-Martínez and Sanchis-Trilles, 2010). Four NN LMs with different values for the projection of each word (128, 192, 256, 320) were linearly combined for the final NN LM. Each NN LM had 320 units in the hidden layer. The combination weights were computed maximizing the perplexity over the News2009 set. The training procedure was conducted by means of the stochastic back-propagation algorithm with weight decay, with a replacement of $300K$ training samples and $200K$ validation samples in each training epoch, selecting the random sample using a different distribution weight for each corpus. The validation set was the News2009 set. The networks were stopped after 99, 70, 53, and 42 epochs respectively (unfortunately, without achieving convergence, due to the competition timings). This resulted in very few training samples compared with the size of the training set: $29M$ in the best case, versus more than $500M$ of the full set. The training of the NN LMs was accomplished with the April toolkit (España-Boquera et al., 2007; Zamora-Martínez et al., 2009). The perplexity achieved by the 6-gram NN LM in the Spanish News2009 set was 281, versus 145 obtained with the standard 6-gram language model with interpolation and Kneser-Ney smoothing (Kneser and Ney, 1995).

The number of sentences in the N-best list was set to 2 000 unique output sentences. Results can be seen in Table 3. In order to assess the reliability of such results, we computed pairwise improvement intervals as described in (Koehn, 2004), by means of bootstrapping with 1 000 bootstrap iterations and at a 95% confidence level. Such confidence test reported the improvements to be statistically significant. A difference of more than 0.3 points of BLEU is considered significant in the pairwise comparison. The final results leads to 31.5 points of BLEU, positioning this system as second in the final classification.

Table 3: Main results of the experimentation

System	News2010 BLEU	News2010 TER	News2011 BLEU	News2011 TER
Baseline	29.2	60.0	30.5	58.9
Smooth1	29.3	59.9	–	–
Smooth2	29.2	59.9	–	–
Smooth3	29.5	59.6	30.9	58.5
+ NN LM	29.9	59.2	31.4	58.0
Linear	29.5	59.5	30.9	58.7
+ NN LM	**30.2**	**58.8**	**31.5**	**57.9**

6 Conclusions and future work

The presented CEU-UPV system, using phrase translation models combinations and NN LMs, leads an improvement of 0.4 points of BLEU in the two cases: the count smoothing approach (Smooth3 system) and the linear interpolation approach (Linear system). The incorporation of NN LMs in both systems gets an additional improvement of 0.5 BLEU points for the Smooth3 system, and 0.6 BLEU points for the Linear system. The final result for the primary system is 31.5 BLEU points.

The combination of translation models could be enhanced optimizing the β_t weights over the BLEU score. Currently the weights are manually set for the Smooth[1,2,3] systems, and fixed to the LM weights for the Linear system. Nevertheless, both approaches achieve similar results. Finally, it is important to emphasize that the use of NN LMs implies an interesting improvement, though this year's gain is lower than that obtained by our 2010 system.[1]

[1]Note that the NN LMs didn't achieve convergence due to

Acknowledgments

This work has been partially supported by the Spanish Goverment under project TIN2010-1958.

References

L. R. Bahl, F. Jelinek, and R. L. Mercer. 1983. A Maximum Likelihood Approach to Continuous Speech Recognition. *IEEE Trans. on Pat. Anal. and Mach. Intel.*, 5(2):179–190.

Y. Bengio, R. Ducharme, P. Vincent, and C. Jauvin. 2003. A Neural Probabilistic Language Model. *Journal of Machine Learning Research*, 3(2):1137–1155.

Y. Bengio. 2008. Neural net language models. *Scholarpedia*, 3(1):3881.

C. M. Bishop. 1995. *Neural networks for pattern recognition*. Oxford University Press.

Peter F. Brown, Vincent J. Della Pietra, Stephen A. Della Pietra, and Robert L. Mercer. 1993. The mathematics of statistical machine translation: parameter estimation. *Comput. Linguist.*, 19(2):263–311.

M.J. Castro-Bleda and F. Prat. 2003. New Directions in Connectionist Language Modeling. In *Computational Methods in Neural Modeling*, volume 2686 of *LNCS*, pages 598–605. Springer-Verlag.

S. España-Boquera, F. Zamora-Martínez, M.J. Castro-Bleda, and J. Gorbe-Moya. 2007. Efficient BP Algorithms for General Feedforward Neural Networks. In *Bio-inspired Modeling of Cognitive Tasks*, volume 4527 of *LNCS*, pages 327–336. Springer.

George Foster, Cyril Goutte, and Roland Kuhn. 2010. Discriminative instance weighting for domain adaptation in statistical machine translation. In *Proc. of EMNLP*, EMNLP'10, pages 451–459, Stroudsburg, PA, USA. Association for Computational Linguistics.

F. Jelinek. 1997. *Statistical Methods for Speech Recognition*. Language, Speech, and Communication. The MIT Press.

R. Kneser and H. Ney. 1995. Improved backing-off for m-gram language modeling. In *Proc. of the International Conference on Acoustics, Speech, and Signal Processing (ICASSP'95)*, volume II, pages 181–184, May.

Philipp Koehn and Josh Schroeder. 2007. Experiments in domain adaptation for statistical machine translation. In *Proc. of WMT'07*, pages 224–227.

P. Koehn et al. 2007. Moses: Open Source Toolkit for Statistical Machine Translation. In *Proc. of the ACL'07 Demo and Poster Sessions*, pages 177–180, Prague, Czech Republic.

competition timings.

P. Koehn. 2004. Statistical significance tests for machine translation evaluation. In *Proc. of EMNLP*, EMNLP'04, pages 388–395. Association for Computational Linguistics.

Spyros Matsoukas, Antti-Veikko I. Rosti, and Bing Zhang. 2009. Discriminative corpus weight estimation for machine translation. In *Proc. of EMNLP'09*, volume 2, pages 708–717, Stroudsburg, PA, USA. Association for Computational Linguistics.

F. Och and H. Ney. 2002. Discriminative training and maximum entropy models for statistical machine translation. In *Proc. of ACL'02*, pages 295–302.

Franz Josef Och and Hermann Ney. 2003. A systematic comparison of various statistical alignment models. *Computational Linguistics*, 29(1):19–51.

F.J. Och. 2003. Minimum Error Rate Training in Statistical Machine Translation. In *Proc. of ACL'03*, pages 160–167, Sapporo, Japan.

K. Papineni, S. Roukos, and T. Ward. 1998. Maximum likelihood and discriminative training of direct translation models. In *Proc. of the International Conference on Acoustics, Speech, and Signal Processing (ICASSP'98)*, pages 189–192.

Philip Resnik and Noah A. Smith. 2003. The web as a parallel corpus. *Computational Linguistics*, 29:349–380.

Germán Sanchis-Trilles and Francisco Casacuberta. 2010. Bayesian adaptation for statistical machine translation. In *Proc. of SSSPR'10*, pages 620–629.

H. Schwenk, D. Déchelotte, and J. L. Gauvain. 2006. Continuous space language models for statistical machine translation. In *Proc. of the COLING/ACL 2006 Main Conference Poster Sessions*, pages 723–730.

H. Schwenk. 2007. Continuous space language models. *Computer Speech and Language*, 21(3):492–518.

H. Schwenk. 2010. Continuous space language models for statistical machine translation. *The Prague Bulletin of Mathematical Linguistics*, 93.

A. Stolcke. 2002. SRILM – an extensible language modeling toolkit. In *Proc. of the International Conference in Spoken Language Processing (ICSLP'02)*, pages 901–904, September.

Keiji Yasuda, Ruiqiang Zhang, Hirofumi Yamamoto, and Eiichiro Sumita. Method of selecting training data to build a compact and efficient translation model. In *Proc. of IJCNLP'10*, pages 655–660.

Francisco Zamora-Martínez and Germán Sanchis-Trilles. 2010. UCH-UPV English–Spanish System for WMT10. In *Proc. of WMT'10*, pages 207–211, July.

F. Zamora-Martínez, M.J. Castro-Bleda, and S. España-Boquera. 2009. Fast Evaluation of Connectionist Language Models. In *IWANN*, volume 5517 of *LNCS*, pages 33–40. Springer.

Hierarchical Phrase-Based MT at the Charles University for the WMT 2011 Shared Task

Daniel Zeman
Charles University in Prague, Institute of Formal and Applied Linguistics (ÚFAL)
Univerzita Karlova v Praze, Ústav formální a aplikované lingvistiky (ÚFAL)
Malostranské náměstí 25, Praha, CZ-11800, Czechia
zeman@ufal.mff.cuni.cz

Abstract

We describe our experiments with hierarchical phrase-based machine translation for the WMT 2011 Shared Task. We trained a system for all 8 translation directions between English on one side and Czech, German, Spanish or French on the other side, though we focused slightly more on the English-to-Czech direction. We provide a detailed description of our configuration and data so the results are replicable.

1 Introduction

With so many official languages, Europe is a paradise for machine translation research. One of the largest bodies of electronically available parallel texts is being nowadays generated by the European Union and its institutions. At the same time, the EU also provides motivation and boosts potential market for machine translation outcomes.

Most of the major European languages belong to one of the following three branches of the Indo-European language family: Germanic, Romance or Slavic. Such relatedness is responsible for many structural similarities in European languages, although significant differences still exist. Within the language portfolio selected for the WMT shared task, English, French and Spanish seem to be closer to each other than to the rest.

German, despite being genetically related to English, differs in many properties. Its word order rules, shifting verbs from one end of the sentence to the other, easily create long-distance dependencies. Long German compound words are notorious for increasing out-of-vocabulary rate, which has led many researchers to devising unsupervised compound-splitting techniques. Also, uppercase/lowercase distinction is more important because all German nouns start with an uppercase letter by the rule.

Czech is a language with rich morphology (both inflectional and derivational) and relatively free word order. In fact, the predicate-argument structure, often encoded by fixed word order in English, is usually captured by inflection (especially the system of 7 grammatical cases) in Czech. While the free word order of Czech is a problem when translating to English (the text should be parsed first in order to determine the syntactic functions and the English word order), generating correct inflectional affixes is indeed a challenge for English-to-Czech systems. Furthermore, the multitude of possible Czech word forms (at least order of magnitude higher than in English) makes the data sparseness problem really severe, hindering both directions.

There are numerous ways how these issues could be addressed. For instance, parsing and syntax-aware reordering of the source-language sentences can help with the word order differences (same goal could be achieved by a reordering model or a synchronous context-free grammar in a hierarchical system). Factored translation, a secondary language model of morphological tags or even a morphological generator are some of the possible solutions to the poor-to-rich translation issues.

Our goal is to run one system under as similar conditions as possible to all eight translation directions, to compare their translation accuracies and see why some directions are easier than others. Future work will benefit from knowing what are the special processing needs for a given language pair. The current version of the system does not include really language-specific techniques: we neither split German compounds, nor do we address the peculiarities of Czech mentioned above. Still, comparability of the results is limited, as the quality and quantity of English-Czech data differs from that of the other pairs.

Proceedings of the 6th Workshop on Statistical Machine Translation, pages 496–500,
Edinburgh, Scotland, UK, July 30–31, 2011.

2 The Translation System

Our translation system belongs to the hierarchical phrase-based class (Chiang, 2007), i.e. phrase pairs with nonterminals (rules of a synchronous context-free grammar) are extracted from symmetrized word alignments and subsequently used by the decoder. We use Joshua, a Java-based open-source implementation of the hierarchical decoder (Li et al., 2009), release 1.3.[1]

Word alignment was computed using the first three steps of the `train-factored-phrase-model.perl` script packed with Moses[2] (Koehn et al., 2007). This includes the usual combination of word clustering using `mkcls`[3] (Och, 1999), two-way word alignment using GIZA++[4] (Och and Ney, 2003), and alignment symmetrization using the *grow-diag-final-and* heuristic (Koehn et al., 2003).

For language modeling we use the SRILM toolkit[5] (Stolcke, 2002) with modified Kneser-Ney smoothing (Kneser and Ney, 1995; Chen and Goodman, 1998).

We use the Z-MERT implementation of minimum error rate training (Zaidan, 2009). The following settings have been used for Joshua and Z-MERT (for the sake of reproducibility, we keep the original names of the options; for their detailed explanation please refer to the documentation available on-line at the Joshua project site). `-ipi` is the number of intermediate initial points per Z-MERT iteration.

- Grammar extraction: `maxPhraseSpan=10` `maxPhraseLength=5` `maxNonterminals=2` `maxNonterminalSpan=2` `requireTightSpans=true` `edgeXViolates=true` `sentenceInitialX=true` `sentenceFinalX=true` `ruleSampleSize=300`
- Language model order: 6 (hexagram)
- Decoding: `span_limit=10` `fuzz1=0.1` `fuzz2=0.1` `max_n_items=30` `relative_threshold=10.0` `max_n_rules=50` `rule_relative_threshold=10.0`
- N-best decoding: `use_unique_nbest=true` `use_tree_nbest=false` `add_combined_cost=true` `top_n=300`
- Z-MERT: `-m BLEU 4 closest -maxIt 5 -ipi 20`

3 Data and Pre-processing Pipeline

We applied our system to all eight language pairs. From the data point of view the experiments were even more constrained than the organizers of the shared task suggested. We used neither the French/Spanish-English UN corpora nor the 10^9 French-English corpus. For 7 translation directions we used the Europarl ver6 and News-Commentary ver6 corpora[6] for training. The target side of the corpora was our only source of monolingual data for training the language model. Table 1 shows the size of the training data.

For the English-Czech direction, we used CzEng 0.9 (Bojar and Žabokrtský, 2009)[7] as our main parallel corpus. Following CzEng authors' request, we did not use sections 8* and 9* reserved for evaluation purposes.

In addition, we also used the EMEA corpus[8] (Tiedemann, 2009).[9]

Czech was also the only language where we used extra monolingual data for the language model. It was the set provided by the organizers of WMT 2010 (13,042,040 sentences, 210,507,305 tokens).

We use a slightly modified tokenization rules compared to CzEng export format. Most notably, we normalize English abbreviated negation and auxiliary verbs ("couldn't" → "could not") and attempt at normalizing quotation marks to distinguish between opening and closing one following proper typesetting rules.

The rest of our pre-processing pipeline matches the processing employed in CzEng (Bojar and Žabokrtský, 2009).[10] We use "supervised truecasing", meaning that we cast the case of the lemma to the form, relying on our morphological analyzers and taggers to identify proper names, all other

[1] `http://sourceforge.net/projects/joshua/`

[2] `http://www.statmt.org/moses/`

[3] `http://fjoch.com/mkcls.html`

[4] `http://fjoch.com/GIZA++.html`

[5] `http://www-speech.sri.com/projects/srilm/`

[6] Available for download at `http://www.statmt.org/wmt11/translation-task.html` using the link "Parallel corpus training data".

[7] `http://ufal.mff.cuni.cz/czeng/`

[8] `http://urd.let.rug.nl/tiedeman/OPUS/EMEA.php`

[9] Unfortunately, the EMEA corpus is badly tokenized on the Czech side with fractional numbers split into several tokens (e.g. "3, 14"). We attempted to reconstruct the original detokenized form using a small set of regular expressions.

Corpus	SentPairs	Tokens xx	Tokens en
cs-en	583,124	13,224,596	15,397,742
de-en	1,857,087	48,834,569	51,243,594
es-en	1,903,562	54,488,621	52,369,658
fr-en	1,920,363	61,030,918	52,686,784
en-cs	7,543,152	79,057,403	89,018,033

Table 1: Number of sentence pairs and tokens for every language pair in the parallel training corpus. Languages are identified by their ISO 639 codes: cs = Czech, de = German, en = English, es = Spanish, fr = French. The en-cs line describes the CzEng + EMEA combined corpus, all other lines correspond to the respective versions of EuroParl + News Commentary.

words are lowercased.

Note that in some cases the grammar extraction algorithm in Joshua fails if the training corpus contains sentences that are too long. Removing sentences of 100 or more tokens (per advice by Joshua developers) effectively healed all failures.[11]

The News Test 2008 data set[12] (2051 sentences in each language) was used as development data for MERT. BLEU scores reported in this paper were computed on the News Test 2011 set (3003 sentences each language). We do not use the News Test 2009 and 2010.

4 Experiments

All BLEU scores were computed directly by Joshua on the News Test 2011 set. Note that they differ from what the official evaluation script would report, due to different tokenization.

4.1 Baseline Experiments

The set of baseline experiments with all translation directions involved running the system on lowercased News Commentary corpora. Word alignments were computed on lowercased 4-character stems. A hexagram language model was trained on the target side of the parallel corpus.

In the en-cs case, word alignments were computed on lemmatized version of the parallel corpus. Hexagram language model was trained on the monolingual data. Truecased data were used for training, as described above; the BLEU score of this experiment in Table 2 is computed on truecased system output.

Direction	$BLEU_J$	$BLEU_l$	$BLEU_t$
en-cs	0.1274	0.141	0.123
en-de	0.1324	0.128	0.052
en-es	0.2756	0.274	0.221
en-fr	0.2727	0.212	0.174
cs-en	0.1782	0.178	0.137
de-en	0.1957	0.187	0.137
es-en	0.2630	0.255	0.197
fr-en	0.2471	0.248	0.193

Table 2: Lowercased BLEU scores of the baseline experiments on News Test 2011 data: $BLEU_J$ is computed by the system, $BLEU_l$ is the official evaluation by `matrix.statmt.org` (it differs because of different tokenization). $BLEU_t$ is official truecased evaluation.

An interesting perspective on the models is provided by the feature weights optimized during MERT. We can see in Table 3 that translation models are trusted significantly more than language models for the en-de, de-en and es-en directions. In fact, the language model has a low relative weight in all language pairs but en-cs, which was the only pair where we used a significant amount of extra monolingual data. In the future, we should probably use the Gigaword corpus for the to-English directions.

Setup	LM	Pt_0	Pt_1	Pt_2	WP
en-cs	1.0	1.04	0.84	−0.06	−1.19
en-de	1.0	2.60	0.57	0.47	−3.17
en-es	1.0	1.67	0.81	0.60	−2.96
en-fr	1.0	1.41	0.92	0.53	−2.80
cs-en	1.0	1.48	0.94	1.08	−4.55
de-en	1.0	2.28	1.11	0.34	−2.88
es-en	1.0	2.26	1.67	0.23	−0.84
fr-en	1.0	1.89	1.32	0.13	−0.04

Table 3: Feature weights are relative to the weight of LM, the score by the language model. Then there are the three translation features: $Pt_0 = P(e|f)$, $Pt_1 = P_{lex}(f|e)$ and $Pt_2 = P_{lex}(e|f)$. WP is the word penalty.

[10] Due to the subsequent processing, incl. parsing, the tokenization of English follows PennTreebenk style. The rather unfortunate convention of treating hyphenated words as single tokens increases our out-of-vocabulary rate.

[11] Table 1 presents statistics *before* removing the long sentences.

[12] `http://www.statmt.org/wmt11/translation-task.html`

4.2 Efficiency

The machines on which the experiments were conducted are 64bit Intel Xeon dual core 2.8 GHz CPUs with 32 GB RAM.

Word alignment of each parallel corpus was the most resource-consuming subtask. It took between 12 and 48 hours, though it could be cut to one half by running both GIZA++ directions in parallel. The time needed for data preprocessing and training of the language model was negligible. Parallelized grammar extraction took 19 processors for about an hour. For decoding the test data were split into 20 chunks that were processed in parallel. One MERT iteration, including decoding, took from 30 minutes to 1 hour.

Training of large models requires some careful engineering. The grammar extraction easily consumes over 20 GB memory so it is important to make sure Java really has access to it. The decoder must use the SWIG-linked SRILM library because Java-based language modeling is too slow and memory-consuming.

4.3 Supervised Truecasing

Our baseline experiments operated on lowercased data, except for en-cs, where truecased word forms were obtained using lemmas from morphological annotation (note that guessing of the true case is only needed for the sentence-initial token, other words can just be left in their original form).

As contrastive runs we applied the supervised truecasing to other directions as well. We used the Morče tagger for English lemmatization, TreeTagger for German and two simple rule-based approaches to Spanish and French lemmatization. All these tools are embedded in the TectoMT analysis framework (Žabokrtský et al., 2008).

The results are in Table 4. $BLEU_t$ has increased in all cases w.r.t. the baseline results.

4.4 Alignment on Lemmas

Once we are able to lemmatize all five languages we can also experiment with word alignments based on lemmas. Table 5 shows that the differences in BLEU are insignificant.

5 Conclusion

We have described the hierarchical phrase-based SMT system we used for the WMT 2011 shared task. We discussed experiments with large data from the point of view of both the translation accuracy and efficiency. We used moderately-sized training data and took advantage from their basic linguistic annotation (lemmas). The truecasing technique helped us to better target named entities.

Direction	$BLEU_J$	$BLEU_l$	$BLEU_t$
en-cs	0.1191	0.126	0.119
en-de	0.1337	0.131	0.127
en-es	0.2573	0.276	0.265
en-fr	0.2591	0.211	0.189
cs-en	0.1692	0.180	0.168
de-en	0.1885	0.191	0.178
es-en	0.2446	0.260	0.236
fr-en	0.2243	0.245	0.221

Table 4: Results of experiments with supervised truecasing. Note that training on truecased corpus slightly influenced even the lowercased BLEU (cf. with Table 2). This is because probabilities of tokens that may appear both uppercased and lowercased (with different meanings) have changed, and thus different translation may have been chosen.

Direction	$BLEU_Jl4$	$BLEU_Jlm$
en-cs	0.1191	0.1193
en-de	0.1337	0.1318
en-es	0.2573	0.2590
en-fr	0.2591	0.2592
cs-en	0.1692	0.1690
de-en	0.1885	0.1892
es-en	0.2446	0.2452
fr-en	0.2243	0.2244

Table 5: Results of experiments with word alignment computed on different factors. $BLEU_Jl4$ is the score computed by Joshua on lowercased test data for the original experiments (alignment based on lowercased 4-character prefixes). $BLEU_Jlm$ is the corresponding score for alignment based on lemmas.

Acknowledgements

The work on this project was supported by the grant P406/11/1499 of the Czech Science Foundation (GAČR).

References

Ondřej Bojar and Zdeněk Žabokrtský. 2009. Czeng 0.9: Large parallel treebank with rich annotation.

The Prague Bulletin of Mathematical Linguistics, 92:63–83.

Stanley F. Chen and Joshua Goodman. 1998. An empirical study of smoothing techniques for language modeling. In *Technical report TR-10-98, Computer Science Group*, Harvard, MA, USA, August. Harvard University.

David Chiang. 2007. Hierarchical Phrase-Based Translation. *Computational Linguistics*, 33(2):201–228.

Reinhard Kneser and Hermann Ney. 1995. Improved backing-off for m-gram language modeling. In *Proceedings of the IEEE International Conference on Acoustics, Speech and Signal Processing*, pages 181–184, Los Alamitos, California, USA. IEEE Computer Society Press.

Philipp Koehn, Franz Josef Och, and Daniel Marcu. 2003. Statistical phrase-based translation. In *NAACL '03: Proceedings of the 2003 Conference of the North American Chapter of the Association for Computational Linguistics on Human Language Technology*, pages 48–54, Morristown, NJ, USA. Association for Computational Linguistics.

Philipp Koehn, Hieu Hoang, Alexandra Birch, Chris Callison-Burch, Marcello Federico, Nicola Bertoldi, Brooke Cowan, Wade Shen, Christine Moran, Richard Zens, Chris Dyer, Ondřej Bojar, Alexandra Constantin, and Evan Herbst. 2007. Moses: Open Source Toolkit for Statistical Machine Translation. In *Proceedings of the 45th Annual Meeting of the Association for Computational Linguistics Companion Volume Proceedings of the Demo and Poster Sessions*, pages 177–180, Praha, Czechia, June. Association for Computational Linguistics.

Zhifei Li, Chris Callison-Burch, Sanjeev Khudanpur, and Wren Thornton. 2009. Decoding in Joshua: Open Source, Parsing-Based Machine Translation. *The Prague Bulletin of Mathematical Linguistics*, 91:47–56, 1.

Franz Josef Och and Hermann Ney. 2003. A systematic comparison of various statistical alignment models. *Computational Linguistics*, 29(1):19–51.

Franz Josef Och. 1999. An efficient method for determining bilingual word classes. In *Proceedings of the Ninth Conference of the European Chapter of the Association for Computational Linguistics (EACL'99)*, pages 71–76, Bergen, Norway, June. Association for Computational Linguistics.

Andreas Stolcke. 2002. Srilm – an extensible language modeling toolkit. In *Proceedings of International Conference on Spoken Language Processing*, Denver, Colorado, USA.

Jörg Tiedemann. 2009. News from opus – a collection of multilingual parallel corpora with tools and interfaces. In *Recent Advances in Natural Language Processing (vol. V)*, pages 237–248. John Benjamins.

Zdeněk Žabokrtský, Jan Ptáček, and Petr Pajas. 2008. TectoMT: Highly modular MT system with tectogrammatics used as transfer layer. In *ACL 2008 WMT: Proceedings of the Third Workshop on Statistical Machine Translation*, pages 167–170, Columbus, OH, USA. Association for Computational Linguistics.

Omar F. Zaidan. 2009. Z-mert: A fully configurable open source tool for minimum error rate training of machine translation systems. *The Prague Bulletin of Mathematical Linguistics*, 91:79–88.

Crisis MT: Developing A Cookbook for MT in Crisis Situations

William D. Lewis
Microsoft Research
Redmond, WA 98052
wilewis@microsoft.com

Robert Munro
Stanford University
Stanford, CA 94305
rmunro@stanford.edu

Stephan Vogel
Carnegie Mellon University
Pittsburgh, PA 15213
stephan.vogel@cmu.edu

Abstract

In this paper, we propose that MT is an important technology in crisis events, something that can and should be an integral part of a rapid-response infrastructure. By integrating MT services directly into a messaging infrastructure (whatever the type of messages being serviced, *e.g.*, text messages, Twitter feeds, blog postings, etc.), MT can be used to provide first pass translations into a majority language, which can be more effectively triaged and then routed to the appropriate aid agencies. If done right, MT can dramatically increase the speed by which relief can be provided. To ensure that MT is a standard tool in the arsenal of tools needed in crisis events, we propose a preliminary *Crisis Cookbook*, the contents of which could be translated into the relevant language(s) by volunteers immediately after a crisis event occurs. The resulting data could then be made available to relief groups on the ground, as well as to providers of MT services. We also note that there are significant contributions that our community can make to relief efforts through continued work on our research, especially that research which makes MT more viable for under-resourced languages.

1 Introduction

The connected world contains approximately 5000 languages – at least that is how many languages you could find at the other end of your phone right now. However, the majority of these languages are under-resourced, and they have few or no digital resources. In the event of a sudden onset crisis, people will immediately begin using their communication technologies – and their languages – to report their situations, request help, and seek out loved ones. Yet, in the event that such a crisis occurs in a region of the world where an under-resourced language is spoken, delivery of support or aid could be affected due to the inability to communicate. This was felt most strongly in the wake of the January 12, 2010 earthquake in Haiti. Local emergency response services were inoperable, but 70-80% of cell-towers were quickly restored. With 83% of men and 67% of women possessing cellphones, the nation remained largely connected. People within Haiti were texting, calling, and interacting with social media, primarily in Haitian Kreyòl (Munro, 2011). Yet, most of the aid that was being delivered to the country – initially, soley by the American Military – was being delivered by groups that did not communicate in Kreyòl. It was the first time that the world has seen a large-scale sudden onset crisis in a region with productive digital communications in an under-resourced language, but it certainly will not be the last.

We strongly believe that MT is an important technology to facilitate communication in crisis situations, crucially since it can make content in a language spoken or written by a local population accessible to those that do not know the language, in particular aid agencies. Multiple groups saw MT as a grand challenge in the Haitian crisis, and they set to work to make MT available as soon as possible after the crisis. Within two weeks of the crisis, the first two MT engines were built and were available to those who needed them. We believe that we can make MT available just as quickly in future crises, and, with the right preparation, tightly integrate MT into the communication infrastructure that is deployed (*e.g.*, the text messaging infrastructure). The challenge is doing the work now to make this vision possible.

In this paper, we describe the technologies that came to play in the Haitian crisis, how Haitian Kreyòl MT was developed, the problems of surprise languages and low resource MT, and detail the research and technologies, cast as a "Crisis MT Cookbook", that will be essential for MT to form a core role in future crises. In Sections 2, 3, and 4 we discuss Mission 4636 and the technologies that came

Proceedings of the 6th Workshop on Statistical Machine Translation, pages 501–511,
Edinburgh, Scotland, UK, July 30–31, 2011.

into play in Haiti and other recent crises, and the role that technologies can and should play in future crises. In Section 5, we discuss what made Haitian Kreyòl a special case of a "surprise language", and how MT was developed for the language. In Section 6, we review the NLP and MT research areas that will likely net big returns for under-resourced languages. In Section 7, we review the need for an MT Crisis Cookbook, and what the data and infrastructural components of the Cookbook should be. Finally, in Section 8 we review a sample crisis timeline, and how a crisis might play out with all the components of the Cookbook available. Section 9 wraps up the paper.

2 Mission 4636

In Haiti, crowdsourced translation enabled communications between the Kreyòl-speaking Haitian population and English-speaking emergency responders. A small group of international aid workers established a phone-number,'4636'[1] , that people were able to send text messages to for free within Haiti. The actual translations were made by about 2000 Kreyòl[2] and French speaking volunteers collaborating on an online microtasking platform that they used to translate, categorize, identify missing people and geolocate information on a map (Munro, 2010).[3] After a month, this work was gradually transferred to paid workers in Mirebalais, Haiti. These messages, about 80,000 in total, were used as part of the shared task for the *2011 Workshop on Machine Translation*. About 3,000 of the messages had the categories and coordinates refined by a third workforce working with the Ushahidi platform out of Boston.[4] They published this information on an online crisis map and worked directly with the main emergency responder, the American Military, to identify actionable information.

The strategy for translation was extremely effective - 80,000 messages equates to about 10 novels of information, translated in real-time, lifting a burden off people in Haiti. One high-ranking official described the translation process as a "perfect match" of social media and traditional emergency response (Anderson, 2010).

To meet the scale of translation needs, machine translation services were quickly shipped. A member of Mission 4636 built a high-precision, low-coverage dictionary-based system that was used by a number of translators. A couple of days later, the world's first publically accessible Stastical Machine Translation (SMT) engine for Kreyòl was developed by Microsoft Research, with Google Research following several days later with their own engine.[5] Although the statistical translation engines were not used directly in the SMS translation effort, there is evidence they were used by those who were involved in the relief effort, as determined by blog postings and a review of translation logs showing relief-centric translations. Although Kreyòl is not a high traffic language—it was not expected that it would be—about 5% of the traffic in the weeks and the months following the earthquake appeared to be relief-related, suggesting that machine translation was being used those who needed it most.[6] Had MT been integrated directly into the text messaging infrastructure used in Haiti, this percentage would have been significantly larger.

3 Translation and crisis response - a quickly changing field

To establish a ready-workforce to aid information processing in relief efforts an organization called the

[1]See the "Mission 4636" website at http://www.mission4636.org for more information about the organization and its efforts in Haiti.

[2]We use the term Kreyòl for the Creole spoken in Haiti to differentiate it from other Creoles. This is also in concord with customary usage in Haiti.

[3]An author of this paper, Robert Munro, coordinated this process and is a founding member and translation coordinator for the Standby Task Force, which is discussed later in the paper.

[4]For more information on Ushahidi, see http://www.ushahidi.org.

[5]A rough timeline of these developments can be seen in the commentary posted to the Language Log website (see specifically the archive at: http://languagelog.ldc.upenn.edu/nll/?p=2068).

[6]The logs output by Microsoft Translator's engine were examined, and categorized roughly into broad categories describing the type of content. These categories were: Relief Related (suspected), Colloquial or Common Expressions (which could, in fact, have been relief related), Chat, and Unknown. The analysis was done by hand on a random sample of 200 messages from the many thousands of messages received within a couple of months of the quake. There were a large number of strings that were difficult to categorize, including many partial strings, and a bias against Relief Related when it was not clear. Thus, the 5% estimate is likely a conservative one.

Standby Task Force was established in late 2010. Its founding members had worked together in the Haiti and/or subsequent Pakistan response efforts. It currently has several hundred members who specialize in tasks like report mapping, verification, media monitoring and translation. Of all the different tasks that volunteers can perform, translation is the *least* transferable from one crisis to the next.

Following from the lessons learned in Haiti, crowdsourced and machine translation have been combined for a number of aid efforts: vote monitoring for the referendem in Southern Sudan (Arabic); a UN-led earthquake simulation in Colombia (Spanish); and for crisis mapping following the tsunami in Japan (Japanese).

When information is immediately translated into a high resource language it can be quickly triaged by a greater number of people. The more time-intensive task of manually correcting any mistranslations can be performed in parallel. This workflow of combining machine and crowdsourced translation is largely a succesful one and is likely to become common practice in humanitarian information processing.

The combination of manual and machine-translation was found to be effective across unpredictable input:

> "An email came into the Sudan Vote Monitor platform in Indonesian - your plugin did a good job of translating it into English and Arabic"
>
> Helena Puig Larrauri, volunteer for Sudan Vote Monitor (P.C.)

But not without errors, especially across vital phrases like location names:

> "Names of neighborhoods such as Salitre or Puerta al Llano were not recognized as such and unnecessarily being translated."
>
> Marta Poblet, volunteer for Colombia earthquake simulation (P.C.)

When the uprisings hit Libya in early 2011 the United Nations did not have the capacity to collect vital ground-truth data in the lead up to their involvement. Information about refugee numbers and needs were on web-accessible articles and social media, as were reports about the movements of government and rebel troops and vunerable populations within the country. But there simply wasn't the workforce within the UN to aggregate and verify so much information. This was the first time the United Nations directly engaged a volunteer workforce for large-scale information processing, requesting the Standby Tasks Force's deployment. It was also the first time that so much information had come from social media, a potentially large but unstructured data source, but it gave the UN a huge head-start in their efforts (Verity, 2011). Crowdsourced and machine translation were also combined here, but in this case by directly engaging Arabic speakers in media monitoring and by using reports from *Meedan*.[7]

In a crisis, it will now be more common than not that the volume of available digital information will surpass the volume of information that aid-workers can collect directly from the ground. This rapid change is being quickly met by a rapid change in cloud-based and automated solutions to language processing, especially machine translation.

4 Translation and low-resource languages

We were fortunate that Arabic, Spanish and Japanese are high resource languages for which online machine translation services already exist. Speakers of low resource languages cannot currently benefit from this kind of translation service and yet low resource languages are disproportionally spoken by the world's most vunerable populations. Over the last 12 months many problems have been solved regarding the workflow of managing crisis data, but one of the biggest remaining problems is the ability to quickly deploy machine-translation systems to augment relief efforts.

While translation is not widely discussed aspect of crisis response, it is "a perennial hidden issue" (Disaster 2.0, 2011):

> "Go and look at any evaluation from the last ten or fifteen years. 'Recommendation: make effective information available

[7] *Meedan* is an NGO that seeks to create greater understanding between the Arabic and English speaking world by translating media reports and blogs between the languages, combining quick machine-translation with corrections by a volunteer community.

> to the government and the population in their own language.' We didn't do it ... It is a consistent thing across emergencies."
>
> Brendan McDonald, UN OCHA in (Disaster 2.0, 2011)

Beyond the particular use case of small-to-medium scale emergency information processing, machine translation can also contribute to aid efforts when the scale of information is beyond any manual processing. In addition to the Libya deployment, a recent Red Cross survey (2010) found that nearly half the respondents would use social media to report emergencies. It simply would not be possible to translate all real-time reports when expressed through social media, but translation into a high resource language could aid semi-automated methods for discovering and prioritizing information.

There is, therefore, a great need to explore methods for rapid deployment of machine-translation systems into minority languages. The questions that we seek to address in this paper is how we as a community can prepare for the eventuality of the next crisis, can draw from the lessons we learned in the Haitian crisis, and might significantly impact the aid effort in the next and future crises.

5 Surprise Languages: What Made Haiti Different?

On January 19th, 2010, the Microsoft Research Translator team received an e-mail from the field requesting that they develop an MT engine for Haitian Kreyòl to assist in the relief effort. At the time, no publically available MT engine existed for Kreyòl. In less than five days, the Microsoft Translator site was supporting the language. Given that it can take weeks to months to develop an MT engine for a new language, it would not seem possible that an engine could be developed so quickly, especially for a low-resource, minority language. The reasons this was possible are varied, and are in some ways unique to Kreyòl.

Haitian Kreyòl, as it turns out, has proven to be an exceptional case for a surprise language. Unlike the languages in Surprise Language Exercises of nearly a decade ago (Oard, 2003; Oard and Och, 2003), in which participants were given a month to collect data and build language technologies for previously unknown languages, including Machine Translation systems, there was a surprising amount of data for Kreyòl at the start of the Haitian crisis, and it became available relatively quickly. Partly, this is due to the growth of the Web, which has proven to be a surpisingly diverse multi-lingual resource. But it also stems crucially from work that had been done in the past on Kreyòl, specifically, the work that was done in the DIPLOMAT and NESPOLE! projects at CMU (Frederking et al., 1997). It was possible to assemble a reasonable sample of data for the language in very short order (*i.e.*, days). Further, since the language itself is fairly reduced morphologically, it is an easier target for SMT. In contrast, if one were to sample a language at random from the set of the 7,000 languages spoken on the earth, one is more likely to find a language that is morphologically richer (*e.g.*, fusional, aggutinating, polysynthetic). Morphological richness compounds the data sparsity problem, reducing the quality of the resulting SMT engines.

In other words, a combination of a simple morphology combined with reasonably accessible sources of data made the rapid deployment of MT for Kreyòl far more likely. That is not to say that there weren't problems. First, Kreyòl is fairly "young" as a written language[8], and is still in the early stages of orthographic standardization and normalization (Allen, 1998). This has led to inconsistencies in the orthography that increases data sparseness and noise. Further, Kreyòl has multiple registers in its written form: a "high" register that uses full forms for pronouns and a set of function words, and a "low" register that corresponds more closely to its spoken form, and is written with many contractions. For example, the Kreyòl word for the first person pronoun is *mwen*. It can be written as *mwen* (the high register), or contracted to *m'* (the low register). The form can either be attached to the succeeding word or written with a following space. Likewise, the first person possessive is also *mwen* which is written following the word that is possessed. This

[8] Although Haitian Kreyòl in written form goes back as far as the late 18th century (see Lefebvre (1998) for material on some of these texts), Kreyòl as a written language did not become more commonplace until the 20th century, not achieving official status in Haiti until 1961.

can be written as *'m*, and can be attached to the word or delimited by a space. Both *m'* and *'m* appear in some texts as just *m*. The same patterns hold for all pronouns, and some function words as well. See Table 1 for a list of these reductions.

Table 1: Sample Pronouns and Reductions

Pronoun	Gloss	Appears as
mwen	I, me, mine	m, 'm, m'
nou	you (pl), us	n, 'n, n'
ou	you	w, w'
li	he, she, it	l, l', 'l

Additionally, writers of Kreyòl use a large number of abbreviated forms for common expressions, a kind of shorthand. For example, *avèn* can be used to represent *avèk nou*, *mandem* can be used for *mande mwen*, etc. Overall, the number of alternations and multi-way ambiguities also increases the level of noise and data sparsity. [9]

So, even with a morphologically reduced language like Kreyòl, one has issues with data sparsity beyond the mere lack of availability of data. This compounds the low-data aspect of the language. Adding in a multitude of morphological variants, as one might encounter in a Turkic language, or worse, in an Inuit language, would only make the problem more severe. The big challenge for Crisis MT is not only to deal with the data availability problem, but once one has the data in hand, to deal with the reduction in the utility of that data caused by noise and the multiplication of word forms. These pose major challenges to our community, which can be countered through additional research, a motivated and active community, and scores of rapidly applied heuristics and data repairs.

6 Research Areas to Counter Data Sparsity

As noted, the major problems with low-resource MT is the lack of data and various data issues that increase the sparsity of data already in short supply. What are the research challenges? How can we make MT viable quickly for low-resource and simultaneously morphologically rich languages?

[9]For more details of the Haitian Kreyòl translation systems developed at Microsoft Research, please see Lewis (2010).

The following constitutes a rough list of solutions, many of which map to very interesting research problems:

- Crowdsourcing – Beyond the use of crowdsourcing in the crisis context itself (*e.g.*, to translate or process text messages, much as what was done by Mission 4636), novel techniques for tapping the crowd could also be used to add or repair data:
  - Repairing and evaluation – In this scenario, the crowd would be used to repair data that is obviously noisy, evaluate problems with particular data points, or even make simple determinations as to whether the data in question is actually in the language(s) of interest or too noisy to use.
  - Translating content, generating new data – Given crowd sourced, micro-tasking platforms such as Amazon's Mechanical Turk and Crowdflower, one can now easily tap the crowd to generate new data. The major challenge will be identifying if speakers of the target language(s) are available on the desired platform, and if not, if they could be motivated to particpate.[10] Likewise, infrastructure and resources will be needed to evaluate the quality of the resulting translations (Zaidan and Callison-Burch, 2011).
  - Active Crowd Translation – This method combines active learning with crowdsourcing for annotation of parallel data in comparable resources, and can be used to increase the amount of data that is found (Ambati et al., 2011). Active learning might be applicable to other crowdsourcing tasks as well, such as being used in crowdsourcing for translating content or repairing translated content.

- Tapping non-traditional sources – Critical to traditional approaches of SMT is parallel training data. Parallel data is difficult to impossible to come by for a large number of the world's

[10]Based on the results of an informal survey, there may be speakers of a hundred or more languages on Mechanical Turk. See http://www.junglelightspeed.com/amt_language/ for a list of the languages that may be available on Turk.

languages. Tapping non-traditional sources of data can help increase the supply of ever valuable training data for a language:

- Mining comparable sources of data – mining comparable data for parallel data has a long history, including mining comparable sources for named entities (Udupa et al., 2009; Irvine et al., 2010; Hewavitharana and Vogel, 2008; Hewavitharana and Vogel, 2011), mining Wikipedia for parallel content, including sentences (Smith et al., 2010), and many more too numerous to list. There is always room for improvement and hybridization in this space, as well as tapping additional sources of data, such as the volumes of noisy comparable data on the Web.
- Monolingual – More recent work has focused on mining monolingual sources of data, treating MT as a decipherment problem (Ravi and Knight, 2011), rather than a source-target mapping problem.
- Dictionary bootstraps and backoffs – Despite the absence of context, dictionaries can be useful, especially for resolving out-of-vocabulary items (OOVs). Many bilingual dictionaries also contain example sentences, which can be harvested and used in training.
- Field data from linguists – Given that linguists have variously studied a large percentage of the world's languages, tapping the supply of data that they have accumulated could prove quite fruitful. Some recent work tapping annotated bitexts (at this time, for over 1,200 languages) produced by linguists may prove useful in the future (Lewis and Xia, 2010), if for nothing more than to provide information about linguistic structure (*e.g.*, morphological complexity or divergences, potential distortion rates, and structural divergence (*a la* Fox (2002))). Engaging with the documentary linguistic community and providing tools to facilitate the collection of data might produce additional data, especially data where alignment is assisted through human input (Monson et al., 2008).

- Novel ways of countering data sparsity
  - Systematizing data cleaning heuristics – Undoubtedly, the same kinds of filtration and data cleaning heuristics used for Kreyòl could prove useful for speeding up the processing of data for new languages. Applying Machine Learning techniques to data filtration and data cleaning could aid and generalize the process, thus decreasing overall latency from acquisition to training.
  - Strategies to make the source look more like the target (or vice versa) – A corollary to data sparsity is faulty word alignment, where low frequency words fail to get good alignments because there is not enough data to reinforce fairly weak hypotheses, or where source-target distortion is high. Both problems disfavor what alignments do exist. If the source and target are reordered so that one side more closely matches the other, or one side is "enriched" to be more like the other, one can reduce distortion related effects, and might also counter the large number of forms in morphologically rich languages (*e.g.*, (Yeniterzi and Oflazer, 2010; Genzel, 2010), and many others).

- Strategies to systematically deal with complex morphology – this is one on-going area of research that could still net large returns, since, even with some relatively high-data languages, such as Finnish, data is made sparser due to the multiplication of possible forms. There is too long a literature to really do justice here, but some recent work includes discrimitative lexicons (Jeong et al., 2010), sub-word alignment strategies (Bodrumlu et al., 2009), learning the morphological variants in a language (Oflazer and El-kahlout, 2007), using off-the-shelf morphological tools, *e.g.*, Morfessor [11], etc.

- Use syntax or linguistic knowledge in the translation task – By reducing the hypothesis space for possible alignments, syntax-based

[11] http://www.cis.hut.fi/projects/morpho/

approaches can do better in lower-data situations and can handle source-target discontinuities better than straight phrase-based systems (*e.g.*, (Quirk and Menezes, 2006; Li et al., 2010)).

7 The MT Crisis Cookbook

Given the relatively narrow domain context of Crisis MT—generally the needed vocabulary and data should be centered on relief work, medical interactions, and communicating with the affected populations—it may be possible to approach Crisis MT as we would MT for any domain (*e.g.*, news, government, etc.). With enough data relevant to a particular domain or sub-domain (*e.g.*, earthquake, tsunami, nuclear disaster, flooding, etc.), it would be possible to build the relevant translation memories (TMs) and train highly domain-specific MT engines to produce translations of reasonable quality and utility. Even with highly inflected languages, a domain-specific approach may get around many of the data sparsity issues.

It is also crucial that no data be thrown out. Relief specific content that was relevant to an earlier crisis can certainly contribute to subsequent crises. Among these data are difficult to replicate sources of data, such as SMS messages. This data would constitute a highly domain specific set of data which would only grow over time.

7.1 Outline of the Cookbook

The recipe for the MT Crisis Cookbook consists of two parts:

1. The **content** that would be most useful in crisis situations. This consists of relief-centric vocabulary, phrases, sentences, and other material. It should be in some common "source" language, likely English (English is a reasonable "pivot" in and out of many other languages, given the ubiquity of English-to-X content).
2. The **infrastructure** to support relief workers, aid agencies, and the affected population. As made obvious in Haiti, an SMS messaging infrastructure integrated into a crowd-sourced translation infrastructure, proved to be crucial. For future crises, this infrastructure should be streamlined and have public MT APIs integrated directly into it (to support first pass MT).

7.2 Cookbook Data

As noted in Section 5, one way to counter the data sparsity problem is to build domain specific engines, with a set of data ready-to-go in the event of a crisis. This data, which would exist in English and possibly other languages, would be translated into the target language (if needed), distributed to to aid organizations (as needed), and used to train MT engines and other language processing resources. The following list constitutes a set of possible sources. It is by no means complete (for instance, some resources specific to particular crisis types, *e.g.*, floods, nuclear disasters, etc. are not included), but it does represent a good central core of resources that should be part of any Crisis Cookbook[12] :

- Where There is No Doctor – This is one of the most recognized and widely used and useful references in under-resourced regions around the world. The publisher of the text, the Hesperian Foundation, has already had the text translated into 75 languages, and it is available in PDF as a free download from their website.[13]
- CMU Medical Domain Phrases, Sentences, and Glossary – Collected under the jointly NSF/EU funded NESPOLE! and DIPLOMAT projects (Frederking et al., 1997), this data consists of common phrases and sentences that would be useful in a crisis medical scenario, and would be quite useful for training MT, as it was for training the Kreyòl engines. Only the English side of this data would be relevant to future crises.
- Anonymized Crisis-related SMS Messages – Relief-related SMS messages may be particularly useful in future crises, since those collected in a crisis scenario are likely to contain content that transfers readily to similar crises. A selected sample of the 80,000+ messages resulting from the Haitian crisis could constitute

[12]Some of the resources listed here are under copyright. There may need to be some negotiation with the copyright owners to ensure that the texts can be used, and how they can be used (*e.g.*, to train MT, to be used in TMs, to be distributed in hardcopy form, etc.).

[13]http://hesperian.org/

a reasonable core of SMS messages that could be added to over time.

- Red Cross Emergency Multilingual Phrasebook – A small, but highly focused, set of phrases and questions useful in an emergency medical context. Available in multiple languages.
- Emergency and Crisis Communication Vocabulary – An example bilingual set was prepared by the Canadian Government in both French and English[14] , consisting of a small list of "official" terms needed in crisis situations, and their associated descriptions. Although the terms on the Canadian site are translated and defined only in English and French and have a bias to the Canadian government nomeclature, having such a list of terms from multiple government agencies and their definitions could prove useful for relief vocabulary as well as for vocabulary needed for official announcements.
- High Frequency Wikipedia Disaster Content – This would consist of vocabulary that recurs across multiple related crisis pages on wikipedia. The idea is to harvest those terms that repeat across multiple pages of the same "sub-domain" (*e.g.*, those that cover events with floods, earthquakes, nuclear disasters, etc.), but document disasters in different locales, where cross-page repeated vocabulary is favored (substracting out high-frequency vocabulary that occurs elsewhere). This vocabulary could be distilled automatically from a set of relevant pages, and would likely contain core vocabulary for specific crisis and disaster contexts. For instance, shared vocabulary between the Japanese, Indonesian, Pakistani, and Haitian Earthquake pages might contain a reasonable set of vocabulary relevant to earthquake crises as a whole.

7.3 Cookbook Infrastructure

The Cookbook infrastructure draws directly on what was found to be useful in the Haitian Crisis. Here are the infrastructural components we see as crucial:

- A crowd sourced microtasking infrastructure to translate and route messages from the field. This proved to be essential in Haiti. Having such an infrastructure ready-to-go for future crises would shave days off implementation and likely have profound effects on the rapidity of the response.
- Integration of the APIs for the publically available MT services, such as Microsoft Translator and Google Translate, into the microtasking and messaging infrastructure, enabling processing of SMS messages, Twitter feeds, etc. In this way, when any of these services deploy MT for a given crisis language, the switch can be flipped and first-pass can be MT activated at a moment's notice.
- A ready-to-go smart phone app that acts as a crisis Translation Memory, which can be populated with Cookbook content as it becomes available. In this manner, rather than relying on the distribution of paper copies of Cookbook materials, relief workers on the ground could just sync-up their mobile devices to get the latest content. This is particularly important in crisis locales where "data plan" access is limited, and phones will thus not necessarily have online access to cloud based resources on a regular basis.

8 A Sample Crisis Timeline

The following timeline is only meant to demonstrate what might be possible with the right infrastructure in place and the community fully engaged. The mantra of "every crisis is different" applies, and this timeline should not be interpreted as a "cookbook" for a future event. All place and entity names are intended to add realism; there was no intention to leave anyone in or out.

Day 0 – A massive earthquake hits the island nation of Palladi.

Day 1 – The first aid organizations arrive on the island with food and humanitarian aid, although only the two major cities are directly accessible. Thousands of Palladians are not reachable by aid organizations, and the exact numbers that are affected and their locations are not known.

[14]http://www.btb.gc.ca/publications/documents/crise-crisis.pdf

The native population of Palladians is nearly 80% monolingual. There is a dire need for Palladian interpreters, but also of translated Palladian content. Notified of the need for Palladian translations, MT community volunteers begin efforts to collect and license data in Palladian. The relief community responds by activating the crowd sourcing infrastructure used in other relief scenarios. Researchers and disaster response teams are notified at Microsoft Research and Google Research of the critical need for crisis content to be translated into Palladian. Native Palladian speakers are being looked for by all parties.

Day 2 – As with the Haitian crisis, a text messaging infrastructure is put in place such that text messages can be received from the population and routed to a crowd of rapidly assembling volunteers. Since there is some internet access, including via mobile phones, twitter feeds are monitored. Until messages start arriving, a small crowd of Palladian speakers begin translating content into Palladian, focused specifically on the Cookbook and off-the-shelf SMS content.

The first text messages start arriving by late afternoon. These text messages are routed directly to the text messaging and microtasking infrastructure. The small but growing crowd of Palladian translators begin translating this growing tide of messages.

Day 3 – The humanitarian information processing community, with the support of many organizations and volunteers, releases the first sections of the Crisis Cookbook. The Crisis Cookbook is transmitted directly to aid organizations on the ground in Palladi, and soft- and hard-copies are distributed to aid workers as quickly as feasible.

AT&T puts into place several cell towers with satellite connectivity for areas that do not have cell coverage. Within hours, text and twitter messages from the field increase dramatically.

Day 4 – Microsoft and Google release the first versions of their Palladian-English translators, with ready access via their public APIs. Since the text messaging infrastructure already has both APIs integrated directly into the microtasking and message processing infrastructure, both engines are activated immediately, and all messages are translated first by one or the other engine, and the MT'd content along with the original message are handed to volunteers.[15] Translations are repaired, and routed directly to aid organizations, and to the Google and Microsoft teams (for retraining models).

Day 5 – Additional cookbook materials are translated. Researchers at Johns Hopkins locate a stash of Palladian data at the Palladian Central University. This data is posted at the CMU site, and is immediately consumed by all parties working on the MT problem.

Day 6 – Researchers at University of Edinburgh develop a novel algorithm for dealing with Palladian vowel harmony, which has been a major problem with Palladian MT, since data sparsity is exacerbated by the problem. The Edinburgh researchers publish the algorithm immediately to their Web site, and notify both Microsoft and Google.

Day 10 – Armed with algorithmic improvements and an increasing volume of data, machine translated content is now achieving sufficient quality to warrant passing it directly to aid organizations. Palladian volunteers now work principally on the hard to translate cases (those with high OOVs), and on post-response data clean-up. The fruits of their labor result in iterative improvements on the various MT engines that have been deployed.

Day 11+ – The deployment of language technologies, specifically MT, in the Palladian crisis results in saving untold thousands of lives. The lessons learned in the Palladian earthquake will be applied to future crises, and the translated content produced by volunteers will be added to the cookbook for use in the next crisis.

[15]Determining which engine to send translations to is a problem that should be resolved in advance. A combination of either random selection or on-the-fly OOV calculations could be used to determine routing.

9 Conclusion

In this paper, we propose that MT is an important technology in crisis events, something that can and should be an integral part of the rapid-response infrastructure. By integrating MT services directly into a messaging infrastructure (whatever the type of messages being serviced, *e.g.*, text messages, Twitter feeds, blog postings, etc.), MT can be used to provide first pass translations into a majority language, which can assist in triaging messages and routing them to appropriate aid agencies. If done right, MT can dramatically increase the speed by which relief can be provided. To ensure that MT is a standard tool in the arsenal of tools used in crisis events, we propose a preliminary *Crisis Cookbook*, the data contents of which could be translated into the relevant language(s) by volunteers immediately after a crisis event takes place. The resulting data can then be made available to relief groups on the ground, as well as to providers of MT services. We also note that there are significant contributions that our community can make to relief efforts through continued work on our research, especially that research which makes MT more viable for under-resourced languages.

Credits

This paper is dedicated to the thousands of volunteers who worked selflessly for many, many hours in aid of the people of Haiti. Without their help, many hundreds more would have perished. We also wish to express our deepest appreciation to all those who have devoted their lives to aid people in need, especially the first responders in crisis events. It is our sincerest hope that that the small measures our community can take to assist in relief efforts will help make your jobs more effective, and that our efforts will ultimately assist you and those you strive to help.

References

Jeffrey Allen. 1998. Lexical variation in Haitian Creole and orthographic issues for Machine Translation (MT) and Optical Character Recognition (OCR) applications. In *Association for Machine Translation in the Americas (AMTA) Workshop on Embedded MT Systems: Design, Construction, and Evaluation of Systems with an MT Component*, Langhorne, Pennsylvania.

Vamshi Ambati, Sanjika Hewavitharana, Stephan Vogel, and Jaime Carbonell. 2011. Active Learning with Multiple Annotations for Comparable Data Classification Task. In *Proceedings of ACL 2011*, Portland, Oregon, June.

Sharon Anderson. 2010. Talking with Adm. James G. Stavridis Supreme Allied Commander, Europe Commander, U.S. European Command. *CHIPS - The Department of the Navy Information Technology Magazine*, 28.

Tugba Bodrumlu, Kevin Knight, and Sujith Ravi. 2009. A New Objective Function for Word Alignment. In *Proceedings of the NAACL/HLT Workshop on Integer Programming for Natural Language Processing*, Boulder, Colorado.

Disaster 2.0. 2011. *Disaster Relief 2.0: The Future of Information Sharing in Humanitarian Emergencies.* United Nations Foundation, UN Office for the Coordination of Humanitarian Affairs (UN OCHA), Vodafone Foundation, Harvard Humanitarian Initiative.

Heidi Fox. 2002. Phrasal cohesion and statistical machine translation. In *Proceedings of EMNLP 2002*, Philadelphia, Pennsylvania.

Robert Frederking, Alexander Rudnicky, and Christopher Hogan. 1997. Interactive speech translation in the diplomat project. In *Workshop on Spoken Language Translation at ACL-97*, Madrid.

Dmitriy Genzel. 2010. Automatically Learning Source-side Reordering Rules for Large Scale Machine Translation. In *Proceedings of COLING 2010*, Beijing, August.

Sanjika Hewavitharana and Stephan Vogel. 2008. Enhancing a Statistical Machine Translation System by using an Automatically Extracted Parallel Corpus from Comparable Sources. In *Proceedings of the 6th International Conference on Language Resources and Evaluation (LREC 2008), Workshop on Comparable Corpora*, Marrakech, Morocco, May.

Sanjika Hewavitharana and Stephan Vogel. 2011. Extracting Parallel Phrases from Comparable Data. In *Proceedings of ACL 2011*, Portland, Oregon, June.

Ann Irvine, Chris Callison-Burch, and Alexandre Klementiev. 2010. Transliterating from all languages. In

Proceedings of the Ninth Conference of the Association for Machine Translation in the Americas (AMTA 2010), Denver.

Minwoo Jeong, Kristina Toutanova, Hisami Suzuki, and Chris Quirk. 2010. A Discriminative Lexicon Model for Complex Morphology. In *Proceedings of the Ninth Conference of the Association for Machine Translation in the Americas (AMTA 2010)*, Denver.

Claire Lefebvre. 1998. *Creole Genesis and the Acquisition of Grammar: The case of Haitian Creole*. Cambridge University Press, Cambridge, England.

William D. Lewis and Fei Xia. 2010. Developing ODIN: A Multilingual Repository of Annotated Language Data for Hundreds of the World's Languages. *Literary and Linguistic Computing*. See: http://research.microsoft.com/apps/pubs/default.aspx?id=138757.

William D. Lewis. 2010. Haitian Creole: How to Build and Ship an MT Engine from Scratch in 4 Days, 17 Hours, & 30 Minutes. In *EAMT 2010: Proceedings of the 14th Annual conference of the European Association for Machine Translation*, Saint Raphaël, France, May.

Zhifei Li, Chris Callison-Burch, Chris Dyer, Juri Ganitkevitch, Ann Irvine, Lane Schwartz, Wren N. G. Thornton, Ziyuan Wang, Jonathan Weese, and Omar F. Zaidan. 2010. Joshua 2.0: A Toolkit for Parsing-Based Machine Translation with Syntax, Semirings, Discriminative Training and Other Goodies. In *In Proceedings of Workshop on Statistical Machine Translation (WMT10)*, Uppsala, Sweden.

Christian Monson, Ariadna Font Llitjos, Vamshi Ambati, Lori Levin, Alon Lavie, Alison Alvarez, Robert Frederking Roberto Aranovich, Jaime Carbonell, Erik Peterson, and Katharina Probst. 2008. Linguistic Structure and Bilingual Informants Help Induce Machine Translation of Lesser-Resourced Languages. In *Proceedings of the 6th International Conference on Language Resources and Evaluation (LREC 2008)*, Marrakech, Morocco.

Robert Munro. 2010. Crowdsourced translation for emergency response in Haiti: the global collaboration of local knowledge. In *AMTA Workshop on Collaborative Crowdsourcing for Translation*.

Robert Munro. 2011. Subword and spatiotemporal models for identifying actionable information in Haitian Kreyol. In *Fifteenth Conference on Computational Natural Language Learning (CoNLL 2011)*, Portland.

Douglas W. Oard and Franz Josef Och. 2003. Rapid-Response Machine Translation for Unexpected Languages. In *MT Summit IX*, New Orleans.

Douglas W. Oard. 2003. The Surprise Language Exercises. *ACM Transactions on Asian Language Information Processing - TALIP*, 2(2):79–84.

Kemal Oflazer and Ilknur Durgar El-kahlout. 2007. Exploring Different Representational Units in English-to-Turkish Statistical Machine Translation. In *In Proceedings of the Statistical Machine Translation Workshop, ACL 2007*, Prague.

Chris Quirk and Arul Menezes. 2006. Dependency Treelet Translation: The convergence of statistical and example-based machine translation? *Machine Translation*, 20:43–65.

Sujith Ravi and Kevin Knight. 2011. Deciphering foreign language. In *Proceedings of ACL 2011*, Portland, Oregon, June.

RC. 2010. The American Red Cross: Social Media in Disasters and Emergencies. Presentation.

Jason Smith, Chris Quirk, and Kristina Toutanova. 2010. Extracting parallel sentences from comparable corpora using document level alignment. In *Proceedings of Human Language Technologies: The 2010 Annual Conference of the North American Chapter of the ACL*, Los Angeles.

Raghavendra Udupa, K Saravanan, A Kumaran, and Jagadeesh Jagarlamudi. 2009. MINT: A Method for Effective and Scalable Mining of Named Entity Transliterations from Large Comparable Corpora. In *Proceedings of the 12th Conference of the European Chapter of the Association for Computational Linguistics (EACL 2009)*, Athens, Greece.

Andrej Verity. 2011. What the UN could not have done without the Volunteer Technical Community. In *United Nations Dispatch*. The Disaster Relief 2.0 Blog Series.

Reyyan Yeniterzi and Kemal Oflazer. 2010. Syntax-to-Morphology Mapping in Factored Phrase-Based Statistical Machine Translation from English to Turkish. In *Proceedings of the ACL 2010*, Uppsala, Sweden.

Omar Zaidan and Chris Callison-Burch. 2011. Crowdsourcing Translation: Professional Quality from Non-Professionals. In *Proceedings of ACL 2011*, Portland, Oregon, June.

Generative Models of Monolingual and Bilingual Gappy Patterns

Kevin Gimpel Noah A. Smith
Language Technologies Institute
Carnegie Mellon University
Pittsburgh, PA 15213, USA
{kgimpel,nasmith}@cs.cmu.edu

Abstract

A growing body of machine translation research aims to exploit lexical patterns (e.g., n-grams and phrase pairs) with *gaps* (Simard et al., 2005; Chiang, 2005; Xiong et al., 2011). Typically, these "gappy patterns" are discovered using heuristics based on word alignments or local statistics such as mutual information. In this paper, we develop generative models of monolingual and parallel text that build sentences using gappy patterns of arbitrary length and with arbitrarily many gaps. We exploit Bayesian nonparametrics and collapsed Gibbs sampling to discover salient patterns in a corpus. We evaluate the patterns qualitatively and also add them as features to an MT system, reporting promising preliminary results.

1 Introduction

Beginning with the success of phrase-based translation models (Koehn et al., 2003), a trend arose of modeling larger and increasingly complex structural units in translation. One thread of work has focused on the use of lexical patterns with *gaps*. Simard et al. (2005) proposed using phrase pairs with gaps in a phrase-based translation model, providing a heuristic method to extract gappy phrase pairs from word-aligned parallel corpora. The widely-used hierarchical phrase-based translation framework was introduced by Chiang (2005) and also relies on a simple heuristic for phrase pair extraction. On the monolingual side, researchers have taken inspiration from trigger-based language modeling for speech recognition (Rosenfeld, 1996). Recently Xiong et al. (2011) used monolingual trigger pairs to improve handling of long-distance dependencies in machine translation output.

All of this previous work used heuristics or local statistical tests to extract patterns from corpora. In this paper, we present probabilistic models that generate text using gappy patterns of arbitrary length and with arbitrarily-many gaps. We exploit nonparametric priors and use Bayesian inference to discover the most salient gappy patterns in monolingual and parallel text. We first inspect these patterns manually and discuss the categories of phenomena that they capture. We also add them as features in a discriminatively-trained phrase-based MT system, using standard techniques to train their weights (Arun and Koehn, 2007; Watanabe et al., 2007) and incorporate them during decoding (Chiang, 2007). We present experiments for Spanish-English and Chinese-English translation, reporting encouraging preliminary results.

2 Related Work

There is a rich history of trigger-based language modeling in the speech recognition community, typically involving the use of statistical tests to discover useful trigger-word pairs (Rosenfeld, 1996; Jelinek, 1997). Xiong et al. (2011) used Rosenfeld's mutual information procedure to discover trigger pairs and added a single feature to a phrase-based MT system that scores new words based on all potential triggers from previous parts of the derivation. We are not aware of prior work that uses generative modeling and Bayesian nonparametrics to discover these same types of patterns automatically; doing so allows us to discover larger patterns with more words and gaps if they are warranted by the data.

In addition to the gappy phrase-based (Simard et al., 2005) and hierarchical phrase-based (Chiang, 2005) models mentioned earlier, other researchers have explored the use of bilingual gappy structures for machine translation. Crego and Yvon (2009) and

Proceedings of the 6th Workshop on Statistical Machine Translation, pages 512–522,
Edinburgh, Scotland, UK, July 30–31, 2011.

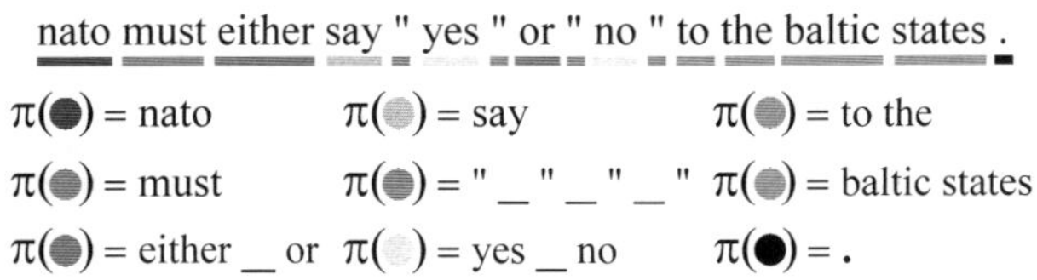

Figure 1: A sentence from the news commentary corpus, along with color assignments for the words and the π function for each color.

Galley and Manning (2010) proposed ways of incorporating phrase pairs with gaps into standard left-to-right decoding algorithms familiar to phrase-based and N-gram-based MT; both used heuristics to extract phrase pairs. Bansal et al. (2011) presented a model and training procedure for word alignment that uses phrase pairs with gaps. They use a semi-Markov model with an enlarged dynamic programming state in order to represent alignment between gappy phrases. Their model permits up to one gap per phrase while our models permit an arbitrary number.

3 Monolingual Pattern Models

We first present a model that generates a sentence as a set of lexical items that we will refer to as **gappy patterns**, or simply **patterns**. A pattern is defined as a sequence containing elements of two types: **words** and **gaps**. All patterns must obey the regular expression `w+ (_ w+)*`, where `w` is a word and `_` is a gap. That is, patterns must begin and end with words and may not contain consecutive gaps.

We assume that we have an n-word sentence $\boldsymbol{w}_{1:n}$.[1] We represent patterns in a sentence by associating each word with a **color**. To do so, we introduce a vector of color assignment variables $\boldsymbol{c}_{1:n}$, with one for each word. We represent a color C_j as a set in terms of the c_i variables: $C_j = \{i : c_i = j\}$. Each color corresponds to a pattern that is obtained by concatenating its words from left to right in the sentence, inserting gaps when necessary. We denote the pattern for a color C_j by $\pi(C_j)$; Figure 1 shows examples of the correspondence between colors and patterns.

The generative story for a single sentence follows:

1. Sample the number of words: $n \sim \text{Poisson}(\beta)$
2. Sample the number of unique colors in the sentence given n: $m \sim \text{Uniform}(1, n)$
3. For each word index $i = 1 \ldots n$, sample the color of word i: $c_i \sim \text{Uniform}(1, m)$. If any of the m colors has no words, repeat this step.
4. For each color $j = 1 \ldots m$, sample from a multinomial distribution over patterns: $\boldsymbol{w}_{C_j} \sim \text{Mult}(\mu)$. If the words $\boldsymbol{w}_{C_j}$ are not consistent with the color assignments, i.e., wrong number of words or gaps, gaps not in the correct locations, repeat this step.

Thus, the probability of generating number of words n, words $\boldsymbol{w}_{1:n}$, color assignments $\boldsymbol{c}_{1:n}$, and number of colors m is

$$p(\boldsymbol{w}_{1:n}, \boldsymbol{c}_{1:n}, m \mid \beta, \mu) = \frac{1}{Z}\left(\frac{\beta^n}{n!}e^{-\beta}\right)\left(\frac{1}{n}\right)\left(\frac{1}{m}\right)^n \prod_{j=1}^{m} p_\mu(\pi(C_j)) \quad (1)$$

where Z is a normalization constant required by the potential repetition of sampling in the final two steps of the generative story. Without Z, the model would be deficient as we would waste probability mass on internally inconsistent color assignments.

The core of the model is a single multinomial distribution $p_\mu(\cdot)$ over patterns. We use a Dirichlet process (DP) prior for this multinomial so that we can model an unbounded set of patterns: $\mu \sim \text{DP}(\alpha, P_0)$, where α is the concentration parameter and P_0 is the base distribution. The base distribution includes a $\text{Poisson}(\nu)$ over the number of words in the pattern, a uniform distribution (over word types in the vocabulary) for each word, a uniform distribution over the number of gaps given the number of words, and a uniform distribution over the arrangement of gaps given the numbers of gaps and words.[2]

Inference We use collapsed Gibbs sampling for inference. Our goal is to obtain samples from the posterior distribution $p(\{\boldsymbol{c}^{(i)}, m^{(i)}\}_{i=1}^S \mid \{\boldsymbol{w}^{(i)}\}_{i=1}^S, \nu, \alpha)$, where S is the total number of sentences in the corpus and μ is marginalized out.[3]

[1] We use boldface lowercase letters to denote vectors (e.g., $\boldsymbol{f}$), denote entry i as f_i, and denote the range from i to j as $\boldsymbol{f}_{i:j}$.

[2] The number of ways of arranging y gaps among x words is "$(x-1)$ choose y".

[3] Since we assume the words are given, β is irrelevant.

During each iteration of Gibbs sampling, we proceed through the corpus and sample a new value for each c_i variable conditioned on the values of all others in the corpus. The m variables are determined by the c_i variables and therefore do not need to be sampled directly. When sampling c_i, we first remove c_i from the corpus (and its color if the color only contained i). Where the remaining colors in the sentence are numbered from 1 to m, there are $m + 1$ possibilities for c_i: m for each of the existing colors and one for choosing a new color.

Since choosing a new color corresponds to creating a new instance of the pattern $\pi(\{i\})$, the probability of choosing a new color $m + 1$ is proportional to

$$\frac{\#_{\pi(\{i\})} + \alpha P_0(\pi(\{i\}))}{\# + \alpha} \tag{2}$$

where $\#_\pi$ is the count of pattern π in the rest of the sentence and all other sentences in the corpus, and $\#$ is the total count of all patterns in this same set. The probability of choosing the existing color j (for $1 \le j \le m$) is proportional to

$$\frac{\#_{\pi(C_j \cup \{i\})} + \alpha P_0(\pi(C_j \cup \{i\}))}{\#_{\pi(C_j)} + \alpha P_0(\pi(C_j))} \tag{3}$$

where the denominator encodes the fact that the move will cause an instance of the pattern for the color C_j to be removed from the corpus as the new pattern for $C_j \cup \{i\}$ is added.

We note that, even though these two types of moves will result in different numbers of colors (m) in the sentence, we do not have to include a term for this in the sampler because we use a uniform distribution for m and therefore all (valid) numbers of colors have the same probability. The normalization constant Z in Equation 1 does not affect inference because our sampler is designed to only consider valid (i.e., internally consistent) settings for the $\boldsymbol{c}^{(i)}$ and $m^{(i)}$ variables.

This model makes few assumptions, using uniform distributions whenever possible. This simplifies inference and causes the resulting lexicon to be influenced primarily by the "rich-get-richer" effect of the DP prior. Despite its simplicity, we will show later that this model discovers patterns that capture a variety of linguistic phenomena.

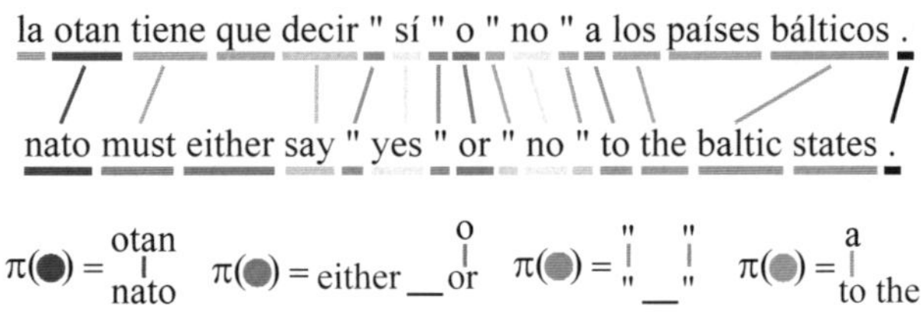

Figure 2: A Spanish-English sentence pair with the intersection of automatic word alignments in each direction. Some source words accept the colors of target words aligned to them while others (light gray) do not. Bilingual patterns for a few colors are shown.

4 Bilingual Pattern Models

We now present a generative model for a sentence *pair* that will enable us to discover *bilingual* patterns. In this section we present one example of extending the previous model to be bilingual, but we note that many other extensions are possible; indeed, flexibility is one of the key advantages of working within the framework of probabilistic modeling.

We assume that we are given sentence pairs and one-to-one word alignments. That is, in addition to an n-word target sentence $\boldsymbol{w}_{1:n}$, we assume we have an n'-word source sentence $\boldsymbol{w}'_{1:n'}$ and word alignments $\boldsymbol{a}_{1:n'}$ where $a_i = j$ iff w'_i is aligned to w_j and $a_i = 0$ if w'_i is aligned to null.

To model bilingual patterns, we distinguish **source colors** from **target colors**. A target-language word can only be colored with a target color, but a source word can be colored with either a source color or with the target color of the target word it is aligned to (if any). We have m target colors as before and now add m' source colors. We introduce additional random variables in the form of a binary vector $\boldsymbol{g}$ of length n' that indicates, for each source word, whether or not it accepts the color of its aligned target word. We introduce an additional parameter γ for the probability that a source word will accept the color of its aligned word. We fix its value to 0.5 and do not learn it during inference. Figure 2 shows an example Spanish-English sentence pair with automatic word alignments and color assignments. The bilingual patterns for a few target colors are shown.

The generative story for a sentence pair follows:

1. Sample the numbers of words in the source and target sentences: $n', n \sim \text{Poisson}(\beta)$

2. Sample the numbers of source and target colors given n', n: $m' \sim \text{Uniform}(1, n'), m \sim \text{Uniform}(1, n)$

3. Sample the alignment vector from any distribution that ensures links are 1-to-1:[4] $\boldsymbol{a}_{1:n'} \sim p(\boldsymbol{a})$

4. For each target word index $i = 1 \ldots n$, sample the color of target word i from a uniform distribution over all target colors: $c_i \sim \text{Uniform}(1, m)$. While any of the m colors has no words, repeat this step.

5. For each source word index $i = 1 \ldots n'$:

   1. Decide whether to use a source color or to use the target color of the aligned target word: $g_i \sim p_\gamma(g_i \mid a_i)$
   2. If $g_i = 1$, set $c'_i = c_{a_i}$; otherwise, sample a source color: $c'_i \sim \text{Uniform}(1, m')$

6. If any source color has no words, repeat Step 5.

7. For each source color $j = 1 \ldots m'$:

   1. Sample from a multinomial over source patterns: $\boldsymbol{w}_{C'_j} \sim \text{Mult}(\mu')$. While the words $\boldsymbol{w}_{C'_j}$ are not consistent with the color assignments, repeat this step.

8. For each target color $j = 1 \ldots m$:

   1. Sample from a multinomial over bilingual patterns: $\boldsymbol{w}_{C_j} \sim \text{Mult}(\mu)$. While the words $\boldsymbol{w}_{C_j}$ are not consistent with the color assignments, repeat this step.

The distribution $p_\gamma(g_i \mid a_i)$ is defined below:

$$p_\gamma(g_i = 1 \mid a_i \neq -1) = \gamma$$
$$p_\gamma(g_i = 1 \mid a_i = -1) = 0$$

where γ determines how frequently source tokens will be added to target patterns.

The probability of generating target words $\boldsymbol{w}_{1:n}$, source words $\boldsymbol{w}'_{1:n'}$, alignments $\boldsymbol{a}_{1:n'}$, target color assignments $\boldsymbol{c}_{1:n}$, source color assignments $\boldsymbol{c}'_{1:n'}$, color propagation variables $\boldsymbol{g}_{1:n'}$, number of target colors m, and number of source colors m' is

$$\frac{1}{Z} p(n) p(n') p(m \mid n) p(m' \mid n') p(\boldsymbol{a}_{1:n'}) \times \left(\prod_{i=1}^{n} p(c_i \mid m) \right) \times \left(\prod_{i=1}^{n'} p_\gamma(g_i \mid a_i) p(c'_i \mid m')^{I[g_i == 0]} \right) \times \left(\prod_{j=1}^{m'} p'_\mu(\pi(C'_j)) \right) \left(\prod_{j=1}^{m} p_\mu(\pi(C_j)) \right)$$

where Z again serves as a normalization constant to prevent the model from leaking probability mass on internally inconsistent configurations.

There are now two multinomial distributions over patterns with parameter vectors μ and μ'. They both use DP priors with identical concentration parameters α and differing base distributions P_0 and P'_0. The base distribution for source patterns, P'_0, takes the same form as the base distribution for the model described in §3.

For target patterns with aligned source words, P_0 generates the target part of the pattern like the base distribution in §3 and then generates the number of aligned source words to each target word with a $\text{Poisson}(1)$ distribution; the number of aligned source words can only be 0 or 1 when all word links are 1-to-1. If it is 1, the base distribution generates the aligned source word by sampling uniformly from among all source types.

While there are connections between this model and work on performing translation using phrase pairs with gaps, the patterns we discover are not guaranteed to be bilingual translation units. Rather, they typically contain additional target-side words that have no explicit correlate on the source side. They can be used to assist an existing translation model by helping to choose the best phrase translation for each source phrase. To define a generative model for phrase pairs with gaps, changes would have to be made to the bilingual model we presented.

Inference As before, we use collapsed Gibbs sampling for inference. Our goal is to obtain samples from the posterior $p(\{\langle \boldsymbol{c}, \boldsymbol{c}', \boldsymbol{g}, m, m' \rangle^{(i)}\}_{i=1}^{S} \mid \{\langle \boldsymbol{w}, \boldsymbol{w}', \boldsymbol{a} \rangle^{(i)}\}_{i=1}^{S})$.

[4]Since we assume alignments are provided during inference, it does not matter what distribution is used, so long as only 1-to-1 links are permitted.

We go through each sentence pair and sample new color assignment variables for each word. For an aligned word pair (w'_i, w_j), we sample a new value for the tuple (g_i, c'_i, c_j). The possible values for c_j include all target colors, including a new target color. The possible values for g_i are 0, in which case c'_i can be any of the source colors, including a new source color, and 1, for which c'_i must be c_j. For an unaligned target word w_j, c_j can be any target color, including a new one, and for an unaligned source word w'_i, c'_i can be any source color, including a new one. The full equations for sampling can be easily derived using the equations from §3.

" __ "	as __ as	" __ " __ " __ "
– __ –	the __ of __ in	why __ ?
(__)	the __ is	, __ the __ of
the __ of	not only __ but	from __ to
, __ , __ ,	it is __ that	the __ between __ and
the __ (__)	of __ " __ "	such as __ ,
both __ and	not __ , but	either __ or
the __ of __ and	in __ , __ in	but __ is
more __ than	the __ of __ ,	" __ " __ the
- __ -	what __ ?	has __ been
, __ " __ "	between __ and	in __ , __ ,
the __ " __ "	the __ of __ 's	an __ of

Table 1: Top-ranked gappy patterns from samples according to $p(\pi)$; patterns without gaps are omitted. The special string "__" represents a gap that can be filled by any nonempty sequence of words.

5 Evaluation

We conducted evaluation to determine (1) what types of phenomena are captured by the most probable patterns discovered by our models, and (2) whether including the patterns as features can improve translation quality.

5.1 Qualitative Evaluation

5.1.1 Monolingual Model

Since inference is computationally expensive, we used the 126K-sentence English news commentary corpus provided for the WMT shared tasks (Callison-Burch et al., 2010). We ran Gibbs sampling for 600 iterations through the data, discarding the first 300 samples for burn-in and computing statistics of the patterns using the remaining 300 samples. Each iteration took approximately 3 minutes on a single 2.2GHz CPU. When looking primarily at the most frequent patterns, we found that this list did not vary much when only using half of the data instead. We set $\nu = 3$ and $\alpha = 100$; we found these hyperparameters to have only minor effects on the results.

Since many frequent patterns include the period (.), we found it useful to constrain the model to treat this token differently: we modify the base distribution so that it assigns zero probability to patterns that contain a period along with other words and we force each occurrence of a period to be alone in its own pattern during initialization. We do not need to change the inference procedure at all; with the modified base distribution and with no patterns including a period with other words, the probability of creating a new illegal pattern during inference is always zero (Eq. 3).

We also perform inference on a transformed version of the corpus in which every word is replaced with its hard word class obtained from Brown clustering (Brown et al., 1992). One property of Brown clusters is that each function word effectively receives its own class, as each ends up in a cluster in which it occupies $\geq$95% of the token counts of all types in the cluster. We call clusters that satisfy this property **singleton clusters**.

To obtain Brown clusters for the source and target languages, we used code from Liang (2005).[5] We used the data from the news commentary corpus along with the first 500K sentences of the additional monolingual newswire data also provided for the WMT shared tasks. We used 300 clusters, ignoring words that appeared only once in this corpus. We did not use the hierarchical information from the clusters but merely converted each cluster name into a unique integer, using one additional integer for unknown words.

We used the same values for ν and α as above but ran Gibbs sampling for 1,300 iterations, again using the last 300 for collecting statistics on patterns. Judging by the number of color assignments changed on each iteration, the sampler takes longer to converge when run on word clusters than on words. As above, we constrain the singleton word cluster corresponding to the period to be alone during both initialization and inference.

[5] http://www.cs.berkeley.edu/~pliang/software

academy _ sciences	regulators _ supervisors
beijing _ shanghai	sine _ non
booms _ busts	stalin _ mao
council _ advisers	treasury secretary _ geithner
dominicans _ haitian	sooner _ later
flemish _ walloons	first _ foremost
gref _ program	played _ role
heat _ droughts	down _ road
humanitarian _ displaced	freedom _ expression
karnofsky _ hassenfeld	at _ disposal
kazakhstan _ kyrgyzstan	take _ granted
portugal _ greece	- _ -

Table 2: Gappy patterns with highest conditional probability $p(\pi|\boldsymbol{w}(\pi))$.

– _ –	whether _ or	france _ germany
(_)	around _ world	he _ his
- _ -	has _ been	allow _ to
both _ and	how _ ?	for _ first time
not only _ but	the _ (_)	china _ india
" _ "	on _ basis	what _ do
more _ than	less _ than	we _ our
either _ or	on _ other hand	over _ past
why _ ?	at _ level	prevent _ from
neither _ nor	it is _ that	in _ way
what _ ?	not _ , but	one _ another
rule _ law	play _ role	political _ economic

Table 3: Top-ranked gappy patterns according to $p(\pi)p(\pi|\boldsymbol{w}(\pi))$.

Pattern Ranking Statistics Several choices exist for ranking patterns. The simplest is to take the pattern count from the posterior samples, averaged over all sampling iterations after burn-in. We refer to this criterion as the **marginal probability**:

$$p(\pi) = \frac{\#_\pi}{\#}$$

where $\#_\pi$ is the average count of the pattern across the posterior samples and $\#$ is the count of all patterns. The top-ranked gappy patterns under this criterion are shown in Table 1. While many of these patterns match our intuitions, there are also several that are highly-ranked simply because their constituent words are frequent.

Alternatively, we can rank patterns by the **conditional probability** of the pattern given the words that comprise it:

$$p(\pi|\boldsymbol{w}(\pi)) = \frac{\#_\pi}{\#_{\boldsymbol{w}(\pi)}}$$

where $\boldsymbol{w}(\pi)$ returns the sequence of words in the pattern π and $\#_{\boldsymbol{w}(\pi)}$ is the number of occurrences of this sequence of words in the corpus that are compatible with pattern π. The ranking of patterns under this criterion is shown in Table 2. This method favors precision but also causes very rare patterns to be highly ranked.

To address this, we also consider a product-of-experts model by simply multiplying together the two probabilities, resulting in the ranking shown in Table 3. This ranking is similar to that in Table 1 but penalizes patterns that are only ranked highly because they consist of common words. Table 4 shows a manual grouping of these highly-ranked patterns into several categories. We show both lexical and Brown cluster patterns.[6]

It is common in both types of patterns to find long-distance dependencies involving punctuation near the top of the ranking. Among agreement patterns, the lexical model finds relationships between pronouns and their associated possessive adjectives while the cluster model finds more general patterns involving classes of nouns. Cluster patterns are more likely to capture topicality within a sentence, while the finer granularity of the lexical model is required to identify constructions like those shown (verbs triggering particular prepositions).

There are also many probable patterns without gaps, shown at the bottom of Table 4. From these patterns we can see that our models can also be used to find collocations, but we note that these are discovered in the context of the gappy patterns. That is, due to the use of latent variables in our models (the color assignments), there is a natural trading-off effect whereby the gappy patterns encourage particular non-gappy patterns to be used, and vice versa.

5.1.2 Bilingual Model

We use the news commentary corpus for each language and take the intersection of GIZA++ (Och and Ney, 2003) word alignments in each direction, thereby ensuring that they are 1-to-1 alignments. We ran Gibbs sampling for 300 iterations, averaging pattern counts from the last 200. We set $\alpha = 100$, $\lambda = 3$, and $\gamma = 0.5$. We ran the model in 3 conditions: source words, target words; source clusters, target clusters; and source clusters, target words. We

[6]We filter Brown cluster patterns in which every cluster is a singleton, since these patterns are typically already accounted for in the lexical patterns.

	Rank	Gappy Lexical Patterns	Rank	Gappy Brown Cluster Patterns
Punctuation	1	-- __ --	2	{what, why, whom, whatever} __ {?, !}
	2	(__)	6	{--, -, –} __ {--, -, –}
	6	" __ "	28	{according, compared, subscribe, thanks, referring} to __ ,
	9	why __ ?	178	{–, -, –} {even, especially, particularly, mostly, mainly} __ {–, -, –}
	63	according to __ ,	239	{obama, bush, clinton, mccain, brown} __ " __ "
Agreement	26	he __ his	8	{people, things, americans, journalists, europeans} __ their
	31	we __ our	12	we __ {our, my}
	46	his __ his	21	{children, women, others, men, students} __ their
	86	china __ its	23	{china, europe, america, russia, iran} 's __ its
	90	his __ he	43	{obama, bush, clinton, mccain, brown} __ his
	99	you __ your	46	{our, my} __ {our, my}
	136	leaders __ their	149	{people, things, americans, journalists, europeans} __ they
	140	we __ ourselves	172	{president, bill, sen., king, senator} {obama, bush, clinton, mccain, brown} __ his
	165	these __ are	180	{all, both, either} __ {countries, companies, banks, groups, issues}
Connectives	4	both __ and	5	{more, less} __ {more, less}
	5	not only __ but	9	if __ , __ {will, would, could, should, might}
	8	either __ or	19	{deal, plan, vote, decision, talks} {against, between, involving} __ and
	10	neither __ nor	40	a __ {against, between, involving} __ and
	13	whether __ or	45	{better, different, further, higher, lower} __ than
	19	less __ than	50	{much, far, slightly, significantly, substantially} __ than
	23	not __ , but	56	{yet, instead, perhaps, thus, neither} __ but
	54	if __ then	68	not {only, necessarily} __ {also, hardly}
	109	between __ and	98	as {much, far, slightly, significantly, substantially} __ as
	192	relationship between __ and	131	is __ {more, less} __ than
Topicality	25	france __ germany	1	⟨UNK⟩ __ ⟨UNK⟩
	29	china __ india	15	{china, europe, ...} 's __ {system, crisis, program, recession, situation}
	36	political __ economic	30	{health, security, defense, safety, intelligence} __ {health, ...}
	43	rich __ poor	47	{china, europe, ...} __ {china, europe, ...} __ {china, europe, ...}
	50	oil __ gas	62	{power, growth, interest, development} __ {10, 1, 20, 30, 2} {percent, %, p.m., a.m.}
	62	billions __ dollars	72	in {iraq, washington, london, 2008, 2009} __ {iraq, washington, london, 2008, 2009}
	96	economic __ social	73	the {end, cost, head, rules, average} of __ {prices, markets, services, problems, costs}
	106	the us __ europe	113	{china, europe, ...} 's __ {economy, election, elections, population, investigation}
	181	public __ private	119	{prices, markets, ...} __ {oil, energy, tax, food, investment} __ {oil, energy, ...}
Prepositions	14	around __ world	14	for __ {first, second, third, final, whole} {time, period, term, class, avenue}
	18	on __ basis	17	in __ {last, next, 20th} {year, week, month, season, summer}
	38	at __ time	51	at __ {end, cost, head, rules, average} of
	42	in __ region	71	at __ {group, rate, leader, level, manager}
	80	in __ manner	112	for __ {times, points, games, goals, reasons}
	85	at __ expense	126	{over, around, across, behind, above} __ {country, company, region, nation, virus}
	112	during __ period	190	{one, none} of __ {best, top, largest, main, biggest}
Constructions	33	prevent __ from		
	84	enable __ to		
	114	provide __ for		
	123	impose __ on		
	177	turn __ into		

Non-Gappy Lexical Patterns		Non-Gappy Brown Cluster Patterns	
as well	their own	as {well, soon, quickly, seriously, slowly} as	{rather, please} than
the united states	prime minister	the united {states, nations, airlines}	{don, didn, doesn, isn, wasn} 't
have been	climate change	{president, bill, sen., king, senator} {mr., mr, john, david, michael} {obama, bush, clinton, ...}	
rather than	the bush administration	{order, plans, needs, efforts, failed} to {make, take, give, keep, provide}	
based on	developing countries	{will, would, could, should, might} not be	{can, 'll} be

Table 4: Gappy patterns manually divided into categories of long-distance dependencies. Patterns were ranked according to $p(\pi)p(\pi|\boldsymbol{w}(\pi))$ and manually selected from the top 300 to exemplify categories. Lower pane shows top ranked non-gappy patterns. Clusters are shown as enough words to cover 95% of the token counts of the cluster, up to a maximum of 5.

again ensured that the period and its word class remained isolated in their own patterns for each condition. We note that no source-side word order information is contained within these bilingual patterns; aligned source words can be in any order in the source sentence and the pattern will still match. The most probable patterns included many monolingual source-only and target-only patterns that are similar to those shown in Table 4. There were also many phrase pairs with gaps like those that are commonly extracted by heuristics (Galley and Manning, 2010). Additionally we noted examples of source words triggering more target-side information than merely one word. There were several examples of patterns that encouraged inclusion of the subject in English when translating from Spanish, as Spanish often drops the subject when it is clear from context, e.g., "we are(estamos)". Also, one probable pattern for German-English was "the _ of the(des)" (*des* is aligned to the final *the*). The German determiner *des* is in the genitive case, so this pattern helps to encourage its object to also be in the genitive case when translated.

5.2 Quantitative Evaluation

We consider the Spanish-to-English (ES→EN) translation task from the ACL-2010 Workshop on Statistical Machine Translation (Callison-Burch et al., 2010). We trained a Moses system (Koehn et al., 2007) following the baseline training instructions for the shared task.[7] In particular, we performed word alignment in each direction using GIZA++ (Och and Ney, 2003), used the "grow-diag-final-and" heuristic for symmetrization, and extracted phrase pairs up to a maximum length of seven. After filtering sentence pairs with one sentence longer than 50 words, we ended up with 1.45M sentence pairs of Europarl data and 91K sentence pairs of news commentary data. Language models ($N = 5$) were estimated using the SRI language modeling toolkit (Stolcke, 2002) with modified Kneser-Ney smoothing (Chen and Goodman, 1998). Language models were trained on the target side of the parallel corpus as well as the first 5 million additional sentences from the extra English monolingual newswire data provided for the shared tasks. We used `news-test2008` for tuning and `news-test2009` for testing.

We also consider Chinese-English (ZH→EN) and followed a similar training procedure as above. We used 303K sentence pairs from the FBIS corpus (LDC2003E14) and segmented the Chinese data using the Stanford Chinese segmenter in "CTB" mode (Chang et al., 2008), giving us 7.9M Chinese words and 9.4M English words. A trigram language model was estimated using modified Kneser-Ney smoothing from the English side of the parallel corpus concatenated with 200M words of randomly-selected sentences from the Gigaword v4 corpus (excluding the NY Times and LA Times). We used NIST MT03 for tuning and NIST MT05 for testing. For evaluation, we used case-insensitive IBM BLEU (Papineni et al., 2001).

5.2.1 Training and Decoding

Unlike n-gram language models, our models have latent structure (the color assignments), making it difficult to compute the probability of a translation during decoding. We leave this problem for future work and instead simply add a feature for each of the most probable patterns discovered by our models. Each feature counts the number of occurrences of its pattern in the translation.

We wish to add thousands of features to our model, but the standard training algorithm – minimum error rate training (MERT; Och, 2003) – cannot handle large numbers of features. So, we leverage recent work on feature-rich training for MT using online discriminative learning algorithms. Our training procedure is shown as Algorithm 1. We find it convenient to notationally distinguish feature weights for the standard Moses features ($\boldsymbol{\lambda}$) from weights for our pattern features ($\boldsymbol{\theta}$). We use $\boldsymbol{h}(e)$ to denote the feature vector for translation e. The function $B_i(t)$ returns the sentence BLEU score for translation t given reference e_i (i.e., treating the sentence pair as a corpus).[8]

MERT is run to convergence on the tuning set to obtain weights for the standard Moses features (line 1). Phrase lattices (Ueffing et al., 2002) are generated for all source sentences in the tuning set using the trained weights $\boldsymbol{\lambda}_M$ (line 2). The lattices are used within a modified version of the margin-infused relaxed algorithm (MIRA; Crammer et al., 2006) for structured max-margin learning (lines 5-15). A k-best list is extracted from the current lattice (line 7), then the translations on the k-best list with the highest and lowest sentence-level BLEU scores are found (lines 8 and 9). The step size is then computed using the standard MIRA formula (lines 10-11) and the update is made (line 12). The returned weights are averaged over all updates.

This training procedure is inspired by several

[7] `www.statmt.org/wmt10/baseline.html`.

[8] When computing sentence BLEU, we smooth by replacing precisions of 0.0 with 0.01.

Input: input sentences $F = \{f_i\}_{i=1}^N$, references $E = \{e_i\}_{i=1}^N$, initial weights $\boldsymbol{\lambda}_0$, size of k-best list k, MIRA max step size C, num. iterations T

Output: learned weights: $\boldsymbol{\lambda}_M$, $\langle \boldsymbol{\lambda}^*, \boldsymbol{\theta}^* \rangle$

$\boldsymbol{\lambda}_M \leftarrow \texttt{MERT}(F, E, \boldsymbol{\lambda}_0)$;

$\{\ell_i\}_{i=1}^N \leftarrow \texttt{generateLattices}(F, \boldsymbol{\lambda}_M)$;

$\boldsymbol{\lambda} \leftarrow \boldsymbol{\lambda}_M$; $\boldsymbol{\theta} \leftarrow \mathbf{0}$;

$\langle \bar{\boldsymbol{\lambda}}, \bar{\boldsymbol{\theta}} \rangle \leftarrow \langle \boldsymbol{\lambda}, \boldsymbol{\theta} \rangle$;

for $iter \leftarrow 1$ **to** T **do**

    for $i \leftarrow 1$ **to** N **do**

        $\{t_j\}_{j=1}^k \leftarrow \texttt{Decode}(\ell_i, \langle \boldsymbol{\lambda}, \boldsymbol{\theta} \rangle)$;

        $e^+ \leftarrow \text{argmax}_{1 \le j \le k} B_i(t_j)$;

        $e^- \leftarrow \text{argmin}_{1 \le j \le k} B_i(t_j)$;

        $\Delta \leftarrow \max(0, \langle \boldsymbol{\lambda}, \boldsymbol{\theta} \rangle^\top [\boldsymbol{h}(e^-) - \boldsymbol{h}(e^+)] + B_i(e^+) - B_i(e^-))$;

        $\eta \leftarrow \min(C, \frac{\Delta}{\|\boldsymbol{h}(e^+) - \boldsymbol{h}(e^-)\|^2})$;

        $\boldsymbol{\theta} \leftarrow \boldsymbol{\theta} + \eta [\boldsymbol{h}(e^+) - \boldsymbol{h}(e^-)]$;

        $\langle \bar{\boldsymbol{\lambda}}, \bar{\boldsymbol{\theta}} \rangle \leftarrow \langle \bar{\boldsymbol{\lambda}}, \bar{\boldsymbol{\theta}} \rangle + \langle \boldsymbol{\lambda}, \boldsymbol{\theta} \rangle$;

    end

end

$\langle \boldsymbol{\lambda}^*, \boldsymbol{\theta}^* \rangle \leftarrow \langle \bar{\boldsymbol{\lambda}}, \bar{\boldsymbol{\theta}} \rangle \times \frac{1}{T \times N + 1}$;

return $\boldsymbol{\lambda}_M$, $\langle \boldsymbol{\lambda}^*, \boldsymbol{\theta}^* \rangle$;

Algorithm 1: `Train`

others that have been shown to be effective for MT (Liang et al., 2006; Arun and Koehn, 2007; Watanabe et al., 2007; Chiang et al., 2008). Though not shown in the algorithm, in practice we store the BLEU-best translation on each k-best list from all previous iterations and use it as e^+ if it has a higher BLEU score than any on the k-best list on the current iteration.

At decoding time, we follow a procedure similar to training: we generate lattices for each source sentence using Moses with its standard set of features and using weights $\boldsymbol{\lambda}_M$. We rescore the lattices using $\boldsymbol{\lambda}^*$ and use cube pruning (Chiang, 2007; Huang and Chiang, 2007) to incorporate the gappy pattern features with weights $\boldsymbol{\theta}^*$. Cube pruning is necessary because the pattern features may match anywhere in the translation; thus they are *non-local* in the phrase lattice and require approximate inference.

5.3 Training Algorithm Comparison

Before adding pattern features, we evaluate our training algorithm by comparing it to MERT using the same standard Moses features. As the initial weights $\boldsymbol{\lambda}_0$, we used the default Moses feature weights. We used $k = 100$, $C = 0.0001$, and $T = 15$. For the n-best list size used during cube pruning during both training and decoding, we used $n = 100$. There are several Moses parameters that affect the scope of the search during decoding and therefore the size of the phrase lattices. We used default values for these except for the stack size parameter, for which we used 100. The resulting lattices encode up to 10^{50} derivations for ES→EN and 10^{65} derivations for ZH→EN.

	ES→EN	ZH→EN
MERT	25.64	32.47
Alg. 1	25.85	32.33

Table 5: Comparing MERT to our training procedure. All numbers are %BLEU.

Table 5 shows test set %BLEU for each language pair and training algorithm. Our procedure performs comparably to MERT. Therefore we use it as our baseline for subsequent experiments since it can handle a large number of feature weights; this allows us to observe the contribution of the additional gappy pattern features more clearly.

5.4 Feature Preparation

We chose monolingual and bilingual pattern features using the posterior samples obtained via the inference procedures described above. We ranked patterns using the product-of-experts formula, removed patterns consisting of only a single token, and added the top 10K patterns from the lexical model and the top 15K patterns from the Brown cluster model. For simplicity of implementation, we skipped over patterns with 3 or more gaps and patterns with 2 gaps and more than 3 total words; this procedure skipped fewer than 1% of the top patterns. For results with bilingual pattern features, we added 15K pattern features (5K word-word, 5K cluster-cluster, and 5K cluster-word).

5.5 Results

The first set of results is shown in Table 6. The first row is the same as in Table 5, the second row adds monolingual pattern features, the third adds bilingual pattern features, and the final row includes both sets. While gains are modest overall,

	ES→EN	ZH→EN
Baseline	25.85	32.33
MonoPats	25.84	32.81
BiPats	25.92	32.68
MonoPats + BiPats	25.59	32.80

Table 6: Adding gappy pattern features. All numbers are %BLEU.

	Ranking	%BLEU
Baseline	N/A	32.33
MonoPats	$p(\pi)$	32.65
MonoPats	$p(\pi \| \boldsymbol{w}(\pi))$	32.53
MonoPats	$p(\pi)p(\pi \| \boldsymbol{w}(\pi))$	32.81
BiPats	$p(\pi)$	32.68
MonoPats + BiPats	$p(\pi)$	32.78
MonoPats + BiPats	$p(\pi)p(\pi \| \boldsymbol{w}(\pi))$	32.80

Table 7: Comparing ways of ranking patterns from posterior samples. Scores are on MT05 for ZH→EN translation.

the pattern features show an encouraging improvement of 0.48 BLEU for ZH→EN. This is similar to the improvement reported by Xiong et al. (2011) (+0.4 BLEU when adding their trigger pair language model). While bilingual patterns give an improvement of 0.35 BLEU, using both monolingual and bilingual features in the same model does not provide additional improvement over monolingual features alone.

For ES→EN, the pattern features have only small effects on BLEU; we suspect that the decreased BLEU score for the full feature set is due to overfitting. It is unclear why the results differ for the two language pairs. One possibility is the use of only a single reference translation when tuning and testing with ES→EN while four references were used for ZH→EN. Another possibility is that our pattern features are correcting some of the mid- to long-range reorderings that are known to be problematic for phrase-based modeling of ZH→EN translation. ES→EN exhibits less long-range reordering and therefore may not benefit as much from our patterns.

Table 7 shows additional ZH→EN results when varying the method of ranking patterns. When using both sets of features, the "Ranking" column contains the criterion for ranking monolingual patterns; bilingual patterns are always ranked using

said that __ the	however , __ the	agence france __ presse
's __ , __ 's	us __ iraq	reported __ the
of __ million	, __ likely	said that __ and
added __ "	- __ -	rate __ percent
the __ {media, school, university, election, bank} __ {made, established, given, taken, reached}		
{said, stressed, stated, indicated, noted} that __ in		
{meeting, report, conference, reports} __ {1, july, june, march, april}		
{news, press, spokesman, reporter} {meeting, ...} __ {1, july, ...}		
{news, press, spokesman, reporter} __ {1, july, june, march, april}		
the __ {enterprises, companies, students, customers, others} __ {enterprises, companies, students, customers, others}		
{japan, russia, europe, 2003, 2004} __ {us, japanese, russian, u.s.}		

Table 8: Selected features from the 15 most highly-weighted lexical and cluster pattern features in the best ZH→EN model.

$p(\pi)$. The results show that ranking monolingual patterns using the product-of-experts method results in the highest BLEU scores, validating our intuitions from observing Tables 1-3. Table 8 shows the most highly-weighted pattern features for the best ZH→EN model.

6 Conclusion

We have presented generative models for monolingual and bilingual gappy patterns. A qualitative analysis shows that the models discover patterns that match our intuitions in capturing linguistic phenomena. Our experimental results show promise for the ability of these patterns to improve translation for certain language pairs. A key advantage of generative models is the ability to rapidly develop and experiment with variations, especially when using Gibbs sampling for inference. In order to encourage modifications and extensions to these models we have made our source code available at `www.ark.cs.cmu.edu/MT`.

Acknowledgments

The authors thank Chris Dyer, Qin Gao, Alon Lavie, Nathan Schneider, Stephan Vogel, and the anonymous reviewers for helpful comments. This research was supported in part by the NSF through grant IIS-0844507, the U. S. Army Research Laboratory and the U. S. Army Research Office under contract/grant number W911NF-10-1-0533, and Sandia National Laboratories (fellowship to K. Gimpel).

References

A. Arun and P. Koehn. 2007. Online learning methods for discriminative training of phrase based statistical machine translation. In *Proc. of MT Summit XI*.

M. Bansal, C. Quirk, and R. Moore. 2011. Gappy phrasal alignment by agreement. In *Proc. of ACL*.

P. F. Brown, P. V. deSouza, R. L. Mercer, V. J. Della Pietra, and J. C. Lai. 1992. Class-based N-gram models of natural language. *Computational Linguistics*, 18.

C. Callison-Burch, P. Koehn, C. Monz, K. Peterson, M. Przybocki, and O. Zaidan. 2010. Findings of the 2010 joint workshop on statistical machine translation and metrics for machine translation. In *Proc. of the 5th Workshop on Statistical Machine Translation*.

P. Chang, M. Galley, and C. Manning. 2008. Optimizing Chinese word segmentation for machine translation performance. In *Proc. of the Third Workshop on Statistical Machine Translation*.

S. Chen and J. Goodman. 1998. An empirical study of smoothing techniques for language modeling. Technical report 10-98, Harvard University.

D. Chiang, Y. Marton, and P. Resnik. 2008. Online large-margin training of syntactic and structural translation features. In *Proc. of EMNLP*.

D. Chiang. 2005. A hierarchical phrase-based model for statistical machine translation. In *Proc. of ACL*.

D. Chiang. 2007. Hierarchical phrase-based translation. *Computational Linguistics*, 33(2):201–228.

K. Crammer, O. Dekel, J. Keshet, S. Shalev-Shwartz, and Y. Singer. 2006. Online passive-aggressive algorithms. *Journal of Machine Learning Research*, 7:551–585.

J. M. Crego and F. Yvon. 2009. Gappy translation units under left-to-right SMT decoding. In *Proc. of EAMT*.

M. Galley and C. D. Manning. 2010. Accurate non-hierarchical phrase-based translation. In *Proc. of NAACL*.

L. Huang and D. Chiang. 2007. Forest rescoring: Faster decoding with integrated language models. In *Proc. of ACL*.

F. Jelinek. 1997. *Statistical methods for speech recognition*. MIT Press.

P. Koehn, F. J. Och, and D. Marcu. 2003. Statistical phrase-based translation. In *Proc. of HLT-NAACL*.

P. Koehn, H. Hoang, A. Birch, C. Callison-Burch, M. Federico, N. Bertoldi, B. Cowan, W. Shen, C. Moran, R. Zens, C. Dyer, O. Bojar, A. Constantin, and E. Herbst. 2007. Moses: Open source toolkit for statistical machine translation. In *Proc. of ACL (demo session)*.

P. Liang, A. Bouchard-Côté, D. Klein, and B. Taskar. 2006. An end-to-end discriminative approach to machine translation. In *Proc. of COLING-ACL*.

P. Liang. 2005. Semi-supervised learning for natural language. Master's thesis, Massachusetts Institute of Technology.

F. J. Och and H. Ney. 2003. A systematic comparison of various statistical alignment models. *Computational Linguistics*, 29(1).

F. J. Och. 2003. Minimum error rate training for statistical machine translation. In *Proc. of ACL*.

K. Papineni, S. Roukos, T. Ward, and W.J. Zhu. 2001. BLEU: a method for automatic evaluation of machine translation. In *Proc. of ACL*.

R. Rosenfeld. 1996. A maximum entropy approach to adaptive statistical language modeling. *Computer, Speech and Language*, 10(3).

M. Simard, N. Cancedda, B. Cavestro, M. Dymetman, É. Gaussier, C. Goutte, K. Yamada, P. Langlais, and A. Mauser. 2005. Translating with non-contiguous phrases. In *Proc. of HLT-EMNLP*.

A. Stolcke. 2002. SRILM—an extensible language modeling toolkit. In *Proc. of ICSLP*.

N. Ueffing, F. J. Och, and H. Ney. 2002. Generation of word graphs in statistical machine translation. In *Proc. of EMNLP*.

T. Watanabe, J. Suzuki, H. Tsukada, and H. Isozaki. 2007. Online large-margin training for statistical machine translation. In *Proc. of EMNLP-CoNLL*.

D. Xiong, M. Zhang, and H. Li. 2011. Enhancing language models in statistical machine translation with backward N-grams and mutual information triggers. In *Proc. of ACL*.

Extraction Programs: A Unified Approach to Translation Rule Extraction

Mark Hopkins and Greg Langmead and Tai Vo
SDL Language Technologies Division
6060 Center Drive, Suite 150
Los Angeles, CA 90045
{mhopkins,glangmead,tvo}@sdl.com

Abstract

We provide a general algorithmic schema for translation rule extraction and show that several popular extraction methods (including phrase pair extraction, hierarchical phrase pair extraction, and GHKM extraction) can be viewed as specific instances of this schema. This work is primarily intended as a survey of the dominant extraction paradigms, in which we make explicit the close relationship between these approaches, and establish a language for future hybridizations. This facilitates a generic and extensible implementation of alignment-based extraction methods.

1 Introduction

The tradition of extracting translation rules from aligned sentence pairs dates back more than a decade. A prominent early example is phrase-based extraction (Och et al., 1999).

Around the middle of the last decade, two extraction paradigms were proposed for syntax-based machine translation: the Hiero paradigm of (Chiang, 2005) and the GHKM paradigm of (Galley et al., 2004). From these papers followed two largely independent lines of research, respectively dubbed *formally syntax-based machine translation* (Chiang, 2007; Zollmann and Venugopal, 2006; Venugopal et al., 2007; Lopez, 2007; Marton and Resnik, 2008; Li et al., 2009; de Gispert et al., 2010) and *linguistically syntax-based machine translation* (Galley et al., 2006; Marcu et al., 2006; Liu et al., 2006; Huang et al., 2006; Liu et al., 2007; Mi and Huang, 2008; Zhang et al., 2008; Liu et al., 2009).

In this paper, we unify these strands of research by showing how to express Hiero extraction, GHKM extraction, and phrase-based extraction as instances of a single master extraction method. Specifically, we express each technique as a simple "program" given to a generic "evaluator". Table 1 summarizes how to express several popular extraction methods as "extraction programs."

Besides providing a unifying survey of popular alignment-based extraction methods, this work has the practical benefit of facilitating the implementation of these methods. By specifying the appropriate input program, the generic evaluator (coded, say, as a Python module) can be used to execute any of the extraction techniques in Table 1. New extraction techniques and hybridizations of existing techniques can be supported with minimal additional programming.

2 Building Blocks

The family of extraction algorithms under consideration share a common setup: they extract translation rules from a sentence pair and an alignment. In this section, we define these concepts.

2.1 Patterns and Sentences

Assume we have a global vocabulary of atomic *symbols*, containing the reserved *substitution symbol* ∇. Define a *pattern* as a sequence of symbols. Define the *rank* of a pattern as the count of its ∇ symbols.

Let $\nabla^k \triangleq \langle \overbrace{\nabla, \nabla, ..., \nabla}^{k} \rangle$.

We will typically use space-delimited quotations to represent example patterns, e.g. "ne ∇ pas" rather than $\langle$ne, ∇, pas$\rangle$. We will use the dot operator to represent the concatenation of patterns, e.g. "il ne" $\cdot$ "va pas" = "il ne va pas".

Proceedings of the 6th Workshop on Statistical Machine Translation, pages 523–532,
Edinburgh, Scotland, UK, July 30–31, 2011.

	Extraction Program		
Method	Primary Protocol	Secondary Protocol	Labeling Protocol
PBMT (Och et al., 1999)	RANKPP_0	$\text{TRIVSP}_{\mathcal{A}}$	TRIVLP
Hiero (Chiang, 2005)	RANKPP_∞	$\text{TRIVSP}_{\mathcal{A}}$	TRIVLP
GHKM (Galley et al., 2004)	MAPPP_t	$\text{TRIVSP}_{\mathcal{A}}$	PMAPLP_t
SAMT (Zollmann and Venugopal, 2006)	RANKPP_∞	$\text{TRIVSP}_{\mathcal{A}}$	$\text{PMAPLP}_{\tilde{t}}$
Forest GHKM (Mi and Huang, 2008)	MAPPP_T	$\text{TRIVSP}_{\mathcal{A}}$	PMAPLP_T
Tree-to-Tree GHKM (Liu et al., 2009)	MAPPP_t	$\text{MAPSP}_{\tau,\mathcal{A}}$	$\text{IMAPLP}_{\{t\},\{\tau\}}$
Forest-to-Forest GHKM (Liu et al., 2009)	MAPPP_T	$\text{MAPSP}_{\mathcal{T},\mathcal{A}}$	$\text{IMAPLP}_{T,\mathcal{T}}$
Fuzzy Dual Syntax (Chiang, 2010)	$\text{MAPPP}_{\tilde{t}}$	$\text{MAPSP}_{\tilde{\tau},\mathcal{A}}$	$\text{IMAPLP}_{\{\tilde{t}\},\{\tilde{\tau}\}}$

Table 1: Various rule extraction methods, expressed as extraction programs. Boldfaced methods are proven in this paper; the rest are left as conjecture. Parameters: t, τ are spanmaps (see Section 3); $\tilde{t}, \tilde{\tau}$ are fuzzy spanmaps (see Section 7); $T, \mathcal{T}$ are sets of spanmaps (typically encoded as forests); $\mathcal{A}$ is an alignment (see Section 2).

We refer to a contiguous portion of a pattern with a *span*, defined as either the *null span* ϕ , or a pair $[b, c]$ of positive integers such that $b \leq c$. We will treat span $[b, c]$ as the implicit encoding of the set $\{b, b+1, ..., c\}$, and employ set-theoretic operations on spans, e.g. $[3, 8] \cap [6, 11] = [6, 8]$. Note that the null span encodes the empty set.

If a set I of positive integers is non-empty, then it has a unique *minimal enclosing span*, defined by the operator $\mathsf{span}(I) = [\mathsf{min}(I), \mathsf{max}(I)]$. For instance, $\mathsf{span}(\{1, 3, 4\}) = [1, 4]$. Define $\mathsf{span}(\{\}) = \phi$.

Finally, define a *sentence* as a pattern of rank 0.

2.2 Alignments

An *alignment* is a triple $\langle m, n, \mathfrak{A}\rangle$, where m and n are positive integers, and $\mathfrak{A}$ is a set of ordered integer pairs (i, j) such that $1 \leq i \leq m$ and $1 \leq j \leq n$.

In Figure 1(a), we show a graphical depiction of alignment $\langle 4, 6, \{(1, 1), (2, 3), (4, 3), (3, 5)\}\rangle$. Observe that alignments have a *primary* side (top) and a *secondary* side (bottom)[1]. For alignment $\mathcal{A} = \langle m, n, \mathfrak{A}\rangle$, define $|\mathcal{A}|_p = m$ and $|\mathcal{A}|_s = n$. A *primary index* (resp., *secondary index*) of $\mathcal{A}$ is any positive integer less than or equal to $|\mathcal{A}|_p$ (resp., $|\mathcal{A}|_s$). A *primary span* (resp., *secondary span*) of $\mathcal{A}$ is any span $[b, c]$ such that $1 \leq b \leq c \leq |\mathcal{A}|_p$ (resp., $|\mathcal{A}|_s$).

Define $a \overset{\mathcal{A}}{\sim} \alpha$ to mean that $(a, \alpha) \in \mathfrak{A}$ (in words, we say that $\mathcal{A}$ *aligns* primary index a to secondary index α), and define $a \overset{\mathcal{A}}{\not\sim} \alpha$ to mean that $(a, \alpha) \notin \mathfrak{A}$.

[1]The terms *primary* and *secondary* allow us to be agnostic about how the extracted rules are used in a translation system, i.e. the primary side can refer to the source or target language.

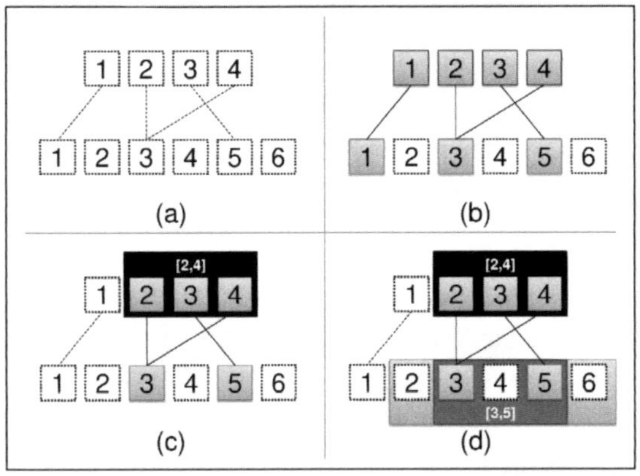

Figure 1: A demonstration of alignment terminology. (a) An alignment is a relation between positive integer sets. (b) The *primary domain* of the example alignment is {1,2,3,4} and the *secondary domain* is {1,3,5}. (c) The *image* of primary span [2,4] is {3,5}. (d) The *minimal projection* of primary span [2,4] is [3,5]. Secondary spans [2,5], [3,6], and [2,6] are also *projections* of primary span [2,4].

Define an *aligned sentence pair* as a triple $\langle s, \sigma, \mathcal{A}\rangle$ where $\mathcal{A}$ is an alignment and s, σ are sentences of length $|\mathcal{A}|_p$ and $|\mathcal{A}|_s$, respectively.

Primary and Secondary Domain: The *primary domain* of alignment $\mathcal{A}$ is the set of primary indices that are aligned to some secondary index, i.e. $\mathsf{pdom}(\mathcal{A}) = \{a | \exists \alpha \text{ s.t. } a \overset{\mathcal{A}}{\sim} \alpha\}$. Analogously, define $\mathsf{sdom}(\mathcal{A}) = \{\alpha | \exists a \text{ s.t. } a \overset{\mathcal{A}}{\sim} \alpha\}$. For the example alignment of Figure 1(b), $\mathsf{pdom}(\mathcal{A}) =$

$\{1, 2, 3, 4\}$ and $\mathsf{sdom}(\mathcal{A}) = \{1, 3, 5\}$.

Image: The *image* of a set I of primary indices (denoted $\mathsf{pimage}_{\mathcal{A}}(I)$) is the set of secondary indices to which the primary indices of I align. In Figure 1(c), for instance, the image of primary span $[2, 4]$ is the set $\{3, 5\}$. Formally, for a set I of primary indices of alignment $\mathcal{A}$, define:

$$\mathsf{pimage}_{\mathcal{A}}(I) = \{\alpha | \exists a \in I \text{ s.t. } (a, \alpha) \in \mathfrak{A}\}$$

Projection: The *minimal projection* of a set I of primary indices (denoted $\mathsf{pmproj}_{\mathcal{A}}(I)$) is the minimal enclosing span of the image of I. In other words, $\mathsf{pmproj}_{\mathcal{A}}(I) = \mathsf{span}(\mathsf{pimage}_{\mathcal{A}}(I))$. In Figure 1(d), for instance, the minimal projection of primary span $[2, 4]$ is the secondary span $[3, 5]$.

Consider Figure 1(d). We will also allow a more relaxed type of projection, in which we allow the broadening of the minimal projection to include unaligned secondary indices. In the example, secondary spans $[2, 5]$, $[3, 6]$, and $[2, 6]$ (in addition to the minimal projection $[3, 5]$) are all considered *projections* of primary span $[2, 4]$. Formally, define $\mathsf{pproj}_{\mathcal{A}}([b, c])$ as the set of superspans $[\beta, \gamma]$ of $\mathsf{pmproj}_{\mathcal{A}}([b, c])$ such that $[\beta, \gamma] \cap \mathsf{sdom}(\mathcal{A}) \subseteq \mathsf{pmproj}_{\mathcal{A}}([b, c])$.

2.3 Rules

We define an *unlabeled rule* as a tuple $\langle k, s^*, \sigma^*, \pi \rangle$ where k is a nonnegative integer, s^* and σ^* are patterns of rank k, and π is a permutation of the sequence $\langle 1, 2, ..., k \rangle$. Such rules can be rewritten using a more standard Synchronous Context-Free Grammar (SCFG) format, e.g. $\langle 3$, "le ∇ ∇ de ∇", "∇ 's ∇ ∇", $\langle 3, 2, 1 \rangle\rangle$ can be written: $\nabla \rightarrow \langle$le ∇_1 ∇_2 de ∇_3, ∇_3 's ∇_2 $\nabla_1\rangle$.

A *labeled rule* is a pair $\langle r, l \rangle$, where r is an unlabeled rule, and l is a "label". The unlabeled rule defines the essential structure of a rule. The label gives us auxiliary information we can use as decoding constraints or rule features. This deliberate modularization lets us unify sequence-based and tree-based extraction methods.

Labels can take many forms. Two examples (depicted in Figure 2) are:

1. An *SCFG label* is a $(k + 1)$-length sequence of symbols.

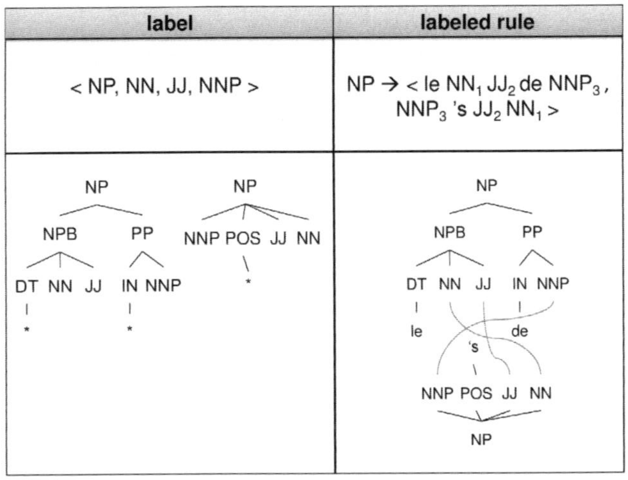

Figure 2: An example SCFG label (top) and STSG label (bottom) for unlabeled rule $\nabla \rightarrow \langle$le ∇_1 ∇_2 de ∇_3, ∇_3 's ∇_2 $\nabla_1\rangle$.

2. An *STSG label* (from Synchronous Tree Substitution Grammar (Eisner, 2003)) is a pair of trees.

STSG labels subsume SCFG labels. Thus STSG extraction techniques can be used as SCFG extraction techniques by ignoring the extra hierarchical structure of the STSG label. Due to space constraints, we will restrict our focus to SCFG labels. When considering techniques originally formulated to extract STSG rules (GHKM, for instance), we will consider their SCFG equivalents.

3 A General Rule Extraction Schema

In this section, we develop a general algorithmic schema for extracting rules from aligned sentence pairs. We will do so by generalizing the GHKM algorithm (Galley et al., 2004). The process goes as follows:

- Repeatedly:
    - Choose a "construction request," which consists of a "primary subrequest" (see Figure 3a) and a "secondary subrequest" (see Figure 3b).
    - Construct the unlabeled rule corresponding to this request (see Figure 3, bottom).
    - Label the rule (see Figure 2).

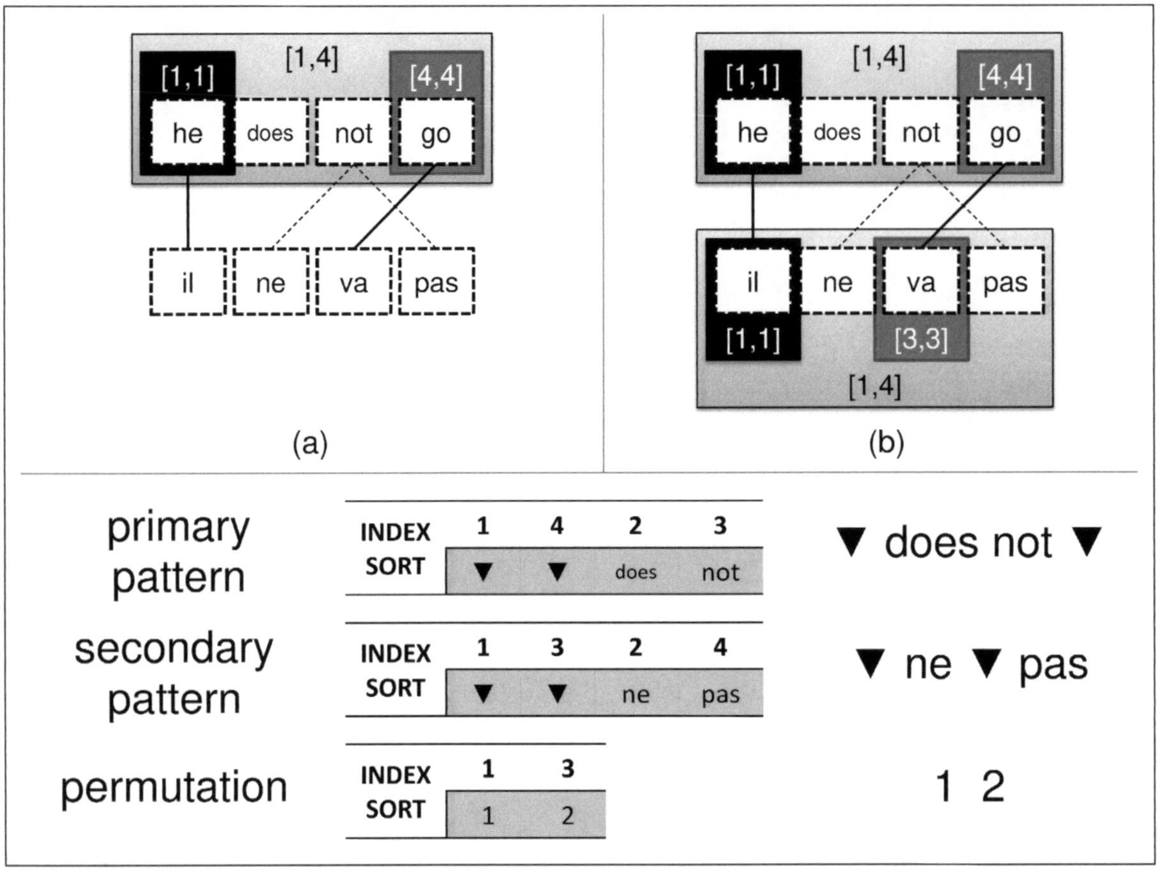

Figure 3: Extraction of the unlabeled rule $\nabla \rightarrow \langle \nabla_1$ does not ∇_2, ∇_1 ne ∇_2 pas$\rangle$. (a) Choose primary subrequest $[1,4] \rightsquigarrow [1,1][4,4]$. (b) Choose secondary subrequest $[1,4] \rightsquigarrow [1,1][3,3]$. (bottom) Construct the rule $\nabla \rightarrow \langle \nabla_1$ does not ∇_2, ∇_1 ne ∇_2 pas$\rangle$.

3.1 Choose a Construction Request

The first step in the extraction process is to choose a "construction request," which directs the algorithm about which unlabeled rule(s) we wish to construct. A "construction request" consists of two "subrequests."

Subrequests: A *subrequest* is a nonempty sequence of non-null spans $\langle [b_0, c_0], [b_1, c_1], ..., [b_k, c_k] \rangle$ such that, for all $1 \leq i < j \leq k$, $[b_i, c_i]$ and $[b_j, c_j]$ are disjoint proper[2] subsets of $[b_0, c_0]$. If it also true that $c_i < b_j$, for all $1 \leq i < j \leq k$, then the subrequest is called *monotonic*. We refer to k as the *rank* of the subrequest.

We typically write subrequest $\langle [b_0, c_0], [b_1, c_1], ..., [b_k, c_k] \rangle$ using the notation:

$$[b_0, c_0] \rightsquigarrow [b_1, c_1]...[b_k, c_k]$$

or as $[b_0, c_0] \rightsquigarrow \epsilon$ if $k = 0$.

For subrequest $x = [b_0, c_0] \rightsquigarrow [b_1, c_1]...[b_k, c_k]$, define:

$$\mathsf{covered}(x) = \cup_{i=1}^{k} [b_i, c_i]$$
$$\mathsf{uncovered}(x) = [b_0, c_0] \backslash \mathsf{covered}(x)$$

Primary Subrequests: Given an alignment $\mathcal{A}$, define the set $\mathsf{frontier}(\mathcal{A})$ as the set of primary spans $[b, c]$ of alignment $\mathcal{A}$ such that $\mathsf{pmproj}_{\mathcal{A}}([b, c]))$ is nonempty and disjoint from $\mathsf{pimage}_{\mathcal{A}}([1, b-1]) \cup \mathsf{pimage}_{\mathcal{A}}([c+1, |\mathcal{A}|_p])$.[3]

[2] If unary rules are desired, i.e. rules of the form $\nabla \rightarrow \nabla$, then this condition can be relaxed.

[3] Our definition of the frontier property is an equivalent reexpression of that given in (Galley et al., 2004). We reexpress it in these terms in order to highlight the fact that the frontier

Algorithm CONSTRUCTRULE$_{s,\sigma,\mathcal{A}}(x, \xi)$:

if construction request $\langle x, \xi\rangle$ matches alignment $\mathcal{A}$ **then**

$\{u_1, ..., u_p\} = \mathsf{uncovered}([b_0, c_0] \rightsquigarrow [b_1, c_1]...[b_k, c_k])$

$\{v_1, ..., v_q\} = \mathsf{uncovered}([\beta_0, \gamma_0] \rightsquigarrow [\beta_1, \gamma_1]...[\beta_k, \gamma_k])$

$s^* = \text{INDEXSORT}(\langle b_1, b_2, ..., b_k, u_1, u_2, ..., u_p\rangle, \langle \overbrace{\nabla, \nabla, ..., \nabla}^{k}, s_{u_1}, s_{u_2}, ..., s_{u_p}\rangle)$

$\sigma^* = \text{INDEXSORT}(\langle \beta_1, \beta_2, ..., \beta_k, v_1, v_2, ..., v_q\rangle, \langle \overbrace{\nabla, \nabla, ..., \nabla}^{k}, \sigma_{v_1}, \sigma_{v_2}, ..., \sigma_{v_q}\rangle)$

$\pi = \text{INDEXSORT}(\langle \beta_1, \beta_2, ..., \beta_k\rangle, \langle 1, 2, ..., k\rangle)$

return $\{\langle k, s^*, \sigma^*, \pi\rangle\}$

else

return $\{\}$

end if

Figure 4: Pseudocode for rule construction. Arguments: $s =$ "$s_1\ s_2\ ...\ s_m$" and $\sigma =$ "$\sigma_1\ \sigma_2\ ...\ \sigma_n$" are sentences, $\mathcal{A} = \langle m, n, \mathfrak{A}\rangle$ is an alignment, $x = [b_0, c_0] \rightsquigarrow [b_1, c_1]...[b_k, c_k]$ and $\xi = [\beta_0, \gamma_0] \rightsquigarrow [\beta_1, \gamma_1]...[\beta_k, \gamma_k]$ are subrequests.

Define $\mathsf{preqs}(\mathcal{A})$ as the set of monotonic subrequests whose spans are all in $\mathsf{frontier}(\mathcal{A})$. We refer to members of $\mathsf{preqs}(\mathcal{A})$ as *primary subrequests* of alignment $\mathcal{A}$. Figure 3a shows a primary subrequest of an example alignment.

Secondary Subrequests: Given a primary subrequest $x = [b_0, c_0] \rightsquigarrow [b_1, c_1]...[b_k, c_k]$ of alignment $\mathcal{A}$, define $\mathsf{sreqs}(x, \mathcal{A})$ as the set of subrequests $[\beta_0, \gamma_0] \rightsquigarrow [\beta_1, \gamma_1]...[\beta_k, \gamma_k]$ such that $[\beta_i, \gamma_i] \in \mathsf{pproj}_{\mathcal{A}}([b_i, c_i])$, for all $0 \leq i \leq k$. We refer to members of $\mathsf{sreqs}(x, \mathcal{A})$ as *secondary subrequests* of primary subrequest x and alignment $\mathcal{A}$. Figure 3b shows a secondary subrequest of the primary subrequest selected in Figure 3a.

Construction Requests: A *construction request* is a pair of subrequests of equivalent rank. Construction request $\langle x, \xi\rangle$ *matches* alignment $\mathcal{A}$ if $x \in \mathsf{preqs}(\mathcal{A})$ and $\xi \in \mathsf{sreqs}(x, \mathcal{A})$.

3.2 Construct the Unlabeled Rule

The basis of rule construction is the INDEXSORT operator, which takes as input a sequence of integers $I = \langle i_1, i_2, ..., i_k\rangle$, and an equivalent-length sequence of arbitrary values $\langle v_1, v_2, ..., v_k\rangle$, and returns a sequence $\langle v_{j_1}, v_{j_2}, ..., v_{j_k}\rangle$, where $\langle j_1, j_2, ..., j_k\rangle$ is a permutation of sequence I in ascending order. For instance, INDEXSORT$(\langle 4, 1, 50, 2\rangle, \langle$"a", "b", "c", "d"$\rangle) =$ $\langle$"b", "d", "a", "c"$\rangle$. Note that the output of INDEXSORT(I, V) is nondeterministic if sequence I has repetitions. In Figure 4, we show the pseudocode for rule construction. We show an example construction in Figure 3 (bottom).

property is a property *of the alignment alone*. It is independent of the auxiliary information that GHKM uses, in particular the tree.

Primary Protocol RANKPP$_k$:

$$\{[b_0, c_0] \rightsquigarrow [b_1, c_1]...[b_j, c_j] \text{ s.t. } 1 \leq b_0 \leq c_0 \text{ and } 0 \leq j \leq k\}$$

Primary Protocol MAPPP$_t$:

$$\{[b_0, c_0] \rightsquigarrow [b_1, c_1]...[b_k, c_k] \text{ s.t. } \forall 0 \leq i \leq k\ [b_i, c_i] \in \mathsf{spans}(t)\}$$

Primary Protocol MAPPP$_T$:

$$\bigcup_{t \in T} \text{MAPPP}_t$$

Figure 5: Various primary protocols. Parameters: k is a nonnegative integer; t is a spanmap; T is a set of spanmaps (typically encoded as a forest).

3.3 Label the Rule

Rule construction produces unlabeled rules. To label these rules, we use a *labeling protocol*, defined as a function that takes a construction request as input, and returns a set of labels.

Figure 7 defines a number of general-purpose la-

Secondary Protocol $\text{TRIVSP}_{\mathcal{A}}(x)$:
  return $\mathsf{sreqs}(x, \mathcal{A})$

Secondary Protocol $\text{MAPSP}_{\tau,\mathcal{A}}(x)$:

$$\{[\beta_0, \gamma_0] \rightsquigarrow [\beta_1, \gamma_1]...[\beta_k, \gamma_k] \in \mathsf{sreqs}(x, \mathcal{A}) \text{ s.t. } \forall 0 \leq i \leq k : [\beta_i, \gamma_i] \in \mathsf{spans}(\tau)\}$$

Figure 6: Various secondary protocols. Parameters: τ is a spanmap; $\mathcal{A}$ is an alignment; $x = [b_0, c_0] \rightsquigarrow [b_1, c_1]...[b_k, c_k]$ is a subrequest.

beling protocols. Some of these are driven by trees. We will represent a tree as a *spanmap*, defined as a function that maps spans to symbol sequences. For instance, if a parse tree has constituent NP over span $[4, 7]$, then the corresponding spanmap t has $t([4, 7]) = \langle \text{NP} \rangle$. We map spans to *sequences* in order to accommodate unary chains in the parse tree. Nonconstituent spans are mapped to the empty sequence. For spanmap t, let $\mathsf{spans}(t)$ be the set of spans $[b, c]$ for which $t([b, c])$ is a nonempty sequence.

4 Extraction Programs

In the previous section, we developed a general technique for extracting labeled rules from aligned sentence pairs. Note that this was not an algorithm, but rather an algorithmic schema, as it left two questions unanswered:

1. What construction requests do we make?
2. What labeling protocol do we use?

We answer these questions with an *extraction program*, defined as a triple $\langle \mathcal{X}, \Xi, \mathcal{L} \rangle$, where:

- $\mathcal{X}$ is a set of subrequests, referred to as the *primary protocol*. It specifies the set of primary subrequests that interest us. Figure 5 defines some general-purpose primary protocols.
- Ξ maps every subrequest to a set of subrequests. We refer to Ξ as the *secondary protocol*. It specifies the set of secondary subrequests that interest us, given a particular primary subrequest. Figure 6 defines some general-purpose secondary protocols.

Labeling Protocol $\text{TRIVLP}(x, \xi)$:
  return ∇^{k+1}

Labeling Protocol $\text{PMAPLP}_t(x, \xi)$:

$$\{\langle l_0, ..., l_k \rangle \text{ s.t. } \forall 0 \leq i \leq k : l_i \in t([b_i, c_i])\}$$

Labeling Protocol $\text{PMAPLP}_T(x, \xi)$:

$$\bigcup_{t \in T} \text{PMAPLP}_t(x, \xi)$$

Labeling Protocol $\text{SMAPLP}_\tau(x, \xi)$:

$$\{\langle \lambda_0, ..., \lambda_k \rangle \text{ s.t. } \forall 0 \leq i \leq k : \lambda_i \in \tau([\beta_i, \gamma_i])\}$$

Labeling Protocol $\text{SMAPLP}_{\mathcal{T}}(x, \xi)$:

$$\bigcup_{\tau \in \mathcal{T}} \text{SMAPLP}_\tau(x, \xi)$$

Labeling Protocol $\text{IMAPLP}_{T,\mathcal{T}}(x, \xi)$:

$$\{\langle (l_0, \lambda_0), ..., (l_k, \lambda_k) \rangle \text{ s.t. } \langle l_0, ..., l_k \rangle \in \text{PMAPLP}_T(x, \xi) \text{ and } \langle \lambda_0, ..., \lambda_k \rangle \in \text{SMAPLP}_{\mathcal{T}}(x, \xi)\}$$

Figure 7: Various labeling protocols. Parameters: t, τ are spanmaps; $T, \mathcal{T}$ are sets of spanmaps; $x = [b_0, c_0] \rightsquigarrow [b_1, c_1]...[b_k, c_k]$ and $\xi = [\beta_0, \gamma_0] \rightsquigarrow [\beta_1, \gamma_1]...[\beta_k, \gamma_k]$ are subrequests.

- $\mathcal{L}$ is a labeling protocol. Figure 7 defines some general-purpose labeling protocols.

Figure 8 shows the pseudocode for an "evaluator" that takes an extraction program (and an aligned sentence pair) as input and returns a set of labeled rules.

4.1 The GHKM Extraction Program

As previously stated, we developed our extraction schema by generalizing the GHKM algorithm (Galley et al., 2004). To recover GHKM as an instance of this schema, use the following program:

$$\text{EXTRACT}_{s,\sigma,\mathcal{A}}(\text{MAPPP}_t, \text{TRIVSP}_{\mathcal{A}}, \text{PMAPLP}_t)$$

where t is a spanmap encoding a parse tree over the primary sentence.

Algorithm $\textsc{Extract}_{s,\sigma,\mathcal{A}}(\mathcal{X}, \Xi, \mathcal{L})$:
  $R = \{\}$
  for all subrequests $x \in \mathcal{X}$ **do**
    for all subrequests $\xi \in \Xi(x)$ **do**
      $U = \textsc{ConstructRule}_{s,\sigma,\mathcal{A}}(x, \xi)$
      $L = \mathcal{L}(x, \xi)$
      $R = R \cup (U \times L)$
    end for
  end for
  return R

Figure 8: Evaluator for extraction programs. Parameters: $\langle s, \sigma, \mathcal{A}\rangle$ is an aligned sentence pair; $\mathcal{X}$ is a primary protocol; Ξ is a secondary protocol; $\mathcal{L}$ is a labeling protocol.

5 The Phrase Pair Extraction Program

In this section, we express phrase pair extraction (Och et al., 1999) as an extraction program.

For primary span $[b, c]$ and secondary span $[\beta, \gamma]$ of alignment $\mathcal{A}$, let $[b, c] \overset{\mathcal{A}}{\approx} [\beta, \gamma]$ if the following three conditions hold:

1. $a \overset{\mathcal{A}}{\sim} \alpha$ for some $a \in [b, c]$ and $\alpha \in [\beta, \gamma]$
2. $a \overset{\mathcal{A}}{\not\sim} \alpha$ for all $a \in [b, c]$ and $\alpha \notin [\beta, \gamma]$
3. $a \overset{\mathcal{A}}{\not\sim} \alpha$ for all $a \notin [b, c]$ and $\alpha \in [\beta, \gamma]$

Define the ruleset $\textsc{Pbmt}(s, \sigma, \mathcal{A})$ to be the set of labeled rules $\langle r, \nabla^1\rangle$ such that:

- $r = \langle 0, \text{“}s_b ... s_c\text{”}, \text{“}\sigma_\beta ... \sigma_\gamma\text{”}, \emptyset\rangle$
- $[b, c] \overset{\mathcal{A}}{\approx} [\beta, \gamma]$

We want to express $\textsc{Pbmt}(s, \sigma, \mathcal{A})$ as an extraction program. First we establish a useful lemma and corollary.

Lemma 1. *$[b, c] \overset{\mathcal{A}}{\approx} [\beta, \gamma]$ iff $[b, c] \in \mathsf{frontier}(\mathcal{A})$ and $[\beta, \gamma] \in \mathsf{pproj}_{\mathcal{A}}([b, c])$.*

Proof. Let $[b, c]^c = [1, b-1] \cup [c+1, |\mathcal{A}|_p]$.

$$[b, c] \in \mathsf{frontier}(\mathcal{A}) \text{ and } [\beta, \gamma] \in \mathsf{pproj}_{\mathcal{A}}([b, c])$$

$$\overset{(1)}{\iff} \begin{cases} \mathsf{pmproj}_{\mathcal{A}}([b, c]) \cap \mathsf{pimage}_{\mathcal{A}}([b, c]^c) = \{\} \\ [\beta, \gamma] \in \mathsf{pproj}_{\mathcal{A}}([b, c]) \end{cases}$$

$$\overset{(2)}{\iff} \begin{cases} [\beta, \gamma] \cap \mathsf{pimage}_{\mathcal{A}}([b, c]^c) = \{\} \\ [\beta, \gamma] \in \mathsf{pproj}_{\mathcal{A}}([b, c]) \end{cases}$$

$$\overset{(3)}{\iff} \begin{cases} [\beta, \gamma] \cap \mathsf{pimage}_{\mathcal{A}}([b, c]^c) = \{\} \\ \mathsf{pimage}_{\mathcal{A}}([b, c]) \subseteq [\beta, \gamma] \end{cases}$$

$$\overset{(4)}{\iff} \begin{cases} \text{conditions 2 and 3 hold} \\ [\beta, \gamma] \neq \{\} \end{cases}$$

$$\overset{(5)}{\iff} \text{conditions 1, 2 and 3 hold}$$

Equivalence 1 holds by definition of $\mathsf{frontier}(\mathcal{A})$. Equivalence 2 holds because $[\beta, \gamma]$ differs from $\mathsf{pmproj}_{\mathcal{A}}([b, c])$ only in unaligned indices. Equivalence 3 holds because given the disjointness from $\mathsf{pimage}_{\mathcal{A}}([b, c]^c)$, $[\beta, \gamma]$ differs from $\mathsf{pimage}_{\mathcal{A}}([b, c])$ only in unaligned indices. Equivalences 4 and 5 are a restatement of conditions 2 and 3 plus the observation that empty spans can satisfy conditions 2 and 3. □

Corollary 2. *Consider monotonic subrequest $x = [b_0, c_0] \rightsquigarrow [b_1, c_1] ... [b_k, c_k]$ and arbitary subrequest $\xi = [\beta_0, \gamma_0] \rightsquigarrow [\beta_1, \gamma_1] ... [\beta_k, \gamma_k]$. Construction request $\langle x, \xi\rangle$ matches alignment $\mathcal{A}$ iff $[b_i, c_i] \overset{\mathcal{A}}{\approx} [\beta_i, \gamma_i]$ for all $0 \leq i \leq k$.*

We are now ready to express the rule set $\textsc{Pbmt}(s, \sigma, \mathcal{A})$ as an extraction program.

Theorem 3. $\textsc{Pbmt}(s, \sigma, \mathcal{A}) = \textsc{Extract}_{s,\sigma,\mathcal{A}}(\textsc{RankPP}_0, \textsc{TrivSP}_{\mathcal{A}}, \textsc{TrivLP})$

Proof.

$$\langle r, l\rangle \in \textsc{Ext}_{s,\sigma,\mathcal{A}}(\textsc{RankPP}_0, \textsc{TrivSP}_{\mathcal{A}}, \textsc{TrivLP})$$

$$\overset{(1)}{\iff} \begin{cases} x = [b, c] \rightsquigarrow \epsilon \text{ and } \xi = [\beta, \gamma] \rightsquigarrow \epsilon \\ \langle x, \xi\rangle \text{ matches alignment } \mathcal{A} \\ \{r\} = \textsc{ConstructRule}_{s,\sigma,\mathcal{A}}(x, \xi) \\ l = \nabla^1 \end{cases}$$

$$\overset{(2)}{\iff} \begin{cases} x = [b, c] \rightsquigarrow \epsilon \text{ and } \xi = [\beta, \gamma] \rightsquigarrow \epsilon \\ \langle x, \xi\rangle \text{ matches alignment } \mathcal{A} \\ r = \langle 0, \text{“}s_b ... s_c\text{”}, \text{“}\sigma_\beta ... \sigma_\gamma\text{”}, \emptyset\rangle \\ l = \nabla^1 \end{cases}$$

$$\overset{(3)}{\iff} \begin{cases} [b, c] \overset{\mathcal{A}}{\approx} [\beta, \gamma] \\ r = \langle 0, \text{“}s_b ... s_c\text{”}, \text{“}\sigma_\beta ... \sigma_\gamma\text{”}, \emptyset\rangle \\ l = \nabla^1 \end{cases}$$

$$\overset{(4)}{\iff} \langle r, l\rangle \in \textsc{Pbmt}(s, \sigma, \mathcal{A})$$

Equivalence 1 holds by the definition of EXTRACT and RANKPP_0. Equivalence 2 holds by the pseudocode of CONSTRUCTRULE. Equivalence 3 holds from Corollary 2. Equivalence 4 holds from the definition of $\text{PBMT}(s, \sigma, \mathcal{A})$. □

6 The Hiero Extraction Program

In this section, we express the hierarchical phrase-based extraction technique of (Chiang, 2007) as an extraction program. Define $\text{HIERO}_0(s, \sigma, \mathcal{A}) = \text{PBMT}(s, \sigma, \mathcal{A})$. For positive integer k, define $\text{HIERO}_k(s, \sigma, \mathcal{A})$ as the smallest superset of $\text{HIERO}_{k-1}(s, \sigma, \mathcal{A})$ satisfying the following condition:

- For any labeled rule $\langle\langle k-1, s^*, \sigma^*, \pi\rangle, \nabla^k\rangle \in \text{HIERO}_{k-1}(s, \sigma, \mathcal{A})$ such that:
  1. $s^* = s_1^* \cdot \text{"}s_b...s_c\text{"} \cdot s_2^*$
  2. $\sigma^* = \sigma_1^* \cdot \text{"}\sigma_\beta...\sigma_\gamma\text{"} \cdot \sigma_2^*$
  3. $\pi = \langle \pi_1, \pi_2, ..., \pi_{k-1}\rangle$
  4. s_2^* has rank 0.[4]
  5. σ_1^* has rank j.
  6. $[b, c] \overset{\mathcal{A}}{\sim} [\beta, \gamma]$

  it holds that labeled rule $\langle r, \nabla^{k+1}\rangle$ is a member of $\text{HIERO}_k(s, \sigma, \mathcal{A})$, where r is:

  $$\langle k, s_1^* \cdot \text{"}\nabla\text{"} \cdot s_2^*, \sigma_1^* \cdot \text{"}\nabla\text{"} \cdot \sigma_2^*, \langle \pi_1, ..., \pi_j, k, \pi_{j+1}, ..., \pi_{k-1}\rangle\rangle$$

Theorem 4. $\text{HIERO}_k(s, \sigma, \mathcal{A}) = \text{EXTRACT}_{s,\sigma,\mathcal{A}}(\text{RANKPP}_k, \text{TRIVSP}_{\mathcal{A}}, \text{TRIVLP})$

Proof. By induction. Define $\text{ext}(k)$ to mean $\text{EXTRACT}_{s,\sigma,\mathcal{A}}(\text{RANKPP}_k, \text{TRIVSP}_{\mathcal{A}}, \text{TRIVLP})$. From Theorem 3, $\text{HIERO}_0(s, \sigma, \mathcal{A}) = \text{ext}(0)$. Assume that $\text{HIERO}_{k-1}(s, \sigma, \mathcal{A}) = \text{ext}(k-1)$ and prove that $\text{HIERO}_k(s, \sigma, \mathcal{A}) \backslash \text{HIERO}_{k-1}(s, \sigma, \mathcal{A}) = \text{ext}(k) \backslash \text{ext}(k-1)$.

$$\langle r', l'\rangle \in \text{ext}(k) \backslash \text{ext}(k-1)$$

$$\overset{(1)}{\Longleftrightarrow} \begin{cases} x' = [b_0, c_0] \rightsquigarrow [b_1, c_1]...[b_k, c_k] \\ \xi' = [\beta_0, \gamma_0] \rightsquigarrow [\beta_1, \gamma_1]...[\beta_k, \gamma_k] \\ \langle x', \xi'\rangle \text{ matches alignment } \mathcal{A} \\ \{r'\} = \text{CONSTRUCTRULE}_{s,\sigma,\mathcal{A}}(x', \xi') \\ l' = \nabla^{k+1} \end{cases}$$

$$\overset{(2)}{\Longleftrightarrow} \begin{cases} x = [b_0, c_0] \rightsquigarrow [b_1, c_1]...[b_{k-1}, c_{k-1}] \\ \xi = [\beta_0, \gamma_0] \rightsquigarrow [\beta_1, \gamma_1]...[\beta_{k-1}, \gamma_{k-1}] \\ \{r\} = \text{CONSTRUCTRULE}_{s,\sigma,\mathcal{A}}(x, \xi) \\ \pi = \langle \pi_1, ..., \pi_{k-1}\rangle \\ r = \begin{matrix}\langle k-1, s_1^* \cdot \text{"}s_{b_k}...s_{c_k}\text{"} \cdot s_2^*, \\ \sigma_1^* \cdot \text{"}\sigma_{\beta_k}...\sigma_{\gamma_k}\text{"} \cdot \sigma_2^*, \pi\rangle\end{matrix} \\ s_2^* \text{ has rank 0 and } \sigma_1^* \text{ has rank } j \\ x' = [b_0, c_0] \rightsquigarrow [b_1, c_1]...[b_k, c_k] \\ \xi' = [\beta_0, \gamma_0] \rightsquigarrow [\beta_1, \gamma_1]...[\beta_k, \gamma_k] \\ \langle x', \xi'\rangle \text{ matches alignment } \mathcal{A} \\ \pi' = \langle \pi_1, ..., \pi_j, k, \pi_{j+1}, ..., \pi_{k-1}\rangle \\ r' = \langle k, s_1^* \cdot \text{"}\nabla\text{"} \cdot s_2^*, \sigma_1^* \cdot \text{"}\nabla\text{"} \cdot \sigma_2^*, \pi'\rangle \\ l' = \nabla^{k+1} \end{cases}$$

$$\overset{(3)}{\Longleftrightarrow} \begin{cases} \pi = \langle \pi_1, ..., \pi_{k-1}\rangle \\ r = \begin{matrix}\langle k-1, s_1^* \cdot \text{"}s_{b_k}...s_{c_k}\text{"} \cdot s_2^*, \\ \sigma_1^* \cdot \text{"}\sigma_{\beta_k}...\sigma_{\gamma_k}\text{"} \cdot \sigma_2^*, \pi\rangle\end{matrix} \\ s_2^* \text{ has rank 0 and } \sigma_1^* \text{ has rank } j \\ \langle r, \nabla^k\rangle \in \text{HIERO}_{k-1}(s, \sigma, \mathcal{A}) \\ \pi' = \langle \pi_1, ..., \pi_j, k, \pi_{j+1}, ..., \pi_{k-1}\rangle \\ r' = \langle k, s_1^* \cdot \text{"}\nabla\text{"} \cdot s_2^*, \sigma_1^* \cdot \text{"}\nabla\text{"} \cdot \sigma_2^*, \pi'\rangle \\ [b_i, c_i] \overset{\mathcal{A}}{\sim} [\beta_i, \gamma_i] \text{ for all } 0 \leq i \leq k \\ l' = \nabla^{k+1} \end{cases}$$

$$\overset{(4)}{\Longleftrightarrow} \langle r', l'\rangle \in \text{HIERO}_k(s, \sigma, \mathcal{A}) \backslash \text{HIERO}_{k-1}(s, \sigma, \mathcal{A})$$

Equivalence 1 holds by the definition of $\text{ext}(k) \backslash \text{ext}(k-1)$. Equivalence 2 holds by the pseudocode of CONSTRUCTRULE. Equivalence 3 holds by the inductive hypothesis and Corollary 2. Equivalence 4 holds by the definition of $\text{HIERO}_k(s, \sigma, \mathcal{A}) \backslash \text{HIERO}_{k-1}(s, \sigma, \mathcal{A})$. □

7 Discussion

In this paper, we have created a framework that allows us to express a desired rule extraction method as a set of construction requests and a labeling protocol. This enables a modular, "mix-and-match" approach to rule extraction. In Table 1, we summarize the results of this paper, as well as our conjectured extraction programs for several other methods. For instance, Syntax-Augmented Machine Translation (SAMT) (Zollmann and Venugopal, 2006) is a

[4] This condition is not in the original definition. It is a cosmetic addition, to enforce the consecutive ordering of variable indices on the rule LHS.

hybridization of Hiero and GHKM that uses the primary protocol of Hiero and the labeling protocol of GHKM. To bridge the approaches, SAMT employs a fuzzy version[5] of the spanmap t that assigns a trivial label to non-constituent primary spans:

$$\tilde{t}([b,c]) = \begin{cases} t([b,c]) & \text{if } [b,c] \in \mathsf{spans}(t) \\ \langle \nabla \rangle & \text{otherwise} \end{cases}$$

Other approaches can be similarly expressed as straightforward variants of the extraction programs we have developed in this paper.

Although we have focused on idealized methods, this framework also allows a compact and precise characterization of practical restrictions of these techniques. For instance, (Chiang, 2007) lists six criteria that he uses in practice to restrict the generation of Hiero rules. His condition 4 ("Rules can have at most two nonterminals.") and condition 5 ("It is prohibited for nonterminals to be adjacent on the French side.") can be jointly captured by replacing Hiero's primary protocol with the following:

$$\{[b_0, c_0] \rightsquigarrow [b_1, c_1]...[b_j, c_j] \text{ s.t. } 1 \leq b_0 \leq c_0 \quad 0 \leq j \leq \mathbf{2} \quad \mathbf{b_2 > c_1 + 1}\}$$

His other conditions can be similarly captured with appropriate changes to Hiero's primary and secondary protocols.

This work is primarily intended as a survey of the dominant translation rule extraction paradigms, in which we make explicit the close relationship between these approaches, and establish a language for future hybridizations. From a practical perspective, we facilitate a generic and extensible implementation which supports a wide variety of existing methods, and which permits the precise expression of practical extraction heuristics.

[5]This corresponds with the original formulation of Syntax Augmented Machine Translation (Zollmann and Venugopal, 2006). More recent versions of SAMT adopt a more refined "fuzzifier" that assigns hybrid labels to non-constituent primary spans.

References

David Chiang. 2005. A hierarchical phrase-based model for statistical machine translation. In *Proceedings of ACL*, pages 263–270.

David Chiang. 2007. Hierarchical phrase-based translation. *Computational Linguistics*, 33(2):201–228.

David Chiang. 2010. Learning to translate with source and target syntax. In *Proceedings of ACL*, pages 1443–1452.

A. de Gispert, G. Iglesias, G. Blackwood, E.R. Banga, and W. Byrne. 2010. Hierarchical phrase-based translation with weighted finite state transducers and shallow-n grammars. *Computational Linguistics*, 36(3):505–533.

Jason Eisner. 2003. Learning non-isomorphic tree mappings for machine translation. In *Proceedings of ACL*, pages 205–208.

Michel Galley, Mark Hopkins, Kevin Knight, and Daniel Marcu. 2004. What's in a translation rule? In *Proceedings of HLT/NAACL*.

Michel Galley, Jonathan Graehl, Kevin Knight, Daniel Marcu, Steve DeNeefe, Wei Wang, and Ignacio Thayer. 2006. Scalable inference and training of context-rich syntactic models. In *Proceedings of ACL-COLING*.

Liang Huang, Kevin Knight, and Aravind Joshi. 2006. Statistical syntax-directed translation with extended domain of locality. In *Proceedings of AMTA*.

Zhifei Li, Chris Callison-Burch, Chris Dyer, Juri Ganitkevitch, Sanjeev Khudanpur, Lane Schwartz, Wren Thornton, Jonathan Weese, and Omar Zaidan. 2009. Joshua: An open source toolkit for parsing-based machine translation. In *Proceedings of the Fourth ACL Workshop on Statistical Machine Translation*, pages 135–139.

Yang Liu, Qun Liu, and Shouxun Lin. 2006. Tree-to-string alignment template for statistical machine translation. In *Proceedings of ACL/COLING*, pages 609–616.

Yang Liu, Yun Huang, Qun Liu, and Shouxun Lin. 2007. Forest-to-string statistical translation rules. In *Proceedings of ACL*.

Yang Liu, Yajuan Lu, and Qun Liu. 2009. Improving tree-to-tree translation with packed forests. In *Proceedings of ACL/IJCNLP*, pages 558–566.

Adam Lopez. 2007. Hierarchical phrase-based translation with suffix arrays. In *Proceedings of EMNLP-CoNLL*.

Daniel Marcu, Wei Wang, Abdessamad Echihabi, and Kevin Knight. 2006. Spmt: Statistical machine translation with syntactified target language phrases. In *Proceedings of EMNLP*, pages 44–52.

Yuval Marton and Philip Resnik. 2008. Soft syntactic constraints for hierarchical phrased-based translation. In *Proceedings of ACL*.

Haitao Mi and Liang Huang. 2008. Forest-based translation rule extraction. In *Proceedings of EMNLP*.

Franz J. Och, Christof Tillmann, and Hermann Ney. 1999. Improved alignment models for statistical machine translation. In *Proceedings of the Joint Conf. of Empirical Methods in Natural Language Processing and Very Large Corpora*, pages 20–28.

Ashish Venugopal, Andreas Zollmann, and Stephan Vogel. 2007. An efficient two-pass approach to synchronous-cfg driven statistical mt. In *Proceedings of HLT/NAACL*.

Min Zhang, Hongfei Jiang, Aiti Aw, Haizhou Li, Chew Lim Tan, and Sheng Li. 2008. A tree sequence alignment-based tree-to-tree translation model. In *Proceedings of ACL*.

Andreas Zollmann and Ashish Venugopal. 2006. Syntax augmented machine translation via chart parsing. In *Proceedings of NAACL Workshop on Statistical Machine Translation*.

Bayesian Extraction of Minimal SCFG Rules for Hierarchical Phrase-based Translation

Baskaran Sankaran
Simon Fraser University
Burnaby BC, Canada
baskaran@cs.sfu.ca

Gholamreza Haffari
Monash University
Melbourne, Australia
reza@monash.edu

Anoop Sarkar
Simon Fraser University
Burnaby BC, Canada
anoop@cs.sfu.ca

Abstract

We present a novel approach for extracting a minimal synchronous context-free grammar (SCFG) for Hiero-style statistical machine translation using a non-parametric Bayesian framework. Our approach is designed to extract rules that are licensed by the word alignments and heuristically extracted phrase pairs. Our Bayesian model limits the number of SCFG rules extracted, by sampling from the space of all possible hierarchical rules; additionally our informed prior based on the lexical alignment probabilities biases the grammar to extract high quality rules leading to improved generalization and the automatic identification of commonly re-used rules. We show that our Bayesian model is able to extract minimal set of hierarchical phrase rules without impacting the translation quality as measured by the BLEU score.

1 Introduction

Hierarchical phrase-based (Hiero) machine translation (Chiang, 2007) has attracted significant interest within the Machine Translation community. It extends phrase-based translation by automatically inferring a synchronous grammar from an aligned bitext. The synchronous context-free grammar links non-terminals in source and target languages. Decoding in such systems employ a modified CKY-parser that is integrated with a language model.

The primary advantage of Hiero-style systems lie in their unsupervised model of syntax for translation: allowing long-distance reordering and capturing certain syntactic constructions, particularly those that involve discontiguous phrases. It has been demonstrated to be a successful framework with comparable performance with other statistical frameworks and suitable for large-scale corpora (Zollmann et al., 2008). However, one of the major difficulties in Hiero-style systems has been on learning a concise and general synchronous grammar from the bitext.

While most of the research in Hiero-style systems is focused on the improving the decoder, and in particular the link to the language model, comparatively few papers have considered the inference of the probabilistic SCFG from the word alignments. A majority of the systems employ the classic rule-extraction algorithm (Chiang, 2007) which extracts rules by replacing possible sub-spans (permitted by the word alignments) with a non-terminal and then using relative frequencies to estimate the probabilistic synchronous context-free grammar. One of the issues in building Hiero-style systems is in managing the size of the synchronous grammar. The original approach extracts a larger number of rules when compared to a phrase-based system on the same data leading to practical issues in terms of memory requirements and decoding speed.

Extremely large Hiero phrase tables may also lead to statistical issues, where the probability mass has to be shared by more rules: the probability $p(e|f)$ has to be shared by all the rules having the same source side string f, leading to fragmentation and resulting in many rules having very poor probability.

Approaches to improve the inference (the induction of the SCFG rules from the bitext) typically follows two streams. One focusses on filtering the extracted hierarchical rules either by removing redundancy (He et al., 2009) or by filtering rules based on certain patterns (Iglesias et al., 2009), while the other stream is concerned about alternative approaches for learning the synchronous grammar (Blunsom et al., 2008; Blunsom et al., 2009; de Gispert et al., 2010). This paper falls under the latter category and we use a non-parametric Bayesian approach for rule extraction for Hiero-style systems. Our objective in this paper is to provide a principled

Proceedings of the 6th Workshop on Statistical Machine Translation, pages 533–541,
Edinburgh, Scotland, UK, July 30–31, 2011.

rule extraction method using a Bayesian framework that can extract the minimal SCFG rules without reducing the BLEU score.

2 Motivation and Related Work

The large number of rules in Hiero-style systems leads to slow decoding and increased memory requirements. The heuristic rule extraction algorithm (Chiang, 2007) introduces redundant monotone composed rules (He et al., 2009) in the SCFG grammar. The research on Hiero rule extraction falls into two broad categories: i) rule reduction by eliminating a subset of rules extracted by the heuristic approach and ii) alternate approaches for rule extraction.

There have been approaches to reduce the size of Hiero phrase table, without significantly affecting the translation quality. He et. al. (2009) proposed the idea of discarding monotone composed rules from the phrase table that can instead be obtained dynamically by combining the minimal rules in the same order. They achieve up to 70% reduction in the phrase table by discarding these redundant rules, without appreciable reduction in the performance as measured by BLEU. Empirically analyzing the effectiveness of specific rule patterns, (Iglesias et al., 2009) show that some patterns having over 95% of the total SCFG rules can be safely eliminated without any reduction in the BLEU score.

Along a different track, some prior works have employed alternate rule extraction approaches using a Bayesian framework (DeNero et al., 2008; Blunsom et al., 2008; Blunsom et al., 2009). (DeNero et al., 2008) use a Maximum likelihood model of learning phrase pairs (Marcu and Wong, 2002), but use sampling to compute the expected counts of the phrase pairs for the E-step. Other recent approaches use Gibbs sampler for learning the SCFG by exploring a fixed grammar having pre-defined rule templates (Blunsom et al., 2008) or by reasoning over the space of derivations (Blunsom et al., 2009).

We differ from earlier Bayesian approaches in that our model is guided by the word alignments to reason over the space of the SCFG rules and this restricts the search space of our model. We believe the word alignments to encode information, useful for identifying the good phrase-pairs. For example, several attempts have been made to learn a phrasal translation model directly from the bitext without the word alignments (Marcu and Wong, 2002; DeNero et al., 2008; Blunsom et al., 2008), but without any clear breakthrough that can scale to larger corpora.

Our model exploits the word alignment information in the form of lexical alignment probability in order to construct an informative prior over SCFG rules and it moves away from a heuristic framework, instead using a Bayesian non-parametric model to infer a minimal, high-quality grammar from the data.

3 Model

Our model is based on similar assumptions as the original Hiero system. We assume that the bitext has been word aligned, and that we can use that word alignment to extract *phrase pairs*.

Given the word alignments and the heuristically extracted phrase pairs R_p, our goal is to extract the minimal set of *hierarchical* rules R_g that would best explain R_p. This is achieved by inferring a distribution over the derivations for each phrase pair, where the set of derivations collectively specify the grammar. In the following, we denote the sequence of derivations for the set of phrase pairs by $\mathbf{r}$, which is composed of grammar rules r. We will essentially read off our learned grammar from the sequence of derivations $\mathbf{r}$.

Our non-parametric model reasons over the space of the (hierarchical and terminal) rules and samples a set of rules by employing a prior based on the alignment probability of the words in the phrase pairs. We hypothesize that the resulting grammar will be compact and also will explain the phrase pairs better (the SCFG rules will maximize the likelihood of producing the entire set of observed phrase pairs).

Using Bayes' rule, the posterior over the derivations $\mathbf{r}$ given the phrase pairs R_p can be written as:

$$P(\mathbf{r}|R_p) \propto P(R_p|\mathbf{r})P(\mathbf{r}) \quad (1)$$

where $P(R_p|\mathbf{r})$ is equal to one when the sequence of rules $\mathbf{r}$ and phrase-pairs R_p are consistent, i.e. $\mathbf{r}$ can be partitioned into derivations to compose the set of phrase-pairs such that the derivations respect the given word alignments; otherwise $P(R_p|\mathbf{r})$ is zero. The overall structure of the model is analogous to the Bayesian model for inducing Tree Substitution Grammars proposed by Cohn et al. (2009). Note that, our model extracts hierarchical rules for the word-aligned phrase pairs and not for the sentences.

Similar to the other Hiero-style systems, we use two types of rules: *terminal* and *hierarchical* rules. For each phrase-pair, our model either generates a terminal rule by *not* segmenting the phrase-pair, or decides to *segment* the phrase-pair and extract some rules.

Though it is possible to segment phrase-pairs by two (or more) non-overlapping spans, we propose a simpler model in this paper and restrict the hierarchical rules to contain only one non-terminal (unlike the case of classic Hiero-style grammars containing two non-terminals). This simpler model, samples the space of derivations and identifies a sub-span for introducing the non-terminal, which can be expressed as *terminal rules* (it is *not* decomposed further). Figure 1 shows an example phrase-pair with the Viterbi-best word alignment and Figure 2 shows two possible derivations for the same phrase-pair with the non-terminals introduced at different sub-spans. It can be seen that the sub-phrase corresponding to the non-terminal span X_1 is directly written as a terminal rule and is not decomposed further.

While the resulting model is slightly weaker than the original Hiero grammar, it should be noted our simpler model *does* allow reordering and discontiguous alignments. For example our model includes rules such as, $X \rightarrow (\alpha X_1 \beta, \alpha' \beta' X_1)$, which can capture phrases like (*not* X_1, *ne* X_1 *pas*) in the case of English-French translation. In terms of the reordering, our model lies in between the hierarchical phrase-based and phrase-based models. To summarize, the segmentation of each phrase-pair in our model results in two rules: a hierarchical rule with one nonterminal as well as a terminal rule.

More specifically, the generative process for generating a phrase pair x from the grammar rules may have two steps as follows. In the first step, the model decides on the type of the rule $t_x \in \{\text{TERMINAL}, \text{HIERARCHICAL}\}$ used to generate the phrase-pair based on a Bernoulli distribution, having a prior γ coming from a Beta distribution:

$$t_x \sim \text{Bernoulli}(\gamma)$$
$$\gamma \sim \text{Beta}(l_x, 0.5)$$

The lexical alignment probability l_x controls the tendency for extracting hierarchical rules from the phrase-pair x. For a given phrase-pair, l_x is computed by taking the (geometric or arithmetic) average of the reverse and forward alignment probabilities, which we explain later in this section. Integrating out γ gives us the conditional probabilities of choosing the rule type t_x as:

$$p(t_{term}|x) \propto n^x_{term} + l_x \quad (2)$$
$$p(t_{hier}|x) \propto n^x_{hier} + 0.5 \quad (3)$$

where n^x_{term} and n^x_{hier} denote the number of terminal or hierarchical rules, among the rules extracted so far from the phrase-pair x during the sampling.

In the second step, if the rule type $t_x = \text{HIERARCHICAL}$, the model generates the phrase-pair by sampling from the hierarchical and terminal rules. We use a Dirichlet Process (DP) to model the generation of hierarchical rules r:

$$G \sim DP(\alpha_h, P_0(r))$$
$$r \sim G$$

Integrating out the grammar G, the predictive distribution of a hierarchical rule r_x for generating the current phrase-pair (conditioned on the rules from the rest of the phrase-pairs) is:

$$p(r_x|r^{-x}, \alpha_h, P_0) \propto n^{-x}_{r_x} + \alpha_h P_0(r_x) \quad (4)$$

where $n^{-x}_{r_x}$ is the count of the rule r_x in the rest of the phrase-pairs that is represented by r^{-x}, P_0 is the base measure, and α_h is the concentration parameter controlling the model's preference towards using an existing hierarchical rule from the cache or to create a new rule sanctioned by the base distribution. We use the lexical alignment probabilities of the component rules as our base measure P_0:

$$P_0(r) = \Big[\Big(\prod_{(k,l)\in a} p(e_l|f_k)\Big)^{\frac{1}{|a|}} \Big(\prod_{(k,l)\in a} p(f_k|e_l)\Big)^{\frac{1}{|a|}}\Big]^{\frac{1}{2}} \quad (5)$$

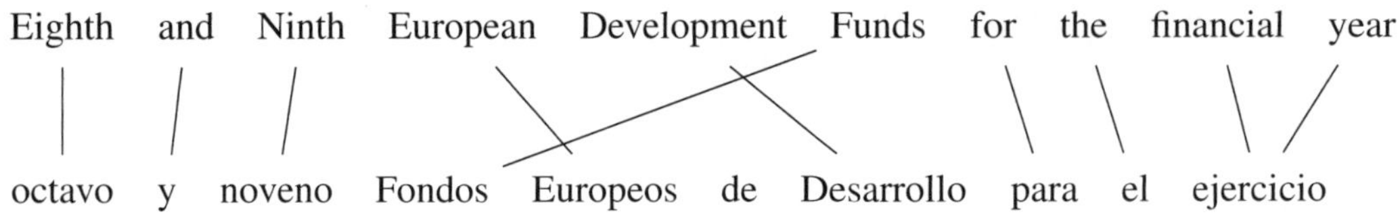

Figure 1: An example *phrase-pair* with Viterbi alignments

$X \rightarrow$ (Eighth and Ninth X_1 for the financial year, octavo y noveno X_1 para el ejercicio)

$X \rightarrow$ (*European Development Funds, Fondos Europeos de Desarrollo*)

$X \rightarrow$ (Eighth and Ninth X_1, octavo y noveno X_1)

$X \rightarrow$ (*European Development Funds for the financial year,*
Fondos Europeos de Desarrollo para el ejercicio)

Figure 2: Two possible derivations of the phrase-pair in Figure 1

where a is the set of alignments in the given sub-span; if the sub-span has multiple Viterbi alignments from different phrase-pairs, we consider the union of all such alignments. DeNero et al. (2008) use a similar prior- geometric mean of the forward and reverse IBM-1 alignments. However, we use the product of geometric means of the forward and reverse alignment scores. We also experimented with the arithmetic mean of the lexical alignment probabilities. The lexical prior l_x in the first step can be defined similarly. We found the particular combination of, 'arithmetic mean' for the lexical prior l_x (in the first step) and 'geometric mean' for the base distribution P_0 (in the second step) to work better, as we discuss later in Section 5.

Assuming the heuristically extracted phrase pairs to be the input to our inference algorithm, our approach samples the space of rules to find the best possible segmentation for the sentences as defined by the cache and base distribution. We explore a subset of the space of rules being considered by (Blunsom et al., 2009) — i.e., only those rules satisfying the word alignments and heuristically grown phrase alignments.

4 Inference

We train our model by using a Gibbs sampler – a Markov Chain Monte Carlo (MCMC) method for sampling one variable in the model, conditional to the other variables. The sampling procedure is repeated for what is called a long Gibbs chain spanning several iterations, while the counts are collected at fixed *thin* intervals in the chain. As is common in the MCMC procedures, we ignore samples from a fixed number of initial *burn-in* iterations, allowing the model to move away from the initial bias. The rules in the final sampler state at the end of the Gibbs chain along with their counts averaged by the number of thin iterations become our translation model.

In our model, a sample for a given phrase pair corresponds either to its terminal derivation or two rules in a hierarchical derivation. The model samples a derivation from the space of derivations that are consistent with the word alignments. In order to achieve this, we need an efficient way to enumerate the derivations for a phrase pair such that they are consistent with the alignments. We use the linear time algorithm to maximally decompose a word-aligned phrase pair, so as to encode it as a compact alignment tree (Zhang et al., 2008).

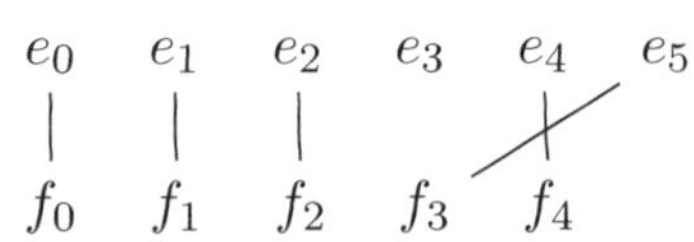

Figure 3: Example phrase pair with alignments.

For a phrase-pair with a given alignment as shown in Figure 3, Zhang et al. (2008) generalize the $\mathcal{O}(n+K)$ time algorithm for computing all K common intervals of two different permutations of length n. The contiguous blocks of the alignment are captured as the nodes in the alignment tree and the tree structure for the example phrase pair in Figure 3 is shown in Figure 4. The italicized nodes form a left-branching chain in the alignment tree and the sub-spans of this chain also lead to alignment nodes that are not explicitly captured in the tree (Please refer to Zhang et al. (2008) for details). In our work, each node in the tree (and also each sub-span in the left-branching chain) corresponds to an *aligned source-target sub-span* within the phrase-pair, and is a potential site for introducing the non-terminal X to generate hierarchical rules.

Given this alignment tree for a phrase pair, a derivation can be obtained by introducing a non-terminal at some node n_d in the tree and re-writing the span rooted at n_d as a separate rule. As mentioned earlier, we compute the derivation probability as a product of the probabilities of the component rules, which are computed using the Equation 4.

We initialize the sampler by using our lexical alignment prior and sampling from the distribution of derivations as suggested by the priors. We found this to perform better in practice, than a naive sampler without an initializer.

At each iteration, the Gibbs sampler processes the phrase pairs in random order. For each phrase pair R_p, it visits the nodes in the corresponding alignment tree and computes the posterior probability of the derivations and samples from this posterior distribution. To speedup the sampling, we store the pre-computed alignment tree for the phrase pairs and just recompute the derivation probabilities based on the sampler state at every iteration. While the sampler state is updated with the counts at each iteration, we accumulate the counts only at fixed intervals in the Gibbs chain. In applying the model for decoding, we use the grammar from the final sampler state.

Since our model includes only one hyperparameter α_h, we tune its value manually by empirically experimenting on a small set of initial phrase pairs. We keep for future work the task of automatically tuning for hyper-parameter values by sampling.

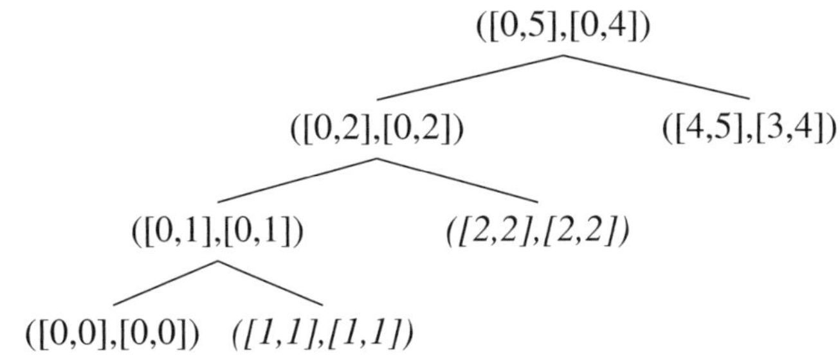

Figure 4: Decomposed alignment tree for the example alignment in Fig. 3.

5 Experiments

We use the English-Spanish data from WMT-10 shared task for the experiments to evaluate the effectiveness of our Bayesian rule extraction approach. We used the entire shared task training set except the UN data for training translation model and the language model was trained with the same set and an additional 2 million sentences from the UN data, using SRILM toolkit with Knesser-Ney discounting. We tuned the feature weights on the WMT-10 devset using MERT (Och, 2003) and evaluate on the test set by computing lower-cased BLEU score (Papineni et al., 2002) using the WMT-10 standard evaluation script.

We use *Kriya* – an in-house implementation of hierarchical phrase-based translation written predominantly in Python. Kriya supports the entire translation pipeline of SCFG rule extraction and decoding with cube pruning (Huang and Chiang, 2007) and LM integration (Chiang, 2007). We use the 7 features (4 translation model features, extracted rules penalty, word penalty and language model) as is typical in Hiero-style systems. For tuning the feature weights, we have adapted the MERT implementation in Moses[1] for use with Kriya as the decoder.

We started by training and evaluating the two baseline systems using i) two non-terminals and ii) one non-terminal, which were trained using the conventional heuristic extraction approach. For the baseline with one non-terminal, we modified the heuristic rule extraction algorithm appropriately[2].

[1]www.statmt.org/moses/

[2]Given an initial phrase pair, the algorithm would introduce a non-terminal for each sub-span consistent with the alignments and extract rules corresponding to each sub-span. The con-

Experiment	# of rules filtered for devset (in millions)	BLEU
Baseline (w/ 2 non-terminals)	52.36	**27.45**
Baseline (w/ 1 non-terminal)	22.09	26.71
Pattern-based filtering†	18.78	24.61
1 non-terminal; monotone & non-monotone	10.36	24.17
1 non-terminal; non-monotone	3.62	23.99

Table 1: Kriya: Baseline and Filtering experiments. †: This is the initial rule set used in Iglesias et al. (2009) obtained by greedy filtering. Rows 4 and 5 represents the filtering that uses single non-terminal rules with row 4 allowing monotone rules in addition to the non-monotone (reordering) rules.

As part of the baseline methods to be applied to minimize the number of SCFG rules, We also wanted to assess the effect of a simpler rule filtering, where the idea is to filter the heuristically extracted rules based on certain patterns. Our first baseline filtering strategy uses the heuristic methods in Iglesias et al. (2009) in order to minimize the number of rules[3]. For the other baseline filtering experiments, we retained only one non-terminal rules and then further limited it by retaining only non-monotone one non-terminal rules; in both cases the terminal rules were retained.

Table 1 shows the results for baseline and the rule filtering experiments. Restricting rule extraction to just one non-terminal doesn't affect the BLEU score significantly and this justifies the simpler model used in this paper. Secondly, we find significant reduction in the BLEU for the pattern-based filtering strategy and this is because we only use the initial rule set obtained by greedy filtering without augmenting it with other specific patterns. The other two filtering methods reduced the BLEU further but not significantly. The second column in the table gives the number of SCFG rules filtered for the devset, which is typically much less than the full set of rules. We later use this to put in perspective the effective reduction in the model size achieved by our Bayesian model. We can ideally compare our Bayesian rule extraction using Gibbs sampling with the baselines and the filtering approaches. However, running our Gibbs sampler on the full set of phrase pairs demand sampling to be distributed, possibly with approximation (?; ?), which we reserve for our future work.

In this work, we focus on evaluating our Gibbs sampler on reasonable sized set of phrase pairs with corresponding baselines. We filter the initial phrase pairs based on their frequency using three different thresholds, viz. 20, 10 and 3- resulting in smaller sets of initial phrase pairs because we throw out infrequent phrase pairs (the threshold-20 case is the smallest initial set of phrase pairs). This allows us to run our sampler as a stand-alone instance for the three sets, obviating the need for distributed sampling.

Table 2 shows the number of unique phrase pairs in each set. While, the filtering reduces the number of phrase pairs to a small fraction of the total phrase pairs, it also increases the unknown words (OOV) in the test set by a factor between 1.8 and 3. In order to address this issue due to the OOV words, we additionally added *non-decomposable phrase pairs* having just one word at either source or target side,

Phrase-pairs set	# of Unique phrase-pairs	Testset OOV
All phrase-pairs	110782174	1136
Threshold-20	292336	3735
Threshold-10	606590	3056
Threshold-3	2689855	2067

Table 2: Phrase-pair statistics for different frequency threshold

straints relating to two non-terminals (such as, no adjacent non-terminals in source side) does not apply for the one non-terminal case.

[3]It should be noted that we didn't use the augmentations to the initial rule set (Iglesias et al., 2009) and our objective is to find the impact of the filtering approaches.

Experiment	Threshold-20	Threshold-10	Threshold-3
Baseline (w/ 2 non-terminals)	24.30	25.96	26.34
Baseline (w/ 1 non-terminal)	**24.00**	**25.90**	**26.83**
Bayesian rule extraction	23.39	24.30	25.22

Table 3: BLEU scores: Heuristic vs Bayesian rule extraction

Experiment	Rules Extracted (in millions)		Reduction
	Heuristic (1 nt)	Bayesian	
Threshold-20	1.93 (0.117)	1.86 (0.07)	3.57 (38.34)
Threshold-10	2.91 (1.09)	2.10 (0.28)	27.7 (73.95)
Threshold-3	7.46 (5.64)	2.45 (0.71)	**67.17 (87.28)**

Table 4: Model compression: Heuristic vs Bayesian rule extraction

Priors	α_h	BLEU
Arith + Arith means	0.5	22.46
Arith + Geom means	0.5	**23.39**
Geom + Arith means	0.5	22.96
Arith + Geom means	0.5	22.83
Arith + Geom means	0.1	22.88
Arith + Geom means	0.2	22.97
Arith + Geom means	0.3	22.98
Arith + Geom means	0.4	22.69
Arith + Geom means	0.5	**23.39**
Arith + Geom means	0.6	22.89
Arith + Geom means	0.7	22.82
Arith + Geom means	0.8	22.82
Arith + Geom means	0.9	22.67

Table 5: Effect of different priors and α_h on Threshold-20 set. The two priors correspond to the lexical prior l_x in the first step and the base distribution P_0 in the second step.

as coverage rules. The coverage rules (about 1.8 million) were added separately to the SCFG rules induced by both heuristic algorithm and Gibbs sampler. This is justified because we only add the rules that can not be decomposed further by both rule extraction approaches. However, note that both approaches can independently induce rules that overlap with the coverage rules set and in such cases we simply add the original corpus count to the counts returned by the respective rule extraction method.

The Gibbs sampler considers the phrase pairs in random order at each iteration and induces SCFG rules by sampling a derivation for each phrase pair. Given a phrase pair x with raw corpus frequency f_x, we simply scale the count for its sampled derivation $\mathbf{r}$ by its frequency f_x. Alternately, we also experimented with independently sampling for each instance of the phrase pair and found their performances to be comparable. Sampling phrase pairs once and then scaling the sampled derivation, help us to speed up the sampling process. In our experiments, we ran the Gibbs sampler for 2000 iterations with a burn-in period of 200, collecting counts every 50 iterations. We set the concentration parameter α_h to be 0.5 based on our experiments detailed later in this section.

The BLEU scores for the SCFG learned from the Gibbs sampler are shown in Table 3. We first note that, the threshold-20 set has lower baseline BLEU than threshold-10 and threshold-3 sets, as can be expected because threshold-20 set uses a much smaller subset of the full set of phrase pairs to extract hierarchical rules. The Bayesian approach results in a maximum BLEU score reduction of 1.6 for the sets using thresholds 10 and 3, compared to the one non-terminal baseline. The two non-terminal baseline is also provided to place our results in perspective.

Table 4 shows the model size, including the coverage rules for the two rule extraction approaches. The number of extracted rules, excluding the coverage rules are shown within the parenthesis. The last column shows the reduction in the model size for both with and without the coverage rules; yielding a maximum absolute reduction of 67.17% for the threshold-3 phrase pairs set. It can be seen that the number of rules are far fewer than the rules extracted using the baseline heuristic methods for filtering detailed in Table 1. Interestingly, we obtain a smaller model size, even as we decrease the threshold to include more initial phrase pairs used as input to the inference procedure, e.g. a 67.17% reduction over the rules extracted from the threshold-3 phrase pairs v.s. a 27.7% reduction for threshold-10.

These results show that our model is capable of extracting high-value Hiero-style SCFG rules, albeit with a reduction in the BLEU score. However, our current approach offers scope for improvement in several avenues, for example we can use annealing to perturb the initial sampling iterations to encourage the Gibbs sampler to explore several derivations for each phrase pair. Though this might result in slightly large models than the current ones, we still expect substantial reduction than the original Hiero rule extraction. In future, we also plan to sample the hyperparameter α_h, instead of using a fixed value.

Table 5 shows the effect of different values of the concentration parameter α_h and the priors used in the model. The order of priors in each setting correspond to the prior used in deciding the rule-type and identifying the non-terminal span for sampling a derivation. We found the geometric mean to work better in both cases. We further found that the concentration parameter α_h value 0.5 gives the best BLEU score.

6 Conclusion and Future Work

We proposed a novel method for extracting minimal set of hierarchical rules using non-parametric Bayesian framework. We demonstrated substantial reduction in the size of extracted grammar with the best case reduction of 67.17%, as compared to the heuristic approach, albeit with a slight reduction in the BLEU scores.

We plan to extend our model to handle two non-terminals to allow for better reordering. We also plan to run our sampler on the full set of phrase pairs using distributed sampling and our preliminary results in this direction are encouraging. Finally, we would like to directly sample from the Viterbi aligned sentence pairs instead of relying on the heuristically extracted phrase pairs. This can be accomplished by using a model that is closer to the Tree Substitution Grammar induction model in (Cohn et al., 2009) but in our case the model would infer a Hiero-style SCFG from word-aligned sentence pairs.

References

Phil Blunsom, Trevor Cohn, and Miles Osborne. 2008. Bayesian synchronous grammar induction. In *Proceedings of Neural Information Processing Systems-08*.

Phil Blunsom, Trevor Cohn, Chris Dyer, and Miles Osborne. 2009. A gibbs sampler for phrasal synchronous grammar induction. In *Proceedings of Association of Computational Linguistics-09*, pages 782–790. Association for Computational Linguistics.

David Chiang. 2007. Hierarchical phrase-based translation. *Computational Linguistics*, 33.

Trevor Cohn, Sharon Goldwater, and Phil Blunsom. 2009. Inducing compact but accurate tree-substitution grammars. In *Proceedings of Human Language Technologies: North American Chapter of the Association for Computational Linguistics-09*, pages 548–556. Association for Computational Linguistics.

Adrià de Gispert, Juan Pino, and William Byrne. 2010. Hierarchical phrase-based translation grammars extracted from alignment posterior probabilities. In *Proceedings of the 2010 Conference on Empirical Methods in Natural Language Processing*, pages 545–554. Association for Computational Linguistics.

John DeNero, Alexandre Bouchard-Cote, and Klein Dan. 2008. Sampling alignment structure under a bayesian translation model. In *In Proceedings of Empirical Methods in Natural Language Processing-08*, pages 314–323. Association for Computational Linguistics.

Zhongjun He, Yao Meng, and Hao Yu. 2009. Discarding monotone composed rule for hierarchical phrase-based statistical machine translation. In *Proceedings of the 3rd International Universal Communication Symposium*, pages 25–29. ACM.

Liang Huang and David Chiang. 2007. Forest rescoring: Faster decoding with integrated language models. In *Proceedings of the 45th Annual Meeting of the Association of Computational Linguistics*, pages 144–151. Association for Computational Linguistics.

Gonzalo Iglesias, Adrià de Gispert, Eduardo R. Banga, and William Byrne. 2009. Rule filtering by pattern for efficient hierarchical translation. In *Proceedings of the 12th Conference of the European Chapter of the ACL (EACL 2009)*, pages 380–388. Association for Computational Linguistics.

Daniel Marcu and William Wong. 2002. A phrase-based, joint probability model for statistical machine translation. In *In Proceedings of Empirical Methods in Natural Language Processing-02*, pages 133–139. Association for Computational Linguistics.

Franz Josef Och. 2003. Minimum error rate training in statistical machine translation. In *Proceedings of the 41st Annual Meeting of the Association for Computational Linguistics*, pages 160–167. Association for Computational Linguistics.

Kishore Papineni, Salim Roukos, Todd Ward, and Wie-Jing Zhu. 2002. BLEU: a method for automatic evaluation of machine translation. In *In Proceedings of Association of Computational Linguistics*, pages 311–318. Association for Computational Linguistics.

Hao Zhang, Daniel Gildea, and David Chiang. 2008. Extracting synchronous grammar rules from word-level alignments in linear time. In *In Proceedings of the 22nd International Conference on Computational Linguistics (COLING) - Volume 1*, pages 1081–1088. Association for Computational Linguistics.

Andreas Zollmann, Ashish Venugopal, Franz Och, and Jay Ponte. 2008. A systematic comparison of phrase-based, hierarchical and syntax-augmented statistical mt. In *Proceedings of the 22nd International Conference on Computational Linguistics (COLING) - Volume 1*, pages 1145–1152. Association for Computational Linguistics.

From n-gram-based to CRF-based Translation Models

Thomas Lavergne **Josep Maria Crego**
LIMSI/CNRS
BP 133
F-91 403 Orsay Cédex
{lavergne, jmcrego}@limsi.fr

Alexandre Allauzen **François Yvon**
LIMSI/CNRS & Uni. Paris Sud
BP 133
F-91 403 Orsay Cédex
{allauzen, yvon}@limsi.fr

Abstract

A major weakness of extant statistical machine translation (SMT) systems is their lack of a proper training procedure. Phrase extraction and scoring processes rely on a chain of crude heuristics, a situation judged problematic by many. In this paper, we recast the machine translation problem in the familiar terms of a sequence labeling task, thereby enabling the use of enriched feature sets and exact training and inference procedures. The tractability of the whole enterprise is achieved through an efficient implementation of the conditional random fields (CRFs) model using a weighted finite-state transducers library. This approach is experimentally contrasted with several conventional phrase-based systems.

1 Introduction

A weakness of existing phrase-based SMT systems, that has been repeatedly highlighted, is their lack of a proper training procedure. Attempts to design probabilistic models of phrase-to-phrase alignments (e.g. (Marcu and Wong, 2002)) have thus far failed to overcome the related combinatorial problems (DeNero and Klein, 2008) and/or to yield improved training heuristics (DeNero et al., 2006).

Phrase extraction and scoring thus rely on a chain of heuristics see (Koehn et al., 2003), which evolve phrase alignments from "symmetrized" word-to-word alignments obtained with IBM models (Brown et al., 1990) and the like (Liang et al., 2006b; Deng and Byrne, 2006; Ganchev et al., 2008). Phrase scoring is also mostly heuristic and relies on an optimized interpolation of several simple frequency-based scores. Overall, the training procedure of translation models within conventional phrase-based (or hierarchical) systems is generally considered unsatisfactory and the design of better estimation procedures remains an active research area (Wuebker et al., 2010).

To overcome the NP-hard problems that derive from the need to consider all possible permutations of the source sentence, we make here a radical simplification and consider training the translation model given a fixed segmentation and reordering. This idea is not new, and is one of the grounding principle of n-gram-based approaches (Casacuberta and Vidal, 2004; Mariño et al., 2006) in SMT. The novelty here is that we will use this assumption to recast machine translation (MT) in the familiar terms of a sequence labeling task.

This reformulation allows us to make use of the efficient training and inference tools that exists for such tasks, most notably linear CRFs (Lafferty et al., 2001; Sutton and McCallum, 2006). It also enables to easily integrate linguistically informed (describing morphological or morpho-syntactical properties of phrases) and/or contextual features into the translation model. In return, in addition to having a better trained model, we also expect (i) to make estimation less sensible to data sparsity issues and (ii) to improve the ability of our system to make the correct lexical choices based on the neighboring source words. As explained in Section 2, this reformulation borrows much from the general architecture of n-gram MT systems and implies to solve several computational challenges. In our ap-

Proceedings of the 6th Workshop on Statistical Machine Translation, pages 542–553,
Edinburgh, Scotland, UK, July 30–31, 2011.

proach, the tractability of the whole enterprise is achieved through an efficient reimplementation of CRFs using a public domain library for weighted finite-state transducers (WFSTs) (see details in Section 3). This approach is experimentally contrasted with more conventional n-gram based and phrase-based approaches on a standard benchmark in Section 4, where we also evaluate the benefits of various feature sets and training regimes. We finally relate our new system with alternative proposals for training discriminatively SMT systems in Section 5, before drawing some lessons and discussing possible extensions of this work.

The main contribution of this work are thus (i) a detailed presentation of the CRF in translation including all necessary implementation details and (ii) an experimental study of various feature functions and of various ways to integrate target side LM information.

2 MT as sequence labeling

In this section, we briefly review the n-gram based approach to SMT, originally introduced in (Casacuberta and Vidal, 2004; Mariño et al., 2006), which constitutes our starting point. We then describe our new proposal, which, in essence, consists in replacing the modeling of compound source-target translation units by a conditional model where the probability of each target side phrase is conditioned on the source sentence.

2.1 The n-gram based approach in SMT

The n-gram based approach of (Mariño et al., 2006) is a variation of the standard phrase-based model, characterized by the peculiar form of the translation model. In this approach, the translation model is based on bilingual units called *tuples*. Tuples are the analogous of phrase pairs, as they represent a matching $u = (e, f)$ between a source f and a target e word sequence. The probability of a sequence of tuples is computed using a conventional n-gram model as:

$$p(u_1 \dots u_I) = \prod_{i=1}^{I} p(u_l | u_{i-1} \dots u_{i-n+1}).$$

The probability of a sentence pair $(\mathbf{f}, \mathbf{e})$ is then either recovered by marginalization, or approximated by maximization, over all possible joint segmentations of $\mathbf{f}$ and $\mathbf{e}$ into tuples.

As for any n-gram model, the parameters are estimated using statistics collected in a training corpus made of *sequences of tuples* derived from the parallel sentences in a two step process. First, a word alignment is computed using a standard alignment pipeline[1] based on the IBM models. Source words are then reordered so as to disentangle the alignment links and to synchronize the source and target texts. Special care has to be paid to non-aligned source words, which have to be collapsed with their neighbor words. A byproduct of this process is a *deterministic joint segmentation* of parallel sentences into minimal bilingual units, the tuples, that constitute the basic elements in the model. This process is illustrated on Figure 1, where the unfolding process enables the extraction of tuples such as: (*demanda*, *said*) or (*de nouveau*, *again*).

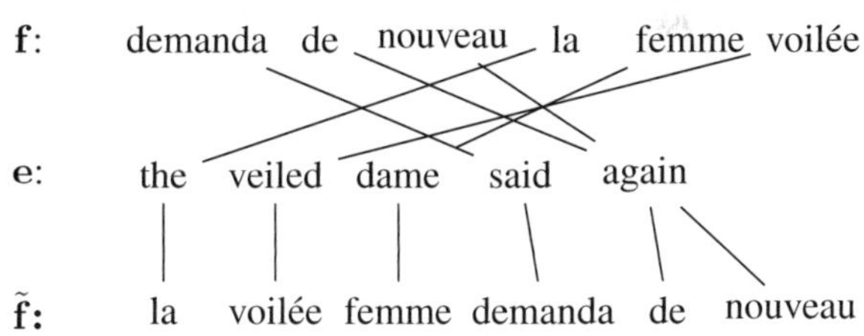

Figure 1: The tuple extraction process
The original (top) and reordered (bottom) French sentence aligned with its translation.

At test time, the source text is reordered so as to match the reordering implied by the disentanglement procedure. Various proposals has been made to perform such source side reordering (Collins et al., 2005; Xia and McCord, 2004), or even learning reordering rules based on syntactic or morphosyntactic information (Crego and Mariño, 2007). The latter approach amounts to accumulate reordering patterns during the training; test source sentences are then non-deterministically reordered *in all possible ways* yielding a word graph. This graph is then monotonously decoded, where the score of a translation hypothesis combines information from the translation models as well as from other information sources (lexicalized reordering model, target

[1]Here, using the MGIZA++ package (Gao and Vogel, 2008).

side language model (LM), word and phrase penalties, etc).

2.2 Translating with CRFs

A discriminative version of the n-gram approach consists in modeling $P(\mathbf{e}|\mathbf{f})$ instead of $P(\mathbf{e},\mathbf{f})$, which can be efficiently performed with CRFs (Lafferty et al., 2001; Sutton and McCallum, 2006). Assuming matched sequences of observations ($\mathbf{x} = x_1^L$) and labels ($\mathbf{y} = y_1^L$), CRFs express the conditional probability of labels as:

$$P(y_1^L|x_1^L) = \frac{1}{Z(x_1^L;\theta)} \exp(\theta^T G(x_1^L, y_1^L)),$$

where θ is a parameter vector and G denotes a vector of *feature functions* testing various properties of $\mathbf{x}$ and $\mathbf{y}$. In the *linear-chain* CRF, each component $G_k(x_1^I, y_1^I)$ of G is decomposed as a sum of local features: $G_k(x_1^I, y_1^I) = \sum_i g_k(x_1^I, y_{i-1}, y_i)$[2]. CRFs are trained by maximizing the (penalized) log-likelihood of a corpus containing observations and their labels.

In principle, the data used to train n-gram translation models provide all the necessary information required to train a CRF[3]. It suffices to consider that the alphabet of possible observations ranges over all possible source side fragments, and that each target side of a tuple is a potential label. The model thus defines the probability of a segmented target $\widetilde{\mathbf{e}} = \widetilde{e}_1^I$ given the segmented and reordered source sentence $\tilde{\mathbf{f}} = \tilde{f}_1^I$. To complete the model, one just needs to define a distribution over source segmentations $P(\tilde{\mathbf{f}}|\mathbf{f})$. Given the deterministic relationship between $\mathbf{e}$ and $\widetilde{\mathbf{e}}$ expressed by the "unsegmentation" function ϕ which maps $\widetilde{\mathbf{e}}$ with $\mathbf{e} = \phi(\widetilde{\mathbf{e}})$, we then have:

$$\begin{aligned} P(\mathbf{e}|\mathbf{f}) &= \sum_{\tilde{\mathbf{f}},\widetilde{\mathbf{e}}|\phi(\widetilde{\mathbf{e}})=\mathbf{e}} P(\widetilde{\mathbf{e}},\tilde{\mathbf{f}}|\mathbf{f}) \\ &= \sum_{\tilde{\mathbf{f}},\widetilde{\mathbf{e}}|\phi(\widetilde{\mathbf{e}})=\mathbf{e}} P(\widetilde{\mathbf{e}},|\tilde{\mathbf{f}},\mathbf{f})P(\tilde{\mathbf{f}}|\mathbf{f}) \\ &= \sum_{\tilde{\mathbf{f}},\widetilde{\mathbf{e}}|\phi(\widetilde{\mathbf{e}})=\mathbf{e}} P(\widetilde{\mathbf{e}},|\tilde{\mathbf{f}})P(\tilde{\mathbf{f}}|\mathbf{f}) \end{aligned}$$

[2] Assuming first order dependencies.

[3] This is a significant difference with (Blunsom et al., 2008), as we do not need to introduce latent variables during training.

In practice, we will only consider a restricted number of possible segmentation/reorderings of the source, denoted $\mathcal{L}(\mathbf{f})$, and compute the best translation $\mathbf{e}^*$ as $\phi(\widetilde{\mathbf{e}}^*)$, where:

$$\begin{aligned} \widetilde{\mathbf{e}}^* &= \arg\max_{\widetilde{\mathbf{e}}} P(\widetilde{\mathbf{e}}|\mathbf{f}) \\ &\approx \arg\max_{\tilde{\mathbf{f}}\in\mathcal{L}(\mathbf{f}),\widetilde{\mathbf{e}}} P(\widetilde{\mathbf{e}},|\tilde{\mathbf{f}},\mathbf{f})P(\tilde{\mathbf{f}}|\mathbf{f}) \qquad (1) \end{aligned}$$

Even with these simplifying assumptions, this approach raises several challenging computational problems. First, training a CRF is quadratic in the number of labels, of which we will have plenty (typically hundreds of thousands). A second issue is decoding: as we need to consider at test time a combinatorial number of possible source reorderings and segmentations, we can no longer dispense with the computation of the normalizer $Z(\tilde{\mathbf{f}};\theta)$ which is required to compute $P(\widetilde{\mathbf{e}},\tilde{\mathbf{f}}|\mathbf{f})$ as $P(\tilde{\mathbf{f}}|\mathbf{f})P(\widetilde{\mathbf{e}}|\tilde{\mathbf{f}})$ and to compare hypotheses associated with different values of $\tilde{\mathbf{f}}$. We discuss our solutions to these problems in the next section.

3 Implementation issues

3.1 Training

Basic training The main difficulties in training are caused by the unusually large number of labels, each of which corresponds to a (small) sequence of target words. Hopefully, each observation (source side tuple) occurs with a very small number of different labels. A first simplification is thus to consider that the set of possible "labels" $\widetilde{e}$ for a source sequence $\widetilde{f}$ is limited to those that are seen in training: all the other associations $(\widetilde{f},\widetilde{e})$ are deemed impossible, which amounts to setting the corresponding parameter value to $-\infty$.

A second speed-up is to enforce sparsity in the model, through the use of a ℓ_1 regularization term (Tibshirani, 1996): on the one hand, this greatly reduces the memory usage; furthermore, sparse models are also prone to various optimization of the forward-backward computations (Lavergne et al., 2010). As discussed in (Ng, 2004; Turian et al., 2007), this feature selection strategy is well suited to the task at hand, where the number of possible features is extremely large. Optimization is performed using the Rprop algorithm[4] (Riedmiller and Braun, 1993), which provides the memory efficiency needed to cope with the very large feature sets considered here.

Training with a target language model One of the main strength of the phrase-based "log-linear" models is their ability to make use of powerful target side language models trained on very large amounts of monolingual texts. This ability is crucial to achieve good performance and has to be preserved no matter the difficulties that occur when one moves away from conventional phrase-based systems (Chiang, 2005; Huang and Chiang, 2007; Blunsom and Osborne, 2008; Kääriäinen, 2009). It thus seems appropriate to include a LM feature function in our model or alternatively to define:

$$P(\widetilde{\mathbf{e}}|\tilde{\mathbf{f}}) = \frac{1}{Z(\tilde{\mathbf{f}};\theta)} P_{LM}(\widetilde{\mathbf{e}}) \exp(\theta^T G(\tilde{\mathbf{f}}, \widetilde{\mathbf{e}})),$$

where P_{LM} is the target language model and $Z(\tilde{\mathbf{f}};\theta) = \sum_{\widetilde{\mathbf{e}}} P_{LM}(\widetilde{\mathbf{e}}) \exp(\theta^T G(\tilde{\mathbf{f}}, \widetilde{\mathbf{e}}))$. Implementing this approach implies to deal with the lack of synchronization between the units of the translation models, which are variable-length (possibly empty) tuples, and the units of the language models, which are plain words.

In practice, this extension is implemented by performing training and inference over a graph whose nodes are not only indexed by their position and the left target context, but also by the required n-gram (target) history. In most cases, for small values of n such as considered in this study, the n-gram history can be deduced from the left target tuple. The most problematic case is when the left target tuple is NULL, which require to copy the history from the previous states. As a consequence, for the values of n considered here, the impact of this extension on the total training time is limited.

Reference reachability A recurring problem for discriminative training approaches is *reference unreachability* (Liang et al., 2006a): this happens when the model cannot predict the reference translation, which means in our case that the probability of the reference cannot be computed. In our implementation, this only happens when the reference involves a tuple $(\widetilde{f},\widetilde{e})$ that is too rare to be included in the model. As a practical workaround, when this happens for a given training sentence, we make sure to "locally" augment the tuple dictionary with the missing part of the reference, which is then removed for processing the rest of the training corpus.

[4] Adapted to handle a locally non-differentiable objective.

3.2 Inference

Our decoder is implemented as a cascade of weighted finite-state transducers (WFSTs) using the functionalities of the OpenFst library (Allauzen et al., 2007). This library provides many basic operation for WFSTs, notably the left (π_1) and right (π_2) projections as well as the composition operation ($\circ$). The related notions and algorithms are presented in detail in (Mohri, 2009), to which we refer the reader.

In essence, our decoder is implemented of a finite-state cascade involoving the following steps: (i) source reordering and segmentation (ii) application of the translation model and (optionally) (iii) composition with a target side language model, an architecture that is closely related to the proposal of (Kumar et al., 2006). A more precise account of these various steps is given below, where we describe the main finite-state transducers involved in our decoder:

- S, the acceptor for the source sentence $\mathbf{f}$;
- R, which implements segmentation and reordering rules;
- T, the tuple dictionary, associating source side sequences with possible translations based on the inventory of tuples;
- F, the feature matcher, mapping each feature with the corresponding parameter value;

Source reordering The computation of R mainly follows the approach of (Crego and Mariño, 2007) and uses a part-of-speech tagged version of the reordered training data. Each reordering pattern seen in training is generalized as a non-deterministic reordering rule which expresses a possible rearrangement of some subpart of the source sentence. Each rule is implemented as an elementary finite-state transducer, and the set of possible word reorderings is computed as the composition of these transducers. R is finally obtained by composing the result with a transducer computing all the possible segmentations of its input into sequences of source side tuples[5].

The output of $S \circ R$ are sequences of source side tuples $\tilde{\mathbf{f}}$; each path in this transducer is additionally weighted with a simplistic n-tuple segmentation model, estimated using the source side of the parallel training corpus. Note that these scores are normalized, so that the weight of each path labelled $\tilde{\mathbf{f}}$ in $S \circ R$ is $\log P(\tilde{\mathbf{f}}|f)$.

The feature matcher F The feature matcher is also implemented as a series of elementary weighted transducers, each transducer being responsible for a given *class of feature functions*. The simplest transducer in this family deals with the class of *unigram feature functions*, ie. feature functions that only test the current observation and label. It is represented on the left part of Figure 3.2, where for the sake of readability we only display one example for each test pattern (here: an unconditional feature that always returns true for a given label, a test on the source word, and a test on the source POS label). As long as dependencies between source and/or target symbols remain local, they can be captured by finite-state transducers such as the ones on the mid and right part of Figure 3.2, which respectively compute *bigram* target features, and joint bigram source and target features.

The feature matcher F is computed as the composition of these elementary transducers, where we only include source and target labels that can occur given the current input sentence. Weights in F are interpreted in the tropical semiring. $\exp(F)$ is obtained by replacing weights w in F with $\exp(w)$ in the real semiring.

Decoding a word graph If the input segmentation and reordering were deterministically set, meaning that the automaton $I = \pi_1(S \circ R \circ T)$ would only contain one path, decoding would amount to finding the best path in $S \circ R \circ T \circ F$. However, we need to compute:

$$\arg\max_{\tilde{\mathbf{e}}} P(\tilde{\mathbf{e}}|\mathbf{f}) = \arg\max_{\tilde{\mathbf{e}}} \sum_{\tilde{\mathbf{f}}} P(\tilde{\mathbf{e}}, \tilde{\mathbf{f}}|\mathbf{f}) = \arg\max_{\tilde{\mathbf{e}}} \sum_{\tilde{\mathbf{f}}} P(\tilde{\mathbf{e}}|\tilde{\mathbf{f}}) P(\tilde{\mathbf{f}}|\mathbf{f}).$$

This requires to compare model scores for multiple source segmentations and reorderings $\tilde{\mathbf{f}}$, hence to compute $P(\tilde{\mathbf{f}}|\mathbf{f})$ and $P(\tilde{\mathbf{e}}|\tilde{\mathbf{f}})$, rather than just the non-normalized value that is usually used in CRFs.

Computing the normalizer $Z(\tilde{\mathbf{f}};\theta)$ for all sequences in $S \circ R$ is performed efficiently using standard finite-state operations as :

$$D = \det(\pi_1(\pi_2(S \circ R) \circ T \circ \exp(F))).$$

In fact, determinization (in the real semiring) has the effect of accumulating for each $\tilde{\mathbf{f}}$ the corresponding normalizer $Z(\tilde{\mathbf{f}};\theta)$. Replacing each weight w in D by $-\log(w)$ and using the log semiring enables to compute $-\log(Z(\tilde{\mathbf{f}};\theta))$. The best translation is then obtained as: $\mathrm{bestpath}(\pi_2(S \circ R) \circ -\log(D) \circ T \circ F)$ in the tropical semiring.

Decoding and Rescoring with a target language model An alternative manner of using a (large) target side language model is to use it for rescoring purposes. The consistent use of finite-state machines and operations makes it fairly easy to include one during decoding : it suffices to perform the search in $\pi_2(S \circ R) \circ -\log(D) \circ T \circ F \circ L$, where L represents a n-gram language model. When combining several models, notably a source segmentation model and/or a target language model for rescoring, we have made sure to rescale the (log)probabilities so as to balance the language model scores with the CRF scores, and to use a fixed word bonus to make hypotheses of different length more comparable. All these parameters are tuned as part of the decoder development process. It is finally noteworthy that, in our architecture, alternative decoding strategies, such as MBR (Kumar and Byrne, 2004) are also readily implemented.

4 Experiments

4.1 Corpora and metrics

For these experiments, we have used a medium size training corpus, extracted from the datasets made available for WMT 2011[6] evaluation campaign, and have focused on one translation direction, from French to English[7].

Translation model training uses the entire *News-Commentary* subpart of the WMT'2011 training

[5]When none is found, we also consider a maximal segmentation into isolated words.

[6]`statmt.org/wmt11`

[7]Results in the other direction suggest similar conclusions.

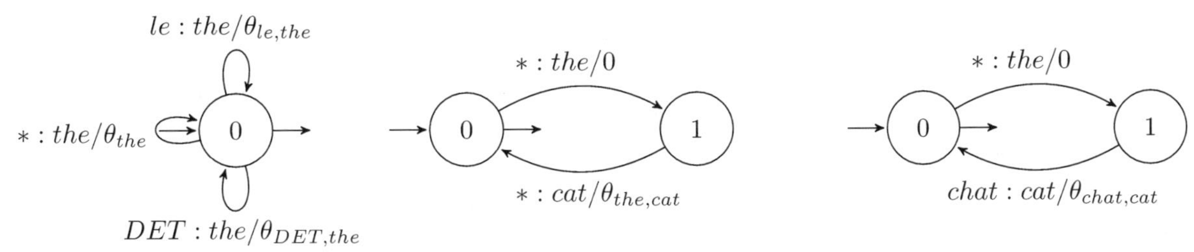

Figure 2: Feature matchers. The star symbol (*) matches any possible observation.

		French		English	
	sent˙	token	types	token	types
train	115 K	3 339 K	60 K	2 816 K	58 K
test 2008	2.0 K	55 K	9 K	49 K	8 K
test 2009	2.5 K	72 K	11 K	65 K	10 K
test 2010	2.5 K	69 K	10 K	61 K	9 K

Table 1: Corpora used for the experiments

data; for language models, we have considered two approaches (i) a "large" bigram model highly optimized using all the available monolingual data and (ii) a "small" trigram language model trained on just the English side of the NewsCommentary corpus. The regularization parameters used in training are tuned using the WMT 2009 test set; the various parameters implied in the decoding are tuned (for BLEU) on WMT 2008 test set; the internal tests reported below are performed on the 2010 test lines (see Table 1) using the best parameters found during tuning. Various statistics regarding these corpora are reproduced on Table 1.

All the training corpora were aligned using MGIZA++ with standard parameters[8], and processed in the standard tuple extraction pipeline. The development and test corpora were also processed analogously. For the sake of comparison, we also trained a standard n-gram-based and a Moses system (Koehn et al., 2007) with default parameters and a 3-gram target LM trained using only the target side of our parallel corpus. The development set (test 2009) was used to tune these two systems. All performance are measured using BLEU (Papineni et al., 2002).

[8]As part of a much larger batch of texts.

4.2 Features

The baseline system is composed only of *translation features* **[trs]** and *target bigram features* **[t2g]**. The former correspond to functions of the form $\mathrm{gu}_{s,t}(\tilde{\mathbf{f}}, \tilde{\mathbf{e}}, i) = \mathbb{I}(\tilde{f}_i = s \wedge \tilde{e}_i = t)$, where s and t respectively denote source and target phrases and $\mathbb{I}()$ is the indicator function. These are also generalized to part-of-speech and also to any possible source phrase, giving rise to features such as $\mathrm{gu}_{*,t} = (\tilde{\mathbf{f}}, \tilde{\mathbf{e}}, i) = \mathbb{I}(\tilde{e}_i = t)$. Target bigram features correspond to functions of the form $\mathrm{gb}_{t,t'}(\tilde{\mathbf{f}}, \tilde{\mathbf{e}}, i) = \mathbb{I}(\tilde{e}_{i-1} = t \wedge \tilde{e}_i = t')$. The last baseline feature is the *copy* feature, which fires whenever the source and target segments are identical.

Supplementary groups of features are considered in further stages:

- suffix/prefix features **[ix]**. These features allow to generalize baseline features on the source side to fixed length prefixes and suffixes, thus smoothing the parameters.
- context features **[ctx]**. These features are similar to unigram features, but also test the left *source* tuple and the corresponding part-of-speech.
- segmentation features **[seg]**. These features are meant to express a preference for longer tuples and to regulate the number of target words per source word. We consider the following feature functions ($|e|$ denotes the length of e):
  - target length features : $\mathrm{gl}_{*,l}(\tilde{\mathbf{f}}, \tilde{\mathbf{e}}, i) = \mathbb{I}(|\tilde{e}_i| = l)$
  - source-target length features : $\mathrm{gl}_{l,l'}(\tilde{\mathbf{f}}, \tilde{\mathbf{e}}, i) = \mathbb{I}(|\tilde{f}_i| = l \wedge |\tilde{e}_i| = l')$
  - source-target length ratio : $\mathrm{gl}_{l}(\tilde{\mathbf{f}}, \tilde{\mathbf{e}}, i) = \mathbb{I}(\mathrm{round}(\frac{|\tilde{f}_i|}{|\tilde{e}_i|}) = l)$

Note that all these features are further conditioned on the *target* label.

- reordering features [**ord**]. These features are meant to model preferences for specific local reordering patterns and take into account neighbor source fragments in $\widetilde{\mathbf{e}}$ together with the current label. Each source side segment $\widetilde{f}_i$ is made of some source words that, prior to source reordering, were located at indices $i_1 \ldots i_l$, so that $\widetilde{f}_i = f_{i_1} \ldots f_{i_l}$. The highest (resp. lowest) index in this sequence is $\lceil \widetilde{f}_i \rceil$ (resp. $\lfloor \widetilde{f}_i \rfloor$). The leftmost (resp. rightmost) index is $[\widetilde{f}_i[$ (resp. $]\widetilde{f}_i]$).

  Using these notations, our model includes the following patterns:

  – distortion features, measuring the gaps between consecutive source fragments : $\mathrm{go}_{l,t}(\widetilde{\mathbf{f}}, \widetilde{\mathbf{e}}, i) = \mathbb{I}(\Delta(\widetilde{f}_i, \widetilde{e}_i) = l \wedge \widetilde{e}_i = t)$, where $\Delta(\widetilde{f}_i, \widetilde{e}_i) =$ $\begin{cases} \lfloor \widetilde{f}_i \rfloor - \lceil \widetilde{f}_{i-1} \rceil \text{ if } (\lceil \widetilde{f}_{i-1} \rceil \leq \lfloor \widetilde{f}_i \rfloor) \\ \lceil \widetilde{f}_i \rceil - \lfloor \widetilde{f}_{i-1} \rfloor \text{ otherwise .} \end{cases}$

  – lexicalized reordering, identifying monotone, swap and discontinuous configurations (Tillman, 2004). The monotonous test is defined as: $\mathrm{go}_m(\widetilde{\mathbf{f}}, \widetilde{\mathbf{e}}, i) = \mathbb{I}(]e_{i-1}] = [e_i[)$; the swap and discontinuous configurations are defined analogously.

  – "gappiness" test : this feature is activated whenever the source indices $i_1 ... i_l$ contain one or several gaps.

4.3 Experiments and lessons learned

Training time The first lesson learned is that training can be performed efficiently. Our baseline system, which only contains **trs** and **trg** contains approximately 87 million features, out of which a little bit more than 600K are selected. Adding up all supplementary features raises the number of parameters to about 130M features, out of which 1.5M are found useful. All these systems require between 3 and 5 hours to train[9]. These numbers are obtained with a ℓ^1 penalty term ≈ 1, which offers a good balance between accuracy and sparsity.

[9] All experiments run on a server with 64G of memory and two Xeon processors with 4 cores at 2.27 Ghz.

Test conditions In order to better assess the strengths and weaknesses of our approach, we compare several test settings: the most favorable considers only one possible segmentation/reordering $\widetilde{\mathbf{f}}$ for each $\mathbf{f}$, obtained through forced alignment with the reference; we then consider the more challenging case where the reordering is fixed, but several segmentations are considered; then the regular decoding task, where both segmentation and reordering are unknown and where the entire space of all segmentations and reordering is searched. For each condition, we also vary (i) the set of features used and (ii) the target language model used, if any. Wherever applicable, we also report contrasts with n-gram-based systems subject to the same input and comparable resources, varying the order of the tuple language model, as well as with Moses. Results are in Table 2.

	dev	test	# feat.
decoding with optimal segmentation/reordering			
CRF (**trs,trg**)	23.8	25.1	660K
CRF +**ctx**	24.1	25.4	1.5M
CRF +**ix,ord,seg**	24.3	25.6	1.5M
decoding with optimal reordering			
n-gram (2g,3g)	20.6	24.1	755K
n-gram (3g,3g)	21.5	25.2	755K
CRF **trs,trg**	-	22.8	660K
CRF +**ctx**	-	23.1	1.5M
CRF +**ix,ord,seg**	-	23.5	1.5M
regular decoding			
Moses (3g)	21.2	20.5	
n-gram (2g,3g)	20.6	20.2	755K
n-gram (3g,3g)	21.5	21.2	755K
CRF (**trs,trg**)	-	18.3	660K
CRF +**ctx**	-	18.8	1.5M
CRF +**ix,ord,seg**	-	19.1	1.5M
CRF +**ix,ord,seg**+3g	-	19.1	1.5M

Table 2: Translation performance

Extending the feature set As expected, the use of increasingly complex feature sets seems beneficial in all experimented conditions. It is noteworthy that throwing in reordering and contextual features is helping, *even when decoding one single segmentation and reordering*. This is because these features do not help to select the best input reordering, but help choose the best target phrase.

Searching a larger space Going from the simpler to the more difficult conditions yields significant degradations in the model, as our best score drops down from 25.6 to 23.5 (with known reordering) then to 19.1 (regular decoding). This is a clear indication that our current segmentation/reordering model is not delivering very useful scores. A similar loss is incurred by the n-gram system, which loses 4 bleu points between the two conditions.

LM rescoring Our results to date with target side language models have proven inconclusive, which might explain why our best results remain between one and two BLEU points behind the n-gram based system using comparable information. Note also that preliminary experiments with incorporating a large bigram during training have also failed to date to provide us with improvements over the baseline.

Summary In sum, the results accumulated during this first round of experiments tend to show that our CRF model is still underperforming the more established baseline by approximately 1 to 1.5 BLEU point, when provided with comparable resources. Sources of improvements that have been clearly identified is the scoring of reordering and segmentations, and the use of a target language model in training and/or decoding.

5 Related work

Discriminative learning approaches have proven successful for many NLP tasks, notably thanks to their ability to cope with flexible linguistic representations and to accommodate potentially redundant descriptions. This is especially appealing for machine translation, where the mapping between a source word or phrase and its target correlate(s) seems to involve an large array of factors, such as its morphology, its syntactic role, its meaning, its lexical context, etc. (see eg. (Och et al., 2004; Gimpel and Smith, 2008; Chiang et al., 2009), for inspiration regarding potentially useful features in SMT).

Discriminative learning requires (i) a parameterized scoring function and (ii) a training objective. The scoring function is usually assumed to be linear and ranks candidate outputs y for input x according to $\theta^T G(x, y)$, where θ is the parameter vector. θ and G deterministically imply the input/output mapping as $x \rightarrow \arg\max_y \theta^T G(x, y)$. Given a set of training pairs $\{x^i, y^i, i = 1 \dots N\}$, parameters are learned by optimizing some regularized loss function of θ, so as to make the inferred input/output mapping faithfully replicate the observed instances.

Machine translation, like most NLP tasks, does not easily lend itself to that approach, due to the complexity of the input/output objects (word or label strings, parse trees, dependency structures, etc). This complexity makes inference and learning intractable, as both steps imply the resolution of the $\arg\max$ problem over a combinatorially large space of candidates y. Structured learning techniques (Bakir et al., 2007), developed over the last decade, rely on decompositions of these objects into sub-parts as part of a *derivation* process, and use conditional independence assumptions between sub-parts to render the learning and inference problem tractable. For machine translation, this only provides part of the solution, as the training data only contain pairs of word aligned sentences $(\mathbf{f}, \mathbf{e})$, but lack the explicit derivation $\mathbf{h}$ from $\mathbf{f}$ to $\mathbf{e}$ that is required to train the model in a fully supervised way.

The approach of (Liang et al., 2006a) circumvents the issue by assuming that the hidden derivation $\mathbf{h}$ can be approximated through forced decoding. Assuming that $\mathbf{h}$ is in fact observed as the optimal (Viterbi) derivation $\mathbf{h}^*$ from $\mathbf{f}$ to $\mathbf{e}$ given the current parameter value[10], it is straightforward to recast the training of a phrase-based system as a standard structured learning problem, thus amenable to training algorithms such as the averaged perceptron of (Collins, 2002). This approximation is however not genuine, and the choice of the most appropriate derivation seems to raises intriguing issues (Watanabe et al., 2007; Chiang et al., 2008).

The authors of (Blunsom et al., 2008; Blunsom and Osborne, 2008) consider models for which it is computationally possible to marginalize out all possible derivations of a given translation. As demonstrated in these papers, this approach is tractable even when the derivation process is a based on synchronous context-free grammars, rather that finite-state devices. However, the computational cost as-

[10] If one actually exists in the model, thus raising the issue of *reference reachability*, see discussion in Section 3.

sociated with training and inference remains very high, especially when using a target side language model, which seems to preclude the application to large-scale translation tasks[11]. The recent work of (Dyer and Resnik, 2010) proceeds from a similar vein: translation is however modeled as a two step process, where a set of possible source reorderings, represented as a parse forest, are associated with possible target sentences, using, as we do, a finite-state translation model. This translation model is trained discriminatively by marginalizing out the (unobserved) reordering variables; inference can be performed effectively by intersecting the input parse forest with a transducer representing translation options.

A third strategy is to consider a simpler class of derivation process, which only *partly* describe the mapping between $\mathbf{f}$ and $\mathbf{e}$. This is, for instance, the approach of (Bangalore et al., 2007), where a simple *bag-of-word* representation of the target sentence is computed using a battery of boolean classifiers (one for each target word). In this approach, discriminative training is readily applicable, as the required supervision is overtly present in example source-target pairs $(\mathbf{f}, \mathbf{e})$; however, a complementary reshaping/reordering step is necessary to turn the bag-of-word into a full-fledged translation. This work was recently revisited in (Mauser et al., 2009), where a conditional model predicting the presence of each target phrase provides a supplementary score for the standard "log-linear" model.

This line of research has been continued notably in (Kääriäinen, 2009), which introduces an exponential model of *bag of phrases* (allowing some overlap), that enables to capture localized dependencies between target words, while preserving (to some extend) the efficiency of training and inference. Supervision is here indirectly provided by word alignment and correlated phrase extraction processes implemented in conventional phrase-based systems (Koehn et al., 2003). If this model seems to deliver state-of-the-art performance on large-scale tasks, it does so at a very high computational cost. Moreover, for lack of an internal modeling of reordering processes, this approach, like the bag-of-word approach, seems only appropriate for language pairs with similar or related word ordering.

[11] For instance, the experiments reported in (Blunsom and Osborne, 2008) use the English-Chinese BTEC, where the average sentence length is lesser than 10.

The approach developed in this paper fills a gap between the hierarchical model of (Blunsom et al., 2008) and the phrase-based model (Kääriäinen, 2009), with whom we share several important assumptions, such as the use of alignment information to provide supervision, and the resort to a an "external", albeit a more powerful, reordering component. Using a finite-state model enables to process reasonably large corpora, and gives some hopes as to the scalability of the whole enterprise; it also makes the integration of a target side language model much easier than in hierarchical models.

6 Discussion and future work

In this paper, we have given detailed description of an original phrase-based system implementing a discriminative version of the n-gram model, where the translation model probabilities are computed with conditional random fields. We have showed how to implement this approach using a memory efficient implementation of the optimization algorithms needed for training: in our approach, training a mid-scale translation system with hundred of thousands sentence pairs and millions of features only takes a couple of hours on a standalone desktop machine. Using ℓ_1 regularization has enabled to assess the usefulness of various families of features.

We have also detailed a complete decoder implemented as a pipeline of finite-state transducers, which allows to efficiently combine several models, to produce n-best lists and word lattices.

The results obtained in a series of preliminary experiments show that our system is already delivering competitive translations, as acknowledged by a comparison with two strong phrase-based baselines. We have already started to implement various optimizations and to experiment with somewhat larger datasets (up to 500K sentence pairs) and larger feature sets, notably incorporating word sense disambiguation features: this work needs to be continued. In addition, we intend to explore a number of extensions of this architecture, such as implementing MBR decoding (Kumar and Byrne, 2004) or adapting the translation model to new domains and conditions, using, for instance, the proposal of

(Daume III, 2007)[12].

One positive side effect of experimenting with new translation models is that they help reevaluate the performance of the whole translation system pipeline: in particular, discriminative training seems to be more sensible to alignments errors than the corresponding n-gram system, which suggests to pay more attention to possible errors in the training data; we have also seen that the current reordering model defines a too narrow search space and delivers insufficiently discriminant scores: we will investigate various ways to further improve the computation and scoring of hypothetical source reorderings.

Acknowledgements

The authors wish to thank the reviewers for comments and suggestions. This work was achieved as part of the *Quaero* Programme, funded by OSEO, French State agency for innovation.

References

Cyril Allauzen, Michael Riley, Johan Schalkwyk, Wojciech Skut, and Mehryar Mohri. 2007. OpenFst: A general and efficient weighted finite-state transducer library. In *Proceedings of the Ninth International Conference on Implementation and Application of Automata, (CIAA 2007)*, volume 4783 of *Lecture Notes in Computer Science*, pages 11–23. Springer. http://www.openfst.org.

Gökhan Bakir, Thomas Hofmann, Bernhard Schölkopf, Alexander J.Smola, Ben Taskar, and S.V.N. Vishwanathan. 2007. *Predicting structured output*. MIT Press.

Srinivas Bangalore, Patrick Haffner, and Stephan Kanthak. 2007. Statistical machine translation through global lexical selection and sentence reconstruction. In *Proceedings of the 45th Annual Meeting of the Association of Computational Linguistics*, pages 152–159, Prague, Czech Republic.

Phil Blunsom and Miles Osborne. 2008. Probabilistic inference for machine translation. In *Proceedings of the 2008 Conference on Empirical Methods in Natural Language Processing*, pages 215–223, Honolulu, Hawaii.

[12]In a nutshell, this proposal amounts to having three different parameters for each feature; one parameter is trained as usual; the other two parameters are updated conditionally, depending whether the training instance comes from the in-domain or from the out-domain training dataset.

Phil Blunsom, Trevor Cohn, and Miles Osborne. 2008. A discriminative latent variable model for statistical machine translation. In *Proceedings of ACL-08: HLT*, pages 200–208, Columbus, Ohio.

Peter F. Brown, John Cocke, Stephen Della Pietra, Vincent J. Della Pietra, Frederick Jelinek, John D. Lafferty, Robert L. Mercer, and Paul S. Roossin. 1990. A statistical approach to machine translation. *Computational Linguistics*, 16(2):79–85.

Francesco Casacuberta and Enrique Vidal. 2004. Machine translation with inferred stochastic finite-state transducers. *Computational Linguistics*, 30(3):205–225.

David Chiang, Yuval Marton, and Philip Resnik. 2008. Online large-margin training of syntactic and structural translation features. In *Proceedings of the 2008 Conference on Empirical Methods in Natural Language Processing*, pages 224–233, Honolulu, Hawaii.

D. Chiang, K. Knight, and W. Wang. 2009. 11,001 new features for statistical machine translation. In *Proceedings of Human Language Technologies: The 2009 Annual Conference of the North American Chapter of the Association for Computational Linguistics*, pages 218–226. Association for Computational Linguistics.

David Chiang. 2005. A hierarchical phrase-based model for statistical machine translation. In *Proceedings of the 43rd Annual Meeting of the Association for Computational Linguistics (ACL'05)*, pages 263–270, Ann Arbor, Michigan.

Michael Collins, Philipp Koehn, and Ivona Kucerova. 2005. Clause restructuring for statistical machine translation. In *Proceedings of the 43rd Annual Meeting of the Association for Computational Linguistics (ACL'05)*, pages 531–540, Ann Arbor, Michigan.

Michael Collins. 2002. Discriminative training methods for hidden markov models: Theory and experiments with perceptron algorithms. In *Proceedings of the 2002 Conference on Empirical Methods in Natural Language Processing*, pages 1–8. Association for Computational Linguistics, July.

Josep M. Crego and José B. Mariño. 2007. Improving SMT by coupling reordering and decoding. *Machine Translation*, 20(3):199–215.

Hal Daume III. 2007. Frustratingly easy domain adaptation. In *Proceedings of the 45th Annual Meeting of the Association of Computational Linguistics*, pages 256–263, Prague, Czech Republic. Association for Computational Linguistics.

John DeNero and Dan Klein. 2008. The complexity of phrase alignment problems. In *Proceedings of ACL-08: HLT, Short Papers*, pages 25–28, Columbus, Ohio.

John DeNero, Dan Gillick, James Zhang, and Dan Klein. 2006. Why generative phrase models underperform surface heuristics. In *Proceedings of the ACL workshop on Statistical Machine Translation*, pages 31–38, New York City, NY.

Yonggang Deng and William Byrne. 2006. MTTK: An alignment toolkit for statistical machine translation. In *Proceedings of the Human Language Technology Conference of the NAACL, Companion Volume: Demonstrations*, pages 265–268, New York City, USA.

Chris Dyer and Philip Resnik. 2010. Context-free reordering, finite-state translation. In *Human Language Technologies: The 2010 Annual Conference of the North American Chapter of the Association for Computational Linguistics*, pages 858–866, Los Angeles, California. Association for Computational Linguistics.

Kuzman Ganchev, João V. Graça, and Ben Taskar. 2008. Better alignments = better translations ? In *Proceedings of ACL-08: HLT*, pages 986–993, Columbus, Ohio.

Qin Gao and Stephan Vogel. 2008. Parallel implementations of word alignment tool. In *SETQA-NLP '08*.

Kevin Gimpel and Noah A. Smith. 2008. Rich source-side context for statistical machine translation. In *Proceedings of the Third Workshop on Statistical Machine Translation*, pages 9–17, Columbus, Ohio, June.

Liang Huang and David Chiang. 2007. Forest rescoring: Faster decoding with integrated language models. In *Proceedings of the 45th Annual Meeting of the Association of Computational Linguistics*, pages 144–151, Prague, Czech Republic.

Matti Kääriäinen. 2009. Sinuhe – statistical machine translation using a globally trained conditional exponential family translation model. In *Proceedings of the 2009 Conference on Empirical Methods in Natural Language Processing*, pages 1027–1036, Singapore.

Philipp Koehn, Franz Josef Och, and Daniel Marcu. 2003. Statistical phrase-based translation. In *Proceedings of the Human Language Technology Conference of the North American Chapter of the Association for Computational Linguistic*, pages 127–133, Edmonton, Canada.

Philipp Koehn, Hieu Hoang, Alexandra Birch, Chris Callison-Burch, Marcello Federico, Nicola Bertoldi, Brooke Cowan, Wade Shen, Christine Moran, Richard Zens, Chris Dyer, Ondrej Bojar, Alexandra Constantin, and Evan Herbst. 2007. Moses: Open source toolkit for statistical machine translation. In *Proc. Annual Meeting of the Association for Computational Linguistics (ACL), demonstration session*, pages 177–180, Prague, Czech Republic.

Shankar Kumar and William Byrne. 2004. Minimum bayes-risk decoding for statistical machine translation. In Daniel Marcu Susan Dumais and Salim Roukos, editors, *HLT-NAACL 2004: Main Proceedings*, pages 169–176, Boston, Massachusetts, USA. Association for Computational Linguistics.

Shankar Kumar, Yonggang Deng, and William Byrne. 2006. A weighted finite state transducer translation template model for statistical machine translation. *Natural Language Engineering*, 12(1):35–75.

John Lafferty, Andrew McCallum, and Fernando Pereira. 2001. Conditional random fields: probabilistic models for segmenting and labeling sequence data. In *Proceedings of the International Conference on Machine Learning*, pages 282–289. Morgan Kaufmann, San Francisco, CA.

Thomas Lavergne, Olivier Capp, and Franois Yvon. 2010. Practical very large scale crfs. In *Proceedings of the 48th Annual Meeting of the Association for Computational Linguistics*, pages 504–513, Uppsala, Sweden.

Percy Liang, Alexandre Bouchard-Côté, Dan Klein, and Ben Taskar. 2006a. An end-to-end discriminative approach to machine translation. In *Proceedings of the 21st International Conference on Computational Linguistics and 44th Annual Meeting of the Association for Computational Linguistics*, pages 761–768, Sydney, Australia.

Percy Liang, Ben Taskar, and Dan Klein. 2006b. Alignment by agreement. In *Proceedings of the Human Language Technology Conference of the NAACL, Main Conference*, pages 104–111, New York City, USA.

Daniel Marcu and Daniel Wong. 2002. A phrase-based, joint probability model for statistical machine translation. In *Proceedings of the 2002 Conference on Empirical Methods in Natural Language Processing*, pages 133–139.

José B. Mariño, Rafael E. Banchs, Josep M. Crego, Adrià de Gispert, Patrick Lambert, José A.R. Fonollosa, and Marta R. Costa-Jussà. 2006. N-gram-based machine translation. *Computational Linguistics*, 32(4):527–549.

Arne Mauser, Saša Hasan, and Hermann Ney. 2009. Extending statistical machine translation with discriminative and trigger-based lexicon models. In *Proceedings of the 2009 Conference on Empirical Methods in Natural Language Processing*, pages 210–218, Singapore.

Mehryar Mohri. 2009. Weighted automata algorithms. In Manfred Droste, Werner Kuich, and Heiko Vogler, editors, *Handbook of Weighted Automata*, chapter 6, pages 213–254. Springer Verlag.

Andrew Y. Ng. 2004. Feature selection, l1 vs. l2 regularization, and rotational invariance. In *Proceedings of the twenty-first international conference on Machine learning*, pages 78–86.

Franz J. Och, Daniel Gildea, Sanjeev Khudanpur, Anoop Sarkar, Kenji Yamada, Alex Fraser, Shankar Kumar,

Libin Shen, David Smith, Katherine Eng, Viren Jain, Zhen Jin, and Dragomir Radev. 2004. A smorgasbord of features for statistical machine translation. In *HLT-NAACL 2004: Main Proceedings*, pages 161–168, Boston, Massachusetts, USA. Association for Computational Linguistics.

Kishore Papineni, Salim Roukos, Todd Ward, and Wei-Jing Zhu. 2002. BLEU: a method for automatic evaluation of machine translation. In *Proceedings of the 40th Annual Meeting on Association for Computational Linguistics*, pages 311–318.

Martin Riedmiller and Heinrich Braun. 1993. A direct adaptive method for faster backpropagation learning: The RPROP algorithm. In *Proceedings of the IEEE International Conference on Neural Networks*, pages 586–591, San Francisco, USA.

Charles Sutton and Andrew McCallum. 2006. An introduction to conditional random fields for relational learning. In Lise Getoor and Ben Taskar, editors, *Introduction to Statistical Relational Learning*, Cambridge, MA. The MIT Press.

Robert Tibshirani. 1996. Regression shrinkage and selection via the lasso. *J.R.Statist.Soc.B*, 58(1):267–288.

Christoph Tillman. 2004. A unigram orientation model for statistical machine translation. In Susan Dumais, Daniel Marcu, and Salim Roukos, editors, *HLT-NAACL 2004: Short Papers*, pages 101–104, Boston, Massachusetts, USA.

J. Turian, B. Wellington, and I.D. Melamed. 2007. Scalable discriminative learning for natural language parsing and translation. In *Proc. Neural Information Processing Systems (NIPS)*, volume 19, pages 1409–1417.

Taro Watanabe, Jun Suzuki, Hajime Tsukada, and Hideki Isozaki. 2007. Online large-margin training for statistical machine translation. In *Proceedings of the 2007 Joint Conference on Empirical Methods in Natural Language Processing and Computational Natural Language Learning (EMNLP-CoNLL)*, pages 764–773, Prague, Czech Republic.

Joern Wuebker, Arne Mauser, and Hermann Ney. 2010. Training phrase translation models with leaving-one-out. In *Proceedings of the 48th Annual Meeting of the Association for Computational Linguistics*, pages 475–484, Uppsala, Sweden.

Fei Xia and Michael McCord. 2004. Improving a statistical mt system with automatically learned rewrite patterns. In *Proceedings of the 20th International Conference on Computational Linguistics (COLING)*, pages 508–514, Geneva, Switzerland.

Author Index

Association for Computational Linguistics
209 N. Eighth Street
Stroudsburg, Pennsylvania 18360

CURRAN ASSOCIATES INC
proceedings.com

Combined Proceedings, International Plant Propagators' Society 2019

IPPS Volume 69

2019

IPPS

Sharing Plant Production Knowledge Globally